America's
Top-Rated Cities:
A Statistical Handbook

Volume 4

2014

Twenty-First Edition

America's
Top-Rated Cities:
A Statistical Handbook

Volume 4: Eastern Region

PUBLISHER:	Leslie Mackenzie
EDITORIAL DIRECTOR:	Laura Mars
EDITOR:	David Garoogian

RESEARCHERS & WRITERS:	Allison Blake; Denise Lenchner; Veronica Towers
PRODUCTION MANAGER:	Kristen Thatcher
MARKETING DIRECTOR:	Jessica Moody

A Universal Reference Book
Grey House Publishing, Inc.
4919 Route 22
Amenia, NY 12501
518.789.8700
Fax 845.373.6390
www.greyhouse.com
e-mail: books @greyhouse.com

Twenty-first Edition
Printed in Canada

Publisher's Cataloging-in-Publication Data
(Prepared by The Donohue Group, Inc.)

America's top-rated cities. Vol. IV, Eastern region : a statistical handbook. — 1992-

v. : ill. ; cm.
Annual, 1995-
Irregular, 1992-1993
ISSN: 1082-7102

1. Cities and towns--Ratings--Eastern States--Statistics--Periodicals. 2. Cities and towns--Eastern States--Statistics--Periodicals. 3. Social indicators--Eastern States--Periodicals. 4. Quality of life--Eastern States--Statistics--Periodicals. 5. Eastern States--Social conditions--Statistics--Periodicals. I. Title: America's top rated cities. II. Title: Eastern region

HT123.5.S6 A44
307.76/0973/05

95644648

4-Volume Set	ISBN: 978-1-61925-264-6
Volume 1	ISBN: 978-1-61925-265-3
Volume 2	ISBN: 978-1-61925-266-0
Volume 3	ISBN: 978-1-61925-267-7
Volume 4	**ISBN: 978-1-61925-268-4**

Baltimore, Maryland

Boston, Massachusetts

Charlotte, North Carolina

Cincinnati, Ohio

Columbus, Ohio

Durham, North Carolina

Erie, Pennsylvania

Fayetteville, North Carolina

Wilmington, North Carolina

Worcester, Massachusetts

Introduction

This twenty-first edition of *America's Top Rated Cities* is a concise, statistical, 4-volume work identifying America's top-rated cities with populations of at least 100,000. It profiles 100 cities that have received high marks for business and living from prominent sources such as *Forbes, U.S. News & World Report, BusinessWeek, Inc., Fortune, Men's Health, The Wall Street Journal, Cosmopolitan,* and *CNNMoney.*

Each volume covers a different region of the country—Southern, Western, Central and Eastern—and includes a detailed Table of Contents, City Chapters, Appendices, and Maps. Each City Chapter incorporates information from hundreds of resources to create the following major sections:

- **Background**—lively narrative of significant, up-to-date news for both businesses and residents. These combine historical facts with current developments, "known-for" annual events, and climate data.
- **Rankings**—fun-to-read, bulleted survey results from over 300 books, magazines, and online articles, ranging from general (Great Places to Live), to specific (Best Cities for Newlyweds), and everything in between.
- **Statistical Tables**—121 tables and detailed topics—several new and expanded—that offer an unparalleled view of each city's Business and Living Environments. They are carefully organized with data that is easy to read and understand.
- **Appendices**—five in all, follow each volume of City Chapters. These range from listings of Metropolitan Statistical Areas to Comparative Statistics for all 100 cities.

This new edition of *America's Top Rated Cities* includes cities that not only surveyed well, but ranked highest using our unique weighting system. We looked at violent crime, property crime, population growth, median household income, educational attainment, and unemployment. You'll find that a number of American cities remain "top-rated" despite less-than-stellar numbers. Miami, for example, is known for high crime and unemployment, but also for its unique location—as both a valuable business port and popular vacation spot. New York and Los Angeles have relatively low high school graduation rates, but both of these cities make up for it in other ways. A final consideration is location—we strive to include as many states in the country as possible.

Part of this year's city criteria is that it be the "primary" city in a given metropolitan area. For example, if the metro area is Raleigh-Cary, NC, we would consider Raleigh, not Cary. This allows for a more equitable core city to core city comparison. In general, the core city of a metro area is defined as having substantial influence on neighboring cities.

The following 14 cities have never before appeared as a top-rated city:

- SOUTHERN: Abilene, TX; Lafayette, LA; Lubbock, TX; Midland, TX; Montgomery, AL
- WESTERN: Salem, OR
- CENTRAL: Davenport, IA; Peoria, IL; Rochester, MN; Topeka, KS
- EASTERN: Erie, PA; Fayetteville, NC; Wilmington, NC; Worcester, MA

The following 21 cities have regained their top-city status after being removed from the list for one, or many, years:

- SOUTHERN: Gainesville, FL; Tallahassee, FL
- WESTERN: Oxnard, CA; Phoenix, AZ; Reno, NV; Riverside, CA; Salt Lake City, UT; Santa Rosa, CA; Spokane, WA
- CENTRAL: Des Moines, IA; Grand Rapids, MI; Green Bay, WI; Minnepolis, MN; Oklahoma City, OK; Springfield, MO; Tulsa, OK; Wichita, KS
- EASTERN: Baltimore, MD; Cincinnati, OH; Louisville, KY; Richmond, VA

Praise for previous editions:

> "...[ATRC] has...proven its worth to a wide audience...from businesspeople and corporations planning to launch, relocate, or expand their operations to market researchers, real estate professionals, urban planners, job-seekers, students...interested in...reliable, attractively presented statistical information about larger U.S. cities."
> —ARBA

> "...For individuals or businesses looking to relocate, this resource conveniently reports rankings from more than 300 sources for the top 100 US cities. Recommended..."
> —Choice

> "...While patrons are becoming increasingly comfortable locating statistical data online, there is still something to be said for the ease associated with such a compendium of otherwise scattered data. A well-organized and appropriate update..."
> —Library Journal

BACKGROUND

Each city begins with an informative Background that combines history with current events. These narratives often reflect changes that have occurred during the past year, and touch on the city's environment, politics, employment, cultural offerings, and climate, often including interesting trivia. For example: The unique craft of cowboy boot making is demonstrated at the Abilene Historical Museum; Peregrine Falcons were rehabilitated and released into the wild from Boise City's World Center for Birds of Prey; Gainesville is home to a 6,800 square-foot living Butterfly Rainforest, and Grand Rapids was the first city to introduce fluoride into its drinking water in 1945.

RANKINGS

This section has rankings from a possible 327 books, articles, and reports. For easy reference, these Rankings are categorized into 17 topics including Business/Finance, Dating/Romance, and Health/Fitness.

The Rankings are presented in an easy-to-read, bulleted format and include results from both annual surveys and one-shot studies. **Fastest-Growing Wages . . . Most Well-Read . . . Most Playful . . . Most Wired. . . Healthiest for Women . . . Best for Minority Entrepreneurs . . . Safest . . . Best to Grow Old . . . Most Polite . . . Best for Moviemakers . . . Most Frugal . . . Noisiest . . . Sex Happy . . . Most Vegetarian-Friendly . . . Least Stressful . . . Hottest Cities of the Future . . . Most Political . . . Most Charitable . . . Most Tax Friendly . . . Best for Telecommuters . . . Best for Singles . . . Greediest . . . Gayest . . . Best for Cats . . . Most Tattooed . . . Best for Wheelchair Users,** and more.

Sources for these Rankings include both well-known magazines and other media, including *Forbes, Fortune, Inc. Magazine, Working Mother, BusinessWeek, Kiplinger's Personal Finance, Men's Journal,* and *Travel + Leisure,* as well as resources not as well known, such as the *Asthma & Allergy Foundation of America, Christopher & Dana Reeve Foundation, The Advocate, Black Enterprise, National Civic League, The National Coalition for the Homeless, MovieMaker Magazine, Center for Digital Government, U.S. Conference of Mayors,* and the *Milken Institute.*

Since rankings cover a variety of geographic areas-metropolitan statistical areas, metropolitan divisions, cities, etc.- rankings can apply to one or all of these areas; see Appendix B for full geographic definitions.

STATISTICAL TABLES

Each city chapter includes a possible 121 tables and detailed topics—67 in BUSINESS and 54 in LIVING. Over 90% of statistical data has been updated. New topics include *Chronic Health Indicators, Air Quality Trends: Ozone,* and *Gross Rent.* Expanded topics include the addition of podiatrists, chiropractors, and optometrists to *Number of Medical Professionals* and the year established to *Professional Sports Teams.*

Business Environment includes hard facts and figures on 12 topics, including City Finances, Demographics, Income, Economy, Employment, and Real Estate. *Living Environment* includes 11 topics, such as Cost of Living, Housing, Health, Education, Safety, Recreation, and Climate.

To compile the Statistical Tables, our editors have again turned to a wide range of sources, some well known, such as the *U.S. Census Bureau, U.S. Environmental Protection Agency, Bureau of Labor Statistics, Centers for Disease Control and Prevention,* and the *Federal Bureau of Investigation,* and some more obscure, like *The Council for Community and Economic Research, Texas Transportation Institute,* and *Federation of Tax Administrators.*

APPENDICES: Data for all cities appear in all volumes.
* **Appendix A**—*Comparative Statistics*
* **Appendix B**—*Metropolitan Area Definitions*
* **Appendix C**—*Government Type and County*
* **Appendix D**—*Chambers of Commerce and Economic Development Organizations*
* **Appendix E**—*State Departments of Labor and Employment*

Material provided by public and private agencies and organizations was supplemented by original research, numerous library sources and Internet sites. *America's Top-Rated Cities, 2014,* is designed for a wide range of readers: private individuals considering relocating a residence or business; professionals considering expanding their businesses or changing careers; corporations considering relocation, opening up additional offices or creating new divisions; government agencies; general and market researchers; real estate consultants; human resource personnel; urban planners; investors; and urban government students.

Customers who purchase the four-volume set receive free online access to *America's Top Rated Cities* to: download city reports; sort and rank by 50-plus data points; and access data for 200 more cities than in the print version.

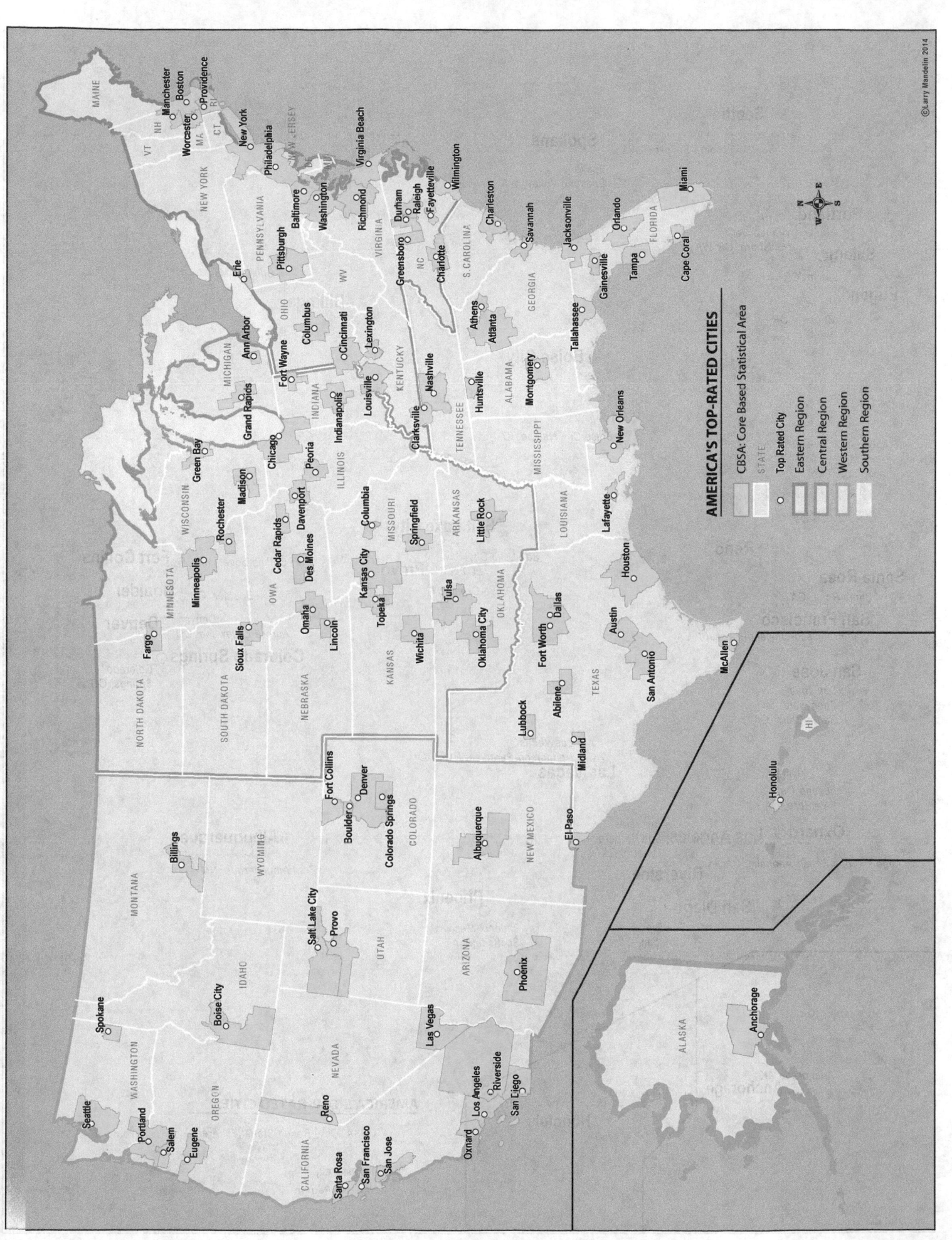

AMERICA'S TOP-RATED CITIES

CBSA: Core Based Statistical Area

STATE

○ Top Rated City

Eastern Region

Central Region

Western Region

Southern Region

Seattle
Seattle-Tacoma-Bellevue, WA

Spokane
Spokane-
Spokane Valley, WA

WASHINGTON

MONTANA

NORTH
DAKOTA

Portland
Portland-
Vancouver-
Hillsboro, OR-WA

Salem
Salem, OR

Eugene
Eugene, OR

OREGON

Billings, MT

Billings

SOUTH
DAKOTA

Boise City

IDAHO

Boise City-Nampa, ID

WYOMING

NEBRASKA

Reno, NV

CALIFORNIA

Reno

NEVADA

Salt Lake City

Salt Lake City, UT

Provo

Provo-Orem, UT

Fort Collins-Loveland, CO   Fort Collins

Boulder, CO   Boulder

Denver-
Aurora-Lakewood, CO   Denver

Colorado Springs

Colorado
Springs, CO

KS

Santa Rosa
Santa Rosa, CA

San Francisco
San Francisco-Oakland-Hayward, CA

San Jose
San Jose-
Sunnyvale-
Santa Clara, CA

UTAH

COLORADO

Las Vegas-
Henderson-Paradise, NV

Oxnard-
Thousand Oaks-
Ventura, CA

Oxnard   Los Angeles

Las Vegas

Riverside-
San Bernardino-
Ontario, CA

ARIZONA

Albuquerque

Albuquerque, NM

Los Angeles-Long Beach-Anaheim, CA   Riverside

San Diego

San Diego-
Carlsbad, CA

Phoenix

Phoenix-Mesa-
Scottsdale, AZ

NEW MEXICO

TEXAS

ALASKA

Anchorage, AK

Anchorage

Urban Honolulu, HI

Honolulu

HAWAII

AMERICA'S TOP-RATED CITIES

CBSA: Core Based Statistical Area

STATE

○ Top Rated City

Western Region

©Larry Mandelin 2014

N
W ○ E
S

AMERICA'S TOP- RATED CITIES

CBSA: Core Based Statistical Area

STATE

○ Top Rated City

Central Region

©Larry Mandelin 2014

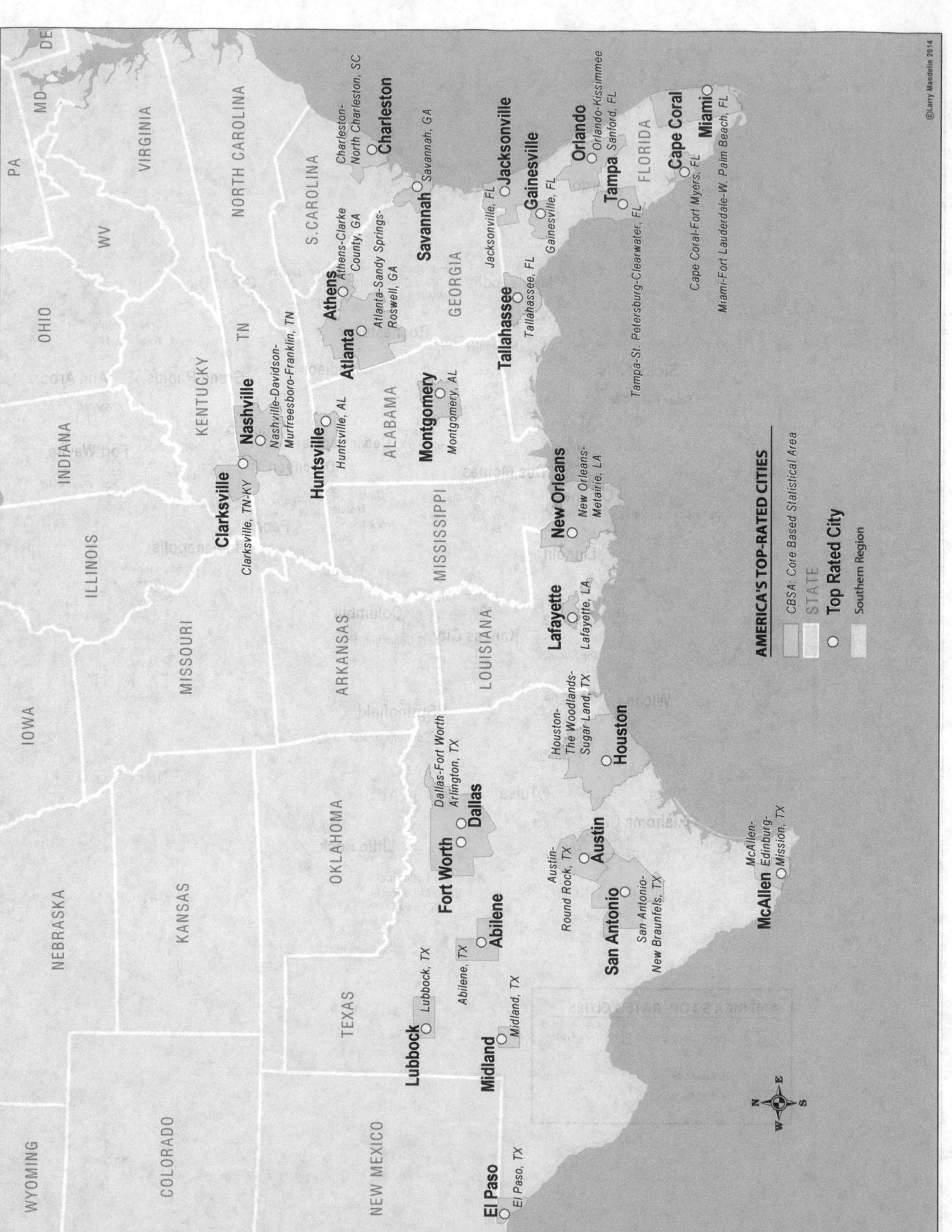

AMERICA'S TOP-RATED CITIES

CBSA: Core Based Statistical Area

STATE

○ Top Rated City

Southern Region

©Larry Mandelin 2014

AMERICA'S TOP-RATED CITIES

CBSA: Core Based Statistical Area
STATE
○ Top Rated City
Eastern Region

MAINE

VT   NH

Manchester
Manchester-Nashua, NH

Boston-Cambridge-Newton, MA-NH
Boston

Worcester
Worcester, MA-CT
Providence
Providence-Warwick, RI-MA

MA

CT

RI

NEW YORK

Erie
Erie, PA

PENNSYLVANIA

NJ

New York
New York-Newark-Jersey City, NY-NJ-PA

Philadelphia

Pittsburgh
Pittsburgh, PA

OHIO

Baltimore-Columbia-Towson, MD

Philadelphia-Camden-Wilmington, PA-NJ-DE-MD

Columbus
Columbus, OH

Baltimore

DE

INDIANA

MD

Washington
Washington-Arlington-Alexandria, DC-VA-MD-WV

WV

IL

Cincinnati
Cincinnati, OH-KY-IN

Richmond
Richmond, VA

Virginia Beach-Norfolk-Newport News, VA-NC

Louisville/Jefferson County, KY-IN

Lexington
Lexington-Fayette, KY

Virginia Beach

VIRGINIA

Louisville

KENTUCKY

Durham-Chapel Hill, NC

Greensboro-High Point, NC   **Durham**
Greensboro   **Raleigh**
Raleigh, NC

MICHIGAN

Charlotte-Concord-Gastonia, NC-SC

Fayetteville
Charlotte   Fayetteville, NC   **Wilmington**
Wilmington, NC

TENNESSEE

NC

S.CAROLINA

MS   ALABAMA   GEORGIA

©Larry Mandelin 2014

Baltimore, Maryland

Background

No one industry dominates Baltimore, but many of them have one thing in common: Baltimore's waterfront. These port facilities provide companies in the city's municipal area with access to domestic and international markets. Not only that, the port also has the advantage of being 150 miles closer to the Midwest than other eastern U.S. port cities.

With its easily accessible harbor, reached via a 42-foot-deep main channel from the Chesapeake Bay, Baltimore boasts strong roots in maritime commerce dating to the "Baltimore Clippers" built here that outran the British during wartime. In 2013, the Port of Baltimore handled $52.6 billion in foreign commerce. A 50-foot berth also was recently completed at the port, making Baltimore the East Coast's second port to have both a 50-foot channel and a 50-foot berth.

The city was founded in 1729 and named for the Lords Baltimore, Cecil and Charles Calvert, the first proprietors of colonial Maryland in the seventeenth century. In 1812, poet and attorney Francis Scott Key wrote "The Star-Spangled Banner" while watching from a warship the bombardment of the city by the British. Baltimore is the site of the first Roman Catholic cathedral in the country, the Basilica of the Assumption of the Blessed Virgin Mary, which was designed by Benjamin H. Latrobe. The first telegraph line in the United States was installed in Baltimore, and the nation's first gas streetlamp was lit here.

Despite the urban decay experienced from the 1950s through the 1970s, reconstruction of many of the city's old areas in the ensuing years has brought people back to Baltimore neighborhoods such as the Inner Harbor, Fells Point, Federal Hill and Canton. The more recent, upscale Harbor East neighborhood has extended the walkability and attraction of the waterside area between the Inner Harbor and Fells Point, bringing new dining, hotels, homes and shopping.

Healthcare and higher education are the city's major employers, with Johns Hopkins University, Johns Hopkins Hospital and Health System, the University of Maryland-Baltimore, and the University of Maryland Medical System providing nearly 60,000 jobs.

Slated for a 2014 opening is the Horseshoe Casino Baltimore, located on Russell Street, a city gateway near the M&T Bank Stadium—home to the NFL's Baltimore Ravens—and Oriole Park at Camden Yards. The $442 million development will feature a two-story casino and a 20,000 square foot Baltimore Marketplace offering food outlets, restaurants, and bars and lounges.

Baltimore's light rail transportation services the Hunt Valley corporate, hotel, and shopping area north of the city, and passes through downtown on its way to Oriole Park and Anne Arundel County. There is also service to BWI Thurgood Marshall Airport and Amtrak's Baltimore Penn Station, as well as public subway and bus transportation. BWI is a major international airport, with 18 major carriers providing over 320 nonstop flights to 79 cities in the U.S., Canada, and Europe.

The Baltimore waterfront area is a retail and entertainment district, including the historic power plant complex located in the heart of the Inner Harbor. Located in Baltimore are several museums, including Port Discovery children's museum, the Edgar Allen Poe House and Museum, the Baltimore Museum of Art and the American Visionary Art Museum, to name only a few. Some other attractions include the Baltimore Symphony Orchestra, Fort McHenry, Maryland Science Center, and the National Aquarium in Baltimore. The Peabody Conservatory, founded in 1857, is located north of the harbor in picturesque Mount Vernon Square, while the Maryland Institute College of Art boasts alumnae such as Jeff Koons. Of MICA's BFA graduates who take jobs immediately after graduation, 86 percent work in an art-related field.

The region is subject to frequent changes in weather, although the mountains to the west, and the Chesapeake Bay and ocean to the east produce a more equable climate compared with other locations farther inland at the same latitude. In the summer, the area is under the influence of the high-pressure system commonly known as the "Bermuda High" which brings warm, humid air. In winter, snow is frequently mixed with rain and sleet, but seldom remains on the ground for more than a few days. Severe thunderstorms are generally confined to summer and fall, and hurricanes during the same period are possible.

Rankings

General Rankings

- Baltimore was selected as one of America's best cities by *Bloomberg Businessweek*. The city ranked #29 out of 50. Criteria: leisure attributes (the number of restaurants, bars, libraries, museums, professional sports teams, and park acres by population); educational attributes (public school performance, the number of colleges, and graduate degree holders); economic factors (2011 income and June and July 2012 unemployment); crime; and air quality. *Bloomberg BusinessWeek, "America's Best Cities," September 26, 2012*

- Baltimore appeared on RelocateAmerica's list of best places to live in America. The annual "Top 100 Places to Live" list recognizes the top communities as nominated by their residents & local businesses. RelocateAmerica's Research Group determined the list based on review of various data gathered for economic, employment, housing, education, industry, opportunity, environment and recreation along with feedback from area leaders and residents. *RelocateAmerica.com, "Top 100 Places to Live for 2011"*

- Baltimore was selected as one of "America's Favorite Cities." The city ranked #34 in the "Quality of Life and Visitor Experience: Cleanliness" category. Respondents to an online survey were asked to rate 35 top urban destinations in the U.S. from a visitor's perspective. Criteria: cleanliness. *Travel + Leisure, "America's Favorite Cities 2013"*

- Baltimore was selected as one of "America's Favorite Cities." The city ranked #28 in the "Type of Trip: Gay-friendly" category. Respondents to an online survey were asked to rate 35 top urban destinations in the U.S. from a visitor's perspective. Criteria: gay-friendly. *Travel + Leisure, "America's Favorite Cities 2013"*

Business/Finance Rankings

- The personal finance site NerdWallet scored the nation's 20 largest American cities according to how friendly a business climate they offer to would-be entrepreneurs. Criteria inlcuded local taxes (state, city, payroll, property), growth rate, and the regulatory environment as judged by small business owners. On the resulting list of most welcoming cities, Baltimore ranked #4. *www.nerdwallet.com, "Top 10 Best Cities for Small Business," August 26, 2013*

- Building on the U.S. Department of Labor's Occupational Information Network Data Collection Program, the Brookings Institution defined STEM occupations and job opportunities for STEM workers at various levels of educational attainment. The Baltimore metro area was placed among the ten large metro areas with the highest demand for high-level STEM knowledge. *www.brookings.edu, "The Hidden Stem Economy," June 10, 2013*

- Analysts for the business website 24/7 Wall Street looked at the local government report "Tax Rates and Tax Burdens in the District of Columbia—A Nationwide Comparison" to determine where a family of three at two different income levels would pay the least and the most in state and local taxes. Among the ten cities with the highest state and local tax burdens was Baltimore, at #10. *247wallst.com, American Cities with the Highest (and Lowest) Taxes, February 25, 2013*

- The business website 24/7 Wall Street drew on the Brookings Institution's report "The Hidden STEM Economy" to identify the proportion of workers in the nation's largest metropolitan areas that were employed in jobs requiring knowledge in the science, technology, engineering, or math (STEM) fields. The Baltimore metro area was #8. *247wallst.com, "The Best Cities for High-Tech Jobs," June 10, 2013*

- Based on a minimum of 500 social media reviews per metro area, the employment opinion group Glassdoor surveyed 50 of the largest U.S. metro areas on measures including compensation and benefits, satisfaction with management, business outlook, and number of employers hiring. The Baltimore metro area was ranked #30 in overall employee satisfaction. *www.glassdoor.com, "Employment Satisfaction Report Card by City," June 21, 2013*

- In its Competitive Alternatives report, consulting firm KPMG analyzed the 27 largest metropolitan statistical areas according to 26 cost components (such as taxes, labor costs, and utilities) and 30 non-cost-related variables (such as crime rates and number of universities). The business website 24/7 Wall Street examined the KPMG findings, adding to the mix current unemployment rates, GDP, median income, and employment decline during the last recession and "projected" recovery. It identified the Baltimore metro area as #6 among the ten best American cities for business. *247wallst.com, "Best American Cities for Business," April 4, 2012*

- The Brookings Institution ranked the 50 largest cities in the U.S. based on income inequality. Baltimore was ranked #10. (#1 = greatest ineqality). Criteria: the cities were ranked based on the "95/20 ratio." This figure represents the income at which a household earns more than 95 percent of all other households, divided by the income at which a household earns more than only 20 percent of all other households. *Brookings Institution, "Income Inequality in America's 50 Largest Cities, 2007-2012," February 20, 2014*

- MarketWatch shared a *24/7 Wall St.* analysis of the District of Columbia's Office of Revenue Analysis report on the estimated property, sales, auto, and income taxes paid in the largest city of each state in 2011. Of the U.S. cities with the highest tax burden, Baltimore ranked #10. *Marketwatch.com, "10 U.S. Cities with the Highest Taxes," March 2, 2013*

- CareerBliss, an employment and careers website, analyzed U.S. Bureau of Labor Statistics data, more than 14,000 company reviews from employees and former employees, and job openings over a six-month period to arrive at its list of the 20 worst places in the United States to look for a job. Baltimore was ranked #18. *CareerBliss.com, "20 Worst Cities to Find a Job for 2012," October 11, 2012*

- Baltimore was ranked #49 out of 100 metro areas in terms of economic performance (#1 = best) during the recession and recovery from trough quarter through the second quarter of 2013. Criteria: percent change in employment; percentage point change in unemployment rate; percent change in gross metropolitan product; percent change in House Price Index. *Brookings Institution, MetroMonitor: Tracking Economic Recession and Recovery in America's 100 Largest Metropolitan Areas, September 2013*

- Payscale.com ranked the 20 largest metro areas in terms of wage growth. The Baltimore metro area ranked #3. Criteria: private-sector wage growth between the 4th quarter of 2012 and the 4th quarter of 2013. *PayScale, "Wage Trends by Metro Area," 4th Quarter, 2013*

- Baltimore was identified as one of "America's Hardest-Working Towns." The city ranked #24 out of 25. Criteria: average hours worked per capita; willingness to work during personal time; number of dual income households; local employment rate. *Parade, "What is America's Hardest-Working Town?," April 15, 2012*

- Baltimore was identified as one of America's "10 Best Cities to Get a Job" by *U.S. News & World Report.* The city ranked #7. Criteria: number of available jobs; unemployment rate. *U.S. News & World Report, "10 Best Cities to Get a Job," February 1, 2011*

- Baltimore was identified as one of the top 25 U.S. cities with the most credit card debt by credit reporting bureau Experian. The city was ranked #11. *Experian, March 4, 2011*

- Baltimore was identified as one of the best cities for college graduates to find work—and live. The city ranked #10 out of 15. Criteria: job availability; average salary; average rent. *CareerBuilder.com, "15 Best Cities for College Grads to Find Work—and Live," June 5, 2012*

- The Baltimore metro area appeared on the Milken Institute "2013 Best Performing Cities" list. Rank: #36 out of 200 large metro areas. Criteria: job growth; wage and salary growth; high-tech output growth. *Milken Institute, "Best-Performing Cities 2013," December 2013*

- *Forbes* ranked the 200 most populous metro areas in the U.S. in terms of the "Best Places for Business and Careers." The Baltimore metro area was ranked #31. Criteria: costs (business and living); job growth (past and projected); income growth; educational attainment (college and high school); projected economic growth; cultural and recreational opportunities; net migration patterns; number of highly ranked colleges. *Forbes, "The Best Places for Business and Careers," August 7, 2013*

Children/Family Rankings

- Baltimore was selected as one of the best cities for families to live by *Parenting* magazine. The city ranked #41 out of 100. Criteria: education; health; community; *Parenting's* Culture & Charm Index. *Parenting.com, "The 2012 Best Cities for Families List"*

Culture/Performing Arts Rankings

- Baltimore was selected as one of "America's Favorite Cities." The city ranked #28 in the "Culture: Museum/Galleries" category. Respondents to an online survey were asked to rate 35 top urban destinations in the U.S. from a visitor's perspective. Criteria: number and quality of museums and galleries. *Travelandleisure.com, "America's Favorite Cities 2013"*

- Baltimore was selected as one of America's top cities for the arts. The city ranked #10 in the big city (population 500,000 and over) category. Criteria: readers' top choices for arts travel destinations based on the richness and variety of visual arts sites, activities and events. *American Style, "2012 Top 25 Arts Destinations," June 2012*

Dating/Romance Rankings

- A *Cosmopolitan* magazine article surveyed the gender balance and other factors to arrive at a list of the best and worst cities for women to meet single guys. Baltimore placed #4 among the worst for single women looking for dates. *www.cosmopolitan.com, "Working the Ratio," October 1, 2013*

- Baltimore took the #5 spot on NerdWallet's list of best cities for singles wanting to date, based on the availability of singles; "date-friendliness," as determined by a city's walkability and the number of bars and restaurants per thousand residents; and the affordability of dating in terms of the cost of movie tickets, pizza, and wine for two. *www.nerdwallet.com, "Best Cities for Singles," February 5, 2014*

- Of the 100 U.S. cities surveyed by *Men's Health* in its quest to identify the nation's best cities for dating and forming relationships, Baltimore was ranked #25 for online dating (#1 = best). *Men's Health, "The Best and Worst Cities for Online Dating," January 30, 2013*

- Baltimore ranked #2 among cities congenial to singles, according to Kiplinger, which searched for "dating scenes as financially attractive as they are romantically promising." High percentages of unmarried people, above-average household incomes, and cost-of-living factors determined the rankings. *Kiplinger.com, "10 Best Cities for Singles," February 2013*

- Baltimore was selected as one of the best cities for single men by *Rent.com*. Criteria: high single female-to-male ratio. *Rent.com, "Top Cities for Single Men," March 14, 2013*

- Baltimore was selected as one of the best cities for newlyweds by *Rent.com*. The city ranked #10 of 10. Criteria: cost of living; mean annual income; unemployment rate. *Rent.com, "10 Best Cities for Newlyweds," March 20, 2012*

Education Rankings

- *Men's Health* ranked 100 U.S. cities in terms of their education levels. Baltimore was ranked #84 (#1 = most educated city). Criteria: high school graduation rates; school enrollment; educational attainment; number of households who have outstanding student loans; number of households whose members have taken adult-education courses. *Men's Health, "Where School Is In: The Most and Least Educated Cities," September 12, 2011*

- Baltimore was selected as one of America's most literate cities. The city ranked #15 out of the 77 largest U.S. cities. Criteria: number of booksellers; library resources; Internet resources; educational attainment; periodical publishing resources; newspaper circulation. *Central Connecticut State University, "America's Most Literate Cities, 2013"*

- Baltimore was identified as one of "America's Smartest Cities" by *The Daily Beast* using data from Lumos Labs. The metro area ranked #25 out of 25. Criteria: with data collected from more than 1 million users as part of its human cognition project, Lumos Labs was able to analyze performance for nearly 200 metro areas in five cognitive areas: memory, processing speed, flexibility, attention, and problem solving. The median Lumos Lab score was worth 50 percent of the final, weighted ranking. The other half of the ranking was based on the percentage of adults over age 25 with a bachelor's and/or master's degree. *The Daily Beast, "America's Smartest Cities 2012" August 16, 2012*

Environmental Rankings

- The Baltimore metro area came in at #223 for the relative comfort of its climate on Sperling's list of "chill cities," as measured by the Sperling Heat Index. All 361 metro areas are included. Criteria included daytime high temperatures, nighttime low temperatures, dew point, and relative humidity at the high temperatures. *www.bertsperling.com, "Sperling's Chill Cities," July 18, 2013*

- Sperling's BestPlaces assessed 379 metropolitan areas of the United States for the likelihood of dangerously extreme weather events or earthquakes. In general the Southeast and South-Central regions have the highest risk of weather extremes and earthquakes, while the Pacific Northwest enjoys the lowest risk. Of the least risky metropolitan areas, the Baltimore metro area was ranked #200. *www.bestplaces.net, "Safest Places from Natural Disasters," April 2011*

- Baltimore was identified as one of America's dirtiest metro areas by *Forbes*. The area ranked #18 out of 20. Criteria: air quality; water quality; toxic releases; superfund sites. *Forbes, "America's 20 Dirtiest Cities," December 10, 2012*

- Baltimore was selected as one of 22 "Smarter Cities" for energy by the Natural Resources Defense Council. Criteria: investment in green power; energy efficiency measures; conservation. *Natural Resources Defense Council, "2010 Smarter Cities," July 19, 2010*

Food/Drink Rankings

- *Men's Health* ranked 100 major U.S. cities in terms of alcohol intoxication. Baltimore ranked #24 (#1 = most sober).Criteria: binge drinking; alcohol-related traffic accidents, arrests, and fatalities. *Men's Health, "The Drunkest Cities in America," November 19, 2013*

Health/Fitness Rankings

- For each of the 50 most populous metro areas in the United States, the American College of Sports Medicine's American Fitness Index evaluated infrastructure, community assets, and policies that encourage healthy and fit lifestyles, including preventive health behaviors, levels of chronic disease conditions, health care access, and community resources and policies that support physical activity. The Baltimore metro area ranked #17 for "community fitness." Personal health indicators were considered as well as community and environmental indicators. *www.americanfitnessindex.org, "ACSM American Fitness Index Health and Community Fitness Status of the 50 Largest Metropolitan Areas," May 2013*

- Baltimore was identified as one of the 10 most walkable cities in the U.S. by Walk Score, a Seattle-based service that rates the convenience and transit access of 10,000 neighborhoods in 3,000 cities. The area ranked #10 out of the 50 largest U.S. cities. Walk Score measures walkability by analyzing hundreds of walking routes to nearby amenities. Walk Score also measures pedestrian friendliness by analyzing population density and road metrics such as block length and intersection density. *WalkScore.com, March 20, 2014*

- The Baltimore metro area was identified as one of the worst cities for bed bugs in America by pest control company Orkin. The area ranked #27 out of 50 based on the number of bed bug treatments Orkin performed from January to December 2013. *Orkin, "Chicago Tops Bed Bug Cities List for Second Year in a Row," January 16, 2014*

- Baltimore was identified as one of 15 cities with the highest increase in bed bug activity in the U.S. by pest control provider Terminix. The city ranked #5.Criteria: cities with the largest percentage gains in bed bug customer calls from January–May 2013 compared to the same time period in 2012. *Terminix, "Cities with Highest Increases in Bed Bug Activity," July 9, 2013*

- Baltimore was selected as one of the 25 fattest cities in America by *Men's Fitness Online*. It ranked #8 out of America's 50 largest cities. Criteria: fitness centers and sport stores; nutrition; sports participation; TV viewing; overweight/sedentary; junk food; air quality; geography; commute; parks and open space; city recreational facilities; access to healthcare; motivation; mayor and city initiatives; state obesity initiatives. *Men's Fitness, "The Fittest and Fattest Cities in America," March 5, 2012*

- Baltimore was identified as a "2013 Spring Allergy Capital." The area ranked #67 out of 100. Three groups of factors were used to identify the most severe cities for people with allergies during the spring season: annual pollen levels; medicine utilization; access to board-certified allergists. *Asthma and Allergy Foundation of America, "Spring Allergy Capitals 2013"*

- Baltimore was identified as a "2013 Fall Allergy Capital." The area ranked #81 out of 100. Three groups of factors were used to identify the most severe cities for people with allergies during the fall season: annual pollen levels; medicine utilization; access to board-certified allergists. *Asthma and Allergy Foundation of America, "Fall Allergy Capitals 2013"*

- Baltimore was identified as a "2013 Asthma Capital." The area ranked #80 out of the nation's 100 largest metropolitan areas. Twelve factors were used to identify the most challenging places to live for people with asthma: estimated prevalence; self-reported prevalence; crude death rate for asthma; annual pollen score; annual air quality; public smoking laws; number of board-certified asthma specialists; school inhaler access laws; rescue medication use; controller medication use; uninsured rate; poverty rate. *Asthma and Allergy Foundation of America, "Asthma Capitals 2013"*

- *Men's Health* ranked 100 major U.S. cities in terms of the best and worst cities for men. Baltimore ranked #89. Criteria: thirty-three data points were examined covering health, fitness, and quality of life. *Men's Health, "The Best & Worst Cities for Men 2014," December 6, 2013*

- *Men's Health* ranked 100 U.S. cities in terms of the best and worst cities for women. Baltimore was ranked among the ten worst at #5. Criteria: dozens of statistical parameters of long life in the categories of health, quality of life, and fitness. *Men's Health, "The 10 Best and Worst Cities for Women 2011," January/February 2011*

- Baltimore was selected as one of the best metropolitan areas for hospital care in America by *HealthGrades.com*. The rankings are based on a comprehensive study of patient death and complication rates in the nation's nearly 5,000 hospitals. Hospitals performing in the top 5% nationwide across 26 different medical procedures and diagnoses were identified. *HealthGrades.com* then ranked cities by the highest percentage of these Distinguished Hospitals for Clinical Excellence™. The Baltimore metro area ranked #1. *HealthGrades.com, "America's Top 50 Cities for Hospital Care," January 21, 2012*

- The American Academy of Dermatology ranked 26 U.S. metropolitan regions in terms of their residents knowledge, attitude and behaviors towards tanning, sun protection and skin cancer detection. The Baltimore metro area ranked #10. The results of the study are based on an online survey of over 7,000 adults nationwide. *American Academy of Dermatology, "Suntelligence: How Sun Smart is Your City?," May 3, 2010*

- The Baltimore metro area appeared in the 2013 Gallup-Healthways Well-Being Index. The area ranked #98 out of 189. The Gallup-Healthways Well-Being Index score is an average of six sub-indexes, which individually examine life evaluation, emotional health, work environment, physical health, healthy behaviors, and access to basic necessities. Results are based on telephone interviews conducted as part of the Gallup-Healthways Well-Being Index survey January 2–December 29, 2012, and January 2–December 30, 2013, with a random sample of 531,630 adults, aged 18 and older, living in metropolitan areas in the 50 U.S. states and the District of Columbia. *Gallup-Healthways, "State of American Well-Being," March 25, 2014*

- The Baltimore metro area was identified as one of "America's Most Stressful Cities" by *Sperling's BestPlaces*. The metro area ranked #34 out of 50. Criteria: unemployment rate; suicide rate; commute time; mental health; poor rest; alcohol use; violent crime rate; property crime rate; cloudy days annually. *Sperling's BestPlaces, www.BestPlaces.net, "Stressful Cities 2012*

- The Baltimore metro area was identified as one of "America's Most Stressful Cities" by *Forbes*. The metro area ranked #12 out of 40. Criteria: housing affordability; unemployment rate; cost of living; air quality; traffic congestion; sunny days; population density. *Forbes.com, "America's Most Stressful Cities," September 23, 2011*

- *Men's Health* ranked 100 U.S. cities in terms of their activity levels. Baltimore was ranked #30 (#1 = most active city). Criteria: where and how often residents exercise; percentage of households that watch more than 15 hours of cable television a week and buy more than 11 video games a year; death rate from deep-vein thrombosis, a condition linked to sitting for extended periods of time. *Men's Health, "Where Sit Happens: The Most and Least Active Cities in America," June 20, 2011*

- Baltimore was selected as one of the "20 Most Livable U.S. Cities for Wheelchair Users" by the Christopher & Dana Reeve Foundation. The city ranked #17. Criteria: Medicaid eligibility and spending; access to physicians and rehabilitation facilities; access to fitness facilities and recreation; access to paratransit; percentage of people living with disabilities who are employed; clean air; climate. *Christopher & Dana Reeve Foundation, "20 Most Livable U.S. Cities for Wheelchair Users," July 26, 2010*

Real Estate Rankings

- Based on the home-price forecasts compiled by the real-estate valuation firm CoreLogic Case-Shiller, the finance website CNNMoney reported that in 2014, the Baltimore metro area is expected to place #7 among American metro areas in terms of increases in residential real estate prices. *money.cnn.com, "10 Hottest Housing Markets for 2014," January 23, 2014*

- NerdWallet identified the 10 U.S. cities among the 25 largest, most hospitable for recent college graduates, based on demographics; social life; accessibility; cost of living; and economic opportunity. Baltimore placed #4 as a destination for new young graduates. *http://www.nerdwallet.com, "Best Cities for Fresh College Graduates," May 30, 2013*

- Baltimore was ranked #144 out of 283 metro areas in terms of house price appreciation in 2013 (#1 = highest rate). *Federal Housing Finance Agency, House Price Index, 4th Quarter 2013*

- Baltimore was ranked #125 out of 224 metro areas in terms of housing affordability in 2013 by the National Association of Home Builders (#1 = most affordable). The NAHB-Wells Fargo Housing Opportunity Index (HOI) for a given area is defined as the share of homes sold in that area that would have been affordable to a family earning the local median income, based on standard mortgage underwriting criteria. *National Association of Home Builders®, NAHB-Wells Fargo Housing Opportunity Index, 4th Quarter 2013*

Safety Rankings

- Business Insider looked at the FBI's Uniform Crime Report to identify the U.S. cities with the most violent crime per capita, excluding localities with fewer than 100,000 residents. To judge by its relatively high murder, rape, and robbery data, Baltimore was ranked #9 (#1 = worst) among the 25 most dangerous cities. *www.businessinsider.com, "The 25 Most Dangerous Cities in America," June 13, 2013*

- To identify the most dangerous cities in America, 24/7 Wall Street focused on four categories—murder, rape, robbery, and aggravated assault—as reported in the FBI's June 2013 Preliminary Annual Uniform Crime Report. Criteria also included median income from American Community Survey and unemployment figures from Bureau of Labor Statistics. For cities with populations over 100,000, Baltimore was ranked #9. *247wallst.com, "The Most Dangerous Cities in America." June 13, 2013*

- Symantec, in partnership with Sperling's BestPlaces, ranked the 50 largest cities in the U.S. in terms of their vulnerability to cybercrime. The city ranked #18. Criteria: number of cyberattacks and potential infections; level of Internet access; expenditures on smartphones and computer hardware/software; wireless hotspots; broadband connectivity; Internet usage; online purchases. *Symantec, "Riskiest Online Cities of 2012" February 15, 2012*

- Allstate ranked the 200 largest cities in America in terms of driver safety. Baltimore ranked #193. Allstate researchers analyzed internal property damage claims over a two-year period from January 2010 to December 2011. A weighted average of the two-year numbers determined the annual percentages. *Allstate, "Allstate America's Best Drivers Report®, August 27, 2013"*

- The Baltimore metro area was identified as one of "America's Most Dangerous Cities" by *Forbes*. The area ranked #7 out of 10. Criteria: violent crime (murder and non-negligent manslaughter, forcible rape, robbery, and aggravated assault) rates per capita. The editors only considered metropolitan areas with populations above 200,000. *Forbes, "America's Most Dangerous Cities 2013," October 22, 2013*

- Baltimore was identified as one of the most dangerous large cities in America by CQ Press. All 32 cities with populations of 500,000 or more that reported crime rates in 2012 for murder, rape, robbery, aggravated assault, burglary, and motor vehicle thefts were ranked. The city ranked #2 out of the top 10. *CQ Press, City Crime Rankings 2014*

- Baltimore was identified as one of the most dangerous cities in America by *The Business Insider*. Criteria: cities with 100,000 residents or more were ranked by violent crime rate in 2011. Violent crimes include for murder, rape, robbery, and aggravated assault. The city ranked #9 out of 25. *The Business Insider, "The 25 Most Dangerous Cities in America," November 4, 2012*

- The National Insurance Crime Bureau ranked 380 metro areas in the U.S. in terms of per capita rates of vehicle theft. The Baltimore metro area ranked #93 (#1 = highest rate). Criteria: number of vehicle theft offenses per 100,000 inhabitants in 2012. *National Insurance Crime Bureau, "Hot Spots 2012," June 26, 2013*

- The Baltimore metro area was identified as one of the most dangerous metro areas for pedestrians by Transportation for America. The metro area ranked #32 out of 52 metro areas with over 1 million residents. Criteria: area's population divided by the number of pedestrian fatalities in that area. *Transportation for America, "Dangerous by Design 2011"*

Seniors/Retirement Rankings

- From its Best Cities for Successful Aging indexes, the Milken Institute generated rankings for metropolitan areas, weighing data in eight categories—general indicators, health care, wellness, living arrangements, transportation and general accessibility, financial well-being, education and employment, and community participation. The Baltimore metro area was ranked #13 overall in the large metro area category. *Milken Institute, "Best Cities for Successful Aging," July 2012*

- Bankers Life and Casualty Company, in partnership with Sperling's BestPlaces, ranked the nation's 50 largest metro areas in terms of the "Best U.S. Cities for Seniors." The Baltimore metro area ranked #15. Criteria: healthcare; transportation; housing; environment; economy; health and longevity; social and spiritual life; crime. *Bankers Life and Casualty Company, Center for a Secure Retirement, "Best U.S. Cities for Seniors 2011," September 2011*

Sports/Recreation Rankings

- *Card Player* magazine scoured North America to identify the top five metropolitan areas where a player can access the types of games that make launching a poker career possible. The Baltimore metro area ranked #5. *Card Player, "The Top Five Cities to Launch Your Poker Career," April 2, 2014*

- Baltimore appeared on the *Sporting News* list of the "Best Sports Cities" for 2011. The area ranked #29 out of 271. Criteria: the magazine takes a 12-month snapshot of each city's sports, putting a heavy premium on regular-season won-lost records (from the most recently completed season). Other criteria include: playoff berths, bowl appearances and tournament bids; championships; applicable power ratings; quality of competition; overall fan fervor (measured in part by attendance); abundance of teams (rewarding quality over quantity); stadium and arena quality; ticket availability and prices; franchise ownership; and marquee appeal of athletes. *Sporting News, "Best Sports Cities 2011," October 4, 2011*

- Baltimore appeared on the *Sporting News* list of the "Best Sports Cities" for 2011. The area ranked #29 out of 271. Criteria: a 12-month snapshot of regular-season won-lost records (from the most recently completed season). Other criteria include: playoff berths, bowl appearances and tournament bids; championships; applicable power ratings; quality of competition; overall fan fervor (measured in part by attendance); abundance of teams (quality over quantity); stadium and arena quality; ticket availability and prices; franchise ownership; and marquee appeal of athletes. *Sporting News, "Best Sports Cities 2011," October 4, 2011*

- Baltimore was chosen as a bicycle friendly community by the League of American Bicyclists. A "Bicycle Friendly Community" welcomes cyclists by providing safe accommodation for cycling and encouraging people to bike for transportation and recreation. There are four award levels: Platinum; Gold; Silver; and Bronze. The community achieved an award level of Bronze. *League of American Bicyclists, "Bicycle Friendly Community Master List," Fall 2013*

- Baltimore was selected as one of the most playful cities in the U.S. by KaBOOM! The organization's Playful City USA initiative honors cities and towns across the nation for a vision, plan and commitment to creating an agenda for play. Criteria: creating a local play commission or task force; designing an annual action plan for play; conducting a play space audit; outlining a financial investment in play for the current fiscal year; and proclaiming and celebrating an annual "play day." *KaBOOM! National Campaign for Play, "2013 Playful City USA Communities"*

Transportation Rankings

- Business Insider presented a Walk Score ranking of public transportation in 316 U.S. cities and thousands of city neighborhoods in which Baltimore earned the #8-ranked "Transit Score," awarded for frequency, type of route, and distance between stops. *www.businessinsider.com, "The US Cities with the Best Public Transportation Systems," January 30, 2014*

- NerdWallet surveyed average annual car insurance premiums in 125 U.S. cities to identify the least expensive U.S. cities in which to insure a car. Locations with no-fault insurance laws was a strong determinant. Baltimore came in at #30 for the most expensive rates. *www.nerdwallet.com, "Best Cities for Cheap Car Insurance," February 3, 2014*

- More U.S. households choose not to have a car in 2012 than in prior years, according to a study by the University of Michigan Transportation Research Institute. The business website 24/7 Wall Street examined that study, along with a 2010 Census Special Report to arrive at its ranking of cities in which the fewest households had a vehicle. Baltimore held the #6 position. *247wallst.com, "Cities Where No One Wants to Drive," February 6, 2014*

Women/Minorities Rankings

- The Daily Beast surveyed the nation's cities for highest percentage of singles and lowest divorce rate, plus other measures, to determine "emotional intelligence"—happiness, confidence, kindness—which, researchers say, has a strong correlation with people's satisfaction with their romantic relationships. Baltimore placed #15. *www.thedailybeast.com, "Best Cities to Find Love and Stay in Love," February 14, 2014*

- *Women's Health* examined U.S. cities and identified the 100 best cities for women. Baltimore was ranked #88. Criteria: 30 categories were examined from obesity and breast cancer rates to commuting times and hours spent working out. *Women's Health, "Best Cities for Women 2012"*

- The Baltimore metro area appeared on *Forbes'* list of the "Best Cities for Minority Entrepreneurs." The area ranked #88 out of 10. Criteria: 52 metropolitan statistical areas were examined. For each ethnicity (African Americans, Asians and Hispanics), the editors measured housing affordability, population growth, income growth, and entrepreneurship (per capita self-employment). *Forbes, "Best Cities for Minority Entrepreneurs," March 23, 2011*

Miscellaneous Rankings

- Baltimore was selected as a 2013 Digital Cities Survey winner. The city ranked #9 in the large city (250,000 or more population) category. The survey examined and assessed how city governments are utilizing information technology to operate and deliver quality service to their customers and citizens. Survey questions focused on implementation and adoption of online service delivery; planning and governance; and the infrastructure and architecture that make the transformation to digital government possible. *Center for Digital Government, "2013 Digital Cities Survey," November 7, 2013*

- The watchdog site Charity Navigator conducts an annual study of charities in the nation's major markets both to analyze statistical differences in their financial, accountability, and transparency practices and to track year-to-year variations in individual communities. The Baltimore metro area was ranked #19 among the 30 metro markets. *www.charitynavigator.org, "Metro Market Study 2013," June 1, 2013*

- Business Insider reports on the 2013 Trick-or-Treat Index compiled by the real estate site Zillow, which used its own Home Value Index and Walk Score along with population density and local crime stats to determine that Baltimore ranked #19 for "how much candy it gives out versus how far kids have to walk to get it." Zillow also zeroes in on the best neighborhoods in its top 20 cities. *www.businessinsider.com, "These Are the Best Cities for Trick-or-Treating," October 15, 2013*

- Baltimore appeared on *Travel + Leisure's* list of America's least attractive people. Criteria: cities were selected by readers in their annual America's Favorite Cities survey. The city ranked #7 out of 10. *Travel + Leisure, "America's Most and Least Attractive People," November 2013*

- *Men's Health* ranked 100 U.S. cities by their level of sadness. Baltimore was ranked #52 (#1 = saddest city). Criteria: suicide rates; unemployment rates; percentage of households that use antidepressants; percent of population who report feeling blue all or most of the time. *Men's Health, "Frown Towns," November 28, 2011*

- The Baltimore metro area was selected as one of "The Best U.S. Cities for Bargain Shopping" by *Forbes*. The area ranked #5 out of 10. Criteria: number of outlet stores; gross leasable retail space in major malls; low consumer price index; low sales tax rate. Indicators were examined in the nation's 50 largest metropolitan areas. *Forbes, "The Best U.S. Cities for Bargain Shopping," January 20, 2012*

- Energizer Personal Care, the makers of Edge® shave gel, in partnership with Sperling's BestPlaces, ranked 50 major metro areas in terms of everyday irritations. The Baltimore metro area ranked #3. Criteria: high male-to-female ratio; poor sports team performance and high ticket prices; slow traffic; lack of job availability; unaffordable housing; extreme weather; lack of nightlife and fitness options. *Energizer Personal Care, "Most Irritatng Cities for Guys," August 26, 2013*

- Mars Chocolate North America, the makers of COMBOS®, in partnership with Sperling's BestPlaces, ranked 50 major metro areas in terms of their "manliness." The Baltimore metro area ranked #35. Criteria: number of professional sports teams; number of nearby NASCAR tracks and racing events; manly lifestyle; concentration of manly retail stores; manly occupations per capita; salty snack sales; "Board of Manliness" rankings. *Mars Chocolate North America, "America's Manliest Cities 2012"*

- The National Alliance to End Homelessness ranked the 100 most populous metro areas in terms the rate of homelessness. The Baltimore metro area ranked #23. Criteria: number of homeless people per 10,000 population in 2011. *National Alliance to End Homelessness, The State of Homelessness in America 2012*

Business Environment

CITY FINANCES

City Government Finances

Component	2011 ($000)	2011 ($ per capita)
Total Revenues	4,141,733	6,497
Total Expenditures	3,962,407	6,216
Debt Outstanding	2,881,863	4,521
Cash and Securities[1]	4,530,018	7,106

Note: (1) Cash and security holdings of a government at the close of its fiscal year, including those of its dependent agencies, utilities, and liquor stores.
Source: U.S Census Bureau, State & Local Government Finances 2011

City Government Revenue by Source

Source	2011 ($000)	2011 ($ per capita)
General Revenue		
From Federal Government	228,925	359
From State Government	1,408,110	2,209
From Local Governments	38,005	60
Taxes		
Property	797,717	1,251
Sales and Gross Receipts	106,366	167
Personal Income	234,955	369
Corporate Income	0	0
Motor Vehicle License	0	0
Other Taxes	83,399	131
Current Charges	301,358	473
Liquor Store	0	0
Utility	129,292	203
Employee Retirement	600,165	942

Source: U.S Census Bureau, State & Local Government Finances 2011

City Government Expenditures by Function

Function	2011 ($000)	2011 ($ per capita)	2011 (%)
General Direct Expenditures			
Air Transportation	0	0	0.0
Corrections	0	0	0.0
Education	1,308,415	2,053	33.0
Employment Security Administration	0	0	0.0
Financial Administration	29,083	46	0.7
Fire Protection	148,966	234	3.8
General Public Buildings	39	< 1	< 0.1
Governmental Administration, Other	104,803	164	2.6
Health	133,396	209	3.4
Highways	194,088	304	4.9
Hospitals	0	0	0.0
Housing and Community Development	102,085	160	2.6
Interest on General Debt	45,472	71	1.1
Judicial and Legal	52,544	82	1.3
Libraries	23,890	37	0.6
Parking	13,165	21	0.3
Parks and Recreation	48,059	75	1.2
Police Protection	357,510	561	9.0
Public Welfare	0	0	0.0
Sewerage	149,673	235	3.8
Solid Waste Management	74,509	117	1.9
Veterans' Services	0	0	0.0
Liquor Store	0	0	0.0
Utility	120,980	190	3.1
Employee Retirement	301,919	474	7.6

Source: U.S Census Bureau, State & Local Government Finances 2011

DEMOGRAPHICS

Population Growth

Area	1990 Census	2000 Census	2010 Census	Population Growth (%)	
				1990-2000	2000-2010
City	736,014	651,154	620,961	-11.5	-4.6
MSA[1]	2,382,172	2,552,994	2,710,489	7.2	6.2
U.S.	248,709,873	281,421,906	308,745,538	13.2	9.7

Note: (1) Figures cover the Baltimore-Columbia-Towson, MD Metropolitan Statistical Area—see Appendix B
for areas included
Source: U.S. Census Bureau, Census 1990, 2000, 2010

Household Size

Area	Persons in Household (%)							Average Household Size
	One	Two	Three	Four	Five	Six	Seven or More	
City	39.4	28.1	15.2	9.1	4.9	1.8	1.6	2.48
MSA[1]	28.6	32.4	16.5	13.2	6.1	2.0	1.2	2.60
U.S.	27.6	33.5	15.7	13.2	6.1	2.4	1.5	2.63

Note: (1) Figures cover the Baltimore-Columbia-Towson, MD Metropolitan Statistical Area—see Appendix B
for areas included
Source: U.S. Census Bureau, 2010-2012 American Community Survey 3-Year Estimates

Race

Area	White Alone[2] (%)	Black Alone[2] (%)	Asian Alone[2] (%)	AIAN[3] Alone[2] (%)	NHOPI[4] Alone[2] (%)	Other Race Alone[2] (%)	Two or More Races (%)
City	30.1	63.4	2.4	0.3	0.0	1.5	2.3
MSA[1]	62.2	28.7	4.7	0.2	0.0	1.5	2.5
U.S.	74.0	12.6	4.9	0.8	0.2	4.7	2.8

Note: (1) Figures cover the Baltimore-Columbia-Towson, MD Metropolitan Statistical Area—see Appendix B
for areas included; (2) Alone is defined as not being in combination with one or more other races; (3) American
Indian and Alaska Native; (4) Native Hawaiian and Other Pacific Islander
Source: U.S. Census Bureau, 2010-2012 American Community Survey 3-Year Estimates

Hispanic or Latino Origin

Area	Total (%)	Mexican (%)	Puerto Rican (%)	Cuban (%)	Other (%)
City	4.3	1.3	0.6	0.2	2.3
MSA[1]	4.8	1.3	0.7	0.1	2.6
U.S.	16.6	10.7	1.6	0.6	3.7

Note: Persons of Hispanic or Latino origin can be of any race; (1) Figures cover the
Baltimore-Columbia-Towson, MD Metropolitan Statistical Area—see Appendix B for areas included
Source: U.S. Census Bureau, 2010-2012 American Community Survey 3-Year Estimates

Segregation

Type	Segregation Indices[1]				Percent Change		
	1990	2000	2010	2010 Rank[2]	1990-2000	1990-2010	2000-2010
Black/White	71.4	68.2	65.4	19	-3.2	-5.9	-2.8
Asian/White	38.3	41.1	43.6	33	2.8	5.3	2.5
Hispanic/White	30.2	35.8	39.8	67	5.6	9.6	4.0

Note: All figures cover the Metropolitan Statistical Area—see Appendix B for areas included; Figures are based
on an analysis of 1990, 2000, and 2010 Census Decennial Census tract data by William H. Frey, Brookings
Institution and the University of Michigan Social Science Data Analysis Network. In this analysis all racial
groups (whites, blacks, and asians) are non-Hispanic members of those races. Hispanics are shown as a
separate category;
(1) Segregation Indices are Dissimilarity Indices that measure the degree to which the minority group is
distributed differently than whites across census tracts. They range from 0 (complete integration) to 100
(complete segregation) where the value indicates the percentage of the minority group that needs to move to be
distributed exactly like whites; (2) Ranges from 1 (most segregated) to 102 (least segregated); n/a not available.
Source: www.CensusScope.org

Ancestry

Area	German	Irish	English	American	Italian	Polish	French[2]	Scottish	Dutch
City	7.5	6.6	3.5	2.3	3.4	2.5	0.7	0.8	0.6
MSA[1]	18.2	13.6	8.6	5.3	6.5	4.6	1.7	1.7	1.0
U.S.	15.2	11.1	8.2	7.2	5.6	3.1	2.8	1.7	1.4

Note: Figures are the percentage of the total population reporting a particular ancestry. The nine most commonly reported ancestries in the U.S. are shown. Figures include multiple ancestries (e.g. if a person reported being Irish and Italian, they were included in both columns); (1) Figures cover the Baltimore-Columbia-Towson, MD Metropolitan Statistical Area—see Appendix B for areas included; (2) Excludes Basque
Source: U.S. Census Bureau, 2010-2012 American Community Survey 3-Year Estimates

Foreign-Born Population

Area	Percent of Population Born in								
	Any Foreign Country	Mexico	Asia	Europe	Carribean	South America	Central America[2]	Africa	Canada
City	7.3	0.7	1.9	1.0	1.1	0.5	1.0	1.0	0.1
MSA[1]	9.3	0.5	3.7	1.3	0.7	0.5	1.1	1.2	0.2
U.S.	13.0	3.7	3.7	1.6	1.2	0.9	1.0	0.5	0.3

Note: (1) Figures cover the Baltimore-Columbia-Towson, MD Metropolitan Statistical Area—see Appendix B for areas included; (2) Excludes Mexico.
Source: U.S. Census Bureau, 2010-2012 American Community Survey 3-Year Estimates

Marital Status

Area	Never Married	Now Married[2]	Separated	Widowed	Divorced
City	52.1	25.9	4.2	7.1	10.8
MSA[1]	35.5	45.7	2.6	6.2	10.1
U.S.	32.4	48.4	2.2	6.0	11.0

Note: Figures are percentages and cover the population 15 years of age and older; (1) Figures cover the Baltimore-Columbia-Towson, MD Metropolitan Statistical Area—see Appendix B for areas included; (2) Excludes separated
Source: U.S. Census Bureau, 2010-2012 American Community Survey 3-Year Estimates

Age

Area	Percent of Population									Median Age
	Under Age 5	Age 5–19	Age 20–34	Age 35–44	Age 45–54	Age 55–64	Age 65–74	Age 75–84	Age 85+	
City	6.7	18.0	26.2	12.1	13.8	11.4	6.3	3.8	1.6	34.3
MSA[1]	6.2	19.4	20.8	13.0	15.3	12.4	7.0	4.1	1.8	38.2
U.S.	6.4	20.1	20.5	13.1	14.3	12.2	7.3	4.2	1.8	37.3

Note: (1) Figures cover the Baltimore-Columbia-Towson, MD Metropolitan Statistical Area—see Appendix B for areas included
Source: U.S. Census Bureau, 2010-2012 American Community Survey 3-Year Estimates

Gender

Area	Males	Females	Males per 100 Females
City	292,411	328,432	89.0
MSA[1]	1,316,630	1,417,508	92.9
U.S.	153,276,055	158,333,314	96.8

Note: (1) Figures cover the Baltimore-Columbia-Towson, MD Metropolitan Statistical Area—see Appendix B for areas included
Source: U.S. Census Bureau, 2010-2012 American Community Survey 3-Year Estimates

Religious Groups by Family

Area	Catholic	Baptist	Non-Den.	Methodist[2]	Lutheran	LDS[3]	Pente-costal	Presby-terian[4]	Muslim[5]	Judaism
MSA[1]	16.7	4.2	4.8	6.1	2.1	0.5	1.1	1.3	0.5	1.8
U.S.	19.1	9.3	4.0	4.0	2.3	2.0	1.9	1.6	0.8	0.7

Note: Figures are the number of adherents as a percentage of the total population; (1) Figures cover the Baltimore-Columbia-Towson, MD Metropolitan Statistical Area—see Appendix B for areas included; (2) Methodist/Pietist; (3) Latter Day Saints; (4) Reformed; (5) Figures are estimates
Source: Association of Statisticians of American Religious Bodies, 2010 U.S. Religion Census: Religious Congregations & Membership Study

Religious Groups by Tradition

Area	Catholic	Evangelical Protestant	Mainline Protestant	Other Tradition	Black Protestant	Orthodox
MSA[1]	16.7	9.9	8.3	3.2	3.5	0.5
U.S.	19.1	16.2	7.3	4.3	1.6	0.3

Note: Figures are the number of adherents as a percentage of the total population; (1) Figures cover the Baltimore-Columbia-Towson, MD Metropolitan Statistical Area—see Appendix B for areas included
Source: Association of Statisticians of American Religious Bodies, 2010 U.S. Religion Census: Religious Congregations & Membership Study

ECONOMY

Gross Metropolitan Product

Area	2011	2012	2013	2014	Rank[2]
MSA[1]	149.8	157.3	162.1	168.7	19

Note: Figures are in billions of dollars; (1) Figures cover the Baltimore-Columbia-Towson, MD Metropolitan Statistical Area—see Appendix B for areas included; (2) Rank is based on 2014 data and ranges from 1 to 363
Source: The United States Conference of Mayors, U.S. Metro Economies: Outlook—Gross Metropolitan Product, with Metro Employment Projections, November 2013

Economic Growth

Area	2011 (%)	2012 (%)	2013 (%)	2014 (%)	Rank[2]
MSA[1]	1.5	3.2	1.6	2.1	102
U.S.	1.6	2.5	1.7	2.5	–

Note: Figures are real gross metropolitan product (GMP) growth rates and represent annual average percent change; (1) Figures cover the Baltimore-Columbia-Towson, MD Metropolitan Statistical Area—see Appendix B for areas included; (2) Rank is based on 2013 data and ranges from 1 to 363
Source: The United States Conference of Mayors, U.S. Metro Economies: Outlook—Gross Metropolitan Product, with Metro Employment Projections, November 2013

Metropolitan Area Exports

Area	2007	2008	2009	2010	2011	2012	Rank[2]
MSA[1]	5,169.7	5,595.0	4,808.7	5,213.1	5,472.1	5,793.2	47

Note: Figures are in millions of dollars; (1) Figures cover the Baltimore-Columbia-Towson, MD Metropolitan Statistical Area—see Appendix B for areas included; (2) Rank is based on 2012 data and ranges from 1 to 369
Source: U.S. Department of Commerce, International Trade Administration, Office of Trade & Industry Information, Manufacturing & Services, data extracted April 1, 2014

INCOME

Income

Area	Per Capita ($)	Median Household ($)	Average Household ($)
City	23,326	39,788	56,287
MSA[1]	34,097	67,340	88,089
U.S.	27,385	51,771	71,579

Note: (1) Figures cover the Baltimore-Columbia-Towson, MD Metropolitan Statistical Area—see Appendix B for areas included
Source: U.S. Census Bureau, 2010-2012 American Community Survey 3-Year Estimates

Household Income Distribution

Area	Percent of Households Earning							
	Under $15,000	$15,000 -24,999	$25,000 -34,999	$35,000 -49,999	$50,000 -74,999	$75,000 -99,000	$100,000 -149,999	$150,000 and up
City	22.0	12.6	10.9	13.5	17.2	9.0	8.9	6.0
MSA[1]	10.3	7.8	8.0	11.1	17.7	13.0	17.1	15.1
U.S.	13.1	11.0	10.5	13.7	18.1	11.9	12.5	9.1

Note: (1) Figures cover the Baltimore-Columbia-Towson, MD Metropolitan Statistical Area—see Appendix B for areas included
Source: U.S. Census Bureau, 2010-2012 American Community Survey 3-Year Estimates

Poverty Rate

Area	All Ages	Under 18 Years Old	18 to 64 Years Old	65 Years and Over
City	25.2	36.5	22.8	18.0
MSA[1]	11.3	15.2	10.4	8.5
U.S.	15.7	22.2	14.6	9.3

Note: Figures are percentage of people whose income during the past 12 months was below the poverty level; (1) Figures cover the Baltimore-Columbia-Towson, MD Metropolitan Statistical Area—see Appendix B for areas included
Source: U.S. Census Bureau, 2010-2012 American Community Survey 3-Year Estimates

Personal Bankruptcy Filing Rate

Area	2008	2009	2010	2011	2012	2013
Baltimore city County	3.08	4.25	5.03	4.87	5.29	5.52
U.S.	3.53	4.61	4.97	4.37	3.76	3.29

Note: Numbers are per 1,000 population and include Chapter 7 and Chapter 13 filings
Source: Federal Deposit Insurance Corporation, Regional Economic Conditions, March 20, 2014

EMPLOYMENT

Labor Force and Employment

Area	Civilian Labor Force			Workers Employed		
	Dec. 2012	Dec. 2013	% Chg.	Dec. 2012	Dec. 2013	% Chg.
City	280,654	276,345	-1.5	253,248	252,991	-0.1
MSA[1]	1,483,033	1,465,478	-1.2	1,380,763	1,379,362	-0.1
U.S.	154,904,000	154,408,000	-0.3	143,060,000	144,423,000	1.0

Note: Data is not seasonally adjusted and covers workers 16 years of age and older; (1) Metropolitan Statistical Area—see Appendix B for areas included
Source: Bureau of Labor Statistics, Local Area Unemployment Statistics

Unemployment Rate

Area	2013											
	Jan.	Feb.	Mar.	Apr.	May	Jun.	Jul.	Aug.	Sep.	Oct.	Nov.	Dec.
City	10.5	9.7	9.5	9.3	10.0	11.1	10.7	10.3	9.4	9.9	9.0	8.5
MSA[1]	7.5	7.1	6.9	6.7	7.2	7.9	7.5	7.1	6.6	7.0	6.3	5.9
U.S.	8.5	8.1	7.6	7.1	7.3	7.8	7.7	7.3	7.0	7.0	6.6	6.5

Note: Data is not seasonally adjusted and covers workers 16 years of age and older; All figures are percentages; (1) Metropolitan Statistical Area—see Appendix B for areas included
Source: Bureau of Labor Statistics, Local Area Unemployment Statistics

Employment by Occupation

Occupation Classification	City (%)	MSA[1] (%)	U.S. (%)
Management, Business, Science, and Arts	37.2	44.2	36.0
Natural Resources, Construction, and Maintenance	6.2	7.3	9.1
Production, Transportation, and Material Moving	10.6	8.2	12.0
Sales and Office	23.9	24.4	24.7
Service	22.0	16.0	18.2

Note: Figures cover employed civilians 16 years of age and older; (1) Figures cover the Baltimore-Columbia-Towson, MD Metropolitan Statistical Area—see Appendix B for areas included
Source: U.S. Census Bureau, 2010-2012 American Community Survey 3-Year Estimates

Employment by Industry

Sector	MSA[1]		U.S.
	Number of Employees	Percent of Total	Percent of Total
Construction	n/a	n/a	4.2
Education and Health Services	255,900	18.9	15.5
Financial Activities	76,800	5.7	5.7
Government	233,000	17.2	16.1
Information	16,500	1.2	1.9
Leisure and Hospitality	122,200	9.0	10.2
Manufacturing	56,400	4.2	8.7
Mining and Logging	n/a	n/a	0.6
Other Services	54,200	4.0	3.9
Professional and Business Services	220,700	16.3	13.7
Retail Trade	146,100	10.8	11.4
Transportation and Utilities	46,200	3.4	3.8
Wholesale Trade	51,500	3.8	4.2

Note: Figures cover non-farm employment as of December 2013 and are not seasonally adjusted;
(1) Metropolitan Statistical Area—see Appendix B for areas included; n/a not available
Source: Bureau of Labor Statistics, Current Employment Statistics, Employment, Hours, and Earnings

Occupations with Greatest Projected Employment Growth: 2010 – 2020

Occupation[1]	2010 Employment	2020 Projected Employment	Numeric Employment Change	Percent Employment Change
Registered Nurses	49,340	62,420	13,090	26.5
Nursing Aides, Orderlies, and Attendants	31,640	39,440	7,790	24.6
Office Clerks, General	58,600	65,800	7,200	12.3
Combined Food Preparation and Serving Workers, Including Fast Food	41,520	48,670	7,150	17.2
Home Health Aides	11,570	18,420	6,850	59.3
Management Analysts	26,340	32,750	6,410	24.3
Business Operations Specialists, All Other	25,450	30,830	5,380	21.1
Retail Salespersons	74,740	80,000	5,260	7.0
Landscaping and Groundskeeping Workers	22,250	27,480	5,230	23.5
Personal Care Aides	9,530	14,680	5,160	54.1

Note: Projections cover Maryland; (1) Sorted by numeric employment change
Source: www.projectionscentral.com, State Occupational Projections, 2010–2020 Long-Term Projections

Fastest Growing Occupations: 2010 – 2020

Occupation[1]	2010 Employment	2020 Projected Employment	Numeric Employment Change	Percent Employment Change
Biomedical Engineers	390	670	280	71.7
Home Health Aides	11,570	18,420	6,850	59.3
Personal Care Aides	9,530	14,680	5,160	54.1
Occupational Therapy Assistants	490	740	240	49.6
Physical Therapist Aides	1,460	2,110	650	44.6
Physical Therapist Assistants	1,320	1,910	590	44.4
Diagnostic Medical Sonographers	1,040	1,480	440	42.6
Interpreters and Translators	860	1,220	360	41.9
Meeting, Convention, and Event Planners	1,820	2,580	760	41.6
Veterinary Technologists and Technicians	2,320	3,280	960	41.5

Note: Projections cover Maryland; (1) Sorted by percent employment change and excludes occupations with numeric employment change less than 100
Source: www.projectionscentral.com, State Occupational Projections, 2010–2020 Long-Term Projections

Average Wages

Occupation	$/Hr.	Occupation	$/Hr.
Accountants and Auditors	36.00	Maids and Housekeeping Cleaners	10.50
Automotive Mechanics	20.24	Maintenance and Repair Workers	19.11
Bookkeepers	20.50	Marketing Managers	56.97
Carpenters	20.24	Nuclear Medicine Technologists	38.66
Cashiers	10.05	Nurses, Licensed Practical	24.87
Clerks, General Office	15.04	Nurses, Registered	34.24
Clerks, Receptionists/Information	13.46	Nursing Assistants	13.96
Clerks, Shipping/Receiving	15.88	Packers and Packagers, Hand	10.58
Computer Programmers	40.57	Physical Therapists	39.05
Computer Systems Analysts	42.83	Postal Service Mail Carriers	24.68
Computer User Support Specialists	25.20	Real Estate Brokers	37.94
Cooks, Restaurant	12.96	Retail Salespersons	11.89
Dentists	88.28	Sales Reps., Exc. Tech./Scientific	33.94
Electrical Engineers	47.30	Sales Reps., Tech./Scientific	42.30
Electricians	26.52	Secretaries, Exc. Legal/Med./Exec.	17.78
Financial Managers	59.94	Security Guards	14.58
First-Line Supervisors/Managers, Sales	21.63	Surgeons	110.84
Food Preparation Workers	11.09	Teacher Assistants	14.30
General and Operations Managers	62.50	Teachers, Elementary School	29.50
Hairdressers/Cosmetologists	13.92	Teachers, Secondary School	29.30
Internists	101.04	Telemarketers	12.90
Janitors and Cleaners	11.93	Truck Drivers, Heavy/Tractor-Trailer	19.80
Landscaping/Groundskeeping Workers	13.56	Truck Drivers, Light/Delivery Svcs.	17.45
Lawyers	58.38	Waiters and Waitresses	9.18

Note: Wage data covers the Baltimore-Towson, MD Metropolitan Statistical Area—see Appendix B for areas included. Hourly wages for elementary/secondary school teachers and teacher assistants were calculated by the editors from annual wage data assuming a 40 hour work week; n/a not available.
Source: Bureau of Labor Statistics, Metro Area Occupational Employment and Wage Estimates, May 2013

RESIDENTIAL REAL ESTATE

Building Permits

Area	Single-Family			Multi-Family			Total		
	2012	2013	Pct. Chg.	2012	2013	Pct. Chg.	2012	2013	Pct. Chg.
City	164	220	34.1	566	1,037	83.2	730	1,257	72.2
MSA[1]	3,895	4,617	18.5	2,061	3,452	67.5	5,956	8,069	35.5
U.S.	518,695	620,802	19.7	310,963	370,020	19.0	829,658	990,822	19.4

Note: (1) Metropolitan Statistical Area—see Appendix B for areas included; figures represent new, privately-owned housing units authorized (unadjusted data); All permit data are based on estimates with imputation.
Source: U.S. Census Bureau, Manufacturing, Mining, and Construction Statistics, Building Permits, 2012, 2013

Homeownership Rate

Area	2006 (%)	2007 (%)	2008 (%)	2009 (%)	2010 (%)	2011 (%)	2012 (%)	2013 (%)
MSA[1]	72.9	71.2	69.3	67.7	65.7	66.8	66.1	66.0
U.S.	68.8	68.1	67.8	67.4	66.9	66.1	65.4	65.1

Note: (1) Figures cover the Baltimore-Columbia-Towson, MD Metropolitan Statistical Area—see Appendix B for areas included
Source: U.S. Census Bureau, Housing Vacancies and Homeownership Annual Statistics: 2013

Housing Vacancy Rates

Area	Gross Vacancy Rate[2] (%)			Year-Round Vacancy Rate[3] (%)			Rental Vacancy Rate[4] (%)			Homeowner Vacancy Rate[5] (%)		
	2011	2012	2013	2011	2012	2013	2011	2012	2013	2011	2012	2013
MSA[1]	11.7	11.7	10.5	11.6	11.4	10.2	10.7	9.7	9.5	2.8	2.2	1.8
U.S.	14.2	13.8	13.8	11.1	10.8	10.7	9.5	8.7	8.3	2.5	2.0	2.0

Note: (1) Figures cover the Baltimore-Columbia-Towson, MD Metropolitan Statistical Area—see Appendix B for areas included; (2) The percentage of the total housing inventory that is vacant; (3) The percentage of the housing inventory (excluding seasonal units) that is year-round vacant; (4) The percentage of rental inventory that is vacant for rent; (5) The percentage of homeowner inventory that is vacant for sale
Source: U.S. Census Bureau, Housing Vacancies and Homeownership Annual Statistics: 2013

TAXES

State Corporate Income Tax Rates

State	Tax Rate (%)	Income Brackets ($)	Num. of Brackets	Financial Institution Tax Rate (%)[a]	Federal Income Tax Ded.
Maryland	8.25	Flat rate	1	8.25	No

Note: Tax rates as of January 1, 2014; (a) Rates listed are the corporate income tax rate applied to financial institutions or excise taxes based on income. Some states have other taxes based upon the value of deposits or shares.
Source: Federation of Tax Administrators, "State Corporate Income Tax Rates, 2014"

State Individual Income Tax Rates

State	Tax Rate (%)	Income Brackets ($)	Num. of Brackets	Personal Exempt. ($)[1]		Fed. Inc. Tax Ded.
				Single	Dependents	
Maryland	2.0 - 5.75	1,000 - 250,000 (l)	8	3,200	3,200	No

Note: Tax rates as of January 1, 2014; Local- and county-level taxes are not included; n/a not applicable; (1) Married joint filers generally receive double the single exemption; (l) The income brackets reported for Maryland are for single individuals. For married couples filing jointly, the same tax rates apply to income brackets ranging from $1,000, to $300,000.
Source: Federation of Tax Administrators, "State Individual Income Tax Rates, 2014"

Various State and Local Tax Rates

State	State and Local Sales and Use (%)	State Sales and Use (%)	Gasoline[1] (¢/gal.)	Cigarette[2] ($/pack)	Spirits[3] ($/gal.)	Wine[4] ($/gal.)	Beer[5] ($/gal.)
Maryland	6.0	6.00	27.00	2.000	4.41 (f)(j)	1.38 (n)	0.45 (r)

Note: All tax rates as of January 1, 2014; (1) The American Petroleum Institute has developed a methodology for determining the average tax rate on a gallon of fuel. Rates may include any of the following: excise taxes, environmental fees, storage tank fees, other fees or taxes, general sales tax, and local taxes. In states where gasoline is subject to the general sales tax, or where the fuel tax is based on the average sale price, the average rate determined by API is sensitive to changes in the price of gasoline. States that fully or partially apply general sales taxes to gasoline: CA, CO, GA, IL, IN, MI, NY; (2) The federal excise tax of $1.0066 per pack and local taxes are not included; (3) Rates are those applicable to off-premise sales of 40% alcohol by volume (a.b.v.) distilled spirits in 750ml containers. Local excise taxes are excluded; (4) Rates are those applicable to off-premise sales of 11% a.b.v. non-carbonated wine in 750ml containers; (5) Rates are those applicable to off-premise sales of 4.7% a.b.v. beer in 12 ounce containers; (f) Different rates also applicable according to alcohol content, place of production, size of container, or place purchased (on- or off-premise or onboard airlines); (j) Includes sales taxes specific to alcoholic beverages; (n) Includes sales taxes specific to alcoholic beverages; (r) Includes sales taxes specific to alcoholic beverages.
Source: Tax Foundation, 2014 Facts & Figures: How Does Your State Compare?

State Business Tax Climate Index Rankings

State	Overall Rank	Corporate Tax Index Rank	Individual Income Tax Index Rank	Sales Tax Index Rank	Unemployment Insurance Tax Index Rank	Property Tax Index Rank
Maryland	41	15	46	8	40	41

Note: The index is a measure of how each state's tax laws affect economic performance. The lower the rank, the more favorable a state's tax system is for business. States without a given tax are given a ranking of 1. The scores/rankings for the District of Columbia do not affect other states. The 2014 index represents the tax climate as of July 1, 2013.
Source: Tax Foundation, State Business Tax Climate Index 2014

COMMERCIAL REAL ESTATE

Office Market

Market Area	Inventory (sq. ft.)	Vacancy Rate (%)	Under Construction (sq. ft.)	YTD Net Absorption (sq. ft.)	Total Average Asking Rent ($/sq. ft./year)
Baltimore	83,715,090	13.9	90,000	682,072	21.40
National	4,726,900,879	15.0	55,419,286	42,829,434	26.27

Source: Newmark Grubb Knight Frank, National Office Market Report, 4th Quarter 2013

Industrial/Warehouse/R&D Market

Market Area	Inventory (sq. ft.)	Vacancy Rate (%)	Under Construction (sq. ft.)	YTD Net Absorption (sq. ft.)	Total Average Asking Rent ($/sq. ft./year)
Baltimore	130,222,260	11.6	2,577,919	1,761,487	5.81
National	14,022,031,238	7.9	83,249,164	156,549,903	5.40

Source: Newmark Grubb Knight Frank, National Industrial Market Report, 4th Quarter 2013

COMMERCIAL UTILITIES

Typical Monthly Electric Bills

Area	Commercial Service ($/month)		Industrial Service ($/month)	
	1,500 kWh	40 kW demand 14,000 kWh	1,000 kW demand 200,000 kWh	50,000 kW demand 15,000,000 kWh
City	200	1,764	n/a	n/a
Average[1]	197	1,636	25,662	1,485,307

Note: Based on total rates in effect July 1, 2013; (1) average based on 180 utilities surveyed; n/a not available
Source: Edison Electric Institute, Typical Bills and Average Rates Report, Summer 2013

TRANSPORTATION

Means of Transportation to Work

Area	Car/Truck/Van		Public Transportation			Bicycle	Walked	Other Means	Worked at Home
	Drove Alone	Car-pooled	Bus	Subway	Railroad				
City	59.8	10.2	15.4	1.5	1.0	0.9	6.8	1.7	2.8
MSA[1]	76.4	9.4	4.4	0.9	0.8	0.2	2.6	1.1	4.1
U.S.	76.4	9.7	2.6	1.7	0.5	0.6	2.8	1.3	4.3

Note: Figures are percentages and cover workers 16 years of age and older; (1) Figures cover the Baltimore-Columbia-Towson, MD Metropolitan Statistical Area—see Appendix B for areas included
Source: U.S. Census Bureau, 2010-2012 American Community Survey 3-Year Estimates

Travel Time to Work

Area	Less Than 10 Minutes	10 to 19 Minutes	20 to 29 Minutes	30 to 44 Minutes	45 to 59 Minutes	60 to 89 Minutes	90 Minutes or More
City	7.2	25.6	23.1	23.8	7.5	7.7	5.2
MSA[1]	8.2	23.7	21.5	24.4	10.2	8.1	3.7
U.S.	13.5	29.8	20.9	20.1	7.5	5.6	2.5

Note: Figures are percentages and include workers 16 years old and over; (1) Figures cover the Baltimore-Columbia-Towson, MD Metropolitan Statistical Area—see Appendix B for areas included
Source: U.S. Census Bureau, 2010-2012 American Community Survey 3-Year Estimates

Travel Time Index

Area	1985	1990	1995	2000	2005	2010	2011
Urban Area[1]	1.07	1.14	1.14	1.17	1.23	1.23	1.23
Average[2]	1.09	1.14	1.16	1.19	1.23	1.18	1.18

Note: Travel Time Index—the ratio of travel time in the peak period to the travel time at free-flow conditions. For example, a value of 1.30 indicates a 20-minute free-flow trip takes 26 minutes in the peak. Free-flow speeds (60 mph on freeways and 35 mph on principal arterials) are used as the comparison threshold; (1) Covers the Baltimore MD urban area; (2) average of 498 urban areas
Source: Texas Transportation Institute, Urban Mobility Report 2012, December 2012

Public Transportation

Agency Name / Mode of Transportation	Vehicles Operated in Maximum Service	Annual Unlinked Passenger Trips (in thous.)	Annual Passenger Miles (in thous.)
Maryland Transit Administration (MTA)			
Bus (directly operated)	599	73,574.8	228,817.7
Commuter Bus (purchased transportation)	192	4,290.5	181,152.0
Commuter Rail (purchased transportation)	132	8,532.2	257,908.1
Demand Response (directly operated)	41	118.6	966.9
Demand Response (purchased transportation)	281	1,419.6	13,010.2
Demand Response Taxi (purchased transportation)	32	345.8	1,516.3
Heavy Rail (directly operated)	54	15,199.1	77,435.6
Light Rail (directly operated)	38	8,796.3	57,500.6

Source: Federal Transit Administration, National Transit Database, 2012

Air Transportation

Airport Name and Code / Type of Service	Passenger Airlines[1]	Passenger Enplanements	Freight Carriers[2]	Freight (lbs.)
Baltimore-Washington International (BWI)				
Domestic service (U.S. carriers - 2013)	37	10,711,204	17	99,732,411
International service (U.S. carriers - 2012)	15	191,621	4	2,773,844

Note: (1) Includes all U.S.-based major, minor and commuter airlines that carried at least one passenger during the year; (2) Includes all U.S.-based airlines and freight carriers that transported at least one lb. of freight during the year.
Source: Bureau of Transportation Statistics, The Intermodal Transportation Database, Air Carriers: T-100 Domestic Market (U.S. Carriers), 2013; Bureau of Transportation Statistics, The Intermodal Transportation Database, Air Carriers: T-100 International Market (U.S. Carriers), 2012

Other Transportation Statistics

Major Highways:	I-70; I-83; I-95; I-97
Amtrak Service:	Yes
Major Waterways/Ports:	Chesapeake Bay; Port of Baltimore

Source: Amtrak.com; Google Maps

BUSINESSES

Major Business Headquarters

Company Name	Rankings	
	Fortune[1]	Forbes[2]
Whiting-Turner Contracting	-	117

Note: (1) Fortune 500—companies that produce a 10-K are ranked 1 to 500 based on 2012 revenue; (2) all private companies with at least $2 billion in annual revenue through the end of their most current fiscal year are ranked 1 to 224; companies listed are headquartered in the city; dashes indicate no ranking
Source: Fortune, "Fortune 500," May 20, 2013; Forbes, "America's Largest Private Companies," December 18, 2013

Fast-Growing Businesses

According to *Inc.*, Baltimore is home to one of America's 500 fastest-growing private companies: **Videology** (#136). Criteria: must be an independent, privately-held, for-profit, U.S. corporation, proprietorship or partnership; revenues must be at least $100,000 in 2009 and $2 million in 2012; must have four-year operating/sales history. Holding companies, regulated banks, and utilities were excluded. *Inc., "America's 500 Fastest-Growing Private Companies," September 2013*

According to *Fortune*, Baltimore is home to one of the 100 fastest-growing companies in the world: **Under Armour** (#53). Companies were ranked by their revenue growth rate; their EPS growth rate; and their three-year annualized total return to investors for the period ending June 30, 2013. Criteria for inclusion: a company, foreign or domestic, must trade on a major U.S. stock exchange; must file quarterly reports with the SEC; must have a minimum market capitalization of $250 million; must have a stock price of at least $5 on June 29, 2013; must have been trading continuously since June 30, 2009; must have revenue and net income for the four quarters ended on or before April 30, 2013, of at least $50 million and $10 million, respectively; and must have posted a compound annual growth in revenue and earnings per share of at least 20% annually over the three years ending on or before April 30, 2013. REITs, limited-liability companies, limited parterships, companies about to be acquired, and companies that lost money in the quarter ending April 30, 2013 were excluded. *Fortune, "100 Fastest-Growing Companies," August 29, 2013*

According to *Initiative for a Competitive Inner City (ICIC)*, Baltimore is home to three of America's 100 fastest-growing "inner city" companies: **Ellicott Dredge Enterprises** (#58); **Intelect Corporation** (#93); **Marlin Steel Wire Products** (#96). Companies were ranked by their five-year compound annual growth rate. Criteria for inclusion: company must be headquartered in or have 51 percent or more of its physical operations in an economically distressed urban area; must be an independent, for-profit corporation, partnership or proprietorship; must have 10 or more employees and have a five-year sales history that includes sales of at least $200,000 in the base year and at least $1 million in the current year with no decrease in sales over the two most recent years. *Initiative for a Competitive Inner City (ICIC), "Inner City 100 Companies, 2013"*

According to Deloitte, Baltimore is home to one of North America's 500 fastest-growing high-technology companies: **Millennial Media** (#73). Companies are ranked by percentage growth in revenue over a five-year period. Criteria for inclusion: company must be headquartered within North America; must own proprietary intellectual property or proprietary technology that contributes to a significant portion of the company's operating revenue, or devote a significant proportion of revenues to research and development of technology; must have been in business for a minumum of five years with 2008 operating revenues of at least $50,000 USD/CD and 2012 operating revenues of at least $5 million USD/CD. *Deloitte Touche Tohmatsu, 2013 Technology Fast 500*[TM]

Minority Business Opportunity

Baltimore is home to one company which is on the *Black Enterprise* Bank 20 list (20 largest banks based on total assets, capital, deposits and loans, including mortgage-backed securities for the calendar year): **Harbor Bancshares Corp. (The Harbor Bank of Maryland)** (#11). Only commercial banks or savings and loans that are classified by the Federal Reserve as black institutions and have been fully operational for the previous calendar year were considered. *Black Enterprise, B.E. 100s, 2013*

Baltimore is home to one company which is on the *Black Enterprise* Asset Manager 15 list (15 largest asset management firms based on assets under management): **Brown Capital Management** (#8). Criteria: company must have been operational in previous calendar year and be at least 51% black-owned. *Black Enterprise, B.E. 100s, 2013*

Minority- and Women-Owned Businesses

Group	All Firms		Firms with Paid Employees			
	Firms	Sales ($000)	Firms	Sales ($000)	Employees	Payroll ($000)
Asian	2,513	927,608	1,253	872,318	5,039	110,334
Black	14,644	871,760	857	629,208	6,537	214,999
Hispanic	893	375,439	271	356,009	1,624	131,983
Women	15,634	1,746,248	1,509	1,491,634	11,804	382,914
All Firms	42,272	83,536,324	10,393	82,403,619	314,323	15,839,540

Note: Figures cover firms located in the city; minority- and women-owned business are defined as firms in which the corresponding group own 51% or more of the stock or equity of the company
Source: U.S. Census Bureau, 2007 Economic Census, Survey of Business Owners (2012 Survey of Business Owners data will be released starting in June 2015)

HOTELS & CONVENTION CENTERS

Hotels/Motels

Area	5 Star		4 Star		3 Star		2 Star		1 Star		Not Rated	
	Num.	Pct.[3]	Num.	Pct.[3]	Num.	Pct.[3]	Num.	Pct.[3]	Num.	Pct.[3]	Num.	Pct.[3]
City[1]	1	0.5	5	2.7	76	40.9	80	43.0	6	3.2	18	9.7
Total[2]	142	0.9	1,005	6.0	5,147	30.9	8,578	51.4	408	2.4	1,397	8.4

Note: (1) Figures cover Baltimore and vicinity; (2) Figures cover all 100 cities in this book; (3) Percentage of hotels which have a given star rating; Star ratings are determined by expedia.com and offer an indication of the general quality of a particular hotel.
Source: expedia.com, April 7, 2014

Major Convention Centers

Name	Overall Space (sq. ft.)	Exhibit Space (sq. ft.)	Meeting Space (sq. ft.)	Meeting Rooms
Baltimore Convention Center	1,225,000	300,000	85,000	50

Note: Table includes convention centers located in the Baltimore-Columbia-Towson, MD metro area; n/a not available

Source: Original research

Living Environment

COST OF LIVING

Cost of Living Index

Composite Index	Groceries	Housing	Utilities	Trans-portation	Health Care	Misc. Goods/ Services
112.6	105.0	154.6	102.5	98.7	95.0	93.4

Note: The Cost of Living Index measures regional differences in the cost of consumer goods and services, excluding taxes and non-consumer expenditures, for professional and managerial households in the top income quintile. It is based on more than 50,000 prices covering almost 60 different items for which prices are collected three times a year by chambers of commerce, economic development organizations or university applied economic centers in each participating urban area. The numbers shown should be read as a percentage above or below the national average of 100. For example, a value of 115.4 in the groceries column indicates that grocery prices are 15.4% higher than the national average. Small differences in the index numbers should not be interpreted as significant; Figures cover the Baltimore MD urban area.
Source: The Council for Community and Economic Research, ACCRA Cost of Living Index, 2013

Grocery Prices

Area[1]	T-Bone Steak ($/pound)	Frying Chicken ($/pound)	Whole Milk ($/half gal.)	Eggs ($/dozen)	Orange Juice ($/64 oz.)	Coffee ($/11.5 oz.)
City[2]	10.49	1.39	2.55	2.28	3.57	4.85
Avg.	10.19	1.28	2.34	1.81	3.48	4.39
Min.	8.56	0.94	1.44	1.19	2.78	3.40
Max.	14.82	2.28	3.56	3.73	6.23	7.32

*Note: (1) Values for the local area are compared with the average, minimum and maximum values for all 327 areas in the Cost of Living Index; (2) Figures cover the Baltimore MD urban area; **T-Bone Steak** (price per pound); **Frying Chicken** (price per pound, whole fryer); **Whole Milk** (half gallon carton); **Eggs** (price per dozen, Grade A, large); **Orange Juice** (64 oz. Tropicana or Florida Natural); **Coffee** (11.5 oz. can, vacuum-packed, Maxwell House, Hills Bros, or Folgers).*
Source: The Council for Community and Economic Research, ACCRA Cost of Living Index, 2013

Housing and Utility Costs

Area[1]	New Home Price ($)	Apartment Rent ($/month)	All Electric ($/month)	Part Electric ($/month)	Other Energy ($/month)	Telephone ($/month)
City[2]	447,890	1,432	-	90.68	78.22	28.11
Avg.	295,864	900	171.38	91.82	70.12	27.73
Min.	185,506	458	117.80	48.81	33.67	17.16
Max.	1,358,917	3,783	441.68	171.40	372.65	39.47

*Note: (1) Values for the local area are compared with the average, minimum and maximum values for all 327 areas in the Cost of Living Index; (2) Figures cover the Baltimore MD urban area; **New Home Price** (2,400 sf living area, 8,000 sf lot, in urban area with full utilities); **Apartment Rent** (950 sf 2 bedroom/1.5 or 2 bath, unfurnished, excluding all utilities except water); **All Electric** (average monthly cost for an all-electric home); **Part Electric** (average monthly cost for a part-electric home); **Other Energy** (average monthly cost for natural gas, fuel oil, coal, wood, and any other forms of energy except electricity); **Telephone** (price includes basic monthly rate for a private residential line plus additional local usage charges incurred by a family of four).*
Source: The Council for Community and Economic Research, ACCRA Cost of Living Index, 2013

Health Care, Transportation, and Other Costs

Area[1]	Doctor ($/visit)	Dentist ($/visit)	Optometrist ($/visit)	Gasoline ($/gallon)	Beauty Salon ($/visit)	Men's Shirt ($)
City[2]	82.09	84.36	70.43	3.48	43.32	26.88
Avg.	101.40	86.48	96.16	3.44	33.87	26.55
Min.	61.67	50.83	50.12	3.08	18.92	12.48
Max.	182.71	152.50	223.78	4.33	68.22	52.03

*Note: (1) Values for the local area are compared with the average, minimum and maximum values for all 327 areas in the Cost of Living Index; (2) Figures cover the Baltimore MD urban area; **Doctor** (general practitioners routine exam of an established patient); **Dentist** (adult teeth cleaning and periodic oral examination); **Optometrist** (full vision eye exam for established adult patient); **Gasoline** (one gallon regular unleaded, national brand, including all taxes, cash price at self-service pump if available); **Beauty Salon** (woman's shampoo, trim, and blow-dry); **Men's Shirt** (cotton/polyester dress shirt, pinpoint weave, long sleeves).*
Source: The Council for Community and Economic Research, ACCRA Cost of Living Index, 2013

HOUSING

House Price Index (HPI)

Area	National Ranking[2]	Quarterly Change (%)	One-Year Change (%)	Five-Year Change (%)
MSA[1]	144	0.25	2.06	-11.68
U.S.[3]	–	1.20	7.69	4.18

Note: The HPI is a weighted repeat sales index. It measures average price changes in repeat sales or refinancings on the same properties. This information is obtained by reviewing repeat mortgage transactions on single-family properties whose mortgages have been purchased or securitized by Fannie Mae or Freddie Mac in January 1975; (1) Baltimore-Columbia-Towson, MD Metropolitan Statistical Area—see Appendix B for areas included; (2) Rankings are based on annual percentage change for all metro areas containing at least 15,000 transactions over the last 10 years and ranges from 1 to 283; (3) figures based on a weighted average of Census Division estimates using a seasonally adjusted, purchase-only index; all figures are for the period ending December 31, 2013
Source: Federal Housing Finance Agency, House Price Index, February 25, 2014

Median Single-Family Home Prices

Area	2011	2012	2013p	Percent Change 2012 to 2013
MSA[1]	230.0	206.0	251.9	22.3
U.S. Average	166.2	177.2	197.4	11.4

Note: Figures are median sales prices of existing single-family homes in thousands of dollars; (p) preliminary; n/a not available; (1) Baltimore-Columbia-Towson, MD Metropolitan Statistical Area—see Appendix B for areas included
Source: National Association of Realtors, Median Sales Price of Existing Single-Family Homes for Metropolitan Areas, 4th Quarter 2013

Qualifying Income Based on Median Sales Price of Existing Single-Family Homes

Area	With 5% Down ($)	With 10% Down ($)	With 20% Down ($)
MSA[1]	55,724	52,791	46,926
U.S. Average	45,395	43,006	38,228

Note: Figures are preliminary; Qualifying income is based on a mortgage rate of 4.4%. Monthly principal and interest payment is limited to 25% of income; n/a not available; (1) Baltimore-Columbia-Towson, MD Metropolitan Statistical Area—see Appendix B for areas included
Source: National Association of Realtors, Qualifying Income Based on Median Sales Price of Existing Single-Family Homes for Metropolitan Areas, 4th Quarter 2013

Median Apartment Condo-Coop Home Prices

Area	2011	2012	2013p	Percent Change 2012 to 2013
MSA[1]	182.8	185.1	196.6	6.2
U.S. Average	165.1	173.7	194.9	12.2

Note: Figures are median sales prices of existing apartment condo-coop homes in thousands of dollars; (p) preliminary; n/a not available; (1) Baltimore-Columbia-Towson, MD Metropolitan Statistical Area—see Appendix B for areas included
Source: National Association of Realtors, Median Sales Price of Existing Apartment Condo-Coop Homes for Metropolitan Areas, 4th Quarter 2013

Gross Monthly Rent

Area	Under $200	$200 -299	$300 -499	$500 -749	$750 -999	$1,000 -1,499	$1,500 and up	Median ($)
City	5.1	6.0	7.9	14.9	26.0	28.5	11.5	900
MSA[1]	2.8	3.4	4.6	9.1	21.5	36.3	22.3	1,099
U.S.	1.7	3.3	8.1	22.7	24.3	25.7	14.3	889

Note: Figures are percentages except for Median; Gross rent is the contract rent plus the estimated average monthly cost of utilities (electricity, gas, and water and sewer) and fuels (oil, coal, kerosene, wood, etc.) if these are paid by the renter (or paid for the renter by someone else); (1) Figures cover the Baltimore-Columbia-Towson, MD Metropolitan Statistical Area—see Appendix B for areas included
Source: U.S. Census Bureau, 2010-2012 American Community Survey 3-Year Estimates

Year Housing Structure Built

Area	2010 or Later	2000 -2009	1990 -1999	1980 -1989	1970 -1979	1960 -1969	1950 -1959	1940 -1949	Before 1940	Median Year
City	0.1	3.6	3.3	4.7	5.8	8.6	15.8	13.8	44.3	1944
MSA[1]	0.4	10.3	13.2	14.2	13.5	10.5	13.9	7.3	16.8	1971
U.S.	0.5	14.9	13.8	13.9	15.9	11.1	10.9	5.5	13.5	1976

Note: Figures are percentages except for Median Year; (1) Figures cover the Baltimore-Columbia-Towson, MD Metropolitan Statistical Area—see Appendix B for areas included
Source: U.S. Census Bureau, 2010-2012 American Community Survey 3-Year Estimates

HEALTH

Health Risk Data

Category	MSA[1] (%)	U.S. (%)
Adults aged 18–64 who have any kind of health care coverage	86.2	79.6
Adults who reported being in good or excellent health	83.5	83.1
Adults who are current smokers	18.5	19.6
Adults who are heavy drinkers[2]	5.3	6.1
Adults who are binge drinkers[3]	17.7	16.9
Adults who are overweight (BMI 25.0 - 29.9)	36.1	35.8
Adults who are obese (BMI 30.0 - 99.8)	27.4	27.6
Adults who participated in any physical activities in the past month	76.6	77.1
Adults 50+ who have ever had a sigmoidoscopy or colonoscopy	72.0	67.3
Women aged 40+ who have had a mammogram within the past two years	79.0	74.0
Men aged 40+ who have had a PSA test within the past two years	49.1	45.2
Adults aged 65+ who have had flu shot within the past year	66.1	60.1
Adults who always wear a seatbelt	96.1	93.8

Note: Data as of 2012 unless otherwise noted; (1) Figures cover the Baltimore-Towson, MD Metropolitan Statistical Area—see Appendix B for areas included; (2) Heavy drinkers are classified as males having more than two drinks per day or females having more than one drink per day; (3) Binge drinkers are classified as males having five or more drinks on one occasion or females having four or more drinks on one occasion
Source: Centers for Disease Control and Prevention, Behaviorial Risk Factor Surveillance System, SMART: Selected Metropolitan/Micropolitan Area Risk Trends, 2012

Chronic Health Indicators

Category	MSA[1] (%)	U.S. (%)
Adults who have ever been told they had a heart attack	4.1	4.5
Adults who have ever been told they had a stroke	2.8	2.9
Adults who have been told they currently have asthma	10.0	8.9
Adults who have ever been told they have arthritis	25.3	25.7
Adults who have ever been told they have diabetes[2]	10.0	9.7
Adults who have ever been told they had skin cancer	4.4	5.7
Adults who have ever been told they had any other types of cancer	5.8	6.5
Adults who have ever been told they have COPD	6.0	6.2
Adults who have ever been told they have kidney disease	2.3	2.5
Adults who have ever been told they have a form of depression	16.3	18.0

Note: Data as of 2012 unless otherwise noted; (1) Figures cover the Baltimore-Towson, MD Metropolitan Statistical Area—see Appendix B for areas included; (2) Figures do not include pregnancy-related, borderline, or pre-diabetes
Source: Centers for Disease Control and Prevention, Behaviorial Risk Factor Surveillance System, SMART: Selected Metropolitan/Micropolitan Area Risk Trends, 2012

Mortality Rates for the Top 10 Causes of Death in the U.S.

ICD-10[a] Sub-Chapter	ICD-10[a] Code	Age-Adjusted Mortality Rate[1] per 100,000 population	
		County[2]	U.S.
Malignant neoplasms	C00-C97	228.8	174.2
Ischaemic heart diseases	I20-I25	177.8	119.1
Other forms of heart disease	I30-I51	49.2	49.6
Chronic lower respiratory diseases	J40-J47	39.7	43.2
Cerebrovascular diseases	I60-I69	51.9	40.3
Organic, including symptomatic, mental disorders	F01-F09	45.0	30.5
Other degenerative diseases of the nervous system	G30-G31	13.1	26.3
Other external causes of accidental injury	W00-X59	19.2	25.1
Diabetes mellitus	E10-E14	32.0	21.3
Hypertensive diseases	I10-I15	45.6	18.8

Note: (a) ICD-10 = International Classification of Diseases 10th Revision; (1) Mortality rates are a three year average covering 2008-2010; (2) Figures cover Baltimore city
Source: Centers for Disease Control and Prevention, National Center for Health Statistics. Compressed Mortality File 1999-2010 on CDC WONDER Online Database, released January 2013. Data are compiled from the Compressed Mortality File 1999-2010, Series 20 No. 2P, 2013.

Mortality Rates for Selected Causes of Death

ICD-10[a] Sub-Chapter	ICD-10[a] Code	Age-Adjusted Mortality Rate[1] per 100,000 population	
		County[2]	U.S.
Assault	X85-Y09	29.9	5.5
Diseases of the liver	K70-K76	16.3	12.4
Human immunodeficiency virus (HIV) disease	B20-B24	31.1	3.0
Influenza and pneumonia	J09-J18	21.8	16.4
Intentional self-harm	X60-X84	7.9	11.8
Malnutrition	E40-E46	*0.9	0.8
Obesity and other hyperalimentation	E65-E68	2.5	1.6
Renal failure	N17-N19	18.6	13.6
Transport accidents	V01-V99	8.5	12.6
Viral hepatitis	B15-B19	5.2	2.2

Note: (a) ICD-10 = International Classification of Diseases 10th Revision; (1) Mortality rates are a three year average covering 2008-2010; (2) Figures cover Baltimore city; (*) Unreliable data as per CDC
Source: Centers for Disease Control and Prevention, National Center for Health Statistics. Compressed Mortality File 1999-2010 on CDC WONDER Online Database, released January 2013. Data are compiled from the Compressed Mortality File 1999-2010, Series 20 No. 2P, 2013.

Health Insurance Coverage

Area	With Health Insurance	With Private Health Insurance	With Public Health Insurance	Without Health Insurance	Population Under Age 18 Without Health Insurance
City	86.6	54.2	42.1	13.4	5.3
MSA[1]	90.8	74.2	28.2	9.2	4.0
U.S.	84.9	65.4	30.4	15.1	7.5

Note: Figures are percentages that cover the civilian noninstitutionalized population; (1) Figures cover the Baltimore-Columbia-Towson, MD Metropolitan Statistical Area—see Appendix B for areas included
Source: U.S. Census Bureau, 2010-2012 American Community Survey 3-Year Estimates

Number of Medical Professionals

Area[1]	MDs[2]	DOs[2,3]	Dentists	Podiatrists	Chiropractors	Optometrists
Local (number)	5,701	99	339	35	61	69
Local (rate[4])	918.1	15.9	54.5	5.6	9.8	11.1
U.S. (rate[4])	267.6	19.6	61.7	5.6	24.7	14.5

Note: Data as of 2012 unless noted; (1) Local data covers Baltimore City; (2) Data as of 2011; (3) Doctor of Osteopathic Medicine; (4) rate per 100,000 population
Source: Area Resource File (ARF) 2012-2013. U.S. Department of Health and Human Services, Health Resources and Services Administration, Bureau of Health Professions

Best Hospitals

According to *U.S. News,* the Baltimore-Columbia-Towson, MD metro area is home to five of the best hospitals in the U.S.: **Johns Hopkins Hospital** (Honor Roll/15 specialties); **Sheppard and Enoch Pratt Hospital** (1 specialty); **MedStar Union Memorial Hospital** (1 specialty); **University of Maryland Medical Center** (5 specialties); **MedStar Franklin Square Medical Center** (1 specialty). The hospitals listed were nationally ranked in at least one adult specialty. Only 147 hospitals nationwide were nationally ranked in one or more specialties. Eighteen hospitals in the U.S. made the Honor Roll by ranking near the top in at least six specialties.*U.S. News Online, "America's Best Hospitals 2013-14"*

According to *U.S. News,* the Baltimore-Columbia-Towson, MD metro area is home to one of the best children's hospitals in the U.S.: **Johns Hopkins Children's Center** (Honor Roll). The hospital listed was highly ranked in at least one pediatric specialty. Eighty-seven hospitals in the U.S. ranked in at least one specialty. Ten children's hospitals in the U.S. made the Honor Roll by ranking near the top in three or more specialties.*U.S. News Online, "America's Best Children's Hospitals 2013-14"*

EDUCATION

Public School District Statistics

District Name	Schls	Pupils	Pupil/ Teacher Ratio	Minority Pupils[1] (%)	Free Lunch Eligible[2] (%)	IEP[3] (%)
Baltimore City Public Schools	195	84,212	15.2	92.0	77.8	16.9

Note: Table includes school districts with 2,000 or more students; (1) Percentage of students that are not non-Hispanic white; (2) Percentage of students that are eligible for the free lunch program; (3) Percentage of students that have an Individualized Education Program.
Source: U.S. Department of Education, National Center for Education Statistics, Common Core of Data, Local Education Agency (School District) Universe Survey: School Year 2011-2012; U.S. Department of Education, National Center for Education Statistics, Common Core of Data, Public Elementary/Secondary School Universe Survey: School Year 2011-2012

Best High Schools

High School Name	Rank[1]	Grad. Rate[2] (%)	Coll.[3] (%)	AP/IB/ AICE Tests[4]	AP/IB/ AICE Score[5]	SAT Score[6]	ACT Score[6]
Baltimore City College	1460	95	80	0.6	2.7	1370	n/a
Baltimore Polytechnic Institute	977	99	93	0.4	2.9	1434	n/a
Baltimore School for the Arts	435	97	100	0.2	4.2	1538	n/a
Loch Raven H.S.	906	92	94	0.5	3.0	1562	23.0
Perry Hall H.S.	1511	92	76	0.4	3.3	1512	20.2
Pikesville H.S.	1270	90	90	0.2	3.2	1514	22.0
Western School of Technology and Environmental Science	1274	99	81	0.4	3.2	1450	n/a

Note: (1) Public schools are ranked from 1 to 2,000 based on the following self-reported statistics (with the corresponding weight used in calculating their overall score). Schools that were newly founded and did not have a graduating senior class in 2012 were excluded; (2) Four-year, on-time graduation rate (25%); (3) Percent of 2011 graduates who were accepted to college (25%); (4) AP/IB/AICE tests taken per student (25%); (5) Average AP/IB/AICE exam score (10%); (6) Average SAT and/or ACT score (10%); Percent of students enrolled in at least one AP/IB/AICE course (5%)—data not shown; n/a not available
Source: Newsweek and The Daily Beast, "America's Best High Schools 2013"

Highest Level of Education

Area	Less than H.S.	H.S. Diploma	Some College, No Deg.	Associate Degree	Bachelor's Degree	Master's Degree	Prof. School Degree	Doctorate Degree
City	20.7	29.4	19.5	4.3	14.1	7.7	2.5	1.7
MSA[1]	11.4	26.5	20.0	6.4	20.4	10.8	2.6	1.9
U.S.	14.1	28.3	21.3	7.8	18.0	7.5	1.9	1.2

Note: Figures cover persons age 25 and over; (1) Figures cover the Baltimore-Columbia-Towson, MD Metropolitan Statistical Area see Appendix B for areas included
Source: U.S. Census Bureau, 2010-2012 American Community Survey 3-Year Estimates

Educational Attainment by Race

Area	High School Graduate or Higher (%)					Bachelor's Degree or Higher (%)				
	Total	White	Black	Asian	Hisp.[2]	Total	White	Black	Asian	Hisp.[2]
City	79.3	84.5	76.7	91.5	57.7	26.1	47.1	13.0	70.4	20.1
MSA[1]	88.6	91.2	83.6	91.1	68.7	35.7	39.9	21.8	61.8	25.4
U.S.	85.9	88.1	82.5	85.5	63.1	28.6	30.0	18.4	50.2	13.4

Note: Figures shown cover persons 25 years old and over; (1) Figures cover the Baltimore-Columbia-Towson, MD Metropolitan Statistical Area—see Appendix B for areas included; (2) People of Hispanic origin can be of any race
Source: U.S. Census Bureau, 2010-2012 American Community Survey 3-Year Estimates

School Enrollment by Grade and Control

Area	Preschool (%)		Kindergarten (%)		Grades 1 - 4 (%)		Grades 5 - 8 (%)		Grades 9 - 12 (%)	
	Public	Private	Public	Private	Public	Private	Public	Private	Public	Private
City	71.0	29.0	83.2	16.8	88.5	11.5	85.3	14.7	87.8	12.2
MSA[1]	48.4	51.6	84.3	15.7	87.1	12.9	85.2	14.8	85.5	14.5
U.S.	56.9	43.1	87.8	12.2	89.9	10.1	90.0	10.0	90.8	9.2

Note: Figures shown cover persons 3 years old and over; (1) Figures cover the Baltimore-Columbia-Towson, MD Metropolitan Statistical Area—see Appendix B for areas included
Source: U.S. Census Bureau, 2010-2012 American Community Survey 3-Year Estimates

Average Salaries of Public School Classroom Teachers

Area	2012-13		2013-14		Percent Change 2012-13 to 2013-14	Percent Change 2003-04 to 2013-14
	Dollars	Rank[1]	Dollars	Rank[1]		
Maryland	64,248	8	64,868	8	0.96	29.1
U.S. Average	56,103	–	56,689	–	1.04	21.8

Note: (1) State rank ranges from 1 to 51 where 1 indicates highest salary.
Source: National Education Association, Rankings & Estimates: Rankings of the States 2013 and Estimates of School Statistics 2014, March 2014

Higher Education

Four-Year Colleges			Two-Year Colleges			Medical Schools[1]	Law Schools[2]	Voc/ Tech[3]
Public	Private Non-profit	Private For-profit	Public	Private Non-profit	Private For-profit			
5	9	0	2	0	2	2	2	7

Note: Figures cover institutions located within the city limits and include main campuses only; (1) includes schools accredited by the Liaison Committee on Medical Education and the American Osteopathic Association's Commission on Osteopathic College Accreditation; (2) includes ABA-accredited schools, schools with provisional ABA accreditation, and state accredited schools; (3) includes all schools with programs that are less than 2 years.
Source: National Center for Education Statistics, Integrated Postsecondary Education System (IPEDS), 2012-13; Association of American Medical Colleges, Member List, April 24, 2014; American Osteopathic Association, Member List, April 24, 2014; Law School Admission Council, Official Guide to ABA-Approved Law Schools Online, April 24, 2014; Wikipedia, List of Medical Schools in the United States, April 24, 2014; Wikipedia, List of Law Schools in the United States, April 24, 2014

According to U.S. News & World Report, the Baltimore-Columbia-Towson, MD metro area is home to two of the best national universities in the U.S.: **Johns Hopkins University** (#12); **University of Maryland–Baltimore County** (#158). The indicators used to capture academic quality fall into a number of categories: assessment by administrators at peer institutions; retention of students; faculty resources; student selectivity; financial resources; alumni giving; high school counselor ratings of colleges; and graduation rate. U.S. News & World Report, "America's Best Colleges 2014"

According to U.S. News & World Report, the Baltimore-Columbia-Towson, MD metro area is home to four of the best liberal arts colleges in the U.S.: **United States Naval Academy** (#12); **Goucher College** (#110); **Saint John's College** (#123); **McDaniel College** (#126). The indicators used to capture academic quality fall into a number of categories: assessment by administrators at peer institutions; retention of students; faculty resources; student selectivity; financial resources; alumni giving; high school counselor ratings of colleges; and graduation rate. U.S. News & World Report, "America's Best Colleges 2014"

According to *U.S. News & World Report,* the Baltimore-Columbia-Towson, MD metro area is home to one of the top 100 law schools in the U.S.: **University of Maryland (Carey) (#41)**. The rankings are based on a weighted average of 12 measures of quality: peer assessment score; assessment score by lawyers/judges; median LSAT scores; median undergrad GPA; acceptance rate; employment rates for graduates; placement success; bar passage rate; faculty resources; expenditures per student; student/faculty ratio; and library resources. *U.S. News & World Report, "America's Best Graduate Schools, Law, 2014"*

PRESIDENTIAL ELECTION

2012 Presidential Election Results

Area	Obama	Romney	Other
Baltimore City	87.0	11.3	1.7
U.S.	51.0	47.2	1.8

Note: Results are percentages and may not add to 100% due to rounding
Source: Dave Leip's Atlas of U.S. Presidential Elections

EMPLOYERS

Major Employers

Company Name	Industry
Baltimore Washington Medical System	General medical and surgical hospitals
Care Source	Employment agencies
CareFirst	Hospital and medical service plans
E2 Acquisition Corporation	Steel foundries
Good Samaritan Hospital of Maryland	General medical and surgical hospitals
Greater Baltimore Medical Center	General medical and surgical hospitals
Howard County of Maryland	County supervisors' and executives' office
Johns Hopkins Bayview Medical Center	General medical and surgical hospitals
Johns Hopkins Medicine	General medical and surgical hospitals
Loyola University in Maryland	Colleges and universities
National Railroad Passenger Corporation	Interurban railways
Northrop Grumman Systems Corporation	Infrared sensors, solid state
Oxford-Columbia Associates	Apartment building operators
Park North-Oxford Associates	Apartment building operators
Social Security Administration	Administration of general economic programs
St Agnes HealthCare	General medical and surgical hospitals
St Joseph Medical Center	General medical and surgical hospitals
State Police, Maryland	State police
The Johns Hopkins University	Colleges and universities
Union Memorial Hospital	General medical and surgical hospitals

Note: Companies shown are located within the Baltimore-Columbia-Towson, MD Metropolitan Statistical Area.
Source: Hoovers.com; Wikipedia

Best Companics to Work For

Erickson Living; Johns Hopkins Medicine, headquartered in Baltimore, are among the "100 Best Places to Work in IT." To qualify, companies, both public and private, had to have a minimum of 50 IT employees and were selected based on average salary and bonus increases, the percentage of IT staffers promoted, IT staff turnover rates, training and development programs, and the percentage of women and minorities in IT staff and management positions. In addition, *Computerworld* looked at retention efforts, programs for recognizing and rewarding outstanding performances, and benefits such as flextime, elder care and child care, and reimbursement for college tuition and the cost of pursuing technology certifications. *Computerworld, "100 Best Places to Work in IT 2013"*

PUBLIC SAFETY

Crime Rate

Area	All Crimes	Violent Crimes				Property Crimes		
		Murder	Forcible Rape	Robbery	Aggrav. Assault	Burglary	Larceny -Theft	Motor Vehicle Theft
City	6,065.5	34.9	50.4	576.4	743.6	1,242.3	2,781.4	636.6
Suburbs[1]	2,883.2	2.1	16.7	107.8	264.4	456.0	1,886.6	149.5
Metro[2]	3,605.5	9.5	24.4	214.2	373.2	634.5	2,089.7	260.1
U.S.	3,246.1	4.7	26.9	112.9	242.3	670.2	1,959.3	229.7

Note: Figures are crimes per 100,000 population; (1) All areas within the metro area that are located outside the city limits; (2) Figures cover the Baltimore-Columbia-Towson, MD Metropolitan Statistical Area—see Appendix B for areas included
Source: FBI Uniform Crime Reports, 2012

Hate Crimes

Area	Number of Quarters Reported	Bias Motivation				
		Race	Religion	Sexual Orientation	Ethnicity	Disability
City	4	1	0	0	0	0
U.S.	4	2,797	1,099	1,135	667	92

Source: Federal Bureau of Investigation, Hate Crime Statistics 2012

Identity Theft Consumer Complaints

Area	Complaints	Complaints per 100,000 Population	Rank[2]
MSA[1]	2,532	93.4	59
U.S.	290,056	91.8	-

Note: (1) Figures cover the Baltimore-Columbia-Towson, MD Metropolitan Statistical Area—see Appendix B for areas included; (2) Rank ranges from 1 to 377 where 1 indicates greatest number of identity theft complaints per 100,000 population
Source: Federal Trade Commission, Consumer Sentinel Network Data Book for January–December 2013

Fraud and Other Consumer Complaints

Area	Complaints	Complaints per 100,000 Population	Rank[2]
MSA[1]	14,242	525.4	12
U.S.	1,811,724	595.2	-

Note: (1) Figures cover the Baltimore-Columbia-Towson, MD Metropolitan Statistical Area—see Appendix B for areas included; (2) Rank ranges from 1 to 377 where 1 indicates greatest number of identity theft complaints per 100,000 population
Source: Federal Trade Commission, Consumer Sentinel Network Data Book for January–December 2013

RECREATION

Culture

Dance[1]	Theatre[1]	Instrumental Music[1]	Vocal Music[1]	Series and Festivals	Museums and Art Galleries[2]	Zoos and Aquariums[3]
1	7	6	5	8	57	2

Note: (1) Number of professional performing groups; (2) Based on organizations with primary SIC code 8412; (3) AZA-accredited
Source: The Grey House Performing Arts Directory, 2013; Association of Zoos & Aquariums, AZA Member Zoos & Aquariums, April 2014; www.AccuLeads.com, May 1, 2014

Professional Sports Teams

Team Name	League	Year Established
Baltimore Orioles	Major League Baseball (MLB)	1954
Baltimore Ravens	National Football League (NFL)	1996

Note: Includes teams located in the Baltimore-Columbia-Towson, MD Metropolitan Statistical Area.
Source: Wikipedia, Major Professional Sports Teams of the United States and Canada

CLIMATE

Average and Extreme Temperatures

Temperature	Jan	Feb	Mar	Apr	May	Jun	Jul	Aug	Sep	Oct	Nov	Dec	Yr.
Extreme High (°F)	75	79	87	94	98	100	104	105	100	92	86	77	105
Average High (°F)	41	44	53	65	74	83	87	85	79	68	56	45	65
Average Temp. (°F)	33	36	44	54	64	73	77	76	69	57	47	37	56
Average Low (°F)	24	26	34	43	53	62	67	66	58	46	37	28	45
Extreme Low (°F)	-7	-3	6	20	32	40	50	45	35	25	13	0	-7

Note: Figures cover the years 1950-1990
Source: National Climatic Data Center, International Station Meteorological Climate Summary, 9/96

Average Precipitation/Snowfall/Humidity

Precip./Humidity	Jan	Feb	Mar	Apr	May	Jun	Jul	Aug	Sep	Oct	Nov	Dec	Yr.
Avg. Precip. (in.)	2.9	3.0	3.5	3.3	3.7	3.7	3.9	4.2	3.4	3.0	3.2	3.3	41.2
Avg. Snowfall (in.)	6	7	4	Tr	Tr	0	0	0	0	Tr	1	4	21
Avg. Rel. Hum. 7am (%)	72	71	71	71	77	79	80	83	85	83	78	74	77
Avg. Rel. Hum. 4pm (%)	56	53	48	47	52	53	53	55	55	54	55	57	53

Note: Figures cover the years 1950-1990; Tr = Trace amounts (<0.05 in. of rain; <0.5 in. of snow)
Source: National Climatic Data Center, International Station Meteorological Climate Summary, 9/96

Weather Conditions

Temperature			Daytime Sky			Precipitation		
10°F & below	32°F & below	90°F & above	Clear	Partly cloudy	Cloudy	0.01 inch or more precip.	0.1 inch or more snow/ice	Thunder-storms
6	97	31	91	143	131	113	13	27

Note: Figures are average number of days per year and cover the years 1950-1990
Source: National Climatic Data Center, International Station Meteorological Climate Summary, 9/96

HAZARDOUS WASTE

Superfund Sites

Baltimore has one hazardous waste site on the EPA's Superfund Final National Priorities List: **Kane & Lombard Street Drums**. *U.S. Environmental Protection Agency, Final National Priorities List, April 26, 2014*

AIR & WATER QUALITY

Air Quality Index

Area	Percent of Days when Air Quality was...[2]					AQI Statistics[2]	
	Good	Moderate	Unhealthy for Sensitive Groups	Unhealthy	Very Unhealthy	Maximum	Median
MSA[1]	58.4	40.3	1.4	0.0	0.0	111	46

Note: (1) Data covers the Baltimore-Columbia-Towson, MD Metropolitan Statistical Area—see Appendix B for areas included; (2) Based on 365 days with AQI data in 2013. Air Quality Index (AQI) is an index for reporting daily air quality. EPA calculates the AQI for five major air pollutants regulated by the Clean Air Act: ground-level ozone, particle pollution (aka particulate matter), carbon monoxide, sulfur dioxide, and nitrogen dioxide. The AQI runs from 0 to 500. The higher the AQI value, the greater the level of air pollution and the greater the health concern. There are six AQI categories: "Good" AQI is between 0 and 50. Air quality is considered satisfactory; "Moderate" AQI is between 51 and 100. Air quality is acceptable; "Unhealthy for Sensitive Groups" When AQI values are between 101 and 150, members of sensitive groups may experience health effects; "Unhealthy" When AQI values are between 151 and 200 everyone may begin to experience health effects; "Very Unhealthy" AQI values between 201 and 300 trigger a health alert; "Hazardous" AQI values over 300 trigger warnings of emergency conditions (not shown).
Source: U.S. Environmental Protection Agency, Air Quality Index Report, 2013

Air Quality Index Pollutants

| Area | Percent of Days when AQI Pollutant was...[2] | | | | | |
	Carbon Monoxide	Nitrogen Dioxide	Ozone	Sulfur Dioxide	Particulate Matter 2.5	Particulate Matter 10
MSA[1]	0.0	4.4	37.5	0.3	57.8	0.0

Note: (1) Data covers the Baltimore-Columbia-Towson, MD Metropolitan Statistical Area—see Appendix B for areas included; (2) Based on 365 days with AQI data in 2013. The Air Quality Index (AQI) is an index for reporting daily air quality. EPA calculates the AQI for five major air pollutants regulated by the Clean Air Act: ground-level ozone, particle pollution (also known as particulate matter), carbon monoxide, sulfur dioxide, and nitrogen dioxide. The AQI runs from 0 to 500. The higher the AQI value, the greater the level of air pollution and the greater the health concern.
Source: U.S. Environmental Protection Agency, Air Quality Index Report, 2013

Air Quality Trends: Ozone

	2003	2004	2005	2006	2007	2008	2009	2010	2011	2012
MSA[1]	0.083	0.082	0.089	0.089	0.086	0.084	0.072	0.085	0.087	0.083

Note: (1) Data covers the Baltimore-Columbia-Towson, MD Metropolitan Statistical Area—see Appendix B for areas included. The values shown are the composite ozone concentration averages among trend sites based on the highest fourth daily maximum 8-hour concentration in parts per million. These trends are based on sites having an adequate record of monitoring data during the trend period. Data from exceptional events are included.
Source: U.S. Environmental Protection Agency, Air Quality Monitoring Information, "Air Quality Trends by City, 2000-2012"

Maximum Air Pollutant Concentrations: Particulate Matter, Ozone, CO and Lead

	Particulate Matter 10 (ug/m^3)	Particulate Matter 2.5 Wtd AM (ug/m^3)	Particulate Matter 2.5 24-Hr (ug/m^3)	Ozone (ppm)	Carbon Monoxide (ppm)	Lead (ug/m^3)
MSA[1] Level	31	11.1	25	0.087	2	n/a
NAAQS[2]	150	15	35	0.075	9	0.15
Met NAAQS[2]	Yes	Yes	Yes	No	Yes	n/a

Note: (1) Data covers the Baltimore-Columbia-Towson, MD Metropolitan Statistical Area—see Appendix B for areas included; Data from exceptional events are included; (2) National Ambient Air Quality Standards; ppm = parts per million; ug/m^3 = micrograms per cubic meter; n/a not available.
Concentrations: Particulate Matter 10 (coarse particulate)—highest second maximum 24-hour concentration; Particulate Matter 2.5 Wtd AM (fine particulate)—highest weighted annual mean concentration; Particulate Matter 2.5 24-Hour (fine particulate)—highest 98th percentile 24-hour concentration; Ozone—highest fourth daily maximum 8-hour concentration; Carbon Monoxide—highest second maximum non-overlapping 8-hour concentration; Lead—maximum running 3-month average
Source: U.S. Environmental Protection Agency, Air Quality Monitoring Information, "Air Quality Statistics by City, 2012"

Maximum Air Pollutant Concentrations: Nitrogen Dioxide and Sulfur Dioxide

	Nitrogen Dioxide AM (ppb)	Nitrogen Dioxide 1-Hr (ppb)	Sulfur Dioxide AM (ppb)	Sulfur Dioxide 1-Hr (ppb)	Sulfur Dioxide 24-Hr (ppb)
MSA[1] Level	16	56	n/a	19	n/a
NAAQS[2]	53	100	30	75	140
Met NAAQS[2]	Yes	Yes	n/a	Yes	n/a

Note: (1) Data covers the Baltimore-Columbia-Towson, MD Metropolitan Statistical Area—see Appendix B for areas included; Data from exceptional events are included; (2) National Ambient Air Quality Standards; ppm = parts per million; ug/m^3 = micrograms per cubic meter; n/a not available.
Concentrations: Nitrogen Dioxide AM—highest arithmetic mean concentration; Nitrogen Dioxide 1-Hr—highest 98th percentile 1-hour daily maximum concentration; Sulfur Dioxide AM—highest annual mean concentration; Sulfur Dioxide 1-Hr—highest 99th percentile 1-hour daily maximum concentration; Sulfur Dioxide 24-Hr—highest second maximum 24-hour concentration
Source: U.S. Environmental Protection Agency, Air Quality Monitoring Information, "Air Quality Statistics by City, 2012"

Drinking Water

Water System Name	Pop. Served	Primary Water Source Type	Violations[1]	
			Health Based	Monitoring/ Reporting
City of Baltimore	1,600,000	Surface	1	0

Note: (1) Based on violation data from January 1, 2013 to December 31, 2013 (includes unresolved violations from earlier years)
Source: U.S. Environmental Protection Agency, Office of Ground Water and Drinking Water, Safe Drinking Water Information System (based on data extracted February 10, 2014)

Drinking Water

Water System Name	Pop. Served	Primary Water Source Type	Violations		
			Health Based	Monitoring Reporting
City of Baltimore	1,600,000	Surface	4	0

Note (†): Based on violation data from January 1, 2011 to December 31, 2014 (includes open and closed violations from current year).

Source: U.S. Environmental Protection Agency, Office of Ground Water and Drinking Water, Safe Drinking Water Information System (based on data extracted February 10, 2014).

Boston, Massachusetts

Background

Who would think that Boston, a city founded upon the Puritan principles of hard work, plain living, sobriety, and unyielding religious conviction, would be known for such a radical act of throwing tea overboard from a ship? The answer lies in the wealth upon which Boston grew: ship trading. Boston sea captains reaped more profits from West Indies molasses, mahogany from Honduras, and slaves from Guinea than did the English, who decided to impose additional taxes upon her colonial subjects. In defiance, Samuel Adams led the Sons of Liberty to throw a precious cargo of tea, so dear to the English, overboard. Events escalated, and the American Revolution began.

After the Revolution, Boston continued to grow into the Yankee capital that it is today. Metropolitan Boston is the site of nearly 80 institutions of higher learning. Boston's largest universities are Boston University, Northeastern University, University of Massachusetts/Boston, and Boston College. Cambridge, across the Charles River, is home to both the Massachusetts Institute of Technology (MIT) and Harvard University, which is undergoing significant expansion into nearby Allston.

Boston's moniker is "The Hub." The largest city in the six-state New England region, it has been recognized not only as a city of historic importance in the American Revolution, but as a leading educational and medical center and as a site for historic architecture and world class cultural institutions.

Historic Faneuil Hall and the nearby Quincy Market have been renovated into a historical attraction and a festival marketplace of food and shopping. The Back Bay and fashionable Newbury Street offers art galleries, fashion boutiques, and open-air cafes draw tourists and local residents. The Fenway neighborhood is home to the Boston Symphony Orchestra, Boston Pops, Berklee College of Music, Gardner Museum, and New England Conservatory. Along the city's downtown waterfront are the Museum of Science, New England Aquarium, and the Children's Museum.

Boston's historic buildings include Trinity Church, with its brilliant stained glass windows, and built in 1877. The African meeting house on Beacon Hill is the oldest surviving black church in North America. Christ Church (Old North Church) is the oldest church in Boston (1723), and was part of Paul Revere's ride. Modern architecture include the John Hancock Tower by I.M. Pei and luxury hotels, including the Ritz Carlton Boston Common and the Four Seasons.

The TD Garden is home to the Boston Bruins and the Boston Celtics and a venue for concerts, shows and conventions. Gillette Stadium, a 68,000 seat outdoor coliseum for football, soccer and other events opened in 2002 in nearby Foxboro. Fenway Park, the oldest major league ballpark still in use, is home to the Boston Red Sox, 2013 World Series winners. In 2011, the legendary field completed major renovations. Deep pride in their sports teams is a known characteristic of Bostonians. In addition to Red Sox victories, the Celtics won the 2008 NBA championship, and the city established a team in Women's Professional Soccer League in 2009, the Boston Breakers.

The Boston Marathon is the world's oldest annual marathon and best-known road racing event. During the 2013 race, nearly three hours after the winners crossed the finish line, two explosions occurred close to the end of the course, halting the race and preventing many from finishing. Three spectators were killed and more than 200 people were injured. Two brothers, allegedly motivated by extremist Islamist beliefs, planted the two bombs. One brother was later killed by police and the other was taken into custody after an extensive search.

Boston's colleges and universities have a major impact on the city's economy, attracting high-tech industries including computer hardware and software and biotech companies such as Genzyme, Biogen Idec, Millennium Pharmaceuticals, and Millipore. Boston receives the largest amount of annual funding from the National Institutes of Health of all cities in the United States.

Boston's weather is influenced by both tropical and polar air masses; proximity to several low-pressure storm tracks, and by its moderating East Coast location. Summer heat is relieved by sea breezes. Cold winters are often alleviated by the relatively warm ocean. In October 2012, Hurricane Sandy delivered severe winds and power outages throughout the city, interrupting train and air service.

Rankings

General Rankings

- Among the 50 largest U.S. cities, Boston placed #12 in Vocativ's "semi-exhaustive, mostly scientific" city Livability Index for people aged 35 and under. Average salary, unemployment rates, rents, and other living costs were considered, along with bike lanes, low-cost broadband, cheap takeout, self-service laundries, the price of a pint of Guinness, music venues, and vintage clothing stores. *vocative.com, "The Livability Index: The Best U.S. Cities for People 35 and Under," November 7, 2013*

- Boston was selected as one of America's best cities by *Bloomberg Businessweek*. The city ranked #4 out of 50. Criteria: leisure attributes (the number of restaurants, bars, libraries, museums, professional sports teams, and park acres by population); educational attributes (public school performance, the number of colleges, and graduate degree holders); economic factors (2011 income and June and July 2012 unemployment); crime; and air quality. *Bloomberg BusinessWeek, "America's Best Cities," September 26, 2012*

- Boston appeared on RelocateAmerica's list of best places to live in America. The annual "Top 100 Places to Live" list recognizes the top communities as nominated by their residents & local businesses. RelocateAmerica's Research Group determined the list based on review of various data gathered for economic, employment, housing, education, industry, opportunity, environment and recreation along with feedback from area leaders and residents. *RelocateAmerica.com, "Top 100 Places to Live for 2011"*

- Boston was selected as one the best places to live in America by *Outside Magazine*. Criteria: ample trailheads; nearby adventure; great farmers' markets; competitive gear-shop scene. *Outside Magazine, "Outside's Best Towns 2013," September 2013*

- Boston was selected as one of "America's Favorite Cities." The city ranked #19 in the "Quality of Life and Visitor Experience: Cleanliness" category. Respondents to an online survey were asked to rate 35 top urban destinations in the U.S. from a visitor's perspective. Criteria: cleanliness. *Travel + Leisure, "America's Favorite Cities 2013"*

- Boston was selected as one of "America's Favorite Cities." The city ranked #15 in the "Type of Trip: Gay-friendly" category. Respondents to an online survey were asked to rate 35 top urban destinations in the U.S. from a visitor's perspective. Criteria: gay-friendly. *Travel + Leisure, "America's Favorite Cities 2013"*

- Mercer Human Resources Consulting ranked 221 cities worldwide in terms of overall quality of life. Boston ranked #35. Criteria: political, social, economic, and socio-cultural factors; medical and health considerations; schools and education; public services and transportation; recreation; consumer goods; housing; and natural environment. *Mercer Human Resources Consulting, "Mercer 2012 Quality of Living Survey,"December 4, 2012*

- The U.S. Conference of Mayors and Waste Management sponsor the City Livability Awards Program. The awards recognize and honor mayors for exemplary leadership in developing and implementing programs that improve the quality of life in America's cities. Boston received an Outstanding Achievement Award in the large cities category. *U.S. Conference of Mayors, "2012 City Livability Awards"*

Business/Finance Rankings

- Measuring indicators of "tolerance"—the nonjudgmental environment that "attracts open-minded and new-thinking kinds of people"— as well as concentrations of technological and economic innovators, analysts identified the most creative American metro areas. On the resulting 2012 Creativity Index, the Boston metro area placed #3. *www.thedailybeast.com, "Boulder, Ann Arbor, Tucson & More: 20 Most Creative U.S. Cities," June 26, 2012*

- TransUnion ranked the nation's metro areas by average credit score, calculated on the VantageScore system, developed by the three major credit-reporting bureaus—TransUnion, Experian, and Equifax. The Boston metro area was among the ten cities with the highest collective credit score, meaning that its residents posed the lowest average consumer credit risk. *www.usatoday.com, "Metro Areas' Average Credit Rating Revealed," February 7, 2013*

- Building on the U.S. Department of Labor's Occupational Information Network Data Collection Program, the Brookings Institution defined STEM occupations and job opportunities for STEM workers at various levels of educational attainment. The Boston metro area was placed among the ten large metro areas with the highest demand for high-level STEM knowledge. *www.brookings.edu, "The Hidden Stem Economy," June 10, 2013*

- Boston was the #5-ranked city in a Seedtable analysis of the world's most active cities for start-up companies, as reported by Statista. *www.statista.com, "San Francisco Has the Most Active Start-Up Scene," August 21, 2013*

- The business website 24/7 Wall Street drew on the Brookings Institution's report "The Hidden STEM Economy" to identify the proportion of workers in the nation's largest metropolitan areas that were employed in jobs requiring knowledge in the science, technology, engineering, or math (STEM) fields. The Boston metro area was #6. *247wallst.com, "The Best Cities for High-Tech Jobs," June 10, 2013*

- Based on a minimum of 500 social media reviews per metro area, the employment opinion group Glassdoor surveyed 50 of the largest U.S. metro areas on measures including compensation and benefits, satisfaction with management, business outlook, and number of employers hiring. The Boston metro area was ranked #8 in overall employee satisfaction. *www.glassdoor.com, "Employment Satisfaction Report Card by City," June 21, 2013*

- The Brookings Institution ranked the 50 largest cities in the U.S. based on income inequality. Boston was ranked #4. (#1 = greatest ineqality). Criteria: the cities were ranked based on the "95/20 ratio." This figure represents the income at which a household earns more than 95 percent of all other households, divided by the income at which a household earns more than only 20 percent of all other households. *Brookings Institution, "Income Inequality in America's 50 Largest Cities, 2007-2012," February 20, 2014*

- *Forbes* ranked the largest metro areas in the U.S. in terms of the "Best Cities for Young Professionals." The Boston metro area ranked #12 out of 15. Criteria: job growth; unemployment rate; median salary of college graduates age 24 to 34; cost of living; number of small businesses per capita; number of large companies; percentage of population 25 years of age and older with college degrees. *Forbes.com, "America's Best Cities for Young Professionals," July 12, 2011*

- Boston was ranked #53 out of 100 metro areas in terms of economic performance (#1 = best) during the recession and recovery from trough quarter through the second quarter of 2013. Criteria: percent change in employment; percentage point change in unemployment rate; percent change in gross metropolitan product; percent change in House Price Index. *Brookings Institution, MetroMonitor: Tracking Economic Recession and Recovery in America's 100 Largest Metropolitan Areas, September 2013*

- Payscale.com ranked the 20 largest metro areas in terms of wage growth. The Boston metro area ranked #9. Criteria: private-sector wage growth between the 4th quarter of 2012 and the 4th quarter of 2013. *PayScale, "Wage Trends by Metro Area," 4th Quarter, 2013*

- For its annual survey of the "10 Most Expensive U.S. Cities to Live In," Kiplinger applied Cost of Living Index statistics developed by the Council for Community and Economic Research to U.S. Census Bureau population and median household income data for cities with populations above 50,000. In the resulting ranking, Boston ranked #7. *Kiplinger.com, "10 Most Expensive U.S. Cities to Live In," June 2013*

- Boston was identified as one of America's most frugal metro areas by *Coupons.com*. The city ranked #7 out of 25. Criteria: online coupon usage. *Coupons.com, "Top 25 Most Frugal Cities of 2012," February 19, 2013*

- Boston was identified as one of America's most frugal metro areas by *Coupons.com*. The city ranked #12 out of 25. Criteria: Grocery IQ and coupons.com mobile app usage. *Coupons.com, "Top 25 Most On-the-Go Frugal Cities of 2012," February 19, 2013*

- Boston was identified as one of America's "10 Best Cities to Get a Job" by *U.S. News & World Report*. The city ranked #3. Criteria: number of available jobs; unemployment rate. *U.S. News & World Report, "10 Best Cities to Get a Job," February 1, 2011*

- Boston was identified as one of the best cities for college graduates to find work—and live. The city ranked #3 out of 15. Criteria: job availability; average salary; average rent. *CareerBuilder.com, "15 Best Cities for College Grads to Find Work—and Live," June 5, 2012*

- Boston was identified as one of the happiest cities to work in by CareerBliss.com, an online community for career advancement. The city ranked #7 out of 10. Criteria: independent company reviews from employees all over the country on: relationship with their boss and co-workers; work environment; job resources; compensation; growth opportunities; company culture; company reputation; daily tasks; job control over work performed on a daily basis. *CareerBliss.com, "Top 10 Happiest and Unhappiest Cities to Work in 2014," February 10, 2014*

- Boston was identified as one of the happiest cities for young professionals by *CareerBliss.com,* an online community for career advancement. The city ranked #10. Criteria: more than 45,000 young professionals were asked to rate key factors that affect workplace happiness including: work-life balance; compensation; company culture; overall work environment; company reputation; relationships with managers and co-workers; opportunities for growth; job resources; daily tasks; job autonomy. Young professionals are defined as having less than 10 years of work experience. *CareerBliss.com, "Happiest Cities for Young Professionals," April 26, 2013*

- The Boston metro area appeared on the Milken Institute "2013 Best Performing Cities" list. Rank: #46 out of 200 large metro areas. Criteria: job growth; wage and salary growth; high-tech output growth. *Milken Institute, "Best-Performing Cities 2013," December 2013*

- *Forbes* ranked the 200 most populous metro areas in the U.S. in terms of the "Best Places for Business and Careers." The Boston metro area was ranked #38. Criteria: costs (business and living); job growth (past and projected); income growth; educational attainment (college and high school); projected economic growth; cultural and recreational opportunities; net migration patterns; number of highly ranked colleges. *Forbes, "The Best Places for Business and Careers," August 7, 2013*

Children/Family Rankings

- Boston was selected as one of the best cities for families to live by *Parenting* magazine. The city ranked #1 out of 100. Criteria: education; health; community; *Parenting's* Culture & Charm Index. *Parenting.com, "The 2012 Best Cities for Families List"*

Culture/Performing Arts Rankings

- Boston was selected as one of 10 best U.S. cities to be a moviemaker. The city was ranked #7. Criteria: film community; access to new films; access to equipment; cost of living; tax incentives. *MovieMaker Magazine, "Top 10 Cities to be a Moviemaker: 2013," March 5, 2013*

- Boston was selected as one of "America's Favorite Cities." The city ranked #9 in the "Culture: Museum/Galleries" category. Respondents to an online survey were asked to rate 35 top urban destinations in the U.S. from a visitor's perspective. Criteria: number and quality of museums and galleries. *Travelandleisure.com, "America's Favorite Cities 2013"*

- Boston was selected as one of America's top cities for the arts. The city ranked #5 in the big city (population 500,000 and over) category. Criteria: readers' top choices for arts travel destinations based on the richness and variety of visual arts sites, activities and events. *American Style, "2012 Top 25 Arts Destinations," June 2012*

Dating/Romance Rankings

- A *Cosmopolitan* magazine article surveyed the gender balance and other factors to arrive at a list of the best and worst cities for women to meet single guys. Boston placed #6 among the worst for single women looking for dates. *www.cosmopolitan.com, "Working the Ratio," October 1, 2013*

- CreditDonkey, a financial education website, sought out the ten best U.S. cities for newlyweds, considering the number of married couples, divorce rate, average credit score, and average number of hours worked per week in metro areas with a million or more residents. The Boston metro area placed #3. *www.creditdonkey.com, "Study: Best Cities for Newlyweds," November 30, 2013*

- Boston took the #1 spot on NerdWallet's list of best cities for singles wanting to date, based on the availability of singles; "date-friendliness," as determined by a city's walkability and the number of bars and restaurants per thousand residents; and the affordability of dating in terms of the cost of movie tickets, pizza, and wine for two. *www.nerdwallet.com, "Best Cities for Singles," February 5, 2014*

- Of the 100 U.S. cities surveyed by *Men's Health* in its quest to identify the nation's best cities for dating and forming relationships, Boston was ranked #30 for online dating (#1 = best). *Men's Health, "The Best and Worst Cities for Online Dating," January 30, 2013*

- Boston was selected as one of America's best cities for singles by the readers of *Travel + Leisure* in their annual "America's Favorite Cities" survey. The city was ranked #18 out of 20. *Travel + Leisure, "America's Best Cities for Singles," July 2012*

- Boston was selected as one of the best cities for single men by *Rent.com*. Criteria: high single female-to-male ratio. *Rent.com, "Top Cities for Single Men," March 14, 2013*

- Boston was selected as one of "America's Best Cities for Dating" by *Yahoo! Travel*. Criteria: high proportion of singles; excellent dating venues and/or stunning natural settings. *Yahoo! Travel, "America's Best Cities for Dating," February 7, 2012*

- Boston was selected as one of the best cities for single women in America by *SingleMindedWomen.com*. The city ranked #3. Criteria: ratio of women to men; singles population; healthy lifestyle; employment opportunities; cost of living; access to travel; entertainment options; social opportunities. *SingleMindedWomen.com, "Top 10 Cities for Single Women," 2011*

Education Rankings

- The Boston metro area was selected as one of the world's most inventive cities by *Forbes*. The area was ranked #7 out of 15. Criteria: patent applications per capita. *Forbes, "World's 15 Most Inventive Cities," July 9, 2013*

- *Fast Company* magazine measured six key components of "smart" cities and three "drivers" for each component to reveal the top ten "Smartest Cities in North America." By these complex metrics, Boston ranked #2. *Fastcoexist.com, "The Top 10 Smartest Cities in North America," November 15, 2013*

- Boston was identified as one of America's "smartest" metropolitan areas by *The Business Journals*. The area ranked #4 out of 10. Criteria: percentage of adults (25 and older) with high school diplomas, bachelor's degrees and graduate degrees. *The Business Journals, "Where the Brainpower Is: Exclusive U.S. Rankings, Insights," February 27, 2014*

- *Men's Health* ranked 100 U.S. cities in terms of their education levels. Boston was ranked #21 (#1 = most educated city). Criteria: high school graduation rates; school enrollment; educational attainment; number of households who have outstanding student loans; number of households whose members have taken adult-education courses. *Men's Health, "Where School Is In: The Most and Least Educated Cities," September 12, 2011*

- Boston was selected as one of "America's Geekiest Cities" by *Forbes.com*. The city ranked #15 of 20. Criteria: percentage of workers with jobs in science, technology, engineering and mathematics. *Forbes.com, "America's Geekiest Cities," August 5, 2011*

- Boston was selected as one of America's most literate cities. The city ranked #8 out of the 77 largest U.S. cities. Criteria: number of booksellers; library resources; Internet resources; educational attainment; periodical publishing resources; newspaper circulation. *Central Connecticut State University, "America's Most Literate Cities, 2013"*

- Boston was identified as one of "America's Smartest Cities" by *The Daily Beast* using data from Lumos Labs. The metro area ranked #6 out of 25. Criteria: with data collected from more than 1 million users as part of its human cognition project, Lumos Labs was able to analyze performance for nearly 200 metro areas in five cognitive areas: memory, processing speed, flexibility, attention, and problem solving. The median Lumos Lab score was worth 50 percent of the final, weighted ranking. The other half of the ranking was based on the percentage of adults over age 25 with a bachelor's and/or master's degree. *The Daily Beast, "America's Smartest Cities 2012" August 16, 2012*

Environmental Rankings

- The Boston metro area came in at #107 for the relative comfort of its climate on Sperling's list of "chill cities," as measured by the Sperling Heat Index. All 361 metro areas are included. Criteria included daytime high temperatures, nighttime low temperatures, dew point, and relative humidity at the high temperatures. *www.bertsperling.com, "Sperling's Chill Cities," July 18, 2013*

- Sperling's BestPlaces assessed 379 metropolitan areas of the United States for the likelihood of dangerously extreme weather events or earthquakes. In general the Southeast and South-Central regions have the highest risk of weather extremes and earthquakes, while the Pacific Northwest enjoys the lowest risk. Of the least risky metropolitan areas, the Boston metro area was ranked #243. *www.bestplaces.net, "Safest Places from Natural Disasters," April 2011*

- Boston was identified as one of North America's greenest metropolitan areas. The area ranked #6. The Green City Index is comprised of 31 indicators, and scores cities across nine categories: carbon dioxide; energy; land use; buildings; transport; water; waste; air quality; environmental governance. The 27 largest metropolitan areas in the U.S. and Canada were considered. *Economist Intelligence Unit, sponsored by Siemens, "U.S. and Canada Green City Index, 2011".*

- The U.S. Environmental Protection Agency (EPA) released a list of U.S. metropolitan areas with the most ENERGY STAR certified buildings in 2012. The Boston metro area was ranked #10 out of 25. *U.S. Environmental Protection Agency, "Top Cities With the Most ENERGY STAR Certified Buildings in 2012," March 12, 2013*

- The Boston metro area was identified as one of the snowiest major metropolitan areas in the U.S. by *Forbes*. The metro area ranked #6 out of 10. Criteria: average annual snowfall. *Forbes, "America's Snowiest Cities," January 12, 2011*

- Boston was selected as one of 22 "Smarter Cities" for energy by the Natural Resources Defense Council. The city appeared as one of 12 cities in the large city (population 250,000 and over) category. Criteria: investment in green power; energy efficiency measures; conservation. *Natural Resources Defense Council, "2010 Smarter Cities," July 19, 2010*

Food/Drink Rankings

- According to Fodor's Travel, Boston placed #6 among the best U.S. cities for food-truck cuisine. *www.fodors.com, "America's Best Food Truck Cities," December 20, 2013*

- *Men's Health* ranked 100 major U.S. cities in terms of alcohol intoxication. Boston ranked #7 (#1 = most sober).Criteria: binge drinking; alcohol-related traffic accidents, arrests, and fatalities. *Men's Health, "The Drunkest Cities in America," November 19, 2013*

- Boston was identified as one of "America's Drunkest Cities of 2011" by *The Daily Beast*. The city ranked #1 out of 25. Criteria: binge drinking; drinks consumed per month. *The Daily Beast, "Tipsy Towns: Where are America's Drunkest Cities?," December 31, 2011*

- Fenway Park (Boston Red Sox) was selected as one of PETA's "Top 10 Vegetarian-Friendly Major League Ballparks" for 2013. The park ranked #8. *People for the Ethical Treatment of Animals, "Top 10 Vegetarian-Friendly Major League Ballparks," June 12, 2013*

- The Boston metro area was selected as one of the best cities for "foodies" in America by Sperling's BestPlaces. The metro area ranked #7 out of 10. A "foodie" is defined as a person whose hobby is food—not just eating it, but also learning about its origins and preparation. Criteria: ratio of local restaurants to chain restaurants; number of local and accessible CSA (Community Supported Agriculture) and farmers markets; number of Whole Foods stores; number of cookware stores; number of craft breweries, brew pubs, wine shops, and wine bars. *Sperling's BestPlaces, www.BestPlaces.net, "America's Best Cities for Foodies," January 2011*

Health/Fitness Rankings

- Analysts who tracked obesity rates in the nation's largest metro areas (those with populations above one million) found that the Boston metro area was one of the ten major metros where residents were least likely to be obese, defined as a BMI score of 30 or above. *www.gallup.com, "Boulder, Colo., Residents Still Least Likely to Be Obese," April 4, 2014*

- For each of the 50 most populous metro areas in the United States, the American College of Sports Medicine's American Fitness Index evaluated infrastructure, community assets, and policies that encourage healthy and fit lifestyles, including preventive health behaviors, levels of chronic disease conditions, health care access, and community resources and policies that support physical activity. The Boston metro area ranked #6 for "community fitness." Personal health indicators were considered as well as community and environmental indicators. *www.americanfitnessindex.org, "ACSM American Fitness Index Health and Community Fitness Status of the 50 Largest Metropolitan Areas," May 2013*

- *Business Insider* reported Trulia's analysis of the 100 largest U.S. metro areas to identify the nation's best cities for weight loss, based on healthful food options, access to outdoor activities, weight-loss centers, gyms, and opportunities to bike or walk to work. Boston ranked #4. *Businessinsider.com, "These Are the Best US Cities for Weight loss," January 17, 2013*

- Boston was identified as one of the 10 most walkable cities in the U.S. by Walk Score, a Seattle-based service that rates the convenience and transit access of 10,000 neighborhoods in 3,000 cities. The area ranked #3 out of the 50 largest U.S. cities. Walk Score measures walkability by analyzing hundreds of walking routes to nearby amenities. Walk Score also measures pedestrian friendliness by analyzing population density and road metrics such as block length and intersection density. *WalkScore.com, March 20, 2014*

- The Boston metro area was identified as one of the worst cities for bed bugs in America by pest control company Orkin. The area ranked #20 out of 50 based on the number of bed bug treatments Orkin performed from January to December 2013. *Orkin, "Chicago Tops Bed Bug Cities List for Second Year in a Row," January 16, 2014*

- Boston was selected as one of the 25 fittest cities in America by *Men's Fitness Online*. It ranked #5 out of America's 50 largest cities. Criteria: fitness centers and sport stores; nutrition; sports participation; TV viewing; overweight/sedentary; junk food; air quality; geography; commute; parks and open space; city recreational facilities; access to healthcare; motivation; mayor and city initiatives; state obesity initiatives. *Men's Fitness, "The Fittest and Fattest Cities in America," March 5, 2012*

- Boston was identified as a "2013 Spring Allergy Capital." The area ranked #83 out of 100. Three groups of factors were used to identify the most severe cities for people with allergies during the spring season: annual pollen levels; medicine utilization; access to board-certified allergists. *Asthma and Allergy Foundation of America, "Spring Allergy Capitals 2013"*

- Boston was identified as a "2013 Fall Allergy Capital." The area ranked #75 out of 100. Three groups of factors were used to identify the most severe cities for people with allergies during the fall season: annual pollen levels; medicine utilization; access to board-certified allergists. *Asthma and Allergy Foundation of America, "Fall Allergy Capitals 2013"*

- Boston was identified as a "2013 Asthma Capital." The area ranked #69 out of the nation's 100 largest metropolitan areas. Twelve factors were used to identify the most challenging places to live for people with asthma: estimated prevalence; self-reported prevalence; crude death rate for asthma; annual pollen score; annual air quality; public smoking laws; number of board-certified asthma specialists; school inhaler access laws; rescue medication use; controller medication use; uninsured rate; poverty rate. *Asthma and Allergy Foundation of America, "Asthma Capitals 2013"*

- *Men's Health* ranked 100 major U.S. cities in terms of the best and worst cities for men. Boston ranked #16. Criteria: thirty-three data points were examined covering health, fitness, and quality of life. *Men's Health, "The Best & Worst Cities for Men 2014," December 6, 2013*

- The American Academy of Dermatology ranked 26 U.S. metropolitan regions in terms of their residents knowledge, attitude and behaviors towards tanning, sun protection and skin cancer detection. The Boston metro area ranked #5. The results of the study are based on an online survey of over 7,000 adults nationwide. *American Academy of Dermatology, "Suntelligence: How Sun Smart is Your City?," May 3, 2010*

- The Boston metro area appeared in the 2013 Gallup-Healthways Well-Being Index. The area ranked #23 out of 189. The Gallup-Healthways Well-Being Index score is an average of six sub-indexes, which individually examine life evaluation, emotional health, work environment, physical health, healthy behaviors, and access to basic necessities. Results are based on telephone interviews conducted as part of the Gallup-Healthways Well-Being Index survey January 2–December 29, 2012, and January 2–December 30, 2013, with a random sample of 531,630 adults, aged 18 and older, living in metropolitan areas in the 50 U.S. states and the District of Columbia. *Gallup-Healthways, "State of American Well-Being," March 25, 2014*

- The Boston metro area was identified as one of "America's Most Stressful Cities" by *Sperling's BestPlaces*. The metro area ranked #35 out of 50. Criteria: unemployment rate; suicide rate; commute time; mental health; poor rest; alcohol use; violent crime rate; property crime rate; cloudy days annually. *Sperling's BestPlaces, www.BestPlaces.net, "Stressful Cities 2012*

- The Boston metro area was identified as one of "America's Most Stressful Cities" by *Forbes*. The metro area ranked #8 out of 40. Criteria: housing affordability; unemployment rate; cost of living; air quality; traffic congestion; sunny days; population density. *Forbes.com, "America's Most Stressful Cities," September 23, 2011*

- *Men's Health* ranked 100 U.S. cities in terms of their activity levels. Boston was ranked #18 (#1 = most active city). Criteria: where and how often residents exercise; percentage of households that watch more than 15 hours of cable television a week and buy more than 11 video games a year; death rate from deep-vein thrombosis, a condition linked to sitting for extended periods of time. *Men's Health, "Where Sit Happens: The Most and Least Active Cities in America," June 20, 2011*

Pet Rankings

- Boston was selected as one of the best cities for dogs by real estate website Estately.com. The city was ranked #8. Criteria: weather; walkability; yard sizes; dog activities; meetup groups; availability of dogsitters. *Estately.com, "17 Best U.S. Cities for Dogs," May 14, 2013*

Real Estate Rankings

- ApartmentList.com calculated the most expensive American cities for renters, comparing median rental prices for studios, one-bedroom units, and two-bedroom units in the nation's 50 most populated cities. Boston placed #3 in the ApartmentList.com ranking. *www.cbsnews.com, "Top 10 Priciest U.S. Cities to Rent an Apartment," July 15, 2013*

- NerdWallet identified the 10 U.S. cities among the 25 largest, most hospitable for recent college graduates, based on demographics; social life; accessibility; cost of living; and economic opportunity. Boston placed #1 as a destination for new young graduates. *http://www.nerdwallet.com, "Best Cities for Fresh College Graduates," May 30, 2013*

- The PricewaterhouseCoopers and Urban Land Institute report *Emerging Trends in Real Estate* forecasts that improvements in leasing, rents, and pricing will fuel recovery in all property sectors in 2013. Boston was ranked #6 among the top ten markets to watch in 2013. *PricewaterhouseCoopers/Urban Land Institute, "U.S. Commercial Real Estate Recovery to Advance in 2013," October 17, 2012*

- The Boston metro area was identified as one of the top 20 housing markets to invest in for 2014 by *Forbes*. The area ranked #15. Criteria: high population and job growth; relatively low home prices which are below equilibrium home price (EHP). The EHP is what the average price for a market should be, if speculation, weird distortions in local income, and other factors (like the housing collapse) weren't present in the market. *Forbes.com, "Best Buy Cities: Where to Invest in Housing in 2014," December 25, 2013*

- Boston ranked #5 in a *Forbes* study of the rental housing market in the nation's 44 largest metropolitan areas to determine the cities that are worst for renters. Criteria: average rent in 2012's first quarter, year-over-year change in that figure, vacancy rate, and average monthly rent payment compared with average monthly mortgage payment. *Forbes.com, "The Best and Worst Cities for Renters," June 14, 2012*

- Boston was identified as one of the priciest cities to rent in the U.S. The area ranked #6 out of 10. Criteria: rent-to-income ratio. *CNBC, "Priciest Cities to Rent," March 14, 2012*

- Boston was ranked #92 out of 283 metro areas in terms of house price appreciation in 2013 (#1 = highest rate). *Federal Housing Finance Agency, House Price Index, 4th Quarter 2013*

- Boston was selected as one of the eight best cities in the U.S. for real estate investment. The city ranked #6. *Association of Foreign Investors in Real Estate, "Ranking of USA Cities for Real Estate Investment, 2013"*

- The Boston metro area was identified as one of the 20 least affordable housing markets in the U.S. in 2013. The area ranked #16 out of 173 markets. Criteria: whether or not a typical family could qualify for a mortgage loan on a typical home. *National Association of Realtors®, Affordability Index of Existing Single-Family Homes for Metropolitan Areas, 2013*

- Boston was ranked #199 out of 224 metro areas in terms of housing affordability in 2013 by the National Association of Home Builders (#1 = most affordable). The NAHB-Wells Fargo Housing Opportunity Index (HOI) for a given area is defined as the share of homes sold in that area that would have been affordable to a family earning the local median income, based on standard mortgage underwriting criteria. *National Association of Home Builders®, NAHB-Wells Fargo Housing Opportunity Index, 4th Quarter 2013*

- Boston was selected as one of the best college towns for renters by ApartmentRatings.com." The area ranked #87 out of 87. Overall satisfaction ratings were ranked using thousands of user submitted scores for hundreds of apartment complexes located in cities and towns that are home to the 100 largest four-year institutions in the U.S. *ApartmentRatings.com, "2011 College Town Renter Satisfaction Rankings"*

Safety Rankings

- Symantec, in partnership with Sperling's BestPlaces, ranked the 50 largest cities in the U.S. in terms of their vulnerability to cybercrime. The city ranked #5. Criteria: number of cyberattacks and potential infections; level of Internet access; expenditures on smartphones and computer hardware/software; wireless hotspots; broadband connectivity; Internet usage; online purchases. *Symantec, "Riskiest Online Cities of 2012" February 15, 2012*

- The National Insurance Crime Bureau ranked 380 metro areas in the U.S. in terms of per capita rates of vehicle theft. The Boston metro area ranked #232 (#1 = highest rate). Criteria: number of vehicle theft offenses per 100,000 inhabitants in 2012. *National Insurance Crime Bureau, "Hot Spots 2012," June 26, 2013*

- The Boston metro area was identified as one of the most dangerous metro areas for pedestrians by Transportation for America. The metro area ranked #52 out of 52 metro areas with over 1 million residents. Criteria: area's population divided by the number of pedestrian fatalities in that area. *Transportation for America, "Dangerous by Design 2011"*

Seniors/Retirement Rankings

- From its Best Cities for Successful Aging indexes, the Milken Institute generated rankings for metropolitan areas, weighing data in eight categories—general indicators, health care, wellness, living arrangements, transportation and general accessibility, financial well-being, education and employment, and community participation. The Boston metro area was ranked #4 overall in the large metro area category. *Milken Institute, "Best Cities for Successful Aging," July 2012*

- Bankers Life and Casualty Company, in partnership with Sperling's BestPlaces, ranked the nation's 50 largest metro areas in terms of the "Best U.S. Cities for Seniors." The Boston metro area ranked #2. Criteria: healthcare; transportation; housing; environment; economy; health and longevity; social and spiritual life; crime. *Bankers Life and Casualty Company, Center for a Secure Retirement, "Best U.S. Cities for Seniors 2011," September 2011*

Sports/Recreation Rankings

- According to the personal finance website NerdWallet, the Boston metro area, at #11, is one of the nation's top dozen metro areas for sports fans. Criteria included the presence of all four major sports—MLB, NFL, NHL, and NBA, fan enthusiasm (as measured by game attendance), ticket affordability, and "sports culture," that is, number of sports bars. *www.nerdwallet.com, "Best Cities for Sports Fans," May 5, 2013*

- Boston appeared on the *Sporting News* list of the "Best Sports Cities" for 2011. The area ranked #2 out of 271. Criteria: the magazine takes a 12-month snapshot of each city's sports, putting a heavy premium on regular-season won-lost records (from the most recently completed season). Other criteria include: playoff berths, bowl appearances and tournament bids; championships; applicable power ratings; quality of competition; overall fan fervor (measured in part by attendance); abundance of teams (rewarding quality over quantity); stadium and arena quality; ticket availability and prices; franchise ownership; and marquee appeal of athletes. *Sporting News, "Best Sports Cities 2011," October 4, 2011*

- Boston appeared on the *Sporting News* list of the "Best Sports Cities" for 2011. The area ranked #2 out of 271. Criteria: a 12-month snapshot of regular-season won-lost records (from the most recently completed season). Other criteria include: playoff berths, bowl appearances and tournament bids; championships; applicable power ratings; quality of competition; overall fan fervor (measured in part by attendance); abundance of teams (quality over quantity); stadium and arena quality; ticket availability and prices; franchise ownership; and marquee appeal of athletes. *Sporting News, "Best Sports Cities 2011," October 4, 2011*

- Boston was chosen as a bicycle friendly community by the League of American Bicyclists. A "Bicycle Friendly Community" welcomes cyclists by providing safe accommodation for cycling and encouraging people to bike for transportation and recreation. There are four award levels: Platinum; Gold; Silver; and Bronze. The community achieved an award level of Silver. *League of American Bicyclists, "Bicycle Friendly Community Master List," Fall 2013*

- Boston was chosen as one of America's best cities for bicycling. The city ranked #16 out of 50. Criteria: robust cycling infrastructure; vibrant bike culture. The editors only considered cities with populations of 95,000 or more. *Bicycling, "America's Top 50 Bike-Friendly Cities," May 23, 2012*

Transportation Rankings

- Business Insider presented a Walk Score ranking of public transportation in 316 U.S. cities and thousands of city neighborhoods in which Boston earned the #3-ranked "Transit Score," awarded for frequency, type of route, and distance between stops. *www.businessinsider.com, "The US Cities with the Best Public Transportation Systems," January 30, 2014*

- NerdWallet surveyed average annual car insurance premiums in 125 U.S. cities to identify the least expensive U.S. cities in which to insure a car. Locations with no-fault insurance laws was a strong determinant. Boston came in at #14 for the most expensive rates. *www.nerdwallet.com, "Best Cities for Cheap Car Insurance," February 3, 2014*

- More U.S. households choose not to have a car in 2012 than in prior years, according to a study by the University of Michigan Transportation Research Institute. The business website 24/7 Wall Street examined that study, along with a 2010 Census Special Report to arrive at its ranking of cities in which the fewest households had a vehicle. Boston held the #3 position. *247wallst.com, "Cities Where No One Wants to Drive," February 6, 2014*

- Boston was identified as one of America's "10 Best Cities for Public Transportation" by *U.S. News & World Report*. The city ranked #4. The ten cities selected had the best combination of public transportation investment, ridership, and safety. *U.S. News & World Report, "10 Best Cities for Public Transportation," February 8, 2011*

- The Boston metro area was identified as one of the best U.S. cities to live in without a car by *24/7 Wall St.* The area ranked #10 out of 10. Criteria: percentage of neighborhoods covered by public transit; frequency of service for those neighborhoods; share of jobs reachable within 90 minutes or less by public transit; how accessible amenities are for residents on foot; percentage of commuters who bike to work. The 100 largest metropolitan areas in the U.S. were examined. *24/7 Wall St., "The Best Cities to Live in Car-Free," November 28, 2011*

- Boston was identified as one of the most congested metro areas in the U.S. The area ranked #5 out of 10. Criteria: yearly delay per auto commuter in hours. *Texas A&M Transportation Institute, "2012 Urban Mobility Report," December 2012*

- The Boston metro area was selected as one of 15 "Smarter Cities" for transportation by the Natural Resources Defense Council. The area appeared in the large metro area (population greater than one million) category. Criteria: public transit availability and use; household automobile ownership and use; innovative, sustainable and affordable transportation programs. *Natural Resources Defense Council, "2011 Smarter Cities," February 23, 2011*

- The Boston metro area appeared on *Forbes* list of places with the most extreme commutes. The metro area ranked #6 out of 10. Criteria: average travel time; percentage of mega commuters. Mega-commuters travel more than 90 minutes and 50 miles each way to work. *Forbes.com, "The Cities with the Most Extreme Commutes," March 5, 2013*

Women/Minorities Rankings

- The Daily Beast surveyed the nation's cities for highest percentage of singles and lowest divorce rate, plus other measures, to determine "emotional intelligence"—happiness, confidence, kindness—which, researchers say, has a strong correlation with people's satisfaction with their romantic relationships. Boston placed #2. *www.thedailybeast.com, "Best Cities to Find Love and Stay in Love," February 14, 2014*

- *Women's Health* examined U.S. cities and identified the 100 best cities for women. Boston was ranked #19. Criteria: 30 categories were examined from obesity and breast cancer rates to commuting times and hours spent working out. *Women's Health, "Best Cities for Women 2012"*

- Boston was selected as one of the 25 healthiest cities for Latinas by *Latina Magazine*. The city ranked #1. Criteria: U.S. cities with populations over 500,000 residents were evaluated on the following criteria: percentage of 18-34 year-olds per city; Latino college graduation rates; number of colleges and universities; affordability; housing costs; income growth over time; average salary; percentage of singles; climate; safety; how the city's diversity compares to the national average; opportunities for minority entrepreneurs. *Latina Magazine, "Top 15 U.S. Cities for Young Latinos to Live In," August 19, 2011*

- Boston was selected as one of the best cities for young Latinos in 2013 by mun2, a national cable television broadcast network. The city ranked #10. Criteria: U.S. cities with populations over 500,000 residents were evaluated on the following criteria: number of young latinos; jobs; friendliness; cost of living; fun. *mun2.tv, "Best Cities for Young Latinos 2013*

- The Boston metro area appeared on *Forbes'* list of the "Best Cities for Minority Entrepreneurs." The area ranked #10 out of 10. Criteria: 52 metropolitan statistical areas were examined. For each ethnicity (African Americans, Asians and Hispanics), the editors measured housing affordability, population growth, income growth, and entrepreneurship (per capita self-employment). *Forbes, "Best Cities for Minority Entrepreneurs," March 23, 2011*

Miscellaneous Rankings

- Boston was selected as a 2013 Digital Cities Survey winner. The city ranked #1 in the large city (250,000 or more population) category. The survey examined and assessed how city governments are utilizing information technology to operate and deliver quality service to their customers and citizens. Survey questions focused on implementation and adoption of online service delivery; planning and governance; and the infrastructure and architecture that make the transformation to digital government possible. *Center for Digital Government, "2013 Digital Cities Survey," November 7, 2013*

- *Travel + Leisure* invited readers to rate cities on indicators such as aloofness, "smarty-pants residents," highbrow cultural offerings, high-end shopping, artisanal coffeehouses, conspicuous eco-consciousness, and more in order to identify the nation's snobbiest cities. Cities large and small made the list; among them was Boston, at #3. *www.travelandleisure.com, "America's Snobbiest Cities, June 2013*

- The watchdog site Charity Navigator conducts an annual study of charities in the nation's major markets both to analyze statistical differences in their financial, accountability, and transparency practices and to track year-to-year variations in individual communities. The Boston metro area was ranked #15 among the 30 metro markets. *www.charitynavigator.org, "Metro Market Study 2013," June 1, 2013*

- Business Insider reports on the 2013 Trick-or-Treat Index compiled by the real estate site Zillow, which used its own Home Value Index and Walk Score along with population density and local crime stats to determine that Boston ranked #2 for "how much candy it gives out versus how far kids have to walk to get it." Zillow also zeroes in on the best neighborhoods in its top 20 cities. *www.businessinsider.com, "These Are the Best Cities for Trick-or-Treating," October 15, 2013*

- The Harris Poll's Happiness Index survey revealed that of the top ten U.S. markets, the Boston metro area residents ranked #9 in happiness. Criteria included strong assent to positive statements and strong disagreement with negative ones, and degree of agreement with a series of statements about respondents' personal relationships and general outlook. The online survey was conducted between July 14 and July 30, 2013. *www.harrisinteractive.com, "Dallas/Fort Worth Is "Happiest" City among America's Top Ten Markets," September 4, 2013*

- Boston was selected as one of America's funniest cities by the Humor Research Lab at the University of Colorado. The city ranked #2 out of 10. Criteria: frequency of visits to comedy websites; number of comedy clubs per square mile; traveling comedians' ratings of each city's comedy-club audiences; number of famous comedians born in each city per capita; number of famous funny tweeters living in each city per capita; number of comedy radio stations available in each city; frequency of humor-related web searches originating in each city. *The New York Times, "So These Professors Walk Into a Comedy Club...," April 20, 2014*

- *Men's Health* ranked 100 U.S. cities by their level of sadness. Boston was ranked #5 (#1 = saddest city). Criteria: suicide rates; unemployment rates; percentage of households that use antidepressants; percent of population who report feeling blue all or most of the time. *Men's Health, "Frown Towns," November 28, 2011*

- Scarborough Research, a leading market research firm, identified the top local markets for lottery ticket purchasers. The Boston DMA (Designated Market Area) ranked in the top 13 with 49% of adults 18+ reporting that they purchased lottery tickets in the past 30 days. *Scarborough Research, January 30, 2012*

- Energizer Personal Care, the makers of Edge® shave gel, in partnership with Sperling's BestPlaces, ranked 50 major metro areas in terms of everyday irritations. The Boston metro area ranked #10. Criteria: high male-to-female ratio; poor sports team performance and high ticket prices; slow traffic; lack of job availability; unaffordable housing; extreme weather; lack of nightlife and fitness options. *Energizer Personal Care, "Most Irritatng Cities for Guys," August 26, 2013*

- Mars Chocolate North America, the makers of COMBOS®, in partnership with Sperling's BestPlaces, ranked 50 major metro areas in terms of their "manliness." The Boston metro area ranked #47. Criteria: number of professional sports teams; number of nearby NASCAR tracks and racing events; manly lifestyle; concentration of manly retail stores; manly occupations per capita; salty snack sales; "Board of Manliness" rankings. *Mars Chocolate North America, "America's Manliest Cities 2012"*

- Boston was selected as one of "America's Best Cities for Hipsters" by *Travel + Leisure*. The city was ranked #14 out of 20. Criteria: live music; coffee bars; independent boutiques; best microbrews; offbeat and tech-savvy locals. *Travel + Leisure, "America's Best Cities for Hipsters," November 2013*

- The National Alliance to End Homelessness ranked the 100 most populous metro areas in terms the rate of homelessness. The Boston metro area ranked #20. Criteria: number of homeless people per 10,000 population in 2011. *National Alliance to End Homelessness, The State of Homelessness in America 2012*

Business Environment

CITY FINANCES

City Government Finances

Component	2011 ($000)	2011 ($ per capita)
Total Revenues	3,969,447	6,623
Total Expenditures	3,562,037	5,943
Debt Outstanding	1,589,023	2,651
Cash and Securities[1]	5,744,405	9,584

Note: (1) Cash and security holdings of a government at the close of its fiscal year, including those of its dependent agencies, utilities, and liquor stores.
Source: U.S Census Bureau, State & Local Government Finances 2011

City Government Revenue by Source

Source	2011 ($000)	2011 ($ per capita)
General Revenue		
From Federal Government	88,717	148
From State Government	891,142	1,487
From Local Governments	0	0
Taxes		
Property	1,609,146	2,685
Sales and Gross Receipts	58,012	97
Personal Income	0	0
Corporate Income	0	0
Motor Vehicle License	0	0
Other Taxes	39,887	67
Current Charges	226,037	377
Liquor Store	0	0
Utility	122,265	204
Employee Retirement	674,327	1,125

Source: U.S Census Bureau, State & Local Government Finances 2011

City Government Expenditures by Function

Function	2011 ($000)	2011 ($ per capita)	2011 (%)
General Direct Expenditures			
Air Transportation	0	0	0.0
Corrections	0	0	0.0
Education	1,034,175	1,725	29.0
Employment Security Administration	0	0	0.0
Financial Administration	37,541	63	1.1
Fire Protection	178,802	298	5.0
General Public Buildings	78,362	131	2.2
Governmental Administration, Other	11,774	20	0.3
Health	11,060	18	0.3
Highways	58,617	98	1.6
Hospitals	257,826	430	7.2
Housing and Community Development	88,614	148	2.5
Interest on General Debt	60,143	100	1.7
Judicial and Legal	5,199	9	0.1
Libraries	41,288	69	1.2
Parking	3,187	5	0.1
Parks and Recreation	54,354	91	1.5
Police Protection	309,096	516	8.7
Public Welfare	5,129	9	0.1
Sewerage	52,070	87	1.5
Solid Waste Management	54,901	92	1.5
Veterans' Services	0	0	0.0
Liquor Store	0	0	0.0
Utility	48,065	80	1.3
Employee Retirement	487,161	813	13.7

Source: U.S Census Bureau, State & Local Government Finances 2011

DEMOGRAPHICS

Population Growth

Area	1990 Census	2000 Census	2010 Census	Population Growth (%) 1990-2000	Population Growth (%) 2000-2010
City	574,283	589,141	617,594	2.6	4.8
MSA[1]	4,133,895	4,391,344	4,552,402	6.2	3.7
U.S.	248,709,873	281,421,906	308,745,538	13.2	9.7

Note: (1) Figures cover the Boston-Cambridge-Newton, MA-NH Metropolitan Statistical Area—see Appendix B for areas included
Source: U.S. Census Bureau, Census 1990, 2000, 2010

Household Size

Area	Persons in Household (%) One	Two	Three	Four	Five	Six	Seven or More	Average Household Size
City	38.2	31.0	14.5	9.8	3.8	1.7	1.0	2.34
MSA[1]	28.7	32.3	16.0	14.4	5.8	1.9	0.9	2.53
U.S.	27.6	33.5	15.7	13.2	6.1	2.4	1.5	2.63

Note: (1) Figures cover the Boston-Cambridge-Newton, MA-NH Metropolitan Statistical Area—see Appendix B for areas included
Source: U.S. Census Bureau, 2010-2012 American Community Survey 3-Year Estimates

Race

Area	White Alone[2] (%)	Black Alone[2] (%)	Asian Alone[2] (%)	AIAN[3] Alone[2] (%)	NHOPI[4] Alone[2] (%)	Other Race Alone[2] (%)	Two or More Races (%)
City	53.8	25.6	9.2	0.3	0.0	6.7	4.5
MSA[1]	78.7	7.7	6.7	0.2	0.0	3.9	2.8
U.S.	74.0	12.6	4.9	0.8	0.2	4.7	2.8

Note: (1) Figures cover the Boston-Cambridge-Newton, MA-NH Metropolitan Statistical Area—see Appendix B for areas included; (2) Alone is defined as not being in combination with one or more other races; (3) American Indian and Alaska Native; (4) Native Hawaiian and Other Pacific Islander
Source: U.S. Census Bureau, 2010-2012 American Community Survey 3-Year Estimates

Hispanic or Latino Origin

Area	Total (%)	Mexican (%)	Puerto Rican (%)	Cuban (%)	Other (%)
City	17.7	1.1	5.0	0.4	11.2
MSA[1]	9.3	0.6	2.6	0.2	5.8
U.S.	16.6	10.7	1.6	0.6	3.7

Note: Persons of Hispanic or Latino origin can be of any race; (1) Figures cover the Boston-Cambridge-Newton, MA-NH Metropolitan Statistical Area—see Appendix B for areas included
Source: U.S. Census Bureau, 2010-2012 American Community Survey 3-Year Estimates

Segregation

Type	Segregation Indices[1] 1990	2000	2010	2010 Rank[2]	Percent Change 1990-2000	Percent Change 1990-2010	Percent Change 2000-2010
Black/White	68.5	67.6	64.0	27	-0.9	-4.5	-3.5
Asian/White	45.5	47.8	45.4	23	2.3	-0.2	-2.5
Hispanic/White	59.3	62.5	59.6	5	3.2	0.3	-2.9

Note: All figures cover the Metropolitan Statistical Area—see Appendix B for areas included; Figures are based on an analysis of 1990, 2000, and 2010 Census Decennial Census tract data by William H. Frey, Brookings Institution and the University of Michigan Social Science Data Analysis Network. In this analysis all racial groups (whites, blacks, and asians) are non-Hispanic members of those races. Hispanics are shown as a separate category;
(1) Segregation Indices are Dissimilarity Indices that measure the degree to which the minority group is distributed differently than whites across census tracts. They range from 0 (complete integration) to 100 (complete segregation) where the value indicates the percentage of the minority group that needs to move to be distributed exactly like whites; (2) Ranges from 1 (most segregated) to 102 (least segregated); n/a not available.
Source: www.CensusScope.org

Ancestry

Area	German	Irish	English	American	Italian	Polish	French[2]	Scottish	Dutch
City	4.8	15.5	5.3	4.8	8.4	2.6	1.9	1.3	0.5
MSA[1]	6.4	24.2	10.9	4.5	15.0	3.8	5.7	2.6	0.6
U.S.	15.2	11.1	8.2	7.2	5.6	3.1	2.8	1.7	1.4

Note: Figures are the percentage of the total population reporting a particular ancestry. The nine most commonly reported ancestries in the U.S. are shown. Figures include multiple ancestries (e.g. if a person reported being Irish and Italian, they were included in both columns); (1) Figures cover the Boston-Cambridge-Newton, MA-NH Metropolitan Statistical Area—see Appendix B for areas included; (2) Excludes Basque
Source: U.S. Census Bureau, 2010-2012 American Community Survey 3-Year Estimates

Foreign-Born Population

Area	Any Foreign Country	Percent of Population Born in							
		Mexico	Asia	Europe	Carribean	South America	Central America[2]	Africa	Canada
City	26.6	0.4	6.9	3.6	7.9	2.0	2.8	2.6	0.4
MSA[1]	16.8	0.2	5.3	3.3	2.9	1.9	1.4	1.3	0.5
U.S.	13.0	3.7	3.7	1.6	1.2	0.9	1.0	0.5	0.3

Note: (1) Figures cover the Boston-Cambridge-Newton, MA-NH Metropolitan Statistical Area—see Appendix B for areas included; (2) Excludes Mexico.
Source: U.S. Census Bureau, 2010-2012 American Community Survey 3-Year Estimates

Marital Status

Area	Never Married	Now Married[2]	Separated	Widowed	Divorced
City	56.8	28.3	2.9	4.1	7.9
MSA[1]	36.2	47.3	1.9	5.6	9.1
U.S.	32.4	48.4	2.2	6.0	11.0

Note: Figures are percentages and cover the population 15 years of age and older; (1) Figures cover the Boston-Cambridge-Newton, MA-NH Metropolitan Statistical Area—see Appendix B for areas included; (2) Excludes separated
Source: U.S. Census Bureau, 2010-2012 American Community Survey 3-Year Estimates

Age

Area	Percent of Population									Median Age
	Under Age 5	Age 5–19	Age 20–34	Age 35–44	Age 45–54	Age 55–64	Age 65–74	Age 75–84	Age 85+	
City	5.3	16.8	34.7	12.3	11.3	9.2	5.4	3.3	1.6	30.9
MSA[1]	5.6	18.8	21.1	13.5	15.3	12.3	7.0	4.3	2.1	38.7
U.S.	6.4	20.1	20.5	13.1	14.3	12.2	7.3	4.2	1.8	37.3

Note: (1) Figures cover the Boston-Cambridge-Newton, MA-NH Metropolitan Statistical Area—see Appendix B for areas included
Source: U.S. Census Bureau, 2010-2012 American Community Survey 3-Year Estimates

Gender

Area	Males	Females	Males per 100 Females
City	299,769	328,596	91.2
MSA[1]	2,229,374	2,373,295	93.9
U.S.	153,276,055	158,333,314	96.8

Note: (1) Figures cover the Boston-Cambridge-Newton, MA-NH Metropolitan Statistical Area—see Appendix B for areas included
Source: U.S. Census Bureau, 2010-2012 American Community Survey 3-Year Estimates

Religious Groups by Family

Area	Catholic	Baptist	Non-Den.	Methodist[2]	Lutheran	LDS[3]	Pente-costal	Presby-terian[4]	Muslim[5]	Judaism
MSA[1]	44.4	1.2	1.0	1.0	0.4	0.4	0.6	1.6	0.4	1.4
U.S.	19.1	9.3	4.0	4.0	2.3	2.0	1.9	1.6	0.8	0.7

Note: Figures are the number of adherents as a percentage of the total population; (1) Figures cover the Boston-Cambridge-Newton, MA-NH Metropolitan Statistical Area—see Appendix B for areas included; (2) Methodist/Pietist; (3) Latter Day Saints; (4) Reformed; (5) Figures are estimates
Source: Association of Statisticians of American Religious Bodies, 2010 U.S. Religion Census: Religious Congregations & Membership Study

Religious Groups by Tradition

Area	Catholic	Evangelical Protestant	Mainline Protestant	Other Tradition	Black Protestant	Orthodox
MSA[1]	44.4	3.2	4.5	3.4	0.2	1.1
U.S.	19.1	16.2	7.3	4.3	1.6	0.3

Note: Figures are the number of adherents as a percentage of the total population; (1) Figures cover the Boston-Cambridge-Newton, MA-NH Metropolitan Statistical Area—see Appendix B for areas included
Source: Association of Statisticians of American Religious Bodies, 2010 U.S. Religion Census: Religious Congregations & Membership Study

ECONOMY

Gross Metropolitan Product

Area	2011	2012	2013	2014	Rank[2]
MSA[1]	323.3	336.2	346.4	361.4	9

Note: Figures are in billions of dollars; (1) Figures cover the Boston-Cambridge-Newton, MA-NH Metropolitan Statistical Area—see Appendix B for areas included; (2) Rank is based on 2014 data and ranges from 1 to 363
Source: The United States Conference of Mayors, U.S. Metro Economies: Outlook—Gross Metropolitan Product, with Metro Employment Projections, November 2013

Economic Growth

Area	2011 (%)	2012 (%)	2013 (%)	2014 (%)	Rank[2]
MSA[1]	2.0	2.3	1.7	2.4	92
U.S.	1.6	2.5	1.7	2.5	–

Note: Figures are real gross metropolitan product (GMP) growth rates and represent annual average percent change; (1) Figures cover the Boston-Cambridge-Newton, MA-NH Metropolitan Statistical Area—see Appendix B for areas included; (2) Rank is based on 2013 data and ranges from 1 to 363
Source: The United States Conference of Mayors, U.S. Metro Economies: Outlook—Gross Metropolitan Product, with Metro Employment Projections, November 2013

Metropolitan Area Exports

Area	2007	2008	2009	2010	2011	2012	Rank[2]
MSA[1]	21,030.7	22,955.2	18,972.6	21,804.5	22,292.8	21,234.8	14

Note: Figures are in millions of dollars; (1) Figures cover the Boston-Cambridge-Newton, MA-NH Metropolitan Statistical Area—see Appendix B for areas included; (2) Rank is based on 2012 data and ranges from 1 to 369
Source: U.S. Department of Commerce, International Trade Administration, Office of Trade & Industry Information, Manufacturing & Services, data extracted April 1, 2014

INCOME

Income

Area	Per Capita ($)	Median Household ($)	Average Household ($)
City	32,886	51,452	78,420
MSA[1]	37,800	71,375	96,583
U.S.	27,385	51,771	71,579

Note: (1) Figures cover the Boston-Cambridge-Newton, MA-NH Metropolitan Statistical Area—see Appendix B for areas included
Source: U.S. Census Bureau, 2010-2012 American Community Survey 3-Year Estimates

Household Income Distribution

Area	Percent of Households Earning							
	Under $15,000	$15,000 -24,999	$25,000 -34,999	$35,000 -49,999	$50,000 -74,999	$75,000 -99,000	$100,000 -149,999	$150,000 and up
City	20.6	10.2	7.5	10.8	14.8	10.6	13.1	12.6
MSA[1]	10.9	7.9	7.3	10.3	15.7	12.8	17.5	17.6
U.S.	13.1	11.0	10.5	13.7	18.1	11.9	12.5	9.1

Note: (1) Figures cover the Boston-Cambridge-Newton, MA-NH Metropolitan Statistical Area—see Appendix B for areas included
Source: U.S. Census Bureau, 2010-2012 American Community Survey 3-Year Estimates

Poverty Rate

Area	All Ages	Under 18 Years Old	18 to 64 Years Old	65 Years and Over
City	22.7	30.4	21.2	20.4
MSA[1]	10.5	12.8	10.1	9.1
U.S.	15.7	22.2	14.6	9.3

Note: Figures are percentage of people whose income during the past 12 months was below the poverty level; (1) Figures cover the Boston-Cambridge-Newton, MA-NH Metropolitan Statistical Area—see Appendix B for areas included
Source: U.S. Census Bureau, 2010-2012 American Community Survey 3-Year Estimates

Personal Bankruptcy Filing Rate

Area	2008	2009	2010	2011	2012	2013
Suffolk County	1.95	2.32	2.70	2.32	1.89	1.30
U.S.	3.53	4.61	4.97	4.37	3.76	3.29

Note: Numbers are per 1,000 population and include Chapter 7 and Chapter 13 filings
Source: Federal Deposit Insurance Corporation, Regional Economic Conditions, March 20, 2014

EMPLOYMENT

Labor Force and Employment

Area	Civilian Labor Force			Workers Employed		
	Dec. 2012	Dec. 2013	% Chg.	Dec. 2012	Dec. 2013	% Chg.
City	320,515	322,960	0.8	301,058	303,051	0.7
MD[1]	1,550,680	1,562,753	0.8	1,466,586	1,476,295	0.7
U.S.	154,904,000	154,408,000	-0.3	143,060,000	144,423,000	1.0

Note: Data is not seasonally adjusted and covers workers 16 years of age and older; (1) Metropolitan Division—see Appendix B for areas included
Source: Bureau of Labor Statistics, Local Area Unemployment Statistics

Unemployment Rate

Area	2013											
	Jan.	Feb.	Mar.	Apr.	May	Jun.	Jul.	Aug.	Sep.	Oct.	Nov.	Dec.
City	6.7	5.8	5.8	5.9	6.8	7.8	7.5	7.1	7.0	6.9	6.3	6.2
MD[1]	6.0	5.4	5.3	5.2	5.7	6.5	6.2	5.8	6.0	6.0	5.5	5.5
U.S.	8.5	8.1	7.6	7.1	7.3	7.8	7.7	7.3	7.0	7.0	6.6	6.5

Note: Data is not seasonally adjusted and covers workers 16 years of age and older; All figures are percentages; (1) Metropolitan Division—see Appendix B for areas included
Source: Bureau of Labor Statistics, Local Area Unemployment Statistics

Employment by Occupation

Occupation Classification	City (%)	MSA[1] (%)	U.S. (%)
Management, Business, Science, and Arts	46.5	46.2	36.0
Natural Resources, Construction, and Maintenance	4.2	6.6	9.1
Production, Transportation, and Material Moving	6.2	7.7	12.0
Sales and Office	21.9	23.2	24.7
Service	21.2	16.4	18.2

Note: Figures cover employed civilians 16 years of age and older; (1) Figures cover the Boston-Cambridge-Newton, MA-NH Metropolitan Statistical Area—see Appendix B for areas included
Source: U.S. Census Bureau, 2010-2012 American Community Survey 3-Year Estimates

Employment by Industry

Sector	NECTAD[1]		U.S.
	Number of Employees	Percent of Total	Percent of Total
Construction	55,400	3.1	4.2
Education and Health Services	411,300	22.9	15.5
Financial Activities	142,800	8.0	5.7
Government	202,100	11.3	16.1
Information	59,700	3.3	1.9
Leisure and Hospitality	168,600	9.4	10.2
Manufacturing	92,500	5.2	8.7
Mining and Logging	300	<0.1	0.6
Other Services	70,600	3.9	3.9
Professional and Business Services	332,800	18.6	13.7
Retail Trade	155,400	8.7	11.4
Transportation and Utilities	41,900	2.3	3.8
Wholesale Trade	59,400	3.3	4.2

Note: Figures cover non-farm employment as of December 2013 and are not seasonally adjusted;
(1) New England City and Town Area Division—see Appendix B for areas included
Source: Bureau of Labor Statistics, Current Employment Statistics, Employment, Hours, and Earnings

Occupations with Greatest Projected Employment Growth: 2010 – 2020

Occupation[1]	2010 Employment	2020 Projected Employment	Numeric Employment Change	Percent Employment Change
Registered Nurses	87,520	110,100	22,580	25.8
Customer Service Representatives	46,390	59,660	13,260	28.6
Personal Care Aides	21,860	31,780	9,920	45.4
Management Analysts	27,280	37,060	9,780	35.8
Software Developers, Systems Software	27,460	37,070	9,620	35.0
Home Health Aides	17,440	26,810	9,370	53.7
Accountants and Auditors	35,760	45,040	9,280	26.0
Office Clerks, General	58,820	68,010	9,190	15.6
Financial Analysts	13,930	22,270	8,340	59.8
Nursing Aides, Orderlies, and Attendants	41,790	49,880	8,100	19.4

Note: Projections cover Massachusetts; (1) Sorted by numeric employment change
Source: www.projectionscentral.com, State Occupational Projections, 2010–2020 Long-Term Projections

Fastest Growing Occupations: 2010 – 2020

Occupation[1]	2010 Employment	2020 Projected Employment	Numeric Employment Change	Percent Employment Change
Biomedical Engineers	1,400	2,630	1,230	87.8
Actuaries	990	1,780	790	79.5
Personal Financial Advisors	7,180	12,660	5,490	76.5
Insurance Sales Agents	7,900	13,820	5,920	74.9
Loan Officers	5,210	8,660	3,440	66.1
Financial Examiners	1,410	2,290	880	62.5
Financial Analysts	13,930	22,270	8,340	59.8
Dental Laboratory Technicians	670	1,060	390	58.1
Securities, Commodities, and Financial Services Sales Agents	9,440	14,850	5,410	57.4
Meeting, Convention, and Event Planners	2,010	3,150	1,140	56.9

Note: Projections cover Massachusetts; (1) Sorted by percent employment change and excludes occupations
with numeric employment change less than 100
Source: www.projectionscentral.com, State Occupational Projections, 2010–2020 Long-Term Projections

Average Wages

Occupation	$/Hr.	Occupation	$/Hr.
Accountants and Auditors	38.28	Maids and Housekeeping Cleaners	13.66
Automotive Mechanics	21.67	Maintenance and Repair Workers	22.26
Bookkeepers	21.66	Marketing Managers	67.72
Carpenters	28.99	Nuclear Medicine Technologists	37.12
Cashiers	10.63	Nurses, Licensed Practical	25.49
Clerks, General Office	17.12	Nurses, Registered	42.35
Clerks, Receptionists/Information	15.11	Nursing Assistants	14.96
Clerks, Shipping/Receiving	17.35	Packers and Packagers, Hand	10.99
Computer Programmers	40.17	Physical Therapists	38.80
Computer Systems Analysts	41.42	Postal Service Mail Carriers	25.95
Computer User Support Specialists	30.58	Real Estate Brokers	63.74
Cooks, Restaurant	13.94	Retail Salespersons	12.39
Dentists	83.35	Sales Reps., Exc. Tech./Scientific	43.10
Electrical Engineers	49.66	Sales Reps., Tech./Scientific	44.47
Electricians	32.11	Secretaries, Exc. Legal/Med./Exec.	21.16
Financial Managers	64.39	Security Guards	15.06
First-Line Supervisors/Managers, Sales	22.24	Surgeons	n/a
Food Preparation Workers	11.68	Teacher Assistants	14.50
General and Operations Managers	67.32	Teachers, Elementary School	34.30
Hairdressers/Cosmetologists	15.96	Teachers, Secondary School	35.10
Internists	98.46	Telemarketers	17.08
Janitors and Cleaners	15.25	Truck Drivers, Heavy/Tractor-Trailer	23.41
Landscaping/Groundskeeping Workers	16.90	Truck Drivers, Light/Delivery Svcs.	18.17
Lawyers	67.33	Waiters and Waitresses	13.50

Note: Wage data covers the Boston-Cambridge-Quincy, MA NECTA Division—see Appendix B for areas included. Hourly wages for elementary/secondary school teachers and teacher assistants were calculated by the editors from annual wage data assuming a 40 hour work week; n/a not available.
Source: Bureau of Labor Statistics, Metro Area Occupational Employment and Wage Estimates, May 2013

RESIDENTIAL REAL ESTATE

Building Permits

Area	Single-Family 2012	Single-Family 2013	Single-Family Pct. Chg.	Multi-Family 2012	Multi-Family 2013	Multi-Family Pct. Chg.	Total 2012	Total 2013	Total Pct. Chg.
City	40	34	-15.0	1,736	2,527	45.6	1,776	2,561	44.2
MSA[1]	4,126	4,953	20.0	4,725	7,068	49.6	8,851	12,021	35.8
U.S.	518,695	620,802	19.7	310,963	370,020	19.0	829,658	990,822	19.4

Note: (1) Metropolitan Statistical Area—see Appendix B for areas included; figures represent new, privately-owned housing units authorized (unadjusted data); All permit data are based on estimates with imputation.
Source: U.S. Census Bureau, Manufacturing, Mining, and Construction Statistics, Building Permits, 2012, 2013

Homeownership Rate

Area	2006 (%)	2007 (%)	2008 (%)	2009 (%)	2010 (%)	2011 (%)	2012 (%)	2013 (%)
MSA[1]	64.7	64.8	66.2	65.5	66.0	65.5	66.0	66.3
U.S.	68.8	68.1	67.8	67.4	66.9	66.1	65.4	65.1

Note: (1) Figures cover the Boston-Cambridge-Newton, MA-NH Metropolitan Statistical Area—see Appendix B for areas included
Source: U.S. Census Bureau, Housing Vacancies and Homeownership Annual Statistics: 2013

Housing Vacancy Rates

Area	Gross Vacancy Rate[2] (%) 2011	2012	2013	Year-Round Vacancy Rate[3] (%) 2011	2012	2013	Rental Vacancy Rate[4] (%) 2011	2012	2013	Homeowner Vacancy Rate[5] (%) 2011	2012	2013
MSA[1]	8.7	8.6	7.8	6.9	6.9	6.2	5.5	5.9	6.8	1.4	1.3	1.1
U.S.	14.2	13.8	13.8	11.1	10.8	10.7	9.5	8.7	8.3	2.5	2.0	2.0

Note: (1) Figures cover the Boston-Cambridge-Newton, MA-NH Metropolitan Statistical Area—see Appendix B for areas included; (2) The percentage of the total housing inventory that is vacant; (3) The percentage of the housing inventory (excluding seasonal units) that is year-round vacant; (4) The percentage of rental inventory that is vacant for rent; (5) The percentage of homeowner inventory that is vacant for sale
Source: U.S. Census Bureau, Housing Vacancies and Homeownership Annual Statistics: 2013

TAXES

State Corporate Income Tax Rates

State	Tax Rate (%)	Income Brackets ($)	Num. of Brackets	Financial Institution Tax Rate (%)[a]	Federal Income Tax Ded.
Massachusetts	8.0 (n)	Flat rate	1	9.0 (n)	No

Note: Tax rates as of January 1, 2014; (a) Rates listed are the corporate income tax rate applied to financial institutions or excise taxes based on income. Some states have other taxes based upon the value of deposits or shares; (n) Business and manufacturing corporations pay an additional tax of $2.60 per $1,000 on either taxable Massachusetts tangible property or taxable net worth allocable to the state (for intangible property corporations). The minimum tax for both corporations and financial institutions is $456.
Source: Federation of Tax Administrators, "State Corporate Income Tax Rates, 2014"

State Individual Income Tax Rates

State	Tax Rate (%)	Income Brackets ($)	Num. of Brackets	Personal Exempt. ($)[1] Single	Personal Exempt. ($)[1] Dependents	Fed. Inc. Tax Ded.
Massachusetts (a)	5.20	Flat rate	1	4,400	1,000	No

Note: Tax rates as of January 1, 2014; Local- and county-level taxes are not included; n/a not applicable; (1) Married joint filers generally receive double the single exemption; (a) 17 states have statutory provision for automatically adjusting to the rate of inflation the dollar values of the income tax brackets, standard deductions, and/or personal exemptions. Massachusetts, Michigan, and Nebraska index the personal exemptiononly. Oregon does not index the income brackets for $125,000 and over. Maine has suspended indexing for 2014 and 2015.
Source: Federation of Tax Administrators, "State Individual Income Tax Rates, 2014"

Various State and Local Tax Rates

State	State and Local Sales and Use (%)	State Sales and Use (%)	Gasoline[1] (¢/gal.)	Cigarette[2] ($/pack)	Spirits[3] ($/gal.)	Wine[4] ($/gal.)	Beer[5] ($/gal.)
Massachusetts	6.25	6.25	26.50	3.510	4.05 (f)	0.55	0.11

Note: All tax rates as of January 1, 2014; (1) The American Petroleum Institute has developed a methodology for determining the average tax rate on a gallon of fuel. Rates may include any of the following: excise taxes, environmental fees, storage tank fees, other fees or taxes, general sales tax, and local taxes. In states where gasoline is subject to the general sales tax, or where the fuel tax is based on the average sale price, the average rate determined by API is sensitive to changes in the price of gasoline. States that fully or partially apply general sales taxes to gasoline: CA, CO, GA, IL, IN, MI, NY; (2) The federal excise tax of $1.0066 per pack and local taxes are not included; (3) Rates are those applicable to off-premise sales of 40% alcohol by volume (a.b.v.) distilled spirits in 750ml containers. Local excise taxes are excluded; (4) Rates are those applicable to off-premise sales of 11% a.b.v. non-carbonated wine in 750ml containers; (5) Rates are those applicable to off-premise sales of 4.7% a.b.v. beer in 12 ounce containers; (f) Different rates also applicable according to alcohol content, place of production, size of container, or place purchased (on- or off-premise or onboard airlines).
Source: Tax Foundation, 2014 Facts & Figures: How Does Your State Compare?

State Business Tax Climate Index Rankings

State	Overall Rank	Corporate Tax Index Rank	Individual Income Tax Index Rank	Sales Tax Index Rank	Unemployment Insurance Tax Index Rank	Property Tax Index Rank
Massachusetts	25	34	13	17	49	47

Note: The index is a measure of how each state's tax laws affect economic performance. The lower the rank, the more favorable a state's tax system is for business. States without a given tax are given a ranking of 1. The scores/rankings for the District of Columbia do not affect other states. The 2014 index represents the tax climate as of July 1, 2013.
Source: Tax Foundation, State Business Tax Climate Index 2014

COMMERCIAL REAL ESTATE

Office Market

Market Area	Inventory (sq. ft.)	Vacancy Rate (%)	Under Construction (sq. ft.)	YTD Net Absorption (sq. ft.)	Total Average Asking Rent ($/sq. ft./year)
Boston	176,970,760	12.2	3,348,148	1,890,273	34.46
National	4,726,900,879	15.0	55,419,286	42,829,434	26.27

Source: Newmark Grubb Knight Frank, National Office Market Report, 4th Quarter 2013

Industrial/Warehouse/R&D Market

Market Area	Inventory (sq. ft.)	Vacancy Rate (%)	Under Construction (sq. ft.)	YTD Net Absorption (sq. ft.)	Total Average Asking Rent ($/sq. ft./year)
Boston	236,427,383	10.7	70,441	2,558,252	7.40
National	14,022,031,238	7.9	83,249,164	156,549,903	5.40

Source: Newmark Grubb Knight Frank, National Industrial Market Report, 4th Quarter 2013

COMMERCIAL UTILITIES

Typical Monthly Electric Bills

Area	Commercial Service ($/month)		Industrial Service ($/month)	
	1,500 kWh	40 kW demand 14,000 kWh	1,000 kW demand 200,000 kWh	50,000 kW demand 15,000,000 kWh
City	291	2,570	42,023	2,510,937
Average[1]	197	1,636	25,662	1,485,307

Note: Based on total rates in effect July 1, 2013; (1) average based on 180 utilities surveyed
Source: Edison Electric Institute, Typical Bills and Average Rates Report, Summer 2013

TRANSPORTATION

Means of Transportation to Work

Area	Car/Truck/Van		Public Transportation			Bicycle	Walked	Other Means	Worked at Home
	Drove Alone	Car-pooled	Bus	Subway	Railroad				
City	38.1	7.2	13.3	17.7	1.1	1.8	15.3	1.8	3.8
MSA[1]	68.8	7.7	4.0	5.5	2.0	0.8	5.4	1.3	4.5
U.S.	76.4	9.7	2.6	1.7	0.5	0.6	2.8	1.3	4.3

Note: Figures are percentages and cover workers 16 years of age and older; (1) Figures cover the Boston-Cambridge-Newton, MA-NH Metropolitan Statistical Area—see Appendix B for areas included
Source: U.S. Census Bureau, 2010-2012 American Community Survey 3-Year Estimates

Travel Time to Work

Area	Less Than 10 Minutes	10 to 19 Minutes	20 to 29 Minutes	30 to 44 Minutes	45 to 59 Minutes	60 to 89 Minutes	90 Minutes or More
City	7.9	22.5	20.8	28.3	10.4	8.3	1.8
MSA[1]	10.6	24.1	18.7	24.0	10.9	8.9	2.7
U.S.	13.5	29.8	20.9	20.1	7.5	5.6	2.5

Note: Figures are percentages and include workers 16 years old and over; (1) Figures cover the Boston-Cambridge-Newton, MA-NH Metropolitan Statistical Area—see Appendix B for areas included
Source: U.S. Census Bureau, 2010-2012 American Community Survey 3-Year Estimates

Travel Time Index

Area	1985	1990	1995	2000	2005	2010	2011
Urban Area[1]	1.17	1.27	1.29	1.34	1.42	1.28	1.28
Average[2]	1.09	1.14	1.16	1.19	1.23	1.18	1.18

Note: Travel Time Index—the ratio of travel time in the peak period to the travel time at free-flow conditions. For example, a value of 1.30 indicates a 20-minute free-flow trip takes 26 minutes in the peak. Free-flow speeds (60 mph on freeways and 35 mph on principal arterials) are used as the comparison threshold; (1) Covers the Boston MA-NH-RI urban area; (2) average of 498 urban areas
Source: Texas Transportation Institute, Urban Mobility Report 2012, December 2012

Public Transportation

Agency Name / Mode of Transportation	Vehicles Operated in Maximum Service	Annual Unlinked Passenger Trips (in thous.)	Annual Passenger Miles (in thous.)
Massachusetts Bay Transportation Authority (MBTA)			
Bus (directly operated)	767	115,340.0	299,014.2
Bus (purchased transportation)	17	1,128.4	2,798.7
Commuter Rail (purchased transportation)	416	36,083.9	729,727.6
Demand Response (purchased transportation)	641	2,609.4	17,724.3
Ferryboat (purchased transportation)	9	1,399.7	11,250.1
Heavy Rail (directly operated)	336	166,961.1	581,700.4
Light Rail (directly operated)	144	74,816.0	196,463.7
Trolleybus (directly operated)	22	3,278.2	6,894.9

Source: Federal Transit Administration, National Transit Database, 2012

Air Transportation

Airport Name and Code / Type of Service	Passenger Airlines[1]	Passenger Enplanements	Freight Carriers[2]	Freight (lbs.)
Logan International (BOS)				
Domestic service (U.S. carriers - 2013)	32	12,724,462	17	189,487,389
International service (U.S. carriers - 2012)	15	595,073	7	10,704,123

Note: (1) Includes all U.S.-based major, minor and commuter airlines that carried at least one passenger during the year; (2) Includes all U.S.-based airlines and freight carriers that transported at least one lb. of freight during the year.
Source: Bureau of Transportation Statistics, The Intermodal Transportation Database, Air Carriers: T-100 Domestic Market (U.S. Carriers), 2013; Bureau of Transportation Statistics, The Intermodal Transportation Database, Air Carriers: T-100 International Market (U.S. Carriers), 2012

Other Transportation Statistics

Major Highways:	I-90; I-93; I-95
Amtrak Service:	Yes
Major Waterways/Ports:	Boston Harbor; Port of Boston

Source: Amtrak.com; Google Maps

BUSINESSES

Major Business Headquarters

Company Name	Rankings	
	Fortune[1]	Forbes[2]
Bain & Co	-	220
Boston Consulting Group	-	121
Fidelity Investments	-	23
International Data Group	-	128
Liberty Mutual Insurance Group	81	-
New Balance Athletic Shoe	-	197
State Street Corp	268	-

Note: (1) Fortune 500—companies that produce a 10-K are ranked 1 to 500 based on 2012 revenue; (2) all private companies with at least $2 billion in annual revenue through the end of their most current fiscal year are ranked 1 to 224; companies listed are headquartered in the city; dashes indicate no ranking
Source: Fortune, "Fortune 500," May 20, 2013; Forbes, "America's Largest Private Companies," December 18, 2013

Fast-Growing Businesses

According to *Inc.*, Boston is home to seven of America's 500 fastest-growing private companies: **DataXu** (#5); **Next Step Living** (#84); **WordStream** (#184); **Target Logistics** (#194); **Dane Street** (#221); **InviCRO** (#327); **Brafton** (#453). Criteria: must be an independent, privately-held, for-profit, U.S. corporation, proprietorship or partnership; revenues must be at least $100,000 in 2009 and $2 million in 2012; must have four-year operating/sales history. Holding companies, regulated banks, and utilities were excluded. *Inc., "America's 500 Fastest-Growing Private Companies," September 2013*

According to *Initiative for a Competitive Inner City (ICIC)*, Boston is home to four of America's 100 fastest-growing "inner city" companies: **Luggage Forward** (#30); **Fennick McCredie Architecture** (#36); **The Locator Services Group** (#84); **Brown, Richardson + Rowe** (#88). Companies were ranked by their five-year compound annual growth rate. Criteria for inclusion: company must be headquartered in or have 51 percent or more of its physical operations in an economically distressed urban area; must be an independent, for-profit corporation, partnership or proprietorship; must have 10 or more employees and have a five-year sales history that includes sales of at least $200,000 in the base year and at least $1 million in the current year with no decrease in sales over the two most recent years. *Initiative for a Competitive Inner City (ICIC), "Inner City 100 Companies, 2013"*

According to Deloitte, Boston is home to eight of North America's 500 fastest-growing high-technology companies: **Carbonite** (#142); **RAMP** (#209); **AlgoSec** (#221); **Brightcove** (#314); **Veson Nautical** (#327); **Trace One** (#426); **LogMeIn** (#437); **EnerNOC** (#446). Companies are ranked by percentage growth in revenue over a five-year period. Criteria for inclusion: company must be headquartered within North America; must own proprietary intellectual property or proprietary technology that contributes to a significant portion of the company's operating revenue, or devote a significant proportion of revenues to research and development of technology; must have been in business for a minumum of five years with 2008 operating revenues of at least $50,000 USD/CD and 2012 operating revenues of at least $5 million USD/CD. *Deloitte Touche Tohmatsu, 2013 Technology Fast 500*[TM]

Minority Business Opportunity

Boston is home to one company which is on the *Black Enterprise* Bank 20 list (20 largest banks based on total assets, capital, deposits and loans, including mortgage-backed securities for the calendar year): **OneUnited Bank** (#2). Only commercial banks or savings and loans that are classified by the Federal Reserve as black institutions and have been fully operational for the previous calendar year were considered. *Black Enterprise, B.E. 100s, 2013*

Minority- and Women-Owned Businesses

Group	All Firms		Firms with Paid Employees			
	Firms	Sales ($000)	Firms	Sales ($000)	Employees	Payroll ($000)
Asian	3,947	1,278,788	1,133	1,173,216	8,902	208,172
Black	5,739	427,611	472	315,717	2,790	79,718
Hispanic	3,589	283,446	348	205,039	1,568	52,271
Women	14,764	2,484,726	1,713	2,103,933	16,828	619,700
All Firms	49,667	163,405,628	13,330	161,652,861	555,416	38,237,342

Note: Figures cover firms located in the city; minority- and women-owned business are defined as firms in which the corresponding group own 51% or more of the stock or equity of the company
Source: U.S. Census Bureau, 2007 Economic Census, Survey of Business Owners (2012 Survey of Business Owners data will be released starting in June 2015)

HOTELS & CONVENTION CENTERS

Hotels/Motels

Area	5 Star		4 Star		3 Star		2 Star		1 Star		Not Rated	
	Num.	Pct.[3]	Num.	Pct.[3]	Num.	Pct.[3]	Num.	Pct.[3]	Num.	Pct.[3]	Num.	Pct.[3]
City[1]	5	2.0	37	14.6	109	43.1	75	29.6	4	1.6	23	9.1
Total[2]	142	0.9	1,005	6.0	5,147	30.9	8,578	51.4	408	2.4	1,397	8.4

Note: (1) Figures cover Boston and vicinity; (2) Figures cover all 100 cities in this book; (3) Percentage of hotels which have a given star rating; Star ratings are determined by expedia.com and offer an indication of the general quality of a particular hotel.
Source: expedia.com, April 7, 2014

Major Convention Centers

Name	Overall Space (sq. ft.)	Exhibit Space (sq. ft.)	Meeting Space (sq. ft.)	Meeting Rooms
Boston Convention & Exhibition Center	n/a	516,000	300,000	84
John B. Hynes Veterans Memorial Convention Center	n/a	193,000	71,600	38

Note: Table includes convention centers located in the Boston-Cambridge-Newton, MA-NH metro area; n/a not available
Source: Original research

Living Environment

COST OF LIVING

Cost of Living Index

Composite Index	Groceries	Housing	Utilities	Trans-portation	Health Care	Misc. Goods/ Services
139.1	125.5	175.3	144.3	104.1	126.1	129.7

Note: The Cost of Living Index measures regional differences in the cost of consumer goods and services, excluding taxes and non-consumer expenditures, for professional and managerial households in the top income quintile. It is based on more than 50,000 prices covering almost 60 different items for which prices are collected three times a year by chambers of commerce, economic development organizations or university applied economic centers in each participating urban area. The numbers shown should be read as a percentage above or below the national average of 100. For example, a value of 115.4 in the groceries column indicates that grocery prices are 15.4% higher than the national average. Small differences in the index numbers should not be interpreted as significant; Figures cover the Boston MA urban area.
Source: The Council for Community and Economic Research, ACCRA Cost of Living Index, 2013

Grocery Prices

Area[1]	T-Bone Steak ($/pound)	Frying Chicken ($/pound)	Whole Milk ($/half gal.)	Eggs ($/dozen)	Orange Juice ($/64 oz.)	Coffee ($/11.5 oz.)
City[2]	11.49	1.64	2.79	2.99	3.85	5.07
Avg.	10.19	1.28	2.34	1.81	3.48	4.39
Min.	8.56	0.94	1.44	1.19	2.78	3.40
Max.	14.82	2.28	3.56	3.73	6.23	7.32

Note: (1) Values for the local area are compared with the average, minimum and maximum values for all 327 areas in the Cost of Living Index; (2) Figures cover the Boston MA urban area; **T-Bone Steak** *(price per pound);* **Frying Chicken** *(price per pound, whole fryer);* **Whole Milk** *(half gallon carton);* **Eggs** *(price per dozen, Grade A, large);* **Orange Juice** *(64 oz. Tropicana or Florida Natural);* **Coffee** *(11.5 oz. can, vacuum-packed, Maxwell House, Hills Bros, or Folgers).*
Source: The Council for Community and Economic Research, ACCRA Cost of Living Index, 2013

Housing and Utility Costs

Area[1]	New Home Price ($)	Apartment Rent ($/month)	All Electric ($/month)	Part Electric ($/month)	Other Energy ($/month)	Telephone ($/month)
City[2]	482,267	1,863	-	105.74	137.62	38.25
Avg.	295,864	900	171.38	91.82	70.12	27.73
Min.	185,506	458	117.80	48.81	33.67	17.16
Max.	1,358,917	3,783	441.68	171.40	372.65	39.47

Note: (1) Values for the local area are compared with the average, minimum and maximum values for all 327 areas in the Cost of Living Index; (2) Figures cover the Boston MA urban area; **New Home Price** *(2,400 sf living area, 8,000 sf lot, in urban area with full utilities);* **Apartment Rent** *(950 sf 2 bedroom/1.5 or 2 bath, unfurnished, excluding all utilities except water);* **All Electric** *(average monthly cost for an all-electric home);* **Part Electric** *(average monthly cost for a part-electric home);* **Other Energy** *(average monthly cost for natural gas, fuel oil, coal, wood, and any other forms of energy except electricity);* **Telephone** *(price includes basic monthly rate for a private residential line plus additional local usage charges incurred by a family of four).*
Source: The Council for Community and Economic Research, ACCRA Cost of Living Index, 2013

Health Care, Transportation, and Other Costs

Area[1]	Doctor ($/visit)	Dentist ($/visit)	Optometrist ($/visit)	Gasoline ($/gallon)	Beauty Salon ($/visit)	Men's Shirt ($)
City[2]	149.00	114.07	120.73	3.61	44.00	36.52
Avg.	101.40	86.48	96.16	3.44	33.87	26.55
Min.	61.67	50.83	50.12	3.08	18.92	12.48
Max.	182.71	152.50	223.78	4.33	68.22	52.03

Note: (1) Values for the local area are compared with the average, minimum and maximum values for all 327 areas in the Cost of Living Index; (2) Figures cover the Boston MA urban area; **Doctor** *(general practitioners routine exam of an established patient);* **Dentist** *(adult teeth cleaning and periodic oral examination);* **Optometrist** *(full vision eye exam for established adult patient);* **Gasoline** *(one gallon regular unleaded, national brand, including all taxes, cash price at self-service pump if available);* **Beauty Salon** *(woman's shampoo, trim, and blow-dry);* **Men's Shirt** *(cotton/polyester dress shirt, pinpoint weave, long sleeves).*
Source: The Council for Community and Economic Research, ACCRA Cost of Living Index, 2013

HOUSING

House Price Index (HPI)

Area	National Ranking[2]	Quarterly Change (%)	One-Year Change (%)	Five-Year Change (%)
MD[1]	92	1.62	4.78	-0.62
U.S.[3]	–	1.20	7.69	4.18

Note: The HPI is a weighted repeat sales index. It measures average price changes in repeat sales or refinancings on the same properties. This information is obtained by reviewing repeat mortgage transactions on single-family properties whose mortgages have been purchased or securitized by Fannie Mae or Freddie Mac in January 1975; (1) Boston, MA Metropolitan Division—see Appendix B for areas included; (2) Rankings are based on annual percentage change for all metro areas containing at least 15,000 transactions over the last 10 years and ranges from 1 to 283; (3) figures based on a weighted average of Census Division estimates using a seasonally adjusted, purchase-only index; all figures are for the period ending December 31, 2013
Source: Federal Housing Finance Agency, House Price Index, February 25, 2014

Median Single-Family Home Prices

Area	2011	2012	2013p	Percent Change 2012 to 2013
MSA[1]	346.2	351.2	375.9	7.0
U.S. Average	166.2	177.2	197.4	11.4

Note: Figures are median sales prices of existing single-family homes in thousands of dollars; (p) preliminary; n/a not available; (1) Boston-Cambridge-Newton, MA-NH Metropolitan Statistical Area—see Appendix B for areas included
Source: National Association of Realtors, Median Sales Price of Existing Single-Family Homes for Metropolitan Areas, 4th Quarter 2013

Qualifying Income Based on Median Sales Price of Existing Single-Family Homes

Area	With 5% Down ($)	With 10% Down ($)	With 20% Down ($)
MSA[1]	85,603	81,098	72,087
U.S. Average	45,395	43,006	38,228

Note: Figures are preliminary; Qualifying income is based on a mortgage rate of 4.4%. Monthly principal and interest payment is limited to 25% of income; n/a not available; (1) Boston-Cambridge-Newton, MA-NH Metropolitan Statistical Area—see Appendix B for areas included
Source: National Association of Realtors, Qualifying Income Based on Median Sales Price of Existing Single-Family Homes for Metropolitan Areas, 4th Quarter 2013

Median Apartment Condo-Coop Home Prices

Area	2011	2012	2013p	Percent Change 2012 to 2013
MSA[1]	296.1	308.6	327.5	6.1
U.S. Average	165.1	173.7	194.9	12.2

Note: Figures are median sales prices of existing apartment condo-coop homes in thousands of dollars; (p) preliminary; n/a not available; (1) Boston-Cambridge-Newton, MA-NH Metropolitan Statistical Area—see Appendix B for areas included
Source: National Association of Realtors, Median Sales Price of Existing Apartment Condo-Coop Homes for Metropolitan Areas, 4th Quarter 2013

Gross Monthly Rent

Area	Under $200	$200 -299	$300 -499	$500 -749	$750 -999	$1,000 -1,499	$1,500 and up	Median ($)
City	3.5	8.4	7.6	6.4	9.3	29.4	35.3	1,260
MSA[1]	2.2	5.8	6.5	7.5	14.7	34.6	28.7	1,177
U.S.	1.7	3.3	8.1	22.7	24.3	25.7	14.3	889

Note: Figures are percentages except for Median; Gross rent is the contract rent plus the estimated average monthly cost of utilities (electricity, gas, and water and sewer) and fuels (oil, coal, kerosene, wood, etc.) if these are paid by the renter (or paid for the renter by someone else); (1) Figures cover the Boston-Cambridge-Newton, MA-NH Metropolitan Statistical Area—see Appendix B for areas included
Source: U.S. Census Bureau, 2010-2012 American Community Survey 3-Year Estimates

Year Housing Structure Built

Area	2010 or Later	2000 -2009	1990 -1999	1980 -1989	1970 -1979	1960 -1969	1950 -1959	1940 -1949	Before 1940	Median Year
City	0.3	6.7	4.2	5.6	7.0	7.5	7.3	5.9	55.5	<1940
MSA[1]	0.3	8.1	7.1	10.6	11.0	10.4	11.2	5.5	35.8	1958
U.S.	0.5	14.9	13.8	13.9	15.9	11.1	10.9	5.5	13.5	1976

Note: Figures are percentages except for Median Year; (1) Figures cover the Boston-Cambridge-Newton, MA-NH Metropolitan Statistical Area—see Appendix B for areas included
Source: U.S. Census Bureau, 2010-2012 American Community Survey 3-Year Estimates

HEALTH

Health Risk Data

Category	MD[1] (%)	U.S. (%)
Adults aged 18–64 who have any kind of health care coverage	93.4	79.6
Adults who reported being in good or excellent health	87.1	83.1
Adults who are current smokers	14.9	19.6
Adults who are heavy drinkers[2]	8.1	6.1
Adults who are binge drinkers[3]	20.5	16.9
Adults who are overweight (BMI 25.0 - 29.9)	35.1	35.8
Adults who are obese (BMI 30.0 - 99.8)	21.1	27.6
Adults who participated in any physical activities in the past month	80.1	77.1
Adults 50+ who have ever had a sigmoidoscopy or colonoscopy	74.8	67.3
Women aged 40+ who have had a mammogram within the past two years	85.3	74.0
Men aged 40+ who have had a PSA test within the past two years	43.3	45.2
Adults aged 65+ who have had flu shot within the past year	61.9	60.1
Adults who always wear a seatbelt	89.1	93.8

Note: Data as of 2012 unless otherwise noted; (1) Figures cover the Boston, MA Metropolitan Division—see Appendix B for areas included; (2) Heavy drinkers are classified as males having more than two drinks per day or females having more than one drink per day; (3) Binge drinkers are classified as males having five or more drinks on one occasion or females having four or more drinks on one occasion
Source: Centers for Disease Control and Prevention, Behaviorial Risk Factor Surveillance System, SMART: Selected Metropolitan/Micropolitan Area Risk Trends, 2012

Chronic Health Indicators

Category	MD[1] (%)	U.S. (%)
Adults who have ever been told they had a heart attack	3.6	4.5
Adults who have ever been told they had a stroke	1.5	2.9
Adults who have been told they currently have asthma	9.2	8.9
Adults who have ever been told they have arthritis	21.1	25.7
Adults who have ever been told they have diabetes[2]	7.3	9.7
Adults who have ever been told they had skin cancer	5.1	5.7
Adults who have ever been told they had any other types of cancer	5.8	6.5
Adults who have ever been told they have COPD	4.4	6.2
Adults who have ever been told they have kidney disease	1.5	2.5
Adults who have ever been told they have a form of depression	16.6	18.0

Note: Data as of 2012 unless otherwise noted; (1) Figures cover the Boston, MA Metropolitan Division—see Appendix B for areas included; (2) Figures do not include pregnancy-related, borderline, or pre-diabetes
Source: Centers for Disease Control and Prevention, Behaviorial Risk Factor Surveillance System, SMART: Selected Metropolitan/Micropolitan Area Risk Trends, 2012

Mortality Rates for the Top 10 Causes of Death in the U.S.

ICD-10[a] Sub-Chapter	ICD-10[a] Code	Age-Adjusted Mortality Rate[1] per 100,000 population	
		County[2]	U.S.
Malignant neoplasms	C00-C97	185.7	174.2
Ischaemic heart diseases	I20-I25	93.9	119.1
Other forms of heart disease	I30-I51	46.3	49.6
Chronic lower respiratory diseases	J40-J47	29.6	43.2
Cerebrovascular diseases	I60-I69	32.9	40.3
Organic, including symptomatic, mental disorders	F01-F09	45.2	30.5
Other degenerative diseases of the nervous system	G30-G31	19.5	26.3
Other external causes of accidental injury	W00-X59	26.5	25.1
Diabetes mellitus	E10-E14	16.4	21.3
Hypertensive diseases	I10-I15	17.5	18.8

Note: (a) ICD-10 = International Classification of Diseases 10th Revision; (1) Mortality rates are a three year average covering 2008-2010; (2) Figures cover Suffolk County
Source: Centers for Disease Control and Prevention, National Center for Health Statistics. Compressed Mortality File 1999-2010 on CDC WONDER Online Database, released January 2013. Data are compiled from the Compressed Mortality File 1999-2010, Series 20 No. 2P, 2013.

Mortality Rates for Selected Causes of Death

ICD-10[a] Sub-Chapter	ICD-10[a] Code	Age-Adjusted Mortality Rate[1] per 100,000 population	
		County[2]	U.S.
Assault	X85-Y09	7.2	5.5
Diseases of the liver	K70-K76	13.0	12.4
Human immunodeficiency virus (HIV) disease	B20-B24	5.0	3.0
Influenza and pneumonia	J09-J18	17.5	16.4
Intentional self-harm	X60-X84	6.6	11.8
Malnutrition	E40-E46	*0.5	0.8
Obesity and other hyperalimentation	E65-E68	1.3	1.6
Renal failure	N17-N19	19.3	13.6
Transport accidents	V01-V99	4.1	12.6
Viral hepatitis	B15-B19	3.2	2.2

Note: (a) ICD-10 = International Classification of Diseases 10th Revision; (1) Mortality rates are a three year average covering 2008-2010; (2) Figures cover Suffolk County; (*) Unreliable data as per CDC
Source: Centers for Disease Control and Prevention, National Center for Health Statistics. Compressed Mortality File 1999-2010 on CDC WONDER Online Database, released January 2013. Data are compiled from the Compressed Mortality File 1999-2010, Series 20 No. 2P, 2013.

Health Insurance Coverage

Area	With Health Insurance	With Private Health Insurance	With Public Health Insurance	Without Health Insurance	Population Under Age 18 Without Health Insurance
City	94.6	66.0	35.6	5.4	1.5
MSA[1]	95.4	77.1	29.4	4.6	1.7
U.S.	84.9	65.4	30.4	15.1	7.5

Note: Figures are percentages that cover the civilian noninstitutionalized population; (1) Figures cover the Boston-Cambridge-Newton, MA-NH Metropolitan Statistical Area—see Appendix B for areas included
Source: U.S. Census Bureau, 2010-2012 American Community Survey 3-Year Estimates

Number of Medical Professionals

Area[1]	MDs[2]	DOs[2,3]	Dentists	Podiatrists	Chiropractors	Optometrists
Local (number)	10,019	100	1,243	66	107	215
Local (rate[4])	1,362.0	13.6	166.6	8.8	14.3	28.8
U.S. (rate[4])	267.6	19.6	61.7	5.6	24.7	14.5

Note: Data as of 2012 unless noted; (1) Local data covers Suffolk County; (2) Data as of 2011; (3) Doctor of Osteopathic Medicine; (4) rate per 100,000 population
Source: Area Resource File (ARF) 2012-2013. U.S. Department of Health and Human Services, Health Resources and Services Administration, Bureau of Health Professions

Best Hospitals

According to *U.S. News,* the Boston, MA metro area is home to six of the best hospitals in the U.S.: **Beth Israel Deaconess Medical Center** (2 specialties); **Brigham and Women's Hospital** (Honor Roll/12 specialties); **Beth Israel Deaconess Medical Center** (2 specialties); **Massachusetts General Hospital** (Honor Roll/16 specialties); **New England Baptist Hospital** (1 specialty); **South Shore Hospital** (1 specialty). The hospitals listed were nationally ranked in at least one adult specialty. Only 147 hospitals nationwide were nationally ranked in one or more specialties. Eighteen hospitals in the U.S. made the Honor Roll by ranking near the top in at least six specialties.*U.S. News Online, "America's Best Hospitals 2013-14"*

According to *U.S. News,* the Boston, MA metro area is home to two of the best children's hospitals in the U.S.: **Boston Children's Hospital** (Honor Roll); **Massachusetts General Hospital for Children.** The hospitals listed were highly ranked in at least one pediatric specialty. Eighty-seven hospitals in the U.S. ranked in at least one specialty. Ten children's hospitals in the U.S. made the Honor Roll by ranking near the top in three or more specialties.*U.S. News Online, "America's Best Children's Hospitals 2013-14"*

EDUCATION

Public School District Statistics

District Name	Schls	Pupils	Pupil/ Teacher Ratio	Minority Pupils[1] (%)	Free Lunch Eligible[2] (%)	IEP[3] (%)
Boston	118	55,027	12.9	87.4	63.6	19.3

Note: Table includes school districts with 2,000 or more students; (1) Percentage of students that are not non-Hispanic white; (2) Percentage of students that are eligible for the free lunch program; (3) Percentage of students that have an Individualized Education Program.
Source: U.S. Department of Education, National Center for Education Statistics, Common Core of Data, Local Education Agency (School District) Universe Survey: School Year 2011-2012; U.S. Department of Education, National Center for Education Statistics, Common Core of Data, Public Elementary/Secondary School Universe Survey: School Year 2011-2012

Best High Schools

High School Name	Rank[1]	Grad. Rate[2] (%)	Coll.[3] (%)	AP/IB/ AICE Tests[4]	AP/IB/ AICE Score[5]	SAT Score[6]	ACT Score[6]
Boston Latin School	116	97	100	1.0	3.4	1876	25.8

Note: (1) Public schools are ranked from 1 to 2,000 based on the following self-reported statistics (with the corresponding weight used in calculating their overall score). Schools that were newly founded and did not have a graduating senior class in 2012 were excluded; (2) Four-year, on-time graduation rate (25%); (3) Percent of 2011 graduates who were accepted to college (25%); (4) AP/IB/AICE tests taken per student (25%); (5) Average AP/IB/AICE exam score (10%); (6) Average SAT and/or ACT score (10%); Percent of students enrolled in at least one AP/IB/AICE course (5%)—data not shown
Source: Newsweek and The Daily Beast, "America's Best High Schools 2013"

Highest Level of Education

Area	Less than H.S.	H.S. Diploma	Some College, No Deg.	Associate Degree	Bachelor's Degree	Master's Degree	Prof. School Degree	Doctorate Degree
City	15.2	22.7	14.3	4.4	23.8	12.6	4.3	2.7
MSA[1]	9.4	24.7	15.7	7.2	24.0	13.1	3.2	2.7
U.S.	14.1	28.3	21.3	7.8	18.0	7.5	1.9	1.2

Note: Figures cover persons age 25 and over; (1) Figures cover the Boston-Cambridge-Newton, MA-NH Metropolitan Statistical Area—see Appendix B for areas included
Source: U.S. Census Bureau, 2010-2012 American Community Survey 3-Year Estimates

Educational Attainment by Race

Area	High School Graduate or Higher (%)					Bachelor's Degree or Higher (%)				
	Total	White	Black	Asian	Hisp.[2]	Total	White	Black	Asian	Hisp.[2]
City	84.8	91.9	79.7	75.8	66.1	43.4	58.5	17.3	45.8	17.0
MSA[1]	90.6	93.3	82.1	83.4	68.5	43.0	45.2	22.6	56.7	19.2
U.S.	85.9	88.1	82.5	85.5	63.1	28.6	30.0	18.4	50.2	13.4

Note: Figures shown cover persons 25 years old and over; (1) Figures cover the Boston-Cambridge-Newton, MA-NH Metropolitan Statistical Area—see Appendix B for areas included; (2) People of Hispanic origin can be of any race
Source: U.S. Census Bureau, 2010-2012 American Community Survey 3-Year Estimates

School Enrollment by Grade and Control

Area	Preschool (%)		Kindergarten (%)		Grades 1 - 4 (%)		Grades 5 - 8 (%)		Grades 9 - 12 (%)	
	Public	Private	Public	Private	Public	Private	Public	Private	Public	Private
City	53.7	46.3	79.9	20.1	84.8	15.2	84.9	15.1	86.5	13.5
MSA[1]	41.6	58.4	86.1	13.9	90.4	9.6	88.9	11.1	86.8	13.2
U.S.	56.9	43.1	87.8	12.2	89.9	10.1	90.0	10.0	90.8	9.2

Note: Figures shown cover persons 3 years old and over; (1) Figures cover the Boston-Cambridge-Newton,
MA-NH Metropolitan Statistical Area—see Appendix B for areas included
Source: U.S. Census Bureau, 2010-2012 American Community Survey 3-Year Estimates

Average Salaries of Public School Classroom Teachers

Area	2012-13		2013-14		Percent Change 2012-13 to 2013-14	Percent Change 2003-04 to 2013-14
	Dollars	Rank[1]	Dollars	Rank[1]		
Massachusetts	72,334	2	73,736	2	1.94	37.2
U.S. Average	56,103	–	56,689	–	1.04	21.8

Note: (1) State rank ranges from 1 to 51 where 1 indicates highest salary.
Source: National Education Association, Rankings & Estimates: Rankings of the States 2013 and Estimates of
School Statistics 2014, March 2014

Higher Education

Four-Year Colleges			Two-Year Colleges			Medical Schools[1]	Law Schools[2]	Voc/ Tech[3]
Public	Private Non-profit	Private For-profit	Public	Private Non-profit	Private For-profit			
2	22	2	1	2	2	3	4	2

Note: Figures cover institutions located within the city limits and include main campuses only; (1) includes
schools accredited by the Liaison Committee on Medical Education and the American Osteopathic Association's
Commission on Osteopathic College Accreditation; (2) includes ABA-accredited schools, schools with
provisional ABA accreditation, and state accredited schools; (3) includes all schools with programs that are less
than 2 years.
Source: National Center for Education Statistics, Integrated Postsecondary Education System (IPEDS),
2012-13; Association of American Medical Colleges, Member List, April 24, 2014; American Osteopathic
Association, Member List, April 24, 2014; Law School Admission Council, Official Guide to ABA-Approved
Law Schools Online, April 24, 2014; Wikipedia, List of Medical Schools in the United States, April 24, 2014;
Wikipedia, List of Law Schools in the United States, April 24, 2014

According to *U.S. News & World Report,* the Boston, MA metro division is home to three of the
best national universities in the U.S.: **Boston College** (#31); **Boston University** (#41);
Northeastern University (#49). The indicators used to capture academic quality fall into a
number of categories: assessment by administrators at peer institutions; retention of students;
faculty resources; student selectivity; financial resources; alumni giving; high school counselor
ratings of colleges; and graduation rate. *U.S. News & World Report, "America's Best Colleges
2014"*

According to *U.S. News & World Report,* the Boston, MA metro division is home to one of the
best liberal arts colleges in the U.S.: **Wellesley College** (#7). The indicators used to capture
academic quality fall into a number of categories: assessment by administrators at peer institutions;
retention of students; faculty resources; student selectivity; financial resources; alumni giving; high
school counselor ratings of colleges; and graduation rate. *U.S. News & World Report, "America's
Best Colleges 2014"*

According to *U.S. News & World Report,* the Boston, MA metro division is home to two of the top
100 law schools in the U.S.: **Boston University** (#29); **Northeastern University** (#86). The
rankings are based on a weighted average of 12 measures of quality: peer assessment score;
assessment score by lawyers/judges; median LSAT scores; median undergrad GPA; acceptance
rate; employment rates for graduates; placement success; bar passage rate; faculty resources;
expenditures per student; student/faculty ratio; and library resources. *U.S. News & World Report,
"America's Best Graduate Schools, Law, 2014"*

According to *U.S. News & World Report,* the Boston, MA metro division is home to five of the top
100 business schools in the U.S.: **Harvard University** (#1); **Boston College (Carroll)** (#40);
Boston University (#40); **Babson College (Olin)** (#56); **Northeastern University** (#61). The
rankings are based on a weighted average of the following nine measures: quality assessment; peer
assessment; recruiter assessment; placement success; mean starting salary and bonus; student
selectivity; mean GMAT and GRE scores; mean undergraduate GPA; and acceptance rate. *U.S.
News & World Report, "America's Best Graduate Schools, Business, 2014"*

**PRESIDENTIAL
ELECTION**

2012 Presidential Election Results

Area	Obama	Romney	Other
Suffolk County	77.6	20.8	1.6
U.S.	51.0	47.2	1.8

Note: Results are percentages and may not add to 100% due to rounding
Source: Dave Leip's Atlas of U.S. Presidential Elections

EMPLOYERS

Major Employers

Company Name	Industry
Beth Israel Deaconess Medical Center	General medical and surgical hospitals
Boston University	Colleges and universities
Children's Hospital Corporation	Specialty hospitals, except psychiatric
City of Lowell	City and town managers' office
Federal Deposit Insurance Corporation	Federal deposit insurance corporation (FDIC)
General Electric Company	Aircraft engines and engine parts
Harvard University	Colleges and universities
Internal Revenue Service	Taxation department, government
John Hancock Corp Tax Credit Fund I	Personal service agents, brokers & bureaus
Lahey Clinic	General medical and surgical hospitals
Massachusetts General Hospital	General medical and surgical hospitals
Massachusetts Institute of Technology	Colleges and universities
State Street Bank and Trust Company	State trust companies accepting deposits, commercial
Sun Healthcare Group	Accident and health insurance
The Admins of the Tulane Educational Fund	Hospital, medical school affiliation
Tufts Medical Center	Hospital management

Note: Companies shown are located within the Boston-Cambridge-Newton, MA-NH Metropolitan Statistical Area.
Source: Hoovers.com; Wikipedia

Best Companies to Work For

Bingham McCutchen LLP; The Boston Consulting Group, headquartered in Boston, are among "The 100 Best Companies to Work For." To pick the 100 Best Companies to Work For, *Fortune* partnered with the Great Place to Work Institute. Two hundred fifty seven firms participated in this year's survey. Two-thirds of a company's score is based on the results of the Institute's Trust Index survey, which is sent to a random sample of employees from each company. The questions related to attitudes about management's credibility, job satisfaction, and camaraderie. The other third of the scoring is based on the company's responses to the Institute's Culture Audit, which includes detailed questions about pay and benefit programs, and a series of open-ended questions about hiring practices, internal communication, training, recognition programs, and diversity efforts. Any company that is at least five years old with more than 1,000 U.S. employees is eligible. *Fortune, "The 100 Best Companies to Work For," 2014*

Bain & Co; State Street; The Boston Consulting Group, headquartered in Boston, are among the "100 Best Companies for Working Mothers." Criteria: workforce representation; child care; flexibility programs; and leave policies. This year *Working Mother* gave particular weight to flexible work arrangements, women's advancement programs, and paid maternity leave. *Working Mother, "100 Best Companies 2013"*

Massachusetts General Hospital, headquartered in Boston, is among the "50 Best Employers for Workers Over 50." Criteria: recruiting practices; opportunities for training, education, and career development; workplace accommodations; alternative work options, such as flexible scheduling, job sharing, and phased retirement; employee health and pension benefits; and retiree benefits. Employers with at least 50 employees based in the U.S. are eligible, including for-profit companies, not-for-profit organizations, and government employers. *AARP, "2013 AARP Best Employers for Workers Over 50"*

PUBLIC SAFETY

Crime Rate

Area	All Crimes	Violent Crimes				Property Crimes		
		Murder	Forcible Rape	Robbery	Aggrav. Assault	Burglary	Larceny -Theft	Motor Vehicle Theft
City	3,744.6	9.0	39.5	302.9	483.6	527.2	2,124.8	257.5
Suburbs[1]	2,153.3	1.1	20.2	74.3	235.1	417.0	1,304.8	100.9
Metro[2]	2,675.7	3.7	26.5	149.4	316.7	453.2	1,574.0	152.3
U.S.	3,246.1	4.7	26.9	112.9	242.3	670.2	1,959.3	229.7

Note: Figures are crimes per 100,000 population; (1) All areas within the metro area that are located outside the city limits; (2) Figures cover the Boston, MA Metropolitan Division—see Appendix B for areas included
Source: FBI Uniform Crime Reports, 2012

Hate Crimes

Area	Number of Quarters Reported	Bias Motivation				
		Race	Religion	Sexual Orientation	Ethnicity	Disability
City	4	52	19	43	9	0
U.S.	4	2,797	1,099	1,135	667	92

Source: Federal Bureau of Investigation, Hate Crime Statistics 2012

Identity Theft Consumer Complaints

Area	Complaints	Complaints per 100,000 Population	Rank[2]
MSA[1]	2,975	65.4	166
U.S.	290,056	91.8	-

Note: (1) Figures cover the Boston-Cambridge-Newton, MA-NH Metropolitan Statistical Area—see Appendix B for areas included; (2) Rank ranges from 1 to 377 where 1 indicates greatest number of identity theft complaints per 100,000 population
Source: Federal Trade Commission, Consumer Sentinel Network Data Book for January–December 2013

Fraud and Other Consumer Complaints

Area	Complaints	Complaints per 100,000 Population	Rank[2]
MSA[1]	17,680	388.4	138
U.S.	1,811,724	595.2	-

Note: (1) Figures cover the Boston-Cambridge-Newton, MA-NH Metropolitan Statistical Area—see Appendix B for areas included; (2) Rank ranges from 1 to 377 where 1 indicates greatest number of identity theft complaints per 100,000 population
Source: Federal Trade Commission, Consumer Sentinel Network Data Book for January–December 2013

RECREATION

Culture

Dance[1]	Theatre[1]	Instrumental Music[1]	Vocal Music[1]	Series and Festivals	Museums and Art Galleries[2]	Zoos and Aquariums[3]
3	6	9	5	8	53	4

Note: (1) Number of professional perfoming groups; (2) Based on organizations with primary SIC code 8412; (3) AZA-accredited
Source: The Grey House Performing Arts Directory, 2013; Association of Zoos & Aquariums, AZA Member Zoos & Aquariums, April 2014; www.AccuLeads.com, May 1, 2014

Professional Sports Teams

Team Name	League	Year Established
Boston Bruins	National Hockey League (NHL)	1924
Boston Celtics	National Basketball Association (NBA)	1946
Boston Red Sox	Major League Baseball (MLB)	1901
New England Patriots	National Football League (NFL)	1960
New England Revolution	Major League Soccer (MLS)	1996

Note: Includes teams located in the Boston-Cambridge-Newton, MA-NH Metropolitan Statistical Area.
Source: Wikipedia, Major Professional Sports Teams of the United States and Canada

CLIMATE

Average and Extreme Temperatures

Temperature	Jan	Feb	Mar	Apr	May	Jun	Jul	Aug	Sep	Oct	Nov	Dec	Yr.
Extreme High (°F)	72	70	85	94	95	100	102	102	100	90	83	73	102
Average High (°F)	36	38	46	56	67	76	82	80	73	63	52	41	59
Average Temp. (°F)	30	31	39	48	58	68	74	72	65	55	45	34	52
Average Low (°F)	22	23	31	40	50	59	65	64	57	47	38	27	44
Extreme Low (°F)	-12	-4	1	16	34	45	50	47	37	28	15	-7	-12

Note: Figures cover the years 1945-1990
Source: National Climatic Data Center, International Station Meteorological Climate Summary, 9/96

Average Precipitation/Snowfall/Humidity

Precip./Humidity	Jan	Feb	Mar	Apr	May	Jun	Jul	Aug	Sep	Oct	Nov	Dec	Yr.
Avg. Precip. (in.)	3.8	3.6	3.8	3.7	3.5	3.1	2.9	3.6	3.1	3.3	4.4	4.1	42.9
Avg. Snowfall (in.)	12	12	8	1	Tr	0	0	0	0	Tr	1	8	41
Avg. Rel. Hum. 7am (%)	68	68	69	68	71	72	73	76	79	77	74	70	72
Avg. Rel. Hum. 4pm (%)	58	57	56	56	58	58	58	61	61	59	61	60	59

Note: Figures cover the years 1945-1990; Tr = Trace amounts (<0.05 in. of rain; <0.5 in. of snow)
Source: National Climatic Data Center, International Station Meteorological Climate Summary, 9/96

Weather Conditions

Temperature			Daytime Sky			Precipitation		
5°F & below	32°F & below	90°F & above	Clear	Partly cloudy	Cloudy	0.01 inch or more precip.	0.1 inch or more snow/ice	Thunder-storms
4	97	12	88	127	150	253	48	18

Note: Figures are average number of days per year and cover the years 1945-1990
Source: National Climatic Data Center, International Station Meteorological Climate Summary, 9/96

HAZARDOUS WASTE

Superfund Sites

Boston has no sites on the EPA's Superfund Final National Priorities List.
U.S. Environmental Protection Agency, Final National Priorities List, April 26, 2014

AIR & WATER QUALITY

Air Quality Index

Area	Percent of Days when Air Quality was...[2]					AQI Statistics[2]	
	Good	Moderate	Unhealthy for Sensitive Groups	Unhealthy	Very Unhealthy	Maximum	Median
MSA[1]	61.1	37.5	1.4	0.0	0.0	116	47

Note: (1) Data covers the Boston-Cambridge-Newton, MA-NH Metropolitan Statistical Area—see Appendix B for areas included; (2) Based on 365 days with AQI data in 2013. Air Quality Index (AQI) is an index for reporting daily air quality. EPA calculates the AQI for five major air pollutants regulated by the Clean Air Act: ground-level ozone, particle pollution (aka particulate matter), carbon monoxide, sulfur dioxide, and nitrogen dioxide. The AQI runs from 0 to 500. The higher the AQI value, the greater the level of air pollution and the greater the health concern. There are six AQI categories: "Good" AQI is between 0 and 50. Air quality is considered satisfactory; "Moderate" AQI is between 51 and 100. Air quality is acceptable; "Unhealthy for Sensitive Groups" When AQI values are between 101 and 150, members of sensitive groups may experience health effects; "Unhealthy" When AQI values are between 151 and 200 everyone may begin to experience health effects; "Very Unhealthy" AQI values between 201 and 300 trigger a health alert; "Hazardous" AQI values over 300 trigger warnings of emergency conditions (not shown).
Source: U.S. Environmental Protection Agency, Air Quality Index Report, 2013

Air Quality Index Pollutants

Area	Percent of Days when AQI Pollutant was...[2]					
	Carbon Monoxide	Nitrogen Dioxide	Ozone	Sulfur Dioxide	Particulate Matter 2.5	Particulate Matter 10
MSA[1]	0.0	5.5	21.4	0.8	72.1	0.3

Note: (1) Data covers the Boston-Cambridge-Newton, MA-NH Metropolitan Statistical Area—see Appendix B for areas included; (2) Based on 365 days with AQI data in 2013. The Air Quality Index (AQI) is an index for reporting daily air quality. EPA calculates the AQI for five major air pollutants regulated by the Clean Air Act: ground-level ozone, particle pollution (also known as particulate matter), carbon monoxide, sulfur dioxide, and nitrogen dioxide. The AQI runs from 0 to 500. The higher the AQI value, the greater the level of air pollution and the greater the health concern.
Source: U.S. Environmental Protection Agency, Air Quality Index Report, 2013

Air Quality Trends: Ozone

	2003	2004	2005	2006	2007	2008	2009	2010	2011	2012
MSA[1]	0.079	0.075	0.082	0.077	0.081	0.072	0.070	0.069	0.066	0.068

Note: (1) Data covers the Boston-Cambridge-Newton, MA-NH Metropolitan Statistical Area—see Appendix B for areas included. The values shown are the composite ozone concentration averages among trend sites based on the highest fourth daily maximum 8-hour concentration in parts per million. These trends are based on sites having an adequate record of monitoring data during the trend period. Data from exceptional events are included.
Source: U.S. Environmental Protection Agency, Air Quality Monitoring Information, "Air Quality Trends by City, 2000-2012"

Maximum Air Pollutant Concentrations: Particulate Matter, Ozone, CO and Lead

	Particulate Matter 10 (ug/m^3)	Particulate Matter 2.5 Wtd AM (ug/m^3)	Particulate Matter 2.5 24-Hr (ug/m^3)	Ozone (ppm)	Carbon Monoxide (ppm)	Lead (ug/m^3)
MSA[1] Level	37	9.5	24	0.074	2	n/a
NAAQS[2]	150	15	35	0.075	9	0.15
Met NAAQS[2]	Yes	Yes	Yes	Yes	Yes	n/a

Note: (1) Data covers the Boston-Cambridge-Newton, MA-NH Metropolitan Statistical Area—see Appendix B for areas included; Data from exceptional events are included; (2) National Ambient Air Quality Standards; ppm = parts per million; ug/m^3 = micrograms per cubic meter; n/a not available.
Concentrations: Particulate Matter 10 (coarse particulate)—highest second maximum 24-hour concentration; Particulate Matter 2.5 Wtd AM (fine particulate)—highest weighted annual mean concentration; Particulate Matter 2.5 24-Hour (fine particulate)—highest 98th percentile 24-hour concentration; Ozone—highest fourth daily maximum 8-hour concentration; Carbon Monoxide—highest second maximum non-overlapping 8-hour concentration; Lead—maximum running 3-month average
Source: U.S. Environmental Protection Agency, Air Quality Monitoring Information, "Air Quality Statistics by City, 2012"

Maximum Air Pollutant Concentrations: Nitrogen Dioxide and Sulfur Dioxide

	Nitrogen Dioxide AM (ppb)	Nitrogen Dioxide 1-Hr (ppb)	Sulfur Dioxide AM (ppb)	Sulfur Dioxide 1-Hr (ppb)	Sulfur Dioxide 24-Hr (ppb)
MSA[1] Level	19	49	n/a	21	n/a
NAAQS[2]	53	100	30	75	140
Met NAAQS[2]	Yes	Yes	n/a	Yes	n/a

Note: (1) Data covers the Boston-Cambridge-Newton, MA-NH Metropolitan Statistical Area—see Appendix B for areas included; Data from exceptional events are included; (2) National Ambient Air Quality Standards; ppm = parts per million; ug/m^3 = micrograms per cubic meter; n/a not available.
Concentrations: Nitrogen Dioxide AM—highest arithmetic mean concentration; Nitrogen Dioxide 1-Hr—highest 98th percentile 1-hour daily maximum concentration; Sulfur Dioxide AM—highest annual mean concentration; Sulfur Dioxide 1-Hr—highest 99th percentile 1-hour daily maximum concentration; Sulfur Dioxide 24-Hr—highest second maximum 24-hour concentration
Source: U.S. Environmental Protection Agency, Air Quality Monitoring Information, "Air Quality Statistics by City, 2012"

Drinking Water

Water System Name	Pop. Served	Primary Water Source Type	Violations[1]	
			Health Based	Monitoring/ Reporting
Boston Water & Sewer Commission	617,594	Purchased Surface	0	0

Note: (1) Based on violation data from January 1, 2013 to December 31, 2013 (includes unresolved violations from earlier years)
Source: U.S. Environmental Protection Agency, Office of Ground Water and Drinking Water, Safe Drinking Water Information System (based on data extracted February 10, 2014)

Charlotte, North Carolina

Background

Charlotte's relationship with England began amiably enough. Settled by Scotch-Irish and German migrants from Pennsylvania, New Jersey, and Virginia in 1750, the area was named for Charlotte Sophia of Mecklenburg-Strelitz, queen to England's King George III. The county in which Charlotte lies was named for Queen Charlotte Sophia's duchy of Mecklenburg.

Trouble started in 1775, however, when the citizens of Charlotte signed the Mecklenburg Resolves, a document invalidating the power of the king and the English Parliament over their lives. The British General Lord Cornwallis found subduing these "treasoners" so difficult, he called Charlotte a "hornet's nest of rebellion."

Today, a better-behaved Charlotte is a thriving metropolitan area, with large employers in banking and finance, manufacturing; retail, education, government, health care, transportation, and telecommunications.

The city is known as a center for the banking industry. Its role as the nucleus of the Carolinas crescent, an industrial arc extending from Raleigh, North Carolina, to Greenville, South Carolina, adds to its prosperity as well. Over 300 Fortune 500 companies have a presence in the Charlotte area.

Charlotte offers a thriving cultural scene and exciting nightlife, sports, and recreation. The National Football League's Carolina Panthers are the hometown football team. Charlotte is also a center of NASCAR racing; many of the scenes from the film "Talladega Nights" were filmed in and around Charlotte. The NASCAR Hall of Fame opened in Charlotte in 2010.

Attractions include the $62 million N.C. Blumenthal Performing Arts Center, which offers Broadway theater, ballet and music productions; the U.S. National Whitewater Center, the world's largest artificial whitewater river; ImaginOn: The Joe & Joan Martin Center, the newest educational facility; and the Mint Museum of Art and Discovery Place, one of America's top hands-on science museums with a planetarium and IMAX® Dome theater. The expanded Levine Museum of the New South offers the nation's most comprehensive exhibits on post-Civil War southern society. Charlotte hosted the 2012 Democratic Convention.

Significant institutions of higher education in the region include Queens University, the University of North Carolina at Charlotte, Davidson College and nearby Winthrop University.

Charlotte is located in the Piedmont of the Carolinas, a transitional area of rolling country between the mountains to the west and the Coastal Plain to the east. The city enjoys a moderate climate, characterized by cool winters and warm summers. Winter weather is changeable, with occasional cold periods, but extreme cold is rare. Snow is infrequent. Summer afternoons can be hot. Rainfall is generally evenly distributed throughout the year. Hurricanes that do strike the Carolina coast can produce heavy rain, but seldom cause dangerous winds.

Rankings

General Rankings

- Charlotte was identified as one of America's fastest-growing cities in terms of population and economy by *Forbes*. The area ranked #8 out of 20. The 100 most populous metro areas in the U.S. were evaluated on the following criteria: estimated population growth; job growth; gross metropolitan product growth; unemployment; median salaries for college-educated workers. *Forbes, "America's Fastest-Growing Cities 2014," February 14, 2014*

- Charlotte was identified as one of America's fastest-growing major metropolitan areas in terms of population by CNNMoney.com. The area ranked #8 out of 10. Criteria: population growth between July 2012 and July 2013. *CNNMoney, "10 Fastest-Growing Cities," March 28, 2014*

- Among the 50 largest U.S. cities, Charlotte placed #27 in Vocativ's "semi-exhaustive, mostly scientific" city Livability Index for people aged 35 and under. Average salary, unemployment rates, rents, and other living costs were considered, along with bike lanes, low-cost broadband, cheap takeout, self-service laundries, the price of a pint of Guinness, music venues, and vintage clothing stores. *vocative.com, "The Livability Index: The Best U.S. Cities for People 35 and Under," November 7, 2013*

- Charlotte was selected as one of America's best cities by *Bloomberg Businessweek*. The city ranked #39 out of 50. Criteria: leisure attributes (the number of restaurants, bars, libraries, museums, professional sports teams, and park acres by population); educational attributes (public school performance, the number of colleges, and graduate degree holders); economic factors (2011 income and June and July 2012 unemployment); crime; and air quality. *Bloomberg BusinessWeek, "America's Best Cities," September 26, 2012*

- Charlotte appeared on RelocateAmerica's list of best places to live in America. The annual "Top 100 Places to Live" list recognizes the top communities as nominated by their residents & local businesses. RelocateAmerica's Research Group determined the list based on review of various data gathered for economic, employment, housing, education, industry, opportunity, environment and recreation along with feedback from area leaders and residents. *RelocateAmerica.com, "Top 100 Places to Live for 2011"*

- The Charlotte metro area was selected as one of 10 "Best Value Cities" for 2011 by *Kiplinger.com* The area ranked #2. Criteria: vibrant economy; low cost of living; abundant lifestyle amenities. *Kiplinger.com, "Best Value Cities 2011"*

Business/Finance Rankings

- The personal finance site NerdWallet scored the nation's 20 largest American cities according to how friendly a business climate they offer to would-be entrepreneurs. Criteria inlcuded local taxes (state, city, payroll, property), growth rate, and the regulatory environment as judged by small business owners. On the resulting list of most welcoming cities, Charlotte ranked #7. *www.nerdwallet.com, "Top 10 Best Cities for Small Business," August 26, 2013*

- Based on a minimum of 500 social media reviews per metro area, the employment opinion group Glassdoor surveyed 50 of the largest U.S. metro areas on measures including compensation and benefits, satisfaction with management, business outlook, and number of employers hiring. The Charlotte metro area was ranked #46 in overall employee satisfaction. *www.glassdoor.com, "Employment Satisfaction Report Card by City," June 21, 2013*

- The financial literacy site NerdWallet.com set out to identify the 20 most promising cities for job seekers, analyzing data for the nation's 50 largest cities. Charlotte was ranked #5. Criteria: unemployment rate; population growth; median income; selected monthly owner costs. *NerdWallet.com, "Best Cities for Job Seekers," January 7, 2014*

- The Brookings Institution ranked the 50 largest cities in the U.S. based on income inequality. Charlotte was ranked #21. (#1 = greatest ineqality). Criteria: the cities were ranked based on the "95/20 ratio." This figure represents the income at which a household earns more than 95 percent of all other households, divided by the income at which a household earns more than only 20 percent of all other households. *Brookings Institution, "Income Inequality in America's 50 Largest Cities, 2007-2012," February 20, 2014*

- Charlotte was ranked #23 out of 100 metro areas in terms of economic performance (#1 = best) during the recession and recovery from trough quarter through the second quarter of 2013. Criteria: percent change in employment; percentage point change in unemployment rate; percent change in gross metropolitan product; percent change in House Price Index. *Brookings Institution, MetroMonitor: Tracking Economic Recession and Recovery in America's 100 Largest Metropolitan Areas, September 2013*

- Charlotte was identified as one of America's most frugal metro areas by *Coupons.com*. The city ranked #5 out of 25. Criteria: online coupon usage. *Coupons.com, "Top 25 Most Frugal Cities of 2012," February 19, 2013*

- Charlotte was identified as one of America's most frugal metro areas by *Coupons.com*. The city ranked #10 out of 25. Criteria: Grocery IQ and coupons.com mobile app usage. *Coupons.com, "Top 25 Most On-the-Go Frugal Cities of 2012," February 19, 2013*

- Charlotte was identified as one of the happiest cities to work in by CareerBliss.com, an online community for career advancement. The city ranked #10 out of 10. Criteria: independent company reviews from employees all over the country on: relationship with their boss and co-workers; work environment; job resources; compensation; growth opportunities; company culture; company reputation; daily tasks; job control over work performed on a daily basis. *CareerBliss.com, "Top 10 Happiest and Unhappiest Cities to Work in 2014," February 10, 2014*

- The Charlotte metro area appeared on the Milken Institute "2013 Best Performing Cities" list. Rank: #27 out of 200 large metro areas. Criteria: job growth; wage and salary growth; high-tech output growth. *Milken Institute, "Best-Performing Cities 2013," December 2013*

- *Forbes* ranked the 200 most populous metro areas in the U.S. in terms of the "Best Places for Business and Careers." The Charlotte metro area was ranked #19. Criteria: costs (business and living); job growth (past and projected); income growth; educational attainment (college and high school); projected economic growth; cultural and recreational opportunities; net migration patterns; number of highly ranked colleges. *Forbes, "The Best Places for Business and Careers," August 7, 2013*

Children/Family Rankings

- Charlotte was selected as one of the best cities for families to live by *Parenting* magazine. The city ranked #86 out of 100. Criteria: education; health; community; *Parenting's* Culture & Charm Index. *Parenting.com, "The 2012 Best Cities for Families List"*

Culture/Performing Arts Rankings

- Charlotte was selected as one of America's top cities for the arts. The city ranked #18 in the big city (population 500,000 and over) category. Criteria: readers' top choices for arts travel destinations based on the richness and variety of visual arts sites, activities and events. *American Style, "2012 Top 25 Arts Destinations," June 2012*

Dating/Romance Rankings

- *Forbes* reports that the Charlotte metro area made Rent.com's Best Cities for Newlyweds survey for 2013, based on Bureau of Labor Statistics and Census Bureau data on number of married couples, percentage of families with children under age six, average annual income, cost of living, and availability of rentals. *www.forbes.com, "The 10 Best Cities for Newlyweds to Live and Work In," May 30, 2013*

- Of the 100 U.S. cities surveyed by *Men's Health* in its quest to identify the nation's best cities for dating and forming relationships, Charlotte was ranked #9 for online dating (#1 = best). *Men's Health, "The Best and Worst Cities for Online Dating," January 30, 2013*

Education Rankings

- *Men's Health* ranked 100 U.S. cities in terms of their education levels. Charlotte was ranked #28 (#1 = most educated city). Criteria: high school graduation rates; school enrollment; educational attainment; number of households who have outstanding student loans; number of households whose members have taken adult-education courses. *Men's Health, "Where School Is In: The Most and Least Educated Cities," September 12, 2011*

- Charlotte was selected as one of America's most literate cities. The city ranked #52 out of the 77 largest U.S. cities. Criteria: number of booksellers; library resources; Internet resources; educational attainment; periodical publishing resources; newspaper circulation. *Central Connecticut State University, "America's Most Literate Cities, 2013"*

Environmental Rankings

- The Charlotte metro area came in at #263 for the relative comfort of its climate on Sperling's list of "chill cities," as measured by the Sperling Heat Index. All 361 metro areas are included. Criteria included daytime high temperatures, nighttime low temperatures, dew point, and relative humidity at the high temperatures. *www.bertsperling.com, "Sperling's Chill Cities," July 18, 2013*

- Sperling's BestPlaces assessed 379 metropolitan areas of the United States for the likelihood of dangerously extreme weather events or earthquakes. In general the Southeast and South-Central regions have the highest risk of weather extremes and earthquakes, while the Pacific Northwest enjoys the lowest risk. Of the least risky metropolitan areas, the Charlotte metro area was ranked #284. *www.bestplaces.net, "Safest Places from Natural Disasters," April 2011*

- Charlotte was identified as one of North America's greenest metropolitan areas. The area ranked #20. The Green City Index is comprised of 31 indicators, and scores cities across nine categories: carbon dioxide; energy; land use; buildings; transport; water; waste; air quality; environmental governance. The 27 largest metropolitan areas in the U.S. and Canada were considered. *Economist Intelligence Unit, sponsored by Siemens, "U.S. and Canada Green City Index, 2011"*

- The U.S. Environmental Protection Agency (EPA) released a list of U.S. metropolitan areas with the most ENERGY STAR certified buildings in 2012. The Charlotte metro area was ranked #14 out of 25. *U.S. Environmental Protection Agency, "Top Cities With the Most ENERGY STAR Certified Buildings in 2012," March 12, 2013*

- Charlotte was selected as one of 22 "Smarter Cities" for energy by the Natural Resources Defense Council. Criteria: investment in green power; energy efficiency measures; conservation. *Natural Resources Defense Council, "2010 Smarter Cities," July 19, 2010*

- Charlotte was highlighted as one of the 25 most ozone-polluted metro areas in the U.S. during 2008 through 2010. The area ranked #19. *American Lung Association, State of the Air 2012*

- Charlotte was highlighted as one of the top 25 cleanest metro areas for short-term particle pollution (24-hour PM 2.5) in the U.S. during 2008 through 2010. Monitors in these cities reported no days with unhealthful PM 2.5 levels. *American Lung Association, State of the Air 2012*

Food/Drink Rankings

- *Men's Health* ranked 100 major U.S. cities in terms of alcohol intoxication. Charlotte ranked #23 (#1 = most sober).Criteria: binge drinking; alcohol-related traffic accidents, arrests, and fatalities. *Men's Health, "The Drunkest Cities in America," November 19, 2013*

Health/Fitness Rankings

- For each of the 50 most populous metro areas in the United States, the American College of Sports Medicine's American Fitness Index evaluated infrastructure, community assets, and policies that encourage healthy and fit lifestyles, including preventive health behaviors, levels of chronic disease conditions, health care access, and community resources and policies that support physical activity. The Charlotte metro area ranked #36 for "community fitness." Personal health indicators were considered as well as community and environmental indicators. *www.americanfitnessindex.org, "ACSM American Fitness Index Health and Community Fitness Status of the 50 Largest Metropolitan Areas," May 2013*

- The Charlotte metro area was identified as one of the worst cities for bed bugs in America by pest control company Orkin. The area ranked #25 out of 50 based on the number of bed bug treatments Orkin performed from January to December 2013. *Orkin, "Chicago Tops Bed Bug Cities List for Second Year in a Row," January 16, 2014*

- Charlotte was selected as one of the 25 fattest cities in America by *Men's Fitness Online*. It ranked #17 out of America's 50 largest cities. Criteria: fitness centers and sport stores; nutrition; sports participation; TV viewing; overweight/sedentary; junk food; air quality; geography; commute; parks and open space; city recreational facilities; access to healthcare; motivation; mayor and city initiatives; state obesity initiatives. *Men's Fitness, "The Fittest and Fattest Cities in America," March 5, 2012*

- Charlotte was identified as a "2013 Spring Allergy Capital." The area ranked #40 out of 100. Three groups of factors were used to identify the most severe cities for people with allergies during the spring season: annual pollen levels; medicine utilization; access to board-certified allergists. *Asthma and Allergy Foundation of America, "Spring Allergy Capitals 2013"*

- Charlotte was identified as a "2013 Fall Allergy Capital." The area ranked #44 out of 100. Three groups of factors were used to identify the most severe cities for people with allergies during the fall season: annual pollen levels; medicine utilization; access to board-certified allergists. *Asthma and Allergy Foundation of America, "Fall Allergy Capitals 2013"*

- Charlotte was identified as a "2013 Asthma Capital." The area ranked #86 out of the nation's 100 largest metropolitan areas. Twelve factors were used to identify the most challenging places to live for people with asthma: estimated prevalence; self-reported prevalence; crude death rate for asthma; annual pollen score; annual air quality; public smoking laws; number of board-certified asthma specialists; school inhaler access laws; rescue medication use; controller medication use; uninsured rate; poverty rate. *Asthma and Allergy Foundation of America, "Asthma Capitals 2013"*

- *Men's Health* ranked 100 major U.S. cities in terms of the best and worst cities for men. Charlotte ranked #19. Criteria: thirty-three data points were examined covering health, fitness, and quality of life. *Men's Health, "The Best & Worst Cities for Men 2014," December 6, 2013*

- Breathe Right Nasal Strips, in partnership with Sperling's BestPlaces, analyzed 50 metro areas and identified those U.S. cities most challenged by chronic nasal congestion. The Charlotte metro area ranked #8. Criteria: tree, grass and weed pollens; molds and spores; air pollution; climate; smoking; purchase habits of congestion products; prescriptions of drugs for congestion relief; incidence of influenza. *Breathe Right Nasal Strips, "Most Congested Cities," October 3, 2011*

- The Charlotte metro area appeared in the 2013 Gallup-Healthways Well-Being Index. The area ranked #53 out of 189. The Gallup-Healthways Well-Being Index score is an average of six sub-indexes, which individually examine life evaluation, emotional health, work environment, physical health, healthy behaviors, and access to basic necessities. Results are based on telephone interviews conducted as part of the Gallup-Healthways Well-Being Index survey January 2–December 29, 2012, and January 2–December 30, 2013, with a random sample of 531,630 adults, aged 18 and older, living in metropolitan areas in the 50 U.S. states and the District of Columbia. *Gallup-Healthways, "State of American Well-Being," March 25, 2014*

- The Charlotte metro area was identified as one of "America's Most Stressful Cities" by *Sperling's BestPlaces*. The metro area ranked #24 out of 50. Criteria: unemployment rate; suicide rate; commute time; mental health; poor rest; alcohol use; violent crime rate; property crime rate; cloudy days annually. *Sperling's BestPlaces, www.BestPlaces.net, "Stressful Cities 2012*

- *Men's Health* ranked 100 U.S. cities in terms of their activity levels. Charlotte was ranked #90 (#1 = most active city). Criteria: where and how often residents exercise; percentage of households that watch more than 15 hours of cable television a week and buy more than 11 video games a year; death rate from deep-vein thrombosis, a condition linked to sitting for extended periods of time. *Men's Health*, *"Where Sit Happens: The Most and Least Active Cities in America," June 20, 2011*

- *The Daily Beast* identified the 30 U.S. metro areas with the worst smoking habits. The Charlotte metro area ranked #21. Sixty urban centers with populations of more than one million were ranked based on the following criteria: number of smokers; number of cigarettes smoked per day; fewest attempts to quit. *The Daily Beast, "30 Cities With Smoking Problems," January 3, 2011*

Real Estate Rankings

- The Charlotte metro area was identified as one of the top 20 housing markets to invest in for 2014 by *Forbes*. The area ranked #3. Criteria: high population and job growth; relatively low home prices which are below equilibrium home price (EHP). The EHP is what the average price for a market should be, if speculation, weird distortions in local income, and other factors (like the housing collapse) weren't present in the market. *Forbes.com, "Best Buy Cities: Where to Invest in Housing in 2014," December 25, 2013*

- Charlotte ranked #7 in a *Forbes* study of the rental housing market in the nation's 44 largest metropolitan areas to determine the cities that are best for renters. Criteria: average rent in 2012's first quarter, year-over-year change in that figure, vacancy rate, and average monthly rent payment compared with average monthly mortgage payment. *Forbes.com, "The Best and Worst Cities for Renters," June 14, 2012*

- *Kiplinger* looked at metro areas with populations above 250,000 to identify the places in which home prices have declined most, drawing on sales, supply, foreclosure, and market data from Realtors' associations and industry analysts. U.S. Bureau of Labor Statistics unemployment figures were also considered. Charlotte ranked #10. *Kiplinger, "12 Cities Where Home Prices Have Fallen Most," May 2013*

- Charlotte was ranked #91 out of 283 metro areas in terms of house price appreciation in 2013 (#1 = highest rate). *Federal Housing Finance Agency, House Price Index, 4th Quarter 2013*

- Charlotte was ranked #139 out of 224 metro areas in terms of housing affordability in 2013 by the National Association of Home Builders (#1 = most affordable). The NAHB-Wells Fargo Housing Opportunity Index (HOI) for a given area is defined as the share of homes sold in that area that would have been affordable to a family earning the local median income, based on standard mortgage underwriting criteria. *National Association of Home Builders®, NAHB-Wells Fargo Housing Opportunity Index, 4th Quarter 2013*

- The Charlotte metro area was identified as one of the 10 best U.S. markets to invest in single-family homes as rental properties by HomeVestors and Local Market Monitor. The area ranked #3. Criteria: risk-return premium relative to national average. *HomeVestors and Local Market Monitor, "Year-End Top 10 Real Estate Markets," December 20, 2013*

Safety Rankings

- Symantec, in partnership with Sperling's BestPlaces, ranked the 50 largest cities in the U.S. in terms of their vulnerability to cybercrime. The city ranked #25. Criteria: number of cyberattacks and potential infections; level of Internet access; expenditures on smartphones and computer hardware/software; wireless hotspots; broadband connectivity; Internet usage; online purchases. *Symantec, "Riskiest Online Cities of 2012" February 15, 2012*

- Allstate ranked the 200 largest cities in America in terms of driver safety. Charlotte ranked #123. Allstate researchers analyzed internal property damage claims over a two-year period from January 2010 to December 2011. A weighted average of the two-year numbers determined the annual percentages. *Allstate, "Allstate America's Best Drivers Report®, August 27, 2013"*

- Charlotte was identified as one of the safest large cities in America by CQ Press. All 32 cities with populations of 500,000 or more that reported crime rates in 2012 for murder, rape, robbery, aggravated assault, burglary, and motor vehicle thefts were ranked. The city ranked #6 out of the top 10. *CQ Press, City Crime Rankings 2014*

- The National Insurance Crime Bureau ranked 380 metro areas in the U.S. in terms of per capita rates of vehicle theft. The Charlotte metro area ranked #161 (#1 = highest rate). Criteria: number of vehicle theft offenses per 100,000 inhabitants in 2012. *National Insurance Crime Bureau, "Hot Spots 2012," June 26, 2013*

- The Charlotte metro area was identified as one of the most dangerous metro areas for pedestrians by Transportation for America. The metro area ranked #17 out of 52 metro areas with over 1 million residents. Criteria: area's population divided by the number of pedestrian fatalities in that area. *Transportation for America, "Dangerous by Design 2011"*

Seniors/Retirement Rankings

- From its Best Cities for Successful Aging indexes, the Milken Institute generated rankings for metropolitan areas, weighing data in eight categories—general indicators, health care, wellness, living arrangements, transportation and general accessibility, financial well-being, education and employment, and community participation. The Charlotte metro area was ranked #60 overall in the large metro area category. *Milken Institute, "Best Cities for Successful Aging," July 2012*

- Bankers Life and Casualty Company, in partnership with Sperling's BestPlaces, ranked the nation's 50 largest metro areas in terms of the "Best U.S. Cities for Seniors." The Charlotte metro area ranked #38. Criteria: healthcare; transportation; housing; environment; economy; health and longevity; social and spiritual life; crime. *Bankers Life and Casualty Company, Center for a Secure Retirement, "Best U.S. Cities for Seniors 2011," September 2011*

- Charlotte was identified as one of the most popular places to retire by *Topretirements.com*. The list reflects the 100 cities (out of 900+ total cities reviewed) that visitors to the website are most interested in for retirement. *Topretirements.com, "Most Popular Places to Retire for 2014," February 25, 2014*

- Charlotte was selected as one of "The Best Retirement Places" by *Forbes*. The magazine considered a wide range of factors such as climate, availability of doctors, driving environment, and crime rates, but focused especially on tax burden and cost of living. *Forbes, "The Best Retirement Places," March 27, 2011*

Sports/Recreation Rankings

- Charlotte appeared on the *Sporting News* list of the "Best Sports Cities" for 2011. The area ranked #47 out of 271. Criteria: the magazine takes a 12-month snapshot of each city's sports, putting a heavy premium on regular-season won-lost records (from the most recently completed season). Other criteria include: playoff berths, bowl appearances and tournament bids; championships; applicable power ratings; quality of competition; overall fan fervor (measured in part by attendance); abundance of teams (rewarding quality over quantity); stadium and arena quality; ticket availability and prices; franchise ownership; and marquee appeal of athletes. *Sporting News, "Best Sports Cities 2011," October 4, 2011*

- Charlotte appeared on the *Sporting News* list of the "Best Sports Cities" for 2011. The area ranked #47 out of 271. Criteria: a 12-month snapshot of regular-season won-lost records (from the most recently completed season). Other criteria include: playoff berths, bowl appearances and tournament bids; championships; applicable power ratings; quality of competition; overall fan fervor (measured in part by attendance); abundance of teams (quality over quantity); stadium and arena quality; ticket availability and prices; franchise ownership; and marquee appeal of athletes. *Sporting News, "Best Sports Cities 2011," October 4, 2011*

- Charlotte was chosen as a bicycle friendly community by the League of American Bicyclists. A "Bicycle Friendly Community" welcomes cyclists by providing safe accommodation for cycling and encouraging people to bike for transportation and recreation. There are four award levels: Platinum; Gold; Silver; and Bronze. The community achieved an award level of Bronze. *League of American Bicyclists, "Bicycle Friendly Community Master List," Fall 2013*

Transportation Rankings

- NerdWallet surveyed average annual car insurance premiums in 125 U.S. cities to identify the least expensive U.S. cities in which to insure a car. Locations without no-fault insurance laws was a strong determinant. Charlotte came in at #5 for the least expensive rates. *www.nerdwallet.com, "Best Cities for Cheap Car Insurance," February 3, 2014*

Women/Minorities Rankings

- *Women's Health* examined U.S. cities and identified the 100 best cities for women. Charlotte was ranked #28. Criteria: 30 categories were examined from obesity and breast cancer rates to commuting times and hours spent working out. *Women's Health, "Best Cities for Women 2012"*

- The Charlotte metro area appeared on *Forbes'* list of the "Best Cities for Minority Entrepreneurs." The area ranked #28 out of 10. Criteria: 52 metropolitan statistical areas were examined. For each ethnicity (African Americans, Asians and Hispanics), the editors measured housing affordability, population growth, income growth, and entrepreneurship (per capita self-employment). *Forbes, "Best Cities for Minority Entrepreneurs," March 23, 2011*

Miscellaneous Rankings

- According to the World Giving Index, the United States is the fifth most generous nation in the world. The finance and lifestyle site NerdWallet looked for the U.S. cities that topped the list in donating money and time to good causes. The Charlotte metro area proved to be the #19-ranked metro area, judged by culture of volunteerism, depth of commitment in terms of volunteer hours per year, and monetary contributions. *www.nerdwallet.com, "Most Generous Cities," September 22, 2013*

- *Men's Health* ranked 100 U.S. cities by their level of sadness. Charlotte was ranked #57 (#1 = saddest city). Criteria: suicide rates; unemployment rates; percentage of households that use antidepressants; percent of population who report feeling blue all or most of the time. *Men's Health, "Frown Towns," November 28, 2011*

- Mars Chocolate North America, the makers of COMBOS®, in partnership with Sperling's BestPlaces, ranked 50 major metro areas in terms of their "manliness." The Charlotte metro area ranked #10. Criteria: number of professional sports teams; number of nearby NASCAR tracks and racing events; manly lifestyle; concentration of manly retail stores; manly occupations per capita; salty snack sales; "Board of Manliness" rankings. *Mars Chocolate North America, "America's Manliest Cities 2012"*

- The National Alliance to End Homelessness ranked the 100 most populous metro areas in terms the rate of homelessness. The Charlotte metro area ranked #34. Criteria: number of homeless people per 10,000 population in 2011. *National Alliance to End Homelessness, The State of Homelessness in America 2012*

Business Environment

CITY FINANCES

City Government Finances

Component	2011 ($000)	2011 ($ per capita)
Total Revenues	1,670,110	2,487
Total Expenditures	1,412,396	2,103
Debt Outstanding	3,280,411	4,885
Cash and Securities[1]	2,076,938	3,093

Note: (1) Cash and security holdings of a government at the close of its fiscal year, including those of its dependent agencies, utilities, and liquor stores.
Source: U.S Census Bureau, State & Local Government Finances 2011

City Government Revenue by Source

Source	2011 ($000)	2011 ($ per capita)
General Revenue		
From Federal Government	125,294	187
From State Government	114,692	171
From Local Governments	25,002	37
Taxes		
Property	363,334	541
Sales and Gross Receipts	183,439	273
Personal Income	0	0
Corporate Income	0	0
Motor Vehicle License	14,942	22
Other Taxes	28,168	42
Current Charges	420,057	625
Liquor Store	0	0
Utility	157,770	235
Employee Retirement	85,478	127

Source: U.S Census Bureau, State & Local Government Finances 2011

City Government Expenditures by Function

Function	2011 ($000)	2011 ($ per capita)	2011 (%)
General Direct Expenditures			
Air Transportation	158,967	237	11.3
Corrections	0	0	0.0
Education	0	0	0.0
Employment Security Administration	0	0	0.0
Financial Administration	8,607	13	0.6
Fire Protection	98,835	147	7.0
General Public Buildings	6,017	9	0.4
Governmental Administration, Other	14,909	22	1.1
Health	4,594	7	0.3
Highways	127,210	189	9.0
Hospitals	0	0	0.0
Housing and Community Development	48,853	73	3.5
Interest on General Debt	124,322	185	8.8
Judicial and Legal	1,952	3	0.1
Libraries	1,167	2	0.1
Parking	652	1	0.0
Parks and Recreation	16,856	25	1.2
Police Protection	198,988	296	14.1
Public Welfare	0	0	0.0
Sewerage	141,140	210	10.0
Solid Waste Management	46,912	70	3.3
Veterans' Services	0	0	0.0
Liquor Store	0	0	0.0
Utility	275,685	410	19.5
Employee Retirement	20,328	30	1.4

Source: U.S Census Bureau, State & Local Government Finances 2011

DEMOGRAPHICS

Population Growth

Area	1990 Census	2000 Census	2010 Census	Population Growth (%) 1990-2000	Population Growth (%) 2000-2010
City	428,283	540,828	731,424	26.3	35.2
MSA[1]	1,024,331	1,330,448	1,758,038	29.9	32.1
U.S.	248,709,873	281,421,906	308,745,538	13.2	9.7

Note: (1) Figures cover the Charlotte-Concord-Gastonia, NC-SC Metropolitan Statistical Area—see Appendix B for areas included
Source: U.S. Census Bureau, Census 1990, 2000, 2010

Household Size

Area	Persons in Household (%) One	Two	Three	Four	Five	Six	Seven or More	Average Household Size
City	31.4	31.2	16.0	12.7	5.7	2.2	0.9	2.54
MSA[1]	27.1	32.6	17.0	13.7	6.1	2.3	1.1	2.64
U.S.	27.6	33.5	15.7	13.2	6.1	2.4	1.5	2.63

Note: (1) Figures cover the Charlotte-Concord-Gastonia, NC-SC Metropolitan Statistical Area—see Appendix B for areas included
Source: U.S. Census Bureau, 2010-2012 American Community Survey 3-Year Estimates

Race

Area	White Alone[2] (%)	Black Alone[2] (%)	Asian Alone[2] (%)	AIAN[3] Alone[2] (%)	NHOPI[4] Alone[2] (%)	Other Race Alone[2] (%)	Two or More Races (%)
City	53.1	34.8	5.2	0.5	0.1	3.7	2.7
MSA[1]	67.1	23.9	3.3	0.4	0.1	2.8	2.3
U.S.	74.0	12.6	4.9	0.8	0.2	4.7	2.8

Note: (1) Figures cover the Charlotte-Concord-Gastonia, NC-SC Metropolitan Statistical Area—see Appendix B for areas included; (2) Alone is defined as not being in combination with one or more other races; (3) American Indian and Alaska Native; (4) Native Hawaiian and Other Pacific Islander
Source: U.S. Census Bureau, 2010-2012 American Community Survey 3-Year Estimates

Hispanic or Latino Origin

Area	Total (%)	Mexican (%)	Puerto Rican (%)	Cuban (%)	Other (%)
City	13.2	5.4	1.1	0.4	6.4
MSA[1]	10.0	4.8	0.9	0.3	4.1
U.S.	16.6	10.7	1.6	0.6	3.7

Note: Persons of Hispanic or Latino origin can be of any race; (1) Figures cover the Charlotte-Concord-Gastonia, NC-SC Metropolitan Statistical Area—see Appendix B for areas included
Source: U.S. Census Bureau, 2010-2012 American Community Survey 3-Year Estimates

Segregation

Type	Segregation Indices[1] 1990	2000	2010	2010 Rank[2]	Percent Change 1990-2000	Percent Change 1990-2010	Percent Change 2000-2010
Black/White	54.7	54.2	53.8	56	-0.5	-0.8	-0.4
Asian/White	41.8	42.6	43.6	34	0.8	1.8	1.0
Hispanic/White	32.8	50.8	47.6	35	18.0	14.8	-3.2

Note: All figures cover the Metropolitan Statistical Area—see Appendix B for areas included; Figures are based on an analysis of 1990, 2000, and 2010 Census Decennial Census tract data by William H. Frey, Brookings Institution and the University of Michigan Social Science Data Analysis Network. In this analysis all racial groups (whites, blacks, and asians) are non-Hispanic members of those races. Hispanics are shown as a separate category;
(1) Segregation Indices are Dissimilarity Indices that measure the degree to which the minority group is distributed differently than whites across census tracts. They range from 0 (complete integration) to 100 (complete segregation) where the value indicates the percentage of the minority group that needs to move to be distributed exactly like whites; (2) Ranges from 1 (most segregated) to 102 (least segregated); n/a not available.
Source: www.CensusScope.org

Ancestry

Area	German	Irish	English	American	Italian	Polish	French[2]	Scottish	Dutch
City	9.9	7.8	7.8	5.0	3.5	1.7	1.5	2.3	0.8
MSA[1]	11.8	9.5	8.6	8.8	3.8	1.7	1.7	2.5	1.0
U.S.	15.2	11.1	8.2	7.2	5.6	3.1	2.8	1.7	1.4

Note: Figures are the percentage of the total population reporting a particular ancestry. The nine most commonly reported ancestries in the U.S. are shown. Figures include multiple ancestries (e.g. if a person reported being Irish and Italian, they were included in both columns); (1) Figures cover the Charlotte-Concord-Gastonia, NC-SC Metropolitan Statistical Area—see Appendix B for areas included; (2) Excludes Basque
Source: U.S. Census Bureau, 2010-2012 American Community Survey 3-Year Estimates

Foreign-Born Population

Area	Any Foreign Country	Mexico	Asia	Europe	Carribean	South America	Central America[2]	Africa	Canada
City	14.7	3.0	4.1	1.5	0.9	1.3	2.4	1.2	0.2
MSA[1]	10.2	2.6	2.5	1.2	0.6	0.9	1.4	0.7	0.2
U.S.	13.0	3.7	3.7	1.6	1.2	0.9	1.0	0.5	0.3

Note: (1) Figures cover the Charlotte-Concord-Gastonia, NC-SC Metropolitan Statistical Area—see Appendix B for areas included; (2) Excludes Mexico.
Source: U.S. Census Bureau, 2010-2012 American Community Survey 3-Year Estimates

Marital Status

Area	Never Married	Now Married[2]	Separated	Widowed	Divorced
City	38.7	43.1	3.2	4.6	10.5
MSA[1]	32.1	49.7	3.0	5.1	10.1
U.S.	32.4	48.4	2.2	6.0	11.0

Note: Figures are percentages and cover the population 15 years of age and older; (1) Figures cover the Charlotte-Concord-Gastonia, NC-SC Metropolitan Statistical Area—see Appendix B for areas included; (2) Excludes separated
Source: U.S. Census Bureau, 2010-2012 American Community Survey 3-Year Estimates

Age

Area	Under Age 5	Age 5–19	Age 20–34	Age 35–44	Age 45–54	Age 55–64	Age 65–74	Age 75–84	Age 85+	Median Age
City	7.6	20.1	24.8	15.5	13.3	9.9	4.9	2.7	1.2	33.4
MSA[1]	7.0	21.3	20.8	15.5	14.3	10.9	6.0	3.1	1.3	35.6
U.S.	6.4	20.1	20.5	13.1	14.3	12.2	7.3	4.2	1.8	37.3

Note: (1) Figures cover the Charlotte-Concord-Gastonia, NC-SC Metropolitan Statistical Area—see Appendix B for areas included
Source: U.S. Census Bureau, 2010-2012 American Community Survey 3-Year Estimates

Gender

Area	Males	Females	Males per 100 Females
City	363,181	393,544	92.3
MSA[1]	872,208	924,551	94.3
U.S.	153,276,055	158,333,314	96.8

Note: (1) Figures cover the Charlotte-Concord-Gastonia, NC-SC Metropolitan Statistical Area—see Appendix B for areas included
Source: U.S. Census Bureau, 2010-2012 American Community Survey 3-Year Estimates

Religious Groups by Family

Area	Catholic	Baptist	Non-Den.	Methodist[2]	Lutheran	LDS[3]	Pente-costal	Presby-terian[4]	Muslim[5]	Judaism
MSA[1]	5.9	17.3	6.8	8.6	1.3	0.8	3.3	4.5	0.2	0.3
U.S.	19.1	9.3	4.0	4.0	2.3	2.0	1.9	1.6	0.8	0.7

Note: Figures are the number of adherents as a percentage of the total population; (1) Figures cover the Charlotte-Concord-Gastonia, NC-SC Metropolitan Statistical Area—see Appendix B for areas included; (2) Methodist/Pietist; (3) Latter Day Saints; (4) Reformed; (5) Figures are estimates
Source: Association of Statisticians of American Religious Bodies, 2010 U.S. Religion Census: Religious Congregations & Membership Study

Religious Groups by Tradition

Area	Catholic	Evangelical Protestant	Mainline Protestant	Other Tradition	Black Protestant	Orthodox
MSA[1]	5.9	27.6	13.3	1.7	2.8	0.5
U.S.	19.1	16.2	7.3	4.3	1.6	0.3

Note: Figures are the number of adherents as a percentage of the total population; (1) Figures cover the Charlotte-Concord-Gastonia, NC-SC Metropolitan Statistical Area—see Appendix B for areas included
Source: Association of Statisticians of American Religious Bodies, 2010 U.S. Religion Census: Religious Congregations & Membership Study

ECONOMY

Gross Metropolitan Product

Area	2011	2012	2013	2014	Rank[2]
MSA[1]	117.4	125.2	130.5	137.0	22

Note: Figures are in billions of dollars; (1) Figures cover the Charlotte-Concord-Gastonia, NC-SC Metropolitan Statistical Area—see Appendix B for areas included; (2) Rank is based on 2014 data and ranges from 1 to 363
Source: The United States Conference of Mayors, U.S. Metro Economies: Outlook—Gross Metropolitan Product, with Metro Employment Projections, November 2013

Economic Growth

Area	2011 (%)	2012 (%)	2013 (%)	2014 (%)	Rank[2]
MSA[1]	1.7	4.9	2.9	3.1	28
U.S.	1.6	2.5	1.7	2.5	–

Note: Figures are real gross metropolitan product (GMP) growth rates and represent annual average percent change; (1) Figures cover the Charlotte-Concord-Gastonia, NC-SC Metropolitan Statistical Area—see Appendix B for areas included; (2) Rank is based on 2013 data and ranges from 1 to 363
Source: The United States Conference of Mayors, U.S. Metro Economies: Outlook—Gross Metropolitan Product, with Metro Employment Projections, November 2013

Metropolitan Area Exports

Area	2007	2008	2009	2010	2011	2012	Rank[2]
MSA[1]	4,269.2	5,036.3	4,133.4	5,424.6	6,253.3	6,322.6	42

Note: Figures are in millions of dollars; (1) Figures cover the Charlotte-Concord-Gastonia, NC-SC Metropolitan Statistical Area—see Appendix B for areas included; (2) Rank is based on 2012 data and ranges from 1 to 369
Source: U.S. Department of Commerce, International Trade Administration, Office of Trade & Industry Information, Manufacturing & Services, data extracted April 1, 2014

INCOME

Income

Area	Per Capita ($)	Median Household ($)	Average Household ($)
City	30,710	51,209	76,914
MSA[1]	28,421	52,346	74,162
U.S.	27,385	51,771	71,579

Note: (1) Figures cover the Charlotte-Concord-Gastonia, NC-SC Metropolitan Statistical Area—see Appendix B for areas included
Source: U.S. Census Bureau, 2010-2012 American Community Survey 3-Year Estimates

Household Income Distribution

Area	Percent of Households Earning							
	Under $15,000	$15,000 -24,999	$25,000 -34,999	$35,000 -49,999	$50,000 -74,999	$75,000 -99,000	$100,000 -149,999	$150,000 and up
City	12.8	10.5	10.9	14.6	18.3	11.0	11.7	10.2
MSA[1]	12.2	10.5	10.4	14.5	18.6	11.8	12.4	9.5
U.S.	13.1	11.0	10.5	13.7	18.1	11.9	12.5	9.1

Note: (1) Figures cover the Charlotte-Concord-Gastonia, NC-SC Metropolitan Statistical Area—see Appendix B for areas included
Source: U.S. Census Bureau, 2010-2012 American Community Survey 3-Year Estimates

Poverty Rate

Area	All Ages	Under 18 Years Old	18 to 64 Years Old	65 Years and Over
City	17.8	24.9	16.3	8.2
MSA[1]	15.2	20.7	14.1	8.0
U.S.	15.7	22.2	14.6	9.3

Note: Figures are percentage of people whose income during the past 12 months was below the poverty level; (1) Figures cover the Charlotte-Concord-Gastonia, NC-SC Metropolitan Statistical Area—see Appendix B for areas included
Source: U.S. Census Bureau, 2010-2012 American Community Survey 3-Year Estimates

Personal Bankruptcy Filing Rate

Area	2008	2009	2010	2011	2012	2013
Mecklenburg County	1.98	2.50	2.67	2.23	2.02	1.76
U.S.	3.53	4.61	4.97	4.37	3.76	3.29

Note: Numbers are per 1,000 population and include Chapter 7 and Chapter 13 filings
Source: Federal Deposit Insurance Corporation, Regional Economic Conditions, March 20, 2014

EMPLOYMENT

Labor Force and Employment

Area	Civilian Labor Force			Workers Employed		
	Dec. 2012	Dec. 2013	% Chg.	Dec. 2012	Dec. 2013	% Chg.
City	394,698	391,422	-0.8	363,056	368,591	1.5
MSA[1]	928,564	916,145	-1.3	841,635	855,842	1.7
U.S.	154,904,000	154,408,000	-0.3	143,060,000	144,423,000	1.0

Note: Data is not seasonally adjusted and covers workers 16 years of age and older; (1) Metropolitan Statistical Area—see Appendix B for areas included
Source: Bureau of Labor Statistics, Local Area Unemployment Statistics

Unemployment Rate

Area	2013											
	Jan.	Feb.	Mar.	Apr.	May	Jun.	Jul.	Aug.	Sep.	Oct.	Nov.	Dec.
City	8.5	8.0	7.7	7.4	7.9	8.4	8.4	7.5	6.8	6.9	6.1	5.8
MSA[1]	10.0	9.4	8.8	8.4	8.9	9.3	9.2	8.3	7.6	7.5	6.9	6.6
U.S.	8.5	8.1	7.6	7.1	7.3	7.8	7.7	7.3	7.0	7.0	6.6	6.5

Note: Data is not seasonally adjusted and covers workers 16 years of age and older; All figures are percentages; (1) Metropolitan Statistical Area—see Appendix B for areas included
Source: Bureau of Labor Statistics, Local Area Unemployment Statistics

Employment by Occupation

Occupation Classification	City (%)	MSA[1] (%)	U.S. (%)
Management, Business, Science, and Arts	39.8	37.8	36.0
Natural Resources, Construction, and Maintenance	6.9	8.2	9.1
Production, Transportation, and Material Moving	10.5	11.8	12.0
Sales and Office	26.0	25.9	24.7
Service	16.9	16.2	18.2

Note: Figures cover employed civilians 16 years of age and older; (1) Figures cover the Charlotte-Concord-Gastonia, NC-SC Metropolitan Statistical Area—see Appendix B for areas included
Source: U.S. Census Bureau, 2010-2012 American Community Survey 3-Year Estimates

Employment by Industry

Sector	MSA[1]		U.S.
	Number of Employees	Percent of Total	Percent of Total
Construction	n/a	n/a	4.2
Education and Health Services	90,100	10.1	15.5
Financial Activities	75,300	8.4	5.7
Government	125,400	14.0	16.1
Information	22,300	2.5	1.9
Leisure and Hospitality	96,500	10.8	10.2
Manufacturing	73,400	8.2	8.7
Mining and Logging	n/a	n/a	0.6
Other Services	32,000	3.6	3.9
Professional and Business Services	148,500	16.6	13.7
Retail Trade	101,700	11.4	11.4
Transportation and Utilities	38,900	4.4	3.8
Wholesale Trade	47,200	5.3	4.2

Note: Figures cover non-farm employment as of December 2013 and are not seasonally adjusted;
(1) Metropolitan Statistical Area—see Appendix B for areas included; n/a not available
Source: Bureau of Labor Statistics, Current Employment Statistics, Employment, Hours, and Earnings

Occupations with Greatest Projected Employment Growth: 2010 – 2020

Occupation[1]	2010 Employment	2020 Projected Employment	Numeric Employment Change	Percent Employment Change
Combined Food Preparation and Serving Workers, Including Fast Food	114,040	132,650	18,610	16.3
Registered Nurses	92,540	109,790	17,250	18.6
Retail Salespersons	131,650	145,910	14,270	10.8
Home Health Aides	55,560	67,570	12,010	21.6
Customer Service Representatives	74,700	84,800	10,090	13.5
Postsecondary Teachers	49,850	59,780	9,930	19.9
Landscaping and Groundskeeping Workers	33,610	43,450	9,830	29.3
Janitors and Cleaners, Except Maids and Housekeeping Cleaners	52,290	61,160	8,870	17.0
Cashiers	101,410	110,200	8,790	8.7
Elementary School Teachers, Except Special Education	37,090	45,730	8,650	23.3

Note: Projections cover North Carolina; (1) Sorted by numeric employment change
Source: www.projectionscentral.com, State Occupational Projections, 2010–2020 Long-Term Projections

Fastest Growing Occupations: 2010 – 2020

Occupation[1]	2010 Employment	2020 Projected Employment	Numeric Employment Change	Percent Employment Change
Biomedical Engineers	250	480	230	90.5
Medical Scientists, Except Epidemiologists	4,270	6,550	2,280	53.4
Biochemists and Biophysicists	460	670	210	44.9
Interpreters and Translators	3,000	4,210	1,220	40.6
Veterinary Technologists and Technicians	3,060	4,300	1,240	40.4
Market Research Analysts and Marketing Specialists	9,750	13,580	3,830	39.3
Helpers—Brickmasons, Blockmasons, Stonemasons, and Tile and Marble Setters	1,900	2,630	740	38.8
Helpers—Carpenters	1,850	2,560	710	38.4
Diagnostic Medical Sonographers	1,660	2,280	620	37.3
Audiologists	350	460	120	33.6

Note: Projections cover North Carolina; (1) Sorted by percent employment change and excludes occupations
with numeric employment change less than 100
Source: www.projectionscentral.com, State Occupational Projections, 2010–2020 Long-Term Projections

Average Wages

Occupation	$/Hr.	Occupation	$/Hr.
Accountants and Auditors	35.75	Maids and Housekeeping Cleaners	8.93
Automotive Mechanics	20.32	Maintenance and Repair Workers	18.46
Bookkeepers	17.69	Marketing Managers	63.83
Carpenters	17.12	Nuclear Medicine Technologists	32.42
Cashiers	9.50	Nurses, Licensed Practical	19.86
Clerks, General Office	13.74	Nurses, Registered	28.52
Clerks, Receptionists/Information	13.53	Nursing Assistants	11.23
Clerks, Shipping/Receiving	14.93	Packers and Packagers, Hand	10.76
Computer Programmers	39.57	Physical Therapists	37.91
Computer Systems Analysts	42.61	Postal Service Mail Carriers	24.31
Computer User Support Specialists	24.91	Real Estate Brokers	35.01
Cooks, Restaurant	10.66	Retail Salespersons	12.10
Dentists	75.21	Sales Reps., Exc. Tech./Scientific	31.41
Electrical Engineers	42.52	Sales Reps., Tech./Scientific	40.29
Electricians	18.07	Secretaries, Exc. Legal/Med./Exec.	17.10
Financial Managers	67.43	Security Guards	11.31
First-Line Supervisors/Managers, Sales	21.23	Surgeons	n/a
Food Preparation Workers	9.65	Teacher Assistants	11.20
General and Operations Managers	63.70	Teachers, Elementary School	22.10
Hairdressers/Cosmetologists	13.62	Teachers, Secondary School	22.40
Internists	116.54	Telemarketers	13.66
Janitors and Cleaners	10.35	Truck Drivers, Heavy/Tractor-Trailer	19.37
Landscaping/Groundskeeping Workers	10.88	Truck Drivers, Light/Delivery Svcs.	16.05
Lawyers	55.60	Waiters and Waitresses	9.34

Note: Wage data covers the Charlotte-Gastonia-Rock Hill, NC-SC Metropolitan Statistical Area—see Appendix B for areas included. Hourly wages for elementary/secondary school teachers and teacher assistants were calculated by the editors from annual wage data assuming a 40 hour work week; n/a not available.
Source: Bureau of Labor Statistics, Metro Area Occupational Employment and Wage Estimates, May 2013

RESIDENTIAL REAL ESTATE

Building Permits

Area	Single-Family			Multi-Family			Total		
	2012	2013	Pct. Chg.	2012	2013	Pct. Chg.	2012	2013	Pct. Chg.
City	n/a	n/a	n/a	n/a	n/a	n/a	n/a	n/a	n/a
MSA[1]	6,703	8,792	31.2	5,544	5,217	-5.9	12,247	14,009	14.4
U.S.	518,695	620,802	19.7	310,963	370,020	19.0	829,658	990,822	19.4

Note: (1) Metropolitan Statistical Area—see Appendix B for areas included; figures represent new, privately-owned housing units authorized (unadjusted data); All permit data are based on estimates with imputation.
Source: U.S. Census Bureau, Manufacturing, Mining, and Construction Statistics, Building Permits, 2012, 2013

Homeownership Rate

Area	2006 (%)	2007 (%)	2008 (%)	2009 (%)	2010 (%)	2011 (%)	2012 (%)	2013 (%)
MSA[1]	66.1	66.5	65.4	66.1	66.1	63.6	58.3	58.9
U.S.	68.8	68.1	67.8	67.4	66.9	66.1	65.4	65.1

Note: (1) Figures cover the Charlotte-Concord-Gastonia, NC-SC Metropolitan Statistical Area—see Appendix B for areas included
Source: U.S. Census Bureau, Housing Vacancies and Homeownership Annual Statistics: 2013

Housing Vacancy Rates

Area	Gross Vacancy Rate[2] (%)			Year-Round Vacancy Rate[3] (%)			Rental Vacancy Rate[4] (%)			Homeowner Vacancy Rate[5] (%)		
	2011	2012	2013	2011	2012	2013	2011	2012	2013	2011	2012	2013
MSA[1]	9.2	8.0	9.3	9.1	7.7	8.7	10.1	6.4	6.4	1.9	1.3	3.5
U.S.	14.2	13.8	13.8	11.1	10.8	10.7	9.5	8.7	8.3	2.5	2.0	2.0

Note: (1) Figures cover the Charlotte-Concord-Gastonia, NC-SC Metropolitan Statistical Area—see Appendix B for areas included; (2) The percentage of the total housing inventory that is vacant; (3) The percentage of the housing inventory (excluding seasonal units) that is year-round vacant; (4) The percentage of rental inventory that is vacant for rent; (5) The percentage of homeowner inventory that is vacant for sale
Source: U.S. Census Bureau, Housing Vacancies and Homeownership Annual Statistics: 2013

TAXES

State Corporate Income Tax Rates

State	Tax Rate (%)	Income Brackets ($)	Num. of Brackets	Financial Institution Tax Rate (%)[a]	Federal Income Tax Ded.
North Carolina	6.0	Flat rate	1	6.0 (t)	No

Note: Tax rates as of January 1, 2014; (a) Rates listed are the corporate income tax rate applied to financial institutions or excise taxes based on income. Some states have other taxes based upon the value of deposits or shares; (t) In North Carolina financial institutions are also subject to a tax equal to $30 per one million in assets.
Source: Federation of Tax Administrators, "State Corporate Income Tax Rates, 2014"

State Individual Income Tax Rates

State	Tax Rate (%)	Income Brackets ($)	Num. of Brackets	Personal Exempt. ($)[1] Single	Personal Exempt. ($)[1] Dependents	Fed. Inc. Tax Ded.
North Carolina	5.8	Flat rate	1	None	None	No

Note: Tax rates as of January 1, 2014; Local- and county-level taxes are not included; n/a not applicable;
(1) Married joint filers generally receive double the single exemption
Source: Federation of Tax Administrators, "State Individual Income Tax Rates, 2014"

Various State and Local Tax Rates

State	State and Local Sales and Use (%)	State Sales and Use (%)	Gasoline[1] (¢/gal.)	Cigarette[2] ($/pack)	Spirits[3] ($/gal.)	Wine[4] ($/gal.)	Beer[5] ($/gal.)
North Carolina	7.25	4.75	37.75	0.450	12.36 (g)	1.00	0.62

Note: All tax rates as of January 1, 2014; (1) The American Petroleum Institute has developed a methodology for determining the average tax rate on a gallon of fuel. Rates may include any of the following: excise taxes, environmental fees, storage tank fees, other fees or taxes, general sales tax, and local taxes. In states where gasoline is subject to the general sales tax, or where the fuel tax is based on the average sale price, the average rate determined by API is sensitive to changes in the price of gasoline. States that fully or partially apply general sales taxes to gasoline: CA, CO, GA, IL, IN, MI, NY; (2) The federal excise tax of $1.0066 per pack and local taxes are not included; (3) Rates are those applicable to off-premise sales of 40% alcohol by volume (a.b.v.) distilled spirits in 750ml containers. Local excise taxes are excluded; (4) Rates are those applicable to off-premise sales of 11% a.b.v. non-carbonated wine in 750ml containers; (5) Rates are those applicable to off-premise sales of 4.7% a.b.v. beer in 12 ounce containers; (g) States where the government controls sales. In these "control states," products are subject to ad valorem mark-up and excise taxes. The excise tax rate is calculated using a methodology developed by the Distilled Spirits Council of the United States.
Source: Tax Foundation, 2014 Facts & Figures: How Does Your State Compare?

State Business Tax Climate Index Rankings

State	Overall Rank	Corporate Tax Index Rank	Individual Income Tax Index Rank	Sales Tax Index Rank	Unemployment Insurance Tax Index Rank	Property Tax Index Rank
North Carolina	44	29	42	47	7	30

Note: The index is a measure of how each state's tax laws affect economic performance. The lower the rank, the more favorable a state's tax system is for business. States without a given tax are given a ranking of 1. The scores/rankings for the District of Columbia do not affect other states. The 2014 index represents the tax climate as of July 1, 2013.
Source: Tax Foundation, State Business Tax Climate Index 2014

COMMERCIAL REAL ESTATE

Office Market

Market Area	Inventory (sq. ft.)	Vacancy Rate (%)	Under Construction (sq. ft.)	YTD Net Absorption (sq. ft.)	Total Average Asking Rent ($/sq. ft./year)
Charlotte	62,291,151	13.6	338,851	965,046	20.35
National	4,726,900,879	15.0	55,419,286	42,829,434	26.27

Source: Newmark Grubb Knight Frank, National Office Market Report, 4th Quarter 2013

Industrial/Warehouse/R&D Market

Market Area	Inventory (sq. ft.)	Vacancy Rate (%)	Under Construction (sq. ft.)	YTD Net Absorption (sq. ft.)	Total Average Asking Rent ($/sq. ft./year)
Charlotte	323,079,566	11.8	261,844	4,405,611	3.51
National	14,022,031,238	7.9	83,249,164	156,549,903	5.40

Source: Newmark Grubb Knight Frank, National Industrial Market Report, 4th Quarter 2013

COMMERCIAL UTILITIES

Typical Monthly Electric Bills

Area	Commercial Service ($/month)		Industrial Service ($/month)	
	1,500 kWh	40 kW demand 14,000 kWh	1,000 kW demand 200,000 kWh	50,000 kW demand 15,000,000 kWh
City	197	1,123	16,763	1,091,630
Average[1]	197	1,636	25,662	1,485,307

Note: Based on total rates in effect July 1, 2013; (1) average based on 180 utilities surveyed
Source: Edison Electric Institute, Typical Bills and Average Rates Report, Summer 2013

TRANSPORTATION

Means of Transportation to Work

Area	Car/Truck/Van Drove Alone	Car-pooled	Public Transportation Bus	Subway	Railroad	Bicycle	Walked	Other Means	Worked at Home
City	76.8	10.1	3.3	0.4	0.1	0.2	2.2	1.1	5.8
MSA[1]	79.8	10.0	1.8	0.2	0.1	0.2	1.5	0.9	5.4
U.S.	76.4	9.7	2.6	1.7	0.5	0.6	2.8	1.3	4.3

Note: Figures are percentages and cover workers 16 years of age and older; (1) Figures cover the Charlotte-Concord-Gastonia, NC-SC Metropolitan Statistical Area—see Appendix B for areas included
Source: U.S. Census Bureau, 2010-2012 American Community Survey 3-Year Estimates

Travel Time to Work

Area	Less Than 10 Minutes	10 to 19 Minutes	20 to 29 Minutes	30 to 44 Minutes	45 to 59 Minutes	60 to 89 Minutes	90 Minutes or More
City	10.0	30.2	26.5	23.2	5.4	2.5	2.2
MSA[1]	10.3	28.8	23.8	24.1	7.6	3.3	2.0
U.S.	13.5	29.8	20.9	20.1	7.5	5.6	2.5

Note: Figures are percentages and include workers 16 years old and over; (1) Figures cover the Charlotte-Concord-Gastonia, NC-SC Metropolitan Statistical Area—see Appendix B for areas included
Source: U.S. Census Bureau, 2010-2012 American Community Survey 3-Year Estimates

Travel Time Index

Area	1985	1990	1995	2000	2005	2010	2011
Urban Area[1]	1.10	1.14	1.13	1.22	1.23	1.20	1.20
Average[2]	1.09	1.14	1.16	1.19	1.23	1.18	1.18

Note: Travel Time Index—the ratio of travel time in the peak period to the travel time at free-flow conditions. For example, a value of 1.30 indicates a 20-minute free-flow trip takes 26 minutes in the peak. Free-flow speeds (60 mph on freeways and 35 mph on principal arterials) are used as the comparison threshold; (1) Covers the Charlotte NC-SC urban area; (2) average of 498 urban areas
Source: Texas Transportation Institute, Urban Mobility Report 2012, December 2012

Public Transportation

Agency Name / Mode of Transportation	Vehicles Operated in Maximum Service	Annual Unlinked Passenger Trips (in thous.)	Annual Passenger Miles (in thous.)
Charlotte Area Transit System (CATS)			
Bus (directly operated)	258	22,870.4	102,261.7
Demand Response (directly operated)	71	228.0	2,120.5
Light Rail (directly operated)	14	4,889.5	25,735.4
Vanpool (directly operated)	80	255.8	12,592.3

Source: Federal Transit Administration, National Transit Database, 2012

Air Transportation

Airport Name and Code / Type of Service	Passenger Airlines[1]	Passenger Enplanements	Freight Carriers[2]	Freight (lbs.)
Charlotte-Douglas International (CLT)				
Domestic service (U.S. carriers - 2013)	31	19,838,664	22	89,317,742
International service (U.S. carriers - 2012)	11	1,346,375	5	10,254,644

Note: (1) Includes all U.S.-based major, minor and commuter airlines that carried at least one passenger during the year; (2) Includes all U.S.-based airlines and freight carriers that transported at least one lb. of freight during the year.
Source: Bureau of Transportation Statistics, The Intermodal Transportation Database, Air Carriers: T-100 Domestic Market (U.S. Carriers), 2013; Bureau of Transportation Statistics, The Intermodal Transportation Database, Air Carriers: T-100 International Market (U.S. Carriers), 2012

Other Transportation Statistics

Major Highways:	I-77; I-85
Amtrak Service:	Yes
Major Waterways/Ports:	None

Source: Amtrak.com; Google Maps

BUSINESSES

Major Business Headquarters

Company Name	Rankings	
	Fortune[1]	Forbes[2]
Bank of America Corp.	21	-
Belk	-	108
Duke Energy	145	-
Nucor	146	-
SPX	431	-
Sonic Automotive	307	-

Note: (1) Fortune 500—companies that produce a 10-K are ranked 1 to 500 based on 2012 revenue; (2) all private companies with at least $2 billion in annual revenue through the end of their most current fiscal year are ranked 1 to 224; companies listed are headquartered in the city; dashes indicate no ranking
Source: Fortune, "Fortune 500," May 20, 2013; Forbes, "America's Largest Private Companies," December 18, 2013

Fast-Growing Businesses

According to *Inc.*, Charlotte is home to three of America's 500 fastest-growing private companies: **Titan Electric Company** (#224); **Movement Mortgage** (#272); **In-Flight Crew Connections** (#415). Criteria: must be an independent, privately-held, for-profit, U.S. corporation, proprietorship or partnership; revenues must be at least $100,000 in 2009 and $2 million in 2012; must have four-year operating/sales history. Holding companies, regulated banks, and utilities were excluded. *Inc., "America's 500 Fastest-Growing Private Companies," September 2013*

According to *Initiative for a Competitive Inner City (ICIC)*, Charlotte is home to one of America's 100 fastest-growing "inner city" companies: **Park Inc.** (#61). Companies were ranked by their five-year compound annual growth rate. Criteria for inclusion: company must be headquartered in or have 51 percent or more of its physical operations in an economically distressed urban area; must be an independent, for-profit corporation, partnership or proprietorship; must have 10 or more employees and have a five-year sales history that includes sales of at least $200,000 in the base year and at least $1 million in the current year with no decrease in sales over the two most recent years. *Initiative for a Competitive Inner City (ICIC), "Inner City 100 Companies, 2013"*

Minority Business Opportunity

Charlotte is home to two companies which are on the *Black Enterprise* Industrial/Service 100 list (100 largest companies based on gross sales): **NDR Energy Group** (#57); **American Product Distributors** (#78). Criteria: operational in previous calendar year; at least 51% black-owned and manufactures/owns the product it sells or provides industrial or consumer services. Brokerages, real estate firms and firms that provide professional services are not eligible. *Black Enterprise, B.E. 100s, 2013*

Charlotte is home to one company which is on the *Hispanic Business* 500 list (500 largest U.S. Hispanic-owned companies based on 2012 revenue): **ROJO Marketing / RED F Marketing** (#342). Companies included must show at least 51 percent ownership by Hispanic U.S. citizens, and must maintain headquarters in one of the 50 states or Washington, D.C. *Hispanic Business, "Hispanic Business 500," June 20, 2013*

Minority- and Women-Owned Businesses

Group	All Firms		Firms with Paid Employees			
	Firms	Sales ($000)	Firms	Sales ($000)	Employees	Payroll ($000)
Asian	3,093	955,472	990	887,161	7,194	148,988
Black	12,219	876,207	605	648,448	5,856	153,088
Hispanic	3,526	570,726	282	423,809	2,083	64,718
Women	21,332	3,553,085	2,235	3,015,006	24,133	792,510
All Firms	68,545	143,882,230	16,440	141,276,500	509,528	25,270,229

Note: Figures cover firms located in the city; minority- and women-owned business are defined as firms in which the corresponding group own 51% or more of the stock or equity of the company
Source: U.S. Census Bureau, 2007 Economic Census, Survey of Business Owners (2012 Survey of Business Owners data will be released starting in June 2015)

HOTELS & CONVENTION CENTERS

Hotels/Motels

Area	5 Star		4 Star		3 Star		2 Star		1 Star		Not Rated	
	Num.	Pct.[3]	Num.	Pct.[3]	Num.	Pct.[3]	Num.	Pct.[3]	Num.	Pct.[3]	Num.	Pct.[3]
City[1]	1	0.4	4	1.5	75	28.8	151	58.1	12	4.6	17	6.5
Total[2]	142	0.9	1,005	6.0	5,147	30.9	8,578	51.4	408	2.4	1,397	8.4

Note: (1) Figures cover Charlotte and vicinity; (2) Figures cover all 100 cities in this book; (3) Percentage of hotels which have a given star rating; Star ratings are determined by expedia.com and offer an indication of the general quality of a particular hotel.
Source: expedia.com, April 7, 2014

The Charlotte-Concord-Gastonia, NC-SC metro area is home to one of the best hotels in the world according to *Condé Nast Traveler*: **Ritz-Carlton**. The selections are based on over 79,000 responses to the magazine's annual Readers' Choice Survey. The list includes the top 200 hotels in the U.S. *Condé Nast Traveler, "Gold List 2014, The World's Best Places to Stay"*

Major Convention Centers

Name	Overall Space (sq. ft.)	Exhibit Space (sq. ft.)	Meeting Space (sq. ft.)	Meeting Rooms
Charlotte Convention Center	n/a	280,000	90,000	46

Note: Table includes convention centers located in the Charlotte-Concord-Gastonia, NC-SC metro area; n/a not available
Source: Original research

Living Environment

COST OF LIVING

Cost of Living Index

Composite Index	Groceries	Housing	Utilities	Trans-portation	Health Care	Misc. Goods/Services
95.4	101.6	83.7	106.6	98.4	98.2	97.0

Note: The Cost of Living Index measures regional differences in the cost of consumer goods and services, excluding taxes and non-consumer expenditures, for professional and managerial households in the top income quintile. It is based on more than 50,000 prices covering almost 60 different items for which prices are collected three times a year by chambers of commerce, economic development organizations or university applied economic centers in each participating urban area. The numbers shown should be read as a percentage above or below the national average of 100. For example, a value of 115.4 in the groceries column indicates that grocery prices are 15.4% higher than the national average. Small differences in the index numbers should not be interpreted as significant; Figures cover the Charlotte NC urban area.
Source: The Council for Community and Economic Research, ACCRA Cost of Living Index, 2013

Grocery Prices

Area[1]	T-Bone Steak ($/pound)	Frying Chicken ($/pound)	Whole Milk ($/half gal.)	Eggs ($/dozen)	Orange Juice ($/64 oz.)	Coffee ($/11.5 oz.)
City[2]	9.59	1.42	2.71	1.79	3.44	3.85
Avg.	10.19	1.28	2.34	1.81	3.48	4.39
Min.	8.56	0.94	1.44	1.19	2.78	3.40
Max.	14.82	2.28	3.56	3.73	6.23	7.32

Note: (1) Values for the local area are compared with the average, minimum and maximum values for all 327 areas in the Cost of Living Index; (2) Figures cover the Charlotte NC urban area; **T-Bone Steak** (price per pound); **Frying Chicken** (price per pound, whole fryer); **Whole Milk** (half gallon carton); **Eggs** (price per dozen, Grade A, large); **Orange Juice** (64 oz. Tropicana or Florida Natural); **Coffee** (11.5 oz. can, vacuum-packed, Maxwell House, Hills Bros, or Folgers).
Source: The Council for Community and Economic Research, ACCRA Cost of Living Index, 2013

Housing and Utility Costs

Area[1]	New Home Price ($)	Apartment Rent ($/month)	All Electric ($/month)	Part Electric ($/month)	Other Energy ($/month)	Telephone ($/month)
City[2]	244,676	829	164.64	-	-	31.94
Avg.	295,864	900	171.38	91.82	70.12	27.73
Min.	185,506	458	117.80	48.81	33.67	17.16
Max.	1,358,917	3,783	441.68	171.40	372.65	39.47

Note: (1) Values for the local area are compared with the average, minimum and maximum values for all 327 areas in the Cost of Living Index; (2) Figures cover the Charlotte NC urban area; **New Home Price** (2,400 sf living area, 8,000 sf lot, in urban area with full utilities); **Apartment Rent** (950 sf 2 bedroom/1.5 or 2 bath, unfurnished, excluding all utilities except water); **All Electric** (average monthly cost for an all-electric home); **Part Electric** (average monthly cost for a part-electric home); **Other Energy** (average monthly cost for natural gas, fuel oil, coal, wood, and any other forms of energy except electricity); **Telephone** (price includes basic monthly rate for a private residential line plus additional local usage charges incurred by a family of four).
Source: The Council for Community and Economic Research, ACCRA Cost of Living Index, 2013

Health Care, Transportation, and Other Costs

Area[1]	Doctor ($/visit)	Dentist ($/visit)	Optometrist ($/visit)	Gasoline ($/gallon)	Beauty Salon ($/visit)	Men's Shirt ($)
City[2]	98.80	85.07	114.83	3.47	38.80	18.52
Avg.	101.40	86.48	96.16	3.44	33.87	26.55
Min.	61.67	50.83	50.12	3.08	18.92	12.48
Max.	182.71	152.50	223.78	4.33	68.22	52.03

Note: (1) Values for the local area are compared with the average, minimum and maximum values for all 327 areas in the Cost of Living Index; (2) Figures cover the Charlotte NC urban area; **Doctor** (general practitioners routine exam of an established patient); **Dentist** (adult teeth cleaning and periodic oral examination); **Optometrist** (full vision eye exam for established adult patient); **Gasoline** (one gallon regular unleaded, national brand, including all taxes, cash price at self-service pump if available); **Beauty Salon** (woman's shampoo, trim, and blow-dry); **Men's Shirt** (cotton/polyester dress shirt, pinpoint weave, long sleeves).
Source: The Council for Community and Economic Research, ACCRA Cost of Living Index, 2013

HOUSING

House Price Index (HPI)

Area	National Ranking[2]	Quarterly Change (%)	One-Year Change (%)	Five-Year Change (%)
MSA[1]	91	0.84	4.85	-8.42
U.S.[3]	–	1.20	7.69	4.18

Note: The HPI is a weighted repeat sales index. It measures average price changes in repeat sales or refinancings on the same properties. This information is obtained by reviewing repeat mortgage transactions on single-family properties whose mortgages have been purchased or securitized by Fannie Mae or Freddie Mac in January 1975; (1) Charlotte-Concord-Gastonia, NC-SC Metropolitan Statistical Area—see Appendix B for areas included; (2) Rankings are based on annual percentage change for all metro areas containing at least 15,000 transactions over the last 10 years and ranges from 1 to 283; (3) figures based on a weighted average of Census Division estimates using a seasonally adjusted, purchase-only index; all figures are for the period ending December 31, 2013
Source: Federal Housing Finance Agency, House Price Index, February 25, 2014

Median Single-Family Home Prices

Area	2011	2012	2013[p]	Percent Change 2012 to 2013
MSA[1]	148.9	156.6	174.2	11.2
U.S. Average	166.2	177.2	197.4	11.4

Note: Figures are median sales prices of existing single-family homes in thousands of dollars; (p) preliminary; n/a not available; (1) Charlotte-Concord-Gastonia, NC-SC Metropolitan Statistical Area—see Appendix B for areas included
Source: National Association of Realtors, Median Sales Price of Existing Single-Family Homes for Metropolitan Areas, 4th Quarter 2013

Qualifying Income Based on Median Sales Price of Existing Single-Family Homes

Area	With 5% Down ($)	With 10% Down ($)	With 20% Down ($)
MSA[1]	39,770	37,677	33,491
U.S. Average	45,395	43,006	38,228

Note: Figures are preliminary; Qualifying income is based on a mortgage rate of 4.4%. Monthly principal and interest payment is limited to 25% of income; n/a not available; (1) Charlotte-Concord-Gastonia, NC-SC Metropolitan Statistical Area—see Appendix B for areas included
Source: National Association of Realtors, Qualifying Income Based on Median Sales Price of Existing Single-Family Homes for Metropolitan Areas, 4th Quarter 2013

Median Apartment Condo-Coop Home Prices

Area	2011	2012	2013[p]	Percent Change 2012 to 2013
MSA[1]	n/a	n/a	n/a	n/a
U.S. Average	165.1	173.7	194.9	12.2

Note: Figures are median sales prices of existing apartment condo-coop homes in thousands of dollars; (p) preliminary; n/a not available; (1) Charlotte-Concord-Gastonia, NC-SC Metropolitan Statistical Area—see Appendix B for areas included
Source: National Association of Realtors, Median Sales Price of Existing Apartment Condo-Coop Homes for Metropolitan Areas, 4th Quarter 2013

Gross Monthly Rent

Area	Under $200	$200 -299	$300 -499	$500 -749	$750 -999	$1,000 -1,499	$1,500 and up	Median ($)
City	1.1	1.5	3.6	26.3	34.6	25.8	7.0	868
MSA[1]	1.0	1.8	5.3	29.6	33.0	22.6	6.7	833
U.S.	1.7	3.3	8.1	22.7	24.3	25.7	14.3	889

Note: Figures are percentages except for Median; Gross rent is the contract rent plus the estimated average monthly cost of utilities (electricity, gas, and water and sewer) and fuels (oil, coal, kerosene, wood, etc.) if these are paid by the renter (or paid for the renter by someone else); (1) Figures cover the Charlotte-Concord-Gastonia, NC-SC Metropolitan Statistical Area—see Appendix B for areas included
Source: U.S. Census Bureau, 2010-2012 American Community Survey 3-Year Estimates

Year Housing Structure Built

Area	2010 or Later	2000 -2009	1990 -1999	1980 -1989	1970 -1979	1960 -1969	1950 -1959	1940 -1949	Before 1940	Median Year
City	0.7	25.4	20.6	15.7	13.8	10.4	7.3	3.1	3.0	1988
MSA[1]	0.8	27.0	20.8	15.4	12.5	9.2	7.0	3.2	4.1	1989
U.S.	0.5	14.9	13.8	13.9	15.9	11.1	10.9	5.5	13.5	1976

Note: Figures are percentages except for Median Year; (1) Figures cover the Charlotte-Concord-Gastonia, NC-SC Metropolitan Statistical Area—see Appendix B for areas included
Source: U.S. Census Bureau, 2010-2012 American Community Survey 3-Year Estimates

HEALTH

Health Risk Data

Category	MSA[1] (%)	U.S. (%)
Adults aged 18–64 who have any kind of health care coverage	76.3	79.6
Adults who reported being in good or excellent health	82.6	83.1
Adults who are current smokers	18.6	19.6
Adults who are heavy drinkers[2]	4.5	6.1
Adults who are binge drinkers[3]	13.1	16.9
Adults who are overweight (BMI 25.0 - 29.9)	36.4	35.8
Adults who are obese (BMI 30.0 - 99.8)	27.9	27.6
Adults who participated in any physical activities in the past month	78.6	77.1
Adults 50+ who have ever had a sigmoidoscopy or colonoscopy	69.3	67.3
Women aged 40+ who have had a mammogram within the past two years	71.0	74.0
Men aged 40+ who have had a PSA test within the past two years	51.1	45.2
Adults aged 65+ who have had flu shot within the past year	63.2	60.1
Adults who always wear a seatbelt	96.6	93.8

Note: Data as of 2012 unless otherwise noted; (1) Figures cover the Charlotte-Gastonia-Concord, NC-SC Metropolitan Statistical Area—see Appendix B for areas included; (2) Heavy drinkers are classified as males having more than two drinks per day or females having more than one drink per day; (3) Binge drinkers are classified as males having five or more drinks on one occasion or females having four or more drinks on one occasion
Source: Centers for Disease Control and Prevention, Behaviorial Risk Factor Surveillance System, SMART: Selected Metropolitan/Micropolitan Area Risk Trends, 2012

Chronic Health Indicators

Category	MSA[1] (%)	U.S. (%)
Adults who have ever been told they had a heart attack	3.9	4.5
Adults who have ever been told they had a stroke	2.5	2.9
Adults who have been told they currently have asthma	7.3	8.9
Adults who have ever been told they have arthritis	23.0	25.7
Adults who have ever been told they have diabetes[2]	10.0	9.7
Adults who have ever been told they had skin cancer	6.1	5.7
Adults who have ever been told they had any other types of cancer	5.9	6.5
Adults who have ever been told they have COPD	6.5	6.2
Adults who have ever been told they have kidney disease	2.4	2.5
Adults who have ever been told they have a form of depression	14.6	18.0

Note: Data as of 2012 unless otherwise noted; (1) Figures cover the Charlotte-Gastonia-Concord, NC-SC Metropolitan Statistical Area—see Appendix B for areas included; (2) Figures do not include pregnancy-related, borderline, or pre-diabetes
Source: Centers for Disease Control and Prevention, Behaviorial Risk Factor Surveillance System, SMART: Selected Metropolitan/Micropolitan Area Risk Trends, 2012

Mortality Rates for the Top 10 Causes of Death in the U.S.

ICD-10[a] Sub-Chapter	ICD-10[a] Code	Age-Adjusted Mortality Rate[1] per 100,000 population	
		County[2]	U.S.
Malignant neoplasms	C00-C97	167.8	174.2
Ischaemic heart diseases	I20-I25	76.6	119.1
Other forms of heart disease	I30-I51	52.6	49.6
Chronic lower respiratory diseases	J40-J47	38.1	43.2
Cerebrovascular diseases	I60-I69	41.0	40.3
Organic, including symptomatic, mental disorders	F01-F09	42.3	30.5
Other degenerative diseases of the nervous system	G30-G31	47.1	26.3
Other external causes of accidental injury	W00-X59	18.5	25.1
Diabetes mellitus	E10-E14	17.1	21.3
Hypertensive diseases	I10-I15	15.1	18.8

Note: (a) ICD-10 = International Classification of Diseases 10th Revision; (1) Mortality rates are a three year average covering 2008-2010; (2) Figures cover Mecklenburg County
Source: Centers for Disease Control and Prevention, National Center for Health Statistics. Compressed Mortality File 1999-2010 on CDC WONDER Online Database, released January 2013. Data are compiled from the Compressed Mortality File 1999-2010, Series 20 No. 2P, 2013.

Mortality Rates for Selected Causes of Death

ICD-10[a] Sub-Chapter	ICD-10[a] Code	Age-Adjusted Mortality Rate[1] per 100,000 population	
		County[2]	U.S.
Assault	X85-Y09	7.1	5.5
Diseases of the liver	K70-K76	10.6	12.4
Human immunodeficiency virus (HIV) disease	B20-B24	6.2	3.0
Influenza and pneumonia	J09-J18	13.5	16.4
Intentional self-harm	X60-X84	9.6	11.8
Malnutrition	E40-E46	*0.7	0.8
Obesity and other hyperalimentation	E65-E68	1.6	1.6
Renal failure	N17-N19	17.5	13.6
Transport accidents	V01-V99	8.7	12.6
Viral hepatitis	B15-B19	1.9	2.2

Note: (a) ICD-10 = International Classification of Diseases 10th Revision; (1) Mortality rates are a three year average covering 2008-2010; (2) Figures cover Mecklenburg County; (*) Unreliable data as per CDC
Source: Centers for Disease Control and Prevention, National Center for Health Statistics. Compressed Mortality File 1999-2010 on CDC WONDER Online Database, released January 2013. Data are compiled from the Compressed Mortality File 1999-2010, Series 20 No. 2P, 2013.

Health Insurance Coverage

Area	With Health Insurance	With Private Health Insurance	With Public Health Insurance	Without Health Insurance	Population Under Age 18 Without Health Insurance
City	82.4	64.7	25.0	17.6	6.9
MSA[1]	83.5	66.7	25.5	16.5	7.2
U.S.	84.9	65.4	30.4	15.1	7.5

Note: Figures are percentages that cover the civilian noninstitutionalized population; (1) Figures cover the Charlotte-Concord-Gastonia, NC-SC Metropolitan Statistical Area—see Appendix B for areas included
Source: U.S. Census Bureau, 2010-2012 American Community Survey 3-Year Estimates

Number of Medical Professionals

Area[1]	MDs[2]	DOs[2,3]	Dentists	Podiatrists	Chiropractors	Optometrists
Local (number)	2,826	84	629	32	295	122
Local (rate[4])	299.1	8.9	65.0	3.3	30.5	12.6
U.S. (rate[4])	267.6	19.6	61.7	5.6	24.7	14.5

Note: Data as of 2012 unless noted; (1) Local data covers Mecklenburg County; (2) Data as of 2011; (3) Doctor of Osteopathic Medicine; (4) rate per 100,000 population
Source: Area Resource File (ARF) 2012-2013. U.S. Department of Health and Human Services, Health Resources and Services Administration, Bureau of Health Professions

Best Hospitals

According to *U.S. News*, the Charlotte-Concord-Gastonia, NC-SC metro area is home to one of the best children's hospitals in the U.S.: **Levine Children's Hospital**. The hospital listed was highly ranked in at least one pediatric specialty. Eighty-seven hospitals in the U.S. ranked in at least one specialty. Ten children's hospitals in the U.S. made the Honor Roll by ranking near the top in three or more specialties.*U.S. News Online, "America's Best Children's Hospitals 2013-14"*

EDUCATION

Public School District Statistics

District Name	Schls	Pupils	Pupil/ Teacher Ratio	Minority Pupils[1] (%)	Free Lunch Eligible[2] (%)	IEP[3] (%)
Charlotte-Mecklenburg Schools	174	141,728	16.1	68.0	48.8	9.6

Note: Table includes school districts with 2,000 or more students; (1) Percentage of students that are not non-Hispanic white; (2) Percentage of students that are eligible for the free lunch program; (3) Percentage of students that have an Individualized Education Program.
Source: U.S. Department of Education, National Center for Education Statistics, Common Core of Data, Local Education Agency (School District) Universe Survey: School Year 2011-2012; U.S. Department of Education, National Center for Education Statistics, Common Core of Data, Public Elementary/Secondary School Universe Survey: School Year 2011-2012

Best High Schools

High School Name	Rank[1]	Grad. Rate[2] (%)	Coll.[3] (%)	AP/IB/ AICE Tests[4]	AP/IB/ AICE Score[5]	SAT Score[6]	ACT Score[6]
Ardrey Kell High	473	94	95	0.5	3.9	1641	n/a
Biotechnology, Health and Public Administration at Olympic HS	1570	88	100	0.2	2.0	1389	n/a
Cato Middle College High	207	100	100	0.8	2.7	1605	n/a
East Mecklenburg H.S.	1771	80	90	0.3	3.1	1463	21.9
International Studies and Global Economics at Olympic H.S.	1952	72	100	0.1	2.3	1335	n/a
Mallard Creek High	1177	93	96	0.2	3.1	1410	n/a
Math, Engineering, Technology and Science at Olympic H.S.	1430	88	100	0.1	2.6	1456	n/a
Myers Park High	652	89	98	0.5	3.5	1641	n/a
Northwest School of the Arts	1362	93	89	0.3	3.0	1569	19.0
Providence H.S.	446	95	96	0.5	3.9	1708	23.2
South Mecklenburg High	1006	88	100	0.4	3.1	1512	n/a

Note: (1) Public schools are ranked from 1 to 2,000 based on the following self-reported statistics (with the corresponding weight used in calculating their overall score). Schools that were newly founded and did not have a graduating senior class in 2012 were excluded; (2) Four-year, on-time graduation rate (25%); (3) Percent of 2011 graduates who were accepted to college (25%); (4) AP/IB/AICE tests taken per student (25%); (5) Average AP/IB/AICE exam score (10%); (6) Average SAT and/or ACT score (10%); Percent of students enrolled in at least one AP/IB/AICE course (5%)—data not shown; n/a not available
Source: Newsweek and The Daily Beast, "America's Best High Schools 2013"

Highest Level of Education

Area	Less than H.S.	H.S. Diploma	Some College, No Deg.	Associate Degree	Bachelor's Degree	Master's Degree	Prof. School Degree	Doctorate Degree
City	11.7	20.4	21.0	7.1	27.3	9.3	2.3	0.8
MSA[1]	12.8	24.3	21.8	8.1	22.9	7.7	1.7	0.8
U.S.	14.1	28.3	21.3	7.8	18.0	7.5	1.9	1.2

Note: Figures cover persons age 25 and over; (1) Figures cover the Charlotte-Concord-Gastonia, NC-SC Metropolitan Statistical Area—see Appendix B for areas included
Source: U.S. Census Bureau, 2010-2012 American Community Survey 3-Year Estimates

Educational Attainment by Race

Area	High School Graduate or Higher (%)					Bachelor's Degree or Higher (%)				
	Total	White	Black	Asian	Hisp.[2]	Total	White	Black	Asian	Hisp.[2]
City	88.3	91.5	86.9	84.4	57.5	39.8	50.0	22.8	55.2	15.5
MSA[1]	87.2	89.1	85.3	84.3	59.0	33.1	36.6	21.7	53.3	15.3
U.S.	85.9	88.1	82.5	85.5	63.1	28.6	30.0	18.4	50.2	13.4

Note: Figures shown cover persons 25 years old and over; (1) Figures cover the Charlotte-Concord-Gastonia, NC-SC Metropolitan Statistical Area—see Appendix B for areas included; (2) People of Hispanic origin can be of any race
Source: U.S. Census Bureau, 2010-2012 American Community Survey 3-Year Estimates

School Enrollment by Grade and Control

Area	Preschool (%)		Kindergarten (%)		Grades 1 - 4 (%)		Grades 5 - 8 (%)		Grades 9 - 12 (%)	
	Public	Private	Public	Private	Public	Private	Public	Private	Public	Private
City	39.9	60.1	89.8	10.2	89.0	11.0	87.2	12.8	89.4	10.6
MSA[1]	43.5	56.5	90.2	9.8	89.9	10.1	89.3	10.7	89.6	10.4
U.S.	56.9	43.1	87.8	12.2	89.9	10.1	90.0	10.0	90.8	9.2

Note: Figures shown cover persons 3 years old and over; (1) Figures cover the Charlotte-Concord-Gastonia, NC-SC Metropolitan Statistical Area—see Appendix B for areas included
Source: U.S. Census Bureau, 2010-2012 American Community Survey 3-Year Estimates

Average Salaries of Public School Classroom Teachers

Area	2012-13		2013-14		Percent Change 2012-13 to 2013-14	Percent Change 2003-04 to 2013-14
	Dollars	Rank[1]	Dollars	Rank[1]		
North Carolina	45,737	46	45,355	48	-0.84	5.0
U.S. Average	56,103	–	56,689	–	1.04	21.8

Note: (1) State rank ranges from 1 to 51 where 1 indicates highest salary.
Source: National Education Association, Rankings & Estimates: Rankings of the States 2013 and Estimates of School Statistics 2014, March 2014

Higher Education

Four-Year Colleges			Two-Year Colleges			Medical Schools[1]	Law Schools[2]	Voc/ Tech[3]
Public	Private Non-profit	Private For-profit	Public	Private Non-profit	Private For-profit			
1	4	7	3	0	2	0	1	7

Note: Figures cover institutions located within the city limits and include main campuses only; (1) includes schools accredited by the Liaison Committee on Medical Education and the American Osteopathic Association's Commission on Osteopathic College Accreditation; (2) includes ABA-accredited schools, schools with provisional ABA accreditation, and state accredited schools; (3) includes all schools with programs that are less than 2 years.
Source: National Center for Education Statistics, Integrated Postsecondary Education System (IPEDS), 2012-13; Association of American Medical Colleges, Member List, April 24, 2014; American Osteopathic Association, Member List, April 24, 2014; Law School Admission Council, Official Guide to ABA-Approved Law Schools Online, April 24, 2014; Wikipedia, List of Medical Schools in the United States, April 24, 2014; Wikipedia, List of Law Schools in the United States, April 24, 2014

According to *U.S. News & World Report,* the Charlotte-Concord-Gastonia, NC-SC metro area is home to one of the best national universities in the U.S.: **University of North Carolina–Charlotte** (#201). The indicators used to capture academic quality fall into a number of categories: assessment by administrators at peer institutions; retention of students; faculty resources; student selectivity; financial resources; alumni giving; high school counselor ratings of colleges; and graduation rate. *U.S. News & World Report, "America's Best Colleges 2014"*

According to *U.S. News & World Report,* the Charlotte-Concord-Gastonia, NC-SC metro area is home to one of the best liberal arts colleges in the U.S.: **Davidson College** (#9). The indicators used to capture academic quality fall into a number of categories: assessment by administrators at peer institutions; retention of students; faculty resources; student selectivity; financial resources; alumni giving; high school counselor ratings of colleges; and graduation rate. *U.S. News & World Report, "America's Best Colleges 2014"*

PRESIDENTIAL ELECTION

2012 Presidential Election Results

Area	Obama	Romney	Other
Mecklenburg County	60.7	38.2	1.1
U.S.	51.0	47.2	1.8

Note: Results are percentages and may not add to 100% due to rounding
Source: Dave Leip's Atlas of U.S. Presidential Elections

EMPLOYERS

Major Employers

Company Name	Industry
Bank of America National Association	National commercial banks
Carlisle Companies Incorporated	Fabricated rubber products
Carolina Medical Center Northeast	General medical and surgical hospitals
Carolina Medical Center Union	General medical and surgical hospitals
Charlotte Mecklenburg Hosp Auth	General medical and surgical hospitals
Compass Group North America	Services
Duke Energy Corporation	Electric services
IBM	Office equipment
IBM	Banking machines
Insource Performance Solutions	Help supply services
Medcath Incorporated	Specialty hospitals, except psychiatric
Merchandising Corporation of America	Business consulting
Microsoft Corporation	Computer peripheral equipment
Polymer Group	Nonwoven fabrics
Presbyterian Hospital	General medical and surgical hospitals
Rohr Inc Credit Corporation	Aircraft engines and engine parts
University of NC at Chapel Hill	Colleges and universities
Wachovia Corporation	National commercial banks
Wells Fargo Bank	Banking and finance consultant

Note: Companies shown are located within the Charlotte-Concord-Gastonia, NC-SC Metropolitan Statistical Area.
Source: Hoovers.com; Wikipedia

Best Companies to Work For

Bank of America, headquartered in Charlotte, is among the "100 Best Companies for Working Mothers." Criteria: workforce representation; child care; flexibility programs; and leave policies. This year *Working Mother* gave particular weight to flexible work arrangements, women's advancement programs, and paid maternity leave. *Working Mother, "100 Best Companies 2013"*

Carolinas HealthCare System, headquartered in Charlotte, is among the "100 Best Places to Work in IT." To qualify, companies, both public and private, had to have a minimum of 50 IT employees and were selected based on average salary and bonus increases, the percentage of IT staffers promoted, IT staff turnover rates, training and development programs, and the percentage of women and minorities in IT staff and management positions. In addition, *Computerworld* looked at retention efforts, programs for recognizing and rewarding outstanding performances, and benefits such as flextime, elder care and child care, and reimbursement for college tuition and the cost of pursuing technology certifications. *Computerworld, "100 Best Places to Work in IT 2013"*

Bank of America, headquartered in Charlotte, is among the "Top Companies for Executive Women." To be named to the list, companies with a minimum of two women on the board complete a comprehensive application that focuses on the number of women in senior ranks. In addition to assessing corporate programs and policies dedicated to advancing women, NAFE examined the number of women in each company overall, in senior management, and on its board of directors, paying particular attention to the number of women with profit-and-loss responsibility. *National Association for Female Executives, "2013 NAFE Top 50 Companies for Executive Women"*

PUBLIC SAFETY

Crime Rate

Area	All Crimes	Violent Crimes				Property Crimes		
		Murder	Forcible Rape	Robbery	Aggrav. Assault	Burglary	Larceny -Theft	Motor Vehicle Theft
City	4,660.7	7.1	27.6	204.2	367.5	1,081.2	2,707.0	266.1
Suburbs[1]	3,228.5	3.0	22.2	60.5	200.4	686.7	2,117.4	138.3
Metro[2]	3,863.7	4.8	24.6	124.2	274.5	861.7	2,378.9	195.0
U.S.	3,292.5	4.7	27.0	113.9	241.5	701.3	1,974.1	230.0

Note: Figures are crimes per 100,000 population; (1) All areas within the metro area that are located outside the city limits; (2) Figures cover the Charlotte-Concord-Gastonia, NC-SC Metropolitan Statistical Area—see Appendix B for areas included
Source: FBI Uniform Crime Reports, 2011 (data for 2012 was not available)

Hate Crimes

Area	Number of Quarters Reported	Bias Motivation				
		Race	Religion	Sexual Orientation	Ethnicity	Disability
Area[2]	4	7	1	2	4	0
U.S.	4	2,797	1,099	1,135	667	92

Note: (2) Figures cover Charlotte-Mecklenburg.
Source: Federal Bureau of Investigation, Hate Crime Statistics 2012

Identity Theft Consumer Complaints

Area	Complaints	Complaints per 100,000 Population	Rank[2]
MSA[1]	1,812	81.7	102
U.S.	290,056	91.8	-

Note: (1) Figures cover the Charlotte-Concord-Gastonia, NC-SC Metropolitan Statistical Area—see Appendix B for areas included; (2) Rank ranges from 1 to 377 where 1 indicates greatest number of identity theft complaints per 100,000 population
Source: Federal Trade Commission, Consumer Sentinel Network Data Book for January–December 2013

Fraud and Other Consumer Complaints

Area	Complaints	Complaints per 100,000 Population	Rank[2]
MSA[1]	9,782	441.2	62
U.S.	1,811,724	595.2	-

Note: (1) Figures cover the Charlotte-Concord-Gastonia, NC-SC Metropolitan Statistical Area—see Appendix B for areas included; (2) Rank ranges from 1 to 377 where 1 indicates greatest number of identity theft complaints per 100,000 population
Source: Federal Trade Commission, Consumer Sentinel Network Data Book for January–December 2013

RECREATION

Culture

Dance[1]	Theatre[1]	Instrumental Music[1]	Vocal Music[1]	Series and Festivals	Museums and Art Galleries[2]	Zoos and Aquariums[3]
1	4	5	2	3	29	0

Note: (1) Number of professional perfoming groups; (2) Based on organizations with primary SIC code 8412; (3) AZA-accredited
Source: The Grey House Performing Arts Directory, 2013; Association of Zoos & Aquariums, AZA Member Zoos & Aquariums, April 2014; www.AccuLeads.com, May 1, 2014

Professional Sports Teams

Team Name	League	Year Established
Carolina Panthers	National Football League (NFL)	1995
Charlotte Bobcats (Hornets in 2014)	National Basketball Association (NBA)	2004

Note: Includes teams located in the Charlotte-Concord-Gastonia, NC-SC Metropolitan Statistical Area.
Source: Wikipedia, Major Professional Sports Teams of the United States and Canada

CLIMATE

Average and Extreme Temperatures

Temperature	Jan	Feb	Mar	Apr	May	Jun	Jul	Aug	Sep	Oct	Nov	Dec	Yr.
Extreme High (°F)	78	81	86	93	97	103	103	103	104	98	85	77	104
Average High (°F)	51	54	62	72	80	86	89	88	82	72	62	53	71
Average Temp. (°F)	41	44	51	61	69	76	79	78	72	61	51	43	61
Average Low (°F)	31	33	40	48	57	65	69	68	62	50	40	33	50
Extreme Low (°F)	-5	5	4	25	32	45	53	53	39	24	11	2	-5

Note: Figures cover the years 1948-1990
Source: National Climatic Data Center, International Station Meteorological Climate Summary, 9/96

Average Precipitation/Snowfall/Humidity

Precip./Humidity	Jan	Feb	Mar	Apr	May	Jun	Jul	Aug	Sep	Oct	Nov	Dec	Yr.
Avg. Precip. (in.)	3.6	3.8	4.5	3.0	3.7	3.4	3.9	3.9	3.4	3.2	3.1	3.4	42.8
Avg. Snowfall (in.)	2	2	1	Tr	0	0	0	0	0	0	Tr	1	6
Avg. Rel. Hum. 7am (%)	78	77	78	78	82	83	86	89	89	87	83	79	82
Avg. Rel. Hum. 4pm (%)	53	49	46	43	49	51	54	55	54	50	50	54	51

Note: Figures cover the years 1948-1990; Tr = Trace amounts (<0.05 in. of rain; <0.5 in. of snow)
Source: National Climatic Data Center, International Station Meteorological Climate Summary, 9/96

Weather Conditions

Temperature			Daytime Sky			Precipitation		
10°F & below	32°F & below	90°F & above	Clear	Partly cloudy	Cloudy	0.01 inch or more precip.	0.1 inch or more snow/ice	Thunder-storms
1	65	44	98	142	125	113	3	41

Note: Figures are average number of days per year and cover the years 1948-1990
Source: National Climatic Data Center, International Station Meteorological Climate Summary, 9/96

HAZARDOUS WASTE

Superfund Sites

Charlotte has one hazardous waste site on the EPA's Superfund Final National Priorities List: **Ram Leather Care**. *U.S. Environmental Protection Agency, Final National Priorities List, April 26, 2014*

AIR & WATER QUALITY

Air Quality Index

Area	Percent of Days when Air Quality was...[2]					AQI Statistics[2]	
	Good	Moderate	Unhealthy for Sensitive Groups	Unhealthy	Very Unhealthy	Maximum	Median
MSA[1]	76.2	23.8	0.0	0.0	0.0	87	42

Note: (1) Data covers the Charlotte-Concord-Gastonia, NC-SC Metropolitan Statistical Area—see Appendix B for areas included; (2) Based on 365 days with AQI data in 2013. Air Quality Index (AQI) is an index for reporting daily air quality. EPA calculates the AQI for five major air pollutants regulated by the Clean Air Act: ground-level ozone, particle pollution (aka particulate matter), carbon monoxide, sulfur dioxide, and nitrogen dioxide. The AQI runs from 0 to 500. The higher the AQI value, the greater the level of air pollution and the greater the health concern. There are six AQI categories: "Good" AQI is between 0 and 50. Air quality is considered satisfactory; "Moderate" AQI is between 51 and 100. Air quality is acceptable; "Unhealthy for Sensitive Groups" When AQI values are between 101 and 150, members of sensitive groups may experience health effects; "Unhealthy" When AQI values are between 151 and 200 everyone may begin to experience health effects; "Very Unhealthy" AQI values between 201 and 300 trigger a health alert; "Hazardous" AQI values over 300 trigger warnings of emergency conditions (not shown).
Source: U.S. Environmental Protection Agency, Air Quality Index Report, 2013

Air Quality Index Pollutants

Area	Percent of Days when AQI Pollutant was...[2]					
	Carbon Monoxide	Nitrogen Dioxide	Ozone	Sulfur Dioxide	Particulate Matter 2.5	Particulate Matter 10
MSA[1]	0.0	2.7	41.4	0.0	55.3	0.5

Note: (1) Data covers the Charlotte-Concord-Gastonia, NC-SC Metropolitan Statistical Area—see Appendix B for areas included; (2) Based on 365 days with AQI data in 2013. The Air Quality Index (AQI) is an index for reporting daily air quality. EPA calculates the AQI for five major air pollutants regulated by the Clean Air Act: ground-level ozone, particle pollution (also known as particulate matter), carbon monoxide, sulfur dioxide, and nitrogen dioxide. The AQI runs from 0 to 500. The higher the AQI value, the greater the level of air pollution and the greater the health concern.
Source: U.S. Environmental Protection Agency, Air Quality Index Report, 2013

Air Quality Trends: Ozone

	2003	2004	2005	2006	2007	2008	2009	2010	2011	2012
MSA[1]	0.081	0.078	0.085	0.084	0.088	0.081	0.067	0.076	0.078	0.076

Note: (1) Data covers the Charlotte-Concord-Gastonia, NC-SC Metropolitan Statistical Area—see Appendix B for areas included. The values shown are the composite ozone concentration averages among trend sites based on the highest fourth daily maximum 8-hour concentration in parts per million. These trends are based on sites having an adequate record of monitoring data during the trend period. Data from exceptional events are included.
Source: U.S. Environmental Protection Agency, Air Quality Monitoring Information, "Air Quality Trends by City, 2000-2012"

Maximum Air Pollutant Concentrations: Particulate Matter, Ozone, CO and Lead

	Particulate Matter 10 (ug/m^3)	Particulate Matter 2.5 Wtd AM (ug/m^3)	Particulate Matter 2.5 24-Hr (ug/m^3)	Ozone (ppm)	Carbon Monoxide (ppm)	Lead (ug/m^3)
MSA[1] Level	38	9.6	21	0.085	2	n/a
NAAQS[2]	150	15	35	0.075	9	0.15
Met NAAQS[2]	Yes	Yes	Yes	No	Yes	n/a

Note: (1) Data covers the Charlotte-Concord-Gastonia, NC-SC Metropolitan Statistical Area—see Appendix B for areas included; Data from exceptional events are included; (2) National Ambient Air Quality Standards; ppm = parts per million; ug/m^3 = micrograms per cubic meter; n/a not available.
Concentrations: Particulate Matter 10 (coarse particulate)—highest second maximum 24-hour concentration; Particulate Matter 2.5 Wtd AM (fine particulate)—highest weighted annual mean concentration; Particulate Matter 2.5 24-Hour (fine particulate)—highest 98th percentile 24-hour concentration; Ozone—highest fourth daily maximum 8-hour concentration; Carbon Monoxide—highest second maximum non-overlapping 8-hour concentration; Lead—maximum running 3-month average
Source: U.S. Environmental Protection Agency, Air Quality Monitoring Information, "Air Quality Statistics by City, 2012"

Maximum Air Pollutant Concentrations: Nitrogen Dioxide and Sulfur Dioxide

	Nitrogen Dioxide AM (ppb)	Nitrogen Dioxide 1-Hr (ppb)	Sulfur Dioxide AM (ppb)	Sulfur Dioxide 1-Hr (ppb)	Sulfur Dioxide 24-Hr (ppb)
MSA[1] Level	9	n/a	n/a	8	n/a
NAAQS[2]	53	100	30	75	140
Met NAAQS[2]	Yes	n/a	n/a	Yes	n/a

Note: (1) Data covers the Charlotte-Concord-Gastonia, NC-SC Metropolitan Statistical Area—see Appendix B for areas included; Data from exceptional events are included; (2) National Ambient Air Quality Standards; ppm = parts per million; ug/m^3 = micrograms per cubic meter; n/a not available.
Concentrations: Nitrogen Dioxide AM—highest arithmetic mean concentration; Nitrogen Dioxide 1-Hr—highest 98th percentile 1-hour daily maximum concentration; Sulfur Dioxide AM—highest annual mean concentration; Sulfur Dioxide 1-Hr—highest 99th percentile 1-hour daily maximum concentration; Sulfur Dioxide 24-Hr—highest second maximum 24-hour concentration
Source: U.S. Environmental Protection Agency, Air Quality Monitoring Information, "Air Quality Statistics by City, 2012"

Drinking Water

Water System Name	Pop. Served	Primary Water Source Type	Violations[1]	
			Health Based	Monitoring/ Reporting
Charlotte-Mecklenburg Utility	805,242	Surface	0	0

Note: (1) Based on violation data from January 1, 2013 to December 31, 2013 (includes unresolved violations from earlier years)
Source: U.S. Environmental Protection Agency, Office of Ground Water and Drinking Water, Safe Drinking Water Information System (based on data extracted February 10, 2014)

Cincinnati, Ohio

Background

Cincinnati's name has a long history. After the American Revolution, former Continental Army soldiers formed a fraternal organization called the Society of Cincinnati, alluding to the Roman General Lucius Quinctius Cincinnatus. In 1790, General Arthur St. Clair, a member of that society and the first governor of the Northwest Territory, felt that this lovely city overlooking the Ohio River could only be called Cincinnati. As if that were not enough, he had to pay homage to fellow fraternal member Alexander Hamilton, so St. Clair named the county in which Cincinnati lies after him.

Since its incorporation as a city in 1819, the Miami and Erie canals have played great roles in Cincinnati's economic growth. Because of these waterways, farmers had the transportation necessary to sell their produce in town. From there, businesses would process the farmers' wares such as corn, pigs, and wheat into whiskey, pork, and flour.

Incidentally, the South, which was Cincinnati's greatest market for pork, made the city's loyalties difficult to declare during the Civil War. However, Cincinnati finally chose sides when its political climate made it a major station of the Underground Railroad, as well as the haven where Harriet Beecher Stowe could write her classic, *Uncle Tom's Cabin*. The National Underground Railroad Freedom Center here offers programs and exhibits highlighting the Railroad's true stories of courage in the quest for freedom.

Today, the city's major economic sectors include aerospace, automotive, chemistry and plastics, and financial services, although newer sectors are emerging such as advanced energy and consumer products. The city is home to the University of Cincinnati and Xavier University, and its centralized location has attracted Fortune 500 corporate headquarters. Major employers headquartered here include Proctor & Gamble, The Kroger Company, and Macy's. Five interstate highways converge at Cincinnati, providing present-day transportation access just as the canals did early in the city's growth. Work is underway by the Ohio Rail Development Corp to build a passenger rail line linking Cincinnati and other major Ohio cities that is anticipated to serve nearly a half-million people in its first year of operation. The federal government will spend $400 million to back the project.

The city blends Old World charm with modern business savvy. Investments of more than $700 million in the last decade are drawing tourists, conventioneers, and residents downtown—the Cincinnati Center City Development Corp., charged with supporting the area's renaissance, has seen to that. Improvements include new entertainment districts, called The Banks and Over the Rhine that have either opened or undergone gentrification and redevelopment. In addition, three new hotels are slated to open by the end of 2014, joining three other new hotels that have opened in recent years. They include the 21c Museum Hotel, which has an 8,000 square foot art museum. On top of that, Horseshoe Casino Cincinnati opened in March 2013. It boasts a 31-table World Series Poker Room in addition to entertainment venues and restaurants. All of these amenities are situated in close proximity to the Duke Energy Convention Center or the city's two professional sports stadiums: the Cincinnati Reds MLB team plays at the Great American Ball Park and the NFL's Cincinnati Bengals call the Paul Brown Stadium home.

The arts thrive in Cincinnati. The Rosenthal Center for Contemporary Art celebrates its 75th anniversary in 2014, and is housed in an acclaimed, Zaha Hadid-designed building; she won the Pritzker Architecture Award in 2004, the year after the building opened. The famed Cincinnati Opera, founded in 1920 and the second-oldest opera company in the U.S., features a complete season of productions as well as a summer program. The Cincinnati Symphony Orchestra, founded in 1905, is the nation's fifth-oldest orchestra. Both organizations perform in the historic Music Hall, whose Springer Auditorium is renowned for its acoustics.

To celebrate its German heritage, Cincinnati hosts the second largest Oktoberfest in the world.

But perhaps Cincinnati most celebrated tradition is its chili. "Cincinnati Chili" is unique in that it's served over spaghetti or as a "coney" sauce on a hotdog. It's served in independent restaurants all over the city, but is most famously found in chain restaurants like Skyline Chili, Empress, and Gold Star.

Cincinnati experiences a rather wide range of temperatures from winter to summer. Summers are warm and quite humid, with brief periods of very high temperatures every two or three years. Winters are moderately cold with numerous periods of extensive cloudiness.

Rankings

General Rankings

- Cincinnati was selected as one of America's best cities by *Bloomberg Businessweek*. The city ranked #21 out of 50. Criteria: leisure attributes (the number of restaurants, bars, libraries, museums, professional sports teams, and park acres by population); educational attributes (public school performance, the number of colleges, and graduate degree holders); economic factors (2011 income and June and July 2012 unemployment); crime; and air quality. *Bloomberg BusinessWeek, "America's Best Cities," September 26, 2012*

- The Cincinnati metro area was selected as one of 10 "Best Value Cities" for 2011 by *Kiplinger.com* The area ranked #10. Criteria: vibrant economy; low cost of living; abundant lifestyle amenities. *Kiplinger.com, "Best Value Cities 2011"*

Business/Finance Rankings

- Based on a minimum of 500 social media reviews per metro area, the employment opinion group Glassdoor surveyed 50 of the largest U.S. metro areas on measures including compensation and benefits, satisfaction with management, business outlook, and number of employers hiring. The Cincinnati metro area was ranked #21 in overall employee satisfaction. *www.glassdoor.com, "Employment Satisfaction Report Card by City," June 21, 2013*

- In its Competitive Alternatives report, consulting firm KPMG analyzed the 27 largest metropolitan statistical areas according to 26 cost components (such as taxes, labor costs, and utilities) and 30 non-cost-related variables (such as crime rates and number of universities). The business website 24/7 Wall Street examined the KPMG findings, adding to the mix current unemployment rates, GDP, median income, and employment decline during the last recession and "projected" recovery. It identified the Cincinnati metro area as #1 among the ten best American cities for business. *247wallst.com, "Best American Cities for Business," April 4, 2012*

- Cincinnati was ranked #65 out of 100 metro areas in terms of economic performance (#1 = best) during the recession and recovery from trough quarter through the second quarter of 2013. Criteria: percent change in employment; percentage point change in unemployment rate; percent change in gross metropolitan product; percent change in House Price Index. *Brookings Institution, MetroMonitor: Tracking Economic Recession and Recovery in America's 100 Largest Metropolitan Areas, September 2013*

- The Cincinnati metro area was identified as one of the most affordable metropolitan areas in America by *Forbes*. The area ranked #3 out of 20. Criteria: the 100 largest metro areas in the U.S. were analyzed based on housing affordability and cost-of-living. *Forbes.com, "America's Most Affordable Cities," March 11, 2014*

- Cincinnati was identified as one of America's most frugal metro areas by *Coupons.com*. The city ranked #13 out of 25. Criteria: online coupon usage. *Coupons.com, "Top 25 Most Frugal Cities of 2012," February 19, 2013*

- Cincinnati was identified as one of America's most frugal metro areas by *Coupons.com*. The city ranked #17 out of 25. Criteria: Grocery IQ and coupons.com mobile app usage. *Coupons.com, "Top 25 Most On-the-Go Frugal Cities of 2012," February 19, 2013*

- Cincinnati was cited as one of America's top metros for new and expanded facility projects in 2013. The area ranked #6 in the large metro area category (population over 1 million). *Site Selection, "Top Metros of 2013," March 2014*

- Cincinnati was identified as one of the uhappiest cities to work in by CareerBliss.com, an online community for career advancement. The city ranked #1 out of 10. Criteria: independent company reviews from employees all over the country on: relationship with their boss and co-workers; work environment; job resources; compensation; growth opportunities; company culture; company reputation; daily tasks; job control over work performed on a daily basis. *CareerBliss.com, "Top 10 Happiest and Unhappiest Cities to Work in 2014," February 10, 2014*

- The Cincinnati metro area appeared on the Milken Institute "2013 Best Performing Cities" list. Rank: #113 out of 200 large metro areas. Criteria: job growth; wage and salary growth; high-tech output growth. *Milken Institute, "Best-Performing Cities 2013," December 2013*

- *Forbes* ranked the 200 most populous metro areas in the U.S. in terms of the "Best Places for Business and Careers." The Cincinnati metro area was ranked #115. Criteria: costs (business and living); job growth (past and projected); income growth; educational attainment (college and high school); projected economic growth; cultural and recreational opportunities; net migration patterns; number of highly ranked colleges. *Forbes, "The Best Places for Business and Careers," August 7, 2013*

Children/Family Rankings

- *Forbes* ranked the 100 largest metropolitan areas in the U.S. in terms of the "The Best Cities for Raising a Family." The Cincinnati metro area was ranked #9. Criteria: median income; overall cost of living; housing affordability; commuting delays; percentage of families owning homes; crime rate; education quality (mainly test scores). *Forbes, "The Best Cities for Raising a Family," April 4, 2012*

- Cincinnati was selected as one of the best cities for families to live by *Parenting* magazine. The city ranked #30 out of 100. Criteria: education; health; community; *Parenting's* Culture & Charm Index. *Parenting.com, "The 2012 Best Cities for Families List"*

- Cincinnati was chosen as one of America's 100 best communities for young people. The winners were selected based upon detailed information provided about each community's efforts to fulfill five essential promises critical to the well-being of young people: caring adults who are actively involved in their lives; safe places in which to learn and grow; a healthy start toward adulthood; an effective education that builds marketable skills; and opportunities to help others. *America's Promise Alliance, "100 Best Communities for Young People, 2012"*

Culture/Performing Arts Rankings

- Cincinnati was selected as one of America's top cities for the arts. The city ranked #9 in the mid-sized city (population 100,000 to 499,999) category. Criteria: readers' top choices for arts travel destinations based on the richness and variety of visual arts sites, activities and events. *American Style, "2012 Top 25 Arts Destinations," June 2012*

Dating/Romance Rankings

- Of the 100 U.S. cities surveyed by *Men's Health* in its quest to identify the nation's best cities for dating and forming relationships, Cincinnati was ranked #26 for online dating (#1 = best). *Men's Health, "The Best and Worst Cities for Online Dating," January 30, 2013*

- Cincinnati was selected as one of the most romantic cities in America by Amazon.com. The city ranked #8 of 20. Criteria: cities with 100,000 or more residents were ranked on their per capita sales of romance novels and relationship books, romantic comedy movies, romantic music, and sexual wellness products. *Amazon.com, "Top 20 Most Romantic Cities in America," February 3, 2014*

Education Rankings

- *Men's Health* ranked 100 U.S. cities in terms of their education levels. Cincinnati was ranked #48 (#1 = most educated city). Criteria: high school graduation rates; school enrollment; educational attainment; number of households who have outstanding student loans; number of households whose members have taken adult-education courses. *Men's Health, "Where School Is In: The Most and Least Educated Cities," September 12, 2011*

- Cincinnati was selected as one of the most well-read cities in America by Amazon.com. The city ranked #8 of 20. Cities with populations greater than 100,000 were evaluated based on per capita sales of books, magazines and newspapers. *Amazon.com, "The 20 Most Well-Read Cities in America," April 28, 2013*

- Cincinnati was selected as one of America's most literate cities. The city ranked #12 out of the 77 largest U.S. cities. Criteria: number of booksellers; library resources; Internet resources; educational attainment; periodical publishing resources; newspaper circulation. *Central Connecticut State University, "America's Most Literate Cities, 2013"*

- Cincinnati was identified as one of America's most inventive cities by *The Daily Beast.* The city ranked #13 out of 25. The 200 largest cities in the U.S. were ranked by the number of patents (applied and approved) per capita. *The Daily Beast, "The 25 Most Inventive Cities," October 2, 2011*

Environmental Rankings

- CNNMoney based its list of the nation's ten most polluted cities on the annual State of the Air report prepared by the American Lung Association, which noted that the cities with the worst air pollution also had some of the highest incidences of heart and lung disease. At #10 (#1 = worst), Cincinnati was among those with the poorest air quality. *money.cnn.com, "10 Most Polluted Cities," April 24, 2013*

- The Cincinnati metro area came in at #184 for the relative comfort of its climate on Sperling's list of "chill cities," as measured by the Sperling Heat Index. All 361 metro areas are included. Criteria included daytime high temperatures, nighttime low temperatures, dew point, and relative humidity at the high temperatures. *www.bertsperling.com, "Sperling's Chill Cities," July 18, 2013*

- Sperling's BestPlaces assessed 379 metropolitan areas of the United States for the likelihood of dangerously extreme weather events or earthquakes. In general the Southeast and South-Central regions have the highest risk of weather extremes and earthquakes, while the Pacific Northwest enjoys the lowest risk. Of the least risky metropolitan areas, the Cincinnati metro area was ranked #249. *www.bestplaces.net, "Safest Places from Natural Disasters," April 2011*

- The U.S. Environmental Protection Agency (EPA) released a list of U.S. metropolitan areas with the most ENERGY STAR certified buildings in 2012. The Cincinnati metro area was ranked #13 out of 25. *U.S. Environmental Protection Agency, "Top Cities With the Most ENERGY STAR Certified Buildings in 2012," March 12, 2013*

- Cincinnati was selected as one of 22 "Smarter Cities" for energy by the Natural Resources Defense Council. Criteria: investment in green power; energy efficiency measures; conservation. *Natural Resources Defense Council, "2010 Smarter Cities," July 19, 2010*

- Cincinnati was highlighted as one of the 25 most ozone-polluted metro areas in the U.S. during 2008 through 2010. The area ranked #14. *American Lung Association, State of the Air 2012*

- Cincinnati was highlighted as one of the 25 metro areas most polluted by year-round particle pollution (Annual PM 2.5) in the U.S. during 2008 through 2010. The area ranked #10. *American Lung Association, State of the Air 2012*

Food/Drink Rankings

- *Men's Health* ranked 100 major U.S. cities in terms of alcohol intoxication. Cincinnati ranked #68 (#1 = most sober).Criteria: binge drinking; alcohol-related traffic accidents, arrests, and fatalities. *Men's Health, "The Drunkest Cities in America," November 19, 2013*

Health/Fitness Rankings

- For each of the 50 most populous metro areas in the United States, the American College of Sports Medicine's American Fitness Index evaluated infrastructure, community assets, and policies that encourage healthy and fit lifestyles, including preventive health behaviors, levels of chronic disease conditions, health care access, and community resources and policies that support physical activity. The Cincinnati metro area ranked #13 for "community fitness." Personal health indicators were considered as well as community and environmental indicators. *www.americanfitnessindex.org, "ACSM American Fitness Index Health and Community Fitness Status of the 50 Largest Metropolitan Areas," May 2013*

- The Cincinnati metro area was identified as one of the worst cities for bed bugs in America by pest control company Orkin. The area ranked #5 out of 50 based on the number of bed bug treatments Orkin performed from January to December 2013. *Orkin, "Chicago Tops Bed Bug Cities List for Second Year in a Row," January 16, 2014*

- Cincinnati was identified as a "2013 Spring Allergy Capital." The area ranked #69 out of 100. Three groups of factors were used to identify the most severe cities for people with allergies during the spring season: annual pollen levels; medicine utilization; access to board-certified allergists. *Asthma and Allergy Foundation of America, "Spring Allergy Capitals 2013"*

- Cincinnati was identified as a "2013 Fall Allergy Capital." The area ranked #55 out of 100. Three groups of factors were used to identify the most severe cities for people with allergies during the fall season: annual pollen levels; medicine utilization; access to board-certified allergists. *Asthma and Allergy Foundation of America, "Fall Allergy Capitals 2013"*

- Cincinnati was identified as a "2013 Asthma Capital." The area ranked #29 out of the nation's 100 largest metropolitan areas. Twelve factors were used to identify the most challenging places to live for people with asthma: estimated prevalence; self-reported prevalence; crude death rate for asthma; annual pollen score; annual air quality; public smoking laws; number of board-certified asthma specialists; school inhaler access laws; rescue medication use; controller medication use; uninsured rate; poverty rate. *Asthma and Allergy Foundation of America, "Asthma Capitals 2013"*

- *Men's Health* ranked 100 major U.S. cities in terms of the best and worst cities for men. Cincinnati ranked #80. Criteria: thirty-three data points were examined covering health, fitness, and quality of life. *Men's Health, "The Best & Worst Cities for Men 2014," December 6, 2013*

- Breathe Right Nasal Strips, in partnership with Sperling's BestPlaces, analyzed 50 metro areas and identified those U.S. cities most challenged by chronic nasal congestion. The Cincinnati metro area ranked #20. Criteria: tree, grass and weed pollens; molds and spores; air pollution; climate; smoking; purchase habits of congestion products; prescriptions of drugs for congestion relief; incidence of influenza. *Breathe Right Nasal Strips, "Most Congested Cities," October 3, 2011*

- Cincinnati was selected as one of the best metropolitan areas for hospital care in America by *HealthGrades.com.* The rankings are based on a comprehensive study of patient death and complication rates in the nation's nearly 5,000 hospitals. Hospitals performing in the top 5% nationwide across 26 different medical procedures and diagnoses were identified. *HealthGrades.com* then ranked cities by the highest percentage of these Distinguished Hospitals for Clinical Excellence™. The Cincinnati metro area ranked #5. *HealthGrades.com, "America's Top 50 Cities for Hospital Care," January 21, 2012*

- The American Academy of Dermatology ranked 26 U.S. metropolitan regions in terms of their residents knowledge, attitude and behaviors towards tanning, sun protection and skin cancer detection. The Cincinnati metro area ranked #18. The results of the study are based on an online survey of over 7,000 adults nationwide. *American Academy of Dermatology, "Suntelligence: How Sun Smart is Your City?," May 3, 2010*

- The Cincinnati metro area appeared in the 2013 Gallup-Healthways Well-Being Index. The area ranked #142 out of 189. The Gallup-Healthways Well-Being Index score is an average of six sub-indexes, which individually examine life evaluation, emotional health, work environment, physical health, healthy behaviors, and access to basic necessities. Results are based on telephone interviews conducted as part of the Gallup-Healthways Well-Being Index survey January 2–December 29, 2012, and January 2–December 30, 2013, with a random sample of 531,630 adults, aged 18 and older, living in metropolitan areas in the 50 U.S. states and the District of Columbia. *Gallup-Healthways, "State of American Well-Being," March 25, 2014*

- The Cincinnati metro area was identified as one of "America's Most Stressful Cities" by *Sperling's BestPlaces.* The metro area ranked #22 out of 50. Criteria: unemployment rate; suicide rate; commute time; mental health; poor rest; alcohol use; violent crime rate; property crime rate; cloudy days annually. *Sperling's BestPlaces, www.BestPlaces.net, "Stressful Cities 2012*

- *Men's Health* ranked 100 U.S. cities in terms of their activity levels. Cincinnati was ranked #76 (#1 = most active city). Criteria: where and how often residents exercise; percentage of households that watch more than 15 hours of cable television a week and buy more than 11 video games a year; death rate from deep-vein thrombosis, a condition linked to sitting for extended periods of time. *Men's Health, "Where Sit Happens: The Most and Least Active Cities in America," June 20, 2011*

- *The Daily Beast* identified the 30 U.S. metro areas with the worst smoking habits. The Cincinnati metro area ranked #18. Sixty urban centers with populations of more than one million were ranked based on the following criteria: number of smokers; number of cigarettes smoked per day; fewest attempts to quit. *The Daily Beast, "30 Cities With Smoking Problems," January 3, 2011*

Real Estate Rankings

- Cincinnati ranked #9 in a *Forbes* study of the rental housing market in the nation's 44 largest metropolitan areas to determine the cities that are best for renters. Criteria: average rent in 2012's first quarter, year-over-year change in that figure, vacancy rate, and average monthly rent payment compared with average monthly mortgage payment. *Forbes.com, "The Best and Worst Cities for Renters," June 14, 2012*

- Cincinnati was ranked #232 out of 283 metro areas in terms of house price appreciation in 2013 (#1 = highest rate). *Federal Housing Finance Agency, House Price Index, 4th Quarter 2013*

- Cincinnati was ranked #46 out of 224 metro areas in terms of housing affordability in 2013 by the National Association of Home Builders (#1 = most affordable). The NAHB-Wells Fargo Housing Opportunity Index (HOI) for a given area is defined as the share of homes sold in that area that would have been affordable to a family earning the local median income, based on standard mortgage underwriting criteria. *National Association of Home Builders®, NAHB-Wells Fargo Housing Opportunity Index, 4th Quarter 2013*

- Cincinnati was selected as one of the best college towns for renters by ApartmentRatings.com." The area ranked #39 out of 87. Overall satisfaction ratings were ranked using thousands of user submitted scores for hundreds of apartment complexes located in cities and towns that are home to the 100 largest four-year institutions in the U.S. *ApartmentRatings.com, "2011 College Town Renter Satisfaction Rankings"*

- The Cincinnati metro area was identified as one of America's most undervalued cities in 2011 by *CNNMoney.com* based on data from Local Market Monitor. Criteria: median home prices; local interest rates; economic and population growth; construction costs; vacancies; household income. *CNNMoney.com, "America's Most Overvalued (and Undervalued) Cities," January 16, 2011*

Safety Rankings

- Business Insider looked at the FBI's Uniform Crime Report to identify the U.S. cities with the most violent crime per capita, excluding localities with fewer than 100,000 residents. To judge by its relatively high murder, rape, and robbery data, Cincinnati was ranked #16 (#1 = worst) among the 25 most dangerous cities. *www.businessinsider.com, "The 25 Most Dangerous Cities in America," June 13, 2013*

- Symantec, in partnership with Sperling's BestPlaces, ranked the 50 largest cities in the U.S. in terms of their vulnerability to cybercrime. The city ranked #26. Criteria: number of cyberattacks and potential infections; level of Internet access; expenditures on smartphones and computer hardware/software; wireless hotspots; broadband connectivity; Internet usage; online purchases. *Symantec, "Riskiest Online Cities of 2012" February 15, 2012*

- Allstate ranked the 200 largest cities in America in terms of driver safety. Cincinnati ranked #115. Allstate researchers analyzed internal property damage claims over a two-year period from January 2010 to December 2011. A weighted average of the two-year numbers determined the annual percentages. *Allstate, "Allstate America's Best Drivers Report®, August 27, 2013"*

- The National Insurance Crime Bureau ranked 380 metro areas in the U.S. in terms of per capita rates of vehicle theft. The Cincinnati metro area ranked #210 (#1 = highest rate). Criteria: number of vehicle theft offenses per 100,000 inhabitants in 2012. *National Insurance Crime Bureau, "Hot Spots 2012," June 26, 2013*

- The Cincinnati metro area was identified as one of the most dangerous metro areas for pedestrians by Transportation for America. The metro area ranked #42 out of 52 metro areas with over 1 million residents. Criteria: area's population divided by the number of pedestrian fatalities in that area. *Transportation for America, "Dangerous by Design 2011"*

Seniors/Retirement Rankings

- From its Best Cities for Successful Aging indexes, the Milken Institute generated rankings for metropolitan areas, weighing data in eight categories—general indicators, health care, wellness, living arrangements, transportation and general accessibility, financial well-being, education and employment, and community participation. The Cincinnati metro area was ranked #72 overall in the large metro area category. *Milken Institute, "Best Cities for Successful Aging," July 2012*

- Bankers Life and Casualty Company, in partnership with Sperling's BestPlaces, ranked the nation's 50 largest metro areas in terms of the "Best U.S. Cities for Seniors." The Cincinnati metro area ranked #21. Criteria: healthcare; transportation; housing; environment; economy; health and longevity; social and spiritual life; crime. *Bankers Life and Casualty Company, Center for a Secure Retirement, "Best U.S. Cities for Seniors 2011," September 2011*

Sports/Recreation Rankings

- *24/7 Wall St.* analysts isolated the ten cities that spent the most public money per capita on sports stadiums, according to 2010 data. Cincinnati ranked #3. *24/7 Wall St., "Cities Paying the Most for Sports Teams," January 30, 2013*

- Cincinnati appeared on the *Sporting News* list of the "Best Sports Cities" for 2011. The area ranked #21 out of 271. Criteria: the magazine takes a 12-month snapshot of each city's sports, putting a heavy premium on regular-season won-lost records (from the most recently completed season). Other criteria include: playoff berths, bowl appearances and tournament bids; championships; applicable power ratings; quality of competition; overall fan fervor (measured in part by attendance); abundance of teams (rewarding quality over quantity); stadium and arena quality; ticket availability and prices; franchise ownership; and marquee appeal of athletes. *Sporting News, "Best Sports Cities 2011," October 4, 2011*

- Cincinnati appeared on the *Sporting News* list of the "Best Sports Cities" for 2011. The area ranked #21 out of 271. Criteria: a 12-month snapshot of regular-season won-lost records (from the most recently completed season). Other criteria include: playoff berths, bowl appearances and tournament bids; championships; applicable power ratings; quality of competition; overall fan fervor (measured in part by attendance); abundance of teams (quality over quantity); stadium and arena quality; ticket availability and prices; franchise ownership; and marquee appeal of athletes. *Sporting News, "Best Sports Cities 2011," October 4, 2011*

- Cincinnati was chosen as a bicycle friendly community by the League of American Bicyclists. A "Bicycle Friendly Community" welcomes cyclists by providing safe accommodation for cycling and encouraging people to bike for transportation and recreation. There are four award levels: Platinum; Gold; Silver; and Bronze. The community achieved an award level of Bronze. *League of American Bicyclists, "Bicycle Friendly Community Master List," Fall 2013*

- The Cincinnati was selected as one of the best metro areas for golf in America by *Golf Digest*. The Cincinnati area was ranked #3 out of 20. Criteria: climate; cost of public golf; quality of public golf; accessibility. *Golf Digest, "The Top 20 Cities for Golf," October 2011*

Women/Minorities Rankings

- The Daily Beast surveyed the nation's cities for highest percentage of singles and lowest divorce rate, plus other measures, to determine "emotional intelligence"—happiness, confidence, kindness—which, researchers say, has a strong correlation with people's satisfaction with their romantic relationships. Cincinnati placed #23. *www.thedailybeast.com, "Best Cities to Find Love and Stay in Love," February 14, 2014*

- *Women's Health* examined U.S. cities and identified the 100 best cities for women. Cincinnati was ranked #82. Criteria: 30 categories were examined from obesity and breast cancer rates to commuting times and hours spent working out. *Women's Health, "Best Cities for Women 2012"*

- The Cincinnati metro area appeared on *Forbes'* list of the "Best Cities for Minority Entrepreneurs." The area ranked #82 out of 10. Criteria: 52 metropolitan statistical areas were examined. For each ethnicity (African Americans, Asians and Hispanics), the editors measured housing affordability, population growth, income growth, and entrepreneurship (per capita self-employment). *Forbes, "Best Cities for Minority Entrepreneurs," March 23, 2011*

Miscellaneous Rankings

- The watchdog site Charity Navigator conducts an annual study of charities in the nation's major markets both to analyze statistical differences in their financial, accountability, and transparency practices and to track year-to-year variations in individual communities. The Cincinnati metro area was ranked #4 among the 30 metro markets. *www.charitynavigator.org, "Metro Market Study 2013," June 1, 2013*

- Business Insider reports on the 2013 Trick-or-Treat Index compiled by the real estate site Zillow, which used its own Home Value Index and Walk Score along with population density and local crime stats to determine that Cincinnati ranked #18 for "how much candy it gives out versus how far kids have to walk to get it." Zillow also zeroes in on the best neighborhoods in its top 20 cities. *www.businessinsider.com, "These Are the Best Cities for Trick-or-Treating," October 15, 2013*

- Market analyst Scarborough Research surveyed adults who had done volunteer work over the previous 12 months to find out where volunteers are concentrated. The Cincinnati metro area made the list for highest volunteer participation. *Scarborough Research, "Salt Lake City, UT; Minneapolis, MN; and Des Moines, IA Lend a Helping Hand," November 27, 2012*

- *Men's Health* ranked 100 U.S. cities by their level of sadness. Cincinnati was ranked #84 (#1 = saddest city). Criteria: suicide rates; unemployment rates; percentage of households that use antidepressants; percent of population who report feeling blue all or most of the time. *Men's Health, "Frown Towns," November 28, 2011*

- The Cincinnati metro area was selected as one of "The Best U.S. Cities for Bargain Shopping" by *Forbes*. The area ranked #8 out of 10. Criteria: number of outlet stores; gross leasable retail space in major malls; low consumer price index; low sales tax rate. Indicators were examined in the nation's 50 largest metropolitan areas. *Forbes, "The Best U.S. Cities for Bargain Shopping," January 20, 2012*

- Mars Chocolate North America, the makers of COMBOS®, in partnership with Sperling's BestPlaces, ranked 50 major metro areas in terms of their "manliness." The Cincinnati metro area ranked #12. Criteria: number of professional sports teams; number of nearby NASCAR tracks and racing events; manly lifestyle; concentration of manly retail stores; manly occupations per capita; salty snack sales; "Board of Manliness" rankings. *Mars Chocolate North America, "America's Manliest Cities 2012"*

- The National Alliance to End Homelessness ranked the 100 most populous metro areas in terms the rate of homelessness. The Cincinnati metro area ranked #96. Criteria: number of homeless people per 10,000 population in 2011. *National Alliance to End Homelessness, The State of Homelessness in America 2012*

Business Environment

CITY FINANCES

City Government Finances

Component	2011 ($000)	2011 ($ per capita)
Total Revenues	1,331,173	4,004
Total Expenditures	1,373,939	4,133
Debt Outstanding	922,265	2,774
Cash and Securities[1]	2,676,661	8,051

Note: (1) Cash and security holdings of a government at the close of its fiscal year, including those of its dependent agencies, utilities, and liquor stores.
Source: U.S Census Bureau, State & Local Government Finances 2011

City Government Revenue by Source

Source	2011 ($000)	2011 ($ per capita)
General Revenue		
From Federal Government	64,850	195
From State Government	76,431	230
From Local Governments	242,289	729
Taxes		
Property	61,664	185
Sales and Gross Receipts	7,416	22
Personal Income	317,588	955
Corporate Income	0	0
Motor Vehicle License	2,098	6
Other Taxes	25,431	76
Current Charges	101,842	306
Liquor Store	0	0
Utility	123,443	371
Employee Retirement	278,131	837

Source: U.S Census Bureau, State & Local Government Finances 2011

City Government Expenditures by Function

Function	2011 ($000)	2011 ($ per capita)	2011 (%)
General Direct Expenditures			
Air Transportation	6,027	18	0.4
Corrections	0	0	0.0
Education	0	0	0.0
Employment Security Administration	0	0	0.0
Financial Administration	28,275	85	2.1
Fire Protection	67,435	203	4.9
General Public Buildings	17,654	53	1.3
Governmental Administration, Other	24,755	74	1.8
Health	35,671	107	2.6
Highways	83,229	250	6.1
Hospitals	0	0	0.0
Housing and Community Development	52,195	157	3.8
Interest on General Debt	23,173	70	1.7
Judicial and Legal	4,963	15	0.4
Libraries	0	0	0.0
Parking	19,008	57	1.4
Parks and Recreation	72,071	217	5.2
Police Protection	112,342	338	8.2
Public Welfare	0	0	0.0
Sewerage	237,995	716	17.3
Solid Waste Management	15,623	47	1.1
Veterans' Services	0	0	0.0
Liquor Store	0	0	0.0
Utility	198,591	597	14.5
Employee Retirement	187,292	563	13.6

Source: U.S Census Bureau, State & Local Government Finances 2011

DEMOGRAPHICS

Population Growth

Area	1990 Census	2000 Census	2010 Census	Population Growth (%) 1990-2000	Population Growth (%) 2000-2010
City	363,974	331,285	296,943	-9.0	-10.4
MSA[1]	1,844,917	2,009,632	2,130,151	8.9	6.0
U.S.	248,709,873	281,421,906	308,745,538	13.2	9.7

Note: (1) Figures cover the Cincinnati, OH-KY-IN Metropolitan Statistical Area—see Appendix B for areas included
Source: U.S. Census Bureau, Census 1990, 2000, 2010

Household Size

Area	Persons in Household (%) One	Two	Three	Four	Five	Six	Seven or More	Average Household Size
City	43.4	29.1	13.0	8.1	3.2	2.0	1.1	2.22
MSA[1]	28.1	33.8	15.9	13.1	5.7	2.2	1.1	2.57
U.S.	27.6	33.5	15.7	13.2	6.1	2.4	1.5	2.63

Note: (1) Figures cover the Cincinnati, OH-KY-IN Metropolitan Statistical Area—see Appendix B for areas included
Source: U.S. Census Bureau, 2010-2012 American Community Survey 3-Year Estimates

Race

Area	White Alone[2] (%)	Black Alone[2] (%)	Asian Alone[2] (%)	AIAN[3] Alone[2] (%)	NHOPI[4] Alone[2] (%)	Other Race Alone[2] (%)	Two or More Races (%)
City	50.1	44.2	1.9	0.4	0.0	0.9	2.5
MSA[1]	83.1	12.1	2.0	0.2	0.0	0.8	1.8
U.S.	74.0	12.6	4.9	0.8	0.2	4.7	2.8

Note: (1) Figures cover the Cincinnati, OH-KY-IN Metropolitan Statistical Area—see Appendix B for areas included; (2) Alone is defined as not being in combination with one or more other races; (3) American Indian and Alaska Native; (4) Native Hawaiian and Other Pacific Islander
Source: U.S. Census Bureau, 2010-2012 American Community Survey 3-Year Estimates

Hispanic or Latino Origin

Area	Total (%)	Mexican (%)	Puerto Rican (%)	Cuban (%)	Other (%)
City	2.9	1.3	0.3	0.1	1.2
MSA[1]	2.7	1.4	0.3	0.1	0.9
U.S.	16.6	10.7	1.6	0.6	3.7

Note: Persons of Hispanic or Latino origin can be of any race; (1) Figures cover the Cincinnati, OH-KY-IN Metropolitan Statistical Area—see Appendix B for areas included
Source: U.S. Census Bureau, 2010-2012 American Community Survey 3-Year Estimates

Segregation

Type	Segregation Indices[1] 1990	2000	2010	2010 Rank[2]	Percent Change 1990-2000	Percent Change 1990-2010	Percent Change 2000-2010
Black/White	75.9	73.7	69.4	8	-2.2	-6.5	-4.3
Asian/White	42.7	44.6	46.0	21	1.9	3.4	1.5
Hispanic/White	25.8	29.0	36.9	77	3.2	11.1	7.9

Note: All figures cover the Metropolitan Statistical Area—see Appendix B for areas included; Figures are based on an analysis of 1990, 2000, and 2010 Census Decennial Census tract data by William H. Frey, Brookings Institution and the University of Michigan Social Science Data Analysis Network. In this analysis all racial groups (whites, blacks, and asians) are non-Hispanic members of those races. Hispanics are shown as a separate category;
(1) Segregation Indices are Dissimilarity Indices that measure the degree to which the minority group is distributed differently than whites across census tracts. They range from 0 (complete integration) to 100 (complete segregation) where the value indicates the percentage of the minority group that needs to move to be distributed exactly like whites; (2) Ranges from 1 (most segregated) to 102 (least segregated); n/a not available.
Source: www.CensusScope.org

Ancestry

Area	German	Irish	English	American	Italian	Polish	French[2]	Scottish	Dutch
City	19.1	10.3	5.3	5.2	3.5	1.4	1.5	1.1	0.9
MSA[1]	29.9	14.4	9.2	11.3	4.1	1.5	2.1	1.8	1.2
U.S.	15.2	11.1	8.2	7.2	5.6	3.1	2.8	1.7	1.4

Note: Figures are the percentage of the total population reporting a particular ancestry. The nine most commonly reported ancestries in the U.S. are shown. Figures include multiple ancestries (e.g. if a person reported being Irish and Italian, they were included in both columns); (1) Figures cover the Cincinnati, OH-KY-IN Metropolitan Statistical Area—see Appendix B for areas included; (2) Excludes Basque
Source: U.S. Census Bureau, 2010-2012 American Community Survey 3-Year Estimates

Foreign-Born Population

Area	Any Foreign Country	Mexico	Asia	Europe	Carribean	South America	Central America[2]	Africa	Canada
City	5.3	0.5	1.6	0.6	0.2	0.2	0.6	1.5	0.2
MSA[1]	4.0	0.5	1.6	0.8	0.1	0.2	0.3	0.5	0.1
U.S.	13.0	3.7	3.7	1.6	1.2	0.9	1.0	0.5	0.3

Note: (1) Figures cover the Cincinnati, OH-KY-IN Metropolitan Statistical Area—see Appendix B for areas included; (2) Excludes Mexico.
Source: U.S. Census Bureau, 2010-2012 American Community Survey 3-Year Estimates

Marital Status

Area	Never Married	Now Married[2]	Separated	Widowed	Divorced
City	51.1	27.7	3.0	5.7	12.6
MSA[1]	31.1	49.6	1.9	5.9	11.6
U.S.	32.4	48.4	2.2	6.0	11.0

Note: Figures are percentages and cover the population 15 years of age and older; (1) Figures cover the Cincinnati, OH-KY-IN Metropolitan Statistical Area—see Appendix B for areas included; (2) Excludes separated
Source: U.S. Census Bureau, 2010-2012 American Community Survey 3-Year Estimates

Age

Area	Under Age 5	Age 5–19	Age 20–34	Age 35–44	Age 45–54	Age 55–64	Age 65–74	Age 75–84	Age 85+	Median Age
City	7.2	19.0	27.4	11.3	13.1	11.1	5.8	3.5	1.9	32.4
MSA[1]	6.7	20.8	19.7	13.1	15.0	12.3	6.8	3.9	1.7	37.3
U.S.	6.4	20.1	20.5	13.1	14.3	12.2	7.3	4.2	1.8	37.3

Note: (1) Figures cover the Cincinnati, OH-KY-IN Metropolitan Statistical Area—see Appendix B for areas included
Source: U.S. Census Bureau, 2010-2012 American Community Survey 3-Year Estimates

Gender

Area	Males	Females	Males per 100 Females
City	140,714	155,729	90.4
MSA[1]	1,046,009	1,092,127	95.8
U.S.	153,276,055	158,333,314	96.8

Note: (1) Figures cover the Cincinnati, OH-KY-IN Metropolitan Statistical Area—see Appendix B for areas included
Source: U.S. Census Bureau, 2010-2012 American Community Survey 3-Year Estimates

Religious Groups by Family

Area	Catholic	Baptist	Non-Den.	Methodist[2]	Lutheran	LDS[3]	Pente-costal	Presby-terian[4]	Muslim[5]	Judaism
MSA[1]	19.1	9.6	3.7	3.9	1.2	0.6	2.2	1.6	0.2	0.5
U.S.	19.1	9.3	4.0	4.0	2.3	2.0	1.9	1.6	0.8	0.7

Note: Figures are the number of adherents as a percentage of the total population; (1) Figures cover the Cincinnati, OH-KY-IN Metropolitan Statistical Area—see Appendix B for areas included; (2) Methodist/Pietist; (3) Latter Day Saints; (4) Reformed; (5) Figures are estimates
Source: Association of Statisticians of American Religious Bodies, 2010 U.S. Religion Census: Religious Congregations & Membership Study

Religious Groups by Tradition

Area	Catholic	Evangelical Protestant	Mainline Protestant	Other Tradition	Black Protestant	Orthodox
MSA[1]	19.1	15.5	7.2	1.6	1.2	0.2
U.S.	19.1	16.2	7.3	4.3	1.6	0.3

Note: Figures are the number of adherents as a percentage of the total population; (1) Figures cover the Cincinnati, OH-KY-IN Metropolitan Statistical Area—see Appendix B for areas included
Source: Association of Statisticians of American Religious Bodies, 2010 U.S. Religion Census: Religious Congregations & Membership Study

ECONOMY

Gross Metropolitan Product

Area	2011	2012	2013	2014	Rank[2]
MSA[1]	103.8	108.4	111.2	115.7	29

Note: Figures are in billions of dollars; (1) Figures cover the Cincinnati, OH-KY-IN Metropolitan Statistical Area—see Appendix B for areas included; (2) Rank is based on 2014 data and ranges from 1 to 363
Source: The United States Conference of Mayors, U.S. Metro Economies: Outlook—Gross Metropolitan Product, with Metro Employment Projections, November 2013

Economic Growth

Area	2011 (%)	2012 (%)	2013 (%)	2014 (%)	Rank[2]
MSA[1]	1.9	2.7	1.3	2.1	128
U.S.	1.6	2.5	1.7	2.5	–

Note: Figures are real gross metropolitan product (GMP) growth rates and represent annual average percent change; (1) Figures cover the Cincinnati, OH-KY-IN Metropolitan Statistical Area—see Appendix B for areas included; (2) Rank is based on 2013 data and ranges from 1 to 363
Source: The United States Conference of Mayors, U.S. Metro Economies: Outlook—Gross Metropolitan Product, with Metro Employment Projections, November 2013

Metropolitan Area Exports

Area	2007	2008	2009	2010	2011	2012	Rank[2]
MSA[1]	15,359.2	17,533.9	15,488.7	17,598.5	18,744.2	19,966.8	16

Note: Figures are in millions of dollars; (1) Figures cover the Cincinnati, OH-KY-IN Metropolitan Statistical Area—see Appendix B for areas included; (2) Rank is based on 2012 data and ranges from 1 to 369
Source: U.S. Department of Commerce, International Trade Administration, Office of Trade & Industry Information, Manufacturing & Services, data extracted April 1, 2014

INCOME

Income

Area	Per Capita ($)	Median Household ($)	Average Household ($)
City	24,106	32,591	53,215
MSA[1]	27,761	53,475	70,905
U.S.	27,385	51,771	71,579

Note: (1) Figures cover the Cincinnati, OH-KY-IN Metropolitan Statistical Area—see Appendix B for areas included
Source: U.S. Census Bureau, 2010-2012 American Community Survey 3-Year Estimates

Household Income Distribution

Area	Under $15,000	$15,000 -24,999	$25,000 -34,999	$35,000 -49,999	$50,000 -74,999	$75,000 -99,000	$100,000 -149,999	$150,000 and up
				Percent of Households Earning				
City	27.1	14.3	10.7	12.3	14.4	8.2	7.3	5.7
MSA[1]	12.9	10.6	10.0	13.4	18.7	12.7	12.8	8.8
U.S.	13.1	11.0	10.5	13.7	18.1	11.9	12.5	9.1

Note: (1) Figures cover the Cincinnati, OH-KY-IN Metropolitan Statistical Area—see Appendix B for areas included
Source: U.S. Census Bureau, 2010-2012 American Community Survey 3-Year Estimates

Poverty Rate

Area	All Ages	Under 18 Years Old	18 to 64 Years Old	65 Years and Over
City	31.4	48.1	28.6	13.3
MSA[1]	14.3	20.3	13.3	7.4
U.S.	15.7	22.2	14.6	9.3

Note: Figures are percentage of people whose income during the past 12 months was below the poverty level; (1) Figures cover the Cincinnati, OH-KY-IN Metropolitan Statistical Area—see Appendix B for areas included
Source: U.S. Census Bureau, 2010-2012 American Community Survey 3-Year Estimates

Personal Bankruptcy Filing Rate

Area	2008	2009	2010	2011	2012	2013
Hamilton County	4.67	5.49	5.78	5.14	4.70	4.10
U.S.	3.53	4.61	4.97	4.37	3.76	3.29

Note: Numbers are per 1,000 population and include Chapter 7 and Chapter 13 filings
Source: Federal Deposit Insurance Corporation, Regional Economic Conditions, March 20, 2014

EMPLOYMENT

Labor Force and Employment

Area	Civilian Labor Force			Workers Employed		
	Dec. 2012	Dec. 2013	% Chg.	Dec. 2012	Dec. 2013	% Chg.
City	139,839	139,879	0.0	130,211	130,389	0.1
MSA[1]	1,081,111	1,073,366	-0.7	1,011,041	1,006,980	-0.4
U.S.	154,904,000	154,408,000	-0.3	143,060,000	144,423,000	1.0

Note: Data is not seasonally adjusted and covers workers 16 years of age and older; (1) Metropolitan Statistical Area—see Appendix B for areas included
Source: Bureau of Labor Statistics, Local Area Unemployment Statistics

Unemployment Rate

Area	2013											
	Jan.	Feb.	Mar.	Apr.	May	Jun.	Jul.	Aug.	Sep.	Oct.	Nov.	Dec.
City	8.6	7.8	7.4	6.9	7.6	8.3	8.0	7.7	8.1	8.1	7.8	6.8
MSA[1]	8.0	7.5	7.2	6.5	6.8	7.3	7.1	6.8	7.1	7.0	6.8	6.2
U.S.	8.5	8.1	7.6	7.1	7.3	7.8	7.7	7.3	7.0	7.0	6.6	6.5

Note: Data is not seasonally adjusted and covers workers 16 years of age and older; All figures are percentages; (1) Metropolitan Statistical Area—see Appendix B for areas included
Source: Bureau of Labor Statistics, Local Area Unemployment Statistics

Employment by Occupation

Occupation Classification	City (%)	MSA[1] (%)	U.S. (%)
Management, Business, Science, and Arts	39.0	37.1	36.0
Natural Resources, Construction, and Maintenance	4.2	7.0	9.1
Production, Transportation, and Material Moving	10.3	13.1	12.0
Sales and Office	24.0	25.8	24.7
Service	22.5	17.0	18.2

Note: Figures cover employed civilians 16 years of age and older; (1) Figures cover the Cincinnati, OH-KY-IN Metropolitan Statistical Area—see Appendix B for areas included
Source: U.S. Census Bureau, 2010-2012 American Community Survey 3-Year Estimates

Employment by Industry

Sector	MSA[1]		U.S.
	Number of Employees	Percent of Total	Percent of Total
Construction	n/a	n/a	4.2
Education and Health Services	159,100	15.4	15.5
Financial Activities	65,600	6.4	5.7
Government	130,200	12.6	16.1
Information	14,000	1.4	1.9
Leisure and Hospitality	105,700	10.2	10.2
Manufacturing	106,800	10.3	8.7
Mining and Logging	n/a	n/a	0.6
Other Services	39,900	3.9	3.9
Professional and Business Services	165,900	16.1	13.7
Retail Trade	107,600	10.4	11.4
Transportation and Utilities	40,000	3.9	3.8
Wholesale Trade	59,900	5.8	4.2

Note: Figures cover non-farm employment as of December 2013 and are not seasonally adjusted;
(1) Metropolitan Statistical Area—see Appendix B for areas included; n/a not available
Source: Bureau of Labor Statistics, Current Employment Statistics, Employment, Hours, and Earnings

Occupations with Greatest Projected Employment Growth: 2010 – 2020

Occupation[1]	2010 Employment	2020 Projected Employment	Numeric Employment Change	Percent Employment Change
Home Health Aides	71,140	110,490	39,360	55.3
Registered Nurses	126,130	152,380	26,260	20.8
Combined Food Preparation and Serving Workers, Including Fast Food	142,570	160,140	17,580	12.3
Retail Salespersons	156,370	170,890	14,530	9.3
Medical Secretaries	39,140	51,780	12,640	32.3
Office Clerks, General	105,750	117,610	11,860	11.2
Heavy and Tractor-Trailer Truck Drivers	67,070	78,510	11,440	17.1
Laborers and Freight, Stock, and Material Movers, Hand	97,960	109,350	11,390	11.6
Nursing Aides, Orderlies, and Attendants	75,590	85,550	9,950	13.2
Personal Care Aides	15,590	23,150	7,570	48.5

Note: Projections cover Ohio; (1) Sorted by numeric employment change
Source: www.projectionscentral.com, State Occupational Projections, 2010–2020 Long-Term Projections

Fastest Growing Occupations: 2010 – 2020

Occupation[1]	2010 Employment	2020 Projected Employment	Numeric Employment Change	Percent Employment Change
Gaming Managers	10	110	100	1,428.6
Gaming Cage Workers	30	190	170	589.3
Gaming and Sports Book Writers and Runners	230	470	240	102.6
Home Health Aides	71,140	110,490	39,360	55.3
Biomedical Engineers	300	470	160	53.0
Personal Care Aides	15,590	23,150	7,570	48.5
Helpers—Carpenters	660	980	320	47.9
Veterinary Technologists and Technicians	2,260	3,240	980	43.2
Helpers—Brickmasons, Blockmasons, Stonemasons, and Tile and Marble Setters	810	1,150	350	43.1
Meeting, Convention, and Event Planners	1,710	2,370	660	38.4

Note: Projections cover Ohio; (1) Sorted by percent employment change and excludes occupations with numeric employment change less than 100
Source: www.projectionscentral.com, State Occupational Projections, 2010–2020 Long-Term Projections

Average Wages

Occupation	$/Hr.	Occupation	$/Hr.
Accountants and Auditors	32.92	Maids and Housekeeping Cleaners	10.52
Automotive Mechanics	16.95	Maintenance and Repair Workers	19.13
Bookkeepers	17.65	Marketing Managers	57.28
Carpenters	20.92	Nuclear Medicine Technologists	30.29
Cashiers	9.78	Nurses, Licensed Practical	20.64
Clerks, General Office	14.81	Nurses, Registered	30.08
Clerks, Receptionists/Information	12.84	Nursing Assistants	12.21
Clerks, Shipping/Receiving	14.76	Packers and Packagers, Hand	10.64
Computer Programmers	34.51	Physical Therapists	38.29
Computer Systems Analysts	40.85	Postal Service Mail Carriers	24.51
Computer User Support Specialists	23.82	Real Estate Brokers	23.98
Cooks, Restaurant	10.04	Retail Salespersons	11.78
Dentists	84.46	Sales Reps., Exc. Tech./Scientific	31.64
Electrical Engineers	38.69	Sales Reps., Tech./Scientific	39.93
Electricians	23.81	Secretaries, Exc. Legal/Med./Exec.	15.94
Financial Managers	54.26	Security Guards	16.47
First-Line Supervisors/Managers, Sales	18.37	Surgeons	109.54
Food Preparation Workers	10.45	Teacher Assistants	12.70
General and Operations Managers	54.22	Teachers, Elementary School	27.20
Hairdressers/Cosmetologists	12.62	Teachers, Secondary School	27.40
Internists	71.31	Telemarketers	13.51
Janitors and Cleaners	11.35	Truck Drivers, Heavy/Tractor-Trailer	20.10
Landscaping/Groundskeeping Workers	12.28	Truck Drivers, Light/Delivery Svcs.	16.71
Lawyers	54.21	Waiters and Waitresses	9.15

Note: Wage data covers the Cincinnati-Middletown, OH-KY-IN Metropolitan Statistical Area—see Appendix B for areas included. Hourly wages for elementary/secondary school teachers and teacher assistants were calculated by the editors from annual wage data assuming a 40 hour work week; n/a not available.
Source: Bureau of Labor Statistics, Metro Area Occupational Employment and Wage Estimates, May 2013

RESIDENTIAL REAL ESTATE

Building Permits

Area	Single-Family			Multi-Family			Total		
	2012	2013	Pct. Chg.	2012	2013	Pct. Chg.	2012	2013	Pct. Chg.
City	83	90	8.4	367	74	-79.8	450	164	-63.6
MSA[1]	2,641	3,308	25.3	963	1,022	6.1	3,604	4,330	20.1
U.S.	518,695	620,802	19.7	310,963	370,020	19.0	829,658	990,822	19.4

Note: (1) Metropolitan Statistical Area—see Appendix B for areas included; figures represent new, privately-owned housing units authorized (unadjusted data); All permit data are based on estimates with imputation.
Source: U.S. Census Bureau, Manufacturing, Mining, and Construction Statistics, Building Permits, 2012, 2013

Homeownership Rate

Area	2006 (%)	2007 (%)	2008 (%)	2009 (%)	2010 (%)	2011 (%)	2012 (%)	2013 (%)
MSA[1]	65.5	67.6	64.7	62.4	62.8	65.2	63.4	63.3
U.S.	68.8	68.1	67.8	67.4	66.9	66.1	65.4	65.1

Note: (1) Figures cover the Cincinnati, OH-KY-IN Metropolitan Statistical Area—see Appendix B for areas included
Source: U.S. Census Bureau, Housing Vacancies and Homeownership Annual Statistics: 2013

Housing Vacancy Rates

Area	Gross Vacancy Rate[2] (%)			Year-Round Vacancy Rate[3] (%)			Rental Vacancy Rate[4] (%)			Homeowner Vacancy Rate[5] (%)		
	2011	2012	2013	2011	2012	2013	2011	2012	2013	2011	2012	2013
MSA[1]	13.2	11.2	11.2	11.8	9.6	10.0	11.1	9.3	8.9	3.0	1.8	2.6
U.S.	14.2	13.8	13.8	11.1	10.8	10.7	9.5	8.7	8.3	2.5	2.0	2.0

Note: (1) Figures cover the Cincinnati, OH-KY-IN Metropolitan Statistical Area—see Appendix B for areas included; (2) The percentage of the total housing inventory that is vacant; (3) The percentage of the housing inventory (excluding seasonal units) that is year-round vacant; (4) The percentage of rental inventory that is vacant for rent; (5) The percentage of homeowner inventory that is vacant for sale
Source: U.S. Census Bureau, Housing Vacancies and Homeownership Annual Statistics: 2013

TAXES

State Corporate Income Tax Rates

State	Tax Rate (%)	Income Brackets ($)	Num. of Brackets	Financial Institution Tax Rate (%)[a]	Federal Income Tax Ded.
Ohio	(u)	–	–	(u)	No

Note: Tax rates as of January 1, 2014; (a) Rates listed are the corporate income tax rate applied to financial institutions or excise taxes based on income. Some states have other taxes based upon the value of deposits or shares; (u) Ohio no longer levies a tax based on income (except for a particular subset of corporations), but instead imposes a Commercial Activity Tax (CAT) equal to $150 for gross receipts sitused to Ohio of between $150,000 and $1 million, plus 0.26% of gross receipts over $1 million. Banks continue to pay a franchise tax of 1.3% of net worth. For those few corporations for whom the franchise tax on net worth or net income still applies, a litter tax also applies.
Source: Federation of Tax Administrators, "State Corporate Income Tax Rates, 2014"

State Individual Income Tax Rates

State	Tax Rate (%)	Income Brackets ($)	Num. of Brackets	Personal Exempt. ($)[1] Single	Personal Exempt. ($)[1] Dependents	Fed. Inc. Tax Ded.
Ohio (a)	0.534 - 5.392	5,000 - 200,000	9	1,700 (r)	1,700 (r)	No

Note: Tax rates as of January 1, 2014; Local- and county-level taxes are not included; n/a not applicable; (1) Married joint filers generally receive double the single exemption; (a) 17 states have statutory provision for automatically adjusting to the rate of inflation the dollar values of the income tax brackets, standard deductions, and/or personal exemptions. Massachusetts, Michigan, and Nebraska index the personal exemption only. Oregon does not index the income brackets for $125,000 and over. Maine has suspended indexing for 2014 and 2015; (r) Ohio provides an additional tax credit of $20 per exemption.
Source: Federation of Tax Administrators, "State Individual Income Tax Rates, 2014"

Various State and Local Tax Rates

State	State and Local Sales and Use (%)	State Sales and Use (%)	Gasoline[1] (¢/gal.)	Cigarette[2] ($/pack)	Spirits[3] ($/gal.)	Wine[4] ($/gal.)	Beer[5] ($/gal.)
Ohio	6.75	5.75	28.00	1.250	9.32 (g)	0.32	0.18

Note: All tax rates as of January 1, 2014; (1) The American Petroleum Institute has developed a methodology for determining the average tax rate on a gallon of fuel. Rates may include any of the following: excise taxes, environmental fees, storage tank fees, other fees or taxes, general sales tax, and local taxes. In states where gasoline is subject to the general sales tax, or where the fuel tax is based on the average sale price, the average rate determined by API is sensitive to changes in the price of gasoline. States that fully or partially apply general sales taxes to gasoline: CA, CO, GA, IL, IN, MI, NY; (2) The federal excise tax of $1.0066 per pack and local taxes are not included; (3) Rates are those applicable to off-premise sales of 40% alcohol by volume (a.b.v.) distilled spirits in 750ml containers. Local excise taxes are excluded; (4) Rates are those applicable to off-premise sales of 11% a.b.v. non-carbonated wine in 750ml containers; (5) Rates are those applicable to off-premise sales of 4.7% a.b.v. beer in 12 ounce containers; (g) States where the government controls sales. In these "control states," products are subject to ad valorem mark-up and excise taxes. The excise tax rate is calculated using a methodology developed by the Distilled Spirits Council of the United States.
Source: Tax Foundation, 2014 Facts & Figures: How Does Your State Compare?

State Business Tax Climate Index Rankings

State	Overall Rank	Corporate Tax Index Rank	Individual Income Tax Index Rank	Sales Tax Index Rank	Unemployment Insurance Tax Index Rank	Property Tax Index Rank
Ohio	39	23	44	30	10	20

Note: The index is a measure of how each state's tax laws affect economic performance. The lower the rank, the more favorable a state's tax system is for business. States without a given tax are given a ranking of 1. The scores/rankings for the District of Columbia do not affect other states. The 2014 index represents the tax climate as of July 1, 2013.
Source: Tax Foundation, State Business Tax Climate Index 2014

COMMERCIAL REAL ESTATE

Office Market

Market Area	Inventory (sq. ft.)	Vacancy Rate (%)	Under Construction (sq. ft.)	YTD Net Absorption (sq. ft.)	Total Average Asking Rent ($/sq. ft./year)
Cincinnati	58,372,122	17.2	633,410	630,627	15.18
National	4,726,900,879	15.0	55,419,286	42,829,434	26.27

Source: Newmark Grubb Knight Frank, National Office Market Report, 4th Quarter 2013

Industrial/Warehouse/R&D Market

Market Area	Inventory (sq. ft.)	Vacancy Rate (%)	Under Construction (sq. ft.)	YTD Net Absorption (sq. ft.)	Total Average Asking Rent ($/sq. ft./year)
Cincinnati	393,437,244	9.3	890,168	4,458,215	3.18
National	14,022,031,238	7.9	83,249,164	156,549,903	5.40

Source: Newmark Grubb Knight Frank, National Industrial Market Report, 4th Quarter 2013

COMMERCIAL UTILITIES

Typical Monthly Electric Bills

Area	Commercial Service ($/month)		Industrial Service ($/month)	
	1,500 kWh	40 kW demand 14,000 kWh	1,000 kW demand 200,000 kWh	50,000 kW demand 15,000,000 kWh
City	211	1,327	25,171	1,218,086
Average[1]	197	1,636	25,662	1,485,307

Note: Based on total rates in effect July 1, 2013; (1) average based on 180 utilities surveyed
Source: Edison Electric Institute, Typical Bills and Average Rates Report, Summer 2013

TRANSPORTATION

Means of Transportation to Work

Area	Car/Truck/Van Drove Alone	Car-pooled	Public Transportation Bus	Subway	Railroad	Bicycle	Walked	Other Means	Worked at Home
City	72.1	9.7	7.8	0.0	0.0	0.4	5.0	0.8	4.1
MSA[1]	83.3	8.2	2.0	0.0	0.0	0.1	2.1	0.6	3.7
U.S.	76.4	9.7	2.6	1.7	0.5	0.6	2.8	1.3	4.3

Note: Figures are percentages and cover workers 16 years of age and older; (1) Figures cover the Cincinnati, OH-KY-IN Metropolitan Statistical Area—see Appendix B for areas included
Source: U.S. Census Bureau, 2010-2012 American Community Survey 3-Year Estimates

Travel Time to Work

Area	Less Than 10 Minutes	10 to 19 Minutes	20 to 29 Minutes	30 to 44 Minutes	45 to 59 Minutes	60 to 89 Minutes	90 Minutes or More
City	11.7	35.1	26.7	17.7	4.2	2.6	2.0
MSA[1]	11.4	29.1	25.4	22.6	6.9	3.3	1.4
U.S.	13.5	29.8	20.9	20.1	7.5	5.6	2.5

Note: Figures are percentages and include workers 16 years old and over; (1) Figures cover the Cincinnati, OH-KY-IN Metropolitan Statistical Area—see Appendix B for areas included
Source: U.S. Census Bureau, 2010-2012 American Community Survey 3-Year Estimates

Travel Time Index

Area	1985	1990	1995	2000	2005	2010	2011
Urban Area[1]	1.06	1.14	1.20	1.23	1.21	1.20	1.20
Average[2]	1.09	1.14	1.16	1.19	1.23	1.18	1.18

Note: Travel Time Index—the ratio of travel time in the peak period to the travel time at free-flow conditions. For example, a value of 1.30 indicates a 20-minute free-flow trip takes 26 minutes in the peak. Free-flow speeds (60 mph on freeways and 35 mph on principal arterials) are used as the comparison threshold; (1) Covers the Cincinnati OH-KY-IN urban area; (2) average of 498 urban areas
Source: Texas Transportation Institute, Urban Mobility Report 2012, December 2012

Public Transportation

Agency Name / Mode of Transportation	Vehicles Operated in Maximum Service	Annual Unlinked Passenger Trips (in thous.)	Annual Passenger Miles (in thous.)
Southwest Ohio Regional Transit Authority (SORTA/Metro)			
Bus (directly operated)	289	17,390.3	86,595.7
Demand Response (purchased transportation)	48	162.8	1,816.5

Source: Federal Transit Administration, National Transit Database, 2012

Air Transportation

Airport Name and Code / Type of Service	Passenger Airlines[1]	Passenger Enplanements	Freight Carriers[2]	Freight (lbs.)
Cincinnati-Northern Kentucky International (CVG)				
Domestic service (U.S. carriers - 2013)	24	2,675,685	19	376,580,677
International service (U.S. carriers - 2012)	6	90,036	9	151,189,186

Note: (1) Includes all U.S.-based major, minor and commuter airlines that carried at least one passenger during the year; (2) Includes all U.S.-based airlines and freight carriers that transported at least one lb. of freight during the year.
Source: Bureau of Transportation Statistics, The Intermodal Transportation Database, Air Carriers: T-100 Domestic Market (U.S. Carriers), 2013; Bureau of Transportation Statistics, The Intermodal Transportation Database, Air Carriers: T-100 International Market (U.S. Carriers), 2012

Other Transportation Statistics

Major Highways:	I-71; I-74; I-75
Amtrak Service:	Yes
Major Waterways/Ports:	Ohio River; Port of Cincinnati

Source: Amtrak.com; Google Maps

BUSINESSES

Major Business Headquarters

Company Name	Rankings	
	Fortune[1]	Forbes[2]
American Financial Group	485	-
Fifth Third Bancorp	361	-
Kroger	23	-
Macy's	109	-
Procter & Gamble	28	-
Western & Southern Financial Group	471	-

Note: (1) Fortune 500—companies that produce a 10-K are ranked 1 to 500 based on 2012 revenue; (2) all private companies with at least $2 billion in annual revenue through the end of their most current fiscal year are ranked 1 to 224; companies listed are headquartered in the city; dashes indicate no ranking Source: Fortune, "Fortune 500," May 20, 2013; Forbes, "America's Largest Private Companies," December 18, 2013

Fast-Growing Businesses

According to *Inc.*, Cincinnati is home to one of America's 500 fastest-growing private companies: **US Logistics** (#34). Criteria: must be an independent, privately-held, for-profit, U.S. corporation, proprietorship or partnership; revenues must be at least $100,000 in 2009 and $2 million in 2012; must have four-year operating/sales history. Holding companies, regulated banks, and utilities were excluded. *Inc., "America's 500 Fastest-Growing Private Companies," September 2013*

According to *Initiative for a Competitive Inner City (ICIC)*, Cincinnati is home to one of America's 100 fastest-growing "inner city" companies: **World Pac Paper** (#69). Companies were ranked by their five-year compound annual growth rate. Criteria for inclusion: company must be headquartered in or have 51 percent or more of its physical operations in an economically distressed urban area; must be an independent, for-profit corporation, partnership or proprietorship; must have 10 or more employees and have a five-year sales history that includes sales of at least $200,000 in the base year and at least $1 million in the current year with no decrease in sales over the two most recent years. *Initiative for a Competitive Inner City (ICIC), "Inner City 100 Companies, 2013"*

Minority Business Opportunity

Cincinnati is home to three companies which are on the *Black Enterprise* Industrial/Service 100 list (100 largest companies based on gross sales): **World Pac Paper** (#59); **Megen Construction Co.** (#72); **Che International Group** (#81). Criteria: operational in previous calendar year; at least 51% black-owned and manufactures/owns the product it sells or provides industrial or consumer services. Brokerages, real estate firms and firms that provide professional services are not eligible. *Black Enterprise, B.E. 100s, 2013*

Cincinnati is home to one company which is on the *Hispanic Business* 500 list (500 largest U.S. Hispanic-owned companies based on 2012 revenue): **Best Upon Request Corporate** (#393). Companies included must show at least 51 percent ownership by Hispanic U.S. citizens, and must maintain headquarters in one of the 50 states or Washington, D.C. *Hispanic Business, "Hispanic Business 500," June 20, 2013*

Minority- and Women-Owned Businesses

Group	All Firms		Firms with Paid Employees			
	Firms	Sales ($000)	Firms	Sales ($000)	Employees	Payroll ($000)
Asian	566	367,879	205	346,382	1,127	40,852
Black	4,844	245,402	204	165,641	1,555	36,787
Hispanic	316	41,968	28	34,524	390	13,047
Women	7,808	1,219,372	849	1,071,775	9,848	266,750
All Firms	26,491	60,197,147	6,642	59,323,274	226,554	10,811,280

Note: Figures cover firms located in the city; minority- and women-owned business are defined as firms in which the corresponding group own 51% or more of the stock or equity of the company
Source: U.S. Census Bureau, 2007 Economic Census, Survey of Business Owners (2012 Survey of Business Owners data will be released starting in June 2015)

HOTELS & CONVENTION CENTERS

Hotels/Motels

Area	5 Star		4 Star		3 Star		2 Star		1 Star		Not Rated	
	Num.	Pct.[3]	Num.	Pct.[3]	Num.	Pct.[3]	Num.	Pct.[3]	Num.	Pct.[3]	Num.	Pct.[3]
City[1]	0	0.0	5	2.6	51	27.0	108	57.1	6	3.2	19	10.1
Total[2]	142	0.9	1,005	6.0	5,147	30.9	8,578	51.4	408	2.4	1,397	8.4

Note: (1) Figures cover Cincinnati and vicinity; (2) Figures cover all 100 cities in this book; (3) Percentage of hotels which have a given star rating; Star ratings are determined by expedia.com and offer an indication of the general quality of a particular hotel.
Source: expedia.com, April 7, 2014

The Cincinnati, OH-KY-IN metro area is home to one of the best hotels in the world according to *Condé Nast Traveler*: **21C Museum Hotel**. The selections are based on over 79,000 responses to the magazine's annual Readers' Choice Survey. The list includes the top 200 hotels in the U.S. *Condé Nast Traveler, "Gold List 2014, The World's Best Places to Stay"*

Major Convention Centers

Name	Overall Space (sq. ft.)	Exhibit Space (sq. ft.)	Meeting Space (sq. ft.)	Meeting Rooms
Duke Energy Convention Center	750,000	n/a	n/a	n/a

Note: Table includes convention centers located in the Cincinnati, OH KY IN metro area; n/a not available
Source: Original research

Living Environment

COST OF LIVING

Cost of Living Index

Composite Index	Groceries	Housing	Utilities	Trans-portation	Health Care	Misc. Goods/Services
91.4	92.0	79.0	86.8	105.2	99.8	95.8

Note: The Cost of Living Index measures regional differences in the cost of consumer goods and services, excluding taxes and non-consumer expenditures, for professional and managerial households in the top income quintile. It is based on more than 50,000 prices covering almost 60 different items for which prices are collected three times a year by chambers of commerce, economic development organizations or university applied economic centers in each participating urban area. The numbers shown should be read as a percentage above or below the national average of 100. For example, a value of 115.4 in the groceries column indicates that grocery prices are 15.4% higher than the national average. Small differences in the index numbers should not be interpreted as significant; Figures cover the Cincinnati OH urban area.
Source: The Council for Community and Economic Research, ACCRA Cost of Living Index, 2013

Grocery Prices

Area[1]	T-Bone Steak ($/pound)	Frying Chicken ($/pound)	Whole Milk ($/half gal.)	Eggs ($/dozen)	Orange Juice ($/64 oz.)	Coffee ($/11.5 oz.)
City[2]	10.80	1.40	1.86	1.69	3.62	4.77
Avg.	10.19	1.28	2.34	1.81	3.48	4.39
Min.	8.56	0.94	1.44	1.19	2.78	3.40
Max.	14.82	2.28	3.56	3.73	6.23	7.32

*Note: (1) Values for the local area are compared with the average, minimum and maximum values for all 327 areas in the Cost of Living Index; (2) Figures cover the Cincinnati OH urban area; **T-Bone Steak** (price per pound); **Frying Chicken** (price per pound, whole fryer); **Whole Milk** (half gallon carton); **Eggs** (price per dozen, Grade A, large); **Orange Juice** (64 oz. Tropicana or Florida Natural); **Coffee** (11.5 oz. can, vacuum-packed, Maxwell House, Hills Bros, or Folgers).*
Source: The Council for Community and Economic Research, ACCRA Cost of Living Index, 2013

Housing and Utility Costs

Area[1]	New Home Price ($)	Apartment Rent ($/month)	All Electric ($/month)	Part Electric ($/month)	Other Energy ($/month)	Telephone ($/month)
City[2]	217,051	847	-	84.01	61.24	23.27
Avg.	295,864	900	171.38	91.82	70.12	27.73
Min.	185,506	458	117.80	48.81	33.67	17.16
Max.	1,358,917	3,783	441.68	171.40	372.65	39.47

*Note: (1) Values for the local area are compared with the average, minimum and maximum values for all 327 areas in the Cost of Living Index; (2) Figures cover the Cincinnati OH urban area; **New Home Price** (2,400 sf living area, 8,000 sf lot, in urban area with full utilities); **Apartment Rent** (950 sf 2 bedroom/1.5 or 2 bath, unfurnished, excluding all utilities except water); **All Electric** (average monthly cost for an all-electric home); **Part Electric** (average monthly cost for a part-electric home); **Other Energy** (average monthly cost for natural gas, fuel oil, coal, wood, and any other forms of energy except electricity); **Telephone** (price includes basic monthly rate for a private residential line plus additional local usage charges incurred by a family of four).*
Source: The Council for Community and Economic Research, ACCRA Cost of Living Index, 2013

Health Care, Transportation, and Other Costs

Area[1]	Doctor ($/visit)	Dentist ($/visit)	Optometrist ($/visit)	Gasoline ($/gallon)	Beauty Salon ($/visit)	Men's Shirt ($)
City[2]	98.24	84.06	91.67	3.53	37.20	23.38
Avg.	101.40	86.48	96.16	3.44	33.87	26.55
Min.	61.67	50.83	50.12	3.08	18.92	12.48
Max.	182.71	152.50	223.78	4.33	68.22	52.03

*Note: (1) Values for the local area are compared with the average, minimum and maximum values for all 327 areas in the Cost of Living Index; (2) Figures cover the Cincinnati OH urban area; **Doctor** (general practitioners routine exam of an established patient); **Dentist** (adult teeth cleaning and periodic oral examination); **Optometrist** (full vision eye exam for established adult patient); **Gasoline** (one gallon regular unleaded, national brand, including all taxes, cash price at self-service pump if available); **Beauty Salon** (woman's shampoo, trim, and blow-dry); **Men's Shirt** (cotton/polyester dress shirt, pinpoint weave, long sleeves).*
Source: The Council for Community and Economic Research, ACCRA Cost of Living Index, 2013

HOUSING

House Price Index (HPI)

Area	National Ranking[2]	Quarterly Change (%)	One-Year Change (%)	Five-Year Change (%)
MSA[1]	232	-0.85	-0.23	-6.61
U.S.[3]	–	1.20	7.69	4.18

Note: The HPI is a weighted repeat sales index. It measures average price changes in repeat sales or refinancings on the same properties. This information is obtained by reviewing repeat mortgage transactions on single-family properties whose mortgages have been purchased or securitized by Fannie Mae or Freddie Mac in January 1975; (1) Cincinnati, OH-KY-IN Metropolitan Statistical Area—see Appendix B for areas included; (2) Rankings are based on annual percentage change for all metro areas containing at least 15,000 transactions over the last 10 years and ranges from 1 to 283; (3) figures based on a weighted average of Census Division estimates using a seasonally adjusted, purchase-only index; all figures are for the period ending December 31, 2013
Source: Federal Housing Finance Agency, House Price Index, February 25, 2014

Median Single-Family Home Prices

Area	2011	2012	2013p	Percent Change 2012 to 2013
MSA[1]	122.3	128.3	135.9	5.9
U.S. Average	166.2	177.2	197.4	11.4

Note: Figures are median sales prices of existing single-family homes in thousands of dollars; (p) preliminary; n/a not available; (1) Cincinnati, OH-KY-IN Metropolitan Statistical Area—see Appendix B for areas included
Source: National Association of Realtors, Median Sales Price of Existing Single-Family Homes for Metropolitan Areas, 4th Quarter 2013

Qualifying Income Based on Median Sales Price of Existing Single-Family Homes

Area	With 5% Down ($)	With 10% Down ($)	With 20% Down ($)
MSA[1]	29,672	28,110	24,987
U.S. Average	45,395	43,006	38,228

Note: Figures are preliminary; Qualifying income is based on a mortgage rate of 4.4%. Monthly principal and interest payment is limited to 25% of income; n/a not available; (1) Cincinnati, OH-KY-IN Metropolitan Statistical Area—see Appendix B for areas included
Source: National Association of Realtors, Qualifying Income Based on Median Sales Price of Existing Single-Family Homes for Metropolitan Areas, 4th Quarter 2013

Median Apartment Condo-Coop Home Prices

Area	2011	2012	2013p	Percent Change 2012 to 2013
MSA[1]	104.0	105.6	109.6	3.8
U.S. Average	165.1	173.7	194.9	12.2

Note: Figures are median sales prices of existing apartment condo-coop homes in thousands of dollars; (p) preliminary; n/a not available; (1) Cincinnati, OH-KY-IN Metropolitan Statistical Area—see Appendix B for areas included
Source: National Association of Realtors, Median Sales Price of Existing Apartment Condo-Coop Homes for Metropolitan Areas, 4th Quarter 2013

Gross Monthly Rent

Area	Under $200	$200 -299	$300 -499	$500 -749	$750 -999	$1,000 -1,499	$1,500 and up	Median ($)
City	4.9	5.3	16.0	40.5	17.3	12.6	3.4	632
MSA[1]	2.6	3.4	11.6	34.8	24.6	18.0	4.9	731
U.S.	1.7	3.3	8.1	22.7	24.3	25.7	14.3	889

Note: Figures are percentages except for Median; Gross rent is the contract rent plus the estimated average monthly cost of utilities (electricity, gas, and water and sewer) and fuels (oil, coal, kerosene, wood, etc.) if these are paid by the renter (or paid for the renter by someone else); (1) Figures cover the Cincinnati, OH-KY-IN Metropolitan Statistical Area—see Appendix B for areas included
Source: U.S. Census Bureau, 2010-2012 American Community Survey 3-Year Estimates

Year Housing Structure Built

Area	2010 or Later	2000 -2009	1990 -1999	1980 -1989	1970 -1979	1960 -1969	1950 -1959	1940 -1949	Before 1940	Median Year
City	0.3	4.0	3.3	4.2	8.1	14.2	13.0	9.5	43.4	1947
MSA[1]	0.4	12.8	14.4	10.8	13.3	11.5	12.7	5.5	18.7	1971
U.S.	0.5	14.9	13.8	13.9	15.9	11.1	10.9	5.5	13.5	1976

Note: Figures are percentages except for Median Year; (1) Figures cover the Cincinnati, OH-KY-IN Metropolitan Statistical Area—see Appendix B for areas included
Source: U.S. Census Bureau, 2010-2012 American Community Survey 3-Year Estimates

HEALTH

Health Risk Data

Category	MSA[1] (%)	U.S. (%)
Adults aged 18–64 who have any kind of health care coverage	84.5	79.6
Adults who reported being in good or excellent health	82.3	83.1
Adults who are current smokers	23.3	19.6
Adults who are heavy drinkers[2]	5.8	6.1
Adults who are binge drinkers[3]	19.4	16.9
Adults who are overweight (BMI 25.0 - 29.9)	35.3	35.8
Adults who are obese (BMI 30.0 - 99.8)	28.3	27.6
Adults who participated in any physical activities in the past month	75.9	77.1
Adults 50+ who have ever had a sigmoidoscopy or colonoscopy	66.7	67.3
Women aged 40+ who have had a mammogram within the past two years	72.4	74.0
Men aged 40+ who have had a PSA test within the past two years	47.1	45.2
Adults aged 65+ who have had flu shot within the past year	63.3	60.1
Adults who always wear a seatbelt	92.4	93.8

Note: Data as of 2012 unless otherwise noted; (1) Figures cover the Cincinnati-Middletown, OH-KY-IN Metropolitan Statistical Area—see Appendix B for areas included; (2) Heavy drinkers are classified as males having more than two drinks per day or females having more than one drink per day; (3) Binge drinkers are classified as males having five or more drinks on one occasion or females having four or more drinks on one occasion
Source: Centers for Disease Control and Prevention, Behavioral Risk Factor Surveillance System, SMART: Selected Metropolitan/Micropolitan Area Risk Trends, 2012

Chronic Health Indicators

Category	MSA[1] (%)	U.S. (%)
Adults who have ever been told they had a heart attack	5.2	4.5
Adults who have ever been told they had a stroke	4.1	2.9
Adults who have been told they currently have asthma	10.3	8.9
Adults who have ever been told they have arthritis	27.6	25.7
Adults who have ever been told they have diabetes[2]	11.9	9.7
Adults who have ever been told they had skin cancer	6.1	5.7
Adults who have ever been told they had any other types of cancer	6.8	6.5
Adults who have ever been told they have COPD	7.5	6.2
Adults who have ever been told they have kidney disease	2.8	2.5
Adults who have ever been told they have a form of depression	20.2	18.0

Note: Data as of 2012 unless otherwise noted; (1) Figures cover the Cincinnati-Middletown, OH-KY-IN Metropolitan Statistical Area—see Appendix B for areas included; (2) Figures do not include pregnancy-related, borderline, or pre-diabetes
Source: Centers for Disease Control and Prevention, Behavioral Risk Factor Surveillance System, SMART: Selected Metropolitan/Micropolitan Area Risk Trends, 2012

Mortality Rates for the Top 10 Causes of Death in the U.S.

ICD-10[a] Sub-Chapter	ICD-10[a] Code	Age-Adjusted Mortality Rate[1] per 100,000 population	
		County[2]	U.S.
Malignant neoplasms	C00-C97	188.6	174.2
Ischaemic heart diseases	I20-I25	105.7	119.1
Other forms of heart disease	I30-I51	52.5	49.6
Chronic lower respiratory diseases	J40-J47	50.7	43.2
Cerebrovascular diseases	I60-I69	50.4	40.3
Organic, including symptomatic, mental disorders	F01-F09	42.9	30.5
Other degenerative diseases of the nervous system	G30-G31	35.1	26.3
Other external causes of accidental injury	W00-X59	27.1	25.1
Diabetes mellitus	E10-E14	28.5	21.3
Hypertensive diseases	I10-I15	22.1	18.8

Note: (a) ICD-10 = International Classification of Diseases 10th Revision; (1) Mortality rates are a three year average covering 2008-2010; (2) Figures cover Hamilton County
Source: Centers for Disease Control and Prevention, National Center for Health Statistics. Compressed Mortality File 1999-2010 on CDC WONDER Online Database, released January 2013. Data are compiled from the Compressed Mortality File 1999-2010, Series 20 No. 2P, 2013.

Mortality Rates for Selected Causes of Death

ICD-10[a] Sub-Chapter	ICD-10[a] Code	Age-Adjusted Mortality Rate[1] per 100,000 population	
		County[2]	U.S.
Assault	X85-Y09	9.4	5.5
Diseases of the liver	K70-K76	12.8	12.4
Human immunodeficiency virus (HIV) disease	B20-B24	2.3	3.0
Influenza and pneumonia	J09-J18	18.3	16.4
Intentional self-harm	X60-X84	10.8	11.8
Malnutrition	E40-E46	1.8	0.8
Obesity and other hyperalimentation	E65-E68	2.2	1.6
Renal failure	N17-N19	13.6	13.6
Transport accidents	V01-V99	8.0	12.6
Viral hepatitis	B15-B19	2.5	2.2

Note: (a) ICD-10 = International Classification of Diseases 10th Revision; (1) Mortality rates are a three year average covering 2008-2010; (2) Figures cover Hamilton County
Source: Centers for Disease Control and Prevention, National Center for Health Statistics. Compressed Mortality File 1999-2010 on CDC WONDER Online Database, released January 2013. Data are compiled from the Compressed Mortality File 1999-2010, Series 20 No. 2P, 2013.

Health Insurance Coverage

Area	With Health Insurance	With Private Health Insurance	With Public Health Insurance	Without Health Insurance	Population Under Age 18 Without Health Insurance
City	84.2	56.3	36.1	15.8	6.2
MSA[1]	88.9	72.6	26.7	11.1	4.9
U.S.	84.9	65.4	30.4	15.1	7.5

Note: Figures are percentages that cover the civilian noninstitutionalized population; (1) Figures cover the Cincinnati, OH-KY-IN Metropolitan Statistical Area—see Appendix B for areas included
Source: U.S. Census Bureau, 2010-2012 American Community Survey 3-Year Estimates

Number of Medical Professionals

Area[1]	MDs[2]	DOs[2,3]	Dentists	Podiatrists	Chiropractors	Optometrists
Local (number)	4,390	172	537	62	152	131
Local (rate[4])	548.1	21.5	66.9	7.7	18.9	16.3
U.S. (rate[4])	267.6	19.6	61.7	5.6	24.7	14.5

Note: Data as of 2012 unless noted; (1) Local data covers Hamilton County; (2) Data as of 2011; (3) Doctor of Osteopathic Medicine; (4) rate per 100,000 population
Source: Area Resource File (ARF) 2012-2013. U.S. Department of Health and Human Services, Health Resources and Services Administration, Bureau of Health Professions

Best Hospitals

According to *U.S. News,* the Cincinnati, OH-KY-IN metro area is home to two of the best hospitals in the U.S.: **Christ Hospital** (3 specialties); **Bethesda North Hospital** (2 specialties). The hospitals listed were nationally ranked in at least one adult specialty. Only 147 hospitals nationwide were nationally ranked in one or more specialties. Eighteen hospitals in the U.S. made the Honor Roll by ranking near the top in at least six specialties.*U.S. News Online, "America's Best Hospitals 2013-14"*

According to *U.S. News,* the Cincinnati, OH-KY-IN metro area is home to one of the best children's hospitals in the U.S.: **Cincinnati Children's Hospital Medical Center** (Honor Roll). The hospital listed was highly ranked in at least one pediatric specialty. Eighty-seven hospitals in the U.S. ranked in at least one specialty. Ten children's hospitals in the U.S. made the Honor Roll by ranking near the top in three or more specialties.*U.S. News Online, "America's Best Children's Hospitals 2013-14"*

EDUCATION

Public School District Statistics

District Name	Schls	Pupils	Pupil/ Teacher Ratio	Minority Pupils[1] (%)	Free Lunch Eligible[2] (%)	IEP[3] (%)
Cincinnati City	57	32,154	19.1	75.2	63.5	21.3
Forest Hills Local	9	7,484	19.7	8.8	9.3	10.3
Indian Hill Exempted Village	4	2,004	13.9	16.6	5.1	10.1
Mt Healthy City	5	3,396	17.0	80.0	70.4	20.0
Northwest Local	14	9,212	19.5	36.8	39.6	16.5
Oak Hills Local	9	7,938	19.4	7.2	5.2	15.2
Princeton City	11	5,336	18.1	66.9	55.5	15.3
Sycamore Community City	7	5,306	16.6	30.1	14.2	12.3
Winton Woods City	6	3,419	18.3	84.4	54.5	17.9

Note: Table includes school districts with 2,000 or more students; (1) Percentage of students that are not non-Hispanic white; (2) Percentage of students that are eligible for the free lunch program; (3) Percentage of students that have an Individualized Education Program.
Source: U.S. Department of Education, National Center for Education Statistics, Common Core of Data, Local Education Agency (School District) Universe Survey: School Year 2011-2012; U.S. Department of Education, National Center for Education Statistics, Common Core of Data, Public Elementary/Secondary School Universe Survey: School Year 2011-2012

Best High Schools

High School Name	Rank[1]	Grad. Rate[2] (%)	Coll.[3] (%)	AP/IB/ AICE Tests[4]	AP/IB/ AICE Score[5]	SAT Score[6]	ACT Score[6]
Anderson H.S.	1093	95	88	0.2	3.4	1617	24.4
Indian Hill H.S.	82	99	96	1.1	3.9	1741	25.0
Madeira H.S.	131	100	95	0.8	4.1	1700	25.3
Mariemont H.S.	812	97	79	0.5	3.9	1719	26.0
Sycamore H.S.	674	95	88	0.5	3.8	1682	25.3
Turpin H.S.	400	99	96	0.4	3.8	1651	24.6
Walnut Hills H.S.	53	100	100	1.3	3.6	1788	26.0
Wyoming H.S.	120	97	94	1.2	3.5	1920	26.1

Note: (1) Public schools are ranked from 1 to 2,000 based on the following self-reported statistics (with the corresponding weight used in calculating their overall score). Schools that were newly founded and did not have a graduating senior class in 2012 were excluded; (2) Four-year, on-time graduation rate (25%); (3) Percent of 2011 graduates who were accepted to college (25%); (4) AP/IB/AICE tests taken per student (25%); (5) Average AP/IB/AICE exam score (10%); (6) Average SAT and/or ACT score (10%); Percent of students enrolled in at least one AP/IB/AICE course (5%)—data not shown
Source: Newsweek and The Daily Beast, "America's Best High Schools 2013"

Highest Level of Education

Area	Less than H.S.	H.S. Diploma	Some College, No Deg.	Associate Degree	Bachelor's Degree	Master's Degree	Prof. School Degree	Doctorate Degree
City	15.5	26.4	20.2	6.7	18.5	8.5	2.6	1.7
MSA[1]	11.2	31.3	20.2	7.8	18.7	7.9	1.7	1.2
U.S.	14.1	28.3	21.3	7.8	18.0	7.5	1.9	1.2

Note: Figures cover persons age 25 and over; (1) Figures cover the Cincinnati, OH-KY-IN Metropolitan Statistical Area—see Appendix B for areas included
Source: U.S. Census Bureau, 2010-2012 American Community Survey 3-Year Estimates

Educational Attainment by Race

Area	High School Graduate or Higher (%)					Bachelor's Degree or Higher (%)				
	Total	White	Black	Asian	Hisp.[2]	Total	White	Black	Asian	Hisp.[2]
City	84.5	89.2	78.3	96.4	57.4	31.3	45.2	11.2	78.1	25.9
MSA[1]	88.8	89.7	82.8	92.0	69.9	29.5	30.6	15.5	63.8	24.1
U.S.	85.9	88.1	82.5	85.5	63.1	28.6	30.0	18.4	50.2	13.4

Note: Figures shown cover persons 25 years old and over; (1) Figures cover the Cincinnati, OH-KY-IN Metropolitan Statistical Area—see Appendix B for areas included; (2) People of Hispanic origin can be of any race
Source: U.S. Census Bureau, 2010-2012 American Community Survey 3-Year Estimates

School Enrollment by Grade and Control

Area	Preschool (%)		Kindergarten (%)		Grades 1 - 4 (%)		Grades 5 - 8 (%)		Grades 9 - 12 (%)	
	Public	Private	Public	Private	Public	Private	Public	Private	Public	Private
City	62.9	37.1	88.1	11.9	78.1	21.9	79.4	20.6	82.1	17.9
MSA[1]	48.7	51.3	84.3	15.7	83.4	16.6	82.5	17.5	83.6	16.4
U.S.	56.9	43.1	87.8	12.2	89.9	10.1	90.0	10.0	90.8	9.2

Note: Figures shown cover persons 3 years old and over; (1) Figures cover the Cincinnati, OH-KY-IN Metropolitan Statistical Area—see Appendix B for areas included
Source: U.S. Census Bureau, 2010-2012 American Community Survey 3-Year Estimates

Average Salaries of Public School Classroom Teachers

Area	2012-13		2013-14		Percent Change 2012-13 to 2013-14	Percent Change 2003-04 to 2013-14
	Dollars	Rank[1]	Dollars	Rank[1]		
Ohio	56,307	16	57,270	17	1.71	20.6
U.S. Average	56,103	–	56,689	–	1.04	21.8

Note: (1) State rank ranges from 1 to 51 where 1 indicates highest salary.
Source: National Education Association, Rankings & Estimates: Rankings of the States 2013 and Estimates of School Statistics 2014, March 2014

Higher Education

Four-Year Colleges			Two-Year Colleges			Medical Schools[1]	Law Schools[2]	Voc/ Tech[3]
Public	Private Non-profit	Private For-profit	Public	Private Non-profit	Private For-profit			
1	10	2	2	1	12	1	1	5

Note: Figures cover institutions located within the city limits and include main campuses only; (1) includes schools accredited by the Liaison Committee on Medical Education and the American Osteopathic Association's Commission on Osteopathic College Accreditation; (2) includes ABA-accredited schools, schools with provisional ABA accreditation, and state accredited schools; (3) includes all schools with programs that are less than 2 years.
Source: National Center for Education Statistics, Integrated Postsecondary Education System (IPEDS), 2012-13; Association of American Medical Colleges, Member List, April 24, 2014; American Osteopathic Association, Member List, April 24, 2014; Law School Admission Council, Official Guide to ABA-Approved Law Schools Online, April 24, 2014; Wikipedia, List of Medical Schools in the United States, April 24, 2014; Wikipedia, List of Law Schools in the United States, April 24, 2014

According to U.S. News & World Report, the Cincinnati, OH-KY-IN metro area is home to two of the best national universities in the U.S.: **Miami University–Oxford** (#75); **University of Cincinnati** (#135). The indicators used to capture academic quality fall into a number of categories: assessment by administrators at peer institutions; retention of students; faculty resources; student selectivity; financial resources; alumni giving; high school counselor ratings of colleges; and graduation rate. U.S. News & World Report, "America's Best Colleges 2014"

According to *U.S. News & World Report*, the Cincinnati, OH-KY-IN metro area is home to one of the top 100 law schools in the U.S.: **University of Cincinnati** (#80). The rankings are based on a weighted average of 12 measures of quality: peer assessment score; assessment score by lawyers/judges; median LSAT scores; median undergrad GPA; acceptance rate; employment rates for graduates; placement success; bar passage rate; faculty resources; expenditures per student; student/faculty ratio; and library resources. *U.S. News & World Report*, *"America's Best Graduate Schools, Law, 2014"*

According to *U.S. News & World Report*, the Cincinnati, OH-KY-IN metro area is home to one of the top 100 business schools in the U.S.: **University of Cincinnati (Lindner)** (#99). The rankings are based on a weighted average of the following nine measures: quality assessment; peer assessment; recruiter assessment; placement success; mean starting salary and bonus; student selectivity; mean GMAT and GRE scores; mean undergraduate GPA; and acceptance rate. *U.S. News & World Report*, *"America's Best Graduate Schools, Business, 2014"*

PRESIDENTIAL ELECTION

2012 Presidential Election Results

Area	Obama	Romney	Other
Hamilton County	51.8	46.9	1.3
U.S.	51.0	47.2	1.8

Note: Results are percentages and may not add to 100% due to rounding
Source: Dave Leip's Atlas of U.S. Presidential Elections

EMPLOYERS

Major Employers

Company Name	Industry
Archdiocese of Cincinnati	Religious
Christ Hospital	Medical
Cincinnati Children's Hospital Med Ctr	Medical
Cincinnati Public Schools	Education
City of Cincinnati	Government
Fifth Third Bancorp	Banking
Frisch's Restaurants	Restaurant
GE Aviation	Aviation
Hamilton County	Government
Internal Revenue Service	Government
Kroger Company	Supermarket
Macy's	Retail
Mercy Health Partners	Medical
Miami University	Education
Procter & Gamble Company	Consumer products
St. Elizabeth Healthcare	Medical
TriHealth	Medical
University of Cincinnati	Education
US Postal Service	Government
Wal-Mart Stores	Retail

Note: Companies shown are located within the Cincinnati, OH-KY-IN Metropolitan Statistical Area.
Source: Hoovers.com; Wikipedia

Best Companies to Work For

Procter & Gamble; TriHealth, headquartered in Cincinnati, are among the "100 Best Companies for Working Mothers." Criteria: workforce representation; child care; flexibility programs; and leave policies. This year *Working Mother* gave particular weight to flexible work arrangements, women's advancement programs, and paid maternity leave. *Working Mother*, *"100 Best Companies 2013"*

TriHealth, headquartered in Cincinnati, is among the "50 Best Employers for Workers Over 50." Criteria: recruiting practices; opportunities for training, education, and career development; workplace accommodations; alternative work options, such as flexible scheduling, job sharing, and phased retirement; employee health and pension benefits; and retiree benefits. Employers with at least 50 employees based in the U.S. are eligible, including for-profit companies, not-for-profit organizations, and government employers. *AARP*, *"2013 AARP Best Employers for Workers Over 50"*

Macy's; Procter & Gamble, headquartered in Cincinnati, are among the "Best Companies for Multicultural Women." *Working Mother* selected 25 companies based on a detailed application completed by public and private firms based in the United States, excluding government agencies, companies in the human resources field and non-autonomous divisions. Companies supplied data about the hiring, pay, and promotion of multicultural employees. Applications focused on representation of multicultural women, recruitment, retention and advancement programs, and company culture. *Working Mother, "2013 Best Companies for Multicultural Women"*

Procter & Gamble, headquartered in Cincinnati, is among the "Top Companies for Executive Women." To be named to the list, companies with a minimum of two women on the board complete a comprehensive application that focuses on the number of women in senior ranks. In addition to assessing corporate programs and policies dedicated to advancing women, NAFE examined the number of women in each company overall, in senior management, and on its board of directors, paying particular attention to the number of women with profit-and-loss responsibility. *National Association for Female Executives, "2013 NAFE Top 50 Companies for Executive Women"*

PUBLIC SAFETY

Crime Rate

Area	All Crimes	Violent Crimes				Property Crimes		
		Murder	Forcible Rape	Robbery	Aggrav. Assault	Burglary	Larceny -Theft	Motor Vehicle Theft
City	7,110.0	15.5	63.5	582.4	313.3	1,851.1	3,912.8	371.4
Suburbs[1]	3,035.0	1.6	27.1	58.7	85.3	623.0	2,145.0	94.3
Metro[2]	3,603.4	3.5	32.2	131.8	117.1	794.3	2,391.6	133.0
U.S.	3,246.1	4.7	26.9	112.9	242.3	670.2	1,959.3	229.7

Note: Figures are crimes per 100,000 population; (1) All areas within the metro area that are located outside the city limits; (2) Figures cover the Cincinnati, OH-KY-IN Metropolitan Statistical Area—see Appendix B for areas included
Source: FBI Uniform Crime Reports, 2012

Hate Crimes

Area	Number of Quarters Reported	Bias Motivation				
		Race	Religion	Sexual Orientation	Ethnicity	Disability
City	4	5	1	5	0	0
U.S.	4	2,797	1,099	1,135	667	92

Source: Federal Bureau of Investigation, Hate Crime Statistics 2012

Identity Theft Consumer Complaints

Area	Complaints	Complaints per 100,000 Population	Rank[2]
MSA[1]	1,261	59.6	210
U.S.	290,056	91.8	-

Note: (1) Figures cover the Cincinnati, OH-KY-IN Metropolitan Statistical Area—see Appendix B for areas included; (2) Rank ranges from 1 to 377 where 1 indicates greatest number of identity theft complaints per 100,000 population
Source: Federal Trade Commission, Consumer Sentinel Network Data Book for January–December 2013

Fraud and Other Consumer Complaints

Area	Complaints	Complaints per 100,000 Population	Rank[2]
MSA[1]	8,343	394.5	130
U.S.	1,811,724	595.2	-

Note: (1) Figures cover the Cincinnati, OH-KY-IN Metropolitan Statistical Area—see Appendix B for areas included; (2) Rank ranges from 1 to 377 where 1 indicates greatest number of identity theft complaints per 100,000 population
Source: Federal Trade Commission, Consumer Sentinel Network Data Book for January–December 2013

RECREATION

Culture

Dance[1]	Theatre[1]	Instrumental Music[1]	Vocal Music[1]	Series and Festivals	Museums and Art Galleries[2]	Zoos and Aquariums[3]
3	7	5	2	13	52	1

Note: (1) Number of professional performing groups; (2) Based on organizations with primary SIC code 8412; (3) AZA-accredited
Source: The Grey House Performing Arts Directory, 2013; Association of Zoos & Aquariums, AZA Member Zoos & Aquariums, April 2014; www.AccuLeads.com, May 1, 2014

Professional Sports Teams

Team Name	League	Year Established
Cincinnati Bengals	National Football League (NFL)	1968
Cincinnati Reds	Major League Baseball (MLB)	1882

Note: Includes teams located in the Cincinnati, OH-KY-IN Metropolitan Statistical Area.
Source: Wikipedia, Major Professional Sports Teams of the United States and Canada

CLIMATE

Average and Extreme Temperatures

Temperature	Jan	Feb	Mar	Apr	May	Jun	Jul	Aug	Sep	Oct	Nov	Dec	Yr.
Extreme High (°F)	74	72	84	89	93	102	103	102	102	89	81	75	103
Average High (°F)	38	42	52	64	74	82	86	85	78	67	53	42	64
Average Temp. (°F)	30	33	43	54	63	72	76	74	68	56	44	34	54
Average Low (°F)	21	24	33	43	52	61	65	63	56	45	35	26	44
Extreme Low (°F)	-25	-15	-11	17	27	39	47	43	33	16	0	-20	-25

Note: Figures cover the years 1948-1990
Source: National Climatic Data Center, International Station Meteorological Climate Summary, 9/96

Average Precipitation/Snowfall/Humidity

Precip./Humidity	Jan	Feb	Mar	Apr	May	Jun	Jul	Aug	Sep	Oct	Nov	Dec	Yr.
Avg. Precip. (in.)	3.2	2.9	3.9	3.5	4.0	3.9	4.2	3.1	2.8	2.8	3.4	3.1	40.9
Avg. Snowfall (in.)	7	5	4	1	Tr	0	0	0	0	Tr	2	4	23
Avg. Rel. Hum. 7am (%)	79	78	77	76	79	82	85	87	87	83	79	79	81
Avg. Rel. Hum. 4pm (%)	65	60	55	50	51	53	54	52	52	51	58	65	55

Note: Figures cover the years 1948-1990; Tr = Trace amounts (<0.05 in. of rain; <0.5 in. of snow)
Source: National Climatic Data Center, International Station Meteorological Climate Summary, 9/96

Weather Conditions

Temperature			Daytime Sky			Precipitation		
10°F & below	32°F & below	90°F & above	Clear	Partly cloudy	Cloudy	0.01 inch or more precip.	0.1 inch or more snow/ice	Thunder-storms
14	107	23	80	126	159	127	25	39

Note: Figures are average number of days per year and cover the years 1948-1990
Source: National Climatic Data Center, International Station Meteorological Climate Summary, 9/96

HAZARDOUS WASTE

Superfund Sites

Cincinnati has no sites on the EPA's Superfund Final National Priorities List.
U.S. Environmental Protection Agency, Final National Priorities List, April 26, 2014

AIR & WATER QUALITY

Air Quality Index

| Area | Percent of Days when Air Quality was...[2] | | | | | AQI Statistics[2] | |
	Good	Moderate	Unhealthy for Sensitive Groups	Unhealthy	Very Unhealthy	Maximum	Median
MSA[1]	42.7	54.2	3.0	0.0	0.0	123	54

Note: (1) Data covers the Cincinnati, OH-KY-IN Metropolitan Statistical Area—see Appendix B for areas included; (2) Based on 365 days with AQI data in 2013. Air Quality Index (AQI) is an index for reporting daily air quality. EPA calculates the AQI for five major air pollutants regulated by the Clean Air Act: ground-level ozone, particle pollution (aka particulate matter), carbon monoxide, sulfur dioxide, and nitrogen dioxide. The AQI runs from 0 to 500. The higher the AQI value, the greater the level of air pollution and the greater the health concern. There are six AQI categories: "Good" AQI is between 0 and 50. Air quality is considered satisfactory; "Moderate" AQI is between 51 and 100. Air quality is acceptable; "Unhealthy for Sensitive Groups" When AQI values are between 101 and 150, members of sensitive groups may experience health effects; "Unhealthy" When AQI values are between 151 and 200 everyone may begin to experience health effects; "Very Unhealthy" AQI values between 201 and 300 trigger a health alert; "Hazardous" AQI values over 300 trigger warnings of emergency conditions (not shown).
Source: U.S. Environmental Protection Agency, Air Quality Index Report, 2013

Air Quality Index Pollutants

| Area | Percent of Days when AQI Pollutant was...[2] | | | | | |
	Carbon Monoxide	Nitrogen Dioxide	Ozone	Sulfur Dioxide	Particulate Matter 2.5	Particulate Matter 10
MSA[1]	0.0	0.8	23.8	15.9	58.1	1.4

Note: (1) Data covers the Cincinnati, OH-KY-IN Metropolitan Statistical Area—see Appendix B for areas included; (2) Based on 365 days with AQI data in 2013. The Air Quality Index (AQI) is an index for reporting daily air quality. EPA calculates the AQI for five major air pollutants regulated by the Clean Air Act: ground-level ozone, particle pollution (also known as particulate matter), carbon monoxide, sulfur dioxide, and nitrogen dioxide. The AQI runs from 0 to 500. The higher the AQI value, the greater the level of air pollution and the greater the health concern.
Source: U.S. Environmental Protection Agency, Air Quality Index Report, 2013

Air Quality Trends: Ozone

	2003	2004	2005	2006	2007	2008	2009	2010	2011	2012
MSA[1]	0.088	0.075	0.085	0.078	0.086	0.075	0.070	0.076	0.080	0.083

Note: (1) Data covers the Cincinnati, OH-KY-IN Metropolitan Statistical Area—see Appendix B for areas included. The values shown are the composite ozone concentration averages among trend sites based on the highest fourth daily maximum 8-hour concentration in parts per million. These trends are based on sites having an adequate record of monitoring data during the trend period. Data from exceptional events are included.
Source: U.S. Environmental Protection Agency, Air Quality Monitoring Information, "Air Quality Trends by City, 2000-2012"

Maximum Air Pollutant Concentrations: Particulate Matter, Ozone, CO and Lead

	Particulate Matter 10 (ug/m³)	Particulate Matter 2.5 Wtd AM (ug/m³)	Particulate Matter 2.5 24-Hr (ug/m³)	Ozone (ppm)	Carbon Monoxide (ppm)	Lead (ug/m³)
MSA[1] Level	105	13.9	28	0.091	1	0.01
NAAQS[2]	150	15	35	0.075	9	0.15
Met NAAQS[2]	Yes	Yes	Yes	No	Yes	Yes

Note: (1) Data covers the Cincinnati, OH-KY-IN Metropolitan Statistical Area—see Appendix B for areas included; Data from exceptional events are included; (2) National Ambient Air Quality Standards; ppm = parts per million; ug/m³ = micrograms per cubic meter; n/a not available.
Concentrations: Particulate Matter 10 (coarse particulate)—highest second maximum 24-hour concentration; Particulate Matter 2.5 Wtd AM (fine particulate)—highest weighted annual mean concentration; Particulate Matter 2.5 24-Hour (fine particulate)—highest 98th percentile 24-hour concentration; Ozone—highest fourth daily maximum 8-hour concentration; Carbon Monoxide—highest second maximum non-overlapping 8-hour concentration; Lead—maximum running 3-month average
Source: U.S. Environmental Protection Agency, Air Quality Monitoring Information, "Air Quality Statistics by City, 2012"

Maximum Air Pollutant Concentrations: Nitrogen Dioxide and Sulfur Dioxide

	Nitrogen Dioxide AM (ppb)	Nitrogen Dioxide 1-Hr (ppb)	Sulfur Dioxide AM (ppb)	Sulfur Dioxide 1-Hr (ppb)	Sulfur Dioxide 24-Hr (ppb)
MSA[1] Level	4	29	n/a	85	n/a
NAAQS[2]	53	100	30	75	140
Met NAAQS[2]	Yes	Yes	n/a	No	n/a

Note: (1) Data covers the Cincinnati, OH-KY-IN Metropolitan Statistical Area—see Appendix B for areas included; Data from exceptional events are included; (2) National Ambient Air Quality Standards; ppm = parts per million; ug/m[3] = micrograms per cubic meter; n/a not available.
Concentrations: Nitrogen Dioxide AM—highest arithmetic mean concentration; Nitrogen Dioxide 1-Hr—highest 98th percentile 1-hour daily maximum concentration; Sulfur Dioxide AM—highest annual mean concentration; Sulfur Dioxide 1-Hr—highest 99th percentile 1-hour daily maximum concentration; Sulfur Dioxide 24-Hr—highest second maximum 24-hour concentration
Source: U.S. Environmental Protection Agency, Air Quality Monitoring Information, "Air Quality Statistics by City, 2012"

Drinking Water

Water System Name	Pop. Served	Primary Water Source Type	Violations[1] Health Based	Violations[1] Monitoring/ Reporting
Cincinnati Public Water System	827,727	Surface	0	0

Note: (1) Based on violation data from January 1, 2013 to December 31, 2013 (includes unresolved violations from earlier years)
Source: U.S. Environmental Protection Agency, Office of Ground Water and Drinking Water, Safe Drinking Water Information System (based on data extracted February 10, 2014)

Columbus, Ohio

Background

Columbus is the capital of Ohio, and centrally located in the watershed of the Ohio River. The largest city in the state, it was not the first choice for a state capital, but in 1812, residents of Franklinton, a county seat in the heart of Ohio, offered the government 1,200 acres of land and $50,000 with which to build a capitol building and state penitentiary.

Columbus grew steadily throughout the nineteenth century; its prosperity bolstered by the construction of a feeder link into the Ohio and Erie canals, which connected the town to the Great Lakes system and the Ohio River. By 1834, Columbus had attained a population of about 20,000. The railroad was established in 1850, bringing trade opportunities from the East.

Columbus became a major staging area for Union armies during the Civil War and was also home to Camp Chase, the largest military prison for Rebel soldiers. Both before and after the war, manufacturing in the city developed dramatically, based primarily on agricultural processing and packing, shoes, hardware, and heavy equipment. A specialty of Columbus was the buggy, and the Iron Buggy Company was the largest of its kind in the world.

Ohio State University, originally Ohio Agricultural and Mechanical University (1870), is in Columbus, and other colleges and universities include Franklin University (1902), Capital University (1830), Ohio Dominican University (1911), the Columbus College of Art and Design (1879), and Pontifical College Josephinum (1888). One of the first schools for the blind in the U.S., the Ohio State School for the Blind, was founded in Columbus in 1832.

Cultural resources include the Wexner Center for the Arts of Ohio State University, noted for its innovative architecture, and the Columbus Museum of Art, housing one of the nation's finest collections of 19th and 20th-century paintings. Columbus is also home to a symphony orchestra, and opera and ballet companies. The Columbus Zoo is nationally famous both for its success in the breeding of endangered species and for its large coral reef aquarium.

Columbus fans support Ohio State University's Buckeye football, a major league soccer team (Columbus Crew), an expansion National Hockey League franchise (Columbus Blue Jackets), and a minor league baseball team (Columbus Clippers). The Clippers played in Cooper Stadium from 1977 to the 2008 season. April 2009 marked the opening of the new ballpark, Huntington Park. Bodybuilding has long played an important role in Columbus sports. Arnold Fitness Weekend (formerly The Arnold Classic) is a bodybuilding and fitness competition held annually in Columbus, and named for Arnold Schwarzenegger.

The largest employers in Columbus are state government and Ohio State University. Other major employers include Nationwide Insurance, and Proctor & Gamble Company. Columbus is increasingly a digital city, and the Online Computer Library Center operates from here, as do CompuServe (a subsidiary of AOL) and the world's largest databases of chemical information. The multi-jurisdictional 315 Research + Technology Corridor was set up in 2006 to promote the area nationally and internationally, in hopes of achieving something similar to Research Triangle Park in North Carolina.

Columbus has a widespread municipal bus service, but the city remains the largest metropolitan area in the United States without passenger rail service. Preliminary projects for a light rail service are under consideration, but no firm dates for the project have been set.

Port Columbus International Airport, built in the 1920s, today serves national and international carriers. Rickenbacker Airport, named for famed Columbus resident Eddie Rickenbacker, World War I ace and airline pioneer, is a major center for air cargo. Columbus has also been home to other famous Americans, most notably Red Barber, beloved sports announcer, and James Thurber, perhaps the nation's most widely read humorist after Mark Twain. In *More Alarms at Night,* Thurber wrote of Columbus: "It's a town in which almost anything is likely to happen, and in which almost everything has."

Columbus has the usual four seasons associated with a continental climate, but extremes of high and low temperatures are possible. Summers are pleasant and mild. Though variable from year to year, rainfall is slightly in excess of the national average. Floods have occurred, and steps are being taken to limit their impact on the city.

Rankings

General Rankings

- Among the 50 largest U.S. cities, Columbus placed #19 in Vocativ's "semi-exhaustive, mostly scientific" city Livability Index for people aged 35 and under. Average salary, unemployment rates, rents, and other living costs were considered, along with bike lanes, low-cost broadband, cheap takeout, self-service laundries, the price of a pint of Guinness, music venues, and vintage clothing stores. *vocative.com, "The Livability Index: The Best U.S. Cities for People 35 and Under," November 7, 2013*

- Columbus was selected as one of America's best cities by *Bloomberg Businessweek*. The city ranked #20 out of 50. Criteria: leisure attributes (the number of restaurants, bars, libraries, museums, professional sports teams, and park acres by population); educational attributes (public school performance, the number of colleges, and graduate degree holders); economic factors (2011 income and June and July 2012 unemployment); crime; and air quality. *Bloomberg BusinessWeek, "America's Best Cities," September 26, 2012*

- Columbus appeared on RelocateAmerica's list of best places to live in America. The annual "Top 100 Places to Live" list recognizes the top communities as nominated by their residents & local businesses. RelocateAmerica's Research Group determined the list based on review of various data gathered for economic, employment, housing, education, industry, opportunity, environment and recreation along with feedback from area leaders and residents. *RelocateAmerica.com, "Top 100 Places to Live for 2011"*

Business/Finance Rankings

- Analysts for the business website 24/7 Wall Street looked at the local government report "Tax Rates and Tax Burdens in the District of Columbia—A Nationwide Comparison" to determine where a family of three at two different income levels would pay the least and the most in state and local taxes. Among the ten cities with the highest state and local tax burdens was Columbus, at #3. *247wallst.com, American Cities with the Highest (and Lowest) Taxes, February 25, 2013*

- Based on a minimum of 500 social media reviews per metro area, the employment opinion group Glassdoor surveyed 50 of the largest U.S. metro areas on measures including compensation and benefits, satisfaction with management, business outlook, and number of employers hiring. The Columbus metro area was ranked #25 in overall employee satisfaction. *www.glassdoor.com, "Employment Satisfaction Report Card by City," June 21, 2013*

- A *Fiscal Times* analysis balancing cost of living with average income to find the cities where residents' dollars go furthest was published by the *Huffington Post*. Based on the Census Bureau's 2010 Cost of Living Index and the National Compensation Survey, Columbus was ranked the #4 metro area where you can "actually spend less and make more." *Fiscal Times/Huffington Post, "The Best Bang for Your Buck Cities in the United States," June 26, 2012*

- The Brookings Institution ranked the 50 largest cities in the U.S. based on income inequality. Columbus was ranked #40. (#1 = greatest inequality). Criteria: the cities were ranked based on the "95/20 ratio." This figure represents the income at which a household earns more than 95 percent of all other households, divided by the income at which a household earns more than only 20 percent of all other households. *Brookings Institution, "Income Inequality in America's 50 Largest Cities, 2007-2012," February 20, 2014*

- MarketWatch shared a *24/7 Wall St.* analysis of the District of Columbia's Office of Revenue Analysis report on the estimated property, sales, auto, and income taxes paid in the largest city of each state in 2011. Of the U.S. cities with the highest tax burden, Columbus ranked #3. *Marketwatch.com, "10 U.S. Cities with the Highest Taxes," March 2, 2013*

- CareerBliss, an employment and careers website, analyzed U.S. Bureau of Labor Statistics data, more than 14,000 company reviews from employees and former employees, and job openings over a six-month period to arrive at its list of the 20 worst places in the United States to look for a job. Columbus was ranked #17. *CareerBliss.com, "20 Worst Cities to Find a Job for 2012," October 11, 2012*

- Columbus was ranked #41 out of 100 metro areas in terms of economic performance (#1 = best) during the recession and recovery from trough quarter through the second quarter of 2013. Criteria: percent change in employment; percentage point change in unemployment rate; percent change in gross metropolitan product; percent change in House Price Index. *Brookings Institution, MetroMonitor: Tracking Economic Recession and Recovery in America's 100 Largest Metropolitan Areas, September 2013*

- Columbus was identified as one of the best places for finding a job by *U.S. News & World Report*. The city ranked #8 out of 10. Criteria: strong job market. *U.S. News & World Report, "The 10 Best Cities to Find Jobs," June 17, 2013*

- The Columbus metro area was identified as one of the most affordable metropolitan areas in America by *Forbes*. The area ranked #20 out of 20. Criteria: the 100 largest metro areas in the U.S. were analyzed based on housing affordability and cost-of-living. *Forbes.com, "America's Most Affordable Cities," March 11, 2014*

- Columbus was identified as one of America's most frugal metro areas by *Coupons.com*. The city ranked #12 out of 25. Criteria: online coupon usage. *Coupons.com, "Top 25 Most Frugal Cities of 2012," February 19, 2013*

- Columbus was identified as one of America's most frugal metro areas by *Coupons.com*. The city ranked #9 out of 25. Criteria: Grocery IQ and coupons.com mobile app usage. *Coupons.com, "Top 25 Most On-the-Go Frugal Cities of 2012," February 19, 2013*

- Columbus was identified as one of the top 25 U.S. cities with the most credit card debt by credit reporting bureau Experian. The city was ranked #12. *Experian, March 4, 2011*

- Columbus was cited as one of America's top metros for new and expanded facility projects in 2013. The area ranked #8 in the large metro area category (population over 1 million). *Site Selection, "Top Metros of 2013," March 2014*

- Columbus was identified as one of the uhappiest cities to work in by CareerBliss.com, an online community for career advancement. The city ranked #7 out of 10. Criteria: independent company reviews from employees all over the country on: relationship with their boss and co-workers; work environment; job resources; compensation; growth opportunities; company culture; company reputation; daily tasks; job control over work performed on a daily basis. *CareerBliss.com, "Top 10 Happiest and Unhappiest Cities to Work in 2014," February 10, 2014*

- The Columbus metro area appeared on the Milken Institute "2013 Best Performing Cities" list. Rank: #37 out of 200 large metro areas. Criteria: job growth; wage and salary growth; high-tech output growth. *Milken Institute, "Best-Performing Cities 2013," December 2013*

- *Forbes* ranked the 200 most populous metro areas in the U.S. in terms of the "Best Places for Business and Careers." The Columbus metro area was ranked #20. Criteria: costs (business and living); job growth (past and projected); income growth; educational attainment (college and high school); projected economic growth; cultural and recreational opportunities; net migration patterns; number of highly ranked colleges. *Forbes, "The Best Places for Business and Careers," August 7, 2013*

Children/Family Rankings

- Columbus was selected as one of the best cities for families to live by *Parenting* magazine. The city ranked #62 out of 100. Criteria: education; health; community; *Parenting's* Culture & Charm Index. *Parenting.com, "The 2012 Best Cities for Families List"*

Culture/Performing Arts Rankings

- Columbus was selected as one of America's top cities for the arts. The city ranked #13 in the big city (population 500,000 and over) category. Criteria: readers' top choices for arts travel destinations based on the richness and variety of visual arts sites, activities and events. *American Style, "2012 Top 25 Arts Destinations," June 2012*

Dating/Romance Rankings

- Of the 100 U.S. cities surveyed by *Men's Health* in its quest to identify the nation's best cities for dating and forming relationships, Columbus was ranked #32 for online dating (#1 = best). *Men's Health, "The Best and Worst Cities for Online Dating," January 30, 2013*

Education Rankings

- *Men's Health* ranked 100 U.S. cities in terms of their education levels. Columbus was ranked #29 (#1 = most educated city). Criteria: high school graduation rates; school enrollment; educational attainment; number of households who have outstanding student loans; number of households whose members have taken adult-education courses. *Men's Health, "Where School Is In: The Most and Least Educated Cities," September 12, 2011*

- Columbus was selected as one of America's most literate cities. The city ranked #26 out of the 77 largest U.S. cities. Criteria: number of booksellers; library resources; Internet resources; educational attainment; periodical publishing resources; newspaper circulation. *Central Connecticut State University, "America's Most Literate Cities, 2013"*

Environmental Rankings

- The Columbus metro area came in at #158 for the relative comfort of its climate on Sperling's list of "chill cities," as measured by the Sperling Heat Index. All 361 metro areas are included. Criteria included daytime high temperatures, nighttime low temperatures, dew point, and relative humidity at the high temperatures. *www.bertsperling.com, "Sperling's Chill Cities," July 18, 2013*

- Sperling's BestPlaces assessed 379 metropolitan areas of the United States for the likelihood of dangerously extreme weather events or earthquakes. In general the Southeast and South-Central regions have the highest risk of weather extremes and earthquakes, while the Pacific Northwest enjoys the lowest risk. Of the least risky metropolitan areas, the Columbus metro area was ranked #144. *www.bestplaces.net, "Safest Places from Natural Disasters," April 2011*

- *The Daily Beast* identifed the snowiest among the 100 largest U.S. cities, looking at average snowfall per month from December 2011 through March 2012 and from December 1, 2012 to December 21, 2012. Number of days with maximum and minimum temperatures of 32 degrees or less contributed to the rankings. Columbus ranked #22. *The Daily Beast, "25 Snowiest Cities in America," December 21, 2012*

- Columbus was selected as one of 22 "Smarter Cities" for energy by the Natural Resources Defense Council. The city appeared as one of 12 cities in the large city (population 250,000 and over) category. Criteria: investment in green power; energy efficiency measures; conservation. *Natural Resources Defense Council, "2010 Smarter Cities," July 19, 2010*

Food/Drink Rankings

- *Men's Health* ranked 100 major U.S. cities in terms of alcohol intoxication. Columbus ranked #64 (#1 = most sober).Criteria: binge drinking; alcohol-related traffic accidents, arrests, and fatalities. *Men's Health, "The Drunkest Cities in America," November 19, 2013*

Health/Fitness Rankings

- Analysts who tracked obesity rates in the nation's largest metro areas (those with populations above one million) found that the Columbus metro area was one of the ten major metros where residents were most likely to be obese, defined as a BMI score of 30 or above. *www.gallup.com, "Boulder, Colo., Residents Still Least Likely to Be Obese," April 4, 2014*

- For each of the 50 most populous metro areas in the United States, the American College of Sports Medicine's American Fitness Index evaluated infrastructure, community assets, and policies that encourage healthy and fit lifestyles, including preventive health behaviors, levels of chronic disease conditions, health care access, and community resources and policies that support physical activity. The Columbus metro area ranked #30 for "community fitness." Personal health indicators were considered as well as community and environmental indicators. *www.americanfitnessindex.org, "ACSM American Fitness Index Health and Community Fitness Status of the 50 Largest Metropolitan Areas," May 2013*

- The Columbus metro area was identified as one of the worst cities for bed bugs in America by pest control company Orkin. The area ranked #3 out of 50 based on the number of bed bug treatments Orkin performed from January to December 2013. *Orkin, "Chicago Tops Bed Bug Cities List for Second Year in a Row," January 16, 2014*

- Columbus was identified as one of 15 cities with the highest increase in bed bug activity in the U.S. by pest control provider Terminix. The city ranked #4.Criteria: cities with the largest percentage gains in bed bug customer calls from January–May 2013 compared to the same time period in 2012. *Terminix, "Cities with Highest Increases in Bed Bug Activity," July 9, 2013*

- Columbus was selected as one of the 25 fattest cities in America by *Men's Fitness Online*. It ranked #16 out of America's 50 largest cities. Criteria: fitness centers and sport stores; nutrition; sports participation; TV viewing; overweight/sedentary; junk food; air quality; geography; commute; parks and open space; city recreational facilities; access to healthcare; motivation; mayor and city initiatives; state obesity initiatives. *Men's Fitness, "The Fittest and Fattest Cities in America," March 5, 2012*

- Columbus was identified as a "2013 Spring Allergy Capital." The area ranked #56 out of 100. Three groups of factors were used to identify the most severe cities for people with allergies during the spring season: annual pollen levels; medicine utilization; access to board-certified allergists. *Asthma and Allergy Foundation of America, "Spring Allergy Capitals 2013"*

- Columbus was identified as a "2013 Fall Allergy Capital." The area ranked #40 out of 100. Three groups of factors were used to identify the most severe cities for people with allergies during the fall season: annual pollen levels; medicine utilization; access to board-certified allergists. *Asthma and Allergy Foundation of America, "Fall Allergy Capitals 2013"*

- Columbus was identified as a "2013 Asthma Capital." The area ranked #54 out of the nation's 100 largest metropolitan areas. Twelve factors were used to identify the most challenging places to live for people with asthma: estimated prevalence; self-reported prevalence; crude death rate for asthma; annual pollen score; annual air quality; public smoking laws; number of board-certified asthma specialists; school inhaler access laws; rescue medication use; controller medication use; uninsured rate; poverty rate. *Asthma and Allergy Foundation of America, "Asthma Capitals 2013"*

- *Men's Health* ranked 100 major U.S. cities in terms of the best and worst cities for men. Columbus ranked #56. Criteria: thirty-three data points were examined covering health, fitness, and quality of life. *Men's Health, "The Best & Worst Cities for Men 2014," December 6, 2013*

- The Columbus metro area appeared in the 2013 Gallup-Healthways Well-Being Index. The area ranked #59 out of 189. The Gallup-Healthways Well-Being Index score is an average of six sub-indexes, which individually examine life evaluation, emotional health, work environment, physical health, healthy behaviors, and access to basic necessities. Results are based on telephone interviews conducted as part of the Gallup-Healthways Well-Being Index survey January 2–December 29, 2012, and January 2–December 30, 2013, with a random sample of 531,630 adults, aged 18 and older, living in metropolitan areas in the 50 U.S. states and the District of Columbia. *Gallup-Healthways, "State of American Well-Being," March 25, 2014*

- The Columbus metro area was identified as one of "America's Most Stressful Cities" by *Sperling's BestPlaces*. The metro area ranked #37 out of 50. Criteria: unemployment rate; suicide rate; commute time; mental health; poor rest; alcohol use; violent crime rate; property crime rate; cloudy days annually. *Sperling's BestPlaces, www.BestPlaces.net, "Stressful Cities 2012*

- *Men's Health* ranked 100 U.S. cities in terms of their activity levels. Columbus was ranked #78 (#1 = most active city). Criteria: where and how often residents exercise; percentage of households that watch more than 15 hours of cable television a week and buy more than 11 video games a year; death rate from deep-vein thrombosis, a condition linked to sitting for extended periods of time. *Men's Health, "Where Sit Happens: The Most and Least Active Cities in America," June 20, 2011*

- *The Daily Beast* identified the 30 U.S. metro areas with the worst smoking habits. The Columbus metro area ranked #22. Sixty urban centers with populations of more than one million were ranked based on the following criteria: number of smokers; number of cigarettes smoked per day; fewest attempts to quit. *The Daily Beast, "30 Cities With Smoking Problems," January 3, 2011*

Real Estate Rankings

- *Forbes* reported that Columbus ranked #8 on its list of cities where renters could get the best value for their money, based on current rental prices, price per square foot, year-over-year changes in rent cost, and cost of renting compared with the cost of purchasing a home. *www.forbes.com, "Renting? Cities to Get the Most Bang for Your Buck," July 19, 2013*

- NerdWallet identified the 10 U.S. cities among the 25 largest, most hospitable for recent college graduates, based on demographics; social life; accessibility; cost of living; and economic opportunity. Columbus placed #7 as a destination for new young graduates. *http://www.nerdwallet.com, "Best Cities for Fresh College Graduates," May 30, 2013*

- Columbus was ranked #125 out of 283 metro areas in terms of house price appreciation in 2013 (#1 = highest rate). *Federal Housing Finance Agency, House Price Index, 4th Quarter 2013*

- Columbus was ranked #138 out of 224 metro areas in terms of housing affordability in 2013 by the National Association of Home Builders (#1 = most affordable). The NAHB-Wells Fargo Housing Opportunity Index (HOI) for a given area is defined as the share of homes sold in that area that would have been affordable to a family earning the local median income, based on standard mortgage underwriting criteria. *National Association of Home Builders®, NAHB-Wells Fargo Housing Opportunity Index, 4th Quarter 2013*

- Columbus was selected as one of the best college towns for renters by ApartmentRatings.com." The area ranked #50 out of 87. Overall satisfaction ratings were ranked using thousands of user submitted scores for hundreds of apartment complexes located in cities and towns that are home to the 100 largest four-year institutions in the U.S. *ApartmentRatings.com, "2011 College Town Renter Satisfaction Rankings"*

- The Columbus metro area was identified as one of America's most undervalued cities in 2011 by *CNNMoney.com* based on data from Local Market Monitor. Criteria: median home prices; local interest rates; economic and population growth; construction costs; vacancies; household income. *CNNMoney.com, "America's Most Overvalued (and Undervalued) Cities," January 16, 2011*

Safety Rankings

- Symantec, in partnership with Sperling's BestPlaces, ranked the 50 largest cities in the U.S. in terms of their vulnerability to cybercrime. The city ranked #28. Criteria: number of cyberattacks and potential infections; level of Internet access; expenditures on smartphones and computer hardware/software; wireless hotspots; broadband connectivity; Internet usage; online purchases. *Symantec, "Riskiest Online Cities of 2012" February 15, 2012*

- Allstate ranked the 200 largest cities in America in terms of driver safety. Columbus ranked #139. Allstate researchers analyzed internal property damage claims over a two-year period from January 2010 to December 2011. A weighted average of the two-year numbers determined the annual percentages. *Allstate, "Allstate America's Best Drivers Report®, August 27, 2013"*

- The National Insurance Crime Bureau ranked 380 metro areas in the U.S. in terms of per capita rates of vehicle theft. The Columbus metro area ranked #107 (#1 = highest rate). Criteria: number of vehicle theft offenses per 100,000 inhabitants in 2012. *National Insurance Crime Bureau, "Hot Spots 2012," June 26, 2013*

- The Columbus metro area was identified as one of the most dangerous metro areas for pedestrians by Transportation for America. The metro area ranked #35 out of 52 metro areas with over 1 million residents. Criteria: area's population divided by the number of pedestrian fatalities in that area. *Transportation for America, "Dangerous by Design 2011"*

Seniors/Retirement Rankings

- From its Best Cities for Successful Aging indexes, the Milken Institute generated rankings for metropolitan areas, weighing data in eight categories—general indicators, health care, wellness, living arrangements, transportation and general accessibility, financial well-being, education and employment, and community participation. The Columbus metro area was ranked #80 overall in the large metro area category. *Milken Institute, "Best Cities for Successful Aging," July 2012*

- Bankers Life and Casualty Company, in partnership with Sperling's BestPlaces, ranked the nation's 50 largest metro areas in terms of the "Best U.S. Cities for Seniors." The Columbus metro area ranked #22. Criteria: healthcare; transportation; housing; environment; economy; health and longevity; social and spiritual life; crime. *Bankers Life and Casualty Company, Center for a Secure Retirement, "Best U.S. Cities for Seniors 2011," September 2011*

Sports/Recreation Rankings

- Columbus appeared on the *Sporting News* list of the "Best Sports Cities" for 2011. The area ranked #36 out of 271. Criteria: the magazine takes a 12-month snapshot of each city's sports, putting a heavy premium on regular-season won-lost records (from the most recently completed season). Other criteria include: playoff berths, bowl appearances and tournament bids; championships; applicable power ratings; quality of competition; overall fan fervor (measured in part by attendance); abundance of teams (rewarding quality over quantity); stadium and arena quality; ticket availability and prices; franchise ownership; and marquee appeal of athletes. *Sporting News, "Best Sports Cities 2011," October 4, 2011*

- Columbus appeared on the *Sporting News* list of the "Best Sports Cities" for 2011. The area ranked #36 out of 271. Criteria: a 12-month snapshot of regular-season won-lost records (from the most recently completed season). Other criteria include: playoff berths, bowl appearances and tournament bids; championships; applicable power ratings; quality of competition; overall fan fervor (measured in part by attendance); abundance of teams (quality over quantity); stadium and arena quality; ticket availability and prices; franchise ownership; and marquee appeal of athletes. *Sporting News, "Best Sports Cities 2011," October 4, 2011*

- Columbus was chosen as a bicycle friendly community by the League of American Bicyclists. A "Bicycle Friendly Community" welcomes cyclists by providing safe accommodation for cycling and encouraging people to bike for transportation and recreation. There are four award levels: Platinum; Gold; Silver; and Bronze. The community achieved an award level of Bronze. *League of American Bicyclists, "Bicycle Friendly Community Master List," Fall 2013*

- Columbus was selected as one of the most playful cities in the U.S. by KaBOOM! The organization's Playful City USA initiative honors cities and towns across the nation for a vision, plan and commitment to creating an agenda for play. Criteria: creating a local play commission or task force; designing an annual action plan for play; conducting a play space audit; outlining a financial investment in play for the current fiscal year; and proclaiming and celebrating an annual "play day." *KaBOOM! National Campaign for Play, "2013 Playful City USA Communities"*

Women/Minorities Rankings

- *Women's Health* examined U.S. cities and identified the 100 best cities for women. Columbus was ranked #67. Criteria: 30 categories were examined from obesity and breast cancer rates to commuting times and hours spent working out. *Women's Health, "Best Cities for Women 2012"*

- The Columbus metro area appeared on *Forbes'* list of the "Best Cities for Minority Entrepreneurs." The area ranked #67 out of 10. Criteria: 52 metropolitan statistical areas were examined. For each ethnicity (African Americans, Asians and Hispanics), the editors measured housing affordability, population growth, income growth, and entrepreneurship (per capita self-employment). *Forbes, "Best Cities for Minority Entrepreneurs," March 23, 2011*

Miscellaneous Rankings

- Market analyst Scarborough Research surveyed adults who had done volunteer work over the previous 12 months to find out where volunteers are concentrated. The Columbus metro area made the list for highest volunteer participation. *Scarborough Research, "Salt Lake City, UT; Minneapolis, MN; and Des Moines, IA Lend a Helping Hand," November 27, 2012*

- *Men's Health* ranked 100 U.S. cities by their level of sadness. Columbus was ranked #36 (#1 = saddest city). Criteria: suicide rates; unemployment rates; percentage of households that use antidepressants; percent of population who report feeling blue all or most of the time. *Men's Health, "Frown Towns," November 28, 2011*

- Mars Chocolate North America, the makers of COMBOS®, in partnership with Sperling's BestPlaces, ranked 50 major metro areas in terms of their "manliness." The Columbus metro area ranked #27. Criteria: number of professional sports teams; number of nearby NASCAR tracks and racing events; manly lifestyle; concentration of manly retail stores; manly occupations per capita; salty snack sales; "Board of Manliness" rankings. *Mars Chocolate North America, "America's Manliest Cities 2012"*

- The National Alliance to End Homelessness ranked the 100 most populous metro areas in terms the rate of homelessness. The Columbus metro area ranked #92. Criteria: number of homeless people per 10,000 population in 2011. *National Alliance to End Homelessness, The State of Homelessness in America 2012*

Business Environment

CITY FINANCES

City Government Finances

Component	2011 ($000)	2011 ($ per capita)
Total Revenues	1,598,525	2,138
Total Expenditures	1,383,685	1,850
Debt Outstanding	2,524,558	3,376
Cash and Securities[1]	1,212,525	1,622

Note: (1) Cash and security holdings of a government at the close of its fiscal year, including those of its dependent agencies, utilities, and liquor stores.
Source: U.S Census Bureau, State & Local Government Finances 2011

City Government Revenue by Source

Source	2011 ($000)	2011 ($ per capita)
General Revenue		
From Federal Government	105,948	142
From State Government	124,293	166
From Local Governments	13,763	18
Taxes		
Property	47,185	63
Sales and Gross Receipts	17,067	23
Personal Income	637,752	853
Corporate Income	0	0
Motor Vehicle License	0	0
Other Taxes	36,195	48
Current Charges	316,375	423
Liquor Store	0	0
Utility	229,098	306
Employee Retirement	0	0

Source: U.S Census Bureau, State & Local Government Finances 2011

City Government Expenditures by Function

Function	2011 ($000)	2011 ($ per capita)	2011 (%)
General Direct Expenditures			
Air Transportation	0	0	0.0
Corrections	2,372	3	0.2
Education	0	0	0.0
Employment Security Administration	0	0	0.0
Financial Administration	33,443	45	2.4
Fire Protection	168,853	226	12.2
General Public Buildings	13,472	18	1.0
Governmental Administration, Other	22,773	30	1.6
Health	34,265	46	2.5
Highways	87,701	117	6.3
Hospitals	0	0	0.0
Housing and Community Development	19,082	26	1.4
Interest on General Debt	149,895	200	10.8
Judicial and Legal	32,997	44	2.4
Libraries	0	0	0.0
Parking	2,505	3	0.2
Parks and Recreation	110,740	148	8.0
Police Protection	235,144	314	17.0
Public Welfare	0	0	0.0
Sewerage	169,020	226	12.2
Solid Waste Management	29,870	40	2.2
Veterans' Services	0	0	0.0
Liquor Store	0	0	0.0
Utility	192,302	257	13.9
Employee Retirement	0	0	0.0

Source: U.S Census Bureau, State & Local Government Finances 2011

DEMOGRAPHICS

Population Growth

Area	1990 Census	2000 Census	2010 Census	Population Growth (%) 1990-2000	Population Growth (%) 2000-2010
City	648,656	711,470	787,033	9.7	10.6
MSA[1]	1,405,176	1,612,694	1,836,536	14.8	13.9
U.S.	248,709,873	281,421,906	308,745,538	13.2	9.7

Note: (1) Figures cover the Columbus, OH Metropolitan Statistical Area—see Appendix B for areas included
Source: U.S. Census Bureau, Census 1990, 2000, 2010

Household Size

Area	Persons in Household (%) One	Two	Three	Four	Five	Six	Seven or More	Average Household Size
City	36.4	30.7	14.3	10.1	5.4	1.8	1.2	2.40
MSA[1]	29.3	32.8	15.4	13.3	6.0	2.0	1.1	2.54
U.S.	27.6	33.5	15.7	13.2	6.1	2.4	1.5	2.63

Note: (1) Figures cover the Columbus, OH Metropolitan Statistical Area—see Appendix B for areas included
Source: U.S. Census Bureau, 2010-2012 American Community Survey 3-Year Estimates

Race

Area	White Alone[2] (%)	Black Alone[2] (%)	Asian Alone[2] (%)	AIAN[3] Alone[2] (%)	NHOPI[4] Alone[2] (%)	Other Race Alone[2] (%)	Two or More Races (%)
City	62.1	27.7	4.4	0.2	0.0	2.1	3.5
MSA[1]	77.7	14.9	3.2	0.2	0.0	1.3	2.7
U.S.	74.0	12.6	4.9	0.8	0.2	4.7	2.8

Note: (1) Figures cover the Columbus, OH Metropolitan Statistical Area—see Appendix B for areas included;
(2) Alone is defined as not being in combination with one or more other races; (3) American Indian and Alaska Native; (4) Native Hawaiian and Other Pacific Islander
Source: U.S. Census Bureau, 2010-2012 American Community Survey 3-Year Estimates

Hispanic or Latino Origin

Area	Total (%)	Mexican (%)	Puerto Rican (%)	Cuban (%)	Other (%)
City	5.6	3.2	0.7	0.1	1.6
MSA[1]	3.7	2.1	0.5	0.1	1.0
U.S.	16.6	10.7	1.6	0.6	3.7

Note: Persons of Hispanic or Latino origin can be of any race; (1) Figures cover the Columbus, OH Metropolitan Statistical Area—see Appendix B for areas included
Source: U.S. Census Bureau, 2010-2012 American Community Survey 3-Year Estimates

Segregation

Type	Segregation Indices[1] 1990	2000	2010	2010 Rank[2]	Percent Change 1990-2000	1990-2010	2000-2010
Black/White	67.6	63.4	62.2	33	-4.2	-5.5	-1.2
Asian/White	44.7	43.3	43.3	35	-1.4	-1.4	0.0
Hispanic/White	27.9	36.9	41.5	59	9.0	13.6	4.6

Note: All figures cover the Metropolitan Statistical Area—see Appendix B for areas included; Figures are based on an analysis of 1990, 2000, and 2010 Census Decennial Census tract data by William H. Frey, Brookings Institution and the University of Michigan Social Science Data Analysis Network. In this analysis all racial groups (whites, blacks, and asians) are non-Hispanic members of those races. Hispanics are shown as a separate category;
(1) Segregation Indices are Dissimilarity Indices that measure the degree to which the minority group is distributed differently than whites across census tracts. They range from 0 (complete integration) to 100 (complete segregation) where the value indicates the percentage of the minority group that needs to move to be distributed exactly like whites; (2) Ranges from 1 (most segregated) to 102 (least segregated); n/a not available.
Source: www.CensusScope.org

Ancestry

Area	German	Irish	English	American	Italian	Polish	French[2]	Scottish	Dutch
City	20.4	12.6	6.8	4.9	5.4	2.2	1.8	1.6	1.2
MSA[1]	25.5	14.5	9.6	8.0	5.7	2.4	2.2	2.1	1.6
U.S.	15.2	11.1	8.2	7.2	5.6	3.1	2.8	1.7	1.4

Note: Figures are the percentage of the total population reporting a particular ancestry. The nine most commonly reported ancestries in the U.S. are shown. Figures include multiple ancestries (e.g. if a person reported being Irish and Italian, they were included in both columns); (1) Figures cover the Columbus, OH Metropolitan Statistical Area—see Appendix B for areas included; (2) Excludes Basque
Source: U.S. Census Bureau, 2010-2012 American Community Survey 3-Year Estimates

Foreign-Born Population

Area	Any Foreign Country	Mexico	Asia	Europe	Carribean	South America	Central America[2]	Africa	Canada
City	10.9	1.6	3.8	0.9	0.5	0.5	0.4	3.1	0.1
MSA[1]	7.0	0.9	2.7	0.8	0.2	0.3	0.3	1.6	0.2
U.S.	13.0	3.7	3.7	1.6	1.2	0.9	1.0	0.5	0.3

Note: (1) Figures cover the Columbus, OH Metropolitan Statistical Area—see Appendix B for areas included; (2) Excludes Mexico.
Source: U.S. Census Bureau, 2010-2012 American Community Survey 3-Year Estimates

Marital Status

Area	Never Married	Now Married[2]	Separated	Widowed	Divorced
City	43.2	36.8	2.6	4.5	12.8
MSA[1]	33.4	47.8	2.0	5.0	11.9
U.S.	32.4	48.4	2.2	6.0	11.0

Note: Figures are percentages and cover the population 15 years of age and older; (1) Figures cover the Columbus, OH Metropolitan Statistical Area—see Appendix B for areas included; (2) Excludes separated
Source: U.S. Census Bureau, 2010-2012 American Community Survey 3-Year Estimates

Age

Area	Under Age 5	Age 5–19	Age 20–34	Age 35–44	Age 45–54	Age 55–64	Age 65–74	Age 75–84	Age 85+	Median Age
City	7.7	18.8	29.2	13.6	12.2	9.8	4.9	2.7	1.2	31.7
MSA[1]	6.8	20.4	22.2	14.0	14.2	11.4	6.1	3.4	1.4	35.3
U.S.	6.4	20.1	20.5	13.1	14.3	12.2	7.3	4.2	1.8	37.3

Note: (1) Figures cover the Columbus, OH Metropolitan Statistical Area—see Appendix B for areas included
Source: U.S. Census Bureau, 2010-2012 American Community Survey 3-Year Estimates

Gender

Area	Males	Females	Males per 100 Females
City	389,045	410,312	94.8
MSA[1]	912,971	946,726	96.4
U.S.	153,276,055	158,333,314	96.8

Note: (1) Figures cover the Columbus, OH Metropolitan Statistical Area—see Appendix B for areas included
Source: U.S. Census Bureau, 2010-2012 American Community Survey 3-Year Estimates

Religious Groups by Family

Area	Catholic	Baptist	Non-Den.	Methodist[2]	Lutheran	LDS[3]	Pentecostal	Presbyterian[4]	Muslim[5]	Judaism
MSA[1]	11.8	5.3	3.6	4.7	2.4	0.7	2.0	2.0	0.8	0.5
U.S.	19.1	9.3	4.0	4.0	2.3	2.0	1.9	1.6	0.8	0.7

Note: Figures are the number of adherents as a percentage of the total population; (1) Figures cover the Columbus, OH Metropolitan Statistical Area—see Appendix B for areas included; (2) Methodist/Pietist; (3) Latter Day Saints; (4) Reformed; (5) Figures are estimates
Source: Association of Statisticians of American Religious Bodies, 2010 U.S. Religion Census: Religious Congregations & Membership Study

Religious Groups by Tradition

Area	Catholic	Evangelical Protestant	Mainline Protestant	Other Tradition	Black Protestant	Orthodox
MSA[1]	11.8	11.9	9.5	3.1	1.1	0.3
U.S.	19.1	16.2	7.3	4.3	1.6	0.3

Note: Figures are the number of adherents as a percentage of the total population; (1) Figures cover the Columbus, OH Metropolitan Statistical Area—see Appendix B for areas included
Source: Association of Statisticians of American Religious Bodies, 2010 U.S. Religion Census: Religious Congregations & Membership Study

ECONOMY

Gross Metropolitan Product

Area	2011	2012	2013	2014	Rank[2]
MSA[1]	95.3	99.7	102.1	106.7	32

Note: Figures are in billions of dollars; (1) Figures cover the Columbus, OH Metropolitan Statistical Area—see Appendix B for areas included; (2) Rank is based on 2014 data and ranges from 1 to 363
Source: The United States Conference of Mayors, U.S. Metro Economies: Outlook—Gross Metropolitan Product, with Metro Employment Projections, November 2013

Economic Growth

Area	2011 (%)	2012 (%)	2013 (%)	2014 (%)	Rank[2]
MSA[1]	2.9	2.7	1.1	2.5	149
U.S.	1.6	2.5	1.7	2.5	–

Note: Figures are real gross metropolitan product (GMP) growth rates and represent annual average percent change; (1) Figures cover the Columbus, OH Metropolitan Statistical Area—see Appendix B for areas included; (2) Rank is based on 2013 data and ranges from 1 to 363
Source: The United States Conference of Mayors, U.S. Metro Economies: Outlook—Gross Metropolitan Product, with Metro Employment Projections, November 2013

Metropolitan Area Exports

Area	2007	2008	2009	2010	2011	2012	Rank[2]
MSA[1]	3,489.3	3,881.8	2,872.7	3,554.4	4,327.5	5,488.6	48

Note: Figures are in millions of dollars; (1) Figures cover the Columbus, OH Metropolitan Statistical Area—see Appendix B for areas included; (2) Rank is based on 2012 data and ranges from 1 to 369
Source: U.S. Department of Commerce, International Trade Administration, Office of Trade & Industry Information, Manufacturing & Services, data extracted April 1, 2014

INCOME

Income

Area	Per Capita ($)	Median Household ($)	Average Household ($)
City	23,609	42,491	55,908
MSA[1]	28,259	53,717	71,707
U.S.	27,385	51,771	71,579

Note: (1) Figures cover the Columbus, OH Metropolitan Statistical Area—see Appendix B for areas included
Source: U.S. Census Bureau, 2010-2012 American Community Survey 3-Year Estimates

Household Income Distribution

Area	Percent of Households Earning							
	Under $15,000	$15,000 -24,999	$25,000 -34,999	$35,000 -49,999	$50,000 -74,999	$75,000 -99,000	$100,000 -149,999	$150,000 and up
City	17.3	12.2	11.8	15.3	18.9	10.8	9.3	4.5
MSA[1]	12.5	10.2	10.1	13.7	18.9	12.5	13.0	9.0
U.S.	13.1	11.0	10.5	13.7	18.1	11.9	12.5	9.1

Note: (1) Figures cover the Columbus, OH Metropolitan Statistical Area—see Appendix B for areas included
Source: U.S. Census Bureau, 2010-2012 American Community Survey 3-Year Estimates

Poverty Rate

Area	All Ages	Under 18 Years Old	18 to 64 Years Old	65 Years and Over
City	22.4	31.9	20.7	10.4
MSA[1]	15.3	21.0	14.6	7.0
U.S.	15.7	22.2	14.6	9.3

Note: Figures are percentage of people whose income during the past 12 months was below the poverty level;
(1) Figures cover the Columbus, OH Metropolitan Statistical Area—see Appendix B for areas included
Source: U.S. Census Bureau, 2010-2012 American Community Survey 3-Year Estimates

Personal Bankruptcy Filing Rate

Area	2008	2009	2010	2011	2012	2013
Franklin County	5.41	6.20	6.22	5.47	4.80	4.46
U.S.	3.53	4.61	4.97	4.37	3.76	3.29

Note: Numbers are per 1,000 population and include Chapter 7 and Chapter 13 filings
Source: Federal Deposit Insurance Corporation, Regional Economic Conditions, March 20, 2014

EMPLOYMENT

Labor Force and Employment

Area	Civilian Labor Force			Workers Employed		
	Dec. 2012	Dec. 2013	% Chg.	Dec. 2012	Dec. 2013	% Chg.
City	426,552	430,423	0.9	403,825	407,115	0.8
MSA[1]	967,106	975,987	0.9	915,289	922,747	0.8
U.S.	154,904,000	154,408,000	-0.3	143,060,000	144,423,000	1.0

Note: Data is not seasonally adjusted and covers workers 16 years of age and older; (1) Metropolitan Statistical Area—see Appendix B for areas included
Source: Bureau of Labor Statistics, Local Area Unemployment Statistics

Unemployment Rate

Area	2013											
	Jan.	Feb.	Mar.	Apr.	May	Jun.	Jul.	Aug.	Sep.	Oct.	Nov.	Dec.
City	6.8	6.3	6.1	5.7	6.0	6.4	6.3	6.1	6.5	6.2	6.1	5.4
MSA[1]	7.0	6.4	6.2	5.7	6.0	6.4	6.3	6.0	6.4	6.1	6.1	5.5
U.S.	8.5	8.1	7.6	7.1	7.3	7.8	7.7	7.3	7.0	7.0	6.6	6.5

Note: Data is not seasonally adjusted and covers workers 16 years of age and older; All figures are percentages;
(1) Metropolitan Statistical Area—see Appendix B for areas included
Source: Bureau of Labor Statistics, Local Area Unemployment Statistics

Employment by Occupation

Occupation Classification	City (%)	MSA[1] (%)	U.S. (%)
Management, Business, Science, and Arts	37.4	39.4	36.0
Natural Resources, Construction, and Maintenance	5.4	6.3	9.1
Production, Transportation, and Material Moving	11.2	11.3	12.0
Sales and Office	27.6	26.4	24.7
Service	18.4	16.5	18.2

Note: Figures cover employed civilians 16 years of age and older; (1) Figures cover the Columbus, OH
Metropolitan Statistical Area—see Appendix B for areas included
Source: U.S. Census Bureau, 2010-2012 American Community Survey 3-Year Estimates

Employment by Industry

Sector	MSA[1]		U.S.
	Number of Employees	Percent of Total	Percent of Total
Construction	n/a	n/a	4.2
Education and Health Services	138,800	14.0	15.5
Financial Activities	75,500	7.6	5.7
Government	165,900	16.7	16.1
Information	18,300	1.8	1.9
Leisure and Hospitality	97,500	9.8	10.2
Manufacturing	67,300	6.8	8.7
Mining and Logging	n/a	n/a	0.6
Other Services	37,600	3.8	3.9
Professional and Business Services	164,200	16.5	13.7
Retail Trade	106,100	10.7	11.4
Transportation and Utilities	49,200	5.0	3.8
Wholesale Trade	40,100	4.0	4.2

Note: Figures cover non-farm employment as of December 2013 and are not seasonally adjusted;
(1) Metropolitan Statistical Area—see Appendix B for areas included; n/a not available
Source: Bureau of Labor Statistics, Current Employment Statistics, Employment, Hours, and Earnings

Occupations with Greatest Projected Employment Growth: 2010 – 2020

Occupation[1]	2010 Employment	2020 Projected Employment	Numeric Employment Change	Percent Employment Change
Home Health Aides	71,140	110,490	39,360	55.3
Registered Nurses	126,130	152,380	26,260	20.8
Combined Food Preparation and Serving Workers, Including Fast Food	142,570	160,140	17,580	12.3
Retail Salespersons	156,370	170,890	14,530	9.3
Medical Secretaries	39,140	51,780	12,640	32.3
Office Clerks, General	105,750	117,610	11,860	11.2
Heavy and Tractor-Trailer Truck Drivers	67,070	78,510	11,440	17.1
Laborers and Freight, Stock, and Material Movers, Hand	97,960	109,350	11,390	11.6
Nursing Aides, Orderlies, and Attendants	75,590	85,550	9,950	13.2
Personal Care Aides	15,590	23,150	7,570	48.5

Note: Projections cover Ohio; (1) Sorted by numeric employment change
Source: www.projectionscentral.com, State Occupational Projections, 2010–2020 Long-Term Projections

Fastest Growing Occupations: 2010 – 2020

Occupation[1]	2010 Employment	2020 Projected Employment	Numeric Employment Change	Percent Employment Change
Gaming Managers	10	110	100	1,428.6
Gaming Cage Workers	30	190	170	589.3
Gaming and Sports Book Writers and Runners	230	470	240	102.6
Home Health Aides	71,140	110,490	39,360	55.3
Biomedical Engineers	300	470	160	53.0
Personal Care Aides	15,590	23,150	7,570	48.5
Helpers—Carpenters	660	980	320	47.9
Veterinary Technologists and Technicians	2,260	3,240	980	43.2
Helpers—Brickmasons, Blockmasons, Stonemasons, and Tile and Marble Setters	810	1,150	350	43.1
Meeting, Convention, and Event Planners	1,710	2,370	660	38.4

Note: Projections cover Ohio; (1) Sorted by percent employment change and excludes occupations with numeric employment change less than 100
Source: www.projectionscentral.com, State Occupational Projections, 2010–2020 Long-Term Projections

Average Wages

Occupation	$/Hr.	Occupation	$/Hr.
Accountants and Auditors	32.32	Maids and Housekeeping Cleaners	9.76
Automotive Mechanics	18.75	Maintenance and Repair Workers	18.14
Bookkeepers	20.46	Marketing Managers	63.14
Carpenters	21.36	Nuclear Medicine Technologists	31.93
Cashiers	9.64	Nurses, Licensed Practical	20.13
Clerks, General Office	14.62	Nurses, Registered	30.64
Clerks, Receptionists/Information	12.91	Nursing Assistants	12.13
Clerks, Shipping/Receiving	13.64	Packers and Packagers, Hand	11.04
Computer Programmers	34.99	Physical Therapists	36.90
Computer Systems Analysts	38.04	Postal Service Mail Carriers	24.08
Computer User Support Specialists	24.30	Real Estate Brokers	34.29
Cooks, Restaurant	11.15	Retail Salespersons	12.03
Dentists	91.49	Sales Reps., Exc. Tech./Scientific	29.62
Electrical Engineers	35.80	Sales Reps., Tech./Scientific	36.19
Electricians	22.13	Secretaries, Exc. Legal/Med./Exec.	16.87
Financial Managers	60.47	Security Guards	12.43
First-Line Supervisors/Managers, Sales	18.15	Surgeons	119.77
Food Preparation Workers	10.62	Teacher Assistants	13.10
General and Operations Managers	53.60	Teachers, Elementary School	29.10
Hairdressers/Cosmetologists	12.27	Teachers, Secondary School	29.90
Internists	87.91	Telemarketers	11.74
Janitors and Cleaners	11.87	Truck Drivers, Heavy/Tractor-Trailer	19.02
Landscaping/Groundskeeping Workers	11.91	Truck Drivers, Light/Delivery Svcs.	16.63
Lawyers	55.29	Waiters and Waitresses	9.37

Note: Wage data covers the Columbus, OH Metropolitan Statistical Area—see Appendix B for areas included. Hourly wages for elementary/secondary school teachers and teacher assistants were calculated by the editors from annual wage data assuming a 40 hour work week; n/a not available.
Source: Bureau of Labor Statistics, Metro Area Occupational Employment and Wage Estimates, May 2013

RESIDENTIAL REAL ESTATE

Building Permits

Area	Single-Family			Multi-Family			Total		
	2012	2013	Pct. Chg.	2012	2013	Pct. Chg.	2012	2013	Pct. Chg.
City	723	770	6.5	3,286	3,565	8.5	4,009	4,335	8.1
MSA[1]	2,913	3,495	20.0	3,898	4,868	24.9	6,811	8,363	22.8
U.S.	518,695	620,802	19.7	310,963	370,020	19.0	829,658	990,822	19.4

Note: (1) Metropolitan Statistical Area—see Appendix B for areas included; figures represent new, privately-owned housing units authorized (unadjusted data); All permit data are based on estimates with imputation.
Source: U.S. Census Bureau, Manufacturing, Mining, and Construction Statistics, Building Permits, 2012, 2013

Homeownership Rate

Area	2006 (%)	2007 (%)	2008 (%)	2009 (%)	2010 (%)	2011 (%)	2012 (%)	2013 (%)
MSA[1]	65.8	66.1	61.2	61.5	62.2	59.7	60.7	60.5
U.S.	68.8	68.1	67.8	67.4	66.9	66.1	65.4	65.1

Note: (1) Figures cover the Columbus, OH Metropolitan Statistical Area—see Appendix B for areas included
Source: U.S. Census Bureau, Housing Vacancies and Homeownership Annual Statistics: 2013

Housing Vacancy Rates

Area	Gross Vacancy Rate[2] (%)			Year-Round Vacancy Rate[3] (%)			Rental Vacancy Rate[4] (%)			Homeowner Vacancy Rate[5] (%)		
	2011	2012	2013	2011	2012	2013	2011	2012	2013	2011	2012	2013
MSA[1]	11.8	13.7	9.8	11.7	13.7	9.8	8.2	8.3	6.3	3.2	2.3	1.1
U.S.	14.2	13.8	13.8	11.1	10.8	10.7	9.5	8.7	8.3	2.5	2.0	2.0

Note: (1) Figures cover the Columbus, OH Metropolitan Statistical Area—see Appendix B for areas included; (2) The percentage of the total housing inventory that is vacant; (3) The percentage of the housing inventory (excluding seasonal units) that is year-round vacant; (4) The percentage of rental inventory that is vacant for rent; (5) The percentage of homeowner inventory that is vacant for sale
Source: U.S. Census Bureau, Housing Vacancies and Homeownership Annual Statistics: 2013

TAXES

State Corporate Income Tax Rates

State	Tax Rate (%)	Income Brackets ($)	Num. of Brackets	Financial Institution Tax Rate (%)[a]	Federal Income Tax Ded.
Ohio	(u)	–	–	(u)	No

Note: Tax rates as of January 1, 2014; (a) Rates listed are the corporate income tax rate applied to financial institutions or excise taxes based on income. Some states have other taxes based upon the value of deposits or shares; (u) Ohio no longer levies a tax based on income (except for a particular subset of corporations), but instead imposes a Commercial Activity Tax (CAT) equal to $150 for gross receipts sitused to Ohio of between $150,000 and $1 million, plus 0.26% of gross receipts over $1 million. Banks continue to pay a franchise tax of 1.3% of net worth. For those few corporations for whom the franchise tax on net worth or net income still applies, a litter tax also applies.
Source: Federation of Tax Administrators, "State Corporate Income Tax Rates, 2014"

State Individual Income Tax Rates

State	Tax Rate (%)	Income Brackets ($)	Num. of Brackets	Personal Exempt. ($)[1] Single	Personal Exempt. ($)[1] Dependents	Fed. Inc. Tax Ded.
Ohio (a)	0.534 - 5.392	5,000 - 200,000	9	1,700 (r)	1,700 (r)	No

Note: Tax rates as of January 1, 2014; Local- and county-level taxes are not included; n/a not applicable; (1) Married joint filers generally receive double the single exemption; (a) 17 states have statutory provision for automatically adjusting to the rate of inflation the dollar values of the income tax brackets, standard deductions, and/or personal exemptions. Massachusetts, Michigan, and Nebraska index the personal exemptiononly. Oregon does not index the income brackets for $125,000 and over. Maine has suspended indexing for 2014 and 2015; (r) Ohio provides an additional tax credit of $20 per exemption.
Source: Federation of Tax Administrators, "State Individual Income Tax Rates, 2014"

Various State and Local Tax Rates

State	State and Local Sales and Use (%)	State Sales and Use (%)	Gasoline[1] (¢/gal.)	Cigarette[2] ($/pack)	Spirits[3] ($/gal.)	Wine[4] ($/gal.)	Beer[5] ($/gal.)
Ohio	7.5	5.75	28.00	1.250	9.32 (g)	0.32	0.18

Note: All tax rates as of January 1, 2014; (1) The American Petroleum Institute has developed a methodology for determining the average tax rate on a gallon of fuel. Rates may include any of the following: excise taxes, environmental fees, storage tank fees, other fees or taxes, general sales tax, and local taxes. In states where gasoline is subject to the general sales tax, or where the fuel tax is based on the average sale price, the average rate determined by API is sensitive to changes in the price of gasoline. States that fully or partially apply general sales taxes to gasoline: CA, CO, GA, IL, IN, MI, NY; (2) The federal excise tax of $1.0066 per pack and local taxes are not included; (3) Rates are those applicable to off-premise sales of 40% alcohol by volume (a.b.v.) distilled spirits in 750ml containers. Local excise taxes are excluded; (4) Rates are those applicable to off-premise sales of 11% a.b.v. non-carbonated wine in 750ml containers; (5) Rates are those applicable to off-premise sales of 4.7% a.b.v. beer in 12 ounce containers; (g) States where the government controls sales. In these "control states," products are subject to ad valorem mark-up and excise taxes. The excise tax rate is calculated using a methodology developed by the Distilled Spirits Council of the United States.
Source: Tax Foundation, 2014 Facts & Figures: How Does Your State Compare?

State Business Tax Climate Index Rankings

State	Overall Rank	Corporate Tax Index Rank	Individual Income Tax Index Rank	Sales Tax Index Rank	Unemployment Insurance Tax Index Rank	Property Tax Index Rank
Ohio	39	23	44	30	10	20

Note: The index is a measure of how each state's tax laws affect economic performance. The lower the rank, the more favorable a state's tax system is for business. States without a given tax are given a ranking of 1. The scores/rankings for the District of Columbia do not affect other states. The 2014 index represents the tax climate as of July 1, 2013.
Source: Tax Foundation, State Business Tax Climate Index 2014

COMMERCIAL REAL ESTATE

Office Market

Market Area	Inventory (sq. ft.)	Vacancy Rate (%)	Under Construction (sq. ft.)	YTD Net Absorption (sq. ft.)	Total Average Asking Rent ($/sq. ft./year)
Columbus	53,358,865	12.9	621,323	1,199,057	16.28
National	4,726,900,879	15.0	55,419,286	42,829,434	26.27

Source: Newmark Grubb Knight Frank, National Office Market Report, 4th Quarter 2013

Industrial/Warehouse/R&D Market

Market Area	Inventory (sq. ft.)	Vacancy Rate (%)	Under Construction (sq. ft.)	YTD Net Absorption (sq. ft.)	Total Average Asking Rent ($/sq. ft./year)
Columbus	255,552,600	7.8	4,037,280	5,568,848	2.91
National	14,022,031,238	7.9	83,249,164	156,549,903	5.40

Source: Newmark Grubb Knight Frank, National Industrial Market Report, 4th Quarter 2013

COMMERCIAL UTILITIES

Typical Monthly Electric Bills

Area	Commercial Service ($/month)		Industrial Service ($/month)	
	1,500 kWh	40 kW demand 14,000 kWh	1,000 kW demand 200,000 kWh	50,000 kW demand 15,000,000 kWh
City	213	1,823	27,224	1,056,285
Average[1]	197	1,636	25,662	1,485,307

Note: Based on total rates in effect July 1, 2013; (1) average based on 180 utilities surveyed
Source: Edison Electric Institute, Typical Bills and Average Rates Report, Summer 2013

TRANSPORTATION

Means of Transportation to Work

Area	Car/Truck/Van Drove Alone	Car-pooled	Bus	Subway	Railroad	Bicycle	Walked	Other Means	Worked at Home
City	80.3	8.6	3.0	0.0	0.0	0.7	3.0	1.0	3.4
MSA[1]	82.4	8.0	1.6	0.0	0.0	0.4	2.2	0.9	4.4
U.S.	76.4	9.7	2.6	1.7	0.5	0.6	2.8	1.3	4.3

Note: Figures are percentages and cover workers 16 years of age and older; (1) Figures cover the Columbus, OH Metropolitan Statistical Area—see Appendix B for areas included
Source: U.S. Census Bureau, 2010-2012 American Community Survey 3-Year Estimates

Travel Time to Work

Area	Less Than 10 Minutes	10 to 19 Minutes	20 to 29 Minutes	30 to 44 Minutes	45 to 59 Minutes	60 to 89 Minutes	90 Minutes or More
City	10.3	34.7	30.7	18.6	2.8	1.7	1.2
MSA[1]	12.2	30.3	27.0	21.3	5.3	2.5	1.3
U.S.	13.5	29.8	20.9	20.1	7.5	5.6	2.5

Note: Figures are percentages and include workers 16 years old and over; (1) Figures cover the Columbus, OH Metropolitan Statistical Area—see Appendix B for areas included
Source: U.S. Census Bureau, 2010-2012 American Community Survey 3-Year Estimates

Travel Time Index

Area	1985	1990	1995	2000	2005	2010	2011
Urban Area[1]	1.03	1.08	1.13	1.15	1.18	1.18	1.18
Average[2]	1.09	1.14	1.16	1.19	1.23	1.18	1.18

Note: Travel Time Index—the ratio of travel time in the peak period to the travel time at free-flow conditions. For example, a value of 1.30 indicates a 20-minute free-flow trip takes 26 minutes in the peak. Free-flow speeds (60 mph on freeways and 35 mph on principal arterials) are used as the comparison threshold; (1) Covers the Columbus OH urban area; (2) average of 498 urban areas
Source: Texas Transportation Institute, Urban Mobility Report 2012, December 2012

Public Transportation

Agency Name / Mode of Transportation	Vehicles Operated in Maximum Service	Annual Unlinked Passenger Trips (in thous.)	Annual Passenger Miles (in thous.)
Central Ohio Transit Authority (COTA)			
Bus (directly operated)	257	18,423.4	70,809.4
Demand Response (purchased transportation)	68	269.0	2,696.1

Source: Federal Transit Administration, National Transit Database, 2012

Air Transportation

Airport Name and Code / Type of Service	Passenger Airlines[1]	Passenger Enplanements	Freight Carriers[2]	Freight (lbs.)
Port Columbus International (CMH)				
Domestic service (U.S. carriers - 2013)	30	3,041,249	16	3,090,717
International service (U.S. carriers - 2012)	8	1,795	2	20,015

Note: (1) Includes all U.S.-based major, minor and commuter airlines that carried at least one passenger during the year; (2) Includes all U.S.-based airlines and freight carriers that transported at least one lb. of freight during the year.
Source: Bureau of Transportation Statistics, The Intermodal Transportation Database, Air Carriers: T-100 Domestic Market (U.S. Carriers), 2013; Bureau of Transportation Statistics, The Intermodal Transportation Database, Air Carriers: T-100 International Market (U.S. Carriers), 2012

Other Transportation Statistics

Major Highways:	I-70; I-71
Amtrak Service:	Bus connection
Major Waterways/Ports:	None

Source: Amtrak.com; Google Maps

BUSINESSES

Major Business Headquarters

Company Name	Rankings	
	Fortune[1]	Forbes[2]
American Electric Power	185	-
Big Lots	466	-
L Brands	258	-
Momentive Performance Materials Holdings	-	49
Nationwide	100	-

Note: (1) Fortune 500—companies that produce a 10-K are ranked 1 to 500 based on 2012 revenue; (2) all private companies with at least $2 billion in annual revenue through the end of their most current fiscal year are ranked 1 to 224; companies listed are headquartered in the city; dashes indicate no ranking Source: Fortune, "Fortune 500," May 20, 2013; Forbes, "America's Largest Private Companies," December 18, 2013

Fast-Growing Businesses

According to *Inc.*, Columbus is home to two of America's 500 fastest-growing private companies: **Vertex Body Sciences** (#19); **Plug Smart** (#290). Criteria: must be an independent, privately-held, for-profit, U.S. corporation, proprietorship or partnership; revenues must be at least $100,000 in 2009 and $2 million in 2012; must have four-year operating/sales history. Holding companies, regulated banks, and utilities were excluded. *Inc., "America's 500 Fastest-Growing Private Companies," September 2013*

According to *Initiative for a Competitive Inner City (ICIC)*, Columbus is home to one of America's 100 fastest-growing "inner city" companies: **Navigator Management Partners** (#33). Companies were ranked by their five-year compound annual growth rate. Criteria for inclusion: company must be headquartered in or have 51 percent or more of its physical operations in an economically distressed urban area; must be an independent, for-profit corporation, partnership or proprietorship; must have 10 or more employees and have a five-year sales history that includes sales of at least $200,000 in the base year and at least $1 million in the current year with no decrease in sales over the two most recent years. *Initiative for a Competitive Inner City (ICIC), "Inner City 100 Companies, 2013"*

Minority Business Opportunity

Columbus is home to three companies which are on the *Black Enterprise* Industrial/Service 100 list (100 largest companies based on gross sales): **Miles-McClellan Construction Co.** (#61); **IAP Government Services Group** (#83); **Moody Nolan** (#89). Criteria: operational in previous calendar year; at least 51% black-owned and manufactures/owns the product it sells or provides industrial or consumer services. Brokerages, real estate firms and firms that provide professional services are not eligible. *Black Enterprise, B.E. 100s, 2013*

Minority- and Women-Owned Businesses

Group	All Firms		Firms with Paid Employees			
	Firms	Sales ($000)	Firms	Sales ($000)	Employees	Payroll ($000)
Asian	2,147	719,988	680	671,731	7,200	188,801
Black	9,464	663,434	443	488,398	4,642	130,328
Hispanic	1,380	310,528	117	257,723	919	40,257
Women	18,952	2,240,978	1,619	1,820,661	20,898	489,712
All Firms	56,954	120,659,673	12,404	118,921,486	482,279	18,614,103

Note: Figures cover firms located in the city; minority- and women-owned business are defined as firms in which the corresponding group own 51% or more of the stock or equity of the company
Source: U.S. Census Bureau, 2007 Economic Census, Survey of Business Owners (2012 Survey of Business Owners data will be released starting in June 2015)

HOTELS & CONVENTION CENTERS

Hotels/Motels

Area	5 Star		4 Star		3 Star		2 Star		1 Star		Not Rated	
	Num.	Pct.[3]	Num.	Pct.[3]	Num.	Pct.[3]	Num.	Pct.[3]	Num.	Pct.[3]	Num.	Pct.[3]
City[1]	0	0.0	5	2.5	56	28.3	108	54.5	10	5.1	19	9.6
Total[2]	142	0.9	1,005	6.0	5,147	30.9	8,578	51.4	408	2.4	1,397	8.4

Note: (1) Figures cover Columbus and vicinity; (2) Figures cover all 100 cities in this book; (3) Percentage of hotels which have a given star rating; Star ratings are determined by expedia.com and offer an indication of the general quality of a particular hotel.
Source: expedia.com, April 7, 2014

Major Convention Centers

Name	Overall Space (sq. ft.)	Exhibit Space (sq. ft.)	Meeting Space (sq. ft.)	Meeting Rooms
Greater Columbus Convention Center	1,700,000	426,000	90,943	61

Note: Table includes convention centers located in the Columbus, OH metro area; n/a not available
Source: Original research

Living Environment

COST OF LIVING

Cost of Living Index

Composite Index	Groceries	Housing	Utilities	Trans- portation	Health Care	Misc. Goods/ Services
86.9	86.5	77.1	96.4	96.2	95.1	87.2

Note: The Cost of Living Index measures regional differences in the cost of consumer goods and services, excluding taxes and non-consumer expenditures, for professional and managerial households in the top income quintile. It is based on more than 50,000 prices covering almost 60 different items for which prices are collected three times a year by chambers of commerce, economic development organizations or university applied economic centers in each participating urban area. The numbers shown should be read as a percentage above or below the national average of 100. For example, a value of 115.4 in the groceries column indicates that grocery prices are 15.4% higher than the national average. Small differences in the index numbers should not be interpreted as significant; Figures cover the Columbus OH urban area.
Source: The Council for Community and Economic Research, ACCRA Cost of Living Index, 2013

Grocery Prices

Area[1]	T-Bone Steak ($/pound)	Frying Chicken ($/pound)	Whole Milk ($/half gal.)	Eggs ($/dozen)	Orange Juice ($/64 oz.)	Coffee ($/11.5 oz.)
City[2]	10.70	1.11	1.99	1.74	3.27	4.70
Avg.	10.19	1.28	2.34	1.81	3.48	4.39
Min.	8.56	0.94	1.44	1.19	2.78	3.40
Max.	14.82	2.28	3.56	3.73	6.23	7.32

Note: (1) Values for the local area are compared with the average, minimum and maximum values for all 327 areas in the Cost of Living Index; (2) Figures cover the Columbus OH urban area; **T-Bone Steak** *(price per pound);* **Frying Chicken** *(price per pound, whole fryer);* **Whole Milk** *(half gallon carton);* **Eggs** *(price per dozen, Grade A, large);* **Orange Juice** *(64 oz. Tropicana or Florida Natural);* **Coffee** *(11.5 oz. can, vacuum-packed, Maxwell House, Hills Bros, or Folgers).*
Source: The Council for Community and Economic Research, ACCRA Cost of Living Index, 2013

Housing and Utility Costs

Area[1]	New Home Price ($)	Apartment Rent ($/month)	All Electric ($/month)	Part Electric ($/month)	Other Energy ($/month)	Telephone ($/month)
City[2]	217,589	784	-	90.95	61.53	27.99
Avg.	295,864	900	171.38	91.82	70.12	27.73
Min.	185,506	458	117.80	48.81	33.67	17.16
Max.	1,358,917	3,783	441.68	171.40	372.65	39.47

Note: (1) Values for the local area are compared with the average, minimum and maximum values for all 327 areas in the Cost of Living Index; (2) Figures cover the Columbus OH urban area; **New Home Price** *(2,400 sf living area, 8,000 sf lot, in urban area with full utilities);* **Apartment Rent** *(950 sf 2 bedroom/1.5 or 2 bath, unfurnished, excluding all utilities except water);* **All Electric** *(average monthly cost for an all-electric home);* **Part Electric** *(average monthly cost for a part-electric home);* **Other Energy** *(average monthly cost for natural gas, fuel oil, coal, wood, and any other forms of energy except electricity);* **Telephone** *(price includes basic monthly rate for a private residential line plus additional local usage charges incurred by a family of four).*
Source: The Council for Community and Economic Research, ACCRA Cost of Living Index, 2013

Health Care, Transportation, and Other Costs

Area[1]	Doctor ($/visit)	Dentist ($/visit)	Optometrist ($/visit)	Gasoline ($/gallon)	Beauty Salon ($/visit)	Men's Shirt ($)
City[2]	99.04	79.19	63.62	3.39	35.40	24.51
Avg.	101.40	86.48	96.16	3.44	33.87	26.55
Min.	61.67	50.83	50.12	3.08	18.92	12.48
Max.	182.71	152.50	223.78	4.33	68.22	52.03

Note: (1) Values for the local area are compared with the average, minimum and maximum values for all 327 areas in the Cost of Living Index; (2) Figures cover the Columbus OH urban area; **Doctor** *(general practitioners routine exam of an established patient);* **Dentist** *(adult teeth cleaning and periodic oral examination);* **Optometrist** *(full vision eye exam for established adult patient);* **Gasoline** *(one gallon regular unleaded, national brand, including all taxes, cash price at self-service pump if available);* **Beauty Salon** *(woman's shampoo, trim, and blow-dry);* **Men's Shirt** *(cotton/polyester dress shirt, pinpoint weave, long sleeves).*
Source: The Council for Community and Economic Research, ACCRA Cost of Living Index, 2013

HOUSING

House Price Index (HPI)

Area	National Ranking[2]	Quarterly Change (%)	One-Year Change (%)	Five-Year Change (%)
MSA[1]	125	0.05	2.90	-2.47
U.S.[3]	–	1.20	7.69	4.18

Note: The HPI is a weighted repeat sales index. It measures average price changes in repeat sales or refinancings on the same properties. This information is obtained by reviewing repeat mortgage transactions on single-family properties whose mortgages have been purchased or securitized by Fannie Mae or Freddie Mac in January 1975; (1) Columbus, OH Metropolitan Statistical Area—see Appendix B for areas included; (2) Rankings are based on annual percentage change for all metro areas containing at least 15,000 transactions over the last 10 years and ranges from 1 to 283; (3) figures based on a weighted average of Census Division estimates using a seasonally adjusted, purchase-only index; all figures are for the period ending December 31, 2013
Source: Federal Housing Finance Agency, House Price Index, February 25, 2014

Median Single-Family Home Prices

Area	2011	2012	2013p	Percent Change 2012 to 2013
MSA[1]	123.9	136.5	142.8	4.6
U.S. Average	166.2	177.2	197.4	11.4

Note: Figures are median sales prices of existing single-family homes in thousands of dollars; (p) preliminary; n/a not available; (1) Columbus, OH Metropolitan Statistical Area—see Appendix B for areas included
Source: National Association of Realtors, Median Sales Price of Existing Single-Family Homes for Metropolitan Areas, 4th Quarter 2013

Qualifying Income Based on Median Sales Price of Existing Single-Family Homes

Area	With 5% Down ($)	With 10% Down ($)	With 20% Down ($)
MSA[1]	31,355	29,705	26,404
U.S. Average	45,395	43,006	38,228

Note: Figures are preliminary; Qualifying income is based on a mortgage rate of 4.4%. Monthly principal and interest payment is limited to 25% of income; n/a not available; (1) Columbus, OH Metropolitan Statistical Area—see Appendix B for areas included
Source: National Association of Realtors, Qualifying Income Based on Median Sales Price of Existing Single-Family Homes for Metropolitan Areas, 4th Quarter 2013

Median Apartment Condo-Coop Home Prices

Area	2011	2012	2013p	Percent Change 2012 to 2013
MSA[1]	106.0	111.8	118.8	6.3
U.S. Average	165.1	173.7	194.9	12.2

Note: Figures are median sales prices of existing apartment condo-coop homes in thousands of dollars; (p) preliminary; n/a not available; (1) Columbus, OH Metropolitan Statistical Area—see Appendix B for areas included
Source: National Association of Realtors, Median Sales Price of Existing Apartment Condo-Coop Homes for Metropolitan Areas, 4th Quarter 2013

Gross Monthly Rent

Area	Under $200	$200 -299	$300 -499	$500 -749	$750 -999	$1,000 -1,499	$1,500 and up	Median ($)
City	2.0	2.4	6.5	32.0	33.5	19.5	4.1	792
MSA[1]	1.8	2.4	7.3	31.3	32.9	19.4	5.0	794
U.S.	1.7	3.3	8.1	22.7	24.3	25.7	14.3	889

Note: Figures are percentages except for Median; Gross rent is the contract rent plus the estimated average monthly cost of utilities (electricity, gas, and water and sewer) and fuels (oil, coal, kerosene, wood, etc.) if these are paid by the renter (or paid for the renter by someone else); (1) Figures cover the Columbus, OH Metropolitan Statistical Area—see Appendix B for areas included
Source: U.S. Census Bureau, 2010-2012 American Community Survey 3-Year Estimates

Year Housing Structure Built

Area	2010 or Later	2000 -2009	1990 -1999	1980 -1989	1970 -1979	1960 -1969	1950 -1959	1940 -1949	Before 1940	Median Year
City	0.4	12.4	15.7	13.3	14.8	13.5	11.7	5.3	12.9	1974
MSA[1]	0.4	15.5	17.0	11.9	14.6	12.5	11.0	4.5	12.7	1976
U.S.	0.5	14.9	13.8	13.9	15.9	11.1	10.9	5.5	13.5	1976

Note: Figures are percentages except for Median Year; (1) Figures cover the Columbus, OH Metropolitan Statistical Area—see Appendix B for areas included
Source: U.S. Census Bureau, 2010-2012 American Community Survey 3-Year Estimates

HEALTH

Health Risk Data

Category	MSA[1] (%)	U.S. (%)
Adults aged 18–64 who have any kind of health care coverage	82.9	79.6
Adults who reported being in good or excellent health	84.6	83.1
Adults who are current smokers	20.0	19.6
Adults who are heavy drinkers[2]	6.1	6.1
Adults who are binge drinkers[3]	17.7	16.9
Adults who are overweight (BMI 25.0 - 29.9)	33.0	35.8
Adults who are obese (BMI 30.0 - 99.8)	30.6	27.6
Adults who participated in any physical activities in the past month	77.2	77.1
Adults 50+ who have ever had a sigmoidoscopy or colonoscopy	67.4	67.3
Women aged 40+ who have had a mammogram within the past two years	78.3	74.0
Men aged 40+ who have had a PSA test within the past two years	44.9	45.2
Adults aged 65+ who have had flu shot within the past year	67.4	60.1
Adults who always wear a seatbelt	90.2	93.8

Note: Data as of 2012 unless otherwise noted; (1) Figures cover the Columbus, OH Metropolitan Statistical Area—see Appendix B for areas included; (2) Heavy drinkers are classified as males having more than two drinks per day or females having more than one drink per day; (3) Binge drinkers are classified as males having five or more drinks on one occasion or females having four or more drinks on one occasion
Source: Centers for Disease Control and Prevention, Behaviorial Risk Factor Surveillance System, SMART: Selected Metropolitan/Micropolitan Area Risk Trends, 2012

Chronic Health Indicators

Category	MSA[1] (%)	U.S. (%)
Adults who have ever been told they had a heart attack	4.8	4.5
Adults who have ever been told they had a stroke	2.8	2.9
Adults who have been told they currently have asthma	9.3	8.9
Adults who have ever been told they have arthritis	27.4	25.7
Adults who have ever been told they have diabetes[2]	9.3	9.7
Adults who have ever been told they had skin cancer	5.7	5.7
Adults who have ever been told they had any other types of cancer	5.4	6.5
Adults who have ever been told they have COPD	6.7	6.2
Adults who have ever been told they have kidney disease	1.9	2.5
Adults who have ever been told they have a form of depression	18.5	18.0

Note: Data as of 2012 unless otherwise noted; (1) Figures cover the Columbus, OH Metropolitan Statistical Area—see Appendix B for areas included; (2) Figures do not include pregnancy-related, borderline, or pre-diabetes
Source: Centers for Disease Control and Prevention, Behaviorial Risk Factor Surveillance System, SMART: Selected Metropolitan/Micropolitan Area Risk Trends, 2012

Mortality Rates for the Top 10 Causes of Death in the U.S.

ICD-10[a] Sub-Chapter	ICD-10[a] Code	Age-Adjusted Mortality Rate[1] per 100,000 population	
		County[2]	U.S.
Malignant neoplasms	C00-C97	189.8	174.2
Ischaemic heart diseases	I20-I25	115.5	119.1
Other forms of heart disease	I30-I51	53.5	49.6
Chronic lower respiratory diseases	J40-J47	53.9	43.2
Cerebrovascular diseases	I60-I69	46.4	40.3
Organic, including symptomatic, mental disorders	F01-F09	47.8	30.5
Other degenerative diseases of the nervous system	G30-G31	27.9	26.3
Other external causes of accidental injury	W00-X59	29.6	25.1
Diabetes mellitus	E10-E14	24.2	21.3
Hypertensive diseases	I10-I15	21.9	18.8

Note: (a) ICD-10 = International Classification of Diseases 10th Revision; (1) Mortality rates are a three year average covering 2008-2010; (2) Figures cover Franklin County
Source: Centers for Disease Control and Prevention, National Center for Health Statistics. Compressed Mortality File 1999-2010 on CDC WONDER Online Database, released January 2013. Data are compiled from the Compressed Mortality File 1999-2010, Series 20 No. 2P, 2013.

Mortality Rates for Selected Causes of Death

ICD-10[a] Sub-Chapter	ICD-10[a] Code	Age-Adjusted Mortality Rate[1] per 100,000 population	
		County[2]	U.S.
Assault	X85-Y09	8.5	5.5
Diseases of the liver	K70-K76	12.7	12.4
Human immunodeficiency virus (HIV) disease	B20-B24	2.7	3.0
Influenza and pneumonia	J09-J18	19.8	16.4
Intentional self-harm	X60-X84	10.9	11.8
Malnutrition	E40-E46	1.7	0.8
Obesity and other hyperalimentation	E65-E68	2.0	1.6
Renal failure	N17-N19	13.9	13.6
Transport accidents	V01-V99	8.7	12.6
Viral hepatitis	B15-B19	1.5	2.2

Note: (a) ICD-10 = International Classification of Diseases 10th Revision; (1) Mortality rates are a three year average covering 2008-2010; (2) Figures cover Franklin County
Source: Centers for Disease Control and Prevention, National Center for Health Statistics. Compressed Mortality File 1999-2010 on CDC WONDER Online Database, released January 2013. Data are compiled from the Compressed Mortality File 1999-2010, Series 20 No. 2P, 2013.

Health Insurance Coverage

Area	With Health Insurance	With Private Health Insurance	With Public Health Insurance	Without Health Insurance	Population Under Age 18 Without Health Insurance
City	84.5	63.2	29.0	15.5	6.6
MSA[1]	88.3	71.4	26.4	11.7	5.0
U.S.	84.9	65.4	30.4	15.1	7.5

Note: Figures are percentages that cover the civilian noninstitutionalized population; (1) Figures cover the Columbus, OH Metropolitan Statistical Area—see Appendix B for areas included
Source: U.S. Census Bureau, 2010-2012 American Community Survey 3-Year Estimates

Number of Medical Professionals

Area[1]	MDs[2]	DOs[2,3]	Dentists	Podiatrists	Chiropractors	Optometrists
Local (number)	4,700	704	963	80	268	290
Local (rate[4])	398.5	59.7	80.5	6.7	22.4	24.2
U.S. (rate[4])	267.6	19.6	61.7	5.6	24.7	14.5

Note: Data as of 2012 unless noted; (1) Local data covers Franklin County; (2) Data as of 2011; (3) Doctor of Osteopathic Medicine; (4) rate per 100,000 population
Source: Area Resource File (ARF) 2012-2013. U.S. Department of Health and Human Services, Health Resources and Services Administration, Bureau of Health Professions

Best Hospitals

According to *U.S. News*, the Columbus, OH metro area is home to one of the best hospitals in the U.S.: **Ohio State University Wexner Medical Center** (10 specialties). The hospital listed was nationally ranked in at least one adult specialty. Only 147 hospitals nationwide were nationally ranked in one or more specialties. Eighteen hospitals in the U.S. made the Honor Roll by ranking near the top in at least six specialties.*U.S. News Online, "America's Best Hospitals 2013-14"*

According to *U.S. News*, the Columbus, OH metro area is home to one of the best children's hospitals in the U.S.: **Nationwide Children's Hospital**. The hospital listed was highly ranked in at least one pediatric specialty. Eighty-seven hospitals in the U.S. ranked in at least one specialty. Ten children's hospitals in the U.S. made the Honor Roll by ranking near the top in three or more specialties.*U.S. News Online, "America's Best Children's Hospitals 2013-14"*

EDUCATION

Public School District Statistics

District Name	Schls	Pupils	Pupil/ Teacher Ratio	Minority Pupils[1] (%)	Free Lunch Eligible[2] (%)	IEP[3] (%)
Columbus City SD	119	50,488	15.8	72.6	68.8	17.5
Electronic Classroom of Tomorrow	1	10,840	37.6	24.0	n/a	21.5
Hamilton Local	4	3,094	19.9	21.5	52.6	10.9

Note: Table includes school districts with 2,000 or more students; (1) Percentage of students that are not non-Hispanic white; (2) Percentage of students that are eligible for the free lunch program; (3) Percentage of students that have an Individualized Education Program.
Source: U.S. Department of Education, National Center for Education Statistics, Common Core of Data, Local Education Agency (School District) Universe Survey: School Year 2011-2012; U.S. Department of Education, National Center for Education Statistics, Common Core of Data, Public Elementary/Secondary School Universe Survey: School Year 2011-2012

Best High Schools

High School Name	Rank[1]	Grad. Rate[2] (%)	Coll.[3] (%)	AP/IB/ AICE Tests[4]	AP/IB/ AICE Score[5]	SAT Score[6]	ACT Score[6]
Columbus Alternative H.S.	1668	98	71	0.2	2.7	972	21.0
Eastmoor Academy H.S.	1962	93	86	0.1	1.6	n/a	18.0
Grandview Heights H.S.	564	97	98	0.2	3.5	1703	26.0
Worthington Kilbourne H.S.	1582	95	70	0.2	3.5	1727	25.0

Note: (1) Public schools are ranked from 1 to 2,000 based on the following self-reported statistics (with the corresponding weight used in calculating their overall score). Schools that were newly founded and did not have a graduating senior class in 2012 were excluded; (2) Four-year, on-time graduation rate (25%); (3) Percent of 2011 graduates who were accepted to college (25%); (4) AP/IB/AICE tests taken per student (25%); (5) Average AP/IB/AICE exam score (10%); (6) Average SAT and/or ACT score (10%); Percent of students enrolled in at least one AP/IB/AICE course (5%)—data not shown; n/a not available
Source: Newsweek and The Daily Beast, "America's Best High Schools 2013"

Highest Level of Education

Area	Less than H.S.	H.S. Diploma	Some College, No Deg.	Associate Degree	Bachelor's Degree	Master's Degree	Prof. School Degree	Doctorate Degree
City	11.7	26.7	22.3	6.9	21.4	7.7	1.8	1.4
MSA[1]	9.9	28.7	20.8	7.3	21.6	8.2	2.0	1.5
U.S.	14.1	28.3	21.3	7.8	18.0	7.5	1.9	1.2

Note: Figures cover persons age 25 and over; (1) Figures cover the Columbus, OH Metropolitan Statistical Area—see Appendix B for areas included
Source: U.S. Census Bureau, 2010-2012 American Community Survey 3-Year Estimates

Educational Attainment by Race

Area	High School Graduate or Higher (%)					Bachelor's Degree or Higher (%)				
	Total	White	Black	Asian	Hisp.[2]	Total	White	Black	Asian	Hisp.[2]
City	88.3	90.3	85.6	88.6	64.4	32.4	37.2	16.3	63.5	18.5
MSA[1]	90.1	91.3	85.9	90.2	69.2	33.3	34.7	18.9	67.2	21.8
U.S.	85.9	88.1	82.5	85.5	63.1	28.6	30.0	18.4	50.2	13.4

Note: Figures shown cover persons 25 years old and over; (1) Figures cover the Columbus, OH Metropolitan Statistical Area—see Appendix B for areas included; (2) People of Hispanic origin can be of any race
Source: U.S. Census Bureau, 2010-2012 American Community Survey 3-Year Estimates

School Enrollment by Grade and Control

Area	Preschool (%)		Kindergarten (%)		Grades 1 - 4 (%)		Grades 5 - 8 (%)		Grades 9 - 12 (%)	
	Public	Private	Public	Private	Public	Private	Public	Private	Public	Private
City	52.3	47.7	88.4	11.6	87.6	12.4	87.4	12.6	88.6	11.4
MSA[1]	47.8	52.2	86.4	13.6	88.3	11.7	88.2	11.8	89.8	10.2
U.S.	56.9	43.1	87.8	12.2	89.9	10.1	90.0	10.0	90.8	9.2

Note: Figures shown cover persons 3 years old and over; (1) Figures cover the Columbus, OH Metropolitan Statistical Area—see Appendix B for areas included
Source: U.S. Census Bureau, 2010-2012 American Community Survey 3-Year Estimates

Average Salaries of Public School Classroom Teachers

Area	2012-13		2013-14		Percent Change 2012-13 to 2013-14	Percent Change 2003-04 to 2013-14
	Dollars	Rank[1]	Dollars	Rank[1]		
Ohio	56,307	16	57,270	17	1.71	20.6
U.S. Average	56,103	–	56,689	–	1.04	21.8

Note: (1) State rank ranges from 1 to 51 where 1 indicates highest salary.
Source: National Education Association, Rankings & Estimates: Rankings of the States 2013 and Estimates of School Statistics 2014, March 2014

Higher Education

Four-Year Colleges			Two-Year Colleges			Medical Schools[1]	Law Schools[2]	Voc/ Tech[3]
Public	Private Non-profit	Private For-profit	Public	Private Non-profit	Private For-profit			
1	8	5	1	0	11	1	2	9

Note: Figures cover institutions located within the city limits and include main campuses only; (1) includes schools accredited by the Liaison Committee on Medical Education and the American Osteopathic Association's Commission on Osteopathic College Accreditation; (2) includes ABA-accredited schools, schools with provisional ABA accreditation, and state accredited schools; (3) includes all schools with programs that are less than 2 years.
Source: National Center for Education Statistics, Integrated Postsecondary Education System (IPEDS), 2012-13; Association of American Medical Colleges, Member List, April 24, 2014; American Osteopathic Association, Member List, April 24, 2014; Law School Admission Council, Official Guide to ABA-Approved Law Schools Online, April 24, 2014; Wikipedia, List of Medical Schools in the United States, April 24, 2014; Wikipedia, List of Law Schools in the United States, April 24, 2014

According to *U.S. News & World Report,* the Columbus, OH metro area is home to one of the best national universities in the U.S.: **Ohio State University–Columbus** (#52). The indicators used to capture academic quality fall into a number of categories: assessment by administrators at peer institutions; retention of students; faculty resources; student selectivity; financial resources; alumni giving; high school counselor ratings of colleges; and graduation rate. *U.S. News & World Report,* "America's Best Colleges 2014"

According to *U.S. News & World Report,* the Columbus, OH metro area is home to two of the best liberal arts colleges in the U.S.: **Denison University** (#50); **Ohio Wesleyan University** (#100). The indicators used to capture academic quality fall into a number of categories: assessment by administrators at peer institutions; retention of students; faculty resources; student selectivity; financial resources; alumni giving; high school counselor ratings of colleges; and graduation rate. *U.S. News & World Report,* "America's Best Colleges 2014"

According to *U.S. News & World Report,* the Columbus, OH metro area is home to one of the top 100 law schools in the U.S.: **Ohio State University (Moritz)** (#36). The rankings are based on a weighted average of 12 measures of quality: peer assessment score; assessment score by lawyers/judges; median LSAT scores; median undergrad GPA; acceptance rate; employment rates for graduates; placement success; bar passage rate; faculty resources; expenditures per student; student/faculty ratio; and library resources. *U.S. News & World Report,* "America's Best Graduate Schools, Law, 2014"

According to *U.S. News & World Report,* the Columbus, OH metro area is home to one of the top 100 business schools in the U.S.: **Ohio State University (Fisher)** (#27). The rankings are based on a weighted average of the following nine measures: quality assessment; peer assessment; recruiter assessment; placement success; mean starting salary and bonus; student selectivity; mean GMAT and GRE scores; mean undergraduate GPA; and acceptance rate. *U.S. News & World Report,* "America's Best Graduate Schools, Business, 2014"

**PRESIDENTIAL
ELECTION**

2012 Presidential Election Results

Area	Obama	Romney	Other
Franklin County	60.1	38.4	1.5
U.S.	51.0	47.2	1.8

Note: Results are percentages and may not add to 100% due to rounding
Source: Dave Leip's Atlas of U.S. Presidential Elections

EMPLOYERS

Major Employers

Company Name	Industry
Abbott Laboratories	Druggists' preparations (pharmaceuticals)
Banc One Services Corporation	Financial services
Battelle Memorial Institute	Noncommercial research organizations
Chase Manhattan Mortgage Corp.	Mortgage bankers and loan correspondents
Defense Finance & Accounting Svc	Accounting services, except auditing
Indiana Michigan Power Company	Electric services
JPMorgan Chase Bank, NA	State commercial banks
Liebert North America	Electrical equipment and supplies
Limited Brands	Women's clothing stores
MWH Americas	Engineering services
Nationwide Children's Hospital	Childrens' hospital
Nationwide Mutual Insurance Company	Fire, marine and casualty insurance
Ohio Bureau of Workers' Compensation	Workmen's compensation office, government
Safelite Solutions	Management consulting services
The Ohio State University	Colleges and universities
The Ohio State University Hospital	Medical centers

Note: Companies shown are located within the Columbus, OH Metropolitan Statistical Area.
Source: Hoovers.com; Wikipedia

Best Companies to Work For

OhioHealth, headquartered in Columbus, is among "The 100 Best Companies to Work For." To pick the 100 Best Companies to Work For, *Fortune* partnered with the Great Place to Work Institute. Two hundred fifty seven firms participated in this year's survey. Two-thirds of a company's score is based on the results of the Institute's Trust Index survey, which is sent to a random sample of employees from each company. The questions related to attitudes about management's credibility, job satisfaction, and camaraderie. The other third of the scoring is based on the company's responses to the Institute's Culture Audit, which includes detailed questions about pay and benefit programs, and a series of open-ended questions about hiring practices, internal communication, training, recognition programs, and diversity efforts. Any company that is at least five years old with more than 1,000 U.S. employees is eligible. *Fortune, "The 100 Best Companies to Work For," 2014*

Nationwide Mutual Insurance; OhioHealth, headquartered in Columbus, are among the "100 Best Places to Work in IT." To qualify, companies, both public and private, had to have a minimum of 50 IT employees and were selected based on average salary and bonus increases, the percentage of IT staffers promoted, IT staff turnover rates, training and development programs, and the percentage of women and minorities in IT staff and management positions. In addition, *Computerworld* looked at retention efforts, programs for recognizing and rewarding outstanding performances, and benefits such as flextime, elder care and child care, and reimbursement for college tuition and the cost of pursuing technology certifications. *Computerworld, "100 Best Places to Work in IT 2013"*

PUBLIC SAFETY

Crime Rate

Area	All Crimes	Violent Crimes				Property Crimes		
		Murder	Forcible Rape	Robbery	Aggrav. Assault	Burglary	Larceny -Theft	Motor Vehicle Theft
City	6,885.1	11.0	71.7	411.9	163.7	1,926.0	3,841.9	459.0
Suburbs[1]	2,783.7	1.6	24.5	49.9	64.8	593.9	1,979.6	69.3
Metro[2]	4,541.3	5.7	44.7	205.0	107.2	1,164.8	2,777.7	236.3
U.S.	3,292.5	4.7	27.0	113.9	241.5	701.3	1,974.1	230.0

Note: Figures are crimes per 100,000 population; (1) All areas within the metro area that are located outside the city limits; (2) Figures cover the Columbus, OH Metropolitan Statistical Area—see Appendix B for areas included
Source: FBI Uniform Crime Reports, 2011 (data for 2012 was not available)

Hate Crimes

Area	Number of Quarters Reported	Bias Motivation				
		Race	Religion	Sexual Orientation	Ethnicity	Disability
City	4	19	4	14	7	0
U.S.	4	2,797	1,099	1,135	667	92

Source: Federal Bureau of Investigation, Hate Crime Statistics 2012

Identity Theft Consumer Complaints

Area	Complaints	Complaints per 100,000 Population	Rank[2]
MSA[1]	1,250	65.7	164
U.S.	290,056	91.8	-

Note: (1) Figures cover the Columbus, OH Metropolitan Statistical Area—see Appendix B for areas included; (2) Rank ranges from 1 to 377 where 1 indicates greatest number of identity theft complaints per 100,000 population
Source: Federal Trade Commission, Consumer Sentinel Network Data Book for January–December 2013

Fraud and Other Consumer Complaints

Area	Complaints	Complaints per 100,000 Population	Rank[2]
MSA[1]	9,351	491.6	21
U.S.	1,811,724	595.2	-

Note: (1) Figures cover the Columbus, OH Metropolitan Statistical Area—see Appendix B for areas included; (2) Rank ranges from 1 to 377 where 1 indicates greatest number of identity theft complaints per 100,000 population
Source: Federal Trade Commission, Consumer Sentinel Network Data Book for January–December 2013

RECREATION

Culture

Dance[1]	Theatre[1]	Instrumental Music[1]	Vocal Music[1]	Series and Festivals	Museums and Art Galleries[2]	Zoos and Aquariums[3]
2	11	5	1	10	41	1

Note: (1) Number of professional perfoming groups; (2) Based on organizations with primary SIC code 8412; (3) AZA-accredited
Source: The Grey House Performing Arts Directory, 2013; Association of Zoos & Aquariums, AZA Member Zoos & Aquariums, April 2014; www.AccuLeads.com, May 1, 2014

Professional Sports Teams

Team Name	League	Year Established
Columbus Blue Jackets	National Hockey League (NHL)	2000
Columbus Crew	Major League Soccer (MLS)	1996

Note: Includes teams located in the Columbus, OH Metropolitan Statistical Area.
Source: Wikipedia, Major Professional Sports Teams of the United States and Canada

CLIMATE

Average and Extreme Temperatures

Temperature	Jan	Feb	Mar	Apr	May	Jun	Jul	Aug	Sep	Oct	Nov	Dec	Yr.
Extreme High (°F)	74	73	82	89	93	101	104	101	100	90	80	76	104
Average High (°F)	36	39	50	62	73	82	85	83	77	65	51	40	62
Average Temp. (°F)	28	31	41	52	62	70	74	73	66	54	43	32	52
Average Low (°F)	20	22	31	40	50	59	63	62	55	43	34	24	42
Extreme Low (°F)	-19	-13	-6	14	25	35	43	39	31	17	-4	-17	-19

Note: Figures cover the years 1948-1990
Source: National Climatic Data Center, International Station Meteorological Climate Summary, 9/96

Average Precipitation/Snowfall/Humidity

Precip./Humidity	Jan	Feb	Mar	Apr	May	Jun	Jul	Aug	Sep	Oct	Nov	Dec	Yr.
Avg. Precip. (in.)	2.8	2.4	3.1	3.3	3.9	4.0	4.3	3.3	2.7	2.1	3.0	2.8	37.9
Avg. Snowfall (in.)	8	6	5	1	Tr	0	0	0	Tr	Tr	2	6	28
Avg. Rel. Hum. 7am (%)	78	78	76	76	79	81	84	87	87	83	80	79	81
Avg. Rel. Hum. 4pm (%)	66	62	55	51	52	53	53	54	53	53	61	68	57

Note: Figures cover the years 1948-1990; Tr = Trace amounts (<0.05 in. of rain; <0.5 in. of snow)
Source: National Climatic Data Center, International Station Meteorological Climate Summary, 9/96

Weather Conditions

Temperature			Daytime Sky			Precipitation		
5°F & below	32°F & below	90°F & above	Clear	Partly cloudy	Cloudy	0.01 inch or more precip.	0.1 inch or more snow/ice	Thunder-storms
10	118	19	72	137	156	136	29	40

Note: Figures are average number of days per year and cover the years 1948-1990
Source: National Climatic Data Center, International Station Meteorological Climate Summary, 9/96

HAZARDOUS WASTE

Superfund Sites

Columbus has no sites on the EPA's Superfund Final National Priorities List.
U.S. Environmental Protection Agency, Final National Priorities List, April 26, 2014

AIR & WATER QUALITY

Air Quality Index

Area	Percent of Days when Air Quality was...[2]					AQI Statistics[2]	
	Good	Moderate	Unhealthy for Sensitive Groups	Unhealthy	Very Unhealthy	Maximum	Median
MSA[1]	66.6	32.9	0.5	0.0	0.0	114	43

Note: (1) Data covers the Columbus, OH Metropolitan Statistical Area—see Appendix B for areas included; (2) Based on 365 days with AQI data in 2013. Air Quality Index (AQI) is an index for reporting daily air quality. EPA calculates the AQI for five major air pollutants regulated by the Clean Air Act: ground-level ozone, particle pollution (aka particulate matter), carbon monoxide, sulfur dioxide, and nitrogen dioxide. The AQI runs from 0 to 500. The higher the AQI value, the greater the level of air pollution and the greater the health concern. There are six AQI categories: "Good" AQI is between 0 and 50. Air quality is considered satisfactory; "Moderate" AQI is between 51 and 100. Air quality is acceptable; "Unhealthy for Sensitive Groups" When AQI values are between 101 and 150, members of sensitive groups may experience health effects; "Unhealthy" When AQI values are between 151 and 200 everyone may begin to experience health effects; "Very Unhealthy" AQI values between 201 and 300 trigger a health alert; "Hazardous" AQI values over 300 trigger warnings of emergency conditions (not shown).
Source: U.S. Environmental Protection Agency, Air Quality Index Report, 2013

Air Quality Index Pollutants

| Area | Percent of Days when AQI Pollutant was...[2] | | | | | |
	Carbon Monoxide	Nitrogen Dioxide	Ozone	Sulfur Dioxide	Particulate Matter 2.5	Particulate Matter 10
MSA[1]	0.0	1.1	34.8	0.0	64.1	0.0

Note: (1) Data covers the Columbus, OH Metropolitan Statistical Area—see Appendix B for areas included;
(2) Based on 365 days with AQI data in 2013. The Air Quality Index (AQI) is an index for reporting daily air
quality. EPA calculates the AQI for five major air pollutants regulated by the Clean Air Act: ground-level ozone,
particle pollution (also known as particulate matter), carbon monoxide, sulfur dioxide, and nitrogen dioxide.
The AQI runs from 0 to 500. The higher the AQI value, the greater the level of air pollution and the greater the
health concern.
Source: U.S. Environmental Protection Agency, Air Quality Index Report, 2013

Air Quality Trends: Ozone

	2003	2004	2005	2006	2007	2008	2009	2010	2011	2012
MSA[1]	0.088	0.075	0.085	0.077	0.081	0.073	0.070	0.074	0.078	0.079

Note: (1) Data covers the Columbus, OH Metropolitan Statistical Area—see Appendix B for areas included. The
values shown are the composite ozone concentration averages among trend sites based on the highest fourth
daily maximum 8-hour concentration in parts per million. These trends are based on sites having an adequate
record of monitoring data during the trend period. Data from exceptional events are included.
Source: U.S. Environmental Protection Agency, Air Quality Monitoring Information, "Air Quality Trends by
City, 2000-2012"

Maximum Air Pollutant Concentrations: Particulate Matter, Ozone, CO and Lead

	Particulate Matter 10 (ug/m^3)	Particulate Matter 2.5 Wtd AM (ug/m^3)	Particulate Matter 2.5 24-Hr (ug/m^3)	Ozone (ppm)	Carbon Monoxide (ppm)	Lead (ug/m^3)
MSA[1] Level	62	10.7	22	0.082	2	0.01
NAAQS[2]	150	15	35	0.075	9	0.15
Met NAAQS[2]	Yes	Yes	Yes	No	Yes	Yes

Note: (1) Data covers the Columbus, OH Metropolitan Statistical Area—see Appendix B for areas included;
Data from exceptional events are included; (2) National Ambient Air Quality Standards; ppm = parts per
million; ug/m^3 = micrograms per cubic meter; n/a not available.
Concentrations: Particulate Matter 10 (coarse particulate)—highest second maximum 24-hour concentration;
Particulate Matter 2.5 Wtd AM (fine particulate)—highest weighted annual mean concentration; Particulate
Matter 2.5 24-Hour (fine particulate)—highest 98th percentile 24-hour concentration; Ozone—highest fourth
daily maximum 8-hour concentration; Carbon Monoxide—highest second maximum non-overlapping 8-hour
concentration; Lead—maximum running 3-month average
Source: U.S. Environmental Protection Agency, Air Quality Monitoring Information, "Air Quality Statistics by
City, 2012"

Maximum Air Pollutant Concentrations: Nitrogen Dioxide and Sulfur Dioxide

	Nitrogen Dioxide AM (ppb)	Nitrogen Dioxide 1-Hr (ppb)	Sulfur Dioxide AM (ppb)	Sulfur Dioxide 1-Hr (ppb)	Sulfur Dioxide 24-Hr (ppb)
MSA[1] Level	n/a	n/a	n/a	n/a	n/a
NAAQS[2]	53	100	30	75	140
Met NAAQS[2]	n/a	n/a	n/a	n/a	n/a

Note: (1) Data covers the Columbus, OH Metropolitan Statistical Area—see Appendix B for areas included;
Data from exceptional events are included; (2) National Ambient Air Quality Standards; ppm = parts per
million; ug/m^3 = micrograms per cubic meter; n/a not available.
Concentrations: Nitrogen Dioxide AM—highest arithmetic mean concentration; Nitrogen Dioxide
1-Hr—highest 98th percentile 1-hour daily maximum concentration; Sulfur Dioxide AM—highest annual mean
concentration; Sulfur Dioxide 1-Hr—highest 99th percentile 1-hour daily maximum concentration; Sulfur
Dioxide 24-Hr—highest second maximum 24-hour concentration
Source: U.S. Environmental Protection Agency, Air Quality Monitoring Information, "Air Quality Statistics by
City, 2012"

Drinking Water

Water System Name	Pop. Served	Primary Water Source Type	Violations[1]	
			Health Based	Monitoring/ Reporting
Columbus Public Water System	1,163,128	Surface	0	0

Note: (1) Based on violation data from January 1, 2013 to December 31, 2013 (includes unresolved violations from earlier years)
Source: U.S. Environmental Protection Agency, Office of Ground Water and Drinking Water, Safe Drinking Water Information System (based on data extracted February 10, 2014)

Durham, North Carolina

Background

Durham, on the Eno River in north-central North Carolina, is known as the "City of Medicine," and forms a corner of the region's famous Research Triangle, one of the nation's earliest and most successful planned centers for research and development. The economy is deeply interlinked with area universities and businesses specializing in medicine, biopharmaceuticals, computer technology and software, and telecommunications.

The original inhabitants of the area were Eno and Occaneechi Indians, who were mostly settled, horticulturist villagers. An English explorer, John Lawson, visited the site in 1701, and called it the "flower of the Carolinas" for its scenic beauty. By the mid-eighteenth century, Scottish, Irish, and English settlers had established farms in the site of the present city.

Durham began as a station for the North Carolina Railroad, which had been built on land originally owned by the city's namesake, Bartlett Durham. Prior to the Civil War, a number of extensive plantations were established in the area.

Throughout the prewar period and beyond, Durham continued its growth as a center for tobacco farming and processing, with emphasis on "brightleaf" tobacco. One tobacco entrepreneur, Washington Duke, was of particular importance to the growth of Durham, and his own and others' efforts established Durham as a major regional economic center. The textile industry also grew and prospered in the post-Civil War years, giving rise to many clothing innovations: the nation's first denim and sheer hosiery mills were established there.

In 1910, the popular B.C. Headache Powders was produced in Durham; the city's connection with health care deepened considerably when, in 1939, Duke University's Medical School opened.

Durham's economy is both high-tech and broad-based. Hundreds of private companies in the area employ thousands of highly skilled workers in a variety of high-technology enterprises.

Durham boasts a vibrant African-American community, the center of which was an area once known as Hayti, just south of the center of town, where some of the most prominent and successful black-owned businesses in the country were established during the early 20th century. These businesses would come to be known as "Black Wall Street." Portions of the Hayti district, along with the loss of large parts of other historic neighborhoods, were demolished for the construction of the Durham Freeway during the late 1960s. Although downtown revitalization heated up in the '70s and '80s, economic progress continues to butt heads with historic preservation.

Durham's downtown draws many residents and out-of-town visitors for its architecture, shops, and restaurants. For some years, former tobacco warehouses and factories have been undergoing conversion to residential, office, retail or entertainment uses. The American Tobacco Company Historic District now features historic preservation projects, as well as offices, restaurants, stores and residences. At the center of Durham's cultural scene is The Carolina Theatre, a historic building currently owned by the city and maintained by The Carolina Theatre of Durham Incorporated, a nonprofit. Durham is home to the renowned annual Full Frame Documentary Film Festival, which celebrated its 15th anniversary in 2013.

Beyond the influence of the historic theater, Durham maintains a vibrant arts scene. Many of Durham's substantial cultural assets are linked to Duke University, including the Nasher Museum of Art at Duke University, which opened its Rafael Vinoly-designed building on the campus in 2005. The Nasher Museum of Art hosts traveling exhibitions from cutting-edge contemporary artists. Duke University also hosts The American Dance Festival each summer.

The city is also home to North Carolina Central University (1910), the nation's first publicly supported liberal arts college for African-Americans.

Durham is serviced by the 5,000-acre Raleigh-Durham International Airport, one of the country's fastest-growing terminals. A new, second passenger terminal opened in 2011.

Durham lies between coastal plain and piedmont plateau, giving it a moderate climate. The mountains to the west partially protect the area from excess cold winter winds, although temperatures fall below freezing some days. Summers are hot and humid. July and August see the most rain, often in the form of thunderstorms, while October and November see the least.

Rankings

Business/Finance Rankings

- Measuring indicators of "tolerance"—the nonjudgmental environment that "attracts open-minded and new-thinking kinds of people"— as well as concentrations of technological and economic innovators, analysts identified the most creative American metro areas. On the resulting 2012 Creativity Index, the Durham metro area placed #8. *www.thedailybeast.com*, *"Boulder, Ann Arbor, Tucson & More: 20 Most Creative U.S. Cities," June 26, 2012*

- Based on a minimum of 500 social media reviews per metro area, the employment opinion group Glassdoor surveyed 50 of the largest U.S. metro areas on measures including compensation and benefits, satisfaction with management, business outlook, and number of employers hiring. The Durham metro area was ranked #14 in overall employee satisfaction. *www.glassdoor.com, "Employment Satisfaction Report Card by City," June 21, 2013*

- A *Fiscal Times* analysis balancing cost of living with average income to find the cities where residents' dollars go furthest was published by the *Huffington Post*. Based on the Census Bureau's 2010 Cost of Living Index and the National Compensation Survey, Durham was ranked the #7 metro area where you can "actually spend less and make more." *Fiscal Times/Huffington Post, "The Best Bang for Your Buck Cities in the United States," June 26, 2012*

- The Durham metro area appeared on the Milken Institute "2013 Best Performing Cities" list. Rank: #60 out of 200 large metro areas. Criteria: job growth; wage and salary growth; high-tech output growth. *Milken Institute, "Best-Performing Cities 2013," December 2013*

- *Forbes* ranked the 200 most populous metro areas in the U.S. in terms of the "Best Places for Business and Careers." The Durham metro area was ranked #10. Criteria: costs (business and living); job growth (past and projected); income growth; educational attainment (college and high school); projected economic growth; cultural and recreational opportunities; net migration patterns; number of highly ranked colleges. *Forbes, "The Best Places for Business and Careers," August 7, 2013*

Children/Family Rankings

- Durham was selected as one of the best cities for families to live by *Parenting* magazine. The city ranked #39 out of 100. Criteria: education; health; community; *Parenting's* Culture & Charm Index. *Parenting.com, "The 2012 Best Cities for Families List"*

Dating/Romance Rankings

- A *Cosmopolitan* magazine article surveyed the gender balance and other factors to arrive at a list of the best and worst cities for women to meet single guys. Durham placed #8 among the worst for single women looking for dates. *www.cosmopolitan.com, "Working the Ratio," October 1, 2013*

- Of the 100 U.S. cities surveyed by *Men's Health* in its quest to identify the nation's best cities for dating and forming relationships, Durham was ranked #80 for online dating (#1 = best). *Men's Health, "The Best and Worst Cities for Online Dating," January 30, 2013*

- Durham was selected as one of the best cities for newlyweds by *Rent.com*. The city ranked #2 of 10. Criteria: cost of living; mean annual income; unemployment rate. *Rent.com, "10 Best Cities for Newlyweds," March 20, 2012*

Education Rankings

- The Durham metro area was selected as one of America's most innovative cities" by *The Business Insider*. The metro area was ranked #14 out of 20. Criteria: patents per capita. *The Business Insider, "The 20 Most Innovative Cities in the U.S.," February 1, 2013*

- Durham was identified as one of America's "smartest" metropolitan areas by *The Business Journals*. The area ranked #6 out of 10. Criteria: percentage of adults (25 and older) with high school diplomas, bachelor's degrees and graduate degrees. *The Business Journals, "Where the Brainpower Is: Exclusive U.S. Rankings, Insights," February 27, 2014*

- *Men's Health* ranked 100 U.S. cities in terms of their education levels. Durham was ranked #24 (#1 = most educated city). Criteria: high school graduation rates; school enrollment; educational attainment; number of households who have outstanding student loans; number of households whose members have taken adult-education courses. *Men's Health, "Where School Is In: The Most and Least Educated Cities," September 12, 2011*

- Durham was selected as one of "America's Geekiest Cities" by *Forbes.com*. The city ranked #5 of 20. Criteria: percentage of workers with jobs in science, technology, engineering and mathematics. *Forbes.com, "America's Geekiest Cities," August 5, 2011*

- Durham was identified as one of "America's Smartest Cities" by *The Daily Beast* using data from Lumos Labs. The metro area ranked #21 out of 25. Criteria: with data collected from more than 1 million users as part of its human cognition project, Lumos Labs was able to analyze performance for nearly 200 metro areas in five cognitive areas: memory, processing speed, flexibility, attention, and problem solving. The median Lumos Lab score was worth 50 percent of the final, weighted ranking. The other half of the ranking was based on the percentage of adults over age 25 with a bachelor's and/or master's degree. *The Daily Beast, "America's Smartest Cities 2012" August 16, 2012*

- Durham was identified as one of America's most inventive cities by *The Daily Beast*. The city ranked #16 out of 25. The 200 largest cities in the U.S. were ranked by the number of patents (applied and approved) per capita. *The Daily Beast, "The 25 Most Inventive Cities," October 2, 2011*

Environmental Rankings

- The Durham metro area came in at #236 for the relative comfort of its climate on Sperling's list of "chill cities," as measured by the Sperling Heat Index. All 361 metro areas are included. Criteria included daytime high temperatures, nighttime low temperatures, dew point, and relative humidity at the high temperatures. *www.bertsperling.com, "Sperling's Chill Cities," July 18, 2013*

- Sperling's BestPlaces assessed 379 metropolitan areas of the United States for the likelihood of dangerously extreme weather events or earthquakes. In general the Southeast and South-Central regions have the highest risk of weather extremes and earthquakes, while the Pacific Northwest enjoys the lowest risk. Of the least risky metropolitan areas, the Durham metro area was ranked #240. *www.bestplaces.net, "Safest Places from Natural Disasters," April 2011*

- Durham was selected as one of 22 "Smarter Cities" for energy by the Natural Resources Defense Council. Criteria: investment in green power; energy efficiency measures; conservation. *Natural Resources Defense Council, "2010 Smarter Cities," July 19, 2010*

Food/Drink Rankings

- *Men's Health* ranked 100 major U.S. cities in terms of alcohol intoxication. Durham ranked #30 (#1 = most sober).Criteria: binge drinking; alcohol-related traffic accidents, arrests, and fatalities. *Men's Health, "The Drunkest Cities in America," November 19, 2013*

Health/Fitness Rankings

- The Durham metro area was identified as one of the worst cities for bed bugs in America by pest control company Orkin. The area ranked #12 out of 50 based on the number of bed bug treatments Orkin performed from January to December 2013. *Orkin, "Chicago Tops Bed Bug Cities List for Second Year in a Row," January 16, 2014*

- *Men's Health* ranked 100 major U.S. cities in terms of the best and worst cities for men. Durham ranked #21. Criteria: thirty-three data points were examined covering health, fitness, and quality of life. *Men's Health, "The Best & Worst Cities for Men 2014," December 6, 2013*

- The Durham metro area appeared in the 2013 Gallup-Healthways Well-Being Index. The area ranked #31 out of 189. The Gallup-Healthways Well-Being Index score is an average of six sub-indexes, which individually examine life evaluation, emotional health, work environment, physical health, healthy behaviors, and access to basic necessities. Results are based on telephone interviews conducted as part of the Gallup-Healthways Well-Being Index survey January 2–December 29, 2012, and January 2–December 30, 2013, with a random sample of 531,630 adults, aged 18 and older, living in metropolitan areas in the 50 U.S. states and the District of Columbia. *Gallup-Healthways, "State of American Well-Being," March 25, 2014*

- *Men's Health* ranked 100 U.S. cities in terms of their activity levels. Durham was ranked #51 (#1 = most active city). Criteria: where and how often residents exercise; percentage of households that watch more than 15 hours of cable television a week and buy more than 11 video games a year; death rate from deep-vein thrombosis, a condition linked to sitting for extended periods of time. *Men's Health, "Where Sit Happens: The Most and Least Active Cities in America," June 20, 2011*

- Durham was selected as one of the "20 Most Livable U.S. Cities for Wheelchair Users" by the Christopher & Dana Reeve Foundation. The city ranked #13. Criteria: Medicaid eligibility and spending; access to physicians and rehabilitation facilities; access to fitness facilities and recreation; access to paratransit; percentage of people living with disabilities who are employed; clean air; climate. *Christopher & Dana Reeve Foundation, "20 Most Livable U.S. Cities for Wheelchair Users," July 26, 2010*

- *The Daily Beast* identified the 30 U.S. metro areas with the worst smoking habits. The Durham metro area ranked #26. Sixty urban centers with populations of more than one million were ranked based on the following criteria: number of smokers; number of cigarettes smoked per day; fewest attempts to quit. *The Daily Beast, "30 Cities With Smoking Problems," January 3, 2011*

Real Estate Rankings

- Durham was ranked #166 out of 283 metro areas in terms of house price appreciation in 2013 (#1 = highest rate). *Federal Housing Finance Agency, House Price Index, 4th Quarter 2013*

- Durham was ranked #117 out of 224 metro areas in terms of housing affordability in 2013 by the National Association of Home Builders (#1 = most affordable). The NAHB-Wells Fargo Housing Opportunity Index (HOI) for a given area is defined as the share of homes sold in that area that would have been affordable to a family earning the local median income, based on standard mortgage underwriting criteria. *National Association of Home Builders®, NAHB-Wells Fargo Housing Opportunity Index, 4th Quarter 2013*

Safety Rankings

- Allstate ranked the 200 largest cities in America in terms of driver safety. Durham ranked #89. Allstate researchers analyzed internal property damage claims over a two-year period from January 2010 to December 2011. A weighted average of the two-year numbers determined the annual percentages. *Allstate, "Allstate America's Best Drivers Report®, August 27, 2013"*

- The National Insurance Crime Bureau ranked 380 metro areas in the U.S. in terms of per capita rates of vehicle theft. The Durham metro area ranked #124 (#1 = highest rate). Criteria: number of vehicle theft offenses per 100,000 inhabitants in 2012. *National Insurance Crime Bureau, "Hot Spots 2012," June 26, 2013*

Seniors/Retirement Rankings

- From its Best Cities for Successful Aging indexes, the Milken Institute generated rankings for metropolitan areas, weighing data in eight categories—general indicators, health care, wellness, living arrangements, transportation and general accessibility, financial well-being, education and employment, and community participation. The Durham metro area was ranked #9 overall in the small metro area category. *Milken Institute, "Best Cities for Successful Aging," July 2012*

Sports/Recreation Rankings

- Durham appeared on the *Sporting News* list of the "Best Sports Cities" for 2011. The area ranked #23 out of 271. Criteria: the magazine takes a 12-month snapshot of each city's sports, putting a heavy premium on regular-season won-lost records (from the most recently completed season). Other criteria include: playoff berths, bowl appearances and tournament bids; championships; applicable power ratings; quality of competition; overall fan fervor (measured in part by attendance); abundance of teams (rewarding quality over quantity); stadium and arena quality; ticket availability and prices; franchise ownership; and marquee appeal of athletes. *Sporting News, "Best Sports Cities 2011," October 4, 2011*

- Durham appeared on the *Sporting News* list of the "Best Sports Cities" for 2011. The area ranked #23 out of 271. Criteria: a 12-month snapshot of regular-season won-lost records (from the most recently completed season). Other criteria include: playoff berths, bowl appearances and tournament bids; championships; applicable power ratings; quality of competition; overall fan fervor (measured in part by attendance); abundance of teams (quality over quantity); stadium and arena quality; ticket availability and prices; franchise ownership; and marquee appeal of athletes. *Sporting News, "Best Sports Cities 2011," October 4, 2011*

- Durham was chosen as a bicycle friendly community by the League of American Bicyclists. A "Bicycle Friendly Community" welcomes cyclists by providing safe accommodation for cycling and encouraging people to bike for transportation and recreation. There are four award levels: Platinum; Gold; Silver; and Bronze. The community achieved an award level of Bronze. *League of American Bicyclists, "Bicycle Friendly Community Master List," Fall 2013*

- Durham was selected as one of the most playful cities in the U.S. by KaBOOM! The organization's Playful City USA initiative honors cities and towns across the nation for a vision, plan and commitment to creating an agenda for play. Criteria: creating a local play commission or task force; designing an annual action plan for play; conducting a play space audit; outlining a financial investment in play for the current fiscal year; and proclaiming and celebrating an annual "play day." *KaBOOM! National Campaign for Play, "2013 Playful City USA Communities"*

Transportation Rankings

- NerdWallet surveyed average annual car insurance premiums in 125 U.S. cities to identify the least expensive U.S. cities in which to insure a car. Locations without no-fault insurance laws was a strong determinant. Durham came in at #4 for the least expensive rates. *www.nerdwallet.com, "Best Cities for Cheap Car Insurance," February 3, 2014*

Women/Minorities Rankings

- To determine the best metro areas for working women, the personal finance website NerdWallet considered city size as well as relevant economic metrics—high salaries, narrow pay differential by gender, prevalence of women in the highest-paying industries, and population growth over 2010–2012. Of the medium-sized U.S. cities examined, the Durham metro area held the #1 position. *www.nerdwallet.com, "Best Places for Women in the Workforce," May 19, 2013*

- *Women's Health* examined U.S. cities and identified the 100 best cities for women. Durham was ranked #27. Criteria: 30 categories were examined from obesity and breast cancer rates to commuting times and hours spent working out. *Women's Health, "Best Cities for Women 2012"*

Miscellaneous Rankings

- Durham was selected as a 2013 Digital Cities Survey winner. The city ranked #3 in the mid-sized city (125,000 to 249,999 population) category. The survey examined and assessed how city governments are utilizing information technology to operate and deliver quality service to their customers and citizens. Survey questions focused on implementation and adoption of online service delivery; planning and governance; and the infrastructure and architecture that make the transformation to digital government possible. *Center for Digital Government, "2013 Digital Cities Survey," November 7, 2013*

- *Men's Health* ranked 100 U.S. cities by their level of sadness. Durham was ranked #24 (#1 = saddest city). Criteria: suicide rates; unemployment rates; percentage of households that use antidepressants; percent of population who report feeling blue all or most of the time. *Men's Health, "Frown Towns," November 28, 2011*

Business Environment

CITY FINANCES

City Government Finances

Component	2011 ($000)	2011 ($ per capita)
Total Revenues	353,819	1,624
Total Expenditures	369,901	1,698
Debt Outstanding	461,394	2,118
Cash and Securities[1]	301,102	1,382

Note: (1) Cash and security holdings of a government at the close of its fiscal year, including those of its dependent agencies, utilities, and liquor stores.
Source: U.S Census Bureau, State & Local Government Finances 2011

City Government Revenue by Source

Source	2011 ($000)	2011 ($ per capita)
General Revenue		
From Federal Government	19,690	90
From State Government	25,274	116
From Local Governments	0	0
Taxes		
Property	127,728	586
Sales and Gross Receipts	34,461	158
Personal Income	0	0
Corporate Income	0	0
Motor Vehicle License	2,235	10
Other Taxes	7,792	36
Current Charges	77,347	355
Liquor Store	0	0
Utility	41,338	190
Employee Retirement	0	0

Source: U.S Census Bureau, State & Local Government Finances 2011

City Government Expenditures by Function

Function	2011 ($000)	2011 ($ per capita)	2011 (%)
General Direct Expenditures			
Air Transportation	12	< 1	< 0.1
Corrections	0	0	0.0
Education	0	0	0.0
Employment Security Administration	0	0	0.0
Financial Administration	7,373	34	2.0
Fire Protection	22,866	105	6.2
General Public Buildings	11,685	54	3.2
Governmental Administration, Other	11,406	52	3.1
Health	0	0	0.0
Highways	30,538	140	8.3
Hospitals	0	0	0.0
Housing and Community Development	13,358	61	3.6
Interest on General Debt	9,659	44	2.6
Judicial and Legal	1,555	7	0.4
Libraries	0	0	0.0
Parking	4,195	19	1.1
Parks and Recreation	26,966	124	7.3
Police Protection	51,689	237	14.0
Public Welfare	0	0	0.0
Sewerage	43,581	200	11.8
Solid Waste Management	20,362	93	5.5
Veterans' Services	0	0	0.0
Liquor Store	0	0	0.0
Utility	64,803	297	17.5
Employee Retirement	0	0	0.0

Source: U.S Census Bureau, State & Local Government Finances 2011

DEMOGRAPHICS

Population Growth

Area	1990 Census	2000 Census	2010 Census	Population Growth (%) 1990-2000	Population Growth (%) 2000-2010
City	151,737	187,035	228,330	23.3	22.1
MSA[1]	344,646	426,493	504,357	23.7	18.3
U.S.	248,709,873	281,421,906	308,745,538	13.2	9.7

Note: (1) Figures cover the Durham-Chapel Hill, NC Metropolitan Statistical Area—see Appendix B for areas included
Source: U.S. Census Bureau, Census 1990, 2000, 2010

Household Size

Area	Persons in Household (%) One	Two	Three	Four	Five	Six	Seven or More	Average Household Size
City	32.2	34.0	15.5	10.6	4.7	2.0	1.0	2.34
MSA[1]	29.7	35.7	15.8	11.6	4.7	1.5	1.0	2.41
U.S.	27.6	33.5	15.7	13.2	6.1	2.4	1.5	2.63

Note: (1) Figures cover the Durham-Chapel Hill, NC Metropolitan Statistical Area—see Appendix B for areas included
Source: U.S. Census Bureau, 2010-2012 American Community Survey 3-Year Estimates

Race

Area	White Alone[2] (%)	Black Alone[2] (%)	Asian Alone[2] (%)	AIAN[3] Alone[2] (%)	NHOPI[4] Alone[2] (%)	Other Race Alone[2] (%)	Two or More Races (%)
City	46.8	40.2	4.8	0.5	0.1	4.8	2.9
MSA[1]	62.1	26.8	4.4	0.4	0.0	3.8	2.4
U.S.	74.0	12.6	4.9	0.8	0.2	4.7	2.8

Note: (1) Figures cover the Durham-Chapel Hill, NC Metropolitan Statistical Area—see Appendix B for areas included; (2) Alone is defined as not being in combination with one or more other races; (3) American Indian and Alaska Native; (4) Native Hawaiian and Other Pacific Islander
Source: U.S. Census Bureau, 2010-2012 American Community Survey 3-Year Estimates

Hispanic or Latino Origin

Area	Total (%)	Mexican (%)	Puerto Rican (%)	Cuban (%)	Other (%)
City	13.6	8.0	0.8	0.3	4.6
MSA[1]	11.3	7.0	0.7	0.2	3.4
U.S.	16.6	10.7	1.6	0.6	3.7

Note: Persons of Hispanic or Latino origin can be of any race; (1) Figures cover the Durham-Chapel Hill, NC Metropolitan Statistical Area—see Appendix B for areas included
Source: U.S. Census Bureau, 2010-2012 American Community Survey 3-Year Estimates

Segregation

Type	Segregation Indices[1] 1990	2000	2010	2010 Rank[2]	Percent Change 1990-2000	Percent Change 1990-2010	Percent Change 2000-2010
Black/White	45.7	46.7	48.1	75	1.1	2.4	1.3
Asian/White	45.5	45.4	44.0	30	-0.2	-1.5	-1.3
Hispanic/White	23.4	53.8	48.0	33	30.4	24.6	-5.8

Note: All figures cover the Metropolitan Statistical Area—see Appendix B for areas included; Figures are based on an analysis of 1990, 2000, and 2010 Census Decennial Census tract data by William H. Frey, Brookings Institution and the University of Michigan Social Science Data Analysis Network. In this analysis all racial groups (whites, blacks, and asians) are non-Hispanic members of those races. Hispanics are shown as a separate category;
(1) Segregation Indices are Dissimilarity Indices that measure the degree to which the minority group is distributed differently than whites across census tracts. They range from 0 (complete integration) to 100 (complete segregation) where the value indicates the percentage of the minority group that needs to move to be distributed exactly like whites; (2) Ranges from 1 (most segregated) to 102 (least segregated); n/a not available.
Source: www.CensusScope.org

Ancestry

Area	German	Irish	English	American	Italian	Polish	French[2]	Scottish	Dutch
City	7.3	5.3	7.6	4.3	2.6	1.6	1.5	1.6	0.8
MSA[1]	9.6	8.1	11.4	6.9	2.9	1.7	2.0	2.2	1.0
U.S.	15.2	11.1	8.2	7.2	5.6	3.1	2.8	1.7	1.4

Note: Figures are the percentage of the total population reporting a particular ancestry. The nine most commonly reported ancestries in the U.S. are shown. Figures include multiple ancestries (e.g. if a person reported being Irish and Italian, they were included in both columns); (1) Figures cover the Durham-Chapel Hill, NC Metropolitan Statistical Area—see Appendix B for areas included; (2) Excludes Basque
Source: U.S. Census Bureau, 2010-2012 American Community Survey 3-Year Estimates

Foreign-Born Population

Area	\multicolumn{9}{c}{Percent of Population Born in}
	Any Foreign Country	Mexico	Asia	Europe	Carribean	South America	Central America[2]	Africa	Canada
City	14.5	4.5	3.7	1.0	0.3	0.6	2.5	1.4	0.3
MSA[1]	12.3	3.9	3.3	1.2	0.3	0.5	1.8	0.9	0.3
U.S.	13.0	3.7	3.7	1.6	1.2	0.9	1.0	0.5	0.3

Note: (1) Figures cover the Durham-Chapel Hill, NC Metropolitan Statistical Area—see Appendix B for areas included; (2) Excludes Mexico.
Source: U.S. Census Bureau, 2010-2012 American Community Survey 3-Year Estimates

Marital Status

Area	Never Married	Now Married[2]	Separated	Widowed	Divorced
City	42.0	40.3	2.9	4.7	10.2
MSA[1]	37.4	45.4	2.4	5.0	9.8
U.S.	32.4	48.4	2.2	6.0	11.0

Note: Figures are percentages and cover the population 15 years of age and older; (1) Figures cover the Durham-Chapel Hill, NC Metropolitan Statistical Area—see Appendix B for areas included; (2) Excludes separated
Source: U.S. Census Bureau, 2010-2012 American Community Survey 3-Year Estimates

Age

Area	\multicolumn{9}{c}{Percent of Population}	Median Age
	Under Age 5	Age 5–19	Age 20–34	Age 35–44	Age 45–54	Age 55–64	Age 65–74	Age 75–84	Age 85+	
City	7.7	18.9	28.1	13.9	12.0	10.1	5.1	2.7	1.5	32.2
MSA[1]	6.4	19.2	23.8	13.5	13.4	11.8	6.7	3.5	1.6	35.4
U.S.	6.4	20.1	20.5	13.1	14.3	12.2	7.3	4.2	1.8	37.3

Note: (1) Figures cover the Durham-Chapel Hill, NC Metropolitan Statistical Area—see Appendix B for areas included
Source: U.S. Census Bureau, 2010-2012 American Community Survey 3-Year Estimates

Gender

Area	Males	Females	Males per 100 Females
City	110,168	123,992	88.9
MSA[1]	246,272	267,934	91.9
U.S.	153,276,055	158,333,314	96.8

Note: (1) Figures cover the Durham-Chapel Hill, NC Metropolitan Statistical Area—see Appendix B for areas included
Source: U.S. Census Bureau, 2010-2012 American Community Survey 3-Year Estimates

Religious Groups by Family

Area	Catholic	Baptist	Non-Den.	Methodist[2]	Lutheran	LDS[3]	Pentecostal	Presbyterian[4]	Muslim[5]	Judaism
MSA[1]	5.1	13.9	5.6	8.1	0.5	0.8	1.4	2.5	0.5	0.6
U.S.	19.1	9.3	4.0	4.0	2.3	2.0	1.9	1.6	0.8	0.7

Note: Figures are the number of adherents as a percentage of the total population; (1) Figures cover the Durham-Chapel Hill, NC Metropolitan Statistical Area—see Appendix B for areas included; (2) Methodist/Pietist; (3) Latter Day Saints; (4) Reformed; (5) Figures are estimates
Source: Association of Statisticians of American Religious Bodies, 2010 U.S. Religion Census: Religious Congregations & Membership Study

Religious Groups by Tradition

Area	Catholic	Evangelical Protestant	Mainline Protestant	Other Tradition	Black Protestant	Orthodox
MSA[1]	5.1	19.4	11.7	2.9	3.1	0.1
U.S.	19.1	16.2	7.3	4.3	1.6	0.3

Note: Figures are the number of adherents as a percentage of the total population; (1) Figures cover the Durham-Chapel Hill, NC Metropolitan Statistical Area—see Appendix B for areas included
Source: Association of Statisticians of American Religious Bodies, 2010 U.S. Religion Census: Religious Congregations & Membership Study

ECONOMY

Gross Metropolitan Product

Area	2011	2012	2013	2014	Rank[2]
MSA[1]	38.0	39.7	41.5	43.8	59

Note: Figures are in billions of dollars; (1) Figures cover the Durham-Chapel Hill, NC Metropolitan Statistical Area—see Appendix B for areas included; (2) Rank is based on 2014 data and ranges from 1 to 363
Source: The United States Conference of Mayors, U.S. Metro Economies: Outlook—Gross Metropolitan Product, with Metro Employment Projections, November 2013

Economic Growth

Area	2011 (%)	2012 (%)	2013 (%)	2014 (%)	Rank[2]
MSA[1]	-3.5	2.7	3.0	3.7	23
U.S.	1.6	2.5	1.7	2.5	–

Note: Figures are real gross metropolitan product (GMP) growth rates and represent annual average percent change; (1) Figures cover the Durham-Chapel Hill, NC Metropolitan Statistical Area—see Appendix B for areas included; (2) Rank is based on 2013 data and ranges from 1 to 363
Source: The United States Conference of Mayors, U.S. Metro Economies: Outlook—Gross Metropolitan Product, with Metro Employment Projections, November 2013

Metropolitan Area Exports

Area	2007	2008	2009	2010	2011	2012	Rank[2]
MSA[1]	2,429.7	2,688.4	2,656.1	2,736.6	2,640.3	2,723.2	81

Note: Figures are in millions of dollars; (1) Figures cover the Durham-Chapel Hill, NC Metropolitan Statistical Area—see Appendix B for areas included; (2) Rank is based on 2012 data and ranges from 1 to 369
Source: U.S. Department of Commerce, International Trade Administration, Office of Trade & Industry Information, Manufacturing & Services, data extracted April 1, 2014

INCOME

Income

Area	Per Capita ($)	Median Household ($)	Average Household ($)
City	27,001	46,924	65,249
MSA[1]	29,028	49,965	72,098
U.S.	27,385	51,771	71,579

Note: (1) Figures cover the Durham-Chapel Hill, NC Metropolitan Statistical Area—see Appendix B for areas included
Source: U.S. Census Bureau, 2010-2012 American Community Survey 3-Year Estimates

Household Income Distribution

Area	Percent of Households Earning							
	Under $15,000	$15,000 -24,999	$25,000 -34,999	$35,000 -49,999	$50,000 -74,999	$75,000 -99,000	$100,000 -149,999	$150,000 and up
City	14.6	12.2	11.8	14.8	16.7	10.8	11.5	7.7
MSA[1]	13.8	11.3	11.0	13.9	16.8	11.2	12.2	9.8
U.S.	13.1	11.0	10.5	13.7	18.1	11.9	12.5	9.1

Note: (1) Figures cover the Durham-Chapel Hill, NC Metropolitan Statistical Area—see Appendix B for areas included
Source: U.S. Census Bureau, 2010-2012 American Community Survey 3-Year Estimates

Poverty Rate

Area	All Ages	Under 18 Years Old	18 to 64 Years Old	65 Years and Over
City	21.1	28.7	19.9	10.1
MSA[1]	18.4	24.6	18.1	7.9
U.S.	15.7	22.2	14.6	9.3

Note: Figures are percentage of people whose income during the past 12 months was below the poverty level;
(1) Figures cover the Durham-Chapel Hill, NC Metropolitan Statistical Area—see Appendix B for areas included
Source: U.S. Census Bureau, 2010-2012 American Community Survey 3-Year Estimates

Personal Bankruptcy Filing Rate

Area	2008	2009	2010	2011	2012	2013
Durham County	2.35	2.80	2.97	2.70	2.41	2.08
U.S.	3.53	4.61	4.97	4.37	3.76	3.29

Note: Numbers are per 1,000 population and include Chapter 7 and Chapter 13 filings
Source: Federal Deposit Insurance Corporation, Regional Economic Conditions, March 20, 2014

EMPLOYMENT

Labor Force and Employment

Area	Civilian Labor Force			Workers Employed		
	Dec. 2012	Dec. 2013	% Chg.	Dec. 2012	Dec. 2013	% Chg.
City	123,995	122,692	-1.1	115,431	116,919	1.3
MSA[1]	276,816	273,704	-1.1	257,103	260,417	1.3
U.S.	154,904,000	154,408,000	-0.3	143,060,000	144,423,000	1.0

Note: Data is not seasonally adjusted and covers workers 16 years of age and older; (1) Metropolitan Statistical Area—see Appendix B for areas included
Source: Bureau of Labor Statistics, Local Area Unemployment Statistics

Unemployment Rate

Area	2013											
	Jan.	Feb.	Mar.	Apr.	May	Jun.	Jul.	Aug.	Sep.	Oct.	Nov.	Dec.
City	7.3	6.6	6.4	6.1	6.6	7.0	7.1	6.4	5.6	5.7	4.9	4.7
MSA[1]	7.7	7.0	6.6	6.3	6.8	7.2	7.1	6.4	5.7	5.7	5.1	4.9
U.S.	8.5	8.1	7.6	7.1	7.3	7.8	7.7	7.3	7.0	7.0	6.6	6.5

Note: Data is not seasonally adjusted and covers workers 16 years of age and older; All figures are percentages;
(1) Metropolitan Statistical Area—see Appendix B for areas included
Source: Bureau of Labor Statistics, Local Area Unemployment Statistics

Employment by Occupation

Occupation Classification	City (%)	MSA[1] (%)	U.S. (%)
Management, Business, Science, and Arts	49.7	48.7	36.0
Natural Resources, Construction, and Maintenance	7.4	8.1	9.1
Production, Transportation, and Material Moving	6.9	7.6	12.0
Sales and Office	18.4	19.2	24.7
Service	17.5	16.4	18.2

Note: Figures cover employed civilians 16 years of age and older; (1) Figures cover the Durham-Chapel Hill, NC Metropolitan Statistical Area—see Appendix B for areas included
Source: U.S. Census Bureau, 2010-2012 American Community Survey 3-Year Estimates

Employment by Industry

Sector	MSA[1]		U.S.
	Number of Employees	Percent of Total	Percent of Total
Construction	n/a	n/a	4.2
Education and Health Services	62,900	21.6	15.5
Financial Activities	12,900	4.4	5.7
Government	65,600	22.5	16.1
Information	3,700	1.3	1.9
Leisure and Hospitality	25,400	8.7	10.2
Manufacturing	30,000	10.3	8.7
Mining and Logging	n/a	n/a	0.6
Other Services	10,300	3.5	3.9
Professional and Business Services	36,100	12.4	13.7
Retail Trade	24,300	8.3	11.4
Transportation and Utilities	4,300	1.5	3.8
Wholesale Trade	9,300	3.2	4.2

Note: Figures cover non-farm employment as of December 2013 and are not seasonally adjusted;
(1) Metropolitan Statistical Area—see Appendix B for areas included; n/a not available
Source: Bureau of Labor Statistics, Current Employment Statistics, Employment, Hours, and Earnings

Occupations with Greatest Projected Employment Growth: 2010 – 2020

Occupation[1]	2010 Employment	2020 Projected Employment	Numeric Employment Change	Percent Employment Change
Combined Food Preparation and Serving Workers, Including Fast Food	114,040	132,650	18,610	16.3
Registered Nurses	92,540	109,790	17,250	18.6
Retail Salespersons	131,650	145,910	14,270	10.8
Home Health Aides	55,560	67,570	12,010	21.6
Customer Service Representatives	74,700	84,800	10,090	13.5
Postsecondary Teachers	49,850	59,780	9,930	19.9
Landscaping and Groundskeeping Workers	33,610	43,450	9,830	29.3
Janitors and Cleaners, Except Maids and Housekeeping Cleaners	52,290	61,160	8,870	17.0
Cashiers	101,410	110,200	8,790	8.7
Elementary School Teachers, Except Special Education	37,090	45,730	8,650	23.3

Note: Projections cover North Carolina; (1) Sorted by numeric employment change
Source: www.projectionscentral.com, State Occupational Projections, 2010–2020 Long-Term Projections

Fastest Growing Occupations: 2010 – 2020

Occupation[1]	2010 Employment	2020 Projected Employment	Numeric Employment Change	Percent Employment Change
Biomedical Engineers	250	480	230	90.5
Medical Scientists, Except Epidemiologists	4,270	6,550	2,280	53.4
Biochemists and Biophysicists	460	670	210	44.9
Interpreters and Translators	3,000	4,210	1,220	40.6
Veterinary Technologists and Technicians	3,060	4,300	1,240	40.4
Market Research Analysts and Marketing Specialists	9,750	13,580	3,830	39.3
Helpers—Brickmasons, Blockmasons, Stonemasons, and Tile and Marble Setters	1,900	2,630	740	38.8
Helpers—Carpenters	1,850	2,560	710	38.4
Diagnostic Medical Sonographers	1,660	2,280	620	37.3
Audiologists	350	460	120	33.6

Note: Projections cover North Carolina; (1) Sorted by percent employment change and excludes occupations with numeric employment change less than 100
Source: www.projectionscentral.com, State Occupational Projections, 2010–2020 Long-Term Projections

Average Wages

Occupation	$/Hr.	Occupation	$/Hr.
Accountants and Auditors	35.16	Maids and Housekeeping Cleaners	10.28
Automotive Mechanics	18.90	Maintenance and Repair Workers	20.22
Bookkeepers	18.59	Marketing Managers	70.91
Carpenters	18.11	Nuclear Medicine Technologists	n/a
Cashiers	9.33	Nurses, Licensed Practical	21.76
Clerks, General Office	13.79	Nurses, Registered	31.62
Clerks, Receptionists/Information	13.22	Nursing Assistants	12.82
Clerks, Shipping/Receiving	14.73	Packers and Packagers, Hand	9.49
Computer Programmers	37.11	Physical Therapists	36.49
Computer Systems Analysts	40.26	Postal Service Mail Carriers	24.41
Computer User Support Specialists	27.13	Real Estate Brokers	26.03
Cooks, Restaurant	10.37	Retail Salespersons	10.89
Dentists	65.26	Sales Reps., Exc. Tech./Scientific	31.22
Electrical Engineers	40.44	Sales Reps., Tech./Scientific	45.63
Electricians	19.44	Secretaries, Exc. Legal/Med./Exec.	17.51
Financial Managers	61.38	Security Guards	12.77
First-Line Supervisors/Managers, Sales	19.43	Surgeons	113.39
Food Preparation Workers	11.11	Teacher Assistants	12.20
General and Operations Managers	64.84	Teachers, Elementary School	20.70
Hairdressers/Cosmetologists	16.36	Teachers, Secondary School	21.40
Internists	n/a	Telemarketers	15.76
Janitors and Cleaners	11.12	Truck Drivers, Heavy/Tractor-Trailer	17.58
Landscaping/Groundskeeping Workers	13.26	Truck Drivers, Light/Delivery Svcs.	17.67
Lawyers	53.74	Waiters and Waitresses	9.40

Note: Wage data covers the Durham-Chapel Hill, NC Metropolitan Statistical Area—see Appendix B for areas included. Hourly wages for elementary/secondary school teachers and teacher assistants were calculated by the editors from annual wage data assuming a 40 hour work week; n/a not available.
Source: Bureau of Labor Statistics, Metro Area Occupational Employment and Wage Estimates, May 2013

RESIDENTIAL REAL ESTATE

Building Permits

Area	Single-Family			Multi-Family			Total		
	2012	2013	Pct. Chg.	2012	2013	Pct. Chg.	2012	2013	Pct. Chg.
City	874	1,112	27.2	1,719	2,636	53.3	2,593	3,748	44.5
MSA[1]	1,595	1,969	23.4	1,719	2,725	58.5	3,314	4,694	41.6
U.S.	518,695	620,802	19.7	310,963	370,020	19.0	829,658	990,822	19.4

Note: (1) Metropolitan Statistical Area—see Appendix B for areas included; figures represent new, privately-owned housing units authorized (unadjusted data); All permit data are based on estimates with imputation.
Source: U.S. Census Bureau, Manufacturing, Mining, and Construction Statistics, Building Permits, 2012, 2013

Homeownership Rate

Area	2006 (%)	2007 (%)	2008 (%)	2009 (%)	2010 (%)	2011 (%)	2012 (%)	2013 (%)
MSA[1]	n/a	n/a	n/a	n/a	n/a	n/a	n/a	n/a
U.S.	68.8	68.1	67.8	67.4	66.9	66.1	65.4	65.1

Note: (1) Figures cover the Durham-Chapel Hill, NC Metropolitan Statistical Area—see Appendix B for areas included; n/a not available
Source: U.S. Census Bureau, Housing Vacancies and Homeownership Annual Statistics: 2013

Housing Vacancy Rates

Area	Gross Vacancy Rate[2] (%)			Year-Round Vacancy Rate[3] (%)			Rental Vacancy Rate[4] (%)			Homeowner Vacancy Rate[5] (%)		
	2011	2012	2013	2011	2012	2013	2011	2012	2013	2011	2012	2013
MSA[1]	n/a	n/a	n/a	n/a	n/a	n/a	n/a	n/a	n/a	n/a	n/a	n/a
U.S.	14.2	13.8	13.8	11.1	10.8	10.7	9.5	8.7	8.3	2.5	2.0	2.0

Note: (1) Figures cover the Durham-Chapel Hill, NC Metropolitan Statistical Area—see Appendix B for areas included; (2) The percentage of the total housing inventory that is vacant; (3) The percentage of the housing inventory (excluding seasonal units) that is year-round vacant; (4) The percentage of rental inventory that is vacant for rent; (5) The percentage of homeowner inventory that is vacant for sale; n/a not available
Source: U.S. Census Bureau, Housing Vacancies and Homeownership Annual Statistics: 2013

TAXES

State Corporate Income Tax Rates

State	Tax Rate (%)	Income Brackets ($)	Num. of Brackets	Financial Institution Tax Rate (%)[a]	Federal Income Tax Ded.
North Carolina	6.0	Flat rate	1	6.0 (t)	No

Note: Tax rates as of January 1, 2014; (a) Rates listed are the corporate income tax rate applied to financial institutions or excise taxes based on income. Some states have other taxes based upon the value of deposits or shares; (t) In North Carolina financial institutions are also subject to a tax equal to $30 per one million in assets.
Source: Federation of Tax Administrators, "State Corporate Income Tax Rates, 2014"

State Individual Income Tax Rates

State	Tax Rate (%)	Income Brackets ($)	Num. of Brackets	Personal Exempt. ($)[1] Single	Personal Exempt. ($)[1] Dependents	Fed. Inc. Tax Ded.
North Carolina	5.8	Flat rate	1	None	None	No

Note: Tax rates as of January 1, 2014; Local- and county-level taxes are not included; n/a not applicable; (1) Married joint filers generally receive double the single exemption
Source: Federation of Tax Administrators, "State Individual Income Tax Rates, 2014"

Various State and Local Tax Rates

State	State and Local Sales and Use (%)	State Sales and Use (%)	Gasoline[1] (¢/gal.)	Cigarette[2] ($/pack)	Spirits[3] ($/gal.)	Wine[4] ($/gal.)	Beer[5] ($/gal.)
North Carolina	7.5	4.75	37.75	0.450	12.36 (g)	1.00	0.62

Note: All tax rates as of January 1, 2014; (1) The American Petroleum Institute has developed a methodology for determining the average tax rate on a gallon of fuel. Rates may include any of the following: excise taxes, environmental fees, storage tank fees, other fees or taxes, general sales tax, and local taxes. In states where gasoline is subject to the general sales tax, or where the fuel tax is based on the average sale price, the average rate determined by API is sensitive to changes in the price of gasoline. States that fully or partially apply general sales taxes to gasoline: CA, CO, GA, IL, IN, MI, NY; (2) The federal excise tax of $1.0066 per pack and local taxes are not included; (3) Rates are those applicable to off-premise sales of 40% alcohol by volume (a.b.v.) distilled spirits in 750ml containers. Local excise taxes are excluded; (4) Rates are those applicable to off-premise sales of 11% a.b.v. non-carbonated wine in 750ml containers; (5) Rates are those applicable to off-premise sales of 4.7% a.b.v. beer in 12 ounce containers; (g) States where the government controls sales. In these "control states," products are subject to ad valorem mark-up and excise taxes. The excise tax rate is calculated using a methodology developed by the Distilled Spirits Council of the United States.
Source: Tax Foundation, 2014 Facts & Figures: How Does Your State Compare?

State Business Tax Climate Index Rankings

State	Overall Rank	Corporate Tax Index Rank	Individual Income Tax Index Rank	Sales Tax Index Rank	Unemployment Insurance Tax Index Rank	Property Tax Index Rank
North Carolina	44	29	42	47	7	30

Note: The index is a measure of how each state's tax laws affect economic performance. The lower the rank, the more favorable a state's tax system is for business. States without a given tax are given a ranking of 1. The scores/rankings for the District of Columbia do not affect other states. The 2014 index represents the tax climate as of July 1, 2013.
Source: Tax Foundation, State Business Tax Climate Index 2014

COMMERCIAL REAL ESTATE

Office Market

Market Area	Inventory (sq. ft.)	Vacancy Rate (%)	Under Construction (sq. ft.)	YTD Net Absorption (sq. ft.)	Total Average Asking Rent ($/sq. ft./year)
Raleigh/Durham	58,403,609	13.3	1,168,592	762,016	19.23
National	4,726,900,879	15.0	55,419,286	42,829,434	26.27

Source: Newmark Grubb Knight Frank, National Office Market Report, 4th Quarter 2013

Industrial/Warehouse/R&D Market

Market Area	Inventory (sq. ft.)	Vacancy Rate (%)	Under Construction (sq. ft.)	YTD Net Absorption (sq. ft.)	Total Average Asking Rent ($/sq. ft./year)
Raleigh/Durham	110,978,639	9.6	233,246	117,943	5.28
National	14,022,031,238	7.9	83,249,164	156,549,903	5.40

Source: Newmark Grubb Knight Frank, National Industrial Market Report, 4th Quarter 2013

COMMERCIAL UTILITIES

Typical Monthly Electric Bills

Area	Commercial Service ($/month)		Industrial Service ($/month)	
	1,500 kWh	40 kW demand 14,000 kWh	1,000 kW demand 200,000 kWh	50,000 kW demand 15,000,000 kWh
City	174	1,200	22,258	1,349,994
Average[1]	197	1,636	25,662	1,485,307

Note: Based on total rates in effect July 1, 2013; (1) average based on 180 utilities surveyed
Source: Edison Electric Institute, Typical Bills and Average Rates Report, Summer 2013

TRANSPORTATION

Means of Transportation to Work

Area	Car/Truck/Van		Public Transportation			Bicycle	Walked	Other Means	Worked at Home
	Drove Alone	Car-pooled	Bus	Subway	Railroad				
City	74.8	11.9	3.7	0.0	0.0	1.0	3.3	1.4	4.0
MSA[1]	74.0	11.0	4.0	0.0	0.0	1.1	3.0	1.6	5.2
U.S.	76.4	9.7	2.6	1.7	0.5	0.6	2.8	1.3	4.3

Note: Figures are percentages and cover workers 16 years of age and older; (1) Figures cover the Durham-Chapel Hill, NC Metropolitan Statistical Area—see Appendix B for areas included
Source: U.S. Census Bureau, 2010-2012 American Community Survey 3-Year Estimates

Travel Time to Work

Area	Less Than 10 Minutes	10 to 19 Minutes	20 to 29 Minutes	30 to 44 Minutes	45 to 59 Minutes	60 to 89 Minutes	90 Minutes or More
City	12.7	40.7	23.6	15.8	3.1	2.2	1.8
MSA[1]	11.4	34.6	25.1	18.9	5.6	3.0	1.5
U.S.	13.5	29.8	20.9	20.1	7.5	5.6	2.5

Note: Figures are percentages and include workers 16 years old and over; (1) Figures cover the Durham-Chapel Hill, NC Metropolitan Statistical Area—see Appendix B for areas included
Source: U.S. Census Bureau, 2010-2012 American Community Survey 3-Year Estimates

Travel Time Index

Area	1985	1990	1995	2000	2005	2010	2011
Urban Area[1]	n/a	n/a	n/a	n/a	n/a	n/a	n/a
Average[2]	1.09	1.14	1.16	1.19	1.23	1.18	1.18

Note: Travel Time Index—the ratio of travel time in the peak period to the travel time at free-flow conditions. For example, a value of 1.30 indicates a 20-minute free-flow trip takes 26 minutes in the peak. Free-flow speeds (60 mph on freeways and 35 mph on principal arterials) are used as the comparison threshold; (1) Data for the Durham-Chapel Hill, NC urban area was not available; (2) average of 498 urban areas
Source: Texas Transportation Institute, Urban Mobility Report 2012, December 2012

Public Transportation

Agency Name / Mode of Transportation	Vehicles Operated in Maximum Service	Annual Unlinked Passenger Trips (in thous.)	Annual Passenger Miles (in thous.)
Durham Area Transit Authority (DATA)			
Bus (purchased transportation)	38	6,313.9	22,759.0
Demand Response (purchased transportation)	37	188.3	1,681.6

Source: Federal Transit Administration, National Transit Database, 2012

Air Transportation

Airport Name and Code / Type of Service	Passenger Airlines[1]	Passenger Enplanements	Freight Carriers[2]	Freight (lbs.)
Raleigh-Durham International (RDU)				
Domestic service (U.S. carriers - 2013)	33	4,383,707	14	69,963,046
International service (U.S. carriers - 2012)	12	67,779	3	2,638,951

Note: (1) Includes all U.S.-based major, minor and commuter airlines that carried at least one passenger during the year; (2) Includes all U.S.-based airlines and freight carriers that transported at least one lb. of freight during the year.
Source: Bureau of Transportation Statistics, The Intermodal Transportation Database, Air Carriers: T-100 Domestic Market (U.S. Carriers), 2013; Bureau of Transportation Statistics, The Intermodal Transportation Database, Air Carriers: T-100 International Market (U.S. Carriers), 2012

Other Transportation Statistics

Major Highways:	I-40; I-85
Amtrak Service:	Yes
Major Waterways/Ports:	None

Source: Amtrak.com; Google Maps

BUSINESSES

Major Business Headquarters

Company Name	Rankings	
	Fortune[1]	Forbes[2]
No companies listed	-	-

Note: (1) Fortune 500—companies that produce a 10-K are ranked 1 to 500 based on 2012 revenue; (2) all private companies with at least $2 billion in annual revenue through the end of their most current fiscal year are ranked 1 to 224; companies listed are headquartered in the city; dashes indicate no ranking Source: Fortune, "Fortune 500," May 20, 2013; Forbes, "America's Largest Private Companies," December 18, 2013

Fast-Growing Businesses

According to *Inc.*, Durham is home to one of America's 500 fastest-growing private companies: **ReverbNation** (#345). Criteria: must be an independent, privately-held, for-profit, U.S. corporation, proprietorship or partnership; revenues must be at least $100,000 in 2009 and $2 million in 2012; must have four-year operating/sales history. Holding companies, regulated banks, and utilities were excluded. *Inc., "America's 500 Fastest-Growing Private Companies," September 2013*

According to Deloitte, Durham is home to one of North America's 500 fastest-growing high-technology companies: **Bronto Software** (#270). Companies are ranked by percentage growth in revenue over a five-year period. Criteria for inclusion: company must be headquartered within North America; must own proprietary intellectual property or proprietary technology that contributes to a significant portion of the company's operating revenue, or devote a significant proportion of revenues to research and development of technology; must have been in business for a minumum of five years with 2008 operating revenues of at least $50,000 USD/CD and 2012 operating revenues of at least $5 million USD/CD. *Deloitte Touche Tohmatsu, 2013 Technology Fast 500*[TM]

Minority Business Opportunity

Durham is home to one company which is on the *Black Enterprise* Bank 20 list (20 largest banks based on total assets, capital, deposits and loans, including mortgage-backed securities for the calendar year): **M&F Bancorp (Mechanics & Farmers Bank)** (#10). Only commercial banks or savings and loans that are classified by the Federal Reserve as black institutions and have been fully operational for the previous calendar year were considered. *Black Enterprise, B.E. 100s, 2013*

Durham is home to one company which is on the *Black Enterprise* Asset Manager 15 list (15 largest asset management firms based on assets under management): **Piedmont Investment Advisors** (#10). Criteria: company must have been operational in previous calendar year and be at least 51% black-owned. *Black Enterprise, B.E. 100s, 2013*

Minority- and Women-Owned Businesses

Group	All Firms		Firms with Paid Employees			
	Firms	Sales ($000)	Firms	Sales ($000)	Employees	Payroll ($000)
Asian	787	256,028	284	241,818	2,426	65,742
Black	4,701	293,510	362	212,510	2,620	74,602
Hispanic	726	166,483	93	134,913	492	20,208
Women	6,213	794,723	770	682,328	6,583	183,993
All Firms	18,147	27,036,751	4,718	26,572,440	126,193	5,909,394

Note: Figures cover firms located in the city; minority- and women-owned business are defined as firms in which the corresponding group own 51% or more of the stock or equity of the company
Source: U.S. Census Bureau, 2007 Economic Census, Survey of Business Owners (2012 Survey of Business Owners data will be released starting in June 2015)

HOTELS & CONVENTION CENTERS

Hotels/Motels

Area	5 Star		4 Star		3 Star		2 Star		1 Star		Not Rated	
	Num.	Pct.[3]	Num.	Pct.[3]	Num.	Pct.[3]	Num.	Pct.[3]	Num.	Pct.[3]	Num.	Pct.[3]
City[1]	0	0.0	3	3.5	38	44.2	42	48.8	0	0.0	3	3.5
Total[2]	142	0.9	1,005	6.0	5,147	30.9	8,578	51.4	408	2.4	1,397	8.4

Note: (1) Figures cover Durham and vicinity; (2) Figures cover all 100 cities in this book; (3) Percentage of hotels which have a given star rating; Star ratings are determined by expedia.com and offer an indication of the general quality of a particular hotel.
Source: expedia.com, April 7, 2014

The Durham-Chapel Hill, NC metro area is home to one of the best hotels in the U.S. according to *Travel & Leisure*: **Fearrington House Inn, Restaurant and Spa**. Criteria: service; location; rooms; food; and value. The list includes the top 200 hotels in the U.S. *Travel & Leisure, "T+L 500, The World's Best Hotels 2014"*

The Durham-Chapel Hill, NC metro area is home to one of the best hotels in the world according to *Condé Nast Traveler*: **Fearrington House Country Inn**. The selections are based on over 79,000 responses to the magazine's annual Readers' Choice Survey. The list includes the top 200 hotels in the U.S. *Condé Nast Traveler, "Gold List 2014, The World's Best Places to Stay"*

Major Convention Centers

Name	Overall Space (sq. ft.)	Exhibit Space (sq. ft.)	Meeting Space (sq. ft.)	Meeting Rooms
Durham Convention Center	44,000	n/a	n/a	n/a

Note: Table includes convention centers located in the Durham-Chapel Hill, NC metro area; n/a not available
Source: Original research

Living Environment

COST OF LIVING

Cost of Living Index

Composite Index	Groceries	Housing	Utilities	Transportation	Health Care	Misc. Goods/ Services
92.3	100.4	80.2	83.5	98.6	101.7	97.5

Note: The Cost of Living Index measures regional differences in the cost of consumer goods and services, excluding taxes and non-consumer expenditures, for professional and managerial households in the top income quintile. It is based on more than 50,000 prices covering almost 60 different items for which prices are collected three times a year by chambers of commerce, economic development organizations or university applied economic centers in each participating urban area. The numbers shown should be read as a percentage above or below the national average of 100. For example, a value of 115.4 in the groceries column indicates that grocery prices are 15.4% higher than the national average. Small differences in the index numbers should not be interpreted as significant; Figures cover the Durham NC urban area.
Source: The Council for Community and Economic Research, ACCRA Cost of Living Index, 2013

Grocery Prices

Area[1]	T-Bone Steak ($/pound)	Frying Chicken ($/pound)	Whole Milk ($/half gal.)	Eggs ($/dozen)	Orange Juice ($/64 oz.)	Coffee ($/11.5 oz.)
City[2]	10.14	1.46	2.65	1.85	3.46	4.08
Avg.	10.19	1.28	2.34	1.81	3.48	4.39
Min.	8.56	0.94	1.44	1.19	2.78	3.40
Max.	14.82	2.28	3.56	3.73	6.23	7.32

Note: (1) Values for the local area are compared with the average, minimum and maximum values for all 327 areas in the Cost of Living Index; (2) Figures cover the Durham NC urban area; **T-Bone Steak** *(price per pound);* **Frying Chicken** *(price per pound, whole fryer);* **Whole Milk** *(half gallon carton);* **Eggs** *(price per dozen, Grade A, large);* **Orange Juice** *(64 oz. Tropicana or Florida Natural);* **Coffee** *(11.5 oz. can, vacuum-packed, Maxwell House, Hills Bros, or Folgers).*
Source: The Council for Community and Economic Research, ACCRA Cost of Living Index, 2013

Housing and Utility Costs

Area[1]	New Home Price ($)	Apartment Rent ($/month)	All Electric ($/month)	Part Electric ($/month)	Other Energy ($/month)	Telephone ($/month)
City[2]	232,103	802	148.11	-	-	20.37
Avg.	295,864	900	171.38	91.82	70.12	27.73
Min.	185,506	458	117.80	48.81	33.67	17.16
Max.	1,358,917	3,783	441.68	171.40	372.65	39.47

Note: (1) Values for the local area are compared with the average, minimum and maximum values for all 327 areas in the Cost of Living Index; (2) Figures cover the Durham NC urban area; **New Home Price** *(2,400 sf living area, 8,000 sf lot, in urban area with full utilities);* **Apartment Rent** *(950 sf 2 bedroom/1.5 or 2 bath, unfurnished, excluding all utilities except water);* **All Electric** *(average monthly cost for an all-electric home);* **Part Electric** *(average monthly cost for a part-electric home);* **Other Energy** *(average monthly cost for natural gas, fuel oil, coal, wood, and any other forms of energy except electricity);* **Telephone** *(price includes basic monthly rate for a private residential line plus additional local usage charges incurred by a family of four).*
Source: The Council for Community and Economic Research, ACCRA Cost of Living Index, 2013

Health Care, Transportation, and Other Costs

Area[1]	Doctor ($/visit)	Dentist ($/visit)	Optometrist ($/visit)	Gasoline ($/gallon)	Beauty Salon ($/visit)	Men's Shirt ($)
City[2]	95.42	84.50	115.08	3.46	43.75	19.39
Avg.	101.40	86.48	96.16	3.44	33.87	26.55
Min.	61.67	50.83	50.12	3.08	18.92	12.48
Max.	182.71	152.50	223.78	4.33	68.22	52.03

Note: (1) Values for the local area are compared with the average, minimum and maximum values for all 327 areas in the Cost of Living Index; (2) Figures cover the Durham NC urban area; **Doctor** *(general practitioners routine exam of an established patient);* **Dentist** *(adult teeth cleaning and periodic oral examination);* **Optometrist** *(full vision eye exam for established adult patient);* **Gasoline** *(one gallon regular unleaded, national brand, including all taxes, cash price at self-service pump if available);* **Beauty Salon** *(woman's shampoo, trim, and blow-dry);* **Men's Shirt** *(cotton/polyester dress shirt, pinpoint weave, long sleeves).*
Source: The Council for Community and Economic Research, ACCRA Cost of Living Index, 2013

HOUSING

House Price Index (HPI)

Area	National Ranking[2]	Quarterly Change (%)	One-Year Change (%)	Five-Year Change (%)
MSA[1]	166	0.37	1.51	-2.44
U.S.[3]	–	1.20	7.69	4.18

Note: The HPI is a weighted repeat sales index. It measures average price changes in repeat sales or refinancings on the same properties. This information is obtained by reviewing repeat mortgage transactions on single-family properties whose mortgages have been purchased or securitized by Fannie Mae or Freddie Mac in January 1975; (1) Durham-Chapel Hill, NC Metropolitan Statistical Area—see Appendix B for areas included; (2) Rankings are based on annual percentage change for all metro areas containing at least 15,000 transactions over the last 10 years and ranges from 1 to 283; (3) figures based on a weighted average of Census Division estimates using a seasonally adjusted, purchase-only index; all figures are for the period ending December 31, 2013
Source: Federal Housing Finance Agency, House Price Index, February 25, 2014

Median Single-Family Home Prices

Area	2011	2012	2013[p]	Percent Change 2012 to 2013
MSA[1]	183.3	185.7	192.7	3.8
U.S. Average	166.2	177.2	197.4	11.4

Note: Figures are median sales prices of existing single-family homes in thousands of dollars; (p) preliminary; n/a not available; (1) Durham-Chapel Hill, NC Metropolitan Statistical Area—see Appendix B for areas included
Source: National Association of Realtors, Median Sales Price of Existing Single-Family Homes for Metropolitan Areas, 4th Quarter 2013

Qualifying Income Based on Median Sales Price of Existing Single-Family Homes

Area	With 5% Down ($)	With 10% Down ($)	With 20% Down ($)
MSA[1]	42,398	40,167	35,704
U.S. Average	45,395	43,006	38,228

Note: Figures are preliminary; Qualifying income is based on a mortgage rate of 4.4%. Monthly principal and interest payment is limited to 25% of income; n/a not available; (1) Durham-Chapel Hill, NC Metropolitan Statistical Area—see Appendix B for areas included
Source: National Association of Realtors, Qualifying Income Based on Median Sales Price of Existing Single-Family Homes for Metropolitan Areas, 4th Quarter 2013

Median Apartment Condo-Coop Home Prices

Area	2011	2012	2013[p]	Percent Change 2012 to 2013
MSA[1]	n/a	n/a	n/a	n/a
U.S. Average	165.1	173.7	194.9	12.2

Note: Figures are median sales prices of existing apartment condo-coop homes in thousands of dollars; (p) preliminary; n/a not available; (1) Durham-Chapel Hill, NC Metropolitan Statistical Area—see Appendix B for areas included
Source: National Association of Realtors, Median Sales Price of Existing Apartment Condo-Coop Homes for Metropolitan Areas, 4th Quarter 2013

Gross Monthly Rent

Area	Under $200	$200 -299	$300 -499	$500 -749	$750 -999	$1,000 -1,499	$1,500 and up	Median ($)
City	2.3	2.3	4.7	30.9	32.6	22.4	4.7	825
MSA[1]	2.0	1.9	5.4	29.5	33.3	21.8	6.0	829
U.S.	1.7	3.3	8.1	22.7	24.3	25.7	14.3	889

Note: Figures are percentages except for Median; Gross rent is the contract rent plus the estimated average monthly cost of utilities (electricity, gas, and water and sewer) and fuels (oil, coal, kerosene, wood, etc.) if these are paid by the renter (or paid for the renter by someone else); (1) Figures cover the Durham-Chapel Hill, NC Metropolitan Statistical Area—see Appendix B for areas included
Source: U.S. Census Bureau, 2010-2012 American Community Survey 3-Year Estimates

Year Housing Structure Built

Area	2010 or Later	2000 -2009	1990 -1999	1980 -1989	1970 -1979	1960 -1969	1950 -1959	1940 -1949	Before 1940	Median Year
City	1.1	21.7	18.6	17.9	11.4	11.4	6.9	4.9	6.1	1985
MSA[1]	0.9	20.9	19.5	17.7	13.8	10.7	7.3	4.0	5.3	1985
U.S.	0.5	14.9	13.8	13.9	15.9	11.1	10.9	5.5	13.5	1976

Note: Figures are percentages except for Median Year; (1) Figures cover the Durham-Chapel Hill, NC Metropolitan Statistical Area—see Appendix B for areas included
Source: U.S. Census Bureau, 2010-2012 American Community Survey 3-Year Estimates

HEALTH

Health Risk Data

Category	MSA[1] (%)	U.S. (%)
Adults aged 18–64 who have any kind of health care coverage	72.8	79.6
Adults who reported being in good or excellent health	84.6	83.1
Adults who are current smokers	17.9	19.6
Adults who are heavy drinkers[2]	7.7	6.1
Adults who are binge drinkers[3]	16.8	16.9
Adults who are overweight (BMI 25.0 - 29.9)	33.9	35.8
Adults who are obese (BMI 30.0 - 99.8)	26.9	27.6
Adults who participated in any physical activities in the past month	77.5	77.1
Adults 50+ who have ever had a sigmoidoscopy or colonoscopy	77.1	67.3
Women aged 40+ who have had a mammogram within the past two years	79.2	74.0
Men aged 40+ who have had a PSA test within the past two years	47.7	45.2
Adults aged 65+ who have had flu shot within the past year	72.4	60.1
Adults who always wear a seatbelt	n/a	93.8

Note: Data as of 2012 unless otherwise noted; n/a not available; (1) Figures cover the Durham, NC Metropolitan Statistical Area—see Appendix B for areas included; (2) Heavy drinkers are classified as males having more than two drinks per day or females having more than one drink per day; (3) Binge drinkers are classified as males having five or more drinks on one occasion or females having four or more drinks on one occasion
Source: Centers for Disease Control and Prevention, Behaviorial Risk Factor Surveillance System, SMART: Selected Metropolitan/Micropolitan Area Risk Trends, 2012

Chronic Health Indicators

Category	MSA[1] (%)	U.S. (%)
Adults who have ever been told they had a heart attack	3.0	4.5
Adults who have ever been told they had a stroke	2.3	2.9
Adults who have been told they currently have asthma	7.4	8.9
Adults who have ever been told they have arthritis	18.9	25.7
Adults who have ever been told they have diabetes[2]	8.1	9.7
Adults who have ever been told they had skin cancer	6.8	5.7
Adults who have ever been told they had any other types of cancer	5.4	6.5
Adults who have ever been told they have COPD	3.9	6.2
Adults who have ever been told they have kidney disease	1.2	2.5
Adults who have ever been told they have a form of depression	15.4	18.0

Note: Data as of 2012 unless otherwise noted; (1) Figures cover the Durham, NC Metropolitan Statistical Area—see Appendix B for areas included; (2) Figures do not include pregnancy-related, borderline, or pre-diabetes
Source: Centers for Disease Control and Prevention, Behaviorial Risk Factor Surveillance System, SMART: Selected Metropolitan/Micropolitan Area Risk Trends, 2012

Mortality Rates for the Top 10 Causes of Death in the U.S.

ICD-10[a] Sub-Chapter	ICD-10[a] Code	Age-Adjusted Mortality Rate[1] per 100,000 population	
		County[2]	U.S.
Malignant neoplasms	C00-C97	180.9	174.2
Ischaemic heart diseases	I20-I25	85.8	119.1
Other forms of heart disease	I30-I51	50.2	49.6
Chronic lower respiratory diseases	J40-J47	33.1	43.2
Cerebrovascular diseases	I60-I69	46.4	40.3
Organic, including symptomatic, mental disorders	F01-F09	45.4	30.5
Other degenerative diseases of the nervous system	G30-G31	21.1	26.3
Other external causes of accidental injury	W00-X59	24.5	25.1
Diabetes mellitus	E10-E14	22.0	21.3
Hypertensive diseases	I10-I15	17.4	18.8

Note: (a) ICD-10 = International Classification of Diseases 10th Revision; (1) Mortality rates are a three year average covering 2008-2010; (2) Figures cover Durham County
Source: Centers for Disease Control and Prevention, National Center for Health Statistics. Compressed Mortality File 1999-2010 on CDC WONDER Online Database, released January 2013. Data are compiled from the Compressed Mortality File 1999-2010, Series 20 No. 2P, 2013.

Mortality Rates for Selected Causes of Death

ICD-10[a] Sub-Chapter	ICD-10[a] Code	Age-Adjusted Mortality Rate[1] per 100,000 population	
		County[2]	U.S.
Assault	X85-Y09	9.8	5.5
Diseases of the liver	K70-K76	10.3	12.4
Human immunodeficiency virus (HIV) disease	B20-B24	4.9	3.0
Influenza and pneumonia	J09-J18	20.5	16.4
Intentional self-harm	X60-X84	8.6	11.8
Malnutrition	E40-E46	Suppressed	0.8
Obesity and other hyperalimentation	E65-E68	*2.2	1.6
Renal failure	N17-N19	20.3	13.6
Transport accidents	V01-V99	11.1	12.6
Viral hepatitis	B15-B19	3.0	2.2

Note: (a) ICD-10 = International Classification of Diseases 10th Revision; (1) Mortality rates are a three year average covering 2008-2010; (2) Figures cover Durham County; (*) Unreliable data as per CDC
Source: Centers for Disease Control and Prevention, National Center for Health Statistics. Compressed Mortality File 1999-2010 on CDC WONDER Online Database, released January 2013. Data are compiled from the Compressed Mortality File 1999-2010, Series 20 No. 2P, 2013.

Health Insurance Coverage

Area	With Health Insurance	With Private Health Insurance	With Public Health Insurance	Without Health Insurance	Population Under Age 18 Without Health Insurance
City	81.9	63.6	26.5	18.1	9.4
MSA[1]	84.5	68.3	26.1	15.5	8.4
U.S.	84.9	65.4	30.4	15.1	7.5

Note: Figures are percentages that cover the civilian noninstitutionalized population; (1) Figures cover the Durham-Chapel Hill, NC Metropolitan Statistical Area—see Appendix B for areas included
Source: U.S. Census Bureau, 2010-2012 American Community Survey 3-Year Estimates

Number of Medical Professionals

Area[1]	MDs[2]	DOs[2,3]	Dentists	Podiatrists	Chiropractors	Optometrists
Local (number)	3,087	33	198	14	45	35
Local (rate[4])	1,118.0	12.0	70.2	5.0	16.0	12.4
U.S. (rate[4])	267.6	19.6	61.7	5.6	24.7	14.5

Note: Data as of 2012 unless noted; (1) Local data covers Durham County; (2) Data as of 2011; (3) Doctor of Osteopathic Medicine; (4) rate per 100,000 population
Source: Area Resource File (ARF) 2012-2013. U.S. Department of Health and Human Services, Health Resources and Services Administration, Bureau of Health Professions

Best Hospitals

According to *U.S. News,* the Durham-Chapel Hill, NC metro area is home to three of the best hospitals in the U.S.: **Duke University Medical Center** (Honor Roll/13 specialties); **University of North Carolina Hospitals** (3 specialties); **Duke Regional Hospital** (1 specialty). The hospitals listed were nationally ranked in at least one adult specialty. Only 147 hospitals nationwide were nationally ranked in one or more specialties. Eighteen hospitals in the U.S. made the Honor Roll by ranking near the top in at least six specialties.*U.S. News Online, "America's Best Hospitals 2013-14"*

According to *U.S. News,* the Durham-Chapel Hill, NC metro area is home to two of the best children's hospitals in the U.S.: **Duke Children's Hospital and Health Center**; **North Carolina Children's Hospital at UNC.** The hospitals listed were highly ranked in at least one pediatric specialty. Eighty-seven hospitals in the U.S. ranked in at least one specialty. Ten children's hospitals in the U.S. made the Honor Roll by ranking near the top in three or more specialties.*U.S. News Online, "America's Best Children's Hospitals 2013-14"*

EDUCATION

Public School District Statistics

District Name	Schls	Pupils	Pupil/ Teacher Ratio	Minority Pupils[1] (%)	Free Lunch Eligible[2] (%)	IEP[3] (%)
Durham Public Schools	56	33,256	15.6	79.4	53.9	13.1

Note: Table includes school districts with 2,000 or more students; (1) Percentage of students that are not non-Hispanic white; (2) Percentage of students that are eligible for the free lunch program; (3) Percentage of students that have an Individualized Education Program.
Source: U.S. Department of Education, National Center for Education Statistics, Common Core of Data, Local Education Agency (School District) Universe Survey: School Year 2011-2012; U.S. Department of Education, National Center for Education Statistics, Common Core of Data, Public Elementary/Secondary School Universe Survey: School Year 2011-2012

Best High Schools

High School Name	Rank[1]	Grad. Rate[2] (%)	Coll.[3] (%)	AP/IB/ AICE Tests[4]	AP/IB/ AICE Score[5]	SAT Score[6]	ACT Score[6]
Durham School of the Arts	643	94	94	0.5	3.5	1588	24.6
North Carolina School of Science and Mathematics	23	100	100	1.2	4.0	2034	30.0

Note: (1) Public schools are ranked from 1 to 2,000 based on the following self-reported statistics (with the corresponding weight used in calculating their overall score). Schools that were newly founded and did not have a graduating senior class in 2012 were excluded; (2) Four-year, on-time graduation rate (25%); (3) Percent of 2011 graduates who were accepted to college (25%); (4) AP/IB/AICE tests taken per student (25%); (5) Average AP/IB/AICE exam score (10%); (6) Average SAT and/or ACT score (10%); Percent of students enrolled in at least one AP/IB/AICE course (5%)—data not shown
Source: Newsweek and The Daily Beast, "America's Best High Schools 2013"

Highest Level of Education

Area	Less than H.S.	H.S. Diploma	Some College, No Deg.	Associate Degree	Bachelor's Degree	Master's Degree	Prof. School Degree	Doctorate Degree
City	12.9	17.0	18.2	6.0	25.0	12.8	3.6	4.4
MSA[1]	12.5	20.1	17.7	6.5	22.7	12.1	3.6	4.7
U.S.	14.1	28.3	21.3	7.8	18.0	7.5	1.9	1.2

Note: Figures cover persons age 25 and over; (1) Figures cover the Durham-Chapel Hill, NC Metropolitan Statistical Area—see Appendix B for areas included
Source: U.S. Census Bureau, 2010-2012 American Community Survey 3-Year Estimates

Educational Attainment by Race

Area	High School Graduate or Higher (%)					Bachelor's Degree or Higher (%)				
	Total	White	Black	Asian	Hisp.[2]	Total	White	Black	Asian	Hisp.[2]
City	87.1	90.2	86.7	94.9	45.1	45.9	58.7	29.6	76.9	13.1
MSA[1]	87.5	90.3	84.4	91.7	49.4	43.1	49.8	25.6	76.1	12.7
U.S.	85.9	88.1	82.5	85.5	63.1	28.6	30.0	18.4	50.2	13.4

Note: Figures shown cover persons 25 years old and over; (1) Figures cover the Durham-Chapel Hill, NC Metropolitan Statistical Area—see Appendix B for areas included; (2) People of Hispanic origin can be of any race
Source: U.S. Census Bureau, 2010-2012 American Community Survey 3-Year Estimates

School Enrollment by Grade and Control

Area	Preschool (%)		Kindergarten (%)		Grades 1 - 4 (%)		Grades 5 - 8 (%)		Grades 9 - 12 (%)	
	Public	Private	Public	Private	Public	Private	Public	Private	Public	Private
City	48.6	51.4	93.4	6.6	92.0	8.0	88.8	11.2	92.5	7.5
MSA[1]	42.9	57.1	92.4	7.6	91.9	8.1	89.8	10.2	91.5	8.5
U.S.	56.9	43.1	87.8	12.2	89.9	10.1	90.0	10.0	90.8	9.2

Note: Figures shown cover persons 3 years old and over; (1) Figures cover the Durham-Chapel Hill, NC Metropolitan Statistical Area—see Appendix B for areas included
Source: U.S. Census Bureau, 2010-2012 American Community Survey 3-Year Estimates

Average Salaries of Public School Classroom Teachers

Area	2012-13		2013-14		Percent Change 2012-13 to 2013-14	Percent Change 2003-04 to 2013-14
	Dollars	Rank[1]	Dollars	Rank[1]		
North Carolina	45,737	46	45,355	48	-0.84	5.0
U.S. Average	56,103	–	56,689	–	1.04	21.8

Note: (1) State rank ranges from 1 to 51 where 1 indicates highest salary.
Source: National Education Association, Rankings & Estimates: Rankings of the States 2013 and Estimates of School Statistics 2014, March 2014

Higher Education

Four-Year Colleges			Two-Year Colleges			Medical Schools[1]	Law Schools[2]	Voc/ Tech[3]
Public	Private Non-profit	Private For-profit	Public	Private Non-profit	Private For-profit			
1	2	2	1	1	0	1	2	5

Note: Figures cover institutions located within the city limits and include main campuses only; (1) includes schools accredited by the Liaison Committee on Medical Education and the American Osteopathic Association's Commission on Osteopathic College Accreditation; (2) includes ABA-accredited schools, schools with provisional ABA accreditation, and state accredited schools; (3) includes all schools with programs that are less than 2 years.
Source: National Center for Education Statistics, Integrated Postsecondary Education System (IPEDS), 2012-13; Association of American Medical Colleges, Member List, April 24, 2014; American Osteopathic Association, Member List, April 24, 2014; Law School Admission Council, Official Guide to ABA-Approved Law Schools Online, April 24, 2014; Wikipedia, List of Medical Schools in the United States, April 24, 2014; Wikipedia, List of Law Schools in the United States, April 24, 2014

According to *U.S. News & World Report,* the Durham-Chapel Hill, NC metro area is home to two of the best national universities in the U.S.: **Duke University** (#7); **University of North Carolina–Chapel Hill** (#30). The indicators used to capture academic quality fall into a number of categories: assessment by administrators at peer institutions; retention of students; faculty resources; student selectivity; financial resources; alumni giving; high school counselor ratings of colleges; and graduation rate. *U.S. News & World Report, "America's Best Colleges 2014"*

According to *U.S. News & World Report,* the Durham-Chapel Hill, NC metro area is home to two of the top 100 law schools in the U.S.: **Duke University** (#11); **University of North Carolina–Chapel Hill** (#31). The rankings are based on a weighted average of 12 measures of quality: peer assessment score; assessment score by lawyers/judges; median LSAT scores; median undergrad GPA; acceptance rate; employment rates for graduates; placement success; bar passage rate; faculty resources; expenditures per student; student/faculty ratio; and library resources. *U.S. News & World Report, "America's Best Graduate Schools, Law, 2014"*

According to *U.S. News & World Report,* the Durham-Chapel Hill, NC metro area is home to two of the top 100 business schools in the U.S.: **Duke University (Fuqua)** (#11); **University of North Carolina–Chapel Hill (Kenan-Flagler)** (#20). The rankings are based on a weighted average of the following nine measures: quality assessment; peer assessment; recruiter assessment; placement success; mean starting salary and bonus; student selectivity; mean GMAT and GRE scores; mean undergraduate GPA; and acceptance rate. *U.S. News & World Report, "America's Best Graduate Schools, Business, 2014"*

PRESIDENTIAL
ELECTION

2012 Presidential Election Results

Area	Obama	Romney	Other
Durham County	75.8	23.0	1.2
U.S.	51.0	47.2	1.8

Note: Results are percentages and may not add to 100% due to rounding
Source: Dave Leip's Atlas of U.S. Presidential Elections

EMPLOYERS

Major Employers

Company Name	Industry
CISCO Systems	Data conversion equipment, media-to-media: computer
City of Durham	City and town managers' office
Duke University	Colleges and universities
Duke University Health System	General medical and surgical hospitals
Duke University Health System	Radiologist
Durham County Hospital Corporation	General medical and surgical hospitals
Environmental Protection Agency	Environmental protection agency, government
IBM	Computer peripheral equipment
National Institutes of Health	Environmental health program administration, government
Netapp	Computer integrated systems design
North Carolina Central University	Colleges and universities
Patheon	Pharmaceutical preparations
Phyamerica Government Services	Hospital management
Research Triangle Institute	Commercial physical research
Sports Endeavors	Sporting goods and bicycle shops
University of NC at Chapel Hill	Hospital, med school affiliated with nursing & residency
University of NC at Chapel Hill	University
University of NC at Chapel Hill	Medical centers
University of North Carolina Hospitals	General medical and surgical hospitals

Note: Companies shown are located within the Durham-Chapel Hill, NC Metropolitan Statistical Area.
Source: Hoovers.com; Wikipedia

Best Companies to Work For

Blue Cross Blue Shield of North Carolina, headquartered in Durham, is among the "100 Best Companies for Working Mothers." Criteria: workforce representation; child care; flexibility programs; and leave policies. This year *Working Mother* gave particular weight to flexible work arrangements, women's advancement programs, and paid maternity leave. *Working Mother, "100 Best Companies 2013"*

BlueCross and BlueShield of North Carolina, headquartered in Durham, is among the "50 Best Employers for Workers Over 50." Criteria: recruiting practices; opportunities for training, education, and career development; workplace accommodations; alternative work options, such as flexible scheduling, job sharing, and phased retirement; employee health and pension benefits; and retiree benefits. Employers with at least 50 employees based in the U.S. are eligible, including for-profit companies, not-for-profit organizations, and government employers. *AARP, "2013 AARP Best Employers for Workers Over 50"*

Quintiles, headquartered in Durham, is among the "100 Best Places to Work in IT." To qualify, companies, both public and private, had to have a minimum of 50 IT employees and were selected based on average salary and bonus increases, the percentage of IT staffers promoted, IT staff turnover rates, training and development programs, and the percentage of women and minorities in IT staff and management positions. In addition, *Computerworld* looked at retention efforts, programs for recognizing and rewarding outstanding performances, and benefits such as flextime, elder care and child care, and reimbursement for college tuition and the cost of pursuing technology certifications. *Computerworld, "100 Best Places to Work in IT 2013"*

PUBLIC SAFETY

Crime Rate

Area	All Crimes	Violent Crimes				Property Crimes		
		Murder	Forcible Rape	Robbery	Aggrav. Assault	Burglary	Larceny -Theft	Motor Vehicle Theft
City	5,089.5	8.9	26.7	261.1	429.2	1,394.1	2,670.6	298.9
Suburbs[1]	2,848.2	2.1	16.6	38.9	120.7	845.7	1,724.3	99.8
Metro[2]	3,867.3	5.2	21.2	139.9	261.0	1,095.0	2,154.6	190.3
U.S.	3,246.1	4.7	26.9	112.9	242.3	670.2	1,959.3	229.7

Note: Figures are crimes per 100,000 population; (1) All areas within the metro area that are located outside the city limits; (2) Figures cover the Durham-Chapel Hill, NC Metropolitan Statistical Area—see Appendix B for areas included
Source: FBI Uniform Crime Reports, 2012

Hate Crimes

Area	Number of Quarters Reported	Bias Motivation				
		Race	Religion	Sexual Orientation	Ethnicity	Disability
City	4	2	1	2	0	0
U.S.	4	2,797	1,099	1,135	667	92

Source: Federal Bureau of Investigation, Hate Crime Statistics 2012

Identity Theft Consumer Complaints

Area	Complaints	Complaints per 100,000 Population	Rank[2]
MSA[1]	342	67.8	156
U.S.	290,056	91.8	-

Note: (1) Figures cover the Durham-Chapel Hill, NC Metropolitan Statistical Area—see Appendix B for areas included; (2) Rank ranges from 1 to 377 where 1 indicates greatest number of identity theft complaints per 100,000 population
Source: Federal Trade Commission, Consumer Sentinel Network Data Book for January–December 2013

Fraud and Other Consumer Complaints

Area	Complaints	Complaints per 100,000 Population	Rank[2]
MSA[1]	1,728	342.6	232
U.S.	1,811,724	595.2	-

Note: (1) Figures cover the Durham-Chapel Hill, NC Metropolitan Statistical Area—see Appendix B for areas included; (2) Rank ranges from 1 to 377 where 1 indicates greatest number of identity theft complaints per 100,000 population
Source: Federal Trade Commission, Consumer Sentinel Network Data Book for January–December 2013

RECREATION

Culture

Dance[1]	Theatre[1]	Instrumental Music[1]	Vocal Music[1]	Series and Festivals	Museums and Art Galleries[2]	Zoos and Aquariums[3]
1	2	4	1	5	11	0

Note: (1) Number of professional performing groups; (2) Based on organizations with primary SIC code 8412; (3) AZA-accredited
Source: The Grey House Performing Arts Directory, 2013; Association of Zoos & Aquariums, AZA Member Zoos & Aquariums, April 2014; www.AccuLeads.com, May 1, 2014

Professional Sports Teams

Team Name	League	Year Established
Carolina Hurricanes	National Hockey League (NHL)	1997

Note: Includes teams located in the Durham-Chapel Hill, NC Metropolitan Statistical Area.
Source: Wikipedia, Major Professional Sports Teams of the United States and Canada

CLIMATE

Average and Extreme Temperatures

Temperature	Jan	Feb	Mar	Apr	May	Jun	Jul	Aug	Sep	Oct	Nov	Dec	Yr.
Extreme High (°F)	79	84	90	95	97	104	105	105	104	98	88	79	105
Average High (°F)	50	53	61	72	79	86	89	87	81	72	62	53	71
Average Temp. (°F)	40	43	50	59	67	75	78	77	71	60	51	42	60
Average Low (°F)	29	31	38	46	55	63	68	67	60	48	39	32	48
Extreme Low (°F)	-9	5	11	23	29	38	48	46	37	19	11	4	-9

Note: Figures cover the years 1948-1990
Source: National Climatic Data Center, International Station Meteorological Climate Summary, 9/96

Average Precipitation/Snowfall/Humidity

Precip./Humidity	Jan	Feb	Mar	Apr	May	Jun	Jul	Aug	Sep	Oct	Nov	Dec	Yr.
Avg. Precip. (in.)	3.4	3.6	3.6	2.9	3.9	3.6	4.4	4.4	3.2	2.9	3.0	3.1	42.0
Avg. Snowfall (in.)	2	3	1	Tr	0	0	0	0	0	0	Tr	1	8
Avg. Rel. Hum. 7am (%)	79	79	79	80	84	86	88	91	91	90	84	81	84
Avg. Rel. Hum. 4pm (%)	53	49	46	43	51	54	57	59	57	53	51	53	52

Note: Figures cover the years 1948-1990; Tr = Trace amounts (<0.05 in. of rain; <0.5 in. of snow)
Source: National Climatic Data Center, International Station Meteorological Climate Summary, 9/96

Weather Conditions

Temperature			Daytime Sky			Precipitation		
32°F & below	45°F & below	90°F & above	Clear	Partly cloudy	Cloudy	0.01 inch or more precip.	0.1 inch or more snow/ice	Thunder-storms
77	160	39	98	143	124	110	3	42

Note: Figures are average number of days per year and cover the years 1948-1990
Source: National Climatic Data Center, International Station Meteorological Climate Summary, 9/96

HAZARDOUS WASTE

Superfund Sites

Durham has no sites on the EPA's Superfund Final National Priorities List.
U.S. Environmental Protection Agency, Final National Priorities List, April 26, 2014

AIR & WATER QUALITY

Air Quality Index

Area	Percent of Days when Air Quality was...[2]					AQI Statistics[2]	
	Good	Moderate	Unhealthy for Sensitive Groups	Unhealthy	Very Unhealthy	Maximum	Median
MSA[1]	84.9	15.1	0.0	0.0	0.0	90	35

Note: (1) Data covers the Durham-Chapel Hill, NC Metropolitan Statistical Area—see Appendix B for areas included; (2) Based on 365 days with AQI data in 2013. Air Quality Index (AQI) is an index for reporting daily air quality. EPA calculates the AQI for five major air pollutants regulated by the Clean Air Act: ground-level ozone, particle pollution (aka particulate matter), carbon monoxide, sulfur dioxide, and nitrogen dioxide. The AQI runs from 0 to 500. The higher the AQI value, the greater the level of air pollution and the greater the health concern. There are six AQI categories: "Good" AQI is between 0 and 50. Air quality is considered satisfactory; "Moderate" AQI is between 51 and 100. Air quality is acceptable; "Unhealthy for Sensitive Groups" When AQI values are between 101 and 150, members of sensitive groups may experience health effects; "Unhealthy" When AQI values are between 151 and 200 everyone may begin to experience health effects; "Very Unhealthy" AQI values between 201 and 300 trigger a health alert; "Hazardous" AQI values over 300 trigger warnings of emergency conditions (not shown).
Source: U.S. Environmental Protection Agency, Air Quality Index Report, 2013

Air Quality Index Pollutants

| Area | Percent of Days when AQI Pollutant was...[2] | | | | | |
	Carbon Monoxide	Nitrogen Dioxide	Ozone	Sulfur Dioxide	Particulate Matter 2.5	Particulate Matter 10
MSA[1]	0.0	0.0	31.5	0.3	68.2	0.0

Note: (1) Data covers the Durham-Chapel Hill, NC Metropolitan Statistical Area—see Appendix B for areas included; (2) Based on 365 days with AQI data in 2013. The Air Quality Index (AQI) is an index for reporting daily air quality. EPA calculates the AQI for five major air pollutants regulated by the Clean Air Act: ground-level ozone, particle pollution (also known as particulate matter), carbon monoxide, sulfur dioxide, and nitrogen dioxide. The AQI runs from 0 to 500. The higher the AQI value, the greater the level of air pollution and the greater the health concern.
Source: U.S. Environmental Protection Agency, Air Quality Index Report, 2013

Air Quality Trends: Ozone

	2003	2004	2005	2006	2007	2008	2009	2010	2011	2012
MSA[1]	0.079	0.072	0.079	0.073	0.077	0.075	0.064	0.072	0.070	0.068

Note: (1) Data covers the Durham-Chapel Hill, NC Metropolitan Statistical Area—see Appendix B for areas included. The values shown are the composite ozone concentration averages among trend sites based on the highest fourth daily maximum 8-hour concentration in parts per million. These trends are based on sites having an adequate record of monitoring data during the trend period. Data from exceptional events are included.
Source: U.S. Environmental Protection Agency, Air Quality Monitoring Information, "Air Quality Trends by City, 2000-2012"

Maximum Air Pollutant Concentrations: Particulate Matter, Ozone, CO and Lead

	Particulate Matter 10 (ug/m^3)	Particulate Matter 2.5 Wtd AM (ug/m^3)	Particulate Matter 2.5 24-Hr (ug/m^3)	Ozone (ppm)	Carbon Monoxide (ppm)	Lead (ug/m^3)
MSA[1] Level	30	8.3	18	0.076	n/a	n/a
NAAQS[2]	150	15	35	0.075	9	0.15
Met NAAQS[2]	Yes	Yes	Yes	No	n/a	n/a

Note: (1) Data covers the Durham-Chapel Hill, NC Metropolitan Statistical Area—see Appendix B for areas included; Data from exceptional events are included; (2) National Ambient Air Quality Standards; ppm = parts per million; ug/m^3 = micrograms per cubic meter; n/a not available.
Concentrations: Particulate Matter 10 (coarse particulate)—highest second maximum 24-hour concentration; Particulate Matter 2.5 Wtd AM (fine particulate)—highest weighted annual mean concentration; Particulate Matter 2.5 24-Hour (fine particulate)—highest 98th percentile 24-hour concentration; Ozone—highest fourth daily maximum 8-hour concentration; Carbon Monoxide—highest second maximum non-overlapping 8-hour concentration; Lead—maximum running 3-month average
Source: U.S. Environmental Protection Agency, Air Quality Monitoring Information, "Air Quality Statistics by City, 2012"

Maximum Air Pollutant Concentrations: Nitrogen Dioxide and Sulfur Dioxide

	Nitrogen Dioxide AM (ppb)	Nitrogen Dioxide 1-Hr (ppb)	Sulfur Dioxide AM (ppb)	Sulfur Dioxide 1-Hr (ppb)	Sulfur Dioxide 24-Hr (ppb)
MSA[1] Level	n/a	n/a	n/a	n/a	n/a
NAAQS[2]	53	100	30	75	140
Met NAAQS[2]	n/a	n/a	n/a	n/a	n/a

Note: (1) Data covers the Durham-Chapel Hill, NC Metropolitan Statistical Area—see Appendix B for areas included; Data from exceptional events are included; (2) National Ambient Air Quality Standards; ppm = parts per million; ug/m^3 = micrograms per cubic meter; n/a not available.
Concentrations: Nitrogen Dioxide AM—highest arithmetic mean concentration; Nitrogen Dioxide 1-Hr—highest 98th percentile 1-hour daily maximum concentration; Sulfur Dioxide AM—highest annual mean concentration; Sulfur Dioxide 1-Hr—highest 99th percentile 1-hour daily maximum concentration; Sulfur Dioxide 24-Hr—highest second maximum 24-hour concentration
Source: U.S. Environmental Protection Agency, Air Quality Monitoring Information, "Air Quality Statistics by City, 2012"

Drinking Water

Water System Name	Pop. Served	Primary Water Source Type	Violations[1] Health Based	Monitoring/ Reporting
City of Durham	258,636	Surface	0	0

Note: (1) Based on violation data from January 1, 2013 to December 31, 2013 (includes unresolved violations from earlier years)
Source: U.S. Environmental Protection Agency, Office of Ground Water and Drinking Water, Safe Drinking Water Information System (based on data extracted February 10, 2014)

Erie, Pennsylvania

Background

The name Erie is derived from the Eriez tribe of Native Americans, but the area is more commonly remembered as part of the domain of the Six Nations of the Iroquois Confederacy and the Seneca Nation. The first westerners to land were the French who, in 1753, established Fort Presque Isle, which literally means "almost an island." Presque Isle is a small peninsula jutting out into Lake Erie. By 1760 the French had abandoned the area to the British.

An undercurrent of unrest plagued Erie for much of its early history. Once the land was wrested from the Native Americans and the French, the United States fought the British for ownership of the Great Lakes and surrounding lands in the War of 1812. President James Madison ordered the construction of a naval fleet at Erie to help the war effort. Following the U.S. victory, four U.S. states tried to claim Erie, often referred to as the "Erie Triangle" because of its shape, for themselves. New York, Connecticut, and Massachusetts ultimately ceded their claims to the Federal Government, which, in turn, sold it to Pennsylvania.

Erie was an important railroad hub in the mid-19th Century. At the time, there were no standards for rail gauges—the width of rail tracks. Three rail companies converged in Erie, and Erie made a booming business of transferring passengers and goods from one rail line to another. When the idea of standardizing rail gauges was introduced, the Erie citizenry, including the Mayor, responded by destroying the rail bridges in an effort to thwart the standardization efforts, known as the "Erie Gauge War."

A horse-drawn trolley began operations in 1860—one of the best in the nation. Loesch's trolley line operated without competition until the Erie City Railway Company was chartered. Soon after, Loesch's horses all died mysteriously in one night, and his business collapsed. Iin 1889 The Erie City Passenger Railway Company began running an electric trolley that covered 65 miles of track, with 110 streetcars.

More conflict arose for Erie during the era of prohibition. Because of its location on Lake Erie, with relatively easy access to Canadian markets, illicit smuggling rings arose, bringing organized crime and prostitution. This era of speakeasies and lawlessness would be quashed with the stock market crash in 1929, and Erie would turn its attention to repealing prohibition.

Mill Creek, which runs through town to empty into Lake Erie, has a history of flooding. In May of 1893, 60 hours of constant rain caused the creek to change its course when heaps of timber and debris jammed up against the rail bridges, forming temporary reservoirs. The city tried, unsuccessfully, to dynamite the walls of debris. When the wall finally collapsed, a huge torrent inundated the town, destroying everything in its path. Twenty-five years later, an even more devastating flood, killing 36 and destroying 500 buidlings, swept through the city after 5.77 inches of rain fell over thirteen hours. In 1923, the city completed work on an underground tube to contain the creek. The Mill Creek Tube is 12,280 feet long, 22 feet wide, and 19 feet tall.

Today, Erie is the third largest city in Pennsylvania, and an important port for manufacturing and shipping. About one quarter of the area's jobs are in manufacturing, and Erie has the largest concentration of tool-makers of anywhere in the country. The city has made concerted efforts to restore and revitalize the downtown area with its Erie Downtown Partnership (EDP), a non-profit organization, committed to improving the business climate and making the downtown area a more attractive place to live.

Erie is also a college town with four small colleges and one medical school. The Northwestern Pennsylvania Technical Institute offers training in a number of trades.

The climate of Erie is typical of the Great Lakes, Located in the snow belt that stretches from Cleveland to Syracuse and Watertown, Erie's winters are typically cold, with heavy lake effect snow, but also with occasional stretches of mild weather that cause accumulated snow to melt. The city experiences a full range of weather events, including snow, ice, rain, thunderstorms and fog. The city's lakeside location helps to temper summer heat, with an average of only 3.8 days of 90 °F + highs annually, and an average of 2.5 days with sub-0 °F lows annually.

Rankings

Business/Finance Rankings

- The Erie metro area appeared on the Milken Institute "2013 Best Performing Cities" list. Rank: #96 out of 200 large metro areas. Criteria: job growth; wage and salary growth; high-tech output growth. *Milken Institute, "Best-Performing Cities 2013," December 2013*

- *Forbes* ranked the 200 most populous metro areas in the U.S. in terms of the "Best Places for Business and Careers." The Erie metro area was ranked #182. Criteria: costs (business and living); job growth (past and projected); income growth; educational attainment (college and high school); projected economic growth; cultural and recreational opportunities; net migration patterns; number of highly ranked colleges. *Forbes, "The Best Places for Business and Careers," August 7, 2013*

Dating/Romance Rankings

- Erie was selected as one of the most romantic cities in America by Amazon.com. The city ranked #19 of 20. Criteria: cities with 100,000 or more residents were ranked on their per capita sales of romance novels and relationship books, romantic comedy movies, romantic music, and sexual wellness products. *Amazon.com, "Top 20 Most Romantic Cities in America," February 3, 2014*

Environmental Rankings

- The Weather Channel determined the nation's snowiest cities, based on the National Oceanic and Atmospheric Administration's 30-year average snowfall data. Among cities with a population of at least 100,000, the #2-ranked city was Erie *weather.com, America's 20 Snowiest Major Cities, February 3, 2014*

- The Erie metro area came in at #70 for the relative comfort of its climate on Sperling's list of "chill cities," as measured by the Sperling Heat Index. All 361 metro areas are included. Criteria included daytime high temperatures, nighttime low temperatures, dew point, and relative humidity at the high temperatures. *www.bertsperling.com, "Sperling's Chill Cities," July 18, 2013*

- Sperling's BestPlaces assessed 379 metropolitan areas of the United States for the likelihood of dangerously extreme weather events or earthquakes. In general the Southeast and South-Central regions have the highest risk of weather extremes and earthquakes, while the Pacific Northwest enjoys the lowest risk. Of the least risky metropolitan areas, the Erie metro area was ranked #113. *www.bestplaces.net, "Safest Places from Natural Disasters," April 2011*

- Erie was selected as one of 22 "Smarter Cities" for energy by the Natural Resources Defense Council. Criteria: investment in green power; energy efficiency measures; conservation. *Natural Resources Defense Council, "2010 Smarter Cities," July 19, 2010*

Health/Fitness Rankings

- The Erie metro area appeared in the 2013 Gallup-Healthways Well-Being Index. The area ranked #117 out of 189. The Gallup-Healthways Well-Being Index score is an average of six sub-indexes, which individually examine life evaluation, emotional health, work environment, physical health, healthy behaviors, and access to basic necessities. Results are based on telephone interviews conducted as part of the Gallup-Healthways Well-Being Index survey January 2–December 29, 2012, and January 2–December 30, 2013, with a random sample of 531,630 adults, aged 18 and older, living in metropolitan areas in the 50 U.S. states and the District of Columbia. *Gallup-Healthways, "State of American Well-Being," March 25, 2014*

Real Estate Rankings

- The Erie metro area was identified as one of the 20 most affordable housing markets in the U.S. in 2013. The area ranked #18 out of 173 markets. Criteria: whether or not a typical family could qualify for a mortgage loan on a typical home. *National Association of Realtors®, Affordability Index of Existing Single-Family Homes for Metropolitan Areas, 2013*

- Erie was ranked #31 out of 224 metro areas in terms of housing affordability in 2013 by the National Association of Home Builders (#1 = most affordable). The NAHB-Wells Fargo Housing Opportunity Index (HOI) for a given area is defined as the share of homes sold in that area that would have been affordable to a family earning the local median income, based on standard mortgage underwriting criteria. *National Association of Home Builders®, NAHB-Wells Fargo Housing Opportunity Index, 4th Quarter 2013*

Safety Rankings

- Farmers Insurance, in partnership with Sperling's BestPlaces, ranked metro areas in the U.S. and identified the "Most Secure Places to Live." The Erie metro area ranked #10 out of the top 20 in the mid-size city category (150,000 to 500,000 residents). Criteria: economic stability; crime statistics; extreme weather; risk of natural disasters; housing depreciation; foreclosures; air quality; environmental hazards; life expectancy; motor vehicle fatalities; and employment numbers. *Farmers Insurance Group of Companies, "Most Secure U.S. Places to Live in the U.S.," June 25, 2013*

- The National Insurance Crime Bureau ranked 380 metro areas in the U.S. in terms of per capita rates of vehicle theft. The Erie metro area ranked #333 (#1 = highest rate). Criteria: number of vehicle theft offenses per 100,000 inhabitants in 2012. *National Insurance Crime Bureau, "Hot Spots 2012," June 26, 2013*

Seniors/Retirement Rankings

- *AARP the Magazine* selected Erie as one of the ten of best places in the United States for seniors to live the "good life." For the 2013 list, the magazine looked for cities where seniors could live comfortably on $30,000 annually, considering median home prices, property taxes, and mortgage rates along with amenities such as entertainment and local eateries. *www.aarp.org/magazine, "AARP the Magazine Reveals 2013 List of Best Places to Live the Good Life for Under $30k," October 9, 2013*

- From its Best Cities for Successful Aging indexes, the Milken Institute generated rankings for metropolitan areas, weighing data in eight categories—general indicators, health care, wellness, living arrangements, transportation and general accessibility, financial well-being, education and employment, and community participation. The Erie metro area was ranked #182 overall in the small metro area category. *Milken Institute, "Best Cities for Successful Aging," July 2012*

Business Environment

CITY FINANCES

City Government Finances

Component	2011 ($000)	2011 ($ per capita)
Total Revenues	137,172	1,323
Total Expenditures	119,259	1,151
Debt Outstanding	159,910	1,543
Cash and Securities[1]	210,885	2,035

Note: (1) Cash and security holdings of a government at the close of its fiscal year, including those of its dependent agencies, utilities, and liquor stores.
Source: U.S Census Bureau, State & Local Government Finances 2011

City Government Revenue by Source

Source	2011 ($000)	2011 ($ per capita)
General Revenue		
From Federal Government	8,732	84
From State Government	8,941	86
From Local Governments	11,124	107
Taxes		
Property	28,041	271
Sales and Gross Receipts	0	0
Personal Income	10,783	104
Corporate Income	0	0
Motor Vehicle License	0	0
Other Taxes	6,640	64
Current Charges	31,509	304
Liquor Store	0	0
Utility	0	0
Employee Retirement	24,199	233

Source: U.S Census Bureau, State & Local Government Finances 2011

City Government Expenditures by Function

Function	2011 ($000)	2011 ($ per capita)	2011 (%)
General Direct Expenditures			
Air Transportation	0	0	0.0
Corrections	0	0	0.0
Education	0	0	0.0
Employment Security Administration	0	0	0.0
Financial Administration	483	5	0.4
Fire Protection	10,349	100	8.7
General Public Buildings	5,137	50	4.3
Governmental Administration, Other	2,143	21	1.8
Health	0	0	0.0
Highways	9,567	92	8.0
Hospitals	0	0	0.0
Housing and Community Development	11,227	108	9.4
Interest on General Debt	7,848	76	6.6
Judicial and Legal	391	4	0.3
Libraries	0	0	0.0
Parking	0	0	0.0
Parks and Recreation	1,671	16	1.4
Police Protection	14,212	137	11.9
Public Welfare	0	0	0.0
Sewerage	8,971	87	7.5
Solid Waste Management	4,421	43	3.7
Veterans' Services	0	0	0.0
Liquor Store	0	0	0.0
Utility	0	0	0.0
Employee Retirement	17,933	173	15.0

Source: U.S Census Bureau, State & Local Government Finances 2011

DEMOGRAPHICS

Population Growth

Area	1990 Census	2000 Census	2010 Census	Population Growth (%) 1990-2000	Population Growth (%) 2000-2010
City	108,718	103,717	101,786	-4.6	-1.9
MSA[1]	275,603	280,843	280,566	1.9	-0.1
U.S.	248,709,873	281,421,906	308,745,538	13.2	9.7

Note: (1) Figures cover the Erie, PA Metropolitan Statistical Area—see Appendix B for areas included
Source: U.S. Census Bureau, Census 1990, 2000, 2010

Household Size

Area	Persons in Household (%) One	Two	Three	Four	Five	Six	Seven or More	Average Household Size
City	36.9	31.7	13.9	9.7	4.8	1.5	1.5	2.33
MSA[1]	30.5	34.7	14.8	12.1	5.1	1.7	1.0	2.45
U.S.	27.6	33.5	15.7	13.2	6.1	2.4	1.5	2.63

Note: (1) Figures cover the Erie, PA Metropolitan Statistical Area—see Appendix B for areas included
Source: U.S. Census Bureau, 2010-2012 American Community Survey 3-Year Estimates

Race

Area	White Alone[2] (%)	Black Alone[2] (%)	Asian Alone[2] (%)	AIAN[3] Alone[2] (%)	NHOPI[4] Alone[2] (%)	Other Race Alone[2] (%)	Two or More Races (%)
City	75.7	16.2	2.1	0.5	0.0	1.8	3.7
MSA[1]	88.3	7.1	1.2	0.3	0.0	0.9	2.2
U.S.	74.0	12.6	4.9	0.8	0.2	4.7	2.8

Note: (1) Figures cover the Erie, PA Metropolitan Statistical Area—see Appendix B for areas included; (2)
Alone is defined as not being in combination with one or more other races; (3) American Indian and Alaska
Native; (4) Native Hawaiian and Other Pacific Islander
Source: U.S. Census Bureau, 2010-2012 American Community Survey 3-Year Estimates

Hispanic or Latino Origin

Area	Total (%)	Mexican (%)	Puerto Rican (%)	Cuban (%)	Other (%)
City	6.7	1.4	4.3	0.1	0.9
MSA[1]	3.5	0.9	1.9	0.1	0.6
U.S.	16.6	10.7	1.6	0.6	3.7

Note: Persons of Hispanic or Latino origin can be of any race; (1) Figures cover the Erie, PA Metropolitan
Statistical Area—see Appendix B for areas included
Source: U.S. Census Bureau, 2010-2012 American Community Survey 3-Year Estimates

Segregation

Type	Segregation Indices[1] 1990	2000	2010	2010 Rank[2]	Percent Change 1990-2000	1990-2010	2000-2010
Black/White	n/a	n/a	n/a	n/a	n/a	n/a	n/a
Asian/White	n/a	n/a	n/a	n/a	n/a	n/a	n/a
Hispanic/White	n/a	n/a	n/a	n/a	n/a	n/a	n/a

Note: All figures cover the Metropolitan Statistical Area—see Appendix B for areas included; Figures are based
on an analysis of 1990, 2000, and 2010 Census Decennial Census tract data by William H. Frey, Brookings
Institution and the University of Michigan Social Science Data Analysis Network. In this analysis all racial
groups (whites, blacks, and asians) are non-Hispanic members of those races. Hispanics are shown as a
separate category;
(1) Segregation Indices are Dissimilarity Indices that measure the degree to which the minority group is
distributed differently than whites across census tracts. They range from 0 (complete integration) to 100
(complete segregation) where the value indicates the percentage of the minority group that needs to move to be
distributed exactly like whites; (2) Ranges from 1 (most segregated) to 102 (least segregated); n/a not available.
Source: www.CensusScope.org

Ancestry

Area	German	Irish	English	American	Italian	Polish	French[2]	Scottish	Dutch
City	23.5	14.8	4.5	2.8	12.6	12.6	1.8	0.8	1.3
MSA[1]	29.5	17.4	7.9	4.9	13.2	12.5	1.8	1.6	1.5
U.S.	15.2	11.1	8.2	7.2	5.6	3.1	2.8	1.7	1.4

Note: Figures are the percentage of the total population reporting a particular ancestry. The nine most commonly reported ancestries in the U.S. are shown. Figures include multiple ancestries (e.g. if a person reported being Irish and Italian, they were included in both columns); (1) Figures cover the Erie, PA Metropolitan Statistical Area—see Appendix B for areas included; (2) Excludes Basque
Source: U.S. Census Bureau, 2010-2012 American Community Survey 3-Year Estimates

Foreign-Born Population

Area	Any Foreign Country	Mexico	Asia	Europe	Carribean	South America	Central America[2]	Africa	Canada
				Percent of Population Born in					
City	n/a	n/a	n/a	n/a	n/a	n/a	n/a	n/a	n/a
MSA[1]	4.1	0.2	1.3	1.7	0.1	0.1	0.1	0.4	0.2
U.S.	13.0	3.7	3.7	1.6	1.2	0.9	1.0	0.5	0.3

Note: (1) Figures cover the Erie, PA Metropolitan Statistical Area—see Appendix B for areas included; (2) Excludes Mexico.
Source: U.S. Census Bureau, 2010-2012 American Community Survey 3-Year Estimates

Marital Status

Area	Never Married	Now Married[2]	Separated	Widowed	Divorced
City	42.2	36.4	3.5	6.9	11.1
MSA[1]	34.3	46.4	2.6	6.9	9.8
U.S.	32.4	48.4	2.2	6.0	11.0

Note: Figures are percentages and cover the population 15 years of age and older; (1) Figures cover the Erie, PA Metropolitan Statistical Area—see Appendix B for areas included; (2) Excludes separated
Source: U.S. Census Bureau, 2010-2012 American Community Survey 3-Year Estimates

Age

Area	Under Age 5	Age 5–19	Age 20–34	Age 35–44	Age 45–54	Age 55–64	Age 65–74	Age 75–84	Age 85+	Median Age
					Percent of Population					
City	7.1	20.5	23.7	11.7	12.8	11.1	6.2	4.4	2.5	33.9
MSA[1]	5.9	20.2	19.9	11.8	14.4	13.2	7.5	4.9	2.3	38.7
U.S.	6.4	20.1	20.5	13.1	14.3	12.2	7.3	4.2	1.8	37.3

Note: (1) Figures cover the Erie, PA Metropolitan Statistical Area—see Appendix B for areas included
Source: U.S. Census Bureau, 2010-2012 American Community Survey 3-Year Estimates

Gender

Area	Males	Females	Males per 100 Females
City	49,329	52,090	94.7
MSA[1]	138,077	142,717	96.7
U.S.	153,276,055	158,333,314	96.8

Note: (1) Figures cover the Erie, PA Metropolitan Statistical Area—see Appendix B for areas included
Source: U.S. Census Bureau, 2010-2012 American Community Survey 3-Year Estimates

Religious Groups by Family

Area	Catholic	Baptist	Non-Den.	Methodist[2]	Lutheran	LDS[3]	Pentecostal	Presbyterian[4]	Muslim[5]	Judaism
MSA[1]	33.5	2.2	1.7	5.7	3.0	0.6	2.2	2.1	0.7	0.2
U.S.	19.1	9.3	4.0	4.0	2.3	2.0	1.9	1.6	0.8	0.7

Note: Figures are the number of adherents as a percentage of the total population; (1) Figures cover the Erie, PA Metropolitan Statistical Area—see Appendix B for areas included; (2) Methodist/Pietist; (3) Latter Day Saints; (4) Reformed; (5) Figures are estimates
Source: Association of Statisticians of American Religious Bodies, 2010 U.S. Religion Census: Religious Congregations & Membership Study

Religious Groups by Tradition

Area	Catholic	Evangelical Protestant	Mainline Protestant	Other Tradition	Black Protestant	Orthodox
MSA[1]	33.5	8.4	11.7	1.6	0.9	0.3
U.S.	19.1	16.2	7.3	4.3	1.6	0.3

Note: Figures are the number of adherents as a percentage of the total population; (1) Figures cover the Erie, PA Metropolitan Statistical Area—see Appendix B for areas included
Source: Association of Statisticians of American Religious Bodies, 2010 U.S. Religion Census: Religious Congregations & Membership Study

ECONOMY

Gross Metropolitan Product

Area	2011	2012	2013	2014	Rank[2]
MSA[1]	9.7	10.0	10.1	10.5	182

Note: Figures are in billions of dollars; (1) Figures cover the Erie, PA Metropolitan Statistical Area—see Appendix B for areas included; (2) Rank is based on 2014 data and ranges from 1 to 363
Source: The United States Conference of Mayors, U.S. Metro Economies: Outlook—Gross Metropolitan Product, with Metro Employment Projections, November 2013

Economic Growth

Area	2011 (%)	2012 (%)	2013 (%)	2014 (%)	Rank[2]
MSA[1]	5.3	1.0	0.2	1.7	230
U.S.	1.6	2.5	1.7	2.5	–

Note: Figures are real gross metropolitan product (GMP) growth rates and represent annual average percent change; (1) Figures cover the Erie, PA Metropolitan Statistical Area—see Appendix B for areas included; (2) Rank is based on 2013 data and ranges from 1 to 363
Source: The United States Conference of Mayors, U.S. Metro Economies: Outlook—Gross Metropolitan Product, with Metro Employment Projections, November 2013

Metropolitan Area Exports

Area	2007	2008	2009	2010	2011	2012	Rank[2]
MSA[1]	1,135.3	1,861.9	1,407.8	1,063.3	1,577.7	1,854.2	104

Note: Figures are in millions of dollars; (1) Figures cover the Erie, PA Metropolitan Statistical Area—see Appendix B for areas included; (2) Rank is based on 2012 data and ranges from 1 to 369
Source: U.S. Department of Commerce, International Trade Administration, Office of Trade & Industry Information, Manufacturing & Services, data extracted April 1, 2014

INCOME

Income

Area	Per Capita ($)	Median Household ($)	Average Household ($)
City	18,207	31,838	42,773
MSA[1]	23,650	44,475	58,689
U.S.	27,385	51,771	71,579

Note: (1) Figures cover the Erie, PA Metropolitan Statistical Area—see Appendix B for areas included
Source: U.S. Census Bureau, 2010-2012 American Community Survey 3-Year Estimates

Household Income Distribution

Area	Under $15,000	$15,000 -24,999	$25,000 -34,999	$35,000 -49,999	$50,000 -74,999	$75,000 -99,000	$100,000 -149,999	$150,000 and up
City	24.4	15.9	13.0	15.6	15.6	8.3	5.3	2.0
MSA[1]	15.9	12.6	11.5	14.8	19.2	11.3	9.9	4.6
U.S.	13.1	11.0	10.5	13.7	18.1	11.9	12.5	9.1

Note: (1) Figures cover the Erie, PA Metropolitan Statistical Area—see Appendix B for areas included
Source: U.S. Census Bureau, 2010-2012 American Community Survey 3-Year Estimates

Poverty Rate

Area	All Ages	Under 18 Years Old	18 to 64 Years Old	65 Years and Over
City	28.1	43.1	25.2	14.0
MSA[1]	16.6	24.7	15.4	9.1
U.S.	15.7	22.2	14.6	9.3

Note: Figures are percentage of people whose income during the past 12 months was below the poverty level;
(1) Figures cover the Erie, PA Metropolitan Statistical Area—see Appendix B for areas included
Source: U.S. Census Bureau, 2010-2012 American Community Survey 3-Year Estimates

Personal Bankruptcy Filing Rate

Area	2008	2009	2010	2011	2012	2013
Erie County	3.69	3.33	3.56	3.23	2.70	2.43
U.S.	3.53	4.61	4.97	4.37	3.76	3.29

Note: Numbers are per 1,000 population and include Chapter 7 and Chapter 13 filings
Source: Federal Deposit Insurance Corporation, Regional Economic Conditions, March 20, 2014

EMPLOYMENT

Labor Force and Employment

Area	Civilian Labor Force			Workers Employed		
	Dec. 2012	Dec. 2013	% Chg.	Dec. 2012	Dec. 2013	% Chg.
City	48,156	48,060	-0.2	43,940	44,643	1.6
MSA[1]	140,809	140,694	-0.1	129,605	131,678	1.6
U.S.	154,904,000	154,408,000	-0.3	143,060,000	144,423,000	1.0

Note: Data is not seasonally adjusted and covers workers 16 years of age and older; (1) Metropolitan Statistical Area—see Appendix B for areas included
Source: Bureau of Labor Statistics, Local Area Unemployment Statistics

Unemployment Rate

Area	2013											
	Jan.	Feb.	Mar.	Apr.	May	Jun.	Jul.	Aug.	Sep.	Oct.	Nov.	Dec.
City	10.1	9.1	8.7	7.7	7.8	8.7	8.5	8.6	7.6	7.7	8.0	7.1
MSA[1]	9.2	8.2	7.8	7.2	7.1	7.7	7.5	7.6	6.6	6.7	7.1	6.4
U.S.	8.5	8.1	7.6	7.1	7.3	7.8	7.7	7.3	7.0	7.0	6.6	6.5

Note: Data is not seasonally adjusted and covers workers 16 years of age and older; All figures are percentages;
(1) Metropolitan Statistical Area—see Appendix B for areas included
Source: Bureau of Labor Statistics, Local Area Unemployment Statistics

Employment by Occupation

Occupation Classification	City (%)	MSA[1] (%)	U.S. (%)
Management, Business, Science, and Arts	27.5	32.8	36.0
Natural Resources, Construction, and Maintenance	6.3	7.5	9.1
Production, Transportation, and Material Moving	17.8	16.8	12.0
Sales and Office	23.9	23.4	24.7
Service	24.6	19.5	18.2

Note: Figures cover employed civilians 16 years of age and older; (1) Figures cover the Erie, PA Metropolitan Statistical Area—see Appendix B for areas included
Source: U.S. Census Bureau, 2010-2012 American Community Survey 3-Year Estimates

Employment by Industry

Sector	MSA[1]		U.S.
	Number of Employees	Percent of Total	Percent of Total
Construction	n/a	n/a	4.2
Education and Health Services	27,800	21.3	15.5
Financial Activities	6,300	4.8	5.7
Government	16,700	12.8	16.1
Information	1,300	1.0	1.9
Leisure and Hospitality	13,200	10.1	10.2
Manufacturing	22,100	17.0	8.7
Mining and Logging	n/a	n/a	0.6
Other Services	6,200	4.8	3.9
Professional and Business Services	9,600	7.4	13.7
Retail Trade	15,900	12.2	11.4
Transportation and Utilities	3,300	2.5	3.8
Wholesale Trade	3,900	3.0	4.2

Note: Figures cover non-farm employment as of December 2013 and are not seasonally adjusted;
(1) Metropolitan Statistical Area—see Appendix B for areas included; n/a not available
Source: Bureau of Labor Statistics, Current Employment Statistics, Employment, Hours, and Earnings

Occupations with Greatest Projected Employment Growth: 2010 – 2020

Occupation[1]	2010 Employment	2020 Projected Employment	Numeric Employment Change	Percent Employment Change
Registered Nurses	136,470	159,610	23,140	17.0
Home Health Aides	67,900	89,820	21,920	32.3
Heavy and Tractor-Trailer Truck Drivers	71,510	83,040	11,530	16.1
Combined Food Preparation and Serving Workers, Including Fast Food	115,230	126,100	10,870	9.4
Personal Care Aides	36,860	47,130	10,280	27.9
Retail Salespersons	189,930	199,800	9,870	5.2
Office Clerks, General	151,450	160,950	9,490	6.3
Nursing Aides, Orderlies, and Attendants	78,080	86,470	8,390	10.8
Laborers and Freight, Stock, and Material Movers, Hand	102,590	110,170	7,590	7.4
Landscaping and Groundskeeping Workers	45,700	53,130	7,430	16.3

Note: Projections cover Pennsylvania; (1) Sorted by numeric employment change
Source: www.projectionscentral.com, State Occupational Projections, 2010–2020 Long-Term Projections

Fastest Growing Occupations: 2010 – 2020

Occupation[1]	2010 Employment	2020 Projected Employment	Numeric Employment Change	Percent Employment Change
Service Unit Operators, Oil, Gas, and Mining	1,040	2,130	1,090	104.6
Rotary Drill Operators, Oil and Gas	1,100	2,200	1,110	100.6
Derrick Operators, Oil and Gas	210	420	210	97.2
Roustabouts, Oil and Gas	1,170	2,290	1,120	95.5
Pump Operators, Except Wellhead Pumpers	700	1,250	550	78.5
Wellhead Pumpers	1,080	1,900	820	76.4
Petroleum Engineers	240	420	180	72.9
Gaming Dealers	1,920	3,280	1,360	71.0
Biomedical Engineers	960	1,560	600	62.6
Helpers—Extraction Workers	1,210	1,920	710	58.9

Note: Projections cover Pennsylvania; (1) Sorted by percent employment change and excludes occupations with numeric employment change less than 100
Source: www.projectionscentral.com, State Occupational Projections, 2010–2020 Long-Term Projections

Average Wages

Occupation	$/Hr.	Occupation	$/Hr.
Accountants and Auditors	28.43	Maids and Housekeeping Cleaners	8.84
Automotive Mechanics	15.68	Maintenance and Repair Workers	15.58
Bookkeepers	15.06	Marketing Managers	56.19
Carpenters	18.21	Nuclear Medicine Technologists	n/a
Cashiers	8.83	Nurses, Licensed Practical	18.48
Clerks, General Office	12.89	Nurses, Registered	26.75
Clerks, Receptionists/Information	11.20	Nursing Assistants	12.25
Clerks, Shipping/Receiving	13.62	Packers and Packagers, Hand	11.76
Computer Programmers	36.17	Physical Therapists	37.13
Computer Systems Analysts	30.92	Postal Service Mail Carriers	23.58
Computer User Support Specialists	18.99	Real Estate Brokers	n/a
Cooks, Restaurant	10.73	Retail Salespersons	11.39
Dentists	75.00	Sales Reps., Exc. Tech./Scientific	30.08
Electrical Engineers	37.20	Sales Reps., Tech./Scientific	39.28
Electricians	24.09	Secretaries, Exc. Legal/Med./Exec.	13.84
Financial Managers	48.31	Security Guards	11.23
First-Line Supervisors/Managers, Sales	18.73	Surgeons	115.46
Food Preparation Workers	10.73	Teacher Assistants	10.00
General and Operations Managers	50.50	Teachers, Elementary School	27.00
Hairdressers/Cosmetologists	11.14	Teachers, Secondary School	24.10
Internists	n/a	Telemarketers	8.65
Janitors and Cleaners	10.54	Truck Drivers, Heavy/Tractor-Trailer	18.04
Landscaping/Groundskeeping Workers	11.09	Truck Drivers, Light/Delivery Svcs.	15.28
Lawyers	56.25	Waiters and Waitresses	9.07

Note: Wage data covers the Erie, PA Metropolitan Statistical Area—see Appendix B for areas included. Hourly wages for elementary/secondary school teachers and teacher assistants were calculated by the editors from annual wage data assuming a 40 hour work week; n/a not available.
Source: Bureau of Labor Statistics, Metro Area Occupational Employment and Wage Estimates, May 2013

RESIDENTIAL REAL ESTATE

Building Permits

Area	Single-Family			Multi-Family			Total		
	2012	2013	Pct. Chg.	2012	2013	Pct. Chg.	2012	2013	Pct. Chg.
City	40	2	-95.0	0	0	-	40	2	-95.0
MSA[1]	216	258	19.4	272	209	-23.2	488	467	-4.3
U.S.	518,695	620,802	19.7	310,963	370,020	19.0	829,658	990,822	19.4

Note: (1) Metropolitan Statistical Area—see Appendix B for areas included; figures represent new, privately-owned housing units authorized (unadjusted data); All permit data are based on estimates with imputation.
Source: U.S. Census Bureau, Manufacturing, Mining, and Construction Statistics, Building Permits, 2012, 2013

Homeownership Rate

Area	2006 (%)	2007 (%)	2008 (%)	2009 (%)	2010 (%)	2011 (%)	2012 (%)	2013 (%)
MSA[1]	n/a	n/a	n/a	n/a	n/a	n/a	n/a	n/a
U.S.	68.8	68.1	67.8	67.4	66.9	66.1	65.4	65.1

Note: (1) Figures cover the Erie, PA Metropolitan Statistical Area—see Appendix B for areas included; n/a not available
Source: U.S. Census Bureau, Housing Vacancies and Homeownership Annual Statistics: 2013

Housing Vacancy Rates

Area	Gross Vacancy Rate[2] (%)			Year-Round Vacancy Rate[3] (%)			Rental Vacancy Rate[4] (%)			Homeowner Vacancy Rate[5] (%)		
	2011	2012	2013	2011	2012	2013	2011	2012	2013	2011	2012	2013
MSA[1]	n/a	n/a	n/a	n/a	n/a	n/a	n/a	n/a	n/a	n/a	n/a	n/a
U.S.	14.2	13.8	13.8	11.1	10.8	10.7	9.5	8.7	8.3	2.5	2.0	2.0

Note: (1) Figures cover the Erie, PA Metropolitan Statistical Area—see Appendix B for areas included; (2) The percentage of the total housing inventory that is vacant; (3) The percentage of the housing inventory (excluding seasonal units) that is year-round vacant; (4) The percentage of rental inventory that is vacant for rent; (5) The percentage of homeowner inventory that is vacant for sale; n/a not available
Source: U.S. Census Bureau, Housing Vacancies and Homeownership Annual Statistics: 2013

TAXES

State Corporate Income Tax Rates

State	Tax Rate (%)	Income Brackets ($)	Num. of Brackets	Financial Institution Tax Rate (%)[a]	Federal Income Tax Ded.
Pennsylvania	9.99	Flat rate	1	(a)	No

Note: Tax rates as of January 1, 2014; (a) Rates listed are the corporate income tax rate applied to financial institutions or excise taxes based on income. Some states have other taxes based upon the value of deposits or shares.
Source: Federation of Tax Administrators, "State Corporate Income Tax Rates, 2014"

State Individual Income Tax Rates

State	Tax Rate (%)	Income Brackets ($)	Num. of Brackets	Personal Exempt. ($)[1] Single	Personal Exempt. ($)[1] Dependents	Fed. Inc. Tax Ded.
Pennsylvania	3.07	Flat rate	1	None		No

Note: Tax rates as of January 1, 2014; Local- and county-level taxes are not included; n/a not applicable;
(1) Married joint filers generally receive double the single exemption
Source: Federation of Tax Administrators, "State Individual Income Tax Rates, 2014"

Various State and Local Tax Rates

State	State and Local Sales and Use (%)	State Sales and Use (%)	Gasoline[1] (¢/gal.)	Cigarette[2] ($/pack)	Spirits[3] ($/gal.)	Wine[4] ($/gal.)	Beer[5] ($/gal.)
Pennsylvania	6.0	6.00	41.80	1.600	7.21 (g)	(l)	0.08

Note: All tax rates as of January 1, 2014; (1) The American Petroleum Institute has developed a methodology for determining the average tax rate on a gallon of fuel. Rates may include any of the following: excise taxes, environmental fees, storage tank fees, other fees or taxes, general sales tax, and local taxes. In states where gasoline is subject to the general sales tax, or where the fuel tax is based on the average sale price, the average rate determined by API is sensitive to changes in the price of gasoline. States that fully or partially apply general sales taxes to gasoline: CA, CO, GA, IL, IN, MI, NY; (2) The federal excise tax of $1.0066 per pack and local taxes are not included; (3) Rates are those applicable to off-premise sales of 40% alcohol by volume (a.b.v.) distilled spirits in 750ml containers. Local excise taxes are excluded; (4) Rates are those applicable to off-premise sales of 11% a.b.v. non-carbonated wine in 750ml containers; (5) Rates are those applicable to off-premise sales of 4.7% a.b.v. beer in 12 ounce containers; (g) States where the government controls sales. In these "control states," products are subject to ad valorem mark-up and excise taxes. The excise tax rate is calculated using a methodology developed by the Distilled Spirits Council of the United States; (l) Control states, where the government controls all sales. Products can be subject to ad valorem mark-up and excise taxes.
Source: Tax Foundation, 2014 Facts & Figures: How Does Your State Compare?

State Business Tax Climate Index Rankings

State	Overall Rank	Corporate Tax Index Rank	Individual Income Tax Index Rank	Sales Tax Index Rank	Unemployment Insurance Tax Index Rank	Property Tax Index Rank
Pennsylvania	24	46	16	19	39	43

Note: The index is a measure of how each state's tax laws affect economic performance. The lower the rank, the more favorable a state's tax system is for business. States without a given tax are given a ranking of 1. The scores/rankings for the District of Columbia do not affect other states. The 2014 index represents the tax climate as of July 1, 2013.
Source: Tax Foundation, State Business Tax Climate Index 2014

COMMERCIAL UTILITIES

Typical Monthly Electric Bills

Area	Commercial Service ($/month) 1,500 kWh	Commercial Service ($/month) 40 kW demand 14,000 kWh	Industrial Service ($/month) 1,000 kW demand 200,000 kWh	Industrial Service ($/month) 50,000 kW demand 15,000,000 kWh
City	160	1,409	19,494	1,268,154
Average[1]	197	1,636	25,662	1,485,307

Note: Based on total rates in effect July 1, 2013; (1) average based on 180 utilities surveyed
Source: Edison Electric Institute, Typical Bills and Average Rates Report, Summer 2013

TRANSPORTATION

Means of Transportation to Work

Area	Car/Truck/Van		Public Transportation			Bicycle	Walked	Other Means	Worked at Home
	Drove Alone	Car-pooled	Bus	Subway	Railroad				
City	75.7	10.9	4.7	0.0	0.0	0.3	5.4	1.0	2.0
MSA[1]	81.2	9.0	1.8	0.0	0.0	0.2	3.9	0.8	3.1
U.S.	76.4	9.7	2.6	1.7	0.5	0.6	2.8	1.3	4.3

Note: Figures are percentages and cover workers 16 years of age and older; (1) Figures cover the Erie, PA Metropolitan Statistical Area—see Appendix B for areas included
Source: U.S. Census Bureau, 2010-2012 American Community Survey 3-Year Estimates

Travel Time to Work

Area	Less Than 10 Minutes	10 to 19 Minutes	20 to 29 Minutes	30 to 44 Minutes	45 to 59 Minutes	60 to 89 Minutes	90 Minutes or More
City	20.0	50.8	15.7	8.8	2.5	1.4	0.7
MSA[1]	19.3	39.2	21.9	14.0	3.1	1.4	1.1
U.S.	13.5	29.8	20.9	20.1	7.5	5.6	2.5

Note: Figures are percentages and include workers 16 years old and over; (1) Figures cover the Erie, PA Metropolitan Statistical Area—see Appendix B for areas included
Source: U.S. Census Bureau, 2010-2012 American Community Survey 3-Year Estimates

Travel Time Index

Area	1985	1990	1995	2000	2005	2010	2011
Urban Area[1]	n/a	n/a	n/a	n/a	n/a	n/a	n/a
Average[2]	1.09	1.14	1.16	1.19	1.23	1.18	1.18

Note: Travel Time Index—the ratio of travel time in the peak period to the travel time at free-flow conditions. For example, a value of 1.30 indicates a 20-minute free-flow trip takes 26 minutes in the peak. Free-flow speeds (60 mph on freeways and 35 mph on principal arterials) are used as the comparison threshold; (1) Data for the Erie, PA urban area was not available; (2) average of 498 urban areas
Source: Texas Transportation Institute, Urban Mobility Report 2012, December 2012

Public Transportation

Agency Name / Mode of Transportation	Vehicles Operated in Maximum Service	Annual Unlinked Passenger Trips (in thous.)	Annual Passenger Miles (in thous.)
Erie Metropolitan Transit Authority			
Bus (directly operated)	62	3,408.2	9,838.2
Demand Response (directly operated)	58	246.1	1,663.4

Source: Federal Transit Administration, National Transit Database, 2012

Air Transportation

Airport Name and Code / Type of Service	Passenger Airlines[1]	Passenger Enplanements	Freight Carriers[2]	Freight (lbs.)
Erie International Airport (ERI)				
Domestic service (U.S. carriers - 2013)	6	109,113	3	4,961
International service (U.S. carriers - 2012)	0	0	0	0

Note: (1) Includes all U.S.-based major, minor and commuter airlines that carried at least one passenger during the year; (2) Includes all U.S.-based airlines and freight carriers that transported at least one lb. of freight during the year.
Source: Bureau of Transportation Statistics, The Intermodal Transportation Database, Air Carriers: T-100 Domestic Market (U.S. Carriers), 2013; Bureau of Transportation Statistics, The Intermodal Transportation Database, Air Carriers: T-100 International Market (U.S. Carriers), 2012

Other Transportation Statistics

Major Highways:	I-79; I-86; I-90
Amtrak Service:	Yes
Major Waterways/Ports:	Lake Erie

Source: Amtrak.com; Google Maps

BUSINESSES

Major Business Headquarters

Company Name	Rankings	
	Fortune[1]	Forbes[2]
Erie Insurance Group	455	-

Note: (1) Fortune 500—companies that produce a 10-K are ranked 1 to 500 based on 2012 revenue; (2) all private companies with at least $2 billion in annual revenue through the end of their most current fiscal year are ranked 1 to 224; companies listed are headquartered in the city; dashes indicate no ranking
Source: Fortune, "Fortune 500," May 20, 2013; Forbes, "America's Largest Private Companies," December 18, 2013

Minority Business Opportunity

Erie is home to one company which is on the *Hispanic Business* 500 list (500 largest U.S. Hispanic-owned companies based on 2012 revenue): **McManis & Monsalve Associates** (#337). Companies included must show at least 51 percent ownership by Hispanic U.S. citizens, and must maintain headquarters in one of the 50 states or Washington, D.C. *Hispanic Business, "Hispanic Business 500," June 20, 2013*

Erie is home to one company which is on the *Hispanic Business* Fastest-Growing 100 list (greatest sales growth from 2008 to 2012): **McManis & Monsalve Associates** (#48). Companies included must show at least 51 percent ownership by Hispanic U.S. citizens, and must maintain headquarters in one of the 50 states or Washington, D.C. In addition, companies must have minimum revenues of $200,000 for calendar year 2008. *Hispanic Business, June20, 2013*

Minority- and Women-Owned Businesses

Group	All Firms		Firms with Paid Employees			
	Firms	Sales ($000)	Firms	Sales ($000)	Employees	Payroll ($000)
Asian	(s)	(s)	(s)	(s)	(s)	(s)
Black	591	20,321	31	(s)	(s)	(s)
Hispanic	163	1,920	(s)	(s)	(s)	(s)
Women	1,594	155,141	273	137,949	2,112	47,339
All Firms	6,245	8,891,369	1,928	8,751,291	51,860	1,714,785

Note: Figures cover firms located in the city; minority- and women-owned business are defined as firms in which the corresponding group own 51% or more of the stock or equity of the company; (s) estimates are suppressed when publication standards are not met
Source: U.S. Census Bureau, 2007 Economic Census, Survey of Business Owners (2012 Survey of Business Owners data will be released starting in June 2015)

HOTELS & CONVENTION CENTERS

Hotels/Motels

Area	5 Star		4 Star		3 Star		2 Star		1 Star		Not Rated	
	Num.	Pct.[3]	Num.	Pct.[3]	Num.	Pct.[3]	Num.	Pct.[3]	Num.	Pct.[3]	Num.	Pct.[3]
City[1]	0	0.0	0	0.0	10	18.9	33	62.3	2	3.8	8	15.1
Total[2]	142	0.9	1,005	6.0	5,147	30.9	8,578	51.4	408	2.4	1,397	8.4

Note: (1) Figures cover Erie and vicinity; (2) Figures cover all 100 cities in this book; (3) Percentage of hotels which have a given star rating; Star ratings are determined by expedia.com and offer an indication of the general quality of a particular hotel.
Source: expedia.com, April 7, 2014

Major Convention Centers

Name	Overall Space (sq. ft.)	Exhibit Space (sq. ft.)	Meeting Space (sq. ft.)	Meeting Rooms
Bayfront Convention Center	65,100	n/a	n/a	15

Note: Table Includes convention centers located In the Erle, PA metro area; n/a not available
Source: Original research

Living Environment

COST OF LIVING

Cost of Living Index

Composite Index	Groceries	Housing	Utilities	Trans-portation	Health Care	Misc. Goods/ Services
97.8	97.5	94.8	97.1	100.5	94.6	99.9

Note: The Cost of Living Index measures regional differences in the cost of consumer goods and services, excluding taxes and non-consumer expenditures, for professional and managerial households in the top income quintile. It is based on more than 50,000 prices covering almost 60 different items for which prices are collected three times a year by chambers of commerce, economic development organizations or university applied economic centers in each participating urban area. The numbers shown should be read as a percentage above or below the national average of 100. For example, a value of 115.4 in the groceries column indicates that grocery prices are 15.4% higher than the national average. Small differences in the index numbers should not be interpreted as significant; Figures cover the Erie PA urban area.
Source: The Council for Community and Economic Research, ACCRA Cost of Living Index, 2013

Grocery Prices

Area[1]	T-Bone Steak ($/pound)	Frying Chicken ($/pound)	Whole Milk ($/half gal.)	Eggs ($/dozen)	Orange Juice ($/64 oz.)	Coffee ($/11.5 oz.)
City[2]	10.33	1.33	2.06	1.80	3.29	4.76
Avg.	10.19	1.28	2.34	1.81	3.48	4.39
Min.	8.56	0.94	1.44	1.19	2.78	3.40
Max.	14.82	2.28	3.56	3.73	6.23	7.32

Note: (1) Values for the local area are compared with the average, minimum and maximum values for all 327 areas in the Cost of Living Index; (2) Figures cover the Erie PA urban area; **T-Bone Steak** *(price per pound);* **Frying Chicken** *(price per pound, whole fryer);* **Whole Milk** *(half gallon carton);* **Eggs** *(price per dozen, Grade A, large);* **Orange Juice** *(64 oz. Tropicana or Florida Natural);* **Coffee** *(11.5 oz. can, vacuum-packed, Maxwell House, Hills Bros, or Folgers).*
Source: The Council for Community and Economic Research, ACCRA Cost of Living Index, 2013

Housing and Utility Costs

Area[1]	New Home Price ($)	Apartment Rent ($/month)	All Electric ($/month)	Part Electric ($/month)	Other Energy ($/month)	Telephone ($/month)
City[2]	295,090	684	-	98.71	80.68	21.95
Avg.	295,864	900	171.38	91.82	70.12	27.73
Min.	185,506	458	117.80	48.81	33.67	17.16
Max.	1,358,917	3,783	441.68	171.40	372.65	39.47

Note: (1) Values for the local area are compared with the average, minimum and maximum values for all 327 areas in the Cost of Living Index; (2) Figures cover the Erie PA urban area; **New Home Price** *(2,400 sf living area, 8,000 sf lot, in urban area with full utilities);* **Apartment Rent** *(950 sf 2 bedroom/1.5 or 2 bath, unfurnished, excluding all utilities except water);* **All Electric** *(average monthly cost for an all-electric home);* **Part Electric** *(average monthly cost for a part-electric home);* **Other Energy** *(average monthly cost for natural gas, fuel oil, coal, wood, and any other forms of energy except electricity);* **Telephone** *(price includes basic monthly rate for a private residential line plus additional local usage charges incurred by a family of four).*
Source: The Council for Community and Economic Research, ACCRA Cost of Living Index, 2013

Health Care, Transportation, and Other Costs

Area[1]	Doctor ($/visit)	Dentist ($/visit)	Optometrist ($/visit)	Gasoline ($/gallon)	Beauty Salon ($/visit)	Men's Shirt ($)
City[2]	94.94	78.51	80.86	3.53	35.71	33.33
Avg.	101.40	86.48	96.16	3.44	33.87	26.55
Min.	61.67	50.83	50.12	3.08	18.92	12.48
Max.	182.71	152.50	223.78	4.33	68.22	52.03

Note: (1) Values for the local area are compared with the average, minimum and maximum values for all 327 areas in the Cost of Living Index; (2) Figures cover the Erie PA urban area; **Doctor** *(general practitioners routine exam of an established patient);* **Dentist** *(adult teeth cleaning and periodic oral examination);* **Optometrist** *(full vision eye exam for established adult patient);* **Gasoline** *(one gallon regular unleaded, national brand, including all taxes, cash price at self-service pump if available);* **Beauty Salon** *(woman's shampoo, trim, and blow-dry);* **Men's Shirt** *(cotton/polyester dress shirt, pinpoint weave, long sleeves).*
Source: The Council for Community and Economic Research, ACCRA Cost of Living Index, 2013

HOUSING

House Price Index (HPI)

Area	National Ranking[2]	Quarterly Change (%)	One-Year Change (%)	Five-Year Change (%)
MSA[1]	(a)	n/a	5.98	9.28
U.S.[3]	–	1.20	7.69	4.18

Note: The HPI is a weighted repeat sales index. It measures average price changes in repeat sales or refinancings on the same properties. This information is obtained by reviewing repeat mortgage transactions on single-family properties whose mortgages have been purchased or securitized by Fannie Mae or Freddie Mac in January 1975; (1) Erie, PA Metropolitan Statistical Area—see Appendix B for areas included; (2) Rankings are based on annual percentage change for all metro areas containing at least 15,000 transactions over the last 10 years and ranges from 1 to 283; (3) figures based on a weighted average of Census Division estimates using a seasonally adjusted, purchase-only index; all figures are for the period ending December 31, 2013; n/a not available; (a) Not ranked because of increased index variability due to smaller sample size
Source: Federal Housing Finance Agency, House Price Index, February 25, 2014

Median Single-Family Home Prices

Area	2011	2012	2013p	Percent Change 2012 to 2013
MSA[1]	109.7	114.9	113.3	-1.4
U.S. Average	166.2	177.2	197.4	11.4

Note: Figures are median sales prices of existing single-family homes in thousands of dollars; (p) preliminary; n/a not available; (1) Erie, PA Metropolitan Statistical Area—see Appendix B for areas included
Source: National Association of Realtors, Median Sales Price of Existing Single-Family Homes for Metropolitan Areas, 4th Quarter 2013

Qualifying Income Based on Median Sales Price of Existing Single-Family Homes

Area	With 5% Down ($)	With 10% Down ($)	With 20% Down ($)
MSA[1]	25,776	24,419	21,706
U.S. Average	45,395	43,006	38,228

Note: Figures are preliminary; Qualifying income is based on a mortgage rate of 4.4%. Monthly principal and interest payment is limited to 25% of income; n/a not available; (1) Erie, PA Metropolitan Statistical Area—see Appendix B for areas included
Source: National Association of Realtors, Qualifying Income Based on Median Sales Price of Existing Single-Family Homes for Metropolitan Areas, 4th Quarter 2013

Median Apartment Condo-Coop Home Prices

Area	2011	2012	2013p	Percent Change 2012 to 2013
MSA[1]	n/a	n/a	n/a	n/a
U.S. Average	165.1	173.7	194.9	12.2

Note: Figures are median sales prices of existing apartment condo-coop homes in thousands of dollars; (p) preliminary; n/a not available; (1) Erie, PA Metropolitan Statistical Area—see Appendix B for areas included
Source: National Association of Realtors, Median Sales Price of Existing Apartment Condo-Coop Homes for Metropolitan Areas, 4th Quarter 2013

Gross Monthly Rent

Area	Under $200	$200 -299	$300 -499	$500 -749	$750 -999	$1,000 -1,499	$1,500 and up	Median ($)
City	1.9	7.4	18.2	43.6	19.2	7.6	2.0	610
MSA[1]	1.8	6.0	16.4	40.3	21.4	10.5	3.6	651
U.S.	1.7	3.3	8.1	22.7	24.3	25.7	14.3	889

Note: Figures are percentages except for Median; Gross rent is the contract rent plus the estimated average monthly cost of utilities (electricity, gas, and water and sewer) and fuels (oil, coal, kerosene, wood, etc.) if these are paid by the renter (or paid for the renter by someone else); (1) Figures cover the Erie, PA Metropolitan Statistical Area—see Appendix B for areas included
Source: U.S. Census Bureau, 2010-2012 American Community Survey 3-Year Estimates

Year Housing Structure Built

Area	2010 or Later	2000 -2009	1990 -1999	1980 -1989	1970 -1979	1960 -1969	1950 -1959	1940 -1949	Before 1940	Median Year
City	0.1	3.7	2.6	4.3	10.1	7.7	17.9	10.7	42.9	1947
MSA[1]	0.1	7.1	8.8	8.9	14.7	9.7	15.2	7.7	27.8	1960
U.S.	0.5	14.9	13.8	13.9	15.9	11.1	10.9	5.5	13.5	1976

Note: Figures are percentages except for Median Year; (1) Figures cover the Erie, PA Metropolitan Statistical Area—see Appendix B for areas included
Source: U.S. Census Bureau, 2010-2012 American Community Survey 3-Year Estimates

HEALTH

Health Risk Data

Category	MSA[1] (%)	U.S. (%)
Adults aged 18–64 who have any kind of health care coverage	n/a	79.6
Adults who reported being in good or excellent health	n/a	83.1
Adults who are current smokers	n/a	19.6
Adults who are heavy drinkers[2]	n/a	6.1
Adults who are binge drinkers[3]	n/a	16.9
Adults who are overweight (BMI 25.0 - 29.9)	n/a	35.8
Adults who are obese (BMI 30.0 - 99.8)	n/a	27.6
Adults who participated in any physical activities in the past month	n/a	77.1
Adults 50+ who have ever had a sigmoidoscopy or colonoscopy	n/a	67.3
Women aged 40+ who have had a mammogram within the past two years	n/a	74.0
Men aged 40+ who have had a PSA test within the past two years	n/a	45.2
Adults aged 65+ who have had flu shot within the past year	n/a	60.1
Adults who always wear a seatbelt	n/a	93.8

Note: Data as of 2012 unless otherwise noted; n/a not available; (1) Figures cover the Erie, PA Metropolitan Statistical Area—see Appendix B for areas included; (2) Heavy drinkers are classified as males having more than two drinks per day or females having more than one drink per day; (3) Binge drinkers are classified as males having five or more drinks on one occasion or females having four or more drinks on one occasion
Source: Centers for Disease Control and Prevention, Behaviorial Risk Factor Surveillance System, SMART: Selected Metropolitan/Micropolitan Area Risk Trends, 2012

Chronic Health Indicators

Category	MSA[1] (%)	U.S. (%)
Adults who have ever been told they had a heart attack	n/a	4.5
Adults who have ever been told they had a stroke	n/a	2.9
Adults who have been told they currently have asthma	n/a	8.9
Adults who have ever been told they have arthritis	n/a	25.7
Adults who have ever been told they have diabetes[2]	n/a	9.7
Adults who have ever been told they had skin cancer	n/a	5.7
Adults who have ever been told they had any other types of cancer	n/a	6.5
Adults who have ever been told they have COPD	n/a	6.2
Adults who have ever been told they have kidney disease	n/a	2.5
Adults who have ever been told they have a form of depression	n/a	18.0

Note: Data as of 2012 unless otherwise noted; n/a not available; (1) Figures cover the Erie, PA Metropolitan Statistical Area—see Appendix B for areas included; (2) Figures do not include pregnancy-related, borderline, or pre-diabetes
Source: Centers for Disease Control and Prevention, Behaviorial Risk Factor Surveillance System, SMART: Selected Metropolitan/Micropolitan Area Risk Trends, 2012

Mortality Rates for the Top 10 Causes of Death in the U.S.

ICD-10[a] Sub-Chapter	ICD-10[a] Code	Age-Adjusted Mortality Rate[1] per 100,000 population	
		County[2]	U.S.
Malignant neoplasms	C00-C97	189.5	174.2
Ischaemic heart diseases	I20-I25	105.4	119.1
Other forms of heart disease	I30-I51	85.5	49.6
Chronic lower respiratory diseases	J40-J47	44.3	43.2
Cerebrovascular diseases	I60-I69	40.6	40.3
Organic, including symptomatic, mental disorders	F01-F09	30.2	30.5
Other degenerative diseases of the nervous system	G30-G31	23.7	26.3
Other external causes of accidental injury	W00-X59	23.4	25.1
Diabetes mellitus	E10-E14	24.2	21.3
Hypertensive diseases	I10-I15	9.7	18.8

Note: (a) ICD-10 = International Classification of Diseases 10th Revision; (1) Mortality rates are a three year average covering 2008-2010; (2) Figures cover Erie County
Source: Centers for Disease Control and Prevention, National Center for Health Statistics. Compressed Mortality File 1999-2010 on CDC WONDER Online Database, released January 2013. Data are compiled from the Compressed Mortality File 1999-2010, Series 20 No. 2P, 2013.

Mortality Rates for Selected Causes of Death

ICD-10[a] Sub-Chapter	ICD-10[a] Code	Age-Adjusted Mortality Rate[1] per 100,000 population	
		County[2]	U.S.
Assault	X85-Y09	3.6	5.5
Diseases of the liver	K70-K76	10.8	12.4
Human immunodeficiency virus (HIV) disease	B20-B24	Suppressed	3.0
Influenza and pneumonia	J09-J18	17.6	16.4
Intentional self-harm	X60-X84	13.1	11.8
Malnutrition	E40-E46	*1.3	0.8
Obesity and other hyperalimentation	E65-E68	*1.1	1.6
Renal failure	N17-N19	17.8	13.6
Transport accidents	V01-V99	11.0	12.6
Viral hepatitis	B15-B19	*1.6	2.2

Note: (a) ICD-10 = International Classification of Diseases 10th Revision; (1) Mortality rates are a three year average covering 2008-2010; (2) Figures cover Erie County; (*) Unreliable data as per CDC
Source: Centers for Disease Control and Prevention, National Center for Health Statistics. Compressed Mortality File 1999-2010 on CDC WONDER Online Database, released January 2013. Data are compiled from the Compressed Mortality File 1999-2010, Series 20 No. 2P, 2013.

Health Insurance Coverage

Area	With Health Insurance	With Private Health Insurance	With Public Health Insurance	Without Health Insurance	Population Under Age 18 Without Health Insurance
City	88.5	57.2	44.6	11.5	3.5
MSA[1]	90.9	69.6	35.9	9.1	2.8
U.S.	84.9	65.4	30.4	15.1	7.5

Note: Figures are percentages that cover the civilian noninstitutionalized population; (1) Figures cover the Erie, PA Metropolitan Statistical Area—see Appendix B for areas included
Source: U.S. Census Bureau, 2010-2012 American Community Survey 3-Year Estimates

Number of Medical Professionals

Area[1]	MDs[2]	DOs[2,3]	Dentists	Podiatrists	Chiropractors	Optometrists
Local (number)	476	273	173	31	99	41
Local (rate[4])	169.4	97.2	61.6	11.0	35.3	14.6
U.S. (rate[4])	267.6	19.6	61.7	5.6	24.7	14.5

Note: Data as of 2012 unless noted; (1) Local data covers Erie County; (2) Data as of 2011; (3) Doctor of Osteopathic Medicine; (4) rate per 100,000 population
Source: Area Resource File (ARF) 2012-2013. U.S. Department of Health and Human Services, Health Resources and Services Administration, Bureau of Health Professions

EDUCATION

Public School District Statistics

District Name	Schls	Pupils	Pupil/ Teacher Ratio	Minority Pupils[1] (%)	Free Lunch Eligible[2] (%)	IEP[3] (%)
Erie City SD	23	12,324	13.2	52.7	53.8	19.9
Millcreek Township SD	13	7,350	15.3	9.1	22.8	14.5

Note: Table includes school districts with 2,000 or more students; (1) Percentage of students that are not non-Hispanic white; (2) Percentage of students that are eligible for the free lunch program; (3) Percentage of students that have an Individualized Education Program.
Source: U.S. Department of Education, National Center for Education Statistics, Common Core of Data, Local Education Agency (School District) Universe Survey: School Year 2011-2012; U.S. Department of Education, National Center for Education Statistics, Common Core of Data, Public Elementary/Secondary School Universe Survey: School Year 2011-2012

Best High Schools

High School Name	Rank[1]	Grad. Rate[2] (%)	Coll.[3] (%)	AP/IB/ AICE Tests[4]	AP/IB/ AICE Score[5]	SAT Score[6]	ACT Score[6]
Northwest Pennsylvania Collegiate Academy	123	99	100	1.0	2.5	1667	27.1

Note: (1) Public schools are ranked from 1 to 2,000 based on the following self-reported statistics (with the corresponding weight used in calculating their overall score). Schools that were newly founded and did not have a graduating senior class in 2012 were excluded; (2) Four-year, on-time graduation rate (25%); (3) Percent of 2011 graduates who were accepted to college (25%); (4) AP/IB/AICE tests taken per student (25%); (5) Average AP/IB/AICE exam score (10%); (6) Average SAT and/or ACT score (10%); Percent of students enrolled in at least one AP/IB/AICE course (5%)—data not shown
Source: Newsweek and The Daily Beast, "America's Best High Schools 2013"

Highest Level of Education

Area	Less than H.S.	H.S. Diploma	Some College, No Deg.	Associate Degree	Bachelor's Degree	Master's Degree	Prof. School Degree	Doctorate Degree
City	13.6	42.4	17.1	6.7	13.2	4.9	1.0	1.2
MSA[1]	9.5	41.2	16.9	8.0	15.3	6.4	1.6	1.1
U.S.	14.1	28.3	21.3	7.8	18.0	7.5	1.9	1.2

Note: Figures cover persons age 25 and over; (1) Figures cover the Erie, PA Metropolitan Statistical Area—see Appendix B for areas included
Source: U.S. Census Bureau, 2010-2012 American Community Survey 3-Year Estimates

Educational Attainment by Race

Area	High School Graduate or Higher (%)					Bachelor's Degree or Higher (%)				
	Total	White	Black	Asian	Hisp.[2]	Total	White	Black	Asian	Hisp.[2]
City	86.4	88.3	80.9	62.1	71.6	20.3	21.5	13.6	29.9	11.4
MSA[1]	90.5	91.6	81.7	70.5	74.7	24.4	25.1	13.8	36.3	14.6
U.S.	85.9	88.1	82.5	85.5	63.1	28.6	30.0	18.4	50.2	13.4

Note: Figures shown cover persons 25 years old and over; (1) Figures cover the Erie, PA Metropolitan Statistical Area—see Appendix B for areas included; (2) People of Hispanic origin can be of any race
Source: U.S. Census Bureau, 2010-2012 American Community Survey 3-Year Estimates

School Enrollment by Grade and Control

Area	Preschool (%)		Kindergarten (%)		Grades 1 - 4 (%)		Grades 5 - 8 (%)		Grades 9 - 12 (%)	
	Public	Private	Public	Private	Public	Private	Public	Private	Public	Private
City	48.2	51.8	80.9	19.1	85.4	14.6	85.6	14.4	83.3	16.7
MSA[1]	50.1	49.9	84.9	15.1	89.2	10.8	89.1	10.9	86.8	13.2
U.S.	56.9	43.1	87.8	12.2	89.9	10.1	90.0	10.0	90.8	9.2

Note: Figures shown cover persons 3 years old and over; (1) Figures cover the Erie, PA Metropolitan Statistical Area—see Appendix B for areas included
Source: U.S. Census Bureau, 2010-2012 American Community Survey 3-Year Estimates

Average Salaries of Public School Classroom Teachers

Area	2012-13		2013-14		Percent Change 2012-13 to 2013-14	Percent Change 2003-04 to 2013-14
	Dollars	Rank[1]	Dollars	Rank[1]		
Pennsylvania	62,994	10	64,072	10	1.71	21.8
U.S. Average	56,103	–	56,689	–	1.04	21.8

Note: (1) State rank ranges from 1 to 51 where 1 indicates highest salary.
Source: National Education Association, Rankings & Estimates: Rankings of the States 2013 and Estimates of School Statistics 2014, March 2014

Higher Education

Four-Year Colleges			Two-Year Colleges			Medical Schools[1]	Law Schools[2]	Voc/ Tech[3]
Public	Private Non-profit	Private For-profit	Public	Private Non-profit	Private For-profit			
1	3	0	0	0	6	1	0	0

Note: Figures cover institutions located within the city limits and include main campuses only; (1) includes schools accredited by the Liaison Committee on Medical Education and the American Osteopathic Association's Commission on Osteopathic College Accreditation; (2) includes ABA-accredited schools, schools with provisional ABA accreditation, and state accredited schools; (3) includes all schools with programs that are less than 2 years.
Source: National Center for Education Statistics, Integrated Postsecondary Education System (IPEDS), 2012-13; Association of American Medical Colleges, Member List, April 24, 2014; American Osteopathic Association, Member List, April 24, 2014; Law School Admission Council, Official Guide to ABA-Approved Law Schools Online, April 24, 2014; Wikipedia, List of Medical Schools in the United States, April 24, 2014; Wikipedia, List of Law Schools in the United States, April 24, 2014

PRESIDENTIAL ELECTION

2012 Presidential Election Results

Area	Obama	Romney	Other
Erie County	57.4	41.3	1.3
U.S.	51.0	47.2	1.8

Note: Results are percentages and may not add to 100% due to rounding
Source: Dave Leip's Atlas of U.S. Presidential Elections

EMPLOYERS

Major Employers

Company Name	Industry
City of Erie	Government
County Fair	Convenience stores
Dr. Gertrude A Barber Center	Healthcare
Erie City School District	Education
Erie County	Government
Erie Indemnity Co	Insurance
Federal Government	Government
Gannon University	Education
General Electric Co.	Drilling
Lord Corporation	Adhesives, coatings
Mercyhurst University	Education
Millcreek Community Hospital	Healthcare
Millcreek Township School District	Education
PA State System of Higher Education	Education
Pennsylvania State University	Education
Plastek Industries	Manufacturing
Presque Isle Downs	Finance & investing
Regional Health Services	Healthcare
Saint Vincent Health Center	Healthcare
State Government	Government
The Tamarkin Company	Food processing
UPMC Hamot	Healthcare
Wal-Mart Associates	Grocery
Wegmans Food Market	Supermarket
YMCA of Greater Erie	Nonprofit

Note: Companies shown are located within the Erie, PA Metropolitan Statistical Area.
Source: Hoovers.com; Wikipedia

Best Companies to Work For

Saint Vincent Health System, headquartered in Erie, is among the "50 Best Employers for Workers Over 50." Criteria: recruiting practices; opportunities for training, education, and career development; workplace accommodations; alternative work options, such as flexible scheduling, job sharing, and phased retirement; employee health and pension benefits; and retiree benefits. Employers with at least 50 employees based in the U.S. are eligible, including for-profit companies, not-for-profit organizations, and government employers. *AARP, "2013 AARP Best Employers for Workers Over 50"*

PUBLIC SAFETY

Crime Rate

Area	All Crimes	Violent Crimes				Property Crimes		
		Murder	Forcible Rape	Robbery	Aggrav. Assault	Burglary	Larceny -Theft	Motor Vehicle Theft
City	3,891.3	7.8	62.8	168.7	209.9	1,073.8	2,266.3	102.0
Suburbs[1]	2,267.8	1.7	16.2	28.4	84.7	397.3	1,680.0	59.6
Metro[2]	2,856.0	3.9	33.0	79.2	130.0	642.4	1,892.4	75.0
U.S.	3,246.1	4.7	26.9	112.9	242.3	670.2	1,959.3	229.7

Note: Figures are crimes per 100,000 population; (1) All areas within the metro area that are located outside the city limits; (2) Figures cover the Erie, PA Metropolitan Statistical Area—see Appendix B for areas included
Source: FBI Uniform Crime Reports, 2012

Hate Crimes

Area	Number of Quarters Reported	Bias Motivation				
		Race	Religion	Sexual Orientation	Ethnicity	Disability
City	4	0	0	0	0	0
U.S.	4	2,797	1,099	1,135	667	92

Source: Federal Bureau of Investigation, Hate Crime Statistics 2012

Identity Theft Consumer Complaints

Area	Complaints	Complaints per 100,000 Population	Rank[2]
MSA[1]	154	54.9	250
U.S.	290,056	91.8	-

Note: (1) Figures cover the Erie, PA Metropolitan Statistical Area—see Appendix B for areas included; (2) Rank ranges from 1 to 377 where 1 indicates greatest number of identity theft complaints per 100,000 population
Source: Federal Trade Commission, Consumer Sentinel Network Data Book for January–December 2013

Fraud and Other Consumer Complaints

Area	Complaints	Complaints per 100,000 Population	Rank[2]
MSA[1]	986	351.4	209
U.S.	1,811,724	595.2	-

Note: (1) Figures cover the Erie, PA Metropolitan Statistical Area—see Appendix B for areas included; (2) Rank ranges from 1 to 377 where 1 indicates greatest number of identity theft complaints per 100,000 population
Source: Federal Trade Commission, Consumer Sentinel Network Data Book for January–December 2013

RECREATION

Culture

Dance[1]	Theatre[1]	Instrumental Music[1]	Vocal Music[1]	Series and Festivals	Museums and Art Galleries[2]	Zoos and Aquariums[3]
0	0	1	0	2	11	1

Note: (1) Number of professional performing groups; (2) Based on organizations with primary SIC code 8412; (3) AZA-accredited
Source: The Grey House Performing Arts Directory, 2013; Association of Zoos & Aquariums, AZA Member Zoos & Aquariums, April 2014; www.AccuLeads.com, May 1, 2014

Professional Sports Teams

Team Name	League	Year Established
No teams are located in the metro area		

Source: Wikipedia, Major Professional Sports Teams of the United States and Canada, April 25, 2014

CLIMATE

Average and Extreme Temperatures

Temperature	Jan	Feb	Mar	Apr	May	Jun	Jul	Aug	Sep	Oct	Nov	Dec	Yr.
Extreme High (°F)	72	66	81	89	90	100	99	94	99	88	81	75	100
Average High (°F)	33	34	43	54	65	75	79	78	71	61	49	37	57
Average Temp. (°F)	26	27	35	46	56	66	71	70	63	53	42	32	49
Average Low (°F)	20	19	27	37	47	57	62	61	54	44	36	26	41
Extreme Low (°F)	-18	-17	-10	12	26	32	44	37	33	24	7	-6	-18

Note: Figures cover the years 1948-1995
Source: National Climatic Data Center, International Station Meteorological Climate Summary, 9/96

Average Precipitation/Snowfall/Humidity

Precip./Humidity	Jan	Feb	Mar	Apr	May	Jun	Jul	Aug	Sep	Oct	Nov	Dec	Yr.
Avg. Precip. (in.)	2.5	2.3	3.1	3.3	3.4	3.8	3.3	3.9	4.1	3.6	4.0	3.4	40.5
Avg. Snowfall (in.)	22	16	11	2	Tr	0	0	0	0	Tr	10	22	83
Avg. Rel. Hum. 7am (%)	78	79	78	75	75	78	79	82	81	77	76	77	78
Avg. Rel. Hum. 4pm (%)	73	72	67	60	58	60	61	62	63	64	69	73	65

Note: Figures cover the years 1948-1995; Tr = Trace amounts (<0.05 in. of rain; <0.5 in. of snow)
Source: National Climatic Data Center, International Station Meteorological Climate Summary, 9/96

Weather Conditions

Temperature			Daytime Sky			Precipitation		
5°F & below	32°F & below	90°F & above	Clear	Partly cloudy	Cloudy	0.01 inch or more precip.	0.1 inch or more snow/ice	Thunder-storms
9	124	3	57	128	180	165	55	36

Note: Figures are average number of days per year and cover the years 1948-1995
Source: National Climatic Data Center, International Station Meteorological Climate Summary, 9/96

HAZARDOUS WASTE

Superfund Sites

Erie has one hazardous waste site on the EPA's Superfund Final National Priorities List: **Mill Creek Dump**. *U.S. Environmental Protection Agency, Final National Priorities List, April 26, 2014*

AIR & WATER QUALITY

Air Quality Index

Area	Percent of Days when Air Quality was...[2]					AQI Statistics[2]	
	Good	Moderate	Unhealthy for Sensitive Groups	Unhealthy	Very Unhealthy	Maximum	Median
MSA[1]	54.8	45.2	0.0	0.0	0.0	88	48

Note: (1) Data covers the Erie, PA Metropolitan Statistical Area—see Appendix B for areas included; (2) Based on 365 days with AQI data in 2013. Air Quality Index (AQI) is an index for reporting daily air quality. EPA calculates the AQI for five major air pollutants regulated by the Clean Air Act: ground-level ozone, particle pollution (aka particulate matter), carbon monoxide, sulfur dioxide, and nitrogen dioxide. The AQI runs from 0 to 500. The higher the AQI value, the greater the level of air pollution and the greater the health concern. There are six AQI categories: "Good" AQI is between 0 and 50. Air quality is considered satisfactory; "Moderate" AQI is between 51 and 100. Air quality is acceptable; "Unhealthy for Sensitive Groups" When AQI values are between 101 and 150, members of sensitive groups may experience health effects; "Unhealthy" When AQI values are between 151 and 200 everyone may begin to experience health effects; "Very Unhealthy" AQI values between 201 and 300 trigger a health alert; "Hazardous" AQI values over 300 trigger warnings of emergency conditions (not shown).
Source: U.S. Environmental Protection Agency, Air Quality Index Report, 2013

Air Quality Index Pollutants

Area	Percent of Days when AQI Pollutant was...[2]					
	Carbon Monoxide	Nitrogen Dioxide	Ozone	Sulfur Dioxide	Particulate Matter 2.5	Particulate Matter 10
MSA[1]	0.0	0.8	23.3	0.0	75.9	0.0

Note: (1) Data covers the Erie, PA Metropolitan Statistical Area—see Appendix B for areas included; (2) Based on 365 days with AQI data in 2013. The Air Quality Index (AQI) is an index for reporting daily air quality. EPA calculates the AQI for five major air pollutants regulated by the Clean Air Act: ground-level ozone, particle pollution (also known as particulate matter), carbon monoxide, sulfur dioxide, and nitrogen dioxide. The AQI runs from 0 to 500. The higher the AQI value, the greater the level of air pollution and the greater the health concern.
Source: U.S. Environmental Protection Agency, Air Quality Index Report, 2013

Air Quality Trends: Ozone

	2003	2004	2005	2006	2007	2008	2009	2010	2011	2012
MSA[1]	0.091	0.074	0.086	0.077	0.084	0.074	0.069	0.075	0.072	0.082

Note: (1) Data covers the Erie, PA Metropolitan Statistical Area—see Appendix B for areas included. The values shown are the composite ozone concentration averages among trend sites based on the highest fourth daily maximum 8-hour concentration in parts per million. These trends are based on sites having an adequate record of monitoring data during the trend period. Data from exceptional events are included.
Source: U.S. Environmental Protection Agency, Air Quality Monitoring Information, "Air Quality Trends by City, 2000-2012"

Maximum Air Pollutant Concentrations: Particulate Matter, Ozone, CO and Lead

	Particulate Matter 10 (ug/m^3)	Particulate Matter 2.5 Wtd AM (ug/m^3)	Particulate Matter 2.5 24-Hr (ug/m^3)	Ozone (ppm)	Carbon Monoxide (ppm)	Lead (ug/m^3)
MSA[1] Level	32	11.2	25	0.082	1	n/a
NAAQS[2]	150	15	35	0.075	9	0.15
Met NAAQS[2]	Yes	Yes	Yes	No	Yes	n/a

Note: (1) Data covers the Erie, PA Metropolitan Statistical Area—see Appendix B for areas included; Data from exceptional events are included; (2) National Ambient Air Quality Standards; ppm = parts per million; ug/m^3 = micrograms per cubic meter; n/a not available.
Concentrations: Particulate Matter 10 (coarse particulate)—highest second maximum 24-hour concentration; Particulate Matter 2.5 Wtd AM (fine particulate)—highest weighted annual mean concentration; Particulate Matter 2.5 24-Hour (fine particulate)—highest 98th percentile 24-hour concentration; Ozone—highest fourth daily maximum 8-hour concentration; Carbon Monoxide—highest second maximum non-overlapping 8-hour concentration; Lead—maximum running 3-month average
Source: U.S. Environmental Protection Agency, Air Quality Monitoring Information, "Air Quality Statistics by City, 2012"

Maximum Air Pollutant Concentrations: Nitrogen Dioxide and Sulfur Dioxide

	Nitrogen Dioxide AM (ppb)	Nitrogen Dioxide 1-Hr (ppb)	Sulfur Dioxide AM (ppb)	Sulfur Dioxide 1-Hr (ppb)	Sulfur Dioxide 24-Hr (ppb)
MSA[1] Level	6	31	n/a	19	n/a
NAAQS[2]	53	100	30	75	140
Met NAAQS[2]	Yes	Yes	n/a	Yes	n/a

Note: (1) Data covers the Erie, PA Metropolitan Statistical Area—see Appendix B for areas included; Data from exceptional events are included; (2) National Ambient Air Quality Standards; ppm = parts per million; ug/m^3 = micrograms per cubic meter; n/a not available.
Concentrations: Nitrogen Dioxide AM—highest arithmetic mean concentration; Nitrogen Dioxide 1-Hr—highest 98th percentile 1-hour daily maximum concentration; Sulfur Dioxide AM—highest annual mean concentration; Sulfur Dioxide 1-Hr—highest 99th percentile 1-hour daily maximum concentration; Sulfur Dioxide 24-Hr—highest second maximum 24-hour concentration
Source: U.S. Environmental Protection Agency, Air Quality Monitoring Information, "Air Quality Statistics by City, 2012"

Drinking Water

Water System Name	Pop. Served	Primary Water Source Type	Violations[1]	
			Health Based	Monitoring/ Reporting
Erie City Water Authority	180,000	Surface	0	56

Note: (1) Based on violation data from January 1, 2013 to December 31, 2013 (includes unresolved violations from earlier years)
Source: U.S. Environmental Protection Agency, Office of Ground Water and Drinking Water, Safe Drinking Water Information System (based on data extracted February 10, 2014)

Fayetteville, North Carolina

Background

Fayetteville, the first town named after a revolutionary war hero—Marquis de Lafayette—is located on the Cape Fear River, about 100 miles from the coast. Most rivers in North Carolina flow south into South Carolina, but the Cape Fear flows in a more easterly direction, making it an important inland port of entry for North Carolina. Originally established as a trading post, Fayetteville's location and rich river-bottom soil made the area an important place for early settlement—evidenced by shiploads of Scottish Highlander's who settled in the area around 1739. Later, the community of Scots had divided loyalties with men fighting on either side during the American Revolution. With the *Liberty Point Resolve* of 1775, the local population pledged its allegiance to the revolutionary cause.

In 1793, George Washington chartered the Fayetteville Independent Light Infantry, which is one of the oldest military units in continuous service in the south, though today its role is largely ceremonial. The FILI sparked great controversy in the Spanish-American War by refusing to retire the Confederate Grey—an action that would preclude them from entering the North Carolina state guard. To this day, the military is still the heart and soul of the Fayetteville community.

Following the American Revolution, Fayetteville experienced a boom, both politically and economically. The state Constitution was ratified in Fayetteville, and many thought the city would become the new state capital. In addition, the charter for the University of North Carolina was created, the first of its kind in the country. During these years, free black minister Henry Evans fathered Fayetteville's first church, as he preached to black slaves.

North Carolina had a southern, agrarian culture and, as such, supported the Confederacy during the Civil War. General William Sherman's troop spent two days in Fayetteville, destroying the Confederacy's arsenal manufacturing facilities, as well as the town's foundries, cotton factories, and news organizations. During Reconstruction, Fayetteville created one of three schools dedicated to educating freed slaves. One of these, the Howard School, evolved into today's Fayetteville State University.

The military remains integral, both economically and socially, in Fayetteville. Fort Bragg, named after Confederate commander General Braxton Bragg, was established in 1918 as an artillery training ground. The fort was nearly closed following World War I, but a visit from the Secretary of War, Newton Baker, saved the base. In 1922, the Field Artillery Board was relocated there, and in 1952, the Army established the Psychological Warfare Center at Fort Bragg. Today, Bragg is the largest Army base in the country. Following the 2005 Base Realignment and Closure Commission (BRAC), Fort Bragg absorbed the base at McPherson, GA. Then again, in 2011, Fort Bragg absorbed Pope Air Force Base. Since the year 2000, the population has increased over 65 percent. Fort Bragg remains one of the largest military complexes in the world, employing over 68,000: 57,000 military personnel; 11,000 civilian employees; and 23,000 family members. It occupied nearly 250 square miles.

Following World War II, Fayetteville began a cultural initiative with the Fayetteville Symphony. The Fayetteville Art Museum was established in 1972. It is also home of the Cape Fear Museum of history. In recent years, Fayetteville has honored its past by painstakingly restoring its historic districts—nine in all. The Cape Fear Botanical Garden sits atop land where Fayetteville's early settlers first built their homes. The gardens include two children's gardens. The Lilliput Labyrinth features giant-sized sculptures. The most recent addition to Fayetteville's cultural landscape is the Airborne and Special Operations Museum. In addition, Fayetteville is home to three universities: Fayetteville State University, Methodist College, and Fayetteville Technical Community College.

Fayetteville has a subtropical climate, with mostly moderate temperatures year round. Winters are mild, but can get cool with snow occurring a few days per year. Summers are hot and humid with a risk of thunderstorms and rain showers. Temperatures range from -5 °F on January 21, 1985 to 110 °F on August 21, 1983, the highest temperature ever recorded in the State of North Carolina. On April 16, 2011, Fayetteville was struck by an EF3 tornado during North Carolina's largest tornado outbreak.

Rankings

Business/Finance Rankings

- The Fayetteville metro area was identified as one of the most debt-ridden places in America by credit reporting agency Equifax. The metro area was ranked #3. Criteria: proportion of average yearly income owed to credit card companies. *Equifax, "The Most Debt-Ridden Cities in America," February 23, 2012*

- The Fayetteville metro area appeared on the Milken Institute "2013 Best Performing Cities" list. Rank: #82 out of 200 large metro areas. Criteria: job growth; wage and salary growth; high-tech output growth. *Milken Institute, "Best-Performing Cities 2013," December 2013*

- *Forbes* ranked the 200 most populous metro areas in the U.S. in terms of the "Best Places for Business and Careers." The Fayetteville metro area was ranked #179. Criteria: costs (business and living); job growth (past and projected); income growth; educational attainment (college and high school); projected economic growth; cultural and recreational opportunities; net migration patterns; number of highly ranked colleges. *Forbes, "The Best Places for Business and Careers," August 7, 2013*

Environmental Rankings

- The Fayetteville metro area came in at #280 for the relative comfort of its climate on Sperling's list of "chill cities," as measured by the Sperling Heat Index. All 361 metro areas are included. Criteria included daytime high temperatures, nighttime low temperatures, dew point, and relative humidity at the high temperatures. *www.bertsperling.com, "Sperling's Chill Cities," July 18, 2013*

- Sperling's BestPlaces assessed 379 metropolitan areas of the United States for the likelihood of dangerously extreme weather events or earthquakes. In general the Southeast and South-Central regions have the highest risk of weather extremes and earthquakes, while the Pacific Northwest enjoys the lowest risk. Of the least risky metropolitan areas, the Fayetteville metro area was ranked #338. *www.bestplaces.net, "Safest Places from Natural Disasters," April 2011*

- Fayetteville was selected as one of 22 "Smarter Cities" for energy by the Natural Resources Defense Council. Criteria: investment in green power; energy efficiency measures; conservation. *Natural Resources Defense Council, "2010 Smarter Cities," July 19, 2010*

- Fayetteville was highlighted as one of the top 25 cleanest metro areas for short-term particle pollution (24-hour PM 2.5) in the U.S. during 2008 through 2010. Monitors in these cities reported no days with unhealthful PM 2.5 levels. *American Lung Association, State of the Air 2012*

Health/Fitness Rankings

- For the Gallup-Healthways Well-Being Index, researchers asked at least 300 adult residents in each of 189 U.S. metropolitan areas how satisfied they were with the metro area in which they lived. The Fayetteville metro area was one of the ten metros where residents were least likely to be satisfied. *www.gallup.com, "City Satisfaction Highest in Fort Collins-Loveland, Colo.," April 11, 2014*

- The Fayetteville metro area was identified as one of the worst cities for bed bugs in America by pest control company Orkin. The area ranked #12 out of 50 based on the number of bed bug treatments Orkin performed from January to December 2013. *Orkin, "Chicago Tops Bed Bug Cities List for Second Year in a Row," January 16, 2014*

- The Fayetteville metro area appeared in the 2013 Gallup-Healthways Well-Being Index. The area ranked #162 out of 189. The Gallup-Healthways Well-Being Index score is an average of six sub-indexes, which individually examine life evaluation, emotional health, work environment, physical health, healthy behaviors, and access to basic necessities. Results are based on telephone interviews conducted as part of the Gallup-Healthways Well-Being Index survey January 2–December 29, 2012, and January 2–December 30, 2013, with a random sample of 531,630 adults, aged 18 and older, living in metropolitan areas in the 50 U.S. states and the District of Columbia. *Gallup-Healthways, "State of American Well-Being," March 25, 2014*

Real Estate Rankings

- Fayetteville was ranked #280 out of 283 metro areas in terms of house price appreciation in 2013 (#1 = highest rate). *Federal Housing Finance Agency, House Price Index, 4th Quarter 2013*

- The Fayetteville metro area was identified as one of the 20 worst housing markets in the U.S. in 2013. The area ranked #5 out of 173 markets with a home price appreciation of -8.8%. Criteria: year-over-year change of median sales price of existing single-family homes between the 4th quarter of 2012 and the 4th quarter of 2013. *National Association of Realtors®, Median Sales Price of Existing Single-Family Homes for Metropolitan Areas, 4th Quarter 2013*

- Fayetteville was ranked #73 out of 224 metro areas in terms of housing affordability in 2013 by the National Association of Home Builders (#1 = most affordable). The NAHB-Wells Fargo Housing Opportunity Index (HOI) for a given area is defined as the share of homes sold in that area that would have been affordable to a family earning the local median income, based on standard mortgage underwriting criteria. *National Association of Home Builders®, NAHB-Wells Fargo Housing Opportunity Index, 4th Quarter 2013*

Safety Rankings

- Allstate ranked the 200 largest cities in America in terms of driver safety. Fayetteville ranked #43. Allstate researchers analyzed internal property damage claims over a two-year period from January 2010 to December 2011. A weighted average of the two-year numbers determined the annual percentages. *Allstate, "Allstate America's Best Drivers Report®, August 27, 2013"*

- The National Insurance Crime Bureau ranked 380 metro areas in the U.S. in terms of per capita rates of vehicle theft. The Fayetteville metro area ranked #43 (#1 = highest rate). Criteria: number of vehicle theft offenses per 100,000 inhabitants in 2012. *National Insurance Crime Bureau, "Hot Spots 2012," June 26, 2013*

Seniors/Retirement Rankings

- From its Best Cities for Successful Aging indexes, the Milken Institute generated rankings for metropolitan areas, weighing data in eight categories—general indicators, health care, wellness, living arrangements, transportation and general accessibility, financial well-being, education and employment, and community participation. The Fayetteville metro area was ranked #219 overall in the small metro area category. *Milken Institute, "Best Cities for Successful Aging," July 2012*

Transportation Rankings

- NerdWallet surveyed average annual car insurance premiums in 125 U.S. cities to identify the least expensive U.S. cities in which to insure a car. Locations without no-fault insurance laws was a strong determinant. Fayetteville came in at #8 for the least expensive rates. *www.nerdwallet.com, "Best Cities for Cheap Car Insurance," February 3, 2014*

Miscellaneous Rankings

- Fayetteville was selected as a 2013 Digital Cities Survey winner. The city ranked #9 in the mid-sized city (125,000 to 249,999 population) category. The survey examined and assessed how city governments are utilizing information technology to operate and deliver quality service to their customers and citizens. Survey questions focused on implementation and adoption of online service delivery; planning and governance; and the infrastructure and architecture that make the transformation to digital government possible. *Center for Digital Government, "2013 Digital Cities Survey," November 7, 2013*

- Fayetteville was selected as one of the "Top 10 Cities to Defy Death" by *Livability.com*. The city was ranked #10. Criteria includes: extreme sports; surfing; rock-climbing; haunted cities. *Livability.com, "Top 10 Cities to Defy Death," February 22, 2011*

Business Environment

CITY FINANCES

City Government Finances

Component	2011 ($000)	2011 ($ per capita)
Total Revenues	449,389	2,615
Total Expenditures	408,722	2,378
Debt Outstanding	219,346	1,276
Cash and Securities[1]	290,813	1,692

Note: (1) Cash and security holdings of a government at the close of its fiscal year, including those of its dependent agencies, utilities, and liquor stores.
Source: U.S Census Bureau, State & Local Government Finances 2011

City Government Revenue by Source

Source	2011 ($000)	2011 ($ per capita)
General Revenue		
From Federal Government	14,362	84
From State Government	29,194	170
From Local Governments	5,108	30
Taxes		
Property	58,987	343
Sales and Gross Receipts	32,336	188
Personal Income	0	0
Corporate Income	0	0
Motor Vehicle License	1,270	7
Other Taxes	4,718	27
Current Charges	51,034	297
Liquor Store	0	0
Utility	230,065	1,339
Employee Retirement	0	0

Source: U.S Census Bureau, State & Local Government Finances 2011

City Government Expenditures by Function

Function	2011 ($000)	2011 ($ per capita)	2011 (%)
General Direct Expenditures			
Air Transportation	6,124	36	1.5
Corrections	0	0	0.0
Education	0	0	0.0
Employment Security Administration	0	0	0.0
Financial Administration	1,784	10	0.4
Fire Protection	24,985	145	6.1
General Public Buildings	1,570	9	0.4
Governmental Administration, Other	3,627	21	0.9
Health	0	0	0.0
Highways	13,009	76	3.2
Hospitals	0	0	0.0
Housing and Community Development	4,832	28	1.2
Interest on General Debt	5,066	29	1.2
Judicial and Legal	993	6	0.2
Libraries	0	0	0.0
Parking	2,444	14	0.6
Parks and Recreation	20,841	121	5.1
Police Protection	41,765	243	10.2
Public Welfare	0	0	0.0
Sewerage	34,243	199	8.4
Solid Waste Management	12,211	71	3.0
Veterans' Services	0	0	0.0
Liquor Store	0	0	0.0
Utility	200,183	1,165	49.0
Employee Retirement	0	0	0.0

Source: U.S Census Bureau, State & Local Government Finances 2011

DEMOGRAPHICS

Population Growth

Area	1990 Census	2000 Census	2010 Census	Population Growth (%) 1990-2000	Population Growth (%) 2000-2010
City	118,247	121,015	200,564	2.3	65.7
MSA[1]	297,422	336,609	366,383	13.2	8.8
U.S.	248,709,873	281,421,906	308,745,538	13.2	9.7

Note: (1) Figures cover the Fayetteville, NC Metropolitan Statistical Area—see Appendix B for areas included
Source: U.S. Census Bureau, Census 1990, 2000, 2010

Household Size

Area	Persons in Household (%) One	Two	Three	Four	Five	Six	Seven or More	Average Household Size
City	29.7	33.4	17.2	12.5	4.9	1.2	1.0	2.49
MSA[1]	27.3	32.1	18.3	13.7	5.8	1.7	1.2	2.63
U.S.	27.6	33.5	15.7	13.2	6.1	2.4	1.5	2.63

Note: (1) Figures cover the Fayetteville, NC Metropolitan Statistical Area—see Appendix B for areas included
Source: U.S. Census Bureau, 2010-2012 American Community Survey 3-Year Estimates

Race

Area	White Alone[2] (%)	Black Alone[2] (%)	Asian Alone[2] (%)	AIAN[3] Alone[2] (%)	NHOPI[4] Alone[2] (%)	Other Race Alone[2] (%)	Two or More Races (%)
City	47.1	40.7	2.8	0.8	0.4	2.9	5.2
MSA[1]	51.4	35.8	2.1	2.1	0.3	2.9	5.3
U.S.	74.0	12.6	4.9	0.8	0.2	4.7	2.8

Note: (1) Figures cover the Fayetteville, NC Metropolitan Statistical Area—see Appendix B for areas included;
(2) Alone is defined as not being in combination with one or more other races; (3) American Indian and Alaska
Native; (4) Native Hawaiian and Other Pacific Islander
Source: U.S. Census Bureau, 2010-2012 American Community Survey 3-Year Estimates

Hispanic or Latino Origin

Area	Total (%)	Mexican (%)	Puerto Rican (%)	Cuban (%)	Other (%)
City	10.6	4.2	3.5	0.2	2.7
MSA[1]	10.2	4.1	3.4	0.3	2.4
U.S.	16.6	10.7	1.6	0.6	3.7

Note: Persons of Hispanic or Latino origin can be of any race; (1) Figures cover the Fayetteville, NC
Metropolitan Statistical Area—see Appendix B for areas included
Source: U.S. Census Bureau, 2010-2012 American Community Survey 3-Year Estimates

Segregation

Type	Segregation Indices[1] 1990	2000	2010	2010 Rank[2]	Percent Change 1990-2000	1990-2010	2000-2010
Black/White	n/a	n/a	n/a	n/a	n/a	n/a	n/a
Asian/White	n/a	n/a	n/a	n/a	n/a	n/a	n/a
Hispanic/White	n/a	n/a	n/a	n/a	n/a	n/a	n/a

Note: All figures cover the Metropolitan Statistical Area—see Appendix B for areas included; Figures are based
on an analysis of 1990, 2000, and 2010 Census Decennial Census tract data by William H. Frey, Brookings
Institution and the University of Michigan Social Science Data Analysis Network. In this analysis all racial
groups (whites, blacks, and asians) are non-Hispanic members of those races. Hispanics are shown as a
separate category;
(1) Segregation Indices are Dissimilarity Indices that measure the degree to which the minority group is
distributed differently than whites across census tracts. They range from 0 (complete integration) to 100
(complete segregation) where the value indicates the percentage of the minority group that needs to move to be
distributed exactly like whites; (2) Ranges from 1 (most segregated) to 102 (least segregated); n/a not available.
Source: www.CensusScope.org

Ancestry

Area	German	Irish	English	American	Italian	Polish	French[2]	Scottish	Dutch
City	11.0	8.0	5.2	4.7	2.7	1.3	1.5	2.0	0.7
MSA[1]	9.9	8.1	5.9	7.0	2.9	1.3	1.7	2.1	0.9
U.S.	15.2	11.1	8.2	7.2	5.6	3.1	2.8	1.7	1.4

Note: Figures are the percentage of the total population reporting a particular ancestry. The nine most commonly reported ancestries in the U.S. are shown. Figures include multiple ancestries (e.g. if a person reported being Irish and Italian, they were included in both columns); (1) Figures cover the Fayetteville, NC Metropolitan Statistical Area—see Appendix B for areas included; (2) Excludes Basque
Source: U.S. Census Bureau, 2010-2012 American Community Survey 3-Year Estimates

Foreign-Born Population

Area	Percent of Population Born in								
	Any Foreign Country	Mexico	Asia	Europe	Carribean	South America	Central America[2]	Africa	Canada
City	6.4	0.7	2.2	1.3	0.5	0.6	0.7	0.3	0.1
MSA[1]	5.9	1.1	1.7	1.1	0.5	0.5	0.7	0.3	0.1
U.S.	13.0	3.7	3.7	1.6	1.2	0.9	1.0	0.5	0.3

Note: (1) Figures cover the Fayetteville, NC Metropolitan Statistical Area—see Appendix B for areas included; (2) Excludes Mexico.
Source: U.S. Census Bureau, 2010-2012 American Community Survey 3-Year Estimates

Marital Status

Area	Never Married	Now Married[2]	Separated	Widowed	Divorced
City	32.8	44.4	3.6	5.7	13.5
MSA[1]	31.1	47.2	3.6	5.6	12.6
U.S.	32.4	48.4	2.2	6.0	11.0

Note: Figures are percentages and cover the population 15 years of age and older; (1) Figures cover the Fayetteville, NC Metropolitan Statistical Area—see Appendix B for areas included; (2) Excludes separated
Source: U.S. Census Bureau, 2010-2012 American Community Survey 3-Year Estimates

Age

Area	Percent of Population									Median Age
	Under Age 5	Age 5–19	Age 20–34	Age 35–44	Age 45–54	Age 55–64	Age 65–74	Age 75–84	Age 85+	
City	8.6	19.9	28.3	11.6	11.9	9.5	5.7	3.3	1.0	30.1
MSA[1]	8.6	21.5	25.5	12.5	12.6	9.9	5.5	2.8	1.0	30.9
U.S.	6.4	20.1	20.5	13.1	14.3	12.2	7.3	4.2	1.8	37.3

Note: (1) Figures cover the Fayetteville, NC Metropolitan Statistical Area—see Appendix B for areas included
Source: U.S. Census Bureau, 2010-2012 American Community Survey 3-Year Estimates

Gender

Area	Males	Females	Males per 100 Females
City	98,609	102,725	96.0
MSA[1]	180,157	191,549	94.1
U.S.	153,276,055	158,333,314	96.8

Note: (1) Figures cover the Fayetteville, NC Metropolitan Statistical Area—see Appendix B for areas included
Source: U.S. Census Bureau, 2010-2012 American Community Survey 3-Year Estimates

Religious Groups by Family

Area	Catholic	Baptist	Non-Den.	Methodist[2]	Lutheran	LDS[3]	Pentecostal	Presbyterian[4]	Muslim[5]	Judaism
MSA[1]	2.6	14.1	10.5	6.2	0.2	1.4	4.9	2.1	0.2	<0.1
U.S.	19.1	9.3	4.0	4.0	2.3	2.0	1.9	1.6	0.8	0.7

Note: Figures are the number of adherents as a percentage of the total population; (1) Figures cover the Fayetteville, NC Metropolitan Statistical Area—see Appendix B for areas included; (2) Methodist/Pietist; (3) Latter Day Saints; (4) Reformed; (5) Figures are estimates
Source: Association of Statisticians of American Religious Bodies, 2010 U.S. Religion Census: Religious Congregations & Membership Study

Religious Groups by Tradition

Area	Catholic	Evangelical Protestant	Mainline Protestant	Other Tradition	Black Protestant	Orthodox
MSA[1]	2.6	26.7	7.9	1.8	4.3	0.1
U.S.	19.1	16.2	7.3	4.3	1.6	0.3

Note: Figures are the number of adherents as a percentage of the total population; (1) Figures cover the Fayetteville, NC Metropolitan Statistical Area—see Appendix B for areas included
Source: Association of Statisticians of American Religious Bodies, 2010 U.S. Religion Census: Religious Congregations & Membership Study

ECONOMY

Gross Metropolitan Product

Area	2011	2012	2013	2014	Rank[2]
MSA[1]	18.4	18.7	18.8	19.4	116

Note: Figures are in billions of dollars; (1) Figures cover the Fayetteville, NC Metropolitan Statistical Area—see Appendix B for areas included; (2) Rank is based on 2014 data and ranges from 1 to 363
Source: The United States Conference of Mayors, U.S. Metro Economies: Outlook—Gross Metropolitan Product, with Metro Employment Projections, November 2013

Economic Growth

Area	2011 (%)	2012 (%)	2013 (%)	2014 (%)	Rank[2]
MSA[1]	2.6	-1.0	-0.9	1.2	310
U.S.	1.6	2.5	1.7	2.5	–

Note: Figures are real gross metropolitan product (GMP) growth rates and represent annual average percent change; (1) Figures cover the Fayetteville, NC Metropolitan Statistical Area—see Appendix B for areas included; (2) Rank is based on 2013 data and ranges from 1 to 363
Source: The United States Conference of Mayors, U.S. Metro Economies: Outlook—Gross Metropolitan Product, with Metro Employment Projections, November 2013

Metropolitan Area Exports

Area	2007	2008	2009	2010	2011	2012	Rank[2]
MSA[1]	321.5	300.4	218.4	260.1	307.7	322.3	247

Note: Figures are in millions of dollars; (1) Figures cover the Fayetteville, NC Metropolitan Statistical Area—see Appendix B for areas included; (2) Rank is based on 2012 data and ranges from 1 to 369
Source: U.S. Department of Commerce, International Trade Administration, Office of Trade & Industry Information, Manufacturing & Services, data extracted April 1, 2014

INCOME

Income

Area	Per Capita ($)	Median Household ($)	Average Household ($)
City	22,889	44,472	56,003
MSA[1]	22,026	44,680	56,594
U.S.	27,385	51,771	71,579

Note: (1) Figures cover the Fayetteville, NC Metropolitan Statistical Area—see Appendix B for areas included
Source: U.S. Census Bureau, 2010-2012 American Community Survey 3-Year Estimates

Household Income Distribution

Area	Percent of Households Earning							
	Under $15,000	$15,000 -24,999	$25,000 -34,999	$35,000 -49,999	$50,000 -74,999	$75,000 -99,000	$100,000 -149,999	$150,000 and up
City	14.8	10.3	12.7	17.7	20.9	11.0	8.5	4.1
MSA[1]	14.9	11.2	12.5	16.3	19.7	11.6	9.7	4.0
U.S.	13.1	11.0	10.5	13.7	18.1	11.9	12.5	9.1

Note: (1) Figures cover the Fayetteville, NC Metropolitan Statistical Area—see Appendix B for areas included
Source: U.S. Census Bureau, 2010-2012 American Community Survey 3-Year Estimates

Poverty Rate

Area	All Ages	Under 18 Years Old	18 to 64 Years Old	65 Years and Over
City	18.2	26.2	16.2	10.0
MSA[1]	18.1	25.0	16.1	11.1
U.S.	15.7	22.2	14.6	9.3

Note: Figures are percentage of people whose income during the past 12 months was below the poverty level;
(1) Figures cover the Fayetteville, NC Metropolitan Statistical Area—see Appendix B for areas included
Source: U.S. Census Bureau, 2010-2012 American Community Survey 3-Year Estimates

Personal Bankruptcy Filing Rate

Area	2008	2009	2010	2011	2012	2013
Cumberland County	2.87	3.25	3.25	2.99	2.59	2.60
U.S.	3.53	4.61	4.97	4.37	3.76	3.29

Note: Numbers are per 1,000 population and include Chapter 7 and Chapter 13 filings
Source: Federal Deposit Insurance Corporation, Regional Economic Conditions, March 20, 2014

EMPLOYMENT

Labor Force and Employment

Area	Civilian Labor Force			Workers Employed		
	Dec. 2012	Dec. 2013	% Chg.	Dec. 2012	Dec. 2013	% Chg.
City	89,479	87,203	-2.5	82,694	82,364	-0.4
MSA[1]	165,633	160,669	-3.0	148,798	148,205	-0.4
U.S.	154,904,000	154,408,000	-0.3	143,060,000	144,423,000	1.0

Note: Data is not seasonally adjusted and covers workers 16 years of age and older; (1) Metropolitan Statistical Area—see Appendix B for areas included
Source: Bureau of Labor Statistics, Local Area Unemployment Statistics

Unemployment Rate

Area	2013											
	Jan.	Feb.	Mar.	Apr.	May	Jun.	Jul.	Aug.	Sep.	Oct.	Nov.	Dec.
City	8.2	7.5	7.1	6.8	7.5	8.0	8.1	7.3	6.5	6.5	5.8	5.5
MSA[1]	10.8	10.0	9.6	9.3	9.9	10.4	10.6	9.8	8.9	8.9	8.2	7.8
U.S.	8.5	8.1	7.6	7.1	7.3	7.8	7.7	7.3	7.0	7.0	6.6	6.5

Note: Data is not seasonally adjusted and covers workers 16 years of age and older; All figures are percentages;
(1) Metropolitan Statistical Area—see Appendix B for areas included
Source: Bureau of Labor Statistics, Local Area Unemployment Statistics

Employment by Occupation

Occupation Classification	City (%)	MSA[1] (%)	U.S. (%)
Management, Business, Science, and Arts	35.3	33.2	36.0
Natural Resources, Construction, and Maintenance	8.0	9.5	9.1
Production, Transportation, and Material Moving	10.9	12.2	12.0
Sales and Office	25.1	24.9	24.7
Service	20.8	20.2	18.2

Note: Figures cover employed civilians 16 years of age and older; (1) Figures cover the Fayetteville, NC Metropolitan Statistical Area—see Appendix B for areas included
Source: U.S. Census Bureau, 2010-2012 American Community Survey 3-Year Estimates

Employment by Industry

| Sector | MSA[1] | | U.S. |
	Number of Employees	Percent of Total	Percent of Total
Construction	n/a	n/a	4.2
Education and Health Services	14,600	11.0	15.5
Financial Activities	3,700	2.8	5.7
Government	39,800	29.9	16.1
Information	1,500	1.1	1.9
Leisure and Hospitality	14,900	11.2	10.2
Manufacturing	11,400	8.6	8.7
Mining and Logging	n/a	n/a	0.6
Other Services	5,000	3.8	3.9
Professional and Business Services	12,900	9.7	13.7
Retail Trade	17,400	13.1	11.4
Transportation and Utilities	4,800	3.6	3.8
Wholesale Trade	2,400	1.8	4.2

Note: Figures cover non-farm employment as of December 2013 and are not seasonally adjusted;
(1) Metropolitan Statistical Area—see Appendix B for areas included; n/a not available
Source: Bureau of Labor Statistics, Current Employment Statistics, Employment, Hours, and Earnings

Occupations with Greatest Projected Employment Growth: 2010 – 2020

Occupation[1]	2010 Employment	2020 Projected Employment	Numeric Employment Change	Percent Employment Change
Combined Food Preparation and Serving Workers, Including Fast Food	114,040	132,650	18,610	16.3
Registered Nurses	92,540	109,790	17,250	18.6
Retail Salespersons	131,650	145,910	14,270	10.8
Home Health Aides	55,560	67,570	12,010	21.6
Customer Service Representatives	74,700	84,800	10,090	13.5
Postsecondary Teachers	49,850	59,780	9,930	19.9
Landscaping and Groundskeeping Workers	33,610	43,450	9,830	29.3
Janitors and Cleaners, Except Maids and Housekeeping Cleaners	52,290	61,160	8,870	17.0
Cashiers	101,410	110,200	8,790	8.7
Elementary School Teachers, Except Special Education	37,090	45,730	8,650	23.3

Note: Projections cover North Carolina; (1) Sorted by numeric employment change
Source: www.projectionscentral.com, State Occupational Projections, 2010–2020 Long-Term Projections

Fastest Growing Occupations: 2010 – 2020

Occupation[1]	2010 Employment	2020 Projected Employment	Numeric Employment Change	Percent Employment Change
Biomedical Engineers	250	480	230	90.5
Medical Scientists, Except Epidemiologists	4,270	6,550	2,280	53.4
Biochemists and Biophysicists	460	670	210	44.9
Interpreters and Translators	3,000	4,210	1,220	40.6
Veterinary Technologists and Technicians	3,060	4,300	1,240	40.4
Market Research Analysts and Marketing Specialists	9,750	13,580	3,830	39.3
Helpers—Brickmasons, Blockmasons, Stonemasons, and Tile and Marble Setters	1,900	2,630	740	38.8
Helpers—Carpenters	1,850	2,560	710	38.4
Diagnostic Medical Sonographers	1,660	2,280	620	37.3
Audiologists	350	460	120	33.6

Note: Projections cover North Carolina; (1) Sorted by percent employment change and excludes occupations with numeric employment change less than 100
Source: www.projectionscentral.com, State Occupational Projections, 2010–2020 Long-Term Projections

Average Wages

Occupation	$/Hr.	Occupation	$/Hr.
Accountants and Auditors	31.00	Maids and Housekeeping Cleaners	8.58
Automotive Mechanics	17.52	Maintenance and Repair Workers	17.19
Bookkeepers	15.79	Marketing Managers	n/a
Carpenters	16.06	Nuclear Medicine Technologists	28.73
Cashiers	8.99	Nurses, Licensed Practical	19.57
Clerks, General Office	12.92	Nurses, Registered	29.81
Clerks, Receptionists/Information	10.88	Nursing Assistants	11.33
Clerks, Shipping/Receiving	14.96	Packers and Packagers, Hand	10.02
Computer Programmers	29.95	Physical Therapists	38.64
Computer Systems Analysts	34.22	Postal Service Mail Carriers	24.08
Computer User Support Specialists	22.55	Real Estate Brokers	19.47
Cooks, Restaurant	10.15	Retail Salespersons	10.56
Dentists	96.55	Sales Reps., Exc. Tech./Scientific	24.42
Electrical Engineers	51.65	Sales Reps., Tech./Scientific	39.94
Electricians	20.60	Secretaries, Exc. Legal/Med./Exec.	14.77
Financial Managers	55.58	Security Guards	15.30
First-Line Supervisors/Managers, Sales	17.83	Surgeons	n/a
Food Preparation Workers	10.22	Teacher Assistants	10.00
General and Operations Managers	58.29	Teachers, Elementary School	19.20
Hairdressers/Cosmetologists	11.66	Teachers, Secondary School	19.10
Internists	n/a	Telemarketers	8.90
Janitors and Cleaners	10.01	Truck Drivers, Heavy/Tractor-Trailer	15.43
Landscaping/Groundskeeping Workers	10.33	Truck Drivers, Light/Delivery Svcs.	15.54
Lawyers	53.27	Waiters and Waitresses	9.09

Note: Wage data covers the Fayetteville, NC Metropolitan Statistical Area—see Appendix B for areas included. Hourly wages for elementary/secondary school teachers and teacher assistants were calculated by the editors from annual wage data assuming a 40 hour work week; n/a not available.
Source: Bureau of Labor Statistics, Metro Area Occupational Employment and Wage Estimates, May 2013

RESIDENTIAL REAL ESTATE

Building Permits

Area	Single-Family			Multi-Family			Total		
	2012	2013	Pct. Chg.	2012	2013	Pct. Chg.	2012	2013	Pct. Chg.
City	527	437	-17.1	1,356	288	-78.8	1,883	725	-61.5
MSA[1]	1,376	1,269	-7.8	1,664	621	-62.7	3,040	1,890	-37.8
U.S.	518,695	620,802	19.7	310,963	370,020	19.0	829,658	990,822	19.4

Note: (1) Metropolitan Statistical Area—see Appendix B for areas included; figures represent new, privately-owned housing units authorized (unadjusted data); All permit data are based on estimates with imputation.
Source: U.S. Census Bureau, Manufacturing, Mining, and Construction Statistics, Building Permits, 2012, 2013

Homeownership Rate

Area	2006 (%)	2007 (%)	2008 (%)	2009 (%)	2010 (%)	2011 (%)	2012 (%)	2013 (%)
MSA[1]	n/a	n/a	n/a	n/a	n/a	n/a	n/a	n/a
U.S.	68.8	68.1	67.8	67.4	66.9	66.1	65.4	65.1

Note: (1) Figures cover the Fayetteville, NC Metropolitan Statistical Area—see Appendix B for areas included; n/a not available
Source: U.S. Census Bureau, Housing Vacancies and Homeownership Annual Statistics: 2013

Housing Vacancy Rates

Area	Gross Vacancy Rate[2] (%)			Year-Round Vacancy Rate[3] (%)			Rental Vacancy Rate[4] (%)			Homeowner Vacancy Rate[5] (%)		
	2011	2012	2013	2011	2012	2013	2011	2012	2013	2011	2012	2013
MSA[1]	n/a	n/a	n/a	n/a	n/a	n/a	n/a	n/a	n/a	n/a	n/a	n/a
U.S.	14.2	13.8	13.8	11.1	10.8	10.7	9.5	8.7	8.3	2.5	2.0	2.0

Note: (1) Figures cover the Fayetteville, NC Metropolitan Statistical Area—see Appendix B for areas included; (2) The percentage of the total housing inventory that is vacant; (3) The percentage of the housing inventory (excluding seasonal units) that is year-round vacant; (4) The percentage of rental inventory that is vacant for rent; (5) The percentage of homeowner inventory that is vacant for sale; n/a not available
Source: U.S. Census Bureau, Housing Vacancies and Homeownership Annual Statistics: 2013

TAXES

State Corporate Income Tax Rates

State	Tax Rate (%)	Income Brackets ($)	Num. of Brackets	Financial Institution Tax Rate (%)[a]	Federal Income Tax Ded.
North Carolina	6.0	Flat rate	1	6.0 (t)	No

Note: Tax rates as of January 1, 2014; (a) Rates listed are the corporate income tax rate applied to financial institutions or excise taxes based on income. Some states have other taxes based upon the value of deposits or shares; (t) In North Carolina financial institutions are also subject to a tax equal to $30 per one million in assets.
Source: Federation of Tax Administrators, "State Corporate Income Tax Rates, 2014"

State Individual Income Tax Rates

State	Tax Rate (%)	Income Brackets ($)	Num. of Brackets	Personal Exempt. ($)[1] Single	Dependents	Fed. Inc. Tax Ded.
North Carolina	5.8	Flat rate	1	None	None	No

Note: Tax rates as of January 1, 2014; Local- and county-level taxes are not included; n/a not applicable; (1) Married joint filers generally receive double the single exemption
Source: Federation of Tax Administrators, "State Individual Income Tax Rates, 2014"

Various State and Local Tax Rates

State	State and Local Sales and Use (%)	State Sales and Use (%)	Gasoline[1] (¢/gal.)	Cigarette[2] ($/pack)	Spirits[3] ($/gal.)	Wine[4] ($/gal.)	Beer[5] ($/gal.)
North Carolina	7.0	4.75	37.75	0.450	12.36 (g)	1.00	0.62

Note: All tax rates as of January 1, 2014; (1) The American Petroleum Institute has developed a methodology for determining the average tax rate on a gallon of fuel. Rates may include any of the following: excise taxes, environmental fees, storage tank fees, other fees or taxes, general sales tax, and local taxes. In states where gasoline is subject to the general sales tax, or where the fuel tax is based on the average sale price, the average rate determined by API is sensitive to changes in the price of gasoline. States that fully or partially apply general sales taxes to gasoline: CA, CO, GA, IL, IN, MI, NY; (2) The federal excise tax of $1.0066 per pack and local taxes are not included; (3) Rates are those applicable to off-premise sales of 40% alcohol by volume (a.b.v.) distilled spirits in 750ml containers. Local excise taxes are excluded; (4) Rates are those applicable to off-premise sales of 11% a.b.v. non-carbonated wine in 750ml containers; (5) Rates are those applicable to off-premise sales of 4.7% a.b.v. beer in 12 ounce containers; (g) States where the government controls sales. In these "control states," products are subject to ad valorem mark-up and excise taxes. The excise tax rate is calculated using a methodology developed by the Distilled Spirits Council of the United States.
Source: Tax Foundation, 2014 Facts & Figures: How Does Your State Compare?

State Business Tax Climate Index Rankings

State	Overall Rank	Corporate Tax Index Rank	Individual Income Tax Index Rank	Sales Tax Index Rank	Unemployment Insurance Tax Index Rank	Property Tax Index Rank
North Carolina	44	29	42	47	7	30

Note: The index is a measure of how each state's tax laws affect economic performance. The lower the rank, the more favorable a state's tax system is for business. States without a given tax are given a ranking of 1. The scores/rankings for the District of Columbia do not affect other states. The 2014 index represents the tax climate as of July 1, 2013.
Source: Tax Foundation, State Business Tax Climate Index 2014

COMMERCIAL UTILITIES

Typical Monthly Electric Bills

Area	Commercial Service ($/month) 1,500 kWh	40 kW demand 14,000 kWh	Industrial Service ($/month) 1,000 kW demand 200,000 kWh	50,000 kW demand 15,000,000 kWh
City	n/a	n/a	n/a	n/a
Average[1]	197	1,636	25,662	1,485,307

Note: Based on total rates in effect July 1, 2013; (1) average based on 180 utilities surveyed; n/a not available
Source: Edison Electric Institute, Typical Bills and Average Rates Report, Summer 2013

TRANSPORTATION

Means of Transportation to Work

| Area | Car/Truck/Van | | Public Transportation | | | Bicycle | Walked | Other Means | Worked at Home |
	Drove Alone	Car-pooled	Bus	Subway	Railroad				
City	80.5	9.8	0.8	0.0	0.0	0.2	4.5	1.3	2.9
MSA[1]	82.7	9.6	0.5	0.0	0.0	0.2	3.1	1.5	2.3
U.S.	76.4	9.7	2.6	1.7	0.5	0.6	2.8	1.3	4.3

Note: Figures are percentages and cover workers 16 years of age and older; (1) Figures cover the Fayetteville, NC Metropolitan Statistical Area—see Appendix B for areas included
Source: U.S. Census Bureau, 2010-2012 American Community Survey 3-Year Estimates

Travel Time to Work

Area	Less Than 10 Minutes	10 to 19 Minutes	20 to 29 Minutes	30 to 44 Minutes	45 to 59 Minutes	60 to 89 Minutes	90 Minutes or More
City	17.0	38.5	24.2	12.5	3.8	1.8	2.0
MSA[1]	13.6	33.7	25.7	17.8	4.9	2.1	2.1
U.S.	13.5	29.8	20.9	20.1	7.5	5.6	2.5

Note: Figures are percentages and include workers 16 years old and over; (1) Figures cover the Fayetteville, NC Metropolitan Statistical Area—see Appendix B for areas included
Source: U.S. Census Bureau, 2010-2012 American Community Survey 3-Year Estimates

Travel Time Index

Area	1985	1990	1995	2000	2005	2010	2011
Urban Area[1]	n/a	n/a	n/a	n/a	n/a	n/a	n/a
Average[2]	1.09	1.14	1.16	1.19	1.23	1.18	1.18

Note: Travel Time Index—the ratio of travel time in the peak period to the travel time at free-flow conditions. For example, a value of 1.30 indicates a 20-minute free-flow trip takes 26 minutes in the peak. Free-flow speeds (60 mph on freeways and 35 mph on principal arterials) are used as the comparison threshold; (1) Data for the Fayetteville, NC urban area was not available; (2) average of 498 urban areas
Source: Texas Transportation Institute, Urban Mobility Report 2012, December 2012

Public Transportation

Agency Name / Mode of Transportation	Vehicles Operated in Maximum Service	Annual Unlinked Passenger Trips (in thous.)	Annual Passenger Miles (in thous.)
Fayetteville Area System of Transit			
Bus (directly operated)	17	1,646.2	7,815.7
Demand Response (directly operated)	13	53.1	369.2

Source: Federal Transit Administration, National Transit Database, 2012

Air Transportation

Airport Name and Code / Type of Service	Passenger Airlines[1]	Passenger Enplanements	Freight Carriers[2]	Freight (lbs.)
Fayetteville Regional Airport (FAY)				
Domestic service (U.S. carriers - 2013)	11	243,841	4	10,808
International service (U.S. carriers - 2012)	0	0	0	0

Note: (1) Includes all U.S.-based major, minor and commuter airlines that carried at least one passenger during the year; (2) Includes all U.S.-based airlines and freight carriers that transported at least one lb. of freight during the year.
Source: Bureau of Transportation Statistics, The Intermodal Transportation Database, Air Carriers: T-100 Domestic Market (U.S. Carriers), 2013; Bureau of Transportation Statistics, The Intermodal Transportation Database, Air Carriers: T-100 International Market (U.S. Carriers), 2012

Other Transportation Statistics

Major Highways:	I-95; I-295
Amtrak Service:	Yes
Major Waterways/Ports:	Cape Fear River

Source: Amtrak.com; Google Maps

BUSINESSES

Major Business Headquarters

Company Name	Rankings	
	Fortune[1]	Forbes[2]
No companies listed	–	–

Note: (1) Fortune 500—companies that produce a 10-K are ranked 1 to 500 based on 2012 revenue; (2) all private companies with at least $2 billion in annual revenue through the end of their most current fiscal year are ranked 1 to 224; companies listed are headquartered in the city; dashes indicate no ranking
Source: Fortune, "Fortune 500," May 20, 2013; Forbes, "America's Largest Private Companies," December 18, 2013

Minority- and Women-Owned Businesses

Group	All Firms		Firms with Paid Employees			
	Firms	Sales ($000)	Firms	Sales ($000)	Employees	Payroll ($000)
Asian	823	239,359	237	205,554	2,655	62,395
Black	3,552	233,026	263	150,621	3,202	57,152
Hispanic	347	26,309	17	16,436	237	3,903
Women	4,336	633,772	705	572,048	7,609	150,547
All Firms	12,937	9,891,128	3,745	9,430,170	76,304	1,898,796

Note: Figures cover firms located in the city; minority- and women-owned business are defined as firms in which the corresponding group own 51% or more of the stock or equity of the company
Source: U.S. Census Bureau, 2007 Economic Census, Survey of Business Owners (2012 Survey of Business Owners data will be released starting in June 2015)

HOTELS & CONVENTION CENTERS

Hotels/Motels

Area	5 Star		4 Star		3 Star		2 Star		1 Star		Not Rated	
	Num.	Pct.[3]	Num.	Pct.[3]	Num.	Pct.[3]	Num.	Pct.[3]	Num.	Pct.[3]	Num.	Pct.[3]
City[1]	0	0.0	0	0.0	13	15.9	62	75.6	1	1.2	6	7.3
Total[2]	142	0.9	1,005	6.0	5,147	30.9	8,578	51.4	408	2.4	1,397	8.4

Note: (1) Figures cover Fayetteville and vicinity; (2) Figures cover all 100 cities in this book; (3) Percentage of hotels which have a given star rating; Star ratings are determined by expedia.com and offer an indication of the general quality of a particular hotel.
Source: expedia.com, April 7, 2014

Major Convention Centers

Name	Overall Space (sq. ft.)	Exhibit Space (sq. ft.)	Meeting Space (sq. ft.)	Meeting Rooms
Crown Complex	60,000	n/a	n/a	n/a

Note: Table includes convention centers located in the Fayetteville, NC metro area; n/a not available
Source: Original research

Living Environment

COST OF LIVING

Cost of Living Index

Composite Index	Groceries	Housing	Utilities	Trans-portation	Health Care	Misc. Goods/ Services
n/a	n/a	n/a	n/a	n/a	n/a	n/a

Note: The Cost of Living Index measures regional differences in the cost of consumer goods and services, excluding taxes and non-consumer expenditures, for professional and managerial households in the top income quintile. It is based on more than 50,000 prices covering almost 60 different items for which prices are collected three times a year by chambers of commerce, economic development organizations or university applied economic centers in each participating urban area. The numbers shown should be read as a percentage above or below the national average of 100. For example, a value of 115.4 in the groceries column indicates that grocery prices are 15.4% higher than the national average. Small differences in the index numbers should not be interpreted as significant; n/a not available.
Source: The Council for Community and Economic Research, ACCRA Cost of Living Index, 2013

Grocery Prices

Area[1]	T-Bone Steak ($/pound)	Frying Chicken ($/pound)	Whole Milk ($/half gal.)	Eggs ($/dozen)	Orange Juice ($/64 oz.)	Coffee ($/11.5 oz.)
City[2]	n/a	n/a	n/a	n/a	n/a	n/a
Avg.	10.19	1.28	2.34	1.81	3.48	4.39
Min.	8.56	0.94	1.44	1.19	2.78	3.40
Max.	14.82	2.28	3.56	3.73	6.23	7.32

Note: (1) Values for the local area are compared with the average, minimum and maximum values for all 327 areas in the Cost of Living Index; (2) Figures cover the Fayetteville NC urban area; n/a not available; **T-Bone Steak** *(price per pound);* **Frying Chicken** *(price per pound, whole fryer);* **Whole Milk** *(half gallon carton);* **Eggs** *(price per dozen, Grade A, large);* **Orange Juice** *(64 oz. Tropicana or Florida Natural);* **Coffee** *(11.5 oz. can, vacuum-packed, Maxwell House, Hills Bros, or Folgers).*
Source: The Council for Community and Economic Research, ACCRA Cost of Living Index, 2013

Housing and Utility Costs

Area[1]	New Home Price ($)	Apartment Rent ($/month)	All Electric ($/month)	Part Electric ($/month)	Other Energy ($/month)	Telephone ($/month)
City[2]	n/a	n/a	n/a	n/a	n/a	n/a
Avg.	295,864	900	171.38	91.82	70.12	27.73
Min.	185,506	458	117.80	48.81	33.67	17.16
Max.	1,358,917	3,783	441.68	171.40	372.65	39.47

Note: (1) Values for the local area are compared with the average, minimum and maximum values for all 327 areas in the Cost of Living Index; (2) Figures cover the Fayetteville NC urban area; n/a not available; **New Home Price** *(2,400 sf living area, 8,000 sf lot, in urban area with full utilities);* **Apartment Rent** *(950 sf 2 bedroom/1.5 or 2 bath, unfurnished, excluding all utilities except water);* **All Electric** *(average monthly cost for an all-electric home);* **Part Electric** *(average monthly cost for a part-electric home);* **Other Energy** *(average monthly cost for natural gas, fuel oil, coal, wood, and any other forms of energy except electricity);* **Telephone** *(price includes basic monthly rate for a private residential line plus additional local usage charges incurred by a family of four).*
Source: The Council for Community and Economic Research, ACCRA Cost of Living Index, 2013

Health Care, Transportation, and Other Costs

Area[1]	Doctor ($/visit)	Dentist ($/visit)	Optometrist ($/visit)	Gasoline ($/gallon)	Beauty Salon ($/visit)	Men's Shirt ($)
City[2]	n/a	n/a	n/a	n/a	n/a	n/a
Avg.	101.40	86.48	96.16	3.44	33.87	26.55
Min.	61.67	50.83	50.12	3.08	18.92	12.48
Max.	182.71	152.50	223.78	4.33	68.22	52.03

Note: (1) Values for the local area are compared with the average, minimum and maximum values for all 327 areas in the Cost of Living Index; (2) Figures cover the Fayetteville NC urban area; n/a not available; **Doctor** *(general practitioners routine exam of an established patient);* **Dentist** *(adult teeth cleaning and periodic oral examination);* **Optometrist** *(full vision eye exam for established adult patient);* **Gasoline** *(one gallon regular unleaded, national brand, including all taxes, cash price at self-service pump if available);* **Beauty Salon** *(woman's shampoo, trim, and blow-dry);* **Men's Shirt** *(cotton/polyester dress shirt, pinpoint weave, long sleeves).*
Source: The Council for Community and Economic Research, ACCRA Cost of Living Index, 2013

HOUSING

House Price Index (HPI)

Area	National Ranking[2]	Quarterly Change (%)	One-Year Change (%)	Five-Year Change (%)
MSA[1]	280	1.32	-3.52	-4.73
U.S.[3]	–	1.20	7.69	4.18

Note: The HPI is a weighted repeat sales index. It measures average price changes in repeat sales or refinancings on the same properties. This information is obtained by reviewing repeat mortgage transactions on single-family properties whose mortgages have been purchased or securitized by Fannie Mae or Freddie Mac in January 1975; (1) Fayetteville, NC Metropolitan Statistical Area—see Appendix B for areas included; (2) Rankings are based on annual percentage change for all metro areas containing at least 15,000 transactions over the last 10 years and ranges from 1 to 283; (3) figures based on a weighted average of Census Division estimates using a seasonally adjusted, purchase-only index; all figures are for the period ending December 31, 2013
Source: Federal Housing Finance Agency, House Price Index, February 25, 2014

Median Single-Family Home Prices

Area	2011	2012	2013p	Percent Change 2012 to 2013
MSA[1]	152.3	152.0	146.5	-3.6
U.S. Average	166.2	177.2	197.4	11.4

Note: Figures are median sales prices of existing single-family homes in thousands of dollars; (p) preliminary; n/a not available; (1) Fayetteville, NC Metropolitan Statistical Area—see Appendix B for areas included
Source: National Association of Realtors, Median Sales Price of Existing Single-Family Homes for Metropolitan Areas, 4th Quarter 2013

Qualifying Income Based on Median Sales Price of Existing Single-Family Homes

Area	With 5% Down ($)	With 10% Down ($)	With 20% Down ($)
MSA[1]	32,047	30,360	26,987
U.S. Average	45,395	43,006	38,228

Note: Figures are preliminary; Qualifying income is based on a mortgage rate of 4.4%. Monthly principal and interest payment is limited to 25% of income; n/a not available; (1) Fayetteville, NC Metropolitan Statistical Area—see Appendix B for areas included
Source: National Association of Realtors, Qualifying Income Based on Median Sales Price of Existing Single-Family Homes for Metropolitan Areas, 4th Quarter 2013

Median Apartment Condo-Coop Home Prices

Area	2011	2012	2013p	Percent Change 2012 to 2013
MSA[1]	n/a	n/a	n/a	n/a
U.S. Average	165.1	173.7	194.9	12.2

Note: Figures are median sales prices of existing apartment condo-coop homes in thousands of dollars; (p) preliminary; n/a not available; (1) Fayetteville, NC Metropolitan Statistical Area—see Appendix B for areas included
Source: National Association of Realtors, Median Sales Price of Existing Apartment Condo-Coop Homes for Metropolitan Areas, 4th Quarter 2013

Gross Monthly Rent

Area	Under $200	$200 -299	$300 -499	$500 -749	$750 -999	$1,000 -1,499	$1,500 and up	Median ($)
City	1.5	1.4	5.7	25.1	33.5	29.6	3.1	867
MSA[1]	1.5	2.1	6.8	26.7	31.6	27.7	3.6	848
U.S.	1.7	3.3	8.1	22.7	24.3	25.7	14.3	889

Note: Figures are percentages except for Median; Gross rent is the contract rent plus the estimated average monthly cost of utilities (electricity, gas, and water and sewer) and fuels (oil, coal, kerosene, wood, etc.) if these are paid by the renter (or paid for the renter by someone else); (1) Figures cover the Fayetteville, NC Metropolitan Statistical Area—see Appendix B for areas included
Source: U.S. Census Bureau, 2010-2012 American Community Survey 3-Year Estimates

Year Housing Structure Built

Area	2010 or Later	2000 -2009	1990 -1999	1980 -1989	1970 -1979	1960 -1969	1950 -1959	1940 -1949	Before 1940	Median Year
City	0.7	17.7	18.1	16.7	18.9	14.3	8.7	2.6	2.3	1982
MSA[1]	1.4	21.5	21.1	16.3	17.0	11.2	7.2	2.2	2.1	1986
U.S.	0.5	14.9	13.8	13.9	15.9	11.1	10.9	5.5	13.5	1976

Note: Figures are percentages except for Median Year; (1) Figures cover the Fayetteville, NC Metropolitan Statistical Area—see Appendix B for areas included
Source: U.S. Census Bureau, 2010-2012 American Community Survey 3-Year Estimates

HEALTH

Health Risk Data

Category	MSA[1] (%)	U.S. (%)
Adults aged 18–64 who have any kind of health care coverage	78.6	79.6
Adults who reported being in good or excellent health	83.6	83.1
Adults who are current smokers	22.5	19.6
Adults who are heavy drinkers[2]	n/a	6.1
Adults who are binge drinkers[3]	11.7	16.9
Adults who are overweight (BMI 25.0 - 29.9)	35.8	35.8
Adults who are obese (BMI 30.0 - 99.8)	30.7	27.6
Adults who participated in any physical activities in the past month	76.1	77.1
Adults 50+ who have ever had a sigmoidoscopy or colonoscopy	75.2	67.3
Women aged 40+ who have had a mammogram within the past two years	78.0	74.0
Men aged 40+ who have had a PSA test within the past two years	50.9	45.2
Adults aged 65+ who have had flu shot within the past year	61.5	60.1
Adults who always wear a seatbelt	94.9	93.8

Note: Data as of 2012 unless otherwise noted; n/a not available; (1) Figures cover the Fayetteville, NC Metropolitan Statistical Area—see Appendix B for areas included; (2) Heavy drinkers are classified as males having more than two drinks per day or females having more than one drink per day; (3) Binge drinkers are classified as males having five or more drinks on one occasion or females having four or more drinks on one occasion
Source: Centers for Disease Control and Prevention, Behaviorial Risk Factor Surveillance System, SMART: Selected Metropolitan/Micropolitan Area Risk Trends, 2012

Chronic Health Indicators

Category	MSA[1] (%)	U.S. (%)
Adults who have ever been told they had a heart attack	4.7	4.5
Adults who have ever been told they had a stroke	2.8	2.9
Adults who have been told they currently have asthma	5.6	8.9
Adults who have ever been told they have arthritis	26.2	25.7
Adults who have ever been told they have diabetes[2]	13.4	9.7
Adults who have ever been told they had skin cancer	3.6	5.7
Adults who have ever been told they had any other types of cancer	4.2	6.5
Adults who have ever been told they have COPD	6.3	6.2
Adults who have ever been told they have kidney disease	1.4	2.5
Adults who have ever been told they have a form of depression	16.1	18.0

Note: Data as of 2012 unless otherwise noted; (1) Figures cover the Fayetteville, NC Metropolitan Statistical Area—see Appendix B for areas included; (2) Figures do not include pregnancy-related, borderline, or pre-diabetes
Source: Centers for Disease Control and Prevention, Behaviorial Risk Factor Surveillance System, SMART: Selected Metropolitan/Micropolitan Area Risk Trends, 2012

Mortality Rates for the Top 10 Causes of Death in the U.S.

ICD-10[a] Sub-Chapter	ICD-10[a] Code	Age-Adjusted Mortality Rate[1] per 100,000 population	
		County[2]	U.S.
Malignant neoplasms	C00-C97	194.0	174.2
Ischaemic heart diseases	I20-I25	142.0	119.1
Other forms of heart disease	I30-I51	42.8	49.6
Chronic lower respiratory diseases	J40-J47	50.2	43.2
Cerebrovascular diseases	I60-I69	49.3	40.3
Organic, including symptomatic, mental disorders	F01-F09	42.9	30.5
Other degenerative diseases of the nervous system	G30-G31	26.2	26.3
Other external causes of accidental injury	W00-X59	22.4	25.1
Diabetes mellitus	E10-E14	32.9	21.3
Hypertensive diseases	I10-I15	36.2	18.8

Note: (a) ICD-10 = International Classification of Diseases 10th Revision; (1) Mortality rates are a three year average covering 2008-2010; (2) Figures cover Cumberland County
Source: Centers for Disease Control and Prevention, National Center for Health Statistics. Compressed Mortality File 1999-2010 on CDC WONDER Online Database, released January 2013. Data are compiled from the Compressed Mortality File 1999-2010, Series 20 No. 2P, 2013.

Mortality Rates for Selected Causes of Death

ICD-10[a] Sub-Chapter	ICD-10[a] Code	Age-Adjusted Mortality Rate[1] per 100,000 population	
		County[2]	U.S.
Assault	X85-Y09	9.9	5.5
Diseases of the liver	K70-K76	13.1	12.4
Human immunodeficiency virus (HIV) disease	B20-B24	6.0	3.0
Influenza and pneumonia	J09-J18	16.9	16.4
Intentional self-harm	X60-X84	15.0	11.8
Malnutrition	E40-E46	Suppressed	0.8
Obesity and other hyperalimentation	E65-E68	*1.8	1.6
Renal failure	N17-N19	23.5	13.6
Transport accidents	V01-V99	16.1	12.6
Viral hepatitis	B15-B19	3.6	2.2

Note: (a) ICD-10 = International Classification of Diseases 10th Revision; (1) Mortality rates are a three year average covering 2008-2010; (2) Figures cover Cumberland County; (*) Unreliable data as per CDC
Source: Centers for Disease Control and Prevention, National Center for Health Statistics. Compressed Mortality File 1999-2010 on CDC WONDER Online Database, released January 2013. Data are compiled from the Compressed Mortality File 1999-2010, Series 20 No. 2P, 2013.

Health Insurance Coverage

Area	With Health Insurance	With Private Health Insurance	With Public Health Insurance	Without Health Insurance	Population Under Age 18 Without Health Insurance
City	85.8	66.1	33.0	14.2	5.0
MSA[1]	85.2	64.6	32.9	14.8	5.9
U.S.	84.9	65.4	30.4	15.1	7.5

Note: Figures are percentages that cover the civilian noninstitutionalized population; (1) Figures cover the Fayetteville, NC Metropolitan Statistical Area—see Appendix B for areas included
Source: U.S. Census Bureau, 2010-2012 American Community Survey 3-Year Estimates

Number of Medical Professionals

Area[1]	MDs[2]	DOs[2,3]	Dentists	Podiatrists	Chiropractors	Optometrists
Local (number)	627	63	275	21	31	58
Local (rate[4])	193.6	19.5	85.1	6.5	9.6	18.0
U.S. (rate[4])	267.6	19.6	61.7	5.6	24.7	14.5

Note: Data as of 2012 unless noted; (1) Local data covers Cumberland County; (2) Data as of 2011; (3) Doctor of Osteopathic Medicine; (4) rate per 100,000 population
Source: Area Resource File (ARF) 2012-2013. U.S. Department of Health and Human Services, Health Resources and Services Administration, Bureau of Health Professions

EDUCATION

Public School District Statistics

District Name	Schls	Pupils	Pupil/ Teacher Ratio	Minority Pupils[1] (%)	Free Lunch Eligible[2] (%)	IEP[3] (%)
Cumberland County Schools	88	53,053	14.8	66.3	47.9	13.5

Note: Table includes school districts with 2,000 or more students; (1) Percentage of students that are not non-Hispanic white; (2) Percentage of students that are eligible for the free lunch program; (3) Percentage of students that have an Individualized Education Program.
Source: U.S. Department of Education, National Center for Education Statistics, Common Core of Data, Local Education Agency (School District) Universe Survey: School Year 2011-2012; U.S. Department of Education, National Center for Education Statistics, Common Core of Data, Public Elementary/Secondary School Universe Survey: School Year 2011-2012

Best High Schools

High School Name	Rank[1]	Grad. Rate[2] (%)	Coll.[3] (%)	AP/IB/ AICE Tests[4]	AP/IB/ AICE Score[5]	SAT Score[6]	ACT Score[6]
Terry Sanford H.S.	1863	82	84	0.5	2.1	1505	18.8

Note: (1) Public schools are ranked from 1 to 2,000 based on the following self-reported statistics (with the corresponding weight used in calculating their overall score). Schools that were newly founded and did not have a graduating senior class in 2012 were excluded; (2) Four-year, on-time graduation rate (25%); (3) Percent of 2011 graduates who were accepted to college (25%); (4) AP/IB/AICE tests taken per student (25%); (5) Average AP/IB/AICE exam score (10%); (6) Average SAT and/or ACT score (10%); Percent of students enrolled in at least one AP/IB/AICE course (5%)—data not shown
Source: Newsweek and The Daily Beast, "America's Best High Schools 2013"

Highest Level of Education

Area	Less than H.S.	H.S. Diploma	Some College, No Deg.	Associate Degree	Bachelor's Degree	Master's Degree	Prof. School Degree	Doctorate Degree
City	9.2	25.6	29.5	10.8	16.5	6.1	1.4	1.0
MSA[1]	11.6	27.1	28.4	10.9	14.8	5.4	1.1	0.7
U.S.	14.1	28.3	21.3	7.8	18.0	7.5	1.9	1.2

Note: Figures cover persons age 25 and over; (1) Figures cover the Fayetteville, NC Metropolitan Statistical Area—see Appendix B for areas included
Source: U.S. Census Bureau, 2010-2012 American Community Survey 3-Year Estimates

Educational Attainment by Race

Area	High School Graduate or Higher (%)					Bachelor's Degree or Higher (%)				
	Total	White	Black	Asian	Hisp.[2]	Total	White	Black	Asian	Hisp.[2]
City	90.8	93.5	88.3	83.4	90.1	25.0	27.9	21.2	37.6	17.0
MSA[1]	88.4	90.4	87.4	83.3	82.4	22.0	24.3	19.6	32.9	15.0
U.S.	85.9	88.1	82.5	85.5	63.1	28.6	30.0	18.4	50.2	13.4

Note: Figures shown cover persons 25 years old and over; (1) Figures cover the Fayetteville, NC Metropolitan Statistical Area—see Appendix B for areas included; (2) People of Hispanic origin can be of any race
Source: U.S. Census Bureau, 2010-2012 American Community Survey 3-Year Estimates

School Enrollment by Grade and Control

Area	Preschool (%)		Kindergarten (%)		Grades 1 - 4 (%)		Grades 5 - 8 (%)		Grades 9 - 12 (%)	
	Public	Private	Public	Private	Public	Private	Public	Private	Public	Private
City	81.6	18.4	92.7	7.3	91.7	8.3	90.0	10.0	90.0	10.0
MSA[1]	78.0	22.0	93.6	6.4	91.0	9.0	90.6	9.4	90.4	9.6
U.S.	56.9	43.1	87.8	12.2	89.9	10.1	90.0	10.0	90.8	9.2

Note: Figures shown cover persons 3 years old and over; (1) Figures cover the Fayetteville, NC Metropolitan Statistical Area—see Appendix B for areas included
Source: U.S. Census Bureau, 2010-2012 American Community Survey 3-Year Estimates

Average Salaries of Public School Classroom Teachers

Area	2012-13		2013-14		Percent Change 2012-13 to 2013-14	Percent Change 2003-04 to 2013-14
	Dollars	Rank[1]	Dollars	Rank[1]		
North Carolina	45,737	46	45,355	48	-0.84	5.0
U.S. Average	56,103	–	56,689	–	1.04	21.8

Note: (1) State rank ranges from 1 to 51 where 1 indicates highest salary.
Source: National Education Association, Rankings & Estimates: Rankings of the States 2013 and Estimates of School Statistics 2014, March 2014

Higher Education

Four-Year Colleges			Two-Year Colleges			Medical Schools[1]	Law Schools[2]	Voc/ Tech[3]
Public	Private Non-profit	Private For-profit	Public	Private Non-profit	Private For-profit			
1	3	0	1	0	1	0	0	2

Note: Figures cover institutions located within the city limits and include main campuses only; (1) includes schools accredited by the Liaison Committee on Medical Education and the American Osteopathic Association's Commission on Osteopathic College Accreditation; (2) includes ABA-accredited schools, schools with provisional ABA accreditation, and state accredited schools; (3) includes all schools with programs that are less than 2 years.
Source: National Center for Education Statistics, Integrated Postsecondary Education System (IPEDS), 2012-13; Association of American Medical Colleges, Member List, April 24, 2014; American Osteopathic Association, Member List, April 24, 2014; Law School Admission Council, Official Guide to ABA-Approved Law Schools Online, April 24, 2014; Wikipedia, List of Medical Schools in the United States, April 24, 2014; Wikipedia, List of Law Schools in the United States, April 24, 2014

PRESIDENTIAL ELECTION

2012 Presidential Election Results

Area	Obama	Romney	Other
Cumberland County	59.4	39.7	0.9
U.S.	51.0	47.2	1.8

Note: Results are percentages and may not add to 100% due to rounding
Source: Dave Leip's Atlas of U.S. Presidential Elections

EMPLOYERS

Major Employers

Company Name	Industry
Army & Air Force Exchange Service	Public administration
AT&T Services	Information
Cape Fear Valley Health Systems	Education & health services
City of Fayetteville	Public administration
County of Cumberland	Public administration
Cumberland County Board of Education	Education & health services
Department of Defense	Public administration
E.I. DuPont De Nemours & Co.	Professional & business services
Eaton Corporation	Manufacturing
Fayetteville State University (18321)	Education & health services
Fayetteville Technical Community College	Education & health services
Food Lion	Trade, transportation & utilities
Goodyear Tire & Rubber	Manufacturing
ITT Systems Corporation	Other services
Linc Government Services	Construction
Lowes Home Centers	Trade, transportation & utilities
Methodist University (Branch)	Education & health services
National Security Solutions	Professional & business services
Non-Appropriated Fund Activity-Army	Leisure & hospitality
Public Works Commission	Public administration
Purolator Filters	Manufacturing
U.S. Postal Service	Trade, transportation & utilities
Veterans Administration	Public administration
Wal-Mart Associates	Trade, transportation & utilities
Worldwide Language Resources	Professional & business services

Note: Companies shown are located within the Fayetteville, NC Metropolitan Statistical Area.
Source: Hoovers.com; Wikipedia

PUBLIC SAFETY

Crime Rate

Area	All Crimes	Violent Crimes				Property Crimes		
		Murder	Forcible Rape	Robbery	Aggrav. Assault	Burglary	Larceny -Theft	Motor Vehicle Theft
City	6,966.7	10.7	34.0	271.9	259.3	1,995.0	4,028.8	367.1
Suburbs[1]	4,535.2	4.7	14.5	112.3	279.8	1,626.5	2,345.6	151.8
Metro[2]	5,860.6	7.9	25.1	199.3	268.6	1,827.4	3,263.1	269.1
U.S.	3,246.1	4.7	26.9	112.9	242.3	670.2	1,959.3	229.7

Note: Figures are crimes per 100,000 population; (1) All areas within the metro area that are located outside the city limits; (2) Figures cover the Fayetteville, NC Metropolitan Statistical Area—see Appendix B for areas included
Source: FBI Uniform Crime Reports, 2012

Hate Crimes

Area	Number of Quarters Reported	Bias Motivation				
		Race	Religion	Sexual Orientation	Ethnicity	Disability
City	4	4	3	1	0	0
U.S.	4	2,797	1,099	1,135	667	92

Source: Federal Bureau of Investigation, Hate Crime Statistics 2012

Identity Theft Consumer Complaints

Area	Complaints	Complaints per 100,000 Population	Rank[2]
MSA[1]	377	102.9	44
U.S.	290,056	91.8	-

Note: (1) Figures cover the Fayetteville, NC Metropolitan Statistical Area—see Appendix B for areas included; (2) Rank ranges from 1 to 377 where 1 indicates greatest number of identity theft complaints per 100,000 population
Source: Federal Trade Commission, Consumer Sentinel Network Data Book for January–December 2013

Fraud and Other Consumer Complaints

Area	Complaints	Complaints per 100,000 Population	Rank[2]
MSA[1]	1,754	478.7	30
U.S.	1,811,724	595.2	-

Note: (1) Figures cover the Fayetteville, NC Metropolitan Statistical Area—see Appendix B for areas included; (2) Rank ranges from 1 to 377 where 1 indicates greatest number of identity theft complaints per 100,000 population
Source: Federal Trade Commission, Consumer Sentinel Network Data Book for January–December 2013

RECREATION

Culture

Dance[1]	Theatre[1]	Instrumental Music[1]	Vocal Music[1]	Series and Festivals	Museums and Art Galleries[2]	Zoos and Aquariums[3]
0	2	2	0	1	7	0

Note: (1) Number of professional perfoming groups; (2) Based on organizations with primary SIC code 8412; (3) AZA-accredited
Source: The Grey House Performing Arts Directory, 2013; Association of Zoos & Aquariums, AZA Member Zoos & Aquariums, April 2014; www.AccuLeads.com, May 1, 2014

Professional Sports Teams

Team Name	League	Year Established
No teams are located in the metro area		

Source: Wikipedia, Major Professional Sports Teams of the United States and Canada, April 25, 2014

CLIMATE

Average and Extreme Temperatures

Temperature	Jan	Feb	Mar	Apr	May	Jun	Jul	Aug	Sep	Oct	Nov	Dec	Yr.
Extreme High (°F)	79	84	90	95	97	104	105	105	104	98	88	79	105
Average High (°F)	50	53	61	72	79	86	89	87	81	72	62	53	71
Average Temp. (°F)	40	43	50	59	67	75	78	77	71	60	51	42	60
Average Low (°F)	29	31	38	46	55	63	68	67	60	48	39	32	48
Extreme Low (°F)	-9	5	11	23	29	38	48	46	37	19	11	4	-9

Note: Figures cover the years 1948-1990
Source: National Climatic Data Center, International Station Meteorological Climate Summary, 9/96

Average Precipitation/Snowfall/Humidity

Precip./Humidity	Jan	Feb	Mar	Apr	May	Jun	Jul	Aug	Sep	Oct	Nov	Dec	Yr.
Avg. Precip. (in.)	3.4	3.6	3.6	2.9	3.9	3.6	4.4	4.4	3.2	2.9	3.0	3.1	42.0
Avg. Snowfall (in.)	2	3	1	Tr	0	0	0	0	0	0	Tr	1	8
Avg. Rel. Hum. 7am (%)	79	79	79	80	84	86	88	91	91	90	84	81	84
Avg. Rel. Hum. 4pm (%)	53	49	46	43	51	54	57	59	57	53	51	53	52

Note: Figures cover the years 1948-1990; Tr = Trace amounts (<0.05 in. of rain; <0.5 in. of snow)
Source: National Climatic Data Center, International Station Meteorological Climate Summary, 9/96

Weather Conditions

Temperature			Daytime Sky			Precipitation		
32°F & below	45°F & below	90°F & above	Clear	Partly cloudy	Cloudy	0.01 inch or more precip.	0.1 inch or more snow/ice	Thunder-storms
77	160	39	98	143	124	110	3	42

Note: Figures are average number of days per year and cover the years 1948-1990
Source: National Climatic Data Center, International Station Meteorological Climate Summary, 9/96

HAZARDOUS WASTE

Superfund Sites

Fayetteville has two hazardous waste sites on the EPA's Superfund Final National Priorities List: **Cape Fear Wood Preserving; Carolina Transformer Co.** *U.S. Environmental Protection Agency, Final National Priorities List, April 26, 2014*

AIR & WATER QUALITY

Air Quality Index

Area	Percent of Days when Air Quality was...[2]					AQI Statistics[2]	
	Good	Moderate	Unhealthy for Sensitive Groups	Unhealthy	Very Unhealthy	Maximum	Median
MSA[1]	84.8	15.2	0.0	0.0	0.0	90	37

Note: (1) Data covers the Fayetteville, NC Metropolitan Statistical Area—see Appendix B for areas included; (2) Based on 336 days with AQI data in 2013. Air Quality Index (AQI) is an index for reporting daily air quality. EPA calculates the AQI for five major air pollutants regulated by the Clean Air Act: ground-level ozone, particle pollution (aka particulate matter), carbon monoxide, sulfur dioxide, and nitrogen dioxide. The AQI runs from 0 to 500. The higher the AQI value, the greater the level of air pollution and the greater the health concern. There are six AQI categories: "Good" AQI is between 0 and 50. Air quality is considered satisfactory; "Moderate" AQI is between 51 and 100. Air quality is acceptable; "Unhealthy for Sensitive Groups" When AQI values are between 101 and 150, members of sensitive groups may experience health effects; "Unhealthy" When AQI values are between 151 and 200 everyone may begin to experience health effects; "Very Unhealthy" AQI values between 201 and 300 trigger a health alert; "Hazardous" AQI values over 300 trigger warnings of emergency conditions (not shown).
Source: U.S. Environmental Protection Agency, Air Quality Index Report, 2013

Air Quality Index Pollutants

Area	Percent of Days when AQI Pollutant was...[2]					
	Carbon Monoxide	Nitrogen Dioxide	Ozone	Sulfur Dioxide	Particulate Matter 2.5	Particulate Matter 10
MSA[1]	0.0	0.0	36.0	0.0	64.0	0.0

Note: (1) Data covers the Fayetteville, NC Metropolitan Statistical Area—see Appendix B for areas included; (2) Based on 336 days with AQI data in 2013. The Air Quality Index (AQI) is an index for reporting daily air quality. EPA calculates the AQI for five major air pollutants regulated by the Clean Air Act: ground-level ozone, particle pollution (also known as particulate matter), carbon monoxide, sulfur dioxide, and nitrogen dioxide. The AQI runs from 0 to 500. The higher the AQI value, the greater the level of air pollution and the greater the health concern.

Source: U.S. Environmental Protection Agency, Air Quality Index Report, 2013

Air Quality Trends: Ozone

	2003	2004	2005	2006	2007	2008	2009	2010	2011	2012
MSA[1]	0.084	0.075	0.088	0.073	0.081	0.075	0.066	0.072	0.075	0.069

Note: (1) Data covers the Fayetteville, NC Metropolitan Statistical Area—see Appendix B for areas included. The values shown are the composite ozone concentration averages among trend sites based on the highest fourth daily maximum 8-hour concentration in parts per million. These trends are based on sites having an adequate record of monitoring data during the trend period. Data from exceptional events are included.

Source: U.S. Environmental Protection Agency, Air Quality Monitoring Information, "Air Quality Trends by City, 2000-2012"

Maximum Air Pollutant Concentrations: Particulate Matter, Ozone, CO and Lead

	Particulate Matter 10 (ug/m^3)	Particulate Matter 2.5 Wtd AM (ug/m^3)	Particulate Matter 2.5 24-Hr (ug/m^3)	Ozone (ppm)	Carbon Monoxide (ppm)	Lead (ug/m^3)
MSA[1] Level	26	8.9	18	0.069	n/a	n/a
NAAQS[2]	150	15	35	0.075	9	0.15
Met NAAQS[2]	Yes	Yes	Yes	Yes	n/a	n/a

Note: (1) Data covers the Fayetteville, NC Metropolitan Statistical Area—see Appendix B for areas included; Data from exceptional events are included; (2) National Ambient Air Quality Standards; ppm = parts per million; ug/m^3 = micrograms per cubic meter; n/a not available.

Concentrations: Particulate Matter 10 (coarse particulate)—highest second maximum 24-hour concentration; Particulate Matter 2.5 Wtd AM (fine particulate)—highest weighted annual mean concentration; Particulate Matter 2.5 24-Hour (fine particulate)—highest 98th percentile 24-hour concentration; Ozone—highest fourth daily maximum 8-hour concentration; Carbon Monoxide—highest second maximum non-overlapping 8-hour concentration; Lead—maximum running 3-month average

Source: U.S. Environmental Protection Agency, Air Quality Monitoring Information, "Air Quality Statistics by City, 2012"

Maximum Air Pollutant Concentrations: Nitrogen Dioxide and Sulfur Dioxide

	Nitrogen Dioxide AM (ppb)	Nitrogen Dioxide 1-Hr (ppb)	Sulfur Dioxide AM (ppb)	Sulfur Dioxide 1-Hr (ppb)	Sulfur Dioxide 24-Hr (ppb)
MSA[1] Level	n/a	n/a	n/a	4	n/a
NAAQS[2]	53	100	30	75	140
Met NAAQS[2]	n/a	n/a	n/a	Yes	n/a

Note: (1) Data covers the Fayetteville, NC Metropolitan Statistical Area—see Appendix B for areas included; Data from exceptional events are included; (2) National Ambient Air Quality Standards; ppm = parts per million; ug/m^3 = micrograms per cubic meter; n/a not available.

Concentrations: Nitrogen Dioxide AM—highest arithmetic mean concentration; Nitrogen Dioxide 1-Hr—highest 98th percentile 1-hour daily maximum concentration; Sulfur Dioxide AM—highest annual mean concentration; Sulfur Dioxide 1-Hr—highest 99th percentile 1-hour daily maximum concentration; Sulfur Dioxide 24-Hr—highest second maximum 24-hour concentration

Source: U.S. Environmental Protection Agency, Air Quality Monitoring Information, "Air Quality Statistics by City, 2012"

Drinking Water

Water System Name	Pop. Served	Primary Water Source Type	Violations[1]	
			Health Based	Monitoring/ Reporting
Fayetteville Public Works Comm.	198,000	Surface	0	0

Note: (1) Based on violation data from January 1, 2013 to December 31, 2013 (includes unresolved violations from earlier years)
Source: U.S. Environmental Protection Agency, Office of Ground Water and Drinking Water, Safe Drinking Water Information System (based on data extracted February 10, 2014)

Greensboro, North Carolina

Background

Greensboro is a quiet community in northern North Carolina. It, along with Winston-Salem and High Point, form an urban triangle. The city was the site of the Battle of Guilford Courthouse on March 15, 1781, during the American Revolution, as well as the birthplace of such notable Americans as Dolly Madison, wife of James Madison, the fourth president of the United States; and William Sydney Porter, otherwise known as author O. Henry.

During the mid- to late nineteenth century, the economy of the city was largely based upon textile production. While that still remains a vital role in Greensboro, petroleum, pharmaceutical products, and furniture have come into prominence as well.

The birth of the American Civil Rights movement can be traced to 1960 in Greensboro when four students from the historically black North Carolina A&T State sat at the white lunch counter at Greensboro's downtown Woolworth's. Their violent removal led to sit-ins all over the south. Today, the former Woolworth Building houses the Civil Rights Center and Museum.

Greensboro is one of the anchors of the center for business opportunities in North Carolina, the Piedmont Triad. Along with Winston-Salem and High Point, it has become a major metro area for attracting new plants and facilities. FedEx opened a Mid-Atlantic air-cargo package-sorting hub in 2009. In 2007, Greensboro broke ground on the Gateway University Research Park, consisting of two 75-acre campuses focusing on nanotechnology, biotechnology, biochemistry, electronics, artificial intelligence, environmental sciences, food and nutrition, health genetics, materials science and engineering, alternate and renewable energy and social sciences. The first building on the South Campus opened in October of 2008. The Research Park's most recent building, the Joint School for Nanoscience and Nanoengineering, opened in 2011.

Greensboro has a thriving cultural scene. The Green Hill Center for North Carolina Art Gallery promotes the visual arts and includes ArtQuest, an interactive gallery. The Greensboro Ballet provides performances, educational programs, the Summer Ballet Festival, and houses student and professional studios. The Greensboro Symphony Orchestra's Masterworks and Chamber Series concerts feature guest artists from around the world.

Greensboro College, Guilford College, and University of North Carolina at Greensboro, North Carolina A&T State, and Bennett College for Women all reside in Greensboro. The Eastern Music Festival and School, part of Guilford College, offers a summer concert series. Elon University School of Law opened its doors in the heart of downtown to its first students in 2006.

In the past 30 years, Greensboro has grown into an internationally diverse community. Today, the city is home to large populations of Vietnamese, West African and Latino immigrants. Such diverse communities have contributed to the local cuisine and flavor, and authentic international specialty stores and restaurants are not hard to come by.

Downtown development, such as the NewBridge Bank Park minor league baseball stadium, and a variety of residential options, have helped transform the city center. The revitalized Southside neighborhood is touted as one of the best planned re-developments in the U.S. The city is famous to college sports fans as the home to the Atlantic Coast Conference. The annual ACC basketball tournament in March often airs from the Greensboro Coliseum Complex.

For general recreation, the Greensboro Parks & Recreation Department has acquired over 3,200 acres of land, with more than 170 parks and special facilities recognized internationally for their culturally diverse athletic, historical, and arts programs. The Bog Garden features more than 8,000 individually labeled trees, shrubs, ferns, bamboo, and wildflowers. Wet 'n' Wild Emerald Pointe Water Park offers one of only four tsunami (giant wave) pools in the U.S. Greensboro Historical Museum, located downtown in a building dating back to 1900, is listed on the National Register of Historic Places. The Battle of Guilford Courthouse National Military Park, with 220 acres of historic fields and forests, monuments, and graves, was the first national park established at a Revolutionary War site.

Greensboro is the largest city in the Piedmont Triad region. Both winter temperatures and rainfall are modified by the Blue Ridge Mountain barrier on the northwest. The summer temperatures vary with cloudiness and shower activity, but are generally mild. Northwesterly winds rarely bring heavy or prolonged winter rain or snow. Damaging storms are infrequent, as are tornadoes.

Rankings

Business/Finance Rankings

- CareerBliss, an employment and careers website, analyzed U.S. Bureau of Labor Statistics data, more than 14,000 company reviews from employees and former employees, and job openings over a six-month period to arrive at its list of the 20 worst places in the United States to look for a job. Greensboro was ranked #4. *CareerBliss.com, "20 Worst Cities to Find a Job for 2012," October 11, 2012*

- Greensboro was ranked #78 out of 100 metro areas in terms of economic performance (#1 = best) during the recession and recovery from trough quarter through the second quarter of 2013. Criteria: percent change in employment; percentage point change in unemployment rate; percent change in gross metropolitan product; percent change in House Price Index. *Brookings Institution, MetroMonitor: Tracking Economic Recession and Recovery in America's 100 Largest Metropolitan Areas, September 2013*

- Greensboro was cited as one of America's top metros for new and expanded facility projects in 2013. The area ranked #4 in the mid-sized metro area category (population 200,000 to 1 million). *Site Selection, "Top Metros of 2013," March 2014*

- The Greensboro metro area appeared on the Milken Institute "2013 Best Performing Cities" list. Rank: #135 out of 200 large metro areas. Criteria: job growth; wage and salary growth; high-tech output growth. *Milken Institute, "Best-Performing Cities 2013," December 2013*

- *Forbes* ranked the 200 most populous metro areas in the U.S. in terms of the "Best Places for Business and Careers." The Greensboro metro area was ranked #71. Criteria: costs (business and living); job growth (past and projected); income growth; educational attainment (college and high school); projected economic growth; cultural and recreational opportunities; net migration patterns; number of highly ranked colleges. *Forbes, "The Best Places for Business and Careers," August 7, 2013*

Children/Family Rankings

- Greensboro was identified as one of the best cities for raising a family by *24/7 Wall St.* The city ranked #10. The nation's 100 largest cities were evaluated on the following criteria: large public outdoor spaces; top hospitals; strong schools; low unemployment; high educational attainment; low violent crime rates. *24/7 Wall St., "The 10 Best U.S. Cities for Raising a Family," January 13, 2012*

- Greensboro was selected as one of the best cities for families to live by *Parenting* magazine. The city ranked #66 out of 100. Criteria: education; health; community; *Parenting's* Culture & Charm Index. *Parenting.com, "The 2012 Best Cities for Families List"*

Dating/Romance Rankings

- A *Cosmopolitan* magazine article surveyed the gender balance and other factors to arrive at a list of the best and worst cities for women to meet single guys. Greensboro placed #7 among the worst for single women looking for dates. *www.cosmopolitan.com, "Working the Ratio," October 1, 2013*

- Of the 100 U.S. cities surveyed by *Men's Health* in its quest to identify the nation's best cities for dating and forming relationships, Greensboro was ranked #56 for online dating (#1 = best). *Men's Health, "The Best and Worst Cities for Online Dating," January 30, 2013*

- Greensboro was selected as one of the most romantic cities in the U.S. by video-rental kiosk company Redbox. The city ranked #5 out of 10. Criteria: number of romance-related rentals in 2012. *Redbox, "10 Most/Least Romantic Cities," February 12, 2013*

Education Rankings

- *Men's Health* ranked 100 U.S. cities in terms of their education levels. Greensboro was ranked #23 (#1 = most educated city). Criteria: high school graduation rates; school enrollment; educational attainment; number of households who have outstanding student loans; number of households whose members have taken adult-education courses. *Men's Health, "Where School Is In: The Most and Least Educated Cities," September 12, 2011*

- Greensboro was selected as one of America's most literate cities. The city ranked #50 out of the 77 largest U.S. cities. Criteria: number of booksellers; library resources; Internet resources; educational attainment; periodical publishing resources; newspaper circulation. *Central Connecticut State University, "America's Most Literate Cities, 2013"*

Environmental Rankings

- The Greensboro metro area came in at #239 for the relative comfort of its climate on Sperling's list of "chill cities," as measured by the Sperling Heat Index. All 361 metro areas are included. Criteria included daytime high temperatures, nighttime low temperatures, dew point, and relative humidity at the high temperatures. *www.bertsperling.com, "Sperling's Chill Cities," July 18, 2013*

- Sperling's BestPlaces assessed 379 metropolitan areas of the United States for the likelihood of dangerously extreme weather events or earthquakes. In general the Southeast and South-Central regions have the highest risk of weather extremes and earthquakes, while the Pacific Northwest enjoys the lowest risk. Of the least risky metropolitan areas, the Greensboro metro area was ranked #217. *www.bestplaces.net, "Safest Places from Natural Disasters," April 2011*

- Greensboro was selected as one of 22 "Smarter Cities" for energy by the Natural Resources Defense Council. Criteria: investment in green power; energy efficiency measures; conservation. *Natural Resources Defense Council, "2010 Smarter Cities," July 19, 2010*

Food/Drink Rankings

- *Men's Health* ranked 100 major U.S. cities in terms of alcohol intoxication. Greensboro ranked #57 (#1 = most sober).Criteria: binge drinking; alcohol-related traffic accidents, arrests, and fatalities. *Men's Health, "The Drunkest Cities in America," November 19, 2013*

Health/Fitness Rankings

- Greensboro was identified as a "2013 Spring Allergy Capital." The area ranked #42 out of 100. Three groups of factors were used to identify the most severe cities for people with allergies during the spring season: annual pollen levels; medicine utilization; access to board-certified allergists. *Asthma and Allergy Foundation of America, "Spring Allergy Capitals 2013"*

- Greensboro was identified as a "2013 Fall Allergy Capital." The area ranked #49 out of 100. Three groups of factors were used to identify the most severe cities for people with allergies during the fall season: annual pollen levels; medicine utilization; access to board-certified allergists. *Asthma and Allergy Foundation of America, "Fall Allergy Capitals 2013"*

- Greensboro was identified as a "2013 Asthma Capital." The area ranked #50 out of the nation's 100 largest metropolitan areas. Twelve factors were used to identify the most challenging places to live for people with asthma: estimated prevalence; self-reported prevalence; crude death rate for asthma; annual pollen score; annual air quality; public smoking laws; number of board-certified asthma specialists; school inhaler access laws; rescue medication use; controller medication use; uninsured rate; poverty rate. *Asthma and Allergy Foundation of America, "Asthma Capitals 2013"*

- *Men's Health* ranked 100 major U.S. cities in terms of the best and worst cities for men. Greensboro ranked #46. Criteria: thirty-three data points were examined covering health, fitness, and quality of life. *Men's Health, "The Best & Worst Cities for Men 2014," December 6, 2013*

- The Greensboro metro area appeared in the 2013 Gallup-Healthways Well-Being Index. The area ranked #118 out of 189. The Gallup-Healthways Well-Being Index score is an average of six sub-indexes, which individually examine life evaluation, emotional health, work environment, physical health, healthy behaviors, and access to basic necessities. Results are based on telephone interviews conducted as part of the Gallup-Healthways Well-Being Index survey January 2–December 29, 2012, and January 2–December 30, 2013, with a random sample of 531,630 adults, aged 18 and older, living in metropolitan areas in the 50 U.S. states and the District of Columbia. *Gallup-Healthways, "State of American Well-Being," March 25, 2014*

- *Men's Health* ranked 100 U.S. cities in terms of their activity levels. Greensboro was ranked #80 (#1 = most active city). Criteria: where and how often residents exercise; percentage of households that watch more than 15 hours of cable television a week and buy more than 11 video games a year; death rate from deep-vein thrombosis, a condition linked to sitting for extended periods of time. *Men's Health, "Where Sit Happens: The Most and Least Active Cities in America," June 20, 2011*

- *The Daily Beast* identified the 30 U.S. metro areas with the worst smoking habits. The Greensboro metro area ranked #23. Sixty urban centers with populations of more than one million were ranked based on the following criteria: number of smokers; number of cigarettes smoked per day; fewest attempts to quit. *The Daily Beast, "30 Cities With Smoking Problems," January 3, 2011*

Real Estate Rankings

- Greensboro was ranked #244 out of 283 metro areas in terms of house price appreciation in 2013 (#1 = highest rate). *Federal Housing Finance Agency, House Price Index, 4th Quarter 2013*

- The Greensboro metro area was identified as one of the 10 worst condo markets in the U.S. in 2013. The area ranked #5 out of 64 markets with a price appreciation of -3.3%. Criteria: year-over-year change of median sales price of existing apartment condo-coop homes between the 4th quarter of 2012 and the 4th quarter of 2013. *National Association of Realtors®, Median Sales Price of Existing Apartment Condo-Coop Homes for Metropolitan Areas, 4th Quarter 2013*

- Greensboro was ranked #83 out of 224 metro areas in terms of housing affordability in 2013 by the National Association of Home Builders (#1 = most affordable). The NAHB-Wells Fargo Housing Opportunity Index (HOI) for a given area is defined as the share of homes sold in that area that would have been affordable to a family earning the local median income, based on standard mortgage underwriting criteria. *National Association of Home Builders®, NAHB-Wells Fargo Housing Opportunity Index, 4th Quarter 2013*

Safety Rankings

- Allstate ranked the 200 largest cities in America in terms of driver safety. Greensboro ranked #68. Allstate researchers analyzed internal property damage claims over a two-year period from January 2010 to December 2011. A weighted average of the two-year numbers determined the annual percentages. *Allstate, "Allstate America's Best Drivers Report®, August 27, 2013"*

- The National Insurance Crime Bureau ranked 380 metro areas in the U.S. in terms of per capita rates of vehicle theft. The Greensboro metro area ranked #136 (#1 = highest rate). Criteria: number of vehicle theft offenses per 100,000 inhabitants in 2012. *National Insurance Crime Bureau, "Hot Spots 2012," June 26, 2013*

Seniors/Retirement Rankings

- From its Best Cities for Successful Aging indexes, the Milken Institute generated rankings for metropolitan areas, weighing data in eight categories—general indicators, health care, wellness, living arrangements, transportation and general accessibility, financial well-being, education and employment, and community participation. The Greensboro metro area was ranked #84 overall in the large metro area category. *Milken Institute, "Best Cities for Successful Aging," July 2012*

Sports/Recreation Rankings

- Greensboro appeared on the *Sporting News* list of the "Best Sports Cities" for 2011. The area ranked #227 out of 271. Criteria: the magazine takes a 12-month snapshot of each city's sports, putting a heavy premium on regular-season won-lost records (from the most recently completed season). Other criteria include: playoff berths, bowl appearances and tournament bids; championships; applicable power ratings; quality of competition; overall fan fervor (measured in part by attendance); abundance of teams (rewarding quality over quantity); stadium and arena quality; ticket availability and prices; franchise ownership; and marquee appeal of athletes. *Sporting News, "Best Sports Cities 2011," October 4, 2011*

- Greensboro appeared on the *Sporting News* list of the "Best Sports Cities" for 2011. The area ranked #227 out of 271. Criteria: a 12-month snapshot of regular-season won-lost records (from the most recently completed season). Other criteria include: playoff berths, bowl appearances and tournament bids; championships; applicable power ratings; quality of competition; overall fan fervor (measured in part by attendance); abundance of teams (quality over quantity); stadium and arena quality; ticket availability and prices; franchise ownership; and marquee appeal of athletes. *Sporting News, "Best Sports Cities 2011," October 4, 2011*

- Greensboro was chosen as a bicycle friendly community by the League of American Bicyclists. A "Bicycle Friendly Community" welcomes cyclists by providing safe accommodation for cycling and encouraging people to bike for transportation and recreation. There are four award levels: Platinum; Gold; Silver; and Bronze. The community achieved an award level of Bronze. *League of American Bicyclists, "Bicycle Friendly Community Master List," Fall 2013*

Transportation Rankings

- NerdWallet surveyed average annual car insurance premiums in 125 U.S. cities to identify the least expensive U.S. cities in which to insure a car. Locations without no-fault insurance laws was a strong determinant. Greensboro came in at #2 for the least expensive rates. *www.nerdwallet.com, "Best Cities for Cheap Car Insurance," February 3, 2014*

Women/Minorities Rankings

- *Women's Health* examined U.S. cities and identified the 100 best cities for women. Greensboro was ranked #54. Criteria: 30 categories were examined from obesity and breast cancer rates to commuting times and hours spent working out. *Women's Health, "Best Cities for Women 2012"*

Miscellaneous Rankings

- *Men's Health* ranked 100 U.S. cities by their level of sadness. Greensboro was ranked #79 (#1 = saddest city). Criteria: suicide rates; unemployment rates; percentage of households that use antidepressants; percent of population who report feeling blue all or most of the time. *Men's Health, "Frown Towns," November 28, 2011*

- The National Alliance to End Homelessness ranked the 100 most populous metro areas in terms the rate of homelessness. The Greensboro metro area ranked #55. Criteria: number of homeless people per 10,000 population in 2011. *National Alliance to End Homelessness, The State of Homelessness in America 2012*

- Scarborough Research, a leading market research firm, identified the top local markets for givers in the U.S. The Greensboro DMA (Designated Market Area) ranked in the top 10 with 61.0% of adults contributing money to an arts/cultural, healthcare/medical, religious or social care/welfare organization in the past 12 months. *Scarborough Research, December 13, 2011*

Business Environment

CITY FINANCES

City Government Finances

Component	2011 ($000)	2011 ($ per capita)
Total Revenues	477,078	1,930
Total Expenditures	490,903	1,986
Debt Outstanding	476,956	1,930
Cash and Securities[1]	295,004	1,193

Note: (1) Cash and security holdings of a government at the close of its fiscal year, including those of its dependent agencies, utilities, and liquor stores.
Source: U.S Census Bureau, State & Local Government Finances 2011

City Government Revenue by Source

Source	2011 ($000)	2011 ($ per capita)
General Revenue		
From Federal Government	16,535	67
From State Government	35,742	145
From Local Governments	4,197	17
Taxes		
Property	144,633	585
Sales and Gross Receipts	42,415	172
Personal Income	0	0
Corporate Income	0	0
Motor Vehicle License	628	3
Other Taxes	5,883	24
Current Charges	110,412	447
Liquor Store	25,975	105
Utility	51,035	206
Employee Retirement	0	0

Source: U.S Census Bureau, State & Local Government Finances 2011

City Government Expenditures by Function

Function	2011 ($000)	2011 ($ per capita)	2011 (%)
General Direct Expenditures			
Air Transportation	0	0	0.0
Corrections	0	0	0.0
Education	0	0	0.0
Employment Security Administration	0	0	0.0
Financial Administration	3,783	15	0.8
Fire Protection	43,645	177	8.9
General Public Buildings	3,996	16	0.8
Governmental Administration, Other	10,072	41	2.1
Health	156	1	0.0
Highways	25,488	103	5.2
Hospitals	0	0	0.0
Housing and Community Development	11,354	46	2.3
Interest on General Debt	12,211	49	2.5
Judicial and Legal	1,030	4	0.2
Libraries	9,389	38	1.9
Parking	1,036	4	0.2
Parks and Recreation	66,042	267	13.5
Police Protection	75,189	304	15.3
Public Welfare	0	0	0.0
Sewerage	54,011	219	11.0
Solid Waste Management	34,855	141	7.1
Veterans' Services	0	0	0.0
Liquor Store	22,414	91	4.6
Utility	74,176	300	15.1
Employee Retirement	0	0	0.0

Source: U.S Census Bureau, State & Local Government Finances 2011

DEMOGRAPHICS

Population Growth

Area	1990 Census	2000 Census	2010 Census	Population Growth (%)	
				1990-2000	2000-2010
City	193,389	223,891	269,666	15.8	20.4
MSA[1]	540,257	643,430	723,801	19.1	12.5
U.S.	248,709,873	281,421,906	308,745,538	13.2	9.7

Note: (1) Figures cover the Greensboro-High Point, NC Metropolitan Statistical Area—see Appendix B for areas included
Source: U.S. Census Bureau, Census 1990, 2000, 2010

Household Size

Area	Persons in Household (%)							Average Household Size
	One	Two	Three	Four	Five	Six	Seven or More	
City	34.7	32.7	14.8	10.6	4.5	1.8	0.9	2.35
MSA[1]	29.2	34.4	16.6	12.1	4.8	1.9	1.0	2.47
U.S.	27.6	33.5	15.7	13.2	6.1	2.4	1.5	2.63

Note: (1) Figures cover the Greensboro-High Point, NC Metropolitan Statistical Area—see Appendix B for areas included
Source: U.S. Census Bureau, 2010-2012 American Community Survey 3-Year Estimates

Race

Area	White Alone[2] (%)	Black Alone[2] (%)	Asian Alone[2] (%)	AIAN[3] Alone[2] (%)	NHOPI[4] Alone[2] (%)	Other Race Alone[2] (%)	Two or More Races (%)
City	49.8	40.5	4.2	0.4	0.1	2.6	2.5
MSA[1]	66.0	25.6	3.1	0.4	0.0	2.6	2.2
U.S.	74.0	12.6	4.9	0.8	0.2	4.7	2.8

Note: (1) Figures cover the Greensboro-High Point, NC Metropolitan Statistical Area—see Appendix B for areas included; (2) Alone is defined as not being in combination with one or more other races; (3) American Indian and Alaska Native; (4) Native Hawaiian and Other Pacific Islander
Source: U.S. Census Bureau, 2010-2012 American Community Survey 3-Year Estimates

Hispanic or Latino Origin

Area	Total (%)	Mexican (%)	Puerto Rican (%)	Cuban (%)	Other (%)
City	7.4	4.6	0.6	0.2	2.1
MSA[1]	7.7	5.4	0.7	0.2	1.4
U.S.	16.6	10.7	1.6	0.6	3.7

Note: Persons of Hispanic or Latino origin can be of any race; (1) Figures cover the Greensboro-High Point, NC Metropolitan Statistical Area—see Appendix B for areas included
Source: U.S. Census Bureau, 2010-2012 American Community Survey 3-Year Estimates

Segregation

Type	Segregation Indices[1]				Percent Change		
	1990	2000	2010	2010 Rank[2]	1990-2000	1990-2010	2000-2010
Black/White	54.3	53.8	54.7	53	-0.5	0.4	0.9
Asian/White	43.3	48.3	47.7	14	5.0	4.4	-0.6
Hispanic/White	24.3	44.4	41.1	61	20.1	16.8	-3.3

Note: All figures cover the Metropolitan Statistical Area—see Appendix B for areas included; Figures are based on an analysis of 1990, 2000, and 2010 Census Decennial Census tract data by William H. Frey, Brookings Institution and the University of Michigan Social Science Data Analysis Network. In this analysis all racial groups (whites, blacks, and asians) are non-Hispanic members of those races. Hispanics are shown as a separate category;
(1) Segregation Indices are Dissimilarity Indices that measure the degree to which the minority group is distributed differently than whites across census tracts. They range from 0 (complete integration) to 100 (complete segregation) where the value indicates the percentage of the minority group that needs to move to be distributed exactly like whites; (2) Ranges from 1 (most segregated) to 102 (least segregated); n/a not available.
Source: www.CensusScope.org

Ancestry

Area	German	Irish	English	American	Italian	Polish	French[2]	Scottish	Dutch
City	7.7	6.1	8.1	5.2	2.4	1.0	1.2	2.2	0.7
MSA[1]	8.9	7.0	9.5	10.0	2.4	0.9	1.3	2.2	0.8
U.S.	15.2	11.1	8.2	7.2	5.6	3.1	2.8	1.7	1.4

Note: Figures are the percentage of the total population reporting a particular ancestry. The nine most commonly reported ancestries in the U.S. are shown. Figures include multiple ancestries (e.g. if a person reported being Irish and Italian, they were included in both columns); (1) Figures cover the Greensboro-High Point, NC Metropolitan Statistical Area—see Appendix B for areas included; (2) Excludes Basque
Source: U.S. Census Bureau, 2010-2012 American Community Survey 3-Year Estimates

Foreign-Born Population

Area	Percent of Population Born in								
	Any Foreign Country	Mexico	Asia	Europe	Carribean	South America	Central America[2]	Africa	Canada
City	11.1	2.6	3.6	1.0	0.3	0.6	0.8	1.9	0.2
MSA[1]	8.4	3.0	2.4	0.7	0.2	0.4	0.6	0.9	0.1
U.S.	13.0	3.7	3.7	1.6	1.2	0.9	1.0	0.5	0.3

Note: (1) Figures cover the Greensboro-High Point, NC Metropolitan Statistical Area—see Appendix B for areas included; (2) Excludes Mexico.
Source: U.S. Census Bureau, 2010-2012 American Community Survey 3-Year Estimates

Marital Status

Area	Never Married	Now Married[2]	Separated	Widowed	Divorced
City	41.2	39.4	2.9	5.7	10.7
MSA[1]	32.2	47.5	3.3	6.3	10.7
U.S.	32.4	48.4	2.2	6.0	11.0

Note: Figures are percentages and cover the population 15 years of age and older; (1) Figures cover the Greensboro-High Point, NC Metropolitan Statistical Area—see Appendix B for areas included; (2) Excludes separated
Source: U.S. Census Bureau, 2010-2012 American Community Survey 3-Year Estimates

Age

Area	Percent of Population									Median Age
	Under Age 5	Age 5–19	Age 20–34	Age 35–44	Age 45–54	Age 55–64	Age 65–74	Age 75–84	Age 85+	
City	6.5	19.8	24.9	13.0	12.7	11.2	6.0	4.3	1.6	34.0
MSA[1]	6.1	20.2	19.8	13.6	14.4	12.4	7.5	4.5	1.5	38.1
U.S.	6.4	20.1	20.5	13.1	14.3	12.2	7.3	4.2	1.8	37.3

Note: (1) Figures cover the Greensboro-High Point, NC Metropolitan Statistical Area—see Appendix B for areas included
Source: U.S. Census Bureau, 2010-2012 American Community Survey 3-Year Estimates

Gender

Area	Males	Females	Males per 100 Females
City	129,218	144,423	89.5
MSA[1]	351,105	379,472	92.5
U.S.	153,276,055	158,333,314	96.8

Note: (1) Figures cover the Greensboro-High Point, NC Metropolitan Statistical Area—see Appendix B for areas included
Source: U.S. Census Bureau, 2010-2012 American Community Survey 3-Year Estimates

Religious Groups by Family

Area	Catholic	Baptist	Non-Den.	Methodist[2]	Lutheran	LDS[3]	Pentecostal	Presbyterian[4]	Muslim[5]	Judaism
MSA[1]	2.7	12.8	7.4	9.9	0.7	0.8	2.5	3.2	0.6	0.4
U.S.	19.1	9.3	4.0	4.0	2.3	2.0	1.9	1.6	0.8	0.7

Note: Figures are the number of adherents as a percentage of the total population; (1) Figures cover the Greensboro-High Point, NC Metropolitan Statistical Area—see Appendix B for areas included; (2) Methodist/Pietist; (3) Latter Day Saints; (4) Reformed; (5) Figures are estimates
Source: Association of Statisticians of American Religious Bodies, 2010 U.S. Religion Census: Religious Congregations & Membership Study

Religious Groups by Tradition

Area	Catholic	Evangelical Protestant	Mainline Protestant	Other Tradition	Black Protestant	Orthodox
MSA[1]	2.7	23.2	14.0	2.2	2.6	0.1
U.S.	19.1	16.2	7.3	4.3	1.6	0.3

Note: Figures are the number of adherents as a percentage of the total population; (1) Figures cover the Greensboro-High Point, NC Metropolitan Statistical Area—see Appendix B for areas included
Source: Association of Statisticians of American Religious Bodies, 2010 U.S. Religion Census: Religious Congregations & Membership Study

ECONOMY

Gross Metropolitan Product

Area	2011	2012	2013	2014	Rank[2]
MSA[1]	35.3	36.9	37.9	39.5	64

Note: Figures are in billions of dollars; (1) Figures cover the Greensboro-High Point, NC Metropolitan Statistical Area—see Appendix B for areas included; (2) Rank is based on 2014 data and ranges from 1 to 363
Source: The United States Conference of Mayors, U.S. Metro Economies: Outlook—Gross Metropolitan Product, with Metro Employment Projections, November 2013

Economic Growth

Area	2011 (%)	2012 (%)	2013 (%)	2014 (%)	Rank[2]
MSA[1]	1.7	2.6	1.4	2.3	119
U.S.	1.6	2.5	1.7	2.5	–

Note: Figures are real gross metropolitan product (GMP) growth rates and represent annual average percent change; (1) Figures cover the Greensboro-High Point, NC Metropolitan Statistical Area—see Appendix B for areas included; (2) Rank is based on 2013 data and ranges from 1 to 363
Source: The United States Conference of Mayors, U.S. Metro Economies: Outlook—Gross Metropolitan Product, with Metro Employment Projections, November 2013

Metropolitan Area Exports

Area	2007	2008	2009	2010	2011	2012	Rank[2]
MSA[1]	3,843.8	3,687.9	3,168.6	4,007.8	4,054.1	4,281.9	58

Note: Figures are in millions of dollars; (1) Figures cover the Greensboro-High Point, NC Metropolitan Statistical Area—see Appendix B for areas included; (2) Rank is based on 2012 data and ranges from 1 to 369
Source: U.S. Department of Commerce, International Trade Administration, Office of Trade & Industry Information, Manufacturing & Services, data extracted April 1, 2014

INCOME

Income

Area	Per Capita ($)	Median Household ($)	Average Household ($)
City	24,608	40,323	58,528
MSA[1]	23,568	42,235	58,207
U.S.	27,385	51,771	71,579

Note: (1) Figures cover the Greensboro-High Point, NC Metropolitan Statistical Area—see Appendix B for areas included
Source: U.S. Census Bureau, 2010-2012 American Community Survey 3-Year Estimates

Household Income Distribution

Area	Percent of Households Earning							
	Under $15,000	$15,000 -24,999	$25,000 -34,999	$35,000 -49,999	$50,000 -74,999	$75,000 -99,000	$100,000 -149,999	$150,000 and up
City	15.9	14.6	13.8	15.5	16.9	8.9	8.5	6.0
MSA[1]	15.2	13.1	13.5	15.1	18.2	10.5	9.2	5.4
U.S.	13.1	11.0	10.5	13.7	18.1	11.9	12.5	9.1

Note: (1) Figures cover the Greensboro-High Point, NC Metropolitan Statistical Area—see Appendix B for areas included
Source: U.S. Census Bureau, 2010-2012 American Community Survey 3-Year Estimates

Poverty Rate

Area	All Ages	Under 18 Years Old	18 to 64 Years Old	65 Years and Over
City	19.9	26.3	19.6	9.4
MSA[1]	18.0	25.6	17.0	9.7
U.S.	15.7	22.2	14.6	9.3

Note: Figures are percentage of people whose income during the past 12 months was below the poverty level; (1) Figures cover the Greensboro-High Point, NC Metropolitan Statistical Area—see Appendix B for areas included
Source: U.S. Census Bureau, 2010-2012 American Community Survey 3-Year Estimates

Personal Bankruptcy Filing Rate

Area	2008	2009	2010	2011	2012	2013
Guilford County	2.28	2.68	2.54	2.27	2.10	1.87
U.S.	3.53	4.61	4.97	4.37	3.76	3.29

Note: Numbers are per 1,000 population and include Chapter 7 and Chapter 13 filings
Source: Federal Deposit Insurance Corporation, Regional Economic Conditions, March 20, 2014

EMPLOYMENT

Labor Force and Employment

Area	Civilian Labor Force			Workers Employed		
	Dec. 2012	Dec. 2013	% Chg.	Dec. 2012	Dec. 2013	% Chg.
City	139,545	136,564	-2.1	127,146	127,851	0.6
MSA[1]	373,892	364,290	-2.6	337,407	339,279	0.6
U.S.	154,904,000	154,408,000	-0.3	143,060,000	144,423,000	1.0

Note: Data is not seasonally adjusted and covers workers 16 years of age and older; (1) Metropolitan Statistical Area—see Appendix B for areas included
Source: Bureau of Labor Statistics, Local Area Unemployment Statistics

Unemployment Rate

Area	2013											
	Jan.	Feb.	Mar.	Apr.	May	Jun.	Jul.	Aug.	Sep.	Oct.	Nov.	Dec.
City	9.8	8.6	8.3	8.0	8.8	9.4	9.2	8.3	7.4	7.6	6.7	6.4
MSA[1]	10.6	9.9	9.4	8.9	9.4	9.7	9.6	8.6	7.9	7.9	7.2	6.9
U.S.	8.5	8.1	7.6	7.1	7.3	7.8	7.7	7.3	7.0	7.0	6.6	6.5

Note: Data is not seasonally adjusted and covers workers 16 years of age and older; All figures are percentages; (1) Metropolitan Statistical Area—see Appendix B for areas included
Source: Bureau of Labor Statistics, Local Area Unemployment Statistics

Employment by Occupation

Occupation Classification	City (%)	MSA[1] (%)	U.S. (%)
Management, Business, Science, and Arts	35.5	32.9	36.0
Natural Resources, Construction, and Maintenance	6.5	8.3	9.1
Production, Transportation, and Material Moving	12.4	15.9	12.0
Sales and Office	27.0	26.0	24.7
Service	18.6	16.9	18.2

Note: Figures cover employed civilians 16 years of age and older; (1) Figures cover the Greensboro-High Point, NC Metropolitan Statistical Area—see Appendix B for areas included
Source: U.S. Census Bureau, 2010-2012 American Community Survey 3-Year Estimates

Employment by Industry

| Sector | MSA[1] | | U.S. |
	Number of Employees	Percent of Total	Percent of Total
Construction	n/a	n/a	4.2
Education and Health Services	49,300	14.0	15.5
Financial Activities	18,100	5.2	5.7
Government	45,700	13.0	16.1
Information	4,900	1.4	1.9
Leisure and Hospitality	30,800	8.8	10.2
Manufacturing	52,700	15.0	8.7
Mining and Logging	n/a	n/a	0.6
Other Services	12,600	3.6	3.9
Professional and Business Services	50,600	14.4	13.7
Retail Trade	38,500	11.0	11.4
Transportation and Utilities	16,400	4.7	3.8
Wholesale Trade	18,900	5.4	4.2

Note: Figures cover non-farm employment as of December 2013 and are not seasonally adjusted;
(1) Metropolitan Statistical Area—see Appendix B for areas included; n/a not available
Source: Bureau of Labor Statistics, Current Employment Statistics, Employment, Hours, and Earnings

Occupations with Greatest Projected Employment Growth: 2010 – 2020

Occupation[1]	2010 Employment	2020 Projected Employment	Numeric Employment Change	Percent Employment Change
Combined Food Preparation and Serving Workers, Including Fast Food	114,040	132,650	18,610	16.3
Registered Nurses	92,540	109,790	17,250	18.6
Retail Salespersons	131,650	145,910	14,270	10.8
Home Health Aides	55,560	67,570	12,010	21.6
Customer Service Representatives	74,700	84,800	10,090	13.5
Postsecondary Teachers	49,850	59,780	9,930	19.9
Landscaping and Groundskeeping Workers	33,610	43,450	9,830	29.3
Janitors and Cleaners, Except Maids and Housekeeping Cleaners	52,290	61,160	8,870	17.0
Cashiers	101,410	110,200	8,790	8.7
Elementary School Teachers, Except Special Education	37,090	45,730	8,650	23.3

Note: Projections cover North Carolina; (1) Sorted by numeric employment change
Source: www.projectionscentral.com, State Occupational Projections, 2010–2020 Long-Term Projections

Fastest Growing Occupations: 2010 – 2020

Occupation[1]	2010 Employment	2020 Projected Employment	Numeric Employment Change	Percent Employment Change
Biomedical Engineers	250	480	230	90.5
Medical Scientists, Except Epidemiologists	4,270	6,550	2,280	53.4
Biochemists and Biophysicists	460	670	210	44.9
Interpreters and Translators	3,000	4,210	1,220	40.6
Veterinary Technologists and Technicians	3,060	4,300	1,240	40.4
Market Research Analysts and Marketing Specialists	9,750	13,580	3,830	39.3
Helpers—Brickmasons, Blockmasons, Stonemasons, and Tile and Marble Setters	1,900	2,630	740	38.8
Helpers—Carpenters	1,850	2,560	710	38.4
Diagnostic Medical Sonographers	1,660	2,280	620	37.3
Audiologists	350	460	120	33.6

Note: Projections cover North Carolina; (1) Sorted by percent employment change and excludes occupations with numeric employment change less than 100
Source: www.projectionscentral.com, State Occupational Projections, 2010–2020 Long-Term Projections

Average Wages

Occupation	$/Hr.	Occupation	$/Hr.
Accountants and Auditors	32.99	Maids and Housekeeping Cleaners	9.06
Automotive Mechanics	20.17	Maintenance and Repair Workers	18.38
Bookkeepers	16.88	Marketing Managers	62.14
Carpenters	14.58	Nuclear Medicine Technologists	31.19
Cashiers	8.85	Nurses, Licensed Practical	19.67
Clerks, General Office	13.23	Nurses, Registered	28.80
Clerks, Receptionists/Information	12.77	Nursing Assistants	10.89
Clerks, Shipping/Receiving	14.49	Packers and Packagers, Hand	9.28
Computer Programmers	36.40	Physical Therapists	35.43
Computer Systems Analysts	39.01	Postal Service Mail Carriers	24.12
Computer User Support Specialists	22.68	Real Estate Brokers	22.44
Cooks, Restaurant	10.21	Retail Salespersons	12.20
Dentists	103.71	Sales Reps., Exc. Tech./Scientific	30.40
Electrical Engineers	45.86	Sales Reps., Tech./Scientific	33.29
Electricians	18.65	Secretaries, Exc. Legal/Med./Exec.	15.60
Financial Managers	59.93	Security Guards	11.06
First-Line Supervisors/Managers, Sales	20.13	Surgeons	n/a
Food Preparation Workers	9.69	Teacher Assistants	10.90
General and Operations Managers	59.17	Teachers, Elementary School	21.60
Hairdressers/Cosmetologists	12.52	Teachers, Secondary School	21.80
Internists	109.09	Telemarketers	11.11
Janitors and Cleaners	9.70	Truck Drivers, Heavy/Tractor-Trailer	18.90
Landscaping/Groundskeeping Workers	11.98	Truck Drivers, Light/Delivery Svcs.	15.37
Lawyers	56.20	Waiters and Waitresses	8.67

Note: Wage data covers the Greensboro-High Point, NC Metropolitan Statistical Area—see Appendix B for areas included. Hourly wages for elementary/secondary school teachers and teacher assistants were calculated by the editors from annual wage data assuming a 40 hour work week; n/a not available.
Source: Bureau of Labor Statistics, Metro Area Occupational Employment and Wage Estimates, May 2013

RESIDENTIAL REAL ESTATE

Building Permits

Area	Single-Family			Multi-Family			Total		
	2012	2013	Pct. Chg.	2012	2013	Pct. Chg.	2012	2013	Pct. Chg.
City	323	354	9.6	481	614	27.7	804	968	20.4
MSA[1]	1,183	1,416	19.7	704	616	-12.5	1,887	2,032	7.7
U.S.	518,695	620,802	19.7	310,963	370,020	19.0	829,658	990,822	19.4

Note: (1) Metropolitan Statistical Area—see Appendix B for areas included; figures represent new, privately-owned housing units authorized (unadjusted data); All permit data are based on estimates with imputation.
Source: U.S. Census Bureau, Manufacturing, Mining, and Construction Statistics, Building Permits, 2012, 2013

Homeownership Rate

Area	2006 (%)	2007 (%)	2008 (%)	2009 (%)	2010 (%)	2011 (%)	2012 (%)	2013 (%)
MSA[1]	62.2	62.1	68.0	70.7	68.8	62.7	64.9	67.9
U.S.	68.8	68.1	67.8	67.4	66.9	66.1	65.4	65.1

Note: (1) Figures cover the Greensboro-High Point, NC Metropolitan Statistical Area—see Appendix B for areas included
Source: U.S. Census Bureau, Housing Vacancies and Homeownership Annual Statistics: 2013

Housing Vacancy Rates

Area	Gross Vacancy Rate[2] (%)			Year-Round Vacancy Rate[3] (%)			Rental Vacancy Rate[4] (%)			Homeowner Vacancy Rate[5] (%)		
	2011	2012	2013	2011	2012	2013	2011	2012	2013	2011	2012	2013
MSA[1]	12.4	12.1	12.5	12.4	12.0	12.4	11.9	7.6	9.6	3.0	3.5	3.0
U.S.	14.2	13.8	13.8	11.1	10.8	10.7	9.5	8.7	8.3	2.5	2.0	2.0

Note: (1) Figures cover the Greensboro-High Point, NC Metropolitan Statistical Area—see Appendix B for areas included; (2) The percentage of the total housing inventory that is vacant; (3) The percentage of the housing inventory (excluding seasonal units) that is year-round vacant; (4) The percentage of rental inventory that is vacant for rent; (5) The percentage of homeowner inventory that is vacant for sale
Source: U.S. Census Bureau, Housing Vacancies and Homeownership Annual Statistics: 2013

TAXES

State Corporate Income Tax Rates

State	Tax Rate (%)	Income Brackets ($)	Num. of Brackets	Financial Institution Tax Rate (%)[a]	Federal Income Tax Ded.
North Carolina	6.0	Flat rate	1	6.0 (t)	No

Note: Tax rates as of January 1, 2014; (a) Rates listed are the corporate income tax rate applied to financial institutions or excise taxes based on income. Some states have other taxes based upon the value of deposits or shares; (t) In North Carolina financial institutions are also subject to a tax equal to $30 per one million in assets.
Source: Federation of Tax Administrators, "State Corporate Income Tax Rates, 2014"

State Individual Income Tax Rates

State	Tax Rate (%)	Income Brackets ($)	Num. of Brackets	Personal Exempt. ($)[1] Single	Personal Exempt. ($)[1] Dependents	Fed. Inc. Tax Ded.
North Carolina	5.8	Flat rate	1	None	None	No

Note: Tax rates as of January 1, 2014; Local- and county-level taxes are not included; n/a not applicable; (1) Married joint filers generally receive double the single exemption
Source: Federation of Tax Administrators, "State Individual Income Tax Rates, 2014"

Various State and Local Tax Rates

State	State and Local Sales and Use (%)	State Sales and Use (%)	Gasoline[1] (¢/gal.)	Cigarette[2] ($/pack)	Spirits[3] ($/gal.)	Wine[4] ($/gal.)	Beer[5] ($/gal.)
North Carolina	6.75	4.75	37.75	0.450	12.36 (g)	1.00	0.62

Note: All tax rates as of January 1, 2014; (1) The American Petroleum Institute has developed a methodology for determining the average tax rate on a gallon of fuel. Rates may include any of the following: excise taxes, environmental fees, storage tank fees, other fees or taxes, general sales tax, and local taxes. In states where gasoline is subject to the general sales tax, or where the fuel tax is based on the average sale price, the average rate determined by API is sensitive to changes in the price of gasoline. States that fully or partially apply general sales taxes to gasoline: CA, CO, GA, IL, IN, MI, NY; (2) The federal excise tax of $1.0066 per pack and local taxes are not included; (3) Rates are those applicable to off-premise sales of 40% alcohol by volume (a.b.v.) distilled spirits in 750ml containers. Local excise taxes are excluded; (4) Rates are those applicable to off-premise sales of 11% a.b.v. non-carbonated wine in 750ml containers; (5) Rates are those applicable to off-premise sales of 4.7% a.b.v. beer in 12 ounce containers; (g) States where the government controls sales. In these "control states," products are subject to ad valorem mark-up and excise taxes. The excise tax rate is calculated using a methodology developed by the Distilled Spirits Council of the United States.
Source: Tax Foundation, 2014 Facts & Figures: How Does Your State Compare?

State Business Tax Climate Index Rankings

State	Overall Rank	Corporate Tax Index Rank	Individual Income Tax Index Rank	Sales Tax Index Rank	Unemployment Insurance Tax Index Rank	Property Tax Index Rank
North Carolina	44	29	42	47	7	30

Note: The index is a measure of how each state's tax laws affect economic performance. The lower the rank, the more favorable a state's tax system is for business. States without a given tax are given a ranking of 1. The scores/rankings for the District of Columbia do not affect other states. The 2014 index represents the tax climate as of July 1, 2013.
Source: Tax Foundation, State Business Tax Climate Index 2014

COMMERCIAL UTILITIES

Typical Monthly Electric Bills

Area	Commercial Service ($/month) 1,500 kWh	Commercial Service ($/month) 40 kW demand 14,000 kWh	Industrial Service ($/month) 1,000 kW demand 200,000 kWh	Industrial Service ($/month) 50,000 kW demand 15,000,000 kWh
City	197	1,123	16,763	1,091,630
Average[1]	197	1,636	25,662	1,485,307

Note: Based on total rates in effect July 1, 2013; (1) average based on 180 utilities surveyed
Source: Edison Electric Institute, Typical Bills and Average Rates Report, Summer 2013

TRANSPORTATION

Means of Transportation to Work

| Area | Car/Truck/Van | | Public Transportation | | | Bicycle | Walked | Other Means | Worked at Home |
	Drove Alone	Car-pooled	Bus	Subway	Railroad				
City	81.2	9.6	2.2	0.0	0.0	0.3	2.3	0.9	3.5
MSA[1]	83.2	9.7	1.1	0.0	0.0	0.1	1.7	0.7	3.6
U.S.	76.4	9.7	2.6	1.7	0.5	0.6	2.8	1.3	4.3

Note: Figures are percentages and cover workers 16 years of age and older; (1) Figures cover the Greensboro-High Point, NC Metropolitan Statistical Area—see Appendix B for areas included
Source: U.S. Census Bureau, 2010-2012 American Community Survey 3-Year Estimates

Travel Time to Work

Area	Less Than 10 Minutes	10 to 19 Minutes	20 to 29 Minutes	30 to 44 Minutes	45 to 59 Minutes	60 to 89 Minutes	90 Minutes or More
City	13.0	45.0	22.6	13.4	2.3	1.8	1.9
MSA[1]	12.6	37.6	24.3	17.2	4.3	2.0	1.9
U.S.	13.5	29.8	20.9	20.1	7.5	5.6	2.5

Note: Figures are percentages and include workers 16 years old and over; (1) Figures cover the Greensboro-High Point, NC Metropolitan Statistical Area—see Appendix B for areas included
Source: U.S. Census Bureau, 2010-2012 American Community Survey 3-Year Estimates

Travel Time Index

Area	1985	1990	1995	2000	2005	2010	2011
Urban Area[1]	1.02	1.03	1.07	1.13	1.12	1.10	1.10
Average[2]	1.09	1.14	1.16	1.19	1.23	1.18	1.18

Note: Travel Time Index—the ratio of travel time in the peak period to the travel time at free-flow conditions. For example, a value of 1.30 indicates a 20-minute free-flow trip takes 26 minutes in the peak. Free-flow speeds (60 mph on freeways and 35 mph on principal arterials) are used as the comparison threshold; (1) Covers the Greensboro NC urban area; (2) average of 498 urban areas
Source: Texas Transportation Institute, Urban Mobility Report 2012, December 2012

Public Transportation

Agency Name / Mode of Transportation	Vehicles Operated in Maximum Service	Annual Unlinked Passenger Trips (in thous.)	Annual Passenger Miles (in thous.)
Greensboro Transit Authority (GTA)			
Bus (purchased transportation)	46	4,662.5	20,048.8
Demand Response (purchased transportation)	36	224.7	1,809.2

Source: Federal Transit Administration, National Transit Database, 2012

Air Transportation

Airport Name and Code / Type of Service	Passenger Airlines[1]	Passenger Enplanements	Freight Carriers[2]	Freight (lbs.)
Piedmont Triad International (GSO)				
Domestic service (U.S. carriers - 2013)	24	858,190	12	82,727,036
International service (U.S. carriers - 2012)	3	678	0	0

Note: (1) Includes all U.S.-based major, minor and commuter airlines that carried at least one passenger during the year; (2) Includes all U.S.-based airlines and freight carriers that transported at least one lb. of freight during the year.
Source: Bureau of Transportation Statistics, The Intermodal Transportation Database, Air Carriers: T-100 Domestic Market (U.S. Carriers), 2013; Bureau of Transportation Statistics, The Intermodal Transportation Database, Air Carriers: T-100 International Market (U.S. Carriers), 2012

Other Transportation Statistics

Major Highways:	I-40; I-85
Amtrak Service:	Yes
Major Waterways/Ports:	None

Source: Amtrak.com; Google Maps

BUSINESSES

Major Business Headquarters

Company Name	Rankings	
	Fortune[1]	Forbes[2]
VF	250	-

Note: (1) Fortune 500—companies that produce a 10-K are ranked 1 to 500 based on 2012 revenue; (2) all private companies with at least $2 billion in annual revenue through the end of their most current fiscal year are ranked 1 to 224; companies listed are headquartered in the city; dashes indicate no ranking
Source: Fortune, "Fortune 500," May 20, 2013; Forbes, "America's Largest Private Companies," December 18, 2013

Fast-Growing Businesses

According to *Inc.*, Greensboro is home to two of America's 500 fastest-growing private companies: **Intellect Resources** (#39); **Adora** (#230). Criteria: must be an independent, privately-held, for-profit, U.S. corporation, proprietorship or partnership; revenues must be at least $100,000 in 2009 and $2 million in 2012; must have four-year operating/sales history. Holding companies, regulated banks, and utilities were excluded. *Inc., "America's 500 Fastest-Growing Private Companies," September 2013*

Minority- and Women-Owned Businesses

Group	All Firms		Firms with Paid Employees			
	Firms	Sales ($000)	Firms	Sales ($000)	Employees	Payroll ($000)
Asian	1,045	252,431	344	215,306	1,634	33,193
Black	4,666	350,081	307	247,198	4,953	89,820
Hispanic	760	155,502	108	119,634	546	14,724
Women	7,178	1,223,497	981	1,062,320	13,962	295,760
All Firms	24,061	56,342,814	6,716	55,531,472	178,706	6,703,932

Note: Figures cover firms located in the city; minority- and women-owned business are defined as firms in which the corresponding group own 51% or more of the stock or equity of the company
Source: U.S. Census Bureau, 2007 Economic Census, Survey of Business Owners (2012 Survey of Business Owners data will be released starting in June 2015)

HOTELS & CONVENTION CENTERS

Hotels/Motels

Area	5 Star		4 Star		3 Star		2 Star		1 Star		Not Rated	
	Num.	Pct.[3]	Num.	Pct.[3]	Num.	Pct.[3]	Num.	Pct.[3]	Num.	Pct.[3]	Num.	Pct.[3]
City[1]	0	0.0	0	0.0	19	19.8	65	67.7	3	3.1	9	9.4
Total[2]	142	0.9	1,005	6.0	5,147	30.9	8,578	51.4	408	2.4	1,397	8.4

Note: (1) Figures cover Greensboro and vicinity; (2) Figures cover all 100 cities in this book; (3) Percentage of hotels which have a given star rating; Star ratings are determined by expedia.com and offer an indication of the general quality of a particular hotel.
Source: expedia.com, April 7, 2014

Major Convention Centers

Name	Overall Space (sq. ft.)	Exhibit Space (sq. ft.)	Meeting Space (sq. ft.)	Meeting Rooms
Joseph S. Koury Convention Center	250,000	n/a	n/a	n/a
Showplace	n/a	37,000	n/a	n/a

Note: Table includes convention centers located in the Greensboro-High Point, NC metro area; n/a not available
Source: Original research

Living Environment

COST OF LIVING

Cost of Living Index

Composite Index	Groceries	Housing	Utilities	Trans- portation	Health Care	Misc. Goods/ Services
88.1	98.0	69.5	100.3	85.3	102.9	94.0

Note: The Cost of Living Index measures regional differences in the cost of consumer goods and services, excluding taxes and non-consumer expenditures, for professional and managerial households in the top income quintile. It is based on more than 50,000 prices covering almost 60 different items for which prices are collected three times a year by chambers of commerce, economic development organizations or university applied economic centers in each participating urban area. The numbers shown should be read as a percentage above or below the national average of 100. For example, a value of 115.4 in the groceries column indicates that grocery prices are 15.4% higher than the national average. Small differences in the index numbers should not be interpreted as significant; Figures cover the Winston-Salem NC urban area.
Source: The Council for Community and Economic Research, ACCRA Cost of Living Index, 2013

Grocery Prices

Area[1]	T-Bone Steak ($/pound)	Frying Chicken ($/pound)	Whole Milk ($/half gal.)	Eggs ($/dozen)	Orange Juice ($/64 oz.)	Coffee ($/11.5 oz.)
City[2]	10.89	1.37	2.68	1.86	3.28	3.75
Avg.	10.19	1.28	2.34	1.81	3.48	4.39
Min.	8.56	0.94	1.44	1.19	2.78	3.40
Max.	14.82	2.28	3.56	3.73	6.23	7.32

*Note: (1) Values for the local area are compared with the average, minimum and maximum values for all 327 areas in the Cost of Living Index; (2) Figures cover the Winston-Salem NC urban area; **T-Bone Steak** (price per pound); **Frying Chicken** (price per pound, whole fryer); **Whole Milk** (half gallon carton); **Eggs** (price per dozen, Grade A, large); **Orange Juice** (64 oz. Tropicana or Florida Natural); **Coffee** (11.5 oz. can, vacuum-packed, Maxwell House, Hills Bros, or Folgers).*
Source: The Council for Community and Economic Research, ACCRA Cost of Living Index, 2013

Housing and Utility Costs

Area[1]	New Home Price ($)	Apartment Rent ($/month)	All Electric ($/month)	Part Electric ($/month)	Other Energy ($/month)	Telephone ($/month)
City[2]	202,750	659	157.77	-	-	29.33
Avg.	295,864	900	171.38	91.82	70.12	27.73
Min.	185,506	458	117.80	48.81	33.67	17.16
Max.	1,358,917	3,783	441.68	171.40	372.65	39.47

*Note: (1) Values for the local area are compared with the average, minimum and maximum values for all 327 areas in the Cost of Living Index; (2) Figures cover the Winston-Salem NC urban area; **New Home Price** (2,400 sf living area, 8,000 sf lot, in urban area with full utilities); **Apartment Rent** (950 sf 2 bedroom/1.5 or 2 bath, unfurnished, excluding all utilities except water); **All Electric** (average monthly cost for an all-electric home); **Part Electric** (average monthly cost for a part-electric home); **Other Energy** (average monthly cost for natural gas, fuel oil, coal, wood, and any other forms of energy except electricity); **Telephone** (price includes basic monthly rate for a private residential line plus additional local usage charges incurred by a family of four).*
Source: The Council for Community and Economic Research, ACCRA Cost of Living Index, 2013

Health Care, Transportation, and Other Costs

Area[1]	Doctor ($/visit)	Dentist ($/visit)	Optometrist ($/visit)	Gasoline ($/gallon)	Beauty Salon ($/visit)	Men's Shirt ($)
City[2]	107.75	83.20	95.40	3.36	36.53	30.24
Avg.	101.40	86.48	96.16	3.44	33.87	26.55
Min.	61.67	50.83	50.12	3.08	18.92	12.48
Max.	182.71	152.50	223.78	4.33	68.22	52.03

*Note: (1) Values for the local area are compared with the average, minimum and maximum values for all 327 areas in the Cost of Living Index; (2) Figures cover the Winston-Salem NC urban area; **Doctor** (general practitioners routine exam of an established patient); **Dentist** (adult teeth cleaning and periodic oral examination); **Optometrist** (full vision eye exam for established adult patient); **Gasoline** (one gallon regular unleaded, national brand, including all taxes, cash price at self-service pump if available); **Beauty Salon** (woman's shampoo, trim, and blow-dry); **Men's Shirt** (cotton/polyester dress shirt, pinpoint weave, long sleeves).*
Source: The Council for Community and Economic Research, ACCRA Cost of Living Index, 2013

HOUSING

House Price Index (HPI)

Area	National Ranking[2]	Quarterly Change (%)	One-Year Change (%)	Five-Year Change (%)
MSA[1]	244	-1.22	-0.57	-6.33
U.S.[3]	–	1.20	7.69	4.18

Note: The HPI is a weighted repeat sales index. It measures average price changes in repeat sales or refinancings on the same properties. This information is obtained by reviewing repeat mortgage transactions on single-family properties whose mortgages have been purchased or securitized by Fannie Mae or Freddie Mac in January 1975; (1) Greensboro-High Point, NC Metropolitan Statistical Area—see Appendix B for areas included; (2) Rankings are based on annual percentage change for all metro areas containing at least 15,000 transactions over the last 10 years and ranges from 1 to 283; (3) figures based on a weighted average of Census Division estimates using a seasonally adjusted, purchase-only index; all figures are for the period ending December 31, 2013
Source: Federal Housing Finance Agency, House Price Index, February 25, 2014

Median Single-Family Home Prices

Area	2011	2012	2013p	Percent Change 2012 to 2013
MSA[1]	123.8	124.8	131.0	5.0
U.S. Average	166.2	177.2	197.4	11.4

Note: Figures are median sales prices of existing single-family homes in thousands of dollars; (p) preliminary; n/a not available; (1) Greensboro-High Point, NC Metropolitan Statistical Area—see Appendix B for areas included
Source: National Association of Realtors, Median Sales Price of Existing Single-Family Homes for Metropolitan Areas, 4th Quarter 2013

Qualifying Income Based on Median Sales Price of Existing Single-Family Homes

Area	With 5% Down ($)	With 10% Down ($)	With 20% Down ($)
MSA[1]	29,257	27,717	24,637
U.S. Average	45,395	43,006	38,228

Note: Figures are preliminary; Qualifying income is based on a mortgage rate of 4.4%. Monthly principal and interest payment is limited to 25% of income; n/a not available; (1) Greensboro-High Point, NC Metropolitan Statistical Area—see Appendix B for areas included
Source: National Association of Realtors, Qualifying Income Based on Median Sales Price of Existing Single-Family Homes for Metropolitan Areas, 4th Quarter 2013

Median Apartment Condo-Coop Home Prices

Area	2011	2012	2013p	Percent Change 2012 to 2013
MSA[1]	69.9	62.4	68.5	9.8
U.S. Average	165.1	173.7	194.9	12.2

Note: Figures are median sales prices of existing apartment condo-coop homes in thousands of dollars; (p) preliminary; n/a not available; (1) Greensboro-High Point, NC Metropolitan Statistical Area—see Appendix B for areas included
Source: National Association of Realtors, Median Sales Price of Existing Apartment Condo-Coop Homes for Metropolitan Areas, 4th Quarter 2013

Gross Monthly Rent

Area	Under $200	$200 -299	$300 -499	$500 -749	$750 -999	$1,000 -1,499	$1,500 and up	Median ($)
City	1.8	3.3	9.5	40.4	28.3	14.0	2.7	723
MSA[1]	1.9	3.9	11.7	39.3	26.5	13.7	3.1	711
U.S.	1.7	3.3	8.1	22.7	24.3	25.7	14.3	889

Note: Figures are percentages except for Median; Gross rent is the contract rent plus the estimated average monthly cost of utilities (electricity, gas, and water and sewer) and fuels (oil, coal, kerosene, wood, etc.) if these are paid by the renter (or paid for the renter by someone else); (1) Figures cover the Greensboro-High Point, NC Metropolitan Statistical Area—see Appendix B for areas included
Source: U.S. Census Bureau, 2010 2012 American Community Survey 3 Year Estimates

Year Housing Structure Built

Area	2010 or Later	2000 -2009	1990 -1999	1980 -1989	1970 -1979	1960 -1969	1950 -1959	1940 -1949	Before 1940	Median Year
City	0.4	15.9	19.2	17.1	16.2	11.7	10.2	4.3	5.1	1982
MSA[1]	0.5	16.4	19.1	15.7	15.4	11.4	10.3	5.0	6.2	1981
U.S.	0.5	14.9	13.8	13.9	15.9	11.1	10.9	5.5	13.5	1976

Note: Figures are percentages except for Median Year; (1) Figures cover the Greensboro-High Point, NC Metropolitan Statistical Area—see Appendix B for areas included
Source: U.S. Census Bureau, 2010-2012 American Community Survey 3-Year Estimates

HEALTH

Health Risk Data

Category	MSA[1] (%)	U.S. (%)
Adults aged 18–64 who have any kind of health care coverage	74.3	79.6
Adults who reported being in good or excellent health	81.5	83.1
Adults who are current smokers	20.0	19.6
Adults who are heavy drinkers[2]	5.0	6.1
Adults who are binge drinkers[3]	13.7	16.9
Adults who are overweight (BMI 25.0 - 29.9)	38.3	35.8
Adults who are obese (BMI 30.0 - 99.8)	32.2	27.6
Adults who participated in any physical activities in the past month	72.7	77.1
Adults 50+ who have ever had a sigmoidoscopy or colonoscopy	70.6	67.3
Women aged 40+ who have had a mammogram within the past two years	73.2	74.0
Men aged 40+ who have had a PSA test within the past two years	43.5	45.2
Adults aged 65+ who have had flu shot within the past year	77.8	60.1
Adults who always wear a seatbelt	95.4	93.8

Note: Data as of 2012 unless otherwise noted; (1) Figures cover the Greensboro-High Point, NC Metropolitan Statistical Area—see Appendix B for areas included; (2) Heavy drinkers are classified as males having more than two drinks per day or females having more than one drink per day; (3) Binge drinkers are classified as males having five or more drinks on one occasion or females having four or more drinks on one occasion
Source: Centers for Disease Control and Prevention, Behaviorial Risk Factor Surveillance System, SMART: Selected Metropolitan/Micropolitan Area Risk Trends, 2012

Chronic Health Indicators

Category	MSA[1] (%)	U.S. (%)
Adults who have ever been told they had a heart attack	4.9	4.5
Adults who have ever been told they had a stroke	2.8	2.9
Adults who have been told they currently have asthma	7.2	8.9
Adults who have ever been told they have arthritis	25.8	25.7
Adults who have ever been told they have diabetes[2]	11.0	9.7
Adults who have ever been told they had skin cancer	5.7	5.7
Adults who have ever been told they had any other types of cancer	7.9	6.5
Adults who have ever been told they have COPD	7.1	6.2
Adults who have ever been told they have kidney disease	2.8	2.5
Adults who have ever been told they have a form of depression	18.6	18.0

Note: Data as of 2012 unless otherwise noted; (1) Figures cover the Greensboro-High Point, NC Metropolitan Statistical Area—see Appendix B for areas included; (2) Figures do not include pregnancy-related, borderline, or pre-diabetes
Source: Centers for Disease Control and Prevention, Behaviorial Risk Factor Surveillance System, SMART: Selected Metropolitan/Micropolitan Area Risk Trends, 2012

Mortality Rates for the Top 10 Causes of Death in the U.S.

ICD-10[a] Sub-Chapter	ICD-10[a] Code	Age-Adjusted Mortality Rate[1] per 100,000 population	
		County[2]	U.S.
Malignant neoplasms	C00-C97	170.0	174.2
Ischaemic heart diseases	I20-I25	95.1	119.1
Other forms of heart disease	I30-I51	46.3	49.6
Chronic lower respiratory diseases	J40-J47	37.4	43.2
Cerebrovascular diseases	I60-I69	44.6	40.3
Organic, including symptomatic, mental disorders	F01-F09	50.0	30.5
Other degenerative diseases of the nervous system	G30-G31	33.1	26.3
Other external causes of accidental injury	W00-X59	28.2	25.1
Diabetes mellitus	E10-E14	14.9	21.3
Hypertensive diseases	I10-I15	17.1	18.8

Note: (a) ICD-10 = International Classification of Diseases 10th Revision; (1) Mortality rates are a three year average covering 2008-2010; (2) Figures cover Guilford County
Source: Centers for Disease Control and Prevention, National Center for Health Statistics. Compressed Mortality File 1999-2010 on CDC WONDER Online Database, released January 2013. Data are compiled from the Compressed Mortality File 1999-2010, Series 20 No. 2P, 2013.

Mortality Rates for Selected Causes of Death

ICD-10[a] Sub-Chapter	ICD-10[a] Code	Age-Adjusted Mortality Rate[1] per 100,000 population	
		County[2]	U.S.
Assault	X85-Y09	6.0	5.5
Diseases of the liver	K70-K76	10.8	12.4
Human immunodeficiency virus (HIV) disease	B20-B24	4.7	3.0
Influenza and pneumonia	J09-J18	17.7	16.4
Intentional self-harm	X60-X84	9.6	11.8
Malnutrition	E40-E46	1.4	0.8
Obesity and other hyperalimentation	E65-E68	2.4	1.6
Renal failure	N17-N19	17.9	13.6
Transport accidents	V01-V99	13.3	12.6
Viral hepatitis	B15-B19	2.0	2.2

Note: (a) ICD-10 = International Classification of Diseases 10th Revision; (1) Mortality rates are a three year average covering 2008-2010; (2) Figures cover Guilford County
Source: Centers for Disease Control and Prevention, National Center for Health Statistics. Compressed Mortality File 1999-2010 on CDC WONDER Online Database, released January 2013. Data are compiled from the Compressed Mortality File 1999-2010, Series 20 No. 2P, 2013.

Health Insurance Coverage

Area	With Health Insurance	With Private Health Insurance	With Public Health Insurance	Without Health Insurance	Population Under Age 18 Without Health Insurance
City	82.6	63.2	28.0	17.4	7.1
MSA[1]	83.2	62.5	30.7	16.8	8.0
U.S.	84.9	65.4	30.4	15.1	7.5

Note: Figures are percentages that cover the civilian noninstitutionalized population; (1) Figures cover the Greensboro-High Point, NC Metropolitan Statistical Area—see Appendix B for areas included
Source: U.S. Census Bureau, 2010-2012 American Community Survey 3-Year Estimates

Number of Medical Professionals

Area[1]	MDs[2]	DOs[2,3]	Dentists	Podiatrists	Chiropractors	Optometrists
Local (number)	1,258	32	264	19	65	51
Local (rate[4])	254.1	6.5	52.7	3.8	13.0	10.2
U.S. (rate[4])	267.6	19.6	61.7	5.6	24.7	14.5

Note: Data as of 2012 unless noted; (1) Local data covers Guilford County; (2) Data as of 2011; (3) Doctor of Osteopathic Medicine; (4) rate per 100,000 population
Source: Area Resource File (ARF) 2012-2013. U.S. Department of Health and Human Services, Health Resources and Services Administration, Bureau of Health Professions

EDUCATION

Public School District Statistics

District Name	Schls	Pupils	Pupil/ Teacher Ratio	Minority Pupils[1] (%)	Free Lunch Eligible[2] (%)	IEP[3] (%)
Guilford County Schools	123	74,086	15.0	62.1	48.6	13.7

Note: Table includes school districts with 2,000 or more students; (1) Percentage of students that are not non-Hispanic white; (2) Percentage of students that are eligible for the free lunch program; (3) Percentage of students that have an Individualized Education Program.
Source: U.S. Department of Education, National Center for Education Statistics, Common Core of Data, Local Education Agency (School District) Universe Survey: School Year 2011-2012; U.S. Department of Education, National Center for Education Statistics, Common Core of Data, Public Elementary/Secondary School Universe Survey: School Year 2011-2012

Best High Schools

High School Name	Rank[1]	Grad. Rate[2] (%)	Coll.[3] (%)	AP/IB/ AICE Tests[4]	AP/IB/ AICE Score[5]	SAT Score[6]	ACT Score[6]
Early College at Guilford	21	100	100	1.3	4.4	2051	30.4
Greensboro College Middle College	1491	100	84	0.4	1.9	1419	18.5
Grimsley H.S.	991	81	95	0.9	3.4	1588	24.7
Northern Guilford H.S.	671	98	90	0.5	3.4	1568	24.4
Northwest Guilford H.S.	526	94	95	0.6	3.4	1605	23.6
Page H.S.	1393	86	91	0.6	2.6	1469	22.3
Southeast Guilford H.S.	1168	97	96	0.3	2.8	1417	17.6
The Academy at Smith	1508	98	98	0.2	1.8	1238	15.1
The Middle College At NC A&T	1783	100	100	0.0	n/a	1139	14.4
The Middle College at Bennett	1916	95	97	0.0	n/a	1158	15.8
The Middle College at GTCC Greensboro	1546	100	100	0.0	n/a	1443	23.3
Weaver Academy	311	100	100	0.8	2.4	1601	23.5
Western Guilford H.S.	1594	81	90	0.5	2.8	1439	20.7

Note: (1) Public schools are ranked from 1 to 2,000 based on the following self-reported statistics (with the corresponding weight used in calculating their overall score). Schools that were newly founded and did not have a graduating senior class in 2012 were excluded; (2) Four-year, on-time graduation rate (25%); (3) Percent of 2011 graduates who were accepted to college (25%); (4) AP/IB/AICE tests taken per student (25%); (5) Average AP/IB/AICE exam score (10%); (6) Average SAT and/or ACT score (10%); Percent of students enrolled in at least one AP/IB/AICE course (5%)—data not shown; n/a not available
Source: Newsweek and The Daily Beast, "America's Best High Schools 2013"

Highest Level of Education

Area	Less than H.S.	H.S. Diploma	Some College, No Deg.	Associate Degree	Bachelor's Degree	Master's Degree	Prof. School Degree	Doctorate Degree
City	12.6	23.7	21.6	6.5	23.9	8.6	1.7	1.4
MSA[1]	15.2	29.1	21.6	7.8	18.1	6.2	1.2	0.9
U.S.	14.1	28.3	21.3	7.8	18.0	7.5	1.9	1.2

Note: Figures cover persons age 25 and over; (1) Figures cover the Greensboro-High Point, NC Metropolitan Statistical Area—see Appendix B for areas included
Source: U.S. Census Bureau, 2010-2012 American Community Survey 3-Year Estimates

Educational Attainment by Race

Area	High School Graduate or Higher (%)					Bachelor's Degree or Higher (%)				
	Total	White	Black	Asian	Hisp.[2]	Total	White	Black	Asian	Hisp.[2]
City	87.4	91.6	85.6	62.0	53.3	35.6	45.1	23.3	31.7	11.8
MSA[1]	84.8	86.7	83.8	70.2	54.2	26.4	28.4	20.8	35.9	10.9
U.S.	85.9	88.1	82.5	85.5	63.1	28.6	30.0	18.4	50.2	13.4

Note: Figures shown cover persons 25 years old and over; (1) Figures cover the Greensboro-High Point, NC Metropolitan Statistical Area—see Appendix B for areas included; (2) People of Hispanic origin can be of any race
Source: U.S. Census Bureau, 2010-2012 American Community Survey 3-Year Estimates

School Enrollment by Grade and Control

Area	Preschool (%)		Kindergarten (%)		Grades 1 - 4 (%)		Grades 5 - 8 (%)		Grades 9 - 12 (%)	
	Public	Private	Public	Private	Public	Private	Public	Private	Public	Private
City	51.9	48.1	90.9	9.1	92.6	7.4	91.0	9.0	91.0	9.0
MSA[1]	57.3	42.7	89.6	10.4	91.8	8.2	91.1	8.9	90.5	9.5
U.S.	56.9	43.1	87.8	12.2	89.9	10.1	90.0	10.0	90.8	9.2

Note: Figures shown cover persons 3 years old and over; (1) Figures cover the Greensboro-High Point, NC Metropolitan Statistical Area—see Appendix B for areas included
Source: U.S. Census Bureau, 2010-2012 American Community Survey 3-Year Estimates

Average Salaries of Public School Classroom Teachers

Area	2012-13		2013-14		Percent Change 2012-13 to 2013-14	Percent Change 2003-04 to 2013-14
	Dollars	Rank[1]	Dollars	Rank[1]		
North Carolina	45,737	46	45,355	48	-0.84	5.0
U.S. Average	56,103	–	56,689	–	1.04	21.8

Note: (1) State rank ranges from 1 to 51 where 1 indicates highest salary.
Source: National Education Association, Rankings & Estimates: Rankings of the States 2013 and Estimates of School Statistics 2014, March 2014

Higher Education

Four-Year Colleges			Two-Year Colleges			Medical Schools[1]	Law Schools[2]	Voc/ Tech[3]
Public	Private Non-profit	Private For-profit	Public	Private Non-profit	Private For-profit			
2	3	0	0	0	0	0	1	4

Note: Figures cover institutions located within the city limits and include main campuses only; (1) includes schools accredited by the Liaison Committee on Medical Education and the American Osteopathic Association's Commission on Osteopathic College Accreditation; (2) includes ABA-accredited schools, schools with provisional ABA accreditation, and state accredited schools; (3) includes all schools with programs that are less than 2 years.
Source: National Center for Education Statistics, Integrated Postsecondary Education System (IPEDS), 2012-13; Association of American Medical Colleges, Member List, April 24, 2014; American Osteopathic Association, Member List, April 24, 2014; Law School Admission Council, Official Guide to ABA-Approved Law Schools Online, April 24, 2014; Wikipedia, List of Medical Schools in the United States, April 24, 2014; Wikipedia, List of Law Schools in the United States, April 24, 2014

According to *U.S. News & World Report*, the Greensboro-High Point, NC metro area is home to one of the best national universities in the U.S.: **University of North Carolina–Greensboro** (#190). The indicators used to capture academic quality fall into a number of categories: assessment by administrators at peer institutions; retention of students; faculty resources; student selectivity; financial resources; alumni giving; high school counselor ratings of colleges; and graduation rate. *U.S. News & World Report, "America's Best Colleges 2014"*

According to *U.S. News & World Report*, the Greensboro-High Point, NC metro area is home to one of the best liberal arts colleges in the U.S.: **Guilford College** (#173). The indicators used to capture academic quality fall into a number of categories: assessment by administrators at peer institutions; retention of students; faculty resources; student selectivity; financial resources; alumni giving; high school counselor ratings of colleges; and graduation rate. *U.S. News & World Report, "America's Best Colleges 2014"*

PRESIDENTIAL ELECTION

2012 Presidential Election Results

Area	Obama	Romney	Other
Guilford County	57.7	41.2	1.1
U.S.	51.0	47.2	1.8

Note: Results are percentages and may not add to 100% due to rounding
Source: Dave Leip's Atlas of U.S. Presidential Elections

EMPLOYERS

Major Employers

Company Name	Industry
CitiGroup	Financial services
City of Greensboro	Public relations services
Cone Denim	Denims
County of Guilford	Executive offices/county government
Daimler Trucks North America	Motor vehicles/car bodies
Gilbarco	Electronic computers
High Point Regional Health System	General medical/surgical hospitals
ITG Holdings	Denims
Kayser- Roth Corporation	Mens. boys, girls, hosiery
Klaussner Corp	Upholstered/household furniture
Klaussner Furniture Industries	Upholstered/household furniture
Lorillard Tobbacco Co	Cigarettes
NC Ag & Technical State University	University
Piedmont Express	Airline ticket offices
RF Micro Devices	Semiconductors and related devices
Technimark	Injection molding of plastics
The Fresh Market	Grocery stores
The Moses H Cone Memorial Hospital	General medical/surgical hospitals
The University of NC at Greensboro	Colleges/universities
Thomas Built Buses	Truck and bus bodies
Zen Hro	Employee leasing

Note: Companies shown are located within the Greensboro-High Point, NC Metropolitan Statistical Area.
Source: Hoovers.com; Wikipedia

PUBLIC SAFETY

Crime Rate

Area	All Crimes	Violent Crimes				Property Crimes		
		Murder	Forcible Rape	Robbery	Aggrav. Assault	Burglary	Larceny -Theft	Motor Vehicle Theft
City	4,932.0	7.6	25.4	201.4	328.8	1,211.4	2,952.6	205.0
Suburbs[1]	3,311.6	5.0	14.5	64.9	169.0	878.4	2,036.5	143.3
Metro[2]	3,917.7	6.0	18.6	116.0	228.8	1,003.0	2,379.1	166.3
U.S.	3,246.1	4.7	26.9	112.9	242.3	670.2	1,959.3	229.7

Note: Figures are crimes per 100,000 population; (1) All areas within the metro area that are located outside the city limits; (2) Figures cover the Greensboro-High Point, NC Metropolitan Statistical Area—see Appendix B for areas included
Source: FBI Uniform Crime Reports, 2012

Hate Crimes

Area	Number of Quarters Reported	Bias Motivation				
		Race	Religion	Sexual Orientation	Ethnicity	Disability
City	4	0	1	1	0	0
U.S.	4	2,797	1,099	1,135	667	92

Source: Federal Bureau of Investigation, Hate Crime Statistics 2012

Identity Theft Consumer Complaints

Area	Complaints	Complaints per 100,000 Population	Rank[2]
MSA[1]	457	63.1	185
U.S.	290,056	91.8	-

Note: (1) Figures cover the Greensboro-High Point, NC Metropolitan Statistical Area—see Appendix B for areas included; (2) Rank ranges from 1 to 377 where 1 indicates greatest number of identity theft complaints per 100,000 population
Source: Federal Trade Commission, Consumer Sentinel Network Data Book for January–December 2013

Fraud and Other Consumer Complaints

Area	Complaints	Complaints per 100,000 Population	Rank[2]
MSA[1]	2,796	386.3	144
U.S.	1,811,724	595.2	-

Note: (1) Figures cover the Greensboro-High Point, NC Metropolitan Statistical Area—see Appendix B for areas included; (2) Rank ranges from 1 to 377 where 1 indicates greatest number of identity theft complaints per 100,000 population
Source: Federal Trade Commission, Consumer Sentinel Network Data Book for January–December 2013

RECREATION

Culture

Dance[1]	Theatre[1]	Instrumental Music[1]	Vocal Music[1]	Series and Festivals	Museums and Art Galleries[2]	Zoos and Aquariums[3]
2	3	2	2	5	19	1

Note: (1) Number of professional performing groups; (2) Based on organizations with primary SIC code 8412; (3) AZA-accredited
Source: The Grey House Performing Arts Directory, 2013; Association of Zoos & Aquariums, AZA Member Zoos & Aquariums, April 2014; www.AccuLeads.com, May 1, 2014

Professional Sports Teams

Team Name	League	Year Established
No teams are located in the metro area		

Source: Wikipedia, Major Professional Sports Teams of the United States and Canada, April 25, 2014

CLIMATE

Average and Extreme Temperatures

Temperature	Jan	Feb	Mar	Apr	May	Jun	Jul	Aug	Sep	Oct	Nov	Dec	Yr.
Extreme High (°F)	78	81	89	91	96	102	102	103	100	95	85	78	103
Average High (°F)	48	51	60	70	78	84	87	86	80	70	60	50	69
Average Temp. (°F)	38	41	49	58	67	74	78	76	70	59	49	40	58
Average Low (°F)	28	30	37	46	55	63	67	66	59	47	37	30	47
Extreme Low (°F)	-8	-1	5	23	32	42	49	45	37	20	10	0	-8

Note: Figures cover the years 1948-1990
Source: National Climatic Data Center, International Station Meteorological Climate Summary, 9/96

Average Precipitation/Snowfall/Humidity

Precip./Humidity	Jan	Feb	Mar	Apr	May	Jun	Jul	Aug	Sep	Oct	Nov	Dec	Yr.
Avg. Precip. (in.)	3.2	3.4	3.7	3.1	3.7	3.8	4.5	4.2	3.4	3.4	2.9	3.3	42.5
Avg. Snowfall (in.)	4	3	2	Tr	0	0	0	0	0	0	Tr	1	10
Avg. Rel. Hum. 7am (%)	80	78	78	77	82	84	87	90	90	88	83	80	83
Avg. Rel. Hum. 4pm (%)	53	50	47	44	51	54	57	58	56	51	51	54	52

Note: Figures cover the years 1948-1990; Tr = Trace amounts (<0.05 in. of rain; <0.5 in. of snow)
Source: National Climatic Data Center, International Station Meteorological Climate Summary, 9/96

Weather Conditions

Temperature			Daytime Sky			Precipitation		
10°F & below	32°F & below	90°F & above	Clear	Partly cloudy	Cloudy	0.01 inch or more precip.	0.1 inch or more snow/ice	Thunder-storms
3	85	32	94	143	128	113	5	43

Note: Figures are average number of days per year and cover the years 1948-1990
Source: National Climatic Data Center, International Station Meteorological Climate Summary, 9/96

HAZARDOUS WASTE

Superfund Sites

Greensboro has no sites on the EPA's Superfund Final National Priorities List.
U.S. Environmental Protection Agency, Final National Priorities List, April 26, 2014

**AIR & WATER
QUALITY**

Air Quality Index

Area	Percent of Days when Air Quality was...[2]					AQI Statistics[2]	
	Good	Moderate	Unhealthy for Sensitive Groups	Unhealthy	Very Unhealthy	Maximum	Median
MSA[1]	81.7	18.3	0.0	0.0	0.0	90	38

Note: (1) Data covers the Greensboro-High Point, NC Metropolitan Statistical Area—see Appendix B for areas included; (2) Based on 338 days with AQI data in 2013. Air Quality Index (AQI) is an index for reporting daily air quality. EPA calculates the AQI for five major air pollutants regulated by the Clean Air Act: ground-level ozone, particle pollution (aka particulate matter), carbon monoxide, sulfur dioxide, and nitrogen dioxide. The AQI runs from 0 to 500. The higher the AQI value, the greater the level of air pollution and the greater the health concern. There are six AQI categories: "Good" AQI is between 0 and 50. Air quality is considered satisfactory; "Moderate" AQI is between 51 and 100. Air quality is acceptable; "Unhealthy for Sensitive Groups" When AQI values are between 101 and 150, members of sensitive groups may experience health effects; "Unhealthy" When AQI values are between 151 and 200 everyone may begin to experience health effects; "Very Unhealthy" AQI values between 201 and 300 trigger a health alert; "Hazardous" AQI values over 300 trigger warnings of emergency conditions (not shown).
Source: U.S. Environmental Protection Agency, Air Quality Index Report, 2013

Air Quality Index Pollutants

Area	Percent of Days when AQI Pollutant was...[2]					
	Carbon Monoxide	Nitrogen Dioxide	Ozone	Sulfur Dioxide	Particulate Matter 2.5	Particulate Matter 10
MSA[1]	0.0	0.0	39.1	0.0	60.7	0.3

Note: (1) Data covers the Greensboro-High Point, NC Metropolitan Statistical Area—see Appendix B for areas included; (2) Based on 338 days with AQI data in 2013. The Air Quality Index (AQI) is an index for reporting daily air quality. EPA calculates the AQI for five major air pollutants regulated by the Clean Air Act: ground-level ozone, particle pollution (also known as particulate matter), carbon monoxide, sulfur dioxide, and nitrogen dioxide. The AQI runs from 0 to 500. The higher the AQI value, the greater the level of air pollution and the greater the health concern.
Source: U.S. Environmental Protection Agency, Air Quality Index Report, 2013

Air Quality Trends: Ozone

	2003	2004	2005	2006	2007	2008	2009	2010	2011	2012
MSA[1]	0.083	0.074	0.078	0.075	0.082	0.084	0.068	0.074	0.071	0.076

Note: (1) Data covers the Greensboro-High Point, NC Metropolitan Statistical Area—see Appendix B for areas included. The values shown are the composite ozone concentration averages among trend sites based on the highest fourth daily maximum 8-hour concentration in parts per million. These trends are based on sites having an adequate record of monitoring data during the trend period. Data from exceptional events are included.
Source: U.S. Environmental Protection Agency, Air Quality Monitoring Information, "Air Quality Trends by City, 2000-2012"

Maximum Air Pollutant Concentrations: Particulate Matter, Ozone, CO and Lead

	Particulate Matter 10 (ug/m^3)	Particulate Matter 2.5 Wtd AM (ug/m^3)	Particulate Matter 2.5 24-Hr (ug/m^3)	Ozone (ppm)	Carbon Monoxide (ppm)	Lead (ug/m^3)
MSA[1] Level	24	8.5	20	0.078	n/a	n/a
NAAQS[2]	150	15	35	0.075	9	0.15
Met NAAQS[2]	Yes	Yes	Yes	No	n/a	n/a

Note: (1) Data covers the Greensboro-High Point, NC Metropolitan Statistical Area—see Appendix B for areas included; Data from exceptional events are included; (2) National Ambient Air Quality Standards; ppm = parts per million; ug/m^3 = micrograms per cubic meter; n/a not available.
Concentrations: Particulate Matter 10 (coarse particulate)—highest second maximum 24-hour concentration; Particulate Matter 2.5 Wtd AM (fine particulate)—highest weighted annual mean concentration; Particulate Matter 2.5 24-Hour (fine particulate)—highest 98th percentile 24-hour concentration; Ozone—highest fourth daily maximum 8-hour concentration; Carbon Monoxide—highest second maximum non-overlapping 8-hour concentration; Lead—maximum running 3-month average
Source: U.S. Environmental Protection Agency, Air Quality Monitoring Information, "Air Quality Statistics by City, 2012"

Maximum Air Pollutant Concentrations: Nitrogen Dioxide and Sulfur Dioxide

	Nitrogen Dioxide AM (ppb)	Nitrogen Dioxide 1-Hr (ppb)	Sulfur Dioxide AM (ppb)	Sulfur Dioxide 1-Hr (ppb)	Sulfur Dioxide 24-Hr (ppb)
MSA[1] Level	n/a	n/a	n/a	n/a	n/a
NAAQS[2]	53	100	30	75	140
Met NAAQS[2]	n/a	n/a	n/a	n/a	n/a

Note: (1) Data covers the Greensboro-High Point, NC Metropolitan Statistical Area—see Appendix B for areas included; Data from exceptional events are included; (2) National Ambient Air Quality Standards; ppm = parts per million; ug/m³ = micrograms per cubic meter; n/a not available.
Concentrations: Nitrogen Dioxide AM—highest arithmetic mean concentration; Nitrogen Dioxide 1-Hr—highest 98th percentile 1-hour daily maximum concentration; Sulfur Dioxide AM—highest annual mean concentration; Sulfur Dioxide 1-Hr—highest 99th percentile 1-hour daily maximum concentration; Sulfur Dioxide 24-Hr—highest second maximum 24-hour concentration
Source: U.S. Environmental Protection Agency, Air Quality Monitoring Information, "Air Quality Statistics by City, 2012"

Drinking Water

Water System Name	Pop. Served	Primary Water Source Type	Violations[1] Health Based	Violations[1] Monitoring/ Reporting
City of Greensboro	250,000	Surface	0	0

Note: (1) Based on violation data from January 1, 2013 to December 31, 2013 (includes unresolved violations from earlier years)
Source: U.S. Environmental Protection Agency, Office of Ground Water and Drinking Water, Safe Drinking Water Information System (based on data extracted February 10, 2014)

Lexington, Kentucky

Background

Lexington has managed to combine the frenzied pace of a major city with the slow tempo of a small town without losing the traditions and gentility of its Southern heritage. It is located in a scenic area of rolling plateaus and small creeks flowing into the Kentucky River.

Since its settlement in 1775, Lexington has grown to become Kentucky's second-largest city and the commercial center of the Bluegrass Region. The town was founded in 1779 and incorporated in 1832. Hemp was Lexington's major antebellum crop until the rope from which it was made was no longer used for ship rigging. After the Civil War the farmers in the area switched to tobacco as their primary crop. The city is also the chief producer of bluegrass seed and white barley in the United States.

Other products manufactured in Lexington include paper products, air-conditioning and heating equipment, electric typewriters, metal products, and bourbon whiskey.

Lexington was once known as the "Athens of the West" when a large number of early American artists, poets, musicians, and architects settled here, all leaving their imprint on the city. The Actor's Guild of Lexington and the Studio Players, Lexington's oldest community theater (1953) reside there, as does the Chamber Music Society of Kentucky. The 1898 Fayette County Courthouse, which operated from 1901 to 2001, has been transformed into the Lexington History Museum.

No discussion of Lexington would be complete without mention of horse racing. Kentucky is synonymous with horses, especially the American Saddlebred—Kentucky's only native breed. The region, with its fertile soil and excellent pastureland, is perfectly suited for breeding horses. Horse racing in Kentucky dates back to 1789, when the first course was laid out in Lexington. In 1787, The Commons, a park-like block near Race Street in Lexington, was used for horse racing, but complaints by citizens led to the formal development of a race meet, organized by Kentucky statesman Henry Clay, who also helped form the commonwealth's first jockey club, now known as the Kentucky Jockey Club. The Kentucky Horse Park, a 1,200-acre educational theme park, highlights 50 different horse breeds and allows visitors the opportunity to pet and ride the horses and talk with riders, while the International Museum of the Horse traces the history of the horse with exhibits and artifacts, and includes online exhibits. Finally, the American Saddle Horse Museum offers exciting exhibits showing the role of the saddle horse in American history.

From race courses to golf courses, Lexington has it all, with many fine courses for golfers to play. The city also has its share of blues, country, and dance clubs for those who prefer musical nightlife. Lexington is also home to many thriving arts organizations including a professional orchestra, two ballet companies, and several museums including a basketball museum, several choral organizations and a highly respected opera program at the University of Kentucky. There are more than 230 churches and synagogues in Lexington, representing 38 denominations. Institutions of higher learning in and around the city include the University of Kentucky, Lexington Theological Seminary, the National College of Business and Technology, Georgetown College, Kentucky State University, and Transylvania University. Since its opening in 1982, the Kentucky World Trade Center has organized high-profile trade programs featuring business and political leaders from Asia, Europe, and the Middle East. The Commonwealth of Kentucky has emerged as a leader among the 50 states in expanding its international trade.

Lexington has a definite continental climate, temperate and well-suited to a varied plant and animal life. The area is subject to rather sudden and sweeping temperature changes, generally of short duration. Temperatures below zero and above 100 degrees are relatively rare.

Rankings

General Rankings

- Lexington was selected as one of America's best cities by *Bloomberg Businessweek*. The city ranked #25 out of 50. Criteria: leisure attributes (the number of restaurants, bars, libraries, museums, professional sports teams, and park acres by population); educational attributes (public school performance, the number of colleges, and graduate degree holders); economic factors (2011 income and June and July 2012 unemployment); crime; and air quality. *Bloomberg BusinessWeek, "America's Best Cities," September 26, 2012*

- Lexington appeared on RelocateAmerica's list of best places to live in America. The annual "Top 100 Places to Live" list recognizes the top communities as nominated by their residents & local businesses. RelocateAmerica's Research Group determined the list based on review of various data gathered for economic, employment, housing, education, industry, opportunity, environment and recreation along with feedback from area leaders and residents. *RelocateAmerica.com, "Top 100 Places to Live for 2011"*

- The Lexington metro area was selected as one of 10 "Best Value Cities" for 2011 by *Kiplinger.com* The area ranked #6. Criteria: vibrant economy; low cost of living; abundant lifestyle amenities. *Kiplinger.com, "Best Value Cities 2011"*

Business/Finance Rankings

- Recognizing the sizeable percentage of American workers who are self-employed, NerdWallet editors assessed the country's cities according to percentage of freelancers, median rental costs, and affordability of median healthcare costs. By these criteria, Lexington placed #7 among the best cities for independent workers. *www.nerdwallet.com, "Best Cities for Freelancers," February 25, 2014*

- Lexington was cited as one of America's top metros for new and expanded facility projects in 2013. The area ranked #8 in the mid-sized metro area category (population 200,000 to 1 million). *Site Selection, "Top Metros of 2013," March 2014*

- The Lexington metro area appeared on the Milken Institute "2013 Best Performing Cities" list. Rank: #44 out of 200 large metro areas. Criteria: job growth; wage and salary growth; high-tech output growth. *Milken Institute, "Best-Performing Cities 2013," December 2013*

- *Forbes* ranked the 200 most populous metro areas in the U.S. in terms of the "Best Places for Business and Careers." The Lexington metro area was ranked #27. Criteria: costs (business and living); job growth (past and projected); income growth; educational attainment (college and high school); projected economic growth; cultural and recreational opportunities; net migration patterns; number of highly ranked colleges. *Forbes, "The Best Places for Business and Careers," August 7, 2013*

Children/Family Rankings

- Lexington was selected as one of the best cities for families to live by *Parenting* magazine. The city ranked #29 out of 100. Criteria: education; health; community; *Parenting's* Culture & Charm Index. *Parenting.com, "The 2012 Best Cities for Families List"*

- Lexington was chosen as one of America's 100 best communities for young people. The winners were selected based upon detailed information provided about each community's efforts to fulfill five essential promises critical to the well-being of young people: caring adults who are actively involved in their lives; safe places in which to learn and grow; a healthy start toward adulthood; an effective education that builds marketable skills; and opportunities to help others. *America's Promise Alliance, "100 Best Communities for Young People, 2012"*

Dating/Romance Rankings

- Of the 100 U.S. cities surveyed by *Men's Health* in its quest to identify the nation's best cities for dating and forming relationships, Lexington was ranked #40 for online dating (#1 = best). *Men's Health, "The Best and Worst Cities for Online Dating," January 30, 2013*

Education Rankings

- *Men's Health* ranked 100 U.S. cities in terms of their education levels. Lexington was ranked #16 (#1 = most educated city). Criteria: high school graduation rates; school enrollment; educational attainment; number of households who have outstanding student loans; number of households whose members have taken adult-education courses. *Men's Health, "Where School Is In: The Most and Least Educated Cities," September 12, 2011*

- Lexington was selected as one of America's most literate cities. The city ranked #18 out of the 77 largest U.S. cities. Criteria: number of booksellers; library resources; Internet resources; educational attainment; periodical publishing resources; newspaper circulation. *Central Connecticut State University, "America's Most Literate Cities, 2013"*

Environmental Rankings

- The Lexington metro area came in at #199 for the relative comfort of its climate on Sperling's list of "chill cities," as measured by the Sperling Heat Index. All 361 metro areas are included. Criteria included daytime high temperatures, nighttime low temperatures, dew point, and relative humidity at the high temperatures. *www.bertsperling.com, "Sperling's Chill Cities," July 18, 2013*

- Sperling's BestPlaces assessed 379 metropolitan areas of the United States for the likelihood of dangerously extreme weather events or earthquakes. In general the Southeast and South-Central regions have the highest risk of weather extremes and earthquakes, while the Pacific Northwest enjoys the lowest risk. Of the least risky metropolitan areas, the Lexington metro area was ranked #228. *www.bestplaces.net, "Safest Places from Natural Disasters," April 2011*

- Lexington was selected as one of 22 "Smarter Cities" for energy by the Natural Resources Defense Council. Criteria: investment in green power; energy efficiency measures; conservation. *Natural Resources Defense Council, "2010 Smarter Cities," July 19, 2010*

Food/Drink Rankings

- *Men's Health* ranked 100 major U.S. cities in terms of alcohol intoxication. Lexington ranked #86 (#1 = most sober).Criteria: binge drinking; alcohol-related traffic accidents, arrests, and fatalities. *Men's Health, "The Drunkest Cities in America," November 19, 2013*

Health/Fitness Rankings

- The Lexington metro area was identified as one of the worst cities for bed bugs in America by pest control company Orkin. The area ranked #40 out of 50 based on the number of bed bug treatments Orkin performed from January to December 2013. *Orkin, "Chicago Tops Bed Bug Cities List for Second Year in a Row," January 16, 2014*

- *Men's Health* ranked 100 major U.S. cities in terms of the best and worst cities for men. Lexington ranked #32. Criteria: thirty-three data points were examined covering health, fitness, and quality of life. *Men's Health, "The Best & Worst Cities for Men 2014," December 6, 2013*

- The Lexington metro area appeared in the 2013 Gallup-Healthways Well-Being Index. The area ranked #87 out of 189. The Gallup-Healthways Well-Being Index score is an average of six sub-indexes, which individually examine life evaluation, emotional health, work environment, physical health, healthy behaviors, and access to basic necessities. Results are based on telephone interviews conducted as part of the Gallup-Healthways Well-Being Index survey January 2–December 29, 2012, and January 2–December 30, 2013, with a random sample of 531,630 adults, aged 18 and older, living in metropolitan areas in the 50 U.S. states and the District of Columbia. *Gallup-Healthways, "State of American Well-Being," March 25, 2014*

- *Men's Health* ranked 100 U.S. cities in terms of their activity levels. Lexington was ranked #100 (#1 = most active city). Criteria: where and how often residents exercise; percentage of households that watch more than 15 hours of cable television a week and buy more than 11 video games a year; death rate from deep-vein thrombosis, a condition linked to sitting for extended periods of time. *Men's Health, "Where Sit Happens: The Most and Least Active Cities in America," June 20, 2011*

Real Estate Rankings

- Lexington was ranked #234 out of 283 metro areas in terms of house price appreciation in 2013 (#1 = highest rate). *Federal Housing Finance Agency, House Price Index, 4th Quarter 2013*

- The Lexington metro area was identified as one of the 20 worst housing markets in the U.S. in 2013. The area ranked #17 out of 173 markets with a home price appreciation of -4.6%. Criteria: year-over-year change of median sales price of existing single-family homes between the 4th quarter of 2012 and the 4th quarter of 2013. *National Association of Realtors®, Median Sales Price of Existing Single-Family Homes for Metropolitan Areas, 4th Quarter 2013*

- Lexington was selected as one of the best college towns for renters by ApartmentRatings.com." The area ranked #69 out of 87. Overall satisfaction ratings were ranked using thousands of user submitted scores for hundreds of apartment complexes located in cities and towns that are home to the 100 largest four-year institutions in the U.S. *ApartmentRatings.com, "2011 College Town Renter Satisfaction Rankings"*

Safety Rankings

- Allstate ranked the 200 largest cities in America in terms of driver safety. Lexington ranked #48. Allstate researchers analyzed internal property damage claims over a two-year period from January 2010 to December 2011. A weighted average of the two-year numbers determined the annual percentages. *Allstate, "Allstate America's Best Drivers Report®, August 27, 2013"*

- The National Insurance Crime Bureau ranked 380 metro areas in the U.S. in terms of per capita rates of vehicle theft. The Lexington metro area ranked #147 (#1 = highest rate). Criteria: number of vehicle theft offenses per 100,000 inhabitants in 2012. *National Insurance Crime Bureau, "Hot Spots 2012," June 26, 2013*

Seniors/Retirement Rankings

- From its Best Cities for Successful Aging indexes, the Milken Institute generated rankings for metropolitan areas, weighing data in eight categories—general indicators, health care, wellness, living arrangements, transportation and general accessibility, financial well-being, education and employment, and community participation. The Lexington metro area was ranked #33 overall in the small metro area category. *Milken Institute, "Best Cities for Successful Aging," July 2012*

Sports/Recreation Rankings

- Lexington appeared on the *Sporting News* list of the "Best Sports Cities" for 2011. The area ranked #70 out of 271. Criteria: the magazine takes a 12-month snapshot of each city's sports, putting a heavy premium on regular-season won-lost records (from the most recently completed season). Other criteria include: playoff berths, bowl appearances and tournament bids; championships; applicable power ratings; quality of competition; overall fan fervor (measured in part by attendance); abundance of teams (rewarding quality over quantity); stadium and arena quality; ticket availability and prices; franchise ownership; and marquee appeal of athletes. *Sporting News, "Best Sports Cities 2011," October 4, 2011*

- Lexington appeared on the *Sporting News* list of the "Best Sports Cities" for 2011. The area ranked #70 out of 271. Criteria: a 12-month snapshot of regular-season won-lost records (from the most recently completed season). Other criteria include: playoff berths, bowl appearances and tournament bids; championships; applicable power ratings; quality of competition; overall fan fervor (measured in part by attendance); abundance of teams (quality over quantity); stadium and arena quality; ticket availability and prices; franchise ownership; and marquee appeal of athletes. *Sporting News, "Best Sports Cities 2011," October 4, 2011*

- Lexington was selected as one of the most playful cities in the U.S. by KaBOOM! The organization's Playful City USA initiative honors cities and towns across the nation for a vision, plan and commitment to creating an agenda for play. Criteria: creating a local play commission or task force; designing an annual action plan for play; conducting a play space audit; outlining a financial investment in play for the current fiscal year; and proclaiming and celebrating an annual "play day." *KaBOOM! National Campaign for Play, "2013 Playful City USA Communities"*

Transportation Rankings

- NerdWallet surveyed average annual car insurance premiums in 125 U.S. cities to identify the least expensive U.S. cities in which to insure a car. Locations with no-fault insurance laws was a strong determinant. Lexington came in at #16 for the most expensive rates. *www.nerdwallet.com, "Best Cities for Cheap Car Insurance," February 3, 2014*

Women/Minorities Rankings

- *Women's Health* examined U.S. cities and identified the 100 best cities for women. Lexington was ranked #51. Criteria: 30 categories were examined from obesity and breast cancer rates to commuting times and hours spent working out. *Women's Health, "Best Cities for Women 2012"*

Miscellaneous Rankings

- Using Musicmetric's Digital Music Index (DMI), CNBC ranked results for music piracy by way of the file-sharing protocol BitTorrent. Lexington was ranked #4 among American cities. *CNBC.com, "Florida City Named 'Pirate Capital' of Music World," October 8, 2012*

- *Men's Health* ranked 100 U.S. cities by their level of sadness. Lexington was ranked #22 (#1 = saddest city). Criteria: suicide rates; unemployment rates; percentage of households that use antidepressants; percent of population who report feeling blue all or most of the time. *Men's Health, "Frown Towns," November 28, 2011*

Business Environment

CITY FINANCES

City Government Finances

Component	2011 ($000)	2011 ($ per capita)
Total Revenues	675,261	2,420
Total Expenditures	517,955	1,856
Debt Outstanding	1,005,907	3,605
Cash and Securities[1]	894,023	3,204

Note: (1) Cash and security holdings of a government at the close of its fiscal year, including those of its dependent agencies, utilities, and liquor stores.
Source: U.S Census Bureau, State & Local Government Finances 2011

City Government Revenue by Source

Source	2011 ($000)	2011 ($ per capita)
General Revenue		
From Federal Government	37,110	133
From State Government	16,546	59
From Local Governments	22,064	79
Taxes		
Property	77,604	278
Sales and Gross Receipts	39,726	142
Personal Income	153,648	551
Corporate Income	30,210	108
Motor Vehicle License	187	1
Other Taxes	2,852	10
Current Charges	168,854	605
Liquor Store	0	0
Utility	2,682	10
Employee Retirement	101,525	364

Source: U.S Census Bureau, State & Local Government Finances 2011

City Government Expenditures by Function

Function	2011 ($000)	2011 ($ per capita)	2011 (%)
General Direct Expenditures			
Air Transportation	11,037	40	2.1
Corrections	23,756	85	4.6
Education	0	0	0.0
Employment Security Administration	0	0	0.0
Financial Administration	4,000	14	0.8
Fire Protection	46,609	167	9.0
General Public Buildings	0	0	0.0
Governmental Administration, Other	115,032	412	22.2
Health	27,849	100	5.4
Highways	17,195	62	3.3
Hospitals	0	0	0.0
Housing and Community Development	3,900	14	0.8
Interest on General Debt	18,833	67	3.6
Judicial and Legal	3,023	11	0.6
Libraries	12,672	45	2.4
Parking	10,318	37	2.0
Parks and Recreation	9,341	33	1.8
Police Protection	49,753	178	9.6
Public Welfare	9,319	33	1.8
Sewerage	38,388	138	7.4
Solid Waste Management	40,308	144	7.8
Veterans' Services	0	0	0.0
Liquor Store	0	0	0.0
Utility	20,853	75	4.0
Employee Retirement	41,939	150	8.1

Source: U.S Census Bureau, State & Local Government Finances 2011

DEMOGRAPHICS

Population Growth

Area	1990 Census	2000 Census	2010 Census	Population Growth (%)	
				1990-2000	2000-2010
City	225,366	260,512	295,803	15.6	13.5
MSA[1]	348,428	408,326	472,099	17.2	15.6
U.S.	248,709,873	281,421,906	308,745,538	13.2	9.7

Note: (1) Figures cover the Lexington-Fayette, KY Metropolitan Statistical Area—see Appendix B for areas included
Source: U.S. Census Bureau, Census 1990, 2000, 2010

Household Size

Area	Persons in Household (%)							Average Household Size
	One	Two	Three	Four	Five	Six	Seven or More	
City	33.2	32.7	16.0	11.8	3.9	1.6	0.7	2.36
MSA[1]	30.1	33.7	16.8	12.5	4.5	1.7	0.8	2.43
U.S.	27.6	33.5	15.7	13.2	6.1	2.4	1.5	2.63

Note: (1) Figures cover the Lexington-Fayette, KY Metropolitan Statistical Area—see Appendix B for areas included
Source: U.S. Census Bureau, 2010-2012 American Community Survey 3-Year Estimates

Race

Area	White Alone[2] (%)	Black Alone[2] (%)	Asian Alone[2] (%)	AIAN[3] Alone[2] (%)	NHOPI[4] Alone[2] (%)	Other Race Alone[2] (%)	Two or More Races (%)
City	76.3	14.1	3.4	0.2	0.0	3.0	2.9
MSA[1]	81.8	10.8	2.4	0.2	0.0	2.5	2.3
U.S.	74.0	12.6	4.9	0.8	0.2	4.7	2.8

Note: (1) Figures cover the Lexington-Fayette, KY Metropolitan Statistical Area—see Appendix B for areas included; (2) Alone is defined as not being in combination with one or more other races; (3) American Indian and Alaska Native; (4) Native Hawaiian and Other Pacific Islander
Source: U.S. Census Bureau, 2010-2012 American Community Survey 3-Year Estimates

Hispanic or Latino Origin

Area	Total (%)	Mexican (%)	Puerto Rican (%)	Cuban (%)	Other (%)
City	6.9	5.3	0.3	0.2	1.2
MSA[1]	5.9	4.6	0.3	0.1	0.9
U.S.	16.6	10.7	1.6	0.6	3.7

Note: Persons of Hispanic or Latino origin can be of any race; (1) Figures cover the Lexington-Fayette, KY Metropolitan Statistical Area—see Appendix B for areas included
Source: U.S. Census Bureau, 2010-2012 American Community Survey 3-Year Estimates

Segregation

Type	Segregation Indices[1]				Percent Change		
	1990	2000	2010	2010 Rank[2]	1990-2000	1990-2010	2000-2010
Black/White	n/a	n/a	n/a	n/a	n/a	n/a	n/a
Asian/White	n/a	n/a	n/a	n/a	n/a	n/a	n/a
Hispanic/White	n/a	n/a	n/a	n/a	n/a	n/a	n/a

Note: All figures cover the Metropolitan Statistical Area—see Appendix B for areas included; Figures are based on an analysis of 1990, 2000, and 2010 Census Decennial Census tract data by William H. Frey, Brookings Institution and the University of Michigan Social Science Data Analysis Network. In this analysis all racial groups (whites, blacks, and asians) are non-Hispanic members of those races. Hispanics are shown as a separate category;
(1) Segregation Indices are Dissimilarity Indices that measure the degree to which the minority group is distributed differently than whites across census tracts. They range from 0 (complete integration) to 100 (complete segregation) where the value indicates the percentage of the minority group that needs to move to be distributed exactly like whites; (2) Ranges from 1 (most segregated) to 102 (least segregated); n/a not available.
Source: www.CensusScope.org

Ancestry

Area	German	Irish	English	American	Italian	Polish	French[2]	Scottish	Dutch
City	13.8	12.6	11.6	15.7	3.0	1.3	2.0	2.5	1.1
MSA[1]	13.9	12.8	11.5	20.0	2.6	1.2	1.9	2.6	1.1
U.S.	15.2	11.1	8.2	7.2	5.6	3.1	2.8	1.7	1.4

Note: Figures are the percentage of the total population reporting a particular ancestry. The nine most commonly reported ancestries in the U.S. are shown. Figures include multiple ancestries (e.g. if a person reported being Irish and Italian, they were included in both columns); (1) Figures cover the Lexington-Fayette, KY Metropolitan Statistical Area—see Appendix B for areas included; (2) Excludes Basque
Source: U.S. Census Bureau, 2010-2012 American Community Survey 3-Year Estimates

Foreign-Born Population

Area	Percent of Population Born in								
	Any Foreign Country	Mexico	Asia	Europe	Carribean	South America	Central America[2]	Africa	Canada
City	8.9	3.0	3.2	0.8	0.2	0.3	0.5	0.6	0.2
MSA[1]	6.8	2.5	2.2	0.7	0.2	0.2	0.4	0.4	0.1
U.S.	13.0	3.7	3.7	1.6	1.2	0.9	1.0	0.5	0.3

Note: (1) Figures cover the Lexington-Fayette, KY Metropolitan Statistical Area—see Appendix B for areas included; (2) Excludes Mexico.
Source: U.S. Census Bureau, 2010-2012 American Community Survey 3-Year Estimates

Marital Status

Area	Never Married	Now Married[2]	Separated	Widowed	Divorced
City	37.5	43.3	1.9	4.5	12.8
MSA[1]	32.9	47.3	2.1	4.9	12.8
U.S.	32.4	48.4	2.2	6.0	11.0

Note: Figures are percentages and cover the population 15 years of age and older; (1) Figures cover the Lexington-Fayette, KY Metropolitan Statistical Area—see Appendix B for areas included; (2) Excludes separated
Source: U.S. Census Bureau, 2010-2012 American Community Survey 3-Year Estimates

Age

Area	Percent of Population									Median Age
	Under Age 5	Age 5–19	Age 20–34	Age 35–44	Age 45–54	Age 55–64	Age 65–74	Age 75–84	Age 85+	
City	6.4	18.3	27.1	13.3	13.1	11.2	5.9	3.4	1.4	33.8
MSA[1]	6.5	19.3	23.8	13.6	13.8	11.7	6.4	3.6	1.4	35.3
U.S.	6.4	20.1	20.5	13.1	14.3	12.2	7.3	4.2	1.8	37.3

Note: (1) Figures cover the Lexington-Fayette, KY Metropolitan Statistical Area—see Appendix B for areas included
Source: U.S. Census Bureau, 2010-2012 American Community Survey 3-Year Estimates

Gender

Area	Males	Females	Males per 100 Females
City	148,398	152,813	97.1
MSA[1]	235,376	243,766	96.6
U.S.	153,276,055	158,333,314	96.8

Note: (1) Figures cover the Lexington-Fayette, KY Metropolitan Statistical Area—see Appendix B for areas included
Source: U.S. Census Bureau, 2010-2012 American Community Survey 3-Year Estimates

Religious Groups by Family

Area	Catholic	Baptist	Non-Den.	Methodist[2]	Lutheran	LDS[3]	Pente-costal	Presby-terian[4]	Muslim[5]	Judaism
MSA[1]	6.8	24.9	2.4	5.9	0.4	1.1	2.1	1.4	0.1	0.3
U.S.	19.1	9.3	4.0	4.0	2.3	2.0	1.9	1.6	0.8	0.7

Note: Figures are the number of adherents as a percentage of the total population; (1) Figures cover the Lexington-Fayette, KY Metropolitan Statistical Area—see Appendix B for areas included; (2) Methodist/Pietist; (3) Latter Day Saints; (4) Reformed; (5) Figures are estimates
Source: Association of Statisticians of American Religious Bodies, 2010 U.S. Religion Census: Religious Congregations & Membership Study

Religious Groups by Tradition

Area	Catholic	Evangelical Protestant	Mainline Protestant	Other Tradition	Black Protestant	Orthodox
MSA[1]	6.8	28.3	10.3	1.7	2.1	0.2
U.S.	19.1	16.2	7.3	4.3	1.6	0.3

Note: Figures are the number of adherents as a percentage of the total population; (1) Figures cover the Lexington-Fayette, KY Metropolitan Statistical Area—see Appendix B for areas included
Source: Association of Statisticians of American Religious Bodies, 2010 U.S. Religion Census: Religious Congregations & Membership Study

ECONOMY

Gross Metropolitan Product

Area	2011	2012	2013	2014	Rank[2]
MSA[1]	23.4	23.9	24.7	25.9	90

Note: Figures are in billions of dollars; (1) Figures cover the Lexington-Fayette, KY Metropolitan Statistical Area—see Appendix B for areas included; (2) Rank is based on 2014 data and ranges from 1 to 363
Source: The United States Conference of Mayors, U.S. Metro Economies: Outlook—Gross Metropolitan Product, with Metro Employment Projections, November 2013

Economic Growth

Area	2011 (%)	2012 (%)	2013 (%)	2014 (%)	Rank[2]
MSA[1]	1.2	0.6	2.0	2.9	73
U.S.	1.6	2.5	1.7	2.5	–

Note: Figures are real gross metropolitan product (GMP) growth rates and represent annual average percent change; (1) Figures cover the Lexington-Fayette, KY Metropolitan Statistical Area—see Appendix B for areas included; (2) Rank is based on 2013 data and ranges from 1 to 363
Source: The United States Conference of Mayors, U.S. Metro Economies: Outlook—Gross Metropolitan Product, with Metro Employment Projections, November 2013

Metropolitan Area Exports

Area	2007	2008	2009	2010	2011	2012	Rank[2]
MSA[1]	2,671.2	2,490.6	2,260.2	2,400.4	2,170.5	2,462.1	86

Note: Figures are in millions of dollars; (1) Figures cover the Lexington-Fayette, KY Metropolitan Statistical Area—see Appendix B for areas included; (2) Rank is based on 2012 data and ranges from 1 to 369
Source: U.S. Department of Commerce, International Trade Administration, Office of Trade & Industry Information, Manufacturing & Services, data extracted April 1, 2014

INCOME

Income

Area	Per Capita ($)	Median Household ($)	Average Household ($)
City	28,369	47,785	68,100
MSA[1]	27,294	48,446	67,120
U.S.	27,385	51,771	71,579

Note: (1) Figures cover the Lexington-Fayette, KY Metropolitan Statistical Area—see Appendix B for areas included
Source: U.S. Census Bureau, 2010-2012 American Community Survey 3-Year Estimates

Household Income Distribution

Area	Percent of Households Earning							
	Under $15,000	$15,000 -24,999	$25,000 -34,999	$35,000 -49,999	$50,000 -74,999	$75,000 -99,000	$100,000 -149,999	$150,000 and up
City	15.9	11.2	10.8	14.0	16.8	11.1	11.9	8.3
MSA[1]	15.3	11.0	10.9	14.2	17.4	11.6	12.2	7.4
U.S.	13.1	11.0	10.5	13.7	18.1	11.9	12.5	9.1

Note: (1) Figures cover the Lexington-Fayette, KY Metropolitan Statistical Area—see Appendix B for areas included
Source: U.S. Census Bureau, 2010-2012 American Community Survey 3-Year Estimates

Poverty Rate

Area	All Ages	Under 18 Years Old	18 to 64 Years Old	65 Years and Over
City	18.5	22.1	19.0	7.9
MSA[1]	17.2	22.1	17.1	8.4
U.S.	15.7	22.2	14.6	9.3

Note: Figures are percentage of people whose income during the past 12 months was below the poverty level;
(1) Figures cover the Lexington-Fayette, KY Metropolitan Statistical Area—see Appendix B for areas included
Source: U.S. Census Bureau, 2010-2012 American Community Survey 3-Year Estimates

Personal Bankruptcy Filing Rate

Area	2008	2009	2010	2011	2012	2013
Fayette County	3.59	4.58	4.57	3.93	3.65	3.42
U.S.	3.53	4.61	4.97	4.37	3.76	3.29

Note: Numbers are per 1,000 population and include Chapter 7 and Chapter 13 filings
Source: Federal Deposit Insurance Corporation, Regional Economic Conditions, March 20, 2014

EMPLOYMENT

Labor Force and Employment

Area	Civilian Labor Force			Workers Employed		
	Dec. 2012	Dec. 2013	% Chg.	Dec. 2012	Dec. 2013	% Chg.
City	159,498	156,989	-1.6	150,161	148,265	-1.3
MSA[1]	247,670	243,841	-1.5	232,678	229,740	-1.3
U.S.	154,904,000	154,408,000	-0.3	143,060,000	144,423,000	1.0

Note: Data is not seasonally adjusted and covers workers 16 years of age and older; (1) Metropolitan Statistical Area—see Appendix B for areas included
Source: Bureau of Labor Statistics, Local Area Unemployment Statistics

Unemployment Rate

Area	2013											
	Jan.	Feb.	Mar.	Apr.	May	Jun.	Jul.	Aug.	Sep.	Oct.	Nov.	Dec.
City	6.5	6.6	6.6	5.9	6.4	7.1	6.4	6.1	6.2	6.4	6.1	5.6
MSA[1]	6.8	6.8	6.8	6.0	6.5	7.3	6.6	6.2	6.4	6.6	6.3	5.8
U.S.	8.5	8.1	7.6	7.1	7.3	7.8	7.7	7.3	7.0	7.0	6.6	6.5

Note: Data is not seasonally adjusted and covers workers 16 years of age and older; All figures are percentages;
(1) Metropolitan Statistical Area—see Appendix B for areas included
Source: Bureau of Labor Statistics, Local Area Unemployment Statistics

Employment by Occupation

Occupation Classification	City (%)	MSA[1] (%)	U.S. (%)
Management, Business, Science, and Arts	42.4	39.6	36.0
Natural Resources, Construction, and Maintenance	6.4	8.2	9.1
Production, Transportation, and Material Moving	8.6	10.9	12.0
Sales and Office	23.9	23.5	24.7
Service	18.7	17.8	18.2

Note: Figures cover employed civilians 16 years of age and older; (1) Figures cover the Lexington-Fayette, KY Metropolitan Statistical Area—see Appendix B for areas included
Source: U.S. Census Bureau, 2010-2012 American Community Survey 3-Year Estimates

Employment by Industry

Sector	MSA[1] Number of Employees	MSA[1] Percent of Total	U.S. Percent of Total
Construction	n/a	n/a	4.2
Education and Health Services	33,600	12.8	15.5
Financial Activities	9,600	3.7	5.7
Government	54,300	20.7	16.1
Information	5,600	2.1	1.9
Leisure and Hospitality	25,600	9.8	10.2
Manufacturing	29,400	11.2	8.7
Mining and Logging	n/a	n/a	0.6
Other Services	9,100	3.5	3.9
Professional and Business Services	37,100	14.1	13.7
Retail Trade	28,800	11.0	11.4
Transportation and Utilities	9,200	3.5	3.8
Wholesale Trade	9,600	3.7	4.2

Note: Figures cover non-farm employment as of December 2013 and are not seasonally adjusted;
(1) Metropolitan Statistical Area—see Appendix B for areas included; n/a not available
Source: Bureau of Labor Statistics, Current Employment Statistics, Employment, Hours, and Earnings

Occupations with Greatest Projected Employment Growth: 2010 – 2020

Occupation[1]	2010 Employment	2020 Projected Employment	Numeric Employment Change	Percent Employment Change
Registered Nurses	47,450	59,370	11,920	25.1
Retail Salespersons	56,670	65,110	8,440	14.9
Laborers and Freight, Stock, and Material Movers, Hand	37,440	43,920	6,480	17.3
Heavy and Tractor-Trailer Truck Drivers	27,810	33,180	5,370	19.3
Combined Food Preparation and Serving Workers, Including Fast Food	52,180	57,220	5,040	9.7
Nursing Aides, Orderlies, and Attendants	25,440	30,470	5,030	19.8
Childcare Workers	19,240	24,140	4,900	25.5
Receptionists and Information Clerks	16,960	21,700	4,740	27.9
Personal Care Aides	6,820	11,430	4,610	67.6
Customer Service Representatives	28,670	33,110	4,440	15.5

Note: Projections cover Kentucky; (1) Sorted by numeric employment change
Source: www.projectionscentral.com, State Occupational Projections, 2010–2020 Long-Term Projections

Fastest Growing Occupations: 2010 – 2020

Occupation[1]	2010 Employment	2020 Projected Employment	Numeric Employment Change	Percent Employment Change
Home Health Aides	3,750	6,310	2,560	68.3
Personal Care Aides	6,820	11,430	4,610	67.6
Helpers—Brickmasons, Blockmasons, Stonemasons, and Tile and Marble Setters	680	1,040	360	52.9
Helpers—Carpenters	730	1,100	370	50.7
Veterinary Technologists and Technicians	1,120	1,670	550	49.1
Marriage and Family Therapists	230	340	110	47.8
Occupational Therapy Assistants	360	530	170	47.2
Athletic Trainers	440	630	190	43.2
Mental Health Counselors	1,190	1,700	510	42.9
Physical Therapist Assistants	1,380	1,970	590	42.8

Note: Projections cover Kentucky; (1) Sorted by percent employment change and excludes occupations with numeric employment change less than 100
Source: www.projectionscentral.com, State Occupational Projections, 2010–2020 Long-Term Projections

Average Wages

Occupation	$/Hr.	Occupation	$/Hr.
Accountants and Auditors	33.61	Maids and Housekeeping Cleaners	9.22
Automotive Mechanics	17.21	Maintenance and Repair Workers	16.36
Bookkeepers	16.87	Marketing Managers	49.27
Carpenters	17.87	Nuclear Medicine Technologists	28.83
Cashiers	9.08	Nurses, Licensed Practical	18.63
Clerks, General Office	14.05	Nurses, Registered	27.91
Clerks, Receptionists/Information	12.73	Nursing Assistants	11.95
Clerks, Shipping/Receiving	14.70	Packers and Packagers, Hand	9.82
Computer Programmers	30.61	Physical Therapists	39.27
Computer Systems Analysts	36.66	Postal Service Mail Carriers	24.65
Computer User Support Specialists	16.81	Real Estate Brokers	n/a
Cooks, Restaurant	10.30	Retail Salespersons	11.71
Dentists	101.69	Sales Reps., Exc. Tech./Scientific	24.93
Electrical Engineers	41.91	Sales Reps., Tech./Scientific	35.03
Electricians	20.66	Secretaries, Exc. Legal/Med./Exec.	15.59
Financial Managers	48.10	Security Guards	10.51
First-Line Supervisors/Managers, Sales	17.37	Surgeons	114.35
Food Preparation Workers	10.18	Teacher Assistants	14.70
General and Operations Managers	45.17	Teachers, Elementary School	24.00
Hairdressers/Cosmetologists	13.08	Teachers, Secondary School	24.60
Internists	78.65	Telemarketers	n/a
Janitors and Cleaners	11.35	Truck Drivers, Heavy/Tractor-Trailer	18.81
Landscaping/Groundskeeping Workers	11.35	Truck Drivers, Light/Delivery Svcs.	16.17
Lawyers	47.19	Waiters and Waitresses	8.84

Note: Wage data covers the Lexington-Fayette, KY Metropolitan Statistical Area—see Appendix B for areas included. Hourly wages for elementary/secondary school teachers and teacher assistants were calculated by the editors from annual wage data assuming a 40 hour work week; n/a not available.
Source: Bureau of Labor Statistics, Metro Area Occupational Employment and Wage Estimates, May 2013

RESIDENTIAL REAL ESTATE

Building Permits

Area	Single-Family			Multi-Family			Total		
	2012	2013	Pct. Chg.	2012	2013	Pct. Chg.	2012	2013	Pct. Chg.
City	750	676	-9.9	1,066	223	-79.1	1,816	899	-50.5
MSA[1]	1,218	1,335	9.6	1,100	319	-71.0	2,318	1,654	-28.6
U.S.	518,695	620,802	19.7	310,963	370,020	19.0	829,658	990,822	19.4

Note: (1) Metropolitan Statistical Area—see Appendix B for areas included; figures represent new, privately-owned housing units authorized (unadjusted data); All permit data are based on estimates with imputation.
Source: U.S. Census Bureau, Manufacturing, Mining, and Construction Statistics, Building Permits, 2012, 2013

Homeownership Rate

Area	2006 (%)	2007 (%)	2008 (%)	2009 (%)	2010 (%)	2011 (%)	2012 (%)	2013 (%)
MSA[1]	n/a	n/a	n/a	n/a	n/a	n/a	n/a	n/a
U.S.	68.8	68.1	67.8	67.4	66.9	66.1	65.4	65.1

Note: (1) Figures cover the Lexington-Fayette, KY Metropolitan Statistical Area—see Appendix B for areas included; n/a not available
Source: U.S. Census Bureau, Housing Vacancies and Homeownership Annual Statistics: 2013

Housing Vacancy Rates

Area	Gross Vacancy Rate[2] (%)			Year-Round Vacancy Rate[3] (%)			Rental Vacancy Rate[4] (%)			Homeowner Vacancy Rate[5] (%)		
	2011	2012	2013	2011	2012	2013	2011	2012	2013	2011	2012	2013
MSA[1]	n/a	n/a	n/a	n/a	n/a	n/a	n/a	n/a	n/a	n/a	n/a	n/a
U.S.	14.2	13.8	13.8	11.1	10.8	10.7	9.5	8.7	8.3	2.5	2.0	2.0

Note: (1) Figures cover the Lexington-Fayette, KY Metropolitan Statistical Area—see Appendix B for areas included; (2) The percentage of the total housing inventory that is vacant; (3) The percentage of the housing inventory (excluding seasonal units) that is year-round vacant; (4) The percentage of rental inventory that is vacant for rent; (5) The percentage of homeowner inventory that is vacant for sale; n/a not available
Source: U.S. Census Bureau, Housing Vacancies and Homeownership Annual Statistics: 2013

TAXES

State Corporate Income Tax Rates

State	Tax Rate (%)	Income Brackets ($)	Num. of Brackets	Financial Institution Tax Rate (%)[a]	Federal Income Tax Ded.
Kentucky	4.0 - 6.0	50,000 - 100,001	3	(a)	No

Note: Tax rates as of January 1, 2014; (a) Rates listed are the corporate income tax rate applied to financial institutions or excise taxes based on income. Some states have other taxes based upon the value of deposits or shares.
Source: Federation of Tax Administrators, "State Corporate Income Tax Rates, 2014"

State Individual Income Tax Rates

State	Tax Rate (%)	Income Brackets ($)	Num. of Brackets	Personal Exempt. ($)[1] Single	Personal Exempt. ($)[1] Dependents	Fed. Inc. Tax Ded.
Kentucky	2.0 - 6.0	3,000 - 75,001	6	20 (c)	20 (c)	No

Note: Tax rates as of January 1, 2014; Local- and county-level taxes are not included; n/a not applicable; (1) Married joint filers generally receive double the single exemption; (c) The personal exemption takes the form of a tax credit instead of a deduction
Source: Federation of Tax Administrators, "State Individual Income Tax Rates, 2014"

Various State and Local Tax Rates

State	State and Local Sales and Use (%)	State Sales and Use (%)	Gasoline[1] (¢/gal.)	Cigarette[2] ($/pack)	Spirits[3] ($/gal.)	Wine[4] ($/gal.)	Beer[5] ($/gal.)
Kentucky	6.0	6.00	30.80	0.600	6.76 (h)	3.56 (o)	0.78

Note: All tax rates as of January 1, 2014; (1) The American Petroleum Institute has developed a methodology for determining the average tax rate on a gallon of fuel. Rates may include any of the following: excise taxes, environmental fees, storage tank fees, other fees or taxes, general sales tax, and local taxes. In states where gasoline is subject to the general sales tax, or where the fuel tax is based on the average sale price, the average rate determined by API is sensitive to changes in the price of gasoline. States that fully or partially apply general sales taxes to gasoline: CA, CO, GA, IL, IN, MI, NY; (2) The federal excise tax of $1.0066 per pack and local taxes are not included; (3) Rates are those applicable to off-premise sales of 40% alcohol by volume (a.b.v.) distilled spirits in 750ml containers. Local excise taxes are excluded; (4) Rates are those applicable to off-premise sales of 11% a.b.v. non-carbonated wine in 750ml containers; (5) Rates are those applicable to off-premise sales of 4.7% a.b.v. beer in 12 ounce containers; (h) Includes the wholesale tax rate of 11%, converted to a gallonage excise tax rate; (o) Includes the wholesale tax rate of 11%, converted into a gallonage excise tax rate.
Source: Tax Foundation, 2014 Facts & Figures: How Does Your State Compare?

State Business Tax Climate Index Rankings

State	Overall Rank	Corporate Tax Index Rank	Individual Income Tax Index Rank	Sales Tax Index Rank	Unemployment Insurance Tax Index Rank	Property Tax Index Rank
Kentucky	27	27	29	10	48	17

Note: The index is a measure of how each state's tax laws affect economic performance. The lower the rank, the more favorable a state's tax system is for business. States without a given tax are given a ranking of 1. The scores/rankings for the District of Columbia do not affect other states. The 2014 index represents the tax climate as of July 1, 2013.
Source: Tax Foundation, State Business Tax Climate Index 2014

COMMERCIAL UTILITIES

Typical Monthly Electric Bills

Area	Commercial Service ($/month) 1,500 kWh	Commercial Service ($/month) 40 kW demand 14,000 kWh	Industrial Service ($/month) 1,000 kW demand 200,000 kWh	Industrial Service ($/month) 50,000 kW demand 15,000,000 kWh
City	167	1,361	18,702	1,071,457
Average[1]	197	1,636	25,662	1,485,307

Note: Based on total rates in effect July 1, 2013; (1) average based on 180 utilities surveyed
Source: Edison Electric Institute, Typical Bills and Average Rates Report, Summer 2013

TRANSPORTATION

Means of Transportation to Work

Area	Car/Truck/Van		Public Transportation			Bicycle	Walked	Other Means	Worked at Home
	Drove Alone	Car-pooled	Bus	Subway	Railroad				
City	79.8	9.8	1.5	0.0	0.0	1.1	3.8	0.7	3.4
MSA[1]	80.7	10.0	1.0	0.0	0.0	0.7	3.2	0.6	3.7
U.S.	76.4	9.7	2.6	1.7	0.5	0.6	2.8	1.3	4.3

Note: Figures are percentages and cover workers 16 years of age and older; (1) Figures cover the
Lexington-Fayette, KY Metropolitan Statistical Area—see Appendix B for areas included
Source: U.S. Census Bureau, 2010-2012 American Community Survey 3-Year Estimates

Travel Time to Work

Area	Less Than 10 Minutes	10 to 19 Minutes	20 to 29 Minutes	30 to 44 Minutes	45 to 59 Minutes	60 to 89 Minutes	90 Minutes or More
City	13.0	42.9	25.6	13.1	2.7	1.8	0.9
MSA[1]	15.0	37.3	24.3	16.2	4.1	1.9	1.2
U.S.	13.5	29.8	20.9	20.1	7.5	5.6	2.5

Note: Figures are percentages and include workers 16 years old and over; (1) Figures cover the
Lexington-Fayette, KY Metropolitan Statistical Area—see Appendix B for areas included
Source: U.S. Census Bureau, 2010-2012 American Community Survey 3-Year Estimates

Travel Time Index

Area	1985	1990	1995	2000	2005	2010	2011
Urban Area[1]	n/a	n/a	n/a	n/a	n/a	n/a	n/a
Average[2]	1.09	1.14	1.16	1.19	1.23	1.18	1.18

Note: Travel Time Index—the ratio of travel time in the peak period to the travel time at free-flow conditions.
For example, a value of 1.30 indicates a 20-minute free-flow trip takes 26 minutes in the peak. Free-flow speeds
(60 mph on freeways and 35 mph on principal arterials) are used as the comparison threshold; (1) Data for the
Lexington-Fayette, KY urban area was not available; (2) average of 498 urban areas
Source: Texas Transportation Institute, Urban Mobility Report 2012, December 2012

Public Transportation

Agency Name / Mode of Transportation	Vehicles Operated in Maximum Service	Annual Unlinked Passenger Trips (in thous.)	Annual Passenger Miles (in thous.)
Lexington Transit Authority (LexTran)			
Bus (directly operated)	58	5,058.8	18,573.3
Demand Response (purchased transportation)	39	162.4	1,419.6

Source: Federal Transit Administration, National Transit Database, 2012

Air Transportation

Airport Name and Code / Type of Service	Passenger Airlines[1]	Passenger Enplanements	Freight Carriers[2]	Freight (lbs.)
Bluegrass Airport (LEX)				
Domestic service (U.S. carriers - 2013)	25	538,244	7	649,052
International service (U.S. carriers - 2012)	1	1	4	504,023

Note: (1) Includes all U.S.-based major, minor and commuter airlines that carried at least one passenger during
the year; (2) Includes all U.S.-based airlines and freight carriers that transported at least one lb. of freight during
the year.
Source: Bureau of Transportation Statistics, The Intermodal Transportation Database, Air Carriers: T-100
Domestic Market (U.S. Carriers), 2013; Bureau of Transportation Statistics, The Intermodal Transportation
Database, Air Carriers: T-100 International Market (U.S. Carriers), 2012

Other Transportation Statistics

Major Highways: I-64; I-75
Amtrak Service: No
Major Waterways/Ports: None
Source: Amtrak.com; Google Maps

BUSINESSES

Major Business Headquarters

Company Name	Rankings	
	Fortune[1]	Forbes[2]
No companies listed	-	-

Note: (1) Fortune 500—companies that produce a 10-K are ranked 1 to 500 based on 2012 revenue; (2) all private companies with at least $2 billion in annual revenue through the end of their most current fiscal year are ranked 1 to 224; companies listed are headquartered in the city; dashes indicate no ranking
Source: Fortune, "Fortune 500," May 20, 2013; Forbes, "America's Largest Private Companies," December 18, 2013

Minority- and Women-Owned Businesses

Group	All Firms		Firms with Paid Employees			
	Firms	Sales ($000)	Firms	Sales ($000)	Employees	Payroll ($000)
Asian	673	126,830	226	110,938	1,201	23,448
Black	(s)	(s)	(s)	(s)	(s)	(s)
Hispanic	613	128,947	101	118,374	1,781	59,332
Women	7,066	1,226,430	1,058	1,079,544	9,735	230,831
All Firms	26,074	29,209,551	6,755	28,334,853	145,105	5,312,820

Note: Figures cover firms located in the city; minority- and women-owned business are defined as firms in which the corresponding group own 51% or more of the stock or equity of the company; (s) estimates are suppressed when publication standards are not met
Source: U.S. Census Bureau, 2007 Economic Census, Survey of Business Owners (2012 Survey of Business Owners data will be released starting in June 2015)

HOTELS & CONVENTION CENTERS

Hotels/Motels

Area	5 Star		4 Star		3 Star		2 Star		1 Star		Not Rated	
	Num.	Pct.[3]	Num.	Pct.[3]	Num.	Pct.[3]	Num.	Pct.[3]	Num.	Pct.[3]	Num.	Pct.[3]
City[1]	0	0.0	1	1.0	26	25.7	61	60.4	5	5.0	8	7.9
Total[2]	142	0.9	1,005	6.0	5,147	30.9	8,578	51.4	408	2.4	1,397	8.4

Note: (1) Figures cover Lexington and vicinity; (2) Figures cover all 100 cities in this book; (3) Percentage of hotels which have a given star rating; Star ratings are determined by expedia.com and offer an indication of the general quality of a particular hotel.
Source: expedia.com, April 7, 2014

Major Convention Centers

Name	Overall Space (sq. ft.)	Exhibit Space (sq. ft.)	Meeting Space (sq. ft.)	Meeting Rooms
Lexington Center	130,000	n/a	n/a	n/a

Note: Table includes convention centers located in the Lexington-Fayette, KY metro area; n/a not available
Source: Original research

Living Environment

COST OF LIVING

Cost of Living Index

Composite Index	Groceries	Housing	Utilities	Trans-portation	Health Care	Misc. Goods/Services
89.4	86.1	75.6	101.0	97.9	94.3	94.1

Note: The Cost of Living Index measures regional differences in the cost of consumer goods and services, excluding taxes and non-consumer expenditures, for professional and managerial households in the top income quintile. It is based on more than 50,000 prices covering almost 60 different items for which prices are collected three times a year by chambers of commerce, economic development organizations or university applied economic centers in each participating urban area. The numbers shown should be read as a percentage above or below the national average of 100. For example, a value of 115.4 in the groceries column indicates that grocery prices are 15.4% higher than the national average. Small differences in the index numbers should not be interpreted as significant; Figures cover the Lexington KY urban area.
Source: The Council for Community and Economic Research, ACCRA Cost of Living Index, 2013

Grocery Prices

Area[1]	T-Bone Steak ($/pound)	Frying Chicken ($/pound)	Whole Milk ($/half gal.)	Eggs ($/dozen)	Orange Juice ($/64 oz.)	Coffee ($/11.5 oz.)
City[2]	9.99	1.01	2.11	1.81	3.44	4.09
Avg.	10.19	1.28	2.34	1.81	3.48	4.39
Min.	8.56	0.94	1.44	1.19	2.78	3.40
Max.	14.82	2.28	3.56	3.73	6.23	7.32

*Note: (1) Values for the local area are compared with the average, minimum and maximum values for all 327 areas in the Cost of Living Index; (2) Figures cover the Lexington KY urban area; **T-Bone Steak** (price per pound); **Frying Chicken** (price per pound, whole fryer); **Whole Milk** (half gallon carton); **Eggs** (price per dozen, Grade A, large); **Orange Juice** (64 oz. Tropicana or Florida Natural); **Coffee** (11.5 oz. can, vacuum-packed, Maxwell House, Hills Bros, or Folgers).*
Source: The Council for Community and Economic Research, ACCRA Cost of Living Index, 2013

Housing and Utility Costs

Area[1]	New Home Price ($)	Apartment Rent ($/month)	All Electric ($/month)	Part Electric ($/month)	Other Energy ($/month)	Telephone ($/month)
City[2]	210,972	792	-	83.74	52.77	34.99
Avg.	295,864	900	171.38	91.82	70.12	27.73
Min.	185,506	458	117.80	48.81	33.67	17.16
Max.	1,358,917	3,783	441.68	171.40	372.65	39.47

*Note: (1) Values for the local area are compared with the average, minimum and maximum values for all 327 areas in the Cost of Living Index; (2) Figures cover the Lexington KY urban area; **New Home Price** (2,400 sf living area, 8,000 sf lot, in urban area with full utilities); **Apartment Rent** (950 sf 2 bedroom/1.5 or 2 bath, unfurnished, excluding all utilities except water); **All Electric** (average monthly cost for an all-electric home); **Part Electric** (average monthly cost for a part-electric home); **Other Energy** (average monthly cost for natural gas, fuel oil, coal, wood, and any other forms of energy except electricity); **Telephone** (price includes basic monthly rate for a private residential line plus additional local usage charges incurred by a family of four).*
Source: The Council for Community and Economic Research, ACCRA Cost of Living Index, 2013

Health Care, Transportation, and Other Costs

Area[1]	Doctor ($/visit)	Dentist ($/visit)	Optometrist ($/visit)	Gasoline ($/gallon)	Beauty Salon ($/visit)	Men's Shirt ($)
City[2]	89.24	89.27	68.33	3.48	37.40	22.79
Avg.	101.40	86.48	96.16	3.44	33.87	26.55
Min.	61.67	50.83	50.12	3.08	18.92	12.48
Max.	182.71	152.50	223.78	4.33	68.22	52.03

*Note: (1) Values for the local area are compared with the average, minimum and maximum values for all 327 areas in the Cost of Living Index; (2) Figures cover the Lexington KY urban area; **Doctor** (general practitioners routine exam of an established patient); **Dentist** (adult teeth cleaning and periodic oral examination); **Optometrist** (full vision eye exam for established adult patient); **Gasoline** (one gallon regular unleaded, national brand, including all taxes, cash price at self-service pump if available); **Beauty Salon** (woman's shampoo, trim, and blow-dry); **Men's Shirt** (cotton/polyester dress shirt, pinpoint weave, long sleeves).*
Source: The Council for Community and Economic Research, ACCRA Cost of Living Index, 2013

HOUSING

House Price Index (HPI)

Area	National Ranking[2]	Quarterly Change (%)	One-Year Change (%)	Five-Year Change (%)
MSA[1]	234	-1.83	-0.28	-2.31
U.S.[3]	–	1.20	7.69	4.18

Note: The HPI is a weighted repeat sales index. It measures average price changes in repeat sales or refinancings on the same properties. This information is obtained by reviewing repeat mortgage transactions on single-family properties whose mortgages have been purchased or securitized by Fannie Mae or Freddie Mac in January 1975; (1) Lexington-Fayette, KY Metropolitan Statistical Area—see Appendix B for areas included; (2) Rankings are based on annual percentage change for all metro areas containing at least 15,000 transactions over the last 10 years and ranges from 1 to 283; (3) figures based on a weighted average of Census Division estimates using a seasonally adjusted, purchase-only index; all figures are for the period ending December 31, 2013
Source: Federal Housing Finance Agency, House Price Index, February 25, 2014

Median Single-Family Home Prices

Area	2011	2012	2013p	Percent Change 2012 to 2013
MSA[1]	138.6	143.2	143.8	0.4
U.S. Average	166.2	177.2	197.4	11.4

Note: Figures are median sales prices of existing single-family homes in thousands of dollars; (p) preliminary; n/a not available; (1) Lexington-Fayette, KY Metropolitan Statistical Area—see Appendix B for areas included
Source: National Association of Realtors, Median Sales Price of Existing Single-Family Homes for Metropolitan Areas, 4th Quarter 2013

Qualifying Income Based on Median Sales Price of Existing Single-Family Homes

Area	With 5% Down ($)	With 10% Down ($)	With 20% Down ($)
MSA[1]	31,977	30,294	26,928
U.S. Average	45,395	43,006	38,228

Note: Figures are preliminary; Qualifying income is based on a mortgage rate of 4.4%. Monthly principal and interest payment is limited to 25% of income; n/a not available; (1) Lexington-Fayette, KY Metropolitan Statistical Area—see Appendix B for areas included
Source: National Association of Realtors, Qualifying Income Based on Median Sales Price of Existing Single-Family Homes for Metropolitan Areas, 4th Quarter 2013

Median Apartment Condo-Coop Home Prices

Area	2011	2012	2013p	Percent Change 2012 to 2013
MSA[1]	n/a	n/a	n/a	n/a
U.S. Average	165.1	173.7	194.9	12.2

Note: Figures are median sales prices of existing apartment condo-coop homes in thousands of dollars; (p) preliminary; n/a not available; (1) Lexington-Fayette, KY Metropolitan Statistical Area—see Appendix B for areas included
Source: National Association of Realtors, Median Sales Price of Existing Apartment Condo-Coop Homes for Metropolitan Areas, 4th Quarter 2013

Gross Monthly Rent

Area	Under $200	$200 -299	$300 -499	$500 -749	$750 -999	$1,000 -1,499	$1,500 and up	Median ($)
City	2.3	3.0	10.9	35.3	26.1	16.5	6.0	737
MSA[1]	2.9	3.9	11.6	35.6	25.7	15.9	4.5	720
U.S.	1.7	3.3	8.1	22.7	24.3	25.7	14.3	889

Note: Figures are percentages except for Median; Gross rent is the contract rent plus the estimated average monthly cost of utilities (electricity, gas, and water and sewer) and fuels (oil, coal, kerosene, wood, etc.) if these are paid by the renter (or paid for the renter by someone else); (1) Figures cover the Lexington-Fayette, KY Metropolitan Statistical Area—see Appendix B for areas included
Source: U.S. Census Bureau, 2010-2012 American Community Survey 3-Year Estimates

Year Housing Structure Built

Area	2010 or Later	2000 -2009	1990 -1999	1980 -1989	1970 -1979	1960 -1969	1950 -1959	1940 -1949	Before 1940	Median Year
City	0.7	16.9	16.2	15.6	15.7	13.4	10.1	3.3	8.0	1980
MSA[1]	0.7	18.5	17.2	15.0	15.6	11.8	8.9	3.3	9.0	1981
U.S.	0.5	14.9	13.8	13.9	15.9	11.1	10.9	5.5	13.5	1976

Note: Figures are percentages except for Median Year; (1) Figures cover the Lexington-Fayette, KY Metropolitan Statistical Area—see Appendix B for areas included
Source: U.S. Census Bureau, 2010-2012 American Community Survey 3-Year Estimates

HEALTH

Health Risk Data

Category	MSA[1] (%)	U.S. (%)
Adults aged 18–64 who have any kind of health care coverage	84.7	79.6
Adults who reported being in good or excellent health	83.5	83.1
Adults who are current smokers	23.2	19.6
Adults who are heavy drinkers[2]	6.4	6.1
Adults who are binge drinkers[3]	17.4	16.9
Adults who are overweight (BMI 25.0 - 29.9)	37.0	35.8
Adults who are obese (BMI 30.0 - 99.8)	22.8	27.6
Adults who participated in any physical activities in the past month	74.5	77.1
Adults 50+ who have ever had a sigmoidoscopy or colonoscopy	71.5	67.3
Women aged 40+ who have had a mammogram within the past two years	76.2	74.0
Men aged 40+ who have had a PSA test within the past two years	39.7	45.2
Adults aged 65+ who have had flu shot within the past year	61.9	60.1
Adults who always wear a seatbelt	91.8	93.8

Note: Data as of 2012 unless otherwise noted; (1) Figures cover the Lexington-Fayette, KY Metropolitan Statistical Area—see Appendix B for areas included; (2) Heavy drinkers are classified as males having more than two drinks per day or females having more than one drink per day; (3) Binge drinkers are classified as males having five or more drinks on one occasion or females having four or more drinks on one occasion
Source: Centers for Disease Control and Prevention, Behaviorial Risk Factor Surveillance System, SMART: Selected Metropolitan/Micropolitan Area Risk Trends, 2012

Chronic Health Indicators

Category	MSA[1] (%)	U.S. (%)
Adults who have ever been told they had a heart attack	5.1	4.5
Adults who have ever been told they had a stroke	2.4	2.9
Adults who have been told they currently have asthma	9.9	8.9
Adults who have ever been told they have arthritis	26.7	25.7
Adults who have ever been told they have diabetes[2]	7.5	9.7
Adults who have ever been told they had skin cancer	7.2	5.7
Adults who have ever been told they had any other types of cancer	7.8	6.5
Adults who have ever been told they have COPD	7.0	6.2
Adults who have ever been told they have kidney disease	3.0	2.5
Adults who have ever been told they have a form of depression	20.8	18.0

Note: Data as of 2012 unless otherwise noted; (1) Figures cover the Lexington-Fayette, KY Metropolitan Statistical Area—see Appendix B for areas included; (2) Figures do not include pregnancy-related, borderline, or pre-diabetes
Source: Centers for Disease Control and Prevention, Behaviorial Risk Factor Surveillance System, SMART: Selected Metropolitan/Micropolitan Area Risk Trends, 2012

Mortality Rates for the Top 10 Causes of Death in the U.S.

ICD-10[a] Sub-Chapter	ICD-10[a] Code	Age-Adjusted Mortality Rate[1] per 100,000 population	
		County[2]	U.S.
Malignant neoplasms	C00-C97	184.9	174.2
Ischaemic heart diseases	I20-I25	78.7	119.1
Other forms of heart disease	I30-I51	55.7	49.6
Chronic lower respiratory diseases	J40-J47	44.3	43.2
Cerebrovascular diseases	I60-I69	31.9	40.3
Organic, including symptomatic, mental disorders	F01-F09	36.0	30.5
Other degenerative diseases of the nervous system	G30-G31	32.7	26.3
Other external causes of accidental injury	W00-X59	28.0	25.1
Diabetes mellitus	E10-E14	21.2	21.3
Hypertensive diseases	I10-I15	23.7	18.8

Note: (a) ICD-10 = International Classification of Diseases 10th Revision; (1) Mortality rates are a three year average covering 2008-2010; (2) Figures cover Fayette County
Source: Centers for Disease Control and Prevention, National Center for Health Statistics. Compressed Mortality File 1999-2010 on CDC WONDER Online Database, released January 2013. Data are compiled from the Compressed Mortality File 1999-2010, Series 20 No. 2P, 2013.

Mortality Rates for Selected Causes of Death

ICD-10[a] Sub-Chapter	ICD-10[a] Code	Age-Adjusted Mortality Rate[1] per 100,000 population	
		County[2]	U.S.
Assault	X85-Y09	5.7	5.5
Diseases of the liver	K70-K76	11.2	12.4
Human immunodeficiency virus (HIV) disease	B20-B24	*1.8	3.0
Influenza and pneumonia	J09-J18	13.2	16.4
Intentional self-harm	X60-X84	12.3	11.8
Malnutrition	E40-E46	Suppressed	0.8
Obesity and other hyperalimentation	E65-E68	*2.1	1.6
Renal failure	N17-N19	18.4	13.6
Transport accidents	V01-V99	9.4	12.6
Viral hepatitis	B15-B19	2.2	2.2

Note; (a) ICD-10 = International Classification of Diseases 10th Revision; (1) Mortality rates are a three year average covering 2008-2010; (2) Figures cover Fayette County; (*) Unreliable data as per CDC
Source: Centers for Disease Control and Prevention, National Center for Health Statistics. Compressed Mortality File 1999-2010 on CDC WONDER Online Database, released January 2013. Data are compiled from the Compressed Mortality File 1999-2010, Series 20 No. 2P, 2013.

Health Insurance Coverage

Area	With Health Insurance	With Private Health Insurance	With Public Health Insurance	Without Health Insurance	Population Under Age 18 Without Health Insurance
City	85.6	71.4	23.5	14.4	6.4
MSA[1]	85.9	70.4	25.4	14.1	5.9
U.S.	84.9	65.4	30.4	15.1	7.5

Note: Figures are percentages that cover the civilian noninstitutionalized population; (1) Figures cover the Lexington-Fayette, KY Metropolitan Statistical Area—see Appendix B for areas included
Source: U.S. Census Bureau, 2010-2012 American Community Survey 3-Year Estimates

Number of Medical Professionals

Area[1]	MDs[2]	DOs[2,3]	Dentists	Podiatrists	Chiropractors	Optometrists
Local (number)	2,046	69	371	22	65	54
Local (rate[4])	679.0	22.9	121.5	7.2	21.3	17.7
U.S. (rate[4])	267.6	19.6	61.7	5.6	24.7	14.5

Note: Data as of 2012 unless noted; (1) Local data covers Fayette County; (2) Data as of 2011; (3) Doctor of Osteopathic Medicine; (4) rate per 100,000 population
Source: Area Resource File (ARF) 2012-2013. U.S. Department of Health and Human Services, Health Resources and Services Administration, Bureau of Health Professions

EDUCATION

Public School District Statistics

District Name	Schls	Pupils	Pupil/ Teacher Ratio	Minority Pupils[1] (%)	Free Lunch Eligible[2] (%)	IEP[3] (%)
Fayette County	73	38,641	14.1	42.8	38.0	10.3

Note: Table includes school districts with 2,000 or more students; (1) Percentage of students that are not non-Hispanic white; (2) Percentage of students that are eligible for the free lunch program; (3) Percentage of students that have an Individualized Education Program.
Source: U.S. Department of Education, National Center for Education Statistics, Common Core of Data, Local Education Agency (School District) Universe Survey: School Year 2011-2012; U.S. Department of Education, National Center for Education Statistics, Common Core of Data, Public Elementary/Secondary School Universe Survey: School Year 2011-2012

Best High Schools

High School Name	Rank[1]	Grad. Rate[2] (%)	Coll.[3] (%)	AP/IB/ AICE Tests[4]	AP/IB/ AICE Score[5]	SAT Score[6]	ACT Score[6]
Henry Clay H.S.	1904	83	77	0.5	3.1	605	21.0
Lafayette Senior H.S.	1488	88	77	0.4	3.6	1710	21.2

Note: (1) Public schools are ranked from 1 to 2,000 based on the following self-reported statistics (with the corresponding weight used in calculating their overall score). Schools that were newly founded and did not have a graduating senior class in 2012 were excluded; (2) Four-year, on-time graduation rate (25%); (3) Percent of 2011 graduates who were accepted to college (25%); (4) AP/IB/AICE tests taken per student (25%); (5) Average AP/IB/AICE exam score (10%); (6) Average SAT and/or ACT score (10%); Percent of students enrolled in at least one AP/IB/AICE course (5%)—data not shown
Source: Newsweek and The Daily Beast, "America's Best High Schools 2013"

Highest Level of Education

Area	Less than H.S.	H.S. Diploma	Some College, No Deg.	Associate Degree	Bachelor's Degree	Master's Degree	Prof. School Degree	Doctorate Degree
City	11.3	21.3	20.5	7.1	22.9	10.1	3.6	3.2
MSA[1]	13.0	25.6	20.7	7.0	19.9	8.7	3.0	2.3
U.S.	14.1	28.3	21.3	7.8	18.0	7.5	1.9	1.2

Note: Figures cover persons age 25 and over; (1) Figures cover the Lexington-Fayette, KY Metropolitan Statistical Area—see Appendix B for areas included
Source: U.S. Census Bureau, 2010-2012 American Community Survey 3-Year Estimates

Educational Attainment by Race

Area	High School Graduate or Higher (%)					Bachelor's Degree or Higher (%)				
	Total	White	Black	Asian	Hisp.[2]	Total	White	Black	Asian	Hisp.[2]
City	88.7	91.0	84.1	90.9	51.8	39.8	43.5	17.3	71.1	13.3
MSA[1]	87.0	88.5	84.3	90.9	51.9	33.8	35.7	16.3	69.2	11.7
U.S.	85.9	88.1	82.5	85.5	63.1	28.6	30.0	18.4	50.2	13.4

Note: Figures shown cover persons 25 years old and over; (1) Figures cover the Lexington-Fayette, KY Metropolitan Statistical Area—see Appendix B for areas included; (2) People of Hispanic origin can be of any race
Source: U.S. Census Bureau, 2010-2012 American Community Survey 3-Year Estimates

School Enrollment by Grade and Control

Area	Preschool (%)		Kindergarten (%)		Grades 1 - 4 (%)		Grades 5 - 8 (%)		Grades 9 - 12 (%)	
	Public	Private	Public	Private	Public	Private	Public	Private	Public	Private
City	41.5	58.5	85.4	14.6	86.8	13.2	85.4	14.6	87.7	12.3
MSA[1]	45.6	54.4	86.4	13.6	86.6	13.4	85.5	14.5	87.0	13.0
U.S.	56.9	43.1	87.8	12.2	89.9	10.1	90.0	10.0	90.8	9.2

Note: Figures shown cover persons 3 years old and over; (1) Figures cover the Lexington-Fayette, KY Metropolitan Statistical Area—see Appendix B for areas included
Source: U.S. Census Bureau, 2010-2012 American Community Survey 3-Year Estimates

Average Salaries of Public School Classroom Teachers

Area	2012-13		2013-14		Percent Change 2012-13 to 2013-14	Percent Change 2003-04 to 2013-14
	Dollars	Rank[1]	Dollars	Rank[1]		
Kentucky	50,203	27	50,705	29	1.00	26.1
U.S. Average	56,103	–	56,689	–	1.04	21.8

Note: (1) State rank ranges from 1 to 51 where 1 indicates highest salary.
Source: National Education Association, Rankings & Estimates: Rankings of the States 2013 and Estimates of School Statistics 2014, March 2014

Higher Education

Four-Year Colleges			Two-Year Colleges			Medical Schools[1]	Law Schools[2]	Voc/ Tech[3]
Public	Private Non-profit	Private For-profit	Public	Private Non-profit	Private For-profit			
1	2	3	1	1	4	1	1	1

Note: Figures cover institutions located within the city limits and include main campuses only; (1) includes schools accredited by the Liaison Committee on Medical Education and the American Osteopathic Association's Commission on Osteopathic College Accreditation; (2) includes ABA-accredited schools, schools with provisional ABA accreditation, and state accredited schools; (3) includes all schools with programs that are less than 2 years.
Source: National Center for Education Statistics, Integrated Postsecondary Education System (IPEDS), 2012-13; Association of American Medical Colleges, Member List, April 24, 2014; American Osteopathic Association, Member List, April 24, 2014; Law School Admission Council, Official Guide to ABA-Approved Law Schools Online, April 24, 2014; Wikipedia, List of Medical Schools in the United States, April 24, 2014; Wikipedia, List of Law Schools in the United States, April 24, 2014

According to *U.S. News & World Report*, the Lexington-Fayette, KY metro area is home to one of the best national universities in the U.S.: **University of Kentucky** (#119). The indicators used to capture academic quality fall into a number of categories: assessment by administrators at peer institutions; retention of students; faculty resources; student selectivity; financial resources; alumni giving; high school counselor ratings of colleges; and graduation rate. *U.S. News & World Report*, *"America's Best Colleges 2014"*

According to *U.S. News & World Report*, the Lexington-Fayette, KY metro area is home to two of the best liberal arts colleges in the U.S.: **Transylvania University** (#76); **Georgetown College** (#146). The indicators used to capture academic quality fall into a number of categories: assessment by administrators at peer institutions; retention of students; faculty resources; student selectivity; financial resources; alumni giving; high school counselor ratings of colleges; and graduation rate. *U.S. News & World Report*, *"America's Best Colleges 2014"*

According to *U.S. News & World Report*, the Lexington-Fayette, KY metro area is home to one of the top 100 law schools in the U.S.: **University of Kentucky** (#58). The rankings are based on a weighted average of 12 measures of quality: peer assessment score; assessment score by lawyers/judges; median LSAT scores; median undergrad GPA; acceptance rate; employment rates for graduates; placement success; bar passage rate; faculty resources; expenditures per student; student/faculty ratio; and library resources. *U.S. News & World Report*, *"America's Best Graduate Schools, Law, 2014"*

According to *U.S. News & World Report*, the Lexington-Fayette, KY metro area is home to one of the top 100 business schools in the U.S.: **University of Kentucky (Gatton)** (#93). The rankings are based on a weighted average of the following nine measures: quality assessment; peer assessment; recruiter assessment; placement success; mean starting salary and bonus; student selectivity; mean GMAT and GRE scores; mean undergraduate GPA; and acceptance rate. *U.S. News & World Report*, *"America's Best Graduate Schools, Business, 2014"*

PRESIDENTIAL ELECTION

2012 Presidential Election Results

Area	Obama	Romney	Other
Fayette County	49.3	48.3	2.3
U.S.	51.0	47.2	1.8

Note: Results are percentages and may not add to 100% due to rounding
Source: Dave Leip's Atlas of U.S. Presidential Elections

EMPLOYERS

Major Employers

Company Name	Industry
Baptist Health Systems	Hospital, ama approved residency
Baptist Healthcare System	Gift shop
Calabash	Ammonium nitrate/sulfate
Central Baptist Hospital Foundation	Specialty hospitals except psychiatric
Integrated Systems	Aircraft/electrical equipment repair
L-3 Communications	Telephone communications
Lexington Fayette Urban County Government	Legislative bodies/government
Lexington Fayette Urban County Government	Police protection
Lexington Fayette Urban County Government	Police protection/county government
Lexmark International	Computer peripheral equipment
Lexmark International	Typewriters and parts
Link Belt Construction Equip Co	Cranes, nec
McLane Midwest	Groceries
OSRAM Sylvania	Electric lamps
Thomas and King of Arizona	American restaurant
Toyota Manufacturing Kentucky	Motor vehicles/car bodies
UK Healthcare Goodsamritan Hospital	General medical/surgical hospitals
University of Kentucky	Colleges/universities
University of Kentucky Chandler Hospital	General medical/surgical hospitals
Veterans Health Administration	General medical/surgical hospitals
Walmart Stores	Department stores/discount

Note: Companies shown are located within the Lexington-Fayette, KY Metropolitan Statistical Area.
Source: Hoovers.com; Wikipedia

PUBLIC SAFETY

Crime Rate

Area	All Crimes	Violent Crimes				Property Crimes		
		Murder	Forcible Rape	Robbery	Aggrav. Assault	Burglary	Larceny -Theft	Motor Vehicle Theft
City	4,784.5	4.0	33.7	200.4	114.4	944.0	3,188.9	299.0
Suburbs[1]	3,732.8	3.4	33.1	53.9	115.1	826.4	2,570.1	130.8
Metro[2]	4,394.6	3.7	33.5	146.1	114.7	900.4	2,959.5	236.6
U.S.	3,246.1	4.7	26.9	112.9	242.3	670.2	1,959.3	229.7

Note: Figures are crimes per 100,000 population; (1) All areas within the metro area that are located outside the city limits; (2) Figures cover the Lexington-Fayette, KY Metropolitan Statistical Area—see Appendix B for areas included
Source: FBI Uniform Crime Reports, 2012

Hate Crimes

Area	Number of Quarters Reported	Bias Motivation				
		Race	Religion	Sexual Orientation	Ethnicity	Disability
City	4	23	4	6	5	4
U.S.	4	2,797	1,099	1,135	667	92

Source: Federal Bureau of Investigation, Hate Crime Statistics 2012

Identity Theft Consumer Complaints

Area	Complaints	Complaints per 100,000 Population	Rank[2]
MSA[1]	262	55.5	245
U.S.	290,056	91.8	-

Note: (1) Figures cover the Lexington-Fayette, KY Metropolitan Statistical Area—see Appendix B for areas included; (2) Rank ranges from 1 to 377 where 1 indicates greatest number of identity theft complaints per 100,000 population
Source: Federal Trade Commission, Consumer Sentinel Network Data Book for January–December 2013

Fraud and Other Consumer Complaints

Area	Complaints	Complaints per 100,000 Population	Rank[2]
MSA[1]	1,901	402.7	115
U.S.	1,811,724	595.2	-

Note: (1) Figures cover the Lexington-Fayette, KY Metropolitan Statistical Area—see Appendix B for areas included; (2) Rank ranges from 1 to 377 where 1 indicates greatest number of identity theft complaints per 100,000 population
Source: Federal Trade Commission, Consumer Sentinel Network Data Book for January–December 2013

RECREATION

Culture

Dance[1]	Theatre[1]	Instrumental Music[1]	Vocal Music[1]	Series and Festivals	Museums and Art Galleries[2]	Zoos and Aquariums[3]
2	4	3	0	2	17	0

Note: (1) Number of professional perfoming groups; (2) Based on organizations with primary SIC code 8412; (3) AZA-accredited
Source: The Grey House Performing Arts Directory, 2013; Association of Zoos & Aquariums, AZA Member Zoos & Aquariums, April 2014; www.AccuLeads.com, May 1, 2014

Professional Sports Teams

Team Name	League	Year Established
No teams are located in the metro area		

Source: Wikipedia, Major Professional Sports Teams of the United States and Canada, April 25, 2014

CLIMATE

Average and Extreme Temperatures

Temperature	Jan	Feb	Mar	Apr	May	Jun	Jul	Aug	Sep	Oct	Nov	Dec	Yr.
Extreme High (°F)	76	75	82	88	92	101	103	103	103	91	83	75	103
Average High (°F)	40	44	54	66	75	83	86	85	79	68	55	44	65
Average Temp. (°F)	32	36	45	55	64	73	76	75	69	57	46	36	55
Average Low (°F)	24	26	34	44	54	62	66	65	58	46	36	28	45
Extreme Low (°F)	-21	-15	-2	18	26	39	47	42	35	20	-3	-19	-21

Note: Figures cover the years 1948-1990
Source: National Climatic Data Center, International Station Meteorological Climate Summary, 9/96

Average Precipitation/Snowfall/Humidity

Precip./Humidity	Jan	Feb	Mar	Apr	May	Jun	Jul	Aug	Sep	Oct	Nov	Dec	Yr.
Avg. Precip. (in.)	3.6	3.4	4.4	3.9	4.3	4.0	4.8	3.7	3.0	2.4	3.5	3.9	45.1
Avg. Snowfall (in.)	6	5	3	Tr	Tr	0	0	0	0	Tr	1	3	17
Avg. Rel. Hum. 7am (%)	81	80	77	75	78	80	83	85	85	83	81	81	81
Avg. Rel. Hum. 4pm (%)	67	61	55	51	54	54	56	55	54	53	60	66	57

Note: Figures cover the years 1948-1990; Tr = Trace amounts (<0.05 in. of rain; <0.5 in. of snow)
Source: National Climatic Data Center, International Station Meteorological Climate Summary, 9/96

Weather Conditions

Temperature			Daytime Sky			Precipitation		
10°F & below	32°F & below	90°F & above	Clear	Partly cloudy	Cloudy	0.01 inch or more precip.	0.1 inch or more snow/ice	Thunderstorms
11	96	22	86	136	143	129	17	44

Note: Figures are average number of days per year and cover the years 1948-1990
Source: National Climatic Data Center, International Station Meteorological Climate Summary, 9/96

HAZARDOUS WASTE

Superfund Sites

Lexington has no sites on the EPA's Superfund Final National Priorities List.
U.S. Environmental Protection Agency, Final National Priorities List, April 26, 2014

AIR & WATER QUALITY

Air Quality Index

Area	Percent of Days when Air Quality was...[2]					AQI Statistics[2]	
	Good	Moderate	Unhealthy for Sensitive Groups	Unhealthy	Very Unhealthy	Maximum	Median
MSA[1]	70.4	29.6	0.0	0.0	0.0	81	42

Note: (1) Data covers the Lexington-Fayette, KY Metropolitan Statistical Area—see Appendix B for areas included; (2) Based on 365 days with AQI data in 2013. Air Quality Index (AQI) is an index for reporting daily air quality. EPA calculates the AQI for five major air pollutants regulated by the Clean Air Act: ground-level ozone, particle pollution (aka particulate matter), carbon monoxide, sulfur dioxide, and nitrogen dioxide. The AQI runs from 0 to 500. The higher the AQI value, the greater the level of air pollution and the greater the health concern. There are six AQI categories: "Good" AQI is between 0 and 50. Air quality is considered satisfactory; "Moderate" AQI is between 51 and 100. Air quality is acceptable; "Unhealthy for Sensitive Groups" When AQI values are between 101 and 150, members of sensitive groups may experience health effects; "Unhealthy" When AQI values are between 151 and 200 everyone may begin to experience health effects; "Very Unhealthy" AQI values between 201 and 300 trigger a health alert; "Hazardous" AQI values over 300 trigger warnings of emergency conditions (not shown).
Source: U.S. Environmental Protection Agency, Air Quality Index Report, 2013

Air Quality Index Pollutants

Area	Percent of Days when AQI Pollutant was...[2]					
	Carbon Monoxide	Nitrogen Dioxide	Ozone	Sulfur Dioxide	Particulate Matter 2.5	Particulate Matter 10
MSA[1]	0.0	6.0	22.2	1.1	70.1	0.5

Note: (1) Data covers the Lexington-Fayette, KY Metropolitan Statistical Area—see Appendix B for areas included; (2) Based on 365 days with AQI data in 2013. The Air Quality Index (AQI) is an index for reporting daily air quality. EPA calculates the AQI for five major air pollutants regulated by the Clean Air Act: ground-level ozone, particle pollution (also known as particulate matter), carbon monoxide, sulfur dioxide, and nitrogen dioxide. The AQI runs from 0 to 500. The higher the AQI value, the greater the level of air pollution and the greater the health concern.
Source: U.S. Environmental Protection Agency, Air Quality Index Report, 2013

Air Quality Trends: Ozone

	2003	2004	2005	2006	2007	2008	2009	2010	2011	2012
MSA[1]	0.071	0.064	0.078	0.070	0.079	0.070	0.064	0.070	0.074	0.078

Note: (1) Data covers the Lexington-Fayette, KY Metropolitan Statistical Area—see Appendix B for areas included. The values shown are the composite ozone concentration averages among trend sites based on the highest fourth daily maximum 8-hour concentration in parts per million. These trends are based on sites having an adequate record of monitoring data during the trend period. Data from exceptional events are included.
Source: U.S. Environmental Protection Agency, Air Quality Monitoring Information, "Air Quality Trends by City, 2000-2012"

Maximum Air Pollutant Concentrations: Particulate Matter, Ozone, CO and Lead

	Particulate Matter 10 (ug/m³)	Particulate Matter 2.5 Wtd AM (ug/m³)	Particulate Matter 2.5 24-Hr (ug/m³)	Ozone (ppm)	Carbon Monoxide (ppm)	Lead (ug/m³)
MSA[1] Level	30	9.8	19	0.078	n/a	n/a
NAAQS[2]	150	15	35	0.075	9	0.15
Met NAAQS[2]	Yes	Yes	Yes	No	n/a	n/a

Note: (1) Data covers the Lexington-Fayette, KY Metropolitan Statistical Area—see Appendix B for areas included; Data from exceptional events are included; (2) National Ambient Air Quality Standards; ppm = parts per million; ug/m³ = micrograms per cubic meter; n/a not available.
Concentrations: Particulate Matter 10 (coarse particulate)—highest second maximum 24-hour concentration; Particulate Matter 2.5 Wtd AM (fine particulate)—highest weighted annual mean concentration; Particulate Matter 2.5 24-Hour (fine particulate)—highest 98th percentile 24-hour concentration; Ozone—highest fourth daily maximum 8-hour concentration; Carbon Monoxide—highest second maximum non-overlapping 8-hour concentration; Lead—maximum running 3-month average
Source: U.S. Environmental Protection Agency, Air Quality Monitoring Information, "Air Quality Statistics by City, 2012"

Maximum Air Pollutant Concentrations: Nitrogen Dioxide and Sulfur Dioxide

	Nitrogen Dioxide AM (ppb)	Nitrogen Dioxide 1-Hr (ppb)	Sulfur Dioxide AM (ppb)	Sulfur Dioxide 1-Hr (ppb)	Sulfur Dioxide 24-Hr (ppb)
MSA[1] Level	8	45	n/a	15	n/a
NAAQS[2]	53	100	30	75	140
Met NAAQS[2]	Yes	Yes	n/a	Yes	n/a

Note: (1) Data covers the Lexington-Fayette, KY Metropolitan Statistical Area—see Appendix B for areas included; Data from exceptional events are included; (2) National Ambient Air Quality Standards; ppm = parts per million; ug/m^3 = micrograms per cubic meter; n/a not available.
Concentrations: Nitrogen Dioxide AM—highest arithmetic mean concentration; Nitrogen Dioxide 1-Hr—highest 98th percentile 1-hour daily maximum concentration; Sulfur Dioxide AM—highest annual mean concentration; Sulfur Dioxide 1-Hr—highest 99th percentile 1-hour daily maximum concentration; Sulfur Dioxide 24-Hr—highest second maximum 24-hour concentration
Source: U.S. Environmental Protection Agency, Air Quality Monitoring Information, "Air Quality Statistics by City, 2012"

Drinking Water

Water System Name	Pop. Served	Primary Water Source Type	Violations[1] Health Based	Violations[1] Monitoring/ Reporting
Kentucky-American Water Co.	321,244	Surface	0	0

Note: (1) Based on violation data from January 1, 2013 to December 31, 2013 (includes unresolved violations from earlier years)
Source: U.S. Environmental Protection Agency, Office of Ground Water and Drinking Water, Safe Drinking Water Information System (based on data extracted February 10, 2014)

Louisville, Kentucky

Background

Louisville was founded in 1778, when George Rogers Clark, on his way to capture British Fort Vincennes, established a base on an island above the Falls of the Ohio River. Shortly thereafter a settlement grew on the south side of the river. Two years later the Virginia state legislature named the town Louisville to pay homage to King Louis XVI of France, who had allied his country with America during the American Revolution.

The Falls forced people traveling down the Ohio to use the portage of Louisville, which helped the town grow in the early nineteenth century. Kentucky incorporated the town as a city in 1828. Two years later, the Portland Canal opened, allowing boats to go around the rapids, thereby increasing river traffic and assisting the city's growth. In the next several years, the arrival of the railroad would link the town to much of the rest of the South. The cultivation of tobacco became important to the state in the 1830s, when Louisville became a prominent processing site.

The Civil War was an interesting period in the city's history, as adherents to both the North and the South walked the city's streets. Yet the North had the upper hand, and Louisville quickly became a supply center for Union armies marching south.

The postwar period saw boom times for Louisville, and by the end of the nineteenth century the population topped 200,000. In 1937, after the Ohio River flooded the city's environs, a floodwall was built to prevent such a catastrophe from recurring. World War II saw Louisville rebound as it became an important center for munitions production. After the war, the city desegregated its schools in a calm fashion, without the trouble seen in so many other areas.

The Kentucky Derby horserace—the annual Run for the Roses-has been held at Churchill Downs in Louisville since 1875, earning the city the nickname, "Derby Town." The fabled track has recently undergone a $14.5 million renovation that adds the Grandstand Terrace and Rooftop Garden, with nearly 2,400 new seats—as well as spiffed-up wagering windows, food and drink offerings, and restrooms. The new venues opened for the 2014 Kentucky Derby.

The city serves as an important corporate command post, hosting the headquarters of three major companies: Humana; Yum! Brands Inc; and Kindred Healthcare Inc. Also, one third of all bourbon whiskey comes from Louisville. The Brown-Forman Corporation is one of the major makers of bourbon, which is headquartered in Louisville.

Louisville has maintained its importance as a vital center of transportation. The metropolitan area has two ports on the Ohio River and three interstate highways intersecting the city. The Louisville International Airport, which serves as the international hub for United Parcel Service, is 75 percent finished with a new 10,000-foot taxiway, a $47.8 million project that has included relocating a road, as well as some FedEx facilities. The Louisville metro area has many incentives to offer new businesses, including a foreign trade zone.

The "NuLu" District, formally called the East Market District, is hopping with new shops, restaurants and breweries established in the old warehouse district. City attractions include the Kentucky Science Center which, in addition to interactive permanent exhibits, includes a Science Education Wing with four science workshop labs for students, parent mentoring, educational camps and teacher training. Other attractions include the Louisville Zoo, the Kentucky Derby Museum, Kentucky Kingdom and Hurricane Bay, the Louisville Slugger Museum & Factor (with the world's largest bat), and the Kentucky Exposition Center.

The city's climate is a typical continental one. Look for cool winters, warm summers, and thunderstorms with intense rainfall during spring and summer. Fall tends to be the driest, and snow can arrive anytime from November through March, although all precipitation varies from year to year.

Rankings

General Rankings

- Louisville was selected as one of the "Best Places to Live" by *Men's Journal*. Criteria: "18 towns were selected that are perfecting the art of living well—places where conservation is more important than development, bike makers and breweries and farmers thrive, and Whole Foods is considered a big-box store." *Men's Journal, "Best Place to Live 2011: Think Small, Live Big," April 2011*

- The U.S. Conference of Mayors and Waste Management sponsor the City Livability Awards Program. The awards recognize and honor mayors for exemplary leadership in developing and implementing programs that improve the quality of life in America's cities. Louisville received First Place Honors in the large cities category. *U.S. Conference of Mayors, "2012 City Livability Awards"*

Business/Finance Rankings

- Analysts for the business website 24/7 Wall Street looked at the local government report "Tax Rates and Tax Burdens in the District of Columbia—A Nationwide Comparison" to determine where a family of three at two different income levels would pay the least and the most in state and local taxes. Among the ten cities with the highest state and local tax burdens was Louisville, at #4. *247wallst.com, American Cities with the Highest (and Lowest) Taxes, February 25, 2013*

- Based on a minimum of 500 social media reviews per metro area, the employment opinion group Glassdoor surveyed 50 of the largest U.S. metro areas on measures including compensation and benefits, satisfaction with management, business outlook, and number of employers hiring. The Louisville metro area was ranked #45 in overall employee satisfaction. *www.glassdoor.com, "Employment Satisfaction Report Card by City," June 21, 2013*

- The Brookings Institution ranked the 50 largest cities in the U.S. based on income inequality. Louisville was ranked #32. (#1 = greatest ineqality). Criteria: the cities were ranked based on the "95/20 ratio." This figure represents the income at which a household earns more than 95 percent of all other households, divided by the income at which a household earns more than only 20 percent of all other households. *Brookings Institution, "Income Inequality in America's 50 Largest Cities, 2007-2012," February 20, 2014*

- MarketWatch shared a *24/7 Wall St.* analysis of the District of Columbia's Office of Revenue Analysis report on the estimated property, sales, auto, and income taxes paid in the largest city of each state in 2011. Of the U.S. cities with the highest tax burden, Louisville ranked #4. *Marketwatch.com, "10 U.S. Cities with the Highest Taxes," March 2, 2013*

- Louisville was ranked #48 out of 100 metro areas in terms of economic performance (#1 = best) during the recession and recovery from trough quarter through the second quarter of 2013. Criteria: percent change in employment; percentage point change in unemployment rate; percent change in gross metropolitan product; percent change in House Price Index. *Brookings Institution, MetroMonitor: Tracking Economic Recession and Recovery in America's 100 Largest Metropolitan Areas, September 2013*

- The Louisville metro area was identified as one of the most affordable metropolitan areas in America by *Forbes*. The area ranked #8 out of 20. Criteria: the 100 largest metro areas in the U.S. were analyzed based on housing affordability and cost-of-living. *Forbes.com, "America's Most Affordable Cities," March 11, 2014*

- The Louisville metro area appeared on the Milken Institute "2013 Best Performing Cities" list. Rank: #58 out of 200 large metro areas. Criteria: job growth; wage and salary growth; high-tech output growth. *Milken Institute, "Best-Performing Cities 2013," December 2013*

- *Forbes* ranked the 200 most populous metro areas in the U.S. in terms of the "Best Places for Business and Careers." The Louisville metro area was ranked #35. Criteria: costs (business and living); job growth (past and projected); income growth; educational attainment (college and high school); projected economic growth; cultural and recreational opportunities; net migration patterns; number of highly ranked colleges. *Forbes, "The Best Places for Business and Careers," August 7, 2013*

Children/Family Rankings

- Louisville was selected as one of the best cities for families to live by *Parenting* magazine. The city ranked #65 out of 100. Criteria: education; health; community; *Parenting's* Culture & Charm Index. *Parenting.com, "The 2012 Best Cities for Families List"*

- Louisville was chosen as one of America's 100 best communities for young people. The winners were selected based upon detailed information provided about each community's efforts to fulfill five essential promises critical to the well-being of young people: caring adults who are actively involved in their lives; safe places in which to learn and grow; a healthy start toward adulthood; an effective education that builds marketable skills; and opportunities to help others. *America's Promise Alliance, "100 Best Communities for Young People, 2012"*

Culture/Performing Arts Rankings

- Louisville was selected as one of America's top cities for the arts. The city ranked #23 in the big city (population 500,000 and over) category. Criteria: readers' top choices for arts travel destinations based on the richness and variety of visual arts sites, activities and events. *American Style, "2012 Top 25 Arts Destinations," June 2012*

Dating/Romance Rankings

- Of the 100 U.S. cities surveyed by *Men's Health* in its quest to identify the nation's best cities for dating and forming relationships, Louisville was ranked #23 for online dating (#1 = best). *Men's Health, "The Best and Worst Cities for Online Dating," January 30, 2013*

Education Rankings

- *Men's Health* ranked 100 U.S. cities in terms of their education levels. Louisville was ranked #71 (#1 = most educated city). Criteria: high school graduation rates; school enrollment; educational attainment; number of households who have outstanding student loans; number of households whose members have taken adult-education courses. *Men's Health, "Where School Is In: The Most and Least Educated Cities," September 12, 2011*

- Louisville was selected as one of America's most literate cities. The city ranked #46 out of the 77 largest U.S. cities. Criteria: number of booksellers; library resources; Internet resources; educational attainment; periodical publishing resources; newspaper circulation. *Central Connecticut State University, "America's Most Literate Cities, 2013"*

Environmental Rankings

- The Louisville metro area came in at #210 for the relative comfort of its climate on Sperling's list of "chill cities," as measured by the Sperling Heat Index. All 361 metro areas are included. Criteria included daytime high temperatures, nighttime low temperatures, dew point, and relative humidity at the high temperatures. *www.bertsperling.com, "Sperling's Chill Cities," July 18, 2013*

- Sperling's BestPlaces assessed 379 metropolitan areas of the United States for the likelihood of dangerously extreme weather events or earthquakes. In general the Southeast and South-Central regions have the highest risk of weather extremes and earthquakes, while the Pacific Northwest enjoys the lowest risk. Of the least risky metropolitan areas, the Louisville metro area was ranked #186. *www.bestplaces.net, "Safest Places from Natural Disasters," April 2011*

- Louisville was identified as one of America's dirtiest metro areas by *Forbes*. The area ranked #16 out of 20. Criteria: air quality; water quality; toxic releases; superfund sites. *Forbes, "America's 20 Dirtiest Cities," December 10, 2012*

- Louisville was selected as one of 22 "Smarter Cities" for energy by the Natural Resources Defense Council. Criteria: investment in green power; energy efficiency measures; conservation. *Natural Resources Defense Council, "2010 Smarter Cities," July 19, 2010*

- Louisville was highlighted as one of the 25 most ozone-polluted metro areas in the U.S. during 2008 through 2010. The area ranked #17. *American Lung Association, State of the Air 2012*

- Louisville was highlighted as one of the 25 metro areas most polluted by year-round particle pollution (Annual PM 2.5) in the U.S. during 2008 through 2010. The area ranked #12. *American Lung Association, State of the Air 2012*

Food/Drink Rankings

- *Men's Health* ranked 100 major U.S. cities in terms of alcohol intoxication. Louisville ranked #45 (#1 = most sober).Criteria: binge drinking; alcohol-related traffic accidents, arrests, and fatalities. *Men's Health, "The Drunkest Cities in America," November 19, 2013*

Health/Fitness Rankings

- Analysts who tracked obesity rates in the nation's largest metro areas (those with populations above one million) found that the Louisville metro area was one of the ten major metros where residents were most likely to be obese, defined as a BMI score of 30 or above. *www.gallup.com, "Boulder, Colo., Residents Still Least Likely to Be Obese," April 4, 2014*

- For each of the 50 most populous metro areas in the United States, the American College of Sports Medicine's American Fitness Index evaluated infrastructure, community assets, and policies that encourage healthy and fit lifestyles, including preventive health behaviors, levels of chronic disease conditions, health care access, and community resources and policies that support physical activity. The Louisville metro area ranked #47 for "community fitness." Personal health indicators were considered as well as community and environmental indicators. *www.americanfitnessindex.org, "ACSM American Fitness Index Health and Community Fitness Status of the 50 Largest Metropolitan Areas," May 2013*

- The Louisville metro area was identified as one of the worst cities for bed bugs in America by pest control company Orkin. The area ranked #32 out of 50 based on the number of bed bug treatments Orkin performed from January to December 2013. *Orkin, "Chicago Tops Bed Bug Cities List for Second Year in a Row," January 16, 2014*

- Louisville was identified as one of 15 cities with the highest increase in bed bug activity in the U.S. by pest control provider Terminix. The city ranked #9.Criteria: cities with the largest percentage gains in bed bug customer calls from January–May 2013 compared to the same time period in 2012. *Terminix, "Cities with Highest Increases in Bed Bug Activity," July 9, 2013*

- Louisville was selected as one of the 25 fattest cities in America by *Men's Fitness Online*. It ranked #10 out of America's 50 largest cities. Criteria: fitness centers and sport stores; nutrition; sports participation; TV viewing; overweight/sedentary; junk food; air quality; geography; commute; parks and open space; city recreational facilities; access to healthcare; motivation; mayor and city initiatives; state obesity initiatives. *Men's Fitness, "The Fittest and Fattest Cities in America," March 5, 2012*

- Louisville was identified as one of "The 8 Most Artery-Clogging Cities in America." The metro area ranked #8. Criteria: obesity rates; heart disease rates. *Prevention, "The 8 Most Artery-Clogging Cities in America," December 2011*

- Louisville was identified as a "2013 Spring Allergy Capital." The area ranked #5 out of 100. Three groups of factors were used to identify the most severe cities for people with allergies during the spring season: annual pollen levels; medicine utilization; access to board-certified allergists. *Asthma and Allergy Foundation of America, "Spring Allergy Capitals 2013"*

- Louisville was identified as a "2013 Fall Allergy Capital." The area ranked #4 out of 100. Three groups of factors were used to identify the most severe cities for people with allergies during the fall season: annual pollen levels; medicine utilization; access to board-certified allergists. *Asthma and Allergy Foundation of America, "Fall Allergy Capitals 2013"*

- Louisville was identified as a "2013 Asthma Capital." The area ranked #19 out of the nation's 100 largest metropolitan areas. Twelve factors were used to identify the most challenging places to live for people with asthma: estimated prevalence; self-reported prevalence; crude death rate for asthma; annual pollen score; annual air quality; public smoking laws; number of board-certified asthma specialists; school inhaler access laws; rescue medication use; controller medication use; uninsured rate; poverty rate. *Asthma and Allergy Foundation of America, "Asthma Capitals 2013"*

- *Men's Health* ranked 100 major U.S. cities in terms of the best and worst cities for men. Louisville ranked #91. Criteria: thirty-three data points were examined covering health, fitness, and quality of life. *Men's Health, "The Best & Worst Cities for Men 2014," December 6, 2013*

- Breathe Right Nasal Strips, in partnership with Sperling's BestPlaces, analyzed 50 metro areas and identified those U.S. cities most challenged by chronic nasal congestion. The Louisville metro area ranked #4. Criteria: tree, grass and weed pollens; molds and spores; air pollution; climate; smoking; purchase habits of congestion products; prescriptions of drugs for congestion relief; incidence of influenza. *Breathe Right Nasal Strips, "Most Congested Cities," October 3, 2011*

- The Louisville metro area appeared in the 2013 Gallup-Healthways Well-Being Index. The area ranked #163 out of 189. The Gallup-Healthways Well-Being Index score is an average of six sub-indexes, which individually examine life evaluation, emotional health, work environment, physical health, healthy behaviors, and access to basic necessities. Results are based on telephone interviews conducted as part of the Gallup-Healthways Well-Being Index survey January 2–December 29, 2012, and January 2–December 30, 2013, with a random sample of 531,630 adults, aged 18 and older, living in metropolitan areas in the 50 U.S. states and the District of Columbia. *Gallup-Healthways, "State of American Well-Being," March 25, 2014*

- *Men's Health* ranked 100 U.S. cities in terms of their activity levels. Louisville was ranked #81 (#1 = most active city). Criteria: where and how often residents exercise; percentage of households that watch more than 15 hours of cable television a week and buy more than 11 video games a year; death rate from deep-vein thrombosis, a condition linked to sitting for extended periods of time. *Men's Health, "Where Sit Happens: The Most and Least Active Cities in America," June 20, 2011*

- *The Daily Beast* identified the 30 U.S. metro areas with the worst smoking habits. The Louisville metro area ranked #5. Sixty urban centers with populations of more than one million were ranked based on the following criteria: number of smokers; number of cigarettes smoked per day; fewest attempts to quit. *The Daily Beast, "30 Cities With Smoking Problems," January 3, 2011*

Pet Rankings

- Louisville was selected as one of the best places to live with pets by *Livability.com*. The city was ranked #10. Criteria: pet-friendly parks and trails; quality veterinary care; active animal welfare groups; abundance of pet boutiques and retail shops; excellent quality of life for pet owners. *Livability.com, "Top 10 Pet Friendly Cities," October 20, 2010*

Real Estate Rankings

- The Louisville metro area was identified as one of the top 20 housing markets to invest in for 2014 by *Forbes*. The area ranked #20. Criteria: high population and job growth; relatively low home prices which are below equilibrium home price (EHP). The EHP is what the average price for a market should be, if speculation, weird distortions in local income, and other factors (like the housing collapse) weren't present in the market. *Forbes.com, "Best Buy Cities: Where to Invest in Housing in 2014," December 25, 2013*

- Louisville was ranked #155 out of 283 metro areas in terms of house price appreciation in 2013 (#1 = highest rate). *Federal Housing Finance Agency, House Price Index, 4th Quarter 2013*

- The Louisville metro area was identified as one of the 10 worst condo markets in the U.S. in 2013. The area ranked #3 out of 64 markets with a price appreciation of -7.3%. Criteria: year-over-year change of median sales price of existing apartment condo-coop homes between the 4th quarter of 2012 and the 4th quarter of 2013. *National Association of Realtors®, Median Sales Price of Existing Apartment Condo-Coop Homes for Metropolitan Areas, 4th Quarter 2013*

- Louisville was ranked #91 out of 224 metro areas in terms of housing affordability in 2013 by the National Association of Home Builders (#1 = most affordable). The NAHB-Wells Fargo Housing Opportunity Index (HOI) for a given area is defined as the share of homes sold in that area that would have been affordable to a family earning the local median income, based on standard mortgage underwriting criteria. *National Association of Home Builders®, NAHB-Wells Fargo Housing Opportunity Index, 4th Quarter 2013*

Safety Rankings

- Allstate ranked the 200 largest cities in America in terms of driver safety. Louisville ranked #91. Allstate researchers analyzed internal property damage claims over a two-year period from January 2010 to December 2011. A weighted average of the two-year numbers determined the annual percentages. *Allstate, "Allstate America's Best Drivers Report®, August 27, 2013"*

- The National Insurance Crime Bureau ranked 380 metro areas in the U.S. in terms of per capita rates of vehicle theft. The Louisville metro area ranked #114 (#1 = highest rate). Criteria: number of vehicle theft offenses per 100,000 inhabitants in 2012. *National Insurance Crime Bureau, "Hot Spots 2012," June 26, 2013*

- The Louisville metro area was identified as one of the most dangerous metro areas for pedestrians by Transportation for America. The metro area ranked #19 out of 52 metro areas with over 1 million residents. Criteria: area's population divided by the number of pedestrian fatalities in that area. *Transportation for America, "Dangerous by Design 2011"*

Seniors/Retirement Rankings

- For *U.S. News & World Report's* Best Places rankings, the editors sought out affordable cities where retirees spend the least on housing and can live on $75 a day while still having easy access to amenities they want and need, such as recreation, services for seniors, and medical facilities. Louisville was among the ten cities that best satisfied their criteria. *money.usnews.com, "The Best Places to Retire on $75 a Day," October 15, 2013*

- *AARP the Magazine* selected Louisville as one of the ten of best places in the United States for seniors to live the "good life." For the 2013 list, the magazine looked for cities where seniors could live comfortably on $30,000 annually, considering median home prices, property taxes, and mortgage rates along with amenities such as entertainment and local eateries. *www.aarp.org/magazine, "AARP the Magazine Reveals 2013 List of Best Places to Live the Good Life for Under $30k," October 9, 2013*

- From its Best Cities for Successful Aging indexes, the Milken Institute generated rankings for metropolitan areas, weighing data in eight categories—general indicators, health care, wellness, living arrangements, transportation and general accessibility, financial well-being, education and employment, and community participation. The Louisville metro area was ranked #69 overall in the large metro area category. *Milken Institute, "Best Cities for Successful Aging," July 2012*

- Louisville was chosen in the "Big City" category of CNNMoney's list of the 25 best places to retire." Criteria include: type of location (big city, small town, resort area, college town); median home prices; top state income tax rate. *CNNMoney, "25 Best Places to Retire," December 17, 2012*

- *U.S. News & World Report* listed the best places to retire on an income of $40,000 per year. Louisville was among the ten cities selected. Criteria: low cost of living; affordable housing; quality of life; accessible major medical facilities; services for seniors; educational institutions; outdoor recreational activities. *U.S. News & World Report, "Best Places to Retire for Under $40,000," October 15, 2012*

Sports/Recreation Rankings

- Louisville appeared on the *Sporting News* list of the "Best Sports Cities" for 2011. The area ranked #65 out of 271. Criteria: the magazine takes a 12-month snapshot of each city's sports, putting a heavy premium on regular-season won-lost records (from the most recently completed season). Other criteria include: playoff berths, bowl appearances and tournament bids; championships; applicable power ratings; quality of competition; overall fan fervor (measured in part by attendance); abundance of teams (rewarding quality over quantity); stadium and arena quality; ticket availability and prices; franchise ownership; and marquee appeal of athletes. *Sporting News, "Best Sports Cities 2011," October 4, 2011*

- Louisville appeared on the *Sporting News* list of the "Best Sports Cities" for 2011. The area ranked #65 out of 271. Criteria: a 12-month snapshot of regular-season won-lost records (from the most recently completed season). Other criteria include: playoff berths, bowl appearances and tournament bids; championships; applicable power ratings; quality of competition; overall fan fervor (measured in part by attendance); abundance of teams (quality over quantity); stadium and arena quality; ticket availability and prices; franchise ownership; and marquee appeal of athletes. *Sporting News, "Best Sports Cities 2011," October 4, 2011*

- Louisville was chosen as one of America's best cities for bicycling. The city ranked #21 out of 50. Criteria: robust cycling infrastructure; vibrant bike culture. The editors only considered cities with populations of 95,000 or more. *Bicycling, "America's Top 50 Bike-Friendly Cities," May 23, 2012*

- The Louisville was selected as one of the best metro areas for golf in America by *Golf Digest*. The Louisville area was ranked #20 out of 20. Criteria: climate; cost of public golf; quality of public golf; accessibility. *Golf Digest, "The Top 20 Cities for Golf," October 2011*

Transportation Rankings

- NerdWallet surveyed average annual car insurance premiums in 125 U.S. cities to identify the least expensive U.S. cities in which to insure a car. Locations with no-fault insurance laws was a strong determinant. Louisville came in at #8 for the most expensive rates. *www.nerdwallet.com, "Best Cities for Cheap Car Insurance," February 3, 2014*

Women/Minorities Rankings

- *Women's Health* examined U.S. cities and identified the 100 best cities for women. Louisville was ranked #89. Criteria: 30 categories were examined from obesity and breast cancer rates to commuting times and hours spent working out. *Women's Health, "Best Cities for Women 2012"*

- The Louisville metro area appeared on *Forbes'* list of the "Best Cities for Minority Entrepreneurs." The area ranked #89 out of 10. Criteria: 52 metropolitan statistical areas were examined. For each ethnicity (African Americans, Asians and Hispanics), the editors measured housing affordability, population growth, income growth, and entrepreneurship (per capita self-employment). *Forbes, "Best Cities for Minority Entrepreneurs," March 23, 2011*

Miscellaneous Rankings

- Louisville was selected as a 2013 Digital Cities Survey winner. The city ranked #2 in the large city (250,000 or more population) category. The survey examined and assessed how city governments are utilizing information technology to operate and deliver quality service to their customers and citizens. Survey questions focused on implementation and adoption of online service delivery; planning and governance; and the infrastructure and architecture that make the transformation to digital government possible. *Center for Digital Government, "2013 Digital Cities Survey," November 7, 2013*

- *Men's Health* ranked 100 U.S. cities by their level of sadness. Louisville was ranked #96 (#1 = saddest city). Criteria: suicide rates; unemployment rates; percentage of households that use antidepressants; percent of population who report feeling blue all or most of the time. *Men's Health, "Frown Towns," November 28, 2011*

- Mars Chocolate North America, the makers of COMBOS®, in partnership with Sperling's BestPlaces, ranked 50 major metro areas in terms of their "manliness." The Louisville metro area ranked #11. Criteria: number of professional sports teams; number of nearby NASCAR tracks and racing events; manly lifestyle; concentration of manly retail stores; manly occupations per capita; salty snack sales; "Board of Manliness" rankings. *Mars Chocolate North America, "America's Manliest Cities 2012"*

- The National Alliance to End Homelessness ranked the 100 most populous metro areas in terms the rate of homelessness. The Louisville metro area ranked #63. Criteria: number of homeless people per 10,000 population in 2011. *National Alliance to End Homelessness, The State of Homelessness in America 2012*

Business Environment

CITY FINANCES

City Government Finances

Component	2011 ($000)	2011 ($ per capita)
Total Revenues	1,152,415	1,625
Total Expenditures	1,273,512	1,796
Debt Outstanding	1,643,121	2,317
Cash and Securities[1]	1,738,505	2,451

Note: (1) Cash and security holdings of a government at the close of its fiscal year, including those of its dependent agencies, utilities, and liquor stores.
Source: U.S Census Bureau, State & Local Government Finances 2011

City Government Revenue by Source

Source	2011 ($000)	2011 ($ per capita)
General Revenue		
From Federal Government	120,755	170
From State Government	56,505	80
From Local Governments	44,802	63
Taxes		
Property	136,323	192
Sales and Gross Receipts	48,100	68
Personal Income	210,716	297
Corporate Income	45,655	64
Motor Vehicle License	321	0
Other Taxes	6,710	9
Current Charges	198,135	279
Liquor Store	0	0
Utility	168,883	238
Employee Retirement	2,416	3

Source: U.S Census Bureau, State & Local Government Finances 2011

City Government Expenditures by Function

Function	2011 ($000)	2011 ($ per capita)	2011 (%)
General Direct Expenditures			
Air Transportation	44,097	62	3.5
Corrections	48,161	68	3.8
Education	32,753	46	2.6
Employment Security Administration	0	0	0.0
Financial Administration	40,191	57	3.2
Fire Protection	73,608	104	5.8
General Public Buildings	0	0	0.0
Governmental Administration, Other	69,322	98	5.4
Health	48,241	68	3.8
Highways	55,266	78	4.3
Hospitals	0	0	0.0
Housing and Community Development	78,190	110	6.1
Interest on General Debt	88,217	124	6.9
Judicial and Legal	7,386	10	0.6
Libraries	17,610	25	1.4
Parking	33,197	47	2.6
Parks and Recreation	36,179	51	2.8
Police Protection	99,352	140	7.8
Public Welfare	21,367	30	1.7
Sewerage	0	0	0.0
Solid Waste Management	14,656	21	1.2
Veterans' Services	0	0	0.0
Liquor Store	0	0	0.0
Utility	367,409	518	28.9
Employee Retirement	6,622	9	0.5

Source: U.S Census Bureau, State & Local Government Finances 2011

DEMOGRAPHICS

Population Growth

Area	1990 Census	2000 Census	2010 Census	Population Growth (%)	
				1990-2000	2000-2010
City	269,160	256,231	597,337	-4.8	133.1
MSA[1]	1,055,973	1,161,975	1,283,566	10.0	10.5
U.S.	248,709,873	281,421,906	308,745,538	13.2	9.7

Note: (1) Figures cover the Louisville/Jefferson County, KY-IN Metropolitan Statistical Area—see Appendix B for areas included
Source: U.S. Census Bureau, Census 1990, 2000, 2010

Household Size

Area	Persons in Household (%)							Average Household Size
	One	Two	Three	Four	Five	Six	Seven or More	
City	32.7	32.0	15.7	11.8	5.1	1.7	0.9	2.43
MSA[1]	28.7	34.2	16.2	13.0	5.4	1.7	0.8	2.51
U.S.	27.6	33.5	15.7	13.2	6.1	2.4	1.5	2.63

Note: (1) Figures cover the Louisville/Jefferson County, KY-IN Metropolitan Statistical Area—see Appendix B for areas included
Source: U.S. Census Bureau, 2010-2012 American Community Survey 3-Year Estimates

Race

Area	White Alone[2] (%)	Black Alone[2] (%)	Asian Alone[2] (%)	AIAN[3] Alone[2] (%)	NHOPI[4] Alone[2] (%)	Other Race Alone[2] (%)	Two or More Races (%)
City	71.4	22.7	2.2	0.1	0.0	0.8	2.7
MSA[1]	81.4	13.7	1.6	0.1	0.0	0.9	2.2
U.S.	74.0	12.6	4.9	0.8	0.2	4.7	2.8

Note: (1) Figures cover the Louisville/Jefferson County, KY-IN Metropolitan Statistical Area—see Appendix B for areas included; (2) Alone is defined as not being in combination with one or more other races; (3) American Indian and Alaska Native; (4) Native Hawaiian and Other Pacific Islander
Source: U.S. Census Bureau, 2010-2012 American Community Survey 3-Year Estimates

Hispanic or Latino Origin

Area	Total (%)	Mexican (%)	Puerto Rican (%)	Cuban (%)	Other (%)
City	4.6	2.0	0.3	1.4	0.9
MSA[1]	4.1	2.2	0.3	0.7	0.8
U.S.	16.6	10.7	1.6	0.6	3.7

Note: Persons of Hispanic or Latino origin can be of any race; (1) Figures cover the Louisville/Jefferson County, KY-IN Metropolitan Statistical Area—see Appendix B for areas included
Source: U.S. Census Bureau, 2010-2012 American Community Survey 3-Year Estimates

Segregation

Type	Segregation Indices[1]				Percent Change		
	1990	2000	2010	2010 Rank[2]	1990-2000	1990-2010	2000-2010
Black/White	68.7	63.8	58.1	43	-4.9	-10.6	-5.7
Asian/White	39.5	43.6	42.2	43	4.0	2.6	-1.4
Hispanic/White	26.1	34.2	38.7	73	8.1	12.6	4.5

Note: All figures cover the Metropolitan Statistical Area—see Appendix B for areas included; Figures are based on an analysis of 1990, 2000, and 2010 Census Decennial Census tract data by William H. Frey, Brookings Institution and the University of Michigan Social Science Data Analysis Network. In this analysis all racial groups (whites, blacks, and asians) are non-Hispanic members of those races. Hispanics are shown as a separate category;
(1) Segregation Indices are Dissimilarity Indices that measure the degree to which the minority group is distributed differently than whites across census tracts. They range from 0 (complete integration) to 100 (complete segregation) where the value indicates the percentage of the minority group that needs to move to be distributed exactly like whites; (2) Ranges from 1 (most segregated) to 102 (least segregated); n/a not available.
Source: www.CensusScope.org

Ancestry

Area	German	Irish	English	American	Italian	Polish	French[2]	Scottish	Dutch
City	17.1	13.0	8.1	13.5	2.6	0.8	2.0	1.6	1.2
MSA[1]	19.0	13.5	9.6	17.4	2.3	1.0	2.2	1.7	1.3
U.S.	15.2	11.1	8.2	7.2	5.6	3.1	2.8	1.7	1.4

Note: Figures are the percentage of the total population reporting a particular ancestry. The nine most commonly reported ancestries in the U.S. are shown. Figures include multiple ancestries (e.g. if a person reported being Irish and Italian, they were included in both columns); (1) Figures cover the Louisville/Jefferson County, KY-IN Metropolitan Statistical Area—see Appendix B for areas included; (2) Excludes Basque
Source: U.S. Census Bureau, 2010-2012 American Community Survey 3-Year Estimates

Foreign-Born Population

Area	Percent of Population Born in								
	Any Foreign Country	Mexico	Asia	Europe	Carribean	South America	Central America[2]	Africa	Canada
City	6.7	0.9	2.1	0.9	1.3	0.2	0.2	0.9	0.1
MSA[1]	4.9	1.0	1.5	0.7	0.7	0.2	0.2	0.5	0.1
U.S.	13.0	3.7	3.7	1.6	1.2	0.9	1.0	0.5	0.3

Note: (1) Figures cover the Louisville/Jefferson County, KY-IN Metropolitan Statistical Area—see Appendix B for areas included; (2) Excludes Mexico.
Source: U.S. Census Bureau, 2010-2012 American Community Survey 3-Year Estimates

Marital Status

Area	Never Married	Now Married[2]	Separated	Widowed	Divorced
City	35.0	42.5	2.4	6.5	13.6
MSA[1]	30.2	48.5	2.0	6.2	13.1
U.S.	32.4	48.4	2.2	6.0	11.0

Note: Figures are percentages and cover the population 15 years of age and older; (1) Figures cover the Louisville/Jefferson County, KY-IN Metropolitan Statistical Area—see Appendix B for areas included; (2) Excludes separated
Source: U.S. Census Bureau, 2010-2012 American Community Survey 3-Year Estimates

Age

Area	Percent of Population									Median Age
	Under Age 5	Age 5–19	Age 20–34	Age 35–44	Age 45–54	Age 55–64	Age 65–74	Age 75–84	Age 85+	
City	6.8	19.3	21.1	12.8	14.6	12.6	6.7	4.2	1.8	37.2
MSA[1]	6.4	19.8	19.6	13.3	15.0	12.8	7.3	4.2	1.7	38.3
U.S.	6.4	20.1	20.5	13.1	14.3	12.2	7.3	4.2	1.8	37.3

Note: (1) Figures cover the Louisville/Jefferson County, KY-IN Metropolitan Statistical Area—see Appendix B for areas included
Source: U.S. Census Bureau, 2010-2012 American Community Survey 3-Year Estimates

Gender

Area	Males	Females	Males per 100 Females
City	291,167	310,503	93.8
MSA[1]	632,215	661,616	95.6
U.S.	153,276,055	158,333,314	96.8

Note: (1) Figures cover the Louisville/Jefferson County, KY-IN Metropolitan Statistical Area—see Appendix B for areas included
Source: U.S. Census Bureau, 2010-2012 American Community Survey 3-Year Estimates

Religious Groups by Family

Area	Catholic	Baptist	Non-Den.	Methodist[2]	Lutheran	LDS[3]	Pentecostal	Presbyterian[4]	Muslim[5]	Judaism
MSA[1]	13.7	25.1	1.7	3.7	0.6	0.8	1.0	1.2	0.5	0.4
U.S.	19.1	9.3	4.0	4.0	2.3	2.0	1.9	1.6	0.8	0.7

Note: Figures are the number of adherents as a percentage of the total population; (1) Figures cover the Louisville/Jefferson County, KY-IN Metropolitan Statistical Area—see Appendix B for areas included; (2) Methodist/Pietist; (3) Latter Day Saints; (4) Reformed; (5) Figures are estimates
Source: Association of Statisticians of American Religious Bodies, 2010 U.S. Religion Census: Religious Congregations & Membership Study

Religious Groups by Tradition

Area	Catholic	Evangelical Protestant	Mainline Protestant	Other Tradition	Black Protestant	Orthodox
MSA[1]	13.7	24.5	7.1	2.0	3.0	0.1
U.S.	19.1	16.2	7.3	4.3	1.6	0.3

Note: Figures are the number of adherents as a percentage of the total population; (1) Figures cover the Louisville/Jefferson County, KY-IN Metropolitan Statistical Area—see Appendix B for areas included
Source: Association of Statisticians of American Religious Bodies, 2010 U.S. Religion Census: Religious Congregations & Membership Study

ECONOMY

Gross Metropolitan Product

Area	2011	2012	2013	2014	Rank[2]
MSA[1]	60.3	63.8	66.5	69.4	46

Note: Figures are in billions of dollars; (1) Figures cover the Louisville/Jefferson County, KY-IN Metropolitan Statistical Area—see Appendix B for areas included; (2) Rank is based on 2014 data and ranges from 1 to 363
Source: The United States Conference of Mayors, U.S. Metro Economies: Outlook—Gross Metropolitan Product, with Metro Employment Projections, November 2013

Economic Growth

Area	2011 (%)	2012 (%)	2013 (%)	2014 (%)	Rank[2]
MSA[1]	2.6	3.8	2.8	2.5	33
U.S.	1.6	2.5	1.7	2.5	–

Note: Figures are real gross metropolitan product (GMP) growth rates and represent annual average percent change; (1) Figures cover the Louisville/Jefferson County, KY-IN Metropolitan Statistical Area—see Appendix B for areas included; (2) Rank is based on 2013 data and ranges from 1 to 363
Source: The United States Conference of Mayors, U.S. Metro Economies: Outlook—Gross Metropolitan Product, with Metro Employment Projections, November 2013

Metropolitan Area Exports

Area	2007	2008	2009	2010	2011	2012	Rank[2]
MSA[1]	5,511.9	5,662.1	5,316.1	6,187.8	6,756.6	7,706.7	39

Note: Figures are in millions of dollars; (1) Figures cover the Louisville/Jefferson County, KY-IN Metropolitan Statistical Area—see Appendix B for areas included; (2) Rank is based on 2012 data and ranges from 1 to 369
Source: U.S. Department of Commerce, International Trade Administration, Office of Trade & Industry Information, Manufacturing & Services, data extracted April 1, 2014

INCOME

Income

Area	Per Capita ($)	Median Household ($)	Average Household ($)
City	25,192	42,609	60,786
MSA[1]	26,032	47,961	64,793
U.S.	27,385	51,771	71,579

Note: (1) Figures cover the Louisville/Jefferson County, KY-IN Metropolitan Statistical Area—see Appendix B for areas included
Source: U.S. Census Bureau, 2010-2012 American Community Survey 3-Year Estimates

Household Income Distribution

Area	Percent of Households Earning							
	Under $15,000	$15,000 -24,999	$25,000 -34,999	$35,000 -49,999	$50,000 -74,999	$75,000 -99,000	$100,000 -149,999	$150,000 and up
City	16.9	13.0	11.8	14.7	17.3	10.2	9.9	6.3
MSA[1]	13.8	11.7	11.2	14.9	18.6	11.9	11.4	6.6
U.S.	13.1	11.0	10.5	13.7	18.1	11.9	12.5	9.1

Note: (1) Figures cover the Louisville/Jefferson County, KY-IN Metropolitan Statistical Area—see Appendix B for areas included
Source: U.S. Census Bureau, 2010-2012 American Community Survey 3-Year Estimates

Poverty Rate

Area	All Ages	Under 18 Years Old	18 to 64 Years Old	65 Years and Over
City	19.3	28.8	17.4	11.1
MSA[1]	15.6	22.9	14.1	9.2
U.S.	15.7	22.2	14.6	9.3

Note: Figures are percentage of people whose income during the past 12 months was below the poverty level; (1) Figures cover the Louisville/Jefferson County, KY-IN Metropolitan Statistical Area—see Appendix B for areas included
Source: U.S. Census Bureau, 2010-2012 American Community Survey 3-Year Estimates

Personal Bankruptcy Filing Rate

Area	2008	2009	2010	2011	2012	2013
Jefferson County	5.43	6.05	6.21	5.90	5.35	4.84
U.S.	3.53	4.61	4.97	4.37	3.76	3.29

Note: Numbers are per 1,000 population and include Chapter 7 and Chapter 13 filings
Source: Federal Deposit Insurance Corporation, Regional Economic Conditions, March 20, 2014

EMPLOYMENT

Labor Force and Employment

Area	Civilian Labor Force			Workers Employed		
	Dec. 2012	Dec. 2013	% Chg.	Dec. 2012	Dec. 2013	% Chg.
City	368,679	359,327	-2.5	339,507	333,783	-1.7
MSA[1]	637,024	626,298	-1.7	588,310	583,770	-0.8
U.S.	154,904,000	154,408,000	-0.3	143,060,000	144,423,000	1.0

Note: Data is not seasonally adjusted and covers workers 16 years of age and older; (1) Metropolitan Statistical Area—see Appendix B for areas included
Source: Bureau of Labor Statistics, Local Area Unemployment Statistics

Unemployment Rate

Area	2013											
	Jan.	Feb.	Mar.	Apr.	May	Jun.	Jul.	Aug.	Sep.	Oct.	Nov.	Dec.
City	8.3	8.3	8.4	7.5	8.4	9.0	8.7	7.8	7.8	7.8	7.6	7.1
MSA[1]	8.4	8.4	8.3	7.4	8.0	8.5	8.2	7.4	7.4	7.6	7.3	6.8
U.S.	8.5	8.1	7.6	7.1	7.3	7.8	7.7	7.3	7.0	7.0	6.6	6.5

Note: Data is not seasonally adjusted and covers workers 16 years of age and older; All figures are percentages; (1) Metropolitan Statistical Area—see Appendix B for areas included
Source: Bureau of Labor Statistics, Local Area Unemployment Statistics

Employment by Occupation

Occupation Classification	City (%)	MSA[1] (%)	U.S. (%)
Management, Business, Science, and Arts	34.6	33.7	36.0
Natural Resources, Construction, and Maintenance	7.2	8.2	9.1
Production, Transportation, and Material Moving	16.2	16.3	12.0
Sales and Office	24.6	25.4	24.7
Service	17.4	16.4	18.2

Note: Figures cover employed civilians 16 years of age and older; (1) Figures cover the Louisville/Jefferson County, KY-IN Metropolitan Statistical Area—see Appendix B for areas included
Source: U.S. Census Bureau, 2010-2012 American Community Survey 3-Year Estimates

Employment by Industry

| Sector | MSA[1] | | U.S. |
	Number of Employees	Percent of Total	Percent of Total
Construction	n/a	n/a	4.2
Education and Health Services	85,700	13.5	15.5
Financial Activities	44,200	7.0	5.7
Government	84,300	13.3	16.1
Information	9,500	1.5	1.9
Leisure and Hospitality	64,100	10.1	10.2
Manufacturing	74,300	11.7	8.7
Mining and Logging	n/a	n/a	0.6
Other Services	25,500	4.0	3.9
Professional and Business Services	82,400	13.0	13.7
Retail Trade	65,300	10.3	11.4
Transportation and Utilities	46,400	7.3	3.8
Wholesale Trade	29,700	4.7	4.2

Note: Figures cover non-farm employment as of December 2013 and are not seasonally adjusted;
(1) Metropolitan Statistical Area—see Appendix B for areas included; n/a not available
Source: Bureau of Labor Statistics, Current Employment Statistics, Employment, Hours, and Earnings

Occupations with Greatest Projected Employment Growth: 2010 – 2020

Occupation[1]	2010 Employment	2020 Projected Employment	Numeric Employment Change	Percent Employment Change
Registered Nurses	47,450	59,370	11,920	25.1
Retail Salespersons	56,670	65,110	8,440	14.9
Laborers and Freight, Stock, and Material Movers, Hand	37,440	43,920	6,480	17.3
Heavy and Tractor-Trailer Truck Drivers	27,810	33,180	5,370	19.3
Combined Food Preparation and Serving Workers, Including Fast Food	52,180	57,220	5,040	9.7
Nursing Aides, Orderlies, and Attendants	25,440	30,470	5,030	19.8
Childcare Workers	19,240	24,140	4,900	25.5
Receptionists and Information Clerks	16,960	21,700	4,740	27.9
Personal Care Aides	6,820	11,430	4,610	67.6
Customer Service Representatives	28,670	33,110	4,440	15.5

Note: Projections cover Kentucky; (1) Sorted by numeric employment change
Source: www.projectionscentral.com, State Occupational Projections, 2010–2020 Long-Term Projections

Fastest Growing Occupations: 2010 – 2020

Occupation[1]	2010 Employment	2020 Projected Employment	Numeric Employment Change	Percent Employment Change
Home Health Aides	3,750	6,310	2,560	68.3
Personal Care Aides	6,820	11,430	4,610	67.6
Helpers—Brickmasons, Blockmasons, Stonemasons, and Tile and Marble Setters	680	1,040	360	52.9
Helpers—Carpenters	730	1,100	370	50.7
Veterinary Technologists and Technicians	1,120	1,670	550	49.1
Marriage and Family Therapists	230	340	110	47.8
Occupational Therapy Assistants	360	530	170	47.2
Athletic Trainers	440	630	190	43.2
Mental Health Counselors	1,190	1,700	510	42.9
Physical Therapist Assistants	1,380	1,970	590	42.8

Note: Projections cover Kentucky; (1) Sorted by percent employment change and excludes occupations with numeric employment change less than 100
Source: www.projectionscentral.com, State Occupational Projections, 2010–2020 Long-Term Projections

Average Wages

Occupation	$/Hr.	Occupation	$/Hr.
Accountants and Auditors	30.07	Maids and Housekeeping Cleaners	9.34
Automotive Mechanics	17.02	Maintenance and Repair Workers	18.32
Bookkeepers	16.92	Marketing Managers	54.14
Carpenters	18.09	Nuclear Medicine Technologists	29.28
Cashiers	9.39	Nurses, Licensed Practical	18.93
Clerks, General Office	14.04	Nurses, Registered	28.80
Clerks, Receptionists/Information	12.93	Nursing Assistants	11.91
Clerks, Shipping/Receiving	14.50	Packers and Packagers, Hand	10.54
Computer Programmers	30.71	Physical Therapists	38.82
Computer Systems Analysts	36.69	Postal Service Mail Carriers	24.11
Computer User Support Specialists	21.44	Real Estate Brokers	n/a
Cooks, Restaurant	9.81	Retail Salespersons	11.51
Dentists	70.32	Sales Reps., Exc. Tech./Scientific	30.69
Electrical Engineers	39.73	Sales Reps., Tech./Scientific	44.89
Electricians	24.00	Secretaries, Exc. Legal/Med./Exec.	15.00
Financial Managers	48.03	Security Guards	13.37
First-Line Supervisors/Managers, Sales	18.48	Surgeons	118.16
Food Preparation Workers	10.02	Teacher Assistants	13.80
General and Operations Managers	46.33	Teachers, Elementary School	26.60
Hairdressers/Cosmetologists	13.37	Teachers, Secondary School	26.90
Internists	89.70	Telemarketers	12.10
Janitors and Cleaners	11.18	Truck Drivers, Heavy/Tractor-Trailer	20.93
Landscaping/Groundskeeping Workers	12.56	Truck Drivers, Light/Delivery Svcs.	17.63
Lawyers	46.86	Waiters and Waitresses	9.31

Note: Wage data covers the Louisville-Jefferson County, KY-IN Metropolitan Statistical Area—see Appendix B for areas included. Hourly wages for elementary/secondary school teachers and teacher assistants were calculated by the editors from annual wage data assuming a 40 hour work week; n/a not available.
Source: Bureau of Labor Statistics, Metro Area Occupational Employment and Wage Estimates, May 2013

RESIDENTIAL REAL ESTATE

Building Permits

Area	Single-Family			Multi-Family			Total		
	2012	2013	Pct. Chg.	2012	2013	Pct. Chg.	2012	2013	Pct. Chg.
City	851	938	10.2	1,185	1,289	8.8	2,036	2,227	9.4
MSA[1]	2,365	2,551	7.9	1,306	1,466	12.3	3,671	4,017	9.4
U.S.	518,695	620,802	19.7	310,963	370,020	19.0	829,658	990,822	19.4

Note: (1) Metropolitan Statistical Area—see Appendix B for areas included; figures represent new, privately-owned housing units authorized (unadjusted data); All permit data are based on estimates with imputation.
Source: U.S. Census Bureau, Manufacturing, Mining, and Construction Statistics, Building Permits, 2012, 2013

Homeownership Rate

Area	2006 (%)	2007 (%)	2008 (%)	2009 (%)	2010 (%)	2011 (%)	2012 (%)	2013 (%)
MSA[1]	66.4	67.2	67.9	67.7	63.4	61.7	63.3	64.5
U.S.	68.8	68.1	67.8	67.4	66.9	66.1	65.4	65.1

Note: (1) Figures cover the Louisville/Jefferson County, KY-IN Metropolitan Statistical Area—see Appendix B for areas included
Source: U.S. Census Bureau, Housing Vacancies and Homeownership Annual Statistics: 2013

Housing Vacancy Rates

Area	Gross Vacancy Rate[2] (%)			Year-Round Vacancy Rate[3] (%)			Rental Vacancy Rate[4] (%)			Homeowner Vacancy Rate[5] (%)		
	2011	2012	2013	2011	2012	2013	2011	2012	2013	2011	2012	2013
MSA[1]	10.8	10.6	11.0	10.8	10.6	11.0	10.2	7.2	7.8	2.4	2.4	0.8
U.S.	14.2	13.8	13.8	11.1	10.8	10.7	9.5	8.7	8.3	2.5	2.0	2.0

Note: (1) Figures cover the Louisville/Jefferson County, KY-IN Metropolitan Statistical Area—see Appendix B for areas included; (2) The percentage of the total housing inventory that is vacant; (3) The percentage of the housing inventory (excluding seasonal units) that is year-round vacant; (4) The percentage of rental inventory that is vacant for rent; (5) The percentage of homeowner inventory that is vacant for sale
Source: U.S. Census Bureau, Housing Vacancies and Homeownership Annual Statistics: 2013

TAXES

State Corporate Income Tax Rates

State	Tax Rate (%)	Income Brackets ($)	Num. of Brackets	Financial Institution Tax Rate (%)[a]	Federal Income Tax Ded.
Kentucky	4.0 - 6.0	50,000 - 100,001	3	(a)	No

Note: Tax rates as of January 1, 2014; (a) Rates listed are the corporate income tax rate applied to financial institutions or excise taxes based on income. Some states have other taxes based upon the value of deposits or shares.
Source: Federation of Tax Administrators, "State Corporate Income Tax Rates, 2014"

State Individual Income Tax Rates

State	Tax Rate (%)	Income Brackets ($)	Num. of Brackets	Personal Exempt. ($)[1] Single	Personal Exempt. ($)[1] Dependents	Fed. Inc. Tax Ded.
Kentucky	2.0 - 6.0	3,000 - 75,001	6	20 (c)	20 (c)	No

Note: Tax rates as of January 1, 2014; Local- and county-level taxes are not included; n/a not applicable;
(1) Married joint filers generally receive double the single exemption; (c) The personal exemption takes the form of a tax credit instead of a deduction
Source: Federation of Tax Administrators, "State Individual Income Tax Rates, 2014"

Various State and Local Tax Rates

State	State and Local Sales and Use (%)	State Sales and Use (%)	Gasoline[1] (¢/gal.)	Cigarette[2] ($/pack)	Spirits[3] ($/gal.)	Wine[4] ($/gal.)	Beer[5] ($/gal.)
Kentucky	6.0	6.00	30.80	0.600	6.76 (h)	3.56 (o)	0.78

Note: All tax rates as of January 1, 2014; (1) The American Petroleum Institute has developed a methodology for determining the average tax rate on a gallon of fuel. Rates may include any of the following: excise taxes, environmental fees, storage tank fees, other fees or taxes, general sales tax, and local taxes. In states where gasoline is subject to the general sales tax, or where the fuel tax is based on the average sale price, the average rate determined by API is sensitive to changes in the price of gasoline. States that fully or partially apply general sales taxes to gasoline: CA, CO, GA, IL, IN, MI, NY; (2) The federal excise tax of $1.0066 per pack and local taxes are not included; (3) Rates are those applicable to off-premise sales of 40% alcohol by volume (a.b.v.) distilled spirits in 750ml containers. Local excise taxes are excluded; (4) Rates are those applicable to off-premise sales of 11% a.b.v. non-carbonated wine in 750ml containers; (5) Rates are those applicable to off-premise sales of 4.7% a.b.v. beer in 12 ounce containers; (h) Includes the wholesale tax rate of 11%, converted to a gallonage excise tax rate; (o) Includes the wholesale tax rate of 11%, converted into a gallonage excise tax rate.
Source: Tax Foundation, 2014 Facts & Figures: How Does Your State Compare?

State Business Tax Climate Index Rankings

State	Overall Rank	Corporate Tax Index Rank	Individual Income Tax Index Rank	Sales Tax Index Rank	Unemployment Insurance Tax Index Rank	Property Tax Index Rank
Kentucky	27	27	29	10	48	17

Note: The index is a measure of how each state's tax laws affect economic performance. The lower the rank, the more favorable a state's tax system is for business. States without a given tax are given a ranking of 1. The scores/rankings for the District of Columbia do not affect other states. The 2014 index represents the tax climate as of July 1, 2013.
Source: Tax Foundation, State Business Tax Climate Index 2014

COMMERCIAL UTILITIES

Typical Monthly Electric Bills

Area	Commercial Service ($/month) 40 kW demand 5,000 kWh	Commercial Service ($/month) 500 kW demand 100,000 kWh	Industrial Service ($/month) 5,000 kW demand 1,500,000 kWh	Industrial Service ($/month) 70,000 kW demand 50,000,000 kWh
City	483	11,438	112,637	n/a

Note: Based on rates in effect January 2, 2013
Source: Memphis Light, Gas and Water, 2013 Utility Bill Comparisons for Selected U.S. Cities

TRANSPORTATION

Means of Transportation to Work

Area	Car/Truck/Van Drove Alone	Car-pooled	Public Transportation Bus	Subway	Railroad	Bicycle	Walked	Other Means	Worked at Home
City	81.6	8.3	3.3	0.0	0.0	0.3	2.1	1.3	3.0
MSA[1]	83.5	8.8	1.9	0.0	0.0	0.2	1.6	1.0	3.0
U.S.	76.4	9.7	2.6	1.7	0.5	0.6	2.8	1.3	4.3

Note: Figures are percentages and cover workers 16 years of age and older; (1) Figures cover the Louisville/Jefferson County, KY-IN Metropolitan Statistical Area—see Appendix B for areas included
Source: U.S. Census Bureau, 2010-2012 American Community Survey 3-Year Estimates

Travel Time to Work

Area	Less Than 10 Minutes	10 to 19 Minutes	20 to 29 Minutes	30 to 44 Minutes	45 to 59 Minutes	60 to 89 Minutes	90 Minutes or More
City	9.9	33.4	29.7	19.7	3.5	2.0	1.7
MSA[1]	10.5	30.5	27.2	21.6	5.9	2.8	1.7
U.S.	13.5	29.8	20.9	20.1	7.5	5.6	2.5

Note: Figures are percentages and include workers 16 years old and over; (1) Figures cover the Louisville/Jefferson County, KY-IN Metropolitan Statistical Area—see Appendix B for areas included
Source: U.S. Census Bureau, 2010-2012 American Community Survey 3-Year Estimates

Travel Time Index

Area	1985	1990	1995	2000	2005	2010	2011
Urban Area[1]	1.11	1.11	1.16	1.20	1.21	1.18	1.18
Average[2]	1.09	1.14	1.16	1.19	1.23	1.18	1.18

Note: Travel Time Index—the ratio of travel time in the peak period to the travel time at free-flow conditions. For example, a value of 1.30 indicates a 20-minute free-flow trip takes 26 minutes in the peak. Free-flow speeds (60 mph on freeways and 35 mph on principal arterials) are used as the comparison threshold; (1) Covers the Louisville KY-IN urban area; (2) average of 498 urban areas
Source: Texas Transportation Institute, Urban Mobility Report 2012, December 2012

Public Transportation

Agency Name / Mode of Transportation	Vehicles Operated in Maximum Service	Annual Unlinked Passenger Trips (in thous.)	Annual Passenger Miles (in thous.)
Transit Authority of River City (TARC)			
Bus (directly operated)	179	16,708.9	65,690.8
Bus (purchased transportation)	2	9.2	40.8
Demand Response (directly operated)	4	10.4	142.9
Demand Response (purchased transportation)	74	383.7	3,636.2
Demand Response Taxi (purchased transportation)	65	73.9	587.2

Source: Federal Transit Administration, National Transit Database, 2012

Air Transportation

Airport Name and Code / Type of Service	Passenger Airlines[1]	Passenger Enplanements	Freight Carriers[2]	Freight (lbs.)
Louisville International-Standiford Field (SDF)				
Domestic service (U.S. carriers - 2013)	29	1,664,131	25	2,388,807,297
International service (U.S. carriers - 2012)	6	2,055	5	111,875,872

Note: (1) Includes all U.S.-based major, minor and commuter airlines that carried at least one passenger during the year; (2) Includes all U.S.-based airlines and freight carriers that transported at least one lb. of freight during the year.
Source: Bureau of Transportation Statistics, The Intermodal Transportation Database, Air Carriers: T-100 Domestic Market (U.S. Carriers), 2013; Bureau of Transportation Statistics, The Intermodal Transportation Database, Air Carriers: T-100 International Market (U.S. Carriers), 2012

Other Transportation Statistics

Major Highways:	I-65; I-64; I-71
Amtrak Service:	Bus connection
Major Waterways/Ports:	Ohio River

Source: Amtrak.com; Google Maps

BUSINESSES

Major Business Headquarters

Company Name	Rankings	
	Fortune[1]	Forbes[2]
Humana	73	-
Kindred Healthcare	410	-
Yum Brands	201	-

Note: (1) Fortune 500—companies that produce a 10-K are ranked 1 to 500 based on 2012 revenue; (2) all private companies with at least $2 billion in annual revenue through the end of their most current fiscal year are ranked 1 to 224; companies listed are headquartered in the city; dashes indicate no ranking
Source: Fortune, "Fortune 500," May 20, 2013; Forbes, "America's Largest Private Companies," December 18, 2013

Fast-Growing Businesses

According to *Inc.*, Louisville is home to one of America's 500 fastest-growing private companies: **Strategic Communications** (#489). Criteria: must be an independent, privately-held, for-profit, U.S. corporation, proprietorship or partnership; revenues must be at least $100,000 in 2009 and $2 million in 2012; must have four-year operating/sales history. Holding companies, regulated banks, and utilities were excluded. *Inc., "America's 500 Fastest-Growing Private Companies," September 2013*

According to *Initiative for a Competitive Inner City (ICIC)*, Louisville is home to two of America's 100 fastest-growing "inner city" companies: **Great Northern Building Products** (#35); **Freedom Metals** (#37). Companies were ranked by their five-year compound annual growth rate. Criteria for inclusion: company must be headquartered in or have 51 percent or more of its physical operations in an economically distressed urban area; must be an independent, for-profit corporation, partnership or proprietorship; must have 10 or more employees and have a five-year sales history that includes sales of at least $200,000 in the base year and at least $1 million in the current year with no decrease in sales over the two most recent years. *Initiative for a Competitive Inner City (ICIC), "Inner City 100 Companies, 2013"*

Minority Business Opportunity

Louisville is home to one company which is on the *Black Enterprise* Industrial/Service 100 list (100 largest companies based on gross sales): **Manna** (#5). Criteria: operational in previous calendar year; at least 51% black-owned and manufactures/owns the product it sells or provides industrial or consumer services. Brokerages, real estate firms and firms that provide professional services are not eligible. *Black Enterprise, B.E. 100s, 2013*

Louisville is home to one company which is on the *Black Enterprise* Auto Dealer 60 list (60 largest dealers based on gross sales): **Winston Pittman Enterprise** (#8). Criteria: company must be operational in previous calendar year and be at least 51% black-owned. *Black Enterprise, B.E. 100s, 2013*

Minority- and Women-Owned Businesses

Group	All Firms		Firms with Paid Employees			
	Firms	Sales ($000)	Firms	Sales ($000)	Employees	Payroll ($000)
Asian	1,434	356,045	260	317,123	2,851	84,598
Black	4,678	315,772	214	239,922	3,784	76,072
Hispanic	1,076	137,201	139	94,902	1,080	21,256
Women	14,580	2,328,471	1,400	1,942,323	15,827	396,955
All Firms	52,754	88,570,624	11,403	86,773,557	296,302	11,631,301

Note: Figures cover firms located in the city; minority- and women-owned business are defined as firms in which the corresponding group own 51% or more of the stock or equity of the company
Source: U.S. Census Bureau, 2007 Economic Census, Survey of Business Owners (2012 Survey of Business Owners data will be released starting in June 2015)

HOTELS & CONVENTION CENTERS

Hotels/Motels

Area	5 Star		4 Star		3 Star		2 Star		1 Star		Not Rated	
	Num.	Pct.[3]	Num.	Pct.[3]	Num.	Pct.[3]	Num.	Pct.[3]	Num.	Pct.[3]	Num.	Pct.[3]
City[1]	0	0.0	4	3.0	35	26.5	80	60.6	4	3.0	9	6.8
Total[2]	142	0.9	1,005	6.0	5,147	30.9	8,578	51.4	408	2.4	1,397	8.4

Note: (1) Figures cover Louisville and vicinity; (2) Figures cover all 100 cities in this book; (3) Percentage of hotels which have a given star rating; Star ratings are determined by expedia.com and offer an indication of the general quality of a particular hotel.
Source: expedia.com, April 7, 2014

The Louisville/Jefferson County, KY-IN metro area is home to one of the best hotels in the world according to *Condé Nast Traveler*: **21c Museum Hotel**. The selections are based on over 79,000 responses to the magazine's annual Readers' Choice Survey. The list includes the top 200 hotels in the U.S. *Condé Nast Traveler, "Gold List 2014, The World's Best Places to Stay"*

Major Convention Centers

Name	Overall Space (sq. ft.)	Exhibit Space (sq. ft.)	Meeting Space (sq. ft.)	Meeting Rooms
Kentucky Exposition Center (KEC)	1,200,000	n/a	n/a	n/a

Note: Table includes convention centers located in the Louisville/Jefferson County, KY-IN metro area; n/a not available
Source: Original research

Living Environment

COST OF LIVING

Cost of Living Index

Composite Index	Groceries	Housing	Utilities	Trans-portation	Health Care	Misc. Goods/Services
91.0	85.3	81.6	87.2	101.0	91.2	98.1

Note: The Cost of Living Index measures regional differences in the cost of consumer goods and services, excluding taxes and non-consumer expenditures, for professional and managerial households in the top income quintile. It is based on more than 50,000 prices covering almost 60 different items for which prices are collected three times a year by chambers of commerce, economic development organizations or university applied economic centers in each participating urban area. The numbers shown should be read as a percentage above or below the national average of 100. For example, a value of 115.4 in the groceries column indicates that grocery prices are 15.4% higher than the national average. Small differences in the index numbers should not be interpreted as significant; Figures cover the Louisville KY urban area.
Source: The Council for Community and Economic Research, ACCRA Cost of Living Index, 2013

Grocery Prices

Area[1]	T-Bone Steak ($/pound)	Frying Chicken ($/pound)	Whole Milk ($/half gal.)	Eggs ($/dozen)	Orange Juice ($/64 oz.)	Coffee ($/11.5 oz.)
City[2]	9.24	0.97	1.99	1.86	3.15	4.42
Avg.	10.19	1.28	2.34	1.81	3.48	4.39
Min.	8.56	0.94	1.44	1.19	2.78	3.40
Max.	14.82	2.28	3.56	3.73	6.23	7.32

*Note: (1) Values for the local area are compared with the average, minimum and maximum values for all 327 areas in the Cost of Living Index; (2) Figures cover the Louisville KY urban area; **T-Bone Steak** (price per pound); **Frying Chicken** (price per pound, whole fryer); **Whole Milk** (half gallon carton); **Eggs** (price per dozen, Grade A, large); **Orange Juice** (64 oz. Tropicana or Florida Natural); **Coffee** (11.5 oz. can, vacuum-packed, Maxwell House, Hills Bros, or Folgers).*
Source: The Council for Community and Economic Research, ACCRA Cost of Living Index, 2013

Housing and Utility Costs

Area[1]	New Home Price ($)	Apartment Rent ($/month)	All Electric ($/month)	Part Electric ($/month)	Other Energy ($/month)	Telephone ($/month)
City[2]	233,107	793	-	58.52	65.67	28.66
Avg.	295,864	900	171.38	91.82	70.12	27.73
Min.	185,506	458	117.80	48.81	33.67	17.16
Max.	1,358,917	3,783	441.68	171.40	372.65	39.47

*Note: (1) Values for the local area are compared with the average, minimum and maximum values for all 327 areas in the Cost of Living Index; (2) Figures cover the Louisville KY urban area; **New Home Price** (2,400 sf living area, 8,000 sf lot, in urban area with full utilities); **Apartment Rent** (950 sf 2 bedroom/1.5 or 2 bath, unfurnished, excluding all utilities except water); **All Electric** (average monthly cost for an all-electric home); **Part Electric** (average monthly cost for a part-electric home); **Other Energy** (average monthly cost for natural gas, fuel oil, coal, wood, and any other forms of energy except electricity); **Telephone** (price includes basic monthly rate for a private residential line plus additional local usage charges incurred by a family of four).*
Source: The Council for Community and Economic Research, ACCRA Cost of Living Index, 2013

Health Care, Transportation, and Other Costs

Area[1]	Doctor ($/visit)	Dentist ($/visit)	Optometrist ($/visit)	Gasoline ($/gallon)	Beauty Salon ($/visit)	Men's Shirt ($)
City[2]	86.27	86.30	78.43	3.58	33.20	27.66
Avg.	101.40	86.48	96.16	3.44	33.87	26.55
Min.	61.67	50.83	50.12	3.08	18.92	12.48
Max.	182.71	152.50	223.78	4.33	68.22	52.03

*Note: (1) Values for the local area are compared with the average, minimum and maximum values for all 327 areas in the Cost of Living Index; (2) Figures cover the Louisville KY urban area; **Doctor** (general practitioners routine exam of an established patient); **Dentist** (adult teeth cleaning and periodic oral examination); **Optometrist** (full vision eye exam for established adult patient); **Gasoline** (one gallon regular unleaded, national brand, including all taxes, cash price at self-service pump if available); **Beauty Salon** (woman's shampoo, trim, and blow-dry); **Men's Shirt** (cotton/polyester dress shirt, pinpoint weave, long sleeves).*
Source: The Council for Community and Economic Research, ACCRA Cost of Living Index, 2013

HOUSING

House Price Index (HPI)

Area	National Ranking[2]	Quarterly Change (%)	One-Year Change (%)	Five-Year Change (%)
MSA[1]	155	0.51	1.79	-0.61
U.S.[3]	–	1.20	7.69	4.18

Note: The HPI is a weighted repeat sales index. It measures average price changes in repeat sales or refinancings on the same properties. This information is obtained by reviewing repeat mortgage transactions on single-family properties whose mortgages have been purchased or securitized by Fannie Mae or Freddie Mac in January 1975; (1) Louisville/Jefferson County, KY-IN Metropolitan Statistical Area—see Appendix B for areas included; (2) Rankings are based on annual percentage change for all metro areas containing at least 15,000 transactions over the last 10 years and ranges from 1 to 283; (3) figures based on a weighted average of Census Division estimates using a seasonally adjusted, purchase-only index; all figures are for the period ending December 31, 2013
Source: Federal Housing Finance Agency, House Price Index, February 25, 2014

Median Single-Family Home Prices

Area	2011	2012	2013p	Percent Change 2012 to 2013
MSA[1]	130.4	137.1	139.5	1.8
U.S. Average	166.2	177.2	197.4	11.4

Note: Figures are median sales prices of existing single-family homes in thousands of dollars; (p) preliminary; n/a not available; (1) Louisville/Jefferson County, KY-IN Metropolitan Statistical Area—see Appendix B for areas included
Source: National Association of Realtors, Median Sales Price of Existing Single-Family Homes for Metropolitan Areas, 4th Quarter 2013

Qualifying Income Based on Median Sales Price of Existing Single-Family Homes

Area	With 5% Down ($)	With 10% Down ($)	With 20% Down ($)
MSA[1]	31,170	29,530	26,249
U.S. Average	45,395	43,006	38,228

Note: Figures are preliminary; Qualifying income is based on a mortgage rate of 4.4%. Monthly principal and interest payment is limited to 25% of income; n/a not available; (1) Louisville/Jefferson County, KY-IN Metropolitan Statistical Area—see Appendix B for areas included
Source: National Association of Realtors, Qualifying Income Based on Median Sales Price of Existing Single-Family Homes for Metropolitan Areas, 4th Quarter 2013

Median Apartment Condo-Coop Home Prices

Area	2011	2012	2013p	Percent Change 2012 to 2013
MSA[1]	119.4	120.5	120.1	-0.3
U.S. Average	165.1	173.7	194.9	12.2

Note: Figures are median sales prices of existing apartment condo-coop homes in thousands of dollars; (p) preliminary; n/a not available; (1) Louisville/Jefferson County, KY-IN Metropolitan Statistical Area—see Appendix B for areas included
Source: National Association of Realtors, Median Sales Price of Existing Apartment Condo-Coop Homes for Metropolitan Areas, 4th Quarter 2013

Gross Monthly Rent

Area	Under $200	$200 -299	$300 -499	$500 -749	$750 -999	$1,000 -1,499	$1,500 and up	Median ($)
City	4.2	3.9	13.4	38.0	25.4	13.2	1.9	683
MSA[1]	3.7	3.9	11.7	36.9	26.8	14.5	2.5	709
U.S.	1.7	3.3	8.1	22.7	24.3	25.7	14.3	889

Note: Figures are percentages except for Median; Gross rent is the contract rent plus the estimated average monthly cost of utilities (electricity, gas, and water and sewer) and fuels (oil, coal, kerosene, wood, etc.) if these are paid by the renter (or paid for the renter by someone else); (1) Figures cover the Louisville/Jefferson County, KY-IN Metropolitan Statistical Area—see Appendix B for areas included
Source: U.S. Census Bureau, 2010-2012 American Community Survey 3-Year Estimates

Year Housing Structure Built

Area	2010 or Later	2000 -2009	1990 -1999	1980 -1989	1970 -1979	1960 -1969	1950 -1959	1940 -1949	Before 1940	Median Year
City	0.2	12.6	11.2	7.2	13.7	14.3	14.8	7.5	18.5	1966
MSA[1]	0.3	15.0	14.6	10.0	15.6	12.7	12.3	6.1	13.3	1974
U.S.	0.5	14.9	13.8	13.9	15.9	11.1	10.9	5.5	13.5	1976

Note: Figures are percentages except for Median Year; (1) Figures cover the Louisville/Jefferson County, KY-IN Metropolitan Statistical Area—see Appendix B for areas included
Source: U.S. Census Bureau, 2010-2012 American Community Survey 3-Year Estimates

HEALTH

Health Risk Data

Category	MSA[1] (%)	U.S. (%)
Adults aged 18–64 who have any kind of health care coverage	79.9	79.6
Adults who reported being in good or excellent health	78.2	83.1
Adults who are current smokers	25.9	19.6
Adults who are heavy drinkers[2]	5.9	6.1
Adults who are binge drinkers[3]	16.8	16.9
Adults who are overweight (BMI 25.0 - 29.9)	35.9	35.8
Adults who are obese (BMI 30.0 - 99.8)	31.8	27.6
Adults who participated in any physical activities in the past month	73.7	77.1
Adults 50+ who have ever had a sigmoidoscopy or colonoscopy	64.6	67.3
Women aged 40+ who have had a mammogram within the past two years	76.3	74.0
Men aged 40+ who have had a PSA test within the past two years	47.3	45.2
Adults aged 65+ who have had flu shot within the past year	62.2	60.1
Adults who always wear a seatbelt	93.5	93.8

Note: Data as of 2012 unless otherwise noted; (1) Figures cover the Louisville, KY-IN Metropolitan Statistical Area—see Appendix B for areas included; (2) Heavy drinkers are classified as males having more than two drinks per day or females having more than one drink per day; (3) Binge drinkers are classified as males having five or more drinks on one occasion or females having four or more drinks on one occasion
Source: Centers for Disease Control and Prevention, Behaviorial Risk Factor Surveillance System, SMART: Selected Metropolitan/Micropolitan Area Risk Trends, 2012

Chronic Health Indicators

Category	MSA[1] (%)	U.S. (%)
Adults who have ever been told they had a heart attack	5.9	4.5
Adults who have ever been told they had a stroke	3.8	2.9
Adults who have been told they currently have asthma	12.0	8.9
Adults who have ever been told they have arthritis	32.3	25.7
Adults who have ever been told they have diabetes[2]	10.1	9.7
Adults who have ever been told they had skin cancer	6.6	5.7
Adults who have ever been told they had any other types of cancer	7.1	6.5
Adults who have ever been told they have COPD	10.9	6.2
Adults who have ever been told they have kidney disease	3.3	2.5
Adults who have ever been told they have a form of depression	22.2	18.0

Note: Data as of 2012 unless otherwise noted; (1) Figures cover the Louisville, KY-IN Metropolitan Statistical Area—see Appendix B for areas included; (2) Figures do not include pregnancy-related, borderline, or pre-diabetes
Source: Centers for Disease Control and Prevention, Behaviorial Risk Factor Surveillance System, SMART: Selected Metropolitan/Micropolitan Area Risk Trends, 2012

Mortality Rates for the Top 10 Causes of Death in the U.S.

ICD-10[a] Sub-Chapter	ICD-10[a] Code	Age-Adjusted Mortality Rate[1] per 100,000 population	
		County[2]	U.S.
Malignant neoplasms	C00-C97	193.8	174.2
Ischaemic heart diseases	I20-I25	105.3	119.1
Other forms of heart disease	I30-I51	61.7	49.6
Chronic lower respiratory diseases	J40-J47	52.1	43.2
Cerebrovascular diseases	I60-I69	39.2	40.3
Organic, including symptomatic, mental disorders	F01-F09	35.1	30.5
Other degenerative diseases of the nervous system	G30-G31	34.5	26.3
Other external causes of accidental injury	W00-X59	27.8	25.1
Diabetes mellitus	E10-E14	28.6	21.3
Hypertensive diseases	I10-I15	20.8	18.8

Note: (a) ICD-10 = International Classification of Diseases 10th Revision; (1) Mortality rates are a three year average covering 2008-2010; (2) Figures cover Jefferson County
Source: Centers for Disease Control and Prevention, National Center for Health Statistics. Compressed Mortality File 1999-2010 on CDC WONDER Online Database, released January 2013. Data are compiled from the Compressed Mortality File 1999-2010, Series 20 No. 2P, 2013.

Mortality Rates for Selected Causes of Death

ICD-10[a] Sub-Chapter	ICD-10[a] Code	Age-Adjusted Mortality Rate[1] per 100,000 population	
		County[2]	U.S.
Assault	X85-Y09	9.1	5.5
Diseases of the liver	K70-K76	12.4	12.4
Human immunodeficiency virus (HIV) disease	B20-B24	3.9	3.0
Influenza and pneumonia	J09-J18	16.7	16.4
Intentional self-harm	X60-X84	12.8	11.8
Malnutrition	E40-E46	1.3	0.8
Obesity and other hyperalimentation	E65-E68	2.5	1.6
Renal failure	N17-N19	21.0	13.6
Transport accidents	V01-V99	12.0	12.6
Viral hepatitis	B15-B19	2.3	2.2

Note: (a) ICD-10 = International Classification of Diseases 10th Revision; (1) Mortality rates are a three year average covering 2008-2010; (2) Figures cover Jefferson County
Source: Centers for Disease Control and Prevention, National Center for Health Statistics. Compressed Mortality File 1999-2010 on CDC WONDER Online Database, released January 2013. Data are compiled from the Compressed Mortality File 1999-2010, Series 20 No. 2P, 2013.

Health Insurance Coverage

Area	With Health Insurance	With Private Health Insurance	With Public Health Insurance	Without Health Insurance	Population Under Age 18 Without Health Insurance
City	85.7	66.1	31.4	14.3	4.9
MSA[1]	87.0	70.6	28.7	13.0	5.3
U.S.	84.9	65.4	30.4	15.1	7.5

Note: Figures are percentages that cover the civilian noninstitutionalized population; (1) Figures cover the Louisville/Jefferson County, KY-IN Metropolitan Statistical Area—see Appendix B for areas included
Source: U.S. Census Bureau, 2010-2012 American Community Survey 3-Year Estimates

Number of Medical Professionals

Area[1]	MDs[2]	DOs[2,3]	Dentists	Podiatrists	Chiropractors	Optometrists
Local (number)	3,463	96	692	57	210	87
Local (rate[4])	464.0	12.9	92.2	7.6	28.0	11.6
U.S. (rate[4])	267.6	19.6	61.7	5.6	24.7	14.5

Note: Data as of 2012 unless noted; (1) Local data covers Jefferson County; (2) Data as of 2011; (3) Doctor of Osteopathic Medicine; (4) rate per 100,000 population
Source: Area Resource File (ARF) 2012-2013. U.S. Department of Health and Human Services, Health Resources and Services Administration, Bureau of Health Professions

Best Hospitals

According to *U.S. News*, the Louisville/Jefferson County, KY-IN metro area is home to one of the best children's hospitals in the U.S.: **Kosair Children's Hospital**. The hospital listed was highly ranked in at least one pediatric specialty. Eighty-seven hospitals in the U.S. ranked in at least one specialty. Ten children's hospitals in the U.S. made the Honor Roll by ranking near the top in three or more specialties.*U.S. News Online, "America's Best Children's Hospitals 2013-14"*

EDUCATION

Public School District Statistics

District Name	Schls	Pupils	Pupil/ Teacher Ratio	Minority Pupils[1] (%)	Free Lunch Eligible[2] (%)	IEP[3] (%)
Jefferson County	173	99,191	16.8	49.1	52.5	13.3

Note: Table includes school districts with 2,000 or more students; (1) Percentage of students that are not non-Hispanic white; (2) Percentage of students that are eligible for the free lunch program; (3) Percentage of students that have an Individualized Education Program.
Source: U.S. Department of Education, National Center for Education Statistics, Common Core of Data, Local Education Agency (School District) Universe Survey: School Year 2011-2012; U.S. Department of Education, National Center for Education Statistics, Common Core of Data, Public Elementary/Secondary School Universe Survey: School Year 2011-2012

Best High Schools

High School Name	Rank[1]	Grad. Rate[2] (%)	Coll.[3] (%)	AP/IB/ AICE Tests[4]	AP/IB/ AICE Score[5]	SAT Score[6]	ACT Score[6]
Ballard H.S.	651	96	98	0.6	2.8	1498	21.2
Eastern H.S.	1778	79	88	0.6	2.4	1082	21.9
J. Graham Brown School	426	95	100	0.4	2.4	n/a	24.0
Louisville Male H.S.	919	100	93	0.5	2.4	n/a	22.3
duPont Manual H.S.	50	99	99	1.1	3.8	1897	26.0

Note: (1) Public schools are ranked from 1 to 2,000 based on the following self-reported statistics (with the corresponding weight used in calculating their overall score). Schools that were newly founded and did not have a graduating senior class in 2012 were excluded; (2) Four-year, on-time graduation rate (25%); (3) Percent of 2011 graduates who were accepted to college (25%); (4) AP/IB/AICE tests taken per student (25%); (5) Average AP/IB/AICE exam score (10%); (6) Average SAT and/or ACT score (10%); Percent of students enrolled in at least one AP/IB/AICE course (5%)—data not shown; n/a not available
Source: Newsweek and The Daily Beast, "America's Best High Schools 2013"

Highest Level of Education

Area	Less than H.S.	H.S. Diploma	Some College, No Deg.	Associate Degree	Bachelor's Degree	Master's Degree	Prof. School Degree	Doctorate Degree
City	13.5	29.9	22.8	6.9	16.0	7.8	2.0	1.2
MSA[1]	12.7	31.4	22.6	7.4	15.8	7.3	1.9	0.9
U.S.	14.1	28.3	21.3	7.8	18.0	7.5	1.9	1.2

Note: Figures cover persons age 25 and over; (1) Figures cover the Louisville/Jefferson County, KY-IN Metropolitan Statistical Area—see Appendix B for areas included
Source: U.S. Census Bureau, 2010-2012 American Community Survey 3-Year Estimates

Educational Attainment by Race

Area	High School Graduate or Higher (%)					Bachelor's Degree or Higher (%)				
	Total	White	Black	Asian	Hisp.[2]	Total	White	Black	Asian	Hisp.[2]
City	86.5	88.2	81.8	74.6	77.0	27.0	29.3	16.5	52.6	22.0
MSA[1]	87.3	88.2	83.1	80.5	70.1	25.9	26.9	17.0	53.9	17.4
U.S.	85.9	88.1	82.5	85.5	63.1	28.6	30.0	18.4	50.2	13.4

Note: Figures shown cover persons 25 years old and over; (1) Figures cover the Louisville/Jefferson County, KY-IN Metropolitan Statistical Area—see Appendix B for areas included; (2) People of Hispanic origin can be of any race
Source: U.S. Census Bureau, 2010-2012 American Community Survey 3-Year Estimates

School Enrollment by Grade and Control

Area	Preschool (%)		Kindergarten (%)		Grades 1 - 4 (%)		Grades 5 - 8 (%)		Grades 9 - 12 (%)	
	Public	Private	Public	Private	Public	Private	Public	Private	Public	Private
City	45.6	54.4	82.8	17.2	80.4	19.6	80.0	20.0	79.9	20.1
MSA[1]	48.3	51.7	84.7	15.3	83.7	16.3	83.2	16.8	83.8	16.2
U.S.	56.9	43.1	87.8	12.2	89.9	10.1	90.0	10.0	90.8	9.2

Note: Figures shown cover persons 3 years old and over; (1) Figures cover the Louisville/Jefferson County,
KY-IN Metropolitan Statistical Area—see Appendix B for areas included
Source: U.S. Census Bureau, 2010-2012 American Community Survey 3-Year Estimates

Average Salaries of Public School Classroom Teachers

Area	2012-13		2013-14		Percent Change 2012-13 to 2013-14	Percent Change 2003-04 to 2013-14
	Dollars	Rank[1]	Dollars	Rank[1]		
Kentucky	50,203	27	50,705	29	1.00	26.1
U.S. Average	56,103	–	56,689	–	1.04	21.8

Note: (1) State rank ranges from 1 to 51 where 1 indicates highest salary.
Source: National Education Association, Rankings & Estimates: Rankings of the States 2013 and Estimates of
School Statistics 2014, March 2014

Higher Education

Four-Year Colleges			Two-Year Colleges			Medical Schools[1]	Law Schools[2]	Voc/ Tech[3]
Public	Private Non-profit	Private For-profit	Public	Private Non-profit	Private For-profit			
1	5	10	1	0	11	1	1	0

Note: Figures cover institutions located within the city limits and include main campuses only; (1) includes
schools accredited by the Liaison Committee on Medical Education and the American Osteopathic Association's
Commission on Osteopathic College Accreditation; (2) includes ABA-accredited schools, schools with
provisional ABA accreditation, and state accredited schools; (3) includes all schools with programs that are less
than 2 years.
Source: National Center for Education Statistics, Integrated Postsecondary Education System (IPEDS),
2012-13; Association of American Medical Colleges, Member List, April 24, 2014; American Osteopathic
Association, Member List, April 24, 2014; Law School Admission Council, Official Guide to ABA-Approved
Law Schools Online, April 24, 2014; Wikipedia, List of Medical Schools in the United States, April 24, 2014;
Wikipedia, List of Law Schools in the United States, April 24, 2014

According to *U.S. News & World Report,* the Louisville/Jefferson County, KY-IN metro area is
home to one of the best national universities in the U.S.: **University of Louisville** (#161). The
indicators used to capture academic quality fall into a number of categories: assessment by
administrators at peer institutions; retention of students; faculty resources; student selectivity;
financial resources; alumni giving; high school counselor ratings of colleges; and graduation rate.
U.S. News & World Report, "America's Best Colleges 2014"

According to *U.S. News & World Report,* the Louisville/Jefferson County, KY-IN metro area is
home to one of the top 100 law schools in the U.S.: **University of Louisville (Brandeis)** (#68).
The rankings are based on a weighted average of 12 measures of quality: peer assessment score;
assessment score by lawyers/judges; median LSAT scores; median undergrad GPA; acceptance
rate; employment rates for graduates; placement success; bar passage rate; faculty resources;
expenditures per student; student/faculty ratio; and library resources. *U.S. News & World Report,
"America's Best Graduate Schools, Law, 2014"*

PRESIDENTIAL ELECTION

2012 Presidential Election Results

Area	Obama	Romney	Other
Jefferson County	54.8	43.7	1.4
U.S.	51.0	47.2	1.8

Note: Results are percentages and may not add to 100% due to rounding
Source: Dave Leip's Atlas of U.S. Presidential Elections

EMPLOYERS

Major Employers

Company Name	Industry
Baptist Healthcare Systems	Healthcare
BF Cos./ERJ Dining	Restaurants
Catholic Archdiocese of Louisville	Schools/churches/related activities
Clark Memorial Hospital	Healthcare
Floyd Memorial Hospital & Health Services	Healthcare
Ford Motor Co.	Automotive manufacturer
GE Appliances & Lighting	Home appliance/lighting products
Horseshoe Southern Indiana	Entertainment
Humana	Health insurance
Jefferson County Public Schools	K-12 public education
Kentucky State Government	Government
KentuckyOne Health	Healthcare
Kindred Healthcare	Healthcare
LG&E and KU Energy	Utility
Louisville/Jefferson County Metro Govt	Government
New Albany-Floyd County School Corp	K-12 public education
Norton Healthcare	Healthcare
Publishers Printing Co.	Printer
Robley Rex VA Medical Center	Healthcare
Securitas Security Services USA	Security services
United Parcel Services	Global commerce services
University of Louisville	Higher education
University of Louisville Hospital	Healthcare
US Government	Government
Yum! Brands	Quick-service restaurants

Note: Companies shown are located within the Louisville/Jefferson County, KY-IN Metropolitan Statistical Area.
Source: Hoovers.com; Wikipedia

Best Companies to Work For

Humana, headquartered in Louisville, is among the "100 Best Places to Work in IT." To qualify, companies, both public and private, had to have a minimum of 50 IT employees and were selected based on average salary and bonus increases, the percentage of IT staffers promoted, IT staff turnover rates, training and development programs, and the percentage of women and minorities in IT staff and management positions. In addition, *Computerworld* looked at retention efforts, programs for recognizing and rewarding outstanding performances, and benefits such as flextime, elder care and child care, and reimbursement for college tuition and the cost of pursuing technology certifications. *Computerworld, "100 Best Places to Work in IT 2013"*

PUBLIC SAFETY

Crime Rate

Area	All Crimes	Violent Crimes				Property Crimes		
		Murder	Forcible Rape	Robbery	Aggrav. Assault	Burglary	Larceny -Theft	Motor Vehicle Theft
City	4,892.7	9.3	27.5	209.2	352.7	1,051.9	2,913.7	328.3
Suburbs[1]	2,765.2	2.7	15.8	54.4	153.8	596.5	1,794.6	147.3
Metro[2]	3,900.3	6.2	22.0	137.0	260.0	839.5	2,391.7	243.9
U.S.	3,246.1	4.7	26.9	112.9	242.3	670.2	1,959.3	229.7

Note: Figures are crimes per 100,000 population; (1) All areas within the metro area that are located outside the city limits; (2) Figures cover the Louisville/Jefferson County, KY-IN Metropolitan Statistical Area—see Appendix B for areas included
Source: FBI Uniform Crime Reports, 2012

Hate Crimes

Area	Number of Quarters Reported	Bias Motivation				
		Race	Religion	Sexual Orientation	Ethnicity	Disability
Area[2]	4	6	1	2	0	0
U.S.	4	2,797	1,099	1,135	667	92

Note: (2) Figures cover Louisville Metro.
Source: Federal Bureau of Investigation, Hate Crime Statistics 2012

Identity Theft Consumer Complaints

Area	Complaints	Complaints per 100,000 Population	Rank[2]
MSA[1]	690	55.8	244
U.S.	290,056	91.8	-

Note: (1) Figures cover the Louisville/Jefferson County, KY-IN Metropolitan Statistical Area—see Appendix B for areas included; (2) Rank ranges from 1 to 377 where 1 indicates greatest number of identity theft complaints per 100,000 population
Source: Federal Trade Commission, Consumer Sentinel Network Data Book for January–December 2013

Fraud and Other Consumer Complaints

Area	Complaints	Complaints per 100,000 Population	Rank[2]
MSA[1]	5,111	413.6	96
U.S.	1,811,724	595.2	-

Note: (1) Figures cover the Louisville/Jefferson County, KY-IN Metropolitan Statistical Area—see Appendix B for areas included; (2) Rank ranges from 1 to 377 where 1 indicates greatest number of identity theft complaints per 100,000 population
Source: Federal Trade Commission, Consumer Sentinel Network Data Book for January–December 2013

RECREATION

Culture

Dance[1]	Theatre[1]	Instrumental Music[1]	Vocal Music[1]	Series and Festivals	Museums and Art Galleries[2]	Zoos and Aquariums[3]
1	4	4	3	1	31	1

Note: (1) Number of professional perfoming groups; (2) Based on organizations with primary SIC code 8412; (3) AZA-accredited
Source: The Grey House Performing Arts Directory, 2013; Association of Zoos & Aquariums, AZA Member Zoos & Aquariums, April 2014; www.AccuLeads.com, May 1, 2014

Professional Sports Teams

Team Name	League	Year Established
No teams are located in the metro area		

Source: Wikipedia, Major Professional Sports Teams of the United States and Canada, April 25, 2014

CLIMATE

Average and Extreme Temperatures

Temperature	Jan	Feb	Mar	Apr	May	Jun	Jul	Aug	Sep	Oct	Nov	Dec	Yr.
Extreme High (°F)	77	77	86	91	95	102	105	101	104	92	84	76	105
Average High (°F)	41	46	56	68	77	85	88	87	80	69	56	45	67
Average Temp. (°F)	33	37	46	57	66	74	78	77	70	58	47	37	57
Average Low (°F)	25	27	36	46	55	64	68	66	59	47	37	29	46
Extreme Low (°F)	-20	-9	-1	22	31	42	50	46	33	23	-1	-15	-20

Note: Figures cover the years 1948-1990
Source: National Climatic Data Center, International Station Meteorological Climate Summary, 9/96

Average Precipitation/Snowfall/Humidity

Precip./Humidity	Jan	Feb	Mar	Apr	May	Jun	Jul	Aug	Sep	Oct	Nov	Dec	Yr.
Avg. Precip. (in.)	3.4	3.5	4.5	4.0	4.5	3.7	4.2	3.2	3.0	2.6	3.7	3.6	43.9
Avg. Snowfall (in.)	5	4	3	Tr	Tr	0	0	0	0	Tr	1	2	17
Avg. Rel. Hum. 7am (%)	78	78	75	75	79	80	82	85	86	84	79	78	80
Avg. Rel. Hum. 4pm (%)	62	58	52	49	52	53	55	53	53	51	57	62	55

Note: Figures cover the years 1948-1990; Tr = Trace amounts (<0.05 in. of rain; <0.5 in. of snow)
Source: National Climatic Data Center, International Station Meteorological Climate Summary, 9/96

Weather Conditions

Temperature			Daytime Sky			Precipitation		
10°F & below	32°F & below	90°F & above	Clear	Partly cloudy	Cloudy	0.01 inch or more precip.	0.1 inch or more snow/ice	Thunderstorms
8	90	35	82	143	140	125	15	45

Note: Figures are average number of days per year and cover the years 1948-1990
Source: National Climatic Data Center, International Station Meteorological Climate Summary, 9/96

HAZARDOUS WASTE

Superfund Sites

Louisville has no sites on the EPA's Superfund Final National Priorities List.

U.S. Environmental Protection Agency, Final National Priorities List, April 26, 2014

AIR & WATER QUALITY

Air Quality Index

Area	Percent of Days when Air Quality was...[2]					AQI Statistics[2]	
	Good	Moderate	Unhealthy for Sensitive Groups	Unhealthy	Very Unhealthy	Maximum	Median
MSA[1]	37.8	57.3	4.9	0.0	0.0	144	55

Note: (1) Data covers the Louisville/Jefferson County, KY-IN Metropolitan Statistical Area—see Appendix B for areas included; (2) Based on 365 days with AQI data in 2013. Air Quality Index (AQI) is an index for reporting daily air quality. EPA calculates the AQI for five major air pollutants regulated by the Clean Air Act: ground-level ozone, particle pollution (aka particulate matter), carbon monoxide, sulfur dioxide, and nitrogen dioxide. The AQI runs from 0 to 500. The higher the AQI value, the greater the level of air pollution and the greater the health concern. There are six AQI categories: "Good" AQI is between 0 and 50. Air quality is considered satisfactory; "Moderate" AQI is between 51 and 100. Air quality is acceptable; "Unhealthy for Sensitive Groups" When AQI values are between 101 and 150, members of sensitive groups may experience health effects; "Unhealthy" When AQI values are between 151 and 200 everyone may begin to experience health effects; "Very Unhealthy" AQI values between 201 and 300 trigger a health alert; "Hazardous" AQI values over 300 trigger warnings of emergency conditions (not shown).
Source: U.S. Environmental Protection Agency, Air Quality Index Report, 2013

Air Quality Index Pollutants

Area	Percent of Days when AQI Pollutant was...[2]					
	Carbon Monoxide	Nitrogen Dioxide	Ozone	Sulfur Dioxide	Particulate Matter 2.5	Particulate Matter 10
MSA[1]	0.0	0.5	12.3	17.5	69.6	0.0

Note: (1) Data covers the Louisville/Jefferson County, KY-IN Metropolitan Statistical Area—see Appendix B for areas included; (2) Based on 365 days with AQI data in 2013. The Air Quality Index (AQI) is an index for reporting daily air quality. EPA calculates the AQI for five major air pollutants regulated by the Clean Air Act: ground-level ozone, particle pollution (also known as particulate matter), carbon monoxide, sulfur dioxide, and nitrogen dioxide. The AQI runs from 0 to 500. The higher the AQI value, the greater the level of air pollution and the greater the health concern.
Source: U.S. Environmental Protection Agency, Air Quality Index Report, 2013

Air Quality Trends: Ozone

	2003	2004	2005	2006	2007	2008	2009	2010	2011	2012
MSA[1]	0.077	0.071	0.083	0.076	0.083	0.074	0.068	0.075	0.081	0.085

Note: (1) Data covers the Louisville/Jefferson County, KY-IN Metropolitan Statistical Area—see Appendix B for areas included. The values shown are the composite ozone concentration averages among trend sites based on the highest fourth daily maximum 8-hour concentration in parts per million. These trends are based on sites having an adequate record of monitoring data during the trend period. Data from exceptional events are included.
Source: U.S. Environmental Protection Agency, Air Quality Monitoring Information, "Air Quality Trends by City, 2000-2012"

Maximum Air Pollutant Concentrations: Particulate Matter, Ozone, CO and Lead

	Particulate Matter 10 (ug/m^3)	Particulate Matter 2.5 Wtd AM (ug/m^3)	Particulate Matter 2.5 24-Hr (ug/m^3)	Ozone (ppm)	Carbon Monoxide (ppm)	Lead (ug/m^3)
MSA[1] Level	46	11.9	24	0.092	2	n/a
NAAQS[2]	150	15	35	0.075	9	0.15
Met NAAQS[2]	Yes	Yes	Yes	No	Yes	n/a

Note: (1) Data covers the Louisville/Jefferson County, KY-IN Metropolitan Statistical Area—see Appendix B for areas included; Data from exceptional events are included; (2) National Ambient Air Quality Standards; ppm = parts per million; ug/m^3 = micrograms per cubic meter; n/a not available.
Concentrations: Particulate Matter 10 (coarse particulate)—highest second maximum 24-hour concentration; Particulate Matter 2.5 Wtd AM (fine particulate)—highest weighted annual mean concentration; Particulate Matter 2.5 24-Hour (fine particulate)—highest 98th percentile 24-hour concentration; Ozone—highest fourth daily maximum 8-hour concentration; Carbon Monoxide—highest second maximum non-overlapping 8-hour concentration; Lead—maximum running 3-month average
Source: U.S. Environmental Protection Agency, Air Quality Monitoring Information, "Air Quality Statistics by City, 2012"

Maximum Air Pollutant Concentrations: Nitrogen Dioxide and Sulfur Dioxide

	Nitrogen Dioxide AM (ppb)	Nitrogen Dioxide 1-Hr (ppb)	Sulfur Dioxide AM (ppb)	Sulfur Dioxide 1-Hr (ppb)	Sulfur Dioxide 24-Hr (ppb)
MSA[1] Level	11	45	n/a	147	n/a
NAAQS[2]	53	100	30	75	140
Met NAAQS[2]	Yes	Yes	n/a	No	n/a

Note: (1) Data covers the Louisville/Jefferson County, KY-IN Metropolitan Statistical Area—see Appendix B for areas included; Data from exceptional events are included; (2) National Ambient Air Quality Standards; ppm = parts per million; ug/m^3 = micrograms per cubic meter; n/a not available.
Concentrations: Nitrogen Dioxide AM—highest arithmetic mean concentration; Nitrogen Dioxide 1-Hr—highest 98th percentile 1-hour daily maximum concentration; Sulfur Dioxide AM—highest annual mean concentration; Sulfur Dioxide 1-Hr—highest 99th percentile 1-hour daily maximum concentration; Sulfur Dioxide 24-Hr—highest second maximum 24-hour concentration
Source: U.S. Environmental Protection Agency, Air Quality Monitoring Information, "Air Quality Statistics by City, 2012"

Drinking Water

Water System Name	Pop. Served	Primary Water Source Type	Violations[1] Health Based	Violations[1] Monitoring/ Reporting
Louisville Water Co.	730,611	Surface	0	0

Note: (1) Based on violation data from January 1, 2013 to December 31, 2013 (includes unresolved violations from earlier years)
Source: U.S. Environmental Protection Agency, Office of Ground Water and Drinking Water, Safe Drinking Water Information System (based on data extracted February 10, 2014)

Manchester, New Hampshire

Background

Manchester, the largest city in northern New England, lies along the Merrimack River in the southern part of the "Live Free or Die" state. Forty-five miles north of Boston, Manchester is a major financial and manufacturing center in its region and a main stop along the way to New Hampshire's many vacation resorts.

Amoskeag Falls, on the Merrimack, had been an important Penacook Indian fishing site for many years prior to the arrival of the first Europeans, who came in 1636 on instructions from Massachusetts Governor John Winthrop. A schoolhouse was built in 1650 by the missionary John Elliot, but for many years the European population was limited to a small number of hunters, trappers, and fishermen. The first permanent settlement was established in 1722 by a tiny group from the Massachusetts Bay Colony. The town was known by a variety of names, including Old Harrytown, Tyngstown, and Derryfield (until 1810).

For many years "Derryfield's" fortunes depended on lumber and fishing, but in 1810, cotton mills relying on water power from the Merrimack River became an economic mainstay. Though the town's population was then only 615, a local resident, Judge Samuel Blodgett, predicted that it would eventually grow to become a mighty center of industry, like England's Manchester. The name change was a result of this unlikely prediction, and by 1846, the new American Manchester had grown to a population of more than 10,000.

Manchester's early industrial history is inextricably linked to the history of the Amoskeag Manufacturing Company, whose 64 mills lined the banks of the river with what came to be the world's largest cotton milling operation. As Amoskeag thrived, so did Manchester, but by the 1920s, Amoskeag had lost some of its leading edge. Its machinery had been allowed to become obsolete, paving the way for cheaper facilities, particularly in the Southern states, to compete. And alternatives to cotton, including silk and rayon, caused Amoskeag to fall further behind. When it declared bankruptcy in 1935, the city's economy was seriously affected, resulting in a decline in jobs and population.

By the mid-1990s, Manchester had recovered from its Depression-era difficulties to become the nation's fastest-growing city. A new development company bought up the old mill buildings, restoring and adapting them to new commercial and residential uses. But the changes were not merely cosmetic; in light of a lesson well-learned from its single-industry past, Manchester's economic renaissance was finely calibrated to fit in with regional and national trends.

To businesses and individuals, the general economic picture in Manchester continues to be bright. The economic attractiveness of the city, and its overall affordability, is also enhanced by New Hampshire's unique reluctance to institute any sales or income tax. In 2009, Manchester was singled out for being "tax friendly" and for being one of the best places in America to launch a business. The city is home to Segway, Inc., manufacturer's of the two-wheeled, self balancing electric vehicle, as well as headquarters for Bank of America and Citizens Bank. In 2011, Dean Kamen, Segway's inventor, proposed a rail loop for downtown.

The city is served by the Manchester-Boston Regional Airport, one of the nation's fastest-growing; it opened a new 74,000-square-foot addition in 2004. Traffic at the airport continues to increase.

The cultural assets of Manchester include the Currier Museum of Art, with its recent expansion, and the New Hampshire Institute of Art. Another major attraction is the Manchester Historical Association's Millyard Museum founded in 1896. Institutions of higher education convenient to Manchester include St. Anselm College, Southern New Hampshire University, Franklin Pierce College, and the University of New Hampshire at Manchester, as well as a community college.

There are four seasons in Manchester, and the climate can be characterized as typical of northern New England. Long winters with considerable snow are to be expected, as are lovely, cool springs and summers.

Rankings

Business/Finance Rankings

- Analysts for the business website 24/7 Wall Street looked at the local government report "Tax Rates and Tax Burdens in the District of Columbia—A Nationwide Comparison" to determine where a family of three at two different income levels would pay the least and the most in state and local taxes. Among the ten cities with the lowest state and local tax burdens was Manchester, at #9. *247wallst.com, American Cities with the Highest (and Lowest) Taxes, February 25, 2013*

- The Manchester metro area appeared on the Milken Institute "2013 Best Performing Cities" list. Rank: #72 out of 200 large metro areas. Criteria: job growth; wage and salary growth; high-tech output growth. *Milken Institute, "Best-Performing Cities 2013," December 2013*

- *Forbes* ranked the 200 most populous metro areas in the U.S. in terms of the "Best Places for Business and Careers." The Manchester metro area was ranked #153. Criteria: costs (business and living); job growth (past and projected); income growth; educational attainment (college and high school); projected economic growth; cultural and recreational opportunities; net migration patterns; number of highly ranked colleges. *Forbes, "The Best Places for Business and Careers," August 7, 2013*

Children/Family Rankings

- Manchester was selected as one of the best cities for families to live by *Parenting* magazine. The city ranked #28 out of 100. Criteria: education; health; community; *Parenting's* Culture & Charm Index. *Parenting.com, "The 2012 Best Cities for Families List"*

Dating/Romance Rankings

- Of the 100 U.S. cities surveyed by *Men's Health* in its quest to identify the nation's best cities for dating and forming relationships, Manchester was ranked #59 for online dating (#1 = best). *Men's Health, "The Best and Worst Cities for Online Dating," January 30, 2013*

Education Rankings

- *Men's Health* ranked 100 U.S. cities in terms of their education levels. Manchester was ranked #49 (#1 = most educated city). Criteria: high school graduation rates; school enrollment; educational attainment; number of households who have outstanding student loans; number of households whose members have taken adult-education courses. *Men's Health, "Where School Is In: The Most and Least Educated Cities," September 12, 2011*

Environmental Rankings

- The Manchester metro area came in at #68 for the relative comfort of its climate on Sperling's list of "chill cities," as measured by the Sperling Heat Index. All 361 metro areas are included. Criteria included daytime high temperatures, nighttime low temperatures, dew point, and relative humidity at the high temperatures. *www.bertsperling.com, "Sperling's Chill Cities," July 18, 2013*

- Sperling's BestPlaces assessed 379 metropolitan areas of the United States for the likelihood of dangerously extreme weather events or earthquakes. In general the Southeast and South-Central regions have the highest risk of weather extremes and earthquakes, while the Pacific Northwest enjoys the lowest risk. Of the least risky metropolitan areas, the Manchester metro area was ranked #273. *www.bestplaces.net, "Safest Places from Natural Disasters," April 2011*

- Manchester was selected as one of 22 "Smarter Cities" for energy by the Natural Resources Defense Council. Criteria: investment in green power; energy efficiency measures; conservation. *Natural Resources Defense Council, "2010 Smarter Cities," July 19, 2010*

Food/Drink Rankings

- *Men's Health* ranked 100 major U.S. cities in terms of alcohol intoxication. Manchester ranked #14 (#1 = most sober).Criteria: binge drinking; alcohol-related traffic accidents, arrests, and fatalities. *Men's Health, "The Drunkest Cities in America," November 19, 2013*

Health/Fitness Rankings

- *Men's Health* ranked 100 major U.S. cities in terms of the best and worst cities for men. Manchester ranked #33. Criteria: thirty-three data points were examined covering health, fitness, and quality of life. *Men's Health, "The Best & Worst Cities for Men 2014," December 6, 2013*

- The Manchester metro area appeared in the 2013 Gallup-Healthways Well-Being Index. The area ranked #114 out of 189. The Gallup-Healthways Well-Being Index score is an average of six sub-indexes, which individually examine life evaluation, emotional health, work environment, physical health, healthy behaviors, and access to basic necessities. Results are based on telephone interviews conducted as part of the Gallup-Healthways Well-Being Index survey January 2–December 29, 2012, and January 2–December 30, 2013, with a random sample of 531,630 adults, aged 18 and older, living in metropolitan areas in the 50 U.S. states and the District of Columbia. *Gallup-Healthways, "State of American Well-Being," March 25, 2014*

- *Men's Health* ranked 100 U.S. cities in terms of their activity levels. Manchester was ranked #16 (#1 = most active city). Criteria: where and how often residents exercise; percentage of households that watch more than 15 hours of cable television a week and buy more than 11 video games a year; death rate from deep-vein thrombosis, a condition linked to sitting for extended periods of time. *Men's Health, "Where Sit Happens: The Most and Least Active Cities in America," June 20, 2011*

Real Estate Rankings

- *Kiplinger* looked at metro areas with populations above 250,000 to identify the places in which home prices have declined most, drawing on sales, supply, foreclosure, and market data from Realtors' associations and industry analysts. U.S. Bureau of Labor Statistics unemployment figures were also considered. Manchester ranked #5. *Kiplinger, "12 Cities Where Home Prices Have Fallen Most," May 2013*

- Manchester was ranked #158 out of 283 metro areas in terms of house price appreciation in 2013 (#1 = highest rate). *Federal Housing Finance Agency, House Price Index, 4th Quarter 2013*

- Manchester was ranked #113 out of 224 metro areas in terms of housing affordability in 2013 by the National Association of Home Builders (#1 = most affordable). The NAHB-Wells Fargo Housing Opportunity Index (HOI) for a given area is defined as the share of homes sold in that area that would have been affordable to a family earning the local median income, based on standard mortgage underwriting criteria. *National Association of Home Builders®, NAHB-Wells Fargo Housing Opportunity Index, 4th Quarter 2013*

Safety Rankings

- The National Insurance Crime Bureau ranked 380 metro areas in the U.S. in terms of per capita rates of vehicle theft. The Manchester metro area ranked #343 (#1 = highest rate). Criteria: number of vehicle theft offenses per 100,000 inhabitants in 2012. *National Insurance Crime Bureau, "Hot Spots 2012," June 26, 2013*

Seniors/Retirement Rankings

- From its Best Cities for Successful Aging indexes, the Milken Institute generated rankings for metropolitan areas, weighing data in eight categories—general indicators, health care, wellness, living arrangements, transportation and general accessibility, financial well-being, education and employment, and community participation. The Manchester metro area was ranked #41 overall in the small metro area category. *Milken Institute, "Best Cities for Successful Aging," July 2012*

Women/Minorities Rankings

- *Women's Health* examined U.S. cities and identified the 100 best cities for women. Manchester was ranked #24. Criteria: 30 categories were examined from obesity and breast cancer rates to commuting times and hours spent working out. *Women's Health, "Best Cities for Women 2012"*

Miscellaneous Rankings

- *Men's Health* ranked 100 U.S. cities by their level of sadness. Manchester was ranked #2 (#1 = saddest city). Criteria: suicide rates; unemployment rates; percentage of households that use antidepressants; percent of population who report feeling blue all or most of the time. *Men's Health, "Frown Towns," November 28, 2011*

Business Environment

CITY FINANCES

City Government Finances

Component	2011 ($000)	2011 ($ per capita)
Total Revenues	439,118	4,033
Total Expenditures	416,462	3,825
Debt Outstanding	607,053	5,576
Cash and Securities[1]	382,641	3,515

Note: (1) Cash and security holdings of a government at the close of its fiscal year, including those of its dependent agencies, utilities, and liquor stores.
Source: U.S Census Bureau, State & Local Government Finances 2011

City Government Revenue by Source

Source	2011 ($000)	2011 ($ per capita)
General Revenue		
From Federal Government	24,667	227
From State Government	115,679	1,063
From Local Governments	867	8
Taxes		
Property	143,505	1,318
Sales and Gross Receipts	0	0
Personal Income	0	0
Corporate Income	0	0
Motor Vehicle License	0	0
Other Taxes	20,400	187
Current Charges	69,191	636
Liquor Store	0	0
Utility	20,316	187
Employee Retirement	21,070	194

Source: U.S Census Bureau, State & Local Government Finances 2011

City Government Expenditures by Function

Function	2011 ($000)	2011 ($ per capita)	2011 (%)
General Direct Expenditures			
Air Transportation	25,262	232	6.1
Corrections	0	0	0.0
Education	165,300	1,518	39.7
Employment Security Administration	0	0	0.0
Financial Administration	3,691	34	0.9
Fire Protection	20,426	188	4.9
General Public Buildings	6,269	58	1.5
Governmental Administration, Other	2,837	26	0.7
Health	4,344	40	1.0
Highways	16,360	150	3.9
Hospitals	0	0	0.0
Housing and Community Development	2,683	25	0.6
Interest on General Debt	22,083	203	5.3
Judicial and Legal	756	7	0.2
Libraries	2,015	19	0.5
Parking	2,583	24	0.6
Parks and Recreation	5,268	48	1.3
Police Protection	22,267	205	5.3
Public Welfare	932	9	0.2
Sewerage	6,856	63	1.6
Solid Waste Management	1,839	17	0.4
Veterans' Services	0	0	0.0
Liquor Store	0	0	0.0
Utility	25,158	231	6.0
Employee Retirement	9,553	88	2.3

Source: U.S Census Bureau, State & Local Government Finances 2011

DEMOGRAPHICS

Population Growth

Area	1990 Census	2000 Census	2010 Census	Population Growth (%) 1990-2000	Population Growth (%) 2000-2010
City	99,567	107,006	109,565	7.5	2.4
MSA[1]	336,073	380,841	400,721	13.3	5.2
U.S.	248,709,873	281,421,906	308,745,538	13.2	9.7

Note: (1) Figures cover the Manchester-Nashua, NH Metropolitan Statistical Area—see Appendix B for areas included
Source: U.S. Census Bureau, Census 1990, 2000, 2010

Household Size

Area	Persons in Household (%) One	Two	Three	Four	Five	Six	Seven or More	Average Household Size
City	31.3	33.7	16.0	11.5	4.9	1.6	1.0	2.40
MSA[1]	25.1	35.2	15.9	15.3	5.9	1.7	0.9	2.56
U.S.	27.6	33.5	15.7	13.2	6.1	2.4	1.5	2.63

Note: (1) Figures cover the Manchester-Nashua, NH Metropolitan Statistical Area—see Appendix B for areas included
Source: U.S. Census Bureau, 2010-2012 American Community Survey 3-Year Estimates

Race

Area	White Alone[2] (%)	Black Alone[2] (%)	Asian Alone[2] (%)	AIAN[3] Alone[2] (%)	NHOPI[4] Alone[2] (%)	Other Race Alone[2] (%)	Two or More Races (%)
City	85.9	4.5	4.2	0.2	0.0	2.7	2.5
MSA[1]	91.1	2.1	3.3	0.2	0.0	1.3	2.0
U.S.	74.0	12.6	4.9	0.8	0.2	4.7	2.8

Note: (1) Figures cover the Manchester-Nashua, NH Metropolitan Statistical Area—see Appendix B for areas included; (2) Alone is defined as not being in combination with one or more other races; (3) American Indian and Alaska Native; (4) Native Hawaiian and Other Pacific Islander
Source: U.S. Census Bureau, 2010-2012 American Community Survey 3-Year Estimates

Hispanic or Latino Origin

Area	Total (%)	Mexican (%)	Puerto Rican (%)	Cuban (%)	Other (%)
City	8.5	3.7	2.0	0.1	2.8
MSA[1]	5.5	1.9	1.5	0.1	2.0
U.S.	16.6	10.7	1.6	0.6	3.7

Note: Persons of Hispanic or Latino origin can be of any race; (1) Figures cover the Manchester-Nashua, NH Metropolitan Statistical Area—see Appendix B for areas included
Source: U.S. Census Bureau, 2010-2012 American Community Survey 3-Year Estimates

Segregation

Type	Segregation Indices[1] 1990	2000	2010	2010 Rank[2]	Percent Change 1990-2000	1990-2010	2000-2010
Black/White	n/a	n/a	n/a	n/a	n/a	n/a	n/a
Asian/White	n/a	n/a	n/a	n/a	n/a	n/a	n/a
Hispanic/White	n/a	n/a	n/a	n/a	n/a	n/a	n/a

Note: All figures cover the Metropolitan Statistical Area—see Appendix B for areas included; Figures are based on an analysis of 1990, 2000, and 2010 Census Decennial Census tract data by William H. Frey, Brookings Institution and the University of Michigan Social Science Data Analysis Network. In this analysis all racial groups (whites, blacks, and asians) are non-Hispanic members of those races. Hispanics are shown as a separate category;
(1) Segregation Indices are Dissimilarity Indices that measure the degree to which the minority group is distributed differently than whites across census tracts. They range from 0 (complete integration) to 100 (complete segregation) where the value indicates the percentage of the minority group that needs to move to be distributed exactly like whites; (2) Ranges from 1 (most segregated) to 102 (least segregated); n/a not available.
Source: www.CensusScope.org

Ancestry

Area	German	Irish	English	American	Italian	Polish	French[2]	Scottish	Dutch
City	7.6	20.5	9.8	3.1	7.9	4.2	18.1	2.1	0.5
MSA[1]	8.5	21.9	14.0	4.3	9.9	4.6	15.8	3.4	1.0
U.S.	15.2	11.1	8.2	7.2	5.6	3.1	2.8	1.7	1.4

Note: Figures are the percentage of the total population reporting a particular ancestry. The nine most commonly reported ancestries in the U.S. are shown. Figures include multiple ancestries (e.g. if a person reported being Irish and Italian, they were included in both columns); (1) Figures cover the Manchester-Nashua, NH Metropolitan Statistical Area—see Appendix B for areas included; (2) Excludes Basque
Source: U.S. Census Bureau, 2010-2012 American Community Survey 3-Year Estimates

Foreign-Born Population

Area	Any Foreign Country	Percent of Population Born in

Area	Any Foreign Country	Mexico	Asia	Europe	Carribean	South America	Central America[2]	Africa	Canada
City	13.0	1.5	3.8	2.5	0.9	1.4	0.3	1.5	1.0
MSA[1]	8.5	0.7	2.7	1.8	0.5	0.9	0.3	0.6	0.9
U.S.	13.0	3.7	3.7	1.6	1.2	0.9	1.0	0.5	0.3

Note: (1) Figures cover the Manchester-Nashua, NH Metropolitan Statistical Area—see Appendix B for areas included; (2) Excludes Mexico.
Source: U.S. Census Bureau, 2010-2012 American Community Survey 3-Year Estimates

Marital Status

Area	Never Married	Now Married[2]	Separated	Widowed	Divorced
City	36.3	43.1	2.2	5.3	13.2
MSA[1]	29.5	52.6	1.5	5.1	11.4
U.S.	32.4	48.4	2.2	6.0	11.0

Note: Figures are percentages and cover the population 15 years of age and older; (1) Figures cover the Manchester-Nashua, NH Metropolitan Statistical Area—see Appendix B for areas included; (2) Excludes separated
Source: U.S. Census Bureau, 2010-2012 American Community Survey 3-Year Estimates

Age

Area	Percent of Population	Median Age

Area	Under Age 5	Age 5–19	Age 20–34	Age 35–44	Age 45–54	Age 55–64	Age 65–74	Age 75–84	Age 85+	Median Age
City	6.3	17.7	23.5	14.5	14.2	11.7	6.7	3.3	2.2	36.6
MSA[1]	5.8	19.8	18.3	14.0	16.9	12.8	6.8	3.8	1.7	39.6
U.S.	6.4	20.1	20.5	13.1	14.3	12.2	7.3	4.2	1.8	37.3

Note: (1) Figures cover the Manchester-Nashua, NH Metropolitan Statistical Area—see Appendix B for areas included
Source: U.S. Census Bureau, 2010-2012 American Community Survey 3-Year Estimates

Gender

Area	Males	Females	Males per 100 Females
City	54,671	55,208	99.0
MSA[1]	198,957	202,976	98.0
U.S.	153,276,055	158,333,314	96.8

Note: (1) Figures cover the Manchester-Nashua, NH Metropolitan Statistical Area—see Appendix B for areas included
Source: U.S. Census Bureau, 2010-2012 American Community Survey 3-Year Estimates

Religious Groups by Family

Area	Catholic	Baptist	Non-Den.	Methodist[2]	Lutheran	LDS[3]	Pentecostal	Presbyterian[4]	Muslim[5]	Judaism
MSA[1]	31.2	1.4	2.4	1.2	0.5	0.6	0.5	2.0	0.3	0.5
U.S.	19.1	9.3	4.0	4.0	2.3	2.0	1.9	1.6	0.8	0.7

Note: Figures are the number of adherents as a percentage of the total population; (1) Figures cover the Manchester-Nashua, NH Metropolitan Statistical Area—see Appendix B for areas included; (2) Methodist/Pietist; (3) Latter Day Saints; (4) Reformed; (5) Figures are estimates
Source: Association of Statisticians of American Religious Bodies, 2010 U.S. Religion Census: Religious Congregations & Membership Study

Religious Groups by Tradition

Area	Catholic	Evangelical Protestant	Mainline Protestant	Other Tradition	Black Protestant	Orthodox
MSA[1]	31.2	5.1	4.4	1.8	<0.1	0.7
U.S.	19.1	16.2	7.3	4.3	1.6	0.3

Note: Figures are the number of adherents as a percentage of the total population; (1) Figures cover the Manchester-Nashua, NH Metropolitan Statistical Area—see Appendix B for areas included
Source: Association of Statisticians of American Religious Bodies, 2010 U.S. Religion Census: Religious Congregations & Membership Study

ECONOMY

Gross Metropolitan Product

Area	2011	2012	2013	2014	Rank[2]
MSA[1]	22.1	22.2	22.3	23.2	97

Note: Figures are in billions of dollars; (1) Figures cover the Manchester-Nashua, NH Metropolitan Statistical Area—see Appendix B for areas included; (2) Rank is based on 2014 data and ranges from 1 to 363
Source: The United States Conference of Mayors, U.S. Metro Economies: Outlook—Gross Metropolitan Product, with Metro Employment Projections, November 2013

Economic Growth

Area	2011 (%)	2012 (%)	2013 (%)	2014 (%)	Rank[2]
MSA[1]	4.6	-1.1	-0.4	2.1	282
U.S.	1.6	2.5	1.7	2.5	–

Note: Figures are real gross metropolitan product (GMP) growth rates and represent annual average percent change; (1) Figures cover the Manchester-Nashua, NH Metropolitan Statistical Area—see Appendix B for areas included; (2) Rank is based on 2013 data and ranges from 1 to 363
Source: The United States Conference of Mayors, U.S. Metro Economies: Outlook—Gross Metropolitan Product, with Metro Employment Projections, November 2013

Metropolitan Area Exports

Area	2007	2008	2009	2010	2011	2012	Rank[2]
MSA[1]	1,450.0	2,005.6	1,743.0	2,612.1	2,494.1	1,634.9	116

Note: Figures are in millions of dollars; (1) Figures cover the Manchester-Nashua, NH Metropolitan Statistical Area—see Appendix B for areas included; (2) Rank is based on 2012 data and ranges from 1 to 369
Source: U.S. Department of Commerce, International Trade Administration, Office of Trade & Industry Information, Manufacturing & Services, data extracted April 1, 2014

INCOME

Income

Area	Per Capita ($)	Median Household ($)	Average Household ($)
City	27,095	54,122	65,035
MSA[1]	33,635	69,395	86,470
U.S.	27,385	51,771	71,579

Note: (1) Figures cover the Manchester-Nashua, NH Metropolitan Statistical Area—see Appendix B for areas included
Source: U.S. Census Bureau, 2010-2012 American Community Survey 3-Year Estimates

Household Income Distribution

Area	Percent of Households Earning							
	Under $15,000	$15,000 -24,999	$25,000 -34,999	$35,000 -49,999	$50,000 -74,999	$75,000 -99,000	$100,000 -149,999	$150,000 and up
City	11.7	10.5	11.5	12.3	21.6	12.7	13.5	6.2
MSA[1]	7.8	8.1	8.3	11.1	18.4	14.5	18.4	13.3
U.S.	13.1	11.0	10.5	13.7	18.1	11.9	12.5	9.1

Note: (1) Figures cover the Manchester-Nashua, NH Metropolitan Statistical Area—see Appendix B for areas included
Source: U.S. Census Bureau, 2010-2012 American Community Survey 3-Year Estimates

Poverty Rate

Area	All Ages	Under 18 Years Old	18 to 64 Years Old	65 Years and Over
City	14.2	24.7	12.0	7.7
MSA[1]	8.3	12.6	7.3	5.9
U.S.	15.7	22.2	14.6	9.3

Note: Figures are percentage of people whose income during the past 12 months was below the poverty level;
(1) Figures cover the Manchester-Nashua, NH Metropolitan Statistical Area—see Appendix B for areas included
Source: U.S. Census Bureau, 2010-2012 American Community Survey 3-Year Estimates

Personal Bankruptcy Filing Rate

Area	2008	2009	2010	2011	2012	2013
Hillsborough County	3.31	3.99	4.62	3.94	3.20	2.50
U.S.	3.53	4.61	4.97	4.37	3.76	3.29

Note: Numbers are per 1,000 population and include Chapter 7 and Chapter 13 filings
Source: Federal Deposit Insurance Corporation, Regional Economic Conditions, March 20, 2014

EMPLOYMENT

Labor Force and Employment

Area	Civilian Labor Force			Workers Employed		
	Dec. 2012	Dec. 2013	% Chg.	Dec. 2012	Dec. 2013	% Chg.
City	62,477	61,692	-1.3	58,772	58,550	-0.4
MSA[1]	107,832	106,653	-1.1	102,005	101,619	-0.4
U.S.	154,904,000	154,408,000	-0.3	143,060,000	144,423,000	1.0

Note: Data is not seasonally adjusted and covers workers 16 years of age and older; (1) Metropolitan Statistical Area—see Appendix B for areas included
Source: Bureau of Labor Statistics, Local Area Unemployment Statistics

Unemployment Rate

Area	2013											
	Jan.	Feb.	Mar.	Apr.	May	Jun.	Jul.	Aug.	Sep.	Oct.	Nov.	Dec.
City	7.0	6.6	6.4	5.5	5.5	5.5	5.4	5.2	5.1	5.2	5.1	5.1
MSA[1]	6.3	6.0	5.8	4.9	4.9	5.0	5.1	4.8	4.7	4.9	4.7	4.7
U.S.	8.5	8.1	7.6	7.1	7.3	7.8	7.7	7.3	7.0	7.0	6.6	6.5

Note: Data is not seasonally adjusted and covers workers 16 years of age and older; All figures are percentages;
(1) Metropolitan Statistical Area—see Appendix B for areas included
Source: Bureau of Labor Statistics, Local Area Unemployment Statistics

Employment by Occupation

Occupation Classification	City (%)	MSA[1] (%)	U.S. (%)
Management, Business, Science, and Arts	34.2	40.8	36.0
Natural Resources, Construction, and Maintenance	8.0	8.2	9.1
Production, Transportation, and Material Moving	14.3	11.7	12.0
Sales and Office	25.6	24.9	24.7
Service	17.9	14.4	18.2

Note: Figures cover employed civilians 16 years of age and older; (1) Figures cover the Manchester-Nashua, NH Metropolitan Statistical Area—see Appendix B for areas included
Source: U.S. Census Bureau, 2010-2012 American Community Survey 3-Year Estimates

Employment by Industry

Sector	NECTA[1]		U.S.
	Number of Employees	Percent of Total	Percent of Total
Construction	n/a	n/a	4.2
Education and Health Services	20,300	19.9	15.5
Financial Activities	7,200	7.1	5.7
Government	11,400	11.2	16.1
Information	3,100	3.0	1.9
Leisure and Hospitality	8,600	8.4	10.2
Manufacturing	7,600	7.5	8.7
Mining and Logging	n/a	n/a	0.6
Other Services	4,600	4.5	3.9
Professional and Business Services	14,600	14.3	13.7
Retail Trade	13,500	13.2	11.4
Transportation and Utilities	2,700	2.6	3.8
Wholesale Trade	4,100	4.0	4.2

Note: Figures cover non-farm employment as of December 2013 and are not seasonally adjusted;
(1) New England City and Town Area—see Appendix B for areas included; n/a not available
Source: Bureau of Labor Statistics, Current Employment Statistics, Employment, Hours, and Earnings

Occupations with Greatest Projected Employment Growth: 2010 – 2020

Occupation[1]	2010 Employment	2020 Projected Employment	Numeric Employment Change	Percent Employment Change
Registered Nurses	13,960	17,060	3,090	22.2
Retail Salespersons	23,080	25,310	2,230	9.7
Personal Care Aides	3,870	6,050	2,190	56.6
Nursing Aides, Orderlies, and Attendants	8,650	10,410	1,760	20.3
Office Clerks, General	11,980	13,470	1,480	12.4
Home Health Aides	2,310	3,750	1,440	62.4
Cashiers	22,690	23,980	1,290	5.7
Combined Food Preparation and Serving Workers, Including Fast Food	10,460	11,680	1,230	11.7
Software Developers, Applications	4,760	5,990	1,230	25.8
Sales Representatives, Wholesale and Manufacturing, Except Technical and Scientific Products	6,790	7,850	1,060	15.6

Note: Projections cover New Hampshire; (1) Sorted by numeric employment change
Source: www.projectionscentral.com, State Occupational Projections, 2010–2020 Long-Term Projections

Fastest Growing Occupations: 2010 – 2020

Occupation[1]	2010 Employment	2020 Projected Employment	Numeric Employment Change	Percent Employment Change
Home Health Aides	2,310	3,750	1,440	62.4
Personal Care Aides	3,870	6,050	2,190	56.6
Helpers—Brickmasons, Blockmasons, Stonemasons, and Tile and Marble Setters	190	290	100	51.3
Health Educators	290	390	110	37.2
Mental Health Counselors	680	910	230	34.1
Physical Therapist Assistants	400	530	140	33.9
Medical Scientists, Except Epidemiologists	360	480	120	33.8
Market Research Analysts and Marketing Specialists	930	1,240	310	33.6
Brickmasons and Blockmasons	290	390	100	32.7
Medical Secretaries	2,530	3,360	830	32.7

Note: Projections cover New Hampshire; (1) Sorted by percent employment change and excludes occupations with numeric employment change less than 100
Source: www.projectionscentral.com, State Occupational Projections, 2010–2020 Long-Term Projections

Average Wages

Occupation	$/Hr.	Occupation	$/Hr.
Accountants and Auditors	34.23	Maids and Housekeeping Cleaners	10.32
Automotive Mechanics	20.10	Maintenance and Repair Workers	20.45
Bookkeepers	19.97	Marketing Managers	50.26
Carpenters	22.32	Nuclear Medicine Technologists	n/a
Cashiers	9.31	Nurses, Licensed Practical	23.10
Clerks, General Office	16.38	Nurses, Registered	31.99
Clerks, Receptionists/Information	13.43	Nursing Assistants	13.91
Clerks, Shipping/Receiving	15.01	Packers and Packagers, Hand	10.50
Computer Programmers	29.13	Physical Therapists	37.48
Computer Systems Analysts	35.94	Postal Service Mail Carriers	25.09
Computer User Support Specialists	23.82	Real Estate Brokers	47.44
Cooks, Restaurant	12.00	Retail Salespersons	11.99
Dentists	99.35	Sales Reps., Exc. Tech./Scientific	31.44
Electrical Engineers	41.16	Sales Reps., Tech./Scientific	38.83
Electricians	25.00	Secretaries, Exc. Legal/Med./Exec.	15.96
Financial Managers	55.30	Security Guards	11.92
First-Line Supervisors/Managers, Sales	21.01	Surgeons	105.45
Food Preparation Workers	13.44	Teacher Assistants	12.90
General and Operations Managers	56.50	Teachers, Elementary School	26.30
Hairdressers/Cosmetologists	13.23	Teachers, Secondary School	26.70
Internists	n/a	Telemarketers	15.57
Janitors and Cleaners	11.87	Truck Drivers, Heavy/Tractor-Trailer	18.63
Landscaping/Groundskeeping Workers	17.02	Truck Drivers, Light/Delivery Svcs.	15.08
Lawyers	61.67	Waiters and Waitresses	11.33

Note: Wage data covers the Manchester, NH Metropolitan Statistical Area—see Appendix B for areas included. Hourly wages for elementary/secondary school teachers and teacher assistants were calculated by the editors from annual wage data assuming a 40 hour work week; n/a not available.
Source: Bureau of Labor Statistics, Metro Area Occupational Employment and Wage Estimates, May 2013

RESIDENTIAL REAL ESTATE

Building Permits

Area	Single-Family			Multi-Family			Total		
	2012	2013	Pct. Chg.	2012	2013	Pct. Chg.	2012	2013	Pct. Chg.
City	61	49	-19.7	61	38	-37.7	122	87	-28.7
MSA[1]	365	468	28.2	255	99	-61.2	620	567	-8.5
U.S.	518,695	620,802	19.7	310,963	370,020	19.0	829,658	990,822	19.4

Note: (1) Metropolitan Statistical Area—see Appendix B for areas included; figures represent new, privately-owned housing units authorized (unadjusted data); All permit data are based on estimates with imputation.
Source: U.S. Census Bureau, Manufacturing, Mining, and Construction Statistics, Building Permits, 2012, 2013

Homeownership Rate

Area	2006 (%)	2007 (%)	2008 (%)	2009 (%)	2010 (%)	2011 (%)	2012 (%)	2013 (%)
MSA[1]	n/a	n/a	n/a	n/a	n/a	n/a	n/a	n/a
U.S.	68.8	68.1	67.8	67.4	66.9	66.1	65.4	65.1

Note: (1) Figures cover the Manchester-Nashua, NH Metropolitan Statistical Area—see Appendix B for areas included; n/a not available
Source: U.S. Census Bureau, Housing Vacancies and Homeownership Annual Statistics: 2013

Housing Vacancy Rates

Area	Gross Vacancy Rate[2] (%)			Year-Round Vacancy Rate[3] (%)			Rental Vacancy Rate[4] (%)			Homeowner Vacancy Rate[5] (%)		
	2011	2012	2013	2011	2012	2013	2011	2012	2013	2011	2012	2013
MSA[1]	n/a	n/a	n/a	n/a	n/a	n/a	n/a	n/a	n/a	n/a	n/a	n/a
U.S.	14.2	13.8	13.8	11.1	10.8	10.7	9.5	8.7	8.3	2.5	2.0	2.0

Note: (1) Figures cover the Manchester-Nashua, NH Metropolitan Statistical Area—see Appendix B for areas included; (2) The percentage of the total housing inventory that is vacant; (3) The percentage of the housing inventory (excluding seasonal units) that is year-round vacant; (4) The percentage of rental inventory that is vacant for rent; (5) The percentage of homeowner inventory that is vacant for sale; n/a not available
Source: U.S. Census Bureau, Housing Vacancies and Homeownership Annual Statistics: 2013

TAXES

State Corporate Income Tax Rates

State	Tax Rate (%)	Income Brackets ($)	Num. of Brackets	Financial Institution Tax Rate (%)[a]	Federal Income Tax Ded.
New Hampshire	8.5 (q)	Flat rate	1	8.5 (q)	No

Note: Tax rates as of January 1, 2014; (a) Rates listed are the corporate income tax rate applied to financial institutions or excise taxes based on income. Some states have other taxes based upon the value of deposits or shares; (q) New Hampshire's 8.5% Business Profits Tax is imposed on both corporations and unincorporated associations with gross income over $50,000. In addition, New Hampshire levies a Business Enterprise Tax of 0.75% on the enterprise base (total compensation, interest and dividends paid) for businesses with gross income over $150,000 or base over $75,000.
Source: Federation of Tax Administrators, "State Corporate Income Tax Rates, 2014"

State Individual Income Tax Rates

State	Tax Rate (%)	Income Brackets ($)	Num. of Brackets	Personal Exempt. ($)[1] Single	Dependents	Fed. Inc. Tax Ded.
New Hampshire		State income tax of 5% on dividends and interest income only				

Note: Tax rates as of January 1, 2014; Local- and county-level taxes are not included; n/a not applicable; (1) Married joint filers generally receive double the single exemption
Source: Federation of Tax Administrators, "State Individual Income Tax Rates, 2014"

Various State and Local Tax Rates

State	State and Local Sales and Use (%)	State Sales and Use (%)	Gasoline[1] (¢/gal.)	Cigarette[2] ($/pack)	Spirits[3] ($/gal.)	Wine[4] ($/gal.)	Beer[5] ($/gal.)
New Hampshire	None	None	19.63	1.780	0.00 (g)	(l)	0.30

Note: All tax rates as of January 1, 2014; (1) The American Petroleum Institute has developed a methodology for determining the average tax rate on a gallon of fuel. Rates may include any of the following: excise taxes, environmental fees, storage tank fees, other fees or taxes, general sales tax, and local taxes. In states where gasoline is subject to the general sales tax, or where the fuel tax is based on the average sale price, the average rate determined by API is sensitive to changes in the price of gasoline. States that fully or partially apply general sales taxes to gasoline: CA, CO, GA, IL, IN, MI, NY; (2) The federal excise tax of $1.0066 per pack and local taxes are not included; (3) Rates are those applicable to off-premise sales of 40% alcohol by volume (a.b.v.) distilled spirits in 750ml containers. Local excise taxes are excluded; (4) Rates are those applicable to off-premise sales of 11% a.b.v. non-carbonated wine in 750ml containers; (5) Rates are those applicable to off-premise sales of 4.7% a.b.v. beer in 12 ounce containers; (g) States where the government controls sales. In these "control states," products are subject to ad valorem mark-up and excise taxes. The excise tax rate is calculated using a methodology developed by the Distilled Spirits Council of the United States; (l) Control states, where the government controls all sales. Products can be subject to ad valorem mark-up and excise taxes.
Source: Tax Foundation, 2014 Facts & Figures: How Does Your State Compare?

State Business Tax Climate Index Rankings

State	Overall Rank	Corporate Tax Index Rank	Individual Income Tax Index Rank	Sales Tax Index Rank	Unemployment Insurance Tax Index Rank	Property Tax Index Rank
New Hampshire	8	48	9	1	46	42

Note: The index is a measure of how each state's tax laws affect economic performance. The lower the rank, the more favorable a state's tax system is for business. States without a given tax are given a ranking of 1. The scores/rankings for the District of Columbia do not affect other states. The 2014 index represents the tax climate as of July 1, 2013.
Source: Tax Foundation, State Business Tax Climate Index 2014

COMMERCIAL UTILITIES

Typical Monthly Electric Bills

Area	Commercial Service ($/month)		Industrial Service ($/month)	
	1,500 kWh	40 kW demand 14,000 kWh	1,000 kW demand 200,000 kWh	50,000 kW demand 15,000,000 kWh
City	217	1,952	30,715	2,049,413
Average[1]	197	1,636	25,662	1,485,307

Note: Based on total rates in effect July 1, 2013; (1) average based on 180 utilities surveyed
Source: Edison Electric Institute, Typical Bills and Average Rates Report, Summer 2013

TRANSPORTATION

Means of Transportation to Work

Area	Car/Truck/Van		Public Transportation			Bicycle	Walked	Other Means	Worked at Home
	Drove Alone	Car-pooled	Bus	Subway	Railroad				
City	81.0	10.4	1.3	0.1	0.0	0.1	2.9	0.7	3.6
MSA[1]	82.1	8.2	0.8	0.0	0.1	0.0	2.0	0.7	6.1
U.S.	76.4	9.7	2.6	1.7	0.5	0.6	2.8	1.3	4.3

Note: Figures are percentages and cover workers 16 years of age and older; (1) Figures cover the Manchester-Nashua, NH Metropolitan Statistical Area—see Appendix B for areas included
Source: U.S. Census Bureau, 2010-2012 American Community Survey 3-Year Estimates

Travel Time to Work

Area	Less Than 10 Minutes	10 to 19 Minutes	20 to 29 Minutes	30 to 44 Minutes	45 to 59 Minutes	60 to 89 Minutes	90 Minutes or More
City	12.5	41.3	19.3	14.6	5.0	5.0	2.2
MSA[1]	11.0	31.0	20.3	20.0	7.9	7.0	2.8
U.S.	13.5	29.8	20.9	20.1	7.5	5.6	2.5

Note: Figures are percentages and include workers 16 years old and over; (1) Figures cover the Manchester-Nashua, NH Metropolitan Statistical Area—see Appendix B for areas included
Source: U.S. Census Bureau, 2010-2012 American Community Survey 3-Year Estimates

Travel Time Index

Area	1985	1990	1995	2000	2005	2010	2011
Urban Area[1]	n/a	n/a	n/a	n/a	n/a	n/a	n/a
Average[2]	1.09	1.14	1.16	1.19	1.23	1.18	1.18

Note: Travel Time Index—the ratio of travel time in the peak period to the travel time at free-flow conditions. For example, a value of 1.30 indicates a 20-minute free-flow trip takes 26 minutes in the peak. Free-flow speeds (60 mph on freeways and 35 mph on principal arterials) are used as the comparison threshold; (1) Data for the Manchester-Nashua, NH urban area was not available; (2) average of 498 urban areas
Source: Texas Transportation Institute, Urban Mobility Report 2012, December 2012

Public Transportation

Agency Name / Mode of Transportation	Vehicles Operated in Maximum Service	Annual Unlinked Passenger Trips (in thous.)	Annual Passenger Miles (in thous.)
Manchester Transit Authority (MTA)			
Bus (directly operated)	14	427.2	958.1
Demand Response (directly operated)	5	14.2	75.5

Source: Federal Transit Administration, National Transit Database, 2012

Air Transportation

Airport Name and Code / Type of Service	Passenger Airlines[1]	Passenger Enplanements	Freight Carriers[2]	Freight (lbs.)
Manchester Municipal (MHT)				
Domestic service (U.S. carriers - 2013)	21	1,189,224	8	85,246,997
International service (U.S. carriers - 2012)	3	342	0	0

Note: (1) Includes all U.S.-based major, minor and commuter airlines that carried at least one passenger during the year; (2) Includes all U.S.-based airlines and freight carriers that transported at least one lb. of freight during the year.
Source: Bureau of Transportation Statistics, The Intermodal Transportation Database, Air Carriers: T-100 Domestic Market (U.S. Carriers), 2013; Bureau of Transportation Statistics, The Intermodal Transportation Database, Air Carriers: T-100 International Market (U.S. Carriers), 2012

Other Transportation Statistics

Major Highways:	I-93
Amtrak Service:	No
Major Waterways/Ports:	Merrimack River

Source: Amtrak.com; Google Maps

BUSINESSES

Major Business Headquarters

Company Name	Rankings	
	Fortune[1]	Forbes[2]
No companies listed	-	-

Note: (1) Fortune 500—companies that produce a 10-K are ranked 1 to 500 based on 2012 revenue; (2) all private companies with at least $2 billion in annual revenue through the end of their most current fiscal year are ranked 1 to 224; companies listed are headquartered in the city; dashes indicate no ranking
Source: Fortune, "Fortune 500," May 20, 2013; Forbes, "America's Largest Private Companies," December 18, 2013

Fast-Growing Businesses

According to *Initiative for a Competitive Inner City (ICIC)*, Manchester is home to one of America's 100 fastest-growing "inner city" companies: **Cellular Specialties** (#51). Companies were ranked by their five-year compound annual growth rate. Criteria for inclusion: company must be headquartered in or have 51 percent or more of its physical operations in an economically distressed urban area; must be an independent, for-profit corporation, partnership or proprietorship; must have 10 or more employees and have a five-year sales history that includes sales of at least $200,000 in the base year and at least $1 million in the current year with no decrease in sales over the two most recent years. *Initiative for a Competitive Inner City (ICIC), "Inner City 100 Companies, 2013"*

According to Deloitte, Manchester is home to one of North America's 500 fastest-growing high-technology companies: **Dyn** (#210). Companies are ranked by percentage growth in revenue over a five-year period. Criteria for inclusion: company must be headquartered within North America; must own proprietary intellectual property or proprietary technology that contributes to a significant portion of the company's operating revenue, or devote a significant proportion of revenues to research and development of technology; must have been in business for a minumum of five years with 2008 operating revenues of at least $50,000 USD/CD and 2012 operating revenues of at least $5 million USD/CD. *Deloitte Touche Tohmatsu, 2013 Technology Fast 500™*

Minority- and Women-Owned Businesses

Group	All Firms		Firms with Paid Employees			
	Firms	Sales ($000)	Firms	Sales ($000)	Employees	Payroll ($000)
Asian	300	81,420	100	71,099	696	21,441
Black	88	3,339	6	1,778	74	506
Hispanic	229	18,361	35	12,728	97	3,438
Women	1,997	265,254	270	219,018	1,808	54,106
All Firms	8,945	14,066,568	2,758	13,759,371	71,869	2,974,158

Note: Figures cover firms located in the city; minority- and women-owned business are defined as firms in which the corresponding group own 51% or more of the stock or equity of the company
Source: U.S. Census Bureau, 2007 Economic Census, Survey of Business Owners (2012 Survey of Business Owners data will be released starting in June 2015)

HOTELS & CONVENTION CENTERS

Hotels/Motels

Area	5 Star		4 Star		3 Star		2 Star		1 Star		Not Rated	
	Num.	Pct.[3]	Num.	Pct.[3]	Num.	Pct.[3]	Num.	Pct.[3]	Num.	Pct.[3]	Num.	Pct.[3]
City[1]	0	0.0	1	1.1	34	37.0	48	52.2	0	0.0	9	9.8
Total[2]	142	0.9	1,005	6.0	5,147	30.9	8,578	51.4	408	2.4	1,397	8.4

Note: (1) Figures cover Manchester and vicinity; (2) Figures cover all 100 cities in this book; (3) Percentage of hotels which have a given star rating; Star ratings are determined by expedia.com and offer an indication of the general quality of a particular hotel.
Source: expedia.com, April 7, 2014

Major Convention Centers

Name	Overall Space (sq. ft.)	Exhibit Space (sq. ft.)	Meeting Space (sq. ft.)	Meeting Rooms

There are no major convention centers located in the metro area
Source: Original research

Living Environment

COST OF LIVING

Cost of Living Index

Composite Index	Groceries	Housing	Utilities	Trans-portation	Health Care	Misc. Goods/ Services
120.2	98.5	137.9	122.7	101.2	117.7	121.9

Note: The Cost of Living Index measures regional differences in the cost of consumer goods and services, excluding taxes and non-consumer expenditures, for professional and managerial households in the top income quintile. It is based on more than 50,000 prices covering almost 60 different items for which prices are collected three times a year by chambers of commerce, economic development organizations or university applied economic centers in each participating urban area. The numbers shown should be read as a percentage above or below the national average of 100. For example, a value of 115.4 in the groceries column indicates that grocery prices are 15.4% higher than the national average. Small differences in the index numbers should not be interpreted as significant; Figures cover the Manchester NH urban area.
Source: The Council for Community and Economic Research, ACCRA Cost of Living Index, 2013

Grocery Prices

Area[1]	T-Bone Steak ($/pound)	Frying Chicken ($/pound)	Whole Milk ($/half gal.)	Eggs ($/dozen)	Orange Juice ($/64 oz.)	Coffee ($/11.5 oz.)
City[2]	10.68	1.26	2.22	1.88	2.88	3.81
Avg.	10.19	1.28	2.34	1.81	3.48	4.39
Min.	8.56	0.94	1.44	1.19	2.78	3.40
Max.	14.82	2.28	3.56	3.73	6.23	7.32

Note: (1) Values for the local area are compared with the average, minimum and maximum values for all 327 areas in the Cost of Living Index; (2) Figures cover the Manchester NH urban area; T-Bone Steak (price per pound); Frying Chicken (price per pound, whole fryer); Whole Milk (half gallon carton); Eggs (price per dozen, Grade A, large); Orange Juice (64 oz. Tropicana or Florida Natural); Coffee (11.5 oz. can, vacuum-packed, Maxwell House, Hills Bros, or Folgers).
Source: The Council for Community and Economic Research, ACCRA Cost of Living Index, 2013

Housing and Utility Costs

Area[1]	New Home Price ($)	Apartment Rent ($/month)	All Electric ($/month)	Part Electric ($/month)	Other Energy ($/month)	Telephone ($/month)
City[2]	389,899	1,378	-	106.64	84.83	36.25
Avg.	295,864	900	171.38	91.82	70.12	27.73
Min.	185,506	458	117.80	48.81	33.67	17.16
Max.	1,358,917	3,783	441.68	171.40	372.65	39.47

Note: (1) Values for the local area are compared with the average, minimum and maximum values for all 327 areas in the Cost of Living Index; (2) Figures cover the Manchester NH urban area; New Home Price (2,400 sf living area, 8,000 sf lot, in urban area with full utilities); Apartment Rent (950 sf 2 bedroom/1.5 or 2 bath, unfurnished, excluding all utilities except water); All Electric (average monthly cost for an all-electric home); Part Electric (average monthly cost for a part-electric home); Other Energy (average monthly cost for natural gas, fuel oil, coal, wood, and any other forms of energy except electricity); Telephone (price includes basic monthly rate for a private residential line plus additional local usage charges incurred by a family of four).
Source: The Council for Community and Economic Research, ACCRA Cost of Living Index, 2013

Health Care, Transportation, and Other Costs

Area[1]	Doctor ($/visit)	Dentist ($/visit)	Optometrist ($/visit)	Gasoline ($/gallon)	Beauty Salon ($/visit)	Men's Shirt ($)
City[2]	149.00	98.13	102.96	3.55	38.13	35.78
Avg.	101.40	86.48	96.16	3.44	33.87	26.55
Min.	61.67	50.83	50.12	3.08	18.92	12.48
Max.	182.71	152.50	223.78	4.33	68.22	52.03

Note: (1) Values for the local area are compared with the average, minimum and maximum values for all 327 areas in the Cost of Living Index; (2) Figures cover the Manchester NH urban area; Doctor (general practitioners routine exam of an established patient); Dentist (adult teeth cleaning and periodic oral examination); Optometrist (full vision eye exam for established adult patient); Gasoline (one gallon regular unleaded, national brand, including all taxes, cash price at self-service pump if available); Beauty Salon (woman's shampoo, trim, and blow-dry); Men's Shirt (cotton/polyester dress shirt, pinpoint weave, long sleeves).
Source: The Council for Community and Economic Research, ACCRA Cost of Living Index, 2013

HOUSING

House Price Index (HPI)

Area	National Ranking[2]	Quarterly Change (%)	One-Year Change (%)	Five-Year Change (%)
MSA[1]	158	0.42	1.76	-10.15
U.S.[3]	–	1.20	7.69	4.18

Note: The HPI is a weighted repeat sales index. It measures average price changes in repeat sales or refinancings on the same properties. This information is obtained by reviewing repeat mortgage transactions on single-family properties whose mortgages have been purchased or securitized by Fannie Mae or Freddie Mac in January 1975; (1) Manchester-Nashua, NH Metropolitan Statistical Area—see Appendix B for areas included; (2) Rankings are based on annual percentage change for all metro areas containing at least 15,000 transactions over the last 10 years and ranges from 1 to 283; (3) figures based on a weighted average of Census Division estimates using a seasonally adjusted, purchase-only index; all figures are for the period ending December 31, 2013
Source: Federal Housing Finance Agency, House Price Index, February 25, 2014

Median Single-Family Home Prices

Area	2011	2012	2013p	Percent Change 2012 to 2013
MSA[1]	213.5	212.8	229.2	7.7
U.S. Average	166.2	177.2	197.4	11.4

Note: Figures are median sales prices of existing single-family homes in thousands of dollars; (p) preliminary; n/a not available; (1) Manchester-Nashua, NH Metropolitan Statistical Area—see Appendix B for areas included
Source: National Association of Realtors, Median Sales Price of Existing Single-Family Homes for Metropolitan Areas, 4th Quarter 2013

Qualifying Income Based on Median Sales Price of Existing Single-Family Homes

Area	With 5% Down ($)	With 10% Down ($)	With 20% Down ($)
MSA[1]	51,159	48,467	43,081
U.S. Average	45,395	43,006	38,228

Note: Figures are preliminary; Qualifying income is based on a mortgage rate of 4.4%. Monthly principal and interest payment is limited to 25% of income; n/a not available; (1) Manchester-Nashua, NH Metropolitan Statistical Area—see Appendix B for areas included
Source: National Association of Realtors, Qualifying Income Based on Median Sales Price of Existing Single-Family Homes for Metropolitan Areas, 4th Quarter 2013

Median Apartment Condo-Coop Home Prices

Area	2011	2012	2013p	Percent Change 2012 to 2013
MSA[1]	149.0	142.8	155.6	9.0
U.S. Average	165.1	173.7	194.9	12.2

Note: Figures are median sales prices of existing apartment condo-coop homes in thousands of dollars; (p) preliminary; n/a not available; (1) Manchester-Nashua, NH Metropolitan Statistical Area—see Appendix B for areas included
Source: National Association of Realtors, Median Sales Price of Existing Apartment Condo-Coop Homes for Metropolitan Areas, 4th Quarter 2013

Gross Monthly Rent

Area	Under $200	$200 -299	$300 -499	$500 -749	$750 -999	$1,000 -1,499	$1,500 and up	Median ($)
City	1.8	5.1	4.0	9.5	32.5	39.4	7.7	980
MSA[1]	1.3	3.6	4.6	11.0	26.4	39.4	13.6	1,028
U.S.	1.7	3.3	8.1	22.7	24.3	25.7	14.3	889

Note: Figures are percentages except for Median; Gross rent is the contract rent plus the estimated average monthly cost of utilities (electricity, gas, and water and sewer) and fuels (oil, coal, kerosene, wood, etc.) if these are paid by the renter (or paid for the renter by someone else); (1) Figures cover the Manchester-Nashua, NH Metropolitan Statistical Area—see Appendix B for areas included
Source: U.S. Census Bureau, 2010-2012 American Community Survey 3-Year Estimates

Year Housing Structure Built

Area	2010 or Later	2000 -2009	1990 -1999	1980 -1989	1970 -1979	1960 -1969	1950 -1959	1940 -1949	Before 1940	Median Year
City	0.1	6.2	6.1	14.2	10.1	6.9	10.1	7.8	38.7	1954
MSA[1]	0.3	10.1	9.7	20.6	15.8	9.5	7.7	4.1	22.3	1974
U.S.	0.5	14.9	13.8	13.9	15.9	11.1	10.9	5.5	13.5	1976

Note: Figures are percentages except for Median Year; (1) Figures cover the Manchester-Nashua, NH Metropolitan Statistical Area—see Appendix B for areas included
Source: U.S. Census Bureau, 2010-2012 American Community Survey 3-Year Estimates

HEALTH

Health Risk Data

Category	MSA[1] (%)	U.S. (%)
Adults aged 18–64 who have any kind of health care coverage	84.8	79.6
Adults who reported being in good or excellent health	87.2	83.1
Adults who are current smokers	17.7	19.6
Adults who are heavy drinkers[2]	7.5	6.1
Adults who are binge drinkers[3]	16.1	16.9
Adults who are overweight (BMI 25.0 - 29.9)	37.2	35.8
Adults who are obese (BMI 30.0 - 99.8)	26.9	27.6
Adults who participated in any physical activities in the past month	78.9	77.1
Adults 50+ who have ever had a sigmoidoscopy or colonoscopy	79.3	67.3
Women aged 40+ who have had a mammogram within the past two years	78.2	74.0
Men aged 40+ who have had a PSA test within the past two years	42.4	45.2
Adults aged 65+ who have had flu shot within the past year	56.8	60.1
Adults who always wear a seatbelt	82.6	93.8

Note: Data as of 2012 unless otherwise noted; (1) Figures cover the Manchester-Nashua, NH Metropolitan Statistical Area—see Appendix B for areas included; (2) Heavy drinkers are classified as males having more than two drinks per day or females having more than one drink per day; (3) Binge drinkers are classified as males having five or more drinks on one occasion or females having four or more drinks on one occasion
Source: Centers for Disease Control and Prevention, Behaviorial Risk Factor Surveillance System, SMART: Selected Metropolitan/Micropolitan Area Risk Trends, 2012

Chronic Health Indicators

Category	MSA[1] (%)	U.S. (%)
Adults who have ever been told they had a heart attack	4.7	4.5
Adults who have ever been told they had a stroke	2.3	2.9
Adults who have been told they currently have asthma	10.6	8.9
Adults who have ever been told they have arthritis	26.4	25.7
Adults who have ever been told they have diabetes[2]	8.7	9.7
Adults who have ever been told they had skin cancer	5.6	5.7
Adults who have ever been told they had any other types of cancer	5.8	6.5
Adults who have ever been told they have COPD	4.7	6.2
Adults who have ever been told they have kidney disease	2.3	2.5
Adults who have ever been told they have a form of depression	19.0	18.0

Note: Data as of 2012 unless otherwise noted; (1) Figures cover the Manchester-Nashua, NH Metropolitan Statistical Area—see Appendix B for areas included; (2) Figures do not include pregnancy-related, borderline, or pre-diabetes
Source: Centers for Disease Control and Prevention, Behaviorial Risk Factor Surveillance System, SMART: Selected Metropolitan/Micropolitan Area Risk Trends, 2012

Mortality Rates for the Top 10 Causes of Death in the U.S.

ICD-10[a] Sub-Chapter	ICD-10[a] Code	Age-Adjusted Mortality Rate[1] per 100,000 population	
		County[2]	U.S.
Malignant neoplasms	C00-C97	169.2	174.2
Ischaemic heart diseases	I20-I25	89.4	119.1
Other forms of heart disease	I30-I51	44.4	49.6
Chronic lower respiratory diseases	J40-J47	45.4	43.2
Cerebrovascular diseases	I60-I69	32.8	40.3
Organic, including symptomatic, mental disorders	F01-F09	36.2	30.5
Other degenerative diseases of the nervous system	G30-G31	30.7	26.3
Other external causes of accidental injury	W00-X59	22.7	25.1
Diabetes mellitus	E10-E14	18.4	21.3
Hypertensive diseases	I10-I15	16.9	18.8

Note: (a) ICD-10 = International Classification of Diseases 10th Revision; (1) Mortality rates are a three year average covering 2008-2010; (2) Figures cover Hillsborough County
Source: Centers for Disease Control and Prevention, National Center for Health Statistics. Compressed Mortality File 1999-2010 on CDC WONDER Online Database, released January 2013. Data are compiled from the Compressed Mortality File 1999-2010, Series 20 No. 2P, 2013.

Mortality Rates for Selected Causes of Death

ICD-10[a] Sub-Chapter	ICD-10[a] Code	Age-Adjusted Mortality Rate[1] per 100,000 population	
		County[2]	U.S.
Assault	X85-Y09	*1.4	5.5
Diseases of the liver	K70-K76	11.6	12.4
Human immunodeficiency virus (HIV) disease	B20-B24	Suppressed	3.0
Influenza and pneumonia	J09-J18	16.8	16.4
Intentional self-harm	X60-X84	12.1	11.8
Malnutrition	E40-E46	Suppressed	0.8
Obesity and other hyperalimentation	E65-E68	2.2	1.6
Renal failure	N17-N19	14.8	13.6
Transport accidents	V01-V99	7.1	12.6
Viral hepatitis	B15-B19	*1.3	2.2

Note: (a) ICD-10 = International Classification of Diseases 10th Revision; (1) Mortality rates are a three year average covering 2008-2010; (2) Figures cover Hillsborough County; (*) Unreliable data as per CDC
Source: Centers for Disease Control and Prevention, National Center for Health Statistics. Compressed Mortality File 1999-2010 on CDC WONDER Online Database, released January 2013. Data are compiled from the Compressed Mortality File 1999-2010, Series 20 No. 2P, 2013.

Health Insurance Coverage

Area	With Health Insurance	With Private Health Insurance	With Public Health Insurance	Without Health Insurance	Population Under Age 18 Without Health Insurance
City	86.0	67.0	29.4	14.0	4.0
MSA[1]	90.3	76.9	23.6	9.7	2.7
U.S.	84.9	65.4	30.4	15.1	7.5

Note: Figures are percentages that cover the civilian noninstitutionalized population; (1) Figures cover the Manchester-Nashua, NH Metropolitan Statistical Area—see Appendix B for areas included
Source: U.S. Census Bureau, 2010-2012 American Community Survey 3-Year Estimates

Number of Medical Professionals

Area[1]	MDs[2]	DOs[2,3]	Dentists	Podiatrists	Chiropractors	Optometrists
Local (number)	911	72	295	19	94	69
Local (rate[4])	226.7	17.9	73.2	4.7	23.3	17.1
U.S. (rate[4])	267.6	19.6	61.7	5.6	24.7	14.5

Note: Data as of 2012 unless noted; (1) Local data covers Hillsborough County; (2) Data as of 2011; (3) Doctor of Osteopathic Medicine; (4) rate per 100,000 population
Source: Area Resource File (ARF) 2012-2013. U.S. Department of Health and Human Services, Health Resources and Services Administration, Bureau of Health Professions

EDUCATION

Public School District Statistics

District Name	Schls	Pupils	Pupil/ Teacher Ratio	Minority Pupils[1] (%)	Free Lunch Eligible[2] (%)	IEP[3] (%)
Manchester SD	21	14,680	13.6	33.5	42.9	17.4

Note: Table includes school districts with 2,000 or more students; (1) Percentage of students that are not non-Hispanic white; (2) Percentage of students that are eligible for the free lunch program; (3) Percentage of students that have an Individualized Education Program.
Source: U.S. Department of Education, National Center for Education Statistics, Common Core of Data, Local Education Agency (School District) Universe Survey: School Year 2011-2012; U.S. Department of Education, National Center for Education Statistics, Common Core of Data, Public Elementary/Secondary School Universe Survey: School Year 2011-2012

Highest Level of Education

Area	Less than H.S.	H.S. Diploma	Some College, No Deg.	Associate Degree	Bachelor's Degree	Master's Degree	Prof. School Degree	Doctorate Degree
City	13.7	33.0	18.7	8.4	17.9	6.4	1.1	0.7
MSA[1]	9.2	27.3	18.4	9.6	22.6	10.2	1.5	1.2
U.S.	14.1	28.3	21.3	7.8	18.0	7.5	1.9	1.2

Note: Figures cover persons age 25 and over; (1) Figures cover the Manchester-Nashua, NH Metropolitan Statistical Area—see Appendix B for areas included
Source: U.S. Census Bureau, 2010-2012 American Community Survey 3-Year Estimates

Educational Attainment by Race

Area	High School Graduate or Higher (%)					Bachelor's Degree or Higher (%)				
	Total	White	Black	Asian	Hisp.[2]	Total	White	Black	Asian	Hisp.[2]
City	86.3	88.2	73.3	68.1	64.7	26.2	26.8	20.2	28.1	13.8
MSA[1]	90.8	91.5	83.5	84.2	70.1	35.5	35.1	29.5	55.3	19.0
U.S.	85.9	88.1	82.5	85.5	63.1	28.6	30.0	18.4	50.2	13.4

Note: Figures shown cover persons 25 years old and over; (1) Figures cover the Manchester-Nashua, NH Metropolitan Statistical Area—see Appendix B for areas included; (2) People of Hispanic origin can be of any race
Source: U.S. Census Bureau, 2010-2012 American Community Survey 3-Year Estimates

School Enrollment by Grade and Control

Area	Preschool (%)		Kindergarten (%)		Grades 1 - 4 (%)		Grades 5 - 8 (%)		Grades 9 - 12 (%)	
	Public	Private	Public	Private	Public	Private	Public	Private	Public	Private
City	50.0	50.0	78.9	21.1	89.9	10.1	91.5	8.5	96.6	3.4
MSA[1]	41.4	58.6	74.9	25.1	89.6	10.4	89.7	10.3	91.3	8.7
U.S.	56.9	43.1	87.8	12.2	89.9	10.1	90.0	10.0	90.8	9.2

Note: Figures shown cover persons 3 years old and over; (1) Figures cover the Manchester-Nashua, NH Metropolitan Statistical Area—see Appendix B for areas included
Source: U.S. Census Bureau, 2010-2012 American Community Survey 3-Year Estimates

Average Salaries of Public School Classroom Teachers

Area	2012-13		2013-14		Percent Change 2012-13 to 2013-14	Percent Change 2003-04 to 2013-14
	Dollars	Rank[1]	Dollars	Rank[1]		
New Hampshire	55,599	19	57,057	19	2.62	33.7
U.S. Average	56,103	–	56,689	–	1.04	21.8

Note: (1) State rank ranges from 1 to 51 where 1 indicates highest salary.
Source: National Education Association, Rankings & Estimates: Rankings of the States 2013 and Estimates of School Statistics 2014, March 2014

Higher Education

Four-Year Colleges			Two-Year Colleges			Medical Schools[1]	Law Schools[2]	Voc/ Tech[3]
Public	Private Non-profit	Private For-profit	Public	Private Non-profit	Private For-profit			
1	3	1	1	0	0	0	0	3

Note: Figures cover institutions located within the city limits and include main campuses only; (1) includes schools accredited by the Liaison Committee on Medical Education and the American Osteopathic Association's Commission on Osteopathic College Accreditation; (2) includes ABA-accredited schools, schools with provisional ABA accreditation, and state accredited schools; (3) includes all schools with programs that are less than 2 years.
Source: National Center for Education Statistics, Integrated Postsecondary Education System (IPEDS), 2012-13; Association of American Medical Colleges, Member List, April 24, 2014; American Osteopathic Association, Member List, April 24, 2014; Law School Admission Council, Official Guide to ABA-Approved Law Schools Online, April 24, 2014; Wikipedia, List of Medical Schools in the United States, April 24, 2014; Wikipedia, List of Law Schools in the United States, April 24, 2014

According to *U.S. News & World Report,* the Manchester-Nashua, NH metro area is home to one of the best liberal arts colleges in the U.S.: **Saint Anselm College** (#120). The indicators used to capture academic quality fall into a number of categories: assessment by administrators at peer institutions; retention of students; faculty resources; student selectivity; financial resources; alumni giving; high school counselor ratings of colleges; and graduation rate. *U.S. News & World Report, "America's Best Colleges 2014"*

PRESIDENTIAL ELECTION

2012 Presidential Election Results

Area	Obama	Romney	Other
Hillsborough County	49.7	48.6	1.6
U.S.	51.0	47.2	1.8

Note: Results are percentages and may not add to 100% due to rounding
Source: Dave Leip's Atlas of U.S. Presidential Elections

EMPLOYERS

Major Employers

Company Name	Industry
Applied research Associates of NM	Engineering services
BAE Systems	Electronic circuits
Catholic Medical Center	General medical/surgical hospitals
Elliot health System	General medical/surgical hospitals
Federal Aviation Administration	Air traffic control operations, government
Framatome Group	Electronic connectors
Hewlett Packard Company	Agents, shipping
Kollsman	Search and navigation equipment
Mary Hitchcock Memorial Hospital	Offices and clinics of medical doctors
Monadnock Health Services	Offices and clinics of medical doctors
OSRAM Sylvania	Electric lamps
Roman Catholic Bishop of Manchester	Religious organizations
Saint Anslem College	Colleges/universities
Southern New Hampshire Medical Center	General medical/surgical hospitals
St Josephs Hospital	General medical/surgical hospitals
The Parkers Maple Barn Com Crib	Restaurant, family independent
Velcro USA	Fabric tapes
Verizon New England	Telephone communication except radio

Note: Companies shown are located within the Manchester-Nashua, NH Metropolitan Statistical Area.
Source: Hoovers.com; Wikipedia

PUBLIC SAFETY

Crime Rate

Area	All Crimes	Violent Crimes				Property Crimes		
		Murder	Forcible Rape	Robbery	Aggrav. Assault	Burglary	Larceny -Theft	Motor Vehicle Theft
City	4,064.0	0.9	65.4	186.3	314.4	771.5	2,588.1	137.2
Suburbs[1]	1,982.7	0.0	24.3	24.3	78.7	302.0	1,486.5	67.0
Metro[2]	2,551.8	0.2	35.5	68.6	143.1	430.3	1,787.7	86.2
U.S.	3,246.1	4.7	26.9	112.9	242.3	670.2	1,959.3	229.7

Note: Figures are crimes per 100,000 population; (1) All areas within the metro area that are located outside the city limits; (2) Figures cover the Manchester-Nashua, NH Metropolitan Statistical Area—see Appendix B for areas included
Source: FBI Uniform Crime Reports, 2012

Hate Crimes

Area	Number of Quarters Reported	Bias Motivation				
		Race	Religion	Sexual Orientation	Ethnicity	Disability
City	4	1	1	0	0	0
U.S.	4	2,797	1,099	1,135	667	92

Source: Federal Bureau of Investigation, Hate Crime Statistics 2012

Identity Theft Consumer Complaints

Area	Complaints	Complaints per 100,000 Population	Rank[2]
MSA[1]	198	49.4	282
U.S.	290,056	91.8	-

Note: (1) Figures cover the Manchester-Nashua, NH Metropolitan Statistical Area—see Appendix B for areas included; (2) Rank ranges from 1 to 377 where 1 indicates greatest number of identity theft complaints per 100,000 population
Source: Federal Trade Commission, Consumer Sentinel Network Data Book for January–December 2013

Fraud and Other Consumer Complaints

Area	Complaints	Complaints per 100,000 Population	Rank[2]
MSA[1]	1,723	430.0	77
U.S.	1,811,724	595.2	-

Note: (1) Figures cover the Manchester-Nashua, NH Metropolitan Statistical Area—see Appendix B for areas included; (2) Rank ranges from 1 to 377 where 1 indicates greatest number of identity theft complaints per 100,000 population
Source: Federal Trade Commission, Consumer Sentinel Network Data Book for January–December 2013

RECREATION

Culture

Dance[1]	Theatre[1]	Instrumental Music[1]	Vocal Music[1]	Series and Festivals	Museums and Art Galleries[2]	Zoos and Aquariums[3]
0	0	2	0	1	7	0

Note: (1) Number of professional perfoming groups; (2) Based on organizations with primary SIC code 8412; (3) AZA-accredited
Source: The Grey House Performing Arts Directory, 2013; Association of Zoos & Aquariums, AZA Member Zoos & Aquariums, April 2014; www.AccuLeads.com, May 1, 2014

Professional Sports Teams

Team Name	League	Year Established

No teams are located in the metro area
Source: Wikipedia, Major Professional Sports Teams of the United States and Canada, April 25, 2014

CLIMATE

Average and Extreme Temperatures

Temperature	Jan	Feb	Mar	Apr	May	Jun	Jul	Aug	Sep	Oct	Nov	Dec	Yr.
Extreme High (°F)	68	66	85	95	97	98	102	101	98	90	80	68	102
Average High (°F)	31	34	43	57	69	77	83	80	72	61	48	35	57
Average Temp. (°F)	20	23	33	44	56	65	70	68	59	48	38	25	46
Average Low (°F)	9	11	22	32	42	51	57	55	46	35	28	15	34
Extreme Low (°F)	-33	-27	-16	8	21	30	35	29	22	10	-5	-22	-33

Note: Figures cover the years 1948-1990
Source: National Climatic Data Center, International Station Meteorological Climate Summary, 9/96

Average Precipitation/Snowfall/Humidity

Precip./Humidity	Jan	Feb	Mar	Apr	May	Jun	Jul	Aug	Sep	Oct	Nov	Dec	Yr.
Avg. Precip. (in.)	2.8	2.5	2.9	3.1	3.2	3.1	3.1	3.3	2.9	3.1	3.8	3.2	36.9
Avg. Snowfall (in.)	18	15	11	2	Tr	0	0	0	0	Tr	4	14	63
Avg. Rel. Hum. 7am (%)	76	76	76	75	75	80	82	87	89	86	83	79	80
Avg. Rel. Hum. 4pm (%)	59	55	52	46	47	52	51	53	55	53	61	63	54

Note: Figures cover the years 1948-1990; Tr = Trace amounts (<0.05 in. of rain; <0.5 in. of snow)
Source: National Climatic Data Center, International Station Meteorological Climate Summary, 9/96

Weather Conditions

Temperature			Daytime Sky			Precipitation		
5°F & below	32°F & below	90°F & above	Clear	Partly cloudy	Cloudy	0.01 inch or more precip.	0.1 inch or more snow/ice	Thunderstorms
32	171	12	87	131	147	125	32	19

Note: Figures are average number of days per year and cover the years 1948-1990
Source: National Climatic Data Center, International Station Meteorological Climate Summary, 9/96

HAZARDOUS WASTE

Superfund Sites

Manchester has no sites on the EPA's Superfund Final National Priorities List.
U.S. Environmental Protection Agency, Final National Priorities List, April 26, 2014

AIR & WATER QUALITY

Air Quality Index

Area	Percent of Days when Air Quality was...[2]					AQI Statistics[2]	
	Good	Moderate	Unhealthy for Sensitive Groups	Unhealthy	Very Unhealthy	Maximum	Median
MSA[1]	89.6	10.4	0.0	0.0	0.0	84	36

Note: (1) Data covers the Manchester-Nashua, NH Metropolitan Statistical Area—see Appendix B for areas included; (2) Based on 365 days with AQI data in 2013. Air Quality Index (AQI) is an index for reporting daily air quality. EPA calculates the AQI for five major air pollutants regulated by the Clean Air Act: ground-level ozone, particle pollution (aka particulate matter), carbon monoxide, sulfur dioxide, and nitrogen dioxide. The AQI runs from 0 to 500. The higher the AQI value, the greater the level of air pollution and the greater the health concern. There are six AQI categories: "Good" AQI is between 0 and 50. Air quality is considered satisfactory; "Moderate" AQI is between 51 and 100. Air quality is acceptable; "Unhealthy for Sensitive Groups" When AQI values are between 101 and 150, members of sensitive groups may experience health effects; "Unhealthy" When AQI values are between 151 and 200 everyone may begin to experience health effects; "Very Unhealthy" AQI values between 201 and 300 trigger a health alert; "Hazardous" AQI values over 300 trigger warnings of emergency conditions (not shown).
Source: U.S. Environmental Protection Agency, Air Quality Index Report, 2013

Air Quality Index Pollutants

Area	Percent of Days when AQI Pollutant was...[2]					
	Carbon Monoxide	Nitrogen Dioxide	Ozone	Sulfur Dioxide	Particulate Matter 2.5	Particulate Matter 10
MSA[1]	0.0	0.0	79.5	0.0	20.5	0.0

Note: (1) Data covers the Manchester-Nashua, NH Metropolitan Statistical Area—see Appendix B for areas included; (2) Based on 365 days with AQI data in 2013. The Air Quality Index (AQI) is an index for reporting daily air quality. EPA calculates the AQI for five major air pollutants regulated by the Clean Air Act: ground-level ozone, particle pollution (also known as particulate matter), carbon monoxide, sulfur dioxide, and nitrogen dioxide. The AQI runs from 0 to 500. The higher the AQI value, the greater the level of air pollution and the greater the health concern.
Source: U.S. Environmental Protection Agency, Air Quality Index Report, 2013

Air Quality Trends: Ozone

	2003	2004	2005	2006	2007	2008	2009	2010	2011	2012
MSA[1]	0.070	0.071	0.071	0.068	0.074	0.064	0.060	0.063	0.063	0.063

Note: (1) Data covers the Manchester-Nashua, NH Metropolitan Statistical Area—see Appendix B for areas included. The values shown are the composite ozone concentration averages among trend sites based on the highest fourth daily maximum 8-hour concentration in parts per million. These trends are based on sites having an adequate record of monitoring data during the trend period. Data from exceptional events are included.
Source: U.S. Environmental Protection Agency, Air Quality Monitoring Information, "Air Quality Trends by City, 2000-2012"

Maximum Air Pollutant Concentrations: Particulate Matter, Ozone, CO and Lead

	Particulate Matter 10 (ug/m³)	Particulate Matter 2.5 Wtd AM (ug/m³)	Particulate Matter 2.5 24-Hr (ug/m³)	Ozone (ppm)	Carbon Monoxide (ppm)	Lead (ug/m³)
MSA[1] Level	20	8.2	23	0.073	0	n/a
NAAQS[2]	150	15	35	0.075	9	0.15
Met NAAQS[2]	Yes	Yes	Yes	Yes	Yes	n/a

Note: (1) Data covers the Manchester-Nashua, NH Metropolitan Statistical Area—see Appendix B for areas included; Data from exceptional events are included; (2) National Ambient Air Quality Standards; ppm = parts per million; ug/m³ = micrograms per cubic meter; n/a not available.
Concentrations: Particulate Matter 10 (coarse particulate)—highest second maximum 24-hour concentration; Particulate Matter 2.5 Wtd AM (fine particulate)—highest weighted annual mean concentration; Particulate Matter 2.5 24-Hour (fine particulate)—highest 98th percentile 24-hour concentration; Ozone—highest fourth daily maximum 8-hour concentration; Carbon Monoxide—highest second maximum non-overlapping 8-hour concentration; Lead—maximum running 3-month average
Source: U.S. Environmental Protection Agency, Air Quality Monitoring Information, "Air Quality Statistics by City, 2012"

Maximum Air Pollutant Concentrations: Nitrogen Dioxide and Sulfur Dioxide

	Nitrogen Dioxide AM (ppb)	Nitrogen Dioxide 1-Hr (ppb)	Sulfur Dioxide AM (ppb)	Sulfur Dioxide 1-Hr (ppb)	Sulfur Dioxide 24-Hr (ppb)
MSA[1] Level	n/a	n/a	n/a	4	n/a
NAAQS[2]	53	100	30	75	140
Met NAAQS[2]	n/a	n/a	n/a	Yes	n/a

Note: (1) Data covers the Manchester-Nashua, NH Metropolitan Statistical Area—see Appendix B for areas included; Data from exceptional events are included; (2) National Ambient Air Quality Standards; ppm = parts per million; ug/m³ = micrograms per cubic meter; n/a not available.
Concentrations: Nitrogen Dioxide AM—highest arithmetic mean concentration; Nitrogen Dioxide 1-Hr—highest 98th percentile 1-hour daily maximum concentration; Sulfur Dioxide AM—highest annual mean concentration; Sulfur Dioxide 1-Hr—highest 99th percentile 1-hour daily maximum concentration; Sulfur Dioxide 24-Hr—highest second maximum 24-hour concentration
Source: U.S. Environmental Protection Agency, Air Quality Monitoring Information, "Air Quality Statistics by City, 2012"

Drinking Water

Water System Name	Pop. Served	Primary Water Source Type	Violations[1]	
			Health Based	Monitoring/ Reporting
Manchester Water Works	133,000	Surface	1	0

Note: (1) Based on violation data from January 1, 2013 to December 31, 2013 (includes unresolved violations from earlier years)
Source: U.S. Environmental Protection Agency, Office of Ground Water and Drinking Water, Safe Drinking Water Information System (based on data extracted February 10, 2014)

New York, New York

Background

Few cities in the world can compare with New York's frenetic excitement. Known for its dramatic skyline and world-famous Brooklyn Bridge, the city is beautiful, mighty, inspiring, loaded with attitude and home to more than 8 million people living within its five boroughs—Bronx, Brooklyn, Queens, Manhattan, and Staten Island.

New York is the largest city in New York State, in the U.S., and one of the largest cities in the world. Located at the mouth of the Hudson River, the area was first explored by Giovanni da Verrazzano in 1524, and then by Henry Hudson in 1609. The first Dutch settlers came in 1624 and by 1625, the area had become the permanent settlement of New Amsterdam. A year later, as the famous story goes, Peter Minuit purchased the island of Manhattan from the local tribes for a mere 60 guilders (24 dollars).

The city continues to offer the very best in the arts—Metropolitan Museum of Art, Museum of Modern Art, Guggenheim Museum, among thousands of others; education—New York University and Columbia University; finance—the New York and the American stock exchanges; plus fashion, theaters, restaurants, political activism, and more.

New York, considered the standard for cultural excellence, is home to The Alvin Ailey American Dance Theater, American Ballet Theater, Brooklyn Academy of Music, Carnegie Hall, and Cunningham Dance Company, among many other world-famous artistic centers.

Professional sports abound in the city, including New York Giants (2012 Super Bowl winners) and Jets football teams, New York Red Bulls soccer team, Knicks basketball team, and New York Yankees (2010 World Series winners) and Mets baseball teams. New stadiums for the Yankees (Yankee Stadium) and the Mets (Citi Field) opened in 2009, and a new MetLife Stadium for the Giants and Jets opened in 2011. MetLife Stadium hosted the Super Bowl in 2014, the first outdoor, cold-weather Super Bowl. In addition, Barclays Arena opened in 2013 in Brooklyn, home of the New Jersey Nets basketball team, and future home of the New York Islanders hockey team.

As host to more Fortune 100 companies than any other U.S. city, New York City clearly remains the business capital of the world. New York's entrepreneurial spirit, highly educated workforce, first-rate transportation system, unequaled telecommunications infrastructure and lowest crime rate of any big city in America all contribute to New York's status as home to the world's leading financial services, advertising, media and entertainment companies. As a center of cultural life, the city has an enduring appeal, and investment in the city is strong.

On September 11, 2001, New York became the site of the deadliest terrorist attack ever to occur in the United States. The deliberate crash of two hijacked commercial airplanes into the famous Twin Towers demolished the complex of seven buildings at the World Trade Center and killed more than 3,500 people.

In its usual show of strength and resilience, the grieving city immediately began the monumental task of moving forward. Construction is ongoing at the new 8-acre World Trade Center Complex that will consist of seven office buildings, a Memorial, and Museum. One World Trade Center, the tallest, will be complete in the summer of 2014. Of the five remaining buildings, two are complete and the others are under construction. The Memorial opened in 2011—the 10th anniversary of the attacks—and consists of two massive pools in the footprints of the Twin Towers, with the largest manmade waterfalls in the country. The Museum is scheduled to open in 2014.

Among New Yorkers, Times Square is as recognized for its severely congested sidewalks as for its spectacular signage. An estimated 80 percent of visitors to the city visit Times Square. Over the last decade, Skadden Arps, Reuters, Ernst & Young, *The New York Times*, and many others, have moved into gleaming new office towers supporting the growth of the once-squalid district. Real estate development in Battery Park also continues unabated. More recent projects include Tribeca Green, which caters to the environmentally conscious.

The New York metro area is close to the path of most storm and frontal systems which move across the continent. The city can experience very high temperatures in summer and very low in winter, despite its coastal location. The passage of many weather systems helps to reduce the duration of both cold and warm spells, circulate the air, and reduce stagnation. In October 2012, New York was hard hit by Hurricane Sandy, which flooded subways and tunnels, shut down hospitals and the NYSE. Fire destroyed 100 homes in Breezy Point, Queens, and areas bordering the New York Harbor, especially Staten Island, were inundated with up to 9 feet of water and damaging winds.

Rankings

General Rankings

- *Business Insider* projected current trends well into the future to compile its list of the "15 Hottest American Cities of the Future." To such metrics as job and population growth, demographics, affordability, livability, and residents' health and welfare, analysts added innovation in technology and sustainability as well as a culture favoring youth and creativity. Judging by these combined factors, Brooklyn ranked #1. *Business Insider, "The Fifteen Hottest American Cities of the Future," June 18, 2012*

- Among the 50 largest U.S. cities, New York placed #23 in Vocativ's "semi-exhaustive, mostly scientific" city Livability Index for people aged 35 and under. Average salary, unemployment rates, rents, and other living costs were considered, along with bike lanes, low-cost broadband, cheap takeout, self-service laundries, the price of a pint of Guinness, music venues, and vintage clothing stores. *vocative.com, "The Livability Index: The Best U.S. Cities for People 35 and Under," November 7, 2013*

- New York was selected as one of America's best cities by *Bloomberg Businessweek*. The city ranked #7 out of 50. Criteria: leisure attributes (the number of restaurants, bars, libraries, museums, professional sports teams, and park acres by population); educational attributes (public school performance, the number of colleges, and graduate degree holders); economic factors (2011 income and June and July 2012 unemployment); crime; and air quality. *Bloomberg BusinessWeek, "America's Best Cities," September 26, 2012*

- New York was selected as one of "America's Favorite Cities." The city ranked #35 in the "Quality of Life and Visitor Experience: Cleanliness" category. Respondents to an online survey were asked to rate 35 top urban destinations in the U.S. from a visitor's perspective. Criteria: cleanliness. *Travel + Leisure, "America's Favorite Cities 2013"*

- New York was selected as one of "America's Favorite Cities." The city ranked #7 in the "Type of Trip: Gay-friendly" category. Respondents to an online survey were asked to rate 35 top urban destinations in the U.S. from a visitor's perspective. Criteria: gay-friendly. *Travel + Leisure, "America's Favorite Cities 2013"*

- Mercer Human Resources Consulting ranked 221 cities worldwide in terms of overall quality of life. New York ranked #44. Criteria: political, social, economic, and socio-cultural factors; medical and health considerations; schools and education; public services and transportation; recreation; consumer goods; housing; and natural environment. *Mercer Human Resources Consulting, "Mercer 2012 Quality of Living Survey," December 4, 2012*

- New York appeared on *Travel + Leisure's* list of the ten best cities in the U.S. and Canada. The city was ranked #3. Criteria: activities/attractions; culture/arts; restaurants/food; people; and value. *Travel + Leisure, "The World's Best Awards 2013"*

- *Condé Nast Traveler* polled 79,268 readers for travel satisfaction. American cities were ranked based on the following criteria: friendliness; atmosphere/ambiance; culture/sites; restaurants; lodging; and shopping. New York appeared in the top 10, ranking #8. *Condé Nast Traveler, Readers' Choice Awards 2013, "Top 10 Cities in the United States"*

Business/Finance Rankings

- Building on the U.S. Department of Labor's Occupational Information Network Data Collection Program, the Brookings Institution defined STEM occupations and job opportunities for STEM workers at various levels of educational attainment. The New York metro area was one of the ten metro areas where workers in low-education-level STEM jobs earn the lowest relative wages. *www.brookings.edu, "The Hidden Stem Economy," June 10, 2013*

- To identify the metro areas with the largest gap in income between rich and poor residents, the 24/7 Wall Street research team used the U.S. Census Bureau's 2012 American Community Survey, an index of income disparity, additional income, poverty, and home-value data. The New York metro area placed #5 among metro areas with the widest wealth gap between rich and poor. *247wallst.com, "Cities with the Widest Gap between Rich and Poor," November 4, 2013*

- The Economist Intelligence Unit (EIU) forecasted the world's "Hot Spots 2025" based on "Benchmarks of Future Competitiveness." The EIU researchers weighted eight factors—economic strength; infrastructure, including telecommunications; financial maturity; institutional character; social and cultural character; human capital; environmental responsibility and ability to respond to hazards; and "global appeal." New York was #1. *247wallst.com, "The Most Competitive Cities of the Future," June 25, 2013*

- Analysts for the business website 24/7 Wall Street looked at the local government report "Tax Rates and Tax Burdens in the District of Columbia—A Nationwide Comparison" to determine where a family of three at two different income levels would pay the least and the most in state and local taxes. Among the ten cities with the highest state and local tax burdens was New York, at #7. *247wallst.com, American Cities with the Highest (and Lowest) Taxes, February 25, 2013*

- New York was the #2-ranked city in a Seedtable analysis of the world's most active cities for start-up companies, as reported by Statista. *www.statista.com, "San Francisco Has the Most Active Start-Up Scene," August 21, 2013*

- Based on a minimum of 500 social media reviews per metro area, the employment opinion group Glassdoor surveyed 50 of the largest U.S. metro areas on measures including compensation and benefits, satisfaction with management, business outlook, and number of employers hiring. The New York metro area was ranked #32 in overall employee satisfaction. *www.glassdoor.com, "Employment Satisfaction Report Card by City," June 21, 2013*

- The Brookings Institution ranked the 50 largest cities in the U.S. based on income inequality. New York was ranked #6. (#1 = greatest ineqality). Criteria: the cities were ranked based on the "95/20 ratio." This figure represents the income at which a household earns more than 95 percent of all other households, divided by the income at which a household earns more than only 20 percent of all other households. *Brookings Institution, "Income Inequality in America's 50 Largest Cities, 2007-2012," February 20, 2014*

- MarketWatch shared a *24/7 Wall St.* analysis of the District of Columbia's Office of Revenue Analysis report on the estimated property, sales, auto, and income taxes paid in the largest city of each state in 2011. Of the U.S. cities with the highest tax burden, New York ranked #7. *Marketwatch.com, "10 U.S. Cities with the Highest Taxes," March 2, 2013*

- New York was ranked #71 out of 100 metro areas in terms of economic performance (#1 = best) during the recession and recovery from trough quarter through the second quarter of 2013. Criteria: percent change in employment; percentage point change in unemployment rate; percent change in gross metropolitan product; percent change in House Price Index. *Brookings Institution, MetroMonitor: Tracking Economic Recession and Recovery in America's 100 Largest Metropolitan Areas, September 2013*

- Payscale.com ranked the 20 largest metro areas in terms of wage growth. The New York metro area ranked #7. Criteria: private-sector wage growth between the 4th quarter of 2012 and the 4th quarter of 2013. *PayScale, "Wage Trends by Metro Area," 4th Quarter, 2013*

- For its annual survey of the "10 Most Expensive U.S. Cities to Live In," Kiplinger applied Cost of Living Index statistics developed by the Council for Community and Economic Research to U.S. Census Bureau population and median household income data for cities with populations above 50,000. In the resulting ranking, New York ranked #1. *Kiplinger.com, "10 Most Expensive U.S. Cities to Live In," June 2013*

- New York was identified as one of America's "10 Best Cities to Get a Job" by *U.S. News & World Report*. The city ranked #9. Criteria: number of available jobs; unemployment rate. *U.S. News & World Report, "10 Best Cities to Get a Job," February 1, 2011*

- New York was cited as one of America's top metros for new and expanded facility projects in 2013. The area ranked #10 in the large metro area category (population over 1 million). *Site Selection, "Top Metros of 2013," March 2014*

- New York was identified as one of the best cities for college graduates to find work—and live. The city ranked #2 out of 15. Criteria: job availability; average salary; average rent. *CareerBuilder.com, "15 Best Cities for College Grads to Find Work—and Live," June 5, 2012*

- The New York metro area appeared on the Milken Institute "2013 Best Performing Cities" list. Rank: #34 out of 200 large metro areas. Criteria: job growth; wage and salary growth; high-tech output growth. *Milken Institute, "Best-Performing Cities 2013," December 2013*

- *Forbes* ranked the 200 most populous metro areas in the U.S. in terms of the "Best Places for Business and Careers." The New York metro area was ranked #50. Criteria: costs (business and living); job growth (past and projected); income growth; educational attainment (college and high school); projected economic growth; cultural and recreational opportunities; net migration patterns; number of highly ranked colleges. *Forbes, "The Best Places for Business and Careers," August 7, 2013*

- Mercer Human Resources Consulting ranked 214 urban areas worldwide in terms of cost-of-living. New York ranked #33 (the lower the ranking, the higher the cost-of-living). The survey measured the comparative cost of over 200 items (i.e. housing, food, clothing, household goods, transportation, and entertainment) in each location. *Mercer Human Resources Consulting, "Worldwide Cost of Living Survey 2012," June 12, 2012*

Children/Family Rankings

- New York was selected as one of the best cities for families to live by *Parenting* magazine. The city ranked #85 out of 100. Criteria: education; health; community; *Parenting's* Culture & Charm Index. *Parenting.com, "The 2012 Best Cities for Families List"*

- New York was chosen as one of America's 100 best communities for young people. The winners were selected based upon detailed information provided about each community's efforts to fulfill five essential promises critical to the well-being of young people: caring adults who are actively involved in their lives; safe places in which to learn and grow; a healthy start toward adulthood; an effective education that builds marketable skills; and opportunities to help others. *America's Promise Alliance, "100 Best Communities for Young People, 2012"*

Culture/Performing Arts Rankings

- New York was selected as one of 10 best U.S. cities to be a moviemaker. The city was ranked #2. Criteria: film community; access to new films; access to equipment; cost of living; tax incentives. *MovieMaker Magazine, "Top 10 Cities to be a Moviemaker: 2013," March 5, 2013*

- New York was selected as one of "America's Favorite Cities." The city ranked #2 in the "Culture: Museum/Galleries" category. Respondents to an online survey were asked to rate 35 top urban destinations in the U.S. from a visitor's perspective. Criteria: number and quality of museums and galleries. *Travelandleisure.com, "America's Favorite Cities 2013"*

- New York was selected as one of America's top cities for the arts. The city ranked #1 in the big city (population 500,000 and over) category. Criteria: readers' top choices for arts travel destinations based on the richness and variety of visual arts sites, activities and events. *American Style, "2012 Top 25 Arts Destinations," June 2012*

Dating/Romance Rankings

- Gizmodo reported on data that Facebook collected on the best American cities for singles. Criteria included highest percentage of single people, the widest single female-to-single male ratio (and vice versa), and the best probability of relationship formation. Among the top 50 American population centers New York ranked #3. *gizmodo.com, "The Best Places to Find Hot Singles (According to Facebook)," February 13, 2014*

- A *Cosmopolitan* magazine article surveyed the gender balance and other factors to arrive at a list of the best and worst cities for women to meet single guys. New York placed #1 among the worst for single women looking for dates. *www.cosmopolitan.com, "Working the Ratio," October 1, 2013*

- CreditDonkey, a financial education website, sought out the ten best U.S. cities for newlyweds, considering the number of married couples, divorce rate, average credit score, and average number of hours worked per week in metro areas with a million or more residents. The New York metro area placed #5. *www.creditdonkey.com, "Study: Best Cities for Newlyweds," November 30, 2013*

- New York took the #3 spot on NerdWallet's list of best cities for singles wanting to date, based on the availability of singles; "date-friendliness," as determined by a city's walkability and the number of bars and restaurants per thousand residents; and the affordability of dating in terms of the cost of movie tickets, pizza, and wine for two. *www.nerdwallet.com, "Best Cities for Singles," February 5, 2014*

- Of the 100 U.S. cities surveyed by *Men's Health* in its quest to identify the nation's best cities for dating and forming relationships, New York was ranked #17 for online dating (#1 = best). *Men's Health, "The Best and Worst Cities for Online Dating," January 30, 2013*

- New York ranked #10 among cities congenial to singles, according to Kiplinger, which searched for "dating scenes as financially attractive as they are romantically promising." High percentages of unmarried people, above-average household incomes, and cost-of-living factors determined the rankings. *Kiplinger.com, "10 Best Cities for Singles," February 2013*

- New York was selected as one of America's best cities for singles by the readers of *Travel + Leisure* in their annual "America's Favorite Cities" survey. The city was ranked #3 out of 20. *Travel + Leisure, "America's Best Cities for Singles," July 2012*

- New York was selected as one of the best cities for single men by *Rent.com*. Criteria: high single female-to-male ratio. *Rent.com, "Top Cities for Single Men," March 14, 2013*

- New York was selected as one of "America's Best Cities for Dating" by *Yahoo! Travel*. Criteria: high proportion of singles; excellent dating venues and/or stunning natural settings. *Yahoo! Travel, "America's Best Cities for Dating," February 7, 2012*

- New York was selected as one of the best cities for single women in America by *SingleMindedWomen.com*. The city ranked #1. Criteria: ratio of women to men; singles population; healthy lifestyle; employment opportunities; cost of living; access to travel; entertainment options; social opportunities. *SingleMindedWomen.com, "Top 10 Cities for Single Women," 2011*

Education Rankings

- *Fast Company* magazine measured six key components of "smart" cities and three "drivers" for each component to reveal the top ten "Smartest Cities in North America." By these complex metrics, New York ranked #5. *Fastcoexist.com, "The Top 10 Smartest Cities in North America," November 15, 2013*

- *Men's Health* ranked 100 U.S. cities in terms of their education levels. New York was ranked #54 (#1 = most educated city). Criteria: high school graduation rates; school enrollment; educational attainment; number of households who have outstanding student loans; number of households whose members have taken adult-education courses. *Men's Health, "Where School Is In: The Most and Least Educated Cities," September 12, 2011*

- New York was selected as one of America's most literate cities. The city ranked #16 out of the 77 largest U.S. cities. Criteria: number of booksellers; library resources; Internet resources; educational attainment; periodical publishing resources; newspaper circulation. *Central Connecticut State University, "America's Most Literate Cities, 2013"*

Environmental Rankings

- The New York metro area came in at #155 for the relative comfort of its climate on Sperling's list of "chill cities," as measured by the Sperling Heat Index. All 361 metro areas are included. Criteria included daytime high temperatures, nighttime low temperatures, dew point, and relative humidity at the high temperatures. *www.bertsperling.com, "Sperling's Chill Cities," July 18, 2013*

- Sperling's BestPlaces assessed 379 metropolitan areas of the United States for the likelihood of dangerously extreme weather events or earthquakes. In general the Southeast and South-Central regions have the highest risk of weather extremes and earthquakes, while the Pacific Northwest enjoys the lowest risk. Of the least risky metropolitan areas, the New York metro area was ranked #207. *www.bestplaces.net, "Safest Places from Natural Disasters," April 2011*

- New York was identified as one of America's dirtiest metro areas by *Forbes*. The area ranked #11 out of 20. Criteria: air quality; water quality; toxic releases; superfund sites. *Forbes, "America's 20 Dirtiest Cities," December 10, 2012*

- New York was identified as one of North America's greenest metropolitan areas. The area ranked #3. The Green City Index is comprised of 31 indicators, and scores cities across nine categories: carbon dioxide; energy; land use; buildings; transport; water; waste; air quality; environmental governance. The 27 largest metropolitan areas in the U.S. and Canada were considered. *Economist Intelligence Unit, sponsored by Siemens, "U.S. and Canada Green City Index, 2011"*

- The U.S. Environmental Protection Agency (EPA) released a list of U.S. metropolitan areas with the most ENERGY STAR certified buildings in 2012. The New York metro area was ranked #4 out of 25. *U.S. Environmental Protection Agency, "Top Cities With the Most ENERGY STAR Certified Buildings in 2012," March 12, 2013*

- The New York metro area was identified as one of the snowiest major metropolitan areas in the U.S. by *Forbes*. The metro area ranked #10 out of 10. Criteria: average annual snowfall. *Forbes, "America's Snowiest Cities," January 12, 2011*

- New York was selected as one of 22 "Smarter Cities" for energy by the Natural Resources Defense Council. The city appeared as one of 12 cities in the large city (population 250,000 and over) category. Criteria: investment in green power; energy efficiency measures; conservation. *Natural Resources Defense Council, "2010 Smarter Cities," July 19, 2010*

- The New York metro area was selected as one of "America's Most Toxic Cities" by *Forbes*. The metro area ranked #4 out of 10. The 80 largest metropolitan areas were ranked on the following criteria: air quality; water quality; Superfund sites; toxic releases. *Forbes, "America's Most Toxic Cities, 2011," February 28, 2011*

- New York was highlighted as one of the 25 most ozone-polluted metro areas in the U.S. during 2008 through 2010. The area ranked #17. *American Lung Association, State of the Air 2012*

Food/Drink Rankings

- According to Fodor's Travel, New York placed #17 among the best U.S. cities for food-truck cuisine. *www.fodors.com, "America's Best Food Truck Cities," December 20, 2013*

- *Men's Health* ranked 100 major U.S. cities in terms of alcohol intoxication. New York ranked #3 (#1 = most sober).Criteria: binge drinking; alcohol-related traffic accidents, arrests, and fatalities. *Men's Health, "The Drunkest Cities in America," November 19, 2013*

- New York was identified as one of "America's Most Caffeinated Cities" by *Bundle.com*. The city was ranked #2 out of 10. The rankings were determined by examining consumer spending at 16 widely known coffee chains during the second quarter of 2011. *Bundle.com, "America's Most Caffeinated Cities," September 19, 2011*

- New York was selected as one of America's best cities for hamburgers by the readers of *Travel + Leisure* in their annual America's Favorite Cities survey. The city was ranked #9 out of 10. *Travel + Leisure, "America's Best Burger Cities," August 25, 2013*

- New York was selected as one of America's 10 most vegan-friendly cities. The city was ranked #4. *People for the Ethical Treatment of Animals, "Top Vegan-Friendly Cities of 2013," June 11, 2013*

- Citi Field (New York Mets) was selected as one of PETA's "Top 10 Vegetarian-Friendly Major League Ballparks" for 2013. The park ranked #7. *People for the Ethical Treatment of Animals, "Top 10 Vegetarian-Friendly Major League Ballparks," June 12, 2013*

Health/Fitness Rankings

- For each of the 50 most populous metro areas in the United States, the American College of Sports Medicine's American Fitness Index evaluated infrastructure, community assets, and policies that encourage healthy and fit lifestyles, including preventive health behaviors, levels of chronic disease conditions, health care access, and community resources and policies that support physical activity. The New York metro area ranked #24 for "community fitness." Personal health indicators were considered as well as community and environmental indicators. *www.americanfitnessindex.org, "ACSM American Fitness Index Health and Community Fitness Status of the 50 Largest Metropolitan Areas," May 2013*

- *Business Insider* reported Trulia's analysis of the 100 largest U.S. metro areas to identify the nation's best cities for weight loss, based on healthful food options, access to outdoor activities, weight-loss centers, gyms, and opportunities to hike or walk to work. New York ranked #6. *Businessinsider.com, "These Are the Best US Cities for Weight loss," January 17, 2013*

- New York was identified as one of the 10 most walkable cities in the U.S. by Walk Score, a Seattle-based service that rates the convenience and transit access of 10,000 neighborhoods in 3,000 cities. The area ranked #1 out of the 50 largest U.S. cities. Walk Score measures walkability by analyzing hundreds of walking routes to nearby amenities. Walk Score also measures pedestrian friendliness by analyzing population density and road metrics such as block length and intersection density. *WalkScore.com, March 20, 2014*

- The New York metro area was identified as one of the worst cities for bed bugs in America by pest control company Orkin. The area ranked #17 out of 50 based on the number of bed bug treatments Orkin performed from January to December 2013. *Orkin, "Chicago Tops Bed Bug Cities List for Second Year in a Row," January 16, 2014*

- New York was selected as one of the 25 fittest cities in America by *Men's Fitness Online*. It ranked #21 out of America's 50 largest cities. Criteria: fitness centers and sport stores; nutrition; sports participation; TV viewing; overweight/sedentary; junk food; air quality; geography; commute; parks and open space; city recreational facilities; access to healthcare; motivation; mayor and city initiatives; state obesity initiatives. *Men's Fitness, "The Fittest and Fattest Cities in America," March 5, 2012*

- New York was identified as a "2013 Spring Allergy Capital." The area ranked #43 out of 100. Three groups of factors were used to identify the most severe cities for people with allergies during the spring season: annual pollen levels; medicine utilization; access to board-certified allergists. *Asthma and Allergy Foundation of America, "Spring Allergy Capitals 2013"*

- New York was identified as a "2013 Fall Allergy Capital." The area ranked #56 out of 100. Three groups of factors were used to identify the most severe cities for people with allergies during the fall season: annual pollen levels; medicine utilization; access to board-certified allergists. *Asthma and Allergy Foundation of America, "Fall Allergy Capitals 2013"*

- New York was identified as a "2013 Asthma Capital." The area ranked #51 out of the nation's 100 largest metropolitan areas. Twelve factors were used to identify the most challenging places to live for people with asthma: estimated prevalence; self-reported prevalence; crude death rate for asthma; annual pollen score; annual air quality; public smoking laws; number of board-certified asthma specialists; school inhaler access laws; rescue medication use; controller medication use; uninsured rate; poverty rate. *Asthma and Allergy Foundation of America, "Asthma Capitals 2013"*

- *Men's Health* ranked 100 major U.S. cities in terms of the best and worst cities for men. New York ranked #43. Criteria: thirty-three data points were examined covering health, fitness, and quality of life. *Men's Health, "The Best & Worst Cities for Men 2014," December 6, 2013*

- The American Academy of Dermatology ranked 26 U.S. metropolitan regions in terms of their residents knowledge, attitude and behaviors towards tanning, sun protection and skin cancer detection. The New York metro area ranked #19. The results of the study are based on an online survey of over 7,000 adults nationwide. *American Academy of Dermatology, "Suntelligence: How Sun Smart is Your City?," May 3, 2010*

- The New York metro area appeared in the 2013 Gallup-Healthways Well-Being Index. The area ranked #110 out of 189. The Gallup-Healthways Well-Being Index score is an average of six sub-indexes, which individually examine life evaluation, emotional health, work environment, physical health, healthy behaviors, and access to basic necessities. Results are based on telephone interviews conducted as part of the Gallup-Healthways Well-Being Index survey January 2–December 29, 2012, and January 2–December 30, 2013, with a random sample of 531,630 adults, aged 18 and older, living in metropolitan areas in the 50 U.S. states and the District of Columbia. *Gallup-Healthways, "State of American Well-Being," March 25, 2014*

- The New York metro area was identified as one of "America's Most Stressful Cities" by *Sperling's BestPlaces*. The metro area ranked #27 out of 50. Criteria: unemployment rate; suicide rate; commute time; mental health; poor rest; alcohol use; violent crime rate; property crime rate; cloudy days annually. *Sperling's BestPlaces, www.BestPlaces.net, "Stressful Cities 2012*

- The New York metro area was identified as one of "America's Most Stressful Cities" by *Forbes*. The metro area ranked #2 out of 40. Criteria: housing affordability; unemployment rate; cost of living; air quality; traffic congestion; sunny days; population density. *Forbes.com, "America's Most Stressful Cities," September 23, 2011*

- *Men's Health* ranked 100 U.S. cities in terms of their activity levels. New York was ranked #33 (#1 = most active city). Criteria: where and how often residents exercise; percentage of households that watch more than 15 hours of cable television a week and buy more than 11 video games a year; death rate from deep-vein thrombosis, a condition linked to sitting for extended periods of time. *Men's Health, "Where Sit Happens: The Most and Least Active Cities in America," June 20, 2011*

Real Estate Rankings

- Based on the home-price forecasts compiled by the real-estate valuation firm CoreLogic Case-Shiller, the finance website CNNMoney reported that in 2014, the New York metro area is expected to place #9 among American metro areas in terms of increases in residential real estate prices. *money.cnn.com, "10 Hottest Housing Markets for 2014," January 23, 2014*

- ApartmentList.com calculated the most expensive American cities for renters, comparing median rental prices for studios, one-bedroom units, and two-bedroom units in the nation's 50 most populated cities. New York placed #2 in the ApartmentList.com ranking. *www.cbsnews.com, "Top 10 Priciest U.S. Cities to Rent an Apartment," July 15, 2013*

- Using data from the housing-market research firm RealtyTrac, Yahoo! Finance researchers listed the housing markets in which housing affordability is deteriorating most, factoring in interest rates as well as median home prices. The New York metro area was among the least affordable housing markets according to the percentage difference in the income required to buy a home in December 2013 as opposed to in December 2012. *news.yahoo.com, "10 Cities Where Ordinary People Can No Longer Afford Homes," March 5, 2014*

- The PricewaterhouseCoopers and Urban Land Institute report *Emerging Trends in Real Estate* forecasts that improvements in leasing, rents, and pricing will fuel recovery in all property sectors in 2013. New York was ranked #2 among the top ten markets to watch in 2013. *PricewaterhouseCoopers/Urban Land Institute, "U.S. Commercial Real Estate Recovery to Advance in 2013," October 17, 2012*

- New York ranked #1 in a *Forbes* study of the rental housing market in the nation's 44 largest metropolitan areas to determine the cities that are worst for renters. Criteria: average rent in 2012's first quarter, year-over-year change in that figure, vacancy rate, and average monthly rent payment compared with average monthly mortgage payment. *Forbes.com, "The Best and Worst Cities for Renters," June 14, 2012*

- New York was identified as one of the priciest cities to rent in the U.S. The area ranked #1 out of 10. Criteria: rent-to-income ratio. *CNBC, "Priciest Cities to Rent," March 14, 2012*

- New York was ranked #146 out of 283 metro areas in terms of house price appreciation in 2013 (#1 = highest rate). *Federal Housing Finance Agency, House Price Index, 4th Quarter 2013*

- New York was selected as one of the eight best cities in the U.S. for real estate investment. The city ranked #1. *Association of Foreign Investors in Real Estate, "Ranking of USA Cities for Real Estate Investment, 2013"*

- The New York metro area was identified as one of the 10 worst condo markets in the U.S. in 2013. The area ranked #8 out of 64 markets with a price appreciation of -1.4%. Criteria: year-over-year change of median sales price of existing apartment condo-coop homes between the 4th quarter of 2012 and the 4th quarter of 2013. *National Association of Realtors®, Median Sales Price of Existing Apartment Condo-Coop Homes for Metropolitan Areas, 4th Quarter 2013*

- The New York metro area was identified as one of the 20 least affordable housing markets in the U.S. in 2013. The area ranked #5 out of 173 markets. Criteria: whether or not a typical family could qualify for a mortgage loan on a typical home. *National Association of Realtors®, Affordability Index of Existing Single-Family Homes for Metropolitan Areas, 2013*

- New York was ranked #220 out of 224 metro areas in terms of housing affordability in 2013 by the National Association of Home Builders (#1 = most affordable). The NAHB-Wells Fargo Housing Opportunity Index (HOI) for a given area is defined as the share of homes sold in that area that would have been affordable to a family earning the local median income, based on standard mortgage underwriting criteria. *National Association of Home Builders®, NAHB-Wells Fargo Housing Opportunity Index, 4th Quarter 2013*

- New York was selected as one of the best college towns for renters by ApartmentRatings.com." The area ranked #30 out of 87. Overall satisfaction ratings were ranked using thousands of user submitted scores for hundreds of apartment complexes located in cities and towns that are home to the 100 largest four-year institutions in the U.S. *ApartmentRatings.com, "2011 College Town Renter Satisfaction Rankings"*

- The nation's largest metro areas were analyzed in terms of the best places to buy foreclosures in 2013. The New York metro area ranked #4 out of 20. Criteria: RealtyTrac scored all metro areas with a population of 500,000 or more by summing up four numbers: months' supply of foreclosure inventory; percentage of foreclosure sales; foreclosure discount; percentage increase in foreclosure activity in 2012. *RealtyTrac, "2012 Year-End Metropolitan Foreclosure Market Report," January 28, 2013*

Safety Rankings

- Symantec, in partnership with Sperling's BestPlaces, ranked the 50 largest cities in the U.S. in terms of their vulnerability to cybercrime. The city ranked #30. Criteria: number of cyberattacks and potential infections; level of Internet access; expenditures on smartphones and computer hardware/software; wireless hotspots; broadband connectivity; Internet usage; online purchases. *Symantec, "Riskiest Online Cities of 2012" February 15, 2012*

- Allstate ranked the 200 largest cities in America in terms of driver safety. New York ranked #172. Allstate researchers analyzed internal property damage claims over a two-year period from January 2010 to December 2011. A weighted average of the two-year numbers determined the annual percentages. *Allstate, "Allstate America's Best Drivers Report®, August 27, 2013"*

- New York was identified as one of the most disaster-proof places in the U.S. in terms of its vulnerability to natural and non-natural disasters. The city ranked #1 out of 5. Rankings are based on the U.S. Center for Disease Control's Cities Readiness Initiative (CRI). As part of the CRI, the CDC and state public health personnel assess local emergency-management plans, protocols and capabilities for 72 Metropolitan Statistical Areas and four non-MSA large cities. *Forbes, "America's Most and Least Disaster-Proof Cities," December 12, 2011*

- New York was identified as one of the safest large cities in America by CQ Press. All 32 cities with populations of 500,000 or more that reported crime rates in 2012 for murder, rape, robbery, aggravated assault, burglary, and motor vehicle thefts were ranked. The city ranked #2 out of the top 10. *CQ Press, City Crime Rankings 2014*

- The National Insurance Crime Bureau ranked 380 metro areas in the U.S. in terms of per capita rates of vehicle theft. The New York metro area ranked #220 (#1 = highest rate). Criteria: number of vehicle theft offenses per 100,000 inhabitants in 2012. *National Insurance Crime Bureau, "Hot Spots 2012," June 26, 2013*

- The New York metro area was identified as one of the most dangerous metro areas for pedestrians by Transportation for America. The metro area ranked #50 out of 52 metro areas with over 1 million residents. Criteria: area's population divided by the number of pedestrian fatalities in that area. *Transportation for America, "Dangerous by Design 2011"*

Seniors/Retirement Rankings

- From its Best Cities for Successful Aging indexes, the Milken Institute generated rankings for metropolitan areas, weighing data in eight categories—general indicators, health care, wellness, living arrangements, transportation and general accessibility, financial well-being, education and employment, and community participation. The New York metro area was ranked #5 overall in the large metro area category. *Milken Institute, "Best Cities for Successful Aging," July 2012*

- Bankers Life and Casualty Company, in partnership with Sperling's BestPlaces, ranked the nation's 50 largest metro areas in terms of the "Best U.S. Cities for Seniors." The New York metro area ranked #26. Criteria: healthcare; transportation; housing; environment; economy; health and longevity; social and spiritual life; crime. *Bankers Life and Casualty Company, Center for a Secure Retirement, "Best U.S. Cities for Seniors 2011," September 2011*

Sports/Recreation Rankings

- According to the personal finance website NerdWallet, the New York metro area, at #4, is one of the nation's top dozen metro areas for sports fans. Criteria included the presence of all four major sports—MLB, NFL, NHL, and NBA, fan enthusiasm (as measured by game attendance), ticket affordability, and "sports culture," that is, number of sports bars. *www.nerdwallet.com, "Best Cities for Sports Fans," May 5, 2013*

- New York appeared on the *Sporting News* list of the "Best Sports Cities" for 2011. The area ranked #5 out of 271. Criteria: the magazine takes a 12-month snapshot of each city's sports, putting a heavy premium on regular-season won-lost records (from the most recently completed season). Other criteria include: playoff berths, bowl appearances and tournament bids; championships; applicable power ratings; quality of competition; overall fan fervor (measured in part by attendance); abundance of teams (rewarding quality over quantity); stadium and arena quality; ticket availability and prices; franchise ownership; and marquee appeal of athletes. *Sporting News, "Best Sports Cities 2011," October 4, 2011*

- New York appeared on the *Sporting News* list of the "Best Sports Cities" for 2011. The area ranked #5 out of 271. Criteria: a 12-month snapshot of regular-season won-lost records (from the most recently completed season). Other criteria include: playoff berths, bowl appearances and tournament bids; championships; applicable power ratings; quality of competition; overall fan fervor (measured in part by attendance); abundance of teams (quality over quantity); stadium and arena quality; ticket availability and prices; franchise ownership; and marquee appeal of athletes. *Sporting News, "Best Sports Cities 2011," October 4, 2011*

- New York was chosen as a bicycle friendly community by the League of American Bicyclists. A "Bicycle Friendly Community" welcomes cyclists by providing safe accommodation for cycling and encouraging people to bike for transportation and recreation. There are four award levels: Platinum; Gold; Silver; and Bronze. The community achieved an award level of Silver. *League of American Bicyclists, "Bicycle Friendly Community Master List," Fall 2013*

- New York was chosen as one of America's best cities for bicycling. The city ranked #7 out of 50. Criteria: robust cycling infrastructure; vibrant bike culture. The editors only considered cities with populations of 95,000 or more. *Bicycling, "America's Top 50 Bike-Friendly Cities," May 23, 2012*

Transportation Rankings

- Business Insider presented a Walk Score ranking of public transportation in 316 U.S. cities and thousands of city neighborhoods in which New York earned the #1-ranked "Transit Score," awarded for frequency, type of route, and distance between stops. *www.businessinsider.com, "The US Cities with the Best Public Transportation Systems," January 30, 2014*

- NerdWallet surveyed average annual car insurance premiums in 125 U.S. cities to identify the least expensive U.S. cities in which to insure a car. Locations with no-fault insurance laws was a strong determinant. New York came in at #13 for the most expensive rates. *www.nerdwallet.com, "Best Cities for Cheap Car Insurance," February 3, 2014*

- More U.S. households choose not to have a car in 2012 than in prior years, according to a study by the University of Michigan Transportation Research Institute. The business website 24/7 Wall Street examined that study, along with a 2010 Census Special Report to arrive at its ranking of cities in which the fewest households had a vehicle. New York held the #1 position. *247wallst.com, "Cities Where No One Wants to Drive," February 6, 2014*

- New York appeared on *Trapster.com's* list of the 10 most-active U.S. cities for speed traps. The city ranked #1 of 10. *Trapster.com* is a community platform accessed online and via smartphone app that alerts drivers to traps, hazards and other traffic issues nearby. *Trapster.com, "Speeders Beware: Cities With the Most Speed Traps," February 10, 2012*

- New York was identified as one of America's "10 Best Cities for Public Transportation" by *U.S. News & World Report*. The city ranked #3. The ten cities selected had the best combination of public transportation investment, ridership, and safety. *U.S. News & World Report, "10 Best Cities for Public Transportation," February 8, 2011*

- New York was identified as one of America's worst cities for speed traps by the National Motorists Association. The city ranked #25 out of 25. Criteria: speed trap locations per 100,000 residents. *National Motorists Association, September 2011*

- The New York metro area was identified as one of the best U.S. cities to live in without a car by *24/7 Wall St.* The area ranked #3 out of 10. Criteria: percentage of neighborhoods covered by public transit; frequency of service for those neighborhoods; share of jobs reachable within 90 minutes or less by public transit; how accessible amenities are for residents on foot; percentage of commuters who bike to work. The 100 largest metropolitan areas in the U.S. were examined. *24/7 Wall St., "The Best Cities to Live in Car-Free," November 28, 2011*

- New York was identified as one of the most congested metro areas in the U.S. The area ranked #4 out of 10. Criteria: yearly delay per auto commuter in hours. *Texas A&M Transportation Institute, "2012 Urban Mobility Report," December 2012*

- The New York metro area was selected as one of 15 "Smarter Cities" for transportation by the Natural Resources Defense Council. The area appeared in the large metro area (population greater than one million) category. Criteria: public transit availability and use; household automobile ownership and use; innovative, sustainable and affordable transportation programs. *Natural Resources Defense Council, "2011 Smarter Cities," February 23, 2011*

- The New York metro area appeared on *Forbes* list of places with the most extreme commutes. The metro area ranked #2 out of 10. Criteria: average travel time; percentage of mega commuters. Mega-commuters travel more than 90 minutes and 50 miles each way to work. *Forbes.com, "The Cities with the Most Extreme Commutes," March 5, 2013*

Women/Minorities Rankings

- The Daily Beast surveyed the nation's cities for highest percentage of singles and lowest divorce rate, plus other measures, to determine "emotional intelligence"—happiness, confidence, kindness—which, researchers say, has a strong correlation with people's satisfaction with their romantic relationships. New York placed #16. *www.thedailybeast.com, "Best Cities to Find Love and Stay in Love," February 14, 2014*

- To determine the best metro areas for working women, the personal finance website NerdWallet considered city size as well as relevant economic metrics—high salaries, narrow pay differential by gender, prevalence of women in the highest-paying industries, and population growth over 2010–2012. Of the large U.S. cities examined, the New York metro area held the #9 position. *www.nerdwallet.com, "Best Places for Women in the Workforce," May 19, 2013*

- *Women's Health* examined U.S. cities and identified the 100 best cities for women. New York was ranked #48. Criteria: 30 categories were examined from obesity and breast cancer rates to commuting times and hours spent working out. *Women's Health, "Best Cities for Women 2012"*

- New York was selected as one of the 25 healthiest cities for Latinas by *Latina Magazine*. The city ranked #4. Criteria: U.S. cities with populations over 500,000 residents were evaluated on the following criteria: percentage of 18-34 year-olds per city; Latino college graduation rates; number of colleges and universities; affordability; housing costs; income growth over time; average salary; percentage of singles; climate; safety; how the city's diversity compares to the national average; opportunities for minority entrepreneurs. *Latina Magazine, "Top 15 U.S. Cities for Young Latinos to Live In," August 19, 2011*

- New York was selected as one of the best cities for young Latinos in 2013 by mun2, a national cable television broadcast network. The city ranked #4. Criteria: U.S. cities with populations over 500,000 residents were evaluated on the following criteria: number of young latinos; jobs; friendliness; cost of living; fun. *mun2.tv, "Best Cities for Young Latinos 2013"*

- The New York metro area appeared on *Forbes'* list of the "Best Cities for Minority Entrepreneurs." The area ranked #4 out of 10. Criteria: 52 metropolitan statistical areas were examined. For each ethnicity (African Americans, Asians and Hispanics), the editors measured housing affordability, population growth, income growth, and entrepreneurship (per capita self-employment). *Forbes, "Best Cities for Minority Entrepreneurs," March 23, 2011*

Miscellaneous Rankings

- *Travel + Leisure* invited readers to rate cities on indicators such as aloofness, "smarty-pants residents," highbrow cultural offerings, high-end shopping, artisanal coffeehouses, conspicuous eco-consciousness, and more in order to identify the nation's snobbiest cities. Cities large and small made the list; among them was New York, at #2. *www.travelandleisure.com, "America's Snobbiest Cities, June 2013*

- Now an international phenomenon, public St. Patrick's Day celebrations of "everything Irish" typically call forth parades and music and green in unexpected places. In its not-particularly-scientific survey of the St. Patrick's Day scene, the Huffington Post chose the festivities in New York as among the world's five best. *www.huffingtonpost.com, "The 5 Best Places to Celebrate St. Patrick's Day," March 10, 2014*

- The watchdog site Charity Navigator conducts an annual study of charities in the nation's major markets both to analyze statistical differences in their financial, accountability, and transparency practices and to track year-to-year variations in individual communities. The New York metro area was ranked #18 among the 30 metro markets. *www.charitynavigator.org, "Metro Market Study 2013," June 1, 2013*

- The Harris Poll's Happiness Index survey revealed that of the top ten U.S. markets, the New York metro area residents ranked #6 in happiness. Criteria included strong assent to positive statements and strong disagreement with negative ones, and degree of agreement with a series of statements about respondents' personal relationships and general outlook. The online survey was conducted between July 14 and July 30, 2013. *www.harrisinteractive.com, "Dallas/Fort Worth Is "Happiest" City among America's Top Ten Markets," September 4, 2013*

- New York was selected as one of America's funniest cities by the Humor Research Lab at the University of Colorado. The city ranked #6 out of 10. Criteria: frequency of visits to comedy websites; number of comedy clubs per square mile; traveling comedians' ratings of each city's comedy-club audiences; number of famous comedians born in each city per capita; number of famous funny tweeters living in each city per capita; number of comedy radio stations available in each city; frequency of humor-related web searches originating in each city. *The New York Times, "So These Professors Walk Into a Comedy Club...," April 20, 2014*

- New York appeared on *Travel + Leisure's* list of America's least attractive people. Criteria: cities were selected by readers in their annual America's Favorite Cities survey. The city ranked #9 out of 10. *Travel + Leisure, "America's Most and Least Attractive People," November 2013*

- *Men's Health* ranked 100 U.S. cities by their level of sadness. New York was ranked #39 (#1 = saddest city). Criteria: suicide rates; unemployment rates; percentage of households that use antidepressants; percent of population who report feeling blue all or most of the time. *Men's Health, "Frown Towns," November 28, 2011*

- Scarborough Research, a leading market research firm, identified the top local markets for lottery ticket purchasers. The New York DMA (Designated Market Area) ranked in the top 13 with 50% of adults 18+ reporting that they purchased lottery tickets in the past 30 days. *Scarborough Research, January 30, 2012*

- The New York metro area was selected as one of "5 Great Cities for Young Adults" by *Kiplinger.com*. Criteria: high starting salaries for college graduates; cost of living near or below national average; affordable monthly rent; percentage of residents ages 20 to 29 near or above national average. *Kiplinger.com, "5 Great Cities for Young Adults," October 25, 2011*

- Energizer Personal Care, the makers of Edge® shave gel, in partnership with Sperling's BestPlaces, ranked 50 major metro areas in terms of everyday irritations. The New York metro area ranked #2. Criteria: high male-to-female ratio; poor sports team performance and high ticket prices; slow traffic; lack of job availability; unaffordable housing; extreme weather; lack of nightlife and fitness options. *Energizer Personal Care, "Most Irritatng Cities for Guys," August 26, 2013*

- Mars Chocolate North America, the makers of COMBOS®, in partnership with Sperling's BestPlaces, ranked 50 major metro areas in terms of their "manliness." The New York metro area ranked #39. Criteria: number of professional sports teams; number of nearby NASCAR tracks and racing events; manly lifestyle; concentration of manly retail stores; manly occupations per capita; salty snack sales; "Board of Manliness" rankings. *Mars Chocolate North America, "America's Manliest Cities 2012"*

- New York was selected as one of "America's Best Cities for Hipsters" by *Travel + Leisure*. The city was ranked #5 out of 20. Criteria: live music; coffee bars; independent boutiques; best microbrews; offbeat and tech-savvy locals. *Travel + Leisure, "America's Best Cities for Hipsters," November 2013*

- The New York metro area was selected as one of "America's Most Miserable Cities" by *Forbes.com*. The metro area ranked #10 out of 20. Criteria: violent crime; unemployment; foreclosures; income and property taxes; home prices; commute times; climate. *Forbes.com, "America's Most Miserable Cities" February 22, 2013*

- The National Alliance to End Homelessness ranked the 100 most populous metro areas in terms the rate of homelessness. The New York metro area ranked #13. Criteria: number of homeless people per 10,000 population in 2011. *National Alliance to End Homelessness, The State of Homelessness in America 2012*

- New York was selected as one of America's best-mannered cities. The area ranked #3. The general public determined the winners by casting votes online. *The Charleston School of Protocol and Etiquette, "2012 Most Mannerly City in America Contest," January 31, 2013*

Business Environment

CITY FINANCES

City Government Finances

Component	2011 ($000)	2011 ($ per capita)
Total Revenues	99,056,242	11,971
Total Expenditures	102,423,894	12,378
Debt Outstanding	127,778,372	15,442
Cash and Securities[1]	118,956,888	14,376

Note: (1) Cash and security holdings of a government at the close of its fiscal year, including those of its dependent agencies, utilities, and liquor stores.
Source: U.S Census Bureau, State & Local Government Finances 2011

City Government Revenue by Source

Source	2011 ($000)	2011 ($ per capita)
General Revenue		
From Federal Government	4,601,392	556
From State Government	27,877,000	3,369
From Local Governments	269,531	33
Taxes		
Property	17,140,631	2,071
Sales and Gross Receipts	7,357,650	889
Personal Income	8,286,164	1,001
Corporate Income	6,151,636	743
Motor Vehicle License	86,768	10
Other Taxes	1,616,389	195
Current Charges	7,879,741	952
Liquor Store	0	0
Utility	4,589,949	555
Employee Retirement	10,068,162	1,217

Source: U.S Census Bureau, State & Local Government Finances 2011

City Government Expenditures by Function

Function	2011 ($000)	2011 ($ per capita)	2011 (%)
General Direct Expenditures			
Air Transportation	0	0	0.0
Corrections	1,525,670	184	1.5
Education	22,117,079	2,673	21.6
Employment Security Administration	0	0	0.0
Financial Administration	625,113	76	0.6
Fire Protection	1,847,496	223	1.8
General Public Buildings	718,589	87	0.7
Governmental Administration, Other	244,246	30	0.2
Health	1,459,931	176	1.4
Highways	2,551,096	308	2.5
Hospitals	6,698,045	809	6.5
Housing and Community Development	4,393,347	531	4.3
Interest on General Debt	4,081,311	493	4.0
Judicial and Legal	587,136	71	0.6
Libraries	341,258	41	0.3
Parking	35,414	4	0.0
Parks and Recreation	1,344,367	162	1.3
Police Protection	4,948,435	598	4.8
Public Welfare	6,827,208	825	6.7
Sewerage	3,113,050	376	3.0
Solid Waste Management	1,369,470	166	1.3
Veterans' Services	0	0	0.0
Liquor Store	0	0	0.0
Utility	12,411,439	1,500	12.1
Employee Retirement	10,907,764	1,318	10.6

Source: U.S Census Bureau, State & Local Government Finances 2011

DEMOGRAPHICS

Population Growth

Area	1990 Census	2000 Census	2010 Census	Population Growth (%) 1990-2000	Population Growth (%) 2000-2010
City	7,322,552	8,008,278	8,175,133	9.4	2.1
MSA[1]	16,845,992	18,323,002	18,897,109	8.8	3.1
U.S.	248,709,873	281,421,906	308,745,538	13.2	9.7

Note: (1) Figures cover the New York-Newark-Jersey City, NY-NJ-PA Metropolitan Statistical Area—see Appendix B for areas included
Source: U.S. Census Bureau, Census 1990, 2000, 2010

Household Size

Area	Persons in Household (%) One	Two	Three	Four	Five	Six	Seven or More	Average Household Size
City	32.7	27.9	16.0	12.5	6.0	2.6	2.2	2.65
MSA[1]	28.0	28.9	16.8	14.8	6.9	2.7	2.0	2.74
U.S.	27.6	33.5	15.7	13.2	6.1	2.4	1.5	2.63

Note: (1) Figures cover the New York-Newark-Jersey City, NY-NJ-PA Metropolitan Statistical Area—see Appendix B for areas included
Source: U.S. Census Bureau, 2010-2012 American Community Survey 3-Year Estimates

Race

Area	White Alone[2] (%)	Black Alone[2] (%)	Asian Alone[2] (%)	AIAN[3] Alone[2] (%)	NHOPI[4] Alone[2] (%)	Other Race Alone[2] (%)	Two or More Races (%)
City	44.0	24.9	12.9	0.4	0.1	14.7	3.1
MSA[1]	59.3	17.4	10.1	0.3	0.0	10.1	2.8
U.S.	74.0	12.6	4.9	0.8	0.2	4.7	2.8

Note: (1) Figures cover the New York-Newark-Jersey City, NY-NJ-PA Metropolitan Statistical Area—see Appendix B for areas included; (2) Alone is defined as not being in combination with one or more other races; (3) American Indian and Alaska Native; (4) Native Hawaiian and Other Pacific Islander
Source: U.S. Census Bureau, 2010-2012 American Community Survey 3-Year Estimates

Hispanic or Latino Origin

Area	Total (%)	Mexican (%)	Puerto Rican (%)	Cuban (%)	Other (%)
City	28.8	3.9	9.0	0.5	15.4
MSA[1]	23.3	3.0	6.4	0.7	13.1
U.S.	16.6	10.7	1.6	0.6	3.7

Note: Persons of Hispanic or Latino origin can be of any race; (1) Figures cover the New York-Newark-Jersey City, NY-NJ-PA Metropolitan Statistical Area—see Appendix B for areas included
Source: U.S. Census Bureau, 2010-2012 American Community Survey 3-Year Estimates

Segregation

Type	Segregation Indices[1] 1990	2000	2010	2010 Rank[2]	Percent Change 1990-2000	1990-2010	2000-2010
Black/White	80.9	80.2	78.0	2	-0.7	-2.9	-2.2
Asian/White	47.4	50.8	51.9	3	3.5	4.5	1.0
Hispanic/White	66.2	65.6	62.0	3	-0.6	-4.2	-3.6

Note: All figures cover the Metropolitan Statistical Area—see Appendix B for areas included; Figures are based on an analysis of 1990, 2000, and 2010 Census Decennial Census tract data by William H. Frey, Brookings Institution and the University of Michigan Social Science Data Analysis Network. In this analysis all racial groups (whites, blacks, and asians) are non-Hispanic members of those races. Hispanics are shown as a separate category;
(1) Segregation Indices are Dissimilarity Indices that measure the degree to which the minority group is distributed differently than whites across census tracts. They range from 0 (complete integration) to 100 (complete segregation) where the value indicates the percentage of the minority group that needs to move to be distributed exactly like whites; (2) Ranges from 1 (most segregated) to 102 (least segregated); n/a not available.
Source: www.CensusScope.org

Ancestry

Area	German	Irish	English	American	Italian	Polish	French[2]	Scottish	Dutch
City	3.1	4.9	1.7	3.7	7.0	2.6	0.8	0.4	0.3
MSA[1]	7.1	10.6	3.1	4.0	13.8	4.4	1.0	0.7	0.6
U.S.	15.2	11.1	8.2	7.2	5.6	3.1	2.8	1.7	1.4

Note: Figures are the percentage of the total population reporting a particular ancestry. The nine most commonly reported ancestries in the U.S. are shown. Figures include multiple ancestries (e.g. if a person reported being Irish and Italian, they were included in both columns); (1) Figures cover the New York-Newark-Jersey City, NY-NJ-PA Metropolitan Statistical Area—see Appendix B for areas included; (2) Excludes Basque
Source: U.S. Census Bureau, 2010-2012 American Community Survey 3-Year Estimates

Foreign-Born Population

Area	Any Foreign Country	Mexico	Asia	Europe	Carribean	South America	Central America[2]	Africa	Canada
City	37.3	2.3	10.3	5.8	10.5	5.1	1.5	1.5	0.3
MSA[1]	29.0	1.7	8.1	4.8	6.7	4.4	1.9	1.1	0.2
U.S.	13.0	3.7	3.7	1.6	1.2	0.9	1.0	0.5	0.3

Note: (1) Figures cover the New York-Newark-Jersey City, NY-NJ-PA Metropolitan Statistical Area—see Appendix B for areas included; (2) Excludes Mexico.
Source: U.S. Census Bureau, 2010-2012 American Community Survey 3-Year Estimates

Marital Status

Area	Never Married	Now Married[2]	Separated	Widowed	Divorced
City	44.1	38.6	3.4	5.7	8.1
MSA[1]	37.8	45.5	2.6	6.1	8.0
U.S.	32.4	48.4	2.2	6.0	11.0

Note: Figures are percentages and cover the population 15 years of age and older; (1) Figures cover the New York-Newark-Jersey City, NY-NJ-PA Metropolitan Statistical Area—see Appendix B for areas included; (2) Excludes separated
Source: U.S. Census Bureau, 2010-2012 American Community Survey 3-Year Estimates

Age

Area	Under Age 5	Age 5–19	Age 20–34	Age 35–44	Age 45–54	Age 55–64	Age 65–74	Age 75–84	Age 85+	Median Age
City	6.4	17.6	25.0	14.0	13.4	11.1	6.7	3.9	1.8	35.5
MSA[1]	6.2	19.0	21.2	13.8	14.7	11.8	7.0	4.3	2.0	37.7
U.S.	6.4	20.1	20.5	13.1	14.3	12.2	7.3	4.2	1.8	37.3

Note: (1) Figures cover the New York-Newark-Jersey City, NY-NJ-PA Metropolitan Statistical Area—see Appendix B for areas included
Source: U.S. Census Bureau, 2010-2012 American Community Survey 3-Year Estimates

Gender

Area	Males	Females	Males per 100 Females
City	3,932,715	4,332,730	90.8
MSA[1]	9,183,572	9,864,595	93.1
U.S.	153,276,055	158,333,314	96.8

Note: (1) Figures cover the New York-Newark-Jersey City, NY-NJ-PA Metropolitan Statistical Area—see Appendix B for areas included
Source: U.S. Census Bureau, 2010-2012 American Community Survey 3-Year Estimates

Religious Groups by Family

Area	Catholic	Baptist	Non-Den.	Methodist[2]	Lutheran	LDS[3]	Pente-costal	Presby-terian[4]	Muslim[5]	Judaism
MSA[1]	36.9	1.9	1.8	1.3	0.8	0.4	0.9	1.1	2.3	4.8
U.S.	19.1	9.3	4.0	4.0	2.3	2.0	1.9	1.6	0.8	0.7

Note: Figures are the number of adherents as a percentage of the total population; (1) Figures cover the New York-Newark-Jersey City, NY-NJ-PA Metropolitan Statistical Area—see Appendix B for areas included; (2) Methodist/Pietist; (3) Latter Day Saints; (4) Reformed; (5) Figures are estimates
Source: Association of Statisticians of American Religious Bodies, 2010 U.S. Religion Census: Religious Congregations & Membership Study

Religious Groups by Tradition

Area	Catholic	Evangelical Protestant	Mainline Protestant	Other Tradition	Black Protestant	Orthodox
MSA[1]	36.9	4.0	4.1	8.4	1.2	1.0
U.S.	19.1	16.2	7.3	4.3	1.6	0.3

Note: Figures are the number of adherents as a percentage of the total population; (1) Figures cover the New York-Newark-Jersey City, NY-NJ-PA Metropolitan Statistical Area—see Appendix B for areas included
Source: Association of Statisticians of American Religious Bodies, 2010 U.S. Religion Census: Religious Congregations & Membership Study

ECONOMY

Gross Metropolitan Product

Area	2011	2012	2013	2014	Rank[2]
MSA[1]	1,294.2	1,335.1	1,379.7	1,431.3	1

Note: Figures are in billions of dollars; (1) Figures cover the New York-Newark-Jersey City, NY-NJ-PA Metropolitan Statistical Area—see Appendix B for areas included; (2) Rank is based on 2014 data and ranges from 1 to 363
Source: The United States Conference of Mayors, U.S. Metro Economies: Outlook—Gross Metropolitan Product, with Metro Employment Projections, November 2013

Economic Growth

Area	2011 (%)	2012 (%)	2013 (%)	2014 (%)	Rank[2]
MSA[1]	1.1	1.4	2.0	1.9	70
U.S.	1.6	2.5	1.7	2.5	—

Note: Figures are real gross metropolitan product (GMP) growth rates and represent annual average percent change; (1) Figures cover the New York-Newark-Jersey City, NY-NJ-PA Metropolitan Statistical Area—see Appendix B for areas included; (2) Rank is based on 2013 data and ranges from 1 to 363
Source: The United States Conference of Mayors, U.S. Metro Economies: Outlook—Gross Metropolitan Product, with Metro Employment Projections, November 2013

Metropolitan Area Exports

Area	2007	2008	2009	2010	2011	2012	Rank[2]
MSA[1]	80,852.0	95,244.3	69,990.3	85,081.2	105,102.0	102,298.0	2

Note: Figures are in millions of dollars; (1) Figures cover the New York-Newark-Jersey City, NY-NJ-PA Metropolitan Statistical Area—see Appendix B for areas included; (2) Rank is based on 2012 data and ranges from 1 to 369
Source: U.S. Department of Commerce, International Trade Administration, Office of Trade & Industry Information, Manufacturing & Services, data extracted April 1, 2014

INCOME

Income

Area	Per Capita ($)	Median Household ($)	Average Household ($)
City	30,826	50,711	79,740
MSA[1]	34,738	64,344	93,767
U.S.	27,385	51,771	71,579

Note: (1) Figures cover the New York-Newark-Jersey City, NY-NJ-PA Metropolitan Statistical Area—see Appendix B for areas included
Source: U.S. Census Bureau, 2010-2012 American Community Survey 3-Year Estimates

Household Income Distribution

Area	Percent of Households Earning							
	Under $15,000	$15,000 -24,999	$25,000 -34,999	$35,000 -49,999	$50,000 -74,999	$75,000 -99,000	$100,000 -149,999	$150,000 and up
City	17.1	11.0	9.4	11.9	15.9	10.5	12.1	12.0
MSA[1]	12.3	9.1	8.2	10.8	15.8	11.7	15.4	16.8
U.S.	13.1	11.0	10.5	13.7	18.1	11.9	12.5	9.1

Note: (1) Figures cover the New York-Newark-Jersey City, NY-NJ-PA Metropolitan Statistical Area—see Appendix B for areas included
Source: U.S. Census Bureau, 2010-2012 American Community Survey 3-Year Estimates

Poverty Rate

Area	All Ages	Under 18 Years Old	18 to 64 Years Old	65 Years and Over
City	20.8	30.4	18.1	18.5
MSA[1]	14.3	20.1	12.8	11.6
U.S.	15.7	22.2	14.6	9.3

Note: Figures are percentage of people whose income during the past 12 months was below the poverty level;
(1) Figures cover the New York-Newark-Jersey City, NY-NJ-PA Metropolitan Statistical Area—see Appendix B for areas included
Source: U.S. Census Bureau, 2010-2012 American Community Survey 3-Year Estimates

Personal Bankruptcy Filing Rate

Area	2008	2009	2010	2011	2012	2013
Bronx County	2.01	2.36	2.34	2.21	1.86	1.74
Kings County	1.49	1.82	1.85	1.65	1.29	1.16
New York County	1.42	2.15	1.96	1.77	1.42	1.06
Queens County	1.99	2.56	2.74	2.41	1.94	1.69
Richmond County	1.92	2.85	3.03	2.73	2.23	1.91
U.S.	3.53	4.61	4.97	4.37	3.76	3.29

Note: Numbers are per 1,000 population and include Chapter 7 and Chapter 13 filings; n/a not available
Source: Federal Deposit Insurance Corporation, Regional Economic Conditions, March 20, 2014

EMPLOYMENT

Labor Force and Employment

Area	Civilian Labor Force			Workers Employed		
	Dec. 2012	Dec. 2013	% Chg.	Dec. 2012	Dec. 2013	% Chg.
City	4,028,164	4,037,749	0.2	3,669,066	3,732,938	1.7
MD[1]	5,745,485	5,742,363	-0.1	5,247,273	5,334,716	1.7
U.S.	154,904,000	154,408,000	-0.3	143,060,000	144,423,000	1.0

Note: Data is not seasonally adjusted and covers workers 16 years of age and older; (1) Metropolitan Division—see Appendix B for areas included
Source: Bureau of Labor Statistics, Local Area Unemployment Statistics

Unemployment Rate

Area	2013											
	Jan.	Feb.	Mar.	Apr.	May	Jun.	Jul.	Aug.	Sep.	Oct.	Nov.	Dec.
City	9.7	9.2	8.6	8.2	8.6	8.9	9.1	8.8	8.5	8.7	8.0	7.5
MD[1]	9.7	9.0	8.4	7.7	8.1	8.5	8.4	8.4	8.2	8.4	7.5	7.1
U.S.	8.5	8.1	7.6	7.1	7.3	7.8	7.7	7.3	7.0	7.0	6.6	6.5

Note: Data is not seasonally adjusted and covers workers 16 years of age and older; All figures are percentages;
(1) Metropolitan Division—see Appendix B for areas included
Source: Bureau of Labor Statistics, Local Area Unemployment Statistics

Employment by Occupation

Occupation Classification	City (%)	MSA[1] (%)	U.S. (%)
Management, Business, Science, and Arts	38.0	40.0	36.0
Natural Resources, Construction, and Maintenance	6.2	6.9	9.1
Production, Transportation, and Material Moving	8.9	9.2	12.0
Sales and Office	23.6	24.5	24.7
Service	23.3	19.4	18.2

Note: Figures cover employed civilians 16 years of age and older; (1) Figures cover the New York-Newark-Jersey City, NY-NJ-PA Metropolitan Statistical Area—see Appendix B for areas included
Source: U.S. Census Bureau, 2010-2012 American Community Survey 3-Year Estimates

Employment by Industry

Sector	MD[1] Number of Employees	MD[1] Percent of Total	U.S. Percent of Total
Construction	n/a	n/a	4.2
Education and Health Services	1,104,400	20.0	15.5
Financial Activities	545,500	9.9	5.7
Government	750,400	13.6	16.1
Information	213,300	3.9	1.9
Leisure and Hospitality	495,900	9.0	10.2
Manufacturing	161,400	2.9	8.7
Mining and Logging	n/a	n/a	0.6
Other Services	235,300	4.3	3.9
Professional and Business Services	874,900	15.9	13.7
Retail Trade	547,900	9.9	11.4
Transportation and Utilities	188,300	3.4	3.8
Wholesale Trade	228,800	4.1	4.2

Note: Figures cover non-farm employment as of December 2013 and are not seasonally adjusted; (1) Metropolitan Division—see Appendix B for areas included; n/a not available
Source: Bureau of Labor Statistics, Current Employment Statistics, Employment, Hours, and Earnings

Occupations with Greatest Projected Employment Growth: 2010 – 2020

Occupation[1]	2010 Employment	2020 Projected Employment	Numeric Employment Change	Percent Employment Change
Personal Care Aides	128,230	191,480	63,250	49.3
Home Health Aides	138,790	200,650	61,860	44.6
Retail Salespersons	285,670	313,770	28,110	9.8
Registered Nurses	178,470	203,360	24,890	13.9
Combined Food Preparation and Serving Workers, Including Fast Food	136,650	159,220	22,570	16.5
Childcare Workers	132,830	152,170	19,340	14.6
Receptionists and Information Clerks	85,290	103,450	18,160	21.3
Office Clerks, General	210,920	228,560	17,640	8.4
Postsecondary Teachers	133,360	148,990	15,630	11.7
Waiters and Waitresses	131,820	147,330	15,500	11.8

Note: Projections cover New York; (1) Sorted by numeric employment change
Source: www.projectionscentral.com, State Occupational Projections, 2010–2020 Long-Term Projections

Fastest Growing Occupations: 2010 – 2020

Occupation[1]	2010 Employment	2020 Projected Employment	Numeric Employment Change	Percent Employment Change
Biomedical Engineers	410	650	240	60.0
Personal Care Aides	128,230	191,480	63,250	49.3
Home Health Aides	138,790	200,650	61,860	44.6
Meeting, Convention, and Event Planners	8,540	12,250	3,710	43.4
Veterinary Technologists and Technicians	3,830	5,390	1,560	40.6
Physical Therapist Aides	2,570	3,560	990	38.3
Health Educators	6,220	8,510	2,290	36.7
Helpers—Carpenters	4,150	5,620	1,480	35.6
Helpers—Brickmasons, Blockmasons, Stonemasons, and Tile and Marble Setters	1,610	2,170	560	34.5
Diagnostic Medical Sonographers	3,600	4,810	1,220	33.8

Note: Projections cover New York; (1) Sorted by percent employment change and excludes occupations with numeric employment change less than 100
Source: www.projectionscentral.com, State Occupational Projections, 2010–2020 Long-Term Projections

Average Wages

Occupation	$/Hr.	Occupation	$/Hr.
Accountants and Auditors	44.94	Maids and Housekeeping Cleaners	17.16
Automotive Mechanics	20.68	Maintenance and Repair Workers	20.80
Bookkeepers	20.95	Marketing Managers	85.29
Carpenters	31.17	Nuclear Medicine Technologists	39.70
Cashiers	10.15	Nurses, Licensed Practical	24.60
Clerks, General Office	14.82	Nurses, Registered	40.44
Clerks, Receptionists/Information	14.70	Nursing Assistants	16.20
Clerks, Shipping/Receiving	15.85	Packers and Packagers, Hand	10.81
Computer Programmers	43.75	Physical Therapists	40.71
Computer Systems Analysts	47.55	Postal Service Mail Carriers	25.37
Computer User Support Specialists	28.67	Real Estate Brokers	54.98
Cooks, Restaurant	13.46	Retail Salespersons	12.84
Dentists	69.88	Sales Reps., Exc. Tech./Scientific	38.77
Electrical Engineers	46.38	Sales Reps., Tech./Scientific	46.37
Electricians	37.44	Secretaries, Exc. Legal/Med./Exec.	19.00
Financial Managers	87.96	Security Guards	15.18
First-Line Supervisors/Managers, Sales	23.97	Surgeons	98.64
Food Preparation Workers	11.96	Teacher Assistants	13.90
General and Operations Managers	77.74	Teachers, Elementary School	35.30
Hairdressers/Cosmetologists	15.36	Teachers, Secondary School	37.40
Internists	80.33	Telemarketers	14.62
Janitors and Cleaners	15.78	Truck Drivers, Heavy/Tractor-Trailer	22.08
Landscaping/Groundskeeping Workers	15.65	Truck Drivers, Light/Delivery Svcs.	17.98
Lawyers	79.66	Waiters and Waitresses	11.50

Note: Wage data covers the New York-White Plains-Wayne, NY-NJ Metropolitan Division—see Appendix B for areas included. Hourly wages for elementary/secondary school teachers and teacher assistants were calculated by the editors from annual wage data assuming a 40 hour work week; n/a not available.
Source: Bureau of Labor Statistics, Metro Area Occupational Employment and Wage Estimates, May 2013

RESIDENTIAL REAL ESTATE

Building Permits

Area	Single-Family			Multi-Family			Total		
	2012	2013	Pct. Chg.	2012	2013	Pct. Chg.	2012	2013	Pct. Chg.
City	280	402	43.6	10,054	17,593	75.0	10,334	17,995	74.1
MSA[1]	6,815	10,139	48.8	20,097	29,685	47.7	26,912	39,824	48.0
U.S.	518,695	620,802	19.7	310,963	370,020	19.0	829,658	990,822	19.4

Note: (1) Metropolitan Statistical Area—see Appendix B for areas included; figures represent new, privately-owned housing units authorized (unadjusted data); All permit data are based on estimates with imputation.
Source: U.S. Census Bureau, Manufacturing, Mining, and Construction Statistics, Building Permits, 2012, 2013

Homeownership Rate

Area	2006 (%)	2007 (%)	2008 (%)	2009 (%)	2010 (%)	2011 (%)	2012 (%)	2013 (%)
MSA[1]	53.6	53.8	52.6	51.7	51.6	50.9	51.5	50.6
U.S.	68.8	68.1	67.8	67.4	66.9	66.1	65.4	65.1

Note: (1) Figures cover the New York-Newark-Jersey City, NY-NJ-PA Metropolitan Statistical Area—see Appendix B for areas included
Source: U.S. Census Bureau, Housing Vacancies and Homeownership Annual Statistics: 2013

Housing Vacancy Rates

Area	Gross Vacancy Rate[2] (%)			Year-Round Vacancy Rate[3] (%)			Rental Vacancy Rate[4] (%)			Homeowner Vacancy Rate[5] (%)		
	2011	2012	2013	2011	2012	2013	2011	2012	2013	2011	2012	2013
MSA[1]	10.0	9.8	9.5	8.7	8.4	8.1	6.4	6.4	5.4	2.6	2.2	2.1
U.S.	14.2	13.8	13.8	11.1	10.8	10.7	9.5	8.7	8.3	2.5	2.0	2.0

Note: (1) Figures cover the New York-Newark-Jersey City, NY-NJ-PA Metropolitan Statistical Area—see Appendix B for areas included; (2) The percentage of the total housing inventory that is vacant; (3) The percentage of the housing inventory (excluding seasonal units) that is year-round vacant; (4) The percentage of rental inventory that is vacant for rent; (5) The percentage of homeowner inventory that is vacant for sale
Source: U.S. Census Bureau, Housing Vacancies and Homeownership Annual Statistics: 2013

TAXES

State Corporate Income Tax Rates

State	Tax Rate (%)	Income Brackets ($)	Num. of Brackets	Financial Institution Tax Rate (%)[a]	Federal Income Tax Ded.
New York	7.1 (s)	Flat rate	1	7.1 (s)	No

Note: Tax rates as of January 1, 2014; (a) Rates listed are the corporate income tax rate applied to financial institutions or excise taxes based on income. Some states have other taxes based upon the value of deposits or shares; (s) New York's General business corporate rate shown. Corporations may also be subject to AMT tax at 1.5% (3% banks), or a capital stocks tax. A minimum tax ranges from $25 to $5,000, depending on receipts ($250 minimum for banks). Certain qualified New York manufacturers pay 6.5%. Small business taxpayers in New York pay rates of 6.5%, 7.1%, and 4.35% on 3 brackets of entire net income up to $390,000.
Source: Federation of Tax Administrators, "State Corporate Income Tax Rates, 2014"

State Individual Income Tax Rates

State	Tax Rate (%)	Income Brackets ($)	Num. of Brackets	Personal Exempt. ($)[1] Single	Personal Exempt. ($)[1] Dependents	Fed. Inc. Tax Ded.
New York	4.0 - 8.82	8,200 - 1,029,250 (b)	8	None	1,000	No

Note: Tax rates as of January 1, 2014; Local- and county-level taxes are not included; n/a not applicable; (1) Married joint filers generally receive double the single exemption; (b) For joint returns, taxes are twice the tax on half the couple's income.
Source: Federation of Tax Administrators, "State Individual Income Tax Rates, 2014"

Various State and Local Tax Rates

State	State and Local Sales and Use (%)	State Sales and Use (%)	Gasoline[1] (¢/gal.)	Cigarette[2] ($/pack)	Spirits[3] ($/gal.)	Wine[4] ($/gal.)	Beer[5] ($/gal.)
New York	8.875	4.00	49.57	4.350	6.44 (f)	0.30	0.14

Note: All tax rates as of January 1, 2014; (1) The American Petroleum Institute has developed a methodology for determining the average tax rate on a gallon of fuel. Rates may include any of the following: excise taxes, environmental fees, storage tank fees, other fees or taxes, general sales tax, and local taxes. In states where gasoline is subject to the general sales tax, or where the fuel tax is based on the average sale price, the average rate determined by API is sensitive to changes in the price of gasoline. States that fully or partially apply general sales taxes to gasoline: CA, CO, GA, IL, IN, MI, NY; (2) The federal excise tax of $1.0066 per pack and local taxes are not included; (3) Rates are those applicable to off-premise sales of 40% alcohol by volume (a.b.v.) distilled spirits in 750ml containers. Local excise taxes are excluded; (4) Rates are those applicable to off-premise sales of 11% a.b.v. non-carbonated wine in 750ml containers; (5) Rates are those applicable to off-premise sales of 4.7% a.b.v. beer in 12 ounce containers; (f) Different rates also applicable according to alcohol content, place of production, size of container, or place purchased (on- or off-premise or onboard airlines).
Source: Tax Foundation, 2014 Facts & Figures: How Does Your State Compare?

State Business Tax Climate Index Rankings

State	Overall Rank	Corporate Tax Index Rank	Individual Income Tax Index Rank	Sales Tax Index Rank	Unemployment Insurance Tax Index Rank	Property Tax Index Rank
New York	50	25	49	38	45	45

Note: The index is a measure of how each state's tax laws affect economic performance. The lower the rank, the more favorable a state's tax system is for business. States without a given tax are given a ranking of 1. The scores/rankings for the District of Columbia do not affect other states. The 2014 index represents the tax climate as of July 1, 2013.
Source: Tax Foundation, State Business Tax Climate Index 2014

**COMMERCIAL
REAL ESTATE**

Office Market

Market Area	Inventory (sq. ft.)	Vacancy Rate (%)	Under Construction (sq. ft.)	YTD Net Absorption (sq. ft.)	Total Average Asking Rent ($/sq. ft./year)
Long Island	55,154,040	12.1	83,799	281,070	26.30
Manhattan	446,543,473	8.9	8,645,586	2,469,181	55.47
Northern New Jersey	219,221,443	19.3	1,075,488	1,976,224	23.94
Westchester County	34,724,994	16.0	345,027	763,287	25.76
National	4,726,900,879	15.0	55,419,286	42,829,434	26.27

Source: Newmark Grubb Knight Frank, National Office Market Report, 4th Quarter 2013

Industrial/Warehouse/R&D Market

Market Area	Inventory (sq. ft.)	Vacancy Rate (%)	Under Construction (sq. ft.)	YTD Net Absorption (sq. ft.)	Total Average Asking Rent ($/sq. ft./year)
Long Island	155,121,947	5.0	592,698	1,706,128	8.42
Northern New Jersey	724,615,373	8.2	4,094,891	8,073,430	5.97
Westchester County	32,475,403	6.7	0	-77,385	9.45
National	14,022,031,238	7.9	83,249,164	156,549,903	5.40

Source: Newmark Grubb Knight Frank, National Industrial Market Report, 4th Quarter 2013

**COMMERCIAL
UTILITIES**

Typical Monthly Electric Bills

Area	Commercial Service ($/month)		Industrial Service ($/month)	
	1,500 kWh	40 kW demand 14,000 kWh	1,000 kW demand 200,000 kWh	50,000 kW demand 15,000,000 kWh
City	446	3,145	53,772	3,821,786
Average[1]	197	1,636	25,662	1,485,307

Note: Based on total rates in effect July 1, 2013; (1) average based on 180 utilities surveyed
Source: Edison Electric Institute, Typical Bills and Average Rates Report, Summer 2013

TRANSPORTATION

Means of Transportation to Work

Area	Car/Truck/Van Drove Alone	Car-pooled	Public Transportation Bus	Subway	Railroad	Bicycle	Walked	Other Means	Worked at Home
City	22.4	4.8	11.7	42.1	1.7	0.9	10.2	2.3	4.0
MSA[1]	50.1	6.7	8.2	18.8	3.6	0.5	6.1	2.0	4.0
U.S.	76.4	9.7	2.6	1.7	0.5	0.6	2.8	1.3	4.3

Note: Figures are percentages and cover workers 16 years of age and older; (1) Figures cover the New York-Newark-Jersey City, NY-NJ-PA Metropolitan Statistical Area—see Appendix B for areas included
Source: U.S. Census Bureau, 2010-2012 American Community Survey 3-Year Estimates

Travel Time to Work

Area	Less Than 10 Minutes	10 to 19 Minutes	20 to 29 Minutes	30 to 44 Minutes	45 to 59 Minutes	60 to 89 Minutes	90 Minutes or More
City	4.5	13.9	14.7	27.4	15.2	17.9	6.4
MSA[1]	7.8	19.9	16.8	23.7	11.9	14.0	5.9
U.S.	13.5	29.8	20.9	20.1	7.5	5.6	2.5

Note: Figures are percentages and include workers 16 years old and over; (1) Figures cover the New York-Newark-Jersey City, NY-NJ-PA Metropolitan Statistical Area—see Appendix B for areas included
Source: U.S. Census Bureau, 2010-2012 American Community Survey 3-Year Estimates

Travel Time Index

Area	1985	1990	1995	2000	2005	2010	2011
Urban Area[1]	1.13	1.23	1.26	1.33	1.43	1.33	1.33
Average[2]	1.09	1.14	1.16	1.19	1.23	1.18	1.18

Note: Travel Time Index—the ratio of travel time in the peak period to the travel time at free-flow conditions. For example, a value of 1.30 indicates a 20-minute free-flow trip takes 26 minutes in the peak. Free-flow speeds (60 mph on freeways and 35 mph on principal arterials) are used as the comparison threshold; (1) Covers the New York-Newark NY-NJ-CT urban area; (2) average of 498 urban areas
Source: Texas Transportation Institute, Urban Mobility Report 2012, December 2012

Public Transportation

Agency Name / Mode of Transportation	Vehicles Operated in Maximum Service	Annual Unlinked Passenger Trips (in thous.)	Annual Passenger Miles (in thous.)
MTA New York City Transit (NYCT)			
Bus (directly operated)	3,772	805,381.5	1,808,151.7
Demand Response (purchased transportation)	1,669	6,137.0	54,417.5
Heavy Rail (directly operated)	5,272	2,569,543.5	10,327,239.9
MTA Metro-North Railroad (MTA-MNCR)			
Bus (purchased transportation)	7	349.0	119.6
Commuter Rail (directly operated)	1,156	82,807.7	2,437,326.7
Ferryboat (purchased transportation)	2	200.6	755.2
MTA Long Island Railroad (MTA-LIRR)			
Commuter Rail (directly operated)	1,007	96,953.1	2,083,399.6
MTA Staten Island Railway (SIRTOA)			
Heavy Rail (directly operated)	46	6,467.9	37,666.9
New York City Department of Transportation (NYCDOT)			
Bus (purchased transportation)	24	655.5	4,230.0
Ferryboat (directly operated)	4	22,178.8	115,330.0
Port Authority Trans-Hudson Corporation (PATH)			
Ferryboat (purchased transportation)	6	1,439.4	3,681.6
Heavy Rail (directly operated)	280	79,852.6	339,698.3

Source: Federal Transit Administration, National Transit Database, 2012

Air Transportation

Airport Name and Code / Type of Service	Passenger Airlines[1]	Passenger Enplanements	Freight Carriers[2]	Freight (lbs.)
John F. Kennedy International (JFK)				
Domestic service (U.S. carriers - 2013)	21	11,970,903	18	255,997,455
International service (U.S. carriers - 2012)	17	5,014,699	14	156,696,289
La Guardia International (LGA)				
Domestic service (U.S. carriers - 2013)	30	12,521,566	11	5,192,775
International service (U.S. carriers - 2012)	10	224,599	2	22,775
Newark International (EWR)				
Domestic service (U.S. carriers - 2013)	36	11,925,977	21	487,340,848
International service (U.S. carriers - 2012)	15	3,897,070	7	82,718,848

Note: (1) Includes all U.S.-based major, minor and commuter airlines that carried at least one passenger during the year; (2) Includes all U.S.-based airlines and freight carriers that transported at least one lb. of freight during the year.
Source: Bureau of Transportation Statistics, The Intermodal Transportation Database, Air Carriers: T-100 Domestic Market (U.S. Carriers), 2013; Bureau of Transportation Statistics, The Intermodal Transportation Database, Air Carriers: T-100 International Market (U.S. Carriers), 2012

Other Transportation Statistics

Major Highways:	I-78; I-87; I-95
Amtrak Service:	Yes
Major Waterways/Ports:	Port of New York/New Jersey

Source: Amtrak.com; Google Maps

BUSINESSES

Major Business Headquarters

Company Name	Rankings	
	Fortune[1]	Forbes[2]
Advance Publications	-	53
Alcoa	128	-
American Express	90	-
American International Group	38	-
Assurant	309	-
Avon Products	252	-
Bank of New York Mellon Corp	180	-
Barnes & Noble	360	-
BlackRock	286	-
Bloomberg	-	42
Bristol-Myers Squibb	158	-
CBS	186	-
Charmer Sunbelt Group	-	80
Citigroup	26	-
Colgate-Palmolive	165	-
Consolidated Edison	226	-
Ernst & Young	-	10
Estee Lauder	279	-
Foot Locker	413	-
Goldman Sachs Group	68	-
Guardian Life Ins. Co. of America	238	-
Hearst	-	111
Hess	75	-
ICC Industries	-	156
INTL FCStone	39	-
Icahn Enterprises	178	-
Interpublic Group	366	-
J.P. Morgan Chase & Co.	18	-
JetBlue Airways	495	-
KKR	277	-
L-3 Communications	197	-
Latham & Watkins	-	206
Leucadia National	289	-
Loews	188	-
Marsh & McLennan	228	-
McGraw-Hill	390	-
McKinsey & Company	-	44
MetLife	40	-
Morgan Stanley	96	-
New York Life Insurance	89	-
News Corp	91	-
Omnicom Group	191	-
PVH	422	-
Pfizer	48	-
Philip Morris International	99	-
PricewaterhouseCoopers	-	6
Ralph Lauren	370	-
Red Apple Group	-	98
Renco Group	-	77
Sequa	-	203
Skadden	Arps	
Structure Tone	-	152
TIAA-CREF	97	-
Time Warner	105	-

Time Warner Cable	134	
Transammonia	-	24
Travelers Cos	116	-
Univision Communications	-	192
Verizon Communications	16	-
Viacom	198	-

Note: (1) Fortune 500—companies that produce a 10-K are ranked 1 to 500 based on 2012 revenue; (2) all private companies with at least $2 billion in annual revenue through the end of their most current fiscal year are ranked 1 to 224; companies listed are headquartered in the city; dashes indicate no ranking Source: Fortune, "Fortune 500," May 20, 2013; Forbes, "America's Largest Private Companies," December 18, 2013

Fast-Growing Businesses

According to *Inc.*, New York is home to 22 of America's 500 fastest-growing private companies: **BeenVerified** (#26); **Sailthru** (#30); **YellowHammer** (#37); **Conductor** (#38); **33Across** (#70); **LiveIntent** (#71); **Quantum Networks** (#124); **Regal Wings** (#153); **Refinery29** (#174); **Rethink Autism** (#232); **Gravity Media** (#250); **MSR Promo** (#264); **NUE Agency** (#267); **RosettaBooks** (#280); **Ivy Exec** (#309); **Panjiva** (#314); **Forward Health** (#400); **Grok** (#418); **Carrot Creative** (#450); **Bustin Boards** (#465); **MASS Communications** (#490); **RCS Capital** (#497). Criteria: must be an independent, privately-held, for-profit, U.S. corporation, proprietorship or partnership; revenues must be at least $100,000 in 2009 and $2 million in 2012; must have four-year operating/sales history. Holding companies, regulated banks, and utilities were excluded. *Inc., "America's 500 Fastest-Growing Private Companies," September 2013*

According to *Fortune*, New York is home to one of the 100 fastest-growing companies in the world: **Steven Madden** (#77). Companies were ranked by their revenue growth rate; their EPS growth rate; and their three-year annualized total return to investors for the period ending June 30, 2013. Criteria for inclusion: a company, foreign or domestic, must trade on a major U.S. stock exchange; must file quarterly reports with the SEC; must have a minimum market capitalization of $250 million; must have a stock price of at least $5 on June 29, 2013; must have been trading continuously since June 30, 2009; must have revenue and net income for the four quarters ended on or before April 30, 2013, of at least $50 million and $10 million, respectively; and must have posted a compound annual growth in revenue and earnings per share of at least 20% annually over the three years ending on or before April 30, 2013. REITs, limited-liability companies, limited parterships, companies about to be acquired, and companies that lost money in the quarter ending April 30, 2013 were excluded. *Fortune, "100 Fastest-Growing Companies," August 29, 2013*

According to *Initiative for a Competitive Inner City (ICIC)*, New York is home to four of America's 100 fastest-growing "inner city" companies: **Happy Family** (#1); **International Asbestos Removal** (#28); **InfoPeople Coporation** (#31); **Tumbador Chocolate** (#52). Companies were ranked by their five-year compound annual growth rate. Criteria for inclusion: company must be headquartered in or have 51 percent or more of its physical operations in an economically distressed urban area; must be an independent, for-profit corporation, partnership or proprietorship; must have 10 or more employees and have a five-year sales history that includes sales of at least $200,000 in the base year and at least $1 million in the current year with no decrease in sales over the two most recent years. *Initiative for a Competitive Inner City (ICIC), "Inner City 100 Companies, 2013"*

According to Deloitte, New York is home to 16 of North America's 500 fastest-growing high-technology companies: **NeoStem** (#11); **Spongecell** (#28); **Dstillery** (#58); **eXelate** (#86); **MediaMath** (#91); **Borderfree** (#112); **Payoneer** (#147); **Usablenet** (#174); **Yodle** (#180); **SNAP Interactive** (#194); **Reval** (#303); **Maesa** (#351); **Shutterstock** (#356); **The Orchard** (#370); **Telx** (#372); **BA Insight** (#393). Companies are ranked by percentage growth in revenue over a five-year period. Criteria for inclusion: company must be headquartered within North America; must own proprietary intellectual property or proprietary technology that contributes to a significant portion of the company's operating revenue, or devote a significant proportion of revenues to research and development of technology; must have been in business for a minumum of five years with 2008 operating revenues of at least $50,000 USD/CD and 2012 operating revenues of at least $5 million USD/CD. *Deloitte Touche Tohmatsu, 2013 Technology Fast 500*[TM]

Minority Business Opportunity

New York is home to two companies which are on the *Black Enterprise* Industrial/Service 100 list (100 largest companies based on gross sales): **Golden Krust Caribbean Bakery & Grill** (#40); **Earl G. Graves** (#74). Criteria: operational in previous calendar year; at least 51% black-owned and manufactures/owns the product it sells or provides industrial or consumer services. Brokerages, real estate firms and firms that provide professional services are not eligible. *Black Enterprise, B.E. 100s, 2013*

New York is home to one company which is on the *Black Enterprise* Auto Dealer 60 list (60 largest dealers based on gross sales): **Kristal Auto Mall Corp.** (#21). Criteria: company must be operational in previous calendar year and be at least 51% black-owned. *Black Enterprise, B.E. 100s, 2013*

New York is home to one company which is on the *Black Enterprise* Bank 20 list (20 largest banks based on total assets, capital, deposits and loans, including mortgage-backed securities for the calendar year): **Carver Bancorp (Carver Federal Savings Bank)** (#1). Only commercial banks or savings and loans that are classified by the Federal Reserve as black institutions and have been fully operational for the previous calendar year were considered. *Black Enterprise, B.E. 100s, 2013*

New York is home to two companies which are on the *Black Enterprise* Asset Manager 15 list (15 largest asset management firms based on assets under management): **Advent Capital Management** (#5); **Williams Capital Management** (#13). Criteria: company must have been operational in previous calendar year and be at least 51% black-owned. *Black Enterprise, B.E. 100s, 2013*

New York is home to three companies which are on the *Black Enterprise* Private Equity 15 list (15 largest private equity firms based on capital under management): **GenNx360 Capital Partners** (#5); **ICV Partners** (#7); **Black Enterprise Greenwich Street Corporate Growth Mgmt** (#14). Criteria: company must be operational in previous calendar year and be at least 51% black-owned. *Black Enterprise, B.E. 100s, 2013*

New York is home to 10 companies which are on the *Hispanic Business* 500 list (500 largest U.S. Hispanic-owned companies based on 2012 revenue): **Pride Technologies** (#25); **Bartlett Dairy** (#47); **Samuel A. Ramirez & Co.** (#104); **LargaVista Companies** (#108); **First in Service Travel** (#148); **La Rosa del Monte Express** (#149); **Mechanical Heating Supply** (#249); **Ideal Interiors** (#288); **Interstate Envelope Mfg.** (#381); **Matiz Architecture and Design** (#473). Companies included must show at least 51 percent ownership by Hispanic U.S. citizens, and must maintain headquarters in one of the 50 states or Washington, D.C. *Hispanic Business, "Hispanic Business 500," June 20, 2013*

New York is home to one company which is on the *Hispanic Business* Fastest-Growing 100 list (greatest sales growth from 2008 to 2012): **First In Service Travel Ltd.** (#47). Companies included must show at least 51 percent ownership by Hispanic U.S. citizens, and must maintain headquarters in one of the 50 states or Washington, D.C. In addition, companies must have minimum revenues of $200,000 for calendar year 2008. *Hispanic Business, June 20, 2013*

Minority- and Women-Owned Businesses

Group	All Firms		Firms with Paid Employees			
	Firms	Sales ($000)	Firms	Sales ($000)	Employees	Payroll ($000)
Asian	153,841	38,064,580	31,534	33,954,049	160,876	5,211,444
Black	154,901	9,044,525	8,067	6,106,801	47,416	1,238,267
Hispanic	143,013	11,872,396	11,244	9,163,482	52,317	1,650,975
Women	305,198	42,278,545	29,706	34,365,449	201,213	8,220,166
All Firms	944,079	1,295,799,894	185,190	1,262,643,863	3,392,770	251,947,158

Note: Figures cover firms located in the city; minority- and women-owned business are defined as firms in which the corresponding group own 51% or more of the stock or equity of the company
Source: U.S. Census Bureau, 2007 Economic Census, Survey of Business Owners (2012 Survey of Business Owners data will be released starting in June 2015)

**HOTELS &
CONVENTION
CENTERS**

Hotels/Motels

Area	5 Star Num.	5 Star Pct.[3]	4 Star Num.	4 Star Pct.[3]	3 Star Num.	3 Star Pct.[3]	2 Star Num.	2 Star Pct.[3]	1 Star Num.	1 Star Pct.[3]	Not Rated Num.	Not Rated Pct.[3]
City[1]	25	4.8	140	26.7	194	37.0	130	24.8	8	1.5	28	5.3
Total[2]	142	0.9	1,005	6.0	5,147	30.9	8,578	51.4	408	2.4	1,397	8.4

*Note: (1) Figures cover New York and vicinity; (2) Figures cover all 100 cities in this book; (3) Percentage of
hotels which have a given star rating; Star ratings are determined by expedia.com and offer an indication of the
general quality of a particular hotel.*
Source: expedia.com, April 7, 2014

Major Convention Centers

Name	Overall Space (sq. ft.)	Exhibit Space (sq. ft.)	Meeting Space (sq. ft.)	Meeting Rooms
Jacob K. Javits Convention Center	n/a	760,000	n/a	75

*Note: Table includes convention centers located in the New York-Newark-Jersey City, NY-NJ-PA metro area; n/a
not available*
Source: Original research

Living Environment

COST OF LIVING

Cost of Living Index

Composite Index	Groceries	Housing	Utilities	Trans-portation	Health Care	Misc. Goods/ Services
170.7	118.7	320.3	124.0	111.9	110.3	119.2

Note: The Cost of Living Index measures regional differences in the cost of consumer goods and services, excluding taxes and non-consumer expenditures, for professional and managerial households in the top income quintile. It is based on more than 50,000 prices covering almost 60 different items for which prices are collected three times a year by chambers of commerce, economic development organizations or university applied economic centers in each participating urban area. The numbers shown should be read as a percentage above or below the national average of 100. For example, a value of 115.4 in the groceries column indicates that grocery prices are 15.4% higher than the national average. Small differences in the index numbers should not be interpreted as significant; Figures cover the New York (Brooklyn) NY urban area.
Source: The Council for Community and Economic Research, ACCRA Cost of Living Index, 2013

Grocery Prices

Area[1]	T-Bone Steak ($/pound)	Frying Chicken ($/pound)	Whole Milk ($/half gal.)	Eggs ($/dozen)	Orange Juice ($/64 oz.)	Coffee ($/11.5 oz.)
City[2]	12.32	1.73	2.26	2.61	4.18	5.13
Avg.	10.19	1.28	2.34	1.81	3.48	4.39
Min.	8.56	0.94	1.44	1.19	2.78	3.40
Max.	14.82	2.28	3.56	3.73	6.23	7.32

Note: (1) Values for the local area are compared with the average, minimum and maximum values for all 327 areas in the Cost of Living Index; (2) Figures cover the New York (Brooklyn) NY urban area; **T-Bone Steak** *(price per pound);* **Frying Chicken** *(price per pound, whole fryer);* **Whole Milk** *(half gallon carton);* **Eggs** *(price per dozen, Grade A, large);* **Orange Juice** *(64 oz. Tropicana or Florida Natural);* **Coffee** *(11.5 oz. can, vacuum-packed, Maxwell House, Hills Bros, or Folgers).*
Source: The Council for Community and Economic Research, ACCRA Cost of Living Index, 2013

Housing and Utility Costs

Area[1]	New Home Price ($)	Apartment Rent ($/month)	All Electric ($/month)	Part Electric ($/month)	Other Energy ($/month)	Telephone ($/month)
City[2]	990,514	2,493	-	116.34	103.28	30.33
Avg.	295,864	900	171.38	91.82	70.12	27.73
Min.	185,506	458	117.80	48.81	33.67	17.16
Max.	1,358,917	3,783	441.68	171.40	372.65	39.47

Note: (1) Values for the local area are compared with the average, minimum and maximum values for all 327 areas in the Cost of Living Index; (2) Figures cover the New York (Brooklyn) NY urban area; **New Home Price** *(2,400 sf living area, 8,000 sf lot, in urban area with full utilities);* **Apartment Rent** *(950 sf 2 bedroom/1.5 or 2 bath, unfurnished, excluding all utilities except water);* **All Electric** *(average monthly cost for an all-electric home);* **Part Electric** *(average monthly cost for a part-electric home);* **Other Energy** *(average monthly cost for natural gas, fuel oil, coal, wood, and any other forms of energy except electricity);* **Telephone** *(price includes basic monthly rate for a private residential line plus additional local usage charges incurred by a family of four).*
Source: The Council for Community and Economic Research, ACCRA Cost of Living Index, 2013

Health Care, Transportation, and Other Costs

Area[1]	Doctor ($/visit)	Dentist ($/visit)	Optometrist ($/visit)	Gasoline ($/gallon)	Beauty Salon ($/visit)	Men's Shirt ($)
City[2]	108.35	114.81	76.87	3.82	57.93	31.16
Avg.	101.40	86.48	96.16	3.44	33.87	26.55
Min.	61.67	50.83	50.12	3.08	18.92	12.48
Max.	182.71	152.50	223.78	4.33	68.22	52.03

Note: (1) Values for the local area are compared with the average, minimum and maximum values for all 327 areas in the Cost of Living Index; (2) Figures cover the New York (Brooklyn) NY urban area; **Doctor** *(general practitioners routine exam of an established patient);* **Dentist** *(adult teeth cleaning and periodic oral examination);* **Optometrist** *(full vision eye exam for established adult patient);* **Gasoline** *(one gallon regular unleaded, national brand, including all taxes, cash price at self-service pump if available);* **Beauty Salon** *(woman's shampoo, trim, and blow-dry);* **Men's Shirt** *(cotton/polyester dress shirt, pinpoint weave, long sleeves).*
Source: The Council for Community and Economic Research, ACCRA Cost of Living Index, 2013

HOUSING

House Price Index (HPI)

Area	National Ranking[2]	Quarterly Change (%)	One-Year Change (%)	Five-Year Change (%)
MD[1]	146	0.50	2.00	-9.63
U.S.[3]	–	1.20	7.69	4.18

Note: The HPI is a weighted repeat sales index. It measures average price changes in repeat sales or refinancings on the same properties. This information is obtained by reviewing repeat mortgage transactions on single-family properties whose mortgages have been purchased or securitized by Fannie Mae or Freddie Mac in January 1975; (1) New York-Jersey City-White Plains, NY-NJ Metropolitan Division—see Appendix B for areas included; (2) Rankings are based on annual percentage change for all metro areas containing at least 15,000 transactions over the last 10 years and ranges from 1 to 283; (3) figures based on a weighted average of Census Division estimates using a seasonally adjusted, purchase-only index; all figures are for the period ending December 31, 2013
Source: Federal Housing Finance Agency, House Price Index, February 25, 2014

Median Single-Family Home Prices

Area	2011	2012	2013[p]	Percent Change 2012 to 2013
MSA[1]	378.7	379.3	391.8	3.3
U.S. Average	166.2	177.2	197.4	11.4

Note: Figures are median sales prices of existing single-family homes in thousands of dollars; (p) preliminary; n/a not available; (1) New York-Newark-Jersey City, NY-NJ-PA Metropolitan Statistical Area—see Appendix B for areas included
Source: National Association of Realtors, Median Sales Price of Existing Single-Family Homes for Metropolitan Areas, 4th Quarter 2013

Qualifying Income Based on Median Sales Price of Existing Single-Family Homes

Area	With 5% Down ($)	With 10% Down ($)	With 20% Down ($)
MSA[1]	89,062	84,374	74,999
U.S. Average	45,395	43,006	38,228

Note: Figures are preliminary; Qualifying income is based on a mortgage rate of 4.4%. Monthly principal and interest payment is limited to 25% of income; n/a not available; (1) New York-Newark-Jersey City, NY-NJ-PA Metropolitan Statistical Area—see Appendix B for areas included
Source: National Association of Realtors, Qualifying Income Based on Median Sales Price of Existing Single-Family Homes for Metropolitan Areas, 4th Quarter 2013

Median Apartment Condo-Coop Home Prices

Area	2011	2012	2013[p]	Percent Change 2012 to 2013
MSA[1]	n/a	n/a	n/a	n/a
U.S. Average	165.1	173.7	194.9	12.2

Note: Figures are median sales prices of existing apartment condo-coop homes in thousands of dollars; (p) preliminary; n/a not available; (1) New York-Newark-Jersey City, NY-NJ-PA Metropolitan Statistical Area—see Appendix B for areas included
Source: National Association of Realtors, Median Sales Price of Existing Apartment Condo-Coop Homes for Metropolitan Areas, 4th Quarter 2013

Gross Monthly Rent

Area	Under $200	$200 -299	$300 -499	$500 -749	$750 -999	$1,000 -1,499	$1,500 and up	Median ($)
City	1.2	4.9	5.8	9.2	14.6	34.1	30.2	1,187
MSA[1]	1.2	4.1	5.0	8.2	14.9	36.1	30.5	1,205
U.S.	1.7	3.3	8.1	22.7	24.3	25.7	14.3	889

Note: Figures are percentages except for Median; Gross rent is the contract rent plus the estimated average monthly cost of utilities (electricity, gas, and water and sewer) and fuels (oil, coal, kerosene, wood, etc.) if these are paid by the renter (or paid for the renter by someone else); (1) Figures cover the New York-Newark-Jersey City, NY-NJ-PA Metropolitan Statistical Area—see Appendix B for areas included
Source: U.S. Census Bureau, 2010-2012 American Community Survey 3-Year Estimates

Year Housing Structure Built

Area	2010 or Later	2000 -2009	1990 -1999	1980 -1989	1970 -1979	1960 -1969	1950 -1959	1940 -1949	Before 1940	Median Year
City	0.3	6.3	3.5	4.4	7.2	12.5	13.8	10.5	41.5	1948
MSA[1]	0.3	7.3	5.8	7.4	9.8	13.9	16.8	9.7	29.0	1957
U.S.	0.5	14.9	13.8	13.9	15.9	11.1	10.9	5.5	13.5	1976

Note: Figures are percentages except for Median Year; (1) Figures cover the New York-Newark-Jersey City, NY-NJ-PA Metropolitan Statistical Area—see Appendix B for areas included
Source: U.S. Census Bureau, 2010-2012 American Community Survey 3-Year Estimates

HEALTH

Health Risk Data

Category	MD[1] (%)	U.S. (%)
Adults aged 18–64 who have any kind of health care coverage	78.3	79.6
Adults who reported being in good or excellent health	81.4	83.1
Adults who are current smokers	14.8	19.6
Adults who are heavy drinkers[2]	4.5	6.1
Adults who are binge drinkers[3]	16.9	16.9
Adults who are overweight (BMI 25.0 - 29.9)	36.8	35.8
Adults who are obese (BMI 30.0 - 99.8)	21.7	27.6
Adults who participated in any physical activities in the past month	74.2	77.1
Adults 50+ who have ever had a sigmoidoscopy or colonoscopy	70.5	67.3
Women aged 40+ who have had a mammogram within the past two years	78.5	74.0
Men aged 40+ who have had a PSA test within the past two years	47.8	45.2
Adults aged 65+ who have had flu shot within the past year	56.0	60.1
Adults who always wear a seatbelt	92.8	93.8

Note: Data as of 2012 unless otherwise noted; (1) Figures cover the New York-Jersey City-White Plains, NY-NJ Metropolitan Division—see Appendix B for areas included; (2) Heavy drinkers are classified as males having more than two drinks per day or females having more than one drink per day; (3) Binge drinkers are classified as males having five or more drinks on one occasion or females having four or more drinks on one occasion
Source: Centers for Disease Control and Prevention, Behaviorial Risk Factor Surveillance System, SMART: Selected Metropolitan/Micropolitan Area Risk Trends, 2012

Chronic Health Indicators

Category	MD[1] (%)	U.S. (%)
Adults who have ever been told they had a heart attack	3.6	4.5
Adults who have ever been told they had a stroke	2.6	2.9
Adults who have been told they currently have asthma	8.0	8.9
Adults who have ever been told they have arthritis	22.2	25.7
Adults who have ever been told they have diabetes[2]	9.9	9.7
Adults who have ever been told they had skin cancer	3.3	5.7
Adults who have ever been told they had any other types of cancer	5.1	6.5
Adults who have ever been told they have COPD	5.3	6.2
Adults who have ever been told they have kidney disease	2.6	2.5
Adults who have ever been told they have a form of depression	13.3	18.0

Note: Data as of 2012 unless otherwise noted; (1) Figures cover the New York-Jersey City-White Plains, NY-NJ Metropolitan Division—see Appendix B for areas included; (2) Figures do not include pregnancy-related, borderline, or pre-diabetes
Source: Centers for Disease Control and Prevention, Behaviorial Risk Factor Surveillance System, SMART: Selected Metropolitan/Micropolitan Area Risk Trends, 2012

Mortality Rates for the Top 10 Causes of Death in the U.S.

ICD-10[a] Sub-Chapter	ICD-10[a] Code	Age-Adjusted Mortality Rate[1] per 100,000 population	
		County[2]	U.S.
Malignant neoplasms	C00-C97	152.5	174.2
Ischaemic heart diseases	I20-I25	224.6	119.1
Other forms of heart disease	I30-I51	12.6	49.6
Chronic lower respiratory diseases	J40-J47	17.4	43.2
Cerebrovascular diseases	I60-I69	18.6	40.3
Organic, including symptomatic, mental disorders	F01-F09	5.4	30.5
Other degenerative diseases of the nervous system	G30-G31	4.5	26.3
Other external causes of accidental injury	W00-X59	13.7	25.1
Diabetes mellitus	E10-E14	22.9	21.3
Hypertensive diseases	I10-I15	38.8	18.8

Note: (a) ICD-10 = International Classification of Diseases 10th Revision; (1) Mortality rates are a three year average covering 2008-2010; (2) Figures cover Kings County
Source: Centers for Disease Control and Prevention, National Center for Health Statistics. Compressed Mortality File 1999-2010 on CDC WONDER Online Database, released January 2013. Data are compiled from the Compressed Mortality File 1999-2010, Series 20 No. 2P, 2013.

Mortality Rates for Selected Causes of Death

ICD-10[a] Sub-Chapter	ICD-10[a] Code	Age-Adjusted Mortality Rate[1] per 100,000 population	
		County[2]	U.S.
Assault	X85-Y09	8.2	5.5
Diseases of the liver	K70-K76	7.4	12.4
Human immunodeficiency virus (HIV) disease	B20-B24	11.3	3.0
Influenza and pneumonia	J09-J18	28.9	16.4
Intentional self-harm	X60-X84	5.1	11.8
Malnutrition	E40-E46	Suppressed	0.8
Obesity and other hyperalimentation	E65-E68	1.5	1.6
Renal failure	N17-N19	5.8	13.6
Transport accidents	V01-V99	4.2	12.6
Viral hepatitis	B15-B19	3.6	2.2

Note: (a) ICD-10 = International Classification of Diseases 10th Revision; (1) Mortality rates are a three year average covering 2008-2010; (2) Figures cover Kings County
Source: Centers for Disease Control and Prevention, National Center for Health Statistics. Compressed Mortality File 1999-2010 on CDC WONDER Online Database, released January 2013. Data are compiled from the Compressed Mortality File 1999-2010, Series 20 No. 2P, 2013.

Health Insurance Coverage

Area	With Health Insurance	With Private Health Insurance	With Public Health Insurance	Without Health Insurance	Population Under Age 18 Without Health Insurance
City	85.5	54.1	39.1	14.5	4.3
MSA[1]	86.8	64.8	31.3	13.2	4.7
U.S.	84.9	65.4	30.4	15.1	7.5

Note: Figures are percentages that cover the civilian noninstitutionalized population; (1) Figures cover the New York-Newark-Jersey City, NY-NJ-PA Metropolitan Statistical Area—see Appendix B for areas included
Source: U.S. Census Bureau, 2010-2012 American Community Survey 3-Year Estimates

Number of Medical Professionals

Area[1]	MDs[2]	DOs[2,3]	Dentists	Podiatrists	Chiropractors	Optometrists
Local (number)	7,629	293	1,519	316	254	232
Local (rate[4])	300.2	11.5	59.1	12.3	9.9	9.0
U.S. (rate[4])	267.6	19.6	61.7	5.6	24.7	14.5

Note: Data as of 2012 unless noted; (1) Local data covers Kings County; (2) Data as of 2011; (3) Doctor of Osteopathic Medicine; (4) rate per 100,000 population
Source: Area Resource File (ARF) 2012-2013. U.S. Department of Health and Human Services, Health Resources and Services Administration, Bureau of Health Professions

Best Hospitals

According to *U.S. News,* the New York-Jersey City-White Plains, NY-NJ metro area is home to 10 of the best hospitals in the U.S.: **Hackensack University Medical Center** (9 specialties); **Hospital for Special Surgery** (3 specialties); **Memorial Sloan-Kettering Cancer Center** (4 specialties); **Montefiore Medical Center-Bronx** (3 specialties); **Mount Sinai Medical Center** (8 specialties); **NYU Langone Medical Center** (Honor Roll/12 specialties); **New York Eye and Ear Infirmary** (1 specialty); **New York-Presbyterian University Hospital of Columbia and Cornell** (Honor Roll/15 specialties); **Lennox Hill Hospital** (2 specialties); **St. Barnabas Hospital** (1 specialty). The hospitals listed were nationally ranked in at least one adult specialty. Only 147 hospitals nationwide were nationally ranked in one or more specialties. Eighteen hospitals in the U.S. made the Honor Roll by ranking near the top in at least six specialties. *U.S. News Online, "America's Best Hospitals 2013-14"*

According to *U.S. News,* the New York-Jersey City-White Plains, NY-NJ metro area is home to six of the best children's hospitals in the U.S.: **Children's Hospital at Montefiore**; **JM Sanzari Children's Hospital at Hackensack University Medical Center**; **Memorial Sloan-Kettering Cancer Center**; **Mount Sinai Kravis Children's Hospital**; **New York-Presbyterian Morgan Stanley-Komansky Children's Hospital**; **Maria Fareri Children's Hospital at Westchester Medical Center**. The hospitals listed were highly ranked in at least one pediatric specialty. Eighty-seven hospitals in the U.S. ranked in at least one specialty. Ten children's hospitals in the U.S. made the Honor Roll by ranking near the top in three or more specialties. *U.S. News Online, "America's Best Children's Hospitals 2013-14"*

EDUCATION

Public School District Statistics

District Name	Schls	Pupils	Pupil/ Teacher Ratio	Minority Pupils[1] (%)	Free Lunch Eligible[2] (%)	IEP[3] (%)
NYC Geo. District # 1 (Manhattan)	31	12,112	13.2	83.6	60.1	19.0
NYC Geo. District # 2 (Manhattan)	109	60,948	16.1	78.4	51.6	16.6
NYC Geo. District # 3 (Manhattan)	46	22,611	15.3	71.9	45.1	16.3
NYC Geo. District # 4 (Manhattan)	35	13,891	13.0	97.0	77.3	25.3
NYC Geo. District # 5 (Manhattan)	31	13,191	14.6	97.1	74.4	26.7
NYC Geo. District # 6 (Manhattan)	45	25,185	14.7	96.7	82.8	17.8
NYC Geo. District # 7 (Bronx)	43	18,401	12.9	n/a	83.3	27.2
NYC Geo. District # 8 (Bronx)	53	30,723	14.7	94.1	72.9	25.7
NYC Geo. District # 9 (Bronx)	67	34,543	14.1	n/a	87.1	22.8
NYC Geo. District #10 (Bronx)	82	55,909	15.1	94.4	76.6	20.2
NYC Geo. District #11 (Bronx)	61	37,883	15.4	92.9	71.0	23.8
NYC Geo. District #12 (Bronx)	55	23,389	14.2	98.9	82.8	23.0
NYC Geo. District #13 (Brooklyn)	46	22,716	16.0	90.6	65.6	13.4
NYC Geo. District #14 (Brooklyn)	42	20,477	14.6	90.5	79.3	21.2
NYC Geo. District #15 (Brooklyn)	45	27,346	14.2	76.6	58.7	19.5
NYC Geo. District #16 (Brooklyn)	26	9,280	13.2	99.0	75.9	29.1
NYC Geo. District #17 (Brooklyn)	52	25,848	15.0	98.3	76.6	20.2
NYC Geo. District #18 (Brooklyn)	34	18,159	15.3	98.5	70.0	18.6
NYC Geo. District #19 (Brooklyn)	45	24,681	15.0	98.9	80.9	20.6
NYC Geo. District #20 (Brooklyn)	43	44,716	16.4	71.4	66.9	19.9
NYC Geo. District #21 (Brooklyn)	40	33,731	15.9	68.4	61.6	20.5
NYC Geo. District #22 (Brooklyn)	38	35,885	16.6	72.5	57.1	19.6
NYC Geo. District #23 (Brooklyn)	28	11,459	14.7	n/a	74.1	23.8
NYC Geo. District #24 (Queens)	51	53,901	16.3	85.6	68.7	16.6
NYC Geo. District #25 (Queens)	43	34,998	16.7	84.3	58.2	15.2
NYC Geo. District #26 (Queens)	31	31,380	18.7	81.2	39.5	14.2
NYC Geo. District #27 (Queens)	58	45,733	15.9	89.7	68.8	19.2
NYC Geo. District #28 (Queens)	47	37,519	16.9	84.1	59.5	17.3
NYC Geo. District #29 (Queens)	45	27,049	16.6	97.9	62.6	19.0
NYC Geo. District #30 (Queens)	43	40,011	16.2	84.8	68.6	15.8
NYC Geo. District #31 (Staten Island)	66	59,629	16.4	47.9	44.6	23.7
NYC Geo. District #32 (Brooklyn)	27	14,839	14.8	98.6	83.4	19.9
NYC Spec. Schls-Dist. 75 (Manhattan)	57	22,002	4.7	86.1	63.7	n/a

Note: Table includes school districts with 2,000 or more students; (1) Percentage of students that are not non-Hispanic white; (2) Percentage of students that are eligible for the free lunch program; (3) Percentage of students that have an Individualized Education Program.
Source: U.S. Department of Education, National Center for Education Statistics, Common Core of Data, Local Education Agency (School District) Universe Survey: School Year 2011-2012; U.S. Department of Education, National Center for Education Statistics, Common Core of Data, Public Elementary/Secondary School Universe Survey: School Year 2011-2012

Best High Schools

High School Name	Rank[1]	Grad. Rate[2] (%)	Coll.[3] (%)	AP/IB/ AICE Tests[4]	AP/IB/ AICE Score[5]	SAT Score[6]	ACT Score[6]
Academy of American Studies (Long Island City)	1223	89	96	0.2	2.8	1516	24.0
Baccalaureate School for Global Education (Astoria)	670	97	97	0.6	n/a	1636	23.8
Bayside H.S. (Bayside)	331	91	99	0.6	2.9	1510	30.0
Benjamin Cardozo H.S. (Bayside)	1153	85	96	0.3	3.4	1545	n/a
Bronx Center for Science and Mathematics (Bronx)	1470	86	100	0.0	2.9	1449	n/a
Bronx H.S. of Science (Bronx)	37	100	100	1.2	3.7	2008	n/a
Brooklyn Technical H.S. (Brooklyn)	126	96	100	0.8	3.4	1880	28.0
Curtis H.S. (Staten Island)	1923	74	93	0.2	2.6	1301	21.0
Edward R. Murrow H.S. (Brooklyn)	1730	80	93	0.2	2.9	1431	n/a
Eleanor Roosevelt H.S. (Manhattan)	212	98	100	0.5	3.6	1812	26.0
Frank Sinatra School of the Arts (Astoria)	1146	97	96	0.2	2.5	1500	n/a
H.S. for Math, Science and Engineering at CCNY (Manhattan)	194	99	100	0.0	3.5	1847	29.3
H.S. of American Studies at Lehman College (Bronx)	48	100	100	1.0	3.7	1920	28.2
H.S. of Telecommunication Arts and Technology (Brooklyn)	1657	86	95	0.2	2.3	1323	21.3
Hunter College H.S. (Manhattan)	46	97	98	0.9	4.2	2207	32.6
Hunter College High School[6]	n/a	n/a	n/a	n/a	n/a	n/a	n/a
It Takes a Village Academy (Manhattan)	1535	87	100	0.0	2.4	1537	n/a
Leon M. Goldstein H.S. for the Sciences (Brooklyn)	349	98	98	0.7	3.0	1667	25.0
Medgar Evers College Preparatory School (Brooklyn)	775	99	99	0.6	2.0	1445	n/a
Michael J. Petrides School (Staten Island)	1605	90	89	0.8	1.6	1463	21.0
Midwood H.S. (Brooklyn)	1457	87	90	0.3	2.9	1473	23.6
NYC Lab School for Collaborative Studies (Manhattan)	848	95	92	0.3	3.2	1660	n/a
New Explorations into Science Technology and Math (Manhattan)	91	98	99	1.1	3.5	1621	25.3
Queens H.S. for the Sciences at York College (Jamaica)	73	98	100	1.0	3.5	1868	n/a
Riverdale Kingsbridge Academy (Bronx)	1342	87	98	0.3	3.0	1333	n/a
Staten Island Technical H.S. (Staten Island)	36	100	100	0.9	3.9	1953	29.4
Stuyvesant H.S. (Manhattan)	38	99	100	0.8	4.3	2068	31.3
Stuyvesant High School[6]	n/a	n/a	n/a	n/a	n/a	n/a	n/a
Thomas A. Edison Career & Technical Education H.S. (Jamaica)	1658	86	81	0.1	3.0	1800	n/a
Townsend Harris H.S. (Flushing)	43	100	100	1.1	3.3	1925	28.8

Note: (1) Public schools are ranked from 1 to 2,000 based on the following self-reported statistics (with the corresponding weight used in calculating their overall score). Schools that were newly founded and did not have a graduating senior class in 2012 were excluded; (2) Four-year, on-time graduation rate (25%); (3) Percent of 2011 graduates who were accepted to college (25%); (4) AP/IB/AICE tests taken per student (25%); (5) Average AP/IB/AICE exam score (10%); (6) Average SAT and/or ACT score (10%); Percent of students enrolled in at least one AP/IB/AICE course (5%)—data not shown; n/a not available
Source: Newsweek and The Daily Beast, "America's Best High Schools 2013"

Highest Level of Education

Area	Less than H.S.	H.S. Diploma	Some College, No Deg.	Associate Degree	Bachelor's Degree	Master's Degree	Prof. School Degree	Doctorate Degree
City	20.4	24.8	14.7	6.1	20.2	9.5	3.0	1.3
MSA[1]	15.2	26.2	15.7	6.4	21.5	10.5	3.0	1.4
U.S.	14.1	28.3	21.3	7.8	18.0	7.5	1.9	1.2

Note: Figures cover persons age 25 and over; (1) Figures cover the New York-Newark-Jersey City, NY-NJ-PA Metropolitan Statistical Area—see Appendix B for areas included
Source: U.S. Census Bureau, 2010-2012 American Community Survey 3-Year Estimates

Educational Attainment by Race

Area	High School Graduate or Higher (%)					Bachelor's Degree or Higher (%)				
	Total	White	Black	Asian	Hisp.[2]	Total	White	Black	Asian	Hisp.[2]
City	79.6	86.2	80.5	74.1	63.6	34.0	45.1	20.9	40.5	15.1
MSA[1]	84.8	89.3	82.4	82.0	66.8	36.5	41.4	21.9	52.3	16.0
U.S.	85.9	88.1	82.5	85.5	63.1	28.6	30.0	18.4	50.2	13.4

Note: Figures shown cover persons 25 years old and over; (1) Figures cover the New York-Newark-Jersey City, NY-NJ-PA Metropolitan Statistical Area—see Appendix B for areas included; (2) People of Hispanic origin can be of any race
Source: U.S. Census Bureau, 2010-2012 American Community Survey 3-Year Estimates

School Enrollment by Grade and Control

Area	Preschool (%)		Kindergarten (%)		Grades 1 - 4 (%)		Grades 5 - 8 (%)		Grades 9 - 12 (%)	
	Public	Private	Public	Private	Public	Private	Public	Private	Public	Private
City	55.0	45.0	79.3	20.7	82.3	17.7	82.3	17.7	83.4	16.6
MSA[1]	49.6	50.4	82.0	18.0	86.1	13.9	86.3	13.7	86.1	13.9
U.S.	56.9	43.1	87.8	12.2	89.9	10.1	90.0	10.0	90.8	9.2

Note: Figures shown cover persons 3 years old and over; (1) Figures cover the New York-Newark-Jersey City, NY-NJ-PA Metropolitan Statistical Area—see Appendix B for areas included
Source: U.S. Census Bureau, 2010-2012 American Community Survey 3-Year Estimates

Average Salaries of Public School Classroom Teachers

Area	2012-13		2013-14		Percent Change 2012-13 to 2013-14	Percent Change 2003-04 to 2013-14
	Dollars	Rank[1]	Dollars	Rank[1]		
New York	75,279	1	76,566	1	1.71	38.8
U.S. Average	56,103	–	56,689	–	1.04	21.8

Note: (1) State rank ranges from 1 to 51 where 1 indicates highest salary.
Source: National Education Association, Rankings & Estimates: Rankings of the States 2013 and Estimates of School Statistics 2014, March 2014

Higher Education

Four-Year Colleges			Two-Year Colleges			Medical Schools[1]	Law Schools[2]	Voc/ Tech[3]
Public	Private Non-profit	Private For-profit	Public	Private Non-profit	Private For-profit			
7	33	9	2	10	10	7	8	23

Note: Figures cover institutions located within the city limits and include main campuses only; (1) includes schools accredited by the Liaison Committee on Medical Education and the American Osteopathic Association's Commission on Osteopathic College Accreditation; (2) includes ABA-accredited schools, schools with provisional ABA accreditation, and state accredited schools; (3) includes all schools with programs that are less than 2 years.
Source: National Center for Education Statistics, Integrated Postsecondary Education System (IPEDS), 2012-13; Association of American Medical Colleges, Member List, April 24, 2014; American Osteopathic Association, Member List, April 24, 2014; Law School Admission Council, Official Guide to ABA-Approved Law Schools Online, April 24, 2014; Wikipedia, List of Medical Schools in the United States, April 24, 2014; Wikipedia, List of Law Schools in the United States, April 24, 2014

According to *U.S. News & World Report*, the New York-Jersey City-White Plains, NY-NJ metro division is home to nine of the best national universities in the U.S.: **Columbia University** (#4); **New York University** (#32); **Yeshiva University** (#47); **Fordham University** (#57); **Stevens Institute of Technology** (#82); **Polytechnic Institute of New York University** (#128); **New School** (#135); **Saint John's University** (#152); **Pace University** (#173). The indicators used to capture academic quality fall into a number of categories: assessment by administrators at peer institutions; retention of students; faculty resources; student selectivity; financial resources; alumni giving; high school counselor ratings of colleges; and graduation rate. *U.S. News & World Report*, *"America's Best Colleges 2014"*

According to *U.S. News & World Report*, the New York-Jersey City-White Plains, NY-NJ metro division is home to one of the best liberal arts colleges in the U.S.: **Barnard College** (#32). The indicators used to capture academic quality fall into a number of categories: assessment by administrators at peer institutions; retention of students; faculty resources; student selectivity; financial resources; alumni giving; high school counselor ratings of colleges; and graduation rate. *U.S. News & World Report*, *"America's Best Colleges 2014"*

According to *U.S. News & World Report*, the New York-Jersey City-White Plains, NY-NJ metro division is home to six of the top 100 law schools in the U.S.: **Columbia University** (#4); **New York University** (#6); **Fordham University** (#38); **Yeshiva University (Cardozo)** (#58); **Brooklyn Law School** (#80); **Saint John's University (Jamaica)** (#98). The rankings are based on a weighted average of 12 measures of quality: peer assessment score; assessment score by lawyers/judges; median LSAT scores; median undergrad GPA; acceptance rate; employment rates for graduates; placement success; bar passage rate; faculty resources; expenditures per student; student/faculty ratio; and library resources. *U.S. News & World Report, "America's Best Graduate Schools, Law, 2014"*

According to *U.S. News & World Report*, the New York-Jersey City-White Plains, NY-NJ metro division is home to four of the top 100 business schools in the U.S.: **Columbia University** (#8); **New York University (Stern)** (#10); **CUNY Bernard M. Baruch College (Zicklin)** (#75); **Fordham University** (#79). The rankings are based on a weighted average of the following nine measures: quality assessment; peer assessment; recruiter assessment; placement success; mean starting salary and bonus; student selectivity; mean GMAT and GRE scores; mean undergraduate GPA; and acceptance rate. *U.S. News & World Report, "America's Best Graduate Schools, Business, 2014"*

PRESIDENTIAL ELECTION

2012 Presidential Election Results

Area	Obama	Romney	Other
Bronx County	91.4	8.1	0.5
Kings County	82.0	16.9	1.1
New York County	83.7	14.9	1.3
Queens County	79.1	19.9	1.0
Richmond County	50.7	48.1	1.2
U.S.	51.0	47.2	1.8

Note: Results are percentages and may not add to 100% due to rounding
Source: Dave Leip's Atlas of U.S. Presidential Elections

EMPLOYERS

Major Employers

Company Name	Industry
American Express Company	Personal credit institutions
American International Group	Life insurance
Deloitte Consulting LLP	Management consulting services
Hackensack University Medical Center	University
Merrill Lynch and Co	Security brokers and dealers
Mount Sinai Hospital	General medical and surgical hospitals
Mount Sinai School of Medicine	Medical training services
NewYork-Presbyterian Hospital	General medical and surgical hospitals
NYC Health and Hospitals Corp	Psychiatric hospitals
NYU School of Medicine	Offices and clinics of medical doctors
Paramount Comm Acq Corp	Investment holding companies, except banks
Patriarch Partners	Investment offices
Rutgers, The State Univ of NJ	Colleges and universities
Standard Americas	Agencies of foreign banks
The Long Island Rail Road Company	Local and suburban transit
U of Med and Dentistry of NJ	Colleges and universities
UMASS Memorial Health Care	Psychiatrist
United States Postal Service	U.s. postal service
WELLCHOICE	Health insurance carriers

Note: Companies shown are located within the New York-Newark-Jersey City, NY-NJ-PA Metropolitan Statistical Area.
Source: Hoovers.com; Wikipedia

Best Companies to Work For

Accenture; American Express; Deloitte; Ernst & Young; Goldman Sachs Group; KPMG; PricewaterhouseCoopers; Teach For America, headquartered in New York, are among "The 100 Best Companies to Work For." To pick the 100 Best Companies to Work For, *Fortune* partnered with the Great Place to Work Institute. Two hundred fifty seven firms participated in this year's survey. Two-thirds of a company's score is based on the results of the Institute's Trust Index survey, which is sent to a random sample of employees from each company. The questions related to attitudes about management's credibility, job satisfaction, and camaraderie. The other third of the scoring is based on the company's responses to the Institute's Culture Audit, which includes detailed questions about pay and benefit programs, and a series of open-ended questions about hiring practices, internal communication, training, recognition programs, and diversity efforts. Any company that is at least five years old with more than 1,000 U.S. employees is eligible. *Fortune, "The 100 Best Companies to Work For," 2014*

AOL; Accenture; American Express; Bristol-Myers Squibb; Citi; Colgate-Palmolive; Credit Suisse; Deloitte; Deutsche Bank; EY; Goldman Sachs; JPMorgan Chase & Co; KPMG; McGraw-Hill Financial; McKinsey & Co; Morgan Stanley; Pfizer; Pillsbury Winthrop Shaw Pittman; PwC; TIAA-CREF; Teach for America; Verizon Communications; Viacom, headquartered in New York, are among the "100 Best Companies for Working Mothers." Criteria: workforce representation; child care; flexibility programs; and leave policies. This year *Working Mother* gave particular weight to flexible work arrangements, women's advancement programs, and paid maternity leave. *Working Mother, "100 Best Companies 2013"*

AXA Equitable; American Express; Citi; Colgate-Palmolive; Deloitte; Goldman Sachs; JPMorgan Chase; KPMG; New York Life Insurance; PwC; The New York Times Company; Verizon Communications, headquartered in New York, are among the "Best Companies for Multicultural Women." *Working Mother* selected 25 companies based on a detailed application completed by public and private firms based in the United States, excluding government agencies, companies in the human resources field and non-autonomous divisions. Companies supplied data about the hiring, pay, and promotion of multicultural employees. Applications focused on representation of multicultural women, recruitment, retention and advancement programs, and company culture. *Working Mother, "2013 Best Companies for Multicultural Women"*

PricewaterhouseCoopers, headquartered in New York, is among the "100 Best Places to Work in IT." To qualify, companies, both public and private, had to have a minimum of 50 IT employees and were selected based on average salary and bonus increases, the percentage of IT staffers promoted, IT staff turnover rates, training and development programs, and the percentage of women and minorities in IT staff and management positions. In addition, *Computerworld* looked at retention efforts, programs for recognizing and rewarding outstanding performances, and benefits such as flextime, elder care and child care, and reimbursement for college tuition and the cost of pursuing technology certifications. *Computerworld, "100 Best Places to Work in IT 2013"*

American Express; Bristol-Myers Squibb; Colgate-Palmolive; HSBC USA; JPMorgan Chase; KPMG; New York Life Insurance Company; Pfizer; Pillsbury Winthrop Shaw Pittman; The New York Times Company; Verizon Communications; Viacom, headquartered in New York, are among the "Top Companies for Executive Women." To be named to the list, companies with a minimum of two women on the board complete a comprehensive application that focuses on the number of women in senior ranks. In addition to assessing corporate programs and policies dedicated to advancing women, NAFE examined the number of women in each company overall, in senior management, and on its board of directors, paying particular attention to the number of women with profit-and-loss responsibility. *National Association for Female Executives, "2013 NAFE Top 50 Companies for Executive Women"*

PUBLIC SAFETY

Crime Rate

Area	All Crimes	Violent Crimes				Property Crimes		
		Murder	Forcible Rape	Robbery	Aggrav. Assault	Burglary	Larceny -Theft	Motor Vehicle Theft
City	2,361.5	5.1	14.0	243.7	376.5	224.8	1,398.6	98.8
Suburbs[1]	n/a	1.9	9.2	94.5	n/a	350.9	1,255.8	102.4
Metro[2]	n/a	3.8	12.0	182.6	n/a	276.5	1,340.1	100.3
U.S.	3,246.1	4.7	26.9	112.9	242.3	670.2	1,959.3	229.7

Note: Figures are crimes per 100,000 population; (1) All areas within the metro area that are located outside the city limits; (2) Figures cover the New York-Jersey City-White Plains, NY-NJ Metropolitan Division—see Appendix B for areas included
Source: FBI Uniform Crime Reports, 2012

Hate Crimes

Area	Number of Quarters Reported	Bias Motivation				
		Race	Religion	Sexual Orientation	Ethnicity	Disability
City	4	45	260	53	14	0
U.S.	4	2,797	1,099	1,135	667	92

Source: Federal Bureau of Investigation, Hate Crime Statistics 2012

Identity Theft Consumer Complaints

Area	Complaints	Complaints per 100,000 Population	Rank[2]
MSA[1]	19,125	97.7	52
U.S.	290,056	91.8	-

Note: (1) Figures cover the New York-Newark-Jersey City, NY-NJ-PA Metropolitan Statistical Area—see Appendix B for areas included; (2) Rank ranges from 1 to 377 where 1 indicates greatest number of identity theft complaints per 100,000 population
Source: Federal Trade Commission, Consumer Sentinel Network Data Book for January–December 2013

Fraud and Other Consumer Complaints

Area	Complaints	Complaints per 100,000 Population	Rank[2]
MSA[1]	78,369	400.5	123
U.S.	1,811,724	595.2	-

Note: (1) Figures cover the New York-Newark-Jersey City, NY-NJ-PA Metropolitan Statistical Area—see Appendix B for areas included; (2) Rank ranges from 1 to 377 where 1 indicates greatest number of identity theft complaints per 100,000 population
Source: Federal Trade Commission, Consumer Sentinel Network Data Book for January–December 2013

RECREATION

Culture

Dance[1]	Theatre[1]	Instrumental Music[1]	Vocal Music[1]	Series and Festivals	Museums and Art Galleries[2]	Zoos and Aquariums[3]
123	139	54	42	72	263	6

Note: (1) Number of professional performing groups; (2) Based on organizations with primary SIC code 8412; (3) AZA-accredited
Source: The Grey House Performing Arts Directory, 2013; Association of Zoos & Aquariums, AZA Member Zoos & Aquariums, April 2014; www.AccuLeads.com, May 1, 2014

Professional Sports Teams

Team Name	League	Year Established
Brooklyn Nets	National Basketball Association (NBA)	1967
New Jersey Devils	National Hockey League (NHL)	1982
New York City FC	Major League Soccer (MLS)	2015
New York Giants	National Football League (NFL)	1925
New York Islanders	National Hockey League (NHL)	1972
New York Jets	National Football League (NFL)	1960
New York Knicks	National Basketball Association (NBA)	1946
New York Mets	Major League Baseball (MLB)	1962
New York Rangers	National Hockey League (NHL)	1926
New York Red Bulls	Major League Soccer (MLS)	1996
New York Yankees	Major League Baseball (MLB)	1903

Note: Includes teams located in the New York-Newark-Jersey City, NY-NJ-PA Metropolitan Statistical Area.
Source: Wikipedia, Major Professional Sports Teams of the United States and Canada

CLIMATE

Average and Extreme Temperatures

Temperature	Jan	Feb	Mar	Apr	May	Jun	Jul	Aug	Sep	Oct	Nov	Dec	Yr.
Extreme High (°F)	68	75	85	96	97	101	104	99	99	88	81	72	104
Average High (°F)	38	41	50	61	72	80	85	84	76	65	54	43	62
Average Temp. (°F)	32	34	43	53	63	72	77	76	68	58	48	37	55
Average Low (°F)	26	27	35	44	54	63	68	67	60	49	41	31	47
Extreme Low (°F)	-2	-2	8	21	36	46	53	50	40	29	17	-1	-2

Note: Figures cover the years 1962-1992
Source: National Climatic Data Center, International Station Meteorological Climate Summary, 9/96

Average Precipitation/Snowfall/Humidity

Precip./Humidity	Jan	Feb	Mar	Apr	May	Jun	Jul	Aug	Sep	Oct	Nov	Dec	Yr.
Avg. Precip. (in.)	3.5	3.1	4.0	3.9	4.5	3.8	4.5	4.1	4.1	3.3	4.5	3.8	47.0
Avg. Snowfall (in.)	7	8	4	Tr	Tr	0	0	0	0	Tr	Tr	3	23
Avg. Rel. Hum. 7am (%)	67	67	66	64	72	74	74	76	78	75	72	69	71
Avg. Rel. Hum. 4pm (%)	55	53	50	45	52	55	53	54	56	55	57	58	53

Note: Figures cover the years 1962-1992; Tr = Trace amounts (<0.05 in. of rain; <0.5 in. of snow)
Source: National Climatic Data Center, International Station Meteorological Climate Summary, 9/96

Weather Conditions

Temperature			Daytime Sky			Precipitation		
32°F & below	45°F & below	90°F & above	Clear	Partly cloudy	Cloudy	0.01 inch or more precip.	0.1 inch or more snow/ice	Thunder-storms
75	170	18	85	166	114	120	11	20

Note: Figures are average number of days per year and cover the years 1962-1992
Source: National Climatic Data Center, International Station Meteorological Climate Summary, 9/96

HAZARDOUS WASTE

Superfund Sites

New York has two hazardous waste sites on the EPA's Superfund Final National Priorities List: **Gowanus Canal; Newtown Creek**. *U.S. Environmental Protection Agency, Final National Priorities List, April 26, 2014*

AIR & WATER QUALITY

Air Quality Index

Area	Percent of Days when Air Quality was...[2]						AQI Statistics[2]	
	Good	Moderate	Unhealthy for Sensitive Groups	Unhealthy	Very Unhealthy		Maximum	Median
MSA[1]	44.1	51.8	4.1	0.0	0.0		135	53

Note: (1) Data covers the New York-Newark-Jersey City, NY-NJ-PA Metropolitan Statistical Area—see Appendix B for areas included; (2) Based on 365 days with AQI data in 2013. Air Quality Index (AQI) is an index for reporting daily air quality. EPA calculates the AQI for five major air pollutants regulated by the Clean Air Act: ground-level ozone, particle pollution (aka particulate matter), carbon monoxide, sulfur dioxide, and nitrogen dioxide. The AQI runs from 0 to 500. The higher the AQI value, the greater the level of air pollution and the greater the health concern. There are six AQI categories: "Good" AQI is between 0 and 50. Air quality is considered satisfactory; "Moderate" AQI is between 51 and 100. Air quality is acceptable; "Unhealthy for Sensitive Groups" When AQI values are between 101 and 150, members of sensitive groups may experience health effects; "Unhealthy" When AQI values are between 151 and 200 everyone may begin to experience health effects; "Very Unhealthy" AQI values between 201 and 300 trigger a health alert; "Hazardous" AQI values over 300 trigger warnings of emergency conditions (not shown).
Source: U.S. Environmental Protection Agency, Air Quality Index Report, 2013

Air Quality Index Pollutants

Area	Percent of Days when AQI Pollutant was...[2]					
	Carbon Monoxide	Nitrogen Dioxide	Ozone	Sulfur Dioxide	Particulate Matter 2.5	Particulate Matter 10
MSA[1]	0.0	15.1	25.2	0.0	59.7	0.0

Note: (1) Data covers the New York-Newark-Jersey City, NY-NJ-PA Metropolitan Statistical Area—see Appendix B for areas included; (2) Based on 365 days with AQI data in 2013. The Air Quality Index (AQI) is an index for reporting daily air quality. EPA calculates the AQI for five major air pollutants regulated by the Clean Air Act: ground-level ozone, particle pollution (also known as particulate matter), carbon monoxide, sulfur dioxide, and nitrogen dioxide. The AQI runs from 0 to 500. The higher the AQI value, the greater the level of air pollution and the greater the health concern.
Source: U.S. Environmental Protection Agency, Air Quality Index Report, 2013

Air Quality Trends: Ozone

	2003	2004	2005	2006	2007	2008	2009	2010	2011	2012
MSA[1]	0.089	0.079	0.092	0.087	0.086	0.081	0.072	0.081	0.081	0.079

Note: (1) Data covers the New York-Newark-Jersey City, NY-NJ-PA Metropolitan Statistical Area—see Appendix B for areas included. The values shown are the composite ozone concentration averages among trend sites based on the highest fourth daily maximum 8-hour concentration in parts per million. These trends are based on sites having an adequate record of monitoring data during the trend period. Data from exceptional events are included.
Source: U.S. Environmental Protection Agency, Air Quality Monitoring Information, "Air Quality Trends by City, 2000-2012"

Maximum Air Pollutant Concentrations: Particulate Matter, Ozone, CO and Lead

	Particulate Matter 10 (ug/m^3)	Particulate Matter 2.5 Wtd AM (ug/m^3)	Particulate Matter 2.5 24-Hr (ug/m^3)	Ozone (ppm)	Carbon Monoxide (ppm)	Lead (ug/m^3)
MSA[1] Level	73	11.7	26	0.085	3	0.03
NAAQS[2]	150	15	35	0.075	9	0.15
Met NAAQS[2]	Yes	Yes	Yes	No	Yes	Yes

Note: (1) Data covers the New York-Newark-Jersey City, NY-NJ-PA Metropolitan Statistical Area—see Appendix B for areas included; Data from exceptional events are included; (2) National Ambient Air Quality Standards; ppm = parts per million; ug/m^3 = micrograms per cubic meter; n/a not available.
Concentrations: Particulate Matter 10 (coarse particulate)—highest second maximum 24-hour concentration; Particulate Matter 2.5 Wtd AM (fine particulate)—highest weighted annual mean concentration; Particulate Matter 2.5 24-Hour (fine particulate)—highest 98th percentile 24-hour concentration; Ozone—highest fourth daily maximum 8-hour concentration; Carbon Monoxide—highest second maximum non-overlapping 8-hour concentration; Lead—maximum running 3-month average
Source: U.S. Environmental Protection Agency, Air Quality Monitoring Information, "Air Quality Statistics by City, 2012"

Maximum Air Pollutant Concentrations: Nitrogen Dioxide and Sulfur Dioxide

	Nitrogen Dioxide AM (ppb)	Nitrogen Dioxide 1-Hr (ppb)	Sulfur Dioxide AM (ppb)	Sulfur Dioxide 1-Hr (ppb)	Sulfur Dioxide 24-Hr (ppb)
MSA[1] Level	22	67	n/a	32	n/a
NAAQS[2]	53	100	30	75	140
Met NAAQS[2]	Yes	Yes	n/a	Yes	n/a

Note: (1) Data covers the New York-Newark-Jersey City, NY-NJ-PA Metropolitan Statistical Area—see Appendix B for areas included; Data from exceptional events are included; (2) National Ambient Air Quality Standards; ppm = parts per million; ug/m^3 = micrograms per cubic meter; n/a not available.
Concentrations: Nitrogen Dioxide AM—highest arithmetic mean concentration; Nitrogen Dioxide 1-Hr—highest 98th percentile 1-hour daily maximum concentration; Sulfur Dioxide AM—highest annual mean concentration; Sulfur Dioxide 1-Hr—highest 99th percentile 1-hour daily maximum concentration; Sulfur Dioxide 24-Hr—highest second maximum 24-hour concentration
Source: U.S. Environmental Protection Agency, Air Quality Monitoring Information, "Air Quality Statistics by City, 2012"

Drinking Water

Water System Name	Pop. Served	Primary Water Source Type	Violations[1] Health Based	Violations[1] Monitoring/ Reporting
New York City System	8,271,000	Surface	0	0

Note: (1) Based on violation data from January 1, 2013 to December 31, 2013 (includes unresolved violations from earlier years)
Source: U.S. Environmental Protection Agency, Office of Ground Water and Drinking Water, Safe Drinking Water Information System (based on data extracted February 10, 2014)

Philadelphia, Pennsylvania

Background

Philadelphia, "The City of Brotherly Love," was not founded upon brotherly love at all. The largest city in Pennsylvania was settled by Swedes and Finns in 1638, in a settlement known as New Sweden. The settlement was seized in 1655 by Peter Stuyvesant, director general of New Amsterdam for the Dutch crown. Inconsiderate of any previous claims by the Dutch, King Charles II of England conferred land between the Connecticut and Delaware rivers upon his brother, the duke of York. Naturally, the two countries went to war. However, thanks to a generous loan by Admiral Sir William Penn, the land fell permanently into English hands. To repay the loan, the king gave Sir William's son, also named William, sole proprietorship of the state of present-day Pennsylvania. At the same time, he was probably glad to be rid of a subject heavily influenced by a dissenting religious sect known as the Society of Friends, or the Quakers.

Pennsylvania's landlord had the vision and the financial means with which to carry out a simple but radical experiment for the times: a city built upon religious tolerance. Amazingly enough, the place of religious outcasts prospered. Thanks to forests abundant in natural resources, and ports busy with international trade, Philadelphia, in the state's southeast corner, was a bustling, ideal American city.

The service sector has emerged as the predominant economic force driving current and future growth in the city. Greater Philadelphia has one of the largest health care industries in the nation. It has also become a major materials development and processing center, with about 100,000 or more individuals involved in the manufacture of chemicals, advanced materials, glass, plastics, industrial gases, metals, composites, and textiles. Philadelphia is fast becoming a national leader in the biotech field. Its "knowledge industry," with over 80 colleges and universities helps to supply a skilled workforce for the growing technical and bio-industries. The city also has its own stock exchange. Because of Philadelphia's importance as a mecca for medical research, the region is a major center for the pharmaceutical industry.

The city claimed firsts in many cultural, educational, and political arenas. The Pennsylvania Academy of Fine Arts is the oldest museum and fine arts school in the country; the University of Pennsylvania, which Benjamin Franklin helped found, is the oldest university in the country; and of course, on July 4, 1776, the United States was born when "longhaired radicals" such as Thomas Jefferson, George Washington, and John Hancock signed the Declaration of Independence in Philadelphia, breaking away from the mother country forever.

The city offers a thriving cultural scene with something for everyone, from chamber music to jazz, from historic Society Hill to South Philadelphia, home of the open-air Italian Market and famous Philly cheesesteak. The historic and waterfront district has many colonial-era homes and cobblestone streets, as well as the Liberty Bell, Independence Hall and Independence National Historic Park. The Avenue of the Arts is home to several theaters, the Kimmel Center for the Performing Arts and the Academy of Music serve as home to eight Resident Company performing arts organizations, including The Philadelphia Orchestra, Opera Company of Philadelphia, Pennsylvania Ballet, Chamber Orchestra of Philadelphia, American Theater Arts for Youth, PHILADANCO, Philadelphia Chamber Music Society and Peter Nero and the Philly Pops.

In 2003, the National Constitution Center Museum, which is devoted to exploring the role and meaning of the United States Constitution, was opened, in a glass, steel, and limestone building designed by Pei, Cobb Freed and Partners. In the same year, a new Liberty Bell Center, designed to enhance the viewing of the nation's iconic Liberty Bell, was also opened. Considerable new construction and expansion has taken place in the city, with more planned.

Sports venues include Lincoln Financial Field for the Philadelphia Eagles football team, and Citizens Bank Park for the Philadelphia Phillies baseball team. These replace the 33-year-old Veterans Stadium, which was razed in a sentimental farewell ceremony.

The Appalachian Mountains to the west and the Atlantic Ocean to the east have a moderating effect on the city's climate and temperatures. Summer does bring humid days, owing to proximity to the ocean. Precipitation is fairly evenly distributed throughout the year, but there are variations within the city: summer rains and winter snows are sometimes heavier in suburbs to the north and west, with their higher elevations, than in the south and east.

Rankings

General Rankings

- *Business Insider* projected current trends well into the future to compile its list of the "15 Hottest American Cities of the Future." To such metrics as job and population growth, demographics, affordability, livability, and residents' health and welfare, analysts added innovation in technology and sustainability as well as a culture favoring youth and creativity. Judging by these combined factors, Philadelphia ranked #8. *Business Insider, "The Fifteen Hottest American Cities of the Future," June 18, 2012*

- Among the 50 largest U.S. cities, Philadelphia placed #33 in Vocativ's "semi-exhaustive, mostly scientific" city Livability Index for people aged 35 and under. Average salary, unemployment rates, rents, and other living costs were considered, along with bike lanes, low-cost broadband, cheap takeout, self-service laundries, the price of a pint of Guinness, music venues, and vintage clothing stores. *vocative.com, "The Livability Index: The Best U.S. Cities for People 35 and Under," November 7, 2013*

- Philadelphia was selected as one of America's best cities by *Bloomberg Businessweek*. The city ranked #24 out of 50. Criteria: leisure attributes (the number of restaurants, bars, libraries, museums, professional sports teams, and park acres by population); educational attributes (public school performance, the number of colleges, and graduate degree holders); economic factors (2011 income and June and July 2012 unemployment); crime; and air quality. *Bloomberg BusinessWeek, "America's Best Cities," September 26, 2012*

- Philadelphia was selected as one of "America's Favorite Cities." The city ranked #33 in the "Quality of Life and Visitor Experience: Cleanliness" category. Respondents to an online survey were asked to rate 35 top urban destinations in the U.S. from a visitor's perspective. Criteria: cleanliness. *Travel + Leisure, "America's Favorite Cities 2013"*

- Philadelphia was selected as one of "America's Favorite Cities." The city ranked #14 in the "Type of Trip: Gay-friendly" category. Respondents to an online survey were asked to rate 35 top urban destinations in the U.S. from a visitor's perspective. Criteria: gay-friendly. *Travel + Leisure, "America's Favorite Cities 2013"*

Business/Finance Rankings

- Analysts for the business website 24/7 Wall Street looked at the local government report "Tax Rates and Tax Burdens in the District of Columbia—A Nationwide Comparison" to determine where a family of three at two different income levels would pay the least and the most in state and local taxes. Among the ten cities with the highest state and local tax burdens was Philadelphia, at #2. *247wallst.com, American Cities with the Highest (and Lowest) Taxes, February 25, 2013*

- Based on a minimum of 500 social media reviews per metro area, the employment opinion group Glassdoor surveyed 50 of the largest U.S. metro areas on measures including compensation and benefits, satisfaction with management, business outlook, and number of employers hiring. The Philadelphia metro area was ranked #34 in overall employee satisfaction. *www.glassdoor.com, "Employment Satisfaction Report Card by City," June 21, 2013*

- The Brookings Institution ranked the 50 largest cities in the U.S. based on income inequality. Philadelphia was ranked #12. (#1 = greatest inequality). Criteria: the cities were ranked based on the "95/20 ratio." This figure represents the income at which a household earns more than 95 percent of all other households, divided by the income at which a household earns more than only 20 percent of all other households. *Brookings Institution, "Income Inequality in America's 50 Largest Cities, 2007-2012," February 20, 2014*

- MarketWatch shared a *24/7 Wall St.* analysis of the District of Columbia's Office of Revenue Analysis report on the estimated property, sales, auto, and income taxes paid in the largest city of each state in 2011. Of the U.S. cities with the highest tax burden, Philadelphia ranked #2. *Marketwatch.com, "10 U.S. Cities with the Highest Taxes," March 2, 2013*

- CareerBliss, an employment and careers website, analyzed U.S. Bureau of Labor Statistics data, more than 14,000 company reviews from employees and former employees, and job openings over a six-month period to arrive at its list of the 20 worst places in the United States to look for a job. Philadelphia was ranked #12. *CareerBliss.com, "20 Worst Cities to Find a Job for 2012," October 11, 2012*

- Philadelphia was ranked #97 out of 100 metro areas in terms of economic performance (#1 = best) during the recession and recovery from trough quarter through the second quarter of 2013. Criteria: percent change in employment; percentage point change in unemployment rate; percent change in gross metropolitan product; percent change in House Price Index. *Brookings Institution, MetroMonitor: Tracking Economic Recession and Recovery in America's 100 Largest Metropolitan Areas, September 2013*

- Payscale.com ranked the 20 largest metro areas in terms of wage growth. The Philadelphia metro area ranked #9. Criteria: private-sector wage growth between the 4th quarter of 2012 and the 4th quarter of 2013. *PayScale, "Wage Trends by Metro Area," 4th Quarter, 2013*

- Philadelphia was identified as one of America's most frugal metro areas by *Coupons.com*. The city ranked #17 out of 25. Criteria: online coupon usage. *Coupons.com, "Top 25 Most Frugal Cities of 2012," February 19, 2013*

- Philadelphia was identified as one of America's most frugal metro areas by *Coupons.com*. The city ranked #15 out of 25. Criteria: Grocery IQ and coupons.com mobile app usage. *Coupons.com, "Top 25 Most On-the-Go Frugal Cities of 2012," February 19, 2013*

- Philadelphia was cited as one of America's top metros for new and expanded facility projects in 2013. The area ranked #9 in the large metro area category (population over 1 million). *Site Selection, "Top Metros of 2013," March 2014*

- Philadelphia was identified as one of the best cities for college graduates to find work—and live. The city ranked #9 out of 15. Criteria: job availability; average salary; average rent. *CareerBuilder.com, "15 Best Cities for College Grads to Find Work—and Live," June 5, 2012*

- Philadelphia was identified as one of the happiest cities to work in by CareerBliss.com, an online community for career advancement. The city ranked #8 out of 10. Criteria: independent company reviews from employees all over the country on: relationship with their boss and co-workers; work environment; job resources; compensation; growth opportunities; company culture; company reputation; daily tasks; job control over work performed on a daily basis. *CareerBliss.com, "Top 10 Happiest and Unhappiest Cities to Work in 2014," February 10, 2014*

- Philadelphia was identified as one of the happiest cities for young professionals by *CareerBliss.com*, an online community for career advancement. The city ranked #7. Criteria: more than 45,000 young professionals were asked to rate key factors that affect workplace happiness including: work-life balance; compensation; company culture; overall work environment; company reputation; relationships with managers and co-workers; opportunities for growth; job resources; daily tasks; job autonomy. Young professionals are defined as having less than 10 years of work experience. *CareerBliss.com, "Happiest Cities for Young Professionals," April 26, 2013*

- The Philadelphia metro area appeared on the Milken Institute "2013 Best Performing Cities" list. Rank: #109 out of 200 large metro areas. Criteria: job growth; wage and salary growth; high-tech output growth. *Milken Institute, "Best-Performing Cities 2013," December 2013*

- *Forbes* ranked the 200 most populous metro areas in the U.S. in terms of the "Best Places for Business and Careers." The Philadelphia metro area was ranked #83. Criteria: costs (business and living); job growth (past and projected); income growth; educational attainment (college and high school); projected economic growth; cultural and recreational opportunities; net migration patterns; number of highly ranked colleges. *Forbes, "The Best Places for Business and Careers," August 7, 2013*

Children/Family Rankings

- Philadelphia was selected as one of the best cities for families to live by *Parenting* magazine. The city ranked #76 out of 100. Criteria: education; health; community; *Parenting's* Culture & Charm Index. *Parenting.com, "The 2012 Best Cities for Families List"*

Culture/Performing Arts Rankings

- Philadelphia was selected as one of "America's Favorite Cities." The city ranked #4 in the "Culture: Museum/Galleries" category. Respondents to an online survey were asked to rate 35 top urban destinations in the U.S. from a visitor's perspective. Criteria: number and quality of museums and galleries. *Travelandleisure.com, "America's Favorite Cities 2013"*

- Philadelphia was selected as one of America's top cities for the arts. The city ranked #6 in the big city (population 500,000 and over) category. Criteria: readers' top choices for arts travel destinations based on the richness and variety of visual arts sites, activities and events. *American Style, "2012 Top 25 Arts Destinations," June 2012*

Dating/Romance Rankings

- A *Cosmopolitan* magazine article surveyed the gender balance and other factors to arrive at a list of the best and worst cities for women to meet single guys. Philadelphia placed #2 among the worst for single women looking for dates. *www.cosmopolitan.com, "Working the Ratio," October 1, 2013*

- CreditDonkey, a financial education website, sought out the ten best U.S. cities for newlyweds, considering the number of married couples, divorce rate, average credit score, and average number of hours worked per week in metro areas with a million or more residents. The Philadelphia metro area placed #6. *www.creditdonkey.com, "Study: Best Cities for Newlyweds," November 30, 2013*

- Of the 100 U.S. cities surveyed by *Men's Health* in its quest to identify the nation's best cities for dating and forming relationships, Philadelphia was ranked #29 for online dating (#1 = best). *Men's Health, "The Best and Worst Cities for Online Dating," January 30, 2013*

- Philadelphia ranked #6 among cities congenial to singles, according to Kiplinger, which searched for "dating scenes as financially attractive as they are romantically promising." High percentages of unmarried people, above-average household incomes, and cost-of-living factors determined the rankings. *Kiplinger.com, "10 Best Cities for Singles," February 2013*

- Philadelphia was selected as one of America's best cities for singles by the readers of *Travel + Leisure* in their annual "America's Favorite Cities" survey. The city was ranked #11 out of 20. *Travel + Leisure, "America's Best Cities for Singles," July 2012*

- Philadelphia was selected as one of the best cities for single men by *Rent.com*. Criteria: high single female-to-male ratio. *Rent.com, "Top Cities for Single Men," March 14, 2013*

- Philadelphia was selected as one of the best cities for single women in America by *SingleMindedWomen.com*. The city ranked #8. Criteria: ratio of women to men; singles population; healthy lifestyle; employment opportunities; cost of living; access to travel; entertainment options; social opportunities. *SingleMindedWomen.com, "Top 10 Cities for Single Women," 2011*

Education Rankings

- *Men's Health* ranked 100 U.S. cities in terms of their education levels. Philadelphia was ranked #89 (#1 = most educated city). Criteria: high school graduation rates; school enrollment; educational attainment; number of households who have outstanding student loans; number of households whose members have taken adult-education courses. *Men's Health, "Where School Is In: The Most and Least Educated Cities," September 12, 2011*

- Philadelphia was selected as one of America's most literate cities. The city ranked #34 out of the 77 largest U.S. cities. Criteria: number of booksellers; library resources; Internet resources; educational attainment; periodical publishing resources; newspaper circulation. *Central Connecticut State University, "America's Most Literate Cities, 2013"*

Environmental Rankings

- The Philadelphia metro area came in at #196 for the relative comfort of its climate on Sperling's list of "chill cities," as measured by the Sperling Heat Index. All 361 metro areas are included. Criteria included daytime high temperatures, nighttime low temperatures, dew point, and relative humidity at the high temperatures. *www.bertsperling.com, "Sperling's Chill Cities," July 18, 2013*

- Sperling's BestPlaces assessed 379 metropolitan areas of the United States for the likelihood of dangerously extreme weather events or earthquakes. In general the Southeast and South-Central regions have the highest risk of weather extremes and earthquakes, while the Pacific Northwest enjoys the lowest risk. Of the least risky metropolitan areas, the Philadelphia metro area was ranked #232. *www.bestplaces.net, "Safest Places from Natural Disasters," April 2011*

- Philadelphia was identified as one of America's dirtiest metro areas by *Forbes*. The area ranked #3 out of 20. Criteria: air quality; water quality; toxic releases; superfund sites. *Forbes, "America's 20 Dirtiest Cities," December 10, 2012*

- Philadelphia was identified as one of North America's greenest metropolitan areas. The area ranked #13. The Green City Index is comprised of 31 indicators, and scores cities across nine categories: carbon dioxide; energy; land use; buildings; transport; water; waste; air quality; environmental governance. The 27 largest metropolitan areas in the U.S. and Canada were considered. *Economist Intelligence Unit, sponsored by Siemens, "U.S. and Canada Green City Index, 2011"*

- The U.S. Environmental Protection Agency (EPA) released a list of U.S. metropolitan areas with the most ENERGY STAR certified buildings in 2012. The Philadelphia metro area was ranked #11 out of 25. *U.S. Environmental Protection Agency, "Top Cities With the Most ENERGY STAR Certified Buildings in 2012," March 12, 2013*

- Philadelphia was selected as one of 22 "Smarter Cities" for energy by the Natural Resources Defense Council. Criteria: investment in green power; energy efficiency measures; conservation. *Natural Resources Defense Council, "2010 Smarter Cities," July 19, 2010*

- The Philadelphia metro area was selected as one of "America's Most Toxic Cities" by *Forbes*. The metro area ranked #1 out of 10. The 80 largest metropolitan areas were ranked on the following criteria: air quality; water quality; Superfund sites; toxic releases. *Forbes, "America's Most Toxic Cities, 2011," February 28, 2011*

- Philadelphia was highlighted as one of the 25 most ozone-polluted metro areas in the U.S. during 2008 through 2010. The area ranked #20. *American Lung Association, State of the Air 2012*

- Philadelphia was highlighted as one of the 25 metro areas most polluted by year-round particle pollution (Annual PM 2.5) in the U.S. during 2008 through 2010. The area ranked #11. *American Lung Association, State of the Air 2012*

Food/Drink Rankings

- *Men's Health* ranked 100 major U.S. cities in terms of alcohol intoxication. Philadelphia ranked #18 (#1 = most sober).Criteria: binge drinking; alcohol-related traffic accidents, arrests, and fatalities. *Men's Health, "The Drunkest Cities in America," November 19, 2013*

- Philadelphia was selected as one of America's best cities for hamburgers by the readers of *Travel + Leisure* in their annual America's Favorite Cities survey. The city was ranked #2 out of 10. *Travel + Leisure, "America's Best Burger Cities," August 25, 2013*

- Citizen Bank Park (Philadelphia Phillies) was selected as one of PETA's "Top 10 Vegetarian-Friendly Major League Ballparks" for 2013. The park ranked #1. *People for the Ethical Treatment of Animals, "Top 10 Vegetarian-Friendly Major League Ballparks, " June 12, 2013*

Health/Fitness Rankings

- For each of the 50 most populous metro areas in the United States, the American College of Sports Medicine's American Fitness Index evaluated infrastructure, community assets, and policies that encourage healthy and fit lifestyles, including preventive health behaviors, levels of chronic disease conditions, health care access, and community resources and policies that support physical activity. The Philadelphia metro area ranked #25 for "community fitness." Personal health indicators were considered as well as community and environmental indicators. *www.americanfitnessindex.org, "ACSM American Fitness Index Health and Community Fitness Status of the 50 Largest Metropolitan Areas," May 2013*

- *Business Insider* reported Trulia's analysis of the 100 largest U.S. metro areas to identify the nation's best cities for weight loss, based on healthful food options, access to outdoor activities, weight-loss centers, gyms, and opportunities to bike or walk to work. Philadelphia ranked #8. *Businessinsider.com, "These Are the Best US Cities for Weight loss," January 17, 2013*

- Philadelphia was identified as one of the 10 most walkable cities in the U.S. by Walk Score, a Seattle-based service that rates the convenience and transit access of 10,000 neighborhoods in 3,000 cities. The area ranked #4 out of the 50 largest U.S. cities. Walk Score measures walkability by analyzing hundreds of walking routes to nearby amenities. Walk Score also measures pedestrian friendliness by analyzing population density and road metrics such as block length and intersection density. *WalkScore.com, March 20, 2014*

- Philadelphia was selected as one of the 25 fattest cities in America by *Men's Fitness Online*. It ranked #14 out of America's 50 largest cities. Criteria: fitness centers and sport stores; nutrition; sports participation; TV viewing; overweight/sedentary; junk food; air quality; geography; commute; parks and open space; city recreational facilities; access to healthcare; motivation; mayor and city initiatives; state obesity initiatives. *Men's Fitness, "The Fittest and Fattest Cities in America," March 5, 2012*

- Philadelphia was identified as a "2013 Spring Allergy Capital." The area ranked #25 out of 100. Three groups of factors were used to identify the most severe cities for people with allergies during the spring season: annual pollen levels; medicine utilization; access to board-certified allergists. *Asthma and Allergy Foundation of America, "Spring Allergy Capitals 2013"*

- Philadelphia was identified as a "2013 Fall Allergy Capital." The area ranked #42 out of 100. Three groups of factors were used to identify the most severe cities for people with allergies during the fall season: annual pollen levels; medicine utilization; access to board-certified allergists. *Asthma and Allergy Foundation of America, "Fall Allergy Capitals 2013"*

- Philadelphia was identified as a "2013 Asthma Capital." The area ranked #4 out of the nation's 100 largest metropolitan areas. Twelve factors were used to identify the most challenging places to live for people with asthma: estimated prevalence; self-reported prevalence; crude death rate for asthma; annual pollen score; annual air quality; public smoking laws; number of board-certified asthma specialists; school inhaler access laws; rescue medication use; controller medication use; uninsured rate; poverty rate. *Asthma and Allergy Foundation of America, "Asthma Capitals 2013"*

- *Men's Health* ranked 100 major U.S. cities in terms of the best and worst cities for men. Philadelphia ranked #100. Criteria: thirty-three data points were examined covering health, fitness, and quality of life. *Men's Health, "The Best & Worst Cities for Men 2014," December 6, 2013*

- *Men's Health* ranked 100 U.S. cities in terms of the best and worst cities for women. Philadelphia was ranked among the ten worst at #1. Criteria: dozens of statistical parameters of long life in the categories of health, quality of life, and fitness. *Men's Health, "The 10 Best and Worst Cities for Women 2011," January/February 2011*

- Breathe Right Nasal Strips, in partnership with Sperling's BestPlaces, analyzed 50 metro areas and identified those U.S. cities most challenged by chronic nasal congestion. The Philadelphia metro area ranked #10. Criteria: tree, grass and weed pollens; molds and spores; air pollution; climate; smoking; purchase habits of congestion products; prescriptions of drugs for congestion relief; incidence of influenza. *Breathe Right Nasal Strips, "Most Congested Cities," October 3, 2011*

- The American Academy of Dermatology ranked 26 U.S. metropolitan regions in terms of their residents knowledge, attitude and behaviors towards tanning, sun protection and skin cancer detection. The Philadelphia metro area ranked #8. The results of the study are based on an online survey of over 7,000 adults nationwide. *American Academy of Dermatology, "Suntelligence: How Sun Smart is Your City?," May 3, 2010*

- The Philadelphia metro area appeared in the 2013 Gallup-Healthways Well-Being Index. The area ranked #100 out of 189. The Gallup-Healthways Well-Being Index score is an average of six sub-indexes, which individually examine life evaluation, emotional health, work environment, physical health, healthy behaviors, and access to basic necessities. Results are based on telephone interviews conducted as part of the Gallup-Healthways Well-Being Index survey January 2–December 29, 2012, and January 2–December 30, 2013, with a random sample of 531,630 adults, aged 18 and older, living in metropolitan areas in the 50 U.S. states and the District of Columbia. *Gallup-Healthways, "State of American Well-Being," March 25, 2014*

- The Philadelphia metro area was identified as one of "America's Most Stressful Cities" by *Sperling's BestPlaces*. The metro area ranked #23 out of 50. Criteria: unemployment rate; suicide rate; commute time; mental health; poor rest; alcohol use; violent crime rate; property crime rate; cloudy days annually. *Sperling's BestPlaces, www.BestPlaces.net, "Stressful Cities 2012*

- The Philadelphia metro area was identified as one of "America's Most Stressful Cities" by *Forbes*. The metro area ranked #6 out of 40. Criteria: housing affordability; unemployment rate; cost of living; air quality; traffic congestion; sunny days; population density. *Forbes.com, "America's Most Stressful Cities," September 23, 2011*

- *Men's Health* ranked 100 U.S. cities in terms of their activity levels. Philadelphia was ranked #38 (#1 = most active city). Criteria: where and how often residents exercise; percentage of households that watch more than 15 hours of cable television a week and buy more than 11 video games a year; death rate from deep-vein thrombosis, a condition linked to sitting for extended periods of time. *Men's Health, "Where Sit Happens: The Most and Least Active Cities in America," June 20, 2011*

Real Estate Rankings

- NerdWallet identified the 10 U.S. cities among the 25 largest, most hospitable for recent college graduates, based on demographics; social life; accessibility; cost of living; and economic opportunity. Philadelphia placed #5 as a destination for new young graduates. *http://www.nerdwallet.com, "Best Cities for Fresh College Graduates," May 30, 2013*

- Philadelphia was ranked #138 out of 283 metro areas in terms of house price appreciation in 2013 (#1 = highest rate). *Federal Housing Finance Agency, House Price Index, 4th Quarter 2013*

- Philadelphia was ranked #156 out of 224 metro areas in terms of housing affordability in 2013 by the National Association of Home Builders (#1 = most affordable). The NAHB-Wells Fargo Housing Opportunity Index (HOI) for a given area is defined as the share of homes sold in that area that would have been affordable to a family earning the local median income, based on standard mortgage underwriting criteria. *National Association of Home Builders®, NAHB-Wells Fargo Housing Opportunity Index, 4th Quarter 2013*

- Philadelphia was selected as one of the best college towns for renters by ApartmentRatings.com." The area ranked #49 out of 87. Overall satisfaction ratings were ranked using thousands of user submitted scores for hundreds of apartment complexes located in cities and towns that are home to the 100 largest four-year institutions in the U.S. *ApartmentRatings.com, "2011 College Town Renter Satisfaction Rankings"*

- The nation's largest metro areas were analyzed in terms of the best places to buy foreclosures in 2013. The Philadelphia metro area ranked #13 out of 20. Criteria: RealtyTrac scored all metro areas with a population of 500,000 or more by summing up four numbers: months' supply of foreclosure inventory; percentage of foreclosure sales; foreclosure discount; percentage increase in foreclosure activity in 2012. *RealtyTrac, "2012 Year-End Metropolitan Foreclosure Market Report," January 28, 2013*

Safety Rankings

- Business Insider looked at the FBI's Uniform Crime Report to identify the U.S. cities with the most violent crime per capita, excluding localities with fewer than 100,000 residents. To judge by its relatively high murder, rape, and robbery data, Philadelphia was ranked #12 (#1 = worst) among the 25 most dangerous cities. *www.businessinsider.com, "The 25 Most Dangerous Cities in America," June 13, 2013*

- Symantec, in partnership with Sperling's BestPlaces, ranked the 50 largest cities in the U.S. in terms of their vulnerability to cybercrime. The city ranked #27. Criteria: number of cyberattacks and potential infections; level of Internet access; expenditures on smartphones and computer hardware/software; wireless hotspots; broadband connectivity; Internet usage; online purchases. *Symantec, "Riskiest Online Cities of 2012" February 15, 2012*

- Allstate ranked the 200 largest cities in America in terms of driver safety. Philadelphia ranked #189. Allstate researchers analyzed internal property damage claims over a two-year period from January 2010 to December 2011. A weighted average of the two-year numbers determined the annual percentages. *Allstate, "Allstate America's Best Drivers Report®, August 27, 2013"*

- Philadelphia was identified as one of the most dangerous large cities in America by CQ Press. All 32 cities with populations of 500,000 or more that reported crime rates in 2012 for murder, rape, robbery, aggravated assault, burglary, and motor vehicle thefts were ranked. The city ranked #5 out of the top 10. *CQ Press, City Crime Rankings 2014*

- Philadelphia was identified as one of the most dangerous cities in America by *The Business Insider.* Criteria: cities with 100,000 residents or more were ranked by violent crime rate in 2011. Violent crimes include for murder, rape, robbery, and aggravated assault. The city ranked #18 out of 25. *The Business Insider, "The 25 Most Dangerous Cities in America," November 4, 2012*

- The National Insurance Crime Bureau ranked 380 metro areas in the U.S. in terms of per capita rates of vehicle theft. The Philadelphia metro area ranked #125 (#1 = highest rate). Criteria: number of vehicle theft offenses per 100,000 inhabitants in 2012. *National Insurance Crime Bureau, "Hot Spots 2012," June 26, 2013*

- The Philadelphia metro area was identified as one of the most dangerous metro areas for pedestrians by Transportation for America. The metro area ranked #39 out of 52 metro areas with over 1 million residents. Criteria: area's population divided by the number of pedestrian fatalities in that area. *Transportation for America, "Dangerous by Design 2011"*

Seniors/Retirement Rankings

- From its Best Cities for Successful Aging indexes, the Milken Institute generated rankings for metropolitan areas, weighing data in eight categories—general indicators, health care, wellness, living arrangements, transportation and general accessibility, financial well-being, education and employment, and community participation. The Philadelphia metro area was ranked #16 overall in the large metro area category. *Milken Institute, "Best Cities for Successful Aging," July 2012*

- Bankers Life and Casualty Company, in partnership with Sperling's BestPlaces, ranked the nation's 50 largest metro areas in terms of the "Best U.S. Cities for Seniors." The Philadelphia metro area ranked #12. Criteria: healthcare; transportation; housing; environment; economy; health and longevity; social and spiritual life; crime. *Bankers Life and Casualty Company, Center for a Secure Retirement, "Best U.S. Cities for Seniors 2011," September 2011*

Sports/Recreation Rankings

- According to the personal finance website NerdWallet, the Philadelphia metro area, at #10, is one of the nation's top dozen metro areas for sports fans. Criteria included the presence of all four major sports—MLB, NFL, NHL, and NBA, fan enthusiasm (as measured by game attendance), ticket affordability, and "sports culture," that is, number of sports bars. *www.nerdwallet.com, "Best Cities for Sports Fans," May 5, 2013*

- Philadelphia appeared on the *Sporting News* list of the "Best Sports Cities" for 2011. The area ranked #3 out of 271. Criteria: the magazine takes a 12-month snapshot of each city's sports, putting a heavy premium on regular-season won-lost records (from the most recently completed season). Other criteria include: playoff berths, bowl appearances and tournament bids; championships; applicable power ratings; quality of competition; overall fan fervor (measured in part by attendance); abundance of teams (rewarding quality over quantity); stadium and arena quality; ticket availability and prices; franchise ownership; and marquee appeal of athletes. *Sporting News, "Best Sports Cities 2011," October 4, 2011*

- Philadelphia appeared on the *Sporting News* list of the "Best Sports Cities" for 2011. The area ranked #3 out of 271. Criteria: a 12-month snapshot of regular-season won-lost records (from the most recently completed season). Other criteria include: playoff berths, bowl appearances and tournament bids; championships; applicable power ratings; quality of competition; overall fan fervor (measured in part by attendance); abundance of teams (quality over quantity); stadium and arena quality; ticket availability and prices; franchise ownership; and marquee appeal of athletes. *Sporting News, "Best Sports Cities 2011," October 4, 2011*

- Philadelphia was chosen as a bicycle friendly community by the League of American Bicyclists. A "Bicycle Friendly Community" welcomes cyclists by providing safe accommodation for cycling and encouraging people to bike for transportation and recreation. There are four award levels: Platinum; Gold; Silver; and Bronze. The community achieved an award level of Silver. *League of American Bicyclists, "Bicycle Friendly Community Master List," Fall 2013*

- Philadelphia was chosen as one of America's best cities for bicycling. The city ranked #17 out of 50. Criteria: robust cycling infrastructure; vibrant bike culture. The editors only considered cities with populations of 95,000 or more. *Bicycling, "America's Top 50 Bike-Friendly Cities," May 23, 2012*

Transportation Rankings

- Business Insider presented a Walk Score ranking of public transportation in 316 U.S. cities and thousands of city neighborhoods in which Philadelphia earned the #5-ranked "Transit Score," awarded for frequency, type of route, and distance between stops. *www.businessinsider.com, "The US Cities with the Best Public Transportation Systems," January 30, 2014*

- NerdWallet surveyed average annual car insurance premiums in 125 U.S. cities to identify the least expensive U.S. cities in which to insure a car. Locations with no-fault insurance laws was a strong determinant. Philadelphia came in at #10 for the most expensive rates. *www.nerdwallet.com, "Best Cities for Cheap Car Insurance," February 3, 2014*

- More U.S. households choose not to have a car in 2012 than in prior years, according to a study by the University of Michigan Transportation Research Institute. The business website 24/7 Wall Street examined that study, along with a 2010 Census Special Report to arrive at its ranking of cities in which the fewest households had a vehicle. Philadelphia held the #4 position. *247wallst.com, "Cities Where No One Wants to Drive," February 6, 2014*

- Philadelphia was identified as one of the most congested metro areas in the U.S. The area ranked #9 out of 10. Criteria: yearly delay per auto commuter in hours. *Texas A&M Transportation Institute, "2012 Urban Mobility Report," December 2012*

- The Philadelphia metro area was selected as one of 15 "Smarter Cities" for transportation by the Natural Resources Defense Council. The area appeared in the large metro area (population greater than one million) category. Criteria: public transit availability and use; household automobile ownership and use; innovative, sustainable and affordable transportation programs. *Natural Resources Defense Council, "2011 Smarter Cities," February 23, 2011*

- The Philadelphia metro area appeared on *Forbes* list of places with the most extreme commutes. The metro area ranked #9 out of 10. Criteria: average travel time; percentage of mega commuters. Mega-commuters travel more than 90 minutes and 50 miles each way to work. *Forbes.com, "The Cities with the Most Extreme Commutes," March 5, 2013*

Women/Minorities Rankings

- The Daily Beast surveyed the nation's cities for highest percentage of singles and lowest divorce rate, plus other measures, to determine "emotional intelligence"—happiness, confidence, kindness—which, researchers say, has a strong correlation with people's satisfaction with their romantic relationships. Philadelphia placed #8. *www.thedailybeast.com, "Best Cities to Find Love and Stay in Love," February 14, 2014*

- *Women's Health* examined U.S. cities and identified the 100 best cities for women. Philadelphia was ranked #97. Criteria: 30 categories were examined from obesity and breast cancer rates to commuting times and hours spent working out. *Women's Health, "Best Cities for Women 2012"*

- Philadelphia was selected as one of the best cities for young Latinos in 2013 by mun2, a national cable television broadcast network. The city ranked #14. Criteria: U.S. cities with populations over 500,000 residents were evaluated on the following criteria: number of young latinos; jobs; friendliness; cost of living; fun. *mun2.tv, "Best Cities for Young Latinos 2013*

- The Philadelphia metro area appeared on *Forbes'* list of the "Best Cities for Minority Entrepreneurs." The area ranked #14 out of 10. Criteria: 52 metropolitan statistical areas were examined. For each ethnicity (African Americans, Asians and Hispanics), the editors measured housing affordability, population growth, income growth, and entrepreneurship (per capita self-employment). *Forbes, "Best Cities for Minority Entrepreneurs," March 23, 2011*

Miscellaneous Rankings

- Philadelphia was selected as a 2013 Digital Cities Survey winner. The city ranked #2 in the large city (250,000 or more population) category. The survey examined and assessed how city governments are utilizing information technology to operate and deliver quality service to their customers and citizens. Survey questions focused on implementation and adoption of online service delivery; planning and governance; and the infrastructure and architecture that make the transformation to digital government possible. *Center for Digital Government, "2013 Digital Cities Survey," November 7, 2013*

- *Travel + Leisure* invited readers to rate cities on indicators such as aloofness, "smarty-pants residents," highbrow cultural offerings, high-end shopping, artisanal coffeehouses, conspicuous eco-consciousness, and more in order to identify the nation's snobbiest cities. Cities large and small made the list; among them was Philadelphia, at #14. *www.travelandleisure.com, "America's Snobbiest Cities, June 2013*

- The watchdog site Charity Navigator conducts an annual study of charities in the nation's major markets both to analyze statistical differences in their financial, accountability, and transparency practices and to track year-to-year variations in individual communities. The Philadelphia metro area was ranked #16 among the 30 metro markets. *www.charitynavigator.org, "Metro Market Study 2013," June 1, 2013*

- Business Insider reports on the 2013 Trick-or-Treat Index compiled by the real estate site Zillow, which used its own Home Value Index and Walk Score along with population density and local crime stats to determine that Philadelphia ranked #10 for "how much candy it gives out versus how far kids have to walk to get it." Zillow also zeroes in on the best neighborhoods in its top 20 cities. *www.businessinsider.com, "These Are the Best Cities for Trick-or-Treating," October 15, 2013*

- The Harris Poll's Happiness Index survey revealed that of the top ten U.S. markets, the Philadelphia metro area residents ranked #3 in happiness. Criteria included strong assent to positive statements and strong disagreement with negative ones, and degree of agreement with a series of statements about respondents' personal relationships and general outlook. The online survey was conducted between July 14 and July 30, 2013. *www.harrisinteractive.com, "Dallas/Fort Worth Is "Happiest" City among America's Top Ten Markets," September 4, 2013*

- *Men's Health* ranked 100 U.S. cities by their level of sadness. Philadelphia was ranked #60 (#1 = saddest city). Criteria: suicide rates; unemployment rates; percentage of households that use antidepressants; percent of population who report feeling blue all or most of the time. *Men's Health, "Frown Towns," November 28, 2011*

- The Philadelphia metro area was selected as one of "The Best U.S. Cities for Bargain Shopping" by *Forbes*. The area ranked #7 out of 10. Criteria: number of outlet stores; gross leasable retail space in major malls; low consumer price index; low sales tax rate. Indicators were examined in the nation's 50 largest metropolitan areas. *Forbes, "The Best U.S. Cities for Bargain Shopping," January 20, 2012*

- Energizer Personal Care, the makers of Edge® shave gel, in partnership with Sperling's BestPlaces, ranked 50 major metro areas in terms of everyday irritations. The Philadelphia metro area ranked #4. Criteria: high male-to-female ratio; poor sports team performance and high ticket prices; slow traffic; lack of job availability; unaffordable housing; extreme weather; lack of nightlife and fitness options. *Energizer Personal Care, "Most Irritatng Cities for Guys," August 26, 2013*

- Mars Chocolate North America, the makers of COMBOS®, in partnership with Sperling's BestPlaces, ranked 50 major metro areas in terms of their "manliness." The Philadelphia metro area ranked #29. Criteria: number of professional sports teams; number of nearby NASCAR tracks and racing events; manly lifestyle; concentration of manly retail stores; manly occupations per capita; salty snack sales; "Board of Manliness" rankings. *Mars Chocolate North America, "America's Manliest Cities 2012"*

- The National Alliance to End Homelessness ranked the 100 most populous metro areas in terms the rate of homelessness. The Philadelphia metro area ranked #27. Criteria: number of homeless people per 10,000 population in 2011. *National Alliance to End Homelessness, The State of Homelessness in America 2012*

Business Environment

CITY FINANCES

City Government Finances

Component	2011 ($000)	2011 ($ per capita)
Total Revenues	8,216,243	5,668
Total Expenditures	6,847,135	4,723
Debt Outstanding	6,775,176	4,674
Cash and Securities[1]	8,295,076	5,722

Note: (1) Cash and security holdings of a government at the close of its fiscal year, including those of its dependent agencies, utilities, and liquor stores.
Source: U.S Census Bureau, State & Local Government Finances 2011

City Government Revenue by Source

Source	2011 ($000)	2011 ($ per capita)
General Revenue		
From Federal Government	522,242	360
From State Government	1,767,210	1,219
From Local Governments	60,218	42
Taxes		
Property	482,716	333
Sales and Gross Receipts	680,188	469
Personal Income	1,494,036	1,031
Corporate Income	300,440	207
Motor Vehicle License	0	0
Other Taxes	181,772	125
Current Charges	695,165	480
Liquor Store	0	0
Utility	960,031	662
Employee Retirement	862,622	595

Source: U.S Census Bureau, State & Local Government Finances 2011

City Government Expenditures by Function

Function	2011 ($000)	2011 ($ per capita)	2011 (%)
General Direct Expenditures			
Air Transportation	186,321	129	2.7
Corrections	328,497	227	4.8
Education	0	0	0.0
Employment Security Administration	0	0	0.0
Financial Administration	47,121	33	0.7
Fire Protection	179,609	124	2.6
General Public Buildings	100,829	70	1.5
Governmental Administration, Other	38,074	26	0.6
Health	1,262,177	871	18.4
Highways	100,358	69	1.5
Hospitals	0	0	0.0
Housing and Community Development	178,606	123	2.6
Interest on General Debt	159,737	110	2.3
Judicial and Legal	251,707	174	3.7
Libraries	37,719	26	0.6
Parking	0	0	0.0
Parks and Recreation	76,717	53	1.1
Police Protection	518,470	358	7.6
Public Welfare	387,673	267	5.7
Sewerage	259,719	179	3.8
Solid Waste Management	88,285	61	1.3
Veterans' Services	0	0	0.0
Liquor Store	0	0	0.0
Utility	958,178	661	14.0
Employee Retirement	947,284	653	13.8

Source: U.S Census Bureau, State & Local Government Finances 2011

DEMOGRAPHICS

Population Growth

Area	1990 Census	2000 Census	2010 Census	Population Growth (%)	
				1990-2000	2000-2010
City	1,585,577	1,517,550	1,526,006	-4.3	0.6
MSA[1]	5,435,470	5,687,147	5,965,343	4.6	4.9
U.S.	248,709,873	281,421,906	308,745,538	13.2	9.7

Note: (1) Figures cover the Philadelphia-Camden-Wilmington, PA-NJ-DE-MD Metropolitan Statistical Area—see Appendix B for areas included
Source: U.S. Census Bureau, Census 1990, 2000, 2010

Household Size

Area	Persons in Household (%)							Average Household Size
	One	Two	Three	Four	Five	Six	Seven or More	
City	39.6	27.7	14.6	9.7	4.9	2.0	1.5	2.58
MSA[1]	29.5	31.3	16.2	13.6	6.2	2.1	1.2	2.62
U.S.	27.6	33.5	15.7	13.2	6.1	2.4	1.5	2.63

Note: (1) Figures cover the Philadelphia-Camden-Wilmington, PA-NJ-DE-MD Metropolitan Statistical Area—see Appendix B for areas included
Source: U.S. Census Bureau, 2010-2012 American Community Survey 3-Year Estimates

Race

Area	White Alone[2] (%)	Black Alone[2] (%)	Asian Alone[2] (%)	AIAN[3] Alone[2] (%)	NHOPI[4] Alone[2] (%)	Other Race Alone[2] (%)	Two or More Races (%)
City	41.3	43.2	6.4	0.3	0.1	6.0	2.6
MSA[1]	68.5	20.8	5.1	0.2	0.1	3.1	2.3
U.S.	74.0	12.6	4.9	0.8	0.2	4.7	2.8

Note: (1) Figures cover the Philadelphia-Camden-Wilmington, PA-NJ-DE-MD Metropolitan Statistical Area—see Appendix B for areas included; (2) Alone is defined as not being in combination with one or more other races; (3) American Indian and Alaska Native; (4) Native Hawaiian and Other Pacific Islander
Source: U.S. Census Bureau, 2010-2012 American Community Survey 3-Year Estimates

Hispanic or Latino Origin

Area	Total (%)	Mexican (%)	Puerto Rican (%)	Cuban (%)	Other (%)
City	12.7	0.9	8.5	0.3	3.0
MSA[1]	8.1	1.7	4.2	0.2	2.0
U.S.	16.6	10.7	1.6	0.6	3.7

Note: Persons of Hispanic or Latino origin can be of any race; (1) Figures cover the Philadelphia-Camden-Wilmington, PA-NJ-DE-MD Metropolitan Statistical Area—see Appendix B for areas included
Source: U.S. Census Bureau, 2010-2012 American Community Survey 3-Year Estimates

Segregation

Type	Segregation Indices[1]				Percent Change		
	1990	2000	2010	2010 Rank[2]	1990-2000	1990-2010	2000-2010
Black/White	75.2	71.0	68.4	9	-4.2	-6.8	-2.6
Asian/White	42.4	44.1	42.3	42	1.7	0.0	-1.8
Hispanic/White	60.9	58.5	55.1	12	-2.5	-5.9	-3.4

Note: All figures cover the Metropolitan Statistical Area—see Appendix B for areas included; Figures are based on an analysis of 1990, 2000, and 2010 Census Decennial Census tract data by William H. Frey, Brookings Institution and the University of Michigan Social Science Data Analysis Network. In this analysis all racial groups (whites, blacks, and asians) are non-Hispanic members of those races. Hispanics are shown as a separate category;
(1) Segregation Indices are Dissimilarity Indices that measure the degree to which the minority group is distributed differently than whites across census tracts. They range from 0 (complete integration) to 100 (complete segregation) where the value indicates the percentage of the minority group that needs to move to be distributed exactly like whites; (2) Ranges from 1 (most segregated) to 102 (least segregated); n/a not available.
Source: www.CensusScope.org

Ancestry

Area	German	Irish	English	American	Italian	Polish	French[2]	Scottish	Dutch
City	7.6	12.3	2.8	2.2	8.0	3.4	0.7	0.6	0.4
MSA[1]	16.8	20.5	7.9	3.5	14.0	5.4	1.5	1.4	1.0
U.S.	15.2	11.1	8.2	7.2	5.6	3.1	2.8	1.7	1.4

Note: Figures are the percentage of the total population reporting a particular ancestry. The nine most commonly reported ancestries in the U.S. are shown. Figures include multiple ancestries (e.g. if a person reported being Irish and Italian, they were included in both columns); (1) Figures cover the Philadelphia-Camden-Wilmington, PA-NJ-DE-MD Metropolitan Statistical Area—see Appendix B for areas included; (2) Excludes Basque
Source: U.S. Census Bureau, 2010-2012 American Community Survey 3-Year Estimates

Foreign-Born Population

Area	Percent of Population Born in								
	Any Foreign Country	Mexico	Asia	Europe	Carribean	South America	Central America[2]	Africa	Canada
City	12.0	0.4	4.7	2.3	2.1	0.8	0.4	1.1	0.1
MSA[1]	9.7	0.9	3.9	2.0	1.1	0.6	0.4	0.8	0.1
U.S.	13.0	3.7	3.7	1.6	1.2	0.9	1.0	0.5	0.3

Note: (1) Figures cover the Philadelphia-Camden-Wilmington, PA-NJ-DE-MD Metropolitan Statistical Area—see Appendix B for areas included; (2) Excludes Mexico.
Source: U.S. Census Bureau, 2010-2012 American Community Survey 3-Year Estimates

Marital Status

Area	Never Married	Now Married[2]	Separated	Widowed	Divorced
City	51.7	28.9	3.5	7.0	8.9
MSA[1]	36.9	45.4	2.3	6.6	8.9
U.S.	32.4	48.4	2.2	6.0	11.0

Note: Figures are percentages and cover the population 15 years of age and older; (1) Figures cover the Philadelphia-Camden-Wilmington, PA-NJ-DE-MD Metropolitan Statistical Area—see Appendix B for areas included; (2) Excludes separated
Source: U.S. Census Bureau, 2010-2012 American Community Survey 3-Year Estimates

Age

Area	Percent of Population									Median Age
	Under Age 5	Age 5–19	Age 20–34	Age 35–44	Age 45–54	Age 55–64	Age 65–74	Age 75–84	Age 85+	
City	6.8	19.1	26.1	12.2	12.7	10.9	6.3	4.0	1.9	33.4
MSA[1]	6.1	19.9	20.3	12.9	15.1	12.2	7.0	4.4	2.1	38.1
U.S.	6.4	20.1	20.5	13.1	14.3	12.2	7.3	4.2	1.8	37.3

Note: (1) Figures cover the Philadelphia-Camden-Wilmington, PA-NJ-DE-MD Metropolitan Statistical Area—see Appendix B for areas included
Source: U.S. Census Bureau, 2010-2012 American Community Survey 3-Year Estimates

Gender

Area	Males	Females	Males per 100 Females
City	726,023	812,188	89.4
MSA[1]	2,894,285	3,101,816	93.3
U.S.	153,276,055	158,333,314	96.8

Note: (1) Figures cover the Philadelphia-Camden-Wilmington, PA-NJ-DE-MD Metropolitan Statistical Area—see Appendix B for areas included
Source: U.S. Census Bureau, 2010-2012 American Community Survey 3-Year Estimates

Religious Groups by Family

Area	Catholic	Baptist	Non-Den.	Methodist[2]	Lutheran	LDS[3]	Pente-costal	Presby-terian[4]	Muslim[5]	Judaism
MSA[1]	33.5	3.9	2.9	3.0	1.9	0.3	0.9	2.1	1.3	1.4
U.S.	19.1	9.3	4.0	4.0	2.3	2.0	1.9	1.6	0.8	0.7

Note: Figures are the number of adherents as a percentage of the total population; (1) Figures cover the Philadelphia-Camden-Wilmington, PA-NJ-DE-MD Metropolitan Statistical Area—see Appendix B for areas included; (2) Methodist/Pietist; (3) Latter Day Saints; (4) Reformed; (5) Figures are estimates
Source: Association of Statisticians of American Religious Bodies, 2010 U.S. Religion Census: Religious Congregations & Membership Study

Religious Groups by Tradition

Area	Catholic	Evangelical Protestant	Mainline Protestant	Other Tradition	Black Protestant	Orthodox
MSA[1]	33.5	6.3	8.9	3.7	1.8	0.4
U.S.	19.1	16.2	7.3	4.3	1.6	0.3

Note: Figures are the number of adherents as a percentage of the total population; (1) Figures cover the Philadelphia-Camden-Wilmington, PA-NJ-DE-MD Metropolitan Statistical Area—see Appendix B for areas included
Source: Association of Statisticians of American Religious Bodies, 2010 U.S. Religion Census: Religious Congregations & Membership Study

ECONOMY

Gross Metropolitan Product

Area	2011	2012	2013	2014	Rank[2]
MSA[1]	352.3	364.0	373.9	388.4	8

Note: Figures are in billions of dollars; (1) Figures cover the Philadelphia-Camden-Wilmington, PA-NJ-DE-MD Metropolitan Statistical Area—see Appendix B for areas included; (2) Rank is based on 2014 data and ranges from 1 to 363
Source: The United States Conference of Mayors, U.S. Metro Economies: Outlook—Gross Metropolitan Product, with Metro Employment Projections, November 2013

Economic Growth

Area	2011 (%)	2012 (%)	2013 (%)	2014 (%)	Rank[2]
MSA[1]	1.1	1.5	1.4	2.0	121
U.S.	1.6	2.5	1.7	2.5	–

Note: Figures are real gross metropolitan product (GMP) growth rates and represent annual average percent change; (1) Figures cover the Philadelphia-Camden-Wilmington, PA-NJ-DE-MD Metropolitan Statistical Area—see Appendix B for areas included; (2) Rank is based on 2013 data and ranges from 1 to 363
Source: The United States Conference of Mayors, U.S. Metro Economies: Outlook—Gross Metropolitan Product, with Metro Employment Projections, November 2013

Metropolitan Area Exports

Area	2007	2008	2009	2010	2011	2012	Rank[2]
MSA[1]	18,881.5	21,683.2	19,067.4	22,710.0	26,155.8	22,991.6	13

Note: Figures are in millions of dollars; (1) Figures cover the Philadelphia-Camden-Wilmington, PA-NJ-DE-MD Metropolitan Statistical Area—see Appendix B for areas included; (2) Rank is based on 2012 data and ranges from 1 to 369
Source: U.S. Department of Commerce, International Trade Administration, Office of Trade & Industry Information, Manufacturing & Services, data extracted April 1, 2014

INCOME

Income

Area	Per Capita ($)	Median Household ($)	Average Household ($)
City	21,292	35,581	52,296
MSA[1]	31,569	60,444	82,361
U.S.	27,385	51,771	71,579

Note: (1) Figures cover the Philadelphia-Camden-Wilmington, PA-NJ-DE-MD Metropolitan Statistical Area—see Appendix B for areas included
Source: U.S. Census Bureau, 2010-2012 American Community Survey 3-Year Estimates

Household Income Distribution

Area	Percent of Households Earning							
	Under $15,000	$15,000 -24,999	$25,000 -34,999	$35,000 -49,999	$50,000 -74,999	$75,000 -99,000	$100,000 -149,999	$150,000 and up
City	23.9	13.6	11.8	13.2	15.9	8.9	7.8	4.8
MSA[1]	12.1	9.2	9.0	11.9	17.0	12.5	15.2	13.0
U.S.	13.1	11.0	10.5	13.7	18.1	11.9	12.5	9.1

Note: (1) Figures cover the Philadelphia-Camden-Wilmington, PA-NJ-DE-MD Metropolitan Statistical Area—see Appendix B for areas included
Source: U.S. Census Bureau, 2010-2012 American Community Survey 3-Year Estimates

Poverty Rate

Area	All Ages	Under 18 Years Old	18 to 64 Years Old	65 Years and Over
City	27.3	37.7	25.6	17.2
MSA[1]	13.2	17.8	12.5	8.7
U.S.	15.7	22.2	14.6	9.3

Note: Figures are percentage of people whose income during the past 12 months was below the poverty level; (1) Figures cover the Philadelphia-Camden-Wilmington, PA-NJ-DE-MD Metropolitan Statistical Area—see Appendix B for areas included
Source: U.S. Census Bureau, 2010-2012 American Community Survey 3-Year Estimates

Personal Bankruptcy Filing Rate

Area	2008	2009	2010	2011	2012	2013
Philadelphia County	2.02	1.88	2.32	2.04	1.97	2.09
U.S.	3.53	4.61	4.97	4.37	3.76	3.29

Note: Numbers are per 1,000 population and include Chapter 7 and Chapter 13 filings
Source: Federal Deposit Insurance Corporation, Regional Economic Conditions, March 20, 2014

EMPLOYMENT

Labor Force and Employment

Area	Civilian Labor Force			Workers Employed		
	Dec. 2012	Dec. 2013	% Chg.	Dec. 2012	Dec. 2013	% Chg.
City	660,276	642,317	-2.7	590,748	588,476	-0.4
MD[1]	2,005,235	1,960,037	-2.3	1,843,376	1,836,286	-0.4
U.S.	154,904,000	154,408,000	-0.3	143,060,000	144,423,000	1.0

Note: Data is not seasonally adjusted and covers workers 16 years of age and older; (1) Metropolitan Division—see Appendix B for areas included
Source: Bureau of Labor Statistics, Local Area Unemployment Statistics

Unemployment Rate

Area	2013											
	Jan.	Feb.	Mar.	Apr.	May	Jun.	Jul.	Aug.	Sep.	Oct.	Nov.	Dec.
City	11.8	10.6	10.1	9.6	10.1	10.4	10.9	11.1	10.2	10.2	9.6	8.4
MD[1]	9.3	8.5	8.0	7.5	7.9	8.2	8.3	8.4	7.5	7.5	7.2	6.3
U.S.	8.5	8.1	7.6	7.1	7.3	7.8	7.7	7.3	7.0	7.0	6.6	6.5

Note: Data is not seasonally adjusted and covers workers 16 years of age and older; All figures are percentages; (1) Metropolitan Division—see Appendix B for areas included
Source: Bureau of Labor Statistics, Local Area Unemployment Statistics

Employment by Occupation

Occupation Classification	City (%)	MSA[1] (%)	U.S. (%)
Management, Business, Science, and Arts	35.6	41.2	36.0
Natural Resources, Construction, and Maintenance	5.5	7.1	9.1
Production, Transportation, and Material Moving	10.5	9.5	12.0
Sales and Office	24.5	25.4	24.7
Service	23.9	16.9	18.2

Note: Figures cover employed civilians 16 years of age and older; (1) Figures cover the Philadelphia-Camden-Wilmington, PA-NJ-DE-MD Metropolitan Statistical Area—see Appendix B for areas included
Source: U.S. Census Bureau, 2010-2012 American Community Survey 3-Year Estimates

Employment by Industry

Sector	MD[1]		U.S.
	Number of Employees	Percent of Total	Percent of Total
Construction	n/a	n/a	4.2
Education and Health Services	438,100	22.8	15.5
Financial Activities	131,300	6.8	5.7
Government	217,000	11.3	16.1
Information	36,500	1.9	1.9
Leisure and Hospitality	165,100	8.6	10.2
Manufacturing	127,200	6.6	8.7
Mining and Logging	n/a	n/a	0.6
Other Services	84,300	4.4	3.9
Professional and Business Services	308,700	16.1	13.7
Retail Trade	200,700	10.4	11.4
Transportation and Utilities	63,700	3.3	3.8
Wholesale Trade	83,100	4.3	4.2

Note: Figures cover non-farm employment as of December 2013 and are not seasonally adjusted;
(1) Metropolitan Division—see Appendix B for areas included; n/a not available
Source: Bureau of Labor Statistics, Current Employment Statistics, Employment, Hours, and Earnings

Occupations with Greatest Projected Employment Growth: 2010 – 2020

Occupation[1]	2010 Employment	2020 Projected Employment	Numeric Employment Change	Percent Employment Change
Registered Nurses	136,470	159,610	23,140	17.0
Home Health Aides	67,900	89,820	21,920	32.3
Heavy and Tractor-Trailer Truck Drivers	71,510	83,040	11,530	16.1
Combined Food Preparation and Serving Workers, Including Fast Food	115,230	126,100	10,870	9.4
Personal Care Aides	36,860	47,130	10,280	27.9
Retail Salespersons	189,930	199,800	9,870	5.2
Office Clerks, General	151,450	160,950	9,490	6.3
Nursing Aides, Orderlies, and Attendants	78,080	86,470	8,390	10.8
Laborers and Freight, Stock, and Material Movers, Hand	102,590	110,170	7,590	7.4
Landscaping and Groundskeeping Workers	45,700	53,130	7,430	16.3

Note: Projections cover Pennsylvania; (1) Sorted by numeric employment change
Source: www.projectionscentral.com, State Occupational Projections, 2010–2020 Long-Term Projections

Fastest Growing Occupations: 2010 – 2020

Occupation[1]	2010 Employment	2020 Projected Employment	Numeric Employment Change	Percent Employment Change
Service Unit Operators, Oil, Gas, and Mining	1,040	2,130	1,090	104.6
Rotary Drill Operators, Oil and Gas	1,100	2,200	1,110	100.6
Derrick Operators, Oil and Gas	210	420	210	97.2
Roustabouts, Oil and Gas	1,170	2,290	1,120	95.5
Pump Operators, Except Wellhead Pumpers	700	1,250	550	78.5
Wellhead Pumpers	1,080	1,900	820	76.4
Petroleum Engineers	240	420	180	72.9
Gaming Dealers	1,920	3,280	1,360	71.0
Biomedical Engineers	960	1,560	600	62.6
Helpers—Extraction Workers	1,210	1,920	710	58.9

Note: Projections cover Pennsylvania; (1) Sorted by percent employment change and excludes occupations with numeric employment change less than 100
Source: www.projectionscentral.com, State Occupational Projections, 2010–2020 Long-Term Projections

Average Wages

Occupation	$/Hr.	Occupation	$/Hr.
Accountants and Auditors	37.58	Maids and Housekeeping Cleaners	11.45
Automotive Mechanics	19.91	Maintenance and Repair Workers	19.63
Bookkeepers	19.61	Marketing Managers	80.57
Carpenters	25.03	Nuclear Medicine Technologists	34.14
Cashiers	10.24	Nurses, Licensed Practical	23.18
Clerks, General Office	16.19	Nurses, Registered	35.07
Clerks, Receptionists/Information	13.60	Nursing Assistants	13.96
Clerks, Shipping/Receiving	16.57	Packers and Packagers, Hand	11.90
Computer Programmers	38.63	Physical Therapists	37.78
Computer Systems Analysts	44.47	Postal Service Mail Carriers	24.81
Computer User Support Specialists	24.11	Real Estate Brokers	64.60
Cooks, Restaurant	13.74	Retail Salespersons	13.07
Dentists	85.38	Sales Reps., Exc. Tech./Scientific	32.23
Electrical Engineers	46.41	Sales Reps., Tech./Scientific	49.82
Electricians	30.89	Secretaries, Exc. Legal/Med./Exec.	17.47
Financial Managers	72.36	Security Guards	12.30
First Line Supervisors/Managers, Sales	25.25	Surgeons	120.27
Food Preparation Workers	11.01	Teacher Assistants	12.90
General and Operations Managers	67.69	Teachers, Elementary School	30.40
Hairdressers/Cosmetologists	13.27	Teachers, Secondary School	31.60
Internists	101.37	Telemarketers	14.56
Janitors and Cleaners	13.88	Truck Drivers, Heavy/Tractor-Trailer	20.89
Landscaping/Groundskeeping Workers	14.88	Truck Drivers, Light/Delivery Svcs.	17.51
Lawyers	68.56	Waiters and Waitresses	10.38

Note: Wage data covers the Philadelphia, PA Metropolitan Division—see Appendix B for areas included. Hourly wages for elementary/secondary school teachers and teacher assistants were calculated by the editors from annual wage data assuming a 40 hour work week; n/a not available.
Source: Bureau of Labor Statistics, Metro Area Occupational Employment and Wage Estimates, May 2013

RESIDENTIAL REAL ESTATE

Building Permits

Area	Single-Family			Multi-Family			Total		
	2012	2013	Pct. Chg.	2012	2013	Pct. Chg.	2012	2013	Pct. Chg.
City	566	632	11.7	1,609	2,183	35.7	2,175	2,815	29.4
MSA[1]	5,175	6,252	20.8	4,095	4,965	21.2	9,270	11,217	21.0
U.S.	518,695	620,802	19.7	310,963	370,020	19.0	829,658	990,822	19.4

Note: (1) Metropolitan Statistical Area—see Appendix B for areas included; figures represent new, privately-owned housing units authorized (unadjusted data); All permit data are based on estimates with imputation.
Source: U.S. Census Bureau, Manufacturing, Mining, and Construction Statistics, Building Permits, 2012, 2013

Homeownership Rate

Area	2006 (%)	2007 (%)	2008 (%)	2009 (%)	2010 (%)	2011 (%)	2012 (%)	2013 (%)
MSA[1]	73.1	73.1	71.8	69.7	70.7	69.7	69.5	69.1
U.S.	68.8	68.1	67.8	67.4	66.9	66.1	65.4	65.1

Note: (1) Figures cover the Philadelphia-Camden-Wilmington, PA-NJ-DE-MD Metropolitan Statistical Area—see Appendix B for areas included
Source: U.S. Census Bureau, Housing Vacancies and Homeownership Annual Statistics: 2013

Housing Vacancy Rates

Area	Gross Vacancy Rate[2] (%)			Year-Round Vacancy Rate[3] (%)			Rental Vacancy Rate[4] (%)			Homeowner Vacancy Rate[5] (%)		
	2011	2012	2013	2011	2012	2013	2011	2012	2013	2011	2012	2013
MSA[1]	10.5	10.2	10.4	10.1	9.8	10.2	12.7	12.6	11.6	1.6	1.9	1.6
U.S.	14.2	13.8	13.8	11.1	10.8	10.7	9.5	8.7	8.3	2.5	2.0	2.0

Note: (1) Figures cover the Philadelphia-Camden-Wilmington, PA-NJ-DE-MD Metropolitan Statistical Area—see Appendix B for areas included; (2) The percentage of the total housing inventory that is vacant; (3) The percentage of the housing inventory (excluding seasonal units) that is year-round vacant; (4) The percentage of rental inventory that is vacant for rent; (5) The percentage of homeowner inventory that is vacant for sale
Source: U.S. Census Bureau, Housing Vacancies and Homeownership Annual Statistics: 2013

TAXES

State Corporate Income Tax Rates

State	Tax Rate (%)	Income Brackets ($)	Num. of Brackets	Financial Institution Tax Rate (%)[a]	Federal Income Tax Ded.
Pennsylvania	9.99	Flat rate	1	(a)	No

Note: Tax rates as of January 1, 2014; (a) Rates listed are the corporate income tax rate applied to financial institutions or excise taxes based on income. Some states have other taxes based upon the value of deposits or shares.
Source: Federation of Tax Administrators, "State Corporate Income Tax Rates, 2014"

State Individual Income Tax Rates

State	Tax Rate (%)	Income Brackets ($)	Num. of Brackets	Personal Exempt. ($)[1]		Fed. Inc. Tax Ded.
				Single	Dependents	
Pennsylvania	3.07	Flat rate	1	None		No

Note: Tax rates as of January 1, 2014; Local- and county-level taxes are not included; n/a not applicable; (1) Married joint filers generally receive double the single exemption
Source: Federation of Tax Administrators, "State Individual Income Tax Rates, 2014"

Various State and Local Tax Rates

State	State and Local Sales and Use (%)	State Sales and Use (%)	Gasoline[1] (¢/gal.)	Cigarette[2] ($/pack)	Spirits[3] ($/gal.)	Wine[4] ($/gal.)	Beer[5] ($/gal.)
Pennsylvania	8.0	6.00	41.80	1.600	7.21 (g)	(l)	0.08

Note: All tax rates as of January 1, 2014; (1) The American Petroleum Institute has developed a methodology for determining the average tax rate on a gallon of fuel. Rates may include any of the following: excise taxes, environmental fees, storage tank fees, other fees or taxes, general sales tax, and local taxes. In states where gasoline is subject to the general sales tax, or where the fuel tax is based on the average sale price, the average rate determined by API is sensitive to changes in the price of gasoline. States that fully or partially apply general sales taxes to gasoline: CA, CO, GA, IL, IN, MI, NY; (2) The federal excise tax of $1.0066 per pack and local taxes are not included; (3) Rates are those applicable to off-premise sales of 40% alcohol by volume (a.b.v.) distilled spirits in 750ml containers. Local excise taxes are excluded; (4) Rates are those applicable to off-premise sales of 11% a.b.v. non-carbonated wine in 750ml containers; (5) Rates are those applicable to off-premise sales of 4.7% a.b.v. beer in 12 ounce containers; (g) States where the government controls sales. In these "control states," products are subject to ad valorem mark-up and excise taxes. The excise tax rate is calculated using a methodology developed by the Distilled Spirits Council of the United States; (l) Control states, where the government controls all sales. Products can be subject to ad valorem mark-up and excise taxes.
Source: Tax Foundation, 2014 Facts & Figures: How Does Your State Compare?

State Business Tax Climate Index Rankings

State	Overall Rank	Corporate Tax Index Rank	Individual Income Tax Index Rank	Sales Tax Index Rank	Unemployment Insurance Tax Index Rank	Property Tax Index Rank
Pennsylvania	24	46	16	19	39	43

Note: The index is a measure of how each state's tax laws affect economic performance. The lower the rank, the more favorable a state's tax system is for business. States without a given tax are given a ranking of 1. The scores/rankings for the District of Columbia do not affect other states. The 2014 index represents the tax climate as of July 1, 2013.
Source: Tax Foundation, State Business Tax Climate Index 2014

COMMERCIAL REAL ESTATE

Office Market

Market Area	Inventory (sq. ft.)	Vacancy Rate (%)	Under Construction (sq. ft.)	YTD Net Absorption (sq. ft.)	Total Average Asking Rent ($/sq. ft./year)
Philadelphia	106,366,429	16.1	1,144,836	534,599	24.98
National	4,726,900,879	15.0	55,419,286	42,829,434	26.27

Source: Newmark Grubb Knight Frank, National Office Market Report, 4th Quarter 2013

Industrial/Warehouse/R&D Market

Market Area	Inventory (sq. ft.)	Vacancy Rate (%)	Under Construction (sq. ft.)	YTD Net Absorption (sq. ft.)	Total Average Asking Rent ($/sq. ft./year)
Philadelphia	483,693,026	9.4	2,093,013	796,571	4.91
National	14,022,031,238	7.9	83,249,164	156,549,903	5.40

Source: Newmark Grubb Knight Frank, National Industrial Market Report, 4th Quarter 2013

COMMERCIAL UTILITIES

Typical Monthly Electric Bills

Area	Commercial Service ($/month)		Industrial Service ($/month)	
	1,500 kWh	40 kW demand 14,000 kWh	1,000 kW demand 200,000 kWh	50,000 kW demand 15,000,000 kWh
City	191	1,410	16,431	1,094,477
Average[1]	197	1,636	25,662	1,485,307

Note: Based on total rates in effect July 1, 2013; (1) average based on 180 utilities surveyed
Source: Edison Electric Institute, Typical Bills and Average Rates Report, Summer 2013

TRANSPORTATION

Means of Transportation to Work

Area	Car/Truck/Van		Public Transportation			Bicycle	Walked	Other Means	Worked at Home
	Drove Alone	Car-pooled	Bus	Subway	Railroad				
City	49.9	9.0	18.7	4.4	2.7	2.0	8.6	1.5	3.0
MSA[1]	73.6	8.0	5.5	1.5	2.2	0.6	3.7	0.9	4.0
U.S.	76.4	9.7	2.6	1.7	0.5	0.6	2.8	1.3	4.3

Note: Figures are percentages and cover workers 16 years of age and older; (1) Figures cover the Philadelphia-Camden-Wilmington, PA-NJ-DE-MD Metropolitan Statistical Area—see Appendix B for areas included
Source: U.S. Census Bureau, 2010-2012 American Community Survey 3-Year Estimates

Travel Time to Work

Area	Less Than 10 Minutes	10 to 19 Minutes	20 to 29 Minutes	30 to 44 Minutes	45 to 59 Minutes	60 to 89 Minutes	90 Minutes or More
City	6.3	20.8	20.1	27.0	12.9	9.2	3.7
MSA[1]	10.2	25.8	20.3	22.9	10.4	7.4	2.9
U.S.	13.5	29.8	20.9	20.1	7.5	5.6	2.5

Note: Figures are percentages and include workers 16 years old and over; (1) Figures cover the Philadelphia-Camden-Wilmington, PA-NJ-DE-MD Metropolitan Statistical Area—see Appendix B for areas included
Source: U.S. Census Bureau, 2010-2012 American Community Survey 3-Year Estimates

Travel Time Index

Area	1985	1990	1995	2000	2005	2010	2011
Urban Area[1]	1.14	1.16	1.17	1.22	1.27	1.26	1.26
Average[2]	1.09	1.14	1.16	1.19	1.23	1.18	1.18

Note: Travel Time Index—the ratio of travel time in the peak period to the travel time at free-flow conditions. For example, a value of 1.30 indicates a 20-minute free-flow trip takes 26 minutes in the peak. Free-flow speeds (60 mph on freeways and 35 mph on principal arterials) are used as the comparison threshold; (1) Covers the Philadelphia PA-NJ-DE-MD urban area; (2) average of 498 urban areas
Source: Texas Transportation Institute, Urban Mobility Report 2012, December 2012

Public Transportation

Agency Name / Mode of Transportation	Vehicles Operated in Maximum Service	Annual Unlinked Passenger Trips (in thous.)	Annual Passenger Miles (in thous.)
Southeastern Pennsylvania Transportation Authority (SEPTA)			
Bus (directly operated)	1,176	189,040.2	561,647.3
Commuter Rail (directly operated)	327	36,899.2	522,945.7
Demand Response (purchased transportation)	368	1,755.6	11,417.5
Heavy Rail (directly operated)	285	102,796.2	456,868.2
Streetcar Rail (directly operated)	126	26,054.9	65,533.7
Trolleybus (directly operated)	30	6,951.6	13,808.2

Source: Federal Transit Administration, National Transit Database, 2012

Air Transportation

Airport Name and Code / Type of Service	Passenger Airlines[1]	Passenger Enplanements	Freight Carriers[2]	Freight (lbs.)
Philadelphia International (PHL)				
Domestic service (U.S. carriers - 2013)	36	12,765,325	21	291,042,676
International service (U.S. carriers - 2012)	10	1,652,711	13	120,019,465

Note: (1) Includes all U.S.-based major, minor and commuter airlines that carried at least one passenger during the year; (2) Includes all U.S.-based airlines and freight carriers that transported at least one lb. of freight during the year.
Source: Bureau of Transportation Statistics, The Intermodal Transportation Database, Air Carriers: T-100 Domestic Market (U.S. Carriers), 2013; Bureau of Transportation Statistics, The Intermodal Transportation Database, Air Carriers: T-100 International Market (U.S. Carriers), 2012

Other Transportation Statistics

Major Highways:	I-76; I-95
Amtrak Service:	Yes
Major Waterways/Ports:	Port of Philadelphia

Source: Amtrak.com; Google Maps

BUSINESSES

Major Business Headquarters

Company Name	Rankings	
	Fortune[1]	Forbes[2]
Aramark	205	20
Cigna	103	-
Comcast	46	-
Crown Holdings	312	-

Note: (1) Fortune 500—companies that produce a 10-K are ranked 1 to 500 based on 2012 revenue; (2) all private companies with at least $2 billion in annual revenue through the end of their most current fiscal year are ranked 1 to 224; companies listed are headquartered in the city; dashes indicate no ranking
Source: Fortune, "Fortune 500," May 20, 2013; Forbes, "America's Largest Private Companies," December 18, 2013

Fast-Growing Businesses

According to *Initiative for a Competitive Inner City (ICIC)*, Philadelphia is home to six of America's 100 fastest-growing "inner city" companies: **Sovereign Security** (#11); **PrintFresh** (#23); **Vynamic** (#27); **SEER Interactive** (#34); **Recovery Networks** (#45); **Azavea** (#79). Companies were ranked by their five-year compound annual growth rate. Criteria for inclusion: company must be headquartered in or have 51 percent or more of its physical operations in an economically distressed urban area; must be an independent, for-profit corporation, partnership or proprietorship; must have 10 or more employees and have a five-year sales history that includes sales of at least $200,000 in the base year and at least $1 million in the current year with no decrease in sales over the two most recent years. *Initiative for a Competitive Inner City (ICIC), "Inner City 100 Companies, 2013"*

According to Deloitte, Philadelphia is home to two of North America's 500 fastest-growing high-technology companies: **InstaMed** (#201); **PHD Virtual** (#353). Companies are ranked by percentage growth in revenue over a five-year period. Criteria for inclusion: company must be headquartered within North America; must own proprietary intellectual property or proprietary technology that contributes to a significant portion of the company's operating revenue, or devote a significant proportion of revenues to research and development of technology; must have been in business for a minumum of five years with 2008 operating revenues of at least $50,000 USD/CD and 2012 operating revenues of at least $5 million USD/CD. *Deloitte Touche Tohmatsu, 2013 Technology Fast 500*[TM]

Minority Business Opportunity

Philadelphia is home to two companies which are on the *Black Enterprise* Industrial/Service 100 list (100 largest companies based on gross sales): **PRWT Services** (#32); **Alpha Office Supplies** (#69). Criteria: operational in previous calendar year; at least 51% black-owned and manufactures/owns the product it sells or provides industrial or consumer services. Brokerages, real estate firms and firms that provide professional services are not eligible. *Black Enterprise, B.E. 100s, 2013*

Philadelphia is home to one company which is on the *Black Enterprise* Bank 20 list (20 largest banks based on total assets, capital, deposits and loans, including mortgage-backed securities for the calendar year): **United Bancshares Inc. (United Bank of Philadelphia)** (#18). Only commercial banks or savings and loans that are classified by the Federal Reserve as black institutions and have been fully operational for the previous calendar year were considered. *Black Enterprise, B.E. 100s, 2013*

Philadelphia is home to one company which is on the *Black Enterprise* Asset Manager 15 list (15 largest asset management firms based on assets under management): **The Swarthmore Group** (#15). Criteria: company must have been operational in previous calendar year and be at least 51% black-owned. *Black Enterprise, B.E. 100s, 2013*

Minority- and Women-Owned Businesses

Group	All Firms		Firms with Paid Employees			
	Firms	Sales ($000)	Firms	Sales ($000)	Employees	Payroll ($000)
Asian	8,494	2,068,234	2,660	1,873,142	11,805	247,319
Black	19,835	1,255,413	1,136	850,136	7,757	236,853
Hispanic	6,877	405,691	517	224,345	2,608	56,746
Women	27,983	3,391,854	3,061	2,745,244	25,673	742,052
All Firms	88,140	139,547,777	20,363	136,959,558	576,631	26,717,495

Note: Figures cover firms located in the city; minority- and women-owned business are defined as firms in which the corresponding group own 51% or more of the stock or equity of the company
Source: U.S. Census Bureau, 2007 Economic Census, Survey of Business Owners (2012 Survey of Business Owners data will be released starting in June 2015)

HOTELS & CONVENTION CENTERS

Hotels/Motels

Area	5 Star		4 Star		3 Star		2 Star		1 Star		Not Rated	
	Num.	Pct.[3]	Num.	Pct.[3]	Num.	Pct.[3]	Num.	Pct.[3]	Num.	Pct.[3]	Num.	Pct.[3]
City[1]	2	0.8	14	5.5	110	43.5	99	39.1	7	2.8	21	8.3
Total[2]	142	0.9	1,005	6.0	5,147	30.9	8,578	51.4	408	2.4	1,397	8.4

Note: (1) Figures cover Philadelphia and vicinity; (2) Figures cover all 100 cities in this book; (3) Percentage of hotels which have a given star rating; Star ratings are determined by expedia.com and offer an indication of the general quality of a particular hotel.
Source: expedia.com, April 7, 2014

The Philadelphia, PA metro area is home to three of the best hotels in the U.S. according to *Travel & Leisure*: **Four Seasons Hotel, Philadelphia**; **Ritz-Carlton, Philadelphia**; **The Rittenhouse Hotel**. Criteria: service; location; rooms; food; and value. The list includes the top 200 hotels in the U.S. *Travel & Leisure, "T+L 500, The World's Best Hotels 2014"*

The Philadelphia, PA metro area is home to one of the best hotels in the world according to *Condé Nast Traveler*: **Rittenhouse Hotel**. The selections are based on over 79,000 responses to the magazine's annual Readers' Choice Survey. The list includes the top 200 hotels in the U.S. *Condé Nast Traveler, "Gold List 2014, The World's Best Places to Stay"*

Major Convention Centers

Name	Overall Space (sq. ft.)	Exhibit Space (sq. ft.)	Meeting Space (sq. ft.)	Meeting Rooms
Pennsylvania Convention Center	1,000,000	700,000	246,000	73

Note: Table includes convention centers located in the Philadelphia-Camden-Wilmington, PA-NJ-DE-MD metro area; n/a not available
Source: Original research

Living Environment

COST OF LIVING

Cost of Living Index

Composite Index	Groceries	Housing	Utilities	Trans-portation	Health Care	Misc. Goods/Services
120.8	112.8	141.9	128.2	105.1	100.0	114.3

Note: The Cost of Living Index measures regional differences in the cost of consumer goods and services, excluding taxes and non-consumer expenditures, for professional and managerial households in the top income quintile. It is based on more than 50,000 prices covering almost 60 different items for which prices are collected three times a year by chambers of commerce, economic development organizations or university applied economic centers in each participating urban area. The numbers shown should be read as a percentage above or below the national average of 100. For example, a value of 115.4 in the groceries column indicates that grocery prices are 15.4% higher than the national average. Small differences in the index numbers should not be interpreted as significant; Figures cover the Philadelphia PA urban area.
Source: The Council for Community and Economic Research, ACCRA Cost of Living Index, 2013

Grocery Prices

Area[1]	T-Bone Steak ($/pound)	Frying Chicken ($/pound)	Whole Milk ($/half gal.)	Eggs ($/dozen)	Orange Juice ($/64 oz.)	Coffee ($/11.5 oz.)
City[2]	10.56	1.73	2.10	2.30	3.89	4.64
Avg.	10.19	1.28	2.34	1.81	3.48	4.39
Min.	8.56	0.94	1.44	1.19	2.78	3.40
Max.	14.82	2.28	3.56	3.73	6.23	7.32

*Note: (1) Values for the local area are compared with the average, minimum and maximum values for all 327 areas in the Cost of Living Index; (2) Figures cover the Philadelphia PA urban area; **T-Bone Steak** (price per pound); **Frying Chicken** (price per pound, whole fryer); **Whole Milk** (half gallon carton); **Eggs** (price per dozen, Grade A, large); **Orange Juice** (64 oz. Tropicana or Florida Natural); **Coffee** (11.5 oz. can, vacuum-packed, Maxwell House, Hills Bros, or Folgers).*
Source: The Council for Community and Economic Research, ACCRA Cost of Living Index, 2013

Housing and Utility Costs

Area[1]	New Home Price ($)	Apartment Rent ($/month)	All Electric ($/month)	Part Electric ($/month)	Other Energy ($/month)	Telephone ($/month)
City[2]	413,372	1,263	-	123.19	74.37	38.50
Avg.	295,864	900	171.38	91.82	70.12	27.73
Min.	185,506	458	117.80	48.81	33.67	17.16
Max.	1,358,917	3,783	441.68	171.40	372.65	39.47

*Note: (1) Values for the local area are compared with the average, minimum and maximum values for all 327 areas in the Cost of Living Index; (2) Figures cover the Philadelphia PA urban area; **New Home Price** (2,400 sf living area, 8,000 sf lot, in urban area with full utilities); **Apartment Rent** (950 sf 2 bedroom/1.5 or 2 bath, unfurnished, excluding all utilities except water); **All Electric** (average monthly cost for an all-electric home); **Part Electric** (average monthly cost for a part-electric home); **Other Energy** (average monthly cost for natural gas, fuel oil, coal, wood, and any other forms of energy except electricity); **Telephone** (price includes basic monthly rate for a private residential line plus additional local usage charges incurred by a family of four).*
Source: The Council for Community and Economic Research, ACCRA Cost of Living Index, 2013

Health Care, Transportation, and Other Costs

Area[1]	Doctor ($/visit)	Dentist ($/visit)	Optometrist ($/visit)	Gasoline ($/gallon)	Beauty Salon ($/visit)	Men's Shirt ($)
City[2]	118.09	94.76	100.24	3.48	52.14	39.08
Avg.	101.40	86.48	96.16	3.44	33.87	26.55
Min.	61.67	50.83	50.12	3.08	18.92	12.48
Max.	182.71	152.50	223.78	4.33	68.22	52.03

*Note: (1) Values for the local area are compared with the average, minimum and maximum values for all 327 areas in the Cost of Living Index; (2) Figures cover the Philadelphia PA urban area; **Doctor** (general practitioners routine exam of an established patient); **Dentist** (adult teeth cleaning and periodic oral examination); **Optometrist** (full vision eye exam for established adult patient); **Gasoline** (one gallon regular unleaded, national brand, including all taxes, cash price at self-service pump if available); **Beauty Salon** (woman's shampoo, trim, and blow-dry); **Men's Shirt** (cotton/polyester dress shirt, pinpoint weave, long sleeves).*
Source: The Council for Community and Economic Research, ACCRA Cost of Living Index, 2013

HOUSING

House Price Index (HPI)

Area	National Ranking[2]	Quarterly Change (%)	One-Year Change (%)	Five-Year Change (%)
MD[1]	138	0.85	2.28	-4.79
U.S.[3]	–	1.20	7.69	4.18

Note: The HPI is a weighted repeat sales index. It measures average price changes in repeat sales or refinancings on the same properties. This information is obtained by reviewing repeat mortgage transactions on single-family properties whose mortgages have been purchased or securitized by Fannie Mae or Freddie Mac in January 1975; (1) Philadelphia, PA Metropolitan Division—see Appendix B for areas included; (2) Rankings are based on annual percentage change for all metro areas containing at least 15,000 transactions over the last 10 years and ranges from 1 to 283; (3) figures based on a weighted average of Census Division estimates using a seasonally adjusted, purchase-only index; all figures are for the period ending December 31, 2013
Source: Federal Housing Finance Agency, House Price Index, February 25, 2014

Median Single-Family Home Prices

Area	2011	2012	2013p	Percent Change 2012 to 2013
MSA[1]	210.1	213.4	220.3	3.2
U.S. Average	166.2	177.2	197.4	11.4

Note: Figures are median sales prices of existing single-family homes in thousands of dollars; (p) preliminary; n/a not available; (1) Philadelphia-Camden-Wilmington, PA-NJ-DE-MD Metropolitan Statistical Area—see Appendix B for areas included
Source: National Association of Realtors, Median Sales Price of Existing Single-Family Homes for Metropolitan Areas, 4th Quarter 2013

Qualifying Income Based on Median Sales Price of Existing Single-Family Homes

Area	With 5% Down ($)	With 10% Down ($)	With 20% Down ($)
MSA[1]	49,407	46,807	41,606
U.S. Average	45,395	43,006	38,228

Note: Figures are preliminary; Qualifying income is based on a mortgage rate of 4.4%. Monthly principal and interest payment is limited to 25% of income; n/a not available; (1) Philadelphia-Camden-Wilmington, PA-NJ-DE-MD Metropolitan Statistical Area—see Appendix B for areas included
Source: National Association of Realtors, Qualifying Income Based on Median Sales Price of Existing Single-Family Homes for Metropolitan Areas, 4th Quarter 2013

Median Apartment Condo-Coop Home Prices

Area	2011	2012	2013p	Percent Change 2012 to 2013
MSA[1]	174.6	170.6	175.5	2.9
U.S. Average	165.1	173.7	194.9	12.2

Note: Figures are median sales prices of existing apartment condo-coop homes in thousands of dollars; (p) preliminary; n/a not available; (1) Philadelphia-Camden-Wilmington, PA-NJ-DE-MD Metropolitan Statistical Area—see Appendix B for areas included
Source: National Association of Realtors, Median Sales Price of Existing Apartment Condo-Coop Homes for Metropolitan Areas, 4th Quarter 2013

Gross Monthly Rent

Area	Under $200	$200 -299	$300 -499	$500 -749	$750 -999	$1,000 -1,499	$1,500 and up	Median ($)
City	3.0	4.2	7.4	19.9	29.7	25.8	9.9	874
MSA[1]	2.0	3.0	5.2	14.7	27.7	32.8	14.7	977
U.S.	1.7	3.3	8.1	22.7	24.3	25.7	14.3	889

Note: Figures are percentages except for Median; Gross rent is the contract rent plus the estimated average monthly cost of utilities (electricity, gas, and water and sewer) and fuels (oil, coal, kerosene, wood, etc.) if these are paid by the renter (or paid for the renter by someone else); (1) Figures cover the Philadelphia-Camden-Wilmington, PA-NJ-DE-MD Metropolitan Statistical Area—see Appendix B for areas included
Source: U.S. Census Bureau, 2010-2012 American Community Survey 3-Year Estimates

Year Housing Structure Built

Area	2010 or Later	2000 -2009	1990 -1999	1980 -1989	1970 -1979	1960 -1969	1950 -1959	1940 -1949	Before 1940	Median Year
City	0.2	3.5	2.7	3.8	7.0	10.7	16.8	15.1	40.3	1946
MSA[1]	0.3	8.4	8.9	10.0	12.5	12.3	16.1	9.2	22.3	1962
U.S.	0.5	14.9	13.8	13.9	15.9	11.1	10.9	5.5	13.5	1976

Note: Figures are percentages except for Median Year; (1) Figures cover the Philadelphia-Camden-Wilmington, PA-NJ-DE-MD Metropolitan Statistical Area—see Appendix B for areas included
Source: U.S. Census Bureau, 2010-2012 American Community Survey 3-Year Estimates

HEALTH

Health Risk Data

Category	MD[1] (%)	U.S. (%)
Adults aged 18–64 who have any kind of health care coverage	79.4	79.6
Adults who reported being in good or excellent health	81.6	83.1
Adults who are current smokers	23.2	19.6
Adults who are heavy drinkers[2]	7.0	6.1
Adults who are binge drinkers[3]	19.3	16.9
Adults who are overweight (BMI 25.0 - 29.9)	35.8	35.8
Adults who are obese (BMI 30.0 - 99.8)	26.9	27.6
Adults who participated in any physical activities in the past month	74.1	77.1
Adults 50+ who have ever had a sigmoidoscopy or colonoscopy	71.0	67.3
Women aged 40+ who have had a mammogram within the past two years	79.3	74.0
Men aged 40+ who have had a PSA test within the past two years	46.3	45.2
Adults aged 65+ who have had flu shot within the past year	54.0	60.1
Adults who always wear a seatbelt	84.5	93.8

Note: Data as of 2012 unless otherwise noted; (1) Figures cover the Philadelphia, PA Metropolitan Division—see Appendix B for areas included; (2) Heavy drinkers are classified as males having more than two drinks per day or females having more than one drink per day; (3) Binge drinkers are classified as males having five or more drinks on one occasion or females having four or more drinks on one occasion
Source: Centers for Disease Control and Prevention, Behaviorial Risk Factor Surveillance System, SMART: Selected Metropolitan/Micropolitan Area Risk Trends, 2012

Chronic Health Indicators

Category	MD[1] (%)	U.S. (%)
Adults who have ever been told they had a heart attack	4.5	4.5
Adults who have ever been told they had a stroke	3.1	2.9
Adults who have been told they currently have asthma	10.8	8.9
Adults who have ever been told they have arthritis	24.8	25.7
Adults who have ever been told they have diabetes[2]	11.2	9.7
Adults who have ever been told they had skin cancer	4.0	5.7
Adults who have ever been told they had any other types of cancer	5.8	6.5
Adults who have ever been told they have COPD	6.3	6.2
Adults who have ever been told they have kidney disease	2.3	2.5
Adults who have ever been told they have a form of depression	17.8	18.0

Note: Data as of 2012 unless otherwise noted; (1) Figures cover the Philadelphia, PA Metropolitan Division—see Appendix B for areas included; (2) Figures do not include pregnancy-related, borderline, or pre-diabetes
Source: Centers for Disease Control and Prevention, Behaviorial Risk Factor Surveillance System, SMART: Selected Metropolitan/Micropolitan Area Risk Trends, 2012

Mortality Rates for the Top 10 Causes of Death in the U.S.

ICD-10[a] Sub-Chapter	ICD-10[a] Code	Age-Adjusted Mortality Rate[1] per 100,000 population	
		County[2]	U.S.
Malignant neoplasms	C00-C97	215.5	174.2
Ischaemic heart diseases	I20-I25	137.4	119.1
Other forms of heart disease	I30-I51	66.5	49.6
Chronic lower respiratory diseases	J40-J47	38.5	43.2
Cerebrovascular diseases	I60-I69	46.3	40.3
Organic, including symptomatic, mental disorders	F01-F09	33.6	30.5
Other degenerative diseases of the nervous system	G30-G31	12.3	26.3
Other external causes of accidental injury	W00-X59	37.5	25.1
Diabetes mellitus	E10-E14	22.1	21.3
Hypertensive diseases	I10-I15	33.0	18.8

Note: (a) ICD-10 = International Classification of Diseases 10th Revision; (1) Mortality rates are a three year average covering 2008-2010; (2) Figures cover Philadelphia County
Source: Centers for Disease Control and Prevention, National Center for Health Statistics. Compressed Mortality File 1999-2010 on CDC WONDER Online Database, released January 2013. Data are compiled from the Compressed Mortality File 1999-2010, Series 20 No. 2P, 2013.

Mortality Rates for Selected Causes of Death

ICD-10[a] Sub-Chapter	ICD-10[a] Code	Age-Adjusted Mortality Rate[1] per 100,000 population	
		County[2]	U.S.
Assault	X85-Y09	18.5	5.5
Diseases of the liver	K70-K76	15.4	12.4
Human immunodeficiency virus (HIV) disease	B20-B24	9.5	3.0
Influenza and pneumonia	J09-J18	16.0	16.4
Intentional self-harm	X60-X84	10.5	11.8
Malnutrition	E40-E46	0.5	0.8
Obesity and other hyperalimentation	E65-E68	1.7	1.6
Renal failure	N17-N19	22.4	13.6
Transport accidents	V01-V99	8.3	12.6
Viral hepatitis	B15-B19	3.9	2.2

Note: (a) ICD-10 = International Classification of Diseases 10th Revision; (1) Mortality rates are a three year average covering 2008-2010; (2) Figures cover Philadelphia County
Source: Centers for Disease Control and Prevention, National Center for Health Statistics. Compressed Mortality File 1999-2010 on CDC WONDER Online Database, released January 2013. Data are compiled from the Compressed Mortality File 1999-2010, Series 20 No. 2P, 2013.

Health Insurance Coverage

Area	With Health Insurance	With Private Health Insurance	With Public Health Insurance	Without Health Insurance	Population Under Age 18 Without Health Insurance
City	85.6	55.1	40.8	14.4	4.8
MSA[1]	90.0	72.3	29.4	10.0	4.1
U.S.	84.9	65.4	30.4	15.1	7.5

Note: Figures are percentages that cover the civilian noninstitutionalized population; (1) Figures cover the Philadelphia-Camden-Wilmington, PA-NJ-DE-MD Metropolitan Statistical Area—see Appendix B for areas included
Source: U.S. Census Bureau, 2010-2012 American Community Survey 3-Year Estimates

Number of Medical Professionals

Area[1]	MDs[2]	DOs[2,3]	Dentists	Podiatrists	Chiropractors	Optometrists
Local (number)	7,985	720	972	244	228	223
Local (rate[4])	519.0	46.8	62.8	15.8	14.7	14.4
U.S. (rate[4])	267.6	19.6	61.7	5.6	24.7	14.5

Note: Data as of 2012 unless noted; (1) Local data covers Philadelphia County; (2) Data as of 2011; (3) Doctor of Osteopathic Medicine; (4) rate per 100,000 population
Source: Area Resource File (ARF) 2012-2013. U.S. Department of Health and Human Services, Health Resources and Services Administration, Bureau of Health Professions

Best Hospitals

According to *U.S. News,* the Philadelphia, PA metro area is home to eight of the best hospitals in the U.S.: **Fox Chase Cancer Center** (1 specialty); **Hospital of the University of Pennsylvania** (Honor Roll/13 specialties); **MossRehab-Elkins Park** (1 specialty); **Pennsylvania Hospital** (1 specialty); **Thomas Jefferson University Hospital** (Honor Roll/12 specialties); **Wills Eye Hospital** (1 specialty); **Penn Presbyterian Medical Center** (2 specialties); **Hahnemann University Hospital** (5 specialties). The hospitals listed were nationally ranked in at least one adult specialty. Only 147 hospitals nationwide were nationally ranked in one or more specialties. Eighteen hospitals in the U.S. made the Honor Roll by ranking near the top in at least six specialties.*U.S. News Online, "America's Best Hospitals 2013-14"*

According to *U.S. News,* the Philadelphia, PA metro area is home to one of the best children's hospitals in the U.S.: **Children's Hospital of Philadelphia** (Honor Roll). The hospital listed was highly ranked in at least one pediatric specialty. Eighty-seven hospitals in the U.S. ranked in at least one specialty. Ten children's hospitals in the U.S. made the Honor Roll by ranking near the top in three or more specialties.*U.S. News Online, "America's Best Children's Hospitals 2013-14"*

EDUCATION

Public School District Statistics

District Name	Schls	Pupils	Pupil/ Teacher Ratio	Minority Pupils[1] (%)	Free Lunch Eligible[2] (%)	IEP[3] (%)
Philadelphia City SD	251	154,262	16.6	86.2	77.5	16.0

Note: Table includes school districts with 2,000 or more students; (1) Percentage of students that are not non-Hispanic white; (2) Percentage of students that are eligible for the free lunch program; (3) Percentage of students that have an Individualized Education Program.
Source: U.S. Department of Education, National Center for Education Statistics, Common Core of Data, Local Education Agency (School District) Universe Survey: School Year 2011-2012; U.S. Department of Education, National Center for Education Statistics, Common Core of Data, Public Elementary/Secondary School Universe Survey: School Year 2011-2012

Best High Schools

High School Name	Rank[1]	Grad. Rate[2] (%)	Coll.[3] (%)	AP/IB/ AICE Tests[4]	AP/IB/ AICE Score[5]	SAT Score[6]	ACT Score[6]
Academy at Palumbo	1114	91	93	0.5	3.0	1385	21.0
Central H.S.	557	98	99	0.5	2.6	1641	23.9
G.W. Carver H.S. of Engineering and Science	1739	94	94	0.0	1.6	1382	20.0
Julia R. Masterman Laboratory and Demonstration School	56	100	100	1.0	4.0	1925	n/a
MaST Community Charter School	702	100	95	0.3	3.5	1495	22.6
Mastery Charter School Thomas Campus	1733	86	99	0.3	1.7	1240	n/a
Mastery Charter Schools Lenfest Campus	1569	88	99	0.2	1.7	1183	28.0

Note: (1) Public schools are ranked from 1 to 2,000 based on the following self-reported statistics (with the corresponding weight used in calculating their overall score). Schools that were newly founded and did not have a graduating senior class in 2012 were excluded; (2) Four-year, on-time graduation rate (25%); (3) Percent of 2011 graduates who were accepted to college (25%); (4) AP/IB/AICE tests taken per student (25%); (5) Average AP/IB/AICE exam score (10%); (6) Average SAT and/or ACT score (10%); Percent of students enrolled in at least one AP/IB/AICE course (5%)—data not shown; n/a not available
Source: Newsweek and The Daily Beast, "America's Best High Schools 2013"

Highest Level of Education

Area	Less than H.S.	H.S. Diploma	Some College, No Deg.	Associate Degree	Bachelor's Degree	Master's Degree	Prof. School Degree	Doctorate Degree
City	19.3	34.7	17.4	5.0	13.6	6.3	2.3	1.3
MSA[1]	11.3	31.0	17.9	6.5	20.2	9.0	2.5	1.6
U.S.	14.1	28.3	21.3	7.8	18.0	7.5	1.9	1.2

Note: Figures cover persons age 25 and over; (1) Figures cover the Philadelphia-Camden-Wilmington, PA-NJ-DE-MD Metropolitan Statistical Area—see Appendix B for areas included
Source: U.S. Census Bureau, 2010-2012 American Community Survey 3-Year Estimates

Educational Attainment by Race

Area	High School Graduate or Higher (%)					Bachelor's Degree or Higher (%)				
	Total	White	Black	Asian	Hisp.[2]	Total	White	Black	Asian	Hisp.[2]
City	80.7	86.1	79.9	67.5	60.6	23.5	33.6	12.8	34.3	10.6
MSA[1]	88.7	91.6	83.6	82.1	66.3	33.4	37.2	17.3	53.5	14.4
U.S.	85.9	88.1	82.5	85.5	63.1	28.6	30.0	18.4	50.2	13.4

Note: Figures shown cover persons 25 years old and over; (1) Figures cover the
Philadelphia-Camden-Wilmington, PA-NJ-DE-MD Metropolitan Statistical Area—see Appendix B for areas
included; (2) People of Hispanic origin can be of any race
Source: U.S. Census Bureau, 2010-2012 American Community Survey 3-Year Estimates

School Enrollment by Grade and Control

Area	Preschool (%)		Kindergarten (%)		Grades 1 - 4 (%)		Grades 5 - 8 (%)		Grades 9 - 12 (%)	
	Public	Private	Public	Private	Public	Private	Public	Private	Public	Private
City	59.2	40.8	82.6	17.4	80.8	19.2	79.1	20.9	82.7	17.3
MSA[1]	43.5	56.5	79.4	20.6	84.3	15.7	83.3	16.7	84.0	16.0
U.S.	56.9	43.1	87.8	12.2	89.9	10.1	90.0	10.0	90.8	9.2

Note: Figures shown cover persons 3 years old and over; (1) Figures cover the
Philadelphia-Camden-Wilmington, PA-NJ-DE-MD Metropolitan Statistical Area—see Appendix B for areas
included
Source: U.S. Census Bureau, 2010-2012 American Community Survey 3-Year Estimates

Average Salaries of Public School Classroom Teachers

Area	2012-13		2013-14		Percent Change 2012-13 to 2013-14	Percent Change 2003-04 to 2013-14
	Dollars	Rank[1]	Dollars	Rank[1]		
Pennsylvania	62,994	10	64,072	10	1.71	21.8
U.S. Average	56,103	–	56,689	–	1.04	21.8

Note: (1) State rank ranges from 1 to 51 where 1 indicates highest salary.
Source: National Education Association, Rankings & Estimates: Rankings of the States 2013 and Estimates of
School Statistics 2014, March 2014

Higher Education

Four-Year Colleges			Two-Year Colleges			Medical Schools[1]	Law Schools[2]	Voc/ Tech[3]
Public	Private Non-profit	Private For-profit	Public	Private Non-profit	Private For-profit			
1	18	2	1	3	11	5	3	6

Note: Figures cover institutions located within the city limits and include main campuses only; (1) includes
schools accredited by the Liaison Committee on Medical Education and the American Osteopathic Association's
Commission on Osteopathic College Accreditation; (2) includes ABA-accredited schools, schools with
provisional ABA accreditation, and state accredited schools; (3) includes all schools with programs that are less
than 2 years.
Source: National Center for Education Statistics, Integrated Postsecondary Education System (IPEDS),
2012-13; Association of American Medical Colleges, Member List, April 24, 2014; American Osteopathic
Association, Member List, April 24, 2014; Law School Admission Council, Official Guide to ABA-Approved
Law Schools Online, April 24, 2014; Wikipedia, List of Medical Schools in the United States, April 24, 2014;
Wikipedia, List of Law Schools in the United States, April 24, 2014

According to U.S. News & World Report, the Philadelphia, PA metro division is home to four of
the best national universities in the U.S.: **University of Pennsylvania** (#7); **Drexel University**
(#97); **Temple University** (#121); **Widener University** (#181). The indicators used to capture
academic quality fall into a number of categories: assessment by administrators at peer institutions;
retention of students; faculty resources; student selectivity; financial resources; alumni giving; high
school counselor ratings of colleges; and graduation rate. U.S. News & World Report, "America's
Best Colleges 2014"

According to U.S. News & World Report, the Philadelphia, PA metro division is home to four of
the best liberal arts colleges in the U.S.: **Swarthmore College** (#3); **Haverford College** (#9);
Bryn Mawr College (#30); **Ursinus College** (#82). The indicators used to capture academic
quality fall into a number of categories: assessment by administrators at peer institutions; retention
of students; faculty resources; student selectivity; financial resources; alumni giving; high school
counselor ratings of colleges; and graduation rate. U.S. News & World Report, "America's Best
Colleges 2014"

According to *U.S. News & World Report,* the Philadelphia, PA metro division is home to three of the top 100 law schools in the U.S.: **University of Pennsylvania** (#7); **Temple University (Beasley)** (#56); **Villanova University** (#98). The rankings are based on a weighted average of 12 measures of quality: peer assessment score; assessment score by lawyers/judges; median LSAT scores; median undergrad GPA; acceptance rate; employment rates for graduates; placement success; bar passage rate; faculty resources; expenditures per student; student/faculty ratio; and library resources. *U.S. News & World Report,* "America's Best Graduate Schools, Law, 2014"

According to *U.S. News & World Report,* the Philadelphia, PA metro division is home to two of the top 100 business schools in the U.S.: **University of Pennsylvania (Wharton)** (#3); **Temple University (Fox)** (#58). The rankings are based on a weighted average of the following nine measures: quality assessment; peer assessment; recruiter assessment; placement success; mean starting salary and bonus; student selectivity; mean GMAT and GRE scores; mean undergraduate GPA; and acceptance rate. *U.S. News & World Report,* "America's Best Graduate Schools, Business, 2014"

PRESIDENTIAL ELECTION

2012 Presidential Election Results

Area	Obama	Romney	Other
Philadelphia County	85.3	14.0	0.7
U.S.	51.0	47.2	1.8

Note: Results are percentages and may not add to 100% due to rounding
Source: Dave Leip's Atlas of U.S. Presidential Elections

EMPLOYERS

Major Employers

Company Name	Industry
Abington Memorial Hospital	General medical and surgical hospitals
AstraZeneca Pharmaceuticals LP	Pharmaceutical preparations
City of Philadelphia	Police protection
Comcast Holdings Corporation	Cable and other pay television services
Cooper Health Care	Hospital management
E.I. du Pont de Nemours and Company	Agricultural chemicals, nec
Einstein Community Health Associates	Offices and clinics of medical doctors
Glaxosmithkline	Commerical physical research
Lockheed Martin Corporation	Defense systems and equipment
Mercy Health System of SE Pennsylvania	General medical and surgical hospitals
On Time Staffing	Employment agencies
Richlieu Associates	Apartment building operators
Temple University	General medical and surgical hospitals
The University of Pennsylvania	Colleges and universities
The US Navy	Navy
The Vanguard Group	Management, investment, open-end
Thomas Jefferson University Hospital	General medical and surgical hospitals
Trustees of the University of Penn	General medical and surgical hospitals
Unisys Corporation	Computer integrated systems design
University of Delaware	Colleges and universities

Note: Companies shown are located within the Philadelphia-Camden-Wilmington, PA-NJ-DE-MD Metropolitan Statistical Area.
Source: Hoovers.com; Wikipedia

Best Companies to Work For

Children's Hospital of Philadelphia, headquartered in Philadelphia, is among the "100 Best Places to Work in IT." To qualify, companies, both public and private, had to have a minimum of 50 IT employees and were selected based on average salary and bonus increases, the percentage of IT staffers promoted, IT staff turnover rates, training and development programs, and the percentage of women and minorities in IT staff and management positions. In addition, *Computerworld* looked at retention efforts, programs for recognizing and rewarding outstanding performances, and benefits such as flextime, elder care and child care, and reimbursement for college tuition and the cost of pursuing technology certifications. *Computerworld, "100 Best Places to Work in IT 2013"*

PUBLIC SAFETY

Crime Rate

Area	All Crimes	Violent Crimes				Property Crimes		
		Murder	Forcible Rape	Robbery	Aggrav. Assault	Burglary	Larceny -Theft	Motor Vehicle Theft
City	4,863.7	21.5	57.2	518.8	562.6	780.0	2,507.7	415.9
Suburbs[1]	n/a	5.0	15.2	143.1	n/a	418.8	1,822.6	107.3
Metro[2]	n/a	16.8	45.3	412.6	n/a	678.0	2,314.1	328.7
U.S.	3,246.1	4.7	26.9	112.9	242.3	670.2	1,959.3	229.7

Note: Figures are crimes per 100,000 population; (1) All areas within the metro area that are located outside the city limits; (2) Figures cover the Philadelphia, PA Metropolitan Division—see Appendix B for areas included
Source: FBI Uniform Crime Reports, 2012

Hate Crimes

Area	Number of Quarters Reported	Bias Motivation				
		Race	Religion	Sexual Orientation	Ethnicity	Disability
City	4	8	1	2	0	0
U.S.	4	2,797	1,099	1,135	667	92

Source: Federal Bureau of Investigation, Hate Crime Statistics 2012

Identity Theft Consumer Complaints

Area	Complaints	Complaints per 100,000 Population	Rank[2]
MSA[1]	5,695	95.5	55
U.S.	290,056	91.8	-

Note: (1) Figures cover the Philadelphia-Camden-Wilmington, PA-NJ-DE-MD Metropolitan Statistical Area—see Appendix B for areas included; (2) Rank ranges from 1 to 377 where 1 indicates greatest number of identity theft complaints per 100,000 population
Source: Federal Trade Commission, Consumer Sentinel Network Data Book for January–December 2013

Fraud and Other Consumer Complaints

Area	Complaints	Complaints per 100,000 Population	Rank[2]
MSA[1]	24,989	418.9	85
U.S.	1,811,724	595.2	-

Note: (1) Figures cover the Philadelphia-Camden-Wilmington, PA-NJ-DE-MD Metropolitan Statistical Area—see Appendix B for areas included; (2) Rank ranges from 1 to 377 where 1 indicates greatest number of identity theft complaints per 100,000 population
Source: Federal Trade Commission, Consumer Sentinel Network Data Book for January–December 2013

RECREATION

Culture

Dance[1]	Theatre[1]	Instrumental Music[1]	Vocal Music[1]	Series and Festivals	Museums and Art Galleries[2]	Zoos and Aquariums[3]
4	15	15	11	14	93	1

Note: (1) Number of professional perfoming groups; (2) Based on organizations with primary SIC code 8412; (3) AZA-accredited
Source: The Grey House Performing Arts Directory, 2013; Association of Zoos & Aquariums, AZA Member Zoos & Aquariums, April 2014; www.AccuLeads.com, May 1, 2014

Professional Sports Teams

Team Name	League	Year Established
Philadelphia 76ers	National Basketball Association (NBA)	1963
Philadelphia Eagles	National Football League (NFL)	1933
Philadelphia Flyers	National Hockey League (NHL)	1967
Philadelphia Phillies	Major League Baseball (MLB)	1883
Philadelphia Union	Major League Soccer (MLS)	2010

Note: Includes teams located in the Philadelphia-Camden-Wilmington, PA-NJ-DE-MD Metropolitan Statistical Area.
Source: Wikipedia, Major Professional Sports Teams of the United States and Canada

CLIMATE

Average and Extreme Temperatures

Temperature	Jan	Feb	Mar	Apr	May	Jun	Jul	Aug	Sep	Oct	Nov	Dec	Yr.
Extreme High (°F)	74	74	85	94	96	100	104	101	100	89	84	72	104
Average High (°F)	39	42	51	63	73	82	86	85	78	67	55	43	64
Average Temp. (°F)	32	34	42	53	63	72	77	76	68	57	47	36	55
Average Low (°F)	24	26	33	43	53	62	67	66	59	47	38	28	45
Extreme Low (°F)	-7	-4	7	19	28	44	51	44	35	25	15	1	-7

Note: Figures cover the years 1948-1990
Source: National Climatic Data Center, International Station Meteorological Climate Summary, 9/96

Average Precipitation/Snowfall/Humidity

Precip./Humidity	Jan	Feb	Mar	Apr	May	Jun	Jul	Aug	Sep	Oct	Nov	Dec	Yr.
Avg. Precip. (in.)	3.2	2.8	3.7	3.5	3.7	3.6	4.1	4.0	3.3	2.7	3.4	3.3	41.4
Avg. Snowfall (in.)	7	7	4	Tr	Tr	0	0	0	0	Tr	1	4	22
Avg. Rel. Hum. 7am (%)	74	73	73	72	75	77	80	82	84	83	79	75	77
Avg. Rel. Hum. 4pm (%)	60	55	51	48	51	52	54	55	55	54	57	60	54

Note: Figures cover the years 1948-1990; Tr = Trace amounts (<0.05 in. of rain; <0.5 in. of snow)
Source: National Climatic Data Center, International Station Meteorological Climate Summary, 9/96

Weather Conditions

Temperature			Daytime Sky			Precipitation		
10°F & below	32°F & below	90°F & above	Clear	Partly cloudy	Cloudy	0.01 inch or more precip.	0.1 inch or more snow/ice	Thunder-storms
5	94	23	81	146	138	117	14	27

Note: Figures are average number of days per year and cover the years 1948-1990
Source: National Climatic Data Center, International Station Meteorological Climate Summary, 9/96

HAZARDOUS WASTE

Superfund Sites

Philadelphia has two hazardous waste sites on the EPA's Superfund Final National Priorities List: **Franklin Slag Pile (MDC); Metal Banks.** *U.S. Environmental Protection Agency, Final National Priorities List, April 26, 2014*

AIR & WATER QUALITY

Air Quality Index

Area	Percent of Days when Air Quality was...[2]					AQI Statistics[2]	
	Good	Moderate	Unhealthy for Sensitive Groups	Unhealthy	Very Unhealthy	Maximum	Median
MSA[1]	30.1	66.8	3.0	0.0	0.0	133	57

Note: (1) Data covers the Philadelphia-Camden-Wilmington, PA-NJ-DE-MD Metropolitan Statistical Area—see Appendix B for areas included; (2) Based on 365 days with AQI data in 2013. Air Quality Index (AQI) is an index for reporting daily air quality. EPA calculates the AQI for five major air pollutants regulated by the Clean Air Act: ground-level ozone, particle pollution (aka particulate matter), carbon monoxide, sulfur dioxide, and nitrogen dioxide. The AQI runs from 0 to 500. The higher the AQI value, the greater the level of air pollution and the greater the health concern. There are six AQI categories: "Good" AQI is between 0 and 50. Air quality is considered satisfactory; "Moderate" AQI is between 51 and 100. Air quality is acceptable; "Unhealthy for Sensitive Groups" When AQI values are between 101 and 150, members of sensitive groups may experience health effects; "Unhealthy" When AQI values are between 151 and 200 everyone may begin to experience health effects; "Very Unhealthy" AQI values between 201 and 300 trigger a health alert; "Hazardous" AQI values over 300 trigger warnings of emergency conditions (not shown).
Source: U.S. Environmental Protection Agency, Air Quality Index Report, 2013

Air Quality Index Pollutants

Area	Carbon Monoxide	Nitrogen Dioxide	Ozone	Sulfur Dioxide	Particulate Matter 2.5	Particulate Matter 10
	Percent of Days when AQI Pollutant was...[2]					
MSA[1]	0.0	1.6	15.6	0.3	81.9	0.5

Note: (1) Data covers the Philadelphia-Camden-Wilmington, PA-NJ-DE-MD Metropolitan Statistical Area—see Appendix B for areas included; (2) Based on 365 days with AQI data in 2013. The Air Quality Index (AQI) is an index for reporting daily air quality. EPA calculates the AQI for five major air pollutants regulated by the Clean Air Act: ground-level ozone, particle pollution (also known as particulate matter), carbon monoxide, sulfur dioxide, and nitrogen dioxide. The AQI runs from 0 to 500. The higher the AQI value, the greater the level of air pollution and the greater the health concern.
Source: U.S. Environmental Protection Agency, Air Quality Index Report, 2013

Air Quality Trends: Ozone

	2003	2004	2005	2006	2007	2008	2009	2010	2011	2012
MSA[1]	0.085	0.080	0.088	0.083	0.086	0.082	0.069	0.082	0.082	0.081

Note: (1) Data covers the Philadelphia-Camden-Wilmington, PA-NJ-DE-MD Metropolitan Statistical Area—see Appendix B for areas included. The values shown are the composite ozone concentration averages among trend sites based on the highest fourth daily maximum 8-hour concentration in parts per million. These trends are based on sites having an adequate record of monitoring data during the trend period. Data from exceptional events are included.
Source: U.S. Environmental Protection Agency, Air Quality Monitoring Information, "Air Quality Trends by City, 2000-2012"

Maximum Air Pollutant Concentrations: Particulate Matter, Ozone, CO and Lead

	Particulate Matter 10 (ug/m³)	Particulate Matter 2.5 Wtd AM (ug/m³)	Particulate Matter 2.5 24-Hr (ug/m³)	Ozone (ppm)	Carbon Monoxide (ppm)	Lead (ug/m³)
MSA[1] Level	66	16.5	31	0.092	2	0.05
NAAQS[2]	150	15	35	0.075	9	0.15
Met NAAQS[2]	Yes	No	Yes	No	Yes	Yes

Note: (1) Data covers the Philadelphia-Camden-Wilmington, PA-NJ-DE-MD Metropolitan Statistical Area—see Appendix B for areas included; Data from exceptional events are included; (2) National Ambient Air Quality Standards; ppm = parts per million; ug/m³ = micrograms per cubic meter; n/a not available.
Concentrations: Particulate Matter 10 (coarse particulate)—highest second maximum 24-hour concentration; Particulate Matter 2.5 Wtd AM (fine particulate)—highest weighted annual mean concentration; Particulate Matter 2.5 24-Hour (fine particulate)—highest 98th percentile 24-hour concentration; Ozone—highest fourth daily maximum 8-hour concentration; Carbon Monoxide—highest second maximum non-overlapping 8-hour concentration; Lead—maximum running 3-month average
Source: U.S. Environmental Protection Agency, Air Quality Monitoring Information, "Air Quality Statistics by City, 2012"

Maximum Air Pollutant Concentrations: Nitrogen Dioxide and Sulfur Dioxide

	Nitrogen Dioxide AM (ppb)	Nitrogen Dioxide 1-Hr (ppb)	Sulfur Dioxide AM (ppb)	Sulfur Dioxide 1-Hr (ppb)	Sulfur Dioxide 24-Hr (ppb)
MSA[1] Level	18	56	n/a	29	n/a
NAAQS[2]	53	100	30	75	140
Met NAAQS[2]	Yes	Yes	n/a	Yes	n/a

Note: (1) Data covers the Philadelphia-Camden-Wilmington, PA-NJ-DE-MD Metropolitan Statistical Area—see Appendix B for areas included; Data from exceptional events are included; (2) National Ambient Air Quality Standards; ppm = parts per million; ug/m³ = micrograms per cubic meter; n/a not available.
Concentrations: Nitrogen Dioxide AM—highest arithmetic mean concentration; Nitrogen Dioxide 1-Hr—highest 98th percentile 1-hour daily maximum concentration; Sulfur Dioxide AM—highest annual mean concentration; Sulfur Dioxide 1-Hr—highest 99th percentile 1-hour daily maximum concentration; Sulfur Dioxide 24-Hr—highest second maximum 24-hour concentration
Source: U.S. Environmental Protection Agency, Air Quality Monitoring Information, "Air Quality Statistics by City, 2012"

Drinking Water

Water System Name	Pop. Served	Primary Water Source Type	Violations[1]	
			Health Based	Monitoring/ Reporting
Philadelphia Water Dept	1,600,000	Surface	0	1

Note: (1) Based on violation data from January 1, 2013 to December 31, 2013 (includes unresolved violations from earlier years)
Source: U.S. Environmental Protection Agency, Office of Ground Water and Drinking Water, Safe Drinking Water Information System (based on data extracted February 10, 2014)

Pittsburgh, Pennsylvania

Background

Pittsburgh was once the creaking, croaking, belching giant of heavy industry. Thanks to a plentiful supply of bituminous coal beds and limestone deposits nearby, the city had forged a prosperous economy based upon steel, glass, rubber, petroleum, and machinery. However, unregulated spews of soot into the air by these factories earned Pittsburgh the title of "Smoky City," prompting concerned citizens and politicians to pass smoke-control laws. Today, Pittsburgh's renaissance is a result of these citizens' unflagging faith in their city.

In the eighteenth century, the area in and around the Ohio Valley and the Allegheny River, where present-day Pittsburgh lies, was claimed by both the British and the French. After being lobbed back and forth between the two, the land finally fell into British hands. The city was named Pittsborough, for the British prime minister at the time, William Pitt.

Almost immediately, the city showed signs of what it was to become. In 1792, the first blast furnace was built by George Anschulz. In 1797, the first glass factory was opened, and in 1804, the first cotton factory was opened. Irish, Scottish, and a smattering of English immigrants provided the labor pool for these factories. During the Civil War, this labor pool was augmented by a wave of German immigrants. Finally, during the late nineteenth century, Poles, Czechs, Slovaks, Italians, Russians, and Hungarians completed the picture in the colorful quilt of Pittsburgh's workforce. The last wave particularly contributed their sweat and toil to the fortunes of captains of industry such as Andrew Carnegie, Henry Clay Frick, and Charles M. Schwab.

Fortunately for Pittsburgh, these industrialists gave back to the city in the form of their cultural and educational patronage. The Carnegie Museum of Natural History has an extensive dinosaur collection and ancient Egypt wing. The Frick Art & Historical Center holds a noted private collection featuring such artists as Rubens, Tintoretto, Fragonard, and Boucher. Other educational and cultural attractions include the Pittsburgh Ballet Theatre, Pittsburgh Opera, Pittsburgh Civic Light Opera, Pittsburgh Symphony Orchestra, Pittsburgh Broadway Across America series, Carnegie Science Center, Phipps Conservatory and Botanical Gardens, Pittsburgh Zoo and PPG Aquarium, Children's Museum of Pittsburgh, Johnstown Flood Museum, Rachel Carson Homestead and the Andy Warhol Museum.

By the late 1990s, Pittsburgh was showing tremendous growth. Technology and health care services, their manufacturing counterparts, and financial institutions were dominant forces behind a steadily diversifying economy. New Internet software and computer software companies have set up operations in or near Pittsburgh, and many major corporations have their headquarters in the city.

An incredible amount of downtown building has occurred in the last ten years. Two downtown stadiums were opened in 2001: PNC Park for the Pittsburgh Pirates baseball team, and Heinz Field for the Steelers football team, 2009 Superbowl XLII champions. PNC Park is built along the lines of traditional two-tier ballparks, providing spectators intimate contact with the game. Heinz Field is an open, natural-turf field with stands in a horseshoe shape, the open end affording visitors a magnificent view of the Pittsburgh skyline.

In September 2003, the city inaugurated its handsome riverfront David L. Lawrence Convention Center, the first and largest certified "green" convention center, which provides 330,000 square feet of exhibition space, meeting rooms, two lecture halls, and a 35,000 square-foot ballroom. The Pittsburgh Cultural Trust completed 700 residential units and multiple towers. This area is home to the PPG Place gothic glass skyscraper complex as well as residents, as condo towers have been constructed and historic office towers have been converted to residential use. Downtown is serviced by a subway, buses and multiple bridges leading north and south.

Pittsburgh is a little over 100 miles southeast of Lake Erie. Its nearness to the Great Lakes and to the Atlantic Seaboard helps to modify its humid, continental climate. Winter is influenced primarily by Canadian air masses that are infrequently tempered by air from the Gulf of Mexico. During the summer, Gulf air brings warm, humid weather. Once every four years, the Monongahela and Ohio rivers combine, causing the Ohio River to reach flood stage.

Rankings

General Rankings

- *Business Insider* projected current trends well into the future to compile its list of the "15 Hottest American Cities of the Future." To such metrics as job and population growth, demographics, affordability, livability, and residents' health and welfare, analysts added innovation in technology and sustainability as well as a culture favoring youth and creativity. Judging by these combined factors, Pittsburgh ranked #13. *Business Insider, "The Fifteen Hottest American Cities of the Future," June 18, 2012*

- Pittsburgh was selected as one of America's best cities by *Bloomberg Businessweek.* The city ranked #11 out of 50. Criteria: leisure attributes (the number of restaurants, bars, libraries, museums, professional sports teams, and park acres by population); educational attributes (public school performance, the number of colleges, and graduate degree holders); economic factors (2011 income and June and July 2012 unemployment); crime; and air quality. *Bloomberg BusinessWeek, "America's Best Cities," September 26, 2012*

- Pittsburgh was identified as one of seven American cities that have lost the most people in the past decade. The city ranked #6. Criteria: population change 2000-2009; percent population change 2000-2009; home vacancy rates. *24/7 Wall St., "American Cities that are Running Out of People," January 1, 2011*

- Pittsburgh appeared on RelocateAmerica's list of best places to live in America. The annual "Top 100 Places to Live" list recognizes the top communities as nominated by their residents & local businesses. RelocateAmerica's Research Group determined the list based on review of various data gathered for economic, employment, housing, education, industry, opportunity, environment and recreation along with feedback from area leaders and residents. *RelocateAmerica.com, "Top 100 Places to Live for 2011"*

Business/Finance Rankings

- The editors of *Kiplinger's Personal Finance Magazine* named Pittsburgh to their list of ten of the best metro areas for start-ups. Criteria included a well-educated workforce and low living costs for self-employed people, as measured by the Council for Community and Economic Research, as well as areas with lots of start-up investment dollars and low business costs. *www.kiplinger.com, "10 Great Cities for Starting a Business," January 2013*

- Based on a minimum of 500 social media reviews per metro area, the employment opinion group Glassdoor surveyed 50 of the largest U.S. metro areas on measures including compensation and benefits, satisfaction with management, business outlook, and number of employers hiring. The Pittsburgh metro area was ranked #43 in overall employee satisfaction. *www.glassdoor.com, "Employment Satisfaction Report Card by City," June 21, 2013*

- In its Competitive Alternatives report, consulting firm KPMG analyzed the 27 largest metropolitan statistical areas according to 26 cost components (such as taxes, labor costs, and utilities) and 30 non-cost-related variables (such as crime rates and number of universities). The business website 24/7 Wall Street examined the KPMG findings, adding to the mix current unemployment rates, GDP, median income, and employment decline during the last recession and "projected" recovery. It identified the Pittsburgh metro area as #9 among the ten best American cities for business. *247wallst.com, "Best American Cities for Business," April 4, 2012*

- In a survey of economic confidence in the nation's 50 largest metropolitan areas conducted January–December 2012, the Pittsburgh metro area placed among the bottom five, according to Gallup's 2013 Economic Confidence Index. *Gallup Economy, "D.C. Metro Area Again Leads U.S. in Economic Confidence," March 28, 2013*

- Pittsburgh was ranked #52 out of 100 metro areas in terms of economic performance (#1 = best) during the recession and recovery from trough quarter through the second quarter of 2013. Criteria: percent change in employment; percentage point change in unemployment rate; percent change in gross metropolitan product; percent change in House Price Index. *Brookings Institution, MetroMonitor: Tracking Economic Recession and Recovery in America's 100 Largest Metropolitan Areas, September 2013*

- The Pittsburgh metro area was identified as one of the most affordable metropolitan areas in America by *Forbes*. The area ranked #16 out of 20. Criteria: the 100 largest metro areas in the U.S. were analyzed based on housing affordability and cost-of-living. *Forbes.com, "America's Most Affordable Cities," March 11, 2014*

- Pittsburgh was identified as one of America's most frugal metro areas by *Coupons.com*. The city ranked #18 out of 25. Criteria: online coupon usage. *Coupons.com, "Top 25 Most Frugal Cities of 2012," February 19, 2013*

- Pittsburgh was identified as one of America's most frugal metro areas by *Coupons.com*. The city ranked #14 out of 25. Criteria: Grocery IQ and coupons.com mobile app usage. *Coupons.com, "Top 25 Most On-the-Go Frugal Cities of 2012," February 19, 2013*

- Pittsburgh was identified as one of the uhappiest cities to work in by CareerBliss.com, an online community for career advancement. The city ranked #5 out of 10. Criteria: independent company reviews from employees all over the country on: relationship with their boss and co-workers; work environment; job resources; compensation; growth opportunities; company culture; company reputation; daily tasks; job control over work performed on a daily basis. *CareerBliss.com, "Top 10 Happiest and Unhappiest Cities to Work in 2014," February 10, 2014*

- The Pittsburgh metro area appeared on the Milken Institute "2013 Best Performing Cities" list. Rank: #31 out of 200 large metro areas. Criteria: job growth; wage and salary growth; high-tech output growth. *Milken Institute, "Best-Performing Cities 2013," December 2013*

- *Forbes* ranked the 200 most populous metro areas in the U.S. in terms of the "Best Places for Business and Careers." The Pittsburgh metro area was ranked #43. Criteria: costs (business and living); job growth (past and projected); income growth; educational attainment (college and high school); projected economic growth; cultural and recreational opportunities; net migration patterns; number of highly ranked colleges. *Forbes, "The Best Places for Business and Careers," August 7, 2013*

Children/Family Rankings

- Pittsburgh was selected as one of the best cities for families to live by *Parenting* magazine. The city ranked #16 out of 100. Criteria: education; health; community; *Parenting's* Culture & Charm Index. *Parenting.com, "The 2012 Best Cities for Families List"*

Culture/Performing Arts Rankings

- Pittsburgh was selected as one of America's top cities for the arts. The city ranked #12 in the mid-sized city (population 100,000 to 499,999) category. Criteria: readers' top choices for arts travel destinations based on the richness and variety of visual arts sites, activities and events. *American Style, "2012 Top 25 Arts Destinations," June 2012*

Dating/Romance Rankings

- Of the 100 U.S. cities surveyed by *Men's Health* in its quest to identify the nation's best cities for dating and forming relationships, Pittsburgh was ranked #14 for online dating (#1 = best). *Men's Health, "The Best and Worst Cities for Online Dating," January 30, 2013*

- Pittsburgh was selected as one of the most romantic cities in America by Amazon.com. The city ranked #17 of 20. Criteria: cities with 100,000 or more residents were ranked on their per capita sales of romance novels and relationship books, romantic comedy movies, romantic music, and sexual wellness products. *Amazon.com, "Top 20 Most Romantic Cities in America," February 3, 2014*

- Pittsburgh was selected as one of the best cities for single women in America by *SingleMindedWomen.com*. The city ranked #7. Criteria: ratio of women to men; singles population; healthy lifestyle; employment opportunities; cost of living; access to travel; entertainment options; social opportunities. *SingleMindedWomen.com, "Top 10 Cities for Single Women," 2011*

Education Rankings

- *Men's Health* ranked 100 U.S. cities in terms of their education levels. Pittsburgh was ranked #17 (#1 = most educated city). Criteria: high school graduation rates; school enrollment; educational attainment; number of households who have outstanding student loans; number of households whose members have taken adult-education courses. *Men's Health, "Where School Is In: The Most and Least Educated Cities," September 12, 2011*

- Pittsburgh was selected as one of the most well-read cities in America by Amazon.com. The city ranked #10 of 20. Cities with populations greater than 100,000 were evaluated based on per capita sales of books, magazines and newspapers. *Amazon.com, "The 20 Most Well-Read Cities in America," April 28, 2013*

- Pittsburgh was selected as one of America's most literate cities. The city ranked #4 out of the 77 largest U.S. cities. Criteria: number of booksellers; library resources; Internet resources; educational attainment; periodical publishing resources; newspaper circulation. *Central Connecticut State University, "America's Most Literate Cities, 2013"*

- Pittsburgh was identified as one of America's most inventive cities by *The Daily Beast*. The city ranked #22 out of 25. The 200 largest cities in the U.S. were ranked by the number of patents (applied and approved) per capita. *The Daily Beast, "The 25 Most Inventive Cities," October 2, 2011*

Environmental Rankings

- CNNMoney based its list of the nation's ten most polluted cities on the annual State of the Air report prepared by the American Lung Association, which noted that the cities with the worst air pollution also had some of the highest incidences of heart and lung disease. At #8 (#1 = worst), Pittsburgh was among those with the poorest air quality. *money.cnn.com, "10 Most Polluted Cities," April 24, 2013*

- The Pittsburgh metro area came in at #105 for the relative comfort of its climate on Sperling's list of "chill cities," as measured by the Sperling Heat Index. All 361 metro areas are included. Criteria included daytime high temperatures, nighttime low temperatures, dew point, and relative humidity at the high temperatures. *www.bertsperling.com, "Sperling's Chill Cities," July 18, 2013*

- Sperling's BestPlaces assessed 379 metropolitan areas of the United States for the likelihood of dangerously extreme weather events or earthquakes. In general the Southeast and South-Central regions have the highest risk of weather extremes and earthquakes, while the Pacific Northwest enjoys the lowest risk. Of the least risky metropolitan areas, the Pittsburgh metro area was ranked #110. *www.bestplaces.net, "Safest Places from Natural Disasters," April 2011*

- *The Daily Beast* identifed the snowiest among the 100 largest U.S. cities, looking at average snowfall per month from December 2011 through March 2012 and from December 1, 2012 to December 21, 2012. Number of days with maximum and minimum temperatures of 32 degrees or less contributed to the rankings. Pittsburgh ranked #9. *The Daily Beast, "25 Snowiest Cities in America," December 21, 2012*

- Pittsburgh was identified as one of North America's greenest metropolitan areas. The area ranked #23. The Green City Index is comprised of 31 indicators, and scores cities across nine categories: carbon dioxide; energy; land use; buildings; transport; water; waste; air quality; environmental governance. The 27 largest metropolitan areas in the U.S. and Canada were considered. *Economist Intelligence Unit, sponsored by Siemens, "U.S. and Canada Green City Index, 2011"*

- The Pittsburgh metro area was identified as one of the snowiest major metropolitan areas in the U.S. by *Forbes*. The metro area ranked #7 out of 10. Criteria: average annual snowfall. *Forbes, "America's Snowiest Cities," January 12, 2011*

- Pittsburgh was selected as one of 22 "Smarter Cities" for energy by the Natural Resources Defense Council. Criteria: investment in green power; energy efficiency measures; conservation. *Natural Resources Defense Council, "2010 Smarter Cities," July 19, 2010*

- Pittsburgh was highlighted as one of the 25 most ozone-polluted metro areas in the U.S. during 2008 through 2010. The area ranked #24. *American Lung Association, State of the Air 2012*

- Pittsburgh was highlighted as one of the 25 metro areas most polluted by year-round particle pollution (Annual PM 2.5) in the U.S. during 2008 through 2010. The area ranked #8. *American Lung Association, State of the Air 2012*

- Pittsburgh was highlighted as one of the 25 metro areas most polluted by short-term particle pollution (24-hour PM 2.5) in the U.S. during 2008 through 2010. The area ranked #7. *American Lung Association, State of the Air 2012*

Food/Drink Rankings

- *Men's Health* ranked 100 major U.S. cities in terms of alcohol intoxication. Pittsburgh ranked #48 (#1 = most sober).Criteria: binge drinking; alcohol-related traffic accidents, arrests, and fatalities. *Men's Health, "The Drunkest Cities in America," November 19, 2013*

Health/Fitness Rankings

- For each of the 50 most populous metro areas in the United States, the American College of Sports Medicine's American Fitness Index evaluated infrastructure, community assets, and policies that encourage healthy and fit lifestyles, including preventive health behaviors, levels of chronic disease conditions, health care access, and community resources and policies that support physical activity. The Pittsburgh metro area ranked #16 for "community fitness." Personal health indicators were considered as well as community and environmental indicators. *www.americanfitnessindex.org, "ACSM American Fitness Index Health and Community Fitness Status of the 50 Largest Metropolitan Areas," May 2013*

- The Pittsburgh metro area was identified as one of the worst cities for bed bugs in America by pest control company Orkin. The area ranked #24 out of 50 based on the number of bed bug treatments Orkin performed from January to December 2013. *Orkin, "Chicago Tops Bed Bug Cities List for Second Year in a Row," January 16, 2014*

- Pittsburgh was identified as a "2013 Spring Allergy Capital." The area ranked #39 out of 100. Three groups of factors were used to identify the most severe cities for people with allergies during the spring season: annual pollen levels; medicine utilization; access to board-certified allergists. *Asthma and Allergy Foundation of America, "Spring Allergy Capitals 2013"*

- Pittsburgh was identified as a "2013 Fall Allergy Capital." The area ranked #46 out of 100. Three groups of factors were used to identify the most severe cities for people with allergies during the fall season: annual pollen levels; medicine utilization; access to board-certified allergists. *Asthma and Allergy Foundation of America, "Fall Allergy Capitals 2013"*

- Pittsburgh was identified as a "2013 Asthma Capital." The area ranked #16 out of the nation's 100 largest metropolitan areas. Twelve factors were used to identify the most challenging places to live for people with asthma: estimated prevalence; self-reported prevalence; crude death rate for asthma; annual pollen score; annual air quality; public smoking laws; number of board-certified asthma specialists; school inhaler access laws; rescue medication use; controller medication use; uninsured rate; poverty rate. *Asthma and Allergy Foundation of America, "Asthma Capitals 2013"*

- *Men's Health* ranked 100 major U.S. cities in terms of the best and worst cities for men. Pittsburgh ranked #70. Criteria: thirty-three data points were examined covering health, fitness, and quality of life. *Men's Health, "The Best & Worst Cities for Men 2014," December 6, 2013*

- Breathe Right Nasal Strips, in partnership with Sperling's BestPlaces, analyzed 50 metro areas and identified those U.S. cities most challenged by chronic nasal congestion. The Pittsburgh metro area ranked #15. Criteria: tree, grass and weed pollens; molds and spores; air pollution; climate; smoking; purchase habits of congestion products; prescriptions of drugs for congestion relief; incidence of influenza. *Breathe Right Nasal Strips, "Most Congested Cities," October 3, 2011*

- The American Academy of Dermatology ranked 26 U.S. metropolitan regions in terms of their residents knowledge, attitude and behaviors towards tanning, sun protection and skin cancer detection. The Pittsburgh metro area ranked #26. The results of the study are based on an online survey of over 7,000 adults nationwide. *American Academy of Dermatology, "Suntelligence: How Sun Smart is Your City?," May 3, 2010*

- The Pittsburgh metro area appeared in the 2013 Gallup-Healthways Well-Being Index. The area ranked #101 out of 189. The Gallup-Healthways Well-Being Index score is an average of six sub-indexes, which individually examine life evaluation, emotional health, work environment, physical health, healthy behaviors, and access to basic necessities. Results are based on telephone interviews conducted as part of the Gallup-Healthways Well-Being Index survey January 2–December 29, 2012, and January 2–December 30, 2013, with a random sample of 531,630 adults, aged 18 and older, living in metropolitan areas in the 50 U.S. states and the District of Columbia. *Gallup-Healthways, "State of American Well-Being," March 25, 2014*

- The Pittsburgh metro area was identified as one of "America's Most Stressful Cities" by *Sperling's BestPlaces*. The metro area ranked #46 out of 50. Criteria: unemployment rate; suicide rate; commute time; mental health; poor rest; alcohol use; violent crime rate; property crime rate; cloudy days annually. *Sperling's BestPlaces, www.BestPlaces.net, "Stressful Cities 2012*

- *Men's Health* ranked 100 U.S. cities in terms of their activity levels. Pittsburgh was ranked #47 (#1 = most active city). Criteria: where and how often residents exercise; percentage of households that watch more than 15 hours of cable television a week and buy more than 11 video games a year; death rate from deep-vein thrombosis, a condition linked to sitting for extended periods of time. *Men's Health, "Where Sit Happens: The Most and Least Active Cities in America," June 20, 2011*

- *The Daily Beast* identified the 30 U.S. metro areas with the worst smoking habits. The Pittsburgh metro area ranked #14. Sixty urban centers with populations of more than one million were ranked based on the following criteria: number of smokers; number of cigarettes smoked per day; fewest attempts to quit. *The Daily Beast, "30 Cities With Smoking Problems," January 3, 2011*

Real Estate Rankings

- Pittsburgh was ranked #132 out of 283 metro areas in terms of house price appreciation in 2013 (#1 = highest rate). *Federal Housing Finance Agency, House Price Index, 4th Quarter 2013*

- Pittsburgh was ranked #53 out of 224 metro areas in terms of housing affordability in 2013 by the National Association of Home Builders (#1 = most affordable). The NAHB-Wells Fargo Housing Opportunity Index (HOI) for a given area is defined as the share of homes sold in that area that would have been affordable to a family earning the local median income, based on standard mortgage underwriting criteria. *National Association of Home Builders®, NAHB-Wells Fargo Housing Opportunity Index, 4th Quarter 2013*

- Pittsburgh was selected as one of the best college towns for renters by ApartmentRatings.com." The area ranked #70 out of 87. Overall satisfaction ratings were ranked using thousands of user submitted scores for hundreds of apartment complexes located in cities and towns that are home to the 100 largest four-year institutions in the U.S. *ApartmentRatings.com, "2011 College Town Renter Satisfaction Rankings"*

Safety Rankings

- Symantec, in partnership with Sperling's BestPlaces, ranked the 50 largest cities in the U.S. in terms of their vulnerability to cybercrime. The city ranked #39. Criteria: number of cyberattacks and potential infections; level of Internet access; expenditures on smartphones and computer hardware/software; wireless hotspots; broadband connectivity; Internet usage; online purchases. *Symantec, "Riskiest Online Cities of 2012" February 15, 2012*

- Farmers Insurance, in partnership with Sperling's BestPlaces, ranked metro areas in the U.S. and identified the "Most Secure Places to Live." The Pittsburgh metro area ranked #3 out of the top 20 in the large metro area category (500,000 or more residents). Criteria: economic stability; crime statistics; extreme weather; risk of natural disasters; housing depreciation; foreclosures; air quality; environmental hazards; life expectancy; motor vehicle fatalities; and employment numbers. *Farmers Insurance Group of Companies, "Most Secure U.S. Places to Live in the U.S.," June 25, 2013*

- Allstate ranked the 200 largest cities in America in terms of driver safety. Pittsburgh ranked #173. Allstate researchers analyzed internal property damage claims over a two-year period from January 2010 to December 2011. A weighted average of the two-year numbers determined the annual percentages. *Allstate, "Allstate America's Best Drivers Report®, August 27, 2013"*

- Pittsburgh was identified as one of the least disaster-proof places in the U.S. in terms of its vulnerability to natural and non-natural disasters. The city ranked #5 out of 5. Rankings are based on the U.S. Center for Disease Control's Cities Readiness Initiative (CRI). As part of the CRI, the CDC and state public health personnel assess local emergency-management plans, protocols and capabilities for 72 Metropolitan Statistical Areas and four non-MSA large cities. *Forbes, "America's Most and Least Disaster-Proof Cities," December 12, 2011*

- The National Insurance Crime Bureau ranked 380 metro areas in the U.S. in terms of per capita rates of vehicle theft. The Pittsburgh metro area ranked #308 (#1 = highest rate). Criteria: number of vehicle theft offenses per 100,000 inhabitants in 2012. *National Insurance Crime Bureau, "Hot Spots 2012," June 26, 2013*

- The Pittsburgh metro area was identified as one of the most dangerous metro areas for pedestrians by Transportation for America. The metro area ranked #49 out of 52 metro areas with over 1 million residents. Criteria: area's population divided by the number of pedestrian fatalities in that area. *Transportation for America, "Dangerous by Design 2011"*

Seniors/Retirement Rankings

- For *U.S. News & World Report's* Best Places rankings, the editors sought out affordable cities where retirees spend the least on housing and can live on $75 a day while still having easy access to amenities they want and need, such as recreation, services for seniors, and medical facilities. Pittsburgh was among the ten cities that best satisfied their criteria. *money.usnews.com, "The Best Places to Retire on $75 a Day," October 15, 2013*

- From its Best Cities for Successful Aging indexes, the Milken Institute generated rankings for metropolitan areas, weighing data in eight categories—general indicators, health care, wellness, living arrangements, transportation and general accessibility, financial well-being, education and employment, and community participation. The Pittsburgh metro area was ranked #10 overall in the large metro area category. *Milken Institute, "Best Cities for Successful Aging," July 2012*

- Pittsburgh made the 2014 *Forbes* list of "25 Best Places to Retire." Criteria include: housing and living costs; tax climate for retirees; weather and air quality; crime rates; doctor availability; active-lifestyle rankings for walkability, bicycling and volunteering. *Forbes.com, "The Best Places to Retire in 2014," January 16, 2014*

- The AARP named Pittsburgh one of the "10 Best Places to Live on $100 a Day." Analysts looked at 200 cities to arrive at their 10-best list. Criteria includes: cost of living; quality-of-life; arts and culture; educational institutions; restaurants; community life; health care; natural setting; sunny days per year; and overall vibe. *AARP The Magazine, "10 Best Places to Live on $100 a Day," July 2012*

- *Forbes* selected the Pittsburgh metro area as one of 25 "Best Places for a Working Retirement." Criteria: affordability; improving, above-average economies and job prospects; and a favorable tax climate for retirees. *Forbes.com, "Best Places for a Working Retirement in 2013," February 4, 2013*

- *U.S. News & World Report* listed the best places to retire on an income of $40,000 per year. Pittsburgh was among the ten cities selected. Criteria: low cost of living; affordable housing; quality of life; accessible major medical facilities; services for seniors; educational institutions; outdoor recreational activities. *U.S. News & World Report, "Best Places to Retire for Under $40,000," October 15, 2012*

- *U.S. News & World Report* selected 10 of the best places to retire in the U.S. in 2012. Pittsburgh was selected as having the "best mix of affordability and amenities." Criteria: ten key attributes that many people look for in a retirement spot, along with a city that excels in meeting each need. *U.S. News & World Report, "The 10 Best Places to Retire in 2012," December 21, 2011*

- Bankers Life and Casualty Company, in partnership with Sperling's BestPlaces, ranked the nation's 50 largest metro areas in terms of the "Best U.S. Cities for Seniors." The Pittsburgh metro area ranked #3. Criteria: healthcare; transportation; housing; environment; economy; health and longevity; social and spiritual life; crime. *Bankers Life and Casualty Company, Center for a Secure Retirement, "Best U.S. Cities for Seniors 2011," September 2011*

- Pittsburgh was identified as one of the most popular places to retire by *Topretirements.com*. The list reflects the 100 cities (out of 900+ total cities reviewed) that visitors to the website are most interested in for retirement. *Topretirements.com, "Most Popular Places to Retire for 2014," February 25, 2014*

- Pittsburgh was selected as one of the best places to retire by *CNNMoney.com*. Criteria: low cost of living; low violent-crime rate; good medical care; large population over age 50; abundant amenities for retirees. *CNNMoney.com, "Best Places to Retire 2011"*

Sports/Recreation Rankings

- *24/7 Wall St.* analysts isolated the ten cities that spent the most public money per capita on sports stadiums, according to 2010 data. Pittsburgh ranked #7. *24/7 Wall St., "Cities Paying the Most for Sports Teams," January 30, 2013*

- Pittsburgh appeared on the *Sporting News* list of the "Best Sports Cities" for 2011. The area ranked #6 out of 271. Criteria: the magazine takes a 12-month snapshot of each city's sports, putting a heavy premium on regular-season won-lost records (from the most recently completed season). Other criteria include: playoff berths, bowl appearances and tournament bids; championships; applicable power ratings; quality of competition; overall fan fervor (measured in part by attendance); abundance of teams (rewarding quality over quantity); stadium and arena quality; ticket availability and prices; franchise ownership; and marquee appeal of athletes. *Sporting News, "Best Sports Cities 2011," October 4, 2011*

- Pittsburgh appeared on the *Sporting News* list of the "Best Sports Cities" for 2011. The area ranked #6 out of 271. Criteria: a 12-month snapshot of regular-season won-lost records (from the most recently completed season). Other criteria include: playoff berths, bowl appearances and tournament bids; championships; applicable power ratings; quality of competition; overall fan fervor (measured in part by attendance); abundance of teams (quality over quantity); stadium and arena quality; ticket availability and prices; franchise ownership; and marquee appeal of athletes. *Sporting News, "Best Sports Cities 2011," October 4, 2011*

- Pittsburgh was selected as one of the most playful cities in the U.S. by KaBOOM! The organization's Playful City USA initiative honors cities and towns across the nation for a vision, plan and commitment to creating an agenda for play. Criteria: creating a local play commission or task force; designing an annual action plan for play; conducting a play space audit; outlining a financial investment in play for the current fiscal year; and proclaiming and celebrating an annual "play day." *KaBOOM! National Campaign for Play, "2013 Playful City USA Communities"*

- Pittsburgh was chosen as one of America's best cities for bicycling. The city ranked #35 out of 50. Criteria: robust cycling infrastructure; vibrant bike culture. The editors only considered cities with populations of 95,000 or more. *Bicycling, "America's Top 50 Bike-Friendly Cities," May 23, 2012*

- The Pittsburgh was selected as one of the best metro areas for golf in America by *Golf Digest*. The Pittsburgh area was ranked #2 out of 20. Criteria: climate; cost of public golf; quality of public golf; accessibility. *Golf Digest, "The Top 20 Cities for Golf," October 2011*

Women/Minorities Rankings

- The Daily Beast surveyed the nation's cities for highest percentage of singles and lowest divorce rate, plus other measures, to determine "emotional intelligence"—happiness, confidence, kindness—which, researchers say, has a strong correlation with people's satisfaction with their romantic relationships. Pittsburgh placed #6. *www.thedailybeast.com, "Best Cities to Find Love and Stay in Love," February 14, 2014*

- Movoto chose five objective criteria to identify the best places for professional women among the largest 100 American cities. Pittsburgh was among the top ten, at #6, based on commute time, recent job growth, unemployment rank, professional women's groups per capita, and average earnings adjusted for the cost of living. *www.movoto.com, "These Are America's Best Cities for Professional Women," March 5, 2014*

- *Women's Health* examined U.S. cities and identified the 100 best cities for women. Pittsburgh was ranked #57. Criteria: 30 categories were examined from obesity and breast cancer rates to commuting times and hours spent working out. *Women's Health, "Best Cities for Women 2012"*

- Pittsburgh was selected as one of the gayest cities in America by *The Advocate*. The city ranked #15 out of 15. This year's criteria include points for a city's LGBT elected officials (and fractional points for the state's elected officials), points for the percentage of the population comprised by lesbian-coupled households, a point for a gay rodeo association, points for bars listed in *Out* magazine's 200 Best Bars list, a point per women's college, and points for concert performances by Mariah Carey, Pink, Lady Gaga, or the Jonas Brothers. The raw score is divided by the population to provide a ranking based on a per capita LGBT quotient. *The Advocate, "2014's Gayest Cities in America" January 6, 2014*

- The Pittsburgh metro area appeared on *Forbes'* list of the "Best Cities for Minority Entrepreneurs." The area ranked #15 out of 10. Criteria: 52 metropolitan statistical areas were examined. For each ethnicity (African Americans, Asians and Hispanics), the editors measured housing affordability, population growth, income growth, and entrepreneurship (per capita self-employment). *Forbes, "Best Cities for Minority Entrepreneurs," March 23, 2011*

Miscellaneous Rankings

- The watchdog site Charity Navigator conducts an annual study of charities in the nation's major markets both to analyze statistical differences in their financial, accountability, and transparency practices and to track year-to-year variations in individual communities. The Pittsburgh metro area was ranked #7 among the 30 metro markets. *www.charitynavigator.org, "Metro Market Study 2013," June 1, 2013*

- Business Insider reports on the 2013 Trick-or-Treat Index compiled by the real estate site Zillow, which used its own Home Value Index and Walk Score along with population density and local crime stats to determine that Pittsburgh ranked #13 for "how much candy it gives out versus how far kids have to walk to get it." Zillow also zeroes in on the best neighborhoods in its top 20 cities. *www.businessinsider.com, "These Are the Best Cities for Trick-or-Treating," October 15, 2013*

- *Men's Health* ranked 100 U.S. cities by their level of sadness. Pittsburgh was ranked #40 (#1 = saddest city). Criteria: suicide rates; unemployment rates; percentage of households that use antidepressants; percent of population who report feeling blue all or most of the time. *Men's Health, "Frown Towns," November 28, 2011*

- Scarborough Research, a leading market research firm, identified the top local markets for lottery ticket purchasers. The Pittsburgh DMA (Designated Market Area) ranked in the top 13 with 50% of adults 18+ reporting that they purchased lottery tickets in the past 30 days. *Scarborough Research, January 30, 2012*

- Mars Chocolate North America, the makers of COMBOS®, in partnership with Sperling's BestPlaces, ranked 50 major metro areas in terms of their "manliness." The Pittsburgh metro area ranked #16. Criteria: number of professional sports teams; number of nearby NASCAR tracks and racing events; manly lifestyle; concentration of manly retail stores; manly occupations per capita; salty snack sales; "Board of Manliness" rankings. *Mars Chocolate North America, "America's Manliest Cities 2012"*

- The National Alliance to End Homelessness ranked the 100 most populous metro areas in terms the rate of homelessness. The Pittsburgh metro area ranked #82. Criteria: number of homeless people per 10,000 population in 2011. *National Alliance to End Homelessness, The State of Homelessness in America 2012*

Business Environment

CITY FINANCES

City Government Finances

Component	2011 ($000)	2011 ($ per capita)
Total Revenues	593,679	1,908
Total Expenditures	640,477	2,058
Debt Outstanding	772,089	2,481
Cash and Securities[1]	471,626	1,515

Note: (1) Cash and security holdings of a government at the close of its fiscal year, including those of its dependent agencies, utilities, and liquor stores.
Source: U.S Census Bureau, State & Local Government Finances 2011

City Government Revenue by Source

Source	2011 ($000)	2011 ($ per capita)
General Revenue		
From Federal Government	24,164	78
From State Government	151,237	486
From Local Governments	4,721	15
Taxes		
Property	131,833	424
Sales and Gross Receipts	92,080	296
Personal Income	70,217	226
Corporate Income	0	0
Motor Vehicle License	0	0
Other Taxes	17,259	55
Current Charges	60,777	195
Liquor Store	0	0
Utility	0	0
Employee Retirement	241	1

Source: U.S Census Bureau, State & Local Government Finances 2011

City Government Expenditures by Function

Function	2011 ($000)	2011 ($ per capita)	2011 (%)
General Direct Expenditures			
Air Transportation	0	0	0.0
Corrections	0	0	0.0
Education	0	0	0.0
Employment Security Administration	0	0	0.0
Financial Administration	7,186	23	1.1
Fire Protection	51,301	165	8.0
General Public Buildings	2,598	8	0.4
Governmental Administration, Other	20,771	67	3.2
Health	13,917	45	2.2
Highways	2,645	8	0.4
Hospitals	0	0	0.0
Housing and Community Development	107,928	347	16.9
Interest on General Debt	37,765	121	5.9
Judicial and Legal	3,009	10	0.5
Libraries	0	0	0.0
Parking	0	0	0.0
Parks and Recreation	14,559	47	2.3
Police Protection	78,726	253	12.3
Public Welfare	0	0	0.0
Sewerage	0	0	0.0
Solid Waste Management	9,622	31	1.5
Veterans' Services	0	0	0.0
Liquor Store	0	0	0.0
Utility	0	0	0.0
Employee Retirement	81,376	261	12.7

Source: U.S Census Bureau, State & Local Government Finances 2011

DEMOGRAPHICS

Population Growth

Area	1990 Census	2000 Census	2010 Census	Population Growth (%) 1990-2000	Population Growth (%) 2000-2010
City	369,785	334,563	305,704	-9.5	-8.6
MSA[1]	2,468,289	2,431,087	2,356,285	-1.5	-3.1
U.S.	248,709,873	281,421,906	308,745,538	13.2	9.7

Note: (1) Figures cover the Pittsburgh, PA Metropolitan Statistical Area—see Appendix B for areas included
Source: U.S. Census Bureau, Census 1990, 2000, 2010

Household Size

Area	Persons in Household (%) One	Two	Three	Four	Five	Six	Seven or More	Average Household Size
City	41.7	32.7	13.2	7.9	2.9	1.0	0.6	2.14
MSA[1]	32.3	35.4	14.8	11.4	4.2	1.3	0.6	2.33
U.S.	27.6	33.5	15.7	13.2	6.1	2.4	1.5	2.63

Note: (1) Figures cover the Pittsburgh, PA Metropolitan Statistical Area—see Appendix B for areas included
Source: U.S. Census Bureau, 2010-2012 American Community Survey 3-Year Estimates

Race

Area	White Alone[2] (%)	Black Alone[2] (%)	Asian Alone[2] (%)	AIAN[3] Alone[2] (%)	NHOPI[4] Alone[2] (%)	Other Race Alone[2] (%)	Two or More Races (%)
City	66.4	25.1	4.7	0.2	0.0	0.5	3.0
MSA[1]	87.6	8.2	1.8	0.1	0.0	0.3	1.9
U.S.	74.0	12.6	4.9	0.8	0.2	4.7	2.8

Note: (1) Figures cover the Pittsburgh, PA Metropolitan Statistical Area—see Appendix B for areas included;
(2) Alone is defined as not being in combination with one or more other races; (3) American Indian and Alaska Native; (4) Native Hawaiian and Other Pacific Islander
Source: U.S. Census Bureau, 2010-2012 American Community Survey 3-Year Estimates

Hispanic or Latino Origin

Area	Total (%)	Mexican (%)	Puerto Rican (%)	Cuban (%)	Other (%)
City	2.6	0.9	0.6	0.2	0.9
MSA[1]	1.4	0.5	0.4	0.1	0.4
U.S.	16.6	10.7	1.6	0.6	3.7

Note: Persons of Hispanic or Latino origin can be of any race; (1) Figures cover the Pittsburgh, PA Metropolitan Statistical Area—see Appendix B for areas included
Source: U.S. Census Bureau, 2010-2012 American Community Survey 3-Year Estimates

Segregation

Type	Segregation Indices[1] 1990	2000	2010	2010 Rank[2]	Percent Change 1990-2000	Percent Change 1990-2010	Percent Change 2000-2010
Black/White	70.8	68.9	65.8	17	-1.9	-5.1	-3.2
Asian/White	51.3	52.1	52.4	2	0.8	1.0	0.3
Hispanic/White	29.5	29.0	28.6	97	-0.5	-0.9	-0.4

Note: All figures cover the Metropolitan Statistical Area—see Appendix B for areas included; Figures are based on an analysis of 1990, 2000, and 2010 Census Decennial Census tract data by William H. Frey, Brookings Institution and the University of Michigan Social Science Data Analysis Network. In this analysis all racial groups (whites, blacks, and asians) are non-Hispanic members of those races. Hispanics are shown as a separate category;
(1) Segregation Indices are Dissimilarity Indices that measure the degree to which the minority group is distributed differently than whites across census tracts. They range from 0 (complete integration) to 100 (complete segregation) where the value indicates the percentage of the minority group that needs to move to be distributed exactly like whites; (2) Ranges from 1 (most segregated) to 102 (least segregated); n/a not available.
Source: www.CensusScope.org

Ancestry

Area	German	Irish	English	American	Italian	Polish	French[2]	Scottish	Dutch
City	19.6	16.0	4.9	3.7	13.1	7.7	1.6	1.5	0.7
MSA[1]	29.0	19.1	8.4	4.6	16.3	9.1	1.9	2.0	1.4
U.S.	15.2	11.1	8.2	7.2	5.6	3.1	2.8	1.7	1.4

Note: Figures are the percentage of the total population reporting a particular ancestry. The nine most commonly reported ancestries in the U.S. are shown. Figures include multiple ancestries (e.g. if a person reported being Irish and Italian, they were included in both columns); (1) Figures cover the Pittsburgh, PA Metropolitan Statistical Area—see Appendix B for areas included; (2) Excludes Basque
Source: U.S. Census Bureau, 2010-2012 American Community Survey 3-Year Estimates

Foreign-Born Population

Area	Percent of Population Born in								
	Any Foreign Country	Mexico	Asia	Europe	Carribean	South America	Central America[2]	Africa	Canada
City	7.2	0.3	3.9	1.7	0.2	0.3	0.1	0.5	0.2
MSA[1]	3.2	0.1	1.5	1.0	0.1	0.1	0.1	0.2	0.1
U.S.	13.0	3.7	3.7	1.6	1.2	0.9	1.0	0.5	0.3

Note: (1) Figures cover the Pittsburgh, PA Metropolitan Statistical Area—see Appendix B for areas included; (2) Excludes Mexico.
Source: U.S. Census Bureau, 2010-2012 American Community Survey 3-Year Estimates

Marital Status

Area	Never Married	Now Married[2]	Separated	Widowed	Divorced
City	51.5	30.4	2.6	6.7	8.8
MSA[1]	31.6	48.5	2.1	8.1	9.7
U.S.	32.4	48.4	2.2	6.0	11.0

Note: Figures are percentages and cover the population 15 years of age and older; (1) Figures cover the Pittsburgh, PA Metropolitan Statistical Area—see Appendix B for areas included; (2) Excludes separated
Source: U.S. Census Bureau, 2010-2012 American Community Survey 3-Year Estimates

Age

Area	Percent of Population									Median Age
	Under Age 5	Age 5–19	Age 20–34	Age 35–44	Age 45–54	Age 55–64	Age 65–74	Age 75–84	Age 85+	
City	5.0	16.7	30.7	10.1	11.8	11.6	6.8	4.5	2.8	33.1
MSA[1]	5.1	17.5	18.4	12.0	15.4	14.3	8.5	6.0	2.9	42.6
U.S.	6.4	20.1	20.5	13.1	14.3	12.2	7.3	4.2	1.8	37.3

Note: (1) Figures cover the Pittsburgh, PA Metropolitan Statistical Area—see Appendix B for areas included
Source: U.S. Census Bureau, 2010-2012 American Community Survey 3-Year Estimates

Gender

Area	Males	Females	Males per 100 Females
City	148,144	157,862	93.8
MSA[1]	1,141,730	1,217,495	93.8
U.S.	153,276,055	158,333,314	96.8

Note: (1) Figures cover the Pittsburgh, PA Metropolitan Statistical Area—see Appendix B for areas included
Source: U.S. Census Bureau, 2010-2012 American Community Survey 3-Year Estimates

Religious Groups by Family

Area	Catholic	Baptist	Non-Den.	Methodist[2]	Lutheran	LDS[3]	Pente-costal	Presby-terian[4]	Muslim[5]	Judaism
MSA[1]	32.8	2.3	2.8	5.7	3.4	0.4	1.1	4.7	0.3	0.7
U.S.	19.1	9.3	4.0	4.0	2.3	2.0	1.9	1.6	0.8	0.7

Note: Figures are the number of adherents as a percentage of the total population; (1) Figures cover the Pittsburgh, PA Metropolitan Statistical Area—see Appendix B for areas included; (2) Methodist/Pietist; (3) Latter Day Saints; (4) Reformed; (5) Figures are estimates
Source: Association of Statisticians of American Religious Bodies, 2010 U.S. Religion Census: Religious Congregations & Membership Study

Religious Groups by Tradition

Area	Catholic	Evangelical Protestant	Mainline Protestant	Other Tradition	Black Protestant	Orthodox
MSA[1]	32.8	7.4	13.8	2.1	0.9	0.7
U.S.	19.1	16.2	7.3	4.3	1.6	0.3

Note: Figures are the number of adherents as a percentage of the total population; (1) Figures cover the Pittsburgh, PA Metropolitan Statistical Area—see Appendix B for areas included
Source: Association of Statisticians of American Religious Bodies, 2010 U.S. Religion Census: Religious Congregations & Membership Study

ECONOMY

Gross Metropolitan Product

Area	2011	2012	2013	2014	Rank[2]
MSA[1]	119.3	123.6	126.5	131.5	23

Note: Figures are in billions of dollars; (1) Figures cover the Pittsburgh, PA Metropolitan Statistical Area—see Appendix B for areas included; (2) Rank is based on 2014 data and ranges from 1 to 363
Source: The United States Conference of Mayors, U.S. Metro Economies: Outlook—Gross Metropolitan Product, with Metro Employment Projections, November 2013

Economic Growth

Area	2011 (%)	2012 (%)	2013 (%)	2014 (%)	Rank[2]
MSA[1]	3.5	2.1	1.0	2.0	152
U.S.	1.6	2.5	1.7	2.5	–

Note: Figures are real gross metropolitan product (GMP) growth rates and represent annual average percent change; (1) Figures cover the Pittsburgh, PA Metropolitan Statistical Area—see Appendix B for areas included; (2) Rank is based on 2013 data and ranges from 1 to 363
Source: The United States Conference of Mayors, U.S. Metro Economies: Outlook—Gross Metropolitan Product, with Metro Employment Projections, November 2013

Metropolitan Area Exports

Area	2007	2008	2009	2010	2011	2012	Rank[2]
MSA[1]	9,750.2	11,309.0	8,343.0	12,160.7	15,165.5	14,134.7	24

Note: Figures are in millions of dollars; (1) Figures cover the Pittsburgh, PA Metropolitan Statistical Area—see Appendix B for areas included; (2) Rank is based on 2012 data and ranges from 1 to 369
Source: U.S. Department of Commerce, International Trade Administration, Office of Trade & Industry Information, Manufacturing & Services, data extracted April 1, 2014

INCOME

Income

Area	Per Capita ($)	Median Household ($)	Average Household ($)
City	25,927	37,280	57,505
MSA[1]	28,881	49,973	67,445
U.S.	27,385	51,771	71,579

Note: (1) Figures cover the Pittsburgh, PA Metropolitan Statistical Area—see Appendix B for areas included
Source: U.S. Census Bureau, 2010-2012 American Community Survey 3-Year Estimates

Household Income Distribution

Area	Under $15,000	$15,000 -24,999	$25,000 -34,999	$35,000 -49,999	$50,000 -74,999	$75,000 -99,000	$100,000 -149,999	$150,000 and up
				Percent of Households Earning				
City	21.4	14.5	11.7	13.2	16.5	8.5	7.8	6.5
MSA[1]	13.2	12.1	11.1	13.7	18.7	11.9	11.8	7.5
U.S.	13.1	11.0	10.5	13.7	18.1	11.9	12.5	9.1

Note: (1) Figures cover the Pittsburgh, PA Metropolitan Statistical Area—see Appendix B for areas included
Source: U.S. Census Bureau, 2010-2012 American Community Survey 3-Year Estimates

Poverty Rate

Area	All Ages	Under 18 Years Old	18 to 64 Years Old	65 Years and Over
City	22.9	31.7	22.7	13.2
MSA[1]	12.3	17.6	11.9	7.8
U.S.	15.7	22.2	14.6	9.3

Note: Figures are percentage of people whose income during the past 12 months was below the poverty level;
(1) Figures cover the Pittsburgh, PA Metropolitan Statistical Area—see Appendix B for areas included
Source: U.S. Census Bureau, 2010-2012 American Community Survey 3-Year Estimates

Personal Bankruptcy Filing Rate

Area	2008	2009	2010	2011	2012	2013
Allegheny County	3.54	3.83	3.70	3.19	2.54	2.39
U.S.	3.53	4.61	4.97	4.37	3.76	3.29

Note: Numbers are per 1,000 population and include Chapter 7 and Chapter 13 filings
Source: Federal Deposit Insurance Corporation, Regional Economic Conditions, March 20, 2014

EMPLOYMENT

Labor Force and Employment

Area	Civilian Labor Force			Workers Employed		
	Dec. 2012	Dec. 2013	% Chg.	Dec. 2012	Dec. 2013	% Chg.
City	155,902	153,811	-1.3	144,809	145,348	0.4
MSA[1]	1,261,313	1,244,990	-1.3	1,170,044	1,174,397	0.4
U.S.	154,904,000	154,408,000	-0.3	143,060,000	144,423,000	1.0

Note: Data is not seasonally adjusted and covers workers 16 years of age and older; (1) Metropolitan Statistical Area—see Appendix B for areas included
Source: Bureau of Labor Statistics, Local Area Unemployment Statistics

Unemployment Rate

Area	2013											
	Jan.	Feb.	Mar.	Apr.	May	Jun.	Jul.	Aug.	Sep.	Oct.	Nov.	Dec.
City	8.2	7.3	6.9	6.5	7.0	7.6	7.6	7.9	6.7	6.5	6.4	5.5
MSA[1]	8.6	7.8	7.1	6.4	6.6	7.2	7.0	7.2	6.2	6.1	6.2	5.7
U.S.	8.5	8.1	7.6	7.1	7.3	7.8	7.7	7.3	7.0	7.0	6.6	6.5

Note: Data is not seasonally adjusted and covers workers 16 years of age and older; All figures are percentages;
(1) Metropolitan Statistical Area—see Appendix B for areas included
Source: Bureau of Labor Statistics, Local Area Unemployment Statistics

Employment by Occupation

Occupation Classification	City (%)	MSA[1] (%)	U.S. (%)
Management, Business, Science, and Arts	43.8	37.7	36.0
Natural Resources, Construction, and Maintenance	4.7	7.9	9.1
Production, Transportation, and Material Moving	7.2	11.8	12.0
Sales and Office	22.9	25.1	24.7
Service	21.3	17.6	18.2

Note: Figures cover employed civilians 16 years of age and older; (1) Figures cover the Pittsburgh, PA Metropolitan Statistical Area—see Appendix B for areas included
Source: U.S. Census Bureau, 2010-2012 American Community Survey 3-Year Estimates

Employment by Industry

Sector	MSA[1]		U.S.
	Number of Employees	Percent of Total	Percent of Total
Construction	51,800	4.5	4.2
Education and Health Services	241,100	20.7	15.5
Financial Activities	71,400	6.1	5.7
Government	121,900	10.5	16.1
Information	18,500	1.6	1.9
Leisure and Hospitality	109,800	9.4	10.2
Manufacturing	88,600	7.6	8.7
Mining and Logging	10,700	0.9	0.6
Other Services	51,600	4.4	3.9
Professional and Business Services	174,700	15.0	13.7
Retail Trade	131,800	11.3	11.4
Transportation and Utilities	45,100	3.9	3.8
Wholesale Trade	45,700	3.9	4.2

Note: Figures cover non-farm employment as of December 2013 and are not seasonally adjusted;
(1) Metropolitan Statistical Area—see Appendix B for areas included
Source: Bureau of Labor Statistics, Current Employment Statistics, Employment, Hours, and Earnings

Occupations with Greatest Projected Employment Growth: 2010 – 2020

Occupation[1]	2010 Employment	2020 Projected Employment	Numeric Employment Change	Percent Employment Change
Registered Nurses	136,470	159,610	23,140	17.0
Home Health Aides	67,900	89,820	21,920	32.3
Heavy and Tractor-Trailer Truck Drivers	71,510	83,040	11,530	16.1
Combined Food Preparation and Serving Workers, Including Fast Food	115,230	126,100	10,870	9.4
Personal Care Aides	36,860	47,130	10,280	27.9
Retail Salespersons	189,930	199,800	9,870	5.2
Office Clerks, General	151,450	160,950	9,490	6.3
Nursing Aides, Orderlies, and Attendants	78,080	86,470	8,390	10.8
Laborers and Freight, Stock, and Material Movers, Hand	102,590	110,170	7,590	7.4
Landscaping and Groundskeeping Workers	45,700	53,130	7,430	16.3

Note: Projections cover Pennsylvania; (1) Sorted by numeric employment change
Source: www.projectionscentral.com, State Occupational Projections, 2010–2020 Long-Term Projections

Fastest Growing Occupations: 2010 – 2020

Occupation[1]	2010 Employment	2020 Projected Employment	Numeric Employment Change	Percent Employment Change
Service Unit Operators, Oil, Gas, and Mining	1,040	2,130	1,090	104.6
Rotary Drill Operators, Oil and Gas	1,100	2,200	1,110	100.6
Derrick Operators, Oil and Gas	210	420	210	97.2
Roustabouts, Oil and Gas	1,170	2,290	1,120	95.5
Pump Operators, Except Wellhead Pumpers	700	1,250	550	78.5
Wellhead Pumpers	1,080	1,900	820	76.4
Petroleum Engineers	240	420	180	72.9
Gaming Dealers	1,920	3,280	1,360	71.0
Biomedical Engineers	960	1,560	600	62.6
Helpers—Extraction Workers	1,210	1,920	710	58.9

Note: Projections cover Pennsylvania; (1) Sorted by percent employment change and excludes occupations with numeric employment change less than 100
Source: www.projectionscentral.com, State Occupational Projections, 2010–2020 Long-Term Projections

Average Wages

Occupation	$/Hr.	Occupation	$/Hr.
Accountants and Auditors	32.64	Maids and Housekeeping Cleaners	10.06
Automotive Mechanics	17.37	Maintenance and Repair Workers	18.75
Bookkeepers	16.84	Marketing Managers	69.89
Carpenters	21.51	Nuclear Medicine Technologists	27.40
Cashiers	9.06	Nurses, Licensed Practical	19.78
Clerks, General Office	14.42	Nurses, Registered	30.04
Clerks, Receptionists/Information	12.31	Nursing Assistants	13.16
Clerks, Shipping/Receiving	15.46	Packers and Packagers, Hand	12.27
Computer Programmers	30.77	Physical Therapists	39.28
Computer Systems Analysts	33.58	Postal Service Mail Carriers	24.65
Computer User Support Specialists	22.75	Real Estate Brokers	71.36
Cooks, Restaurant	11.71	Retail Salespersons	12.50
Dentists	72.66	Sales Reps., Exc. Tech./Scientific	31.81
Electrical Engineers	41.29	Sales Reps., Tech./Scientific	42.81
Electricians	24.73	Secretaries, Exc. Legal/Med./Exec.	15.24
Financial Managers	60.75	Security Guards	11.90
First-Line Supervisors/Managers, Sales	21.60	Surgeons	113.69
Food Preparation Workers	9.91	Teacher Assistants	11.50
General and Operations Managers	57.93	Teachers, Elementary School	27.90
Hairdressers/Cosmetologists	11.63	Teachers, Secondary School	29.00
Internists	105.49	Telemarketers	12.88
Janitors and Cleaners	12.61	Truck Drivers, Heavy/Tractor-Trailer	20.52
Landscaping/Groundskeeping Workers	12.40	Truck Drivers, Light/Delivery Svcs.	15.69
Lawyers	68.07	Waiters and Waitresses	9.69

Note: Wage data covers the Pittsburgh, PA Metropolitan Statistical Area—see Appendix B for areas included. Hourly wages for elementary/secondary school teachers and teacher assistants were calculated by the editors from annual wage data assuming a 40 hour work week; n/a not available.
Source: Bureau of Labor Statistics, Metro Area Occupational Employment and Wage Estimates, May 2013

RESIDENTIAL REAL ESTATE

Building Permits

Area	Single-Family			Multi-Family			Total		
	2012	2013	Pct. Chg.	2012	2013	Pct. Chg.	2012	2013	Pct. Chg.
City	137	100	-27.0	0	0	-	137	100	-27.0
MSA[1]	2,918	3,251	11.4	548	1,312	139.4	3,466	4,563	31.7
U.S.	518,695	620,802	19.7	310,963	370,020	19.0	829,658	990,822	19.4

Note: (1) Metropolitan Statistical Area—see Appendix B for areas included; figures represent new, privately-owned housing units authorized (unadjusted data); All permit data are based on estimates with imputation.
Source: U.S. Census Bureau, Manufacturing, Mining, and Construction Statistics, Building Permits, 2012, 2013

Homeownership Rate

Area	2006 (%)	2007 (%)	2008 (%)	2009 (%)	2010 (%)	2011 (%)	2012 (%)	2013 (%)
MSA[1]	72.2	73.6	73.2	71.7	70.4	70.3	67.9	68.3
U.S.	68.8	68.1	67.8	67.4	66.9	66.1	65.4	65.1

Note: (1) Figures cover the Pittsburgh, PA Metropolitan Statistical Area—see Appendix B for areas included
Source: U.S. Census Bureau, Housing Vacancies and Homeownership Annual Statistics: 2013

Housing Vacancy Rates

Area	Gross Vacancy Rate[2] (%)			Year-Round Vacancy Rate[3] (%)			Rental Vacancy Rate[4] (%)			Homeowner Vacancy Rate[5] (%)		
	2011	2012	2013	2011	2012	2013	2011	2012	2013	2011	2012	2013
MSA[1]	12.3	14.4	12.7	11.6	14.1	12.5	6.3	6.4	7.8	2.2	1.3	1.7
U.S.	14.2	13.8	13.8	11.1	10.8	10.7	9.5	8.7	8.3	2.5	2.0	2.0

Note: (1) Figures cover the Pittsburgh, PA Metropolitan Statistical Area—see Appendix B for areas included; (2) The percentage of the total housing inventory that is vacant; (3) The percentage of the housing inventory (excluding seasonal units) that is year-round vacant; (4) The percentage of rental inventory that is vacant for rent; (5) The percentage of homeowner inventory that is vacant for sale
Source: U.S. Census Bureau, Housing Vacancies and Homeownership Annual Statistics: 2013

TAXES

State Corporate Income Tax Rates

State	Tax Rate (%)	Income Brackets ($)	Num. of Brackets	Financial Institution Tax Rate (%)[a]	Federal Income Tax Ded.
Pennsylvania	9.99	Flat rate	1	(a)	No

Note: Tax rates as of January 1, 2014; (a) Rates listed are the corporate income tax rate applied to financial institutions or excise taxes based on income. Some states have other taxes based upon the value of deposits or shares.
Source: Federation of Tax Administrators, "State Corporate Income Tax Rates, 2014"

State Individual Income Tax Rates

State	Tax Rate (%)	Income Brackets ($)	Num. of Brackets	Personal Exempt. ($)[1] Single	Personal Exempt. ($)[1] Dependents	Fed. Inc. Tax Ded.
Pennsylvania	3.07	Flat rate	1	None		No

Note: Tax rates as of January 1, 2014; Local- and county-level taxes are not included; n/a not applicable;
(1) Married joint filers generally receive double the single exemption
Source: Federation of Tax Administrators, "State Individual Income Tax Rates, 2014"

Various State and Local Tax Rates

State	State and Local Sales and Use (%)	State Sales and Use (%)	Gasoline[1] (¢/gal.)	Cigarette[2] ($/pack)	Spirits[3] ($/gal.)	Wine[4] ($/gal.)	Beer[5] ($/gal.)
Pennsylvania	7.0	6.00	41.80	1.600	7.21 (g)	(l)	0.08

Note: All tax rates as of January 1, 2014; (1) The American Petroleum Institute has developed a methodology for determining the average tax rate on a gallon of fuel. Rates may include any of the following: excise taxes, environmental fees, storage tank fees, other fees or taxes, general sales tax, and local taxes. In states where gasoline is subject to the general sales tax, or where the fuel tax is based on the average sale price, the average rate determined by API is sensitive to changes in the price of gasoline. States that fully or partially apply general sales taxes to gasoline: CA, CO, GA, IL, IN, MI, NY; (2) The federal excise tax of $1.0066 per pack and local taxes are not included; (3) Rates are those applicable to off-premise sales of 40% alcohol by volume (a.b.v.) distilled spirits in 750ml containers. Local excise taxes are excluded; (4) Rates are those applicable to off-premise sales of 11% a.b.v. non-carbonated wine in 750ml containers; (5) Rates are those applicable to off-premise sales of 4.7% a.b.v. beer in 12 ounce containers; (g) States where the government controls sales. In these "control states," products are subject to ad valorem mark-up and excise taxes. The excise tax rate is calculated using a methodology developed by the Distilled Spirits Council of the United States; (l) Control states, where the government controls all sales. Products can be subject to ad valorem mark-up and excise taxes.
Source: Tax Foundation, 2014 Facts & Figures: How Does Your State Compare?

State Business Tax Climate Index Rankings

State	Overall Rank	Corporate Tax Index Rank	Individual Income Tax Index Rank	Sales Tax Index Rank	Unemployment Insurance Tax Index Rank	Property Tax Index Rank
Pennsylvania	24	46	16	19	39	43

Note: The index is a measure of how each state's tax laws affect economic performance. The lower the rank, the more favorable a state's tax system is for business. States without a given tax are given a ranking of 1. The scores/rankings for the District of Columbia do not affect other states. The 2014 index represents the tax climate as of July 1, 2013.
Source: Tax Foundation, State Business Tax Climate Index 2014

COMMERCIAL REAL ESTATE

Office Market

Market Area	Inventory (sq. ft.)	Vacancy Rate (%)	Under Construction (sq. ft.)	YTD Net Absorption (sq. ft.)	Total Average Asking Rent ($/sq. ft./year)
Pittsburgh	52,236,379	14.7	2,087,200	269,910	21.03
National	4,726,900,879	15.0	55,419,286	42,829,434	26.27

Source: Newmark Grubb Knight Frank, National Office Market Report, 4th Quarter 2013

Industrial/Warehouse/R&D Market

Market Area	Inventory (sq. ft.)	Vacancy Rate (%)	Under Construction (sq. ft.)	YTD Net Absorption (sq. ft.)	Total Average Asking Rent ($/sq. ft./year)
Pittsburgh	116,389,193	7.8	700,000	891,241	5.14
National	14,022,031,238	7.9	83,249,164	156,549,903	5.40

Source: Newmark Grubb Knight Frank, National Industrial Market Report, 4th Quarter 2013

COMMERCIAL UTILITIES

Typical Monthly Electric Bills

Area	Commercial Service ($/month)		Industrial Service ($/month)	
	1,500 kWh	40 kW demand 14,000 kWh	1,000 kW demand 200,000 kWh	50,000 kW demand 15,000,000 kWh
City	180	1,220	22,916	903,492
Average[1]	197	1,636	25,662	1,485,307

Note: Based on total rates in effect July 1, 2013; (1) average based on 180 utilities surveyed
Source: Edison Electric Institute, Typical Bills and Average Rates Report, Summer 2013

TRANSPORTATION

Means of Transportation to Work

Area	Car/Truck/Van		Public Transportation			Bicycle	Walked	Other Means	Worked at Home
	Drove Alone	Car-pooled	Bus	Subway	Railroad				
City	54.1	10.4	17.3	0.2	0.0	1.5	10.9	1.8	3.8
MSA[1]	77.1	9.1	5.0	0.1	0.0	0.3	3.5	1.3	3.6
U.S.	76.4	9.7	2.6	1.7	0.5	0.6	2.8	1.3	4.3

Note: Figures are percentages and cover workers 16 years of age and older; (1) Figures cover the Pittsburgh, PA Metropolitan Statistical Area—see Appendix B for areas included
Source: U.S. Census Bureau, 2010-2012 American Community Survey 3-Year Estimates

Travel Time to Work

Area	Less Than 10 Minutes	10 to 19 Minutes	20 to 29 Minutes	30 to 44 Minutes	45 to 59 Minutes	60 to 89 Minutes	90 Minutes or More
City	10.9	32.7	25.6	20.5	5.8	3.1	1.4
MSA[1]	12.8	27.6	21.5	21.6	8.8	5.7	2.0
U.S.	13.5	29.8	20.9	20.1	7.5	5.6	2.5

Note: Figures are percentages and include workers 16 years old and over; (1) Figures cover the Pittsburgh, PA Metropolitan Statistical Area—see Appendix B for areas included
Source: U.S. Census Bureau, 2010-2012 American Community Survey 3-Year Estimates

Travel Time Index

Area	1985	1990	1995	2000	2005	2010	2011
Urban Area[1]	1.21	1.29	1.31	1.29	1.29	1.24	1.24
Average[2]	1.09	1.14	1.16	1.19	1.23	1.18	1.18

Note: Travel Time Index—the ratio of travel time in the peak period to the travel time at free-flow conditions. For example, a value of 1.30 indicates a 20-minute free-flow trip takes 26 minutes in the peak. Free-flow speeds (60 mph on freeways and 35 mph on principal arterials) are used as the comparison threshold; (1) Covers the Pittsburgh PA urban area; (2) average of 498 urban areas
Source: Texas Transportation Institute, Urban Mobility Report 2012, December 2012

Public Transportation

Agency Name / Mode of Transportation	Vehicles Operated in Maximum Service	Annual Unlinked Passenger Trips (in thous.)	Annual Passenger Miles (in thous.)
Port Authority of Allegheny County			
Bus (directly operated)	572	55,704.7	218,677.2
Demand Response (purchased transportation)	325	1,769.5	13,362.9
Inclined Plane (directly operated)	2	723.5	84.5
Inclined Plane (purchased transportation)	2	525.8	78.9
Light Rail (directly operated)	56	7,130.4	33,971.7

Source: Federal Transit Administration, National Transit Database, 2012

Air Transportation

Airport Name and Code / Type of Service	Passenger Airlines[1]	Passenger Enplanements	Freight Carriers[2]	Freight (lbs.)
Pittsburgh International Airport (PIT)				
Domestic service (U.S. carriers - 2013)	32	3,744,473	16	74,196,133
International service (U.S. carriers - 2012)	13	43,135	3	17,875

Note: (1) Includes all U.S.-based major, minor and commuter airlines that carried at least one passenger during the year; (2) Includes all U.S.-based airlines and freight carriers that transported at least one lb. of freight during the year.
Source: Bureau of Transportation Statistics, The Intermodal Transportation Database, Air Carriers: T-100 Domestic Market (U.S. Carriers), 2013; Bureau of Transportation Statistics, The Intermodal Transportation Database, Air Carriers: T-100 International Market (U.S. Carriers), 2012

Other Transportation Statistics

Major Highways:	I-70; I-76; I-79
Amtrak Service:	Yes
Major Waterways/Ports:	Port of Pittsburgh

Source: Amtrak.com; Google Maps

BUSINESSES

Major Business Headquarters

Company Name	Rankings	
	Fortune[1]	Forbes[2]
Allegheny Technologies	490	-
Giant Eagle	-	33
H.J. Heinz	234	-
HJ Heinz	-	26
PNC Financial Services Group	170	-
PPG Industries	182	-
United States Steel	147	-
WESCO International	385	-

Note: (1) Fortune 500—companies that produce a 10-K are ranked 1 to 500 based on 2012 revenue; (2) all private companies with at least $2 billion in annual revenue through the end of their most current fiscal year are ranked 1 to 224; companies listed are headquartered in the city; dashes indicate no ranking
Source: Fortune, "Fortune 500," May 20, 2013; Forbes, "America's Largest Private Companies," December 18, 2013

Fast-Growing Businesses

According to *Inc.*, Pittsburgh is home to three of America's 500 fastest-growing private companies: **Target Freight Management** (#128); **Branding Brand** (#332); **4Moms** (#399). Criteria: must be an independent, privately-held, for-profit, U.S. corporation, proprietorship or partnership; revenues must be at least $100,000 in 2009 and $2 million in 2012; must have four-year operating/sales history. Holding companies, regulated banks, and utilities were excluded. *Inc., "America's 500 Fastest-Growing Private Companies," September 2013*

According to *Fortune*, Pittsburgh is home to one of the 100 fastest-growing companies in the world: **HFF** (#9). Companies were ranked by their revenue growth rate; their EPS growth rate; and their three-year annualized total return to investors for the period ending June 30, 2013. Criteria for inclusion: a company, foreign or domestic, must trade on a major U.S. stock exchange; must file quarterly reports with the SEC; must have a minimum market capitalization of $250 million; must have a stock price of at least $5 on June 29, 2013; must have been trading continuously since June 30, 2009; must have revenue and net income for the four quarters ended on or before April 30, 2013, of at least $50 million and $10 million, respectively; and must have posted a compound annual growth in revenue and earnings per share of at least 20% annually over the three years ending on or before April 30, 2013. REITs, limited-liability companies, limited parterships, companies about to be acquired, and companies that lost money in the quarter ending April 30, 2013 were excluded. *Fortune, "100 Fastest-Growing Companies," August 29, 2013*

According to *Initiative for a Competitive Inner City (ICIC)*, Pittsburgh is home to one of America's 100 fastest-growing "inner city" companies: **Network Deposition Services** (#62). Companies were ranked by their five-year compound annual growth rate. Criteria for inclusion: company must be headquartered in or have 51 percent or more of its physical operations in an economically distressed urban area; must be an independent, for-profit corporation, partnership or proprietorship; must have 10 or more employees and have a five-year sales history that includes sales of at least $200,000 in the base year and at least $1 million in the current year with no decrease in sales over the two most recent years. *Initiative for a Competitive Inner City (ICIC), "Inner City 100 Companies, 2013"*

According to Deloitte, Pittsburgh is home to one of North America's 500 fastest-growing high-technology companies: **FAB Universal Corp.** (#257). Companies are ranked by percentage growth in revenue over a five-year period. Criteria for inclusion: company must be headquartered within North America; must own proprietary intellectual property or proprietary technology that contributes to a significant portion of the company's operating revenue, or devote a significant proportion of revenues to research and development of technology; must have been in business for a minumum of five years with 2008 operating revenues of at least $50,000 USD/CD and 2012 operating revenues of at least $5 million USD/CD. *Deloitte Touche Tohmatsu, 2013 Technology Fast 500*[TM]

Minority Business Opportunity

Pittsburgh is home to one company which is on the *Black Enterprise* Industrial/Service 100 list (100 largest companies based on gross sales): **Urban Lending Solutions** (#16). Criteria: operational in previous calendar year; at least 51% black-owned and manufactures/owns the product it sells or provides industrial or consumer services. Brokerages, real estate firms and firms that provide professional services are not eligible. *Black Enterprise, B.E. 100s, 2013*

Pittsburgh is home to one company which is on the *Hispanic Business* 500 list (500 largest U.S. Hispanic-owned companies based on 2012 revenue): **Novus Staffing Solutions** (#438). Companies included must show at least 51 percent ownership by Hispanic U.S. citizens, and must maintain headquarters in one of the 50 states or Washington, D.C. *Hispanic Business, "Hispanic Business 500," June 20, 2013*

Minority- and Women-Owned Businesses

Group	All Firms		Firms with Paid Employees			
	Firms	Sales ($000)	Firms	Sales ($000)	Employees	Payroll ($000)
Asian	1,001	290,542	267	268,134	2,489	110,962
Black	2,243	161,338	239	136,581	2,278	51,028
Hispanic	(s)	(s)	(s)	(s)	(s)	(s)
Women	6,937	1,091,653	1,138	973,435	10,109	257,251
All Firms	24,581	65,188,095	7,772	64,494,543	290,469	13,852,713

Note: Figures cover firms located in the city; minority- and women-owned business are defined as firms in which the corresponding group own 51% or more of the stock or equity of the company; (s) estimates are suppressed when publication standards are not met
Source: U.S. Census Bureau, 2007 Economic Census, Survey of Business Owners (2012 Survey of Business Owners data will be released starting in June 2015)

HOTELS & CONVENTION CENTERS

Hotels/Motels

Area	5 Star		4 Star		3 Star		2 Star		1 Star		Not Rated	
	Num.	Pct.[3]	Num.	Pct.[3]	Num.	Pct.[3]	Num.	Pct.[3]	Num.	Pct.[3]	Num.	Pct.[3]
City[1]	0	0.0	5	3.4	56	38.6	71	49.0	4	2.8	9	6.2
Total[2]	142	0.9	1,005	6.0	5,147	30.9	8,578	51.4	408	2.4	1,397	8.4

Note: (1) Figures cover Pittsburgh and vicinity; (2) Figures cover all 100 cities in this book; (3) Percentage of hotels which have a given star rating; Star ratings are determined by expedia.com and offer an indication of the general quality of a particular hotel.
Source: expedia.com, April 7, 2014

Major Convention Centers

Name	Overall Space (sq. ft.)	Exhibit Space (sq. ft.)	Meeting Space (sq. ft.)	Meeting Rooms
David L. Lawrence Convention Center	1,500,000	313,400	n/a	53

Note: Table includes convention centers located in the Pittsburgh, PA metro area; n/a not available
Source: Original research

Living Environment

COST OF LIVING

Cost of Living Index

Composite Index	Groceries	Housing	Utilities	Trans-portation	Health Care	Misc. Goods/ Services
93.6	94.2	79.3	94.9	104.2	100.9	99.1

Note: The Cost of Living Index measures regional differences in the cost of consumer goods and services, excluding taxes and non-consumer expenditures, for professional and managerial households in the top income quintile. It is based on more than 50,000 prices covering almost 60 different items for which prices are collected three times a year by chambers of commerce, economic development organizations or university applied economic centers in each participating urban area. The numbers shown should be read as a percentage above or below the national average of 100. For example, a value of 115.4 in the groceries column indicates that grocery prices are 15.4% higher than the national average. Small differences in the index numbers should not be interpreted as significant; Figures cover the Pittsburgh PA urban area.
Source: The Council for Community and Economic Research, ACCRA Cost of Living Index, 2013

Grocery Prices

Area[1]	T-Bone Steak ($/pound)	Frying Chicken ($/pound)	Whole Milk ($/half gal.)	Eggs ($/dozen)	Orange Juice ($/64 oz.)	Coffee ($/11.5 oz.)
City[2]	10.53	1.43	2.05	1.69	3.56	4.51
Avg.	10.19	1.28	2.34	1.81	3.48	4.39
Min.	8.56	0.94	1.44	1.19	2.78	3.40
Max.	14.82	2.28	3.56	3.73	6.23	7.32

*Note: (1) Values for the local area are compared with the average, minimum and maximum values for all 327 areas in the Cost of Living Index; (2) Figures cover the Pittsburgh PA urban area; **T-Bone Steak** (price per pound); **Frying Chicken** (price per pound, whole fryer); **Whole Milk** (half gallon carton); **Eggs** (price per dozen, Grade A, large); **Orange Juice** (64 oz. Tropicana or Florida Natural); **Coffee** (11.5 oz. can, vacuum-packed, Maxwell House, Hills Bros, or Folgers).*
Source: The Council for Community and Economic Research, ACCRA Cost of Living Index, 2013

Housing and Utility Costs

Area[1]	New Home Price ($)	Apartment Rent ($/month)	All Electric ($/month)	Part Electric ($/month)	Other Energy ($/month)	Telephone ($/month)
City[2]	220,334	855	-	83.58	77.16	24.95
Avg.	295,864	900	171.38	91.82	70.12	27.73
Min.	185,506	458	117.80	48.81	33.67	17.16
Max.	1,358,917	3,783	441.68	171.40	372.65	39.47

*Note: (1) Values for the local area are compared with the average, minimum and maximum values for all 327 areas in the Cost of Living Index; (2) Figures cover the Pittsburgh PA urban area; **New Home Price** (2,400 sf living area, 8,000 sf lot, in urban area with full utilities); **Apartment Rent** (950 sf 2 bedroom/1.5 or 2 bath, unfurnished, excluding all utilities except water); **All Electric** (average monthly cost for an all-electric home); **Part Electric** (average monthly cost for a part-electric home); **Other Energy** (average monthly cost for natural gas, fuel oil, coal, wood, and any other forms of energy except electricity); **Telephone** (price includes basic monthly rate for a private residential line plus additional local usage charges incurred by a family of four).*
Source: The Council for Community and Economic Research, ACCRA Cost of Living Index, 2013

Health Care, Transportation, and Other Costs

Area[1]	Doctor ($/visit)	Dentist ($/visit)	Optometrist ($/visit)	Gasoline ($/gallon)	Beauty Salon ($/visit)	Men's Shirt ($)
City[2]	94.13	85.40	97.27	3.63	38.37	23.92
Avg.	101.40	86.48	96.16	3.44	33.87	26.55
Min.	61.67	50.83	50.12	3.08	18.92	12.48
Max.	182.71	152.50	223.78	4.33	68.22	52.03

*Note: (1) Values for the local area are compared with the average, minimum and maximum values for all 327 areas in the Cost of Living Index; (2) Figures cover the Pittsburgh PA urban area; **Doctor** (general practitioners routine exam of an established patient); **Dentist** (adult teeth cleaning and periodic oral examination); **Optometrist** (full vision eye exam for established adult patient); **Gasoline** (one gallon regular unleaded, national brand, including all taxes, cash price at self-service pump if available); **Beauty Salon** (woman's shampoo, trim, and blow-dry); **Men's Shirt** (cotton/polyester dress shirt, pinpoint weave, long sleeves).*
Source: The Council for Community and Economic Research, ACCRA Cost of Living Index, 2013

HOUSING

House Price Index (HPI)

Area	National Ranking[2]	Quarterly Change (%)	One-Year Change (%)	Five-Year Change (%)
MSA[1]	132	-0.32	2.57	7.92
U.S.[3]	–	1.20	7.69	4.18

Note: The HPI is a weighted repeat sales index. It measures average price changes in repeat sales or refinancings on the same properties. This information is obtained by reviewing repeat mortgage transactions on single-family properties whose mortgages have been purchased or securitized by Fannie Mae or Freddie Mac in January 1975; (1) Pittsburgh, PA Metropolitan Statistical Area—see Appendix B for areas included; (2) Rankings are based on annual percentage change for all metro areas containing at least 15,000 transactions over the last 10 years and ranges from 1 to 283; (3) figures based on a weighted average of Census Division estimates using a seasonally adjusted, purchase-only index; all figures are for the period ending December 31, 2013
Source: Federal Housing Finance Agency, House Price Index, February 25, 2014

Median Single-Family Home Prices

Area	2011	2012	2013p	Percent Change 2012 to 2013
MSA[1]	n/a	n/a	n/a	n/a
U.S. Average	166.2	177.2	197.4	11.4

Note: Figures are median sales prices of existing single-family homes in thousands of dollars; (p) preliminary; n/a not available; (1) Pittsburgh, PA Metropolitan Statistical Area—see Appendix B for areas included
Source: National Association of Realtors, Median Sales Price of Existing Single-Family Homes for Metropolitan Areas, 4th Quarter 2013

Qualifying Income Based on Median Sales Price of Existing Single-Family Homes

Area	With 5% Down ($)	With 10% Down ($)	With 20% Down ($)
MSA[1]	n/a	n/a	n/a
U.S. Average	45,395	43,006	38,228

Note: Figures are preliminary; Qualifying income is based on a mortgage rate of 4.4%. Monthly principal and interest payment is limited to 25% of income; n/a not available; (1) Pittsburgh, PA Metropolitan Statistical Area—see Appendix B for areas included
Source: National Association of Realtors, Qualifying Income Based on Median Sales Price of Existing Single-Family Homes for Metropolitan Areas, 4th Quarter 2013

Median Apartment Condo-Coop Home Prices

Area	2011	2012	2013p	Percent Change 2012 to 2013
MSA[1]	n/a	n/a	n/a	n/a
U.S. Average	165.1	173.7	194.9	12.2

Note: Figures are median sales prices of existing apartment condo-coop homes in thousands of dollars; (p) preliminary; n/a not available; (1) Pittsburgh, PA Metropolitan Statistical Area—see Appendix B for areas included
Source: National Association of Realtors, Median Sales Price of Existing Apartment Condo-Coop Homes for Metropolitan Areas, 4th Quarter 2013

Gross Monthly Rent

Area	Under $200	$200 -299	$300 -499	$500 -749	$750 -999	$1,000 -1,499	$1,500 and up	Median ($)
City	4.1	6.0	10.4	30.0	24.3	18.8	6.3	746
MSA[1]	3.0	5.7	14.6	34.2	24.3	13.6	4.5	695
U.S.	1.7	3.3	8.1	22.7	24.3	25.7	14.3	889

Note: Figures are percentages except for Median; Gross rent is the contract rent plus the estimated average monthly cost of utilities (electricity, gas, and water and sewer) and fuels (oil, coal, kerosene, wood, etc.) if these are paid by the renter (or paid for the renter by someone else); (1) Figures cover the Pittsburgh, PA Metropolitan Statistical Area—see Appendix B for areas included
Source: U.S. Census Bureau, 2010-2012 American Community Survey 3-Year Estimates

Year Housing Structure Built

Area	2010 or Later	2000 -2009	1990 -1999	1980 -1989	1970 -1979	1960 -1969	1950 -1959	1940 -1949	Before 1940	Median Year
City	0.1	3.9	2.7	4.5	5.8	8.1	13.0	9.2	52.8	<1940
MSA[1]	0.2	6.7	7.5	7.6	11.9	11.1	16.8	9.8	28.4	1957
U.S.	0.5	14.9	13.8	13.9	15.9	11.1	10.9	5.5	13.5	1976

Note: Figures are percentages except for Median Year; (1) Figures cover the Pittsburgh, PA Metropolitan Statistical Area—see Appendix B for areas included
Source: U.S. Census Bureau, 2010-2012 American Community Survey 3-Year Estimates

HEALTH

Health Risk Data

Category	MSA[1] (%)	U.S. (%)
Adults aged 18–64 who have any kind of health care coverage	85.9	79.6
Adults who reported being in good or excellent health	83.4	83.1
Adults who are current smokers	22.4	19.6
Adults who are heavy drinkers[2]	6.9	6.1
Adults who are binge drinkers[3]	19.0	16.9
Adults who are overweight (BMI 25.0 - 29.9)	37.5	35.8
Adults who are obese (BMI 30.0 - 99.8)	26.9	27.6
Adults who participated in any physical activities in the past month	75.6	77.1
Adults 50+ who have ever had a sigmoidoscopy or colonoscopy	66.6	67.3
Women aged 40+ who have had a mammogram within the past two years	72.6	74.0
Men aged 40+ who have had a PSA test within the past two years	45.7	45.2
Adults aged 65+ who have had flu shot within the past year	60.8	60.1
Adults who always wear a seatbelt	87.5	93.8

Note: Data as of 2012 unless otherwise noted; (1) Figures cover the Pittsburgh, PA Metropolitan Statistical Area—see Appendix B for areas included; (2) Heavy drinkers are classified as males having more than two drinks per day or females having more than one drink per day; (3) Binge drinkers are classified as males having five or more drinks on one occasion or females having four or more drinks on one occasion
Source: Centers for Disease Control and Prevention, Behaviorial Risk Factor Surveillance System, SMART: Selected Metropolitan/Micropolitan Area Risk Trends, 2012

Chronic Health Indicators

Category	MSA[1] (%)	U.S. (%)
Adults who have ever been told they had a heart attack	4.7	4.5
Adults who have ever been told they had a stroke	3.3	2.9
Adults who have been told they currently have asthma	9.3	8.9
Adults who have ever been told they have arthritis	31.2	25.7
Adults who have ever been told they have diabetes[2]	10.9	9.7
Adults who have ever been told they had skin cancer	5.2	5.7
Adults who have ever been told they had any other types of cancer	8.3	6.5
Adults who have ever been told they have COPD	7.8	6.2
Adults who have ever been told they have kidney disease	1.8	2.5
Adults who have ever been told they have a form of depression	18.2	18.0

Note: Data as of 2012 unless otherwise noted; (1) Figures cover the Pittsburgh, PA Metropolitan Statistical Area—see Appendix B for areas included; (2) Figures do not include pregnancy-related, borderline, or pre-diabetes
Source: Centers for Disease Control and Prevention, Behaviorial Risk Factor Surveillance System, SMART: Selected Metropolitan/Micropolitan Area Risk Trends, 2012

Mortality Rates for the Top 10 Causes of Death in the U.S.

ICD-10[a] Sub-Chapter	ICD-10[a] Code	Age-Adjusted Mortality Rate[1] per 100,000 population	
		County[2]	U.S.
Malignant neoplasms	C00-C97	187.8	174.2
Ischaemic heart diseases	I20-I25	137.0	119.1
Other forms of heart disease	I30-I51	46.7	49.6
Chronic lower respiratory diseases	J40-J47	39.6	43.2
Cerebrovascular diseases	I60-I69	41.1	40.3
Organic, including symptomatic, mental disorders	F01-F09	36.3	30.5
Other degenerative diseases of the nervous system	G30-G31	20.4	26.3
Other external causes of accidental injury	W00-X59	34.7	25.1
Diabetes mellitus	E10-E14	17.8	21.3
Hypertensive diseases	I10-I15	12.8	18.8

Note: (a) ICD-10 = International Classification of Diseases 10th Revision; (1) Mortality rates are a three year average covering 2008-2010; (2) Figures cover Allegheny County
Source: Centers for Disease Control and Prevention, National Center for Health Statistics. Compressed Mortality File 1999-2010 on CDC WONDER Online Database, released January 2013. Data are compiled from the Compressed Mortality File 1999-2010, Series 20 No. 2P, 2013.

Mortality Rates for Selected Causes of Death

ICD-10[a] Sub-Chapter	ICD-10[a] Code	Age-Adjusted Mortality Rate[1] per 100,000 population	
		County[2]	U.S.
Assault	X85-Y09	8.4	5.5
Diseases of the liver	K70-K76	14.3	12.4
Human immunodeficiency virus (HIV) disease	B20-B24	1.7	3.0
Influenza and pneumonia	J09-J18	17.6	16.4
Intentional self-harm	X60-X84	10.2	11.8
Malnutrition	E40-E46	0.9	0.8
Obesity and other hyperalimentation	E65-E68	1.3	1.6
Renal failure	N17-N19	17.6	13.6
Transport accidents	V01-V99	7.0	12.6
Viral hepatitis	B15-B19	1.4	2.2

Note: (a) ICD-10 = International Classification of Diseases 10th Revision; (1) Mortality rates are a three year average covering 2008-2010; (2) Figures cover Allegheny County
Source: Centers for Disease Control and Prevention, National Center for Health Statistics. Compressed Mortality File 1999-2010 on CDC WONDER Online Database, released January 2013. Data are compiled from the Compressed Mortality File 1999-2010, Series 20 No. 2P, 2013.

Health Insurance Coverage

Area	With Health Insurance	With Private Health Insurance	With Public Health Insurance	Without Health Insurance	Population Under Age 18 Without Health Insurance
City	89.8	68.7	33.4	10.2	2.9
MSA[1]	91.9	75.5	32.3	8.1	2.8
U.S.	84.9	65.4	30.4	15.1	7.5

Note: Figures are percentages that cover the civilian noninstitutionalized population; (1) Figures cover the Pittsburgh, PA Metropolitan Statistical Area—see Appendix B for areas included
Source: U.S. Census Bureau, 2010-2012 American Community Survey 3-Year Estimates

Number of Medical Professionals

Area[1]	MDs[2]	DOs[2,3]	Dentists	Podiatrists	Chiropractors	Optometrists
Local (number)	7,342	433	1,022	128	479	220
Local (rate[4])	598.2	35.3	83.1	10.4	38.9	17.9
U.S. (rate[4])	267.6	19.6	61.7	5.6	24.7	14.5

Note: Data as of 2012 unless noted; (1) Local data covers Allegheny County; (2) Data as of 2011; (3) Doctor of Osteopathic Medicine; (4) rate per 100,000 population
Source: Area Resource File (ARF) 2012-2013. U.S. Department of Health and Human Services, Health Resources and Services Administration, Bureau of Health Professions

Best Hospitals

According to *U.S. News,* the Pittsburgh, PA metro area is home to three of the best hospitals in the U.S.: **Western Pennsylvania Hospital** (1 specialty); **Magee-Womens Hospital of UPMC** (3 specialties); **UPMC-University of Pittsburgh Medical Center** (Honor Roll/15 specialties). The hospitals listed were nationally ranked in at least one adult specialty. Only 147 hospitals nationwide were nationally ranked in one or more specialties. Eighteen hospitals in the U.S. made the Honor Roll by ranking near the top in at least six specialties.*U.S. News Online, "America's Best Hospitals 2013-14"*

According to *U.S. News,* the Pittsburgh, PA metro area is home to one of the best children's hospitals in the U.S.: **Children's Hospital of Pittsburgh of UPMC** (Honor Roll). The hospital listed was highly ranked in at least one pediatric specialty. Eighty-seven hospitals in the U.S. ranked in at least one specialty. Ten children's hospitals in the U.S. made the Honor Roll by ranking near the top in three or more specialties.*U.S. News Online, "America's Best Children's Hospitals 2013-14"*

EDUCATION

Public School District Statistics

District Name	Schls	Pupils	Pupil/ Teacher Ratio	Minority Pupils[1] (%)	Free Lunch Eligible[2] (%)	IEP[3] (%)
Baldwin-Whitehall SD	5	4,197	16.2	17.4	23.2	10.2
Chartiers Valley SD	4	3,447	14.3	14.7	18.2	12.2
Fox Chapel Area SD	6	4,349	11.3	14.2	14.2	13.5
Keystone Oaks SD	5	2,079	15.1	11.8	24.0	14.5
Mt Lebanon SD	10	5,278	13.4	9.8	6.0	13.4
North Allegheny SD	12	8,199	14.5	13.2	2.6	9.9
North Hills SD	6	4,232	14.1	8.5	14.9	15.2
Penn Hills SD	5	3,987	12.9	63.3	47.8	19.6
Pittsburgh SD	65	26,653	13.5	66.3	67.1	21.8
Upper Saint Clair SD	6	4,138	15.2	11.8	2.7	13.7
Woodland Hills SD	8	4,048	13.0	68.9	63.7	22.4

Note: Table includes school districts with 2,000 or more students; (1) Percentage of students that are not non-Hispanic white; (2) Percentage of students that are eligible for the free lunch program; (3) Percentage of students that have an Individualized Education Program.
Source: U.S. Department of Education, National Center for Education Statistics, Common Core of Data, Local Education Agency (School District) Universe Survey: School Year 2011-2012; U.S. Department of Education, National Center for Education Statistics, Common Core of Data, Public Elementary/Secondary School Universe Survey: School Year 2011-2012

Best High Schools

High School Name	Rank[1]	Grad. Rate[2] (%)	Coll.[3] (%)	AP/IB/ AICE Tests[4]	AP/IB/ AICE Score[5]	SAT Score[6]	ACT Score[6]
Fox Chapel Area H.S.	826	96	90	0.3	4.0	1306	n/a
Mt. Lebanon H.S.	346	97	97	0.3	4.0	1695	24.7
Pittsburgh Allderdice H.S.	1472	85	87	0.3	3.3	1560	23.1
Urban Pathways 6-12 Charter School	1831	97	100	0.1	1.3	807	n/a

Note: (1) Public schools are ranked from 1 to 2,000 based on the following self-reported statistics (with the corresponding weight used in calculating their overall score). Schools that were newly founded and did not have a graduating senior class in 2012 were excluded; (2) Four-year, on-time graduation rate (25%); (3) Percent of 2011 graduates who were accepted to college (25%); (4) AP/IB/AICE tests taken per student (25%); (5) Average AP/IB/AICE exam score (10%); (6) Average SAT and/or ACT score (10%); Percent of students enrolled in at least one AP/IB/AICE course (5%)—data not shown; n/a not available
Source: Newsweek and The Daily Beast, "America's Best High Schools 2013"

Highest Level of Education

Area	Less than H.S.	H.S. Diploma	Some College, No Deg.	Associate Degree	Bachelor's Degree	Master's Degree	Prof. School Degree	Doctorate Degree
City	9.7	29.9	17.3	7.7	18.0	10.3	3.4	3.7
MSA[1]	8.2	35.9	16.9	9.2	18.5	8.0	1.9	1.4
U.S.	14.1	28.3	21.3	7.8	18.0	7.5	1.9	1.2

Note: Figures cover persons age 25 and over; (1) Figures cover the Pittsburgh, PA Metropolitan Statistical Area—see Appendix B for areas included
Source: U.S. Census Bureau, 2010-2012 American Community Survey 3-Year Estimates

Educational Attainment by Race

Area	High School Graduate or Higher (%)					Bachelor's Degree or Higher (%)				
	Total	White	Black	Asian	Hisp.[2]	Total	White	Black	Asian	Hisp.[2]
City	90.3	92.0	84.3	93.0	85.8	35.4	39.8	14.6	79.4	40.6
MSA[1]	91.8	92.3	86.7	89.7	84.1	29.8	30.1	15.8	70.5	34.0
U.S.	85.9	88.1	82.5	85.5	63.1	28.6	30.0	18.4	50.2	13.4

Note: Figures shown cover persons 25 years old and over; (1) Figures cover the Pittsburgh, PA Metropolitan Statistical Area—see Appendix B for areas included; (2) People of Hispanic origin can be of any race
Source: U.S. Census Bureau, 2010-2012 American Community Survey 3-Year Estimates

School Enrollment by Grade and Control

Area	Preschool (%)		Kindergarten (%)		Grades 1 - 4 (%)		Grades 5 - 8 (%)		Grades 9 - 12 (%)	
	Public	Private	Public	Private	Public	Private	Public	Private	Public	Private
City	61.3	38.7	78.9	21.1	80.8	19.2	78.5	21.5	82.4	17.6
MSA[1]	47.4	52.6	86.1	13.9	87.9	12.1	87.8	12.2	90.4	9.6
U.S.	56.9	43.1	87.8	12.2	89.9	10.1	90.0	10.0	90.8	9.2

Note: Figures shown cover persons 3 years old and over; (1) Figures cover the Pittsburgh, PA Metropolitan Statistical Area—see Appendix B for areas included
Source: U.S. Census Bureau, 2010-2012 American Community Survey 3-Year Estimates

Average Salaries of Public School Classroom Teachers

Area	2012-13		2013-14		Percent Change 2012-13 to 2013-14	Percent Change 2003-04 to 2013-14
	Dollars	Rank[1]	Dollars	Rank[1]		
Pennsylvania	62,994	10	64,072	10	1.71	21.8
U.S. Average	56,103	–	56,689	–	1.04	21.8

Note: (1) State rank ranges from 1 to 51 where 1 indicates highest salary.
Source: National Education Association, Rankings & Estimates: Rankings of the States 2013 and Estimates of School Statistics 2014, March 2014

Higher Education

Four-Year Colleges			Two-Year Colleges			Medical Schools[1]	Law Schools[2]	Voc/ Tech[3]
Public	Private Non-profit	Private For-profit	Public	Private Non-profit	Private For-profit			
1	9	3	1	7	12	1	2	3

Note: Figures cover institutions located within the city limits and include main campuses only; (1) includes schools accredited by the Liaison Committee on Medical Education and the American Osteopathic Association's Commission on Osteopathic College Accreditation; (2) includes ABA-accredited schools, schools with provisional ABA accreditation, and state accredited schools; (3) includes all schools with programs that are less than 2 years.
Source: National Center for Education Statistics, Integrated Postsecondary Education System (IPEDS), 2012-13; Association of American Medical Colleges, Member List, April 24, 2014; American Osteopathic Association, Member List, April 24, 2014; Law School Admission Council, Official Guide to ABA-Approved Law Schools Online, April 24, 2014; Wikipedia, List of Medical Schools in the United States, April 24, 2014; Wikipedia, List of Law Schools in the United States, April 24, 2014

According to U.S. News & World Report, the Pittsburgh, PA metro area is home to three of the best national universities in the U.S.: **Carnegie Mellon University** (#23); **University of Pittsburgh** (#62); **Duquesne University** (#121). The indicators used to capture academic quality fall into a number of categories: assessment by administrators at peer institutions; retention of students; faculty resources; student selectivity; financial resources; alumni giving; high school counselor ratings of colleges; and graduation rate. U.S. News & World Report, "America's Best Colleges 2014"

According to U.S. News & World Report, the Pittsburgh, PA metro area is home to two of the best liberal arts colleges in the U.S.: **Washington and Jefferson College** (#97); **Saint Vincent College** (#146). The indicators used to capture academic quality fall into a number of categories: assessment by administrators at peer institutions; retention of students; faculty resources; student selectivity; financial resources; alumni giving; high school counselor ratings of colleges; and graduation rate. U.S. News & World Report, "America's Best Colleges 2014"

According to *U.S. News & World Report*, the Pittsburgh, PA metro area is home to one of the top 100 law schools in the U.S.: **University of Pittsburgh** (#91). The rankings are based on a weighted average of 12 measures of quality: peer assessment score; assessment score by lawyers/judges; median LSAT scores; median undergrad GPA; acceptance rate; employment rates for graduates; placement success; bar passage rate; faculty resources; expenditures per student; student/faculty ratio; and library resources. *U.S. News & World Report, "America's Best Graduate Schools, Law, 2014"*

According to *U.S. News & World Report*, the Pittsburgh, PA metro area is home to two of the top 100 business schools in the U.S.: **Carnegie Mellon University (Tepper)** (#19); **University of Pittsburgh (Katz)** (#61). The rankings are based on a weighted average of the following nine measures: quality assessment; peer assessment; recruiter assessment; placement success; mean starting salary and bonus; student selectivity; mean GMAT and GRE scores; mean undergraduate GPA; and acceptance rate. *U.S. News & World Report, "America's Best Graduate Schools, Business, 2014"*

PRESIDENTIAL ELECTION

2012 Presidential Election Results

Area	Obama	Romney	Other
Allegheny County	56.6	42.2	1.2
U.S.	51.0	47.2	1.8

Note: Results are percentages and may not add to 100% due to rounding
Source: Dave Leip's Atlas of U.S. Presidential Elections

EMPLOYERS

Major Employers

Company Name	Industry
Allegheny General Hospital	Extended care facility
Associated Cleaning Consultants	Janitorial service, contract basis
Bayer Corporation	Pharmaceutical preparations
Children's Hospital of Pittsburgh	Specialty hospitals, except psychiatric
Duquesne University of the Holy Spirit	Colleges and universities
Highmark	Hospital and medical service plans
Jefferson Regional Medical Center	General medical and surgical hospitals
Magee-Womens Hospital of UPMC	Hospital, affiliated with ama residency
Mercy Life Center Corporation	Mental health clinic, outpatient
Mercy Life Center Corporation	Charitable organizations
PNC Bank, National Association	National trust companies with deposits, commercial
United States Steel Corporation	Blast furnaces and steel mills
United States Steel International	Steel
University of Pittsburgh	Colleges and universities
UPMC Mercy	General medical and surgical hospitals
UPMC Shadyside	General medical and surgical hospitals
US Dept of Energy	Noncommercial research organizations
Veterans Health Administration	Administration of veterans' affairs
West Penn Allegheny Health System	Management services

Note: Companies shown are located within the Pittsburgh, PA Metropolitan Statistical Area.
Source: Hoovers.com; Wikipedia

Best Companies to Work For

Bayer; PNC Financial Services Group, headquartered in Pittsburgh, are among the "100 Best Companies for Working Mothers." Criteria: workforce representation; child care; flexibility programs; and leave policies. This year *Working Mother* gave particular weight to flexible work arrangements, women's advancement programs, and paid maternity leave. *Working Mother, "100 Best Companies 2013"*

University of Pittsburgh, headquartered in Pittsburgh, is among the "50 Best Employers for Workers Over 50." Criteria: recruiting practices; opportunities for training, education, and career development; workplace accommodations; alternative work options, such as flexible scheduling, job sharing, and phased retirement; employee health and pension benefits; and retiree benefits. Employers with at least 50 employees based in the U.S. are eligible, including for-profit companies, not-for-profit organizations, and government employers. *AARP, "2013 AARP Best Employers for Workers Over 50"*

PPG Industries, headquartered in Pittsburgh, is among the "100 Best Places to Work in IT." To qualify, companies, both public and private, had to have a minimum of 50 IT employees and were selected based on average salary and bonus increases, the percentage of IT staffers promoted, IT staff turnover rates, training and development programs, and the percentage of women and minorities in IT staff and management positions. In addition, *Computerworld* looked at retention efforts, programs for recognizing and rewarding outstanding performances, and benefits such as flextime, elder care and child care, and reimbursement for college tuition and the cost of pursuing technology certifications. *Computerworld, "100 Best Places to Work in IT 2013"*

The PNC Financial Services Group, headquartered in Pittsburgh, is among the "Top Companies for Executive Women." To be named to the list, companies with a minimum of two women on the board complete a comprehensive application that focuses on the number of women in senior ranks. In addition to assessing corporate programs and policies dedicated to advancing women, NAFE examined the number of women in each company overall, in senior management, and on its board of directors, paying particular attention to the number of women with profit-and-loss responsibility. *National Association for Female Executives, "2013 NAFE Top 50 Companies for Executive Women"*

PUBLIC SAFETY

Crime Rate

| Area | All Crimes | Violent Crimes | | | | Property Crimes | | |
		Murder	Forcible Rape	Robbery	Aggrav. Assault	Burglary	Larceny -Theft	Motor Vehicle Theft
City	4,177.3	13.1	15.1	363.3	360.4	812.8	2,438.2	174.3
Suburbs[1]	n/a	2.9	15.2	48.3	n/a	335.5	1,271.5	61.5
Metro[2]	n/a	4.2	15.2	89.9	n/a	398.5	1,425.6	76.4
U.S.	3,246.1	4.7	26.9	112.9	242.3	670.2	1,959.3	229.7

Note: Figures are crimes per 100,000 population; (1) All areas within the metro area that are located outside the city limits; (2) Figures cover the Pittsburgh, PA Metropolitan Statistical Area—see Appendix B for areas included
Source: FBI Uniform Crime Reports, 2012

Hate Crimes

| Area | Number of Quarters Reported | Bias Motivation | | | | |
		Race	Religion	Sexual Orientation	Ethnicity	Disability
City	2	2	0	0	1	0
U.S.	4	2,797	1,099	1,135	667	92

Source: Federal Bureau of Investigation, Hate Crime Statistics 2012

Identity Theft Consumer Complaints

Area	Complaints	Complaints per 100,000 Population	Rank[2]
MSA[1]	1,367	58.0	223
U.S.	290,056	91.8	-

Note: (1) Figures cover the Pittsburgh, PA Metropolitan Statistical Area—see Appendix B for areas included; (2) Rank ranges from 1 to 377 where 1 indicates greatest number of identity theft complaints per 100,000 population
Source: Federal Trade Commission, Consumer Sentinel Network Data Book for January–December 2013

Fraud and Other Consumer Complaints

Area	Complaints	Complaints per 100,000 Population	Rank[2]
MSA[1]	10,025	425.5	79
U.S.	1,811,724	595.2	-

Note: (1) Figures cover the Pittsburgh, PA Metropolitan Statistical Area—see Appendix B for areas included; (2) Rank ranges from 1 to 377 where 1 indicates greatest number of identity theft complaints per 100,000 population
Source: Federal Trade Commission, Consumer Sentinel Network Data Book for January–December 2013

RECREATION

Culture

Dance[1]	Theatre[1]	Instrumental Music[1]	Vocal Music[1]	Series and Festivals	Museums and Art Galleries[2]	Zoos and Aquariums[3]
5	9	7	7	10	43	2

Note: (1) Number of professional perfoming groups; (2) Based on organizations with primary SIC code 8412; (3) AZA-accredited
Source: The Grey House Performing Arts Directory, 2013; Association of Zoos & Aquariums, AZA Member Zoos & Aquariums, April 2014; www.AccuLeads.com, May 1, 2014

Professional Sports Teams

Team Name	League	Year Established
Pittsburgh Penguins	National Hockey League (NHL)	1967
Pittsburgh Pirates	Major League Baseball (MLB)	1882
Pittsburgh Steelers	National Football League (NFL)	1933

Note: Includes teams located in the Pittsburgh, PA Metropolitan Statistical Area.
Source: Wikipedia, Major Professional Sports Teams of the United States and Canada

CLIMATE

Average and Extreme Temperatures

Temperature	Jan	Feb	Mar	Apr	May	Jun	Jul	Aug	Sep	Oct	Nov	Dec	Yr.
Extreme High (°F)	75	69	83	89	91	98	103	100	97	89	82	74	103
Average High (°F)	35	38	48	61	71	79	83	81	75	63	50	39	60
Average Temp. (°F)	28	30	39	50	60	68	73	71	64	53	42	32	51
Average Low (°F)	20	22	29	39	49	57	62	61	54	43	34	25	41
Extreme Low (°F)	-18	-12	-1	14	26	34	42	39	31	16	-1	-12	-18

Note: Figures cover the years 1948-1990
Source: National Climatic Data Center, International Station Meteorological Climate Summary, 9/96

Average Precipitation/Snowfall/Humidity

Precip./Humidity	Jan	Feb	Mar	Apr	May	Jun	Jul	Aug	Sep	Oct	Nov	Dec	Yr.
Avg. Precip. (in.)	2.8	2.4	3.4	3.3	3.6	3.9	3.8	3.2	2.8	2.4	2.7	2.8	37.1
Avg. Snowfall (in.)	11	9	8	2	Tr	0	0	0	0	Tr	4	8	43
Avg. Rel. Hum. 7am (%)	76	75	75	73	76	79	82	86	85	81	78	77	79
Avg. Rel. Hum. 4pm (%)	64	60	54	49	50	51	53	54	55	53	60	66	56

Note: Figures cover the years 1948-1990; Tr = Trace amounts (<0.05 in. of rain; <0.5 in. of snow)
Source: National Climatic Data Center, International Station Meteorological Climate Summary, 9/96

Weather Conditions

Temperature			Daytime Sky			Precipitation		
5°F & below	32°F & below	90°F & above	Clear	Partly cloudy	Cloudy	0.01 inch or more precip.	0.1 inch or more snow/ice	Thunder-storms
9	121	8	62	137	166	154	42	35

Note: Figures are average number of days per year and cover the years 1948-1990
Source: National Climatic Data Center, International Station Meteorological Climate Summary, 9/96

HAZARDOUS WASTE

Superfund Sites

Pittsburgh has no sites on the EPA's Superfund Final National Priorities List.
U.S. Environmental Protection Agency, Final National Priorities List, April 26, 2014

AIR & WATER QUALITY

Air Quality Index

Area	Percent of Days when Air Quality was...[2]					AQI Statistics[2]	
	Good	Moderate	Unhealthy for Sensitive Groups	Unhealthy	Very Unhealthy	Maximum	Median
MSA[1]	33.7	61.4	4.7	0.3	0.0	164	56

Note: (1) Data covers the Pittsburgh, PA Metropolitan Statistical Area—see Appendix B for areas included; (2) Based on 365 days with AQI data in 2013. Air Quality Index (AQI) is an index for reporting daily air quality. EPA calculates the AQI for five major air pollutants regulated by the Clean Air Act: ground-level ozone, particle pollution (aka particulate matter), carbon monoxide, sulfur dioxide, and nitrogen dioxide. The AQI runs from 0 to 500. The higher the AQI value, the greater the level of air pollution and the greater the health concern. There are six AQI categories: "Good" AQI is between 0 and 50. Air quality is considered satisfactory; "Moderate" AQI is between 51 and 100. Air quality is acceptable; "Unhealthy for Sensitive Groups" When AQI values are between 101 and 150, members of sensitive groups may experience health effects; "Unhealthy" When AQI values are between 151 and 200 everyone may begin to experience health effects; "Very Unhealthy" AQI values between 201 and 300 trigger a health alert; "Hazardous" AQI values over 300 trigger warnings of emergency conditions (not shown).
Source: U.S. Environmental Protection Agency, Air Quality Index Report, 2013

Air Quality Index Pollutants

Area	Percent of Days when AQI Pollutant was...[2]					
	Carbon Monoxide	Nitrogen Dioxide	Ozone	Sulfur Dioxide	Particulate Matter 2.5	Particulate Matter 10
MSA[1]	0.0	0.3	15.6	7.9	76.2	0.0

Note: (1) Data covers the Pittsburgh, PA Metropolitan Statistical Area—see Appendix B for areas included; (2) Based on 365 days with AQI data in 2013. The Air Quality Index (AQI) is an index for reporting daily air quality. EPA calculates the AQI for five major air pollutants regulated by the Clean Air Act: ground-level ozone, particle pollution (also known as particulate matter), carbon monoxide, sulfur dioxide, and nitrogen dioxide. The AQI runs from 0 to 500. The higher the AQI value, the greater the level of air pollution and the greater the health concern.
Source: U.S. Environmental Protection Agency, Air Quality Index Report, 2013

Air Quality Trends: Ozone

	2003	2004	2005	2006	2007	2008	2009	2010	2011	2012
MSA[1]	0.085	0.074	0.085	0.077	0.078	0.075	0.068	0.075	0.072	0.079

Note: (1) Data covers the Pittsburgh, PA Metropolitan Statistical Area—see Appendix B for areas included. The values shown are the composite ozone concentration averages among trend sites based on the highest fourth daily maximum 8-hour concentration in parts per million. These trends are based on sites having an adequate record of monitoring data during the trend period. Data from exceptional events are included.
Source: U.S. Environmental Protection Agency, Air Quality Monitoring Information, "Air Quality Trends by City, 2000-2012"

Maximum Air Pollutant Concentrations: Particulate Matter, Ozone, CO and Lead

	Particulate Matter 10 (ug/m³)	Particulate Matter 2.5 Wtd AM (ug/m³)	Particulate Matter 2.5 24-Hr (ug/m³)	Ozone (ppm)	Carbon Monoxide (ppm)	Lead (ug/m³)
MSA[1] Level	75	14.3	43	0.085	2	0.19
NAAQS[2]	150	15	35	0.075	9	0.15
Met NAAQS[2]	Yes	Yes	No	No	Yes	No

Note: (1) Data covers the Pittsburgh, PA Metropolitan Statistical Area—see Appendix B for areas included; Data from exceptional events are included; (2) National Ambient Air Quality Standards; ppm = parts per million; ug/m³ = micrograms per cubic meter; n/a not available.
Concentrations: Particulate Matter 10 (coarse particulate)—highest second maximum 24-hour concentration; Particulate Matter 2.5 Wtd AM (fine particulate)—highest weighted annual mean concentration; Particulate Matter 2.5 24-Hour (fine particulate)—highest 98th percentile 24-hour concentration; Ozone—highest fourth daily maximum 8-hour concentration; Carbon Monoxide—highest second maximum non-overlapping 8-hour concentration; Lead—maximum running 3-month average
Source: U.S. Environmental Protection Agency, Air Quality Monitoring Information, "Air Quality Statistics by City, 2012"

Maximum Air Pollutant Concentrations: Nitrogen Dioxide and Sulfur Dioxide

	Nitrogen Dioxide AM (ppb)	Nitrogen Dioxide 1-Hr (ppb)	Sulfur Dioxide AM (ppb)	Sulfur Dioxide 1-Hr (ppb)	Sulfur Dioxide 24-Hr (ppb)
MSA[1] Level	14	50	n/a	117	n/a
NAAQS[2]	53	100	30	75	140
Met NAAQS[2]	Yes	Yes	n/a	No	n/a

Note: (1) Data covers the Pittsburgh, PA Metropolitan Statistical Area—see Appendix B for areas included; Data from exceptional events are included; (2) National Ambient Air Quality Standards; ppm = parts per million; ug/m³ = micrograms per cubic meter; n/a not available.
Concentrations: Nitrogen Dioxide AM—highest arithmetic mean concentration; Nitrogen Dioxide 1-Hr—highest 98th percentile 1-hour daily maximum concentration; Sulfur Dioxide AM—highest annual mean concentration; Sulfur Dioxide 1-Hr—highest 99th percentile 1-hour daily maximum concentration; Sulfur Dioxide 24-Hr—highest second maximum 24-hour concentration
Source: U.S. Environmental Protection Agency, Air Quality Monitoring Information, "Air Quality Statistics by City, 2012"

Drinking Water

Water System Name	Pop. Served	Primary Water Source Type	Violations[1] Health Based	Violations[1] Monitoring/ Reporting
PA American Water Co.-Pittsburgh	516,411	Surface	0	0
Pittsburgh Water & Sewer Auth.	250,000	Surface	0	0
West View Boro Muni Authority	200,000	Surface	0	2

Note: (1) Based on violation data from January 1, 2013 to December 31, 2013 (includes unresolved violations from earlier years)
Source: U.S. Environmental Protection Agency, Office of Ground Water and Drinking Water, Safe Drinking Water Information System (based on data extracted February 10, 2014)

Providence, Rhode Island

Background

Providence is the capital of Rhode Island and the Providence County seat. At the head of Narragansett Bay, Providence is one of the nation's most historic cities as well as one of its most fashionable and inviting. It is recognized as having all the qualities of a great city on a more accessible scale.

Providence was founded in 1636 by Roger Williams, the Massachusetts preacher exiled by the Puritans for his radical religious ideas. In a reversal of the usual procedure, Williams first obtained title to the land directly from the Narragansett tribe, and subsequently, in 1644, received a Royal Charter from London for the settlement.

Though the economy originally depended on agriculture, trade soon came to dominate. Whaling, a related maritime economic activity, was as important in Providence as it was to all of Rhode Island's ports. In the course of this trade, a number of Rhode Islanders naturally amassed considerable wealth and endowed many of Providence's enduring public and cultural institutions, including Brown University, one of the nation's oldest.

After the Revolution, Providence underwent a process of industrialization and became a major center for the textile, silver, and jewelry trades. Many industrial innovations came out of Providence workshops, including economical methods of plating base metals with gold or silver. By the time of the Civil War, the economy had almost entirely shifted from the mercantile shipping to the fully industrial mode. As such, the city was a major economic resource to the Union during the Civil War.

By the mid-twentieth century, Providence had fallen very far from its once enviable position as a New England center of commerce and culture, and by 1975, its population had declined by almost one-third. Government mismanagement, along with the general decline and obsolescence of heavy industry throughout the nation, had combined to blemish the city.

Since the 1980s, however, remarkable reforms and improvements have brought to Providence a renaissance in terms of jobs, city services, downtown revitalization, and cultural assets, to the point that it is now regarded, particularly by younger professionals, as one of the most desirable urban locations on the East Coast. Educational and cultural assets include museums, theaters, an award-winning zoo, highly acclaimed restaurants, and renowned venues for arts and entertainment. Providence and the surrounding areas have been used as a backdrop for several movies and television series and the city remains invested in luring filmmakers by offering a 25 percent tax credit to motion picture companies on all Rhode Island spending.

A living testament to Providence's renaissance is WaterFire, a fire sculpture installation by Barnaby Evans which burns anew each spring on downtown Providence's three rivers.

The $1.5 billion downtown facelift of Waterplace Park and Riverwalk is perhaps the most important development in Providence. Parts of the river that had long been paved over with streets were reopened, and park areas were created along the banks. The picturesque river is now used routinely for boating and sculling and by the Brown University crews.

Downtown, the Providence Place Mall, designed by internationally renowned architect Friedrich St. Florian, offers a state-of-the-art emporium that nicely mirrors the historically mercantile character of the city. Nearby, is the Arcade, built in 1828 and generally recognized as America's first indoor shopping mall. In the same neighborhood is the 1922 Biltmore Hotel, a fond and familiar landmark to the city's residents.

Another favorite Providence neighborhood is College Hill, which connects the campuses of Brown University and the Rhode Island School of Design in an array rich with cafes, restaurants, shops, and street vendors.

The energy of Providence is apparent in its choice of sports. The city is home to the American Hockey League's Providence Bruins, and it competed successfully against other cities to host the Gravity Games. Providence is also the birthplace of ESPN's X Games.

Providence enjoys variable southern New England weather with temperatures slightly moderated by the city's proximity to Narragansett Bay and the Atlantic Ocean. The weather is changeable, due to the convergence of weather systems from the west, the Gulf of Mexico, and the North Atlantic. Precipitation is evenly distributed throughout the year. In October 2012, the city was hit by Hurricane Sandy, resulting in storm surges, power outages, and interrupted transportation.

Rankings

General Rankings

- Providence was selected as one of "America's Favorite Cities." The city ranked #13 in the "Quality of Life and Visitor Experience: Cleanliness" category. Respondents to an online survey were asked to rate 35 top urban destinations in the U.S. from a visitor's perspective. Criteria: cleanliness. *Travel + Leisure, "America's Favorite Cities 2013"*

- Providence was selected as one of "America's Favorite Cities." The city ranked #4 in the "Type of Trip: Gay-friendly" category. Respondents to an online survey were asked to rate 35 top urban destinations in the U.S. from a visitor's perspective. Criteria: gay-friendly. *Travel + Leisure, "America's Favorite Cities 2013"*

Business/Finance Rankings

- Based on a minimum of 500 social media reviews per metro area, the employment opinion group Glassdoor surveyed 50 of the largest U.S. metro areas on measures including compensation and benefits, satisfaction with management, business outlook, and number of employers hiring. The Providence metro area was ranked #23 in overall employee satisfaction. *www.glassdoor.com, "Employment Satisfaction Report Card by City," June 21, 2013*

- In a survey of economic confidence in the nation's 50 largest metropolitan areas conducted January–December 2012, the Providence metro area placed among the bottom five, according to Gallup's 2013 Economic Confidence Index. *Gallup Economy, "D.C. Metro Area Again Leads U.S. in Economic Confidence," March 28, 2013*

- Providence was ranked #81 out of 100 metro areas in terms of economic performance (#1 = best) during the recession and recovery from trough quarter through the second quarter of 2013. Criteria: percent change in employment; percentage point change in unemployment rate; percent change in gross metropolitan product; percent change in House Price Index. *Brookings Institution, MetroMonitor: Tracking Economic Recession and Recovery in America's 100 Largest Metropolitan Areas, September 2013*

- The Providence metro area appeared on the Milken Institute "2013 Best Performing Cities" list. Rank: #148 out of 200 large metro areas. Criteria: job growth; wage and salary growth; high-tech output growth. *Milken Institute, "Best-Performing Cities 2013," December 2013*

- *Forbes* ranked the 200 most populous metro areas in the U.S. in terms of the "Best Places for Business and Careers." The Providence metro area was ranked #180. Criteria: costs (business and living); job growth (past and projected); income growth; educational attainment (college and high school); projected economic growth; cultural and recreational opportunities; net migration patterns; number of highly ranked colleges. *Forbes, "The Best Places for Business and Careers," August 7, 2013*

Children/Family Rankings

- Providence was selected as one of the best cities for families to live by *Parenting* magazine. The city ranked #19 out of 100. Criteria: education; health; community; *Parenting's* Culture & Charm Index. *Parenting.com, "The 2012 Best Cities for Families List"*

- Providence was chosen as one of America's 100 best communities for young people. The winners were selected based upon detailed information provided about each community's efforts to fulfill five essential promises critical to the well-being of young people: caring adults who are actively involved in their lives; safe places in which to learn and grow; a healthy start toward adulthood; an effective education that builds marketable skills; and opportunities to help others. *America's Promise Alliance, "100 Best Communities for Young People, 2012"*

Culture/Performing Arts Rankings

- Providence was selected as one of "America's Favorite Cities." The city ranked #13 in the "Culture: Museum/Galleries" category. Respondents to an online survey were asked to rate 35 top urban destinations in the U.S. from a visitor's perspective. Criteria: number and quality of museums and galleries. *Travelandleisure.com, "America's Favorite Cities 2013"*

- Providence was selected as one of America's top cities for the arts. The city ranked #11 in the mid-sized city (population 100,000 to 499,999) category. Criteria: readers' top choices for arts travel destinations based on the richness and variety of visual arts sites, activities and events. *American Style, "2012 Top 25 Arts Destinations," June 2012*

Dating/Romance Rankings

- Of the 100 U.S. cities surveyed by *Men's Health* in its quest to identify the nation's best cities for dating and forming relationships, Providence was ranked #67 for online dating (#1 = best). *Men's Health, "The Best and Worst Cities for Online Dating," January 30, 2013*

- Providence was selected as one of America's best cities for singles by the readers of *Travel + Leisure* in their annual "America's Favorite Cities" survey. The city was ranked #15 out of 20. *Travel + Leisure, "America's Best Cities for Singles," July 2012*

Education Rankings

- *Men's Health* ranked 100 U.S. cities in terms of their education levels. Providence was ranked #59 (#1 = most educated city). Criteria: high school graduation rates; school enrollment; educational attainment; number of households who have outstanding student loans; number of households whose members have taken adult-education courses. *Men's Health, "Where School Is In: The Most and Least Educated Cities," September 12, 2011*

Environmental Rankings

- The Providence metro area came in at #111 for the relative comfort of its climate on Sperling's list of "chill cities," as measured by the Sperling Heat Index. All 361 metro areas are included. Criteria included daytime high temperatures, nighttime low temperatures, dew point, and relative humidity at the high temperatures. *www.bertsperling.com, "Sperling's Chill Cities," July 18, 2013*

- Sperling's BestPlaces assessed 379 metropolitan areas of the United States for the likelihood of dangerously extreme weather events or earthquakes. In general the Southeast and South-Central regions have the highest risk of weather extremes and earthquakes, while the Pacific Northwest enjoys the lowest risk. Of the least risky metropolitan areas, the Providence metro area was ranked #195. *www.bestplaces.net, "Safest Places from Natural Disasters," April 2011*

- Providence was selected as one of 22 "Smarter Cities" for energy by the Natural Resources Defense Council. Criteria: investment in green power; energy efficiency measures; conservation. *Natural Resources Defense Council, "2010 Smarter Cities," July 19, 2010*

Food/Drink Rankings

- *Men's Health* ranked 100 major U.S. cities in terms of alcohol intoxication. Providence ranked #55 (#1 = most sober).Criteria: binge drinking; alcohol-related traffic accidents, arrests, and fatalities. *Men's Health, "The Drunkest Cities in America," November 19, 2013*

- Providence was identified as one of "America's Drunkest Cities of 2011" by *The Daily Beast*. The city ranked #21 out of 25. Criteria: binge drinking; drinks consumed per month. *The Daily Beast, "Tipsy Towns: Where are America's Drunkest Cities?," December 31, 2011*

- Providence was selected as one of America's best cities for hamburgers by the readers of *Travel + Leisure* in their annual America's Favorite Cities survey. The city was ranked #1 out of 10. *Travel + Leisure, "America's Best Burger Cities," August 25, 2013*

- The Providence metro area was selected as one of the best cities for "foodies" in America by Sperling's BestPlaces. The metro area ranked #6 out of 10. A "foodie" is defined as a person whose hobby is food—not just eating it, but also learning about its origins and preparation. Criteria: ratio of local restaurants to chain restaurants; number of local and accessible CSA (Community Supported Agriculture) and farmers markets; number of Whole Foods stores; number of cookware stores; number of craft breweries, brew pubs, wine shops, and wine bars. *Sperling's BestPlaces, www.BestPlaces.net, "America's Best Cities for Foodies," January 2011*

Health/Fitness Rankings

- For each of the 50 most populous metro areas in the United States, the American College of Sports Medicine's American Fitness Index evaluated infrastructure, community assets, and policies that encourage healthy and fit lifestyles, including preventive health behaviors, levels of chronic disease conditions, health care access, and community resources and policies that support physical activity. The Providence metro area ranked #22 for "community fitness." Personal health indicators were considered as well as community and environmental indicators. *www.americanfitnessindex.org, "ACSM American Fitness Index Health and Community Fitness Status of the 50 Largest Metropolitan Areas," May 2013*

- Providence was identified as a "2013 Spring Allergy Capital." The area ranked #16 out of 100. Three groups of factors were used to identify the most severe cities for people with allergies during the spring season: annual pollen levels; medicine utilization; access to board-certified allergists. *Asthma and Allergy Foundation of America, "Spring Allergy Capitals 2013"*

- Providence was identified as a "2013 Fall Allergy Capital." The area ranked #28 out of 100. Three groups of factors were used to identify the most severe cities for people with allergies during the fall season: annual pollen levels; medicine utilization; access to board-certified allergists. *Asthma and Allergy Foundation of America, "Fall Allergy Capitals 2013"*

- Providence was identified as a "2013 Asthma Capital." The area ranked #41 out of the nation's 100 largest metropolitan areas. Twelve factors were used to identify the most challenging places to live for people with asthma: estimated prevalence; self-reported prevalence; crude death rate for asthma; annual pollen score; annual air quality; public smoking laws; number of board-certified asthma specialists; school inhaler access laws; rescue medication use; controller medication use; uninsured rate; poverty rate. *Asthma and Allergy Foundation of America, "Asthma Capitals 2013"*

- *Men's Health* ranked 100 major U.S. cities in terms of the best and worst cities for men. Providence ranked #69. Criteria: thirty-three data points were examined covering health, fitness, and quality of life. *Men's Health, "The Best & Worst Cities for Men 2014," December 6, 2013*

- The Providence metro area appeared in the 2013 Gallup-Healthways Well-Being Index. The area ranked #156 out of 189. The Gallup-Healthways Well-Being Index score is an average of six sub-indexes, which individually examine life evaluation, emotional health, work environment, physical health, healthy behaviors, and access to basic necessities. Results are based on telephone interviews conducted as part of the Gallup-Healthways Well-Being Index survey January 2–December 29, 2012, and January 2–December 30, 2013, with a random sample of 531,630 adults, aged 18 and older, living in metropolitan areas in the 50 U.S. states and the District of Columbia. *Gallup-Healthways, "State of American Well-Being," March 25, 2014*

- The Providence metro area was identified as one of "America's Most Stressful Cities" by *Sperling's BestPlaces*. The metro area ranked #29 out of 50. Criteria: unemployment rate; suicide rate; commute time; mental health; poor rest; alcohol use; violent crime rate; property crime rate; cloudy days annually. *Sperling's BestPlaces, www.BestPlaces.net, "Stressful Cities 2012*

- *Men's Health* ranked 100 U.S. cities in terms of their activity levels. Providence was ranked #41 (#1 = most active city). Criteria: where and how often residents exercise; percentage of households that watch more than 15 hours of cable television a week and buy more than 11 video games a year; death rate from deep-vein thrombosis, a condition linked to sitting for extended periods of time. *Men's Health, "Where Sit Happens: The Most and Least Active Cities in America," June 20, 2011*

Real Estate Rankings

- Providence was ranked #224 out of 283 metro areas in terms of house price appreciation in 2013 (#1 = highest rate). *Federal Housing Finance Agency, House Price Index, 4th Quarter 2013*

- Providence was ranked #130 out of 224 metro areas in terms of housing affordability in 2013 by the National Association of Home Builders (#1 = most affordable). The NAHB-Wells Fargo Housing Opportunity Index (HOI) for a given area is defined as the share of homes sold in that area that would have been affordable to a family earning the local median income, based on standard mortgage underwriting criteria. *National Association of Home Builders®, NAHB-Wells Fargo Housing Opportunity Index, 4th Quarter 2013*

Safety Rankings

- Allstate ranked the 200 largest cities in America in terms of driver safety. Providence ranked #192. Allstate researchers analyzed internal property damage claims over a two-year period from January 2010 to December 2011. A weighted average of the two-year numbers determined the annual percentages. *Allstate, "Allstate America's Best Drivers Report®, August 27, 2013"*

- The National Insurance Crime Bureau ranked 380 metro areas in the U.S. in terms of per capita rates of vehicle theft. The Providence metro area ranked #113 (#1 = highest rate). Criteria: number of vehicle theft offenses per 100,000 inhabitants in 2012. *National Insurance Crime Bureau, "Hot Spots 2012," June 26, 2013*

- The Providence metro area was identified as one of the most dangerous metro areas for pedestrians by Transportation for America. The metro area ranked #40 out of 52 metro areas with over 1 million residents. Criteria: area's population divided by the number of pedestrian fatalities in that area. *Transportation for America, "Dangerous by Design 2011"*

Seniors/Retirement Rankings

- The finance website CNNMoney surveyed small U.S. cities that offer exceptional urban amenities at a cost of living somewhat higher than for the top-ten locations but still affordable for retirees. Median home-price figures were supplied by the residential real-estate website Trulia. Providence was among the eight small cities singled out. *money.cnn.com, "Best Places to Retire with a Nice Nest Egg," October 28, 2013*

- From its Best Cities for Successful Aging indexes, the Milken Institute generated rankings for metropolitan areas, weighing data in eight categories—general indicators, health care, wellness, living arrangements, transportation and general accessibility, financial well-being, education and employment, and community participation. The Providence metro area was ranked #66 overall in the large metro area category. *Milken Institute, "Best Cities for Successful Aging," July 2012*

- Bankers Life and Casualty Company, in partnership with Sperling's BestPlaces, ranked the nation's 50 largest metro areas in terms of the "Best U.S. Cities for Seniors." The Providence metro area ranked #18. Criteria: healthcare; transportation; housing; environment; economy; health and longevity; social and spiritual life; crime. *Bankers Life and Casualty Company, Center for a Secure Retirement, "Best U.S. Cities for Seniors 2011," September 2011*

Sports/Recreation Rankings

- Providence appeared on the *Sporting News* list of the "Best Sports Cities" for 2011. The area ranked #164 out of 271. Criteria: the magazine takes a 12-month snapshot of each city's sports, putting a heavy premium on regular-season won-lost records (from the most recently completed season). Other criteria include: playoff berths, bowl appearances and tournament bids; championships; applicable power ratings; quality of competition; overall fan fervor (measured in part by attendance); abundance of teams (rewarding quality over quantity); stadium and arena quality; ticket availability and prices; franchise ownership; and marquee appeal of athletes. *Sporting News, "Best Sports Cities 2011," October 4, 2011*

- Providence appeared on the *Sporting News* list of the "Best Sports Cities" for 2011. The area ranked #164 out of 271. Criteria: a 12-month snapshot of regular-season won-lost records (from the most recently completed season). Other criteria include: playoff berths, bowl appearances and tournament bids; championships; applicable power ratings; quality of competition; overall fan fervor (measured in part by attendance); abundance of teams (quality over quantity); stadium and arena quality; ticket availability and prices; franchise ownership; and marquee appeal of athletes. *Sporting News, "Best Sports Cities 2011," October 4, 2011*

- Providence was selected as one of the most playful cities in the U.S. by KaBOOM! The organization's Playful City USA initiative honors cities and towns across the nation for a vision, plan and commitment to creating an agenda for play. Criteria: creating a local play commission or task force; designing an annual action plan for play; conducting a play space audit; outlining a financial investment in play for the current fiscal year; and proclaiming and celebrating an annual "play day." *KaBOOM! National Campaign for Play, "2013 Playful City USA Communities"*

Women/Minorities Rankings

- *Women's Health* examined U.S. cities and identified the 100 best cities for women. Providence was ranked #49. Criteria: 30 categories were examined from obesity and breast cancer rates to commuting times and hours spent working out. *Women's Health, "Best Cities for Women 2012"*

- The Providence metro area appeared on *Forbes'* list of the "Best Cities for Minority Entrepreneurs." The area ranked #49 out of 10. Criteria: 52 metropolitan statistical areas were examined. For each ethnicity (African Americans, Asians and Hispanics), the editors measured housing affordability, population growth, income growth, and entrepreneurship (per capita self-employment). *Forbes, "Best Cities for Minority Entrepreneurs," March 23, 2011*

Miscellaneous Rankings

- *Travel + Leisure* invited readers to rate cities on indicators such as aloofness, "smarty-pants residents," highbrow cultural offerings, high-end shopping, artisanal coffeehouses, conspicuous eco-consciousness, and more in order to identify the nation's snobbiest cities. Cities large and small made the list; among them was Providence, at #8. *www.travelandleisure.com, "America's Snobbiest Cities, June 2013*

- Providence appeared on *Travel + Leisure's* list of America's most attractive people. Criteria: cities were selected by readers in their annual America's Favorite Cities survey. The city ranked #2 out of 10. *Travel + Leisure, "America's Most and Least Attractive People," November 2013*

- *Men's Health* ranked 100 U.S. cities by their level of sadness. Providence was ranked #62 (#1 = saddest city). Criteria: suicide rates; unemployment rates; percentage of households that use antidepressants; percent of population who report feeling blue all or most of the time. *Men's Health, "Frown Towns," November 28, 2011*

- Scarborough Research, a leading market research firm, identified the top local markets for lottery ticket purchasers. The Providence DMA (Designated Market Area) ranked in the top 13 with 56% of adults 18+ reporting that they purchased lottery tickets in the past 30 days. *Scarborough Research, January 30, 2012*

- Mars Chocolate North America, the makers of COMBOS®, in partnership with Sperling's BestPlaces, ranked 50 major metro areas in terms of their "manliness." The Providence metro area ranked #24. Criteria: number of professional sports teams; number of nearby NASCAR tracks and racing events; manly lifestyle; concentration of manly retail stores; manly occupations per capita; salty snack sales; "Board of Manliness" rankings. *Mars Chocolate North America, "America's Manliest Cities 2012"*

- Providence was selected as one of "America's Best Cities for Hipsters" by *Travel + Leisure*. The city was ranked #4 out of 20. Criteria: live music; coffee bars; independent boutiques; best microbrews; offbeat and tech-savvy locals. *Travel + Leisure, "America's Best Cities for Hipsters," November 2013*

- The National Alliance to End Homelessness ranked the 100 most populous metro areas in terms the rate of homelessness. The Providence metro area ranked #67. Criteria: number of homeless people per 10,000 population in 2011. *National Alliance to End Homelessness, The State of Homelessness in America 2012*

Business Environment

CITY FINANCES

City Government Finances

Component	2011 ($000)	2011 ($ per capita)
Total Revenues	877,872	5,090
Total Expenditures	900,802	5,223
Debt Outstanding	771,777	4,475
Cash and Securities[1]	483,431	2,803

Note: (1) Cash and security holdings of a government at the close of its fiscal year, including those of its dependent agencies, utilities, and liquor stores.
Source: U.S Census Bureau, State & Local Government Finances 2011

City Government Revenue by Source

Source	2011 ($000)	2011 ($ per capita)
General Revenue		
From Federal Government	27,475	159
From State Government	284,168	1,648
From Local Governments	3,761	22
Taxes		
Property	290,704	1,686
Sales and Gross Receipts	5,454	32
Personal Income	0	0
Corporate Income	0	0
Motor Vehicle License	0	0
Other Taxes	4,902	28
Current Charges	73,536	426
Liquor Store	0	0
Utility	64,017	371
Employee Retirement	79,458	461

Source: U.S Census Bureau, State & Local Government Finances 2011

City Government Expenditures by Function

Function	2011 ($000)	2011 ($ per capita)	2011 (%)
General Direct Expenditures			
Air Transportation	0	0	0.0
Corrections	0	0	0.0
Education	394,603	2,288	43.8
Employment Security Administration	0	0	0.0
Financial Administration	6,810	39	0.8
Fire Protection	69,959	406	7.8
General Public Buildings	47,362	275	5.3
Governmental Administration, Other	10,130	59	1.1
Health	0	0	0.0
Highways	9,283	54	1.0
Hospitals	0	0	0.0
Housing and Community Development	16,789	97	1.9
Interest on General Debt	46,259	268	5.1
Judicial and Legal	6,894	40	0.8
Libraries	3,398	20	0.4
Parking	0	0	0.0
Parks and Recreation	3,418	20	0.4
Police Protection	81,980	475	9.1
Public Welfare	0	0	0.0
Sewerage	727	4	0.1
Solid Waste Management	13,571	79	1.5
Veterans' Services	0	0	0.0
Liquor Store	0	0	0.0
Utility	66,674	387	7.4
Employee Retirement	87,867	509	9.8

Source: U.S Census Bureau, State & Local Government Finances 2011

DEMOGRAPHICS

Population Growth

Area	1990 Census	2000 Census	2010 Census	Population Growth (%) 1990-2000	Population Growth (%) 2000-2010
City	160,734	173,618	178,042	8.0	2.5
MSA[1]	1,509,789	1,582,997	1,600,852	4.8	1.1
U.S.	248,709,873	281,421,906	308,745,538	13.2	9.7

Note: (1) Figures cover the Providence-Warwick, RI-MA Metropolitan Statistical Area—see Appendix B for areas included
Source: U.S. Census Bureau, Census 1990, 2000, 2010

Household Size

Area	Persons in Household (%) One	Two	Three	Four	Five	Six	Seven or More	Average Household Size
City	30.5	26.2	18.4	15.2	5.4	2.7	1.6	2.71
MSA[1]	29.7	32.9	16.3	13.3	5.3	1.6	0.9	2.49
U.S.	27.6	33.5	15.7	13.2	6.1	2.4	1.5	2.63

Note: (1) Figures cover the Providence-Warwick, RI-MA Metropolitan Statistical Area—see Appendix B for areas included
Source: U.S. Census Bureau, 2010-2012 American Community Survey 3-Year Estimates

Race

Area	White Alone[2] (%)	Black Alone[2] (%)	Asian Alone[2] (%)	AIAN[3] Alone[2] (%)	NHOPI[4] Alone[2] (%)	Other Race Alone[2] (%)	Two or More Races (%)
City	50.4	15.3	6.5	0.9	0.2	22.5	4.3
MSA[1]	84.1	5.3	2.7	0.3	0.0	4.9	2.6
U.S.	74.0	12.6	4.9	0.8	0.2	4.7	2.8

Note: (1) Figures cover the Providence-Warwick, RI-MA Metropolitan Statistical Area—see Appendix B for areas included; (2) Alone is defined as not being in combination with one or more other races; (3) American Indian and Alaska Native; (4) Native Hawaiian and Other Pacific Islander
Source: U.S. Census Bureau, 2010-2012 American Community Survey 3-Year Estimates

Hispanic or Latino Origin

Area	Total (%)	Mexican (%)	Puerto Rican (%)	Cuban (%)	Other (%)
City	40.2	2.1	8.3	0.4	29.4
MSA[1]	10.6	0.8	3.4	0.1	6.2
U.S.	16.6	10.7	1.6	0.6	3.7

Note: Persons of Hispanic or Latino origin can be of any race; (1) Figures cover the Providence-Warwick, RI-MA Metropolitan Statistical Area—see Appendix B for areas included
Source: U.S. Census Bureau, 2010-2012 American Community Survey 3-Year Estimates

Segregation

Type	Segregation Indices[1] 1990	2000	2010	2010 Rank[2]	Percent Change 1990-2000	Percent Change 1990-2010	Percent Change 2000-2010
Black/White	60.5	57.2	53.5	57	-3.2	-7.0	-3.8
Asian/White	47.0	44.1	40.1	55	-2.9	-6.9	-4.0
Hispanic/White	57.9	64.5	60.1	4	6.6	2.3	-4.3

Note: All figures cover the Metropolitan Statistical Area—see Appendix B for areas included; Figures are based on an analysis of 1990, 2000, and 2010 Census Decennial Census tract data by William H. Frey, Brookings Institution and the University of Michigan Social Science Data Analysis Network. In this analysis all racial groups (whites, blacks, and asians) are non-Hispanic members of those races. Hispanics are shown as a separate category;
(1) Segregation Indices are Dissimilarity Indices that measure the degree to which the minority group is distributed differently than whites across census tracts. They range from 0 (complete integration) to 100 (complete segregation) where the value indicates the percentage of the minority group that needs to move to be distributed exactly like whites; (2) Ranges from 1 (most segregated) to 102 (least segregated); n/a not available.
Source: www.CensusScope.org

Ancestry

Area	German	Irish	English	American	Italian	Polish	French[2]	Scottish	Dutch
City	3.5	8.8	4.1	1.9	10.1	2.1	3.5	1.2	0.4
MSA[1]	5.2	19.0	11.9	3.0	15.5	4.1	11.6	2.0	0.5
U.S.	15.2	11.1	8.2	7.2	5.6	3.1	2.8	1.7	1.4

Note: Figures are the percentage of the total population reporting a particular ancestry. The nine most commonly reported ancestries in the U.S. are shown. Figures include multiple ancestries (e.g. if a person reported being Irish and Italian, they were included in both columns); (1) Figures cover the Providence-Warwick, RI-MA Metropolitan Statistical Area—see Appendix B for areas included; (2) Excludes Basque
Source: U.S. Census Bureau, 2010-2012 American Community Survey 3-Year Estimates

Foreign-Born Population

Area	Any Foreign Country	Mexico	Asia	Europe	Carribean	South America	Central America[2]	Africa	Canada
City	29.8	0.5	4.6	2.2	10.6	1.6	7.5	2.6	0.2
MSA[1]	12.7	0.2	2.1	4.4	1.8	1.0	1.5	1.4	0.3
U.S.	13.0	3.7	3.7	1.6	1.2	0.9	1.0	0.5	0.3

Note: (1) Figures cover the Providence-Warwick, RI-MA Metropolitan Statistical Area—see Appendix B for areas included; (2) Excludes Mexico.
Source: U.S. Census Bureau, 2010-2012 American Community Survey 3-Year Estimates

Marital Status

Area	Never Married	Now Married[2]	Separated	Widowed	Divorced
City	54.3	28.2	3.6	4.8	9.1
MSA[1]	35.0	45.0	2.0	6.7	11.3
U.S.	32.4	48.4	2.2	6.0	11.0

Note: Figures are percentages and cover the population 15 years of age and older; (1) Figures cover the Providence-Warwick, RI-MA Metropolitan Statistical Area—see Appendix B for areas included; (2) Excludes separated
Source: U.S. Census Bureau, 2010-2012 American Community Survey 3-Year Estimates

Age

Area	Under Age 5	Age 5–19	Age 20–34	Age 35–44	Age 45–54	Age 55–64	Age 65–74	Age 75–84	Age 85+	Median Age
City	6.1	23.3	30.5	11.8	11.0	8.8	4.3	2.6	1.5	28.6
MSA[1]	5.4	19.2	19.6	13.0	15.4	12.7	7.4	4.7	2.5	39.9
U.S.	6.4	20.1	20.5	13.1	14.3	12.2	7.3	4.2	1.8	37.3

Note: (1) Figures cover the Providence-Warwick, RI-MA Metropolitan Statistical Area—see Appendix B for areas included
Source: U.S. Census Bureau, 2010-2012 American Community Survey 3-Year Estimates

Gender

Area	Males	Females	Males per 100 Females
City	86,626	91,673	94.5
MSA[1]	774,756	826,452	93.7
U.S.	153,276,055	158,333,314	96.8

Note: (1) Figures cover the Providence-Warwick, RI-MA Metropolitan Statistical Area—see Appendix B for areas included
Source: U.S. Census Bureau, 2010-2012 American Community Survey 3-Year Estimates

Religious Groups by Family

Area	Catholic	Baptist	Non-Den.	Methodist[2]	Lutheran	LDS[3]	Pentecostal	Presbyterian[4]	Muslim[5]	Judaism
MSA[1]	47.0	1.4	1.2	0.8	0.5	0.3	0.6	1.0	0.1	0.7
U.S.	19.1	9.3	4.0	4.0	2.3	2.0	1.9	1.6	0.8	0.7

Note: Figures are the number of adherents as a percentage of the total population; (1) Figures cover the Providence-Warwick, RI-MA Metropolitan Statistical Area—see Appendix B for areas included; (2) Methodist/Pietist; (3) Latter Day Saints; (4) Reformed; (5) Figures are estimates
Source: Association of Statisticians of American Religious Bodies, 2010 U.S. Religion Census: Religious Congregations & Membership Study

Religious Groups by Tradition

Area	Catholic	Evangelical Protestant	Mainline Protestant	Other Tradition	Black Protestant	Orthodox
MSA[1]	47.0	2.8	4.7	1.6	0.1	0.6
U.S.	19.1	16.2	7.3	4.3	1.6	0.3

Note: Figures are the number of adherents as a percentage of the total population; (1) Figures cover the Providence-Warwick, RI-MA Metropolitan Statistical Area—see Appendix B for areas included
Source: Association of Statisticians of American Religious Bodies, 2010 U.S. Religion Census: Religious Congregations & Membership Study

ECONOMY

Gross Metropolitan Product

Area	2011	2012	2013	2014	Rank[2]
MSA[1]	67.3	69.5	71.2	73.9	44

Note: Figures are in billions of dollars; (1) Figures cover the Providence-Warwick, RI-MA Metropolitan Statistical Area—see Appendix B for areas included; (2) Rank is based on 2014 data and ranges from 1 to 363
Source: The United States Conference of Mayors, U.S. Metro Economies: Outlook—Gross Metropolitan Product, with Metro Employment Projections, November 2013

Economic Growth

Area	2011 (%)	2012 (%)	2013 (%)	2014 (%)	Rank[2]
MSA[1]	0.3	1.7	1.0	1.9	153
U.S.	1.6	2.5	1.7	2.5	–

Note: Figures are real gross metropolitan product (GMP) growth rates and represent annual average percent change; (1) Figures cover the Providence-Warwick, RI-MA Metropolitan Statistical Area—see Appendix B for areas included; (2) Rank is based on 2013 data and ranges from 1 to 363
Source: The United States Conference of Mayors, U.S. Metro Economies: Outlook—Gross Metropolitan Product, with Metro Employment Projections, November 2013

Metropolitan Area Exports

Area	2007	2008	2009	2010	2011	2012	Rank[2]
MSA[1]	3,738.2	5,382.0	5,392.0	5,791.9	7,139.1	5,830.8	44

Note: Figures are in millions of dollars; (1) Figures cover the Providence-Warwick, RI-MA Metropolitan Statistical Area—see Appendix B for areas included; (2) Rank is based on 2012 data and ranges from 1 to 369
Source: U.S. Department of Commerce, International Trade Administration, Office of Trade & Industry Information, Manufacturing & Services, data extracted April 1, 2014

INCOME

Income

Area	Per Capita ($)	Median Household ($)	Average Household ($)
City	21,262	37,654	58,512
MSA[1]	29,018	54,674	72,588
U.S.	27,385	51,771	71,579

Note: (1) Figures cover the Providence-Warwick, RI-MA Metropolitan Statistical Area—see Appendix B for areas included
Source: U.S. Census Bureau, 2010-2012 American Community Survey 3-Year Estimates

Household Income Distribution

Area	Percent of Households Earning							
	Under $15,000	$15,000 -24,999	$25,000 -34,999	$35,000 -49,999	$50,000 -74,999	$75,000 -99,000	$100,000 -149,999	$150,000 and up
City	25.0	12.6	9.8	13.4	16.2	8.8	8.1	6.1
MSA[1]	13.9	10.5	9.1	12.5	17.7	12.4	14.3	9.6
U.S.	13.1	11.0	10.5	13.7	18.1	11.9	12.5	9.1

Note: (1) Figures cover the Providence-Warwick, RI-MA Metropolitan Statistical Area—see Appendix B for areas included
Source: U.S. Census Bureau, 2010-2012 American Community Survey 3-Year Estimates

Poverty Rate

Area	All Ages	Under 18 Years Old	18 to 64 Years Old	65 Years and Over
City	30.0	40.8	27.6	18.2
MSA[1]	13.6	19.1	12.7	9.8
U.S.	15.7	22.2	14.6	9.3

Note: Figures are percentage of people whose income during the past 12 months was below the poverty level; (1) Figures cover the Providence-Warwick, RI-MA Metropolitan Statistical Area—see Appendix B for areas included
Source: U.S. Census Bureau, 2010-2012 American Community Survey 3-Year Estimates

Personal Bankruptcy Filing Rate

Area	2008	2009	2010	2011	2012	2013
Providence County	4.49	5.23	5.59	5.09	4.20	3.62
U.S.	3.53	4.61	4.97	4.37	3.76	3.29

Note: Numbers are per 1,000 population and include Chapter 7 and Chapter 13 filings
Source: Federal Deposit Insurance Corporation, Regional Economic Conditions, March 20, 2014

EMPLOYMENT

Labor Force and Employment

Area	Civilian Labor Force			Workers Employed		
	Dec. 2012	Dec. 2013	% Chg.	Dec. 2012	Dec. 2013	% Chg.
City	81,449	79,843	-2.0	72,508	71,452	-1.5
MSA[1]	698,341	687,582	-1.5	632,386	624,667	-1.2
U.S.	154,904,000	154,408,000	-0.3	143,060,000	144,423,000	1.0

Note: Data is not seasonally adjusted and covers workers 16 years of age and older; (1) Metropolitan Statistical Area—see Appendix B for areas included
Source: Bureau of Labor Statistics, Local Area Unemployment Statistics

Unemployment Rate

Area	2013											
	Jan.	Feb.	Mar.	Apr.	May	Jun.	Jul.	Aug.	Sep.	Oct.	Nov.	Dec.
City	12.1	11.0	11.0	10.4	11.4	11.0	11.7	11.5	10.8	10.4	9.8	10.5
MSA[1]	10.6	10.0	9.9	8.9	9.3	8.7	9.4	9.6	8.9	8.6	8.6	9.2
U.S.	8.5	8.1	7.6	7.1	7.3	7.8	7.7	7.3	7.0	7.0	6.6	6.5

Note: Data is not seasonally adjusted and covers workers 16 years of age and older; All figures are percentages; (1) Metropolitan Statistical Area—see Appendix B for areas included
Source: Bureau of Labor Statistics, Local Area Unemployment Statistics

Employment by Occupation

Occupation Classification	City (%)	MSA[1] (%)	U.S. (%)
Management, Business, Science, and Arts	32.5	35.4	36.0
Natural Resources, Construction, and Maintenance	4.9	7.7	9.1
Production, Transportation, and Material Moving	15.9	11.9	12.0
Sales and Office	22.6	25.3	24.7
Service	24.0	19.7	18.2

Note: Figures cover employed civilians 16 years of age and older; (1) Figures cover the Providence-Warwick, RI-MA Metropolitan Statistical Area—see Appendix B for areas included
Source: U.S. Census Bureau, 2010-2012 American Community Survey 3-Year Estimates

Employment by Industry

Sector	NECTA[1]		U.S.
	Number of Employees	Percent of Total	Percent of Total
Construction	19,700	3.5	4.2
Education and Health Services	123,300	22.0	15.5
Financial Activities	34,900	6.2	5.7
Government	71,500	12.8	16.1
Information	10,000	1.8	1.9
Leisure and Hospitality	60,400	10.8	10.2
Manufacturing	50,900	9.1	8.7
Mining and Logging	200	<0.1	0.6
Other Services	25,800	4.6	3.9
Professional and Business Services	64,400	11.5	13.7
Retail Trade	65,400	11.7	11.4
Transportation and Utilities	13,800	2.5	3.8
Wholesale Trade	20,200	3.6	4.2

Note: Figures cover non-farm employment as of December 2013 and are not seasonally adjusted;
(1) New England City and Town Area—see Appendix B for areas included
Source: Bureau of Labor Statistics, Current Employment Statistics, Employment, Hours, and Earnings

Occupations with Greatest Projected Employment Growth: 2010 – 2020

Occupation[1]	2010 Employment	2020 Projected Employment	Numeric Employment Change	Percent Employment Change
Retail Salespersons	14,700	16,790	2,080	14.2
Registered Nurses	12,960	15,000	2,040	15.7
Home Health Aides	4,610	6,480	1,870	40.5
Combined Food Preparation and Serving Workers, Including Fast Food	8,330	9,880	1,550	18.6
Nursing Aides, Orderlies, and Attendants	9,360	10,810	1,450	15.5
Personal Care Aides	2,980	4,290	1,320	44.2
Customer Service Representatives	8,870	10,070	1,200	13.5
Waiters and Waitresses	8,820	10,010	1,190	13.5
Cashiers	10,890	11,940	1,050	9.6
Office Clerks, General	8,890	9,830	940	10.6

Note: Projections cover Rhode Island; (1) Sorted by numeric employment change
Source: www.projectionscentral.com, State Occupational Projections, 2010–2020 Long-Term Projections

Fastest Growing Occupations: 2010 – 2020

Occupation[1]	2010 Employment	2020 Projected Employment	Numeric Employment Change	Percent Employment Change
Veterinary Technologists and Technicians	470	680	210	45.3
Personal Care Aides	2,980	4,290	1,320	44.2
Home Health Aides	4,610	6,480	1,870	40.5
Market Research Analysts and Marketing Specialists	800	1,120	310	39.2
Logisticians	280	380	100	37.5
Software Developers, Systems Software	1,430	1,910	480	33.7
Medical Scientists, Except Epidemiologists	330	440	110	32.9
Pharmacy Technicians	1,430	1,890	460	32.3
Brickmasons and Blockmasons	500	650	150	30.7
Diagnostic Medical Sonographers	330	430	100	30.4

Note: Projections cover Rhode Island; (1) Sorted by percent employment change and excludes occupations with numeric employment change less than 100
Source: www.projectionscentral.com, State Occupational Projections, 2010–2020 Long-Term Projections

Average Wages

Occupation	$/Hr.	Occupation	$/Hr.
Accountants and Auditors	36.01	Maids and Housekeeping Cleaners	12.21
Automotive Mechanics	18.48	Maintenance and Repair Workers	19.51
Bookkeepers	18.82	Marketing Managers	58.72
Carpenters	22.21	Nuclear Medicine Technologists	40.30
Cashiers	10.02	Nurses, Licensed Practical	24.60
Clerks, General Office	15.77	Nurses, Registered	35.47
Clerks, Receptionists/Information	13.92	Nursing Assistants	13.75
Clerks, Shipping/Receiving	15.08	Packers and Packagers, Hand	10.48
Computer Programmers	38.04	Physical Therapists	38.50
Computer Systems Analysts	38.00	Postal Service Mail Carriers	24.81
Computer User Support Specialists	22.97	Real Estate Brokers	n/a
Cooks, Restaurant	11.89	Retail Salespersons	12.48
Dentists	n/a	Sales Reps., Exc. Tech./Scientific	32.76
Electrical Engineers	45.34	Sales Reps., Tech./Scientific	41.15
Electricians	26.50	Secretaries, Exc. Legal/Med./Exec.	17.93
Financial Managers	62.42	Security Guards	12.83
First-Line Supervisors/Managers, Sales	21.71	Surgeons	116.46
Food Preparation Workers	11.22	Teacher Assistants	14.50
General and Operations Managers	65.06	Teachers, Elementary School	34.70
Hairdressers/Cosmetologists	13.37	Teachers, Secondary School	33.60
Internists	79.79	Telemarketers	15.11
Janitors and Cleaners	13.33	Truck Drivers, Heavy/Tractor-Trailer	20.27
Landscaping/Groundskeeping Workers	13.96	Truck Drivers, Light/Delivery Svcs.	17.91
Lawyers	47.45	Waiters and Waitresses	10.34

Note: Wage data covers the Providence-Fall River-Warwick, RI-MA Metropolitan Statistical Area—see Appendix B for areas included. Hourly wages for elementary/secondary school teachers and teacher assistants were calculated by the editors from annual wage data assuming a 40 hour work week; n/a not available.
Source: Bureau of Labor Statistics, Metro Area Occupational Employment and Wage Estimates, May 2013

RESIDENTIAL REAL ESTATE

Building Permits

Area	Single-Family 2012	2013	Pct. Chg.	Multi-Family 2012	2013	Pct. Chg.	Total 2012	2013	Pct. Chg.
City	12	16	33.3	3	26	766.7	15	42	180.0
MSA[1]	1,144	1,465	28.1	217	509	134.6	1,361	1,974	45.0
U.S.	518,695	620,802	19.7	310,963	370,020	19.0	829,658	990,822	19.4

Note: (1) Metropolitan Statistical Area—see Appendix B for areas included; figures represent new, privately-owned housing units authorized (unadjusted data); All permit data are based on estimates with imputation.
Source: U.S. Census Bureau, Manufacturing, Mining, and Construction Statistics, Building Permits, 2012, 2013

Homeownership Rate

Area	2006 (%)	2007 (%)	2008 (%)	2009 (%)	2010 (%)	2011 (%)	2012 (%)	2013 (%)
MSA[1]	65.5	64.1	63.9	61.7	61.0	61.3	61.7	60.1
U.S.	68.8	68.1	67.8	67.4	66.9	66.1	65.4	65.1

Note: (1) Figures cover the Providence-Warwick, RI-MA Metropolitan Statistical Area—see Appendix B for areas included
Source: U.S. Census Bureau, Housing Vacancies and Homeownership Annual Statistics: 2013

Housing Vacancy Rates

Area	Gross Vacancy Rate[2] (%) 2011	2012	2013	Year-Round Vacancy Rate[3] (%) 2011	2012	2013	Rental Vacancy Rate[4] (%) 2011	2012	2013	Homeowner Vacancy Rate[5] (%) 2011	2012	2013
MSA[1]	13.7	13.8	12.3	10.8	10.9	8.9	8.8	8.0	6.6	2.2	2.9	2.3
U.S.	14.2	13.8	13.8	11.1	10.8	10.7	9.5	8.7	8.3	2.5	2.0	2.0

Note: (1) Figures cover the Providence-Warwick, RI-MA Metropolitan Statistical Area—see Appendix B for areas included; (2) The percentage of the total housing inventory that is vacant; (3) The percentage of the housing inventory (excluding seasonal units) that is year-round vacant; (4) The percentage of rental inventory that is vacant for rent; (5) The percentage of homeowner inventory that is vacant for sale
Source: U.S. Census Bureau, Housing Vacancies and Homeownership Annual Statistics: 2013

TAXES

State Corporate Income Tax Rates

State	Tax Rate (%)	Income Brackets ($)	Num. of Brackets	Financial Institution Tax Rate (%)[a]	Federal Income Tax Ded.
Rhode Island	9.0 (b)	Flat rate	1	9.0 (b)	No

Note: Tax rates as of January 1, 2014; (a) Rates listed are the corporate income tax rate applied to financial institutions or excise taxes based on income. Some states have other taxes based upon the value of deposits or shares; (b) Minimum tax is $50 in Arizona, $100 in District of Columbia, $50 in North Dakota (banks), $500 in Rhode Island, $200 per location in South Dakota (banks), $100 in Utah, $250 in Vermont.
Source: Federation of Tax Administrators, "State Corporate Income Tax Rates, 2014"

State Individual Income Tax Rates

State	Tax Rate (%)	Income Brackets ($)	Num. of Brackets	Personal Exempt. ($)[1] Single	Personal Exempt. ($)[1] Dependents	Fed. Inc. Tax Ded.
Rhode Island (a)	3.75 - 5.99	58,600 - 135,500	3	3,800	3,800	No

Note: Tax rates as of January 1, 2014; Local- and county-level taxes are not included; n/a not applicable; (1) Married joint filers generally receive double the single exemption; (a) 17 states have statutory provision for automatically adjusting to the rate of inflation the dollar values of the income tax brackets, standard deductions, and/or personal exemptions. Massachusetts, Michigan, and Nebraska index the personal exemption only. Oregon does not index the income brackets for $125,000 and over. Maine has suspended indexing for 2014 and 2015.
Source: Federation of Tax Administrators, "State Individual Income Tax Rates, 2014"

Various State and Local Tax Rates

State	State and Local Sales and Use (%)	State Sales and Use (%)	Gasoline[1] (¢/gal.)	Cigarette[2] ($/pack)	Spirits[3] ($/gal.)	Wine[4] ($/gal.)	Beer[5] ($/gal.)
Rhode Island	7.0	7.00	33.00	3.500	3.75 (f)	0.60	0.11 (s)

Note: All tax rates as of January 1, 2014; (1) The American Petroleum Institute has developed a methodology for determining the average tax rate on a gallon of fuel. Rates may include any of the following: excise taxes, environmental fees, storage tank fees, other fees or taxes, general sales tax, and local taxes. In states where gasoline is subject to the general sales tax, or where the fuel tax is based on the average sale price, the average rate determined by API is sensitive to changes in the price of gasoline. States that fully or partially apply general sales taxes to gasoline: CA, CO, GA, IL, IN, MI, NY; (2) The federal excise tax of $1.0066 per pack and local taxes are not included; (3) Rates are those applicable to off-premise sales of 40% alcohol by volume (a.b.v.) distilled spirits in 750ml containers. Local excise taxes are excluded; (4) Rates are those applicable to off-premise sales of 11% a.b.v. non-carbonated wine in 750ml containers; (5) Rates are those applicable to off-premise sales of 4.7% a.b.v. beer in 12 ounce containers; (f) Different rates also applicable according to alcohol content, place of production, size of container, or place purchased (on- or off-premise or onboard airlines); (s) Includes case fees and/or bottle fees which may vary with size of container.
Source: Tax Foundation, 2014 Facts & Figures: How Does Your State Compare?

State Business Tax Climate Index Rankings

State	Overall Rank	Corporate Tax Index Rank	Individual Income Tax Index Rank	Sales Tax Index Rank	Unemployment Insurance Tax Index Rank	Property Tax Index Rank
Rhode Island	46	43	36	27	50	46

Note: The index is a measure of how each state's tax laws affect economic performance. The lower the rank, the more favorable a state's tax system is for business. States without a given tax are given a ranking of 1. The scores/rankings for the District of Columbia do not affect other states. The 2014 index represents the tax climate as of July 1, 2013.
Source: Tax Foundation, State Business Tax Climate Index 2014

COMMERCIAL UTILITIES

Typical Monthly Electric Bills

Area	Commercial Service ($/month) 1,500 kWh	Commercial Service ($/month) 40 kW demand 14,000 kWh	Industrial Service ($/month) 1,000 kW demand 200,000 kWh	Industrial Service ($/month) 50,000 kW demand 15,000,000 kWh
City	233	1,850	26,443	1,686,701
Average[1]	197	1,636	25,662	1,485,307

Note: Based on total rates in effect July 1, 2013; (1) average based on 180 utilities surveyed
Source: Edison Electric Institute, Typical Bills and Average Rates Report, Summer 2013

TRANSPORTATION

Means of Transportation to Work

Area	Car/Truck/Van		Public Transportation			Bicycle	Walked	Other Means	Worked at Home
	Drove Alone	Car-pooled	Bus	Subway	Railroad				
City	58.8	13.8	7.9	0.1	1.0	1.3	10.2	2.4	4.2
MSA[1]	80.7	8.7	1.7	0.2	0.8	0.3	3.2	1.0	3.3
U.S.	76.4	9.7	2.6	1.7	0.5	0.6	2.8	1.3	4.3

Note: Figures are percentages and cover workers 16 years of age and older; (1) Figures cover the
Providence-Warwick, RI-MA Metropolitan Statistical Area—see Appendix B for areas included
Source: U.S. Census Bureau, 2010-2012 American Community Survey 3-Year Estimates

Travel Time to Work

Area	Less Than 10 Minutes	10 to 19 Minutes	20 to 29 Minutes	30 to 44 Minutes	45 to 59 Minutes	60 to 89 Minutes	90 Minutes or More
City	15.9	41.6	18.4	13.4	4.3	4.3	2.1
MSA[1]	13.8	32.2	21.2	18.2	6.8	5.3	2.5
U.S.	13.5	29.8	20.9	20.1	7.5	5.6	2.5

Note: Figures are percentages and include workers 16 years old and over; (1) Figures cover the
Providence-Warwick, RI-MA Metropolitan Statistical Area—see Appendix B for areas included
Source: U.S. Census Bureau, 2010-2012 American Community Survey 3-Year Estimates

Travel Time Index

Area	1985	1990	1995	2000	2005	2010	2011
Urban Area[1]	1.05	1.09	1.12	1.20	1.24	1.16	1.16
Average[2]	1.09	1.14	1.16	1.19	1.23	1.18	1.18

Note: Travel Time Index—the ratio of travel time in the peak period to the travel time at free-flow conditions.
For example, a value of 1.30 indicates a 20-minute free-flow trip takes 26 minutes in the peak. Free-flow speeds
(60 mph on freeways and 35 mph on principal arterials) are used as the comparison threshold; (1) Covers the
Providence RI-MA urban area; (2) average of 498 urban areas
Source: Texas Transportation Institute, Urban Mobility Report 2012, December 2012

Public Transportation

Agency Name / Mode of Transportation	Vehicles Operated in Maximum Service	Annual Unlinked Passenger Trips (in thous.)	Annual Passenger Miles (in thous.)
Rhode Island Public Transit Authority (RIPTA)			
Bus (directly operated)	188	19,762.9	83,518.3
Demand Response (directly operated)	86	482.2	3,183.6
Demand Response (purchased transportation)	18	78.1	690.2
Demand Response Taxi (purchased transportation)	14	146.0	1,439.4

Source: Federal Transit Administration, National Transit Database, 2012

Air Transportation

Airport Name and Code / Type of Service	Passenger Airlines[1]	Passenger Enplanements	Freight Carriers[2]	Freight (lbs.)
Theodore Francis Green State Airport (PVD)				
Domestic service (U.S. carriers - 2013)	29	1,883,316	11	10,247,620
International service (U.S. carriers - 2012)	3	100	0	0

Note: (1) Includes all U.S.-based major, minor and commuter airlines that carried at least one passenger during
the year; (2) Includes all U.S.-based airlines and freight carriers that transported at least one lb. of freight during
the year.
Source: Bureau of Transportation Statistics, The Intermodal Transportation Database, Air Carriers: T-100
Domestic Market (U.S. Carriers), 2013; Bureau of Transportation Statistics, The Intermodal Transportation
Database, Air Carriers: T-100 International Market (U.S. Carriers), 2012

Other Transportation Statistics

Major Highways: I-95; I-195
Amtrak Service: Yes
Major Waterways/Ports: Providence River
Source: Amtrak.com; Google Maps

BUSINESSES

Major Business Headquarters

Company Name	Rankings	
	Fortune[1]	Forbes[2]
Gilbane	-	137
Textron	225	-
United Natural Foods	474	-

Note: (1) Fortune 500—companies that produce a 10-K are ranked 1 to 500 based on 2012 revenue; (2) all private companies with at least $2 billion in annual revenue through the end of their most current fiscal year are ranked 1 to 224; companies listed are headquartered in the city; dashes indicate no ranking
Source: Fortune, "Fortune 500," May 20, 2013; Forbes, "America's Largest Private Companies," December 18, 2013

Minority- and Women-Owned Businesses

Group	All Firms		Firms with Paid Employees			
	Firms	Sales ($000)	Firms	Sales ($000)	Employees	Payroll ($000)
Asian	550	126,018	235	114,889	1,270	23,822
Black	1,615	106,889	70	54,690	283	8,573
Hispanic	3,001	161,518	136	82,916	612	16,098
Women	4,516	535,186	481	451,704	3,801	126,233
All Firms	15,395	20,386,698	4,123	19,873,658	109,057	4,796,327

Note: Figures cover firms located in the city; minority- and women-owned business are defined as firms in which the corresponding group own 51% or more of the stock or equity of the company
Source: U.S. Census Bureau, 2007 Economic Census, Survey of Business Owners (2012 Survey of Business Owners data will be released starting in June 2015)

**HOTELS &
CONVENTION
CENTERS**

Hotels/Motels

Area	5 Star		4 Star		3 Star		2 Star		1 Star		Not Rated	
	Num.	Pct.[3]	Num.	Pct.[3]	Num.	Pct.[3]	Num.	Pct.[3]	Num.	Pct.[3]	Num.	Pct.[3]
City[1]	0	0.0	4	4.2	29	30.2	52	54.2	4	4.2	7	7.3
Total[2]	142	0.9	1,005	6.0	5,147	30.9	8,578	51.4	408	2.4	1,397	8.4

Note: (1) Figures cover Providence and vicinity; (2) Figures cover all 100 cities in this book; (3) Percentage of hotels which have a given star rating; Star ratings are determined by expedia.com and offer an indication of the general quality of a particular hotel.
Source: expedia.com, April 7, 2014

The Providence-Warwick, RI-MA metro area is home to two of the best hotels in the U.S. according to *Travel & Leisure*: **Ocean House, Rhode Island**; **Chanler at Cliff Walk**. Criteria: service; location; rooms; food; and value. The list includes the top 200 hotels in the U.S. *Travel & Leisure, "T+L 500, The World's Best Hotels 2014"*

The Providence-Warwick, RI-MA metro area is home to one of the best hotels in the world according to *Condé Nast Traveler*: **Ocean House**. The selections are based on over 79,000 responses to the magazine's annual Readers' Choice Survey. The list includes the top 200 hotels in the U.S. *Condé Nast Traveler, "Gold List 2014, The World's Best Places to Stay"*

Major Convention Centers

Name	Overall Space (sq. ft.)	Exhibit Space (sq. ft.)	Meeting Space (sq. ft.)	Meeting Rooms
Rhode Island Convention Center	137,000	100,000	n/a	23

Note: Table includes convention centers located in the Providence-Warwick, RI-MA metro area; n/a not available
Source: Original research

Living Environment

COST OF LIVING

Cost of Living Index

Composite Index	Groceries	Housing	Utilities	Trans-portation	Health Care	Misc. Goods/ Services
125.2	106.9	138.8	133.1	104.2	118.2	128.4

Note: The Cost of Living Index measures regional differences in the cost of consumer goods and services, excluding taxes and non-consumer expenditures, for professional and managerial households in the top income quintile. It is based on more than 50,000 prices covering almost 60 different items for which prices are collected three times a year by chambers of commerce, economic development organizations or university applied economic centers in each participating urban area. The numbers shown should be read as a percentage above or below the national average of 100. For example, a value of 115.4 in the groceries column indicates that grocery prices are 15.4% higher than the national average. Small differences in the index numbers should not be interpreted as significant; Figures cover the Providence RI urban area.
Source: The Council for Community and Economic Research, ACCRA Cost of Living Index, 2013

Grocery Prices

Area[1]	T-Bone Steak ($/pound)	Frying Chicken ($/pound)	Whole Milk ($/half gal.)	Eggs ($/dozen)	Orange Juice ($/64 oz.)	Coffee ($/11.5 oz.)
City[2]	11.56	1.36	2.94	2.26	3.29	4.51
Avg.	10.19	1.28	2.34	1.81	3.48	4.39
Min.	8.56	0.94	1.44	1.19	2.78	3.40
Max.	14.82	2.28	3.56	3.73	6.23	7.32

Note: (1) Values for the local area are compared with the average, minimum and maximum values for all 327 areas in the Cost of Living Index; (2) Figures cover the Providence RI urban area; **T-Bone Steak** *(price per pound);* **Frying Chicken** *(price per pound, whole fryer);* **Whole Milk** *(half gallon carton);* **Eggs** *(price per dozen, Grade A, large);* **Orange Juice** *(64 oz. Tropicana or Florida Natural);* **Coffee** *(11.5 oz. can, vacuum-packed, Maxwell House, Hills Bros, or Folgers).*
Source: The Council for Community and Economic Research, ACCRA Cost of Living Index, 2013

Housing and Utility Costs

Area[1]	New Home Price ($)	Apartment Rent ($/month)	All Electric ($/month)	Part Electric ($/month)	Other Energy ($/month)	Telephone ($/month)
City[2]	386,097	1,450	-	117.64	102.89	36.19
Avg.	295,864	900	171.38	91.82	70.12	27.73
Min.	185,506	458	117.80	48.81	33.67	17.16
Max.	1,358,917	3,783	441.68	171.40	372.65	39.47

Note: (1) Values for the local area are compared with the average, minimum and maximum values for all 327 areas in the Cost of Living Index; (2) Figures cover the Providence RI urban area; **New Home Price** *(2,400 sf living area, 8,000 sf lot, in urban area with full utilities);* **Apartment Rent** *(950 sf 2 bedroom/1.5 or 2 bath, unfurnished, excluding all utilities except water);* **All Electric** *(average monthly cost for an all-electric home);* **Part Electric** *(average monthly cost for a part-electric home);* **Other Energy** *(average monthly cost for natural gas, fuel oil, coal, wood, and any other forms of energy except electricity);* **Telephone** *(price includes basic monthly rate for a private residential line plus additional local usage charges incurred by a family of four).*
Source: The Council for Community and Economic Research, ACCRA Cost of Living Index, 2013

Health Care, Transportation, and Other Costs

Area[1]	Doctor ($/visit)	Dentist ($/visit)	Optometrist ($/visit)	Gasoline ($/gallon)	Beauty Salon ($/visit)	Men's Shirt ($)
City[2]	149.00	96.22	116.67	3.68	45.48	39.46
Avg.	101.40	86.48	96.16	3.44	33.87	26.55
Min.	61.67	50.83	50.12	3.08	18.92	12.48
Max.	182.71	152.50	223.78	4.33	68.22	52.03

Note: (1) Values for the local area are compared with the average, minimum and maximum values for all 327 areas in the Cost of Living Index; (2) Figures cover the Providence RI urban area; **Doctor** *(general practitioners routine exam of an established patient);* **Dentist** *(adult teeth cleaning and periodic oral examination);* **Optometrist** *(full vision eye exam for established adult patient);* **Gasoline** *(one gallon regular unleaded, national brand, including all taxes, cash price at self-service pump if available);* **Beauty Salon** *(woman's shampoo, trim, and blow-dry);* **Men's Shirt** *(cotton/polyester dress shirt, pinpoint weave, long sleeves).*
Source: The Council for Community and Economic Research, ACCRA Cost of Living Index, 2013

HOUSING

House Price Index (HPI)

Area	National Ranking[2]	Quarterly Change (%)	One-Year Change (%)	Five-Year Change (%)
MSA[1]	224	-0.59	0.06	-12.41
U.S.[3]	–	1.20	7.69	4.18

Note: The HPI is a weighted repeat sales index. It measures average price changes in repeat sales or refinancings on the same properties. This information is obtained by reviewing repeat mortgage transactions on single-family properties whose mortgages have been purchased or securitized by Fannie Mae or Freddie Mac in January 1975; (1) Providence-Warwick, RI-MA Metropolitan Statistical Area—see Appendix B for areas included; (2) Rankings are based on annual percentage change for all metro areas containing at least 15,000 transactions over the last 10 years and ranges from 1 to 283; (3) figures based on a weighted average of Census Division estimates using a seasonally adjusted, purchase-only index; all figures are for the period ending December 31, 2013
Source: Federal Housing Finance Agency, House Price Index, February 25, 2014

Median Single-Family Home Prices

Area	2011	2012	2013p	Percent Change 2012 to 2013
MSA[1]	217.2	214.7	230.8	7.5
U.S. Average	166.2	177.2	197.4	11.4

Note: Figures are median sales prices of existing single-family homes in thousands of dollars; (p) preliminary; n/a not available; (1) Providence-Warwick, RI-MA Metropolitan Statistical Area—see Appendix B for areas included
Source: National Association of Realtors, Median Sales Price of Existing Single-Family Homes for Metropolitan Areas, 4th Quarter 2013

Qualifying Income Based on Median Sales Price of Existing Single-Family Homes

Area	With 5% Down ($)	With 10% Down ($)	With 20% Down ($)
MSA[1]	52,543	49,777	44,246
U.S. Average	45,395	43,006	38,228

Note: Figures are preliminary; Qualifying income is based on a mortgage rate of 4.4%. Monthly principal and interest payment is limited to 25% of income; n/a not available; (1) Providence-Warwick, RI-MA Metropolitan Statistical Area—see Appendix B for areas included
Source: National Association of Realtors, Qualifying Income Based on Median Sales Price of Existing Single-Family Homes for Metropolitan Areas, 4th Quarter 2013

Median Apartment Condo-Coop Home Prices

Area	2011	2012	2013p	Percent Change 2012 to 2013
MSA[1]	166.3	156.8	178.7	14.0
U.S. Average	165.1	173.7	194.9	12.2

Note: Figures are median sales prices of existing apartment condo-coop homes in thousands of dollars; (p) preliminary; n/a not available; (1) Providence-Warwick, RI-MA Metropolitan Statistical Area—see Appendix B for areas included
Source: National Association of Realtors, Median Sales Price of Existing Apartment Condo-Coop Homes for Metropolitan Areas, 4th Quarter 2013

Gross Monthly Rent

Area	Under $200	$200 -299	$300 -499	$500 -749	$750 -999	$1,000 -1,499	$1,500 and up	Median ($)
City	4.1	7.4	7.4	15.8	27.7	29.5	8.2	888
MSA[1]	2.4	6.8	8.4	19.4	28.5	26.3	8.2	859
U.S.	1.7	3.3	8.1	22.7	24.3	25.7	14.3	889

Note: Figures are percentages except for Median; Gross rent is the contract rent plus the estimated average monthly cost of utilities (electricity, gas, and water and sewer) and fuels (oil, coal, kerosene, wood, etc.) if these are paid by the renter (or paid for the renter by someone else); (1) Figures cover the Providence-Warwick, RI-MA Metropolitan Statistical Area—see Appendix B for areas included
Source: U.S. Census Bureau, 2010-2012 American Community Survey 3-Year Estimates

Year Housing Structure Built

Area	2010 or Later	2000 -2009	1990 -1999	1980 -1989	1970 -1979	1960 -1969	1950 -1959	1940 -1949	Before 1940	Median Year
City	0.1	4.6	2.7	5.3	8.2	6.5	8.4	6.4	58.0	<1940
MSA[1]	0.2	6.7	7.5	10.3	12.1	10.3	11.4	6.8	34.7	1957
U.S.	0.5	14.9	13.8	13.9	15.9	11.1	10.9	5.5	13.5	1976

Note: Figures are percentages except for Median Year; (1) Figures cover the Providence-Warwick, RI-MA Metropolitan Statistical Area—see Appendix B for areas included
Source: U.S. Census Bureau, 2010-2012 American Community Survey 3-Year Estimates

HEALTH

Health Risk Data

Category	MSA[1] (%)	U.S. (%)
Adults aged 18–64 who have any kind of health care coverage	85.1	79.6
Adults who reported being in good or excellent health	83.5	83.1
Adults who are current smokers	18.4	19.6
Adults who are heavy drinkers[2]	6.4	6.1
Adults who are binge drinkers[3]	18.1	16.9
Adults who are overweight (BMI 25.0 - 29.9)	36.8	35.8
Adults who are obese (BMI 30.0 - 99.8)	25.8	27.6
Adults who participated in any physical activities in the past month	77.0	77.1
Adults 50+ who have ever had a sigmoidoscopy or colonoscopy	75.5	67.3
Women aged 40+ who have had a mammogram within the past two years	82.2	74.0
Men aged 40+ who have had a PSA test within the past two years	47.2	45.2
Adults aged 65+ who have had flu shot within the past year	58.7	60.1
Adults who always wear a seatbelt	89.9	93.8

Note: Data as of 2012 unless otherwise noted; (1) Figures cover the Providence-New Bedford-Fall River, RI-MA Metropolitan Statistical Area—see Appendix B for areas included; (2) Heavy drinkers are classified as males having more than two drinks per day or females having more than one drink per day; (3) Binge drinkers are classified as males having five or more drinks on one occasion or females having four or more drinks on one occasion
Source: Centers for Disease Control and Prevention, Behaviorial Risk Factor Surveillance System, SMART: Selected Metropolitan/Micropolitan Area Risk Trends, 2012

Chronic Health Indicators

Category	MSA[1] (%)	U.S. (%)
Adults who have ever been told they had a heart attack	5.0	4.5
Adults who have ever been told they had a stroke	2.4	2.9
Adults who have been told they currently have asthma	11.0	8.9
Adults who have ever been told they have arthritis	26.9	25.7
Adults who have ever been told they have diabetes[2]	10.5	9.7
Adults who have ever been told they had skin cancer	5.7	5.7
Adults who have ever been told they had any other types of cancer	6.7	6.5
Adults who have ever been told they have COPD	6.9	6.2
Adults who have ever been told they have kidney disease	2.3	2.5
Adults who have ever been told they have a form of depression	20.1	18.0

Note: Data as of 2012 unless otherwise noted; (1) Figures cover the Providence-New Bedford-Fall River, RI-MA Metropolitan Statistical Area—see Appendix B for areas included; (2) Figures do not include pregnancy-related, borderline, or pre-diabetes
Source: Centers for Disease Control and Prevention, Behaviorial Risk Factor Surveillance System, SMART: Selected Metropolitan/Micropolitan Area Risk Trends, 2012

Mortality Rates for the Top 10 Causes of Death in the U.S.

ICD-10[a] Sub-Chapter	ICD-10[a] Code	Age-Adjusted Mortality Rate[1] per 100,000 population	
		County[2]	U.S.
Malignant neoplasms	C00-C97	178.2	174.2
Ischaemic heart diseases	I20-I25	142.3	119.1
Other forms of heart disease	I30-I51	31.0	49.6
Chronic lower respiratory diseases	J40-J47	37.5	43.2
Cerebrovascular diseases	I60-I69	33.2	40.3
Organic, including symptomatic, mental disorders	F01-F09	32.9	30.5
Other degenerative diseases of the nervous system	G30-G31	25.4	26.3
Other external causes of accidental injury	W00-X59	32.1	25.1
Diabetes mellitus	E10-E14	18.0	21.3
Hypertensive diseases	I10-I15	12.5	18.8

Note: (a) ICD-10 = International Classification of Diseases 10th Revision; (1) Mortality rates are a three year average covering 2008-2010; (2) Figures cover Providence County
Source: Centers for Disease Control and Prevention, National Center for Health Statistics. Compressed Mortality File 1999-2010 on CDC WONDER Online Database, released January 2013. Data are compiled from the Compressed Mortality File 1999-2010, Series 20 No. 2P, 2013.

Mortality Rates for Selected Causes of Death

ICD-10[a] Sub-Chapter	ICD-10[a] Code	Age-Adjusted Mortality Rate[1] per 100,000 population	
		County[2]	U.S.
Assault	X85-Y09	3.9	5.5
Diseases of the liver	K70-K76	12.3	12.4
Human immunodeficiency virus (HIV) disease	B20-B24	3.1	3.0
Influenza and pneumonia	J09-J18	16.9	16.4
Intentional self-harm	X60-X84	10.8	11.8
Malnutrition	E40-E46	Suppressed	0.8
Obesity and other hyperalimentation	E65-E68	1.7	1.6
Renal failure	N17-N19	11.7	13.6
Transport accidents	V01-V99	7.4	12.6
Viral hepatitis	B15-B19	2.7	2.2

Note: (a) ICD-10 = International Classification of Diseases 10th Revision; (1) Mortality rates are a three year average covering 2008-2010; (2) Figures cover Providence County
Source: Centers for Disease Control and Prevention, National Center for Health Statistics. Compressed Mortality File 1999-2010 on CDC WONDER Online Database, released January 2013. Data are compiled from the Compressed Mortality File 1999-2010, Series 20 No. 2P, 2013.

Health Insurance Coverage

Area	With Health Insurance	With Private Health Insurance	With Public Health Insurance	Without Health Insurance	Population Under Age 18 Without Health Insurance
City	79.3	50.9	35.0	20.7	6.0
MSA[1]	91.0	70.6	33.0	9.0	3.5
U.S.	84.9	65.4	30.4	15.1	7.5

Note: Figures are percentages that cover the civilian noninstitutionalized population; (1) Figures cover the Providence-Warwick, RI-MA Metropolitan Statistical Area—see Appendix B for areas included
Source: U.S. Census Bureau, 2010-2012 American Community Survey 3-Year Estimates

Number of Medical Professionals

Area[1]	MDs[2]	DOs[2,3]	Dentists	Podiatrists	Chiropractors	Optometrists
Local (number)	2,876	97	359	57	116	101
Local (rate[4])	458.5	15.5	57.1	9.1	18.5	16.1
U.S. (rate[4])	267.6	19.6	61.7	5.6	24.7	14.5

Note: Data as of 2012 unless noted; (1) Local data covers Providence County; (2) Data as of 2011; (3) Doctor of Osteopathic Medicine; (4) rate per 100,000 population
Source: Area Resource File (ARF) 2012-2013. U.S. Department of Health and Human Services, Health Resources and Services Administration, Bureau of Health Professions

EDUCATION

Public School District Statistics

District Name	Schls	Pupils	Pupil/ Teacher Ratio	Minority Pupils[1] (%)	Free Lunch Eligible[2] (%)	IEP[3] (%)
Providence	41	23,518	14.3	91.1	76.0	19.2

Note: Table includes school districts with 2,000 or more students; (1) Percentage of students that are not non-Hispanic white; (2) Percentage of students that are eligible for the free lunch program; (3) Percentage of students that have an Individualized Education Program.
Source: U.S. Department of Education, National Center for Education Statistics, Common Core of Data, Local Education Agency (School District) Universe Survey: School Year 2011-2012; U.S. Department of Education, National Center for Education Statistics, Common Core of Data, Public Elementary/Secondary School Universe Survey: School Year 2011-2012

Highest Level of Education

Area	Less than H.S.	H.S. Diploma	Some College, No Deg.	Associate Degree	Bachelor's Degree	Master's Degree	Prof. School Degree	Doctorate Degree
City	28.2	22.5	16.0	5.4	14.6	7.5	2.9	2.9
MSA[1]	16.2	28.1	18.2	8.3	18.0	8.2	1.8	1.2
U.S.	14.1	28.3	21.3	7.8	18.0	7.5	1.9	1.2

Note: Figures cover persons age 25 and over; (1) Figures cover the Providence-Warwick, RI-MA Metropolitan Statistical Area—see Appendix B for areas included
Source: U.S. Census Bureau, 2010-2012 American Community Survey 3-Year Estimates

Educational Attainment by Race

Area	High School Graduate or Higher (%)					Bachelor's Degree or Higher (%)				
	Total	White	Black	Asian	Hisp.[2]	Total	White	Black	Asian	Hisp.[2]
City	71.8	79.5	74.2	63.7	54.0	27.9	40.4	15.5	36.1	7.4
MSA[1]	83.8	85.5	77.3	78.4	60.4	29.2	30.4	18.9	42.2	11.6
U.S.	85.9	88.1	82.5	85.5	63.1	28.6	30.0	18.4	50.2	13.4

Note: Figures shown cover persons 25 years old and over; (1) Figures cover the Providence-Warwick, RI-MA Metropolitan Statistical Area—see Appendix B for areas included; (2) People of Hispanic origin can be of any race
Source: U.S. Census Bureau, 2010-2012 American Community Survey 3-Year Estimates

School Enrollment by Grade and Control

Area	Preschool (%)		Kindergarten (%)		Grades 1 - 4 (%)		Grades 5 - 8 (%)		Grades 9 - 12 (%)	
	Public	Private	Public	Private	Public	Private	Public	Private	Public	Private
City	67.8	32.2	84.1	15.9	90.4	9.6	86.3	13.7	86.6	13.4
MSA[1]	49.7	50.3	85.0	15.0	89.3	10.7	90.3	9.7	87.9	12.1
U.S.	56.9	43.1	87.8	12.2	89.9	10.1	90.0	10.0	90.8	9.2

Note: Figures shown cover persons 3 years old and over; (1) Figures cover the Providence-Warwick, RI-MA Metropolitan Statistical Area—see Appendix B for areas included
Source: U.S. Census Bureau, 2010-2012 American Community Survey 3-Year Estimates

Average Salaries of Public School Classroom Teachers

Area	2012-13		2013-14		Percent Change 2012-13 to 2013-14	Percent Change 2003-04 to 2013-14
	Dollars	Rank[1]	Dollars	Rank[1]		
Rhode Island	63,474	9	64,696	9	1.92	23.8
U.S. Average	56,103	–	56,689	–	1.04	21.8

Note: (1) State rank ranges from 1 to 51 where 1 indicates highest salary.
Source: National Education Association, Rankings & Estimates: Rankings of the States 2013 and Estimates of School Statistics 2014, March 2014

Higher Education

Four-Year Colleges			Two-Year Colleges			Medical Schools[1]	Law Schools[2]	Voc/ Tech[3]
Public	Private Non-profit	Private For-profit	Public	Private Non-profit	Private For-profit			
1	5	0	0	0	0	1	0	1

Note: Figures cover institutions located within the city limits and include main campuses only; (1) includes schools accredited by the Liaison Committee on Medical Education and the American Osteopathic Association's Commission on Osteopathic College Accreditation; (2) includes ABA-accredited schools, schools with provisional ABA accreditation, and state accredited schools; (3) includes all schools with programs that are less than 2 years.
Source: National Center for Education Statistics, Integrated Postsecondary Education System (IPEDS), 2012-13; Association of American Medical Colleges, Member List, April 24, 2014; American Osteopathic Association, Member List, April 24, 2014; Law School Admission Council, Official Guide to ABA-Approved Law Schools Online, April 24, 2014; Wikipedia, List of Medical Schools in the United States, April 24, 2014; Wikipedia, List of Law Schools in the United States, April 24, 2014

According to *U.S. News & World Report*, the Providence-Warwick, RI-MA metro area is home to two of the best national universities in the U.S.: **Brown University** (#14); **University of Rhode Island** (#152). The indicators used to capture academic quality fall into a number of categories: assessment by administrators at peer institutions; retention of students; faculty resources; student selectivity; financial resources; alumni giving; high school counselor ratings of colleges; and graduation rate. *U.S. News & World Report, "America's Best Colleges 2014"*

According to *U.S. News & World Report*, the Providence-Warwick, RI-MA metro area is home to two of the best liberal arts colleges in the U.S.: **Wheaton College** (#65); **Stonehill College** (#115). The indicators used to capture academic quality fall into a number of categories: assessment by administrators at peer institutions; retention of students; faculty resources; student selectivity; financial resources; alumni giving; high school counselor ratings of colleges; and graduation rate. *U.S. News & World Report, "America's Best Colleges 2014"*

PRESIDENTIAL ELECTION

2012 Presidential Election Results

Area	Obama	Romney	Other
Providence County	66.5	31.6	1.9
U.S.	51.0	47.2	1.8

Note: Results are percentages and may not add to 100% due to rounding
Source: Dave Leip's Atlas of U.S. Presidential Elections

EMPLOYERS

Major Employers

Company Name	Industry
A&M Special Purchasing	Payroll accounting service
Acushnet Company	Sporting and recreation goods
Brown University	Colleges and universities
Charlton Memorial Hospital	General medical and surgical hospitals
City of Fall River	Public elementary and secondary schools
City of Providence	General government administration
CVS Pharmacy	Drug stores
Hasbro	Games, toys, and children's vehicles
Hasbro Managerial Services	Management services
Kent Hospital	General medical and surgical hospitals
Providence School Department	Public elementary and secondary schools
Rhode Island Hospital	General medical and surgical hospitals
Roman Catholic Diocese of Fall River	Catholic church
Saint Luke's Hospital of New Bedford	General medical and surgical hospitals
Samsonite International S.A.	Luggage
Southcoast Hospitals Group	General medical and surgical hospitals
University of Rhode Island	Colleges and universities
US Navy	Navy
Women & Infants Hospital of Rhode Island	Specialty outpatient clinics, nec

Note: Companies shown are located within the Providence-Warwick, RI-MA Metropolitan Statistical Area.
Source: Hoovers.com; Wikipedia

PUBLIC SAFETY

Crime Rate

Area	All Crimes	Violent Crimes				Property Crimes		
		Murder	Forcible Rape	Robbery	Aggrav. Assault	Burglary	Larceny -Theft	Motor Vehicle Theft
City	5,121.4	9.6	47.2	203.5	376.7	1,084.4	2,745.6	654.4
Suburbs[1]	2,549.9	1.5	26.8	73.3	201.1	538.3	1,550.7	158.3
Metro[2]	2,835.1	2.4	29.1	87.7	220.6	598.8	1,683.2	213.3
U.S.	3,246.1	4.7	26.9	112.9	242.3	670.2	1,959.3	229.7

Note: Figures are crimes per 100,000 population; (1) All areas within the metro area that are located outside the city limits; (2) Figures cover the Providence-Warwick, RI-MA Metropolitan Statistical Area—see Appendix B for areas included
Source: FBI Uniform Crime Reports, 2012

Hate Crimes

Area	Number of Quarters Reported	Bias Motivation				
		Race	Religion	Sexual Orientation	Ethnicity	Disability
City	4	2	1	1	0	0
U.S.	4	2,797	1,099	1,135	667	92

Source: Federal Bureau of Investigation, Hate Crime Statistics 2012

Identity Theft Consumer Complaints

Area	Complaints	Complaints per 100,000 Population	Rank[2]
MSA[1]	925	57.8	225
U.S.	290,056	91.8	-

Note: (1) Figures cover the Providence-Warwick, RI-MA Metropolitan Statistical Area—see Appendix B for areas included; (2) Rank ranges from 1 to 377 where 1 indicates greatest number of identity theft complaints per 100,000 population
Source: Federal Trade Commission, Consumer Sentinel Network Data Book for January–December 2013

Fraud and Other Consumer Complaints

Area	Complaints	Complaints per 100,000 Population	Rank[2]
MSA[1]	5,196	324.6	263
U.S.	1,811,724	595.2	-

Note: (1) Figures cover the Providence-Warwick, RI-MA Metropolitan Statistical Area—see Appendix B for areas included; (2) Rank ranges from 1 to 377 where 1 indicates greatest number of identity theft complaints per 100,000 population
Source: Federal Trade Commission, Consumer Sentinel Network Data Book for January–December 2013

RECREATION

Culture

Dance[1]	Theatre[1]	Instrumental Music[1]	Vocal Music[1]	Series and Festivals	Museums and Art Galleries[2]	Zoos and Aquariums[3]
2	5	3	1	6	21	1

Note: (1) Number of professional perfoming groups; (2) Based on organizations with primary SIC code 8412; (3) AZA-accredited
Source: The Grey House Performing Arts Directory, 2013; Association of Zoos & Aquariums, AZA Member Zoos & Aquariums, April 2014; www.AccuLeads.com, May 1, 2014

Professional Sports Teams

Team Name	League	Year Established

No teams are located in the metro area
Source: Wikipedia, Major Professional Sports Teams of the United States and Canada, April 25, 2014

CLIMATE

Average and Extreme Temperatures

Temperature	Jan	Feb	Mar	Apr	May	Jun	Jul	Aug	Sep	Oct	Nov	Dec	Yr.
Extreme High (°F)	66	72	80	98	94	97	102	104	100	88	81	70	104
Average High (°F)	37	39	46	58	68	77	82	80	73	63	52	41	60
Average Temp. (°F)	29	30	38	48	58	67	73	71	64	54	44	33	51
Average Low (°F)	20	22	29	39	48	57	63	62	54	43	35	25	42
Extreme Low (°F)	-13	-7	1	14	29	41	48	40	32	20	6	-10	-13

Note: Figures cover the years 1948-1992
Source: National Climatic Data Center, International Station Meteorological Climate Summary, 9/96

Average Precipitation/Snowfall/Humidity

Precip./Humidity	Jan	Feb	Mar	Apr	May	Jun	Jul	Aug	Sep	Oct	Nov	Dec	Yr.
Avg. Precip. (in.)	3.9	3.6	4.2	4.1	3.7	2.9	3.2	4.0	3.5	3.6	4.5	4.3	45.3
Avg. Snowfall (in.)	10	10	7	1	Tr	0	0	0	0	Tr	1	7	35
Avg. Rel. Hum. 7am (%)	71	71	71	70	73	75	78	81	83	81	78	74	75
Avg. Rel. Hum. 4pm (%)	58	56	54	51	55	58	58	60	60	58	60	60	57

Note: Figures cover the years 1948-1992; Tr = Trace amounts (<0.05 in. of rain; <0.5 in. of snow)
Source: National Climatic Data Center, International Station Meteorological Climate Summary, 9/96

Weather Conditions

Temperature			Daytime Sky			Precipitation		
5°F & below	32°F & below	90°F & above	Clear	Partly cloudy	Cloudy	0.01 inch or more precip.	0.1 inch or more snow/ice	Thunder-storms
6	117	9	85	134	146	123	21	21

Note: Figures are average number of days per year and cover the years 1948-1992
Source: National Climatic Data Center, International Station Meteorological Climate Summary, 9/96

HAZARDOUS WASTE

Superfund Sites

Providence has one hazardous waste site on the EPA's Superfund Final National Priorities List: **Centredale Manor Restoration Project (North Providence).** *U.S. Environmental Protection Agency, Final National Priorities List, April 26, 2014*

AIR & WATER QUALITY

Air Quality Index

Area	Percent of Days when Air Quality was...[2]					AQI Statistics[2]	
	Good	Moderate	Unhealthy for Sensitive Groups	Unhealthy	Very Unhealthy	Maximum	Median
MSA[1]	64.1	33.4	2.5	0.0	0.0	145	45

Note: (1) Data covers the Providence-Warwick, RI-MA Metropolitan Statistical Area—see Appendix B for areas included; (2) Based on 365 days with AQI data in 2013. Air Quality Index (AQI) is an index for reporting daily air quality. EPA calculates the AQI for five major air pollutants regulated by the Clean Air Act: ground-level ozone, particle pollution (aka particulate matter), carbon monoxide, sulfur dioxide, and nitrogen dioxide. The AQI runs from 0 to 500. The higher the AQI value, the greater the level of air pollution and the greater the health concern. There are six AQI categories: "Good" AQI is between 0 and 50. Air quality is considered satisfactory; "Moderate" AQI is between 51 and 100. Air quality is acceptable; "Unhealthy for Sensitive Groups" When AQI values are between 101 and 150, members of sensitive groups may experience health effects; "Unhealthy" When AQI values are between 151 and 200 everyone may begin to experience health effects; "Very Unhealthy" AQI values between 201 and 300 trigger a health alert; "Hazardous" AQI values over 300 trigger warnings of emergency conditions (not shown).
Source: U.S. Environmental Protection Agency, Air Quality Index Report, 2013

Air Quality Index Pollutants

Area	Percent of Days when AQI Pollutant was...[2]					
	Carbon Monoxide	Nitrogen Dioxide	Ozone	Sulfur Dioxide	Particulate Matter 2.5	Particulate Matter 10
MSA[1]	0.0	0.5	36.7	3.6	58.6	0.5

Note: (1) Data covers the Providence-Warwick, RI-MA Metropolitan Statistical Area—see Appendix B for areas included; (2) Based on 365 days with AQI data in 2013. The Air Quality Index (AQI) is an index for reporting daily air quality. EPA calculates the AQI for five major air pollutants regulated by the Clean Air Act: ground-level ozone, particle pollution (also known as particulate matter), carbon monoxide, sulfur dioxide, and nitrogen dioxide. The AQI runs from 0 to 500. The higher the AQI value, the greater the level of air pollution and the greater the health concern.
Source: U.S. Environmental Protection Agency, Air Quality Index Report, 2013

Air Quality Trends: Ozone

	2003	2004	2005	2006	2007	2008	2009	2010	2011	2012
MSA[1]	0.089	0.081	0.087	0.082	0.084	0.078	0.068	0.076	0.075	0.077

Note: (1) Data covers the Providence-Warwick, RI-MA Metropolitan Statistical Area—see Appendix B for areas included. The values shown are the composite ozone concentration averages among trend sites based on the highest fourth daily maximum 8-hour concentration in parts per million. These trends are based on sites having an adequate record of monitoring data during the trend period. Data from exceptional events are included.
Source: U.S. Environmental Protection Agency, Air Quality Monitoring Information, "Air Quality Trends by City, 2000-2012"

Maximum Air Pollutant Concentrations: Particulate Matter, Ozone, CO and Lead

	Particulate Matter 10 (ug/m³)	Particulate Matter 2.5 Wtd AM (ug/m³)	Particulate Matter 2.5 24-Hr (ug/m³)	Ozone (ppm)	Carbon Monoxide (ppm)	Lead (ug/m³)
MSA[1] Level	32	7.8	20	0.082	1	n/a
NAAQS[2]	150	15	35	0.075	9	0.15
Met NAAQS[2]	Yes	Yes	Yes	No	Yes	n/a

Note: (1) Data covers the Providence-Warwick, RI-MA Metropolitan Statistical Area—see Appendix B for areas included; Data from exceptional events are included; (2) National Ambient Air Quality Standards; ppm = parts per million; ug/m³ = micrograms per cubic meter; n/a not available.
Concentrations: Particulate Matter 10 (coarse particulate)—highest second maximum 24-hour concentration; Particulate Matter 2.5 Wtd AM (fine particulate)—highest weighted annual mean concentration; Particulate Matter 2.5 24-Hour (fine particulate)—highest 98th percentile 24-hour concentration; Ozone—highest fourth daily maximum 8-hour concentration; Carbon Monoxide—highest second maximum non-overlapping 8-hour concentration; Lead—maximum running 3-month average
Source: U.S. Environmental Protection Agency, Air Quality Monitoring Information, "Air Quality Statistics by City, 2012"

Maximum Air Pollutant Concentrations: Nitrogen Dioxide and Sulfur Dioxide

	Nitrogen Dioxide AM (ppb)	Nitrogen Dioxide 1-Hr (ppb)	Sulfur Dioxide AM (ppb)	Sulfur Dioxide 1-Hr (ppb)	Sulfur Dioxide 24-Hr (ppb)
MSA[1] Level	10	40	n/a	65	n/a
NAAQS[2]	53	100	30	75	140
Met NAAQS[2]	Yes	Yes	n/a	Yes	n/a

Note: (1) Data covers the Providence-Warwick, RI-MA Metropolitan Statistical Area—see Appendix B for areas included; Data from exceptional events are included; (2) National Ambient Air Quality Standards; ppm = parts per million; ug/m³ = micrograms per cubic meter; n/a not available.
Concentrations: Nitrogen Dioxide AM—highest arithmetic mean concentration; Nitrogen Dioxide 1-Hr—highest 98th percentile 1-hour daily maximum concentration; Sulfur Dioxide AM—highest annual mean concentration; Sulfur Dioxide 1-Hr—highest 99th percentile 1-hour daily maximum concentration; Sulfur Dioxide 24-Hr—highest second maximum 24-hour concentration
Source: U.S. Environmental Protection Agency, Air Quality Monitoring Information, "Air Quality Statistics by City, 2012"

Drinking Water

Water System Name	Pop. Served	Primary Water Source Type	Violations[1]	
			Health Based	Monitoring/ Reporting
City of Providence	295,700	Surface	0	0

Note: (1) Based on violation data from January 1, 2013 to December 31, 2013 (includes unresolved violations from earlier years)
Source: U.S. Environmental Protection Agency, Office of Ground Water and Drinking Water, Safe Drinking Water Information System (based on data extracted February 10, 2014)

Raleigh, North Carolina

Background

Raleigh is named for Queen Elizabeth I's swashbuckling favorite, Sir Walter Raleigh. In her name, he plundered Spanish ships for gold in the New World and founded the first English settlement along the North Carolina coast. His excessive piracy led to his execution in 1618.

Raleigh is the capital of North Carolina, and its cultural and educational center, as well. Located 120 miles west of the Atlantic Ocean, Raleigh is the retail and wholesale center of eastern North Carolina. Its numerous federal, state, and local government offices provide jobs for the economy of the surrounding area. The construction of the Research Triangle Park—a complex of research laboratories among the cities of Raleigh, Durham, and Chapel Hill—has pumped money into the local economy.

The city is home to high-tech businesses, including information technology, telecommunications, biomedicine, pharmaceuticals and computer software and hardware. It also boasts first-rate universities such as North Carolina State, Duke University and the University of North Carolina.

The region has a high business startup rate, a low unemployment rate, and average wages above the state level. Research Triangle Park is one of the largest university-affiliated research parks in the world. North Carolina State University's Centennial Campus has also brought major corporate re-locators and thousands of jobs to the area.

Called the "City of Oaks," for its tree-lined streets, Raleigh offers both the modern architecture of the North Carolina Museum of Art, designed by Edward Durrell Stone (architect of Washington DC's John F. Kennedy Center), and antebellum structures such as the Greek Revival Capitol Building. The city's grid-design streets simplify exploration of this fine city. Downtown Raleigh is currently experiencing a windfall of commercial, residential, and public sector development. In 2009, Raleigh became one of three United States cities participating in Project Get Ready—is a non-profit program led by the Rocky Mountain Institute (RMI) to advance Electric Vehicle policies—today 18 cities are involved, but Raleigh leads the East Coast in Electric Vehicle (EV) readiness. Factory-made electric cars have started being purchased by consumers, and RMI looks forward to the day when at least.05 percent of all registered vehicles are plug ins.

Cultural attractions include the North Carolina Symphony, the Opera Company of North Carolina, and the Carolina Ballet, all of which perform at the Progress Energy Center for the Performing Arts. There are numerous other musical, dance and theater groups in the city and the City of Raleigh Arts Commission actively supports the arts. Children enjoy the Marbles Kids Museum & Wachovia IMAX® Theatre.

Because it is centrally located between the mountains on the west and the coast on the south and east, the Raleigh area enjoys a pleasant climate. The mountains form a partial barrier to cold air masses moving from the west. As a result, there are few winter days when the temperature gets seriously cold. In the summer, tropical air is present over the eastern and central sections of North Carolina, bringing warm temperatures and rather high humidity to the area. Raleigh is situated far enough from the coast so that the effects of coastal storms are usually reduced, however, in April 2011, a devastating tornado hit the city, killing 24 people. While snow and sleet usually occur each year, excessive accumulations of snow are rare.

Rankings

General Rankings

- *Business Insider* projected current trends well into the future to compile its list of the "15 Hottest American Cities of the Future." To such metrics as job and population growth, demographics, affordability, livability, and residents' health and welfare, analysts added innovation in technology and sustainability as well as a culture favoring youth and creativity. Judging by these combined factors, Raleigh ranked #6. *Business Insider, "The Fifteen Hottest American Cities of the Future," June 18, 2012*

- Raleigh was identified as one of America's fastest-growing cities in terms of population and economy by *Forbes*. The area ranked #2 out of 20. The 100 most populous metro areas in the U.S. were evaluated on the following criteria: estimated population growth; job growth; gross metropolitan product growth; unemployment; median salaries for college-educated workers. *Forbes, "America's Fastest-Growing Cities 2014," February 14, 2014*

- Raleigh was identified as one of America's fastest-growing major metropolitan areas in terms of population by CNNMoney.com. The area ranked #3 out of 10. Criteria: population growth between July 2012 and July 2013. *CNNMoney, "10 Fastest-Growing Cities," March 28, 2014*

- Among the 50 largest U.S. cities, Raleigh placed #17 in Vocativ's "semi-exhaustive, mostly scientific" city Livability Index for people aged 35 and under. Average salary, unemployment rates, rents, and other living costs were considered, along with bike lanes, low-cost broadband, cheap takeout, self-service laundries, the price of a pint of Guinness, music venues, and vintage clothing stores. *vocative.com, "The Livability Index: The Best U.S. Cities for People 35 and Under," November 7, 2013*

- Raleigh was selected as one of America's best cities by *Bloomberg Businessweek*. The city ranked #18 out of 50. Criteria: leisure attributes (the number of restaurants, bars, libraries, museums, professional sports teams, and park acres by population); educational attributes (public school performance, the number of colleges, and graduate degree holders); economic factors (2011 income and June and July 2012 unemployment); crime; and air quality. *Bloomberg BusinessWeek, "America's Best Cities," September 26, 2012*

- Raleigh appeared on RelocateAmerica's list of best places to live in America. The annual "Top 100 Places to Live" list recognizes the top communities as nominated by their residents & local businesses. RelocateAmerica's Research Group determined the list based on review of various data gathered for economic, employment, housing, education, industry, opportunity, environment and recreation along with feedback from area leaders and residents. *RelocateAmerica.com, "Top 100 Places to Live for 2011"*

- Raleigh was selected as one of "America's Top 10 Places to Live" by *RelocateAmerica.com*. The city ranked #4. Criteria: real estate and housing; economic health; recreation; safety; input from local residents, business and community leaders. *RelocateAmerica.com, "Top 10 Places to Live for 2011"*

Business/Finance Rankings

- The finance website Wall St. Cheat Sheet reported on the prospects for high-wage job creation in the nation's largest metro areas over the next five years and ranked them accordingly, drawing on in-depth analysis by CareerBuilder and Economic Modeling Specialists International (EMSI). The Raleigh metro area placed #6 on the Wall St. Cheat Sheet list. *wallstcheatsheet.com, "Top 10 Cities for High-Wage Job Growth," December 8, 2013*

- Based on a minimum of 500 social media reviews per metro area, the employment opinion group Glassdoor surveyed 50 of the largest U.S. metro areas on measures including compensation and benefits, satisfaction with management, business outlook, and number of employers hiring. The Raleigh metro area was ranked #14 in overall employee satisfaction. *www.glassdoor.com, "Employment Satisfaction Report Card by City," June 21, 2013*

- A *Fiscal Times* analysis balancing cost of living with average income to find the cities where residents' dollars go furthest was published by the *Huffington Post*. Based on the Census Bureau's 2010 Cost of Living Index and the National Compensation Survey, Raleigh was ranked the #7 metro area where you can "actually spend less and make more." *Fiscal Times/Huffington Post, "The Best Bang for Your Buck Cities in the United States," June 26, 2012*

- The financial literacy site NerdWallet.com set out to identify the 20 most promising cities for job seekers, analyzing data for the nation's 50 largest cities. Raleigh was ranked #6. Criteria: unemployment rate; population growth; median income; selected monthly owner costs. *NerdWallet.com, "Best Cities for Job Seekers," January 7, 2014*

- The Brookings Institution ranked the 50 largest cities in the U.S. based on income inequality. Raleigh was ranked #42. (#1 = greatest ineqality). Criteria: the cities were ranked based on the "95/20 ratio." This figure represents the income at which a household earns more than 95 percent of all other households, divided by the income at which a household earns more than only 20 percent of all other households. *Brookings Institution, "Income Inequality in America's 50 Largest Cities, 2007-2012," February 20, 2014*

- CareerBliss, an employment and careers website, analyzed U.S. Bureau of Labor Statistics data, more than 14,000 company reviews from employees and former employees, and job openings over a six-month period to arrive at its list of the 20 worst places in the United States to look for a job. Raleigh was ranked #20. *CareerBliss.com, "20 Worst Cities to Find a Job for 2012," October 11, 2012*

- *Forbes* ranked the largest metro areas in the U.S. in terms of the "Best Cities for Young Professionals." The Raleigh metro area ranked #2 out of 15. Criteria: job growth; unemployment rate; median salary of college graduates age 24 to 34; cost of living; number of small businesses per capita; number of large companies; percentage of population 25 years of age and older with college degrees. *Forbes.com, "America's Best Cities for Young Professionals," July 12, 2011*

- Raleigh was ranked #45 out of 100 metro areas in terms of economic performance (#1 = best) during the recession and recovery from trough quarter through the second quarter of 2013. Criteria: percent change in employment; percentage point change in unemployment rate; percent change in gross metropolitan product; percent change in House Price Index. *Brookings Institution, MetroMonitor: Tracking Economic Recession and Recovery in America's 100 Largest Metropolitan Areas, September 2013*

- The Raleigh metro area appeared on the Milken Institute "2013 Best Performing Cities" list. Rank: #13 out of 200 large metro areas. Criteria: job growth; wage and salary growth; high-tech output growth. *Milken Institute, "Best-Performing Cities 2013," December 2013*

- *Forbes* ranked the 200 most populous metro areas in the U.S. in terms of the "Best Places for Business and Careers." The Raleigh metro area was ranked #3. Criteria: costs (business and living); job growth (past and projected); income growth; educational attainment (college and high school); projected economic growth; cultural and recreational opportunities; net migration patterns; number of highly ranked colleges. *Forbes, "The Best Places for Business and Careers," August 7, 2013*

Children/Family Rankings

- *Forbes* ranked the 100 largest metropolitan areas in the U.S. in terms of the "The Best Cities for Raising a Family." The Raleigh metro area was ranked #5. Criteria: median income; overall cost of living; housing affordability; commuting delays; percentage of families owning homes; crime rate; education quality (mainly test scores). *Forbes, "The Best Cities for Raising a Family," April 4, 2012*

- Raleigh was identified as one of the best cities for raising a family by *24/7 Wall St.* The city ranked #3. The nation's 100 largest cities were evaluated on the following criteria: large public outdoor spaces; top hospitals; strong schools; low unemployment; high educational attainment; low violent crime rates. *24/7 Wall St., "The 10 Best U.S. Cities for Raising a Family," January 13, 2012*

- Raleigh was selected as one of the best cities for families to live by *Parenting* magazine. The city ranked #34 out of 100. Criteria: education; health; community; *Parenting's* Culture & Charm Index. *Parenting.com, "The 2012 Best Cities for Families List"*

Culture/Performing Arts Rankings

- Raleigh was selected as one of America's top cities for the arts. The city ranked #23 in the mid-sized city (population 100,000 to 499,999) category. Criteria: readers' top choices for arts travel destinations based on the richness and variety of visual arts sites, activities and events. *American Style, "2012 Top 25 Arts Destinations," June 2012*

Dating/Romance Rankings

- *Forbes* reports that the Raleigh metro area made Rent.com's Best Cities for Newlyweds survey for 2013, based on Bureau of Labor Statistics and Census Bureau data on number of married couples, percentage of families with children under age six, average annual income, cost of living, and availability of rentals. *www.forbes.com, "The 10 Best Cities for Newlyweds to Live and Work In," May 30, 2013*

- CreditDonkey, a financial education website, sought out the ten best U.S. cities for newlyweds, considering the number of married couples, divorce rate, average credit score, and average number of hours worked per week in metro areas with a million or more residents. The Raleigh metro area placed #8. *www.creditdonkey.com, "Study: Best Cities for Newlyweds," November 30, 2013*

- Of the 100 U.S. cities surveyed by *Men's Health* in its quest to identify the nation's best cities for dating and forming relationships, Raleigh was ranked #15 for online dating (#1 = best). *Men's Health, "The Best and Worst Cities for Online Dating," January 30, 2013*

- Raleigh was selected as one of the best cities for newlyweds by *Rent.com*. The city ranked #2 of 10. Criteria: cost of living; mean annual income; unemployment rate. *Rent.com, "10 Best Cities for Newlyweds," March 20, 2012*

Education Rankings

- The Raleigh metro area was selected as one of the world's most inventive cities by *Forbes*. The area was ranked #15 out of 15. Criteria: patent applications per capita. *Forbes, "World's 15 Most Inventive Cities," July 9, 2013*

- The Raleigh metro area was selected as one of America's most innovative cities" by *The Business Insider*. The metro area was ranked #12 out of 20. Criteria: patents per capita. *The Business Insider, "The 20 Most Innovative Cities in the U.S.," February 1, 2013*

- Raleigh was identified as one of America's "smartest" metropolitan areas by *The Business Journals*. The area ranked #8 out of 10. Criteria: percentage of adults (25 and older) with high school diplomas, bachelor's degrees and graduate degrees. *The Business Journals, "Where the Brainpower Is: Exclusive U.S. Rankings, Insights," February 27, 2014*

- *Men's Health* ranked 100 U.S. cities in terms of their education levels. Raleigh was ranked #3 (#1 = most educated city). Criteria: high school graduation rates; school enrollment; educational attainment; number of households who have outstanding student loans; number of households whose members have taken adult-education courses. *Men's Health, "Where School Is In: The Most and Least Educated Cities," September 12, 2011*

- Raleigh was selected as one of America's most literate cities. The city ranked #23 out of the 77 largest U.S. cities. Criteria: number of booksellers; library resources; Internet resources; educational attainment; periodical publishing resources; newspaper circulation. *Central Connecticut State University, "America's Most Literate Cities, 2013"*

- Raleigh was identified as one of "America's Smartest Cities" by *The Daily Beast* using data from Lumos Labs. The metro area ranked #21 out of 25. Criteria: with data collected from more than 1 million users as part of its human cognition project, Lumos Labs was able to analyze performance for nearly 200 metro areas in five cognitive areas: memory, processing speed, flexibility, attention, and problem solving. The median Lumos Lab score was worth 50 percent of the final, weighted ranking. The other half of the ranking was based on the percentage of adults over age 25 with a bachelor's and/or master's degree. *The Daily Beast, "America's Smartest Cities 2012" August 16, 2012*

- Raleigh was identified as one of America's most inventive cities by *The Daily Beast*. The city ranked #19 out of 25. The 200 largest cities in the U.S. were ranked by the number of patents (applied and approved) per capita. *The Daily Beast, "The 25 Most Inventive Cities," October 2, 2011*

Environmental Rankings

- The Raleigh metro area came in at #254 for the relative comfort of its climate on Sperling's list of "chill cities," as measured by the Sperling Heat Index. All 361 metro areas are included. Criteria included daytime high temperatures, nighttime low temperatures, dew point, and relative humidity at the high temperatures. *www.bertsperling.com, "Sperling's Chill Cities," July 18, 2013*

- Sperling's BestPlaces assessed 379 metropolitan areas of the United States for the likelihood of dangerously extreme weather events or earthquakes. In general the Southeast and South-Central regions have the highest risk of weather extremes and earthquakes, while the Pacific Northwest enjoys the lowest risk. Of the least risky metropolitan areas, the Raleigh metro area was ranked #238. *www.bestplaces.net, "Safest Places from Natural Disasters," April 2011*

- Raleigh was selected as one of 22 "Smarter Cities" for energy by the Natural Resources Defense Council. Criteria: investment in green power; energy efficiency measures; conservation. *Natural Resources Defense Council, "2010 Smarter Cities," July 19, 2010*

- The Raleigh metro area was selected as one of "America's Cleanest Cities" by *Forbes*. The metro area ranked #3 out of 10. Criteria: toxic releases; air and water quality; per capita spending on Superfund site cleanup. *Forbes.com, "America's Cleanest Cities 2011," March 11, 2011*

Food/Drink Rankings

- *Men's Health* ranked 100 major U.S. cities in terms of alcohol intoxication. Raleigh ranked #12 (#1 = most sober).Criteria: binge drinking; alcohol-related traffic accidents, arrests, and fatalities. *Men's Health, "The Drunkest Cities in America," November 19, 2013*

Health/Fitness Rankings

- The Gallup-Healthways Well-Being Index tracks Americans' optimism about their communities in addition to their satisfaction with the metro areas in which they live. Gallup researchers asked at least 300 adult residents in each of 189 U.S. metropolitan areas whether their metro was improving. The Raleigh metro area placed among the top ten in the percentage of residents who were optimistic about their metro area. *www.gallup.com, "City Satisfaction Highest in Fort Collins-Loveland, Colo.," April 11, 2014*

- For each of the 50 most populous metro areas in the United States, the American College of Sports Medicine's American Fitness Index evaluated infrastructure, community assets, and policies that encourage healthy and fit lifestyles, including preventive health behaviors, levels of chronic disease conditions, health care access, and community resources and policies that support physical activity. The Raleigh metro area ranked #15 for "community fitness." Personal health indicators were considered as well as community and environmental indicators. *www.americanfitnessindex.org, "ACSM American Fitness Index Health and Community Fitness Status of the 50 Largest Metropolitan Areas," May 2013*

- The Raleigh metro area was identified as one of the worst cities for bed bugs in America by pest control company Orkin. The area ranked #12 out of 50 based on the number of bed bug treatments Orkin performed from January to December 2013. *Orkin, "Chicago Tops Bed Bug Cities List for Second Year in a Row," January 16, 2014*

- Raleigh was selected as one of the 25 fattest cities in America by *Men's Fitness Online*. It ranked #21 out of America's 50 largest cities. Criteria: fitness centers and sport stores; nutrition; sports participation; TV viewing; overweight/sedentary; junk food; air quality; geography; commute; parks and open space; city recreational facilities; access to healthcare; motivation; mayor and city initiatives; state obesity initiatives. *Men's Fitness, "The Fittest and Fattest Cities in America," March 5, 2012*

- Raleigh was identified as a "2013 Spring Allergy Capital." The area ranked #87 out of 100. Three groups of factors were used to identify the most severe cities for people with allergies during the spring season: annual pollen levels; medicine utilization; access to board-certified allergists. *Asthma and Allergy Foundation of America, "Spring Allergy Capitals 2013"*

- Raleigh was identified as a "2013 Fall Allergy Capital." The area ranked #85 out of 100. Three groups of factors were used to identify the most severe cities for people with allergies during the fall season: annual pollen levels; medicine utilization; access to board-certified allergists. *Asthma and Allergy Foundation of America, "Fall Allergy Capitals 2013"*

- Raleigh was identified as a "2013 Asthma Capital." The area ranked #91 out of the nation's 100 largest metropolitan areas. Twelve factors were used to identify the most challenging places to live for people with asthma: estimated prevalence; self-reported prevalence; crude death rate for asthma; annual pollen score; annual air quality; public smoking laws; number of board-certified asthma specialists; school inhaler access laws; rescue medication use; controller medication use; uninsured rate; poverty rate. *Asthma and Allergy Foundation of America, "Asthma Capitals 2013"*

- *Men's Health* ranked 100 major U.S. cities in terms of the best and worst cities for men. Raleigh ranked #4. Criteria: thirty-three data points were examined covering health, fitness, and quality of life. *Men's Health, "The Best & Worst Cities for Men 2014," December 6, 2013*

- *Men's Health* ranked 100 U.S. cities in terms of the best and worst cities for women. Raleigh was ranked among the ten best at #4. Criteria: dozens of statistical parameters of long life in the categories of health, quality of life, and fitness. *Men's Health, "The 10 Best and Worst Cities for Women 2011," January/February 2011*

- The Raleigh metro area appeared in the 2013 Gallup-Healthways Well-Being Index. The area ranked #19 out of 189. The Gallup-Healthways Well-Being Index score is an average of six sub-indexes, which individually examine life evaluation, emotional health, work environment, physical health, healthy behaviors, and access to basic necessities. Results are based on telephone interviews conducted as part of the Gallup-Healthways Well-Being Index survey January 2–December 29, 2012, and January 2–December 30, 2013, with a random sample of 531,630 adults, aged 18 and older, living in metropolitan areas in the 50 U.S. states and the District of Columbia. *Gallup-Healthways, "State of American Well-Being," March 25, 2014*

- *Men's Health* ranked 100 U.S. cities in terms of their activity levels. Raleigh was ranked #49 (#1 = most active city). Criteria: where and how often residents exercise; percentage of households that watch more than 15 hours of cable television a week and buy more than 11 video games a year; death rate from deep-vein thrombosis, a condition linked to sitting for extended periods of time. *Men's Health, "Where Sit Happens: The Most and Least Active Cities in America," June 20, 2011*

- *The Daily Beast* identified the 30 U.S. metro areas with the worst smoking habits. The Raleigh metro area ranked #26. Sixty urban centers with populations of more than one million were ranked based on the following criteria: number of smokers; number of cigarettes smoked per day; fewest attempts to quit. *The Daily Beast, "30 Cities With Smoking Problems," January 3, 2011*

Real Estate Rankings

- Raleigh was ranked #123 out of 283 metro areas in terms of house price appreciation in 2013 (#1 = highest rate). *Federal Housing Finance Agency, House Price Index, 4th Quarter 2013*

- Raleigh was ranked #132 out of 224 metro areas in terms of housing affordability in 2013 by the National Association of Home Builders (#1 = most affordable). The NAHB-Wells Fargo Housing Opportunity Index (HOI) for a given area is defined as the share of homes sold in that area that would have been affordable to a family earning the local median income, based on standard mortgage underwriting criteria. *National Association of Home Builders®, NAHB-Wells Fargo Housing Opportunity Index, 4th Quarter 2013*

- Raleigh was selected as one of the best college towns for renters by ApartmentRatings.com." The area ranked #8 out of 87. Overall satisfaction ratings were ranked using thousands of user submitted scores for hundreds of apartment complexes located in cities and towns that are home to the 100 largest four-year institutions in the U.S. *ApartmentRatings.com, "2011 College Town Renter Satisfaction Rankings"*

Safety Rankings

- Symantec, in partnership with Sperling's BestPlaces, ranked the 50 largest cities in the U.S. in terms of their vulnerability to cybercrime. The city ranked #9. Criteria: number of cyberattacks and potential infections; level of Internet access; expenditures on smartphones and computer hardware/software; wireless hotspots; broadband connectivity; Internet usage; online purchases. *Symantec, "Riskiest Online Cities of 2012" February 15, 2012*

- Farmers Insurance, in partnership with Sperling's BestPlaces, ranked metro areas in the U.S. and identified the "Most Secure Places to Live." The Raleigh metro area ranked #14 out of the top 20 in the large metro area category (500,000 or more residents). Criteria: economic stability; crime statistics; extreme weather; risk of natural disasters; housing depreciation; foreclosures; air quality; environmental hazards; life expectancy; motor vehicle fatalities; and employment numbers. *Farmers Insurance Group of Companies, "Most Secure U.S. Places to Live in the U.S.," June 25, 2013*

- Allstate ranked the 200 largest cities in America in terms of driver safety. Raleigh ranked #85. Allstate researchers analyzed internal property damage claims over a two-year period from January 2010 to December 2011. A weighted average of the two-year numbers determined the annual percentages. *Allstate, "Allstate America's Best Drivers Report®, August 27, 2013"*

- The National Insurance Crime Bureau ranked 380 metro areas in the U.S. in terms of per capita rates of vehicle theft. The Raleigh metro area ranked #194 (#1 = highest rate). Criteria: number of vehicle theft offenses per 100,000 inhabitants in 2012. *National Insurance Crime Bureau, "Hot Spots 2012," June 26, 2013*

- The Raleigh metro area was identified as one of the most dangerous metro areas for pedestrians by Transportation for America. The metro area ranked #13 out of 52 metro areas with over 1 million residents. Criteria: area's population divided by the number of pedestrian fatalities in that area. *Transportation for America, "Dangerous by Design 2011"*

Seniors/Retirement Rankings

- From its Best Cities for Successful Aging indexes, the Milken Institute generated rankings for metropolitan areas, weighing data in eight categories—general indicators, health care, wellness, living arrangements, transportation and general accessibility, financial well-being, education and employment, and community participation. The Raleigh metro area was ranked #79 overall in the large metro area category. *Milken Institute, "Best Cities for Successful Aging," July 2012*

- Bankers Life and Casualty Company, in partnership with Sperling's BestPlaces, ranked the nation's 50 largest metro areas in terms of the "Best U.S. Cities for Seniors." The Raleigh metro area ranked #36. Criteria: healthcare; transportation; housing; environment; economy; health and longevity; social and spiritual life; crime. *Bankers Life and Casualty Company, Center for a Secure Retirement, "Best U.S. Cities for Seniors 2011," September 2011*

Sports/Recreation Rankings

- Raleigh appeared on the *Sporting News* list of the "Best Sports Cities" for 2011. The area ranked #23 out of 271. Criteria: the magazine takes a 12-month snapshot of each city's sports, putting a heavy premium on regular-season won-lost records (from the most recently completed season). Other criteria include: playoff berths, bowl appearances and tournament bids; championships; applicable power ratings; quality of competition; overall fan fervor (measured in part by attendance); abundance of teams (rewarding quality over quantity); stadium and arena quality; ticket availability and prices; franchise ownership; and marquee appeal of athletes. *Sporting News, "Best Sports Cities 2011," October 4, 2011*

- Raleigh appeared on the *Sporting News* list of the "Best Sports Cities" for 2011. The area ranked #23 out of 271. Criteria: a 12-month snapshot of regular-season won-lost records (from the most recently completed season). Other criteria include: playoff berths, bowl appearances and tournament bids; championships; applicable power ratings; quality of competition; overall fan fervor (measured in part by attendance); abundance of teams (quality over quantity); stadium and arena quality; ticket availability and prices; franchise ownership; and marquee appeal of athletes. *Sporting News, "Best Sports Cities 2011," October 4, 2011*

- Raleigh was chosen as a bicycle friendly community by the League of American Bicyclists. A "Bicycle Friendly Community" welcomes cyclists by providing safe accommodation for cycling and encouraging people to bike for transportation and recreation. There are four award levels: Platinum; Gold; Silver; and Bronze. The community achieved an award level of Bronze. *League of American Bicyclists, "Bicycle Friendly Community Master List," Fall 2013*

- Raleigh was selected as one of the most playful cities in the U.S. by KaBOOM! The organization's Playful City USA initiative honors cities and towns across the nation for a vision, plan and commitment to creating an agenda for play. Criteria: creating a local play commission or task force; designing an annual action plan for play; conducting a play space audit; outlining a financial investment in play for the current fiscal year; and proclaiming and celebrating an annual "play day." *KaBOOM! National Campaign for Play, "2013 Playful City USA Communities"*

Transportation Rankings

- NerdWallet surveyed average annual car insurance premiums in 125 U.S. cities to identify the least expensive U.S. cities in which to insure a car. Locations without no-fault insurance laws was a strong determinant. Raleigh came in at #3 for the least expensive rates. *www.nerdwallet.com, "Best Cities for Cheap Car Insurance," February 3, 2014*

Women/Minorities Rankings

- The Daily Beast surveyed the nation's cities for highest percentage of singles and lowest divorce rate, plus other measures, to determine "emotional intelligence"—happiness, confidence, kindness—which, researchers say, has a strong correlation with people's satisfaction with their romantic relationships. Raleigh placed #25. *www.thedailybeast.com, "Best Cities to Find Love and Stay in Love," February 14, 2014*

- To determine the best metro areas for working women, the personal finance website NerdWallet considered city size as well as relevant economic metrics—high salaries, narrow pay differential by gender, prevalence of women in the highest-paying industries, and population growth over 2010–2012. Of the large U.S. cities examined, the Raleigh metro area held the #8 position. *www.nerdwallet.com, "Best Places for Women in the Workforce," May 19, 2013*

- *Women's Health* examined U.S. cities and identified the 100 best cities for women. Raleigh was ranked #1. Criteria: 30 categories were examined from obesity and breast cancer rates to commuting times and hours spent working out. *Women's Health, "Best Cities for Women 2012"*

- The Raleigh metro area appeared on *Forbes'* list of the "Best Cities for Minority Entrepreneurs." The area ranked #1 out of 10. Criteria: 52 metropolitan statistical areas were examined. For each ethnicity (African Americans, Asians and Hispanics), the editors measured housing affordability, population growth, income growth, and entrepreneurship (per capita self-employment). *Forbes, "Best Cities for Minority Entrepreneurs," March 23, 2011*

Miscellaneous Rankings

- Raleigh was selected as a 2013 Digital Cities Survey winner. The city ranked #10 in the large city (250,000 or more population) category. The survey examined and assessed how city governments are utilizing information technology to operate and deliver quality service to their customers and citizens. Survey questions focused on implementation and adoption of online service delivery; planning and governance; and the infrastructure and architecture that make the transformation to digital government possible. *Center for Digital Government, "2013 Digital Cities Survey," November 7, 2013*

- Market analyst Scarborough Research surveyed adults who had done volunteer work over the previous 12 months to find out where volunteers are concentrated. The Raleigh metro area made the list for highest volunteer participation. *Scarborough Research, "Salt Lake City, UT; Minneapolis, MN; and Des Moines, IA Lend a Helping Hand," November 27, 2012*

- Raleigh was selected as one of the 10 best run cities in America by *24/7 Wall St.* The city ranked #10. Criteria: the 100 largest cities in the U.S. were ranked in terms of economy, job market, crime, and the welfare of its residents. *24/7 Wall St., "The Best and Worst Run Cities in America," January 15, 2013*

- *Men's Health* ranked 100 U.S. cities by their level of sadness. Raleigh was ranked #21 (#1 = saddest city). Criteria: suicide rates; unemployment rates; percentage of households that use antidepressants; percent of population who report feeling blue all or most of the time. *Men's Health, "Frown Towns," November 28, 2011*

- The National Alliance to End Homelessness ranked the 100 most populous metro areas in terms the rate of homelessness. The Raleigh metro area ranked #78. Criteria: number of homeless people per 10,000 population in 2011. *National Alliance to End Homelessness, The State of Homelessness in America 2012*

Business Environment

CITY FINANCES

City Government Finances

Component	2011 ($000)	2011 ($ per capita)
Total Revenues	642,483	1,710
Total Expenditures	674,303	1,794
Debt Outstanding	906,045	2,411
Cash and Securities[1]	660,196	1,757

Note: (1) Cash and security holdings of a government at the close of its fiscal year, including those of its dependent agencies, utilities, and liquor stores.
Source: U.S Census Bureau, State & Local Government Finances 2011

City Government Revenue by Source

Source	2011 ($000)	2011 ($ per capita)
General Revenue		
From Federal Government	37,489	100
From State Government	52,096	139
From Local Governments	17,289	46
Taxes		
Property	186,625	497
Sales and Gross Receipts	62,456	166
Personal Income	0	0
Corporate Income	0	0
Motor Vehicle License	7,554	20
Other Taxes	18,319	49
Current Charges	149,479	398
Liquor Store	0	0
Utility	82,894	221
Employee Retirement	0	0

Source: U.S Census Bureau, State & Local Government Finances 2011

City Government Expenditures by Function

Function	2011 ($000)	2011 ($ per capita)	2011 (%)
General Direct Expenditures			
Air Transportation	0	0	0.0
Corrections	0	0	0.0
Education	0	0	0.0
Employment Security Administration	0	0	0.0
Financial Administration	13,900	37	2.1
Fire Protection	51,705	138	7.7
General Public Buildings	14,817	39	2.2
Governmental Administration, Other	16,593	44	2.5
Health	0	0	0.0
Highways	57,273	152	8.5
Hospitals	0	0	0.0
Housing and Community Development	15,371	41	2.3
Interest on General Debt	28,261	75	4.2
Judicial and Legal	2,193	6	0.3
Libraries	0	0	0.0
Parking	5,902	16	0.9
Parks and Recreation	80,967	215	12.0
Police Protection	84,750	226	12.6
Public Welfare	544	1	0.1
Sewerage	84,486	225	12.5
Solid Waste Management	24,949	66	3.7
Veterans' Services	0	0	0.0
Liquor Store	0	0	0.0
Utility	123,918	330	18.4
Employee Retirement	0	0	0.0

Source: U.S Census Bureau, State & Local Government Finances 2011

DEMOGRAPHICS

Population Growth

Area	1990 Census	2000 Census	2010 Census	Population Growth (%) 1990-2000	Population Growth (%) 2000-2010
City	226,841	276,093	403,892	21.7	46.3
MSA[1]	541,081	797,071	1,130,490	47.3	41.8
U.S.	248,709,873	281,421,906	308,745,538	13.2	9.7

Note: (1) Figures cover the Raleigh, NC Metropolitan Statistical Area—see Appendix B for areas included
Source: U.S. Census Bureau, Census 1990, 2000, 2010

Household Size

Area	Persons in Household (%) One	Two	Three	Four	Five	Six	Seven or More	Average Household Size
City	33.5	30.9	15.8	12.6	4.6	1.7	0.9	2.45
MSA[1]	26.2	32.0	17.3	15.1	6.2	2.0	1.1	2.65
U.S.	27.6	33.5	15.7	13.2	6.1	2.4	1.5	2.63

Note: (1) Figures cover the Raleigh, NC Metropolitan Statistical Area—see Appendix B for areas included
Source: U.S. Census Bureau, 2010-2012 American Community Survey 3-Year Estimates

Race

Area	White Alone[2] (%)	Black Alone[2] (%)	Asian Alone[2] (%)	AIAN[3] Alone[2] (%)	NHOPI[4] Alone[2] (%)	Other Race Alone[2] (%)	Two or More Races (%)
City	61.0	29.8	4.2	0.3	0.0	2.9	1.9
MSA[1]	69.9	20.3	4.5	0.3	0.0	2.7	2.2
U.S.	74.0	12.6	4.9	0.8	0.2	4.7	2.8

Note: (1) Figures cover the Raleigh, NC Metropolitan Statistical Area—see Appendix B for areas included; (2) Alone is defined as not being in combination with one or more other races; (3) American Indian and Alaska Native; (4) Native Hawaiian and Other Pacific Islander
Source: U.S. Census Bureau, 2010-2012 American Community Survey 3-Year Estimates

Hispanic or Latino Origin

Area	Total (%)	Mexican (%)	Puerto Rican (%)	Cuban (%)	Other (%)
City	11.3	5.2	1.2	0.3	4.6
MSA[1]	10.3	6.0	1.0	0.3	3.0
U.S.	16.6	10.7	1.6	0.6	3.7

Note: Persons of Hispanic or Latino origin can be of any race; (1) Figures cover the Raleigh, NC Metropolitan Statistical Area—see Appendix B for areas included
Source: U.S. Census Bureau, 2010-2012 American Community Survey 3-Year Estimates

Segregation

Type	Segregation Indices[1] 1990	2000	2010	2010 Rank[2]	Percent Change 1990-2000	Percent Change 1990-2010	Percent Change 2000-2010
Black/White	41.9	40.8	42.1	87	-1.1	0.2	1.3
Asian/White	42.5	40.1	46.7	16	-2.4	4.2	6.6
Hispanic/White	19.9	34.9	37.1	76	15.1	17.3	2.2

Note: All figures cover the Metropolitan Statistical Area—see Appendix B for areas included; Figures are based on an analysis of 1990, 2000, and 2010 Census Decennial Census tract data by William H. Frey, Brookings Institution and the University of Michigan Social Science Data Analysis Network. In this analysis all racial groups (whites, blacks, and asians) are non-Hispanic members of those races. Hispanics are shown as a separate category;
(1) Segregation Indices are Dissimilarity Indices that measure the degree to which the minority group is distributed differently than whites across census tracts. They range from 0 (complete integration) to 100 (complete segregation) where the value indicates the percentage of the minority group that needs to move to be distributed exactly like whites; (2) Ranges from 1 (most segregated) to 102 (least segregated); n/a not available.
Source: www.CensusScope.org

Ancestry

Area	German	Irish	English	American	Italian	Polish	French[2]	Scottish	Dutch
City	9.7	8.1	9.9	10.0	3.9	1.8	1.8	2.3	0.8
MSA[1]	10.7	9.7	11.3	12.2	4.5	2.2	1.9	2.6	1.1
U.S.	15.2	11.1	8.2	7.2	5.6	3.1	2.8	1.7	1.4

Note: Figures are the percentage of the total population reporting a particular ancestry. The nine most commonly reported ancestries in the U.S. are shown. Figures include multiple ancestries (e.g. if a person reported being Irish and Italian, they were included in both columns); (1) Figures cover the Raleigh, NC Metropolitan Statistical Area—see Appendix B for areas included; (2) Excludes Basque
Source: U.S. Census Bureau, 2010-2012 American Community Survey 3-Year Estimates

Foreign-Born Population

Area	Any Foreign Country	Mexico	Asia	Europe	Carribean	South America	Central America[2]	Africa	Canada
City	13.9	3.1	3.7	1.2	0.8	1.0	1.7	2.1	0.3
MSA[1]	11.8	3.3	3.7	1.1	0.5	0.7	1.1	1.1	0.3
U.S.	13.0	3.7	3.7	1.6	1.2	0.9	1.0	0.5	0.3

Note: (1) Figures cover the Raleigh, NC Metropolitan Statistical Area—see Appendix B for areas included; (2) Excludes Mexico.
Source: U.S. Census Bureau, 2010-2012 American Community Survey 3-Year Estimates

Marital Status

Area	Never Married	Now Married[2]	Separated	Widowed	Divorced
City	41.7	40.8	2.9	4.1	10.5
MSA[1]	31.2	52.2	2.8	4.5	9.4
U.S.	32.4	48.4	2.2	6.0	11.0

Note: Figures are percentages and cover the population 15 years of age and older; (1) Figures cover the Raleigh, NC Metropolitan Statistical Area—see Appendix B for areas included; (2) Excludes separated
Source: U.S. Census Bureau, 2010-2012 American Community Survey 3-Year Estimates

Age

Area	Under Age 5	Age 5–19	Age 20–34	Age 35–44	Age 45–54	Age 55–64	Age 65–74	Age 75–84	Age 85+	Median Age
City	7.2	19.9	27.9	15.3	12.3	9.0	4.7	2.6	1.2	32.3
MSA[1]	7.0	21.6	21.1	15.9	14.5	10.5	5.6	2.7	1.0	35.2
U.S.	6.4	20.1	20.5	13.1	14.3	12.2	7.3	4.2	1.8	37.3

Note: (1) Figures cover the Raleigh, NC Metropolitan Statistical Area—see Appendix B for areas included
Source: U.S. Census Bureau, 2010-2012 American Community Survey 3-Year Estimates

Gender

Area	Males	Females	Males per 100 Females
City	199,292	215,081	92.7
MSA[1]	567,822	595,047	95.4
U.S.	153,276,055	158,333,314	96.8

Note: (1) Figures cover the Raleigh, NC Metropolitan Statistical Area—see Appendix B for areas included
Source: U.S. Census Bureau, 2010-2012 American Community Survey 3-Year Estimates

Religious Groups by Family

Area	Catholic	Baptist	Non-Den.	Methodist[2]	Lutheran	LDS[3]	Pente-costal	Presby-terian[4]	Muslim[5]	Judaism
MSA[1]	9.2	12.1	6.0	6.7	0.9	0.9	2.3	2.3	0.9	0.3
U.S.	19.1	9.3	4.0	4.0	2.3	2.0	1.9	1.6	0.8	0.7

Note: Figures are the number of adherents as a percentage of the total population; (1) Figures cover the Raleigh, NC Metropolitan Statistical Area—see Appendix B for areas included; (2) Methodist/Pietist; (3) Latter Day Saints; (4) Reformed; (5) Figures are estimates
Source: Association of Statisticians of American Religious Bodies, 2010 U.S. Religion Census: Religious Congregations & Membership Study

Religious Groups by Tradition

Area	Catholic	Evangelical Protestant	Mainline Protestant	Other Tradition	Black Protestant	Orthodox
MSA[1]	9.2	19.9	10.1	3.3	1.7	0.2
U.S.	19.1	16.2	7.3	4.3	1.6	0.3

Note: Figures are the number of adherents as a percentage of the total population; (1) Figures cover the Raleigh, NC Metropolitan Statistical Area—see Appendix B for areas included
Source: Association of Statisticians of American Religious Bodies, 2010 U.S. Religion Census: Religious Congregations & Membership Study

ECONOMY

Gross Metropolitan Product

Area	2011	2012	2013	2014	Rank[2]
MSA[1]	59.0	61.4	63.2	66.8	49

Note: Figures are in billions of dollars; (1) Figures cover the Raleigh, NC Metropolitan Statistical Area—see Appendix B for areas included; (2) Rank is based on 2014 data and ranges from 1 to 363
Source: The United States Conference of Mayors, U.S. Metro Economies: Outlook—Gross Metropolitan Product, with Metro Employment Projections, November 2013

Economic Growth

Area	2011 (%)	2012 (%)	2013 (%)	2014 (%)	Rank[2]
MSA[1]	2.2	2.4	1.6	3.8	105
U.S.	1.6	2.5	1.7	2.5	–

Note: Figures are real gross metropolitan product (GMP) growth rates and represent annual average percent change; (1) Figures cover the Raleigh, NC Metropolitan Statistical Area—see Appendix B for areas included; (2) Rank is based on 2013 data and ranges from 1 to 363
Source: The United States Conference of Mayors, U.S. Metro Economies: Outlook—Gross Metropolitan Product, with Metro Employment Projections, November 2013

Metropolitan Area Exports

Area	2007	2008	2009	2010	2011	2012	Rank[2]
MSA[1]	2,129.6	2,076.7	1,799.5	1,912.4	2,254.4	2,308.1	89

Note: Figures are in millions of dollars; (1) Figures cover the Raleigh, NC Metropolitan Statistical Area—see Appendix B for areas included; (2) Rank is based on 2012 data and ranges from 1 to 369
Source: U.S. Department of Commerce, International Trade Administration, Office of Trade & Industry Information, Manufacturing & Services, data extracted April 1, 2014

INCOME

Income

Area	Per Capita ($)	Median Household ($)	Average Household ($)
City	29,277	52,709	72,867
MSA[1]	30,039	60,332	79,164
U.S.	27,385	51,771	71,579

Note: (1) Figures cover the Raleigh, NC Metropolitan Statistical Area—see Appendix B for areas included
Source: U.S. Census Bureau, 2010-2012 American Community Survey 3-Year Estimates

Household Income Distribution

Area	Under $15,000	$15,000 -24,999	$25,000 -34,999	$35,000 -49,999	$50,000 -74,999	$75,000 -99,000	$100,000 -149,999	$150,000 and up
City	11.5	9.4	11.8	14.1	19.2	12.2	12.1	9.6
MSA[1]	9.6	8.5	10.2	13.1	18.8	13.0	15.2	11.7
U.S.	13.1	11.0	10.5	13.7	18.1	11.9	12.5	9.1

Note: (1) Figures cover the Raleigh, NC Metropolitan Statistical Area—see Appendix B for areas included
Source: U.S. Census Bureau, 2010-2012 American Community Survey 3-Year Estimates

Poverty Rate

Area	All Ages	Under 18 Years Old	18 to 64 Years Old	65 Years and Over
City	17.3	24.8	15.9	7.4
MSA[1]	12.6	17.5	11.4	7.4
U.S.	15.7	22.2	14.6	9.3

Note: Figures are percentage of people whose income during the past 12 months was below the poverty level; (1) Figures cover the Raleigh, NC Metropolitan Statistical Area—see Appendix B for areas included
Source: U.S. Census Bureau, 2010-2012 American Community Survey 3-Year Estimates

Personal Bankruptcy Filing Rate

Area	2008	2009	2010	2011	2012	2013
Wake County	2.66	3.45	3.08	2.85	2.68	2.15
U.S.	3.53	4.61	4.97	4.37	3.76	3.29

Note: Numbers are per 1,000 population and include Chapter 7 and Chapter 13 filings
Source: Federal Deposit Insurance Corporation, Regional Economic Conditions, March 20, 2014

EMPLOYMENT

Labor Force and Employment

Area	Civilian Labor Force			Workers Employed		
	Dec. 2012	Dec. 2013	% Chg.	Dec. 2012	Dec. 2013	% Chg.
City	222,597	220,426	-1.0	207,564	210,461	1.4
MSA[1]	602,263	595,803	-1.1	557,064	564,840	1.4
U.S.	154,904,000	154,408,000	-0.3	143,060,000	144,423,000	1.0

Note: Data is not seasonally adjusted and covers workers 16 years of age and older; (1) Metropolitan Statistical Area—see Appendix B for areas included
Source: Bureau of Labor Statistics, Local Area Unemployment Statistics

Unemployment Rate

Area	2013											
	Jan.	Feb.	Mar.	Apr.	May	Jun.	Jul.	Aug.	Sep.	Oct.	Nov.	Dec.
City	7.2	6.6	6.3	6.0	6.6	6.9	6.7	6.2	5.5	5.4	4.8	4.5
MSA[1]	8.0	7.5	7.1	6.7	7.2	7.5	7.3	6.7	6.1	6.0	5.5	5.2
U.S.	8.5	8.1	7.6	7.1	7.3	7.8	7.7	7.3	7.0	7.0	6.6	6.5

Note: Data is not seasonally adjusted and covers workers 16 years of age and older; All figures are percentages; (1) Metropolitan Statistical Area—see Appendix B for areas included
Source: Bureau of Labor Statistics, Local Area Unemployment Statistics

Employment by Occupation

Occupation Classification	City (%)	MSA[1] (%)	U.S. (%)
Management, Business, Science, and Arts	46.4	45.9	36.0
Natural Resources, Construction, and Maintenance	6.1	7.2	9.1
Production, Transportation, and Material Moving	6.7	8.1	12.0
Sales and Office	24.2	23.8	24.7
Service	16.6	15.0	18.2

Note: Figures cover employed civilians 16 years of age and older; (1) Figures cover the Raleigh, NC Metropolitan Statistical Area—see Appendix B for areas included
Source: U.S. Census Bureau, 2010-2012 American Community Survey 3-Year Estimates

Employment by Industry

Sector	MSA[1]		U.S.
	Number of Employees	Percent of Total	Percent of Total
Construction	n/a	n/a	4.2
Education and Health Services	66,200	11.9	15.5
Financial Activities	27,000	4.8	5.7
Government	93,600	16.8	16.1
Information	18,100	3.3	1.9
Leisure and Hospitality	60,900	10.9	10.2
Manufacturing	30,700	5.5	8.7
Mining and Logging	n/a	n/a	0.6
Other Services	22,600	4.1	3.9
Professional and Business Services	109,900	19.7	13.7
Retail Trade	64,100	11.5	11.4
Transportation and Utilities	10,200	1.8	3.8
Wholesale Trade	23,200	4.2	4.2

Note: Figures cover non-farm employment as of December 2013 and are not seasonally adjusted;
(1) Metropolitan Statistical Area—see Appendix B for areas included; n/a not available
Source: Bureau of Labor Statistics, Current Employment Statistics, Employment, Hours, and Earnings

Occupations with Greatest Projected Employment Growth: 2010 – 2020

Occupation[1]	2010 Employment	2020 Projected Employment	Numeric Employment Change	Percent Employment Change
Combined Food Preparation and Serving Workers, Including Fast Food	114,040	132,650	18,610	16.3
Registered Nurses	92,540	109,790	17,250	18.6
Retail Salespersons	131,650	145,910	14,270	10.8
Home Health Aides	55,560	67,570	12,010	21.6
Customer Service Representatives	74,700	84,800	10,090	13.5
Postsecondary Teachers	49,850	59,780	9,930	19.9
Landscaping and Groundskeeping Workers	33,610	43,450	9,830	29.3
Janitors and Cleaners, Except Maids and Housekeeping Cleaners	52,290	61,160	8,870	17.0
Cashiers	101,410	110,200	8,790	8.7
Elementary School Teachers, Except Special Education	37,090	45,730	8,650	23.3

Note: Projections cover North Carolina; (1) Sorted by numeric employment change
Source: www.projectionscentral.com, State Occupational Projections, 2010–2020 Long-Term Projections

Fastest Growing Occupations: 2010 – 2020

Occupation[1]	2010 Employment	2020 Projected Employment	Numeric Employment Change	Percent Employment Change
Biomedical Engineers	250	480	230	90.5
Medical Scientists, Except Epidemiologists	4,270	6,550	2,280	53.4
Biochemists and Biophysicists	460	670	210	44.9
Interpreters and Translators	3,000	4,210	1,220	40.6
Veterinary Technologists and Technicians	3,060	4,300	1,240	40.4
Market Research Analysts and Marketing Specialists	9,750	13,580	3,830	39.3
Helpers—Brickmasons, Blockmasons, Stonemasons, and Tile and Marble Setters	1,900	2,630	740	38.8
Helpers—Carpenters	1,850	2,560	710	38.4
Diagnostic Medical Sonographers	1,660	2,280	620	37.3
Audiologists	350	460	120	33.6

Note: Projections cover North Carolina; (1) Sorted by percent employment change and excludes occupations
with numeric employment change less than 100
Source: www.projectionscentral.com, State Occupational Projections, 2010–2020 Long-Term Projections

Average Wages

Occupation	$/Hr.	Occupation	$/Hr.
Accountants and Auditors	31.96	Maids and Housekeeping Cleaners	9.57
Automotive Mechanics	21.92	Maintenance and Repair Workers	18.32
Bookkeepers	17.94	Marketing Managers	64.08
Carpenters	16.13	Nuclear Medicine Technologists	32.80
Cashiers	9.22	Nurses, Licensed Practical	21.13
Clerks, General Office	14.19	Nurses, Registered	28.43
Clerks, Receptionists/Information	13.40	Nursing Assistants	11.67
Clerks, Shipping/Receiving	14.05	Packers and Packagers, Hand	10.48
Computer Programmers	38.60	Physical Therapists	35.21
Computer Systems Analysts	40.47	Postal Service Mail Carriers	24.14
Computer User Support Specialists	24.88	Real Estate Brokers	25.34
Cooks, Restaurant	10.69	Retail Salespersons	11.79
Dentists	92.29	Sales Reps., Exc. Tech./Scientific	29.45
Electrical Engineers	41.46	Sales Reps., Tech./Scientific	41.18
Electricians	18.70	Secretaries, Exc. Legal/Med./Exec.	16.28
Financial Managers	61.21	Security Guards	12.44
First-Line Supervisors/Managers, Sales	20.55	Surgeons	n/a
Food Preparation Workers	10.38	Teacher Assistants	10.80
General and Operations Managers	64.35	Teachers, Elementary School	21.60
Hairdressers/Cosmetologists	15.50	Teachers, Secondary School	22.00
Internists	120.51	Telemarketers	14.65
Janitors and Cleaners	10.37	Truck Drivers, Heavy/Tractor-Trailer	19.28
Landscaping/Groundskeeping Workers	11.56	Truck Drivers, Light/Delivery Svcs.	16.30
Lawyers	58.36	Waiters and Waitresses	9.47

Note: Wage data covers the Raleigh-Cary, NC Metropolitan Statistical Area—see Appendix B for areas included. Hourly wages for elementary/secondary school teachers and teacher assistants were calculated by the editors from annual wage data assuming a 40 hour work week; n/a not available.
Source: Bureau of Labor Statistics, Metro Area Occupational Employment and Wage Estimates, May 2013

RESIDENTIAL REAL ESTATE

Building Permits

Area	Single-Family			Multi-Family			Total		
	2012	2013	Pct. Chg.	2012	2013	Pct. Chg.	2012	2013	Pct. Chg.
City	1,414	1,662	17.5	3,596	2,138	-40.5	5,010	3,800	-24.2
MSA[1]	6,425	8,034	25.0	6,501	3,397	-47.7	12,926	11,431	-11.6
U.S.	518,695	620,802	19.7	310,963	370,020	19.0	829,658	990,822	19.4

Note: (1) Metropolitan Statistical Area—see Appendix B for areas included; figures represent new, privately-owned housing units authorized (unadjusted data); All permit data are based on estimates with imputation.
Source: U.S. Census Bureau, Manufacturing, Mining, and Construction Statistics, Building Permits, 2012, 2013

Homeownership Rate

Area	2006 (%)	2007 (%)	2008 (%)	2009 (%)	2010 (%)	2011 (%)	2012 (%)	2013 (%)
MSA[1]	71.1	72.8	70.7	65.7	65.9	66.7	67.7	65.5
U.S.	68.8	68.1	67.8	67.4	66.9	66.1	65.4	65.1

Note: (1) Figures cover the Raleigh, NC Metropolitan Statistical Area—see Appendix B for areas included
Source: U.S. Census Bureau, Housing Vacancies and Homeownership Annual Statistics: 2013

Housing Vacancy Rates

Area	Gross Vacancy Rate[2] (%)			Year-Round Vacancy Rate[3] (%)			Rental Vacancy Rate[4] (%)			Homeowner Vacancy Rate[5] (%)		
	2011	2012	2013	2011	2012	2013	2011	2012	2013	2011	2012	2013
MSA[1]	9.2	8.5	7.3	9.1	8.2	7.2	8.9	8.8	6.9	2.9	1.9	1.8
U.S.	14.2	13.8	13.8	11.1	10.8	10.7	9.5	8.7	8.3	2.5	2.0	2.0

Note: (1) Figures cover the Raleigh, NC Metropolitan Statistical Area—see Appendix B for areas included; (2) The percentage of the total housing inventory that is vacant; (3) The percentage of the housing inventory (excluding seasonal units) that is year-round vacant; (4) The percentage of rental inventory that is vacant for rent; (5) The percentage of homeowner inventory that is vacant for sale
Source: U.S. Census Bureau, Housing Vacancies and Homeownership Annual Statistics: 2013

TAXES

State Corporate Income Tax Rates

State	Tax Rate (%)	Income Brackets ($)	Num. of Brackets	Financial Institution Tax Rate (%)[a]	Federal Income Tax Ded.
North Carolina	6.0	Flat rate	1	6.0 (t)	No

Note: Tax rates as of January 1, 2014; (a) Rates listed are the corporate income tax rate applied to financial institutions or excise taxes based on income. Some states have other taxes based upon the value of deposits or shares; (t) In North Carolina financial institutions are also subject to a tax equal to $30 per one million in assets.
Source: Federation of Tax Administrators, "State Corporate Income Tax Rates, 2014"

State Individual Income Tax Rates

State	Tax Rate (%)	Income Brackets ($)	Num. of Brackets	Personal Exempt. ($)[1] Single	Dependents	Fed. Inc. Tax Ded.
North Carolina	5.8	Flat rate	1	None	None	No

Note: Tax rates as of January 1, 2014; Local- and county-level taxes are not included; n/a not applicable;
(1) Married joint filers generally receive double the single exemption
Source: Federation of Tax Administrators, "State Individual Income Tax Rates, 2014"

Various State and Local Tax Rates

State	State and Local Sales and Use (%)	State Sales and Use (%)	Gasoline[1] (¢/gal.)	Cigarette[2] ($/pack)	Spirits[3] ($/gal.)	Wine[4] ($/gal.)	Beer[5] ($/gal.)
North Carolina	6.75	4.75	37.75	0.450	12.36 (g)	1.00	0.62

Note: All tax rates as of January 1, 2014; (1) The American Petroleum Institute has developed a methodology for determining the average tax rate on a gallon of fuel. Rates may include any of the following: excise taxes, environmental fees, storage tank fees, other fees or taxes, general sales tax, and local taxes. In states where gasoline is subject to the general sales tax, or where the fuel tax is based on the average sale price, the average rate determined by API is sensitive to changes in the price of gasoline. States that fully or partially apply general sales taxes to gasoline: CA, CO, GA, IL, IN, MI, NY; (2) The federal excise tax of $1.0066 per pack and local taxes are not included; (3) Rates are those applicable to off-premise sales of 40% alcohol by volume (a.b.v.) distilled spirits in 750ml containers. Local excise taxes are excluded; (4) Rates are those applicable to off-premise sales of 11% a.b.v. non-carbonated wine in 750ml containers; (5) Rates are those applicable to off-premise sales of 4.7% a.b.v. beer in 12 ounce containers; (g) States where the government controls sales. In these "control states," products are subject to ad valorem mark-up and excise taxes. The excise tax rate is calculated using a methodology developed by the Distilled Spirits Council of the United States.
Source: Tax Foundation, 2014 Facts & Figures: How Does Your State Compare?

State Business Tax Climate Index Rankings

State	Overall Rank	Corporate Tax Index Rank	Individual Income Tax Index Rank	Sales Tax Index Rank	Unemployment Insurance Tax Index Rank	Property Tax Index Rank
North Carolina	44	29	42	47	7	30

Note: The index is a measure of how each state's tax laws affect economic performance. The lower the rank, the more favorable a state's tax system is for business. States without a given tax are given a ranking of 1. The scores/rankings for the District of Columbia do not affect other states. The 2014 index represents the tax climate as of July 1, 2013.
Source: Tax Foundation, State Business Tax Climate Index 2014

COMMERCIAL REAL ESTATE

Office Market

Market Area	Inventory (sq. ft.)	Vacancy Rate (%)	Under Construction (sq. ft.)	YTD Net Absorption (sq. ft.)	Total Average Asking Rent ($/sq. ft./year)
Raleigh/Durham	58,403,609	13.3	1,168,592	762,016	19.23
National	4,726,900,879	15.0	55,419,286	42,829,434	26.27

Source: Newmark Grubb Knight Frank, National Office Market Report, 4th Quarter 2013

Industrial/Warehouse/R&D Market

Market Area	Inventory (sq. ft.)	Vacancy Rate (%)	Under Construction (sq. ft.)	YTD Net Absorption (sq. ft.)	Total Average Asking Rent ($/sq. ft./year)
Raleigh/Durham	110,978,639	9.6	233,246	117,943	5.28
National	14,022,031,238	7.9	83,249,164	156,549,903	5.40

Source: Newmark Grubb Knight Frank, National Industrial Market Report, 4th Quarter 2013

COMMERCIAL UTILITIES

Typical Monthly Electric Bills

Area	Commercial Service ($/month)		Industrial Service ($/month)	
	1,500 kWh	40 kW demand 14,000 kWh	1,000 kW demand 200,000 kWh	50,000 kW demand 15,000,000 kWh
City	174	1,200	22,258	1,349,994
Average[1]	197	1,636	25,662	1,485,307

Note: Based on total rates in effect July 1, 2013; (1) average based on 180 utilities surveyed
Source: Edison Electric Institute, Typical Bills and Average Rates Report, Summer 2013

TRANSPORTATION

Means of Transportation to Work

Area	Car/Truck/Van		Public Transportation			Bicycle	Walked	Other Means	Worked at Home
	Drove Alone	Car-pooled	Bus	Subway	Railroad				
City	80.7	9.0	1.8	0.0	0.0	0.6	1.7	1.0	5.1
MSA[1]	81.0	9.1	0.9	0.0	0.0	0.3	1.2	1.2	6.2
U.S.	76.4	9.7	2.6	1.7	0.5	0.6	2.8	1.3	4.3

Note: Figures are percentages and cover workers 16 years of age and older; (1) Figures cover the Raleigh, NC Metropolitan Statistical Area—see Appendix B for areas included
Source: U.S. Census Bureau, 2010-2012 American Community Survey 3-Year Estimates

Travel Time to Work

Area	Less Than 10 Minutes	10 to 19 Minutes	20 to 29 Minutes	30 to 44 Minutes	45 to 59 Minutes	60 to 89 Minutes	90 Minutes or More
City	12.0	36.6	27.3	17.4	3.3	2.2	1.0
MSA[1]	10.6	29.5	25.6	22.2	7.1	3.5	1.5
U.S.	13.5	29.8	20.9	20.1	7.5	5.6	2.5

Note: Figures are percentages and include workers 16 years old and over; (1) Figures cover the Raleigh, NC Metropolitan Statistical Area—see Appendix B for areas included
Source: U.S. Census Bureau, 2010-2012 American Community Survey 3-Year Estimates

Travel Time Index

Area	1985	1990	1995	2000	2005	2010	2011
Urban Area[1]	1.05	1.09	1.10	1.13	1.17	1.14	1.14
Average[2]	1.09	1.14	1.16	1.19	1.23	1.18	1.18

Note: Travel Time Index—the ratio of travel time in the peak period to the travel time at free-flow conditions. For example, a value of 1.30 indicates a 20-minute free-flow trip takes 26 minutes in the peak. Free-flow speeds (60 mph on freeways and 35 mph on principal arterials) are used as the comparison threshold; (1) Covers the Raleigh-Durham NC urban area; (2) average of 498 urban areas
Source: Texas Transportation Institute, Urban Mobility Report 2012, December 2012

Public Transportation

Agency Name / Mode of Transportation	Vehicles Operated in Maximum Service	Annual Unlinked Passenger Trips (in thous.)	Annual Passenger Miles (in thous.)
Capital Area Transit (CAT)			
Bus (directly operated)	65	6,441.6	29,929.4
Demand Response Taxi (purchased transportation)	240	467.1	3,998.9

Source: Federal Transit Administration, National Transit Database, 2012

Air Transportation

Airport Name and Code / Type of Service	Passenger Airlines[1]	Passenger Enplanements	Freight Carriers[2]	Freight (lbs.)
Raleigh-Durham International (RDU)				
Domestic service (U.S. carriers - 2013)	33	4,383,707	14	69,963,046
International service (U.S. carriers - 2012)	12	67,779	3	2,638,951

Note: (1) Includes all U.S.-based major, minor and commuter airlines that carried at least one passenger during the year; (2) Includes all U.S.-based airlines and freight carriers that transported at least one lb. of freight during the year.
Source: Bureau of Transportation Statistics, The Intermodal Transportation Database, Air Carriers: T-100 Domestic Market (U.S. Carriers), 2013; Bureau of Transportation Statistics, The Intermodal Transportation Database, Air Carriers: T-100 International Market (U.S. Carriers), 2012

Other Transportation Statistics

Major Highways:	I-40; I-85
Amtrak Service:	Yes
Major Waterways/Ports:	None

Source: Amtrak.com; Google Maps

BUSINESSES

Major Business Headquarters

Company Name	Rankings	
	Fortune[1]	Forbes[2]
General Parts	-	162

Note: (1) Fortune 500—companies that produce a 10-K are ranked 1 to 500 based on 2012 revenue; (2) all private companies with at least $2 billion in annual revenue through the end of their most current fiscal year are ranked 1 to 224; companies listed are headquartered in the city; dashes indicate no ranking
Source: Fortune, "Fortune 500," May 20, 2013; Forbes, "America's Largest Private Companies," December 18, 2013

Fast-Growing Businesses

According to Deloitte, Raleigh is home to two of North America's 500 fastest-growing high-technology companies: **BioDelivery Sciences International** (#10); **Salix Pharmaceuticals** (#285). Companies are ranked by percentage growth in revenue over a five-year period. Criteria for inclusion: company must be headquartered within North America; must own proprietary intellectual property or proprietary technology that contributes to a significant portion of the company's operating revenue, or devote a significant proportion of revenues to research and development of technology; must have been in business for a minumum of five years with 2008 operating revenues of at least $50,000 USD/CD and 2012 operating revenues of at least $5 million USD/CD. *Deloitte Touche Tohmatsu, 2013 Technology Fast 500*[TM]

Minority Business Opportunity

Raleigh is home to one company which is on the *Black Enterprise* Industrial/Service 100 list (100 largest companies based on gross sales): **Brodie Contractors** (#85). Criteria: operational in previous calendar year; at least 51% black-owned and manufactures/owns the product it sells or provides industrial or consumer services. Brokerages, real estate firms and firms that provide professional services are not eligible. *Black Enterprise, B.E. 100s, 2013*

Raleigh is home to one company which is on the *Hispanic Business* 500 list (500 largest U.S. Hispanic-owned companies based on 2012 revenue): **Stewart** (#278). Companies included must show at least 51 percent ownership by Hispanic U.S. citizens, and must maintain headquarters in one of the 50 states or Washington, D.C. *Hispanic Business, "Hispanic Business 500," June 20, 2013*

Minority- and Women-Owned Businesses

Group	All Firms		Firms with Paid Employees			
	Firms	Sales ($000)	Firms	Sales ($000)	Employees	Payroll ($000)
Asian	1,823	416,462	480	366,680	3,526	80,063
Black	6,138	529,505	446	404,258	6,921	182,791
Hispanic	1,605	498,071	267	437,256	2,437	70,491
Women	11,214	1,925,770	1,532	1,679,320	19,455	517,653
All Firms	39,440	47,569,494	10,609	46,114,283	215,278	8,970,446

Note: Figures cover firms located in the city; minority- and women-owned business are defined as firms in which the corresponding group own 51% or more of the stock or equity of the company
Source: U.S. Census Bureau, 2007 Economic Census, Survey of Business Owners (2012 Survey of Business Owners data will be released starting in June 2015)

HOTELS & CONVENTION CENTERS

Hotels/Motels

Area	5 Star		4 Star		3 Star		2 Star		1 Star		Not Rated	
	Num.	Pct.[3]	Num.	Pct.[3]	Num.	Pct.[3]	Num.	Pct.[3]	Num.	Pct.[3]	Num.	Pct.[3]
City[1]	0	0.0	4	1.9	68	32.7	122	58.7	1	0.5	13	6.3
Total[2]	142	0.9	1,005	6.0	5,147	30.9	8,578	51.4	408	2.4	1,397	8.4

Note: (1) Figures cover Raleigh and vicinity; (2) Figures cover all 100 cities in this book; (3) Percentage of hotels which have a given star rating; Star ratings are determined by expedia.com and offer an indication of the general quality of a particular hotel.
Source: expedia.com, April 7, 2014

The Raleigh, NC metro area is home to one of the best hotels in the world according to *Condé Nast Traveler*: **Umstead Hotel & Spa**. The selections are based on over 79,000 responses to the magazine's annual Readers' Choice Survey. The list includes the top 200 hotels in the U.S. *Condé Nast Traveler, "Gold List 2014, The World's Best Places to Stay"*

Major Convention Centers

Name	Overall Space (sq. ft.)	Exhibit Space (sq. ft.)	Meeting Space (sq. ft.)	Meeting Rooms
Raleigh Convention Center	500,000	150,000	n/a	20

Note: Table includes convention centers located in the Raleigh, NC metro area; n/a not available
Source: Original research

Living Environment

COST OF LIVING

Cost of Living Index

Composite Index	Groceries	Housing	Utilities	Trans-portation	Health Care	Misc. Goods/Services
93.3	101.7	76.1	105.7	97.8	101.7	96.6

Note: The Cost of Living Index measures regional differences in the cost of consumer goods and services, excluding taxes and non-consumer expenditures, for professional and managerial households in the top income quintile. It is based on more than 50,000 prices covering almost 60 different items for which prices are collected three times a year by chambers of commerce, economic development organizations or university applied economic centers in each participating urban area. The numbers shown should be read as a percentage above or below the national average of 100. For example, a value of 115.4 in the groceries column indicates that grocery prices are 15.4% higher than the national average. Small differences in the index numbers should not be interpreted as significant; Figures cover the Raleigh NC urban area.
Source: The Council for Community and Economic Research, ACCRA Cost of Living Index, 2013

Grocery Prices

Area[1]	T-Bone Steak ($/pound)	Frying Chicken ($/pound)	Whole Milk ($/half gal.)	Eggs ($/dozen)	Orange Juice ($/64 oz.)	Coffee ($/11.5 oz.)
City[2]	10.51	1.50	2.61	1.98	3.70	4.00
Avg.	10.19	1.28	2.34	1.81	3.48	4.39
Min.	8.56	0.94	1.44	1.19	2.78	3.40
Max.	14.82	2.28	3.56	3.73	6.23	7.32

Note: (1) Values for the local area are compared with the average, minimum and maximum values for all 327 areas in the Cost of Living Index; (2) Figures cover the Raleigh NC urban area; **T-Bone Steak** (price per pound); **Frying Chicken** (price per pound, whole fryer); **Whole Milk** (half gallon carton); **Eggs** (price per dozen, Grade A, large); **Orange Juice** (64 oz. Tropicana or Florida Natural); **Coffee** (11.5 oz. can, vacuum-packed, Maxwell House, Hills Bros, or Folgers).
Source: The Council for Community and Economic Research, ACCRA Cost of Living Index, 2013

Housing and Utility Costs

Area[1]	New Home Price ($)	Apartment Rent ($/month)	All Electric ($/month)	Part Electric ($/month)	Other Energy ($/month)	Telephone ($/month)
City[2]	228,372	649	-	94.58	65.98	32.33
Avg.	295,864	900	171.38	91.82	70.12	27.73
Min.	185,506	458	117.80	48.81	33.67	17.16
Max.	1,358,917	3,783	441.68	171.40	372.65	39.47

Note: (1) Values for the local area are compared with the average, minimum and maximum values for all 327 areas in the Cost of Living Index; (2) Figures cover the Raleigh NC urban area; **New Home Price** (2,400 sf living area, 8,000 sf lot, in urban area with full utilities); **Apartment Rent** (950 sf 2 bedroom/1.5 or 2 bath, unfurnished, excluding all utilities except water); **All Electric** (average monthly cost for an all-electric home); **Part Electric** (average monthly cost for a part-electric home); **Other Energy** (average monthly cost for natural gas, fuel oil, coal, wood, and any other forms of energy except electricity); **Telephone** (price includes basic monthly rate for a private residential line plus additional local usage charges incurred by a family of four).
Source: The Council for Community and Economic Research, ACCRA Cost of Living Index, 2013

Health Care, Transportation, and Other Costs

Area[1]	Doctor ($/visit)	Dentist ($/visit)	Optometrist ($/visit)	Gasoline ($/gallon)	Beauty Salon ($/visit)	Men's Shirt ($)
City[2]	97.60	104.92	97.55	3.34	36.53	22.47
Avg.	101.40	86.48	96.16	3.44	33.87	26.55
Min.	61.67	50.83	50.12	3.08	18.92	12.48
Max.	182.71	152.50	223.78	4.33	68.22	52.03

Note: (1) Values for the local area are compared with the average, minimum and maximum values for all 327 areas in the Cost of Living Index; (2) Figures cover the Raleigh NC urban area; **Doctor** (general practitioners routine exam of an established patient); **Dentist** (adult teeth cleaning and periodic oral examination); **Optometrist** (full vision eye exam for established adult patient); **Gasoline** (one gallon regular unleaded, national brand, including all taxes, cash price at self-service pump if available); **Beauty Salon** (woman's shampoo, trim, and blow-dry); **Men's Shirt** (cotton/polyester dress shirt, pinpoint weave, long sleeves).
Source: The Council for Community and Economic Research, ACCRA Cost of Living Index, 2013

HOUSING

House Price Index (HPI)

Area	National Ranking[2]	Quarterly Change (%)	One-Year Change (%)	Five-Year Change (%)
MSA[1]	123	-0.09	2.97	-4.52
U.S.[3]	–	1.20	7.69	4.18

Note: The HPI is a weighted repeat sales index. It measures average price changes in repeat sales or refinancings on the same properties. This information is obtained by reviewing repeat mortgage transactions on single-family properties whose mortgages have been purchased or securitized by Fannie Mae or Freddie Mac in January 1975; (1) Raleigh, NC Metropolitan Statistical Area—see Appendix B for areas included; (2) Rankings are based on annual percentage change for all metro areas containing at least 15,000 transactions over the last 10 years and ranges from 1 to 283; (3) figures based on a weighted average of Census Division estimates using a seasonally adjusted, purchase-only index; all figures are for the period ending December 31, 2013
Source: Federal Housing Finance Agency, House Price Index, February 25, 2014

Median Single-Family Home Prices

Area	2011	2012	2013p	Percent Change 2012 to 2013
MSA[1]	185.2	188.5	196.9	4.5
U.S. Average	166.2	177.2	197.4	11.4

Note: Figures are median sales prices of existing single-family homes in thousands of dollars; (p) preliminary; n/a not available; (1) Raleigh, NC Metropolitan Statistical Area—see Appendix B for areas included
Source: National Association of Realtors, Median Sales Price of Existing Single-Family Homes for Metropolitan Areas, 4th Quarter 2013

Qualifying Income Based on Median Sales Price of Existing Single-Family Homes

Area	With 5% Down ($)	With 10% Down ($)	With 20% Down ($)
MSA[1]	46,064	43,640	38,791
U.S. Average	45,395	43,006	38,228

Note: Figures are preliminary; Qualifying income is based on a mortgage rate of 4.4%. Monthly principal and interest payment is limited to 25% of income; n/a not available; (1) Raleigh, NC Metropolitan Statistical Area—see Appendix B for areas included
Source: National Association of Realtors, Qualifying Income Based on Median Sales Price of Existing Single-Family Homes for Metropolitan Areas, 4th Quarter 2013

Median Apartment Condo-Coop Home Prices

Area	2011	2012	2013p	Percent Change 2012 to 2013
MSA[1]	n/a	n/a	n/a	n/a
U.S. Average	165.1	173.7	194.9	12.2

Note: Figures are median sales prices of existing apartment condo-coop homes in thousands of dollars; (p) preliminary; n/a not available; (1) Raleigh, NC Metropolitan Statistical Area—see Appendix B for areas included
Source: National Association of Realtors, Median Sales Price of Existing Apartment Condo-Coop Homes for Metropolitan Areas, 4th Quarter 2013

Gross Monthly Rent

Area	Under $200	$200 -299	$300 -499	$500 -749	$750 -999	$1,000 -1,499	$1,500 and up	Median ($)
City	1.0	1.6	3.5	22.1	39.1	26.0	6.7	873
MSA[1]	1.3	2.1	4.9	22.2	36.2	26.4	6.9	870
U.S.	1.7	3.3	8.1	22.7	24.3	25.7	14.3	889

Note: Figures are percentages except for Median; Gross rent is the contract rent plus the estimated average monthly cost of utilities (electricity, gas, and water and sewer) and fuels (oil, coal, kerosene, wood, etc.) if these are paid by the renter (or paid for the renter by someone else); (1) Figures cover the Raleigh, NC Metropolitan Statistical Area—see Appendix B for areas included
Source: U.S. Census Bureau, 2010-2012 American Community Survey 3-Year Estimates

Year Housing Structure Built

Area	2010 or Later	2000 -2009	1990 -1999	1980 -1989	1970 -1979	1960 -1969	1950 -1959	1940 -1949	Before 1940	Median Year
City	0.8	29.4	21.1	18.4	11.4	8.2	5.3	2.6	3.0	1991
MSA[1]	1.0	30.5	25.4	16.8	10.8	6.5	4.1	2.0	2.9	1993
U.S.	0.5	14.9	13.8	13.9	15.9	11.1	10.9	5.5	13.5	1976

Note: Figures are percentages except for Median Year; (1) Figures cover the Raleigh, NC Metropolitan Statistical Area—see Appendix B for areas included
Source: U.S. Census Bureau, 2010-2012 American Community Survey 3-Year Estimates

HEALTH

Health Risk Data

Category	MSA[1] (%)	U.S. (%)
Adults aged 18–64 who have any kind of health care coverage	78.3	79.6
Adults who reported being in good or excellent health	85.5	83.1
Adults who are current smokers	16.6	19.6
Adults who are heavy drinkers[2]	5.0	6.1
Adults who are binge drinkers[3]	14.3	16.9
Adults who are overweight (BMI 25.0 - 29.9)	36.7	35.8
Adults who are obese (BMI 30.0 - 99.8)	24.3	27.6
Adults who participated in any physical activities in the past month	80.2	77.1
Adults 50+ who have ever had a sigmoidoscopy or colonoscopy	80.3	67.3
Women aged 40+ who have had a mammogram within the past two years	74.5	74.0
Men aged 40+ who have had a PSA test within the past two years	43.4	45.2
Adults aged 65+ who have had flu shot within the past year	74.3	60.1
Adults who always wear a seatbelt	98.5	93.8

Note: Data as of 2012 unless otherwise noted; (1) Figures cover the Raleigh-Cary, NC Metropolitan Statistical Area—see Appendix B for areas included; (2) Heavy drinkers are classified as males having more than two drinks per day or females having more than one drink per day; (3) Binge drinkers are classified as males having five or more drinks on one occasion or females having four or more drinks on one occasion
Source: Centers for Disease Control and Prevention, Behaviorial Risk Factor Surveillance System, SMART: Selected Metropolitan/Micropolitan Area Risk Trends, 2012

Chronic Health Indicators

Category	MSA[1] (%)	U.S. (%)
Adults who have ever been told they had a heart attack	2.7	4.5
Adults who have ever been told they had a stroke	2.1	2.9
Adults who have been told they currently have asthma	7.1	8.9
Adults who have ever been told they have arthritis	19.8	25.7
Adults who have ever been told they have diabetes[2]	8.1	9.7
Adults who have ever been told they had skin cancer	6.0	5.7
Adults who have ever been told they had any other types of cancer	5.9	6.5
Adults who have ever been told they have COPD	4.7	6.2
Adults who have ever been told they have kidney disease	1.6	2.5
Adults who have ever been told they have a form of depression	15.2	18.0

Note: Data as of 2012 unless otherwise noted; (1) Figures cover the Raleigh-Cary, NC Metropolitan Statistical Area—see Appendix B for areas included; (2) Figures do not include pregnancy-related, borderline, or pre-diabetes
Source: Centers for Disease Control and Prevention, Behaviorial Risk Factor Surveillance System, SMART: Selected Metropolitan/Micropolitan Area Risk Trends, 2012

Mortality Rates for the Top 10 Causes of Death in the U.S.

ICD-10[a] Sub-Chapter	ICD-10[a] Code	Age-Adjusted Mortality Rate[1] per 100,000 population	
		County[2]	U.S.
Malignant neoplasms	C00-C97	156.8	174.2
Ischaemic heart diseases	I20-I25	84.4	119.1
Other forms of heart disease	I30-I51	41.2	49.6
Chronic lower respiratory diseases	J40-J47	32.1	43.2
Cerebrovascular diseases	I60-I69	45.6	40.3
Organic, including symptomatic, mental disorders	F01-F09	46.7	30.5
Other degenerative diseases of the nervous system	G30-G31	19.4	26.3
Other external causes of accidental injury	W00-X59	18.8	25.1
Diabetes mellitus	E10-E14	17.9	21.3
Hypertensive diseases	I10-I15	16.3	18.8

Note: (a) ICD-10 = International Classification of Diseases 10th Revision; (1) Mortality rates are a three year average covering 2008-2010; (2) Figures cover Wake County
Source: Centers for Disease Control and Prevention, National Center for Health Statistics. Compressed Mortality File 1999-2010 on CDC WONDER Online Database, released January 2013. Data are compiled from the Compressed Mortality File 1999-2010, Series 20 No. 2P, 2013.

Mortality Rates for Selected Causes of Death

ICD-10[a] Sub-Chapter	ICD-10[a] Code	Age-Adjusted Mortality Rate[1] per 100,000 population	
		County[2]	U.S.
Assault	X85-Y09	3.1	5.5
Diseases of the liver	K70-K76	8.0	12.4
Human immunodeficiency virus (HIV) disease	B20-B24	3.2	3.0
Influenza and pneumonia	J09-J18	10.7	16.4
Intentional self-harm	X60-X84	9.0	11.8
Malnutrition	E40-E46	Suppressed	0.8
Obesity and other hyperalimentation	E65-E68	1.2	1.6
Renal failure	N17-N19	13.7	13.6
Transport accidents	V01-V99	9.1	12.6
Viral hepatitis	B15-B19	1.1	2.2

Note: (a) ICD-10 = International Classification of Diseases 10th Revision; (1) Mortality rates are a three year average covering 2008-2010; (2) Figures cover Wake County
Source: Centers for Disease Control and Prevention, National Center for Health Statistics. Compressed Mortality File 1999-2010 on CDC WONDER Online Database, released January 2013. Data are compiled from the Compressed Mortality File 1999-2010, Series 20 No. 2P, 2013.

Health Insurance Coverage

Area	With Health Insurance	With Private Health Insurance	With Public Health Insurance	Without Health Insurance	Population Under Age 18 Without Health Insurance
City	83.4	68.6	22.5	16.6	9.9
MSA[1]	85.3	71.7	21.9	14.7	8.6
U.S.	84.9	65.4	30.4	15.1	7.5

Note: Figures are percentages that cover the civilian noninstitutionalized population; (1) Figures cover the Raleigh, NC Metropolitan Statistical Area—see Appendix B for areas included
Source: U.S. Census Bureau, 2010-2012 American Community Survey 3-Year Estimates

Number of Medical Professionals

Area[1]	MDs[2]	DOs[2,3]	Dentists	Podiatrists	Chiropractors	Optometrists
Local (number)	2,425	68	605	30	230	147
Local (rate[4])	261.0	7.3	63.5	3.2	24.2	15.4
U.S. (rate[4])	267.6	19.6	61.7	5.6	24.7	14.5

Note: Data as of 2012 unless noted; (1) Local data covers Wake County; (2) Data as of 2011; (3) Doctor of Osteopathic Medicine; (4) rate per 100,000 population
Source: Area Resource File (ARF) 2012-2013. U.S. Department of Health and Human Services, Health Resources and Services Administration, Bureau of Health Professions

EDUCATION

Public School District Statistics

District Name	Schls	Pupils	Pupil/ Teacher Ratio	Minority Pupils[1] (%)	Free Lunch Eligible[2] (%)	IEP[3] (%)
Wake County Schools	170	148,154	15.7	50.8	29.6	13.2

Note: Table includes school districts with 2,000 or more students; (1) Percentage of students that are not non-Hispanic white; (2) Percentage of students that are eligible for the free lunch program; (3) Percentage of students that have an Individualized Education Program.
Source: U.S. Department of Education, National Center for Education Statistics, Common Core of Data, Local Education Agency (School District) Universe Survey: School Year 2011-2012; U.S. Department of Education, National Center for Education Statistics, Common Core of Data, Public Elementary/Secondary School Universe Survey: School Year 2011-2012

Best High Schools

High School Name	Rank[1]	Grad. Rate[2] (%)	Coll.[3] (%)	AP/IB/ AICE Tests[4]	AP/IB/ AICE Score[5]	SAT Score[6]	ACT Score[6]
Leesville Road H.S.	1822	82	75	0.2	3.7	1641	n/a
Millbrook H.S.	1924	81	79	0.3	2.9	1475	n/a
Needham B. Broughton H.S.	1011	87	91	0.6	3.4	1609	23.7
Raleigh Charter H.S.	40	95	100	1.3	4.2	1858	28.7
Sanderson H.S.	1993	79	74	0.2	3.5	1548	n/a
Wake Early College of Health and Sciences	1566	94	80	0.0	3.5	1650	n/a
Wakefield H.S.	1802	86	77	0.2	3.5	1517	n/a
William G. Enloe Magnet H.S.	1450	82	85	0.7	3.7	1692	22.3

Note: (1) Public schools are ranked from 1 to 2,000 based on the following self-reported statistics (with the corresponding weight used in calculating their overall score). Schools that were newly founded and did not have a graduating senior class in 2012 were excluded; (2) Four-year, on-time graduation rate (25%); (3) Percent of 2011 graduates who were accepted to college (25%); (4) AP/IB/AICE tests taken per student (25%); (5) Average AP/IB/AICE exam score (10%); (6) Average SAT and/or ACT score (10%); Percent of students enrolled in at least one AP/IB/AICE course (5%)—data not shown; n/a not available
Source: Newsweek and The Daily Beast, "America's Best High Schools 2013"

Highest Level of Education

Area	Less than H.S.	H.S. Diploma	Some College, No Deg.	Associate Degree	Bachelor's Degree	Master's Degree	Prof. School Degree	Doctorate Degree
City	10.0	16.4	20.1	7.6	30.8	10.5	2.6	1.9
MSA[1]	10.2	20.1	19.6	8.8	27.4	10.0	2.0	1.9
U.S.	14.1	28.3	21.3	7.8	18.0	7.5	1.9	1.2

Note: Figures cover persons age 25 and over; (1) Figures cover the Raleigh, NC Metropolitan Statistical Area—see Appendix B for areas included
Source: U.S. Census Bureau, 2010-2012 American Community Survey 3-Year Estimates

Educational Attainment by Race

Area	High School Graduate or Higher (%)					Bachelor's Degree or Higher (%)				
	Total	White	Black	Asian	Hisp.[2]	Total	White	Black	Asian	Hisp.[2]
City	90.0	93.0	89.0	82.4	50.5	45.9	55.4	28.4	45.0	11.8
MSA[1]	89.8	91.9	86.5	91.1	53.2	41.3	44.8	26.2	66.5	12.9
U.S.	85.9	88.1	82.5	85.5	63.1	28.6	30.0	18.4	50.2	13.4

Note: Figures shown cover persons 25 years old and over; (1) Figures cover the Raleigh, NC Metropolitan Statistical Area—see Appendix B for areas included; (2) People of Hispanic origin can be of any race
Source: U.S. Census Bureau, 2010-2012 American Community Survey 3-Year Estimates

School Enrollment by Grade and Control

Area	Preschool (%)		Kindergarten (%)		Grades 1 - 4 (%)		Grades 5 - 8 (%)		Grades 9 - 12 (%)	
	Public	Private	Public	Private	Public	Private	Public	Private	Public	Private
City	32.1	67.9	88.9	11.1	90.6	9.4	90.7	9.3	93.0	7.0
MSA[1]	33.1	66.9	88.5	11.5	89.9	10.1	89.7	10.3	91.2	8.8
U.S.	56.9	43.1	87.8	12.2	89.9	10.1	90.0	10.0	90.8	9.2

Note: Figures shown cover persons 3 years old and over; (1) Figures cover the Raleigh, NC Metropolitan Statistical Area—see Appendix B for areas included
Source: U.S. Census Bureau, 2010-2012 American Community Survey 3-Year Estimates

Average Salaries of Public School Classroom Teachers

Area	2012-13		2013-14		Percent Change 2012-13 to 2013-14	Percent Change 2003-04 to 2013-14
	Dollars	Rank[1]	Dollars	Rank[1]		
North Carolina	45,737	46	45,355	48	-0.84	5.0
U.S. Average	56,103	–	56,689	–	1.04	21.8

Note: (1) State rank ranges from 1 to 51 where 1 indicates highest salary.
Source: National Education Association, Rankings & Estimates: Rankings of the States 2013 and Estimates of School Statistics 2014, March 2014

Higher Education

Four-Year Colleges			Two-Year Colleges			Medical Schools[1]	Law Schools[2]	Voc/ Tech[3]
Public	Private Non-profit	Private For-profit	Public	Private Non-profit	Private For-profit			
1	4	2	1	0	1	0	1	4

Note: Figures cover institutions located within the city limits and include main campuses only; (1) includes schools accredited by the Liaison Committee on Medical Education and the American Osteopathic Association's Commission on Osteopathic College Accreditation; (2) includes ABA-accredited schools, schools with provisional ABA accreditation, and state accredited schools; (3) includes all schools with programs that are less than 2 years.
Source: National Center for Education Statistics, Integrated Postsecondary Education System (IPEDS), 2012-13; Association of American Medical Colleges, Member List, April 24, 2014; American Osteopathic Association, Member List, April 24, 2014; Law School Admission Council, Official Guide to ABA-Approved Law Schools Online, April 24, 2014; Wikipedia, List of Medical Schools in the United States, April 24, 2014; Wikipedia, List of Law Schools in the United States, April 24, 2014

According to *U.S. News & World Report,* the Raleigh, NC metro area is home to one of the best national universities in the U.S.: **North Carolina State University–Raleigh** (#101). The indicators used to capture academic quality fall into a number of categories: assessment by administrators at peer institutions; retention of students; faculty resources; student selectivity; financial resources; alumni giving; high school counselor ratings of colleges; and graduation rate. *U.S. News & World Report, "America's Best Colleges 2014"*

According to *U.S. News & World Report,* the Raleigh, NC metro area is home to one of the top 100 business schools in the U.S.: **North Carolina State University (Jenkins)** (#88). The rankings are based on a weighted average of the following nine measures: quality assessment; peer assessment; recruiter assessment; placement success; mean starting salary and bonus; student selectivity; mean GMAT and GRE scores; mean undergraduate GPA; and acceptance rate. *U.S. News & World Report, "America's Best Graduate Schools, Business, 2014"*

PRESIDENTIAL ELECTION

2012 Presidential Election Results

Area	Obama	Romney	Other
Wake County	54.9	43.5	1.6
U.S.	51.0	47.2	1.8

Note: Results are percentages and may not add to 100% due to rounding
Source: Dave Leip's Atlas of U.S. Presidential Elections

EMPLOYERS

Major Employers

Company Name	Industry
Carolina Power & Light Company	Electric services
Carter & Burgess	Consulting engineer
County of Wake	Executive offices, county government
Crime Control & Public Safety, NC Dept.	Police protection
First Citizens BancShares	Bank holding companies
Health & Human Services, NC Dept of	Hospital management
Lenovo (United States)	Electronic computers
NC department of Transportation	Regulation, administration of transportation
NC Dept of Environment and Natural Res	Land, mineral and wildlife conservation
North Carolina Executive Branch	Executive offices
Progress Energy Service Company	Electric services
Rex Hospital	General medical and surgical hospitals
SAS Institute	Prepackaged software
Set and Service Resources	Executive placement
Verizon Business Network Services	Telephone communication except radio
Wake County Public School System	School buses
Wake Technical Community College	Community college
Wakemed	General medical and surgical hospitals

Note: Companies shown are located within the Raleigh, NC Metropolitan Statistical Area.
Source: Hoovers.com; Wikipedia

PUBLIC SAFETY

Crime Rate

Area	All Crimes	Violent Crimes				Property Crimes		
		Murder	Forcible Rape	Robbery	Aggrav. Assault	Burglary	Larceny -Theft	Motor Vehicle Theft
City	3,699.3	4.0	26.9	158.1	234.2	721.8	2,332.9	221.4
Suburbs[1]	2,170.5	0.5	12.2	30.2	105.8	557.2	1,379.2	85.4
Metro[2]	2,717.7	1.8	17.4	76.0	151.7	616.1	1,720.5	134.0
U.S.	3,246.1	4.7	26.9	112.9	242.3	670.2	1,959.3	229.7

Note: Figures are crimes per 100,000 population; (1) All areas within the metro area that are located outside the city limits; (2) Figures cover the Raleigh, NC Metropolitan Statistical Area—see Appendix B for areas included
Source: FBI Uniform Crime Reports, 2012

Hate Crimes

Area	Number of Quarters Reported	Bias Motivation				
		Race	Religion	Sexual Orientation	Ethnicity	Disability
City	4	0	0	0	0	0
U.S.	4	2,797	1,099	1,135	667	92

Source: Federal Bureau of Investigation, Hate Crime Statistics 2012

Identity Theft Consumer Complaints

Area	Complaints	Complaints per 100,000 Population	Rank[2]
MSA[1]	773	68.4	154
U.S.	290,056	91.8	-

Note: (1) Figures cover the Raleigh, NC Metropolitan Statistical Area—see Appendix B for areas included; (2) Rank ranges from 1 to 377 where 1 indicates greatest number of identity theft complaints per 100,000 population
Source: Federal Trade Commission, Consumer Sentinel Network Data Book for January–December 2013

Fraud and Other Consumer Complaints

Area	Complaints	Complaints per 100,000 Population	Rank[2]
MSA[1]	4,681	414.1	94
U.S.	1,811,724	595.2	-

Note: (1) Figures cover the Raleigh, NC Metropolitan Statistical Area—see Appendix B for areas included; (2) Rank ranges from 1 to 377 where 1 indicates greatest number of identity theft complaints per 100,000 population
Source: Federal Trade Commission, Consumer Sentinel Network Data Book for January–December 2013

RECREATION

Culture

Dance[1]	Theatre[1]	Instrumental Music[1]	Vocal Music[1]	Series and Festivals	Museums and Art Galleries[2]	Zoos and Aquariums[3]
1	5	3	1	7	21	0

Note: (1) Number of professional perfoming groups; (2) Based on organizations with primary SIC code 8412; (3) AZA-accredited
Source: The Grey House Performing Arts Directory, 2013; Association of Zoos & Aquariums, AZA Member Zoos & Aquariums, April 2014; www.AccuLeads.com, May 1, 2014

Professional Sports Teams

Team Name	League	Year Established
Carolina Hurricanes	National Hockey League (NHL)	1997

Note: Includes teams located in the Raleigh, NC Metropolitan Statistical Area.
Source: Wikipedia, Major Professional Sports Teams of the United States and Canada

CLIMATE

Average and Extreme Temperatures

Temperature	Jan	Feb	Mar	Apr	May	Jun	Jul	Aug	Sep	Oct	Nov	Dec	Yr.
Extreme High (°F)	79	84	90	95	97	104	105	105	104	98	88	79	105
Average High (°F)	50	53	61	72	79	86	89	87	81	72	62	53	71
Average Temp. (°F)	40	43	50	59	67	75	78	77	71	60	51	42	60
Average Low (°F)	29	31	38	46	55	63	68	67	60	48	39	32	48
Extreme Low (°F)	-9	5	11	23	29	38	48	46	37	19	11	4	-9

Note: Figures cover the years 1948-1990
Source: National Climatic Data Center, International Station Meteorological Climate Summary, 9/96

Average Precipitation/Snowfall/Humidity

Precip./Humidity	Jan	Feb	Mar	Apr	May	Jun	Jul	Aug	Sep	Oct	Nov	Dec	Yr.
Avg. Precip. (in.)	3.4	3.6	3.6	2.9	3.9	3.6	4.4	4.4	3.2	2.9	3.0	3.1	42.0
Avg. Snowfall (in.)	2	3	1	Tr	0	0	0	0	0	0	Tr	1	8
Avg. Rel. Hum. 7am (%)	79	79	79	80	84	86	88	91	91	90	84	81	84
Avg. Rel. Hum. 4pm (%)	53	49	46	43	51	54	57	59	57	53	51	53	52

Note: Figures cover the years 1948-1990; Tr = Trace amounts (<0.05 in. of rain; <0.5 in. of snow)
Source: National Climatic Data Center, International Station Meteorological Climate Summary, 9/96

Weather Conditions

Temperature			Daytime Sky			Precipitation		
32°F & below	45°F & below	90°F & above	Clear	Partly cloudy	Cloudy	0.01 inch or more precip.	0.1 inch or more snow/ice	Thunder-storms
77	160	39	98	143	124	110	3	42

Note: Figures are average number of days per year and cover the years 1948-1990
Source: National Climatic Data Center, International Station Meteorological Climate Summary, 9/96

HAZARDOUS WASTE

Superfund Sites

Raleigh has two hazardous waste sites on the EPA's Superfund Final National Priorities List: **North Carolina State University (Lot 86, Farm Unit #1); Ward Transformer.** *U.S. Environmental Protection Agency, Final National Priorities List, April 26, 2014*

AIR & WATER QUALITY

Air Quality Index

Area	Percent of Days when Air Quality was...[2]					AQI Statistics[2]	
	Good	Moderate	Unhealthy for Sensitive Groups	Unhealthy	Very Unhealthy	Maximum	Median
MSA[1]	68.8	31.2	0.0	0.0	0.0	90	43

Note: (1) Data covers the Raleigh, NC Metropolitan Statistical Area—see Appendix B for areas included; (2) Based on 365 days with AQI data in 2013. Air Quality Index (AQI) is an index for reporting daily air quality. EPA calculates the AQI for five major air pollutants regulated by the Clean Air Act: ground-level ozone, particle pollution (aka particulate matter), carbon monoxide, sulfur dioxide, and nitrogen dioxide. The AQI runs from 0 to 500. The higher the AQI value, the greater the level of air pollution and the greater the health concern. There are six AQI categories: "Good" AQI is between 0 and 50. Air quality is considered satisfactory; "Moderate" AQI is between 51 and 100. Air quality is acceptable; "Unhealthy for Sensitive Groups" When AQI values are between 101 and 150, members of sensitive groups may experience health effects; "Unhealthy" When AQI values are between 151 and 200 everyone may begin to experience health effects; "Very Unhealthy" AQI values between 201 and 300 trigger a health alert; "Hazardous" AQI values over 300 trigger warnings of emergency conditions (not shown).
Source: U.S. Environmental Protection Agency, Air Quality Index Report, 2013

Air Quality Index Pollutants

Area	Percent of Days when AQI Pollutant was...[2]					
	Carbon Monoxide	Nitrogen Dioxide	Ozone	Sulfur Dioxide	Particulate Matter 2.5	Particulate Matter 10
MSA[1]	0.0	0.0	26.8	0.0	73.2	0.0

Note: (1) Data covers the Raleigh, NC Metropolitan Statistical Area—see Appendix B for areas included; (2) Based on 365 days with AQI data in 2013. The Air Quality Index (AQI) is an index for reporting daily air quality. EPA calculates the AQI for five major air pollutants regulated by the Clean Air Act: ground-level ozone, particle pollution (also known as particulate matter), carbon monoxide, sulfur dioxide, and nitrogen dioxide. The AQI runs from 0 to 500. The higher the AQI value, the greater the level of air pollution and the greater the health concern.
Source: U.S. Environmental Protection Agency, Air Quality Index Report, 2013

Air Quality Trends: Ozone

	2003	2004	2005	2006	2007	2008	2009	2010	2011	2012
MSA[1]	0.086	0.076	0.083	0.074	0.081	0.078	0.067	0.072	0.075	0.073

Note: (1) Data covers the Raleigh, NC Metropolitan Statistical Area—see Appendix B for areas included. The values shown are the composite ozone concentration averages among trend sites based on the highest fourth daily maximum 8-hour concentration in parts per million. These trends are based on sites having an adequate record of monitoring data during the trend period. Data from exceptional events are included.
Source: U.S. Environmental Protection Agency, Air Quality Monitoring Information, "Air Quality Trends by City, 2000-2012"

Maximum Air Pollutant Concentrations: Particulate Matter, Ozone, CO and Lead

	Particulate Matter 10 (ug/m³)	Particulate Matter 2.5 Wtd AM (ug/m³)	Particulate Matter 2.5 24-Hr (ug/m³)	Ozone (ppm)	Carbon Monoxide (ppm)	Lead (ug/m³)
MSA[1] Level	29	8.5	19	0.075	1	n/a
NAAQS[2]	150	15	35	0.075	9	0.15
Met NAAQS[2]	Yes	Yes	Yes	Yes	Yes	n/a

Note: (1) Data covers the Raleigh, NC Metropolitan Statistical Area—see Appendix B for areas included; Data from exceptional events are included; (2) National Ambient Air Quality Standards; ppm = parts per million; ug/m³ = micrograms per cubic meter; n/a not available.
Concentrations: Particulate Matter 10 (coarse particulate)—highest second maximum 24-hour concentration; Particulate Matter 2.5 Wtd AM (fine particulate)—highest weighted annual mean concentration; Particulate Matter 2.5 24-Hour (fine particulate)—highest 98th percentile 24-hour concentration; Ozone—highest fourth daily maximum 8-hour concentration; Carbon Monoxide—highest second maximum non-overlapping 8-hour concentration; Lead—maximum running 3-month average
Source: U.S. Environmental Protection Agency, Air Quality Monitoring Information, "Air Quality Statistics by City, 2012"

Maximum Air Pollutant Concentrations: Nitrogen Dioxide and Sulfur Dioxide

	Nitrogen Dioxide AM (ppb)	Nitrogen Dioxide 1-Hr (ppb)	Sulfur Dioxide AM (ppb)	Sulfur Dioxide 1-Hr (ppb)	Sulfur Dioxide 24-Hr (ppb)
MSA[1] Level	n/a	n/a	n/a	13	n/a
NAAQS[2]	53	100	30	75	140
Met NAAQS[2]	n/a	n/a	n/a	Yes	n/a

Note: (1) Data covers the Raleigh, NC Metropolitan Statistical Area—see Appendix B for areas included; Data from exceptional events are included; (2) National Ambient Air Quality Standards; ppm = parts per million; ug/m³ = micrograms per cubic meter; n/a not available.
Concentrations: Nitrogen Dioxide AM—highest arithmetic mean concentration; Nitrogen Dioxide 1-Hr—highest 98th percentile 1-hour daily maximum concentration; Sulfur Dioxide AM—highest annual mean concentration; Sulfur Dioxide 1-Hr—highest 99th percentile 1-hour daily maximum concentration; Sulfur Dioxide 24-Hr—highest second maximum 24-hour concentration
Source: U.S. Environmental Protection Agency, Air Quality Monitoring Information, "Air Quality Statistics by City, 2012"

Drinking Water

Water System Name	Pop. Served	Primary Water Source Type	Violations[1] Health Based	Violations[1] Monitoring/ Reporting
City of Raleigh	500,000	Surface	0	0

Note: (1) Based on violation data from January 1, 2013 to December 31, 2013 (includes unresolved violations from earlier years)
Source: U.S. Environmental Protection Agency, Office of Ground Water and Drinking Water, Safe Drinking Water Information System (based on data extracted February 10, 2014)

Richmond, Virginia

Background

Richmond is the capital of Virginia and is located on the James River. Home to blue-blooded old families such as the Byrds and Lees, the city played a central role in both U.S. and Confederate histories.

John Smith (of Pocahontas fame) and Christopher Newport first claimed Richmond in 1607 as English territory. In 1679, the area was granted to William Byrd I, with the understanding that he establish a settlement. His son, William Byrd II, continued his father's work, and, along with William Mayo, surveyed lots for what was to be named Richmond. During the Revolutionary War, Richmond played host to two Virginia Conventions. These conventions, which gathered founding fathers such as George Washington, Thomas Jefferson, and Patrick Henry in the same room, ratified the Constitution as the law of the land for the emerging nation.

Not long after the United States congealed as a nation, however, dissension caused fragmentation and Richmond became the Confederate States' capital. From its Roman temple-inspired capitol designed by Thomas Jefferson, Jefferson Davis presided over the Confederacy.

Not surprisingly, today Richmond is home to authoritative repositories of both Southern and Virginia history, which include the Virginia State Library, the Museum of the Confederacy, and the Virginia Historical Society.

Today, government and higher education are economic mainstays for the city, with Virginia Commonwealth University, the Medical College of Virginia, the University of Richmond, and Virginia Union University all located within the city limits. The Virginia BioTechnology Research Park houses more than 60 life sciences organizations in 1.3 million square feet of research and office space adjacent to the VCU Medical Center. Companies located there include government and VCU labs, young companies nearing mid-stage, and even international bioscience companies. In addition, companies such as Philip Morris USA and Capital One are headquartered in Richmond. The banking and telecommunications sectors are also well represented in the city's economy. In 2014, the Greater Richmond Partnership Inc. launched a plan to grow the region's exports by $1 billion over three years.

The city's James River waterfront continues to undergo change, as major properties such as the 17-acre "Reynolds South Plant," where the packaging group once manufactured foil, are sold. In this case, the property is zoned for mixed-use development.

Richmond's cultural offerings include the Richmond Symphony, Richmond Ballet, and the Virginia Museum of Fine Arts, known for its fine Faberge collection that may be traveling for exhibitions.

Richmond's climate is classified as modified continental with its warm summer and humid, mild winters. Snow only remains on the ground for a day or so. Ice storms are not uncommon, but are not usually severe enough to cause considerable damage. Hurricanes and tropical storms, when they occur, are responsible for flooding during the summer and early fall months. Tornadoes are infrequent, but some notable occurrences have been observed in the Richmond area.

Rankings

General Rankings

- Richmond appeared on RelocateAmerica's list of best places to live in America. The annual "Top 100 Places to Live" list recognizes the top communities as nominated by their residents & local businesses. RelocateAmerica's Research Group determined the list based on review of various data gathered for economic, employment, housing, education, industry, opportunity, environment and recreation along with feedback from area leaders and residents. *RelocateAmerica.com, "Top 100 Places to Live for 2011"*

- Richmond was selected as one of America's best river towns by *Outside Magazine*. Criteria: cost of living; cultural vibrancy; job prospects; environmental stewardship; access to the outdoors. *Outside Magazine, "Best Towns 2012," October 2012*

Business/Finance Rankings

- Based on a minimum of 500 social media reviews per metro area, the employment opinion group Glassdoor surveyed 50 of the largest U.S. metro areas on measures including compensation and benefits, satisfaction with management, business outlook, and number of employers hiring. The Richmond metro area was ranked #29 in overall employee satisfaction. *www.glassdoor.com, "Employment Satisfaction Report Card by City," June 21, 2013*

- Richmond was ranked #61 out of 100 metro areas in terms of economic performance (#1 = best) during the recession and recovery from trough quarter through the second quarter of 2013. Criteria: percent change in employment; percentage point change in unemployment rate; percent change in gross metropolitan product; percent change in House Price Index. *Brookings Institution, MetroMonitor: Tracking Economic Recession and Recovery in America's 100 Largest Metropolitan Areas, September 2013*

- Richmond was identified as one of the best places for finding a job by *U.S. News & World Report*. The city ranked #7 out of 10. Criteria: strong job market. *U.S. News & World Report, "The 10 Best Cities to Find Jobs," June 17, 2013*

- Richmond was identified as one of the top 25 U.S. cities with the most credit card debt by credit reporting bureau Experian. The city was ranked #9. *Experian, March 4, 2011*

- The Richmond metro area appeared on the Milken Institute "2013 Best Performing Cities" list. Rank: #111 out of 200 large metro areas. Criteria: job growth; wage and salary growth; high-tech output growth. *Milken Institute, "Best-Performing Cities 2013," December 2013*

- *Forbes* ranked the 200 most populous metro areas in the U.S. in terms of the "Best Places for Business and Careers." The Richmond metro area was ranked #56. Criteria: costs (business and living); job growth (past and projected); income growth; educational attainment (college and high school); projected economic growth; cultural and recreational opportunities; net migration patterns; number of highly ranked colleges. *Forbes, "The Best Places for Business and Careers," August 7, 2013*

Children/Family Rankings

- Richmond was selected as one of the best cities for families to live by *Parenting* magazine. The city ranked #13 out of 100. Criteria: education; health; community; *Parenting's* Culture & Charm Index. *Parenting.com, "The 2012 Best Cities for Families List"*

Dating/Romance Rankings

- Richmond ranked #9 among cities congenial to singles, according to Kiplinger, which searched for "dating scenes as financially attractive as they are romantically promising." High percentages of unmarried people, above-average household incomes, and cost-of-living factors determined the rankings. *Kiplinger.com, "10 Best Cities for Singles," February 2013*

Education Rankings

- *Men's Health* ranked 100 U.S. cities in terms of their education levels. Richmond was ranked #66 (#1 = most educated city). Criteria: high school graduation rates; school enrollment; educational attainment; number of households who have outstanding student loans; number of households whose members have taken adult-education courses. *Men's Health, "Where School Is In: The Most and Least Educated Cities," September 12, 2011*

- Richmond was selected as one of the most well-read cities in America by Amazon.com. The city ranked #18 of 20. Cities with populations greater than 100,000 were evaluated based on per capita sales of books, magazines and newspapers. *Amazon.com, "The 20 Most Well-Read Cities in America," April 28, 2013*

Environmental Rankings

- The Richmond metro area came in at #241 for the relative comfort of its climate on Sperling's list of "chill cities," as measured by the Sperling Heat Index. All 361 metro areas are included. Criteria included daytime high temperatures, nighttime low temperatures, dew point, and relative humidity at the high temperatures. *www.bertsperling.com, "Sperling's Chill Cities," July 18, 2013*

- Sperling's BestPlaces assessed 379 metropolitan areas of the United States for the likelihood of dangerously extreme weather events or earthquakes. In general the Southeast and South-Central regions have the highest risk of weather extremes and earthquakes, while the Pacific Northwest enjoys the lowest risk. Of the least risky metropolitan areas, the Richmond metro area was ranked #255. *www.bestplaces.net, "Safest Places from Natural Disasters," April 2011*

- Richmond was selected as one of 22 "Smarter Cities" for energy by the Natural Resources Defense Council. Criteria: investment in green power; energy efficiency measures; conservation. *Natural Resources Defense Council, "2010 Smarter Cities," July 19, 2010*

- Richmond was highlighted as one of the top 25 cleanest metro areas for short-term particle pollution (24-hour PM 2.5) in the U.S. during 2008 through 2010. Monitors in these cities reported no days with unhealthful PM 2.5 levels. *American Lung Association, State of the Air 2012*

Food/Drink Rankings

- Richmond was selected as one of America's 10 most vegan-friendly cities. The city was ranked #10. *People for the Ethical Treatment of Animals, "Top Vegan-Friendly Cities of 2013," June 11, 2013*

Health/Fitness Rankings

- Analysts who tracked obesity rates in the nation's largest metro areas (those with populations above one million) found that the Richmond metro area was one of the ten major metros where residents were most likely to be obese, defined as a BMI score of 30 or above. *www.gallup.com, "Boulder, Colo., Residents Still Least Likely to Be Obese," April 4, 2014*

- For each of the 50 most populous metro areas in the United States, the American College of Sports Medicine's American Fitness Index evaluated infrastructure, community assets, and policies that encourage healthy and fit lifestyles, including preventive health behaviors, levels of chronic disease conditions, health care access, and community resources and policies that support physical activity. The Richmond metro area ranked #20 for "community fitness." Personal health indicators were considered as well as community and environmental indicators. *www.americanfitnessindex.org, "ACSM American Fitness Index Health and Community Fitness Status of the 50 Largest Metropolitan Areas," May 2013*

- The Richmond metro area was identified as one of the worst cities for bed bugs in America by pest control company Orkin. The area ranked #11 out of 50 based on the number of bed bug treatments Orkin performed from January to December 2013. *Orkin, "Chicago Tops Bed Bug Cities List for Second Year in a Row," January 16, 2014*

- Richmond was identified as a "2013 Spring Allergy Capital." The area ranked #22 out of 100. Three groups of factors were used to identify the most severe cities for people with allergies during the spring season: annual pollen levels; medicine utilization; access to board-certified allergists. *Asthma and Allergy Foundation of America, "Spring Allergy Capitals 2013"*

- Richmond was identified as a "2013 Fall Allergy Capital." The area ranked #57 out of 100. Three groups of factors were used to identify the most severe cities for people with allergies during the fall season: annual pollen levels; medicine utilization; access to board-certified allergists. *Asthma and Allergy Foundation of America, "Fall Allergy Capitals 2013"*

- Richmond was identified as a "2013 Asthma Capital." The area ranked #1 out of the nation's 100 largest metropolitan areas. Twelve factors were used to identify the most challenging places to live for people with asthma: estimated prevalence; self-reported prevalence; crude death rate for asthma; annual pollen score; annual air quality; public smoking laws; number of board-certified asthma specialists; school inhaler access laws; rescue medication use; controller medication use; uninsured rate; poverty rate. *Asthma and Allergy Foundation of America, "Asthma Capitals 2013"*

- Breathe Right Nasal Strips, in partnership with Sperling's BestPlaces, analyzed 50 metro areas and identified those U.S. cities most challenged by chronic nasal congestion. The Richmond metro area ranked #13. Criteria: tree, grass and weed pollens; molds and spores; air pollution; climate; smoking; purchase habits of congestion products; prescriptions of drugs for congestion relief; incidence of influenza. *Breathe Right Nasal Strips, "Most Congested Cities," October 3, 2011*

- Richmond was selected as one of the best metropolitan areas for hospital care in America by *HealthGrades.com*. The rankings are based on a comprehensive study of patient death and complication rates in the nation's nearly 5,000 hospitals. Hospitals performing in the top 5% nationwide across 26 different medical procedures and diagnoses were identified. *HealthGrades.com* then ranked cities by the highest percentage of these Distinguished Hospitals for Clinical Excellence™. The Richmond metro area ranked #4. *HealthGrades.com, "America's Top 50 Cities for Hospital Care," January 21, 2012*

- The Richmond metro area appeared in the 2013 Gallup-Healthways Well-Being Index. The area ranked #65 out of 189. The Gallup-Healthways Well-Being Index score is an average of six sub-indexes, which individually examine life evaluation, emotional health, work environment, physical health, healthy behaviors, and access to basic necessities. Results are based on telephone interviews conducted as part of the Gallup-Healthways Well-Being Index survey January 2–December 29, 2012, and January 2–December 30, 2013, with a random sample of 531,630 adults, aged 18 and older, living in metropolitan areas in the 50 U.S. states and the District of Columbia. *Gallup-Healthways, "State of American Well-Being," March 25, 2014*

- *Men's Health* ranked 100 U.S. cities in terms of their activity levels. Richmond was ranked #40 (#1 = most active city). Criteria: where and how often residents exercise; percentage of households that watch more than 15 hours of cable television a week and buy more than 11 video games a year; death rate from deep-vein thrombosis, a condition linked to sitting for extended periods of time. *Men's Health, "Where Sit Happens: The Most and Least Active Cities in America," June 20, 2011*

- *The Daily Beast* identified the 30 U.S. metro areas with the worst smoking habits. The Richmond metro area ranked #27. Sixty urban centers with populations of more than one million were ranked based on the following criteria: number of smokers; number of cigarettes smoked per day; fewest attempts to quit. *The Daily Beast, "30 Cities With Smoking Problems," January 3, 2011*

Real Estate Rankings

- Based on the home-price forecasts compiled by the real-estate valuation firm CoreLogic Case-Shiller, the finance website CNNMoney reported that in 2014, the Richmond metro area is expected to place #4 among American metro areas in terms of increases in residential real estate prices. *money.cnn.com, "10 Hottest Housing Markets for 2014," January 23, 2014*

- Richmond was ranked #151 out of 283 metro areas in terms of house price appreciation in 2013 (#1 = highest rate). *Federal Housing Finance Agency, House Price Index, 4th Quarter 2013*

- Richmond was ranked #99 out of 224 metro areas in terms of housing affordability in 2013 by the National Association of Home Builders (#1 = most affordable). The NAHB-Wells Fargo Housing Opportunity Index (HOI) for a given area is defined as the share of homes sold in that area that would have been affordable to a family earning the local median income, based on standard mortgage underwriting criteria. *National Association of Home Builders®, NAHB-Wells Fargo Housing Opportunity Index, 4th Quarter 2013*

- Richmond was selected as one of the best college towns for renters by ApartmentRatings.com." The area ranked #68 out of 87. Overall satisfaction ratings were ranked using thousands of user submitted scores for hundreds of apartment complexes located in cities and towns that are home to the 100 largest four-year institutions in the U.S. *ApartmentRatings.com, "2011 College Town Renter Satisfaction Rankings"*

Safety Rankings

- Allstate ranked the 200 largest cities in America in terms of driver safety. Richmond ranked #55. Allstate researchers analyzed internal property damage claims over a two-year period from January 2010 to December 2011. A weighted average of the two-year numbers determined the annual percentages. *Allstate, "Allstate America's Best Drivers Report®, August 27, 2013"*

- The National Insurance Crime Bureau ranked 380 metro areas in the U.S. in terms of per capita rates of vehicle theft. The Richmond metro area ranked #169 (#1 = highest rate). Criteria: number of vehicle theft offenses per 100,000 inhabitants in 2012. *National Insurance Crime Bureau, "Hot Spots 2012," June 26, 2013*

- The Richmond metro area was identified as one of the most dangerous metro areas for pedestrians by Transportation for America. The metro area ranked #20 out of 52 metro areas with over 1 million residents. Criteria: area's population divided by the number of pedestrian fatalities in that area. *Transportation for America, "Dangerous by Design 2011"*

Seniors/Retirement Rankings

- From its Best Cities for Successful Aging indexes, the Milken Institute generated rankings for metropolitan areas, weighing data in eight categories—general indicators, health care, wellness, living arrangements, transportation and general accessibility, financial well-being, education and employment, and community participation. The Richmond metro area was ranked #45 overall in the large metro area category. *Milken Institute, "Best Cities for Successful Aging," July 2012*

Sports/Recreation Rankings

- Richmond appeared on the *Sporting News* list of the "Best Sports Cities" for 2011. The area ranked #91 out of 271. Criteria: the magazine takes a 12-month snapshot of each city's sports, putting a heavy premium on regular-season won-lost records (from the most recently completed season). Other criteria include: playoff berths, bowl appearances and tournament bids; championships; applicable power ratings; quality of competition; overall fan fervor (measured in part by attendance); abundance of teams (rewarding quality over quantity); stadium and arena quality; ticket availability and prices; franchise ownership; and marquee appeal of athletes. *Sporting News, "Best Sports Cities 2011," October 4, 2011*

- Richmond appeared on the *Sporting News* list of the "Best Sports Cities" for 2011. The area ranked #91 out of 271. Criteria: a 12-month snapshot of regular-season won-lost records (from the most recently completed season). Other criteria include: playoff berths, bowl appearances and tournament bids; championships; applicable power ratings; quality of competition; overall fan fervor (measured in part by attendance); abundance of teams (quality over quantity); stadium and arena quality; ticket availability and prices; franchise ownership; and marquee appeal of athletes. *Sporting News, "Best Sports Cities 2011," October 4, 2011*

- Richmond was chosen as a bicycle friendly community by the League of American Bicyclists. A "Bicycle Friendly Community" welcomes cyclists by providing safe accommodation for cycling and encouraging people to bike for transportation and recreation. There are four award levels: Platinum; Gold; Silver; and Bronze. The community achieved an award level of Bronze. *League of American Bicyclists, "Bicycle Friendly Community Master List," Fall 2013*

Women/Minorities Rankings

- The Daily Beast surveyed the nation's cities for highest percentage of singles and lowest divorce rate, plus other measures, to determine "emotional intelligence"—happiness, confidence, kindness—which, researchers say, has a strong correlation with people's satisfaction with their romantic relationships. Richmond placed #12. *www.thedailybeast.com, "Best Cities to Find Love and Stay in Love," February 14, 2014*

- The Richmond metro area appeared on *Forbes'* list of the "Best Cities for Minority Entrepreneurs." The area ranked #12 out of 10. Criteria: 52 metropolitan statistical areas were examined. For each ethnicity (African Americans, Asians and Hispanics), the editors measured housing affordability, population growth, income growth, and entrepreneurship (per capita self-employment). *Forbes, "Best Cities for Minority Entrepreneurs," March 23, 2011*

Miscellaneous Rankings

- Richmond was selected as a 2013 Digital Cities Survey winner. The city ranked #8 in the mid-sized city (125,000 to 249,999 population) category. The survey examined and assessed how city governments are utilizing information technology to operate and deliver quality service to their customers and citizens. Survey questions focused on implementation and adoption of online service delivery; planning and governance; and the infrastructure and architecture that make the transformation to digital government possible. *Center for Digital Government, "2013 Digital Cities Survey," November 7, 2013*

- Ink Army reported on a survey by the website TotalBeauty calculating the number of tattoo shops per 100,000 residents in order to determine the U.S. cities with the most tattoo acceptance. Richmond took the #3 slot. *inkarmy.com, "Most Tattoo Friendly Cities in the United States," November 1, 2013*

- *Men's Health* ranked 100 U.S. cities by their level of sadness. Richmond was ranked #68 (#1 = saddest city). Criteria: suicide rates; unemployment rates; percentage of households that use antidepressants; percent of population who report feeling blue all or most of the time. *Men's Health, "Frown Towns," November 28, 2011*

- Mars Chocolate North America, the makers of COMBOS®, in partnership with Sperling's BestPlaces, ranked 50 major metro areas in terms of their "manliness." The Richmond metro area ranked #22. Criteria: number of professional sports teams; number of nearby NASCAR tracks and racing events; manly lifestyle; concentration of manly retail stores; manly occupations per capita; salty snack sales; "Board of Manliness" rankings. *Mars Chocolate North America, "America's Manliest Cities 2012"*

- Richmond was selected as one of the most tattooed cities in America by *Lovelyish.com*. The city was ranked #3. Criteria: number of tattoo shops per capita. *Lovelyish.com, "Top Ten: Most Tattooed Cities in America," October 17, 2012*

- The National Alliance to End Homelessness ranked the 100 most populous metro areas in terms the rate of homelessness. The Richmond metro area ranked #84. Criteria: number of homeless people per 10,000 population in 2011. *National Alliance to End Homelessness, The State of Homelessness in America 2012*

Business Environment

CITY FINANCES

City Government Finances

Component	2011 ($000)	2011 ($ per capita)
Total Revenues	1,357,788	6,785
Total Expenditures	1,303,609	6,514
Debt Outstanding	1,347,405	6,733
Cash and Securities[1]	897,573	4,485

Note: (1) Cash and security holdings of a government at the close of its fiscal year, including those of its dependent agencies, utilities, and liquor stores.
Source: U.S Census Bureau, State & Local Government Finances 2011

City Government Revenue by Source

Source	2011 ($000)	2011 ($ per capita)
General Revenue		
From Federal Government	74,112	370
From State Government	324,961	1,624
From Local Governments	17,052	85
Taxes		
Property	277,318	1,386
Sales and Gross Receipts	103,430	517
Personal Income	0	0
Corporate Income	0	0
Motor Vehicle License	3,197	16
Other Taxes	31,287	156
Current Charges	141,643	708
Liquor Store	0	0
Utility	242,518	1,212
Employee Retirement	98,121	490

Source: U.S Census Bureau, State & Local Government Finances 2011

City Government Expenditures by Function

Function	2011 ($000)	2011 ($ per capita)	2011 (%)
General Direct Expenditures			
Air Transportation	0	0	0.0
Corrections	44,432	222	3.4
Education	305,617	1,527	23.4
Employment Security Administration	0	0	0.0
Financial Administration	27,122	136	2.1
Fire Protection	47,296	236	3.6
General Public Buildings	15,783	79	1.2
Governmental Administration, Other	6,616	33	0.5
Health	44,449	222	3.4
Highways	25,941	130	2.0
Hospitals	0	0	0.0
Housing and Community Development	89,148	445	6.8
Interest on General Debt	9,066	45	0.7
Judicial and Legal	15,193	76	1.2
Libraries	5,371	27	0.4
Parking	0	0	0.0
Parks and Recreation	18,516	93	1.4
Police Protection	86,750	433	6.7
Public Welfare	17,424	87	1.3
Sewerage	74,414	372	5.7
Solid Waste Management	24,470	122	1.9
Veterans' Services	0	0	0.0
Liquor Store	0	0	0.0
Utility	285,752	1,428	21.9
Employee Retirement	62,473	312	4.8

Source: U.S Census Bureau, State & Local Government Finances 2011

DEMOGRAPHICS

Population Growth

Area	1990 Census	2000 Census	2010 Census	Population Growth (%)	
				1990-2000	2000-2010
City	202,783	197,790	204,214	-2.5	3.2
MSA[1]	949,244	1,096,957	1,258,251	15.6	14.7
U.S.	248,709,873	281,421,906	308,745,538	13.2	9.7

Note: (1) Figures cover the Richmond, VA Metropolitan Statistical Area—see Appendix B for areas included
Source: U.S. Census Bureau, Census 1990, 2000, 2010

Household Size

Area	Persons in Household (%)							Average Household Size
	One	Two	Three	Four	Five	Six	Seven or More	
City	41.8	31.0	13.7	8.3	3.4	1.0	0.8	2.35
MSA[1]	28.0	34.2	16.4	13.8	5.1	1.6	0.9	2.59
U.S.	27.6	33.5	15.7	13.2	6.1	2.4	1.5	2.63

Note: (1) Figures cover the Richmond, VA Metropolitan Statistical Area—see Appendix B for areas included
Source: U.S. Census Bureau, 2010-2012 American Community Survey 3-Year Estimates

Race

Area	White Alone[2] (%)	Black Alone[2] (%)	Asian Alone[2] (%)	AIAN[3] Alone[2] (%)	NHOPI[4] Alone[2] (%)	Other Race Alone[2] (%)	Two or More Races (%)
City	43.3	49.5	2.2	0.3	0.0	1.3	3.3
MSA[1]	63.0	30.0	3.1	0.4	0.0	1.1	2.3
U.S.	74.0	12.6	4.9	0.8	0.2	4.7	2.8

Note: (1) Figures cover the Richmond, VA Metropolitan Statistical Area—see Appendix B for areas included;
(2) Alone is defined as not being in combination with one or more other races; (3) American Indian and Alaska
Native; (4) Native Hawaiian and Other Pacific Islander
Source: U.S. Census Bureau, 2010-2012 American Community Survey 3-Year Estimates

Hispanic or Latino Origin

Area	Total (%)	Mexican (%)	Puerto Rican (%)	Cuban (%)	Other (%)
City	6.3	2.1	0.5	0.1	3.6
MSA[1]	5.1	1.7	0.8	0.1	2.5
U.S.	16.6	10.7	1.6	0.6	3.7

Note: Persons of Hispanic or Latino origin can be of any race; (1) Figures cover the Richmond, VA
Metropolitan Statistical Area—see Appendix B for areas included
Source: U.S. Census Bureau, 2010-2012 American Community Survey 3-Year Estimates

Segregation

Type	Segregation Indices[1]				Percent Change		
	1990	2000	2010	2010 Rank[2]	1990-2000	1990-2010	2000-2010
Black/White	55.7	53.6	52.4	63	-2.0	-3.2	-1.2
Asian/White	35.3	38.3	43.9	32	3.0	8.6	5.6
Hispanic/White	30.1	39.8	44.9	46	9.7	14.8	5.1

Note: All figures cover the Metropolitan Statistical Area—see Appendix B for areas included; Figures are based
on an analysis of 1990, 2000, and 2010 Census Decennial Census tract data by William H. Frey, Brookings
Institution and the University of Michigan Social Science Data Analysis Network. In this analysis all racial
groups (whites, blacks, and asians) are non-Hispanic members of those races. Hispanics are shown as a
separate category;
(1) Segregation Indices are Dissimilarity Indices that measure the degree to which the minority group is
distributed differently than whites across census tracts. They range from 0 (complete integration) to 100
(complete segregation) where the value indicates the percentage of the minority group that needs to move to be
distributed exactly like whites; (2) Ranges from 1 (most segregated) to 102 (least segregated); n/a not available.
Source: www.CensusScope.org

Ancestry

Area	German	Irish	English	American	Italian	Polish	French[2]	Scottish	Dutch
City	7.0	6.7	8.1	4.0	2.6	1.2	1.6	1.6	0.5
MSA[1]	10.3	8.8	12.3	9.1	3.5	1.8	1.9	2.2	0.8
U.S.	15.2	11.1	8.2	7.2	5.6	3.1	2.8	1.7	1.4

Note: Figures are the percentage of the total population reporting a particular ancestry. The nine most commonly reported ancestries in the U.S. are shown. Figures include multiple ancestries (e.g. if a person reported being Irish and Italian, they were included in both columns); (1) Figures cover the Richmond, VA Metropolitan Statistical Area—see Appendix B for areas included; (2) Excludes Basque
Source: U.S. Census Bureau, 2010-2012 American Community Survey 3-Year Estimates

Foreign-Born Population

Area	Percent of Population Born in								
	Any Foreign Country	Mexico	Asia	Europe	Carribean	South America	Central America[2]	Africa	Canada
City	7.5	1.2	1.6	0.8	0.3	0.3	2.0	1.0	0.2
MSA[1]	7.2	0.8	2.6	1.1	0.3	0.4	1.1	0.7	0.2
U.S.	13.0	3.7	3.7	1.6	1.2	0.9	1.0	0.5	0.3

Note: (1) Figures cover the Richmond, VA Metropolitan Statistical Area—see Appendix B for areas included; (2) Excludes Mexico.
Source: U.S. Census Bureau, 2010-2012 American Community Survey 3-Year Estimates

Marital Status

Area	Never Married	Now Married[2]	Separated	Widowed	Divorced
City	52.3	25.4	4.3	5.9	12.1
MSA[1]	33.7	46.8	2.9	5.8	10.8
U.S.	32.4	48.4	2.2	6.0	11.0

Note: Figures are percentages and cover the population 15 years of age and older; (1) Figures cover the Richmond, VA Metropolitan Statistical Area—see Appendix B for areas included; (2) Excludes separated
Source: U.S. Census Bureau, 2010-2012 American Community Survey 3-Year Estimates

Age

Area	Percent of Population									Median Age
	Under Age 5	Age 5–19	Age 20–34	Age 35–44	Age 45–54	Age 55–64	Age 65–74	Age 75–84	Age 85+	
City	6.5	17.1	30.2	11.5	12.3	11.3	5.8	3.5	1.9	32.3
MSA[1]	6.1	19.7	20.1	13.6	15.1	12.8	7.1	3.7	1.7	38.1
U.S.	6.4	20.1	20.5	13.1	14.3	12.2	7.3	4.2	1.8	37.3

Note: (1) Figures cover the Richmond, VA Metropolitan Statistical Area—see Appendix B for areas included
Source: U.S. Census Bureau, 2010-2012 American Community Survey 3-Year Estimates

Gender

Area	Males	Females	Males per 100 Females
City	98,377	108,559	90.6
MSA[1]	615,392	655,343	93.9
U.S.	153,276,055	158,333,314	96.8

Note: (1) Figures cover the Richmond, VA Metropolitan Statistical Area—see Appendix B for areas included
Source: U.S. Census Bureau, 2010-2012 American Community Survey 3-Year Estimates

Religious Groups by Family

Area	Catholic	Baptist	Non-Den.	Methodist[2]	Lutheran	LDS[3]	Pentecostal	Presbyterian[4]	Muslim[5]	Judaism
MSA[1]	6.0	19.9	5.5	6.1	0.6	1.0	1.8	2.1	2.8	0.4
U.S.	19.1	9.3	4.0	4.0	2.3	2.0	1.9	1.6	0.8	0.7

Note: Figures are the number of adherents as a percentage of the total population; (1) Figures cover the Richmond, VA Metropolitan Statistical Area—see Appendix B for areas included; (2) Methodist/Pietist; (3) Latter Day Saints; (4) Reformed; (5) Figures are estimates
Source: Association of Statisticians of American Religious Bodies, 2010 U.S. Religion Census: Religious Congregations & Membership Study

Religious Groups by Tradition

Area	Catholic	Evangelical Protestant	Mainline Protestant	Other Tradition	Black Protestant	Orthodox
MSA[1]	6.0	23.7	13.3	4.6	2.4	0.2
U.S.	19.1	16.2	7.3	4.3	1.6	0.3

Note: Figures are the number of adherents as a percentage of the total population; (1) Figures cover the Richmond, VA Metropolitan Statistical Area—see Appendix B for areas included
Source: Association of Statisticians of American Religious Bodies, 2010 U.S. Religion Census: Religious Congregations & Membership Study

ECONOMY

Gross Metropolitan Product

Area	2011	2012	2013	2014	Rank[2]
MSA[1]	66.6	70.0	71.7	74.4	43

Note: Figures are in billions of dollars; (1) Figures cover the Richmond, VA Metropolitan Statistical Area—see Appendix B for areas included; (2) Rank is based on 2014 data and ranges from 1 to 363
Source: The United States Conference of Mayors, U.S. Metro Economies: Outlook—Gross Metropolitan Product, with Metro Employment Projections, November 2013

Economic Growth

Area	2011 (%)	2012 (%)	2013 (%)	2014 (%)	Rank[2]
MSA[1]	1.0	3.2	0.9	1.7	166
U.S.	1.6	2.5	1.7	2.5	–

Note: Figures are real gross metropolitan product (GMP) growth rates and represent annual average percent change; (1) Figures cover the Richmond, VA Metropolitan Statistical Area—see Appendix B for areas included; (2) Rank is based on 2013 data and ranges from 1 to 363
Source: The United States Conference of Mayors, U.S. Metro Economies: Outlook—Gross Metropolitan Product, with Metro Employment Projections, November 2013

Metropolitan Area Exports

Area	2007	2008	2009	2010	2011	2012	Rank[2]
MSA[1]	4,952.2	5,162.4	4,096.8	4,606.5	5,072.8	4,328.1	56

Note: Figures are in millions of dollars; (1) Figures cover the Richmond, VA Metropolitan Statistical Area—see Appendix B for areas included; (2) Rank is based on 2012 data and ranges from 1 to 369
Source: U.S. Department of Commerce, International Trade Administration, Office of Trade & Industry Information, Manufacturing & Services, data extracted April 1, 2014

INCOME

Income

Area	Per Capita ($)	Median Household ($)	Average Household ($)
City	26,231	40,001	60,594
MSA[1]	29,527	57,234	76,042
U.S.	27,385	51,771	71,579

Note: (1) Figures cover the Richmond, VA Metropolitan Statistical Area—see Appendix B for areas included
Source: U.S. Census Bureau, 2010-2012 American Community Survey 3-Year Estimates

Household Income Distribution

Area	Under $15,000	$15,000 -24,999	$25,000 -34,999	$35,000 -49,999	$50,000 -74,999	$75,000 -99,000	$100,000 -149,999	$150,000 and up
City	20.9	12.8	11.5	15.1	15.8	9.6	7.7	6.5
MSA[1]	10.5	8.8	9.9	14.2	18.8	13.2	14.8	9.8
U.S.	13.1	11.0	10.5	13.7	18.1	11.9	12.5	9.1

Note: (1) Figures cover the Richmond, VA Metropolitan Statistical Area—see Appendix B for areas included
Source: U.S. Census Bureau, 2010-2012 American Community Survey 3-Year Estimates

Poverty Rate

Area	All Ages	Under 18 Years Old	18 to 64 Years Old	65 Years and Over
City	26.4	39.0	24.7	15.0
MSA[1]	11.8	15.5	11.4	7.4
U.S.	15.7	22.2	14.6	9.3

Note: Figures are percentage of people whose income during the past 12 months was below the poverty level; (1) Figures cover the Richmond, VA Metropolitan Statistical Area—see Appendix B for areas included
Source: U.S. Census Bureau, 2010-2012 American Community Survey 3-Year Estimates

Personal Bankruptcy Filing Rate

Area	2008	2009	2010	2011	2012	2013
Richmond city County	4.41	4.77	5.80	5.13	4.55	4.54
U.S.	3.53	4.61	4.97	4.37	3.76	3.29

Note: Numbers are per 1,000 population and include Chapter 7 and Chapter 13 filings
Source: Federal Deposit Insurance Corporation, Regional Economic Conditions, March 20, 2014

EMPLOYMENT

Labor Force and Employment

Area	Civilian Labor Force			Workers Employed		
	Dec. 2012	Dec. 2013	% Chg.	Dec. 2012	Dec. 2013	% Chg.
City	100,762	101,449	0.7	92,647	94,314	1.8
MSA[1]	659,432	665,236	0.9	619,573	630,722	1.8
U.S.	154,904,000	154,408,000	-0.3	143,060,000	144,423,000	1.0

Note: Data is not seasonally adjusted and covers workers 16 years of age and older; (1) Metropolitan Statistical Area—see Appendix B for areas included
Source: Bureau of Labor Statistics, Local Area Unemployment Statistics

Unemployment Rate

Area	2013											
	Jan.	Feb.	Mar.	Apr.	May	Jun.	Jul.	Aug.	Sep.	Oct.	Nov.	Dec.
City	8.9	8.0	7.4	7.2	7.7	8.2	8.3	8.1	7.6	7.8	7.3	7.0
MSA[1]	6.6	6.1	5.6	5.4	6.0	6.3	6.2	6.0	5.7	5.8	5.3	5.2
U.S.	8.5	8.1	7.6	7.1	7.3	7.8	7.7	7.3	7.0	7.0	6.6	6.5

Note: Data is not seasonally adjusted and covers workers 16 years of age and older; All figures are percentages; (1) Metropolitan Statistical Area—see Appendix B for areas included
Source: Bureau of Labor Statistics, Local Area Unemployment Statistics

Employment by Occupation

Occupation Classification	City (%)	MSA[1] (%)	U.S. (%)
Management, Business, Science, and Arts	38.9	39.7	36.0
Natural Resources, Construction, and Maintenance	6.0	8.4	9.1
Production, Transportation, and Material Moving	9.1	9.6	12.0
Sales and Office	24.6	25.7	24.7
Service	21.4	16.6	18.2

Note: Figures cover employed civilians 16 years of age and older; (1) Figures cover the Richmond, VA Metropolitan Statistical Area—see Appendix B for areas included
Source: U.S. Census Bureau, 2010-2012 American Community Survey 3-Year Estimates

Employment by Industry

| Sector | MSA[1] | | U.S. |
	Number of Employees	Percent of Total	Percent of Total
Construction	n/a	n/a	4.2
Education and Health Services	92,800	14.5	15.5
Financial Activities	48,200	7.5	5.7
Government	114,100	17.9	16.1
Information	7,800	1.2	1.9
Leisure and Hospitality	56,900	8.9	10.2
Manufacturing	32,100	5.0	8.7
Mining and Logging	n/a	n/a	0.6
Other Services	31,100	4.9	3.9
Professional and Business Services	97,900	15.3	13.7
Retail Trade	72,900	11.4	11.4
Transportation and Utilities	21,300	3.3	3.8
Wholesale Trade	28,200	4.4	4.2

Note: Figures cover non-farm employment as of December 2013 and are not seasonally adjusted;
(1) Metropolitan Statistical Area—see Appendix B for areas included; n/a not available
Source: Bureau of Labor Statistics, Current Employment Statistics, Employment, Hours, and Earnings

Occupations with Greatest Projected Employment Growth: 2010 – 2020

Occupation[1]	2010 Employment	2020 Projected Employment	Numeric Employment Change	Percent Employment Change
Retail Salespersons	123,960	146,560	22,600	18.2
Office Clerks, General	95,910	114,570	18,660	19.5
Personal Care Aides	23,440	41,720	18,280	78.0
Combined Food Preparation and Serving Workers, Including Fast Food	87,610	105,340	17,730	20.2
Software Developers, Systems Software	31,370	48,180	16,810	53.6
Registered Nurses	63,120	77,860	14,730	23.3
Management Analysts	57,440	72,140	14,700	25.6
Software Developers, Applications	31,900	44,600	12,700	39.8
Nursing Aides, Orderlies, and Attendants	35,730	46,110	10,380	29.1
Home Health Aides	13,370	23,540	10,170	76.1

Note: Projections cover Virginia; (1) Sorted by numeric employment change
Source: www.projectionscentral.com, State Occupational Projections, 2010–2020 Long-Term Projections

Fastest Growing Occupations: 2010 – 2020

Occupation[1]	2010 Employment	2020 Projected Employment	Numeric Employment Change	Percent Employment Change
Biomedical Engineers	460	910	440	95.9
Personal Care Aides	23,440	41,720	18,280	78.0
Home Health Aides	13,370	23,540	10,170	76.1
Helpers—Brickmasons, Blockmasons, Stonemasons, and Tile and Marble Setters	1,340	2,140	810	60.4
Interpreters and Translators	4,850	7,780	2,930	60.3
Helpers—Carpenters	2,500	3,990	1,490	59.4
Meeting, Convention, and Event Planners	3,660	5,670	2,010	54.8
Software Developers, Systems Software	31,370	48,180	16,810	53.6
Veterinary Technologists and Technicians	1,340	2,040	710	52.8
Reinforcing Iron and Rebar Workers	370	560	190	52.3

Note: Projections cover Virginia; (1) Sorted by percent employment change and excludes occupations with numeric employment change less than 100
Source: www.projectionscentral.com, State Occupational Projections, 2010–2020 Long-Term Projections

Average Wages

Occupation	$/Hr.	Occupation	$/Hr.
Accountants and Auditors	33.61	Maids and Housekeeping Cleaners	9.60
Automotive Mechanics	19.92	Maintenance and Repair Workers	18.31
Bookkeepers	17.74	Marketing Managers	62.98
Carpenters	18.44	Nuclear Medicine Technologists	30.90
Cashiers	9.61	Nurses, Licensed Practical	19.23
Clerks, General Office	14.44	Nurses, Registered	30.32
Clerks, Receptionists/Information	13.22	Nursing Assistants	11.44
Clerks, Shipping/Receiving	15.43	Packers and Packagers, Hand	12.84
Computer Programmers	38.28	Physical Therapists	39.35
Computer Systems Analysts	38.59	Postal Service Mail Carriers	23.71
Computer User Support Specialists	24.88	Real Estate Brokers	27.71
Cooks, Restaurant	10.79	Retail Salespersons	12.43
Dentists	78.56	Sales Reps., Exc. Tech./Scientific	34.63
Electrical Engineers	40.88	Sales Reps., Tech./Scientific	44.28
Electricians	21.48	Secretaries, Exc. Legal/Med./Exec.	16.41
Financial Managers	61.79	Security Guards	12.89
First-Line Supervisors/Managers, Sales	20.33	Surgeons	112.78
Food Preparation Workers	10.36	Teacher Assistants	10.90
General and Operations Managers	58.75	Teachers, Elementary School	26.30
Hairdressers/Cosmetologists	17.09	Teachers, Secondary School	26.40
Internists	98.97	Telemarketers	14.06
Janitors and Cleaners	11.00	Truck Drivers, Heavy/Tractor-Trailer	18.70
Landscaping/Groundskeeping Workers	12.01	Truck Drivers, Light/Delivery Svcs.	16.58
Lawyers	56.65	Waiters and Waitresses	10.48

Note: Wage data covers the Richmond, VA Metropolitan Statistical Area—see Appendix B for areas included. Hourly wages for elementary/secondary school teachers and teacher assistants were calculated by the editors from annual wage data assuming a 40 hour work week; n/a not available.
Source: Bureau of Labor Statistics, Metro Area Occupational Employment and Wage Estimates, May 2013

RESIDENTIAL REAL ESTATE

Building Permits

Area	Single-Family			Multi-Family			Total		
	2012	2013	Pct. Chg.	2012	2013	Pct. Chg.	2012	2013	Pct. Chg.
City	119	106	-10.9	721	743	3.1	840	849	1.1
MSA[1]	2,840	3,555	25.2	1,431	1,450	1.3	4,271	5,005	17.2
U.S.	518,695	620,802	19.7	310,963	370,020	19.0	829,658	990,822	19.4

Note: (1) Metropolitan Statistical Area—see Appendix B for areas included; figures represent new, privately-owned housing units authorized (unadjusted data); All permit data are based on estimates with imputation.
Source: U.S. Census Bureau, Manufacturing, Mining, and Construction Statistics, Building Permits, 2012, 2013

Homeownership Rate

Area	2006 (%)	2007 (%)	2008 (%)	2009 (%)	2010 (%)	2011 (%)	2012 (%)	2013 (%)
MSA[1]	68.9	72.7	72.4	72.2	68.1	65.2	67.0	65.4
U.S.	68.8	68.1	67.8	67.4	66.9	66.1	65.4	65.1

Note: (1) Figures cover the Richmond, VA Metropolitan Statistical Area—see Appendix B for areas included
Source: U.S. Census Bureau, Housing Vacancies and Homeownership Annual Statistics: 2013

Housing Vacancy Rates

Area	Gross Vacancy Rate[2] (%)			Year-Round Vacancy Rate[3] (%)			Rental Vacancy Rate[4] (%)			Homeowner Vacancy Rate[5] (%)		
	2011	2012	2013	2011	2012	2013	2011	2012	2013	2011	2012	2013
MSA[1]	12.4	13.8	14.5	12.0	13.0	13.6	13.7	17.5	11.4	2.4	1.4	2.4
U.S.	14.2	13.8	13.8	11.1	10.8	10.7	9.5	8.7	8.3	2.5	2.0	2.0

Note: (1) Figures cover the Richmond, VA Metropolitan Statistical Area—see Appendix B for areas included; (2) The percentage of the total housing inventory that is vacant; (3) The percentage of the housing inventory (excluding seasonal units) that is year-round vacant; (4) The percentage of rental inventory that is vacant for rent; (5) The percentage of homeowner inventory that is vacant for sale
Source: U.S. Census Bureau, Housing Vacancies and Homeownership Annual Statistics: 2013

TAXES

State Corporate Income Tax Rates

State	Tax Rate (%)	Income Brackets ($)	Num. of Brackets	Financial Institution Tax Rate (%)[a]	Federal Income Tax Ded.
Virginia	6.0	Flat rate	1	6.0	No

Note: Tax rates as of January 1, 2014; (a) Rates listed are the corporate income tax rate applied to financial institutions or excise taxes based on income. Some states have other taxes based upon the value of deposits or shares.
Source: Federation of Tax Administrators, "State Corporate Income Tax Rates, 2014"

State Individual Income Tax Rates

State	Tax Rate (%)	Income Brackets ($)	Num. of Brackets	Personal Exempt. ($)[1] Single	Personal Exempt. ($)[1] Dependents	Fed. Inc. Tax Ded.
Virginia	2.0 - 5.75	3,000 - 17,001	4	930	930	No

Note: Tax rates as of January 1, 2014; Local- and county-level taxes are not included; n/a not applicable;
(1) Married joint filers generally receive double the single exemption
Source: Federation of Tax Administrators, "State Individual Income Tax Rates, 2014"

Various State and Local Tax Rates

State	State and Local Sales and Use (%)	State Sales and Use (%)	Gasoline[1] (¢/gal.)	Cigarette[2] ($/pack)	Spirits[3] ($/gal.)	Wine[4] ($/gal.)	Beer[5] ($/gal.)
Virginia	5.3	5.30 (b)	17.28	0.300	19.19 (g)	1.51	0.26

Note: All tax rates as of January 1, 2014; (1) The American Petroleum Institute has developed a methodology for determining the average tax rate on a gallon of fuel. Rates may include any of the following: excise taxes, environmental fees, storage tank fees, other fees or taxes, general sales tax, and local taxes. In states where gasoline is subject to the general sales tax, or where the fuel tax is based on the average sale price, the average rate determined by API is sensitive to changes in the price of gasoline. States that fully or partially apply general sales taxes to gasoline: CA, CO, GA, IL, IN, MI, NY; (2) The federal excise tax of $1.0066 per pack and local taxes are not included; (3) Rates are those applicable to off-premise sales of 40% alcohol by volume (a.b.v.) distilled spirits in 750ml containers. Local excise taxes are excluded; (4) Rates are those applicable to off-premise sales of 11% a.b.v. non-carbonated wine in 750ml containers; (5) Rates are those applicable to off-premise sales of 4.7% a.b.v. beer in 12 ounce containers; (b) Three states levy mandatory, statewide, local add-on sales taxes at the state level: California (1%), Utah (1.25%), and Virginia (1%). These amounts are included in the state sales tax column; (g) States where the government controls sales. In these "control states," products are subject to ad valorem mark-up and excise taxes. The excise tax rate is calculated using a methodology developed by the Distilled Spirits Council of the United States.
Source: Tax Foundation, 2014 Facts & Figures: How Does Your State Compare?

State Business Tax Climate Index Rankings

State	Overall Rank	Corporate Tax Index Rank	Individual Income Tax Index Rank	Sales Tax Index Rank	Unemployment Insurance Tax Index Rank	Property Tax Index Rank
Virginia	26	6	37	6	35	26

Note: The index is a measure of how each state's tax laws affect economic performance. The lower the rank, the more favorable a state's tax system is for business. States without a given tax are given a ranking of 1. The scores/rankings for the District of Columbia do not affect other states. The 2014 index represents the tax climate as of July 1, 2013.
Source: Tax Foundation, State Business Tax Climate Index 2014

COMMERCIAL UTILITIES

Typical Monthly Electric Bills

Area	Commercial Service ($/month) 1,500 kWh	Commercial Service ($/month) 40 kW demand 14,000 kWh	Industrial Service ($/month) 1,000 kW demand 200,000 kWh	Industrial Service ($/month) 50,000 kW demand 15,000,000 kWh
City	161	1,273	22,650	1,281,975
Average[1]	197	1,636	25,662	1,485,307

Note: Based on total rates in effect July 1, 2013; (1) average based on 180 utilities surveyed
Source: Edison Electric Institute, Typical Bills and Average Rates Report, Summer 2013

TRANSPORTATION

Means of Transportation to Work

| Area | Car/Truck/Van | | Public Transportation | | | Bicycle | Walked | Other Means | Worked at Home |
	Drove Alone	Car-pooled	Bus	Subway	Railroad				
City	71.9	10.5	5.3	0.1	0.0	2.1	4.3	1.4	4.4
MSA[1]	81.7	9.4	1.6	0.0	0.0	0.4	1.3	0.8	4.6
U.S.	76.4	9.7	2.6	1.7	0.5	0.6	2.8	1.3	4.3

Note: Figures are percentages and cover workers 16 years of age and older; (1) Figures cover the Richmond, VA Metropolitan Statistical Area—see Appendix B for areas included
Source: U.S. Census Bureau, 2010-2012 American Community Survey 3-Year Estimates

Travel Time to Work

Area	Less Than 10 Minutes	10 to 19 Minutes	20 to 29 Minutes	30 to 44 Minutes	45 to 59 Minutes	60 to 89 Minutes	90 Minutes or More
City	11.6	38.5	26.8	14.9	3.9	2.4	1.9
MSA[1]	9.4	30.4	27.1	21.9	6.1	2.9	2.2
U.S.	13.5	29.8	20.9	20.1	7.5	5.6	2.5

Note: Figures are percentages and include workers 16 years old and over; (1) Figures cover the Richmond, VA Metropolitan Statistical Area—see Appendix B for areas included
Source: U.S. Census Bureau, 2010-2012 American Community Survey 3-Year Estimates

Travel Time Index

Area	1985	1990	1995	2000	2005	2010	2011
Urban Area[1]	1.05	1.07	1.13	1.11	1.13	1.11	1.11
Average[2]	1.09	1.14	1.16	1.19	1.23	1.18	1.18

Note: Travel Time Index—the ratio of travel time in the peak period to the travel time at free-flow conditions. For example, a value of 1.30 indicates a 20-minute free-flow trip takes 26 minutes in the peak. Free-flow speeds (60 mph on freeways and 35 mph on principal arterials) are used as the comparison threshold; (1) Covers the Richmond VA urban area; (2) average of 498 urban areas
Source: Texas Transportation Institute, Urban Mobility Report 2012, December 2012

Public Transportation

Agency Name / Mode of Transportation	Vehicles Operated in Maximum Service	Annual Unlinked Passenger Trips (in thous.)	Annual Passenger Miles (in thous.)
Greater Richmond Transit Company (GRTC)			
Bus (directly operated)	135	9,353.0	37,675.7
Demand Response (directly operated)	70	119.4	1,344.6
Demand Response (purchased transportation)	61	147.3	1,878.9
Vanpool (purchased transportation)	125	390.6	27,417.6

Source: Federal Transit Administration, National Transit Database, 2012

Air Transportation

Airport Name and Code / Type of Service	Passenger Airlines[1]	Passenger Enplanements	Freight Carriers[2]	Freight (lbs.)
Richmond International (RIC)				
Domestic service (U.S. carriers - 2013)	33	1,591,839	14	58,533,860
International service (U.S. carriers - 2012)	9	2,689	0	0

Note: (1) Includes all U.S.-based major, minor and commuter airlines that carried at least one passenger during the year; (2) Includes all U.S.-based airlines and freight carriers that transported at least one lb. of freight during the year.
Source: Bureau of Transportation Statistics, The Intermodal Transportation Database, Air Carriers: T-100 Domestic Market (U.S. Carriers), 2013; Bureau of Transportation Statistics, The Intermodal Transportation Database, Air Carriers: T-100 International Market (U.S. Carriers), 2012

Other Transportation Statistics

Major Highways:	I-64; I-85; I-95
Amtrak Service:	Yes
Major Waterways/Ports:	Port of Richmond

Source: Amtrak.com; Google Maps

BUSINESSES

Major Business Headquarters

Company Name	Rankings	
	Fortune[1]	Forbes[2]
Altria Group	159	-
CarMax	259	-
Dominion Resources	210	-
Genworth Financial	271	-
MeadWestvaco	448	-
Performance Food Group	-	22

Note: (1) Fortune 500—companies that produce a 10-K are ranked 1 to 500 based on 2012 revenue; (2) all private companies with at least $2 billion in annual revenue through the end of their most current fiscal year are ranked 1 to 224; companies listed are headquartered in the city; dashes indicate no ranking
Source: Fortune, "Fortune 500," May 20, 2013; Forbes, "America's Largest Private Companies," December 18, 2013

Minority- and Women-Owned Businesses

Group	All Firms		Firms with Paid Employees			
	Firms	Sales ($000)	Firms	Sales ($000)	Employees	Payroll ($000)
Asian	532	226,391	246	212,321	1,651	35,150
Black	3,161	295,471	399	237,522	3,441	89,942
Hispanic	182	78,638	27	71,865	347	9,524
Women	4,337	699,800	810	594,847	6,706	169,594
All Firms	15,141	50,228,287	4,971	49,752,855	114,908	5,877,335

Note: Figures cover firms located in the city; minority- and women-owned business are defined as firms in which the corresponding group own 51% or more of the stock or equity of the company
Source: U.S. Census Bureau, 2007 Economic Census, Survey of Business Owners (2012 Survey of Business Owners data will be released starting in June 2015)

HOTELS & CONVENTION CENTERS

Hotels/Motels

Area	5 Star		4 Star		3 Star		2 Star		1 Star		Not Rated	
	Num.	Pct.[3]	Num.	Pct.[3]	Num.	Pct.[3]	Num.	Pct.[3]	Num.	Pct.[3]	Num.	Pct.[3]
City[1]	0	0.0	4	2.3	42	24.1	108	62.1	10	5.7	10	5.7
Total[2]	142	0.9	1,005	6.0	5,147	30.9	8,578	51.4	408	2.4	1,397	8.4

Note: (1) Figures cover Richmond and vicinity; (2) Figures cover all 100 cities in this book; (3) Percentage of hotels which have a given star rating; Star ratings are determined by expedia.com and offer an indication of the general quality of a particular hotel.
Source: expedia.com, April 7, 2014

Major Convention Centers

Name	Overall Space (sq. ft.)	Exhibit Space (sq. ft.)	Meeting Space (sq. ft.)	Meeting Rooms
Greater Richmond Convention Center	n/a	178,159	n/a	36

Note: Table includes convention centers located in the Richmond, VA metro area; n/a not available
Source: Original research

Living Environment

COST OF LIVING

Cost of Living Index

Composite Index	Groceries	Housing	Utilities	Trans-portation	Health Care	Misc. Goods/Services
101.4	98.2	89.4	107.6	99.7	106.5	110.1

Note: The Cost of Living Index measures regional differences in the cost of consumer goods and services, excluding taxes and non-consumer expenditures, for professional and managerial households in the top income quintile. It is based on more than 50,000 prices covering almost 60 different items for which prices are collected three times a year by chambers of commerce, economic development organizations or university applied economic centers in each participating urban area. The numbers shown should be read as a percentage above or below the national average of 100. For example, a value of 115.4 in the groceries column indicates that grocery prices are 15.4% higher than the national average. Small differences in the index numbers should not be interpreted as significant; Figures cover the Richmond VA urban area.
Source: The Council for Community and Economic Research, ACCRA Cost of Living Index, 2013

Grocery Prices

Area[1]	T-Bone Steak ($/pound)	Frying Chicken ($/pound)	Whole Milk ($/half gal.)	Eggs ($/dozen)	Orange Juice ($/64 oz.)	Coffee ($/11.5 oz.)
City[2]	10.12	1.30	2.36	1.74	3.08	4.30
Avg.	10.19	1.28	2.34	1.81	3.48	4.39
Min.	8.56	0.94	1.44	1.19	2.78	3.40
Max.	14.82	2.28	3.56	3.73	6.23	7.32

Note: (1) Values for the local area are compared with the average, minimum and maximum values for all 327 areas in the Cost of Living Index; (2) Figures cover the Richmond VA urban area; **T-Bone Steak** *(price per pound);* **Frying Chicken** *(price per pound, whole fryer);* **Whole Milk** *(half gallon carton);* **Eggs** *(price per dozen, Grade A, large);* **Orange Juice** *(64 oz. Tropicana or Florida Natural);* **Coffee** *(11.5 oz. can, vacuum-packed, Maxwell House, Hills Bros, or Folgers).*
Source: The Council for Community and Economic Research, ACCRA Cost of Living Index, 2013

Housing and Utility Costs

Area[1]	New Home Price ($)	Apartment Rent ($/month)	All Electric ($/month)	Part Electric ($/month)	Other Energy ($/month)	Telephone ($/month)
City[2]	249,778	871	-	85.49	75.66	33.45
Avg.	295,864	900	171.38	91.82	70.12	27.73
Min.	185,506	458	117.80	48.81	33.67	17.16
Max.	1,358,917	3,783	441.68	171.40	372.65	39.47

Note: (1) Values for the local area are compared with the average, minimum and maximum values for all 327 areas in the Cost of Living Index; (2) Figures cover the Richmond VA urban area; **New Home Price** *(2,400 sf living area, 8,000 sf lot, in urban area with full utilities);* **Apartment Rent** *(950 sf 2 bedroom/1.5 or 2 bath, unfurnished, excluding all utilities except water);* **All Electric** *(average monthly cost for an all-electric home);* **Part Electric** *(average monthly cost for a part-electric home);* **Other Energy** *(average monthly cost for natural gas, fuel oil, coal, wood, and any other forms of energy except electricity);* **Telephone** *(price includes basic monthly rate for a private residential line plus additional local usage charges incurred by a family of four).*
Source: The Council for Community and Economic Research, ACCRA Cost of Living Index, 2013

Health Care, Transportation, and Other Costs

Area[1]	Doctor ($/visit)	Dentist ($/visit)	Optometrist ($/visit)	Gasoline ($/gallon)	Beauty Salon ($/visit)	Men's Shirt ($)
City[2]	90.42	103.67	119.17	3.37	51.78	22.08
Avg.	101.40	86.48	96.16	3.44	33.87	26.55
Min.	61.67	50.83	50.12	3.08	18.92	12.48
Max.	182.71	152.50	223.78	4.33	68.22	52.03

Note: (1) Values for the local area are compared with the average, minimum and maximum values for all 327 areas in the Cost of Living Index; (2) Figures cover the Richmond VA urban area; **Doctor** *(general practitioners routine exam of an established patient);* **Dentist** *(adult teeth cleaning and periodic oral examination);* **Optometrist** *(full vision eye exam for established adult patient);* **Gasoline** *(one gallon regular unleaded, national brand, including all taxes, cash price at self-service pump if available);* **Beauty Salon** *(woman's shampoo, trim, and blow-dry);* **Men's Shirt** *(cotton/polyester dress shirt, pinpoint weave, long sleeves).*
Source: The Council for Community and Economic Research, ACCRA Cost of Living Index, 2013

HOUSING

House Price Index (HPI)

Area	National Ranking[2]	Quarterly Change (%)	One-Year Change (%)	Five-Year Change (%)
MSA[1]	151	0.26	1.90	-13.49
U.S.[3]	–	1.20	7.69	4.18

Note: The HPI is a weighted repeat sales index. It measures average price changes in repeat sales or refinancings on the same properties. This information is obtained by reviewing repeat mortgage transactions on single-family properties whose mortgages have been purchased or securitized by Fannie Mae or Freddie Mac in January 1975; (1) Richmond, VA Metropolitan Statistical Area—see Appendix B for areas included; (2) Rankings are based on annual percentage change for all metro areas containing at least 15,000 transactions over the last 10 years and ranges from 1 to 283; (3) figures based on a weighted average of Census Division estimates using a seasonally adjusted, purchase-only index; all figures are for the period ending December 31, 2013

Source: Federal Housing Finance Agency, House Price Index, February 25, 2014

Median Single-Family Home Prices

Area	2011	2012	2013p	Percent Change 2012 to 2013
MSA[1]	n/a	n/a	n/a	n/a
U.S. Average	166.2	177.2	197.4	11.4

Note: Figures are median sales prices of existing single-family homes in thousands of dollars; (p) preliminary; n/a not available; (1) Richmond, VA Metropolitan Statistical Area—see Appendix B for areas included
Source: National Association of Realtors, Median Sales Price of Existing Single-Family Homes for Metropolitan Areas, 4th Quarter 2013

Qualifying Income Based on Median Sales Price of Existing Single-Family Homes

Area	With 5% Down ($)	With 10% Down ($)	With 20% Down ($)
MSA[1]	n/a	n/a	n/a
U.S. Average	45,395	43,006	38,228

Note: Figures are preliminary; Qualifying income is based on a mortgage rate of 4.4%. Monthly principal and interest payment is limited to 25% of income; n/a not available; (1) Richmond, VA Metropolitan Statistical Area—see Appendix B for areas included
Source: National Association of Realtors, Qualifying Income Based on Median Sales Price of Existing Single-Family Homes for Metropolitan Areas, 4th Quarter 2013

Median Apartment Condo-Coop Home Prices

Area	2011	2012	2013p	Percent Change 2012 to 2013
MSA[1]	n/a	n/a	n/a	n/a
U.S. Average	165.1	173.7	194.9	12.2

Note: Figures are median sales prices of existing apartment condo-coop homes in thousands of dollars; (p) preliminary; n/a not available; (1) Richmond, VA Metropolitan Statistical Area—see Appendix B for areas included
Source: National Association of Realtors, Median Sales Price of Existing Apartment Condo-Coop Homes for Metropolitan Areas, 4th Quarter 2013

Gross Monthly Rent

Area	Under $200	$200 -299	$300 -499	$500 -749	$750 -999	$1,000 -1,499	$1,500 and up	Median ($)
City	6.2	4.5	5.3	17.8	32.5	27.2	6.5	870
MSA[1]	3.0	2.6	4.5	15.1	32.2	33.6	9.0	944
U.S.	1.7	3.3	8.1	22.7	24.3	25.7	14.3	889

Note: Figures are percentages except for Median; Gross rent is the contract rent plus the estimated average monthly cost of utilities (electricity, gas, and water and sewer) and fuels (oil, coal, kerosene, wood, etc.) if these are paid by the renter (or paid for the renter by someone else); (1) Figures cover the Richmond, VA Metropolitan Statistical Area—see Appendix B for areas included
Source: U.S. Census Bureau, 2010-2012 American Community Survey 3-Year Estimates

Year Housing Structure Built

Area	2010 or Later	2000 -2009	1990 -1999	1980 -1989	1970 -1979	1960 -1969	1950 -1959	1940 -1949	Before 1940	Median Year
City	0.3	6.4	3.7	6.5	12.2	12.3	16.1	10.0	32.6	1955
MSA[1]	0.6	16.3	15.3	16.5	16.6	11.0	9.7	4.5	9.4	1979
U.S.	0.5	14.9	13.8	13.9	15.9	11.1	10.9	5.5	13.5	1976

Note: Figures are percentages except for Median Year; (1) Figures cover the Richmond, VA Metropolitan Statistical Area—see Appendix B for areas included
Source: U.S. Census Bureau, 2010-2012 American Community Survey 3-Year Estimates

HEALTH

Health Risk Data

Category	MSA[1] (%)	U.S. (%)
Adults aged 18–64 who have any kind of health care coverage	84.3	79.6
Adults who reported being in good or excellent health	84.6	83.1
Adults who are current smokers	19.4	19.6
Adults who are heavy drinkers[2]	6.1	6.1
Adults who are binge drinkers[3]	15.4	16.9
Adults who are overweight (BMI 25.0 - 29.9)	37.3	35.8
Adults who are obese (BMI 30.0 - 99.8)	27.5	27.6
Adults who participated in any physical activities in the past month	78.5	77.1
Adults 50+ who have ever had a sigmoidoscopy or colonoscopy	74.8	67.3
Women aged 40+ who have had a mammogram within the past two years	82.0	74.0
Men aged 40+ who have had a PSA test within the past two years	48.7	45.2
Adults aged 65+ who have had flu shot within the past year	61.1	60.1
Adults who always wear a seatbelt	92.6	93.8

Note: Data as of 2012 unless otherwise noted; (1) Figures cover the Richmond, VA Metropolitan Statistical Area—see Appendix B for areas included; (2) Heavy drinkers are classified as males having more than two drinks per day or females having more than one drink per day; (3) Binge drinkers are classified as males having five or more drinks on one occasion or females having four or more drinks on one occasion
Source: Centers for Disease Control and Prevention, Behavioral Risk Factor Surveillance System, SMART: Selected Metropolitan/Micropolitan Area Risk Trends, 2012

Chronic Health Indicators

Category	MSA[1] (%)	U.S. (%)
Adults who have ever been told they had a heart attack	3.5	4.5
Adults who have ever been told they had a stroke	2.4	2.9
Adults who have been told they currently have asthma	8.9	8.9
Adults who have ever been told they have arthritis	25.9	25.7
Adults who have ever been told they have diabetes[2]	10.9	9.7
Adults who have ever been told they had skin cancer	5.3	5.7
Adults who have ever been told they had any other types of cancer	5.6	6.5
Adults who have ever been told they have COPD	5.4	6.2
Adults who have ever been told they have kidney disease	1.5	2.5
Adults who have ever been told they have a form of depression	13.9	18.0

Note: Data as of 2012 unless otherwise noted; (1) Figures cover the Richmond, VA Metropolitan Statistical Area—see Appendix B for areas included; (2) Figures do not include pregnancy-related, borderline, or pre-diabetes
Source: Centers for Disease Control and Prevention, Behavioral Risk Factor Surveillance System, SMART: Selected Metropolitan/Micropolitan Area Risk Trends, 2012

Mortality Rates for the Top 10 Causes of Death in the U.S.

ICD-10[a] Sub-Chapter	ICD-10[a] Code	Age-Adjusted Mortality Rate[1] per 100,000 population	
		County[2]	U.S.
Malignant neoplasms	C00-C97	214.0	174.2
Ischaemic heart diseases	I20-I25	108.3	119.1
Other forms of heart disease	I30-I51	81.1	49.6
Chronic lower respiratory diseases	J40-J47	43.1	43.2
Cerebrovascular diseases	I60-I69	58.8	40.3
Organic, including symptomatic, mental disorders	F01-F09	35.7	30.5
Other degenerative diseases of the nervous system	G30-G31	20.2	26.3
Other external causes of accidental injury	W00-X59	27.6	25.1
Diabetes mellitus	E10-E14	27.9	21.3
Hypertensive diseases	I10-I15	23.8	18.8

Note: (a) ICD-10 = International Classification of Diseases 10th Revision; (1) Mortality rates are a three year average covering 2008-2010; (2) Figures cover Richmond city
Source: Centers for Disease Control and Prevention, National Center for Health Statistics. Compressed Mortality File 1999-2010 on CDC WONDER Online Database, released January 2013. Data are compiled from the Compressed Mortality File 1999-2010, Series 20 No. 2P, 2013.

Mortality Rates for Selected Causes of Death

ICD-10[a] Sub-Chapter	ICD-10[a] Code	Age-Adjusted Mortality Rate[1] per 100,000 population	
		County[2]	U.S.
Assault	X85-Y09	16.1	5.5
Diseases of the liver	K70-K76	17.1	12.4
Human immunodeficiency virus (HIV) disease	B20-B24	12.4	3.0
Influenza and pneumonia	J09-J18	18.4	16.4
Intentional self-harm	X60-X84	11.9	11.8
Malnutrition	E40-E46	Suppressed	0.8
Obesity and other hyperalimentation	E65-E68	Suppressed	1.6
Renal failure	N17-N19	32.2	13.6
Transport accidents	V01-V99	10.4	12.6
Viral hepatitis	B15-B19	*2.8	2.2

Note: (a) ICD-10 = International Classification of Diseases 10th Revision; (1) Mortality rates are a three year average covering 2008-2010; (2) Figures cover Richmond city; (*) Unreliable data as per CDC
Source: Centers for Disease Control and Prevention, National Center for Health Statistics. Compressed Mortality File 1999-2010 on CDC WONDER Online Database, released January 2013. Data are compiled from the Compressed Mortality File 1999-2010, Series 20 No. 2P, 2013.

Health Insurance Coverage

Area	With Health Insurance	With Private Health Insurance	With Public Health Insurance	Without Health Insurance	Population Under Age 18 Without Health Insurance
City	83.0	59.0	32.9	17.0	4.7
MSA[1]	87.2	73.1	25.0	12.8	6.3
U.S.	84.9	65.4	30.4	15.1	7.5

Note: Figures are percentages that cover the civilian noninstitutionalized population; (1) Figures cover the Richmond, VA Metropolitan Statistical Area—see Appendix B for areas included
Source: U.S. Census Bureau, 2010-2012 American Community Survey 3-Year Estimates

Number of Medical Professionals

Area[1]	MDs[2]	DOs[2,3]	Dentists	Podiatrists	Chiropractors	Optometrists
Local (number)	1,403	37	261	21	14	27
Local (rate[4])	679.8	17.9	123.8	10.0	6.6	12.8
U.S. (rate[4])	267.6	19.6	61.7	5.6	24.7	14.5

Note: Data as of 2012 unless noted; (1) Local data covers Richmond City; (2) Data as of 2011; (3) Doctor of Osteopathic Medicine; (4) rate per 100,000 population
Source: Area Resource File (ARF) 2012-2013. U.S. Department of Health and Human Services, Health Resources and Services Administration, Bureau of Health Professions

Best Hospitals

According to *U.S. News*, the Richmond, VA metro area is home to one of the best hospitals in the U.S.: **Virginia Commonwealth University Medical Center** (2 specialties). The hospital listed was nationally ranked in at least one adult specialty. Only 147 hospitals nationwide were nationally ranked in one or more specialties. Eighteen hospitals in the U.S. made the Honor Roll by ranking near the top in at least six specialties.*U.S. News Online, "America's Best Hospitals 2013-14"*

According to *U.S. News*, the Richmond, VA metro area is home to one of the best children's hospitals in the U.S.: **Children's Hospital of Richmond at VCU**. The hospital listed was highly ranked in at least one pediatric specialty. Eighty-seven hospitals in the U.S. ranked in at least one specialty. Ten children's hospitals in the U.S. made the Honor Roll by ranking near the top in three or more specialties.*U.S. News Online, "America's Best Children's Hospitals 2013-14"*

EDUCATION

Public School District Statistics

District Name	Schls	Pupils	Pupil/ Teacher Ratio	Minority Pupils[1] (%)	Free Lunch Eligible[2] (%)	IEP[3] (%)
Richmond City Public Schs	53	23,336	n/a	90.5	66.7	18.5

Note: Table includes school districts with 2,000 or more students; (1) Percentage of students that are not non-Hispanic white; (2) Percentage of students that are eligible for the free lunch program; (3) Percentage of students that have an Individualized Education Program.
Source: U.S. Department of Education, National Center for Education Statistics, Common Core of Data, Local Education Agency (School District) Universe Survey: School Year 2011-2012; U.S. Department of Education, National Center for Education Statistics, Common Core of Data, Public Elementary/Secondary School Universe Survey: School Year 2011-2012

Best High Schools

High School Name	Rank[1]	Grad. Rate[2] (%)	Coll.[3] (%)	AP/IB/ AICE Tests[4]	AP/IB/ AICE Score[5]	SAT Score[6]	ACT Score[6]
M.L. Walker Governor's School for Govt & Intl Studies[6]	n/a	n/a	n/a	n/a	n/a	n/a	n/a
Maggie L. Walker Governor's School for Government and Intl Studies	14	100	100	1.5	4.3	2128	n/a
Open H.S.	917	100	98	0.7	1.8	1369	19.1
Richmond Community H.S.	313	100	98	1.1	1.8	1489	24.0

Note: (1) Public schools are ranked from 1 to 2,000 based on the following self-reported statistics (with the corresponding weight used in calculating their overall score). Schools that were newly founded and did not have a graduating senior class in 2012 were excluded; (2) Four-year, on-time graduation rate (25%); (3) Percent of 2011 graduates who were accepted to college (25%); (4) AP/IB/AICE tests taken per student (25%); (5) Average AP/IB/AICE exam score (10%); (6) Average SAT and/or ACT score (10%); Percent of students enrolled in at least one AP/IB/AICE course (5%)—data not shown; n/a not available
Source: Newsweek and The Daily Beast, "America's Best High Schools 2013"

Highest Level of Education

Area	Less than H.S.	H.S. Diploma	Some College, No Deg.	Associate Degree	Bachelor's Degree	Master's Degree	Prof. School Degree	Doctorate Degree
City	18.8	22.8	18.7	5.4	21.0	9.0	2.9	1.4
MSA[1]	13.4	27.1	20.9	6.6	20.4	8.5	2.0	1.2
U.S.	14.1	28.3	21.3	7.8	18.0	7.5	1.9	1.2

Note: Figures cover persons age 25 and over; (1) Figures cover the Richmond, VA Metropolitan Statistical Area—see Appendix B for areas included
Source: U.S. Census Bureau, 2010-2012 American Community Survey 3-Year Estimates

Educational Attainment by Race

Area	High School Graduate or Higher (%)					Bachelor's Degree or Higher (%)				
	Total	White	Black	Asian	Hisp.[2]	Total	White	Black	Asian	Hisp.[2]
City	81.2	89.1	74.8	82.9	40.8	34.3	57.1	12.3	59.6	11.2
MSA[1]	86.6	89.9	80.5	85.2	55.5	32.0	37.4	17.9	56.6	16.6
U.S.	85.9	88.1	82.5	85.5	63.1	28.6	30.0	18.4	50.2	13.4

Note: Figures shown cover persons 25 years old and over; (1) Figures cover the Richmond, VA Metropolitan Statistical Area—see Appendix B for areas included; (2) People of Hispanic origin can be of any race
Source: U.S. Census Bureau, 2010-2012 American Community Survey 3-Year Estimates

School Enrollment by Grade and Control

Area	Preschool (%)		Kindergarten (%)		Grades 1 - 4 (%)		Grades 5 - 8 (%)		Grades 9 - 12 (%)	
	Public	Private	Public	Private	Public	Private	Public	Private	Public	Private
City	52.7	47.3	86.4	13.6	87.2	12.8	87.1	12.9	86.7	13.3
MSA[1]	38.5	61.5	89.4	10.6	90.9	9.1	92.0	8.0	91.4	8.6
U.S.	56.9	43.1	87.8	12.2	89.9	10.1	90.0	10.0	90.8	9.2

Note: Figures shown cover persons 3 years old and over; (1) Figures cover the Richmond, VA Metropolitan Statistical Area—see Appendix B for areas included
Source: U.S. Census Bureau, 2010-2012 American Community Survey 3-Year Estimates

Average Salaries of Public School Classroom Teachers

Area	2012-13		2013-14		Percent Change 2012-13 to 2013-14	Percent Change 2003-04 to 2013-14
	Dollars	Rank[1]	Dollars	Rank[1]		
Virginia	48,670	36	49,233	36	1.16	21.1
U.S. Average	56,103	–	56,689	–	1.04	21.8

Note: (1) State rank ranges from 1 to 51 where 1 indicates highest salary.
Source: National Education Association, Rankings & Estimates: Rankings of the States 2013 and Estimates of School Statistics 2014, March 2014

Higher Education

Four-Year Colleges			Two-Year Colleges			Medical Schools[1]	Law Schools[2]	Voc/ Tech[3]
Public	Private Non-profit	Private For-profit	Public	Private Non-profit	Private For-profit			
1	4	2	1	1	4	1	1	2

Note: Figures cover institutions located within the city limits and include main campuses only; (1) includes schools accredited by the Liaison Committee on Medical Education and the American Osteopathic Association's Commission on Osteopathic College Accreditation; (2) includes ABA-accredited schools, schools with provisional ABA accreditation, and state accredited schools; (3) includes all schools with programs that are less than 2 years.
Source: National Center for Education Statistics, Integrated Postsecondary Education System (IPEDS), 2012-13; Association of American Medical Colleges, Member List, April 24, 2014; American Osteopathic Association, Member List, April 24, 2014; Law School Admission Council, Official Guide to ABA-Approved Law Schools Online, April 24, 2014; Wikipedia, List of Medical Schools in the United States, April 24, 2014; Wikipedia, List of Law Schools in the United States, April 24, 2014

According to *U.S. News & World Report*, the Richmond, VA metro area is home to one of the best national universities in the U.S.: **Virginia Commonwealth University** (#167). The indicators used to capture academic quality fall into a number of categories: assessment by administrators at peer institutions; retention of students; faculty resources; student selectivity; financial resources; alumni giving; high school counselor ratings of colleges; and graduation rate. *U.S. News & World Report*, "America's Best Colleges 2014"

According to *U.S. News & World Report*, the Richmond, VA metro area is home to two of the best liberal arts colleges in the U.S.: **University of Richmond** (#25); **Randolph–Macon College** (#134). The indicators used to capture academic quality fall into a number of categories: assessment by administrators at peer institutions; retention of students; faculty resources; student selectivity; financial resources; alumni giving; high school counselor ratings of colleges; and graduation rate. *U.S. News & World Report*, "America's Best Colleges 2014"

According to *U.S. News & World Report*, the Richmond, VA metro area is home to one of the top 100 law schools in the U.S.: **University of Richmond (Williams)** (#53). The rankings are based on a weighted average of 12 measures of quality: peer assessment score; assessment score by lawyers/judges; median LSAT scores; median undergrad GPA; acceptance rate; employment rates for graduates; placement success; bar passage rate; faculty resources; expenditures per student; student/faculty ratio; and library resources. *U.S. News & World Report*, "America's Best Graduate Schools, Law, 2014"

PRESIDENTIAL ELECTION

2012 Presidential Election Results

Area	Obama	Romney	Other
Richmond City	77.0	21.4	1.6
U.S.	51.0	47.2	1.8

Note: Results are percentages and may not add to 100% due to rounding
Source: Dave Leip's Atlas of U.S. Presidential Elections

EMPLOYERS

Major Employers

Company Name	Industry
Altria Group	Cigarettes
Anthem Health Plans of Virginia	Hospital and medical service plans
Bon Secours-St. Mary's Hosp Richmond	General medical and surgical hospitals
Chippenham Hospital	General medical and surgical hospitals
City of Richmond, Virginia	Executive and legislative combined
County of Henrico	General government administration
Defense Logistics Agency	Government national mortgage association
Dominion Resources	Electric services
Dominion Resources Services	Generation, electric power
Federal Bank of Richmond	Public relations services
Federal Reserve Bank of Richmond	Federal reserve banks
National Railroad Passenger Corporation	Interurban railways
Pfizer Consumer Healthcare	Pharmaceutical preparations
Reynolds Consumer Products Holdings	Packaging and labeling services
Reynolds Metals Company	Aluminum cans
Veterans Health Administration	Administration of veterans' affairs
Virginia Commonwealth University	University
Virginia Department of Social Services	Administration of social and manpower programs
Virginia Department of Transportation	Civil engineering
Virginia Electric and Power Company	Electric services

Note: Companies shown are located within the Richmond, VA Metropolitan Statistical Area.
Source: Hoovers.com; Wikipedia

Best Companies to Work For

CarMax, headquartered in Richmond, is among "The 100 Best Companies to Work For." To pick the 100 Best Companies to Work For, *Fortune* partnered with the Great Place to Work Institute. Two hundred fifty seven firms participated in this year's survey. Two-thirds of a company's score is based on the results of the Institute's Trust Index survey, which is sent to a random sample of employees from each company. The questions related to attitudes about management's credibility, job satisfaction, and camaraderie. The other third of the scoring is based on the company's responses to the Institute's Culture Audit, which includes detailed questions about pay and benefit programs, and a series of open-ended questions about hiring practices, internal communication, training, recognition programs, and diversity efforts. Any company that is at least five years old with more than 1,000 U.S. employees is eligible. *Fortune, "The 100 Best Companies to Work For," 2014*

Bon Secours Virginia, headquartered in Richmond, is among the "100 Best Companies for Working Mothers." Criteria: workforce representation; child care; flexibility programs; and leave policies. This year *Working Mother* gave particular weight to flexible work arrangements, women's advancement programs, and paid maternity leave. *Working Mother, "100 Best Companies 2013"*

Bon Secours Virginia; Virginia Commonwealth University, headquartered in Richmond, are among the "50 Best Employers for Workers Over 50." Criteria: recruiting practices; opportunities for training, education, and career development; workplace accommodations; alternative work options, such as flexible scheduling, job sharing, and phased retirement; employee health and pension benefits; and retiree benefits. Employers with at least 50 employees based in the U.S. are eligible, including for-profit companies, not-for-profit organizations, and government employers. *AARP, "2013 AARP Best Employers for Workers Over 50"*

Altria Client Services, headquartered in Richmond, is among the "100 Best Places to Work in IT." To qualify, companies, both public and private, had to have a minimum of 50 IT employees and were selected based on average salary and bonus increases, the percentage of IT staffers promoted, IT staff turnover rates, training and development programs, and the percentage of women and minorities in IT staff and management positions. In addition, *Computerworld* looked at retention efforts, programs for recognizing and rewarding outstanding performances, and benefits such as flextime, elder care and child care, and reimbursement for college tuition and the cost of pursuing technology certifications. *Computerworld, "100 Best Places to Work in IT 2013"*

PUBLIC SAFETY

Crime Rate

Area	All Crimes	Violent Crimes				Property Crimes		
		Murder	Forcible Rape	Robbery	Aggrav. Assault	Burglary	Larceny -Theft	Motor Vehicle Theft
City	5,029.4	20.2	18.3	304.6	305.6	976.9	2,953.8	450.0
Suburbs[1]	2,356.0	4.1	11.9	51.9	93.3	416.8	1,669.2	108.7
Metro[2]	2,806.7	6.8	13.0	94.5	129.1	511.3	1,885.8	166.3
U.S.	3,246.1	4.7	26.9	112.9	242.3	670.2	1,959.3	229.7

Note: Figures are crimes per 100,000 population; (1) All areas within the metro area that are located outside the city limits; (2) Figures cover the Richmond, VA Metropolitan Statistical Area—see Appendix B for areas included
Source: FBI Uniform Crime Reports, 2012

Hate Crimes

Area	Number of Quarters Reported	Bias Motivation				
		Race	Religion	Sexual Orientation	Ethnicity	Disability
City	4	1	0	4	0	0
U.S.	4	2,797	1,099	1,135	667	92

Source: Federal Bureau of Investigation, Hate Crime Statistics 2012

Identity Theft Consumer Complaints

Area	Complaints	Complaints per 100,000 Population	Rank[2]
MSA[1]	883	73.1	137
U.S.	290,056	91.8	-

Note: (1) Figures cover the Richmond, VA Metropolitan Statistical Area—see Appendix B for areas included; (2) Rank ranges from 1 to 377 where 1 indicates greatest number of identity theft complaints per 100,000 population
Source: Federal Trade Commission, Consumer Sentinel Network Data Book for January–December 2013

Fraud and Other Consumer Complaints

Area	Complaints	Complaints per 100,000 Population	Rank[2]
MSA[1]	6,197	513.0	16
U.S.	1,811,724	595.2	-

Note: (1) Figures cover the Richmond, VA Metropolitan Statistical Area—see Appendix B for areas included; (2) Rank ranges from 1 to 377 where 1 indicates greatest number of identity theft complaints per 100,000 population
Source: Federal Trade Commission, Consumer Sentinel Network Data Book for January–December 2013

RECREATION

Culture

Dance[1]	Theatre[1]	Instrumental Music[1]	Vocal Music[1]	Series and Festivals	Museums and Art Galleries[2]	Zoos and Aquariums[3]
3	3	1	0	5	44	0

Note: (1) Number of professional performing groups; (2) Based on organizations with primary SIC code 8412; (3) AZA-accredited
Source: The Grey House Performing Arts Directory, 2013; Association of Zoos & Aquariums, AZA Member Zoos & Aquariums, April 2014; www.AccuLeads.com, May 1, 2014

Professional Sports Teams

Team Name	League	Year Established
No teams are located in the metro area		

Source: Wikipedia, Major Professional Sports Teams of the United States and Canada, April 25, 2014

CLIMATE

Average and Extreme Temperatures

Temperature	Jan	Feb	Mar	Apr	May	Jun	Jul	Aug	Sep	Oct	Nov	Dec	Yr.
Extreme High (°F)	80	82	91	96	98	104	105	103	103	99	86	80	105
Average High (°F)	47	50	59	69	78	85	88	86	81	71	60	50	69
Average Temp. (°F)	38	40	48	58	66	75	78	77	71	60	50	41	58
Average Low (°F)	28	30	37	45	55	63	68	67	60	48	38	31	48
Extreme Low (°F)	-6	-8	11	19	31	40	51	47	35	21	14	1	-8

Note: Figures cover the years 1921-1990
Source: National Climatic Data Center, International Station Meteorological Climate Summary, 9/96

Average Precipitation/Snowfall/Humidity

Precip./Humidity	Jan	Feb	Mar	Apr	May	Jun	Jul	Aug	Sep	Oct	Nov	Dec	Yr.
Avg. Precip. (in.)	3.3	3.0	3.5	3.1	3.7	3.7	5.2	4.9	3.3	3.1	2.9	3.1	43.0
Avg. Snowfall (in.)	5	4	2	Tr	0	0	0	0	0	Tr	1	2	13
Avg. Rel. Hum. 7am (%)	79	79	78	76	81	82	85	89	90	89	84	80	83
Avg. Rel. Hum. 4pm (%)	54	51	46	43	51	53	56	58	57	53	51	55	52

Note: Figures cover the years 1921-1990; Tr = Trace amounts (<0.05 in. of rain; <0.5 in. of snow)
Source: National Climatic Data Center, International Station Meteorological Climate Summary, 9/96

Weather Conditions

Temperature			Daytime Sky			Precipitation		
10°F & below	32°F & below	90°F & above	Clear	Partly cloudy	Cloudy	0.01 inch or more precip.	0.1 inch or more snow/ice	Thunder-storms
3	79	41	90	147	128	115	7	43

Note: Figures are average number of days per year and cover the years 1921-1990
Source: National Climatic Data Center, International Station Meteorological Climate Summary, 9/96

HAZARDOUS WASTE

Superfund Sites

Richmond has one hazardous waste site on the EPA's Superfund Final National Priorities List: **Rentokil, Inc. (Virginia Wood Preserving Division)**. *U.S. Environmental Protection Agency, Final National Priorities List, April 26, 2014*

AIR & WATER QUALITY

Air Quality Index

Area	Percent of Days when Air Quality was...[2]					AQI Statistics[2]	
	Good	Moderate	Unhealthy for Sensitive Groups	Unhealthy	Very Unhealthy	Maximum	Median
MSA[1]	81.6	18.1	0.3	0.0	0.0	124	39

Note: (1) Data covers the Richmond, VA Metropolitan Statistical Area—see Appendix B for areas included; (2) Based on 365 days with AQI data in 2013. Air Quality Index (AQI) is an index for reporting daily air quality. EPA calculates the AQI for five major air pollutants regulated by the Clean Air Act: ground-level ozone, particle pollution (aka particulate matter), carbon monoxide, sulfur dioxide, and nitrogen dioxide. The AQI runs from 0 to 500. The higher the AQI value, the greater the level of air pollution and the greater the health concern. There are six AQI categories: "Good" AQI is between 0 and 50. Air quality is considered satisfactory; "Moderate" AQI is between 51 and 100. Air quality is acceptable; "Unhealthy for Sensitive Groups" When AQI values are between 101 and 150, members of sensitive groups may experience health effects; "Unhealthy" When AQI values are between 151 and 200 everyone may begin to experience health effects; "Very Unhealthy" AQI values between 201 and 300 trigger a health alert; "Hazardous" AQI values over 300 trigger warnings of emergency conditions (not shown).
Source: U.S. Environmental Protection Agency, Air Quality Index Report, 2013

Air Quality Index Pollutants

Area	Percent of Days when AQI Pollutant was...[2]					
	Carbon Monoxide	Nitrogen Dioxide	Ozone	Sulfur Dioxide	Particulate Matter 2.5	Particulate Matter 10
MSA[1]	0.0	8.2	46.3	1.4	44.1	0.0

*Note: (1) Data covers the Richmond, VA Metropolitan Statistical Area—see Appendix B for areas included;
(2) Based on 365 days with AQI data in 2013. The Air Quality Index (AQI) is an index for reporting daily air
quality. EPA calculates the AQI for five major air pollutants regulated by the Clean Air Act: ground-level ozone,
particle pollution (also known as particulate matter), carbon monoxide, sulfur dioxide, and nitrogen dioxide.
The AQI runs from 0 to 500. The higher the AQI value, the greater the level of air pollution and the greater the
health concern.
Source: U.S. Environmental Protection Agency, Air Quality Index Report, 2013*

Air Quality Trends: Ozone

	2003	2004	2005	2006	2007	2008	2009	2010	2011	2012
MSA[1]	0.082	0.076	0.082	0.082	0.081	0.082	0.065	0.078	0.076	0.076

*Note: (1) Data covers the Richmond, VA Metropolitan Statistical Area—see Appendix B for areas included. The
values shown are the composite ozone concentration averages among trend sites based on the highest fourth
daily maximum 8-hour concentration in parts per million. These trends are based on sites having an adequate
record of monitoring data during the trend period. Data from exceptional events are included.
Source: U.S. Environmental Protection Agency, Air Quality Monitoring Information, "Air Quality Trends by
City, 2000-2012"*

Maximum Air Pollutant Concentrations: Particulate Matter, Ozone, CO and Lead

	Particulate Matter 10 (ug/m³)	Particulate Matter 2.5 Wtd AM (ug/m³)	Particulate Matter 2.5 24-Hr (ug/m³)	Ozone (ppm)	Carbon Monoxide (ppm)	Lead (ug/m³)
MSA[1] Level	29	8.9	20	0.078	2	0.01
NAAQS[2]	150	15	35	0.075	9	0.15
Met NAAQS[2]	Yes	Yes	Yes	No	Yes	Yes

*Note: (1) Data covers the Richmond, VA Metropolitan Statistical Area—see Appendix B for areas included;
Data from exceptional events are included; (2) National Ambient Air Quality Standards; ppm = parts per
million; ug/m³ = micrograms per cubic meter; n/a not available.
Concentrations: Particulate Matter 10 (coarse particulate)—highest second maximum 24-hour concentration;
Particulate Matter 2.5 Wtd AM (fine particulate)—highest weighted annual mean concentration; Particulate
Matter 2.5 24-Hour (fine particulate)—highest 98th percentile 24-hour concentration; Ozone—highest fourth
daily maximum 8-hour concentration; Carbon Monoxide—highest second maximum non-overlapping 8-hour
concentration; Lead—maximum running 3-month average
Source: U.S. Environmental Protection Agency, Air Quality Monitoring Information, "Air Quality Statistics by
City, 2012"*

Maximum Air Pollutant Concentrations: Nitrogen Dioxide and Sulfur Dioxide

	Nitrogen Dioxide AM (ppb)	Nitrogen Dioxide 1-Hr (ppb)	Sulfur Dioxide AM (ppb)	Sulfur Dioxide 1-Hr (ppb)	Sulfur Dioxide 24-Hr (ppb)
MSA[1] Level	10	51	n/a	21	n/a
NAAQS[2]	53	100	30	75	140
Met NAAQS[2]	Yes	Yes	n/a	Yes	n/a

*Note: (1) Data covers the Richmond, VA Metropolitan Statistical Area—see Appendix B for areas included;
Data from exceptional events are included; (2) National Ambient Air Quality Standards; ppm = parts per
million; ug/m³ = micrograms per cubic meter; n/a not available.
Concentrations: Nitrogen Dioxide AM—highest arithmetic mean concentration; Nitrogen Dioxide
1-Hr—highest 98th percentile 1-hour daily maximum concentration; Sulfur Dioxide AM—highest annual mean
concentration; Sulfur Dioxide 1-Hr—highest 99th percentile 1-hour daily maximum concentration; Sulfur
Dioxide 24-Hr—highest second maximum 24-hour concentration
Source: U.S. Environmental Protection Agency, Air Quality Monitoring Information, "Air Quality Statistics by
City, 2012"*

Drinking Water

Water System Name	Pop. Served	Primary Water Source Type	Violations[1]	
			Health Based	Monitoring/ Reporting
City of Richmond	197,000	Surface	0	0

Note: (1) Based on violation data from January 1, 2013 to December 31, 2013 (includes unresolved violations from earlier years)
Source: U.S. Environmental Protection Agency, Office of Ground Water and Drinking Water, Safe Drinking Water Information System (based on data extracted February 10, 2014)

Drinking Water

Water System Name	Population Served	Primary Water Source Type	Violations Health Based	Violations Monitoring Reporting
City of Richmond	197,000	Surface	0	0

Note (1): Based on violation data from January 1, 2013 to December 31, 2013. Updates available since the violations from earlier years.

Source: U.S. Environmental Protection Agency, Office of Ground Water and Drinking Water, Safe Drinking Water Information System (based on data extracted on February 10, 2014)

Virginia Beach, Virginia

Background

Virginia Beach, on the shores of the Chesapeake Bay and the Atlantic Ocean, is a paradise for beach lovers. With nearly half a million residents, it is also one of the fastest-growing cities on the East Coast.

The history of Virginia Beach begins in 1607 when English settlers led by Captain John Smith first reached Virginia's shore at Cape Henry aboard the *Susan Constant,* the *Godspeed,* and the *Discovery.* The 100 colonists, sent by the Virginia Company to investigate trade possibilities, shortly moved up the James River to found the first permanent English settlement in America at Jamestown. The first actual settlement within the Virginia Beach city limits was at Lynnhaven Bay in 1621.

With the connection of a railway to Norfolk in the late nineteenth century, Virginia Beach became a popular shore resort and was incorporated as a town in 1906, then as a city in 1952. In 1963, all of neighboring Princess Ann County merged with the city, and today's Virginia Beach covers a territory of 310 square miles, with 38 miles of shoreline. It is the largest city in Virginia and the largest resort city in the world, with tourism still the economic mainstay.

The city naturally enjoys a lifestyle oriented to the water, with 28 miles of public beaches and 79 miles of scenic waterways. The beaches are enjoyed most of the year, while sailing and fishing opportunities are varied and virtually inexhaustible. There are three state and regional parks and three national wildlife refuges in the city, with 208 city parks, making it a municipality with a unique mix of urban, natural, and ecotourist attractions.

Agribusiness also contributes to the vitality of the area, with more than 32,700 acres of land under cultivation, and the construction and real estate industries are robust. Convention and trade shows annually produce millions of dollars in revenues. The labor force is abundant, productive, and energetic, offering a rich range of professional, technical, blue-collar, and clerical skills. Local government receives high grades from residents and visitors alike, and the city received the American Society of Public Administration's first-ever Innovation Recognition Award for excellence in organizational development, strategic planning, quality initiatives, and process improvements.

Virginia Beach is located alongside the Port of Hampton Roads, one of the world's finest harbors. Rail service serves major industrial centers, and nearby Norfolk International Airport serves seven major and seven commuter airlines.

It was at Cape Henry that the French Admiral Comte de Grassein, during the Revolutionary War, came to the aid of American patriots by blockading the British fleet during the final and decisive Battle of Yorktown, and the area to this day has been home to strategically important military bases. The modern phase of this development began during World War II, when the navy built Oceana Naval Air Station in Virginia Beach, which is now home to four bases employing armed-services and civilian workers.

Virginia Beach and its environs are home to 11 colleges and universities, including the Virginia Beach Higher Education Center, the College of William and Mary, Old Dominion University, Norfolk State University, Virginia Wesleyan College, Eastern Virginia Medical School, and Tidewater Community College.

There are more than 200 art and cultural organizations based in the city, including a symphony, opera, theater groups, and many museums. The Virginia Marine Science Museum hosts one of the most attended aquariums in the nation.

Virginia Beach enjoys a temperate maritime climate influenced by the Gulf Stream. Winters are mild, rarely freezing, and splendid beach weather characterizes the area from spring through fall.

Rankings

General Rankings

- Among the 50 largest U.S. cities, Virginia Beach placed #18 in Vocativ's "semi-exhaustive, mostly scientific" city Livability Index for people aged 35 and under. Average salary, unemployment rates, rents, and other living costs were considered, along with bike lanes, low-cost broadband, cheap takeout, self-service laundries, the price of a pint of Guinness, music venues, and vintage clothing stores. *vocative.com, "The Livability Index: The Best U.S. Cities for People 35 and Under," November 7, 2013*

- Virginia Beach was selected as one of America's best cities by *Bloomberg Businessweek*. The city ranked #40 out of 50. Criteria: leisure attributes (the number of restaurants, bars, libraries, museums, professional sports teams, and park acres by population); educational attributes (public school performance, the number of colleges, and graduate degree holders); economic factors (2011 income and June and July 2012 unemployment); crime; and air quality. *Bloomberg BusinessWeek, "America's Best Cities," September 26, 2012*

Business/Finance Rankings

- Building on the U.S. Department of Labor's Occupational Information Network Data Collection Program, the Brookings Institution defined STEM occupations and job opportunities for STEM workers at various levels of educational attainment. The Virginia Beach metro area was one of the ten metro areas where workers in low-education-level STEM jobs earn the highest relative wages. *www.brookings.edu, "The Hidden Stem Economy," June 10, 2013*

- The financial literacy site NerdWallet.com set out to identify the 20 most promising cities for job seekers, analyzing data for the nation's 50 largest cities. Virginia Beach was ranked #20. Criteria: unemployment rate; population growth; median income; selected monthly owner costs. *NerdWallet.com, "Best Cities for Job Seekers," January 7, 2014*

- The Brookings Institution ranked the 50 largest cities in the U.S. based on income inequality. Virginia Beach was ranked #50. (#1 = greatest ineqality). Criteria: the cities were ranked based on the "95/20 ratio." This figure represents the income at which a household earns more than 95 percent of all other households, divided by the income at which a household earns more than only 20 percent of all other households. *Brookings Institution, "Income Inequality in America's 50 Largest Cities, 2007-2012," February 20, 2014*

- Virginia Beach was ranked #92 out of 100 metro areas in terms of economic performance (#1 = best) during the recession and recovery from trough quarter through the second quarter of 2013. Criteria: percent change in employment; percentage point change in unemployment rate; percent change in gross metropolitan product; percent change in House Price Index. *Brookings Institution, MetroMonitor: Tracking Economic Recession and Recovery in America's 100 Largest Metropolitan Areas, September 2013*

- The Virginia Beach metro area was identified as one of the most debt-ridden places in America by credit reporting agency Equifax. The metro area was ranked #1. Criteria: proportion of average yearly income owed to credit card companies. *Equifax, "The Most Debt-Ridden Cities in America," February 23, 2012*

- The Virginia Beach metro area was identified as one of the most affordable metropolitan areas in America by *Forbes*. The area ranked #14 out of 20. Criteria: the 100 largest metro areas in the U.S. were analyzed based on housing affordability and cost-of-living. *Forbes.com, "America's Most Affordable Cities," March 11, 2014*

- Virginia Beach was identified as one of America's most frugal metro areas by *Coupons.com*. The city ranked #15 out of 25. Criteria: online coupon usage. *Coupons.com, "Top 25 Most Frugal Cities of 2012," February 19, 2013*

- Virginia Beach was identified as one of America's most frugal metro areas by *Coupons.com*. The city ranked #13 out of 25. Criteria: Grocery IQ and coupons.com mobile app usage. *Coupons.com, "Top 25 Most On-the-Go Frugal Cities of 2012," February 19, 2013*

- The Virginia Beach metro area appeared on the Milken Institute "2013 Best Performing Cities" list. Rank: #123 out of 200 large metro areas. Criteria: job growth; wage and salary growth; high-tech output growth. *Milken Institute, "Best-Performing Cities 2013," December 2013*

- *Forbes* ranked the 200 most populous metro areas in the U.S. in terms of the "Best Places for Business and Careers." The Virginia Beach metro area was ranked #77. Criteria: costs (business and living); job growth (past and projected); income growth; educational attainment (college and high school); projected economic growth; cultural and recreational opportunities; net migration patterns; number of highly ranked colleges. *Forbes, "The Best Places for Business and Careers," August 7, 2013*

Children/Family Rankings

- Virginia Beach was identified as one of the best cities for raising a family by *24/7 Wall St.* The city ranked #2. The nation's 100 largest cities were evaluated on the following criteria: large public outdoor spaces; top hospitals; strong schools; low unemployment; high educational attainment; low violent crime rates. *24/7 Wall St., "The 10 Best U.S. Cities for Raising a Family," January 13, 2012*

- Virginia Beach was selected as one of the best cities for families to live by *Parenting* magazine. The city ranked #27 out of 100. Criteria: education; health; community; *Parenting's* Culture & Charm Index. *Parenting.com, "The 2012 Best Cities for Families List"*

Dating/Romance Rankings

- Of the 100 U.S. cities surveyed by *Men's Health* in its quest to identify the nation's best cities for dating and forming relationships, Virginia Beach was ranked #39 for online dating (#1 = best). *Men's Health, "The Best and Worst Cities for Online Dating," January 30, 2013*

Education Rankings

- *Men's Health* ranked 100 U.S. cities in terms of their education levels. Virginia Beach was ranked #18 (#1 = most educated city). Criteria: high school graduation rates; school enrollment; educational attainment; number of households who have outstanding student loans; number of households whose members have taken adult-education courses. *Men's Health, "Where School Is In: The Most and Least Educated Cities," September 12, 2011*

- Virginia Beach was selected as one of America's most literate cities. The city ranked #20 out of the 77 largest U.S. cities. Criteria: number of booksellers; library resources; Internet resources; educational attainment; periodical publishing resources; newspaper circulation. *Central Connecticut State University, "America's Most Literate Cities, 2013"*

Environmental Rankings

- The Virginia Beach metro area came in at #255 for the relative comfort of its climate on Sperling's list of "chill cities," as measured by the Sperling Heat Index. All 361 metro areas are included. Criteria included daytime high temperatures, nighttime low temperatures, dew point, and relative humidity at the high temperatures. *www.bertsperling.com, "Sperling's Chill Cities," July 18, 2013*

- Sperling's BestPlaces assessed 379 metropolitan areas of the United States for the likelihood of dangerously extreme weather events or earthquakes. In general the Southeast and South-Central regions have the highest risk of weather extremes and earthquakes, while the Pacific Northwest enjoys the lowest risk. Of the least risky metropolitan areas, the Virginia Beach metro area was ranked #299. *www.bestplaces.net, "Safest Places from Natural Disasters," April 2011*

- The U.S. Environmental Protection Agency (EPA) released a list of U.S. metropolitan areas with the most ENERGY STAR certified buildings in 2012. The Virginia Beach metro area was ranked #25 out of 25. *U.S. Environmental Protection Agency, "Top Cities With the Most ENERGY STAR Certified Buildings in 2012," March 12, 2013*

- Virginia Beach was selected as one of 22 "Smarter Cities" for energy by the Natural Resources Defense Council. Criteria: investment in green power; energy efficiency measures; conservation. *Natural Resources Defense Council, "2010 Smarter Cities," July 19, 2010*

Food/Drink Rankings

- *Men's Health* ranked 100 major U.S. cities in terms of alcohol intoxication. Virginia Beach ranked #8 (#1 = most sober).Criteria: binge drinking; alcohol-related traffic accidents, arrests, and fatalities. *Men's Health, "The Drunkest Cities in America," November 19, 2013*

Health/Fitness Rankings

- For each of the 50 most populous metro areas in the United States, the American College of Sports Medicine's American Fitness Index evaluated infrastructure, community assets, and policies that encourage healthy and fit lifestyles, including preventive health behaviors, levels of chronic disease conditions, health care access, and community resources and policies that support physical activity. The Virginia Beach metro area ranked #18 for "community fitness." Personal health indicators were considered as well as community and environmental indicators. *www.americanfitnessindex.org, "ACSM American Fitness Index Health and Community Fitness Status of the 50 Largest Metropolitan Areas," May 2013*

- Virginia Beach was selected as one of the 25 fittest cities in America by *Men's Fitness Online*. It ranked #18 out of America's 50 largest cities. Criteria: fitness centers and sport stores; nutrition; sports participation; TV viewing; overweight/sedentary; junk food; air quality; geography; commute; parks and open space; city recreational facilities; access to healthcare; motivation; mayor and city initiatives; state obesity initiatives. *Men's Fitness, "The Fittest and Fattest Cities in America," March 5, 2012*

- Virginia Beach was identified as a "2013 Spring Allergy Capital." The area ranked #20 out of 100. Three groups of factors were used to identify the most severe cities for people with allergies during the spring season: annual pollen levels; medicine utilization; access to board-certified allergists. *Asthma and Allergy Foundation of America, "Spring Allergy Capitals 2013"*

- Virginia Beach was identified as a "2013 Fall Allergy Capital." The area ranked #34 out of 100. Three groups of factors were used to identify the most severe cities for people with allergies during the fall season: annual pollen levels; medicine utilization; access to board-certified allergists. *Asthma and Allergy Foundation of America, "Fall Allergy Capitals 2013"*

- Virginia Beach was identified as a "2013 Asthma Capital." The area ranked #26 out of the nation's 100 largest metropolitan areas. Twelve factors were used to identify the most challenging places to live for people with asthma: estimated prevalence; self-reported prevalence; crude death rate for asthma; annual pollen score; annual air quality; public smoking laws; number of board-certified asthma specialists; school inhaler access laws; rescue medication use; controller medication use; uninsured rate; poverty rate. *Asthma and Allergy Foundation of America, "Asthma Capitals 2013"*

- *Men's Health* ranked 100 major U.S. cities in terms of the best and worst cities for men. Virginia Beach ranked #30. Criteria: thirty-three data points were examined covering health, fitness, and quality of life. *Men's Health, "The Best & Worst Cities for Men 2014," December 6, 2013*

- *Men's Health* ranked 100 U.S. cities in terms of the best and worst cities for women. Virginia Beach was ranked among the ten best at #9. Criteria: dozens of statistical parameters of long life in the categories of health, quality of life, and fitness. *Men's Health, "The 10 Best and Worst Cities for Women 2011," January/February 2011*

- The Virginia Beach metro area appeared in the 2013 Gallup-Healthways Well-Being Index. The area ranked #113 out of 189. The Gallup-Healthways Well-Being Index score is an average of six sub-indexes, which individually examine life evaluation, emotional health, work environment, physical health, healthy behaviors, and access to basic necessities. Results are based on telephone interviews conducted as part of the Gallup-Healthways Well-Being Index survey January 2–December 29, 2012, and January 2–December 30, 2013, with a random sample of 531,630 adults, aged 18 and older, living in metropolitan areas in the 50 U.S. states and the District of Columbia. *Gallup-Healthways, "State of American Well-Being," March 25, 2014*

- The Virginia Beach metro area was identified as one of "America's Most Stressful Cities" by *Sperling's BestPlaces.* The metro area ranked #47 out of 50. Criteria: unemployment rate; suicide rate; commute time; mental health; poor rest; alcohol use; violent crime rate; property crime rate; cloudy days annually. *Sperling's BestPlaces, www.BestPlaces.net, "Stressful Cities 2012*

- *Men's Health* ranked 100 U.S. cities in terms of their activity levels. Virginia Beach was ranked #55 (#1 = most active city). Criteria: where and how often residents exercise; percentage of households that watch more than 15 hours of cable television a week and buy more than 11 video games a year; death rate from deep-vein thrombosis, a condition linked to sitting for extended periods of time. *Men's Health, "Where Sit Happens: The Most and Least Active Cities in America," June 20, 2011*

- Virginia Beach was selected as one of the "20 Most Livable U.S. Cities for Wheelchair Users" by the Christopher & Dana Reeve Foundation. The city ranked #15. Criteria: Medicaid eligibility and spending; access to physicians and rehabilitation facilities; access to fitness facilities and recreation; access to paratransit; percentage of people living with disabilities who are employed; clean air; climate. *Christopher & Dana Reeve Foundation, "20 Most Livable U.S. Cities for Wheelchair Users," July 26, 2010*

Real Estate Rankings

- *Forbes* reported that Virginia Beach ranked #5 on its list of cities where renters could get the best value for their money, based on current rental prices, price per square foot, year-over-year changes in rent cost, and cost of renting compared with the cost of purchasing a home. *www.forbes.com, "Renting? Cities to Get the Most Bang for Your Buck," July 19, 2013*

- The Virginia Beach metro area was identified as one of the top 20 housing markets to invest in for 2014 by *Forbes.* The area ranked #18. Criteria: high population and job growth; relatively low home prices which are below equilibrium home price (EHP). The EHP is what the average price for a market should be, if speculation, weird distortions in local income, and other factors (like the housing collapse) weren't present in the market. *Forbes.com, "Best Buy Cities: Where to Invest in Housing in 2014," December 25, 2013*

- Virginia Beach was ranked #237 out of 283 metro areas in terms of house price appreciation in 2013 (#1 = highest rate). *Federal Housing Finance Agency, House Price Index, 4th Quarter 2013*

- Virginia Beach was ranked #66 out of 224 metro areas in terms of housing affordability in 2013 by the National Association of Home Builders (#1 = most affordable). The NAHB-Wells Fargo Housing Opportunity Index (HOI) for a given area is defined as the share of homes sold in that area that would have been affordable to a family earning the local median income, based on standard mortgage underwriting criteria. *National Association of Home Builders®, NAHB-Wells Fargo Housing Opportunity Index, 4th Quarter 2013*

Safety Rankings

- In search of the nation's safest cities, Business Insider looked at the FBI's preliminary Uniform Crime Report, excluding localities with fewer than 200,000 residents. To judge by its low murder, rape, and robbery data, Virginia Beach made the 20 safest cities list, at #12. *www.businessinsider.com, "The 20 Safest Cities in America," July 25, 2013*

- Symantec, in partnership with Sperling's BestPlaces, ranked the 50 largest cities in the U.S. in terms of their vulnerability to cybercrime. The city ranked #42. Criteria: number of cyberattacks and potential infections; level of Internet access; expenditures on smartphones and computer hardware/software; wireless hotspots; broadband connectivity; Internet usage; online purchases. *Symantec, "Riskiest Online Cities of 2012" February 15, 2012*

- Allstate ranked the 200 largest cities in America in terms of driver safety. Virginia Beach ranked #136. Allstate researchers analyzed internal property damage claims over a two-year period from January 2010 to December 2011. A weighted average of the two-year numbers determined the annual percentages. *Allstate, "Allstate America's Best Drivers Report®, August 27, 2013"*

- The National Insurance Crime Bureau ranked 380 metro areas in the U.S. in terms of per capita rates of vehicle theft. The Virginia Beach metro area ranked #189 (#1 = highest rate). Criteria: number of vehicle theft offenses per 100,000 inhabitants in 2012. *National Insurance Crime Bureau, "Hot Spots 2012," June 26, 2013*

- The Virginia Beach metro area was identified as one of the most dangerous metro areas for pedestrians by Transportation for America. The metro area ranked #44 out of 52 metro areas with over 1 million residents. Criteria: area's population divided by the number of pedestrian fatalities in that area. *Transportation for America, "Dangerous by Design 2011"*

Seniors/Retirement Rankings

- The finance website CNNMoney surveyed small U.S. cities that offer exceptional urban amenities at a cost of living somewhat higher than for the top-ten locations but still affordable for retirees. Median home-price figures were supplied by the residential real-estate website Trulia. Virginia Beach was among the eight small cities singled out. *money.cnn.com, "Best Places to Retire with a Nice Nest Egg," October 28, 2013*

- From its Best Cities for Successful Aging indexes, the Milken Institute generated rankings for metropolitan areas, weighing data in eight categories—general indicators, health care, wellness, living arrangements, transportation and general accessibility, financial well-being, education and employment, and community participation. The Virginia Beach metro area was ranked #61 overall in the large metro area category. *Milken Institute, "Best Cities for Successful Aging," July 2012*

- Bankers Life and Casualty Company, in partnership with Sperling's BestPlaces, ranked the nation's 50 largest metro areas in terms of the "Best U.S. Cities for Seniors." The Virginia Beach metro area ranked #41. Criteria: healthcare; transportation; housing; environment; economy; health and longevity; social and spiritual life; crime. *Bankers Life and Casualty Company, Center for a Secure Retirement, "Best U.S. Cities for Seniors 2011," September 2011*

Women/Minorities Rankings

- *Women's Health* examined U.S. cities and identified the 100 best cities for women. Virginia Beach was ranked #7. Criteria: 30 categories were examined from obesity and breast cancer rates to commuting times and hours spent working out. *Women's Health, "Best Cities for Women 2012"*

- The Virginia Beach metro area appeared on *Forbes'* list of the "Best Cities for Minority Entrepreneurs." The area ranked #7 out of 10. Criteria: 52 metropolitan statistical areas were examined. For each ethnicity (African Americans, Asians and Hispanics), the editors measured housing affordability, population growth, income growth, and entrepreneurship (per capita self-employment). *Forbes, "Best Cities for Minority Entrepreneurs," March 23, 2011*

Miscellaneous Rankings

- Virginia Beach was selected as a 2013 Digital Cities Survey winner. The city ranked #5 in the large city (250,000 or more population) category. The survey examined and assessed how city governments are utilizing information technology to operate and deliver quality service to their customers and citizens. Survey questions focused on implementation and adoption of online service delivery; planning and governance; and the infrastructure and architecture that make the transformation to digital government possible. *Center for Digital Government, "2013 Digital Cities Survey," November 7, 2013*

- Business Insider reports on the 2013 Trick-or-Treat Index compiled by the real estate site Zillow, which used its own Home Value Index and Walk Score along with population density and local crime stats to determine that Virginia Beach ranked #20 for "how much candy it gives out versus how far kids have to walk to get it." Zillow also zeroes in on the best neighborhoods in its top 20 cities. *www.businessinsider.com, "These Are the Best Cities for Trick-or-Treating," October 15, 2013*

- Virginia Beach was selected as one of the 10 best run cities in America by *24/7 Wall St.* The city ranked #5. Criteria: the 100 largest cities in the U.S. were ranked in terms of economy, job market, crime, and the welfare of its residents. *24/7 Wall St., "The Best and Worst Run Cities in America," January 15, 2013*

- *Men's Health* ranked 100 U.S. cities by their level of sadness. Virginia Beach was ranked #12 (#1 = saddest city). Criteria: suicide rates; unemployment rates; percentage of households that use antidepressants; percent of population who report feeling blue all or most of the time. *Men's Health, "Frown Towns," November 28, 2011*

- The National Alliance to End Homelessness ranked the 100 most populous metro areas in terms the rate of homelessness. The Virginia Beach metro area ranked #76. Criteria: number of homeless people per 10,000 population in 2011. *National Alliance to End Homelessness, The State of Homelessness in America 2012*

Business Environment

CITY FINANCES

City Government Finances

Component	2011 ($000)	2011 ($ per capita)
Total Revenues	1,708,004	3,929
Total Expenditures	1,826,050	4,200
Debt Outstanding	1,669,399	3,840
Cash and Securities[1]	1,087,178	2,501

Note: (1) Cash and security holdings of a government at the close of its fiscal year, including those of its dependent agencies, utilities, and liquor stores.
Source: U.S Census Bureau, State & Local Government Finances 2011

City Government Revenue by Source

Source	2011 ($000)	2011 ($ per capita)
General Revenue		
From Federal Government	99,876	230
From State Government	537,785	1,237
From Local Governments	245	1
Taxes		
Property	592,363	1,363
Sales and Gross Receipts	194,462	447
Personal Income	0	0
Corporate Income	0	0
Motor Vehicle License	9,018	21
Other Taxes	50,850	117
Current Charges	135,797	312
Liquor Store	0	0
Utility	48,805	112
Employee Retirement	0	0

Source: U.S Census Bureau, State & Local Government Finances 2011

City Government Expenditures by Function

Function	2011 ($000)	2011 ($ per capita)	2011 (%)
General Direct Expenditures			
Air Transportation	0	0	0.0
Corrections	40,997	94	2.2
Education	829,271	1,907	45.4
Employment Security Administration	0	0	0.0
Financial Administration	16,378	38	0.9
Fire Protection	46,311	107	2.5
General Public Buildings	22,548	52	1.2
Governmental Administration, Other	19,869	46	1.1
Health	53,449	123	2.9
Highways	116,200	267	6.4
Hospitals	0	0	0.0
Housing and Community Development	29,878	69	1.6
Interest on General Debt	53,803	124	2.9
Judicial and Legal	16,165	37	0.9
Libraries	15,174	35	0.8
Parking	1,561	4	0.1
Parks and Recreation	101,563	234	5.6
Police Protection	83,603	192	4.6
Public Welfare	69,736	160	3.8
Sewerage	88,422	203	4.8
Solid Waste Management	29,527	68	1.6
Veterans' Services	0	0	0.0
Liquor Store	0	0	0.0
Utility	48,278	111	2.6
Employee Retirement	0	0	0.0

Source: U.S Census Bureau, State & Local Government Finances 2011

DEMOGRAPHICS

Population Growth

Area	1990 Census	2000 Census	2010 Census	Population Growth (%) 1990-2000	Population Growth (%) 2000-2010
City	393,069	425,257	437,994	8.2	3.0
MSA[1]	1,449,389	1,576,370	1,671,683	8.8	6.0
U.S.	248,709,873	281,421,906	308,745,538	13.2	9.7

Note: (1) Figures cover the Virginia Beach-Norfolk-Newport News, VA-NC Metropolitan Statistical Area—see Appendix B for areas included
Source: U.S. Census Bureau, Census 1990, 2000, 2010

Household Size

Area	Persons in Household (%) One	Two	Three	Four	Five	Six	Seven or More	Average Household Size
City	23.7	34.7	18.2	13.8	6.3	2.0	1.3	2.64
MSA[1]	25.9	34.5	17.7	12.9	5.8	1.8	1.3	2.62
U.S.	27.6	33.5	15.7	13.2	6.1	2.4	1.5	2.63

Note: (1) Figures cover the Virginia Beach-Norfolk-Newport News, VA-NC Metropolitan Statistical Area—see Appendix B for areas included
Source: U.S. Census Bureau, 2010-2012 American Community Survey 3-Year Estimates

Race

Area	White Alone[2] (%)	Black Alone[2] (%)	Asian Alone[2] (%)	AIAN[3] Alone[2] (%)	NHOPI[4] Alone[2] (%)	Other Race Alone[2] (%)	Two or More Races (%)
City	68.4	19.2	6.5	0.3	0.1	1.2	4.4
MSA[1]	60.2	31.1	3.7	0.3	0.1	1.1	3.5
U.S.	74.0	12.6	4.9	0.8	0.2	4.7	2.8

Note: (1) Figures cover the Virginia Beach-Norfolk-Newport News, VA-NC Metropolitan Statistical Area—see Appendix B for areas included; (2) Alone is defined as not being in combination with one or more other races; (3) American Indian and Alaska Native; (4) Native Hawaiian and Other Pacific Islander
Source: U.S. Census Bureau, 2010-2012 American Community Survey 3-Year Estimates

Hispanic or Latino Origin

Area	Total (%)	Mexican (%)	Puerto Rican (%)	Cuban (%)	Other (%)
City	6.9	2.1	2.4	0.2	2.3
MSA[1]	5.6	1.8	1.7	0.2	1.9
U.S.	16.6	10.7	1.6	0.6	3.7

Note: Persons of Hispanic or Latino origin can be of any race; (1) Figures cover the Virginia Beach-Norfolk-Newport News, VA-NC Metropolitan Statistical Area—see Appendix B for areas included
Source: U.S. Census Bureau, 2010-2012 American Community Survey 3-Year Estimates

Segregation

Type	Segregation Indices[1] 1990	2000	2010	2010 Rank[2]	Percent Change 1990-2000	Percent Change 1990-2010	Percent Change 2000-2010
Black/White	48.8	46.5	47.8	76	-2.2	-1.0	1.2
Asian/White	35.3	36.3	34.3	79	0.9	-1.0	-2.0
Hispanic/White	30.5	31.6	32.2	90	1.1	1.7	0.6

Note: All figures cover the Metropolitan Statistical Area—see Appendix B for areas included; Figures are based on an analysis of 1990, 2000, and 2010 Census Decennial Census tract data by William H. Frey, Brookings Institution and the University of Michigan Social Science Data Analysis Network. In this analysis all racial groups (whites, blacks, and asians) are non-Hispanic members of those races. Hispanics are shown as a separate category;
(1) Segregation Indices are Dissimilarity Indices that measure the degree to which the minority group is distributed differently than whites across census tracts. They range from 0 (complete integration) to 100 (complete segregation) where the value indicates the percentage of the minority group that needs to move to be distributed exactly like whites; (2) Ranges from 1 (most segregated) to 102 (least segregated); n/a not available.
Source: www.CensusScope.org

Ancestry

Area	German	Irish	English	American	Italian	Polish	French[2]	Scottish	Dutch
City	12.9	11.3	9.2	15.0	6.3	2.7	2.7	2.2	1.2
MSA[1]	10.9	9.6	9.7	11.6	4.5	2.0	2.1	2.2	1.0
U.S.	15.2	11.1	8.2	7.2	5.6	3.1	2.8	1.7	1.4

Note: Figures are the percentage of the total population reporting a particular ancestry. The nine most commonly reported ancestries in the U.S. are shown. Figures include multiple ancestries (e.g. if a person reported being Irish and Italian, they were included in both columns); (1) Figures cover the Virginia Beach-Norfolk-Newport News, VA-NC Metropolitan Statistical Area—see Appendix B for areas included; (2) Excludes Basque
Source: U.S. Census Bureau, 2010-2012 American Community Survey 3-Year Estimates

Foreign-Born Population

Area	Percent of Population Born in								
	Any Foreign Country	Mexico	Asia	Europe	Carribean	South America	Central America[2]	Africa	Canada
City	8.8	0.4	4.6	1.6	0.7	0.5	0.4	0.4	0.2
MSA[1]	6.2	0.4	2.7	1.1	0.5	0.4	0.5	0.4	0.2
U.S.	13.0	3.7	3.7	1.6	1.2	0.9	1.0	0.5	0.3

Note: (1) Figures cover the Virginia Beach-Norfolk-Newport News, VA-NC Metropolitan Statistical Area—see Appendix B for areas included; (2) Excludes Mexico.
Source: U.S. Census Bureau, 2010-2012 American Community Survey 3-Year Estimates

Marital Status

Area	Never Married	Now Married[2]	Separated	Widowed	Divorced
City	30.5	51.0	2.7	4.7	11.0
MSA[1]	32.8	47.6	3.0	5.5	11.0
U.S.	32.4	48.4	2.2	6.0	11.0

Note: Figures are percentages and cover the population 15 years of age and older; (1) Figures cover the Virginia Beach-Norfolk-Newport News, VA-NC Metropolitan Statistical Area—see Appendix B for areas included; (2) Excludes separated
Source: U.S. Census Bureau, 2010-2012 American Community Survey 3-Year Estimates

Age

Area	Percent of Population									Median Age
	Under Age 5	Age 5–19	Age 20–34	Age 35–44	Age 45–54	Age 55–64	Age 65–74	Age 75–84	Age 85+	
City	6.6	19.6	24.0	13.3	14.5	11.1	6.1	3.5	1.3	34.8
MSA[1]	6.5	19.9	23.3	12.5	14.6	11.4	6.7	3.8	1.5	35.4
U.S.	6.4	20.1	20.5	13.1	14.3	12.2	7.3	4.2	1.8	37.3

Note: (1) Figures cover the Virginia Beach-Norfolk-Newport News, VA-NC Metropolitan Statistical Area—see Appendix B for areas included
Source: U.S. Census Bureau, 2010-2012 American Community Survey 3-Year Estimates

Gender

Area	Males	Females	Males per 100 Females
City	217,519	225,583	96.4
MSA[1]	827,442	856,569	96.6
U.S.	153,276,055	158,333,314	96.8

Note: (1) Figures cover the Virginia Beach-Norfolk-Newport News, VA-NC Metropolitan Statistical Area—see Appendix B for areas included
Source: U.S. Census Bureau, 2010-2012 American Community Survey 3-Year Estimates

Religious Groups by Family

Area	Catholic	Baptist	Non-Den.	Methodist[2]	Lutheran	LDS[3]	Pente-costal	Presby-terian[4]	Muslim[5]	Judaism
MSA[1]	6.4	11.6	6.2	5.3	0.7	0.9	1.9	2.0	2.1	0.4
U.S.	19.1	9.3	4.0	4.0	2.3	2.0	1.9	1.6	0.8	0.7

Note: Figures are the number of adherents as a percentage of the total population; (1) Figures cover the Virginia Beach-Norfolk-Newport News, VA-NC Metropolitan Statistical Area—see Appendix B for areas included; (2) Methodist/Pietist; (3) Latter Day Saints; (4) Reformed; (5) Figures are estimates
Source: Association of Statisticians of American Religious Bodies, 2010 U.S. Religion Census: Religious Congregations & Membership Study

Religious Groups by Tradition

Area	Catholic	Evangelical Protestant	Mainline Protestant	Other Tradition	Black Protestant	Orthodox
MSA[1]	6.4	18.0	9.4	4.0	2.3	0.3
U.S.	19.1	16.2	7.3	4.3	1.6	0.3

Note: Figures are the number of adherents as a percentage of the total population; (1) Figures cover the Virginia Beach-Norfolk-Newport News, VA-NC Metropolitan Statistical Area—see Appendix B for areas included
Source: Association of Statisticians of American Religious Bodies, 2010 U.S. Religion Census: Religious Congregations & Membership Study

ECONOMY

Gross Metropolitan Product

Area	2011	2012	2013	2014	Rank[2]
MSA[1]	82.1	85.2	87.2	90.2	39

Note: Figures are in billions of dollars; (1) Figures cover the Virginia Beach-Norfolk-Newport News, VA-NC Metropolitan Statistical Area—see Appendix B for areas included; (2) Rank is based on 2014 data and ranges from 1 to 363
Source: The United States Conference of Mayors, U.S. Metro Economies: Outlook—Gross Metropolitan Product, with Metro Employment Projections, November 2013

Economic Growth

Area	2011 (%)	2012 (%)	2013 (%)	2014 (%)	Rank[2]
MSA[1]	0.5	1.9	0.9	1.4	165
U.S.	1.6	2.5	1.7	2.5	–

Note: Figures are real gross metropolitan product (GMP) growth rates and represent annual average percent change; (1) Figures cover the Virginia Beach-Norfolk-Newport News, VA-NC Metropolitan Statistical Area—see Appendix B for areas included; (2) Rank is based on 2013 data and ranges from 1 to 363
Source: The United States Conference of Mayors, U.S. Metro Economies: Outlook—Gross Metropolitan Product, with Metro Employment Projections, November 2013

Metropolitan Area Exports

Area	2007	2008	2009	2010	2011	2012	Rank[2]
MSA[1]	1,881.2	2,278.8	2,004.5	2,450.7	2,594.6	2,735.0	80

Note: Figures are in millions of dollars; (1) Figures cover the Virginia Beach-Norfolk-Newport News, VA-NC Metropolitan Statistical Area—see Appendix B for areas included; (2) Rank is based on 2012 data and ranges from 1 to 369
Source: U.S. Department of Commerce, International Trade Administration, Office of Trade & Industry Information, Manufacturing & Services, data extracted April 1, 2014

INCOME

Income

Area	Per Capita ($)	Median Household ($)	Average Household ($)
City	31,431	65,169	82,301
MSA[1]	28,418	58,241	73,852
U.S.	27,385	51,771	71,579

Note: (1) Figures cover the Virginia Beach-Norfolk-Newport News, VA-NC Metropolitan Statistical Area—see Appendix B for areas included
Source: U.S. Census Bureau, 2010-2012 American Community Survey 3-Year Estimates

Household Income Distribution

Area	Percent of Households Earning							
	Under $15,000	$15,000 -24,999	$25,000 -34,999	$35,000 -49,999	$50,000 -74,999	$75,000 -99,000	$100,000 -149,999	$150,000 and up
City	7.1	6.6	8.6	14.1	21.1	14.7	16.9	11.1
MSA[1]	10.1	8.8	9.7	14.2	20.0	13.9	14.7	8.8
U.S.	13.1	11.0	10.5	13.7	18.1	11.9	12.5	9.1

Note: (1) Figures cover the Virginia Beach-Norfolk-Newport News, VA-NC Metropolitan Statistical Area—see Appendix B for areas included
Source: U.S. Census Bureau, 2010-2012 American Community Survey 3-Year Estimates

Poverty Rate

Area	All Ages	Under 18 Years Old	18 to 64 Years Old	65 Years and Over
City	8.3	12.8	7.2	5.0
MSA[1]	11.9	18.0	10.7	6.5
U.S.	15.7	22.2	14.6	9.3

Note: Figures are percentage of people whose income during the past 12 months was below the poverty level;
(1) Figures cover the Virginia Beach-Norfolk-Newport News, VA-NC Metropolitan Statistical Area—see Appendix B for areas included
Source: U.S. Census Bureau, 2010-2012 American Community Survey 3-Year Estimates

Personal Bankruptcy Filing Rate

Area	2008	2009	2010	2011	2012	2013
Virginia Beach city County	4.06	4.99	5.46	5.01	4.57	4.03
U.S.	3.53	4.61	4.97	4.37	3.76	3.29

Note: Numbers are per 1,000 population and include Chapter 7 and Chapter 13 filings
Source: Federal Deposit Insurance Corporation, Regional Economic Conditions, March 20, 2014

EMPLOYMENT

Labor Force and Employment

Area	Civilian Labor Force			Workers Employed		
	Dec. 2012	Dec. 2013	% Chg.	Dec. 2012	Dec. 2013	% Chg.
City	226,742	228,375	0.7	214,384	217,580	1.5
MSA[1]	824,175	828,953	0.6	773,629	785,007	1.5
U.S.	154,904,000	154,408,000	-0.3	143,060,000	144,423,000	1.0

Note: Data is not seasonally adjusted and covers workers 16 years of age and older; (1) Metropolitan Statistical Area—see Appendix B for areas included
Source: Bureau of Labor Statistics, Local Area Unemployment Statistics

Unemployment Rate

Area	2013											
	Jan.	Feb.	Mar.	Apr.	May	Jun.	Jul.	Aug.	Sep.	Oct.	Nov.	Dec.
City	5.8	5.4	4.9	4.7	5.3	5.6	5.5	5.2	5.1	5.3	4.9	4.7
MSA[1]	6.8	6.2	5.7	5.4	6.0	6.3	6.2	5.9	5.7	6.0	5.5	5.3
U.S.	8.5	8.1	7.6	7.1	7.3	7.8	7.7	7.3	7.0	7.0	6.6	6.5

Note: Data is not seasonally adjusted and covers workers 16 years of age and older; All figures are percentages;
(1) Metropolitan Statistical Area—see Appendix B for areas included
Source: Bureau of Labor Statistics, Local Area Unemployment Statistics

Employment by Occupation

Occupation Classification	City (%)	MSA[1] (%)	U.S. (%)
Management, Business, Science, and Arts	39.8	36.7	36.0
Natural Resources, Construction, and Maintenance	9.5	10.2	9.1
Production, Transportation, and Material Moving	7.9	10.4	12.0
Sales and Office	25.9	25.2	24.7
Service	16.9	17.6	18.2

Note: Figures cover employed civilians 16 years of age and older; (1) Figures cover the Virginia Beach-Norfolk-Newport News, VA-NC Metropolitan Statistical Area—see Appendix B for areas included
Source: U.S. Census Bureau, 2010-2012 American Community Survey 3-Year Estimates

Employment by Industry

Sector	MSA[1]		U.S.
	Number of Employees	Percent of Total	Percent of Total
Construction	n/a	n/a	4.2
Education and Health Services	107,200	14.2	15.5
Financial Activities	36,500	4.8	5.7
Government	158,200	21.0	16.1
Information	11,200	1.5	1.9
Leisure and Hospitality	80,100	10.6	10.2
Manufacturing	54,300	7.2	8.7
Mining and Logging	n/a	n/a	0.6
Other Services	35,600	4.7	3.9
Professional and Business Services	102,700	13.6	13.7
Retail Trade	90,500	12.0	11.4
Transportation and Utilities	23,900	3.2	3.8
Wholesale Trade	19,900	2.6	4.2

Note: Figures cover non-farm employment as of December 2013 and are not seasonally adjusted;
(1) Metropolitan Statistical Area—see Appendix B for areas included; n/a not available
Source: Bureau of Labor Statistics, Current Employment Statistics, Employment, Hours, and Earnings

Occupations with Greatest Projected Employment Growth: 2010 – 2020

Occupation[1]	2010 Employment	2020 Projected Employment	Numeric Employment Change	Percent Employment Change
Retail Salespersons	123,960	146,560	22,600	18.2
Office Clerks, General	95,910	114,570	18,660	19.5
Personal Care Aides	23,440	41,720	18,280	78.0
Combined Food Preparation and Serving Workers, Including Fast Food	87,610	105,340	17,730	20.2
Software Developers, Systems Software	31,370	48,180	16,810	53.6
Registered Nurses	63,120	77,860	14,730	23.3
Management Analysts	57,440	72,140	14,700	25.6
Software Developers, Applications	31,900	44,600	12,700	39.8
Nursing Aides, Orderlies, and Attendants	35,730	46,110	10,380	29.1
Home Health Aides	13,370	23,540	10,170	76.1

Note: Projections cover Virginia; (1) Sorted by numeric employment change
Source: www.projectionscentral.com, State Occupational Projections, 2010–2020 Long-Term Projections

Fastest Growing Occupations: 2010 – 2020

Occupation[1]	2010 Employment	2020 Projected Employment	Numeric Employment Change	Percent Employment Change
Biomedical Engineers	460	910	440	95.9
Personal Care Aides	23,440	41,720	18,280	78.0
Home Health Aides	13,370	23,540	10,170	76.1
Helpers—Brickmasons, Blockmasons, Stonemasons, and Tile and Marble Setters	1,340	2,140	810	60.4
Interpreters and Translators	4,850	7,780	2,930	60.3
Helpers—Carpenters	2,500	3,990	1,490	59.4
Meeting, Convention, and Event Planners	3,660	5,670	2,010	54.8
Software Developers, Systems Software	31,370	48,180	16,810	53.6
Veterinary Technologists and Technicians	1,340	2,040	710	52.8
Reinforcing Iron and Rebar Workers	370	560	190	52.3

Note: Projections cover Virginia; (1) Sorted by percent employment change and excludes occupations with numeric employment change less than 100
Source: www.projectionscentral.com, State Occupational Projections, 2010–2020 Long-Term Projections

Average Wages

Occupation	$/Hr.	Occupation	$/Hr.
Accountants and Auditors	33.02	Maids and Housekeeping Cleaners	9.68
Automotive Mechanics	20.84	Maintenance and Repair Workers	16.63
Bookkeepers	16.69	Marketing Managers	55.08
Carpenters	18.84	Nuclear Medicine Technologists	32.47
Cashiers	9.04	Nurses, Licensed Practical	18.26
Clerks, General Office	13.39	Nurses, Registered	28.80
Clerks, Receptionists/Information	12.61	Nursing Assistants	11.22
Clerks, Shipping/Receiving	15.44	Packers and Packagers, Hand	10.43
Computer Programmers	32.13	Physical Therapists	39.84
Computer Systems Analysts	39.10	Postal Service Mail Carriers	24.73
Computer User Support Specialists	22.42	Real Estate Brokers	32.08
Cooks, Restaurant	12.75	Retail Salespersons	11.29
Dentists	73.45	Sales Reps., Exc. Tech./Scientific	28.23
Electrical Engineers	38.98	Sales Reps., Tech./Scientific	42.31
Electricians	21.45	Secretaries, Exc. Legal/Med./Exec.	15.60
Financial Managers	57.11	Security Guards	12.89
First-Line Supervisors/Managers, Sales	19.19	Surgeons	111.83
Food Preparation Workers	9.99	Teacher Assistants	11.80
General and Operations Managers	55.74	Teachers, Elementary School	26.30
Hairdressers/Cosmetologists	15.88	Teachers, Secondary School	27.10
Internists	89.75	Telemarketers	10.10
Janitors and Cleaners	10.22	Truck Drivers, Heavy/Tractor-Trailer	17.82
Landscaping/Groundskeeping Workers	11.32	Truck Drivers, Light/Delivery Svcs.	15.15
Lawyers	61.05	Waiters and Waitresses	11.28

Note: Wage data covers the Virginia Beach-Norfolk-Newport News, VA-NC Metropolitan Statistical Area—see Appendix B for areas included. Hourly wages for elementary/secondary school teachers and teacher assistants were calculated by the editors from annual wage data assuming a 40 hour work week; n/a not available.
Source: Bureau of Labor Statistics, Metro Area Occupational Employment and Wage Estimates, May 2013

RESIDENTIAL REAL ESTATE

Building Permits

Area	Single-Family			Multi-Family			Total		
	2012	2013	Pct. Chg.	2012	2013	Pct. Chg.	2012	2013	Pct. Chg.
City	594	733	23.4	523	929	77.6	1,117	1,662	48.8
MSA[1]	3,534	4,104	16.1	1,849	3,273	77.0	5,383	7,377	37.0
U.S.	518,695	620,802	19.7	310,963	370,020	19.0	829,658	990,822	19.4

Note: (1) Metropolitan Statistical Area—see Appendix B for areas included; figures represent new, privately-owned housing units authorized (unadjusted data); All permit data are based on estimates with imputation.
Source: U.S. Census Bureau, Manufacturing, Mining, and Construction Statistics, Building Permits, 2012, 2013

Homeownership Rate

Area	2006 (%)	2007 (%)	2008 (%)	2009 (%)	2010 (%)	2011 (%)	2012 (%)	2013 (%)
MSA[1]	68.3	66.0	63.9	63.5	61.4	62.3	62.0	63.3
U.S.	68.8	68.1	67.8	67.4	66.9	66.1	65.4	65.1

Note: (1) Figures cover the Virginia Beach-Norfolk-Newport News, VA-NC Metropolitan Statistical Area—see Appendix B for areas included
Source: U.S. Census Bureau, Housing Vacancies and Homeownership Annual Statistics: 2013

Housing Vacancy Rates

Area	Gross Vacancy Rate[2] (%)			Year-Round Vacancy Rate[3] (%)			Rental Vacancy Rate[4] (%)			Homeowner Vacancy Rate[5] (%)		
	2011	2012	2013	2011	2012	2013	2011	2012	2013	2011	2012	2013
MSA[1]	10.8	10.8	9.6	10.3	9.5	8.7	9.4	8.7	7.0	3.2	2.9	2.5
U.S.	14.2	13.8	13.8	11.1	10.8	10.7	9.5	8.7	8.3	2.5	2.0	2.0

Note: (1) Figures cover the Virginia Beach-Norfolk-Newport News, VA-NC Metropolitan Statistical Area—see Appendix B for areas included; (2) The percentage of the total housing inventory that is vacant; (3) The percentage of the housing inventory (excluding seasonal units) that is year-round vacant; (4) The percentage of rental inventory that is vacant for rent; (5) The percentage of homeowner inventory that is vacant for sale
Source: U.S. Census Bureau, Housing Vacancies and Homeownership Annual Statistics: 2013

TAXES

State Corporate Income Tax Rates

State	Tax Rate (%)	Income Brackets ($)	Num. of Brackets	Financial Institution Tax Rate (%)[a]	Federal Income Tax Ded.
Virginia	6.0	Flat rate	1	6.0	No

Note: Tax rates as of January 1, 2014; (a) Rates listed are the corporate income tax rate applied to financial institutions or excise taxes based on income. Some states have other taxes based upon the value of deposits or shares.
Source: Federation of Tax Administrators, "State Corporate Income Tax Rates, 2014"

State Individual Income Tax Rates

State	Tax Rate (%)	Income Brackets ($)	Num. of Brackets	Personal Exempt. ($)[1] Single	Personal Exempt. ($)[1] Dependents	Fed. Inc. Tax Ded.
Virginia	2.0 - 5.75	3,000 - 17,001	4	930	930	No

Note: Tax rates as of January 1, 2014; Local- and county-level taxes are not included; n/a not applicable;
(1) Married joint filers generally receive double the single exemption
Source: Federation of Tax Administrators, "State Individual Income Tax Rates, 2014"

Various State and Local Tax Rates

State	State and Local Sales and Use (%)	State Sales and Use (%)	Gasoline[1] (¢/gal.)	Cigarette[2] ($/pack)	Spirits[3] ($/gal.)	Wine[4] ($/gal.)	Beer[5] ($/gal.)
Virginia	6.0	5.30 (b)	17.28	0.300	19.19 (g)	1.51	0.26

Note: All tax rates as of January 1, 2014; (1) The American Petroleum Institute has developed a methodology for determining the average tax rate on a gallon of fuel. Rates may include any of the following: excise taxes, environmental fees, storage tank fees, other fees or taxes, general sales tax, and local taxes. In states where gasoline is subject to the general sales tax, or where the fuel tax is based on the average sale price, the average rate determined by API is sensitive to changes in the price of gasoline. States that fully or partially apply general sales taxes to gasoline: CA, CO, GA, IL, IN, MI, NY; (2) The federal excise tax of $1.0066 per pack and local taxes are not included; (3) Rates are those applicable to off-premise sales of 40% alcohol by volume (a.b.v.) distilled spirits in 750ml containers. Local excise taxes are excluded; (4) Rates are those applicable to off-premise sales of 11% a.b.v. non-carbonated wine in 750ml containers; (5) Rates are those applicable to off-premise sales of 4.7% a.b.v. beer in 12 ounce containers; (b) Three states levy mandatory, statewide, local add-on sales taxes at the state level: California (1%), Utah (1.25%), and Virginia (1%). These amounts are included in the state sales tax column; (g) States where the government controls sales. In these "control states," products are subject to ad valorem mark-up and excise taxes. The excise tax rate is calculated using a methodology developed by the Distilled Spirits Council of the United States.
Source: Tax Foundation, 2014 Facts & Figures: How Does Your State Compare?

State Business Tax Climate Index Rankings

State	Overall Rank	Corporate Tax Index Rank	Individual Income Tax Index Rank	Sales Tax Index Rank	Unemployment Insurance Tax Index Rank	Property Tax Index Rank
Virginia	26	6	37	6	35	26

Note: The index is a measure of how each state's tax laws affect economic performance. The lower the rank, the more favorable a state's tax system is for business. States without a given tax are given a ranking of 1. The scores/rankings for the District of Columbia do not affect other states. The 2014 index represents the tax climate as of July 1, 2013.
Source: Tax Foundation, State Business Tax Climate Index 2014

COMMERCIAL UTILITIES

Typical Monthly Electric Bills

Area	Commercial Service ($/month) 1,500 kWh	Commercial Service ($/month) 40 kW demand 14,000 kWh	Industrial Service ($/month) 1,000 kW demand 200,000 kWh	Industrial Service ($/month) 50,000 kW demand 15,000,000 kWh
City	161	1,273	22,650	1,281,975
Average[1]	197	1,636	25,662	1,485,307

Note: Based on total rates in effect July 1, 2013; (1) average based on 180 utilities surveyed
Source: Edison Electric Institute, Typical Bills and Average Rates Report, Summer 2013

TRANSPORTATION

Means of Transportation to Work

Area	Car/Truck/Van		Public Transportation			Bicycle	Walked	Other Means	Worked at Home
	Drove Alone	Car-pooled	Bus	Subway	Railroad				
City	81.7	8.5	0.8	0.0	0.0	0.6	2.4	1.0	4.9
MSA[1]	80.7	8.7	1.8	0.0	0.0	0.4	2.9	1.1	4.4
U.S.	76.4	9.7	2.6	1.7	0.5	0.6	2.8	1.3	4.3

Note: Figures are percentages and cover workers 16 years of age and older; (1) Figures cover the Virginia Beach-Norfolk-Newport News, VA-NC Metropolitan Statistical Area—see Appendix B for areas included
Source: U.S. Census Bureau, 2010-2012 American Community Survey 3-Year Estimates

Travel Time to Work

Area	Less Than 10 Minutes	10 to 19 Minutes	20 to 29 Minutes	30 to 44 Minutes	45 to 59 Minutes	60 to 89 Minutes	90 Minutes or More
City	10.8	31.5	26.1	23.4	5.0	2.2	1.0
MSA[1]	10.9	32.7	23.6	21.4	6.5	3.3	1.5
U.S.	13.5	29.8	20.9	20.1	7.5	5.6	2.5

Note: Figures are percentages and include workers 16 years old and over; (1) Figures cover the Virginia Beach-Norfolk-Newport News, VA-NC Metropolitan Statistical Area—see Appendix B for areas included
Source: U.S. Census Bureau, 2010-2012 American Community Survey 3-Year Estimates

Travel Time Index

Area	1985	1990	1995	2000	2005	2010	2011
Urban Area[1]	1.14	1.18	1.22	1.23	1.27	1.20	1.20
Average[2]	1.09	1.14	1.16	1.19	1.23	1.18	1.18

Note: Travel Time Index—the ratio of travel time in the peak period to the travel time at free-flow conditions. For example, a value of 1.30 indicates a 20-minute free-flow trip takes 26 minutes in the peak. Free-flow speeds (60 mph on freeways and 35 mph on principal arterials) are used as the comparison threshold; (1) Covers the Virginia Beach VA urban area; (2) average of 498 urban areas
Source: Texas Transportation Institute, Urban Mobility Report 2012, December 2012

Public Transportation

Agency Name / Mode of Transportation	Vehicles Operated in Maximum Service	Annual Unlinked Passenger Trips (in thous.)	Annual Passenger Miles (in thous.)
Hampton Roads Transit (HRT)			
Bus (directly operated)	240	16,166.5	99,459.3
Demand Response (purchased transportation)	84	293.0	2,547.9
Demand Response Taxi (purchased transportation)	75	64.6	885.5
Ferryboat (purchased transportation)	2	380.7	194.4
Light Rail (directly operated)	7	1,360.1	5,648.4
Vanpool (directly operated)	52	194.7	7,077.1

Source: Federal Transit Administration, National Transit Database, 2012

Air Transportation

Airport Name and Code / Type of Service	Passenger Airlines[1]	Passenger Enplanements	Freight Carriers[2]	Freight (lbs.)
Norfolk International (ORF)				
Domestic service (U.S. carriers - 2013)	27	1,557,941	11	26,928,768
International service (U.S. carriers - 2012)	7	177	2	9,525

Note: (1) Includes all U.S.-based major, minor and commuter airlines that carried at least one passenger during the year; (2) Includes all U.S.-based airlines and freight carriers that transported at least one lb. of freight during the year.
Source: Bureau of Transportation Statistics, The Intermodal Transportation Database, Air Carriers: T-100 Domestic Market (U.S. Carriers), 2013; Bureau of Transportation Statistics, The Intermodal Transportation Database, Air Carriers: T-100 International Market (U.S. Carriers), 2012

Other Transportation Statistics

Major Highways:	I-64
Amtrak Service:	No
Major Waterways/Ports:	Atlantic Ocean; Chesapeake Bay

Source: Amtrak.com; Google Maps

BUSINESSES

Major Business Headquarters

Company Name	Rankings	
	Fortune[1]	Forbes[2]
No companies listed	—	—

Note: (1) Fortune 500—companies that produce a 10-K are ranked 1 to 500 based on 2012 revenue; (2) all private companies with at least $2 billion in annual revenue through the end of their most current fiscal year are ranked 1 to 224; companies listed are headquartered in the city; dashes indicate no ranking
Source: Fortune, "Fortune 500," May 20, 2013; Forbes, "America's Largest Private Companies," December 18, 2013

Fast-Growing Businesses

According to *Inc.*, Virginia Beach is home to one of America's 500 fastest-growing private companies: **RMGS** (#144). Criteria: must be an independent, privately-held, for-profit, U.S. corporation, proprietorship or partnership; revenues must be at least $100,000 in 2009 and $2 million in 2012; must have four-year operating/sales history. Holding companies, regulated banks, and utilities were excluded. *Inc.*, *"America's 500 Fastest-Growing Private Companies," September 2013*

Minority Business Opportunity

Virginia Beach is home to three companies which are on the *Hispanic Business* 500 list (500 largest U.S. Hispanic-owned companies based on 2012 revenue): **Dynaric** (#58); **Knowledge Information Solutions** (#141); **Loyola Enterprises** (#390). Companies included must show at least 51 percent ownership by Hispanic U.S. citizens, and must maintain headquarters in one of the 50 states or Washington, D.C. *Hispanic Business, "Hispanic Business 500," June 20, 2013*

Minority- and Women-Owned Businesses

Group	All Firms		Firms with Paid Employees			
	Firms	Sales ($000)	Firms	Sales ($000)	Employees	Payroll ($000)
Asian	2,267	708,943	809	647,450	7,033	227,506
Black	3,257	171,795	271	108,780	1,548	42,873
Hispanic	820	375,856	134	356,746	1,367	45,935
Women	10,971	2,470,105	1,673	2,204,494	13,393	400,784
All Firms	34,768	29,955,218	9,492	28,746,971	158,502	5,063,023

Note: Figures cover firms located in the city; minority- and women-owned business are defined as firms in which the corresponding group own 51% or more of the stock or equity of the company
Source: U.S. Census Bureau, 2007 Economic Census, Survey of Business Owners (2012 Survey of Business Owners data will be released starting in June 2015)

HOTELS & CONVENTION CENTERS

Hotels/Motels

Area	5 Star		4 Star		3 Star		2 Star		1 Star		Not Rated	
	Num.	Pct.[3]	Num.	Pct.[3]	Num.	Pct.[3]	Num.	Pct.[3]	Num.	Pct.[3]	Num.	Pct.[3]
City[1]	0	0.0	3	1.3	60	26.0	126	54.5	15	6.5	27	11.7
Total[2]	142	0.9	1,005	6.0	5,147	30.9	8,578	51.4	408	2.4	1,397	8.4

Note: (1) Figures cover Virginia Beach and vicinity; (2) Figures cover all 100 cities in this book; (3) Percentage of hotels which have a given star rating; Star ratings are determined by expedia.com and offer an indication of the general quality of a particular hotel.
Source: expedia.com, April 7, 2014

The Virginia Beach-Norfolk-Newport News, VA-NC metro area is home to three of the best hotels in the world according to *Condé Nast Traveler*: **Colonial Houses; Williamsburg Inn; Williamsburg Lodge**. The selections are based on over 79,000 responses to the magazine's annual Readers' Choice Survey. The list includes the top 200 hotels in the U.S. *Condé Nast Traveler*, *"Gold List 2014, The World's Best Places to Stay"*

Major Convention Centers

Name	Overall Space (sq. ft.)	Exhibit Space (sq. ft.)	Meeting Space (sq. ft.)	Meeting Rooms
Pavilion/Virginia Beach Convention Center	516,000	150,012	28,929	22

Note: Table includes convention centers located in the Virginia Beach-Norfolk-Newport News, VA-NC metro area; n/a not available
Source: Original research

Living Environment

COST OF LIVING

Cost of Living Index

Composite Index	Groceries	Housing	Utilities	Trans-portation	Health Care	Misc. Goods/Services
n/a	n/a	n/a	n/a	n/a	n/a	n/a

Note: The Cost of Living Index measures regional differences in the cost of consumer goods and services, excluding taxes and non-consumer expenditures, for professional and managerial households in the top income quintile. It is based on more than 50,000 prices covering almost 60 different items for which prices are collected three times a year by chambers of commerce, economic development organizations or university applied economic centers in each participating urban area. The numbers shown should be read as a percentage above or below the national average of 100. For example, a value of 115.4 in the groceries column indicates that grocery prices are 15.4% higher than the national average. Small differences in the index numbers should not be interpreted as significant; n/a not available.
Source: The Council for Community and Economic Research, ACCRA Cost of Living Index, 2013

Grocery Prices

Area[1]	T-Bone Steak ($/pound)	Frying Chicken ($/pound)	Whole Milk ($/half gal.)	Eggs ($/dozen)	Orange Juice ($/64 oz.)	Coffee ($/11.5 oz.)
City[2]	n/a	n/a	n/a	n/a	n/a	n/a
Avg.	10.19	1.28	2.34	1.81	3.48	4.39
Min.	8.56	0.94	1.44	1.19	2.78	3.40
Max.	14.82	2.28	3.56	3.73	6.23	7.32

Note: (1) Values for the local area are compared with the average, minimum and maximum values for all 327 areas in the Cost of Living Index; (2) Figures cover the Virginia Beach VA urban area; n/a not available;
T-Bone Steak *(price per pound)*; **Frying Chicken** *(price per pound, whole fryer)*; **Whole Milk** *(half gallon carton)*; **Eggs** *(price per dozen, Grade A, large)*; **Orange Juice** *(64 oz. Tropicana or Florida Natural)*; **Coffee** *(11.5 oz. can, vacuum-packed, Maxwell House, Hills Bros, or Folgers)*.
Source: The Council for Community and Economic Research, ACCRA Cost of Living Index, 2013

Housing and Utility Costs

Area[1]	New Home Price ($)	Apartment Rent ($/month)	All Electric ($/month)	Part Electric ($/month)	Other Energy ($/month)	Telephone ($/month)
City[2]	n/a	n/a	n/a	n/a	n/a	n/a
Avg.	295,864	900	171.38	91.82	70.12	27.73
Min.	185,506	458	117.80	48.81	33.67	17.16
Max.	1,358,917	3,783	441.68	171.40	372.65	39.47

Note: (1) Values for the local area are compared with the average, minimum and maximum values for all 327 areas in the Cost of Living Index; (2) Figures cover the Virginia Beach VA urban area; n/a not available; **New Home Price** *(2,400 sf living area, 8,000 sf lot, in urban area with full utilities)*; **Apartment Rent** *(950 sf 2 bedroom/1.5 or 2 bath, unfurnished, excluding all utilities except water)*; **All Electric** *(average monthly cost for an all-electric home)*; **Part Electric** *(average monthly cost for a part-electric home)*; **Other Energy** *(average monthly cost for natural gas, fuel oil, coal, wood, and any other forms of energy except electricity)*; **Telephone** *(price includes basic monthly rate for a private residential line plus additional local usage charges incurred by a family of four)*.
Source: The Council for Community and Economic Research, ACCRA Cost of Living Index, 2013

Health Care, Transportation, and Other Costs

Area[1]	Doctor ($/visit)	Dentist ($/visit)	Optometrist ($/visit)	Gasoline ($/gallon)	Beauty Salon ($/visit)	Men's Shirt ($)
City[2]	n/a	n/a	n/a	n/a	n/a	n/a
Avg.	101.40	86.48	96.16	3.44	33.87	26.55
Min.	61.67	50.83	50.12	3.08	18.92	12.48
Max.	182.71	152.50	223.78	4.33	68.22	52.03

Note: (1) Values for the local area are compared with the average, minimum and maximum values for all 327 areas in the Cost of Living Index; (2) Figures cover the Virginia Beach VA urban area; n/a not available; **Doctor** *(general practitioners routine exam of an established patient)*; **Dentist** *(adult teeth cleaning and periodic oral examination)*; **Optometrist** *(full vision eye exam for established adult patient)*; **Gasoline** *(one gallon regular unleaded, national brand, including all taxes, cash price at self-service pump if available)*; **Beauty Salon** *(woman's shampoo, trim, and blow-dry)*; **Men's Shirt** *(cotton/polyester dress shirt, pinpoint weave, long sleeves)*.
Source: The Council for Community and Economic Research, ACCRA Cost of Living Index, 2013

HOUSING

House Price Index (HPI)

Area	National Ranking[2]	Quarterly Change (%)	One-Year Change (%)	Five-Year Change (%)
MSA[1]	237	-0.24	-0.35	-14.40
U.S.[3]	–	1.20	7.69	4.18

Note: The HPI is a weighted repeat sales index. It measures average price changes in repeat sales or refinancings on the same properties. This information is obtained by reviewing repeat mortgage transactions on single-family properties whose mortgages have been purchased or securitized by Fannie Mae or Freddie Mac in January 1975; (1) Virginia Beach-Norfolk-Newport News, VA-NC Metropolitan Statistical Area—see Appendix B for areas included; (2) Rankings are based on annual percentage change for all metro areas containing at least 15,000 transactions over the last 10 years and ranges from 1 to 283; (3) figures based on a weighted average of Census Division estimates using a seasonally adjusted, purchase-only index; all figures are for the period ending December 31, 2013
Source: Federal Housing Finance Agency, House Price Index, February 25, 2014

Median Single-Family Home Prices

Area	2011	2012	2013[p]	Percent Change 2012 to 2013
MSA[1]	182.9	187.5	193.0	2.9
U.S. Average	166.2	177.2	197.4	11.4

Note: Figures are median sales prices of existing single-family homes in thousands of dollars; (p) preliminary; n/a not available; (1) Virginia Beach-Norfolk-Newport News, VA-NC Metropolitan Statistical Area—see Appendix B for areas included
Source: National Association of Realtors, Median Sales Price of Existing Single-Family Homes for Metropolitan Areas, 4th Quarter 2013

Qualifying Income Based on Median Sales Price of Existing Single-Family Homes

Area	With 5% Down ($)	With 10% Down ($)	With 20% Down ($)
MSA[1]	42,652	40,407	35,917
U.S. Average	45,395	43,006	38,228

Note: Figures are preliminary; Qualifying income is based on a mortgage rate of 4.4%. Monthly principal and interest payment is limited to 25% of income; n/a not available; (1) Virginia Beach-Norfolk-Newport News, VA-NC Metropolitan Statistical Area—see Appendix B for areas included
Source: National Association of Realtors, Qualifying Income Based on Median Sales Price of Existing Single-Family Homes for Metropolitan Areas, 4th Quarter 2013

Median Apartment Condo-Coop Home Prices

Area	2011	2012	2013[p]	Percent Change 2012 to 2013
MSA[1]	170.0	165.0	165.0	0.0
U.S. Average	165.1	173.7	194.9	12.2

Note: Figures are median sales prices of existing apartment condo-coop homes in thousands of dollars; (p) preliminary; n/a not available; (1) Virginia Beach-Norfolk-Newport News, VA-NC Metropolitan Statistical Area—see Appendix B for areas included
Source: National Association of Realtors, Median Sales Price of Existing Apartment Condo-Coop Homes for Metropolitan Areas, 4th Quarter 2013

Gross Monthly Rent

Area	Under $200	$200 -299	$300 -499	$500 -749	$750 -999	$1,000 -1,499	$1,500 and up	Median ($)
City	0.5	0.8	1.5	3.7	18.4	49.0	26.1	1,224
MSA[1]	2.0	2.3	3.4	10.3	25.7	38.7	17.5	1,066
U.S.	1.7	3.3	8.1	22.7	24.3	25.7	14.3	889

Note: Figures are percentages except for Median; Gross rent is the contract rent plus the estimated average monthly cost of utilities (electricity, gas, and water and sewer) and fuels (oil, coal, kerosene, wood, etc.) if these are paid by the renter (or paid for the renter by someone else); (1) Figures cover the Virginia Beach-Norfolk-Newport News, VA-NC Metropolitan Statistical Area—see Appendix B for areas included
Source: U.S. Census Bureau, 2010-2012 American Community Survey 3-Year Estimates

Year Housing Structure Built

Area	2010 or Later	2000 -2009	1990 -1999	1980 -1989	1970 -1979	1960 -1969	1950 -1959	1940 -1949	Before 1940	Median Year
City	0.4	11.5	13.6	28.7	23.0	13.7	6.6	1.5	1.1	1981
MSA[1]	0.5	13.3	14.7	19.5	16.9	13.2	10.6	5.3	5.9	1979
U.S.	0.5	14.9	13.8	13.9	15.9	11.1	10.9	5.5	13.5	1976

Note: Figures are percentages except for Median Year; (1) Figures cover the Virginia Beach-Norfolk-Newport News, VA-NC Metropolitan Statistical Area—see Appendix B for areas included
Source: U.S. Census Bureau, 2010-2012 American Community Survey 3-Year Estimates

HEALTH

Health Risk Data

Category	MSA[1] (%)	U.S. (%)
Adults aged 18–64 who have any kind of health care coverage	80.4	79.6
Adults who reported being in good or excellent health	82.8	83.1
Adults who are current smokers	20.6	19.6
Adults who are heavy drinkers[2]	5.9	6.1
Adults who are binge drinkers[3]	15.4	16.9
Adults who are overweight (BMI 25.0 - 29.9)	36.8	35.8
Adults who are obese (BMI 30.0 - 99.8)	29.4	27.6
Adults who participated in any physical activities in the past month	79.3	77.1
Adults 50+ who have ever had a sigmoidoscopy or colonoscopy	73.6	67.3
Women aged 40+ who have had a mammogram within the past two years	79.3	74.0
Men aged 40+ who have had a PSA test within the past two years	50.1	45.2
Adults aged 65+ who have had flu shot within the past year	59.0	60.1
Adults who always wear a seatbelt	95.1	93.8

Note: Data as of 2012 unless otherwise noted; (1) Figures cover the Virginia Beach-Norfolk-Newport News, VA-NC Metropolitan Statistical Area—see Appendix B for areas included; (2) Heavy drinkers are classified as males having more than two drinks per day or females having more than one drink per day; (3) Binge drinkers are classified as males having five or more drinks on one occasion or females having four or more drinks on one occasion
Source: Centers for Disease Control and Prevention, Behaviorial Risk Factor Surveillance System, SMART: Selected Metropolitan/Micropolitan Area Risk Trends, 2012

Chronic Health Indicators

Category	MSA[1] (%)	U.S. (%)
Adults who have ever been told they had a heart attack	4.2	4.5
Adults who have ever been told they had a stroke	3.4	2.9
Adults who have been told they currently have asthma	7.7	8.9
Adults who have ever been told they have arthritis	25.4	25.7
Adults who have ever been told they have diabetes[2]	10.1	9.7
Adults who have ever been told they had skin cancer	4.5	5.7
Adults who have ever been told they had any other types of cancer	5.2	6.5
Adults who have ever been told they have COPD	6.5	6.2
Adults who have ever been told they have kidney disease	1.9	2.5
Adults who have ever been told they have a form of depression	16.7	18.0

Note: Data as of 2012 unless otherwise noted; (1) Figures cover the Virginia Beach-Norfolk-Newport News, VA-NC Metropolitan Statistical Area—see Appendix B for areas included; (2) Figures do not include pregnancy-related, borderline, or pre-diabetes
Source: Centers for Disease Control and Prevention, Behaviorial Risk Factor Surveillance System, SMART: Selected Metropolitan/Micropolitan Area Risk Trends, 2012

Mortality Rates for the Top 10 Causes of Death in the U.S.

ICD-10[a] Sub-Chapter	ICD-10[a] Code	Age-Adjusted Mortality Rate[1] per 100,000 population	
		County[2]	U.S.
Malignant neoplasms	C00-C97	170.8	174.2
Ischaemic heart diseases	I20-I25	84.7	119.1
Other forms of heart disease	I30-I51	56.3	49.6
Chronic lower respiratory diseases	J40-J47	41.8	43.2
Cerebrovascular diseases	I60-I69	33.2	40.3
Organic, including symptomatic, mental disorders	F01-F09	42.3	30.5
Other degenerative diseases of the nervous system	G30-G31	27.1	26.3
Other external causes of accidental injury	W00-X59	20.9	25.1
Diabetes mellitus	E10-E14	14.8	21.3
Hypertensive diseases	I10-I15	12.3	18.8

Note: (a) ICD-10 = International Classification of Diseases 10th Revision; (1) Mortality rates are a three year average covering 2008-2010; (2) Figures cover Virginia Beach city
Source: Centers for Disease Control and Prevention, National Center for Health Statistics. Compressed Mortality File 1999-2010 on CDC WONDER Online Database, released January 2013. Data are compiled from the Compressed Mortality File 1999-2010, Series 20 No. 2P, 2013.

Mortality Rates for Selected Causes of Death

ICD-10[a] Sub-Chapter	ICD-10[a] Code	Age-Adjusted Mortality Rate[1] per 100,000 population	
		County[2]	U.S.
Assault	X85-Y09	4.0	5.5
Diseases of the liver	K70-K76	8.6	12.4
Human immunodeficiency virus (HIV) disease	B20-B24	1.7	3.0
Influenza and pneumonia	J09-J18	17.3	16.4
Intentional self-harm	X60-X84	12.3	11.8
Malnutrition	E40-E46	*1.1	0.8
Obesity and other hyperalimentation	E65-E68	*1.0	1.6
Renal failure	N17-N19	19.1	13.6
Transport accidents	V01-V99	9.0	12.6
Viral hepatitis	B15-B19	*0.8	2.2

Note: (a) ICD-10 = International Classification of Diseases 10th Revision; (1) Mortality rates are a three year average covering 2008-2010; (2) Figures cover Virginia Beach city; (*) Unreliable data as per CDC
Source: Centers for Disease Control and Prevention, National Center for Health Statistics. Compressed Mortality File 1999-2010 on CDC WONDER Online Database, released January 2013. Data are compiled from the Compressed Mortality File 1999-2010, Series 20 No. 2P, 2013.

Health Insurance Coverage

Area	With Health Insurance	With Private Health Insurance	With Public Health Insurance	Without Health Insurance	Population Under Age 18 Without Health Insurance
City	89.3	80.3	20.4	10.7	4.8
MSA[1]	88.1	74.9	25.2	11.9	5.0
U.S.	84.9	65.4	30.4	15.1	7.5

Note: Figures are percentages that cover the civilian noninstitutionalized population; (1) Figures cover the Virginia Beach-Norfolk-Newport News, VA-NC Metropolitan Statistical Area—see Appendix B for areas included
Source: U.S. Census Bureau, 2010-2012 American Community Survey 3-Year Estimates

Number of Medical Professionals

Area[1]	MDs[2]	DOs[2,3]	Dentists	Podiatrists	Chiropractors	Optometrists
Local (number)	1,086	46	309	30	111	62
Local (rate[4])	245.2	10.4	69.4	6.7	24.9	13.9
U.S. (rate[4])	267.6	19.6	61.7	5.6	24.7	14.5

Note: Data as of 2012 unless noted; (1) Local data covers Virginia Beach City; (2) Data as of 2011; (3) Doctor of Osteopathic Medicine; (4) rate per 100,000 population
Source: Area Resource File (ARF) 2012-2013. U.S. Department of Health and Human Services, Health Resources and Services Administration, Bureau of Health Professions

Best Hospitals

According to *U.S. News*, the Virginia Beach-Norfolk-Newport News, VA-NC metro area is home to one of the best hospitals in the U.S.: **Sentara Norfolk General Hospital** (2 specialties). The hospital listed was nationally ranked in at least one adult specialty. Only 147 hospitals nationwide were nationally ranked in one or more specialties. Eighteen hospitals in the U.S. made the Honor Roll by ranking near the top in at least six specialties.*U.S. News Online, "America's Best Hospitals 2013-14"*

EDUCATION

Public School District Statistics

District Name	Schls	Pupils	Pupil/ Teacher Ratio	Minority Pupils[1] (%)	Free Lunch Eligible[2] (%)	IEP[3] (%)
Va Beach City Public Schs	85	70,978	16.1	47.5	28.5	12.2

Note: Table includes school districts with 2,000 or more students; (1) Percentage of students that are not non-Hispanic white; (2) Percentage of students that are eligible for the free lunch program; (3) Percentage of students that have an Individualized Education Program.
Source: U.S. Department of Education, National Center for Education Statistics, Common Core of Data, Local Education Agency (School District) Universe Survey: School Year 2011-2012; U.S. Department of Education, National Center for Education Statistics, Common Core of Data, Public Elementary/Secondary School Universe Survey: School Year 2011-2012

Best High Schools

High School Name	Rank[1]	Grad. Rate[2] (%)	Coll.[3] (%)	AP/IB/ AICE Tests[4]	AP/IB/ AICE Score[5]	SAT Score[6]	ACT Score[6]
Bayside H.S.	1968	80	81	0.3	2.6	1423	21.1
First Colonial H.S.	1358	84	94	0.4	2.7	1543	23.4
Floyd E. Kellam H.S.	1412	92	86	0.4	2.6	1489	22.6
Frank W. Cox H.S.	1302	88	88	0.5	3.0	1561	22.8
Kempsville H.S.	1684	86	84	0.3	3.0	1489	21.5
Landstown H.S.	1915	86	72	0.4	2.9	1434	21.0
Ocean Lakes H.S.	1088	91	86	0.5	3.5	1556	23.8
Princess Anne H.S.	706	89	91	0.8	3.2	1620	24.5
Salem H.S.	1357	90	96	0.4	2.4	1446	19.8
Tallwood H.S.	1770	88	80	0.3	2.6	1446	20.6

Note: (1) Public schools are ranked from 1 to 2,000 based on the following self-reported statistics (with the corresponding weight used in calculating their overall score). Schools that were newly founded and did not have a graduating senior class in 2012 were excluded; (2) Four-year, on-time graduation rate (25%); (3) Percent of 2011 graduates who were accepted to college (25%); (4) AP/IB/AICE tests taken per student (25%); (5) Average AP/IB/AICE exam score (10%); (6) Average SAT and/or ACT score (10%); Percent of students enrolled in at least one AP/IB/AICE course (5%)—data not shown
Source: Newsweek and The Daily Beast, "America's Best High Schools 2013"

Highest Level of Education

Area	Less than H.S.	H.S. Diploma	Some College, No Deg.	Associate Degree	Bachelor's Degree	Master's Degree	Prof. School Degree	Doctorate Degree
City	6.6	23.2	27.6	10.1	21.1	8.4	2.0	0.9
MSA[1]	10.3	26.2	26.0	8.8	18.0	8.0	1.7	1.0
U.S.	14.1	28.3	21.3	7.8	18.0	7.5	1.9	1.2

Note: Figures cover persons age 25 and over; (1) Figures cover the Virginia Beach-Norfolk-Newport News, VA-NC Metropolitan Statistical Area—see Appendix B for areas included
Source: U.S. Census Bureau, 2010-2012 American Community Survey 3-Year Estimates

Educational Attainment by Race

Area	High School Graduate or Higher (%)					Bachelor's Degree or Higher (%)				
	Total	White	Black	Asian	Hisp.[2]	Total	White	Black	Asian	Hisp.[2]
City	93.4	94.6	90.1	90.6	91.2	32.5	34.4	23.8	38.3	20.3
MSA[1]	89.7	92.2	84.5	88.8	83.3	28.6	32.5	18.8	41.9	21.0
U.S.	85.9	88.1	82.5	85.5	63.1	28.6	30.0	18.4	50.2	13.4

Note: Figures shown cover persons 25 years old and over; (1) Figures cover the Virginia Beach-Norfolk-Newport News, VA-NC Metropolitan Statistical Area—see Appendix B for areas included; (2) People of Hispanic origin can be of any race
Source: U.S. Census Bureau, 2010-2012 American Community Survey 3-Year Estimates

School Enrollment by Grade and Control

Area	Preschool (%)		Kindergarten (%)		Grades 1 - 4 (%)		Grades 5 - 8 (%)		Grades 9 - 12 (%)	
	Public	Private	Public	Private	Public	Private	Public	Private	Public	Private
City	32.8	67.2	81.6	18.4	88.6	11.4	90.6	9.4	92.9	7.1
MSA[1]	53.1	46.9	85.7	14.3	90.2	9.8	91.2	8.8	93.1	6.9
U.S.	56.9	43.1	87.8	12.2	89.9	10.1	90.0	10.0	90.8	9.2

Note: Figures shown cover persons 3 years old and over; (1) Figures cover the Virginia Beach-Norfolk-Newport News, VA-NC Metropolitan Statistical Area—see Appendix B for areas included
Source: U.S. Census Bureau, 2010-2012 American Community Survey 3-Year Estimates

Average Salaries of Public School Classroom Teachers

Area	2012-13		2013-14		Percent Change 2012-13 to 2013-14	Percent Change 2003-04 to 2013-14
	Dollars	Rank[1]	Dollars	Rank[1]		
Virginia	48,670	36	49,233	36	1.16	21.1
U.S. Average	56,103	–	56,689	–	1.04	21.8

Note: (1) State rank ranges from 1 to 51 where 1 indicates highest salary.
Source: National Education Association, Rankings & Estimates: Rankings of the States 2013 and Estimates of School Statistics 2014, March 2014

Higher Education

Four-Year Colleges			Two-Year Colleges			Medical Schools[1]	Law Schools[2]	Voc/ Tech[3]
Public	Private Non-profit	Private For-profit	Public	Private Non-profit	Private For-profit			
0	1	5	0	0	1	0	1	5

Note: Figures cover institutions located within the city limits and include main campuses only; (1) includes schools accredited by the Liaison Committee on Medical Education and the American Osteopathic Association's Commission on Osteopathic College Accreditation; (2) includes ABA-accredited schools, schools with provisional ABA accreditation, and state accredited schools; (3) includes all schools with programs that are less than 2 years.
Source: National Center for Education Statistics, Integrated Postsecondary Education System (IPEDS), 2012-13; Association of American Medical Colleges, Member List, April 24, 2014; American Osteopathic Association, Member List, April 24, 2014; Law School Admission Council, Official Guide to ABA-Approved Law Schools Online, April 24, 2014; Wikipedia, List of Medical Schools in the United States, April 24, 2014; Wikipedia, List of Law Schools in the United States, April 24, 2014

According to *U.S. News & World Report,* the Virginia Beach-Norfolk-Newport News, VA-NC metro area is home to one of the best national universities in the U.S.: **College of William and Mary** (#32). The indicators used to capture academic quality fall into a number of categories: assessment by administrators at peer institutions; retention of students; faculty resources; student selectivity; financial resources; alumni giving; high school counselor ratings of colleges; and graduation rate. *U.S. News & World Report, "America's Best Colleges 2014"*

According to *U.S. News & World Report,* the Virginia Beach-Norfolk-Newport News, VA-NC metro area is home to one of the best liberal arts colleges in the U.S.: **Virginia Wesleyan College** (#176). The indicators used to capture academic quality fall into a number of categories: assessment by administrators at peer institutions; retention of students; faculty resources; student selectivity; financial resources; alumni giving; high school counselor ratings of colleges; and graduation rate. *U.S. News & World Report, "America's Best Colleges 2014"*

According to *U.S. News & World Report,* the Virginia Beach-Norfolk-Newport News, VA-NC metro area is home to one of the top 100 law schools in the U.S.: **College of William and Mary (Marshall-Wythe)** (#33). The rankings are based on a weighted average of 12 measures of quality: peer assessment score; assessment score by lawyers/judges; median LSAT scores; median undergrad GPA; acceptance rate; employment rates for graduates; placement success; bar passage rate; faculty resources; expenditures per student; student/faculty ratio; and library resources. *U.S. News & World Report, "America's Best Graduate Schools, Law, 2014"*

According to *U.S. News & World Report,* the Virginia Beach-Norfolk-Newport News, VA-NC metro area is home to one of the top 100 business schools in the U.S.: **College of William and Mary (Mason)** (#70). The rankings are based on a weighted average of the following nine measures: quality assessment; peer assessment; recruiter assessment; placement success; mean starting salary and bonus; student selectivity; mean GMAT and GRE scores; mean undergraduate GPA; and acceptance rate. *U.S. News & World Report, "America's Best Graduate Schools, Business, 2014"*

PRESIDENTIAL ELECTION

2012 Presidential Election Results

Area	Obama	Romney	Other
Virginia Beach City	48.0	50.5	1.6
U.S.	51.0	47.2	1.8

Note: Results are percentages and may not add to 100% due to rounding
Source: Dave Leip's Atlas of U.S. Presidential Elections

EMPLOYERS

Major Employers

Company Name	Industry
Bank of America, National Association	National commerical banks
Chesapeake Hospital Authority	General medical and surgical hospitals
Children's Health System	Specialty hospitals, except psychiatric
City Line Apts.	Apartment building operators
City of Newport News, Virginia	Exeutive and legislative combined
City of Virginia Beach	Exeutive and legislative combined
Cox Communications Hampton Roads	Cable television services
Ford Motor Company	Truck and tractor truck assembly
Gwaltney of Smithfield, LTD	Meat packing plants
Hampton Training School for Nurses	General medical and surgical hospitals
Northrop Grumman Systems Corporation	Systems integration services
Old Dominion University	University
Riverside Hospital	General medical and surgical hospitals
STIHL Incorporated	Power-driven handtools
The College of William & Mary	Colleges and universities
The Colonial Williamsburg Foundation	Management services
The Colonial Williamsburg Foundation	Management consulting services
The Navy United States Department of	Offices and clinics of medical doctors
The Smithfield Packing Company	Hams and picnics, from meat slaughtered on site
Williamsburg James City Co Pub Schls	Schools and educational services, nec

Note: Companies shown are located within the Virginia Beach-Norfolk-Newport News, VA-NC Metropolitan Statistical Area.
Source: Hoovers.com; Wikipedia

PUBLIC SAFETY

Crime Rate

Area	All Crimes	Violent Crimes				Property Crimes		
		Murder	Forcible Rape	Robbery	Aggrav. Assault	Burglary	Larceny -Theft	Motor Vehicle Theft
City	2,787.2	4.7	13.0	72.8	78.9	351.4	2,158.7	107.7
Suburbs[1]	3,622.0	7.6	23.2	112.7	204.1	598.0	2,516.7	159.6
Metro[2]	3,402.7	6.8	20.5	102.3	171.2	533.2	2,422.7	146.0
U.S.	3,246.1	4.7	26.9	112.9	242.3	670.2	1,959.3	229.7

Note: Figures are crimes per 100,000 population; (1) All areas within the metro area that are located outside the city limits; (2) Figures cover the Virginia Beach-Norfolk-Newport News, VA-NC Metropolitan Statistical Area—see Appendix B for areas included
Source: FBI Uniform Crime Reports, 2012

Hate Crimes

Area	Number of Quarters Reported	Bias Motivation				
		Race	Religion	Sexual Orientation	Ethnicity	Disability
City	4	2	0	0	0	0
U.S.	4	2,797	1,099	1,135	667	92

Source: Federal Bureau of Investigation, Hate Crime Statistics 2012

Identity Theft Consumer Complaints

Area	Complaints	Complaints per 100,000 Population	Rank[2]
MSA[1]	1,348	80.4	106
U.S.	290,056	91.8	-

Note: (1) Figures cover the Virginia Beach-Norfolk-Newport News, VA-NC Metropolitan Statistical Area—see Appendix B for areas included; (2) Rank ranges from 1 to 377 where 1 indicates greatest number of identity theft complaints per 100,000 population
Source: Federal Trade Commission, Consumer Sentinel Network Data Book for January–December 2013

Fraud and Other Consumer Complaints

Area	Complaints	Complaints per 100,000 Population	Rank[2]
MSA[1]	7,854	468.4	39
U.S.	1,811,724	595.2	-

Note: (1) Figures cover the Virginia Beach-Norfolk-Newport News, VA-NC Metropolitan Statistical Area—see Appendix B for areas included; (2) Rank ranges from 1 to 377 where 1 indicates greatest number of identity theft complaints per 100,000 population
Source: Federal Trade Commission, Consumer Sentinel Network Data Book for January–December 2013

RECREATION

Culture

Dance[1]	Theatre[1]	Instrumental Music[1]	Vocal Music[1]	Series and Festivals	Museums and Art Galleries[2]	Zoos and Aquariums[3]
1	1	1	0	0	16	1

Note: (1) Number of professional performing groups; (2) Based on organizations with primary SIC code 8412; (3) AZA-accredited
Source: The Grey House Performing Arts Directory, 2013; Association of Zoos & Aquariums, AZA Member Zoos & Aquariums, April 2014; www.AccuLeads.com, May 1, 2014

Professional Sports Teams

Team Name	League	Year Established

No teams are located in the metro area
Source: Wikipedia, Major Professional Sports Teams of the United States and Canada, April 25, 2014

CLIMATE

Average and Extreme Temperatures

Temperature	Jan	Feb	Mar	Apr	May	Jun	Jul	Aug	Sep	Oct	Nov	Dec	Yr.
Extreme High (°F)	78	81	88	97	100	101	103	104	99	95	86	80	104
Average High (°F)	48	51	58	68	76	84	88	86	80	70	61	52	69
Average Temp. (°F)	41	42	49	58	67	75	79	78	72	62	53	44	60
Average Low (°F)	32	33	40	48	57	66	71	70	64	53	44	35	51
Extreme Low (°F)	-3	8	18	28	36	45	54	49	45	27	20	7	-3

Note: Figures cover the years 1948-1995
Source: National Climatic Data Center, International Station Meteorological Climate Summary, 9/96

Average Precipitation/Snowfall/Humidity

Precip./Humidity	Jan	Feb	Mar	Apr	May	Jun	Jul	Aug	Sep	Oct	Nov	Dec	Yr.
Avg. Precip. (in.)	3.6	3.3	3.8	3.0	3.7	3.5	5.2	5.3	3.9	3.3	3.0	3.1	44.8
Avg. Snowfall (in.)	3	3	1	Tr	0	0	0	0	0	0	Tr	1	8
Avg. Rel. Hum. 7am (%)	74	74	74	73	77	79	81	84	83	82	79	75	78
Avg. Rel. Hum. 4pm (%)	59	56	53	50	56	57	60	63	62	60	58	59	58

Note: Figures cover the years 1948-1995; Tr = Trace amounts (<0.05 in. of rain; <0.5 in. of snow)
Source: National Climatic Data Center, International Station Meteorological Climate Summary, 9/96

Weather Conditions

Temperature			Daytime Sky			Precipitation		
10°F & below	32°F & below	90°F & above	Clear	Partly cloudy	Cloudy	0.01 inch or more precip.	0.1 inch or more snow/ice	Thunder-storms
<1	53	33	89	149	127	115	5	38

Note: Figures are average number of days per year and cover the years 1948-1995
Source: National Climatic Data Center, International Station Meteorological Climate Summary, 9/96

HAZARDOUS WASTE

Superfund Sites

Virginia Beach has one hazardous waste site on the EPA's Superfund Final National Priorities List: **Naval Amphibious Base Little Creek.** *U.S. Environmental Protection Agency, Final National Priorities List, April 26, 2014*

AIR & WATER QUALITY

Air Quality Index

Area	Percent of Days when Air Quality was...[2]					AQI Statistics[2]	
	Good	Moderate	Unhealthy for Sensitive Groups	Unhealthy	Very Unhealthy	Maximum	Median
MSA[1]	80.3	19.7	0.0	0.0	0.0	100	39

Note: (1) Data covers the Virginia Beach-Norfolk-Newport News, VA-NC Metropolitan Statistical Area—see Appendix B for areas included; (2) Based on 365 days with AQI data in 2013. Air Quality Index (AQI) is an index for reporting daily air quality. EPA calculates the AQI for five major air pollutants regulated by the Clean Air Act: ground-level ozone, particle pollution, carbon monoxide, sulfur dioxide, and nitrogen dioxide. The AQI runs from 0 to 500. The higher the AQI value, the greater the level of air pollution and the greater the health concern. There are six AQI categories: "Good" AQI is between 0 and 50. Air quality is considered satisfactory; "Moderate" AQI is between 51 and 100. Air quality is acceptable; "Unhealthy for Sensitive Groups" When AQI values are between 101 and 150, members of sensitive groups may experience health effects; "Unhealthy" When AQI values are between 151 and 200 everyone may begin to experience health effects; "Very Unhealthy" AQI values between 201 and 300 trigger a health alert; "Hazardous" AQI values over 300 trigger warnings of emergency conditions (not shown).
Source: U.S. Environmental Protection Agency, Air Quality Index Report, 2013

Air Quality Index Pollutants

Area	Percent of Days when AQI Pollutant was...[2]					
	Carbon Monoxide	Nitrogen Dioxide	Ozone	Sulfur Dioxide	Particulate Matter 2.5	Particulate Matter 10
MSA[1]	0.0	5.8	34.8	9.6	49.9	0.0

Note: (1) Data covers the Virginia Beach-Norfolk-Newport News, VA-NC Metropolitan Statistical Area—see Appendix B for areas included; (2) Based on 365 days with AQI data in 2013. The Air Quality Index (AQI) is an index for reporting daily air quality. EPA calculates the AQI for five major air pollutants regulated by the Clean Air Act: ground-level ozone, particle pollution (also known as particulate matter), carbon monoxide, sulfur dioxide, and nitrogen dioxide. The AQI runs from 0 to 500. The higher the AQI value, the greater the level of air pollution and the greater the health concern.
Source: U.S. Environmental Protection Agency, Air Quality Index Report, 2013

Air Quality Trends: Ozone

	2003	2004	2005	2006	2007	2008	2009	2010	2011	2012
MSA[1]	0.081	0.075	0.078	0.074	0.077	0.078	0.065	0.074	0.075	0.069

Note: (1) Data covers the Virginia Beach-Norfolk-Newport News, VA-NC Metropolitan Statistical Area—see Appendix B for areas included. The values shown are the composite ozone concentration averages among trend sites based on the highest fourth daily maximum 8-hour concentration in parts per million. These trends are based on sites having an adequate record of monitoring data during the trend period. Data from exceptional events are included.
Source: U.S. Environmental Protection Agency, Air Quality Monitoring Information, "Air Quality Trends by City, 2000-2012"

Maximum Air Pollutant Concentrations: Particulate Matter, Ozone, CO and Lead

	Particulate Matter 10 (ug/m³)	Particulate Matter 2.5 Wtd AM (ug/m³)	Particulate Matter 2.5 24-Hr (ug/m³)	Ozone (ppm)	Carbon Monoxide (ppm)	Lead (ug/m³)
MSA[1] Level	32	8.2	23	0.074	1	n/a
NAAQS[2]	150	15	35	0.075	9	0.15
Met NAAQS[2]	Yes	Yes	Yes	Yes	Yes	n/a

Note: (1) Data covers the Virginia Beach-Norfolk-Newport News, VA-NC Metropolitan Statistical Area—see Appendix B for areas included; Data from exceptional events are included; (2) National Ambient Air Quality Standards; ppm = parts per million; ug/m³ = micrograms per cubic meter; n/a not available.
Concentrations: Particulate Matter 10 (coarse particulate)—highest second maximum 24-hour concentration; Particulate Matter 2.5 Wtd AM (fine particulate)—highest weighted annual mean concentration; Particulate Matter 2.5 24-Hour (fine particulate)—highest 98th percentile 24-hour concentration; Ozone—highest fourth daily maximum 8-hour concentration; Carbon Monoxide—highest second maximum non-overlapping 8-hour concentration; Lead—maximum running 3-month average
Source: U.S. Environmental Protection Agency, Air Quality Monitoring Information, "Air Quality Statistics by City, 2012"

Maximum Air Pollutant Concentrations: Nitrogen Dioxide and Sulfur Dioxide

	Nitrogen Dioxide AM (ppb)	Nitrogen Dioxide 1-Hr (ppb)	Sulfur Dioxide AM (ppb)	Sulfur Dioxide 1-Hr (ppb)	Sulfur Dioxide 24-Hr (ppb)
MSA[1] Level	8	41	n/a	56	n/a
NAAQS[2]	53	100	30	75	140
Met NAAQS[2]	Yes	Yes	n/a	Yes	n/a

Note: (1) Data covers the Virginia Beach-Norfolk-Newport News, VA-NC Metropolitan Statistical Area—see Appendix B for areas included; Data from exceptional events are included; (2) National Ambient Air Quality Standards; ppm = parts per million; ug/m³ = micrograms per cubic meter; n/a not available.
Concentrations: Nitrogen Dioxide AM—highest arithmetic mean concentration; Nitrogen Dioxide 1-Hr—highest 98th percentile 1-hour daily maximum concentration; Sulfur Dioxide AM—highest annual mean concentration; Sulfur Dioxide 1-Hr—highest 99th percentile 1-hour daily maximum concentration; Sulfur Dioxide 24-Hr—highest second maximum 24-hour concentration
Source: U.S. Environmental Protection Agency, Air Quality Monitoring Information, "Air Quality Statistics by City, 2012"

Drinking Water

Water System Name	Pop. Served	Primary Water Source Type	Violations[1] Health Based	Violations[1] Monitoring/ Reporting
City of Virginia Beach	446,067	Purchased Surface	0	0

Note: (1) Based on violation data from January 1, 2013 to December 31, 2013 (includes unresolved violations from earlier years)
Source: U.S. Environmental Protection Agency, Office of Ground Water and Drinking Water, Safe Drinking Water Information System (based on data extracted February 10, 2014)

Washington, District of Columbia

Background

The city and federal district of Washington, D.C., with its more than 150 foreign embassies, consulates and ambassadors' residences, is definitely cosmopolitan.

In 1793, the first cornerstone of the White House was laid. In 1800, the north wing was completed, and a drifting Congress found its home. President John Adams was the first president to reside at the White House. The building was burned down by the British in 1814 (during the War of 1812), and its final reconstruction was completed in 1891.

The young capital, which grows more confident and worldly every year, is renowned for its brilliant annual springtime display of cherry blossoms, as well as a breathtaking collection of architectural styles, including Greek Revival, Federal, Victorian, and Baroque. Some of the city's monuments and well-known sites include the Washington Monument, Lincoln Memorial, the White House, Jefferson Memorial, Vietnam Veterans Memorial, and Arlington National Cemetery. In 2004, the National World War II Memorial was dedicated, as part of a four-day WWII Reunion, and the United States Air Force Memorial was completed in 2006.

As the political machine of the country, the main industry is, of course, government. A second major employer for the city proper is the tourism industry. Washington is also home to five major universities: American; Georgetown; George Washington; Howard; and the Catholic University of America.

On September 11, 2001, the city suffered an attack orchestrated by Saudi terrorist Osama bin Laden as part of a wider assault on the U.S. that included the World Trade Center in New York on the same day. An airplane was used (as in the NYC attack) to crash through one side of the Pentagon just across from the Potomac River in Virginia, after, it is believed, terrorists on board were unable to locate their original target—either the White House or the Capitol. Several hundred people were killed in the Pentagon attack, which has led to a major revamping of security procedures on airplanes and in airports throughout the U.S. This has also led to a noticeable tightening of security in the district itself.

Although the months following the tragedy brought economic uncertainty to much of the nation, including the District of Columbia, indicators show a rebound and resumption of the district's urban renaissance, with population now in modest gains.

The Walter E. Washington Convention Center, open since 2004, hosted 191 events and welcomed nearly 1.15 million visitors in 2005. The convention center has sparked a new phase in the economic development of the city's northeast downtown area, which had been devastated by the riots of 1968. In addition to the convention center, a new City Museum opened up across the street at the old Carnegie Library. Just a few blocks south, many new restaurants have opened in the general vicinity of the International Spy Museum and the Verizon Center, home to the NBA Wizards, WNBA Mystics, and the NHL Capitals. The Washington Nationals baseball team plays at Nationals Park, a new state-of-the-art facility with over 41,000 seats.

At the John F. Kennedy Center for the Performing Arts, a $50 million construction project was completed in 2005, which improved access to the center and made its handsome facade more visually compelling. More recently completed was the renovation of the Eisenhower Theater in the JFK Center.

In addition, the Smithsonian Institution's National Air and Space Museum has expanded into a second museum near the Washington Dulles International Airport in Virginia, which is called the Steven F. Udvar-Hazy Center.

The city's numerous museums include the National Gallery of Art, U.S. Holocaust Memorial Museum, the Corcoran Gallery, the Phillips Collection, the Hirshhorn Museum and Sculpture Garden, and the many other Smithsonian museums. One of the city's newest museums, the National Museum of the American Indian, opened in 2004 in a dramatic new building on the National Mall, with a mission to explore and celebrate the histories and cultures of Native Americans from North, Central, and South America.

Washington, a global media center, has bureaus of all worldwide major news outlets. It is also home to Black Entertainment Television, C-SPAN, National Public Radio, the Washington Post Company and XM Satellite Radio.

Summertime in Washington is warm and humid; winters are cold, but usually not severe.

Rankings

General Rankings

- Among the 50 largest U.S. cities, Washington placed #11 in Vocativ's "semi-exhaustive, mostly scientific" city Livability Index for people aged 35 and under. Average salary, unemployment rates, rents, and other living costs were considered, along with bike lanes, low-cost broadband, cheap takeout, self-service laundries, the price of a pint of Guinness, music venues, and vintage clothing stores. *vocative.com, "The Livability Index: The Best U.S. Cities for People 35 and Under," November 7, 2013*

- Washington was selected as one of America's best cities by *Bloomberg Businessweek*. The city ranked #3 out of 50. Criteria: leisure attributes (the number of restaurants, bars, libraries, museums, professional sports teams, and park acres by population); educational attributes (public school performance, the number of colleges, and graduate degree holders); economic factors (2011 income and June and July 2012 unemployment); crime; and air quality. *Bloomberg BusinessWeek, "America's Best Cities," September 26, 2012*

- Washington appeared on RelocateAmerica's list of best places to live in America. The annual "Top 100 Places to Live" list recognizes the top communities as nominated by their residents & local businesses. RelocateAmerica's Research Group determined the list based on review of various data gathered for economic, employment, housing, education, industry, opportunity, environment and recreation along with feedback from area leaders and residents. *RelocateAmerica.com, "Top 100 Places to Live for 2011"*

- Washington was selected as one the best places to live in America by *Outside Magazine*. Criteria: ample trailheads; nearby adventure; great farmers' markets; competitive gear-shop scene. *Outside Magazine, "Outside's Best Towns 2013," September 2013*

- Washington was selected as one of "America's Favorite Cities." The city ranked #21 in the "Quality of Life and Visitor Experience: Cleanliness" category. Respondents to an online survey were asked to rate 35 top urban destinations in the U.S. from a visitor's perspective. Criteria: cleanliness. *Travel + Leisure, "America's Favorite Cities 2013"*

- Washington was selected as one of "America's Favorite Cities." The city ranked #22 in the "Type of Trip: Gay-friendly" category. Respondents to an online survey were asked to rate 35 top urban destinations in the U.S. from a visitor's perspective. Criteria: gay-friendly. *Travel + Leisure, "America's Favorite Cities 2013"*

- Mercer Human Resources Consulting ranked 221 cities worldwide in terms of overall quality of life. Washington ranked #43. Criteria: political, social, economic, and socio-cultural factors; medical and health considerations; schools and education; public services and transportation; recreation; consumer goods; housing; and natural environment. *Mercer Human Resources Consulting, "Mercer 2012 Quality of Living Survey,"December 4, 2012*

- Washington appeared on *Travel + Leisure's* list of the ten best cities in the U.S. and Canada. The city was ranked #10. Criteria: activities/attractions; culture/arts; restaurants/food; people; and value. *Travel + Leisure, "The World's Best Awards 2013"*

Business/Finance Rankings

- Measuring indicators of "tolerance"—the nonjudgmental environment that "attracts open-minded and new-thinking kinds of people"— as well as concentrations of technological and economic innovators, analysts identified the most creative American metro areas. On the resulting 2012 Creativity Index, the Washington metro area placed #9. *www.thedailybeast.com, "Boulder, Ann Arbor, Tucson & More: 20 Most Creative U.S. Cities," June 26, 2012*

- Building on the U.S. Department of Labor's Occupational Information Network Data Collection Program, the Brookings Institution defined STEM occupations and job opportunities for STEM workers at various levels of educational attainment. The Washington metro area was one of the ten metro areas where workers in low-education-level STEM jobs earn the lowest relative wages. *www.brookings.edu, "The Hidden Stem Economy," June 10, 2013*

- Building on the U.S. Department of Labor's Occupational Information Network Data Collection Program, the Brookings Institution defined STEM occupations and job opportunities for STEM workers at various levels of educational attainment. The Washington metro area was placed among the ten large metro areas with the highest demand for high-level STEM knowledge. *www.brookings.edu, "The Hidden Stem Economy," June 10, 2013*

- The business website 24/7 Wall Street drew on the Brookings Institution's report "The Hidden STEM Economy" to identify the proportion of workers in the nation's largest metropolitan areas that were employed in jobs requiring knowledge in the science, technology, engineering, or math (STEM) fields. The Washington metro area was #2. *247wallst.com, "The Best Cities for High-Tech Jobs," June 10, 2013*

- Based on a minimum of 500 social media reviews per metro area, the employment opinion group Glassdoor surveyed 50 of the largest U.S. metro areas on measures including compensation and benefits, satisfaction with management, business outlook, and number of employers hiring. The Washington metro area was ranked #5 in overall employee satisfaction. *www.glassdoor.com, "Employment Satisfaction Report Card by City," June 21, 2013*

- In a survey of economic confidence in the nation's 50 largest metropolitan areas conducted January–December 2012, the Washington metro area placed among the top five, according to Gallup's 2013 Economic Confidence Index. *Gallup Economy, "D.C. Metro Area Again Leads U.S. in Economic Confidence," March 28, 2013*

- The financial literacy site NerdWallet.com set out to identify the 20 most promising cities for job seekers, analyzing data for the nation's 50 largest cities. Washington was ranked #2. Criteria: unemployment rate; population growth; median income; selected monthly owner costs. *NerdWallet.com, "Best Cities for Job Seekers," January 7, 2014*

- The Brookings Institution ranked the 50 largest cities in the U.S. based on income inequality. Washington was ranked #5. (#1 = greatest inequality). Criteria: the cities were ranked based on the "95/20 ratio." This figure represents the income at which a household earns more than 95 percent of all other households, divided by the income at which a household earns more than only 20 percent of all other households. *Brookings Institution, "Income Inequality in America's 50 Largest Cities, 2007-2012," February 20, 2014*

- *Forbes* ranked the largest metro areas in the U.S. in terms of the "Best Cities for Young Professionals." The Washington metro area ranked #9 out of 15. Criteria: job growth; unemployment rate; median salary of college graduates age 24 to 34; cost of living; number of small businesses per capita; number of large companies; percentage of population 25 years of age and older with college degrees. *Forbes.com, "America's Best Cities for Young Professionals," July 12, 2011*

- Washington was ranked #70 out of 100 metro areas in terms of economic performance (#1 = best) during the recession and recovery from trough quarter through the second quarter of 2013. Criteria: percent change in employment; percentage point change in unemployment rate; percent change in gross metropolitan product; percent change in House Price Index. *Brookings Institution, MetroMonitor: Tracking Economic Recession and Recovery in America's 100 Largest Metropolitan Areas, September 2013*

- Washington was identified as one of the best places for finding a job by *U.S. News & World Report.* The city ranked #4 out of 10. Criteria: strong job market. *U.S. News & World Report, "The 10 Best Cities to Find Jobs," June 17, 2013*

- Payscale.com ranked the 20 largest metro areas in terms of wage growth. The Washington metro area ranked #9. Criteria: private-sector wage growth between the 4th quarter of 2012 and the 4th quarter of 2013. *PayScale, "Wage Trends by Metro Area," 4th Quarter, 2013*

- For its annual survey of the "10 Most Expensive U.S. Cities to Live In," Kiplinger applied Cost of Living Index statistics developed by the Council for Community and Economic Research to U.S. Census Bureau population and median household income data for cities with populations above 50,000. In the resulting ranking, Washington ranked #6. *Kiplinger.com, "10 Most Expensive U.S. Cities to Live In," June 2013*

- Washington was identified as one of America's most frugal metro areas by *Coupons.com.* The city ranked #11 out of 25. Criteria: online coupon usage. *Coupons.com, "Top 25 Most Frugal Cities of 2012," February 19, 2013*

- Washington was identified as one of America's most frugal metro areas by *Coupons.com*. The city ranked #11 out of 25. Criteria: Grocery IQ and coupons.com mobile app usage. *Coupons.com, "Top 25 Most On-the-Go Frugal Cities of 2012," February 19, 2013*

- Washington was identified as one of America's "10 Best Cities to Get a Job" by *U.S. News & World Report*. The city ranked #1. Criteria: number of available jobs; unemployment rate. *U.S. News & World Report, "10 Best Cities to Get a Job," February 1, 2011*

- Washington was identified as one of the top 25 U.S. cities with the most credit card debt by credit reporting bureau Experian. The city was ranked #17. *Experian, March 4, 2011*

- Washington was identified as one of the best cities for college graduates to find work—and live. The city ranked #1 out of 15. Criteria: job availability; average salary; average rent. *CareerBuilder.com, "15 Best Cities for College Grads to Find Work—and Live," June 5, 2012*

- Washington was identified as one of the happiest cities to work in by CareerBliss.com, an online community for career advancement. The city ranked #2 out of 10. Criteria: independent company reviews from employees all over the country on: relationship with their boss and co-workers; work environment; job resources; compensation; growth opportunities; company culture; company reputation; daily tasks; job control over work performed on a daily basis. *CareerBliss.com, "Top 10 Happiest and Unhappiest Cities to Work in 2014," February 10, 2014*

- Washington was identified as one of the happiest cities for young professionals by *CareerBliss.com*, an online community for career advancement. The city ranked #3. Criteria: more than 45,000 young professionals were asked to rate key factors that affect workplace happiness including: work-life balance; compensation; company culture; overall work environment; company reputation; relationships with managers and co-workers; opportunities for growth; job resources; daily tasks; job autonomy. Young professionals are defined as having less than 10 years of work experience. *CareerBliss.com, "Happiest Cities for Young Professionals," April 26, 2013*

- The Washington metro area appeared on the Milken Institute "2013 Best Performing Cities" list. Rank: #45 out of 200 large metro areas. Criteria: job growth; wage and salary growth; high-tech output growth. *Milken Institute, "Best-Performing Cities 2013," December 2013*

- *Forbes* ranked the 200 most populous metro areas in the U.S. in terms of the "Best Places for Business and Careers." The Washington metro area was ranked #37. Criteria: costs (business and living); job growth (past and projected); income growth; educational attainment (college and high school); projected economic growth; cultural and recreational opportunities; net migration patterns; number of highly ranked colleges. *Forbes, "The Best Places for Business and Careers," August 7, 2013*

Children/Family Rankings

- Washington was selected as one of the best cities for families to live by *Parenting* magazine. The city ranked #6 out of 100. Criteria: education; health; community; *Parenting's* Culture & Charm Index. *Parenting.com, "The 2012 Best Cities for Families List"*

Culture/Performing Arts Rankings

- Washington was selected as one of "America's Favorite Cities." The city ranked #1 in the "Culture: Museum/Galleries" category. Respondents to an online survey were asked to rate 35 top urban destinations in the U.S. from a visitor's perspective. Criteria: number and quality of museums and galleries. *Travelandleisure.com, "America's Favorite Cities 2013"*

- Washington was selected as one of America's top cities for the arts. The city ranked #2 in the big city (population 500,000 and over) category. Criteria: readers' top choices for arts travel destinations based on the richness and variety of visual arts sites, activities and events. *American Style, "2012 Top 25 Arts Destinations," June 2012*

Dating/Romance Rankings

- A *Cosmopolitan* magazine article surveyed the gender balance and other factors to arrive at a list of the best and worst cities for women to meet single guys. Washington placed #3 among the worst for single women looking for dates. *www.cosmopolitan.com, "Working the Ratio," October 1, 2013*

- *Forbes* reports that the Washington metro area made Rent.com's Best Cities for Newlyweds survey for 2013, based on Bureau of Labor Statistics and Census Bureau data on number of married couples, percentage of families with children under age six, average annual income, cost of living, and availability of rentals. *www.forbes.com, "The 10 Best Cities for Newlyweds to Live and Work In," May 30, 2013*

- CreditDonkey, a financial education website, sought out the ten best U.S. cities for newlyweds, considering the number of married couples, divorce rate, average credit score, and average number of hours worked per week in metro areas with a million or more residents. The Washington metro area placed #7. *www.creditdonkey.com, "Study: Best Cities for Newlyweds," November 30, 2013*

- Washington took the #2 spot on NerdWallet's list of best cities for singles wanting to date, based on the availability of singles; "date-friendliness," as determined by a city's walkability and the number of bars and restaurants per thousand residents; and the affordability of dating in terms of the cost of movie tickets, pizza, and wine for two. *www.nerdwallet.com, "Best Cities for Singles," February 5, 2014*

- Of the 100 U.S. cities surveyed by *Men's Health* in its quest to identify the nation's best cities for dating and forming relationships, Washington was ranked #24 for online dating (#1 = best). *Men's Health, "The Best and Worst Cities for Online Dating," January 30, 2013*

- Washington was selected as one of the best cities for single men by *Rent.com*. Criteria: high single female-to-male ratio. *Rent.com, "Top Cities for Single Men," March 14, 2013*

- Washington was selected as one of the best cities for newlyweds by *Rent.com*. The city ranked #9 of 10. Criteria: cost of living; mean annual income; unemployment rate. *Rent.com, "10 Best Cities for Newlyweds," March 20, 2012*

- Washington was selected as one of the best cities for single women in America by *SingleMindedWomen.com*. The city ranked #5. Criteria: ratio of women to men; singles population; healthy lifestyle; employment opportunities; cost of living; access to travel; entertainment options; social opportunities. *SingleMindedWomen.com, "Top 10 Cities for Single Women," 2011*

Education Rankings

- *Fast Company* magazine measured six key components of "smart" cities and three "drivers" for each component to reveal the top ten "Smartest Cities in North America." By these complex metrics, Washington ranked #4. *Fastcoexist.com, "The Top 10 Smartest Cities in North America," November 15, 2013*

- Washington was identified as one of America's "smartest" metropolitan areas by *The Business Journals*. The area ranked #1 out of 10. Criteria: percentage of adults (25 and older) with high school diplomas, bachelor's degrees and graduate degrees. *The Business Journals, "Where the Brainpower Is: Exclusive U.S. Rankings, Insights," February 27, 2014*

- *Men's Health* ranked 100 U.S. cities in terms of their education levels. Washington was ranked #34 (#1 = most educated city). Criteria: high school graduation rates; school enrollment; educational attainment; number of households who have outstanding student loans; number of households whose members have taken adult-education courses. *Men's Health, "Where School Is In: The Most and Least Educated Cities," September 12, 2011*

- Washington was selected as one of "America's Geekiest Cities" by *Forbes.com*. The city ranked #7 of 20. Criteria: percentage of workers with jobs in science, technology, engineering and mathematics. *Forbes.com, "America's Geekiest Cities," August 5, 2011*

- Washington was selected as one of America's most literate cities. The city ranked #1 out of the 77 largest U.S. cities. Criteria: number of booksellers; library resources; Internet resources; educational attainment; periodical publishing resources; newspaper circulation. *Central Connecticut State University, "America's Most Literate Cities, 2013"*

- Washington was identified as one of "America's Smartest Cities" by *The Daily Beast* using data from Lumos Labs. The metro area ranked #5 out of 25. Criteria: with data collected from more than 1 million users as part of its human cognition project, Lumos Labs was able to analyze performance for nearly 200 metro areas in five cognitive areas: memory, processing speed, flexibility, attention, and problem solving. The median Lumos Lab score was worth 50 percent of the final, weighted ranking. The other half of the ranking was based on the percentage of adults over age 25 with a bachelor's and/or master's degree. *The Daily Beast, "America's Smartest Cities 2012" August 16, 2012*

Environmental Rankings

- The Washington metro area came in at #206 for the relative comfort of its climate on Sperling's list of "chill cities," as measured by the Sperling Heat Index. All 361 metro areas are included. Criteria included daytime high temperatures, nighttime low temperatures, dew point, and relative humidity at the high temperatures. *www.bertsperling.com, "Sperling's Chill Cities," July 18, 2013*

- Sperling's BestPlaces assessed 379 metropolitan areas of the United States for the likelihood of dangerously extreme weather events or earthquakes. In general the Southeast and South-Central regions have the highest risk of weather extremes and earthquakes, while the Pacific Northwest enjoys the lowest risk. Of the least risky metropolitan areas, the Washington metro area was ranked #212. *www.bestplaces.net, "Safest Places from Natural Disasters," April 2011*

- Washington was identified as one of North America's greenest metropolitan areas. The area ranked #8. The Green City Index is comprised of 31 indicators, and scores cities across nine categories: carbon dioxide; energy; land use; buildings; transport; water; waste; air quality; environmental governance. The 27 largest metropolitan areas in the U.S. and Canada were considered. *Economist Intelligence Unit, sponsored by Siemens, "U.S. and Canada Green City Index, 2011"*

- The U.S. Environmental Protection Agency (EPA) released a list of U.S. metropolitan areas with the most ENERGY STAR certified buildings in 2012. The Washington metro area was ranked #2 out of 25. *U.S. Environmental Protection Agency, "Top Cities With the Most ENERGY STAR Certified Buildings in 2012," March 12, 2013*

- Washington was selected as one of 22 "Smarter Cities" for energy by the Natural Resources Defense Council. Criteria: investment in green power; energy efficiency measures; conservation. *Natural Resources Defense Council, "2010 Smarter Cities," July 19, 2010*

- The U.S. Conference of Mayors and Wal-Mart Stores sponsor the Mayors' Climate Protection Awards Program. The awards recognize and honor mayors for outstanding and innovative practices that mayors are taking to increase energy efficiency in their cities, and to help curb global warming. Washington received an Honorable Mention in the large city category. *U.S. Conference of Mayors, "2013 Mayors' Climate Protection Awards Program," June 21, 2013*

- Washington was highlighted as one of the 25 most ozone-polluted metro areas in the U.S. during 2008 through 2010. The area ranked #9. *American Lung Association, State of the Air 2012*

Food/Drink Rankings

- According to Fodor's Travel, Washington placed #9 among the best U.S. cities for food-truck cuisine. *www.fodors.com, "America's Best Food Truck Cities," December 20, 2013*

- *Men's Health* ranked 100 major U.S. cities in terms of alcohol intoxication. Washington ranked #59 (#1 = most sober).Criteria: binge drinking; alcohol-related traffic accidents, arrests, and fatalities. *Men's Health, "The Drunkest Cities in America," November 19, 2013*

- Washington was identified as one of "America's Most Caffeinated Cities" by *Bundle.com*. The city was ranked #6 out of 10. The rankings were determined by examining consumer spending at 16 widely known coffee chains during the second quarter of 2011. *Bundle.com, "America's Most Caffeinated Cities," September 19, 2011*

- National Park (Washington Nationals) was selected as one of PETA's "Top 10 Vegetarian-Friendly Major League Ballparks" for 2013. The park ranked #3. *People for the Ethical Treatment of Animals, "Top 10 Vegetarian-Friendly Major League Ballparks," June 12, 2013*

Health/Fitness Rankings

- Analysts who tracked obesity rates in the nation's largest metro areas (those with populations above one million) found that the Washington metro area was one of the ten major metros where residents were least likely to be obese, defined as a BMI score of 30 or above. *www.gallup.com, "Boulder, Colo., Residents Still Least Likely to Be Obese," April 4, 2014*

- For each of the 50 most populous metro areas in the United States, the American College of Sports Medicine's American Fitness Index evaluated infrastructure, community assets, and policies that encourage healthy and fit lifestyles, including preventive health behaviors, levels of chronic disease conditions, health care access, and community resources and policies that support physical activity. The Washington metro area ranked #2 for "community fitness." Personal health indicators were considered as well as community and environmental indicators. *www.americanfitnessindex.org, "ACSM American Fitness Index Health and Community Fitness Status of the 50 Largest Metropolitan Areas," May 2013*

- Washington was identified as one of the 10 most walkable cities in the U.S. by Walk Score, a Seattle-based service that rates the convenience and transit access of 10,000 neighborhoods in 3,000 cities. The area ranked #7 out of the 50 largest U.S. cities. Walk Score measures walkability by analyzing hundreds of walking routes to nearby amenities. Walk Score also measures pedestrian friendliness by analyzing population density and road metrics such as block length and intersection density. *WalkScore.com, March 20, 2014*

- Washington was identified as one of the top running towns in the southern U.S. by *Running Journal*. The city ranked #1 out of seven. Criteria: training venues; access to running clubs; quality of local running events; specialty running stores; overall social scene. *Running Journal, "Top Running Towns of the South," March 13, 2012*

- The Washington metro area was identified as one of the worst cities for bed bugs in America by pest control company Orkin. The area ranked #8 out of 50 based on the number of bed bug treatments Orkin performed from January to December 2013. *Orkin, "Chicago Tops Bed Bug Cities List for Second Year in a Row," January 16, 2014*

- Washington was selected as one of the 25 fittest cities in America by *Men's Fitness Online*. It ranked #16 out of America's 50 largest cities. Criteria: fitness centers and sport stores; nutrition; sports participation; TV viewing; overweight/sedentary; junk food; air quality; geography; commute; parks and open space; city recreational facilities; access to healthcare; motivation; mayor and city initiatives; state obesity initiatives. *Men's Fitness, "The Fittest and Fattest Cities in America," March 5, 2012*

- Washington was identified as a "2013 Spring Allergy Capital." The area ranked #66 out of 100. Three groups of factors were used to identify the most severe cities for people with allergies during the spring season: annual pollen levels; medicine utilization; access to board-certified allergists. *Asthma and Allergy Foundation of America, "Spring Allergy Capitals 2013"*

- Washington was identified as a "2013 Fall Allergy Capital." The area ranked #83 out of 100. Three groups of factors were used to identify the most severe cities for people with allergies during the fall season: annual pollen levels; medicine utilization; access to board-certified allergists. *Asthma and Allergy Foundation of America, "Fall Allergy Capitals 2013"*

- Washington was identified as a "2013 Asthma Capital." The area ranked #43 out of the nation's 100 largest metropolitan areas. Twelve factors were used to identify the most challenging places to live for people with asthma: estimated prevalence; self-reported prevalence; crude death rate for asthma; annual pollen score; annual air quality; public smoking laws; number of board-certified asthma specialists; school inhaler access laws; rescue medication use; controller medication use; uninsured rate; poverty rate. *Asthma and Allergy Foundation of America, "Asthma Capitals 2013"*

- *Men's Health* ranked 100 major U.S. cities in terms of the best and worst cities for men. Washington ranked #24. Criteria: thirty-three data points were examined covering health, fitness, and quality of life. *Men's Health, "The Best & Worst Cities for Men 2014," December 6, 2013*

- The American Academy of Dermatology ranked 26 U.S. metropolitan regions in terms of their residents knowledge, attitude and behaviors towards tanning, sun protection and skin cancer detection. The Washington metro area ranked #15. The results of the study are based on an online survey of over 7,000 adults nationwide. *American Academy of Dermatology, "Suntelligence: How Sun Smart is Your City?," May 3, 2010*

- The Washington metro area appeared in the 2013 Gallup-Healthways Well-Being Index. The area ranked #11 out of 189. The Gallup-Healthways Well-Being Index score is an average of six sub-indexes, which individually examine life evaluation, emotional health, work environment, physical health, healthy behaviors, and access to basic necessities. Results are based on telephone interviews conducted as part of the Gallup-Healthways Well-Being Index survey January 2–December 29, 2012, and January 2–December 30, 2013, with a random sample of 531,630 adults, aged 18 and older, living in metropolitan areas in the 50 U.S. states and the District of Columbia. *Gallup-Healthways, "State of American Well-Being," March 25, 2014*

- The Washington metro area was identified as one of "America's Most Stressful Cities" by *Sperling's BestPlaces.* The metro area ranked #44 out of 50. Criteria: unemployment rate; suicide rate; commute time; mental health; poor rest; alcohol use; violent crime rate; property crime rate; cloudy days annually. *Sperling's BestPlaces, www.BestPlaces.net, "Stressful Cities 2012*

- The Washington metro area was identified as one of "America's Most Stressful Cities" by *Forbes.* The metro area ranked #4 out of 40. Criteria: housing affordability; unemployment rate; cost of living; air quality; traffic congestion; sunny days; population density. *Forbes.com, "America's Most Stressful Cities," September 23, 2011*

- *Men's Health* ranked 100 U.S. cities in terms of their activity levels. Washington was ranked #4 (#1 = most active city). Criteria: where and how often residents exercise; percentage of households that watch more than 15 hours of cable television a week and buy more than 11 video games a year; death rate from deep-vein thrombosis, a condition linked to sitting for extended periods of time. *Men's Health, "Where Sit Happens: The Most and Least Active Cities in America," June 20, 2011*

Pet Rankings

- Washington was selected as one of the best cities for dogs by real estate website Estately.com. The city was ranked #15. Criteria: weather; walkability; yard sizes; dog activities; meetup groups; availability of dogsitters. *Estately.com, "17 Best U.S. Cities for Dogs," May 14, 2013*

Real Estate Rankings

- ApartmentList.com calculated the most expensive American cities for renters, comparing median rental prices for studios, one-bedroom units, and two-bedroom units in the nation's 50 most populated cities. Washington placed #4 in the ApartmentList.com ranking. *www.cbsnews.com, "Top 10 Priciest U.S. Cities to Rent an Apartment," July 15, 2013*

- NerdWallet identified the 10 U.S. cities among the 25 largest, most hospitable for recent college graduates, based on demographics; social life; accessibility; cost of living; and economic opportunity. Washington placed #6 as a destination for new young graduates. *http://www.nerdwallet.com, "Best Cities for Fresh College Graduates," May 30, 2013*

- The PricewaterhouseCoopers and Urban Land Institute report *Emerging Trends in Real Estate* forecasts that improvements in leasing, rents, and pricing will fuel recovery in all property sectors in 2013. Washington was ranked #8 among the top ten markets to watch in 2013. *PricewaterhouseCoopers/Urban Land Institute, "U.S. Commercial Real Estate Recovery to Advance in 2013," October 17, 2012*

- Washington ranked #6 in a *Forbes* study of the rental housing market in the nation's 44 largest metropolitan areas to determine the cities that are worst for renters. Criteria: average rent in 2012's first quarter, year-over-year change in that figure, vacancy rate, and average monthly rent payment compared with average monthly mortgage payment. *Forbes.com, "The Best and Worst Cities for Renters," June 14, 2012*

- Washington was ranked #90 out of 283 metro areas in terms of house price appreciation in 2013 (#1 = highest rate). *Federal Housing Finance Agency, House Price Index, 4th Quarter 2013*

- Washington was selected as one of the eight best cities in the U.S. for real estate investment. The city ranked #4. *Association of Foreign Investors in Real Estate, "Ranking of USA Cities for Real Estate Investment, 2013"*

- Washington was ranked #153 out of 224 metro areas in terms of housing affordability in 2013 by the National Association of Home Builders (#1 = most affordable). The NAHB-Wells Fargo Housing Opportunity Index (HOI) for a given area is defined as the share of homes sold in that area that would have been affordable to a family earning the local median income, based on standard mortgage underwriting criteria. *National Association of Home Builders®, NAHB-Wells Fargo Housing Opportunity Index, 4th Quarter 2013*

- Washington was selected as one of the best college towns for renters by ApartmentRatings.com." The area ranked #22 out of 87. Overall satisfaction ratings were ranked using thousands of user submitted scores for hundreds of apartment complexes located in cities and towns that are home to the 100 largest four-year institutions in the U.S. *ApartmentRatings.com, "2011 College Town Renter Satisfaction Rankings"*

Safety Rankings

- Symantec, in partnership with Sperling's BestPlaces, ranked the 50 largest cities in the U.S. in terms of their vulnerability to cybercrime. The city ranked #1. Criteria: number of cyberattacks and potential infections; level of Internet access; expenditures on smartphones and computer hardware/software; wireless hotspots; broadband connectivity; Internet usage; online purchases. *Symantec, "Riskiest Online Cities of 2012" February 15, 2012*

- Allstate ranked the 200 largest cities in America in terms of driver safety. Washington ranked #194. Allstate researchers analyzed internal property damage claims over a two-year period from January 2010 to December 2011. A weighted average of the two-year numbers determined the annual percentages. *Allstate, "Allstate America's Best Drivers Report®, August 27, 2013"*

- Washington was identified as one of the most disaster-proof places in the U.S. in terms of its vulnerability to natural and non-natural disasters. The city ranked #5 out of 5. Rankings are based on the U.S. Center for Disease Control's Cities Readiness Initiative (CRI). As part of the CRI, the CDC and state public health personnel assess local emergency-management plans, protocols and capabilities for 72 Metropolitan Statistical Areas and four non-MSA large cities. *Forbes, "America's Most and Least Disaster-Proof Cities," December 12, 2011*

- Washington was identified as one of the most dangerous large cities in America by CQ Press. All 32 cities with populations of 500,000 or more that reported crime rates in 2012 for murder, rape, robbery, aggravated assault, burglary, and motor vehicle thefts were ranked. The city ranked #8 out of the top 10. *CQ Press, City Crime Rankings 2014*

- Washington was identified as one of the most dangerous cities in America by *The Business Insider.* Criteria: cities with 100,000 residents or more were ranked by violent crime rate in 2011. Violent crimes include for murder, rape, robbery, and aggravated assault. The city ranked #21 out of 25. *The Business Insider, "The 25 Most Dangerous Cities in America," November 4, 2012*

- The National Insurance Crime Bureau ranked 380 metro areas in the U.S. in terms of per capita rates of vehicle theft. The Washington metro area ranked #127 (#1 = highest rate). Criteria: number of vehicle theft offenses per 100,000 inhabitants in 2012. *National Insurance Crime Bureau, "Hot Spots 2012," June 26, 2013*

- The Washington metro area was identified as one of the most dangerous metro areas for pedestrians by Transportation for America. The metro area ranked #34 out of 52 metro areas with over 1 million residents. Criteria: area's population divided by the number of pedestrian fatalities in that area. *Transportation for America, "Dangerous by Design 2011"*

Seniors/Retirement Rankings

- From its Best Cities for Successful Aging indexes, the Milken Institute generated rankings for metropolitan areas, weighing data in eight categories—general indicators, health care, wellness, living arrangements, transportation and general accessibility, financial well-being, education and employment, and community participation. The Washington metro area was ranked #9 overall in the large metro area category. *Milken Institute, "Best Cities for Successful Aging," July 2012*

- Bankers Life and Casualty Company, in partnership with Sperling's BestPlaces, ranked the nation's 50 largest metro areas in terms of the "Best U.S. Cities for Seniors." The Washington metro area ranked #23. Criteria: healthcare; transportation; housing; environment; economy; health and longevity; social and spiritual life; crime. *Bankers Life and Casualty Company, Center for a Secure Retirement, "Best U.S. Cities for Seniors 2011," September 2011*

Sports/Recreation Rankings

- According to the personal finance website NerdWallet, the Washington metro area, at #12, is one of the nation's top dozen metro areas for sports fans. Criteria included the presence of all four major sports—MLB, NFL, NHL, and NBA, fan enthusiasm (as measured by game attendance), ticket affordability, and "sports culture," that is, number of sports bars. *www.nerdwallet.com, "Best Cities for Sports Fans," May 5, 2013*

- Washington was selected as one of "America's Most Miserable Sports Cities" by *Forbes*. The city was ranked #9. Criteria: postseason losses; years since last title; ratio of cumulative seasons to championships won. Contenders were limited to cities with at least 75 total seasons of NFL, NBA, NHL and MLB play. *Forbes, "America's Most Miserable Sports Cities," July 31, 2013*

- Washington appeared on the *Sporting News* list of the "Best Sports Cities" for 2011. The area ranked #12 out of 271. Criteria: the magazine takes a 12-month snapshot of each city's sports, putting a heavy premium on regular-season won-lost records (from the most recently completed season). Other criteria include: playoff berths, bowl appearances and tournament bids; championships; applicable power ratings; quality of competition; overall fan fervor (measured in part by attendance); abundance of teams (rewarding quality over quantity); stadium and arena quality; ticket availability and prices; franchise ownership; and marquee appeal of athletes. *Sporting News, "Best Sports Cities 2011," October 4, 2011*

- Washington appeared on the *Sporting News* list of the "Best Sports Cities" for 2011. The area ranked #12 out of 271. Criteria: a 12-month snapshot of regular-season won-lost records (from the most recently completed season). Other criteria include: playoff berths, bowl appearances and tournament bids; championships; applicable power ratings; quality of competition; overall fan fervor (measured in part by attendance); abundance of teams (quality over quantity); stadium and arena quality; ticket availability and prices; franchise ownership; and marquee appeal of athletes. *Sporting News, "Best Sports Cities 2011," October 4, 2011*

- Washington was chosen as a bicycle friendly community by the League of American Bicyclists. A "Bicycle Friendly Community" welcomes cyclists by providing safe accommodation for cycling and encouraging people to bike for transportation and recreation. There are four award levels: Platinum; Gold; Silver; and Bronze. The community achieved an award level of Silver. *League of American Bicyclists, "Bicycle Friendly Community Master List," Fall 2013*

- Washington was chosen as one of America's best cities for bicycling. The city ranked #4 out of 50. Criteria: robust cycling infrastructure; vibrant bike culture. The editors only considered cities with populations of 95,000 or more. *Bicycling, "America's Top 50 Bike-Friendly Cities," May 23, 2012*

Transportation Rankings

- Business Insider presented a Walk Score ranking of public transportation in 316 U.S. cities and thousands of city neighborhoods in which Washington earned the #4-ranked "Transit Score," awarded for frequency, type of route, and distance between stops. *www.businessinsider.com, "The US Cities with the Best Public Transportation Systems," January 30, 2014*

- More U.S. households choose not to have a car in 2012 than in prior years, according to a study by the University of Michigan Transportation Research Institute. The business website 24/7 Wall Street examined that study, along with a 2010 Census Special Report to arrive at its ranking of cities in which the fewest households had a vehicle. Washington held the #2 position. *247wallst.com, "Cities Where No One Wants to Drive," February 6, 2014*

- Washington appeared on *Trapster.com's* list of the 10 most-active U.S. cities for speed traps. The city ranked #5 of 10. *Trapster.com* is a community platform accessed online and via smartphone app that alerts drivers to traps, hazards and other traffic issues nearby. *Trapster.com, "Speeders Beware: Cities With the Most Speed Traps," February 10, 2012*

- Washington was identified as one of the most congested metro areas in the U.S. The area ranked #1 out of 10. Criteria: yearly delay per auto commuter in hours. *Texas A&M Transportation Institute, "2012 Urban Mobility Report," December 2012*

- The Washington metro area was selected as one of 15 "Smarter Cities" for transportation by the Natural Resources Defense Council. The area appeared in the large metro area (population greater than one million) category. Criteria: public transit availability and use; household automobile ownership and use; innovative, sustainable and affordable transportation programs. *Natural Resources Defense Council, "2011 Smarter Cities," February 23, 2011*

- The Washington metro area appeared on *Forbes* list of places with the most extreme commutes. The metro area ranked #3 out of 10. Criteria: average travel time; percentage of mega commuters. Mega-commuters travel more than 90 minutes and 50 miles each way to work. *Forbes.com, "The Cities with the Most Extreme Commutes," March 5, 2013*

Women/Minorities Rankings

- The Daily Beast surveyed the nation's cities for highest percentage of singles and lowest divorce rate, plus other measures, to determine "emotional intelligence"—happiness, confidence, kindness—which, researchers say, has a strong correlation with people's satisfaction with their romantic relationships. Washington placed #1. *www.thedailybeast.com, "Best Cities to Find Love and Stay in Love," February 14, 2014*

- To determine the best metro areas for working women, the personal finance website NerdWallet considered city size as well as relevant economic metrics—high salaries, narrow pay differential by gender, prevalence of women in the highest-paying industries, and population growth over 2010–2012. Of the large U.S. cities examined, the Washington metro area held the #1 position. *www.nerdwallet.com, "Best Places for Women in the Workforce," May 19, 2013*

- *Women's Health* examined U.S. cities and identified the 100 best cities for women. Washington was ranked #50. Criteria: 30 categories were examined from obesity and breast cancer rates to commuting times and hours spent working out. *Women's Health, "Best Cities for Women 2012"*

- Washington was selected as one of the gayest cities in America by *The Advocate*. The city ranked #1 out of 15. This year's criteria include points for a city's LGBT elected officials (and fractional points for the state's elected officials), points for the percentage of the population comprised by lesbian-coupled households, a point for a gay rodeo association, points for bars listed in *Out* magazine's 200 Best Bars list, a point per women's college, and points for concert performances by Mariah Carey, Pink, Lady Gaga, or the Jonas Brothers. The raw score is divided by the population to provide a ranking based on a per capita LGBT quotient. *The Advocate, "2014's Gayest Cities in America" January 6, 2014*

- The Washington metro area appeared on *Forbes'* list of the "Best Cities for Minority Entrepreneurs." The area ranked #1 out of 10. Criteria: 52 metropolitan statistical areas were examined. For each ethnicity (African Americans, Asians and Hispanics), the editors measured housing affordability, population growth, income growth, and entrepreneurship (per capita self-employment). *Forbes, "Best Cities for Minority Entrepreneurs," March 23, 2011*

Miscellaneous Rankings

- *Travel + Leisure* invited readers to rate cities on indicators such as aloofness, "smarty-pants residents," highbrow cultural offerings, high-end shopping, artisanal coffeehouses, conspicuous eco-consciousness, and more in order to identify the nation's snobbiest cities. Cities large and small made the list; among them was Washington, at #9. *www.travelandleisure.com, "America's Snobbiest Cities, June 2013*

- The watchdog site Charity Navigator conducts an annual study of charities in the nation's major markets both to analyze statistical differences in their financial, accountability, and transparency practices and to track year-to-year variations in individual communities. The Washington metro area was ranked #17 among the 30 metro markets. *www.charitynavigator.org, "Metro Market Study 2013," June 1, 2013*

- According to the World Giving Index, the United States is the fifth most generous nation in the world. The finance and lifestyle site NerdWallet looked for the U.S. cities that topped the list in donating money and time to good causes. The Washington metro area proved to be the #17-ranked metro area, judged by culture of volunteerism, depth of commitment in terms of volunteer hours per year, and monetary contributions. *www.nerdwallet.com, "Most Generous Cities," September 22, 2013*

- Business Insider reports on the 2013 Trick-or-Treat Index compiled by the real estate site Zillow, which used its own Home Value Index and Walk Score along with population density and local crime stats to determine that Washington ranked #8 for "how much candy it gives out versus how far kids have to walk to get it." Zillow also zeroes in on the best neighborhoods in its top 20 cities. *www.businessinsider.com, "These Are the Best Cities for Trick-or-Treating," October 15, 2013*

- The Harris Poll's Happiness Index survey revealed that of the top ten U.S. markets, the Washington metro area residents ranked #7 in happiness. Criteria included strong assent to positive statements and strong disagreement with negative ones, and degree of agreement with a series of statements about respondents' personal relationships and general outlook. The online survey was conducted between July 14 and July 30, 2013. *www.harrisinteractive.com, "Dallas/Fort Worth Is "Happiest" City among America's Top Ten Markets," September 4, 2013*

- Market analyst Scarborough Research surveyed adults who had done volunteer work over the previous 12 months to find out where volunteers are concentrated. The Washington metro area made the list for highest volunteer participation. *Scarborough Research, "Salt Lake City, UT; Minneapolis, MN; and Des Moines, IA Lend a Helping Hand," November 27, 2012*

- Washington was selected as one of the best travel desinations in the world during Thanksgiving by *Fodor's Travel*. Criteria: attractions; history; events. *Fodors.com, "10 Best Thanksgiving Destinations for 2013," October 18, 2013*

- Washington was selected as one of America's funniest cities by the Humor Research Lab at the University of Colorado. The city ranked #4 out of 10. Criteria: frequency of visits to comedy websites; number of comedy clubs per square mile; traveling comedians' ratings of each city's comedy-club audiences; number of famous comedians born in each city per capita; number of famous funny tweeters living in each city per capita; number of comedy radio stations available in each city; frequency of humor-related web searches originating in each city. *The New York Times, "So These Professors Walk Into a Comedy Club…," April 20, 2014*

- Washington appeared on *Travel + Leisure's* list of America's least attractive people. Criteria: cities were selected by readers in their annual America's Favorite Cities survey. The city ranked #1 out of 10. *Travel + Leisure, "America's Most and Least Attractive People," November 2013*

- *Men's Health* ranked 100 U.S. cities by their level of sadness. Washington was ranked #81 (#1 = saddest city). Criteria: suicide rates; unemployment rates; percentage of households that use antidepressants; percent of population who report feeling blue all or most of the time. *Men's Health, "Frown Towns," November 28, 2011*

- Energizer Personal Care, the makers of Edge® shave gel, in partnership with Sperling's BestPlaces, ranked 50 major metro areas in terms of everyday irritations. The Washington metro area ranked #9. Criteria: high male-to-female ratio; poor sports team performance and high ticket prices; slow traffic; lack of job availability; unaffordable housing; extreme weather; lack of nightlife and fitness options. *Energizer Personal Care, "Most Irritatng Cities for Guys," August 26, 2013*

- Mars Chocolate North America, the makers of COMBOS®, in partnership with Sperling's BestPlaces, ranked 50 major metro areas in terms of their "manliness." The Washington metro area ranked #43. Criteria: number of professional sports teams; number of nearby NASCAR tracks and racing events; manly lifestyle; concentration of manly retail stores; manly occupations per capita; salty snack sales; "Board of Manliness" rankings. *Mars Chocolate North America, "America's Manliest Cities 2012"*

- The National Alliance to End Homelessness ranked the 100 most populous metro areas in terms the rate of homelessness. The Washington metro area ranked #21. Criteria: number of homeless people per 10,000 population in 2011. *National Alliance to End Homelessness, The State of Homelessness in America 2012*

- Scarborough Research, a leading market research firm, identified the top local markets for volunteers in the U.S. The Washington DMA (Designated Market Area) ranked in the top 10 with 31% of adults 18+ reporting that they have participated in volunteer work in the past 12 months. *Scarborough Research, December 13, 2011*

- Scarborough Research, a leading market research firm, identified the top local markets for givers in the U.S. The Washington DMA (Designated Market Area) ranked in the top 10 with 62.0% of adults contributing money to an arts/cultural, healthcare/medical, religious or social care/welfare organization in the past 12 months. *Scarborough Research, December 13, 2011*

Business Environment

CITY FINANCES

City Government Finances

Component	2011 ($000)	2011 ($ per capita)
Total Revenues	10,640,973	18,088
Total Expenditures	11,520,570	19,583
Debt Outstanding	10,920,295	18,563
Cash and Securities[1]	8,443,195	14,352

Note: (1) Cash and security holdings of a government at the close of its fiscal year, including those of its dependent agencies, utilities, and liquor stores.
Source: U.S Census Bureau, State & Local Government Finances 2011

City Government Revenue by Source

Source	2011 ($000)	2011 ($ per capita)
General Revenue		
From Federal Government	3,229,993	5,490
From State Government	0	0
From Local Governments	0	0
Taxes		
Property	1,757,196	2,987
Sales and Gross Receipts	1,408,712	2,395
Personal Income	1,311,001	2,228
Corporate Income	382,095	649
Motor Vehicle License	32,853	56
Other Taxes	476,946	811
Current Charges	633,417	1,077
Liquor Store	0	0
Utility	128,028	218
Employee Retirement	474,502	807

Source: U.S Census Bureau, State & Local Government Finances 2011

City Government Expenditures by Function

Function	2011 ($000)	2011 ($ per capita)	2011 (%)
General Direct Expenditures			
Air Transportation	0	0	0.0
Corrections	256,760	436	2.2
Education	2,342,304	3,982	20.3
Employment Security Administration	41,146	70	0.4
Financial Administration	282,335	480	2.5
Fire Protection	214,997	365	1.9
General Public Buildings	40,480	69	0.4
Governmental Administration, Other	64,582	110	0.6
Health	395,480	672	3.4
Highways	243,903	415	2.1
Hospitals	226,085	384	2.0
Housing and Community Development	659,416	1,121	5.7
Interest on General Debt	482,039	819	4.2
Judicial and Legal	114,002	194	1.0
Libraries	77,724	132	0.7
Parking	23,491	40	0.2
Parks and Recreation	240,673	409	2.1
Police Protection	591,030	1,005	5.1
Public Welfare	2,824,782	4,802	24.5
Sewerage	404,269	687	3.5
Solid Waste Management	97,977	167	0.9
Veterans' Services	0	0	0.0
Liquor Store	0	0	0.0
Utility	223,132	379	1.9
Employee Retirement	70,831	120	0.6

Source: U.S Census Bureau, State & Local Government Finances 2011

DEMOGRAPHICS

Population Growth

Area	1990 Census	2000 Census	2010 Census	Population Growth (%) 1990-2000	Population Growth (%) 2000-2010
City	606,900	572,059	601,723	-5.7	5.2
MSA[1]	4,122,914	4,796,183	5,582,170	16.3	16.4
U.S.	248,709,873	281,421,906	308,745,538	13.2	9.7

Note: (1) Figures cover the Washington-Arlington-Alexandria, DC-VA-MD-WV Metropolitan Statistical Area—see Appendix B for areas included
Source: U.S. Census Bureau, Census 1990, 2000, 2010

Household Size

Area	Persons in Household (%) One	Two	Three	Four	Five	Six	Seven or More	Average Household Size
City	46.9	29.1	11.6	7.1	3.0	1.5	0.8	2.21
MSA[1]	27.6	30.7	16.6	14.4	6.5	2.6	1.6	2.72
U.S.	27.6	33.5	15.7	13.2	6.1	2.4	1.5	2.63

Note: (1) Figures cover the Washington-Arlington-Alexandria, DC-VA-MD-WV Metropolitan Statistical Area—see Appendix B for areas included
Source: U.S. Census Bureau, 2010-2012 American Community Survey 3-Year Estimates

Race

Area	White Alone[2] (%)	Black Alone[2] (%)	Asian Alone[2] (%)	AIAN[3] Alone[2] (%)	NHOPI[4] Alone[2] (%)	Other Race Alone[2] (%)	Two or More Races (%)
City	39.9	50.3	3.5	0.3	0.0	3.7	2.2
MSA[1]	55.8	25.6	9.4	0.4	0.0	5.3	3.6
U.S.	74.0	12.6	4.9	0.8	0.2	4.7	2.8

Note: (1) Figures cover the Washington-Arlington-Alexandria, DC-VA-MD-WV Metropolitan Statistical Area—see Appendix B for areas included; (2) Alone is defined as not being in combination with one or more other races; (3) American Indian and Alaska Native; (4) Native Hawaiian and Other Pacific Islander
Source: U.S. Census Bureau, 2010-2012 American Community Survey 3-Year Estimates

Hispanic or Latino Origin

Area	Total (%)	Mexican (%)	Puerto Rican (%)	Cuban (%)	Other (%)
City	9.5	1.5	0.6	0.3	7.2
MSA[1]	14.2	2.2	0.9	0.3	10.8
U.S.	16.6	10.7	1.6	0.6	3.7

Note: Persons of Hispanic or Latino origin can be of any race; (1) Figures cover the Washington-Arlington-Alexandria, DC-VA-MD-WV Metropolitan Statistical Area—see Appendix B for areas included
Source: U.S. Census Bureau, 2010-2012 American Community Survey 3-Year Estimates

Segregation

Type	Segregation Indices[1] 1990	2000	2010	2010 Rank[2]	Percent Change 1990-2000	Percent Change 1990-2010	Percent Change 2000-2010
Black/White	65.5	63.8	62.3	32	-1.7	-3.2	-1.5
Asian/White	34.5	38.7	38.9	64	4.2	4.4	0.2
Hispanic/White	41.8	47.4	48.3	32	5.6	6.5	0.9

Note: All figures cover the Metropolitan Statistical Area—see Appendix B for areas included; Figures are based on an analysis of 1990, 2000, and 2010 Census Decennial Census tract data by William H. Frey, Brookings Institution and the University of Michigan Social Science Data Analysis Network. In this analysis all racial groups (whites, blacks, and asians) are non-Hispanic members of those races. Hispanics are shown as a separate category;
(1) Segregation Indices are Dissimilarity Indices that measure the degree to which the minority group is distributed differently than whites across census tracts. They range from 0 (complete integration) to 100 (complete segregation) where the value indicates the percentage of the minority group that needs to move to be distributed exactly like whites; (2) Ranges from 1 (most segregated) to 102 (least segregated); n/a not available.
Source: www.CensusScope.org

Ancestry

Area	German	Irish	English	American	Italian	Polish	French[2]	Scottish	Dutch
City	6.5	6.7	5.3	2.2	3.3	1.8	1.6	1.3	0.5
MSA[1]	10.9	9.5	7.8	4.6	4.4	2.3	1.8	1.8	0.8
U.S.	15.2	11.1	8.2	7.2	5.6	3.1	2.8	1.7	1.4

Note: Figures are the percentage of the total population reporting a particular ancestry. The nine most commonly reported ancestries in the U.S. are shown. Figures include multiple ancestries (e.g. if a person reported being Irish and Italian, they were included in both columns); (1) Figures cover the Washington-Arlington-Alexandria, DC-VA-MD-WV Metropolitan Statistical Area—see Appendix B for areas included; (2) Excludes Basque
Source: U.S. Census Bureau, 2010-2012 American Community Survey 3-Year Estimates

Foreign-Born Population

Area	Any Foreign Country	Mexico	Asia	Europe	Carribean	South America	Central America[2]	Africa	Canada
City	13.8	0.5	2.6	2.5	1.3	1.1	3.2	2.2	0.2
MSA[1]	21.9	0.8	7.8	1.9	1.0	2.3	4.7	3.0	0.2
U.S.	13.0	3.7	3.7	1.6	1.2	0.9	1.0	0.5	0.3

Note: (1) Figures cover the Washington-Arlington-Alexandria, DC-VA-MD-WV Metropolitan Statistical Area—see Appendix B for areas included; (2) Excludes Mexico.
Source: U.S. Census Bureau, 2010-2012 American Community Survey 3-Year Estimates

Marital Status

Area	Never Married	Now Married[2]	Separated	Widowed	Divorced
City	58.0	25.1	2.4	5.0	9.5
MSA[1]	36.1	48.2	2.3	4.5	8.9
U.S.	32.4	48.4	2.2	6.0	11.0

Note: Figures are percentages and cover the population 15 years of age and older; (1) Figures cover the Washington-Arlington-Alexandria, DC-VA-MD-WV Metropolitan Statistical Area—see Appendix B for areas included; (2) Excludes separated
Source: U.S. Census Bureau, 2010-2012 American Community Survey 3-Year Estimates

Age

Area	Under Age 5	Age 5–19	Age 20–34	Age 35–44	Age 45–54	Age 55–64	Age 65–74	Age 75–84	Age 85+	Median Age
City	5.8	15.0	31.4	13.4	12.3	10.7	6.2	3.5	1.7	33.7
MSA[1]	6.7	19.5	22.1	14.8	15.1	11.5	6.0	3.0	1.3	36.0
U.S.	6.4	20.1	20.5	13.1	14.3	12.2	7.3	4.2	1.8	37.3

Note: (1) Figures cover the Washington-Arlington-Alexandria, DC-VA-MD-WV Metropolitan Statistical Area—see Appendix B for areas included
Source: U.S. Census Bureau, 2010-2012 American Community Survey 3-Year Estimates

Gender

Area	Males	Females	Males per 100 Females
City	292,559	326,218	89.7
MSA[1]	2,782,107	2,928,736	95.0
U.S.	153,276,055	158,333,314	96.8

Note: (1) Figures cover the Washington-Arlington-Alexandria, DC-VA-MD-WV Metropolitan Statistical Area—see Appendix B for areas included
Source: U.S. Census Bureau, 2010-2012 American Community Survey 3-Year Estimates

Religious Groups by Family

Area	Catholic	Baptist	Non-Den.	Methodist[2]	Lutheran	LDS[3]	Pentecostal	Presbyterian[4]	Muslim[5]	Judaism
MSA[1]	14.5	7.3	4.9	4.5	1.3	1.2	1.1	1.4	2.4	1.2
U.S.	19.1	9.3	4.0	4.0	2.3	2.0	1.9	1.6	0.8	0.7

Note: Figures are the number of adherents as a percentage of the total population; (1) Figures cover the Washington-Arlington-Alexandria, DC-VA-MD-WV Metropolitan Statistical Area—see Appendix B for areas included; (2) Methodist/Pietist; (3) Latter Day Saints; (4) Reformed; (5) Figures are estimates
Source: Association of Statisticians of American Religious Bodies, 2010 U.S. Religion Census: Religious Congregations & Membership Study

Religious Groups by Tradition

Area	Catholic	Evangelical Protestant	Mainline Protestant	Other Tradition	Black Protestant	Orthodox
MSA[1]	14.5	12.4	8.8	5.9	2.3	0.6
U.S.	19.1	16.2	7.3	4.3	1.6	0.3

Note: Figures are the number of adherents as a percentage of the total population; (1) Figures cover the Washington-Arlington-Alexandria, DC-VA-MD-WV Metropolitan Statistical Area—see Appendix B for areas included
Source: Association of Statisticians of American Religious Bodies, 2010 U.S. Religion Census: Religious Congregations & Membership Study

ECONOMY

Gross Metropolitan Product

Area	2011	2012	2013	2014	Rank[2]
MSA[1]	437.2	446.9	455.8	477.5	5

Note: Figures are in billions of dollars; (1) Figures cover the Washington-Arlington-Alexandria, DC-VA-MD-WV Metropolitan Statistical Area—see Appendix B for areas included; (2) Rank is based on 2014 data and ranges from 1 to 363
Source: The United States Conference of Mayors, U.S. Metro Economies: Outlook—Gross Metropolitan Product, with Metro Employment Projections, November 2013

Economic Growth

Area	2011 (%)	2012 (%)	2013 (%)	2014 (%)	Rank[2]
MSA[1]	1.5	0.6	0.6	2.7	197
U.S.	1.6	2.5	1.7	2.5	–

Note: Figures are real gross metropolitan product (GMP) growth rates and represent annual average percent change; (1) Figures cover the Washington-Arlington-Alexandria, DC-VA-MD-WV Metropolitan Statistical Area—see Appendix B for areas included; (2) Rank is based on 2013 data and ranges from 1 to 363
Source: The United States Conference of Mayors, U.S. Metro Economies: Outlook—Gross Metropolitan Product, with Metro Employment Projections, November 2013

Metropolitan Area Exports

Area	2007	2008	2009	2010	2011	2012	Rank[2]
MSA[1]	9,204.5	9,879.4	9,226.1	11,082.9	10,237.9	14,609.7	23

Note: Figures are in millions of dollars; (1) Figures cover the Washington-Arlington-Alexandria, DC-VA-MD-WV Metropolitan Statistical Area—see Appendix B for areas included; (2) Rank is based on 2012 data and ranges from 1 to 369
Source: U.S. Department of Commerce, International Trade Administration, Office of Trade & Industry Information, Manufacturing & Services, data extracted April 1, 2014

INCOME

Income

Area	Per Capita ($)	Median Household ($)	Average Household ($)
City	44,670	64,610	99,781
MSA[1]	42,624	88,689	114,231
U.S.	27,385	51,771	71,579

Note: (1) Figures cover the Washington-Arlington-Alexandria, DC-VA-MD-WV Metropolitan Statistical Area—see Appendix B for areas included
Source: U.S. Census Bureau, 2010-2012 American Community Survey 3-Year Estimates

Household Income Distribution

Area	Percent of Households Earning							
	Under $15,000	$15,000 -24,999	$25,000 -34,999	$35,000 -49,999	$50,000 -74,999	$75,000 -99,000	$100,000 -149,999	$150,000 and up
City	15.1	7.8	7.1	10.5	14.9	10.8	14.8	19.0
MSA[1]	6.5	5.2	5.5	9.3	15.8	13.3	19.9	24.5
U.S.	13.1	11.0	10.5	13.7	18.1	11.9	12.5	9.1

Note: (1) Figures cover the Washington-Arlington-Alexandria, DC-VA-MD-WV Metropolitan Statistical Area—see Appendix B for areas included
Source: U.S. Census Bureau, 2010-2012 American Community Survey 3-Year Estimates

Poverty Rate

Area	All Ages	Under 18 Years Old	18 to 64 Years Old	65 Years and Over
City	18.8	29.3	17.2	12.6
MSA[1]	8.3	10.7	7.8	6.6
U.S.	15.7	22.2	14.6	9.3

Note: Figures are percentage of people whose income during the past 12 months was below the poverty level;
(1) Figures cover the Washington-Arlington-Alexandria, DC-VA-MD-WV Metropolitan Statistical Area—see Appendix B for areas included
Source: U.S. Census Bureau, 2010-2012 American Community Survey 3-Year Estimates

Personal Bankruptcy Filing Rate

Area	2008	2009	2010	2011	2012	2013
District of Columbia	1.46	1.94	2.13	1.56	1.36	1.27
U.S.	3.53	4.61	4.97	4.37	3.76	3.29

Note: Numbers are per 1,000 population and include Chapter 7 and Chapter 13 filings
Source: Federal Deposit Insurance Corporation, Regional Economic Conditions, March 20, 2014

EMPLOYMENT

Labor Force and Employment

Area	Civilian Labor Force			Workers Employed		
	Dec. 2012	Dec. 2013	% Chg.	Dec. 2012	Dec. 2013	% Chg.
City	371,456	365,540	-1.6	339,415	340,486	0.3
MD[1]	2,521,100	2,514,981	-0.2	2,385,023	2,396,147	0.5
U.S.	154,904,000	154,408,000	-0.3	143,060,000	144,423,000	1.0

Note: Data is not seasonally adjusted and covers workers 16 years of age and older; (1) Metropolitan Division—see Appendix B for areas included
Source: Bureau of Labor Statistics, Local Area Unemployment Statistics

Unemployment Rate

Area	2013											
	Jan.	Feb.	Mar.	Apr.	May	Jun.	Jul.	Aug.	Sep.	Oct.	Nov.	Dec.
City	9.4	8.7	8.4	7.9	8.2	8.9	8.9	8.3	8.1	9.0	7.1	6.9
MD[1]	5.8	5.5	5.2	5.0	5.5	6.0	5.8	5.5	5.4	5.9	4.9	4.7
U.S.	8.5	8.1	7.6	7.1	7.3	7.8	7.7	7.3	7.0	7.0	6.6	6.5

Note: Data is not seasonally adjusted and covers workers 16 years of age and older; All figures are percentages;
(1) Metropolitan Division—see Appendix B for areas included
Source: Bureau of Labor Statistics, Local Area Unemployment Statistics

Employment by Occupation

Occupation Classification	City (%)	MSA[1] (%)	U.S. (%)
Management, Business, Science, and Arts	60.0	50.8	36.0
Natural Resources, Construction, and Maintenance	3.3	6.7	9.1
Production, Transportation, and Material Moving	4.2	5.6	12.0
Sales and Office	17.3	20.7	24.7
Service	15.3	16.2	18.2

Note: Figures cover employed civilians 16 years of age and older; (1) Figures cover the Washington-Arlington-Alexandria, DC-VA-MD-WV Metropolitan Statistical Area—see Appendix B for areas included
Source: U.S. Census Bureau, 2010-2012 American Community Survey 3-Year Estimates

Employment by Industry

Sector	MD[1] Number of Employees	MD[1] Percent of Total	U.S. Percent of Total
Construction	n/a	n/a	4.2
Education and Health Services	320,300	12.7	15.5
Financial Activities	112,700	4.5	5.7
Government	584,500	23.1	16.1
Information	61,600	2.4	1.9
Leisure and Hospitality	239,600	9.5	10.2
Manufacturing	30,100	1.2	8.7
Mining and Logging	n/a	n/a	0.6
Other Services	159,500	6.3	3.9
Professional and Business Services	580,000	22.9	13.7
Retail Trade	221,200	8.7	11.4
Transportation and Utilities	57,100	2.3	3.8
Wholesale Trade	49,800	2.0	4.2

Note: Figures cover non-farm employment as of December 2013 and are not seasonally adjusted;
(1) Metropolitan Division—see Appendix B for areas included; n/a not available
Source: Bureau of Labor Statistics, Current Employment Statistics, Employment, Hours, and Earnings

Occupations with Greatest Projected Employment Growth: 2010 – 2020

Occupation[1]	2010 Employment	2020 Projected Employment	Numeric Employment Change	Percent Employment Change
Lawyers	41,670	48,040	6,370	15.3
Business Operations Specialists, All Other	39,840	43,650	3,820	9.6
Postsecondary Teachers	15,760	18,750	2,990	19.0
Home Health Aides	3,580	6,160	2,580	72.0
Management Analysts	23,610	25,970	2,360	10.0
Janitors and Cleaners, Except Maids and Housekeeping Cleaners	13,520	15,750	2,230	16.5
Security Guards	11,190	13,400	2,210	19.7
Executive Secretaries and Executive Administrative Assistants	13,580	15,710	2,120	15.6
Office Clerks, General	11,910	14,020	2,110	17.7
Registered Nurses	10,080	12,150	2,070	20.5

Note: Projections cover District of Columbia; (1) Sorted by numeric employment change
Source: www.projectionscentral.com, State Occupational Projections, 2010–2020 Long-Term Projections

Fastest Growing Occupations: 2010 – 2020

Occupation[1]	2010 Employment	2020 Projected Employment	Numeric Employment Change	Percent Employment Change
Home Health Aides	3,580	6,160	2,580	72.0
Personal Care Aides	1,730	2,850	1,120	65.0
Software Developers, Systems Software	1,490	2,280	790	53.3
Meeting, Convention, and Event Planners	2,390	3,520	1,130	47.5
Software Developers, Applications	2,390	3,480	1,090	45.7
Database Administrators	1,470	2,120	650	43.9
Market Research Analysts and Marketing Specialists	4,400	6,330	1,920	43.6
Health Educators	730	1,040	310	42.7
Medical Secretaries	1,120	1,570	440	39.6
Interpreters and Translators	500	700	200	39.4

Note: Projections cover District of Columbia; (1) Sorted by percent employment change and excludes occupations with numeric employment change less than 100
Source: www.projectionscentral.com, State Occupational Projections, 2010–2020 Long-Term Projections

Average Wages

Occupation	$/Hr.	Occupation	$/Hr.
Accountants and Auditors	40.82	Maids and Housekeeping Cleaners	11.90
Automotive Mechanics	22.96	Maintenance and Repair Workers	21.37
Bookkeepers	21.52	Marketing Managers	73.15
Carpenters	22.03	Nuclear Medicine Technologists	38.43
Cashiers	10.52	Nurses, Licensed Practical	22.95
Clerks, General Office	17.50	Nurses, Registered	35.74
Clerks, Receptionists/Information	14.93	Nursing Assistants	13.77
Clerks, Shipping/Receiving	16.29	Packers and Packagers, Hand	10.30
Computer Programmers	39.90	Physical Therapists	38.69
Computer Systems Analysts	51.34	Postal Service Mail Carriers	24.66
Computer User Support Specialists	29.12	Real Estate Brokers	34.45
Cooks, Restaurant	12.80	Retail Salespersons	12.12
Dentists	73.33	Sales Reps., Exc. Tech./Scientific	34.08
Electrical Engineers	52.63	Sales Reps., Tech./Scientific	47.52
Electricians	26.69	Secretaries, Exc. Legal/Med./Exec.	20.61
Financial Managers	69.14	Security Guards	17.82
First-Line Supervisors/Managers, Sales	22.09	Surgeons	116.42
Food Preparation Workers	10.87	Teacher Assistants	14.00
General and Operations Managers	68.59	Teachers, Elementary School	32.60
Hairdressers/Cosmetologists	17.40	Teachers, Secondary School	33.60
Internists	103.67	Telemarketers	12.50
Janitors and Cleaners	12.45	Truck Drivers, Heavy/Tractor-Trailer	19.86
Landscaping/Groundskeeping Workers	13.26	Truck Drivers, Light/Delivery Svcs.	19.19
Lawyers	75.70	Waiters and Waitresses	11.87

Note: Wage data covers the Washington-Arlington-Alexandria, DC-VA-MD-WV Metropolitan Division—see Appendix B for areas included. Hourly wages for elementary/secondary school teachers and teacher assistants were calculated by the editors from annual wage data assuming a 40 hour work week; n/a not available.
Source: Bureau of Labor Statistics, Metro Area Occupational Employment and Wage Estimates, May 2013

RESIDENTIAL REAL ESTATE

Building Permits

Area	Single-Family			Multi-Family			Total		
	2012	2013	Pct. Chg.	2012	2013	Pct. Chg.	2012	2013	Pct. Chg.
City	271	333	22.9	3,552	2,922	-17.7	3,823	3,255	-14.9
MSA[1]	10,980	13,274	20.9	11,424	10,759	-5.8	22,404	24,033	7.3
U.S.	518,695	620,802	19.7	310,963	370,020	19.0	829,658	990,822	19.4

Note: (1) Metropolitan Statistical Area—see Appendix B for areas included; figures represent new, privately-owned housing units authorized (unadjusted data); All permit data are based on estimates with imputation.
Source: U.S. Census Bureau, Manufacturing, Mining, and Construction Statistics, Building Permits, 2012, 2013

Homeownership Rate

Area	2006 (%)	2007 (%)	2008 (%)	2009 (%)	2010 (%)	2011 (%)	2012 (%)	2013 (%)
MSA[1]	68.9	69.2	68.1	67.2	67.3	67.6	66.9	66.0
U.S.	68.8	68.1	67.8	67.4	66.9	66.1	65.4	65.1

Note: (1) Figures cover the Washington-Arlington-Alexandria, DC-VA-MD-WV Metropolitan Statistical Area—see Appendix B for areas included
Source: U.S. Census Bureau, Housing Vacancies and Homeownership Annual Statistics: 2013

Housing Vacancy Rates

Area	Gross Vacancy Rate[2] (%)			Year-Round Vacancy Rate[3] (%)			Rental Vacancy Rate[4] (%)			Homeowner Vacancy Rate[5] (%)		
	2011	2012	2013	2011	2012	2013	2011	2012	2013	2011	2012	2013
MSA[1]	9.6	8.1	8.3	9.4	7.9	8.2	7.9	6.4	7.2	1.8	1.3	1.3
U.S.	14.2	13.8	13.8	11.1	10.8	10.7	9.5	8.7	8.3	2.5	2.0	2.0

Note: (1) Figures cover the Washington-Arlington-Alexandria, DC-VA-MD-WV Metropolitan Statistical Area—see Appendix B for areas included; (2) The percentage of the total housing inventory that is vacant; (3) The percentage of the housing inventory (excluding seasonal units) that is year-round vacant; (4) The percentage of rental inventory that is vacant for rent; (5) The percentage of homeowner inventory that is vacant for sale
Source: U.S. Census Bureau, Housing Vacancies and Homeownership Annual Statistics: 2013

TAXES

State Corporate Income Tax Rates

State	Tax Rate (%)	Income Brackets ($)	Num. of Brackets	Financial Institution Tax Rate (%)[a]	Federal Income Tax Ded.
D.C.	9.975 (b)	Flat rate	1	9.975 (b)	No

Note: Tax rates as of January 1, 2014; (a) Rates listed are the corporate income tax rate applied to financial institutions or excise taxes based on income. Some states have other taxes based upon the value of deposits or shares; (b) Minimum tax is $50 in Arizona, $100 in District of Columbia, $50 in North Dakota (banks), $500 in Rhode Island, $200 per location in South Dakota (banks), $100 in Utah, $250 in Vermont.
Source: Federation of Tax Administrators, "State Corporate Income Tax Rates, 2014"

State Individual Income Tax Rates

State	Tax Rate (%)	Income Brackets ($)	Num. of Brackets	Personal Exempt. ($)[1] Single	Personal Exempt. ($)[1] Dependents	Fed. Inc. Tax Ded.
D.C.	4.0 - 8.95	10,000 - 350,000	4	1,675	1,675	No

Note: Tax rates as of January 1, 2014; Local- and county-level taxes are not included; n/a not applicable; (1) Married joint filers generally receive double the single exemption
Source: Federation of Tax Administrators, "State Individual Income Tax Rates, 2014"

Various State and Local Tax Rates

State	State and Local Sales and Use (%)	State Sales and Use (%)	Gasoline[1] (¢/gal.)	Cigarette[2] ($/pack)	Spirits[3] ($/gal.)	Wine[4] ($/gal.)	Beer[5] ($/gal.)
D.C.	5.75	5.75	23.50	2.860	5.37 (j)	1.61 (n)	0.58 (r)

Note: All tax rates as of January 1, 2014; (1) The American Petroleum Institute has developed a methodology for determining the average tax rate on a gallon of fuel. Rates may include any of the following: excise taxes, environmental fees, storage tank fees, other fees or taxes, general sales tax, and local taxes. In states where gasoline is subject to the general sales tax, or where the fuel tax is based on the average sale price, the average rate determined by API is sensitive to changes in the price of gasoline. States that fully or partially apply general sales taxes to gasoline: CA, CO, GA, IL, IN, MI, NY; (2) The federal excise tax of $1.0066 per pack and local taxes are not included; (3) Rates are those applicable to off-premise sales of 40% alcohol by volume (a.b.v.) distilled spirits in 750ml containers. Local excise taxes are excluded; (4) Rates are those applicable to off-premise sales of 11% a.b.v. non-carbonated wine in 750ml containers; (5) Rates are those applicable to off-premise sales of 4.7% a.b.v. beer in 12 ounce containers; (j) Includes sales taxes specific to alcoholic beverages; (n) Includes sales taxes specific to alcoholic beverages; (r) Includes sales taxes specific to alcoholic beverages.
Source: Tax Foundation, 2014 Facts & Figures: How Does Your State Compare?

State Business Tax Climate Index Rankings

State	Overall Rank	Corporate Tax Index Rank	Individual Income Tax Index Rank	Sales Tax Index Rank	Unemployment Insurance Tax Index Rank	Property Tax Index Rank
District of Columbia	44	35	34	41	26	44

Note: The index is a measure of how each state's tax laws affect economic performance. The lower the rank, the more favorable a state's tax system is for business. States without a given tax are given a ranking of 1. The scores/rankings for the District of Columbia do not affect other states. The 2014 index represents the tax climate as of July 1, 2013.
Source: Tax Foundation, State Business Tax Climate Index 2014

COMMERCIAL REAL ESTATE

Office Market

Market Area	Inventory (sq. ft.)	Vacancy Rate (%)	Under Construction (sq. ft.)	YTD Net Absorption (sq. ft.)	Total Average Asking Rent ($/sq. ft./year)
Washington	362,279,252	15.5	4,475,804	397,777	36.56
National	4,726,900,879	15.0	55,419,286	42,829,434	26.27

Source: Newmark Grubb Knight Frank, National Office Market Report, 4th Quarter 2013

Industrial/Warehouse/R&D Market

Market Area	Inventory (sq. ft.)	Vacancy Rate (%)	Under Construction (sq. ft.)	YTD Net Absorption (sq. ft.)	Total Average Asking Rent ($/sq. ft./year)
Washington	267,268,263	10.8	1,147,067	2,602,279	8.05
National	14,022,031,238	7.9	83,249,164	156,549,903	5.40

Source: Newmark Grubb Knight Frank, National Industrial Market Report, 4th Quarter 2013

COMMERCIAL UTILITIES

Typical Monthly Electric Bills

Area	Commercial Service ($/month)		Industrial Service ($/month)	
	1,500 kWh	40 kW demand 14,000 kWh	1,000 kW demand 200,000 kWh	50,000 kW demand 15,000,000 kWh
City	226	2,058	26,564	1,827,360
Average[1]	197	1,636	25,662	1,485,307

Note: Based on total rates in effect July 1, 2013; (1) average based on 180 utilities surveyed
Source: Edison Electric Institute, Typical Bills and Average Rates Report, Summer 2013

TRANSPORTATION

Means of Transportation to Work

Area	Car/Truck/Van		Public Transportation			Bicycle	Walked	Other Means	Worked at Home
	Drove Alone	Car-pooled	Bus	Subway	Railroad				
City	34.0	5.9	17.2	20.9	0.4	3.6	11.9	1.3	4.8
MSA[1]	65.8	10.3	5.7	7.8	0.7	0.7	3.3	1.0	4.8
U.S.	76.4	9.7	2.6	1.7	0.5	0.6	2.8	1.3	4.3

Note: Figures are percentages and cover workers 16 years of age and older; (1) Figures cover the Washington-Arlington-Alexandria, DC-VA-MD-WV Metropolitan Statistical Area—see Appendix B for areas included
Source: U.S. Census Bureau, 2010-2012 American Community Survey 3-Year Estimates

Travel Time to Work

Area	Less Than 10 Minutes	10 to 19 Minutes	20 to 29 Minutes	30 to 44 Minutes	45 to 59 Minutes	60 to 89 Minutes	90 Minutes or More
City	5.3	20.4	23.5	30.8	10.8	6.9	2.2
MSA[1]	6.4	19.1	18.0	25.7	13.7	12.6	4.3
U.S.	13.5	29.8	20.9	20.1	7.5	5.6	2.5

Note: Figures are percentages and include workers 16 years old and over; (1) Figures cover the Washington-Arlington-Alexandria, DC-VA-MD-WV Metropolitan Statistical Area—see Appendix B for areas included
Source: U.S. Census Bureau, 2010-2012 American Community Survey 3-Year Estimates

Travel Time Index

Area	1985	1990	1995	2000	2005	2010	2011
Urban Area[1]	1.17	1.23	1.27	1.30	1.33	1.31	1.32
Average[2]	1.09	1.14	1.16	1.19	1.23	1.18	1.18

Note: Travel Time Index—the ratio of travel time in the peak period to the travel time at free-flow conditions. For example, a value of 1.30 indicates a 20-minute free-flow trip takes 26 minutes in the peak. Free-flow speeds (60 mph on freeways and 35 mph on principal arterials) are used as the comparison threshold; (1) Covers the Washington DC-VA-MD urban area; (2) average of 498 urban areas
Source: Texas Transportation Institute, Urban Mobility Report 2012, December 2012

Public Transportation

Agency Name / Mode of Transportation	Vehicles Operated in Maximum Service	Annual Unlinked Passenger Trips (in thous.)	Annual Passenger Miles (in thous.)
Washington Metropolitan Area Transit Authority (WMATA)			
Bus (directly operated)	1,281	130,889.9	408,162.7
Bus (purchased transportation)	46	5,905.4	7,651.3
Demand Response (purchased transportation)	565	1,981.0	15,108.7
Demand Response Taxi (purchased transportation)	235	101.9	1,546.7
Heavy Rail (directly operated)	868	285,306.7	1,584,631.0

Source: Federal Transit Administration, National Transit Database, 2012

Air Transportation

Airport Name and Code / Type of Service	Passenger Airlines[1]	Passenger Enplanements	Freight Carriers[2]	Freight (lbs.)
Ronald Reagan Washington National (DCA)				
Domestic service (U.S. carriers - 2013)	24	9,645,656	13	2,501,528
International service (U.S. carriers - 2012)	7	87,691	3	2,645
Dulles International (IAD)				
Domestic service (U.S. carriers - 2013)	34	7,193,183	14	98,083,246
International service (U.S. carriers - 2012)	13	1,549,392	6	46,576,279

Note: (1) Includes all U.S.-based major, minor and commuter airlines that carried at least one passenger during the year; (2) Includes all U.S.-based airlines and freight carriers that transported at least one lb. of freight during the year.
Source: Bureau of Transportation Statistics, The Intermodal Transportation Database, Air Carriers: T-100 Domestic Market (U.S. Carriers), 2013; Bureau of Transportation Statistics, The Intermodal Transportation Database, Air Carriers: T-100 International Market (U.S. Carriers), 2012

Other Transportation Statistics

Major Highways:	I-66; I-95
Amtrak Service:	Yes
Major Waterways/Ports:	Potomac River

Source: Amtrak.com; Google Maps

BUSINESSES

Major Business Headquarters

Company Name	Rankings	
	Fortune[1]	Forbes[2]
Danaher	152	-
Fannie Mae	12	-
Pepco Holdings	483	-

Note: (1) Fortune 500—companies that produce a 10-K are ranked 1 to 500 based on 2012 revenue; (2) all private companies with at least $2 billion in annual revenue through the end of their most current fiscal year are ranked 1 to 224; companies listed are headquartered in the city; dashes indicate no ranking
Source: Fortune, "Fortune 500," May 20, 2013; Forbes, "America's Largest Private Companies," December 18, 2013

Fast-Growing Businesses

According to *Inc.*, Washington is home to nine of America's 500 fastest-growing private companies: **LivingSocial** (#15); **Sol Systems** (#91); **Viderity** (#134); **Clinovations** (#175); **Virtual Enterprise Architects** (#195); **FreeAlliance.com** (#215); **Barbaricum** (#322); **Rigil** (#385); **Modus eDiscovery** (#398). Criteria: must be an independent, privately-held, for-profit, U.S. corporation, proprietorship or partnership; revenues must be at least $100,000 in 2009 and $2 million in 2012; must have four-year operating/sales history. Holding companies, regulated banks, and utilities were excluded. *Inc., "America's 500 Fastest-Growing Private Companies," September 2013*

According to *Fortune*, Washington is home to one of the 100 fastest-growing companies in the world: **Liquidity Services** (#48). Companies were ranked by their revenue growth rate; their EPS growth rate; and their three-year annualized total return to investors for the period ending June 30, 2013. Criteria for inclusion: a company, foreign or domestic, must trade on a major U.S. stock exchange; must file quarterly reports with the SEC; must have a minimum market capitalization of

$250 million; must have a stock price of at least $5 on June 29, 2013; must have been trading continuously since June 30, 2009; must have revenue and net income for the four quarters ended on or before April 30, 2013, of at least $50 million and $10 million, respectively; and must have posted a compound annual growth in revenue and earnings per share of at least 20% annually over the three years ending on or before April 30, 2013. REITs, limited-liability companies, limited parterships, companies about to be acquired, and companies that lost money in the quarter ending April 30, 2013 were excluded. *Fortune, "100 Fastest-Growing Companies," August 29, 2013*

According to *Initiative for a Competitive Inner City (ICIC)*, Washington is home to three of America's 100 fastest-growing "inner city" companies: **The Menkiti Group** (#22); **TCG** (#46); **Compass Solutions** (#71). Companies were ranked by their five-year compound annual growth rate. Criteria for inclusion: company must be headquartered in or have 51 percent or more of its physical operations in an economically distressed urban area; must be an independent, for-profit corporation, partnership or proprietorship; must have 10 or more employees and have a five-year sales history that includes sales of at least $200,000 in the base year and at least $1 million in the current year with no decrease in sales over the two most recent years. *Initiative for a Competitive Inner City (ICIC), "Inner City 100 Companies, 2013"*

According to Deloitte, Washington is home to two of North America's 500 fastest-growing high-technology companies: **RepEquity** (#106); **Apprio** (#342). Companies are ranked by percentage growth in revenue over a five-year period. Criteria for inclusion: company must be headquartered within North America; must own proprietary intellectual property or proprietary technology that contributes to a significant portion of the company's operating revenue, or devote a significant proportion of revenues to research and development of technology; must have been in business for a minumum of five years with 2008 operating revenues of at least $50,000 USD/CD and 2012 operating revenues of at least $5 million USD/CD. *Deloitte Touche Tohmatsu, 2013 Technology Fast 500*[TM]

Minority Business Opportunity

Washington is home to one company which is on the *Black Enterprise* Industrial/Service 100 list (100 largest companies based on gross sales): **DKW Communications** (#73). Criteria: operational in previous calendar year; at least 51% black-owned and manufactures/owns the product it sells or provides industrial or consumer services. Brokerages, real estate firms and firms that provide professional services are not eligible. *Black Enterprise, B.E. 100s, 2013*

Washington is home to two companies which are on the *Black Enterprise* Bank 20 list (20 largest banks based on total assets, capital, deposits and loans, including mortgage-backed securities for the calendar year): **Industrial Bank** (#7); **Independence Federal Savings Bank** (#17). Only commercial banks or savings and loans that are classified by the Federal Reserve as black institutions and have been fully operational for the previous calendar year were considered. *Black Enterprise, B.E. 100s, 2013*

Washington is home to one company which is on the *Black Enterprise* Private Equity 15 list (15 largest private equity firms based on capital under management): **Harley Stanfield Global** (#10). Criteria: company must be operational in previous calendar year and be at least 51% black-owned. *Black Enterprise, B.E. 100s, 2013*

Washington is home to one company which is on the *Hispanic Business* 500 list (500 largest U.S. Hispanic-owned companies based on 2012 revenue): **The Keystone Plus Construction Corp.** (#303). Companies included must show at least 51 percent ownership by Hispanic U.S. citizens, and must maintain headquarters in one of the 50 states or Washington, D.C. *Hispanic Business, "Hispanic Business 500," June 20, 2013*

Minority- and Women-Owned Businesses

Group	All Firms		Firms with Paid Employees			
	Firms	Sales ($000)	Firms	Sales ($000)	Employees	Payroll ($000)
Asian	3,278	1,836,669	1,604	1,768,451	11,998	396,211
Black	15,764	2,165,348	1,425	1,808,528	18,968	596,076
Hispanic	3,428	975,041	524	893,415	7,201	227,697
Women	19,291	3,775,077	2,153	3,165,225	25,288	993,919
All Firms	55,887	120,725,735	13,946	118,686,302	389,799	24,255,385

Note: Figures cover firms located in the city; minority- and women-owned business are defined as firms in which the corresponding group own 51% or more of the stock or equity of the company
Source: U.S. Census Bureau, 2007 Economic Census, Survey of Business Owners (2012 Survey of Business Owners data will be released starting in June 2015)

HOTELS & CONVENTION CENTERS

Hotels/Motels

Area	5 Star		4 Star		3 Star		2 Star		1 Star		Not Rated	
	Num.	Pct.[3]	Num.	Pct.[3]	Num.	Pct.[3]	Num.	Pct.[3]	Num.	Pct.[3]	Num.	Pct.[3]
City[1]	9	2.1	38	8.7	205	47.0	120	27.5	3	0.7	61	14.0
Total[2]	142	0.9	1,005	6.0	5,147	30.9	8,578	51.4	408	2.4	1,397	8.4

Note: (1) Figures cover Washington and vicinity; (2) Figures cover all 100 cities in this book; (3) Percentage of hotels which have a given star rating; Star ratings are determined by expedia.com and offer an indication of the general quality of a particular hotel.
Source: expedia.com, April 7, 2014

The Washington-Arlington-Alexandria, DC-VA-MD-WV metro area is home to four of the best hotels in the U.S. according to *Travel & Leisure*: **The Hay-Adams; Ritz-Carlton, Georgetown; Four Seasons Hotel, Washington, D.C.; Ritz-Carlton, Pentagon City**. Criteria: service; location; rooms; food; and value. The list includes the top 200 hotels in the U.S. *Travel & Leisure, "T+L 500, The World's Best Hotels 2014"*

The Washington-Arlington-Alexandria, DC-VA-MD-WV metro area is home to two of the best hotels in the world according to *Condé Nast Traveler*: **Four Seasons; Hay-Adams Hotel**. The selections are based on over 79,000 responses to the magazine's annual Readers' Choice Survey. The list includes the top 200 hotels in the U.S. *Condé Nast Traveler, "Gold List 2014, The World's Best Places to Stay"*

Major Convention Centers

Name	Overall Space (sq. ft.)	Exhibit Space (sq. ft.)	Meeting Space (sq. ft.)	Meeting Rooms
Walter E. Washington Convention Center	2,300,000	703,000	150,000	63

Note: Table includes convention centers located in the Washington-Arlington-Alexandria, DC-VA-MD-WV metro area; n/a not available
Source: Original research

Living Environment

COST OF LIVING

Cost of Living Index

Composite Index	Groceries	Housing	Utilities	Trans-portation	Health Care	Misc. Goods/Services
139.4	107.9	247.5	104.1	105.6	98.6	96.6

Note: The Cost of Living Index measures regional differences in the cost of consumer goods and services, excluding taxes and non-consumer expenditures, for professional and managerial households in the top income quintile. It is based on more than 50,000 prices covering almost 60 different items for which prices are collected three times a year by chambers of commerce, economic development organizations or university applied economic centers in each participating urban area. The numbers shown should be read as a percentage above or below the national average of 100. For example, a value of 115.4 in the groceries column indicates that grocery prices are 15.4% higher than the national average. Small differences in the index numbers should not be interpreted as significant; Figures cover the Washington-Arlington-Alexandria DC-VA urban area.
Source: The Council for Community and Economic Research, ACCRA Cost of Living Index, 2013

Grocery Prices

Area[1]	T-Bone Steak ($/pound)	Frying Chicken ($/pound)	Whole Milk ($/half gal.)	Eggs ($/dozen)	Orange Juice ($/64 oz.)	Coffee ($/11.5 oz.)
City[2]	10.52	1.57	2.58	2.36	3.65	4.93
Avg.	10.19	1.28	2.34	1.81	3.48	4.39
Min.	8.56	0.94	1.44	1.19	2.78	3.40
Max.	14.82	2.28	3.56	3.73	6.23	7.32

Note: (1) Values for the local area are compared with the average, minimum and maximum values for all 327 areas in the Cost of Living Index; (2) Figures cover the Washington-Arlington-Alexandria DC-VA urban area; **T-Bone Steak** *(price per pound);* **Frying Chicken** *(price per pound, whole fryer);* **Whole Milk** *(half gallon carton);* **Eggs** *(price per dozen, Grade A, large);* **Orange Juice** *(64 oz. Tropicana or Florida Natural);* **Coffee** *(11.5 oz. can, vacuum-packed, Maxwell House, Hills Bros, or Folgers).*
Source: The Council for Community and Economic Research, ACCRA Cost of Living Index, 2013

Housing and Utility Costs

Area[1]	New Home Price ($)	Apartment Rent ($/month)	All Electric ($/month)	Part Electric ($/month)	Other Energy ($/month)	Telephone ($/month)
City[2]	767,485	1,961	-	78.65	97.87	27.32
Avg.	295,864	900	171.38	91.82	70.12	27.73
Min.	185,506	458	117.80	48.81	33.67	17.16
Max.	1,358,917	3,783	441.68	171.40	372.65	39.47

Note: (1) Values for the local area are compared with the average, minimum and maximum values for all 327 areas in the Cost of Living Index; (2) Figures cover the Washington-Arlington-Alexandria DC-VA urban area; **New Home Price** *(2,400 sf living area, 8,000 sf lot, in urban area with full utilities);* **Apartment Rent** *(950 sf 2 bedroom/1.5 or 2 bath, unfurnished, excluding all utilities except water);* **All Electric** *(average monthly cost for an all-electric home);* **Part Electric** *(average monthly cost for a part-electric home);* **Other Energy** *(average monthly cost for natural gas, fuel oil, coal, wood, and any other forms of energy except electricity);* **Telephone** *(price includes basic monthly rate for a private residential line plus additional local usage charges incurred by a family of four).*
Source: The Council for Community and Economic Research, ACCRA Cost of Living Index, 2013

Health Care, Transportation, and Other Costs

Area[1]	Doctor ($/visit)	Dentist ($/visit)	Optometrist ($/visit)	Gasoline ($/gallon)	Beauty Salon ($/visit)	Men's Shirt ($)
City[2]	84.40	89.47	72.98	3.73	51.00	26.52
Avg.	101.40	86.48	96.16	3.44	33.87	26.55
Min.	61.67	50.83	50.12	3.08	18.92	12.48
Max.	182.71	152.50	223.78	4.33	68.22	52.03

Note: (1) Values for the local area are compared with the average, minimum and maximum values for all 327 areas in the Cost of Living Index; (2) Figures cover the Washington-Arlington-Alexandria DC-VA urban area; **Doctor** *(general practitioners routine exam of an established patient);* **Dentist** *(adult teeth cleaning and periodic oral examination);* **Optometrist** *(full vision eye exam for established adult patient);* **Gasoline** *(one gallon regular unleaded, national brand, including all taxes, cash price at self-service pump if available);* **Beauty Salon** *(woman's shampoo, trim, and blow-dry);* **Men's Shirt** *(cotton/polyester dress shirt, pinpoint weave, long sleeves).*
Source: The Council for Community and Economic Research, ACCRA Cost of Living Index, 2013

HOUSING

House Price Index (HPI)

Area	National Ranking[2]	Quarterly Change (%)	One-Year Change (%)	Five-Year Change (%)
MD[1]	90	0.58	5.01	1.34
U.S.[3]	–	1.20	7.69	4.18

Note: The HPI is a weighted repeat sales index. It measures average price changes in repeat sales or refinancings on the same properties. This information is obtained by reviewing repeat mortgage transactions on single-family properties whose mortgages have been purchased or securitized by Fannie Mae or Freddie Mac in January 1975; (1) Washington-Arlington-Alexandria, DC-VA-MD-WV Metropolitan Division—see Appendix B for areas included; (2) Rankings are based on annual percentage change for all metro areas containing at least 15,000 transactions over the last 10 years and ranges from 1 to 283; (3) figures based on a weighted average of Census Division estimates using a seasonally adjusted, purchase-only index; all figures are for the period ending December 31, 2013
Source: Federal Housing Finance Agency, House Price Index, February 25, 2014

Median Single-Family Home Prices

Area	2011	2012	2013[p]	Percent Change 2012 to 2013
MSA[1]	325.4	352.0	381.9	8.5
U.S. Average	166.2	177.2	197.4	11.4

Note: Figures are median sales prices of existing single-family homes in thousands of dollars; (p) preliminary; n/a not available; (1) Washington-Arlington-Alexandria, DC-VA-MD-WV Metropolitan Statistical Area—see Appendix B for areas included
Source: National Association of Realtors, Median Sales Price of Existing Single-Family Homes for Metropolitan Areas, 4th Quarter 2013

Qualifying Income Based on Median Sales Price of Existing Single-Family Homes

Area	With 5% Down ($)	With 10% Down ($)	With 20% Down ($)
MSA[1]	84,843	80,377	71,446
U.S. Average	45,395	43,006	38,228

Note: Figures are preliminary; Qualifying income is based on a mortgage rate of 4.4%. Monthly principal and interest payment is limited to 25% of income; n/a not available; (1) Washington-Arlington-Alexandria, DC-VA-MD-WV Metropolitan Statistical Area—see Appendix B for areas included
Source: National Association of Realtors, Qualifying Income Based on Median Sales Price of Existing Single-Family Homes for Metropolitan Areas, 4th Quarter 2013

Median Apartment Condo-Coop Home Prices

Area	2011	2012	2013[p]	Percent Change 2012 to 2013
MSA[1]	230.1	253.9	272.2	7.2
U.S. Average	165.1	173.7	194.9	12.2

Note: Figures are median sales prices of existing apartment condo-coop homes in thousands of dollars; (p) preliminary; n/a not available; (1) Washington-Arlington-Alexandria, DC-VA-MD-WV Metropolitan Statistical Area—see Appendix B for areas included
Source: National Association of Realtors, Median Sales Price of Existing Apartment Condo-Coop Homes for Metropolitan Areas, 4th Quarter 2013

Gross Monthly Rent

Area	Under $200	$200 -299	$300 -499	$500 -749	$750 -999	$1,000 -1,499	$1,500 and up	Median ($)
City	3.1	3.5	4.8	8.7	16.5	27.9	35.5	1,236
MSA[1]	1.4	1.7	2.2	4.5	10.6	35.8	43.8	1,418
U.S.	1.7	3.3	8.1	22.7	24.3	25.7	14.3	889

Note: Figures are percentages except for Median; Gross rent is the contract rent plus the estimated average monthly cost of utilities (electricity, gas, and water and sewer) and fuels (oil, coal, kerosene, wood, etc.) if these are paid by the renter (or paid for the renter by someone else); (1) Figures cover the Washington-Arlington-Alexandria, DC-VA-MD-WV Metropolitan Statistical Area—see Appendix B for areas included
Source: U.S. Census Bureau, 2010-2012 American Community Survey 3-Year Estimates

Year Housing Structure Built

Area	2010 or Later	2000 -2009	1990 -1999	1980 -1989	1970 -1979	1960 -1969	1950 -1959	1940 -1949	Before 1940	Median Year
City	0.3	8.2	3.0	4.4	7.5	12.8	14.0	14.7	35.1	1950
MSA[1]	0.6	15.6	14.1	16.7	15.1	13.2	10.2	5.9	8.6	1978
U.S.	0.5	14.9	13.8	13.9	15.9	11.1	10.9	5.5	13.5	1976

Note: Figures are percentages except for Median Year; (1) Figures cover the Washington-Arlington-Alexandria, DC-VA-MD-WV Metropolitan Statistical Area—see Appendix B for areas included
Source: U.S. Census Bureau, 2010-2012 American Community Survey 3-Year Estimates

HEALTH

Health Risk Data

Category	MD[1] (%)	U.S. (%)
Adults aged 18–64 who have any kind of health care coverage	84.5	79.6
Adults who reported being in good or excellent health	86.5	83.1
Adults who are current smokers	14.6	19.6
Adults who are heavy drinkers[2]	5.6	6.1
Adults who are binge drinkers[3]	17.4	16.9
Adults who are overweight (BMI 25.0 - 29.9)	36.7	35.8
Adults who are obese (BMI 30.0 - 99.8)	24.2	27.6
Adults who participated in any physical activities in the past month	80.8	77.1
Adults 50+ who have ever had a sigmoidoscopy or colonoscopy	70.6	67.3
Women aged 40+ who have had a mammogram within the past two years	80.5	74.0
Men aged 40+ who have had a PSA test within the past two years	45.1	45.2
Adults aged 65+ who have had flu shot within the past year	58.7	60.1
Adults who always wear a seatbelt	95.7	93.8

Note: Data as of 2012 unless otherwise noted; (1) Figures cover the Washington-Arlington-Alexandria, DC-VA-MD-WV Metropolitan Division—see Appendix B for areas included; (2) Heavy drinkers are classified as males having more than two drinks per day or females having more than one drink per day; (3) Binge drinkers are classified as males having five or more drinks on one occasion or females having four or more drinks on one occasion
Source: Centers for Disease Control and Prevention, Behaviorial Risk Factor Surveillance System, SMART: Selected Metropolitan/Micropolitan Area Risk Trends, 2012

Chronic Health Indicators

Category	MD[1] (%)	U.S. (%)
Adults who have ever been told they had a heart attack	2.8	4.5
Adults who have ever been told they had a stroke	2.3	2.9
Adults who have been told they currently have asthma	8.0	8.9
Adults who have ever been told they have arthritis	18.6	25.7
Adults who have ever been told they have diabetes[2]	8.7	9.7
Adults who have ever been told they had skin cancer	3.9	5.7
Adults who have ever been told they had any other types of cancer	4.6	6.5
Adults who have ever been told they have COPD	4.1	6.2
Adults who have ever been told they have kidney disease	2.0	2.5
Adults who have ever been told they have a form of depression	13.3	18.0

Note: Data as of 2012 unless otherwise noted; (1) Figures cover the Washington-Arlington-Alexandria, DC-VA-MD-WV Metropolitan Division—see Appendix B for areas included; (2) Figures do not include pregnancy-related, borderline, or pre-diabetes
Source: Centers for Disease Control and Prevention, Behaviorial Risk Factor Surveillance System, SMART: Selected Metropolitan/Micropolitan Area Risk Trends, 2012

Mortality Rates for the Top 10 Causes of Death in the U.S.

ICD-10[a] Sub-Chapter	ICD-10[a] Code	Age-Adjusted Mortality Rate[1] per 100,000 population	
		County[2]	U.S.
Malignant neoplasms	C00-C97	192.4	174.2
Ischaemic heart diseases	I20-I25	159.0	119.1
Other forms of heart disease	I30-I51	33.4	49.6
Chronic lower respiratory diseases	J40-J47	25.1	43.2
Cerebrovascular diseases	I60-I69	35.3	40.3
Organic, including symptomatic, mental disorders	F01-F09	22.2	30.5
Other degenerative diseases of the nervous system	G30-G31	19.7	26.3
Other external causes of accidental injury	W00-X59	21.1	25.1
Diabetes mellitus	E10-E14	24.9	21.3
Hypertensive diseases	I10-I15	40.9	18.8

Note: (a) ICD-10 = International Classification of Diseases 10th Revision; (1) Mortality rates are a three year average covering 2008-2010; (2) Figures cover District of Columbia
Source: Centers for Disease Control and Prevention, National Center for Health Statistics. Compressed Mortality File 1999-2010 on CDC WONDER Online Database, released January 2013. Data are compiled from the Compressed Mortality File 1999-2010, Series 20 No. 2P, 2013.

Mortality Rates for Selected Causes of Death

ICD-10[a] Sub-Chapter	ICD-10[a] Code	Age-Adjusted Mortality Rate[1] per 100,000 population	
		County[2]	U.S.
Assault	X85-Y09	20.3	5.5
Diseases of the liver	K70-K76	10.7	12.4
Human immunodeficiency virus (HIV) disease	B20-B24	24.1	3.0
Influenza and pneumonia	J09-J18	13.3	16.4
Intentional self-harm	X60-X84	6.2	11.8
Malnutrition	E40-E46	Suppressed	0.8
Obesity and other hyperalimentation	E65-E68	2.2	1.6
Renal failure	N17-N19	11.4	13.6
Transport accidents	V01-V99	7.6	12.6
Viral hepatitis	B15-B19	5.0	2.2

Note: (a) ICD-10 = International Classification of Diseases 10th Revision; (1) Mortality rates are a three year average covering 2008-2010; (2) Figures cover District of Columbia
Source: Centers for Disease Control and Prevention, National Center for Health Statistics. Compressed Mortality File 1999-2010 on CDC WONDER Online Database, released January 2013. Data are compiled from the Compressed Mortality File 1999-2010, Series 20 No. 2P, 2013.

Health Insurance Coverage

Area	With Health Insurance	With Private Health Insurance	With Public Health Insurance	Without Health Insurance	Population Under Age 18 Without Health Insurance
City	93.2	69.9	35.0	6.8	2.6
MSA[1]	88.2	76.9	20.7	11.8	5.2
U.S.	84.9	65.4	30.4	15.1	7.5

Note: Figures are percentages that cover the civilian noninstitutionalized population; (1) Figures cover the Washington-Arlington-Alexandria, DC-VA-MD-WV Metropolitan Statistical Area—see Appendix B for areas included
Source: U.S. Census Bureau, 2010-2012 American Community Survey 3-Year Estimates

Number of Medical Professionals

Area[1]	MDs[2]	DOs[2,3]	Dentists	Podiatrists	Chiropractors	Optometrists
Local (number)	4,943	104	720	53	48	81
Local (rate[4])	797.7	16.8	113.7	8.4	7.6	12.8
U.S. (rate[4])	267.6	19.6	61.7	5.6	24.7	14.5

Note: Data as of 2012 unless noted; (1) Local data covers The District County; (2) Data as of 2011; (3) Doctor of Osteopathic Medicine; (4) rate per 100,000 population
Source: Area Resource File (ARF) 2012-2013. U.S. Department of Health and Human Services, Health Resources and Services Administration, Bureau of Health Professions

Best Hospitals

According to *U.S. News*, the Washington-Arlington-Alexandria, DC-VA-MD-WV metro area is home to three of the best hospitals in the U.S.: **Inova Fairfax Hospital** (1 specialty); **MedStar National Rehabilitation Hospital** (1 specialty); **Medstar Washington Hospital Center** (1 specialty). The hospitals listed were nationally ranked in at least one adult specialty. Only 147 hospitals nationwide were nationally ranked in one or more specialties. Eighteen hospitals in the U.S. made the Honor Roll by ranking near the top in at least six specialties.*U.S. News Online, "America's Best Hospitals 2013-14"*

According to *U.S. News*, the Washington-Arlington-Alexandria, DC-VA-MD-WV metro area is home to two of the best children's hospitals in the U.S.: **Children's National Medical Center**; **Inova Fairfax Hospital for Children**. The hospitals listed were highly ranked in at least one pediatric specialty. Eighty-seven hospitals in the U.S. ranked in at least one specialty. Ten children's hospitals in the U.S. made the Honor Roll by ranking near the top in three or more specialties.*U.S. News Online, "America's Best Children's Hospitals 2013-14"*

EDUCATION

Public School District Statistics

District Name	Schls	Pupils	Pupil/ Teacher Ratio	Minority Pupils[1] (%)	Free Lunch Eligible[2] (%)	IEP[3] (%)
District of Columbia Public Schools	128	44,618	12.8	89.5	50.5	19.6
Friendship Pcs	6	3,979	16.9	n/a	72.4	11.9
Kipp Academy Pcs	9	2,667	13.3	n/a	70.7	11.2

Note: Table includes school districts with 2,000 or more students; (1) Percentage of students that are not non-Hispanic white; (2) Percentage of students that are eligible for the free lunch program; (3) Percentage of students that have an Individualized Education Program.
Source: U.S. Department of Education, National Center for Education Statistics, Common Core of Data, Local Education Agency (School District) Universe Survey: School Year 2011-2012; U.S. Department of Education, National Center for Education Statistics, Common Core of Data, Public Elementary/Secondary School Universe Survey: School Year 2011-2012

Best High Schools

High School Name	Rank[1]	Grad. Rate[2] (%)	Coll.[3] (%)	AP/IB/ AICE Tests[4]	AP/IB/ AICE Score[5]	SAT Score[6]	ACT Score[6]
Benjamin Banneker Academic H.S.	288	98	100	1.0	1.8	1466	20.2
School Without Walls Senior H.S.	210	93	100	1.1	2.9	1706	22.9
Woodrow Wilson H.S.	1317	88	90	0.7	2.5	1477	n/a

Note: (1) Public schools are ranked from 1 to 2,000 based on the following self-reported statistics (with the corresponding weight used in calculating their overall score). Schools that were newly founded and did not have a graduating senior class in 2012 were excluded; (2) Four-year, on-time graduation rate (25%); (3) Percent of 2011 graduates who were accepted to college (25%); (4) AP/IB/AICE tests taken per student (25%); (5) Average AP/IB/AICE exam score (10%); (6) Average SAT and/or ACT score (10%); Percent of students enrolled in at least one AP/IB/AICE course (5%)—data not shown; n/a not available
Source: Newsweek and The Daily Beast, "America's Best High Schools 2013"

Highest Level of Education

Area	Less than H.S.	H.S. Diploma	Some College, No Deg.	Associate Degree	Bachelor's Degree	Master's Degree	Prof. School Degree	Doctorate Degree
City	12.3	19.0	14.0	3.0	23.1	16.7	8.2	3.7
MSA[1]	10.0	19.4	17.4	5.6	24.8	15.5	4.3	2.9
U.S.	14.1	28.3	21.3	7.8	18.0	7.5	1.9	1.2

Note: Figures cover persons age 25 and over; (1) Figures cover the Washington-Arlington-Alexandria, DC-VA-MD-WV Metropolitan Statistical Area—see Appendix B for areas included
Source: U.S. Census Bureau, 2010-2012 American Community Survey 3-Year Estimates

Educational Attainment by Race

Area	High School Graduate or Higher (%)					Bachelor's Degree or Higher (%)				
	Total	White	Black	Asian	Hisp.[2]	Total	White	Black	Asian	Hisp.[2]
City	87.7	95.5	82.0	90.5	64.9	51.7	83.6	22.9	76.8	35.7
MSA[1]	90.0	93.0	89.5	90.4	64.5	47.6	55.3	30.5	61.6	22.7
U.S.	85.9	88.1	82.5	85.5	63.1	28.6	30.0	18.4	50.2	13.4

Note: Figures shown cover persons 25 years old and over; (1) Figures cover the
Washington-Arlington-Alexandria, DC-VA-MD-WV Metropolitan Statistical Area—see Appendix B for areas
included; (2) People of Hispanic origin can be of any race
Source: U.S. Census Bureau, 2010-2012 American Community Survey 3-Year Estimates

School Enrollment by Grade and Control

Area	Preschool (%)		Kindergarten (%)		Grades 1 - 4 (%)		Grades 5 - 8 (%)		Grades 9 - 12 (%)	
	Public	Private	Public	Private	Public	Private	Public	Private	Public	Private
City	71.3	28.7	83.8	16.2	84.0	16.0	79.0	21.0	84.5	15.5
MSA[1]	40.1	59.9	83.6	16.4	87.2	12.8	87.2	12.8	89.0	11.0
U.S.	56.9	43.1	87.8	12.2	89.9	10.1	90.0	10.0	90.8	9.2

Note: Figures shown cover persons 3 years old and over; (1) Figures cover the
Washington-Arlington-Alexandria, DC-VA-MD-WV Metropolitan Statistical Area—see Appendix B for areas
included
Source: U.S. Census Bureau, 2010-2012 American Community Survey 3-Year Estimates

Average Salaries of Public School Classroom Teachers

Area	2012-13		2013-14		Percent Change 2012-13 to 2013-14	Percent Change 2003-04 to 2013-14
	Dollars	Rank[1]	Dollars	Rank[1]		
District of Columbia	70,906	3	73,162	3	3.18	28.3
U.S. Average	56,103	–	56,689	–	1.04	21.8

Note: (1) State rank ranges from 1 to 51 where 1 indicates highest salary.
Source: National Education Association, Rankings & Estimates: Rankings of the States 2013 and Estimates of
School Statistics 2014, March 2014

Higher Education

Four-Year Colleges			Two-Year Colleges			Medical Schools[1]	Law Schools[2]	Voc/ Tech[3]
Public	Private Non-profit	Private For-profit	Public	Private Non-profit	Private For-profit			
2	14	4	0	1	0	3	6	3

Note: Figures cover institutions located within the city limits and include main campuses only; (1) includes
schools accredited by the Liaison Committee on Medical Education and the American Osteopathic Association's
Commission on Osteopathic College Accreditation; (2) includes ABA-accredited schools, schools with
provisional ABA accreditation, and state accredited schools; (3) includes all schools with programs that are less
than 2 years.
Source: National Center for Education Statistics, Integrated Postsecondary Education System (IPEDS),
2012-13; Association of American Medical Colleges, Member List, April 24, 2014; American Osteopathic
Association, Member List, April 24, 2014; Law School Admission Council, Official Guide to ABA-Approved
Law Schools Online, April 24, 2014; Wikipedia, List of Medical Schools in the United States, April 24, 2014;
Wikipedia, List of Law Schools in the United States, April 24, 2014

According to *U.S. News & World Report,* the Washington-Arlington-Alexandria, DC-VA-MD-WV
metro division is home to seven of the best national universities in the U.S.: **Georgetown
University** (#20); **George Washington University** (#52); **University of Maryland–College
Park** (#62); **American University** (#75); **The Catholic University of America** (#121); **George
Mason University** (#141); **Howard University** (#142). The indicators used to capture academic
quality fall into a number of categories: assessment by administrators at peer institutions; retention
of students; faculty resources; student selectivity; financial resources; alumni giving; high school
counselor ratings of colleges; and graduation rate. *U.S. News & World Report, "America's Best
Colleges 2014"*

According to *U.S. News & World Report,* the Washington-Arlington-Alexandria, DC-VA-MD-WV
metro division is home to five of the top 100 law schools in the U.S.: **Georgetown University**
(#14); **George Washington University** (#21); **George Mason University** (#41); **American
University (Washington)** (#56); **Catholic University of America (Columbus)** (#80). The
rankings are based on a weighted average of 12 measures of quality: peer assessment score;

assessment score by lawyers/judges; median LSAT scores; median undergrad GPA; acceptance rate; employment rates for graduates; placement success; bar passage rate; faculty resources; expenditures per student; student/faculty ratio; and library resources. *U.S. News & World Report, "America's Best Graduate Schools, Law, 2014"*

According to *U.S. News & World Report,* the Washington-Arlington-Alexandria, DC-VA-MD-WV metro division is home to three of the top 100 business schools in the U.S.: **Georgetown University (McDonough)** (#25); **University of Maryland–College Park (Smith)** (#37); **George Washington University** (#56). The rankings are based on a weighted average of the following nine measures: quality assessment; peer assessment; recruiter assessment; placement success; mean starting salary and bonus; student selectivity; mean GMAT and GRE scores; mean undergraduate GPA; and acceptance rate. *U.S. News & World Report, "America's Best Graduate Schools, Business, 2014"*

PRESIDENTIAL ELECTION

2012 Presidential Election Results

Area	Obama	Romney	Other
District of Columbia	91.1	7.1	1.8
U.S.	51.0	47.2	1.8

Note: Results are percentages and may not add to 100% due to rounding
Source: Dave Leip's Atlas of U.S. Presidential Elections

EMPLOYERS

Major Employers

Company Name	Industry
Adventist HealthCare	General medical and surgical hospitals
Bechtel National	Engineering services
Computer Sciences Corporation	Computer related consulting services
Federal Aviation Administration	Air traffic control operations, government
Federal Bureau of Investigation	Police protection
Fish and Wildlife Service, United States	Fish and wildlife conservation agency, government
Howard University	Colleges and universities
HR Solutions	Human resource consulting services
Internal Revenue Service	Finance, taxation, and monetary policy
Intl Bank for Recons. & Dev.	Foreign trade and international banks
Natl Inst of Standards & Technology	Administration of general economic programs
Office of the Secretary of Defense	National security
US Department of Agriculture	Regulation of agricultural marketing
US Department of Commerce	Regulation, miscellaneous commercial sectors
US Department of Labor	Administration of social and manpower programs
US Department of the Army	National security
US Department of the Navy	National security
US Department of Transportation	Regulation, administration of transportation
US Environmental Protection Agency	Land, mineral, and wildlife conservation
Washington Hospital Center Corporation	General medical and surgical hospitals

Note: Companies shown are located within the Washington-Arlington-Alexandria, DC-VA-MD-WV Metropolitan Statistical Area.
Source: Hoovers.com; Wikipedia

Best Companies to Work For

Arnold & Porter, headquartered in Washington, is among "The 100 Best Companies to Work For." To pick the 100 Best Companies to Work For, *Fortune* partnered with the Great Place to Work Institute. Two hundred fifty seven firms participated in this year's survey. Two-thirds of a company's score is based on the results of the Institute's Trust Index survey, which is sent to a random sample of employees from each company. The questions related to attitudes about management's credibility, job satisfaction, and camaraderie. The other third of the scoring is based on the company's responses to the Institute's Culture Audit, which includes detailed questions about pay and benefit programs, and a series of open-ended questions about hiring practices, internal communication, training, recognition programs, and diversity efforts. Any company that is at least five years old with more than 1,000 U.S. employees is eligible. *Fortune, "The 100 Best Companies to Work For," 2014*

Arnold & Porter; FINRA; Finnegan, Henderson, Farabow, Garrett & Dunner, headquartered in Washington, are among the "100 Best Companies for Working Mothers." Criteria: workforce representation; child care; flexibility programs; and leave policies. This year *Working Mother* gave particular weight to flexible work arrangements, women's advancement programs, and paid maternity leave. *Working Mother, "100 Best Companies 2013"*

American University; Financial Industry Regulatory Authority (FINRA); U.S. Fish and Wildlife Service; Veterans Health Administration, headquartered in Washington, are among the "50 Best Employers for Workers Over 50." Criteria: recruiting practices; opportunities for training, education, and career development; workplace accommodations; alternative work options, such as flexible scheduling, job sharing, and phased retirement; employee health and pension benefits; and retiree benefits. Employers with at least 50 employees based in the U.S. are eligible, including for-profit companies, not-for-profit organizations, and government employers. *AARP, "2013 AARP Best Employers for Workers Over 50"*

American University; George Washington University, headquartered in Washington, are among the "100 Best Places to Work in IT." To qualify, companies, both public and private, had to have a minimum of 50 IT employees and were selected based on average salary and bonus increases, the percentage of IT staffers promoted, IT staff turnover rates, training and development programs, and the percentage of women and minorities in IT staff and management positions. In addition, *Computerworld* looked at retention efforts, programs for recognizing and rewarding outstanding performances, and benefits such as flextime, elder care and child care, and reimbursement for college tuition and the cost of pursuing technology certifications. *Computerworld, "100 Best Places to Work in IT 2013"*

PUBLIC SAFETY

Crime Rate

Area	All Crimes	Violent Crimes				Property Crimes		
		Murder	Forcible Rape	Robbery	Aggrav. Assault	Burglary	Larceny -Theft	Motor Vehicle Theft
City	5,805.9	13.9	37.3	589.1	537.5	556.5	3,510.2	561.3
Suburbs[1]	2,319.9	2.7	14.9	102.1	118.8	286.0	1,595.7	199.6
Metro[2]	2,800.3	4.3	18.0	169.2	176.5	323.3	1,859.6	249.4
U.S.	3,246.1	4.7	26.9	112.9	242.3	670.2	1,959.3	229.7

Note: Figures are crimes per 100,000 population; (1) All areas within the metro area that are located outside the city limits; (2) Figures cover the Washington-Arlington-Alexandria, DC-VA-MD-WV Metropolitan Division—see Appendix B for areas included
Source: FBI Uniform Crime Reports, 2012

Hate Crimes

Area	Number of Quarters Reported	Bias Motivation				
		Race	Religion	Sexual Orientation	Ethnicity	Disability
City	4	13	6	46	5	1
U.S.	4	2,797	1,099	1,135	667	92

Source: Federal Bureau of Investigation, Hate Crime Statistics 2012

Identity Theft Consumer Complaints

Area	Complaints	Complaints per 100,000 Population	Rank[2]
MSA[1]	5,991	106.3	40
U.S.	290,056	91.8	-

Note: (1) Figures cover the Washington-Arlington-Alexandria, DC-VA-MD-WV Metropolitan Statistical Area—see Appendix B for areas included; (2) Rank ranges from 1 to 377 where 1 indicates greatest number of identity theft complaints per 100,000 population
Source: Federal Trade Commission, Consumer Sentinel Network Data Book for January–December 2013

Fraud and Other Consumer Complaints

Area	Complaints	Complaints per 100,000 Population	Rank[2]
MSA[1]	33,019	585.8	4
U.S.	1,811,724	595.2	-

Note: (1) Figures cover the Washington-Arlington-Alexandria, DC-VA-MD-WV Metropolitan Statistical Area—see Appendix B for areas included; (2) Rank ranges from 1 to 377 where 1 indicates greatest number of identity theft complaints per 100,000 population
Source: Federal Trade Commission, Consumer Sentinel Network Data Book for January–December 2013

RECREATION

Culture

Dance[1]	Theatre[1]	Instrumental Music[1]	Vocal Music[1]	Series and Festivals	Museums and Art Galleries[2]	Zoos and Aquariums[3]
8	22	12	18	20	98	1

Note: (1) Number of professional perfoming groups; (2) Based on organizations with primary SIC code 8412; (3) AZA-accredited
Source: The Grey House Performing Arts Directory, 2013; Association of Zoos & Aquariums, AZA Member Zoos & Aquariums, April 2014; www.AccuLeads.com, May 1, 2014

Professional Sports Teams

Team Name	League	Year Established
D.C. United	Major League Soccer (MLS)	1996
Washington Capitals	National Hockey League (NHL)	1974
Washington Nationals	Major League Baseball (MLB)	2005
Washington Redskins	National Football League (NFL)	1937
Washington Wizards	National Basketball Association (NBA)	1973

Note: Includes teams located in the Washington-Arlington-Alexandria, DC-VA-MD-WV Metropolitan Statistical Area.
Source: Wikipedia, Major Professional Sports Teams of the United States and Canada

CLIMATE

Average and Extreme Temperatures

Temperature	Jan	Feb	Mar	Apr	May	Jun	Jul	Aug	Sep	Oct	Nov	Dec	Yr.
Extreme High (°F)	79	82	89	95	97	101	104	103	101	94	86	75	104
Average High (°F)	43	46	55	67	76	84	88	86	80	69	58	47	67
Average Temp. (°F)	36	38	46	57	66	75	79	78	71	60	49	39	58
Average Low (°F)	28	30	37	46	56	65	70	69	62	50	40	31	49
Extreme Low (°F)	-5	4	14	24	34	47	54	49	39	29	16	3	-5

Note: Figures cover the years 1945-1990
Source: National Climatic Data Center, International Station Meteorological Climate Summary, 9/96

Average Precipitation/Snowfall/Humidity

Precip./Humidity	Jan	Feb	Mar	Apr	May	Jun	Jul	Aug	Sep	Oct	Nov	Dec	Yr.
Avg. Precip. (in.)	2.8	2.6	3.3	2.9	4.0	3.4	4.1	4.2	3.3	2.9	3.0	3.1	39.5
Avg. Snowfall (in.)	6	6	2	Tr	0	0	0	0	0	Tr	1	3	18
Avg. Rel. Hum. 7am (%)	71	70	70	70	74	75	77	80	82	80	76	72	75
Avg. Rel. Hum. 4pm (%)	54	50	46	45	51	52	53	54	54	53	53	55	52

Note: Figures cover the years 1945-1990; Tr = Trace amounts (<0.05 in. of rain; <0.5 in. of snow)
Source: National Climatic Data Center, International Station Meteorological Climate Summary, 9/96

Weather Conditions

Temperature			Daytime Sky			Precipitation		
10°F & below	32°F & below	90°F & above	Clear	Partly cloudy	Cloudy	0.01 inch or more precip.	0.1 inch or more snow/ice	Thunder-storms
2	71	34	84	144	137	112	9	30

Note: Figures are average number of days per year and cover the years 1945-1990
Source: National Climatic Data Center, International Station Meteorological Climate Summary, 9/96

HAZARDOUS WASTE

Superfund Sites

Washington has one hazardous waste site on the EPA's Superfund Final National Priorities List: **Washington Navy Yard**. *U.S. Environmental Protection Agency, Final National Priorities List, April 26, 2014*

AIR & WATER QUALITY

Air Quality Index

Area	Percent of Days when Air Quality was...[2]					AQI Statistics[2]	
	Good	Moderate	Unhealthy for Sensitive Groups	Unhealthy	Very Unhealthy	Maximum	Median
MSA[1]	53.2	45.5	1.4	0.0	0.0	104	49

Note: (1) Data covers the Washington-Arlington-Alexandria, DC-VA-MD-WV Metropolitan Statistical Area—see Appendix B for areas included; (2) Based on 365 days with AQI data in 2013. Air Quality Index (AQI) is an index for reporting daily air quality. EPA calculates the AQI for five major air pollutants regulated by the Clean Air Act: ground-level ozone, particle pollution (aka particulate matter), carbon monoxide, sulfur dioxide, and nitrogen dioxide. The AQI runs from 0 to 500. The higher the AQI value, the greater the level of air pollution and the greater the health concern. There are six AQI categories: "Good" AQI is between 0 and 50. Air quality is considered satisfactory; "Moderate" AQI is between 51 and 100. Air quality is acceptable; "Unhealthy for Sensitive Groups" When AQI values are between 101 and 150, members of sensitive groups may experience health effects; "Unhealthy" When AQI values are between 151 and 200 everyone may begin to experience health effects; "Very Unhealthy" AQI values between 201 and 300 trigger a health alert; "Hazardous" AQI values over 300 trigger warnings of emergency conditions (not shown). Source: U.S. Environmental Protection Agency, Air Quality Index Report, 2013

Air Quality Index Pollutants

Area	Percent of Days when AQI Pollutant was...[2]					
	Carbon Monoxide	Nitrogen Dioxide	Ozone	Sulfur Dioxide	Particulate Matter 2.5	Particulate Matter 10
MSA[1]	0.0	10.1	32.6	0.0	57.3	0.0

Note: (1) Data covers the Washington-Arlington-Alexandria, DC-VA-MD-WV Metropolitan Statistical Area—see Appendix B for areas included; (2) Based on 365 days with AQI data in 2013. The Air Quality Index (AQI) is an index for reporting daily air quality. EPA calculates the AQI for five major air pollutants regulated by the Clean Air Act: ground-level ozone, particle pollution (also known as particulate matter), carbon monoxide, sulfur dioxide, and nitrogen dioxide. The AQI runs from 0 to 500. The higher the AQI value, the greater the level of air pollution and the greater the health concern. Source: U.S. Environmental Protection Agency, Air Quality Index Report, 2013

Air Quality Trends: Ozone

	2003	2004	2005	2006	2007	2008	2009	2010	2011	2012
MSA[1]	0.084	0.080	0.082	0.086	0.084	0.077	0.067	0.080	0.080	0.079

Note: (1) Data covers the Washington-Arlington-Alexandria, DC-VA-MD-WV Metropolitan Statistical Area—see Appendix B for areas included. The values shown are the composite ozone concentration averages among trend sites based on the highest fourth daily maximum 8-hour concentration in parts per million. These trends are based on sites having an adequate record of monitoring data during the trend period. Data from exceptional events are included. Source: U.S. Environmental Protection Agency, Air Quality Monitoring Information, "Air Quality Trends by City, 2000-2012"

Maximum Air Pollutant Concentrations: Particulate Matter, Ozone, CO and Lead

	Particulate Matter 10 (ug/m³)	Particulate Matter 2.5 Wtd AM (ug/m³)	Particulate Matter 2.5 24-Hr (ug/m³)	Ozone (ppm)	Carbon Monoxide (ppm)	Lead (ug/m³)
MSA[1] Level	38	10.3	28	0.09	3	0
NAAQS[2]	150	15	35	0.075	9	0.15
Met NAAQS[2]	Yes	Yes	Yes	No	Yes	Yes

Note: (1) Data covers the Washington-Arlington-Alexandria, DC-VA-MD-WV Metropolitan Statistical Area—see Appendix B for areas included; Data from exceptional events are included; (2) National Ambient Air Quality Standards; ppm = parts per million; ug/m³ = micrograms per cubic meter; n/a not available. Concentrations: Particulate Matter 10 (coarse particulate)—highest second maximum 24-hour concentration; Particulate Matter 2.5 Wtd AM (fine particulate)—highest weighted annual mean concentration; Particulate Matter 2.5 24-Hour (fine particulate)—highest 98th percentile 24-hour concentration; Ozone—highest fourth daily maximum 8-hour concentration; Carbon Monoxide—highest second maximum non-overlapping 8-hour concentration; Lead—maximum running 3-month average
Source: U.S. Environmental Protection Agency, Air Quality Monitoring Information, "Air Quality Statistics by City, 2012"

Maximum Air Pollutant Concentrations: Nitrogen Dioxide and Sulfur Dioxide

	Nitrogen Dioxide AM (ppb)	Nitrogen Dioxide 1-Hr (ppb)	Sulfur Dioxide AM (ppb)	Sulfur Dioxide 1-Hr (ppb)	Sulfur Dioxide 24-Hr (ppb)
MSA[1] Level	17	51	n/a	12	n/a
NAAQS[2]	53	100	30	75	140
Met NAAQS[2]	Yes	Yes	n/a	Yes	n/a

Note: (1) Data covers the Washington-Arlington-Alexandria, DC-VA-MD-WV Metropolitan Statistical Area—see Appendix B for areas included; Data from exceptional events are included; (2) National Ambient Air Quality Standards; ppm = parts per million; ug/m³ = micrograms per cubic meter; n/a not available. Concentrations: Nitrogen Dioxide AM—highest arithmetic mean concentration; Nitrogen Dioxide 1-Hr—highest 98th percentile 1-hour daily maximum concentration; Sulfur Dioxide AM—highest annual mean concentration; Sulfur Dioxide 1-Hr—highest 99th percentile 1-hour daily maximum concentration; Sulfur Dioxide 24-Hr—highest second maximum 24-hour concentration
Source: U.S. Environmental Protection Agency, Air Quality Monitoring Information, "Air Quality Statistics by City, 2012"

Drinking Water

Water System Name	Pop. Served	Primary Water Source Type	Violations[1] Health Based	Violations[1] Monitoring/ Reporting
DC Water and Sewer Authority	632,323	Purchased Surface	0	0

Note: (1) Based on violation data from January 1, 2013 to December 31, 2013 (includes unresolved violations from earlier years)
Source: U.S. Environmental Protection Agency, Office of Ground Water and Drinking Water, Safe Drinking Water Information System (based on data extracted February 10, 2014)

Wilmington, North Carolina

Background

In pre-revolutionary times, Wilmington's importance as a port city was slow to take hold. And while Wilmington played an important early role in the American Revolution, the lack of good roads would remain a hindrance due to the bogs and swamps that surrounded the area. This boggy landscape would later be a boon to the growing economy, providing Wilmington with the natural resources to produce shipbuilding stores (tar, pitch, rosin and Turpentine) for the navy. North Carolina produced about 70% of all U.S. naval stores at its peak. To this day, North Carolina is referred to as the "Tar Heel State." The invention of better navigational tools for sailing, and of the steam-powered engine, helped Wilmington become North Carolina's largest city by 1840, and a major port for U.S. exports of peanuts, rice, flax and cotton.

Wilmington was the site of one of the first rebellions in the United States' revolt against British rule. The Stamp Act required that colonists only use paper produced and stamped in London—a way for the British to earn the necessary revenue to "protect" the colonies. The Colonists objected, claiming it was an unfair tax, and they didn't need protection. In 1765, about 500 Wilmington citizens burned an effigy of their stamp collector, Lord Bute, and forced him to resign.

By the time of the Civil War, Wilmington had become a major port for the eastern seaboard. However, wartime brought Wilmington's normal export industry to an abrupt end. The city turned its attention to importing supplies for the Confederate armies, and was considered the "lifeline of the Confederacy." By late 1864, Wilmington was the only port not captured by Union forces.

Ironically, following the Civil War and the Emancipation Proclamation, Wilmington became home to large numbers of freed slaves, and free people of color, who sought employment in the city's industry. (About two thirds of the population was black.) A large middle-class grew from the black community, prospering in ways few other communities could. A significant number of black men were business professionals, and held important positions in the community, including a police chief, deputy sheriff and a customs collector. In fact, five out of the ten aldermen were black. Wilmington would produce the first black attorney, George Mabson (admitted to the bar in 1871), and the nation's first black architect, Robert R. Taylor, who graduated from Massachusetts Institute of Technology.

Black citizens were achieving near political and social equality with white citizens—a situation white supremacists would not tolerate. Wilmington has the dubious distinction of fomenting the first and only coup d'état in U.S. History. On November 10, 1898, white supremacists overtook the legitimate, bi-racial government and instituted the first Jim Crow laws in North Carolina. By the end of November, 1,400 black residents left Wilmington. Those who stayed were disenfranchised, precluded from voting when the new leadership adopted new literacy requirements.

In 1961, Wilmington became the permanent home of the *U.S.S. North Carolina.* Considered to be the greatest U. S. sea weapon in 1941, it has since become a museum—a major draw in Wilmington's tourism industry.

In the late 70s, Wilmington began aggressive revitalization and restoration efforts, creating a revolving loan fund to draw in new small businesses. By bringing back the "old town feel," Wilmington has created a vibrant tourism industry. Wrightsville Beach, a very popular beach destination for North Carolinians, is only ten miles away.

An important new industry in Wilmington has been the film industry. In 1984, a 32-acre film studio was built. Some of the most notable movies filmed in Wilmington include *The Color Purple, Dirty Dancing* and *Bull Durham.* The television show *Dawson's Creek* was also filmed in Wilmington.

Winters in Wilmington are moderate, and spring is long. Given that Wilmington's climate is sub-tropical, summer can be very hot, and about once every seven years Wilmington finds itself in the path of a hurricane.

Rankings

General Rankings

- Wilmington appeared on RelocateAmerica's list of best places to live in America. The annual "Top 100 Places to Live" list recognizes the top communities as nominated by their residents & local businesses. RelocateAmerica's Research Group determined the list based on review of various data gathered for economic, employment, housing, education, industry, opportunity, environment and recreation along with feedback from area leaders and residents. *RelocateAmerica.com, "Top 100 Places to Live for 2011"*

Business/Finance Rankings

- The Wilmington metro area appeared on the Milken Institute "2013 Best Performing Cities" list. Rank: #77 out of 200 large metro areas. Criteria: job growth; wage and salary growth; high-tech output growth. *Milken Institute, "Best-Performing Cities 2013," December 2013*

- *Forbes* ranked the 200 most populous metro areas in the U.S. in terms of the "Best Places for Business and Careers." The Wilmington metro area was ranked #67. Criteria: costs (business and living); job growth (past and projected); income growth; educational attainment (college and high school); projected economic growth; cultural and recreational opportunities; net migration patterns; number of highly ranked colleges. *Forbes, "The Best Places for Business and Careers," August 7, 2013*

Environmental Rankings

- The Wilmington metro area came in at #281 for the relative comfort of its climate on Sperling's list of "chill cities," as measured by the Sperling Heat Index. All 361 metro areas are included. Criteria included daytime high temperatures, nighttime low temperatures, dew point, and relative humidity at the high temperatures. *www.bertsperling.com, "Sperling's Chill Cities," July 18, 2013*

- Sperling's BestPlaces assessed 379 metropolitan areas of the United States for the likelihood of dangerously extreme weather events or earthquakes. In general the Southeast and South-Central regions have the highest risk of weather extremes and earthquakes, while the Pacific Northwest enjoys the lowest risk. Of the least risky metropolitan areas, the Wilmington metro area was ranked #237. *www.bestplaces.net, "Safest Places from Natural Disasters," April 2011*

- Wilmington was selected as one of 22 "Smarter Cities" for energy by the Natural Resources Defense Council. Criteria: investment in green power; energy efficiency measures; conservation. *Natural Resources Defense Council, "2010 Smarter Cities," July 19, 2010*

Health/Fitness Rankings

- The Wilmington metro area appeared in the 2013 Gallup-Healthways Well-Being Index. The area ranked #126 out of 189. The Gallup-Healthways Well-Being Index score is an average of six sub-indexes, which individually examine life evaluation, emotional health, work environment, physical health, healthy behaviors, and access to basic necessities. Results are based on telephone interviews conducted as part of the Gallup-Healthways Well-Being Index survey January 2–December 29, 2012, and January 2–December 30, 2013, with a random sample of 531,630 adults, aged 18 and older, living in metropolitan areas in the 50 U.S. states and the District of Columbia. *Gallup-Healthways, "State of American Well-Being," March 25, 2014*

Real Estate Rankings

- Wilmington was ranked #179 out of 283 metro areas in terms of house price appreciation in 2013 (#1 = highest rate). *Federal Housing Finance Agency, House Price Index, 4th Quarter 2013*

- The Wilmington metro area was identified as one of 14 best housing markets for the next five years. Criteria: projected annualized change in home prices between the fourth quarter 2012 and the fourth quarter 2017. *The Business Insider, "The 14 Best Housing Markets for the Next Five Years," May 20, 2013*

Safety Rankings

- The National Insurance Crime Bureau ranked 380 metro areas in the U.S. in terms of per capita rates of vehicle theft. The Wilmington metro area ranked #95 (#1 = highest rate). Criteria: number of vehicle theft offenses per 100,000 inhabitants in 2012. *National Insurance Crime Bureau, "Hot Spots 2012," June 26, 2013*

Seniors/Retirement Rankings

- From its Best Cities for Successful Aging indexes, the Milken Institute generated rankings for metropolitan areas, weighing data in eight categories—general indicators, health care, wellness, living arrangements, transportation and general accessibility, financial well-being, education and employment, and community participation. The Wilmington metro area was ranked #178 overall in the small metro area category. *Milken Institute, "Best Cities for Successful Aging," July 2012*

Sports/Recreation Rankings

- Wilmington appeared on the *Sporting News* list of the "Best Sports Cities" for 2011. The area ranked #178 out of 271. Criteria: the magazine takes a 12-month snapshot of each city's sports, putting a heavy premium on regular-season won-lost records (from the most recently completed season). Other criteria include: playoff berths, bowl appearances and tournament bids; championships; applicable power ratings; quality of competition; overall fan fervor (measured in part by attendance); abundance of teams (rewarding quality over quantity); stadium and arena quality; ticket availability and prices; franchise ownership; and marquee appeal of athletes. *Sporting News, "Best Sports Cities 2011," October 4, 2011*

- Wilmington appeared on the *Sporting News* list of the "Best Sports Cities" for 2011. The area ranked #178 out of 271. Criteria: a 12-month snapshot of regular-season won-lost records (from the most recently completed season). Other criteria include: playoff berths, bowl appearances and tournament bids; championships; applicable power ratings; quality of competition; overall fan fervor (measured in part by attendance); abundance of teams (quality over quantity); stadium and arena quality; ticket availability and prices; franchise ownership; and marquee appeal of athletes. *Sporting News, "Best Sports Cities 2011," October 4, 2011*

- Wilmington was chosen as a bicycle friendly community by the League of American Bicyclists. A "Bicycle Friendly Community" welcomes cyclists by providing safe accommodation for cycling and encouraging people to bike for transportation and recreation. There are four award levels: Platinum; Gold; Silver; and Bronze. The community achieved an award level of Bronze. *League of American Bicyclists, "Bicycle Friendly Community Master List," Fall 2013*

Business Environment

CITY FINANCES

City Government Finances

Component	2011 ($000)	2011 ($ per capita)
Total Revenues	124,626	1,251
Total Expenditures	121,833	1,223
Debt Outstanding	212,872	2,137
Cash and Securities[1]	107,261	1,077

Note: (1) Cash and security holdings of a government at the close of its fiscal year, including those of its dependent agencies, utilities, and liquor stores.
Source: U.S Census Bureau, State & Local Government Finances 2011

City Government Revenue by Source

Source	2011 ($000)	2011 ($ per capita)
General Revenue		
From Federal Government	7,129	72
From State Government	9,796	98
From Local Governments	710	7
Taxes		
Property	52,305	525
Sales and Gross Receipts	16,944	170
Personal Income	0	0
Corporate Income	0	0
Motor Vehicle License	341	3
Other Taxes	3,755	38
Current Charges	21,747	218
Liquor Store	0	0
Utility	0	0
Employee Retirement	0	0

Source: U.S Census Bureau, State & Local Government Finances 2011

City Government Expenditures by Function

Function	2011 ($000)	2011 ($ per capita)	2011 (%)
General Direct Expenditures			
Air Transportation	0	0	0.0
Corrections	0	0	0.0
Education	0	0	0.0
Employment Security Administration	0	0	0.0
Financial Administration	2,130	21	1.7
Fire Protection	13,480	135	11.1
General Public Buildings	3,043	31	2.5
Governmental Administration, Other	3,337	33	2.7
Health	0	0	0.0
Highways	13,924	140	11.4
Hospitals	0	0	0.0
Housing and Community Development	1,393	14	1.1
Interest on General Debt	10,692	107	8.8
Judicial and Legal	0	0	0.0
Libraries	0	0	0.0
Parking	1,409	14	1.2
Parks and Recreation	13,077	131	10.7
Police Protection	23,381	235	19.2
Public Welfare	0	0	0.0
Sewerage	5,711	57	4.7
Solid Waste Management	6,813	68	5.6
Veterans' Services	0	0	0.0
Liquor Store	0	0	0.0
Utility	1,175	12	1.0
Employee Retirement	0	0	0.0

Source: U.S Census Bureau, State & Local Government Finances 2011

DEMOGRAPHICS

Population Growth

Area	1990 Census	2000 Census	2010 Census	Population Growth (%) 1990-2000	Population Growth (%) 2000-2010
City	64,609	75,838	106,476	17.4	40.4
MSA[1]	200,124	274,532	362,315	37.2	32.0
U.S.	248,709,873	281,421,906	308,745,538	13.2	9.7

Note: (1) Figures cover the Wilmington, NC Metropolitan Statistical Area—see Appendix B for areas included
Source: U.S. Census Bureau, Census 1990, 2000, 2010

Household Size

Area	Persons in Household (%) One	Two	Three	Four	Five	Six	Seven or More	Average Household Size
City	34.7	35.6	15.7	10.4	2.2	1.0	0.5	2.23
MSA[1]	28.2	39.5	15.7	11.0	4.1	1.1	0.4	2.37
U.S.	27.6	33.5	15.7	13.2	6.1	2.4	1.5	2.63

Note: (1) Figures cover the Wilmington, NC Metropolitan Statistical Area—see Appendix B for areas included
Source: U.S. Census Bureau, 2010-2012 American Community Survey 3-Year Estimates

Race

Area	White Alone[2] (%)	Black Alone[2] (%)	Asian Alone[2] (%)	AIAN[3] Alone[2] (%)	NHOPI[4] Alone[2] (%)	Other Race Alone[2] (%)	Two or More Races (%)
City	75.3	20.1	1.6	0.3	0.0	1.6	1.2
MSA[1]	81.3	13.9	0.9	0.4	0.1	1.5	1.9
U.S.	74.0	12.6	4.9	0.8	0.2	4.7	2.8

Note: (1) Figures cover the Wilmington, NC Metropolitan Statistical Area—see Appendix B for areas included;
(2) Alone is defined as not being in combination with one or more other races; (3) American Indian and Alaska
Native; (4) Native Hawaiian and Other Pacific Islander
Source: U.S. Census Bureau, 2010-2012 American Community Survey 3-Year Estimates

Hispanic or Latino Origin

Area	Total (%)	Mexican (%)	Puerto Rican (%)	Cuban (%)	Other (%)
City	5.1	3.2	0.7	0.1	1.1
MSA[1]	5.4	3.6	0.6	0.1	1.1
U.S.	16.6	10.7	1.6	0.6	3.7

Note: Persons of Hispanic or Latino origin can be of any race; (1) Figures cover the Wilmington, NC
Metropolitan Statistical Area—see Appendix B for areas included
Source: U.S. Census Bureau, 2010-2012 American Community Survey 3-Year Estimates

Segregation

Type	Segregation Indices[1] 1990	2000	2010	2010 Rank[2]	Percent Change 1990-2000	Percent Change 1990-2010	Percent Change 2000-2010
Black/White	n/a	n/a	n/a	n/a	n/a	n/a	n/a
Asian/White	n/a	n/a	n/a	n/a	n/a	n/a	n/a
Hispanic/White	n/a	n/a	n/a	n/a	n/a	n/a	n/a

Note: All figures cover the Metropolitan Statistical Area—see Appendix B for areas included; Figures are based
on an analysis of 1990, 2000, and 2010 Census Decennial Census tract data by William H. Frey, Brookings
Institution and the University of Michigan Social Science Data Analysis Network. In this analysis all racial
groups (whites, blacks, and asians) are non-Hispanic members of those races. Hispanics are shown as a
separate category;
(1) Segregation Indices are Dissimilarity Indices that measure the degree to which the minority group is
distributed differently than whites across census tracts. They range from 0 (complete integration) to 100
(complete segregation) where the value indicates the percentage of the minority group that needs to move to be
distributed exactly like whites; (2) Ranges from 1 (most segregated) to 102 (least segregated); n/a not available.
Source: www.CensusScope.org

Ancestry

Area	German	Irish	English	American	Italian	Polish	French[2]	Scottish	Dutch
City	10.6	10.5	10.5	21.0	4.3	1.5	2.3	3.2	1.5
MSA[1]	12.0	11.9	11.9	17.8	4.8	1.9	2.5	3.1	1.1
U.S.	15.2	11.1	8.2	7.2	5.6	3.1	2.8	1.7	1.4

Note: Figures are the percentage of the total population reporting a particular ancestry. The nine most commonly reported ancestries in the U.S. are shown. Figures include multiple ancestries (e.g. if a person reported being Irish and Italian, they were included in both columns); (1) Figures cover the Wilmington, NC Metropolitan Statistical Area—see Appendix B for areas included; (2) Excludes Basque
Source: U.S. Census Bureau, 2010-2012 American Community Survey 3-Year Estimates

Foreign-Born Population

Area	Percent of Population Born in								
	Any Foreign Country	Mexico	Asia	Europe	Carribean	South America	Central America[2]	Africa	Canada
City	n/a	n/a	n/a	n/a	n/a	n/a	n/a	n/a	n/a
MSA[1]	5.0	2.0	0.7	1.0	0.2	0.2	0.5	0.1	0.2
U.S.	13.0	3.7	3.7	1.6	1.2	0.9	1.0	0.5	0.3

Note: (1) Figures cover the Wilmington, NC Metropolitan Statistical Area—see Appendix B for areas included; (2) Excludes Mexico.
Source: U.S. Census Bureau, 2010-2012 American Community Survey 3-Year Estimates

Marital Status

Area	Never Married	Now Married[2]	Separated	Widowed	Divorced
City	41.9	37.9	3.0	5.1	12.2
MSA[1]	28.2	50.9	2.8	6.0	12.1
U.S.	32.4	48.4	2.2	6.0	11.0

Note: Figures are percentages and cover the population 15 years of age and older; (1) Figures cover the Wilmington, NC Metropolitan Statistical Area—see Appendix B for areas included; (2) Excludes separated
Source: U.S. Census Bureau, 2010-2012 American Community Survey 3-Year Estimates

Age

Area	Percent of Population									Median Age
	Under Age 5	Age 5–19	Age 20–34	Age 35–44	Age 45–54	Age 55–64	Age 65–74	Age 75–84	Age 85+	
City	5.4	18.0	27.6	11.1	12.7	11.6	7.4	4.3	2.0	34.2
MSA[1]	5.4	17.3	19.8	12.5	13.6	14.6	10.4	5.0	1.6	41.1
U.S.	6.4	20.1	20.5	13.1	14.3	12.2	7.3	4.2	1.8	37.3

Note: (1) Figures cover the Wilmington, NC Metropolitan Statistical Area—see Appendix B for areas included
Source: U.S. Census Bureau, 2010-2012 American Community Survey 3-Year Estimates

Gender

Area	Males	Females	Males per 100 Females
City	51,786	56,534	91.6
MSA[1]	180,599	189,112	95.5
U.S.	153,276,055	158,333,314	96.8

Note: (1) Figures cover the Wilmington, NC Metropolitan Statistical Area—see Appendix B for areas included
Source: U.S. Census Bureau, 2010-2012 American Community Survey 3-Year Estimates

Religious Groups by Family

Area	Catholic	Baptist	Non-Den.	Methodist[2]	Lutheran	LDS[3]	Pentecostal	Presbyterian[4]	Muslim[5]	Judaism
MSA[1]	6.2	14.5	4.6	8.5	0.9	1.0	1.1	2.5	0.3	0.1
U.S.	19.1	9.3	4.0	4.0	2.3	2.0	1.9	1.6	0.8	0.7

Note: Figures are the number of adherents as a percentage of the total population; (1) Figures cover the Wilmington, NC Metropolitan Statistical Area—see Appendix B for areas included; (2) Methodist/Pietist; (3) Latter Day Saints; (4) Reformed; (5) Figures are estimates
Source: Association of Statisticians of American Religious Bodies, 2010 U.S. Religion Census: Religious Congregations & Membership Study

Religious Groups by Tradition

Area	Catholic	Evangelical Protestant	Mainline Protestant	Other Tradition	Black Protestant	Orthodox
MSA[1]	6.2	20.4	10.8	1.7	3.1	0.1
U.S.	19.1	16.2	7.3	4.3	1.6	0.3

Note: Figures are the number of adherents as a percentage of the total population; (1) Figures cover the Wilmington, NC Metropolitan Statistical Area—see Appendix B for areas included
Source: Association of Statisticians of American Religious Bodies, 2010 U.S. Religion Census: Religious Congregations & Membership Study

ECONOMY

Gross Metropolitan Product

Area	2011	2012	2013	2014	Rank[2]
MSA[1]	15.1	15.4	15.9	16.6	135

Note: Figures are in billions of dollars; (1) Figures cover the Wilmington, NC Metropolitan Statistical Area—see Appendix B for areas included; (2) Rank is based on 2014 data and ranges from 1 to 363
Source: The United States Conference of Mayors, U.S. Metro Economies: Outlook—Gross Metropolitan Product, with Metro Employment Projections, November 2013

Economic Growth

Area	2011 (%)	2012 (%)	2013 (%)	2014 (%)	Rank[2]
MSA[1]	2.4	0.3	1.7	2.8	93
U.S.	1.6	2.5	1.7	2.5	–

Note: Figures are real gross metropolitan product (GMP) growth rates and represent annual average percent change; (1) Figures cover the Wilmington, NC Metropolitan Statistical Area—see Appendix B for areas included; (2) Rank is based on 2013 data and ranges from 1 to 363
Source: The United States Conference of Mayors, U.S. Metro Economies: Outlook—Gross Metropolitan Product, with Metro Employment Projections, November 2013

Metropolitan Area Exports

Area	2007	2008	2009	2010	2011	2012	Rank[2]
MSA[1]	1,126.9	1,138.8	1,078.6	1,161.9	951.6	923.5	161

Note: Figures are in millions of dollars; (1) Figures cover the Wilmington, NC Metropolitan Statistical Area—see Appendix B for areas included; (2) Rank is based on 2012 data and ranges from 1 to 369
Source: U.S. Department of Commerce, International Trade Administration, Office of Trade & Industry Information, Manufacturing & Services, data extracted April 1, 2014

INCOME

Income

Area	Per Capita ($)	Median Household ($)	Average Household ($)
City	28,552	41,554	64,656
MSA[1]	27,541	47,452	65,184
U.S.	27,385	51,771	71,579

Note: (1) Figures cover the Wilmington, NC Metropolitan Statistical Area—see Appendix B for areas included
Source: U.S. Census Bureau, 2010-2012 American Community Survey 3-Year Estimates

Household Income Distribution

Area	Percent of Households Earning							
	Under $15,000	$15,000 -24,999	$25,000 -34,999	$35,000 -49,999	$50,000 -74,999	$75,000 -99,000	$100,000 -149,999	$150,000 and up
City	18.5	13.3	12.4	13.9	15.7	8.5	9.9	7.9
MSA[1]	14.4	11.5	11.9	14.4	18.5	11.4	11.7	6.2
U.S.	13.1	11.0	10.5	13.7	18.1	11.9	12.5	9.1

Note: (1) Figures cover the Wilmington, NC Metropolitan Statistical Area—see Appendix B for areas included
Source: U.S. Census Bureau, 2010-2012 American Community Survey 3-Year Estimates

Poverty Rate

Area	All Ages	Under 18 Years Old	18 to 64 Years Old	65 Years and Over
City	23.1	34.6	22.9	7.8
MSA[1]	16.8	24.4	17.1	7.0
U.S.	15.7	22.2	14.6	9.3

Note: Figures are percentage of people whose income during the past 12 months was below the poverty level;
(1) Figures cover the Wilmington, NC Metropolitan Statistical Area—see Appendix B for areas included
Source: U.S. Census Bureau, 2010-2012 American Community Survey 3-Year Estimates

Personal Bankruptcy Filing Rate

Area	2008	2009	2010	2011	2012	2013
New Hanover County	1.90	2.95	3.05	3.12	2.77	2.19
U.S.	3.53	4.61	4.97	4.37	3.76	3.29

Note: Numbers are per 1,000 population and include Chapter 7 and Chapter 13 filings
Source: Federal Deposit Insurance Corporation, Regional Economic Conditions, March 20, 2014

EMPLOYMENT

Labor Force and Employment

Area	Civilian Labor Force			Workers Employed		
	Dec. 2012	Dec. 2013	% Chg.	Dec. 2012	Dec. 2013	% Chg.
City	53,923	52,649	-2.4	49,369	49,596	0.5
MSA[1]	184,167	179,204	-2.7	165,773	166,535	0.5
U.S.	154,904,000	154,408,000	-0.3	143,060,000	144,423,000	1.0

Note: Data is not seasonally adjusted and covers workers 16 years of age and older; (1) Metropolitan Statistical Area—see Appendix B for areas included
Source: Bureau of Labor Statistics, Local Area Unemployment Statistics

Unemployment Rate

Area	2013											
	Jan.	Feb.	Mar.	Apr.	May	Jun.	Jul.	Aug.	Sep.	Oct.	Nov.	Dec.
City	9.5	8.8	8.0	7.7	8.2	8.4	8.3	7.4	6.8	7.1	6.1	5.8
MSA[1]	11.1	10.3	9.2	8.7	9.1	9.4	9.1	8.3	7.7	7.7	7.2	7.1
U.S.	8.5	8.1	7.6	7.1	7.3	7.8	7.7	7.3	7.0	7.0	6.6	6.5

Note: Data is not seasonally adjusted and covers workers 16 years of age and older; All figures are percentages;
(1) Metropolitan Statistical Area—see Appendix B for areas included
Source: Bureau of Labor Statistics, Local Area Unemployment Statistics

Employment by Occupation

Occupation Classification	City (%)	MSA[1] (%)	U.S. (%)
Management, Business, Science, and Arts	39.2	35.5	36.0
Natural Resources, Construction, and Maintenance	7.1	10.5	9.1
Production, Transportation, and Material Moving	7.7	9.6	12.0
Sales and Office	23.9	24.8	24.7
Service	22.2	19.6	18.2

Note: Figures cover employed civilians 16 years of age and older; (1) Figures cover the Wilmington, NC Metropolitan Statistical Area—see Appendix B for areas included
Source: U.S. Census Bureau, 2010-2012 American Community Survey 3-Year Estimates

Employment by Industry

Sector	MSA[1] Number of Employees	MSA[1] Percent of Total	U.S. Percent of Total
Construction	n/a	n/a	4.2
Education and Health Services	18,200	12.7	15.5
Financial Activities	6,600	4.6	5.7
Government	27,600	19.3	16.1
Information	2,900	2.0	1.9
Leisure and Hospitality	20,700	14.5	10.2
Manufacturing	7,300	5.1	8.7
Mining and Logging	n/a	n/a	0.6
Other Services	5,300	3.7	3.9
Professional and Business Services	16,700	11.7	13.7
Retail Trade	20,900	14.6	11.4
Transportation and Utilities	4,400	3.1	3.8
Wholesale Trade	4,600	3.2	4.2

Note: Figures cover non-farm employment as of December 2013 and are not seasonally adjusted; (1) Metropolitan Statistical Area—see Appendix B for areas included; n/a not available
Source: Bureau of Labor Statistics, Current Employment Statistics, Employment, Hours, and Earnings

Occupations with Greatest Projected Employment Growth: 2010 – 2020

Occupation[1]	2010 Employment	2020 Projected Employment	Numeric Employment Change	Percent Employment Change
Combined Food Preparation and Serving Workers, Including Fast Food	114,040	132,650	18,610	16.3
Registered Nurses	92,540	109,790	17,250	18.6
Retail Salespersons	131,650	145,910	14,270	10.8
Home Health Aides	55,560	67,570	12,010	21.6
Customer Service Representatives	74,700	84,800	10,090	13.5
Postsecondary Teachers	49,850	59,780	9,930	19.9
Landscaping and Groundskeeping Workers	33,610	43,450	9,830	29.3
Janitors and Cleaners, Except Maids and Housekeeping Cleaners	52,290	61,160	8,870	17.0
Cashiers	101,410	110,200	8,790	8.7
Elementary School Teachers, Except Special Education	37,090	45,730	8,650	23.3

Note: Projections cover North Carolina; (1) Sorted by numeric employment change
Source: www.projectionscentral.com, State Occupational Projections, 2010–2020 Long-Term Projections

Fastest Growing Occupations: 2010 – 2020

Occupation[1]	2010 Employment	2020 Projected Employment	Numeric Employment Change	Percent Employment Change
Biomedical Engineers	250	480	230	90.5
Medical Scientists, Except Epidemiologists	4,270	6,550	2,280	53.4
Biochemists and Biophysicists	460	670	210	44.9
Interpreters and Translators	3,000	4,210	1,220	40.6
Veterinary Technologists and Technicians	3,060	4,300	1,240	40.4
Market Research Analysts and Marketing Specialists	9,750	13,580	3,830	39.3
Helpers—Brickmasons, Blockmasons, Stonemasons, and Tile and Marble Setters	1,900	2,630	740	38.8
Helpers—Carpenters	1,850	2,560	710	38.4
Diagnostic Medical Sonographers	1,660	2,280	620	37.3
Audiologists	350	460	120	33.6

Note: Projections cover North Carolina; (1) Sorted by percent employment change and excludes occupations with numeric employment change less than 100
Source: www.projectionscentral.com, State Occupational Projections, 2010–2020 Long-Term Projections

Average Wages

Occupation	$/Hr.	Occupation	$/Hr.
Accountants and Auditors	32.27	Maids and Housekeeping Cleaners	9.04
Automotive Mechanics	20.30	Maintenance and Repair Workers	17.82
Bookkeepers	16.48	Marketing Managers	50.19
Carpenters	16.21	Nuclear Medicine Technologists	n/a
Cashiers	9.01	Nurses, Licensed Practical	18.86
Clerks, General Office	12.75	Nurses, Registered	26.83
Clerks, Receptionists/Information	12.07	Nursing Assistants	11.21
Clerks, Shipping/Receiving	13.42	Packers and Packagers, Hand	9.61
Computer Programmers	39.39	Physical Therapists	41.89
Computer Systems Analysts	37.39	Postal Service Mail Carriers	23.50
Computer User Support Specialists	22.14	Real Estate Brokers	37.64
Cooks, Restaurant	11.53	Retail Salespersons	11.87
Dentists	87.19	Sales Reps., Exc. Tech./Scientific	29.03
Electrical Engineers	52.57	Sales Reps., Tech./Scientific	35.81
Electricians	18.64	Secretaries, Exc. Legal/Med./Exec.	15.03
Financial Managers	52.06	Security Guards	11.81
First-Line Supervisors/Managers, Sales	21.03	Surgeons	n/a
Food Preparation Workers	10.41	Teacher Assistants	11.60
General and Operations Managers	59.01	Teachers, Elementary School	19.90
Hairdressers/Cosmetologists	10.83	Teachers, Secondary School	19.90
Internists	n/a	Telemarketers	11.55
Janitors and Cleaners	10.91	Truck Drivers, Heavy/Tractor-Trailer	18.87
Landscaping/Groundskeeping Workers	11.00	Truck Drivers, Light/Delivery Svcs.	15.55
Lawyers	45.17	Waiters and Waitresses	8.84

Note: Wage data covers the Wilmington, NC Metropolitan Statistical Area—see Appendix B for areas included. Hourly wages for elementary/secondary school teachers and teacher assistants were calculated by the editors from annual wage data assuming a 40 hour work week; n/a not available.
Source: Bureau of Labor Statistics, Metro Area Occupational Employment and Wage Estimates, May 2013

RESIDENTIAL REAL ESTATE

Building Permits

Area	Single-Family			Multi-Family			Total		
	2012	2013	Pct. Chg.	2012	2013	Pct. Chg.	2012	2013	Pct. Chg.
City	n/a	n/a	n/a	n/a	n/a	n/a	n/a	n/a	n/a
MSA[1]	2,045	3,141	53.6	1,018	916	-10.0	3,063	4,057	32.5
U.S.	518,695	620,802	19.7	310,963	370,020	19.0	829,658	990,822	19.4

Note: (1) Metropolitan Statistical Area—see Appendix B for areas included; figures represent new, privately-owned housing units authorized (unadjusted data); All permit data are based on estimates with imputation.
Source: U.S. Census Bureau, Manufacturing, Mining, and Construction Statistics, Building Permits, 2012, 2013

Homeownership Rate

Area	2006 (%)	2007 (%)	2008 (%)	2009 (%)	2010 (%)	2011 (%)	2012 (%)	2013 (%)
MSA[1]	n/a	n/a	n/a	n/a	n/a	n/a	n/a	n/a
U.S.	68.8	68.1	67.8	67.4	66.9	66.1	65.4	65.1

Note: (1) Figures cover the Wilmington, NC Metropolitan Statistical Area—see Appendix B for areas included; n/a not available
Source: U.S. Census Bureau, Housing Vacancies and Homeownership Annual Statistics: 2013

Housing Vacancy Rates

Area	Gross Vacancy Rate[2] (%)			Year-Round Vacancy Rate[3] (%)			Rental Vacancy Rate[4] (%)			Homeowner Vacancy Rate[5] (%)		
	2011	2012	2013	2011	2012	2013	2011	2012	2013	2011	2012	2013
MSA[1]	n/a	n/a	n/a	n/a	n/a	n/a	n/a	n/a	n/a	n/a	n/a	n/a
U.S.	14.2	13.8	13.8	11.1	10.8	10.7	9.5	8.7	8.3	2.5	2.0	2.0

Note: (1) Figures cover the Wilmington, NC Metropolitan Statistical Area—see Appendix B for areas included; (2) The percentage of the total housing inventory that is vacant; (3) The percentage of the housing inventory (excluding seasonal units) that is year-round vacant; (4) The percentage of rental inventory that is vacant for rent; (5) The percentage of homeowner inventory that is vacant for sale; n/a not available
Source: U.S. Census Bureau, Housing Vacancies and Homeownership Annual Statistics: 2013

TAXES

State Corporate Income Tax Rates

State	Tax Rate (%)	Income Brackets ($)	Num. of Brackets	Financial Institution Tax Rate (%)[a]	Federal Income Tax Ded.
North Carolina	6.0	Flat rate	1	6.0 (t)	No

Note: Tax rates as of January 1, 2014; (a) Rates listed are the corporate income tax rate applied to financial institutions or excise taxes based on income. Some states have other taxes based upon the value of deposits or shares; (t) In North Carolina financial institutions are also subject to a tax equal to $30 per one million in assets.
Source: Federation of Tax Administrators, "State Corporate Income Tax Rates, 2014"

State Individual Income Tax Rates

State	Tax Rate (%)	Income Brackets ($)	Num. of Brackets	Personal Exempt. ($)[1] Single	Dependents	Fed. Inc. Tax Ded.
North Carolina	5.8	Flat rate	1	None	None	No

Note: Tax rates as of January 1, 2014; Local- and county-level taxes are not included; n/a not applicable;
(1) Married joint filers generally receive double the single exemption
Source: Federation of Tax Administrators, "State Individual Income Tax Rates, 2014"

Various State and Local Tax Rates

State	State and Local Sales and Use (%)	State Sales and Use (%)	Gasoline[1] (¢/gal.)	Cigarette[2] ($/pack)	Spirits[3] ($/gal.)	Wine[4] ($/gal.)	Beer[5] ($/gal.)
North Carolina	7.0	4.75	37.75	0.450	12.36 (g)	1.00	0.62

Note: All tax rates as of January 1, 2014; (1) The American Petroleum Institute has developed a methodology for determining the average tax rate on a gallon of fuel. Rates may include any of the following: excise taxes, environmental fees, storage tank fees, other fees or taxes, general sales tax, and local taxes. In states where gasoline is subject to the general sales tax, or where the fuel tax is based on the average sale price, the average rate determined by API is sensitive to changes in the price of gasoline. States that fully or partially apply general sales taxes to gasoline: CA, CO, GA, IL, IN, MI, NY; (2) The federal excise tax of $1.0066 per pack and local taxes are not included; (3) Rates are those applicable to off-premise sales of 40% alcohol by volume (a.b.v.) distilled spirits in 750ml containers. Local excise taxes are excluded; (4) Rates are those applicable to off-premise sales of 11% a.b.v. non-carbonated wine in 750ml containers; (5) Rates are those applicable to off-premise sales of 4.7% a.b.v. beer in 12 ounce containers; (g) States where the government controls sales. In these "control states," products are subject to ad valorem mark-up and excise taxes. The excise tax rate is calculated using a methodology developed by the Distilled Spirits Council of the United States.
Source: Tax Foundation, 2014 Facts & Figures: How Does Your State Compare?

State Business Tax Climate Index Rankings

State	Overall Rank	Corporate Tax Index Rank	Individual Income Tax Index Rank	Sales Tax Index Rank	Unemployment Insurance Tax Index Rank	Property Tax Index Rank
North Carolina	44	29	42	47	7	30

Note: The index is a measure of how each state's tax laws affect economic performance. The lower the rank, the more favorable a state's tax system is for business. States without a given tax are given a ranking of 1. The scores/rankings for the District of Columbia do not affect other states. The 2014 index represents the tax climate as of July 1, 2013.
Source: Tax Foundation, State Business Tax Climate Index 2014

COMMERCIAL UTILITIES

Typical Monthly Electric Bills

Area	Commercial Service ($/month) 1,500 kWh	40 kW demand 14,000 kWh	Industrial Service ($/month) 1,000 kW demand 200,000 kWh	50,000 kW demand 15,000,000 kWh
City	174	1,200	22,258	1,349,994
Average[1]	197	1,636	25,662	1,485,307

Note: Based on total rates in effect July 1, 2013; (1) average based on 180 utilities surveyed
Source: Edison Electric Institute, Typical Bills and Average Rates Report, Summer 2013

TRANSPORTATION

Means of Transportation to Work

Area	Car/Truck/Van		Public Transportation			Bicycle	Walked	Other Means	Worked at Home
	Drove Alone	Car-pooled	Bus	Subway	Railroad				
City	78.2	9.7	0.7	0.0	0.0	1.4	3.1	1.6	5.3
MSA[1]	79.5	11.8	0.4	0.0	0.0	0.6	1.5	1.3	4.8
U.S.	76.4	9.7	2.6	1.7	0.5	0.6	2.8	1.3	4.3

Note: Figures are percentages and cover workers 16 years of age and older; (1) Figures cover the Wilmington, NC Metropolitan Statistical Area—see Appendix B for areas included
Source: U.S. Census Bureau, 2010-2012 American Community Survey 3-Year Estimates

Travel Time to Work

Area	Less Than 10 Minutes	10 to 19 Minutes	20 to 29 Minutes	30 to 44 Minutes	45 to 59 Minutes	60 to 89 Minutes	90 Minutes or More
City	18.3	50.0	18.1	7.3	3.1	2.1	1.1
MSA[1]	13.9	38.2	22.7	15.4	4.9	3.1	1.8
U.S.	13.5	29.8	20.9	20.1	7.5	5.6	2.5

Note: Figures are percentages and include workers 16 years old and over; (1) Figures cover the Wilmington, NC Metropolitan Statistical Area—see Appendix B for areas included
Source: U.S. Census Bureau, 2010-2012 American Community Survey 3-Year Estimates

Travel Time Index

Area	1985	1990	1995	2000	2005	2010	2011
Urban Area[1]	n/a	n/a	n/a	n/a	n/a	n/a	n/a
Average[2]	1.09	1.14	1.16	1.19	1.23	1.18	1.18

Note: Travel Time Index—the ratio of travel time in the peak period to the travel time at free-flow conditions. For example, a value of 1.30 indicates a 20-minute free-flow trip takes 26 minutes in the peak. Free-flow speeds (60 mph on freeways and 35 mph on principal arterials) are used as the comparison threshold; (1) Data for the Wilmington, NC urban area was not available; (2) average of 498 urban areas
Source: Texas Transportation Institute, Urban Mobility Report 2012, December 2012

Public Transportation

Agency Name / Mode of Transportation	Vehicles Operated in Maximum Service	Annual Unlinked Passenger Trips (in thous.)	Annual Passenger Miles (in thous.)
Cape Fear Public Transportation Authority (Wave Transit)			
Bus (purchased transportation)	28	1,530.5	n/a
Demand Response (directly operated)	19	80.5	n/a

Source: Federal Transit Administration, National Transit Database, 2012

Air Transportation

Airport Name and Code / Type of Service	Passenger Airlines[1]	Passenger Enplanements	Freight Carriers[2]	Freight (lbs.)
Wilmington International Airport (ILM)				
Domestic service (U.S. carriers - 2013)	13	396,567	7	1,178,186
International service (U.S. carriers - 2012)	4	49	1	650

Note: (1) Includes all U.S.-based major, minor and commuter airlines that carried at least one passenger during the year; (2) Includes all U.S.-based airlines and freight carriers that transported at least one lb. of freight during the year.
Source: Bureau of Transportation Statistics, The Intermodal Transportation Database, Air Carriers: T-100 Domestic Market (U.S. Carriers), 2013; Bureau of Transportation Statistics, The Intermodal Transportation Database, Air Carriers: T-100 International Market (U.S. Carriers), 2012

Other Transportation Statistics

Major Highways: I-40
Amtrak Service: Bus connection
Major Waterways/Ports: Atlantic Ocean

Source: Amtrak.com; Google Maps

BUSINESSES

Major Business Headquarters

Company Name	Rankings	
	Fortune[1]	Forbes[2]
No companies listed	-	-

Note: (1) Fortune 500—companies that produce a 10-K are ranked 1 to 500 based on 2012 revenue; (2) all private companies with at least $2 billion in annual revenue through the end of their most current fiscal year are ranked 1 to 224; companies listed are headquartered in the city; dashes indicate no ranking
Source: Fortune, "Fortune 500," May 20, 2013; Forbes, "America's Largest Private Companies," December 18, 2013

Minority- and Women-Owned Businesses

Group	All Firms		Firms with Paid Employees			
	Firms	Sales ($000)	Firms	Sales ($000)	Employees	Payroll ($000)
Asian	(s)	(s)	(s)	(s)	(s)	(s)
Black	953	58,307	99	44,935	754	16,232
Hispanic	(s)	(s)	(s)	(s)	(s)	(s)
Women	3,796	744,009	623	675,444	6,362	153,281
All Firms	13,192	13,488,374	4,211	13,059,190	69,278	2,525,758

Note: Figures cover firms located in the city; minority- and women-owned business are defined as firms in which the corresponding group own 51% or more of the stock or equity of the company; (s) estimates are suppressed when publication standards are not met
Source: U.S. Census Bureau, 2007 Economic Census, Survey of Business Owners (2012 Survey of Business Owners data will be released starting in June 2015)

HOTELS & CONVENTION CENTERS

Hotels/Motels

Area	5 Star		4 Star		3 Star		2 Star		1 Star		Not Rated	
	Num.	Pct.[3]	Num.	Pct.[3]	Num.	Pct.[3]	Num.	Pct.[3]	Num.	Pct.[3]	Num.	Pct.[3]
City[1]	0	0.0	0	0.0	15	23.8	42	66.7	0	0.0	6	9.5
Total[2]	142	0.9	1,005	6.0	5,147	30.9	8,578	51.4	408	2.4	1,397	8.4

Note: (1) Figures cover Wilmington and vicinity; (2) Figures cover all 100 cities in this book; (3) Percentage of hotels which have a given star rating; Star ratings are determined by expedia.com and offer an indication of the general quality of a particular hotel.
Source: expedia.com, April 7, 2014

Major Convention Centers

Name	Overall Space (sq. ft.)	Exhibit Space (sq. ft.)	Meeting Space (sq. ft.)	Meeting Rooms
There are no major convention centers located in the metro area				

Source: Original research

Living Environment

COST OF LIVING

Cost of Living Index

Composite Index	Groceries	Housing	Utilities	Trans- portation	Health Care	Misc. Goods/ Services
98.2	104.8	84.9	107.8	97.8	107.4	102.0

Note: The Cost of Living Index measures regional differences in the cost of consumer goods and services, excluding taxes and non-consumer expenditures, for professional and managerial households in the top income quintile. It is based on more than 50,000 prices covering almost 60 different items for which prices are collected three times a year by chambers of commerce, economic development organizations or university applied economic centers in each participating urban area. The numbers shown should be read as a percentage above or below the national average of 100. For example, a value of 115.4 in the groceries column indicates that grocery prices are 15.4% higher than the national average. Small differences in the index numbers should not be interpreted as significant; Figures cover the Wilmington NC urban area.
Source: The Council for Community and Economic Research, ACCRA Cost of Living Index, 2013

Grocery Prices

Area[1]	T-Bone Steak ($/pound)	Frying Chicken ($/pound)	Whole Milk ($/half gal.)	Eggs ($/dozen)	Orange Juice ($/64 oz.)	Coffee ($/11.5 oz.)
City[2]	10.88	1.39	2.62	2.10	3.42	4.33
Avg.	10.19	1.28	2.34	1.81	3.48	4.39
Min.	8.56	0.94	1.44	1.19	2.78	3.40
Max.	14.82	2.28	3.56	3.73	6.23	7.32

*Note: (1) Values for the local area are compared with the average, minimum and maximum values for all 327 areas in the Cost of Living Index; (2) Figures cover the Wilmington NC urban area; **T-Bone Steak** (price per pound); **Frying Chicken** (price per pound, whole fryer); **Whole Milk** (half gallon carton); **Eggs** (price per dozen, Grade A, large); **Orange Juice** (64 oz. Tropicana or Florida Natural); **Coffee** (11.5 oz. can, vacuum-packed, Maxwell House, Hills Bros, or Folgers).*
Source: The Council for Community and Economic Research, ACCRA Cost of Living Index, 2013

Housing and Utility Costs

Area[1]	New Home Price ($)	Apartment Rent ($/month)	All Electric ($/month)	Part Electric ($/month)	Other Energy ($/month)	Telephone ($/month)
City[2]	259,686	713	181.99	-	-	28.53
Avg.	295,864	900	171.38	91.82	70.12	27.73
Min.	185,506	458	117.80	48.81	33.67	17.16
Max.	1,358,917	3,783	441.68	171.40	372.65	39.47

*Note: (1) Values for the local area are compared with the average, minimum and maximum values for all 327 areas in the Cost of Living Index; (2) Figures cover the Wilmington NC urban area; **New Home Price** (2,400 sf living area, 8,000 sf lot, in urban area with full utilities); **Apartment Rent** (950 sf 2 bedroom/1.5 or 2 bath, unfurnished, excluding all utilities except water); **All Electric** (average monthly cost for an all-electric home); **Part Electric** (average monthly cost for a part-electric home); **Other Energy** (average monthly cost for natural gas, fuel oil, coal, wood, and any other forms of energy except electricity); **Telephone** (price includes basic monthly rate for a private residential line plus additional local usage charges incurred by a family of four).*
Source: The Council for Community and Economic Research, ACCRA Cost of Living Index, 2013

Health Care, Transportation, and Other Costs

Area[1]	Doctor ($/visit)	Dentist ($/visit)	Optometrist ($/visit)	Gasoline ($/gallon)	Beauty Salon ($/visit)	Men's Shirt ($)
City[2]	120.42	109.38	94.42	3.45	40.62	31.96
Avg.	101.40	86.48	96.16	3.44	33.87	26.55
Min.	61.67	50.83	50.12	3.08	18.92	12.48
Max.	182.71	152.50	223.78	4.33	68.22	52.03

*Note: (1) Values for the local area are compared with the average, minimum and maximum values for all 327 areas in the Cost of Living Index; (2) Figures cover the Wilmington NC urban area; **Doctor** (general practitioners routine exam of an established patient); **Dentist** (adult teeth cleaning and periodic oral examination); **Optometrist** (full vision eye exam for established adult patient); **Gasoline** (one gallon regular unleaded, national brand, including all taxes, cash price at self-service pump if available); **Beauty Salon** (woman's shampoo, trim, and blow-dry); **Men's Shirt** (cotton/polyester dress shirt, pinpoint weave, long sleeves).*
Source: The Council for Community and Economic Research, ACCRA Cost of Living Index, 2013

HOUSING

House Price Index (HPI)

Area	National Ranking[2]	Quarterly Change (%)	One-Year Change (%)	Five-Year Change (%)
MSA[1]	179	-0.87	1.20	-19.03
U.S.[3]	–	1.20	7.69	4.18

Note: The HPI is a weighted repeat sales index. It measures average price changes in repeat sales or refinancings on the same properties. This information is obtained by reviewing repeat mortgage transactions on single-family properties whose mortgages have been purchased or securitized by Fannie Mae or Freddie Mac in January 1975; (1) Wilmington, NC Metropolitan Statistical Area—see Appendix B for areas included; (2) Rankings are based on annual percentage change for all metro areas containing at least 15,000 transactions over the last 10 years and ranges from 1 to 283; (3) figures based on a weighted average of Census Division estimates using a seasonally adjusted, purchase-only index; all figures are for the period ending December 31, 2013
Source: Federal Housing Finance Agency, House Price Index, February 25, 2014

Median Single-Family Home Prices

Area	2011	2012	2013p	Percent Change 2012 to 2013
MSA[1]	n/a	n/a	n/a	n/a
U.S. Average	166.2	177.2	197.4	11.4

Note: Figures are median sales prices of existing single-family homes in thousands of dollars; (p) preliminary; n/a not available; (1) Wilmington, NC Metropolitan Statistical Area—see Appendix B for areas included
Source: National Association of Realtors, Median Sales Price of Existing Single-Family Homes for Metropolitan Areas, 4th Quarter 2013

Qualifying Income Based on Median Sales Price of Existing Single-Family Homes

Area	With 5% Down ($)	With 10% Down ($)	With 20% Down ($)
MSA[1]	n/a	n/a	n/a
U.S. Average	45,395	43,006	38,228

Note: Figures are preliminary; Qualifying income is based on a mortgage rate of 4.4%. Monthly principal and interest payment is limited to 25% of income; n/a not available; (1) Wilmington, NC Metropolitan Statistical Area—see Appendix B for areas included
Source: National Association of Realtors, Qualifying Income Based on Median Sales Price of Existing Single-Family Homes for Metropolitan Areas, 4th Quarter 2013

Median Apartment Condo-Coop Home Prices

Area	2011	2012	2013p	Percent Change 2012 to 2013
MSA[1]	n/a	n/a	n/a	n/a
U.S. Average	165.1	173.7	194.9	12.2

Note: Figures are median sales prices of existing apartment condo-coop homes in thousands of dollars; (p) preliminary; n/a not available; (1) Wilmington, NC Metropolitan Statistical Area—see Appendix B for areas included
Source: National Association of Realtors, Median Sales Price of Existing Apartment Condo-Coop Homes for Metropolitan Areas, 4th Quarter 2013

Gross Monthly Rent

Area	Under $200	$200 -299	$300 -499	$500 -749	$750 -999	$1,000 -1,499	$1,500 and up	Median ($)
City	2.1	3.0	5.8	27.1	29.2	27.4	5.4	843
MSA[1]	1.5	1.9	5.2	26.0	30.4	27.6	7.5	866
U.S.	1.7	3.3	8.1	22.7	24.3	25.7	14.3	889

Note: Figures are percentages except for Median; Gross rent is the contract rent plus the estimated average monthly cost of utilities (electricity, gas, and water and sewer) and fuels (oil, coal, kerosene, wood, etc.) if these are paid by the renter (or paid for the renter by someone else); (1) Figures cover the Wilmington, NC Metropolitan Statistical Area—see Appendix B for areas included
Source: U.S. Census Bureau, 2010-2012 American Community Survey 3-Year Estimates

Year Housing Structure Built

Area	2010 or Later	2000 -2009	1990 -1999	1980 -1989	1970 -1979	1960 -1969	1950 -1959	1940 -1949	Before 1940	Median Year
City	0.4	15.9	23.3	15.5	10.3	9.5	7.6	7.1	10.4	1983
MSA[1]	0.6	28.2	24.1	18.0	11.3	6.5	4.5	2.8	4.1	1991
U.S.	0.5	14.9	13.8	13.9	15.9	11.1	10.9	5.5	13.5	1976

Note: Figures are percentages except for Median Year; (1) Figures cover the Wilmington, NC Metropolitan Statistical Area—see Appendix B for areas included
Source: U.S. Census Bureau, 2010-2012 American Community Survey 3-Year Estimates

HEALTH

Health Risk Data

Category	MSA[1] (%)	U.S. (%)
Adults aged 18–64 who have any kind of health care coverage	n/a	79.6
Adults who reported being in good or excellent health	n/a	83.1
Adults who are current smokers	n/a	19.6
Adults who are heavy drinkers[2]	n/a	6.1
Adults who are binge drinkers[3]	n/a	16.9
Adults who are overweight (BMI 25.0 - 29.9)	n/a	35.8
Adults who are obese (BMI 30.0 - 99.8)	n/a	27.6
Adults who participated in any physical activities in the past month	n/a	77.1
Adults 50+ who have ever had a sigmoidoscopy or colonoscopy	n/a	67.3
Women aged 40+ who have had a mammogram within the past two years	n/a	74.0
Men aged 40+ who have had a PSA test within the past two years	n/a	45.2
Adults aged 65+ who have had flu shot within the past year	n/a	60.1
Adults who always wear a seatbelt	n/a	93.8

Note: Data as of 2012 unless otherwise noted; n/a not available; (1) Figures cover the Wilmington, NC Metropolitan Statistical Area—see Appendix B for areas included; (2) Heavy drinkers are classified as males having more than two drinks per day or females having more than one drink per day; (3) Binge drinkers are classified as males having five or more drinks on one occasion or females having four or more drinks on one occasion
Source: Centers for Disease Control and Prevention, Behaviorial Risk Factor Surveillance System, SMART: Selected Metropolitan/Micropolitan Area Risk Trends, 2012

Chronic Health Indicators

Category	MSA[1] (%)	U.S. (%)
Adults who have ever been told they had a heart attack	n/a	4.5
Adults who have ever been told they had a stroke	n/a	2.9
Adults who have been told they currently have asthma	n/a	8.9
Adults who have ever been told they have arthritis	n/a	25.7
Adults who have ever been told they have diabetes[2]	n/a	9.7
Adults who have ever been told they had skin cancer	n/a	5.7
Adults who have ever been told they had any other types of cancer	n/a	6.5
Adults who have ever been told they have COPD	n/a	6.2
Adults who have ever been told they have kidney disease	n/a	2.5
Adults who have ever been told they have a form of depression	n/a	18.0

Note: Data as of 2012 unless otherwise noted; n/a not available; (1) Figures cover the Wilmington, NC Metropolitan Statistical Area—see Appendix B for areas included; (2) Figures do not include pregnancy-related, borderline, or pre-diabetes
Source: Centers for Disease Control and Prevention, Behaviorial Risk Factor Surveillance System, SMART: Selected Metropolitan/Micropolitan Area Risk Trends, 2012

Mortality Rates for the Top 10 Causes of Death in the U.S.

ICD-10[a] Sub-Chapter	ICD-10[a] Code	Age-Adjusted Mortality Rate[1] per 100,000 population	
		County[2]	U.S.
Malignant neoplasms	C00-C97	175.7	174.2
Ischaemic heart diseases	I20-I25	115.2	119.1
Other forms of heart disease	I30-I51	45.7	49.6
Chronic lower respiratory diseases	J40-J47	37.1	43.2
Cerebrovascular diseases	I60-I69	39.3	40.3
Organic, including symptomatic, mental disorders	F01-F09	53.0	30.5
Other degenerative diseases of the nervous system	G30-G31	11.4	26.3
Other external causes of accidental injury	W00-X59	29.0	25.1
Diabetes mellitus	E10-E14	15.9	21.3
Hypertensive diseases	I10-I15	11.5	18.8

Note: (a) ICD-10 = International Classification of Diseases 10th Revision; (1) Mortality rates are a three year average covering 2008-2010; (2) Figures cover New Hanover County
Source: Centers for Disease Control and Prevention, National Center for Health Statistics. Compressed Mortality File 1999-2010 on CDC WONDER Online Database, released January 2013. Data are compiled from the Compressed Mortality File 1999-2010, Series 20 No. 2P, 2013.

Mortality Rates for Selected Causes of Death

ICD-10[a] Sub-Chapter	ICD-10[a] Code	Age-Adjusted Mortality Rate[1] per 100,000 population	
		County[2]	U.S.
Assault	X85-Y09	4.2	5.5
Diseases of the liver	K70-K76	12.9	12.4
Human immunodeficiency virus (HIV) disease	B20-B24	5.2	3.0
Influenza and pneumonia	J09-J18	11.8	16.4
Intentional self-harm	X60-X84	12.8	11.8
Malnutrition	E40-E46	Suppressed	0.8
Obesity and other hyperalimentation	E65-E68	Suppressed	1.6
Renal failure	N17-N19	13.1	13.6
Transport accidents	V01-V99	9.3	12.6
Viral hepatitis	B15-B19	*2.8	2.2

Note: (a) ICD-10 = International Classification of Diseases 10th Revision; (1) Mortality rates are a three year average covering 2008-2010; (2) Figures cover New Hanover County; (*) Unreliable data as per CDC
Source: Centers for Disease Control and Prevention, National Center for Health Statistics. Compressed Mortality File 1999-2010 on CDC WONDER Online Database, released January 2013. Data are compiled from the Compressed Mortality File 1999-2010, Series 20 No. 2P, 2013.

Health Insurance Coverage

Area	With Health Insurance	With Private Health Insurance	With Public Health Insurance	Without Health Insurance	Population Under Age 18 Without Health Insurance
City	82.9	65.1	30.3	17.1	6.1
MSA[1]	83.7	66.2	32.5	16.3	7.6
U.S.	84.9	65.4	30.4	15.1	7.5

Note: Figures are percentages that cover the civilian noninstitutionalized population; (1) Figures cover the Wilmington, NC Metropolitan Statistical Area—see Appendix B for areas included
Source: U.S. Census Bureau, 2010-2012 American Community Survey 3-Year Estimates

Number of Medical Professionals

Area[1]	MDs[2]	DOs[2,3]	Dentists	Podiatrists	Chiropractors	Optometrists
Local (number)	704	43	149	14	67	36
Local (rate[4])	341.7	20.9	71.2	6.7	32.0	17.2
U.S. (rate[4])	267.6	19.6	61.7	5.6	24.7	14.5

Note: Data as of 2012 unless noted; (1) Local data covers New Hanover County; (2) Data as of 2011; (3) Doctor of Osteopathic Medicine; (4) rate per 100,000 population
Source: Area Resource File (ARF) 2012-2013. U.S. Department of Health and Human Services, Health Resources and Services Administration, Bureau of Health Professions

EDUCATION

Public School District Statistics

District Name	Schls	Pupils	Pupil/ Teacher Ratio	Minority Pupils[1] (%)	Free Lunch Eligible[2] (%)	IEP[3] (%)
New Hanover County Schools	41	25,131	15.6	37.2	38.2	11.5

Note: Table includes school districts with 2,000 or more students; (1) Percentage of students that are not non-Hispanic white; (2) Percentage of students that are eligible for the free lunch program; (3) Percentage of students that have an Individualized Education Program.
Source: U.S. Department of Education, National Center for Education Statistics, Common Core of Data, Local Education Agency (School District) Universe Survey: School Year 2011-2012; U.S. Department of Education, National Center for Education Statistics, Common Core of Data, Public Elementary/Secondary School Universe Survey: School Year 2011-2012

Best High Schools

High School Name	Rank[1]	Grad. Rate[2] (%)	Coll.[3] (%)	AP/IB/ AICE Tests[4]	AP/IB/ AICE Score[5]	SAT Score[6]	ACT Score[6]
New Hanover H.S.	1774	83	84	0.4	2.7	1424	21.7

Note: (1) Public schools are ranked from 1 to 2,000 based on the following self-reported statistics (with the corresponding weight used in calculating their overall score). Schools that were newly founded and did not have a graduating senior class in 2012 were excluded; (2) Four-year, on-time graduation rate (25%); (3) Percent of 2011 graduates who were accepted to college (25%); (4) AP/IB/AICE tests taken per student (25%); (5) Average AP/IB/AICE exam score (10%); (6) Average SAT and/or ACT score (10%); Percent of students enrolled in at least one AP/IB/AICE course (5%)—data not shown
Source: Newsweek and The Daily Beast, "America's Best High Schools 2013"

Highest Level of Education

Area	Less than H.S.	H.S. Diploma	Some College, No Deg.	Associate Degree	Bachelor's Degree	Master's Degree	Prof. School Degree	Doctorate Degree
City	11.2	19.5	19.1	10.4	26.2	9.5	2.4	1.7
MSA[1]	11.4	25.5	22.6	9.6	20.8	7.3	1.8	1.2
U.S.	14.1	28.3	21.3	7.8	18.0	7.5	1.9	1.2

Note: Figures cover persons age 25 and over; (1) Figures cover the Wilmington, NC Metropolitan Statistical Area—see Appendix B for areas included
Source: U.S. Census Bureau, 2010-2012 American Community Survey 3-Year Estimates

Educational Attainment by Race

Area	High School Graduate or Higher (%)					Bachelor's Degree or Higher (%)				
	Total	White	Black	Asian	Hisp.[2]	Total	White	Black	Asian	Hisp.[2]
City	88.8	92.8	75.0	86.4	56.5	39.8	47.1	10.4	55.7	16.0
MSA[1]	88.6	90.5	80.5	92.0	58.5	31.0	34.3	11.1	61.6	12.3
U.S.	85.9	88.1	82.5	85.5	63.1	28.6	30.0	18.4	50.2	13.4

Note: Figures shown cover persons 25 years old and over; (1) Figures cover the Wilmington, NC Metropolitan Statistical Area—see Appendix B for areas included; (2) People of Hispanic origin can be of any race
Source: U.S. Census Bureau, 2010-2012 American Community Survey 3-Year Estimates

School Enrollment by Grade and Control

Area	Preschool (%)		Kindergarten (%)		Grades 1 - 4 (%)		Grades 5 - 8 (%)		Grades 9 - 12 (%)	
	Public	Private	Public	Private	Public	Private	Public	Private	Public	Private
City	41.8	58.2	82.9	17.1	90.0	10.0	84.2	15.8	86.8	13.2
MSA[1]	46.3	53.7	88.7	11.3	90.2	9.8	91.9	8.1	90.7	9.3
U.S.	56.9	43.1	87.8	12.2	89.9	10.1	90.0	10.0	90.8	9.2

Note: Figures shown cover persons 3 years old and over; (1) Figures cover the Wilmington, NC Metropolitan Statistical Area—see Appendix B for areas included
Source: U.S. Census Bureau, 2010-2012 American Community Survey 3-Year Estimates

Average Salaries of Public School Classroom Teachers

Area	2012-13		2013-14		Percent Change 2012-13 to 2013-14	Percent Change 2003-04 to 2013-14
	Dollars	Rank[1]	Dollars	Rank[1]		
North Carolina	45,737	46	45,355	48	-0.84	5.0
U.S. Average	56,103	–	56,689	–	1.04	21.8

Note: (1) State rank ranges from 1 to 51 where 1 indicates highest salary.
Source: National Education Association, Rankings & Estimates: Rankings of the States 2013 and Estimates of School Statistics 2014, March 2014

Higher Education

Four-Year Colleges			Two-Year Colleges			Medical Schools[1]	Law Schools[2]	Voc/ Tech[3]
Public	Private Non-profit	Private For-profit	Public	Private Non-profit	Private For-profit			
1	0	1	1	0	0	0	0	1

Note: Figures cover institutions located within the city limits and include main campuses only; (1) includes schools accredited by the Liaison Committee on Medical Education and the American Osteopathic Association's Commission on Osteopathic College Accreditation; (2) includes ABA-accredited schools, schools with provisional ABA accreditation, and state accredited schools; (3) includes all schools with programs that are less than 2 years.
Source: National Center for Education Statistics, Integrated Postsecondary Education System (IPEDS), 2012-13; Association of American Medical Colleges, Member List, April 24, 2014; American Osteopathic Association, Member List, April 24, 2014; Law School Admission Council, Official Guide to ABA-Approved Law Schools Online, April 24, 2014; Wikipedia, List of Medical Schools in the United States, April 24, 2014; Wikipedia, List of Law Schools in the United States, April 24, 2014

PRESIDENTIAL ELECTION

2012 Presidential Election Results

Area	Obama	Romney	Other
New Hanover County	47.0	51.5	1.5
U.S.	51.0	47.2	1.8

Note: Results are percentages and may not add to 100% due to rounding
Source: Dave Leip's Atlas of U.S. Presidential Elections

EMPLOYERS

Major Employers

Company Name	Industry
Brunswick County Schools	Education
Cape Fear Community College	Education
City of Wilmington	Government
Corning	Optical fiber
Duke Energy - Southport & Wilmington	Utility
GE Wilmington	GE hitachi and GE aviation
New Hanover County	Government
New Hanover County Schools	Education
New Hanover Reg Med Ctr/Cape Fear Hosp	Healthcare
Novant Medical/Brunswick Community Hosp	Healthcare
PPD	Discovery & development services to pharma/biotech
University of NC Wilmington	Education
Verizon Wireless	Communications
Wal-Mart Stores	Retail

Note: Companies shown are located within the Wilmington, NC Metropolitan Statistical Area.
Source: Hoovers.com; Wikipedia

PUBLIC SAFETY

Crime Rate

Area	All Crimes	Violent Crimes				Property Crimes		
		Murder	Forcible Rape	Robbery	Aggrav. Assault	Burglary	Larceny -Theft	Motor Vehicle Theft
City	5,968.7	7.3	21.0	238.6	298.1	1,548.9	3,513.8	341.0
Suburbs[1]	2,931.5	1.3	22.3	36.0	168.2	641.4	1,949.1	113.2
Metro[2]	4,198.6	3.8	21.7	120.5	222.4	1,020.0	2,601.8	208.3
U.S.	3,246.1	4.7	26.9	112.9	242.3	670.2	1,959.3	229.7

Note: Figures are crimes per 100,000 population; (1) All areas within the metro area that are located outside the city limits; (2) Figures cover the Wilmington, NC Metropolitan Statistical Area—see Appendix B for areas included
Source: FBI Uniform Crime Reports, 2012

Hate Crimes

Area	Number of Quarters Reported	Bias Motivation				
		Race	Religion	Sexual Orientation	Ethnicity	Disability
City	4	4	2	0	0	0
U.S.	4	2,797	1,099	1,135	667	92

Source: Federal Bureau of Investigation, Hate Crime Statistics 2012

Identity Theft Consumer Complaints

Area	Complaints	Complaints per 100,000 Population	Rank[2]
MSA[1]	169	66.3	162
U.S.	290,056	91.8	-

Note: (1) Figures cover the Wilmington, NC Metropolitan Statistical Area—see Appendix B for areas included; (2) Rank ranges from 1 to 377 where 1 indicates greatest number of identity theft complaints per 100,000 population
Source: Federal Trade Commission, Consumer Sentinel Network Data Book for January–December 2013

Fraud and Other Consumer Complaints

Area	Complaints	Complaints per 100,000 Population	Rank[2]
MSA[1]	1,055	413.9	95
U.S.	1,811,724	595.2	-

Note: (1) Figures cover the Wilmington, NC Metropolitan Statistical Area—see Appendix B for areas included; (2) Rank ranges from 1 to 377 where 1 indicates greatest number of identity theft complaints per 100,000 population
Source: Federal Trade Commission, Consumer Sentinel Network Data Book for January–December 2013

RECREATION

Culture

Dance[1]	Theatre[1]	Instrumental Music[1]	Vocal Music[1]	Series and Festivals	Museums and Art Galleries[2]	Zoos and Aquariums[3]
0	1	1	0	1	18	0

Note: (1) Number of professional perfoming groups; (2) Based on organizations with primary SIC code 8412; (3) AZA-accredited
Source: The Grey House Performing Arts Directory, 2013; Association of Zoos & Aquariums, AZA Member Zoos & Aquariums, April 2014; www.AccuLeads.com, May 1, 2014

Professional Sports Teams

Team Name	League	Year Established
No teams are located in the metro area		

Source: Wikipedia, Major Professional Sports Teams of the United States and Canada, April 25, 2014

CLIMATE

Average and Extreme Temperatures

Temperature	Jan	Feb	Mar	Apr	May	Jun	Jul	Aug	Sep	Oct	Nov	Dec	Yr.
Extreme High (°F)	82	85	89	95	98	104	102	102	98	95	87	81	104
Average High (°F)	56	59	65	74	81	86	90	88	84	75	67	59	74
Average Temp. (°F)	46	48	55	63	71	77	81	80	75	65	56	49	64
Average Low (°F)	36	37	43	51	60	67	72	71	65	54	45	37	53
Extreme Low (°F)	5	11	9	30	35	48	55	55	44	27	16	0	0

Note: Figures cover the years 1948-1995
Source: National Climatic Data Center, International Station Meteorological Climate Summary, 9/96

Average Precipitation/Snowfall/Humidity

Precip./Humidity	Jan	Feb	Mar	Apr	May	Jun	Jul	Aug	Sep	Oct	Nov	Dec	Yr.
Avg. Precip. (in.)	3.9	3.5	4.3	2.9	4.3	5.4	7.9	7.0	5.6	3.3	3.3	3.5	55.0
Avg. Snowfall (in.)	Tr	1	Tr	Tr	0	0	0	0	0	0	Tr	1	2
Avg. Rel. Hum. 7am (%)	82	80	82	81	84	85	87	90	90	89	86	82	85
Avg. Rel. Hum. 4pm (%)	58	55	54	51	58	62	66	67	66	60	58	58	59

Note: Figures cover the years 1948-1995; Tr = Trace amounts (<0.05 in. of rain; <0.5 in. of snow)
Source: National Climatic Data Center, International Station Meteorological Climate Summary, 9/96

Weather Conditions

Temperature			Daytime Sky			Precipitation		
10°F & below	32°F & below	90°F & above	Clear	Partly cloudy	Cloudy	0.01 inch or more precip.	0.1 inch or more snow/ice	Thunder-storms
< 1	42	46	96	150	119	115	1	47

Note: Figures are average number of days per year and cover the years 1948-1995
Source: National Climatic Data Center, International Station Meteorological Climate Summary, 9/96

HAZARDOUS WASTE

Superfund Sites

Wilmington has one hazardous waste site on the EPA's Superfund Final National Priorities List: **Horton Iron and Metal.** *U.S. Environmental Protection Agency, Final National Priorities List, April 26, 2014*

AIR & WATER QUALITY

Air Quality Index

Area	Percent of Days when Air Quality was...[2]					AQI Statistics[2]	
	Good	Moderate	Unhealthy for Sensitive Groups	Unhealthy	Very Unhealthy	Maximum	Median
MSA[1]	79.1	20.9	0.0	0.0	0.0	80	38

Note: (1) Data covers the Wilmington, NC Metropolitan Statistical Area—see Appendix B for areas included; (2) Based on 344 days with AQI data in 2013. Air Quality Index (AQI) is an index for reporting daily air quality. EPA calculates the AQI for five major air pollutants regulated by the Clean Air Act: ground-level ozone, particle pollution (aka particulate matter), carbon monoxide, sulfur dioxide, and nitrogen dioxide. The AQI runs from 0 to 500. The higher the AQI value, the greater the level of air pollution and the greater the health concern. There are six AQI categories: "Good" AQI is between 0 and 50. Air quality is considered satisfactory; "Moderate" AQI is between 51 and 100. Air quality is acceptable; "Unhealthy for Sensitive Groups" When AQI values are between 101 and 150, members of sensitive groups may experience health effects; "Unhealthy" When AQI values are between 151 and 200 everyone may begin to experience health effects; "Very Unhealthy" AQI values between 201 and 300 trigger a health alert; "Hazardous" AQI values over 300 trigger warnings of emergency conditions (not shown).
Source: U.S. Environmental Protection Agency, Air Quality Index Report, 2013

Air Quality Index Pollutants

Area	Percent of Days when AQI Pollutant was...[2]					
	Carbon Monoxide	Nitrogen Dioxide	Ozone	Sulfur Dioxide	Particulate Matter 2.5	Particulate Matter 10
MSA[1]	0.0	0.0	29.4	6.7	64.0	0.0

Note: (1) Data covers the Wilmington, NC Metropolitan Statistical Area—see Appendix B for areas included; (2) Based on 344 days with AQI data in 2013. The Air Quality Index (AQI) is an index for reporting daily air quality. EPA calculates the AQI for five major air pollutants regulated by the Clean Air Act: ground-level ozone, particle pollution (also known as particulate matter), carbon monoxide, sulfur dioxide, and nitrogen dioxide. The AQI runs from 0 to 500. The higher the AQI value, the greater the level of air pollution and the greater the health concern.
Source: U.S. Environmental Protection Agency, Air Quality Index Report, 2013

Air Quality Trends: Ozone

	2003	2004	2005	2006	2007	2008	2009	2010	2011	2012
MSA[1]	0.076	0.070	0.075	0.072	0.071	0.063	0.060	0.062	0.064	0.064

Note: (1) Data covers the Wilmington, NC Metropolitan Statistical Area—see Appendix B for areas included. The values shown are the composite ozone concentration averages among trend sites based on the highest fourth daily maximum 8-hour concentration in parts per million. These trends are based on sites having an adequate record of monitoring data during the trend period. Data from exceptional events are included.
Source: U.S. Environmental Protection Agency, Air Quality Monitoring Information, "Air Quality Trends by City, 2000-2012"

Maximum Air Pollutant Concentrations: Particulate Matter, Ozone, CO and Lead

	Particulate Matter 10 (ug/m^3)	Particulate Matter 2.5 Wtd AM (ug/m^3)	Particulate Matter 2.5 24-Hr (ug/m^3)	Ozone (ppm)	Carbon Monoxide (ppm)	Lead (ug/m^3)
MSA[1] Level	n/a	6.6	16	0.064	n/a	n/a
NAAQS[2]	150	15	35	0.075	9	0.15
Met NAAQS[2]	n/a	Yes	Yes	Yes	n/a	n/a

Note: (1) Data covers the Wilmington, NC Metropolitan Statistical Area—see Appendix B for areas included; Data from exceptional events are included; (2) National Ambient Air Quality Standards; ppm = parts per million; ug/m^3 = micrograms per cubic meter; n/a not available.
Concentrations: Particulate Matter 10 (coarse particulate)—highest second maximum 24-hour concentration; Particulate Matter 2.5 Wtd AM (fine particulate)—highest weighted annual mean concentration; Particulate Matter 2.5 24-Hour (fine particulate)—highest 98th percentile 24-hour concentration; Ozone—highest fourth daily maximum 8-hour concentration; Carbon Monoxide—highest second maximum non-overlapping 8-hour concentration; Lead—maximum running 3-month average
Source: U.S. Environmental Protection Agency, Air Quality Monitoring Information, "Air Quality Statistics by City, 2012"

Maximum Air Pollutant Concentrations: Nitrogen Dioxide and Sulfur Dioxide

	Nitrogen Dioxide AM (ppb)	Nitrogen Dioxide 1-Hr (ppb)	Sulfur Dioxide AM (ppb)	Sulfur Dioxide 1-Hr (ppb)	Sulfur Dioxide 24-Hr (ppb)
MSA[1] Level	n/a	n/a	n/a	47	n/a
NAAQS[2]	53	100	30	75	140
Met NAAQS[2]	n/a	n/a	n/a	Yes	n/a

Note: (1) Data covers the Wilmington, NC Metropolitan Statistical Area—see Appendix B for areas included; Data from exceptional events are included; (2) National Ambient Air Quality Standards; ppm = parts per million; ug/m^3 = micrograms per cubic meter; n/a not available.
Concentrations: Nitrogen Dioxide AM—highest arithmetic mean concentration; Nitrogen Dioxide 1-Hr—highest 98th percentile 1-hour daily maximum concentration; Sulfur Dioxide AM—highest annual mean concentration; Sulfur Dioxide 1-Hr—highest 99th percentile 1-hour daily maximum concentration; Sulfur Dioxide 24-Hr—highest second maximum 24-hour concentration
Source: U.S. Environmental Protection Agency, Air Quality Monitoring Information, "Air Quality Statistics by City, 2012"

Drinking Water

Water System Name	Pop. Served	Primary Water Source Type	Violations[1]	
			Health Based	Monitoring/ Reporting
CFPUA-Wilmington	131,089	Surface	0	0

Note: (1) Based on violation data from January 1, 2013 to December 31, 2013 (includes unresolved violations from earlier years)
Source: U.S. Environmental Protection Agency, Office of Ground Water and Drinking Water, Safe Drinking Water Information System (based on data extracted February 10, 2014)

Worcester, Massachusetts

Background

For the first one hundred years following European settlement in central Massachusetts, Worcester was the site of great conflict, making permanent settlement difficult. The Nimpuc Native Americans were Worcester's first inhabitants. In 1673, English settlers established a "praying town" where Christianized Native Americans could settle as a congregation. But the Indian Wars (sometimes referred to as King Phillip's War) broke up any town cohesion as natives left the area to fight. It wasn't until 1713 that Worcester was permanently settled. By 1770, the town played a major role in the American Revolution. The radical Isaiah Thomas moved his *Massachusetts Spy* newspaper to Worcester from Boston, and read the newly penned Declaration of Independence from the step of Worcester's town hall—the declaration's first public reading in New England.

Thomas created the American Antiquarian Society (AAS) in 1812, in part, to protect precious historical documents from destruction in Boston during the War of 1812. AAS membership is by election, and has included 16 U. S. presidents, and 78 Pulitzer Prize winners. It houses the largest collection of pre-1812, American-printed materials in the world, and includes over 4 million documents, covering 25 miles worth of shelf space. Current membership includes such greats at Ken Burns, Doris Kearns Goodwin, David McCullough, and Henry Louis Gates.

Once Worcester established itself as a transportation hub—following the completion of the Blackstone Canal, and the opening of the Worcester and Boston Railroad—manufacturing took root. New industries brought teams of immigrants looking for work. In 1881, Ichabod Washburn established the Washburn & Moen Company that would become the largest wire manufacturer in the country. The Royal Worcester Corset Factory would become the nation's largest employer of women.

Worcester is a city of firsts and foremosts. Besides the first public reading of the Declaration of Independence and formation of the AAS, Worcester hosted the first national women's rights convention in 1850. Worcester's Frances Perkins became the first woman to serve in a President's cabinet, under Franklin Roosevelt. The first ballpoint pen and the first typewriter were each manufactured in Worcester. And in 1963, Worcester native, Harvey Ball, created the ubiquitous, yellow "Smiley Face."

However, not all of the city's firsts were positive. In the early 20th Century, the Ku Klux Klan had more members in Maine and Massachusettes than in any southern state (including Alabama and Mississippi)—a reaction to the influx of Catholic French Canadians looking for work. In 1924, Worcester hosted the largest gathering of the Ku Klux Klan in New England. Later referred to as the "klanvocation," Worcester townspeople rioted following the meeting, burning cars and beating klan members, who had called for police protection. Following the riots, klan membership in the area declined significantly.

In recent years, Worcester has donned the moniker "Wormtown." Though some residents consider it a derogatory term, it has come to represent Worcester's independent, sometimes rebellious, spirit. In 1978, a local radio DJ named L. B. Worm coined the epithet to celebrate original thought in the burgeoning punk music scene. Since then, the underground movement hosts an annual music festival—the Wormtown Music Festival—and publishes the fanzine *Worm Town Punk Punk Press*. Some local businesses, such as the Wormtown Brewery, have adopted the name.

Education and healthcare thrive in Worcester, which boasts 10 universities and over 100 biotech companies. The University of Massassachusetts Medical School is a leader in medical research. Dr. Craig Mello won the Nobel Prize in physiology while teaching at UMMS and conducting research at the Massachusetts Biotechnology Research Park. In 2000, the College of Pharmacy and Health Sciences (CPHS) built a new campus in the heart of downtown Worcester. Worcester Polytechnic Institute, UMMS and CPHS have created a powerful consortium leading the charge in medical research. Clark University, founded in 1887, was the first university in the country to offer graduate degrees.

Like many progressive cities, Worcester has invested in urban renewal. In 2000, Union Station reopened after a $32 million renovation investment. Franklin Square Theater was revived as the Hanover Theatre for the Performing Arts.

Worcester enjoys a temperate climate with warm summers and mild winters generally. However, the city can experience more extreme weather—the winters of 2009-10 and 2010-11 saw prolonged periods of sub-freezing temperatures and heavy snowfalls. In contrast, Worcester recorded 98.6 °F on 3 August 1990.

Rankings

Business/Finance Rankings

- Measuring indicators of "tolerance"—the nonjudgmental environment that "attracts open-minded and new-thinking kinds of people"— as well as concentrations of technological and economic innovators, analysts identified the most creative American metro areas. On the resulting 2012 Creativity Index, the Worcester metro area placed #14. *www.thedailybeast.com, "Boulder, Ann Arbor, Tucson & More: 20 Most Creative U.S. Cities," June 26, 2012*

- Worcester was ranked #67 out of 100 metro areas in terms of economic performance (#1 = best) during the recession and recovery from trough quarter through the second quarter of 2013. Criteria: percent change in employment; percentage point change in unemployment rate; percent change in gross metropolitan product; percent change in House Price Index. *Brookings Institution, MetroMonitor: Tracking Economic Recession and Recovery in America's 100 Largest Metropolitan Areas, September 2013*

- The Worcester metro area appeared on the Milken Institute "2013 Best Performing Cities" list. Rank: #63 out of 200 large metro areas. Criteria: job growth; wage and salary growth; high-tech output growth. *Milken Institute, "Best-Performing Cities 2013," December 2013*

- *Forbes* ranked the 200 most populous metro areas in the U.S. in terms of the "Best Places for Business and Careers." The Worcester metro area was ranked #91. Criteria: costs (business and living); job growth (past and projected); income growth; educational attainment (college and high school); projected economic growth; cultural and recreational opportunities; net migration patterns; number of highly ranked colleges. *Forbes, "The Best Places for Business and Careers," August 7, 2013*

Children/Family Rankings

- *Forbes* ranked the 100 largest metropolitan areas in the U.S. in terms of the "The Best Cities for Raising a Family." The Worcester metro area was ranked #10. Criteria: median income; overall cost of living; housing affordability; commuting delays; percentage of families owning homes; crime rate; education quality (mainly test scores). *Forbes, "The Best Cities for Raising a Family," April 4, 2012*

Environmental Rankings

- The Weather Channel determined the nation's snowiest cities, based on the National Oceanic and Atmospheric Administration's 30-year average snowfall data. Among cities with a population of at least 100,000, the #10-ranked city was Worcester *weather.com, America's 20 Snowiest Major Cities, February 3, 2014*

- The Worcester metro area came in at #60 for the relative comfort of its climate on Sperling's list of "chill cities," as measured by the Sperling Heat Index. All 361 metro areas are included. Criteria included daytime high temperatures, nighttime low temperatures, dew point, and relative humidity at the high temperatures. *www.bertsperling.com, "Sperling's Chill Cities," July 18, 2013*

- Sperling's BestPlaces assessed 379 metropolitan areas of the United States for the likelihood of dangerously extreme weather events or earthquakes. In general the Southeast and South-Central regions have the highest risk of weather extremes and earthquakes, while the Pacific Northwest enjoys the lowest risk. Of the least risky metropolitan areas, the Worcester metro area was ranked #223. *www.bestplaces.net, "Safest Places from Natural Disasters," April 2011*

- Worcester was selected as one of 22 "Smarter Cities" for energy by the Natural Resources Defense Council. Criteria: investment in green power; energy efficiency measures; conservation. *Natural Resources Defense Council, "2010 Smarter Cities," July 19, 2010*

Health/Fitness Rankings

- Worcester was identified as a "2013 Spring Allergy Capital." The area ranked #78 out of 100. Three groups of factors were used to identify the most severe cities for people with allergies during the spring season: annual pollen levels; medicine utilization; access to board-certified allergists. *Asthma and Allergy Foundation of America, "Spring Allergy Capitals 2013"*

- Worcester was identified as a "2013 Fall Allergy Capital." The area ranked #69 out of 100. Three groups of factors were used to identify the most severe cities for people with allergies during the fall season: annual pollen levels; medicine utilization; access to board-certified allergists. *Asthma and Allergy Foundation of America, "Fall Allergy Capitals 2013"*

- Worcester was identified as a "2013 Asthma Capital." The area ranked #83 out of the nation's 100 largest metropolitan areas. Twelve factors were used to identify the most challenging places to live for people with asthma: estimated prevalence; self-reported prevalence; crude death rate for asthma; annual pollen score; annual air quality; public smoking laws; number of board-certified asthma specialists; school inhaler access laws; rescue medication use; controller medication use; uninsured rate; poverty rate. *Asthma and Allergy Foundation of America, "Asthma Capitals 2013"*

- The Worcester metro area appeared in the 2013 Gallup-Healthways Well-Being Index. The area ranked #123 out of 189. The Gallup-Healthways Well-Being Index score is an average of six sub-indexes, which individually examine life evaluation, emotional health, work environment, physical health, healthy behaviors, and access to basic necessities. Results are based on telephone interviews conducted as part of the Gallup-Healthways Well-Being Index survey January 2–December 29, 2012, and January 2–December 30, 2013, with a random sample of 531,630 adults, aged 18 and older, living in metropolitan areas in the 50 U.S. states and the District of Columbia. *Gallup-Healthways, "State of American Well-Being," March 25, 2014*

Real Estate Rankings

- Worcester was ranked #168 out of 283 metro areas in terms of house price appreciation in 2013 (#1 = highest rate). *Federal Housing Finance Agency, House Price Index, 4th Quarter 2013*

- Worcester was ranked #67 out of 224 metro areas in terms of housing affordability in 2013 by the National Association of Home Builders (#1 = most affordable). The NAHB-Wells Fargo Housing Opportunity Index (HOI) for a given area is defined as the share of homes sold in that area that would have been affordable to a family earning the local median income, based on standard mortgage underwriting criteria. *National Association of Home Builders®, NAHB-Wells Fargo Housing Opportunity Index, 4th Quarter 2013*

Safety Rankings

- The National Insurance Crime Bureau ranked 380 metro areas in the U.S. in terms of per capita rates of vehicle theft. The Worcester metro area ranked #313 (#1 = highest rate). Criteria: number of vehicle theft offenses per 100,000 inhabitants in 2012. *National Insurance Crime Bureau, "Hot Spots 2012," June 26, 2013*

Seniors/Retirement Rankings

- From its Best Cities for Successful Aging indexes, the Milken Institute generated rankings for metropolitan areas, weighing data in eight categories—general indicators, health care, wellness, living arrangements, transportation and general accessibility, financial well-being, education and employment, and community participation. The Worcester metro area was ranked #62 overall in the large metro area category. *Milken Institute, "Best Cities for Successful Aging," July 2012*

Sports/Recreation Rankings

- Worcester appeared on the *Sporting News* list of the "Best Sports Cities" for 2011. The area ranked #220 out of 271. Criteria: the magazine takes a 12-month snapshot of each city's sports, putting a heavy premium on regular-season won-lost records (from the most recently completed season). Other criteria include: playoff berths, bowl appearances and tournament bids; championships; applicable power ratings; quality of competition; overall fan fervor (measured in part by attendance); abundance of teams (rewarding quality over quantity); stadium and arena quality; ticket availability and prices; franchise ownership; and marquee appeal of athletes. *Sporting News, "Best Sports Cities 2011," October 4, 2011*

- Worcester appeared on the *Sporting News* list of the "Best Sports Cities" for 2011. The area ranked #220 out of 271. Criteria: a 12-month snapshot of regular-season won-lost records (from the most recently completed season). Other criteria include: playoff berths, bowl appearances and tournament bids; championships; applicable power ratings; quality of competition; overall fan fervor (measured in part by attendance); abundance of teams (quality over quantity); stadium and arena quality; ticket availability and prices; franchise ownership; and marquee appeal of athletes. *Sporting News, "Best Sports Cities 2011," October 4, 2011*

Women/Minorities Rankings

- To determine the best metro areas for working women, the personal finance website NerdWallet considered city size as well as relevant economic metrics—high salaries, narrow pay differential by gender, prevalence of women in the highest-paying industries, and population growth over 2010–2012. Of the medium-sized U.S. cities examined, the Worcester metro area held the #9 position. *www.nerdwallet.com, "Best Places for Women in the Workforce," May 19, 2013*

Miscellaneous Rankings

- The National Alliance to End Homelessness ranked the 100 most populous metro areas in terms the rate of homelessness. The Worcester metro area ranked #44. Criteria: number of homeless people per 10,000 population in 2011. *National Alliance to End Homelessness, The State of Homelessness in America 2012*

Business Environment

CITY FINANCES

City Government Finances

Component	2011 ($000)	2011 ($ per capita)
Total Revenues	814,630	4,683
Total Expenditures	748,077	4,300
Debt Outstanding	633,956	3,644
Cash and Securities[1]	763,535	4,389

Note: (1) Cash and security holdings of a government at the close of its fiscal year, including those of its dependent agencies, utilities, and liquor stores.
Source: U.S Census Bureau, State & Local Government Finances 2011

City Government Revenue by Source

Source	2011 ($000)	2011 ($ per capita)
General Revenue		
From Federal Government	39,449	227
From State Government	325,245	1,870
From Local Governments	0	0
Taxes		
Property	230,642	1,326
Sales and Gross Receipts	2,838	16
Personal Income	0	0
Corporate Income	0	0
Motor Vehicle License	0	0
Other Taxes	4,865	28
Current Charges	58,930	339
Liquor Store	0	0
Utility	27,680	159
Employee Retirement	103,825	597

Source: U.S Census Bureau, State & Local Government Finances 2011

City Government Expenditures by Function

Function	2011 ($000)	2011 ($ per capita)	2011 (%)
General Direct Expenditures			
Air Transportation	1,417	8	0.2
Corrections	0	0	0.0
Education	323,792	1,861	43.3
Employment Security Administration	0	0	0.0
Financial Administration	3,422	20	0.5
Fire Protection	31,723	182	4.2
General Public Buildings	1,585	9	0.2
Governmental Administration, Other	3,780	22	0.5
Health	132	1	0.0
Highways	18,772	108	2.5
Hospitals	0	0	0.0
Housing and Community Development	12,463	72	1.7
Interest on General Debt	26,602	153	3.6
Judicial and Legal	844	5	0.1
Libraries	4,927	28	0.7
Parking	1,831	11	0.2
Parks and Recreation	4,750	27	0.6
Police Protection	38,834	223	5.2
Public Welfare	0	0	0.0
Sewerage	31,482	181	4.2
Solid Waste Management	5,181	30	0.7
Veterans' Services	0	0	0.0
Liquor Store	0	0	0.0
Utility	23,259	134	3.1
Employee Retirement	52,935	304	7.1

Source: U.S Census Bureau, State & Local Government Finances 2011

DEMOGRAPHICS

Population Growth

Area	1990 Census	2000 Census	2010 Census	Population Growth (%) 1990-2000	Population Growth (%) 2000-2010
City	169,759	172,648	181,045	1.7	4.9
MSA[1]	709,728	750,963	798,552	5.8	6.3
U.S.	248,709,873	281,421,906	308,745,538	13.2	9.7

Note: (1) Figures cover the Worcester, MA-CT Metropolitan Statistical Area—see Appendix B for areas included
Source: U.S. Census Bureau, Census 1990, 2000, 2010

Household Size

Area	Persons in Household (%) One	Two	Three	Four	Five	Six	Seven or More	Average Household Size
City	33.4	29.9	15.8	12.4	5.7	1.7	1.1	2.49
MSA[1]	27.0	32.1	16.7	15.5	6.0	1.9	0.8	2.60
U.S.	27.6	33.5	15.7	13.2	6.1	2.4	1.5	2.63

Note: (1) Figures cover the Worcester, MA-CT Metropolitan Statistical Area—see Appendix B for areas included
Source: U.S. Census Bureau, 2010-2012 American Community Survey 3-Year Estimates

Race

Area	White Alone[2] (%)	Black Alone[2] (%)	Asian Alone[2] (%)	AIAN[3] Alone[2] (%)	NHOPI[4] Alone[2] (%)	Other Race Alone[2] (%)	Two or More Races (%)
City	74.3	11.4	6.1	0.3	0.0	3.9	3.9
MSA[1]	85.8	4.1	4.1	0.2	0.0	3.1	2.6
U.S.	74.0	12.6	4.9	0.8	0.2	4.7	2.8

Note: (1) Figures cover the Worcester, MA-CT Metropolitan Statistical Area—see Appendix B for areas included; (2) Alone is defined as not being in combination with one or more other races; (3) American Indian and Alaska Native; (4) Native Hawaiian and Other Pacific Islander
Source: U.S. Census Bureau, 2010-2012 American Community Survey 3-Year Estimates

Hispanic or Latino Origin

Area	Total (%)	Mexican (%)	Puerto Rican (%)	Cuban (%)	Other (%)
City	19.9	0.7	12.3	0.1	6.7
MSA[1]	9.7	0.6	5.3	0.1	3.7
U.S.	16.6	10.7	1.6	0.6	3.7

Note: Persons of Hispanic or Latino origin can be of any race; (1) Figures cover the Worcester, MA-CT Metropolitan Statistical Area—see Appendix B for areas included
Source: U.S. Census Bureau, 2010-2012 American Community Survey 3-Year Estimates

Segregation

Type	Segregation Indices[1] 1990	2000	2010	2010 Rank[2]	Percent Change 1990-2000	Percent Change 1990-2010	Percent Change 2000-2010
Black/White	51.4	52.6	52.6	61	1.2	1.2	0.0
Asian/White	38.6	45.3	45.8	22	6.7	7.2	0.5
Hispanic/White	55.1	55.9	52.7	17	0.8	-2.5	-3.3

Note: All figures cover the Metropolitan Statistical Area—see Appendix B for areas included; Figures are based on an analysis of 1990, 2000, and 2010 Census Decennial Census tract data by William H. Frey, Brookings Institution and the University of Michigan Social Science Data Analysis Network. In this analysis all racial groups (whites, blacks, and asians) are non-Hispanic members of those races. Hispanics are shown as a separate category;
(1) Segregation Indices are Dissimilarity Indices that measure the degree to which the minority group is distributed differently than whites across census tracts. They range from 0 (complete integration) to 100 (complete segregation) where the value indicates the percentage of the minority group that needs to move to be distributed exactly like whites; (2) Ranges from 1 (most segregated) to 102 (least segregated); n/a not available.
Source: www.CensusScope.org

Ancestry

Area	German	Irish	English	American	Italian	Polish	French[2]	Scottish	Dutch
City	3.1	17.3	4.9	2.7	11.1	4.8	8.3	1.2	0.3
MSA[1]	6.3	21.6	10.4	3.9	13.8	6.3	14.7	2.4	0.7
U.S.	15.2	11.1	8.2	7.2	5.6	3.1	2.8	1.7	1.4

Note: Figures are the percentage of the total population reporting a particular ancestry. The nine most commonly reported ancestries in the U.S. are shown. Figures include multiple ancestries (e.g. if a person reported being Irish and Italian, they were included in both columns); (1) Figures cover the Worcester, MA-CT Metropolitan Statistical Area—see Appendix B for areas included; (2) Excludes Basque
Source: U.S. Census Bureau, 2010-2012 American Community Survey 3-Year Estimates

Foreign-Born Population

Area	Percent of Population Born in								
	Any Foreign Country	Mexico	Asia	Europe	Carribean	South America	Central America[2]	Africa	Canada
City	20.3	0.4	5.8	3.7	2.6	2.6	1.0	4.0	0.2
MSA[1]	11.1	0.2	3.4	2.3	1.0	1.6	0.6	1.4	0.6
U.S.	13.0	3.7	3.7	1.6	1.2	0.9	1.0	0.5	0.3

Note: (1) Figures cover the Worcester, MA-CT Metropolitan Statistical Area—see Appendix B for areas included; (2) Excludes Mexico.
Source: U.S. Census Bureau, 2010-2012 American Community Survey 3-Year Estimates

Marital Status

Area	Never Married	Now Married[2]	Separated	Widowed	Divorced
City	43.5	36.0	2.6	6.5	11.4
MSA[1]	32.8	48.6	1.8	6.1	10.7
U.S.	32.4	48.4	2.2	6.0	11.0

Note: Figures are percentages and cover the population 15 years of age and older; (1) Figures cover the Worcester, MA-CT Metropolitan Statistical Area—see Appendix B for areas included; (2) Excludes separated
Source: U.S. Census Bureau, 2010-2012 American Community Survey 3-Year Estimates

Age

Area	Percent of Population									Median Age
	Under Age 5	Age 5–19	Age 20–34	Age 35–44	Age 45–54	Age 55–64	Age 65–74	Age 75–84	Age 85+	
City	7.0	19.6	25.4	12.3	12.8	10.5	6.1	3.8	2.5	33.4
MSA[1]	5.8	20.4	18.5	13.7	16.2	12.5	6.7	4.1	2.2	39.4
U.S.	6.4	20.1	20.5	13.1	14.3	12.2	7.3	4.2	1.8	37.3

Note: (1) Figures cover the Worcester, MA-CT Metropolitan Statistical Area—see Appendix B for areas included
Source: U.S. Census Bureau, 2010-2012 American Community Survey 3-Year Estimates

Gender

Area	Males	Females	Males per 100 Females
City	85,543	96,801	88.4
MSA[1]	396,216	407,213	97.3
U.S.	153,276,055	158,333,314	96.8

Note: (1) Figures cover the Worcester, MA-CT Metropolitan Statistical Area—see Appendix B for areas included
Source: U.S. Census Bureau, 2010-2012 American Community Survey 3-Year Estimates

Religious Groups by Family

Area	Catholic	Baptist	Non-Den.	Methodist[2]	Lutheran	LDS[3]	Pente-costal	Presby-terian[4]	Muslim[5]	Judaism
MSA[1]	38.4	1.2	1.8	1.0	0.9	0.3	1.1	2.1	0.1	0.5
U.S.	19.1	9.3	4.0	4.0	2.3	2.0	1.9	1.6	0.8	0.7

Note: Figures are the number of adherents as a percentage of the total population; (1) Figures cover the Worcester, MA-CT Metropolitan Statistical Area—see Appendix B for areas included; (2) Methodist/Pietist; (3) Latter Day Saints; (4) Reformed; (5) Figures are estimates
Source: Association of Statisticians of American Religious Bodies, 2010 U.S. Religion Census: Religious Congregations & Membership Study

Religious Groups by Tradition

Area	Catholic	Evangelical Protestant	Mainline Protestant	Other Tradition	Black Protestant	Orthodox
MSA[1]	38.4	4.7	5.4	2.4	0.1	1.0
U.S.	19.1	16.2	7.3	4.3	1.6	0.3

Note: Figures are the number of adherents as a percentage of the total population; (1) Figures cover the Worcester, MA-CT Metropolitan Statistical Area—see Appendix B for areas included
Source: Association of Statisticians of American Religious Bodies, 2010 U.S. Religion Census: Religious Congregations & Membership Study

ECONOMY

Gross Metropolitan Product

Area	2011	2012	2013	2014	Rank[2]
MSA[1]	29.7	30.5	31.1	32.2	75

Note: Figures are in billions of dollars; (1) Figures cover the Worcester, MA-CT Metropolitan Statistical Area—see Appendix B for areas included; (2) Rank is based on 2014 data and ranges from 1 to 363
Source: The United States Conference of Mayors, U.S. Metro Economies: Outlook—Gross Metropolitan Product, with Metro Employment Projections, November 2013

Economic Growth

Area	2011 (%)	2012 (%)	2013 (%)	2014 (%)	Rank[2]
MSA[1]	0.9	0.8	0.4	1.7	210
U.S.	1.6	2.5	1.7	2.5	–

Note: Figures are real gross metropolitan product (GMP) growth rates and represent annual average percent change; (1) Figures cover the Worcester, MA-CT Metropolitan Statistical Area—see Appendix B for areas included; (2) Rank is based on 2013 data and ranges from 1 to 363
Source: The United States Conference of Mayors, U.S. Metro Economies: Outlook—Gross Metropolitan Product, with Metro Employment Projections, November 2013

Metropolitan Area Exports

Area	2007	2008	2009	2010	2011	2012	Rank[2]
MSA[1]	2,475.4	2,863.5	2,035.9	2,355.7	2,397.0	2,966.2	73

Note: Figures are in millions of dollars; (1) Figures cover the Worcester, MA-CT Metropolitan Statistical Area—see Appendix B for areas included; (2) Rank is based on 2012 data and ranges from 1 to 369
Source: U.S. Department of Commerce, International Trade Administration, Office of Trade & Industry Information, Manufacturing & Services, data extracted April 1, 2014

INCOME

Income

Area	Per Capita ($)	Median Household ($)	Average Household ($)
City	23,946	43,999	60,512
MSA[1]	30,969	63,687	80,951
U.S.	27,385	51,771	71,579

Note: (1) Figures cover the Worcester, MA-CT Metropolitan Statistical Area—see Appendix B for areas included
Source: U.S. Census Bureau, 2010-2012 American Community Survey 3-Year Estimates

Household Income Distribution

Area	Under $15,000	$15,000 -24,999	$25,000 -34,999	$35,000 -49,999	$50,000 -74,999	$75,000 -99,000	$100,000 -149,999	$150,000 and up
City	18.7	12.6	10.1	13.3	17.5	10.4	10.7	6.7
MSA[1]	11.1	9.3	8.3	11.6	17.0	13.5	16.5	12.7
U.S.	13.1	11.0	10.5	13.7	18.1	11.9	12.5	9.1

Note: (1) Figures cover the Worcester, MA-CT Metropolitan Statistical Area—see Appendix B for areas included
Source: U.S. Census Bureau, 2010-2012 American Community Survey 3-Year Estimates

Poverty Rate

Area	All Ages	Under 18 Years Old	18 to 64 Years Old	65 Years and Over
City	21.3	30.4	19.3	15.1
MSA[1]	11.3	15.1	10.5	8.4
U.S.	15.7	22.2	14.6	9.3

Note: Figures are percentage of people whose income during the past 12 months was below the poverty level;
(1) Figures cover the Worcester, MA-CT Metropolitan Statistical Area—see Appendix B for areas included
Source: U.S. Census Bureau, 2010-2012 American Community Survey 3-Year Estimates

Personal Bankruptcy Filing Rate

Area	2008	2009	2010	2011	2012	2013
Worcester County	3.44	4.37	4.88	3.90	3.24	2.35
U.S.	3.53	4.61	4.97	4.37	3.76	3.29

Note: Numbers are per 1,000 population and include Chapter 7 and Chapter 13 filings
Source: Federal Deposit Insurance Corporation, Regional Economic Conditions, March 20, 2014

EMPLOYMENT

Labor Force and Employment

Area	Civilian Labor Force			Workers Employed		
	Dec. 2012	Dec. 2013	% Chg.	Dec. 2012	Dec. 2013	% Chg.
City	84,235	84,090	-0.2	77,626	77,344	-0.4
MSA[1]	292,613	291,563	-0.4	271,522	270,674	-0.3
U.S.	154,904,000	154,408,000	-0.3	143,060,000	144,423,000	1.0

Note: Data is not seasonally adjusted and covers workers 16 years of age and older; (1) Metropolitan Statistical Area—see Appendix B for areas included
Source: Bureau of Labor Statistics, Local Area Unemployment Statistics

Unemployment Rate

Area	2013											
	Jan.	Feb.	Mar.	Apr.	May	Jun.	Jul.	Aug.	Sep.	Oct.	Nov.	Dec.
City	8.4	7.8	7.9	7.8	8.8	9.8	9.3	8.9	8.7	8.5	8.2	8.0
MSA[1]	7.9	7.3	7.3	7.0	7.4	8.2	8.0	7.6	7.5	7.5	7.1	7.2
U.S.	8.5	8.1	7.6	7.1	7.3	7.8	7.7	7.3	7.0	7.0	6.6	6.5

Note: Data is not seasonally adjusted and covers workers 16 years of age and older; All figures are percentages;
(1) Metropolitan Statistical Area—see Appendix B for areas included
Source: Bureau of Labor Statistics, Local Area Unemployment Statistics

Employment by Occupation

Occupation Classification	City (%)	MSA[1] (%)	U.S. (%)
Management, Business, Science, and Arts	35.5	40.3	36.0
Natural Resources, Construction, and Maintenance	6.2	7.5	9.1
Production, Transportation, and Material Moving	11.9	10.9	12.0
Sales and Office	24.3	23.9	24.7
Service	22.1	17.5	18.2

Note: Figures cover employed civilians 16 years of age and older; (1) Figures cover the Worcester, MA-CT Metropolitan Statistical Area—see Appendix B for areas included
Source: U.S. Census Bureau, 2010-2012 American Community Survey 3-Year Estimates

Employment by Industry

Sector	NECTA[1]		U.S.
	Number of Employees	Percent of Total	Percent of Total
Construction	n/a	n/a	4.2
Education and Health Services	60,800	24.3	15.5
Financial Activities	13,500	5.4	5.7
Government	37,400	14.9	16.1
Information	3,600	1.4	1.9
Leisure and Hospitality	21,200	8.5	10.2
Manufacturing	23,700	9.5	8.7
Mining and Logging	n/a	n/a	0.6
Other Services	7,700	3.1	3.9
Professional and Business Services	25,500	10.2	13.7
Retail Trade	28,900	11.6	11.4
Transportation and Utilities	9,800	3.9	3.8
Wholesale Trade	9,700	3.9	4.2

Note: Figures cover non-farm employment as of December 2013 and are not seasonally adjusted;
(1) New England City and Town Area—see Appendix B for areas included; n/a not available
Source: Bureau of Labor Statistics, Current Employment Statistics, Employment, Hours, and Earnings

Occupations with Greatest Projected Employment Growth: 2010 – 2020

Occupation[1]	2010 Employment	2020 Projected Employment	Numeric Employment Change	Percent Employment Change
Registered Nurses	87,520	110,100	22,580	25.8
Customer Service Representatives	46,390	59,660	13,260	28.6
Personal Care Aides	21,860	31,780	9,920	45.4
Management Analysts	27,280	37,060	9,780	35.8
Software Developers, Systems Software	27,460	37,070	9,620	35.0
Home Health Aides	17,440	26,810	9,370	53.7
Accountants and Auditors	35,760	45,040	9,280	26.0
Office Clerks, General	58,820	68,010	9,190	15.6
Financial Analysts	13,930	22,270	8,340	59.8
Nursing Aides, Orderlies, and Attendants	41,790	49,880	8,100	19.4

Note: Projections cover Massachusetts; (1) Sorted by numeric employment change
Source: www.projectionscentral.com, State Occupational Projections, 2010–2020 Long-Term Projections

Fastest Growing Occupations: 2010 – 2020

Occupation[1]	2010 Employment	2020 Projected Employment	Numeric Employment Change	Percent Employment Change
Biomedical Engineers	1,400	2,630	1,230	87.8
Actuaries	990	1,780	790	79.5
Personal Financial Advisors	7,180	12,660	5,490	76.5
Insurance Sales Agents	7,900	13,820	5,920	74.9
Loan Officers	5,210	8,660	3,440	66.1
Financial Examiners	1,410	2,290	880	62.5
Financial Analysts	13,930	22,270	8,340	59.8
Dental Laboratory Technicians	670	1,060	390	58.1
Securities, Commodities, and Financial Services Sales Agents	9,440	14,850	5,410	57.4
Meeting, Convention, and Event Planners	2,010	3,150	1,140	56.9

Note: Projections cover Massachusetts; (1) Sorted by percent employment change and excludes occupations with numeric employment change less than 100
Source: www.projectionscentral.com, State Occupational Projections, 2010–2020 Long-Term Projections

Average Wages

Occupation	$/Hr.	Occupation	$/Hr.
Accountants and Auditors	35.61	Maids and Housekeeping Cleaners	12.18
Automotive Mechanics	20.23	Maintenance and Repair Workers	20.42
Bookkeepers	19.02	Marketing Managers	62.04
Carpenters	22.84	Nuclear Medicine Technologists	n/a
Cashiers	10.60	Nurses, Licensed Practical	26.36
Clerks, General Office	14.94	Nurses, Registered	43.05
Clerks, Receptionists/Information	14.29	Nursing Assistants	15.10
Clerks, Shipping/Receiving	16.08	Packers and Packagers, Hand	10.06
Computer Programmers	38.85	Physical Therapists	39.78
Computer Systems Analysts	41.52	Postal Service Mail Carriers	24.22
Computer User Support Specialists	23.76	Real Estate Brokers	n/a
Cooks, Restaurant	12.05	Retail Salespersons	11.90
Dentists	88.51	Sales Reps., Exc. Tech./Scientific	35.68
Electrical Engineers	59.16	Sales Reps., Tech./Scientific	38.33
Electricians	32.10	Secretaries, Exc. Legal/Med./Exec.	19.68
Financial Managers	56.15	Security Guards	14.47
First-Line Supervisors/Managers, Sales	21.73	Surgeons	116.75
Food Preparation Workers	10.81	Teacher Assistants	13.60
General and Operations Managers	60.60	Teachers, Elementary School	31.10
Hairdressers/Cosmetologists	16.18	Teachers, Secondary School	32.60
Internists	n/a	Telemarketers	18.18
Janitors and Cleaners	14.17	Truck Drivers, Heavy/Tractor-Trailer	22.87
Landscaping/Groundskeeping Workers	13.49	Truck Drivers, Light/Delivery Svcs.	17.81
Lawyers	60.66	Waiters and Waitresses	12.77

Note: Wage data covers the Worcester, MA-CT Metropolitan Statistical Area—see Appendix B for areas included. Hourly wages for elementary/secondary school teachers and teacher assistants were calculated by the editors from annual wage data assuming a 40 hour work week; n/a not available.
Source: Bureau of Labor Statistics, Metro Area Occupational Employment and Wage Estimates, May 2013

RESIDENTIAL REAL ESTATE

Building Permits

Area	Single-Family			Multi-Family			Total		
	2012	2013	Pct. Chg.	2012	2013	Pct. Chg.	2012	2013	Pct. Chg.
City	44	53	20.5	20	8	-60.0	64	61	-4.7
MSA[1]	867	1,164	34.3	258	177	-31.4	1,125	1,341	19.2
U.S.	518,695	620,802	19.7	310,963	370,020	19.0	829,658	990,822	19.4

Note: (1) Metropolitan Statistical Area—see Appendix B for areas included; figures represent new, privately-owned housing units authorized (unadjusted data); All permit data are based on estimates with imputation.
Source: U.S. Census Bureau, Manufacturing, Mining, and Construction Statistics, Building Permits, 2012, 2013

Homeownership Rate

Area	2006 (%)	2007 (%)	2008 (%)	2009 (%)	2010 (%)	2011 (%)	2012 (%)	2013 (%)
MSA[1]	71.0	67.8	68.5	64.4	64.1	65.8	61.9	63.3
U.S.	68.8	68.1	67.8	67.4	66.9	66.1	65.4	65.1

Note: (1) Figures cover the Worcester, MA-CT Metropolitan Statistical Area—see Appendix B for areas included
Source: U.S. Census Bureau, Housing Vacancies and Homeownership Annual Statistics: 2013

Housing Vacancy Rates

Area	Gross Vacancy Rate[2] (%)			Year-Round Vacancy Rate[3] (%)			Rental Vacancy Rate[4] (%)			Homeowner Vacancy Rate[5] (%)		
	2011	2012	2013	2011	2012	2013	2011	2012	2013	2011	2012	2013
MSA[1]	10.3	10.3	10.8	9.5	9.5	8.6	4.9	3.7	6.4	1.3	2.4	3.1
U.S.	14.2	13.8	13.8	11.1	10.8	10.7	9.5	8.7	8.3	2.5	2.0	2.0

Note: (1) Figures cover the Worcester, MA-CT Metropolitan Statistical Area—see Appendix B for areas included; (2) The percentage of the total housing inventory that is vacant; (3) The percentage of the housing inventory (excluding seasonal units) that is year-round vacant; (4) The percentage of rental inventory that is vacant for rent; (5) The percentage of homeowner inventory that is vacant for sale
Source: U.S. Census Bureau, Housing Vacancies and Homeownership Annual Statistics: 2013

TAXES

State Corporate Income Tax Rates

State	Tax Rate (%)	Income Brackets ($)	Num. of Brackets	Financial Institution Tax Rate (%)[a]	Federal Income Tax Ded.
Massachusetts	8.0 (n)	Flat rate	1	9.0 (n)	No

Note: Tax rates as of January 1, 2014; (a) Rates listed are the corporate income tax rate applied to financial institutions or excise taxes based on income. Some states have other taxes based upon the value of deposits or shares; (n) Business and manufacturing corporations pay an additional tax of $2.60 per $1,000 on either taxable Massachusetts tangible property or taxable net worth allocable to the state (for intangible property corporations). The minimum tax for both corporations and financial institutions is $456.
Source: Federation of Tax Administrators, "State Corporate Income Tax Rates, 2014"

State Individual Income Tax Rates

State	Tax Rate (%)	Income Brackets ($)	Num. of Brackets	Personal Exempt. ($)[1] Single	Personal Exempt. ($)[1] Dependents	Fed. Inc. Tax Ded.
Massachusetts (a)	5.20	Flat rate	1	4,400	1,000	No

Note: Tax rates as of January 1, 2014; Local- and county-level taxes are not included; n/a not applicable; (1) Married joint filers generally receive double the single exemption; (a) 17 states have statutory provision for automatically adjusting to the rate of inflation the dollar values of the income tax brackets, standard deductions, and/or personal exemptions. Massachusetts, Michigan, and Nebraska index the personal exemption only. Oregon does not index the income brackets for $125,000 and over. Maine has suspended indexing for 2014 and 2015.
Source: Federation of Tax Administrators, "State Individual Income Tax Rates, 2014"

Various State and Local Tax Rates

State	State and Local Sales and Use (%)	State Sales and Use (%)	Gasoline[1] (¢/gal.)	Cigarette[2] ($/pack)	Spirits[3] ($/gal.)	Wine[4] ($/gal.)	Beer[5] ($/gal.)
Massachusetts	6.25	6.25	26.50	3.510	4.05 (f)	0.55	0.11

Note: All tax rates as of January 1, 2014; (1) The American Petroleum Institute has developed a methodology for determining the average tax rate on a gallon of fuel. Rates may include any of the following: excise taxes, environmental fees, storage tank fees, other fees or taxes, general sales tax, and local taxes. In states where gasoline is subject to the general sales tax, or where the fuel tax is based on the average sale price, the average rate determined by API is sensitive to changes in the price of gasoline. States that fully or partially apply general sales taxes to gasoline: CA, CO, GA, IL, IN, MI, NY; (2) The federal excise tax of $1.0066 per pack and local taxes are not included; (3) Rates are those applicable to off-premise sales of 40% alcohol by volume (a.b.v.) distilled spirits in 750ml containers. Local excise taxes are excluded; (4) Rates are those applicable to off-premise sales of 11% a.b.v. non-carbonated wine in 750ml containers; (5) Rates are those applicable to off-premise sales of 4.7% a.b.v. beer in 12 ounce containers; (f) Different rates also applicable according to alcohol content, place of production, size of container, or place purchased (on- or off-premise or onboard airlines).
Source: Tax Foundation, 2014 Facts & Figures: How Does Your State Compare?

State Business Tax Climate Index Rankings

State	Overall Rank	Corporate Tax Index Rank	Individual Income Tax Index Rank	Sales Tax Index Rank	Unemployment Insurance Tax Index Rank	Property Tax Index Rank
Massachusetts	25	34	13	17	49	47

Note: The index is a measure of how each state's tax laws affect economic performance. The lower the rank, the more favorable a state's tax system is for business. States without a given tax are given a ranking of 1. The scores/rankings for the District of Columbia do not affect other states. The 2014 index represents the tax climate as of July 1, 2013.
Source: Tax Foundation, State Business Tax Climate Index 2014

COMMERCIAL UTILITIES

Typical Monthly Electric Bills

Area	Commercial Service ($/month) 1,500 kWh	Commercial Service ($/month) 40 kW demand 14,000 kWh	Industrial Service ($/month) 1,000 kW demand 200,000 kWh	Industrial Service ($/month) 50,000 kW demand 15,000,000 kWh
City	n/a	n/a	n/a	n/a
Average[1]	197	1,636	25,662	1,485,307

Note: Based on total rates in effect July 1, 2013; (1) average based on 180 utilities surveyed; n/a not available
Source: Edison Electric Institute, Typical Bills and Average Rates Report, Summer 2013

TRANSPORTATION

Means of Transportation to Work

Area	Car/Truck/Van		Public Transportation			Bicycle	Walked	Other Means	Worked at Home
	Drove Alone	Car-pooled	Bus	Subway	Railroad				
City	74.7	10.3	2.7	0.2	0.6	0.2	6.3	1.1	3.9
MSA[1]	82.0	8.7	0.8	0.1	0.7	0.2	2.8	0.8	3.9
U.S.	76.4	9.7	2.6	1.7	0.5	0.6	2.8	1.3	4.3

Note: Figures are percentages and cover workers 16 years of age and older; (1) Figures cover the Worcester, MA-CT Metropolitan Statistical Area—see Appendix B for areas included
Source: U.S. Census Bureau, 2010-2012 American Community Survey 3-Year Estimates

Travel Time to Work

Area	Less Than 10 Minutes	10 to 19 Minutes	20 to 29 Minutes	30 to 44 Minutes	45 to 59 Minutes	60 to 89 Minutes	90 Minutes or More
City	12.5	39.0	19.2	16.2	6.0	5.2	1.9
MSA[1]	12.7	27.1	19.4	20.5	9.1	8.4	2.9
U.S.	13.5	29.8	20.9	20.1	7.5	5.6	2.5

Note: Figures are percentages and include workers 16 years old and over; (1) Figures cover the Worcester, MA-CT Metropolitan Statistical Area—see Appendix B for areas included
Source: U.S. Census Bureau, 2010-2012 American Community Survey 3-Year Estimates

Travel Time Index

Area	1985	1990	1995	2000	2005	2010	2011
Urban Area[1]	1.09	1.11	1.17	1.19	1.19	1.13	1.13
Average[2]	1.09	1.14	1.16	1.19	1.23	1.18	1.18

Note: Travel Time Index—the ratio of travel time in the peak period to the travel time at free-flow conditions. For example, a value of 1.30 indicates a 20-minute free-flow trip takes 26 minutes in the peak. Free-flow speeds (60 mph on freeways and 35 mph on principal arterials) are used as the comparison threshold; (1) Covers the Worcester MA-CT urban area; (2) average of 498 urban areas
Source: Texas Transportation Institute, Urban Mobility Report 2012, December 2012

Public Transportation

Agency Name / Mode of Transportation	Vehicles Operated in Maximum Service	Annual Unlinked Passenger Trips (in thous.)	Annual Passenger Miles (in thous.)
Worcester Regional Transit Authority			
Bus (directly operated)	35	3,791.5	11,334.8
Demand Response (directly operated)	9	40.6	193.2
Demand Response (purchased transportation)	26	57.3	359.1
Demand Response Taxi (purchased transportation)	10	49.5	235.4

Source: Federal Transit Administration, National Transit Database, 2012

Air Transportation

Airport Name and Code / Type of Service	Passenger Airlines[1]	Passenger Enplanements	Freight Carriers[2]	Freight (lbs.)
Worcester Regional Airport (ORH)				
Domestic service (U.S. carriers - 2013)	3	7,732	1	108
International service (U.S. carriers - 2012)	0	0	0	0
Boston Logan International Airport (50 miles) ()				
Domestic service (U.S. carriers - 2013)	0	0	0	0
International service (U.S. carriers - 2012)	0	0	0	0

Note: (1) Includes all U.S.-based major, minor and commuter airlines that carried at least one passenger during the year; (2) Includes all U.S.-based airlines and freight carriers that transported at least one lb. of freight during the year.
Source: Bureau of Transportation Statistics, The Intermodal Transportation Database, Air Carriers: T-100 Domestic Market (U.S. Carriers), 2013; Bureau of Transportation Statistics, The Intermodal Transportation Database, Air Carriers: T-100 International Market (U.S. Carriers), 2012

Other Transportation Statistics

Major Highways:	I-90; I-190; I-290; I-395
Amtrak Service:	Yes
Major Waterways/Ports:	None

Source: Amtrak.com; Google Maps

BUSINESSES

Major Business Headquarters

Company Name	Rankings	
	Fortune[1]	Forbes[2]
No companies listed	-	-

Note: (1) Fortune 500—companies that produce a 10-K are ranked 1 to 500 based on 2012 revenue; (2) all private companies with at least $2 billion in annual revenue through the end of their most current fiscal year are ranked 1 to 224; companies listed are headquartered in the city; dashes indicate no ranking Source: Fortune, "Fortune 500," May 20, 2013; Forbes, "America's Largest Private Companies," December 18, 2013

Fast-Growing Businesses

According to *Initiative for a Competitive Inner City (ICIC)*, Worcester is home to one of America's 100 fastest-growing "inner city" companies: **TANTARA Corporation** (#42). Companies were ranked by their five-year compound annual growth rate. Criteria for inclusion: company must be headquartered in or have 51 percent or more of its physical operations in an economically distressed urban area; must be an independent, for-profit corporation, partnership or proprietorship; must have 10 or more employees and have a five-year sales history that includes sales of at least $200,000 in the base year and at least $1 million in the current year with no decrease in sales over the two most recent years. *Initiative for a Competitive Inner City (ICIC), "Inner City 100 Companies, 2013"*

Minority- and Women-Owned Businesses

Group	All Firms		Firms with Paid Employees			
	Firms	Sales ($000)	Firms	Sales ($000)	Employees	Payroll ($000)
Asian	1,213	128,747	170	88,118	692	27,331
Black	823	66,198	51	46,664	253	11,347
Hispanic	761	55,987	78	32,589	364	12,362
Women	3,276	1,047,620	480	982,522	4,567	129,979
All Firms	11,798	18,357,964	3,421	18,030,311	85,549	3,638,657

Note: Figures cover firms located in the city; minority- and women-owned business are defined as firms in which the corresponding group own 51% or more of the stock or equity of the company Source: U.S. Census Bureau, 2007 Economic Census, Survey of Business Owners (2012 Survey of Business Owners data will be released starting in June 2015)

HOTELS & CONVENTION CENTERS

Hotels/Motels

Area	5 Star		4 Star		3 Star		2 Star		1 Star		Not Rated	
	Num.	Pct.[3]	Num.	Pct.[3]	Num.	Pct.[3]	Num.	Pct.[3]	Num.	Pct.[3]	Num.	Pct.[3]
City[1]	0	0.0	3	3.3	38	41.8	44	48.4	2	2.2	4	4.4
Total[2]	142	0.9	1,005	6.0	5,147	30.9	8,578	51.4	408	2.4	1,397	8.4

Note: (1) Figures cover Worcester and vicinity; (2) Figures cover all 100 cities in this book; (3) Percentage of hotels which have a given star rating; Star ratings are determined by expedia.com and offer an indication of the general quality of a particular hotel. Source: expedia.com, April 7, 2014

Major Convention Centers

Name	Overall Space (sq. ft.)	Exhibit Space (sq. ft.)	Meeting Space (sq. ft.)	Meeting Rooms

There are no major convention centers located in the metro area
Source: Original research

Living Environment

COST OF LIVING

Cost of Living Index

Composite Index	Groceries	Housing	Utilities	Trans-portation	Health Care	Misc. Goods/Services
104.2	94.3	97.7	117.6	103.8	123.4	106.6

Note: The Cost of Living Index measures regional differences in the cost of consumer goods and services, excluding taxes and non-consumer expenditures, for professional and managerial households in the top income quintile. It is based on more than 50,000 prices covering almost 60 different items for which prices are collected three times a year by chambers of commerce, economic development organizations or university applied economic centers in each participating urban area. The numbers shown should be read as a percentage above or below the national average of 100. For example, a value of 115.4 in the groceries column indicates that grocery prices are 15.4% higher than the national average. Small differences in the index numbers should not be interpreted as significant; Figures cover the Fitchburg-Leominster MA urban area.
Source: The Council for Community and Economic Research, ACCRA Cost of Living Index, 2013

Grocery Prices

Area[1]	T-Bone Steak ($/pound)	Frying Chicken ($/pound)	Whole Milk ($/half gal.)	Eggs ($/dozen)	Orange Juice ($/64 oz.)	Coffee ($/11.5 oz.)
City[2]	9.82	1.41	1.86	1.51	3.28	4.69
Avg.	10.19	1.28	2.34	1.81	3.48	4.39
Min.	8.56	0.94	1.44	1.19	2.78	3.40
Max.	14.82	2.28	3.56	3.73	6.23	7.32

Note: (1) Values for the local area are compared with the average, minimum and maximum values for all 327 areas in the Cost of Living Index; (2) Figures cover the Fitchburg-Leominster MA urban area; **T-Bone Steak** *(price per pound);* **Frying Chicken** *(price per pound, whole fryer);* **Whole Milk** *(half gallon carton);* **Eggs** *(price per dozen, Grade A, large);* **Orange Juice** *(64 oz. Tropicana or Florida Natural);* **Coffee** *(11.5 oz. can, vacuum-packed, Maxwell House, Hills Bros, or Folgers).*
Source: The Council for Community and Economic Research, ACCRA Cost of Living Index, 2013

Housing and Utility Costs

Area[1]	New Home Price ($)	Apartment Rent ($/month)	All Electric ($/month)	Part Electric ($/month)	Other Energy ($/month)	Telephone ($/month)
City[2]	288,809	881	-	93.43	109.81	29.99
Avg.	295,864	900	171.38	91.82	70.12	27.73
Min.	185,506	458	117.80	48.81	33.67	17.16
Max.	1,358,917	3,783	441.68	171.40	372.65	39.47

Note: (1) Values for the local area are compared with the average, minimum and maximum values for all 327 areas in the Cost of Living Index; (2) Figures cover the Fitchburg-Leominster MA urban area; **New Home Price** *(2,400 sf living area, 8,000 sf lot, in urban area with full utilities);* **Apartment Rent** *(950 sf 2 bedroom/1.5 or 2 bath, unfurnished, excluding all utilities except water);* **All Electric** *(average monthly cost for an all-electric home);* **Part Electric** *(average monthly cost for a part-electric home);* **Other Energy** *(average monthly cost for natural gas, fuel oil, coal, wood, and any other forms of energy except electricity);* **Telephone** *(price includes basic monthly rate for a private residential line plus additional local usage charges incurred by a family of four).*
Source: The Council for Community and Economic Research, ACCRA Cost of Living Index, 2013

Health Care, Transportation, and Other Costs

Area[1]	Doctor ($/visit)	Dentist ($/visit)	Optometrist ($/visit)	Gasoline ($/gallon)	Beauty Salon ($/visit)	Men's Shirt ($)
City[2]	178.33	105.00	96.94	3.54	31.52	31.35
Avg.	101.40	86.48	96.16	3.44	33.87	26.55
Min.	61.67	50.83	50.12	3.08	18.92	12.48
Max.	182.71	152.50	223.78	4.33	68.22	52.03

Note: (1) Values for the local area are compared with the average, minimum and maximum values for all 327 areas in the Cost of Living Index; (2) Figures cover the Fitchburg-Leominster MA urban area; **Doctor** *(general practitioners routine exam of an established patient);* **Dentist** *(adult teeth cleaning and periodic oral examination);* **Optometrist** *(full vision eye exam for established adult patient);* **Gasoline** *(one gallon regular unleaded, national brand, including all taxes, cash price at self-service pump if available);* **Beauty Salon** *(woman's shampoo, trim, and blow-dry);* **Men's Shirt** *(cotton/polyester dress shirt, pinpoint weave, long sleeves).*
Source: The Council for Community and Economic Research, ACCRA Cost of Living Index, 2013

HOUSING

House Price Index (HPI)

Area	National Ranking[2]	Quarterly Change (%)	One-Year Change (%)	Five-Year Change (%)
MSA[1]	168	0.84	1.46	-8.55
U.S.[3]	–	1.20	7.69	4.18

Note: The HPI is a weighted repeat sales index. It measures average price changes in repeat sales or refinancings on the same properties. This information is obtained by reviewing repeat mortgage transactions on single-family properties whose mortgages have been purchased or securitized by Fannie Mae or Freddie Mac in January 1975; (1) Worcester, MA-CT Metropolitan Statistical Area—see Appendix B for areas included; (2) Rankings are based on annual percentage change for all metro areas containing at least 15,000 transactions over the last 10 years and ranges from 1 to 283; (3) figures based on a weighted average of Census Division estimates using a seasonally adjusted, purchase-only index; all figures are for the period ending December 31, 2013
Source: Federal Housing Finance Agency, House Price Index, February 25, 2014

Median Single-Family Home Prices

Area	2011	2012	2013p	Percent Change 2012 to 2013
MSA[1]	209.6	206.0	231.3	12.3
U.S. Average	166.2	177.2	197.4	11.4

Note: Figures are median sales prices of existing single-family homes in thousands of dollars; (p) preliminary; n/a not available; (1) Worcester, MA-CT Metropolitan Statistical Area—see Appendix B for areas included
Source: National Association of Realtors, Median Sales Price of Existing Single-Family Homes for Metropolitan Areas, 4th Quarter 2013

Qualifying Income Based on Median Sales Price of Existing Single-Family Homes

Area	With 5% Down ($)	With 10% Down ($)	With 20% Down ($)
MSA[1]	52,612	49,843	44,305
U.S. Average	45,395	43,006	38,228

Note: Figures are preliminary; Qualifying income is based on a mortgage rate of 4.4%. Monthly principal and interest payment is limited to 25% of income; n/a not available; (1) Worcester, MA-CT Metropolitan Statistical Area—see Appendix B for areas included
Source: National Association of Realtors, Qualifying Income Based on Median Sales Price of Existing Single-Family Homes for Metropolitan Areas, 4th Quarter 2013

Median Apartment Condo-Coop Home Prices

Area	2011	2012	2013p	Percent Change 2012 to 2013
MSA[1]	162.0	158.7	182.5	15.0
U.S. Average	165.1	173.7	194.9	12.2

Note: Figures are median sales prices of existing apartment condo-coop homes in thousands of dollars; (p) preliminary; n/a not available; (1) Worcester, MA-CT Metropolitan Statistical Area—see Appendix B for areas included
Source: National Association of Realtors, Median Sales Price of Existing Apartment Condo-Coop Homes for Metropolitan Areas, 4th Quarter 2013

Gross Monthly Rent

Area	Under $200	$200 -299	$300 -499	$500 -749	$750 -999	$1,000 -1,499	$1,500 and up	Median ($)
City	2.0	8.0	7.4	15.3	29.6	31.7	5.9	903
MSA[1]	1.5	6.1	8.3	17.4	29.5	29.2	8.0	895
U.S.	1.7	3.3	8.1	22.7	24.3	25.7	14.3	889

Note: Figures are percentages except for Median; Gross rent is the contract rent plus the estimated average monthly cost of utilities (electricity, gas, and water and sewer) and fuels (oil, coal, kerosene, wood, etc.) if these are paid by the renter (or paid for the renter by someone else); (1) Figures cover the Worcester, MA-CT Metropolitan Statistical Area—see Appendix B for areas included
Source: U.S. Census Bureau, 2010-2012 American Community Survey 3-Year Estimates

Year Housing Structure Built

Area	2010 or Later	2000 -2009	1990 -1999	1980 -1989	1970 -1979	1960 -1969	1950 -1959	1940 -1949	Before 1940	Median Year
City	0.3	4.6	4.4	9.4	8.6	6.3	9.7	8.2	48.5	1942
MSA[1]	0.3	8.8	9.4	12.4	10.9	8.2	10.7	6.2	33.2	1960
U.S.	0.5	14.9	13.8	13.9	15.9	11.1	10.9	5.5	13.5	1976

Note: Figures are percentages except for Median Year; (1) Figures cover the Worcester, MA-CT Metropolitan Statistical Area—see Appendix B for areas included
Source: U.S. Census Bureau, 2010-2012 American Community Survey 3-Year Estimates

HEALTH

Health Risk Data

Category	MSA[1] (%)	U.S. (%)
Adults aged 18–64 who have any kind of health care coverage	91.8	79.6
Adults who reported being in good or excellent health	87.3	83.1
Adults who are current smokers	17.6	19.6
Adults who are heavy drinkers[2]	7.4	6.1
Adults who are binge drinkers[3]	19.6	16.9
Adults who are overweight (BMI 25.0 - 29.9)	33.5	35.8
Adults who are obese (BMI 30.0 - 99.8)	28.5	27.6
Adults who participated in any physical activities in the past month	79.7	77.1
Adults 50+ who have ever had a sigmoidoscopy or colonoscopy	76.4	67.3
Women aged 40+ who have had a mammogram within the past two years	83.5	74.0
Men aged 40+ who have had a PSA test within the past two years	40.8	45.2
Adults aged 65+ who have had flu shot within the past year	63.8	60.1
Adults who always wear a seatbelt	90.4	93.8

Note: Data as of 2012 unless otherwise noted; (1) Figures cover the Worcester, MA Metropolitan Statistical Area—see Appendix B for areas included; (2) Heavy drinkers are classified as males having more than two drinks per day or females having more than one drink per day; (3) Binge drinkers are classified as males having five or more drinks on one occasion or females having four or more drinks on one occasion
Source: Centers for Disease Control and Prevention, Behaviorial Risk Factor Surveillance System, SMART: Selected Metropolitan/Micropolitan Area Risk Trends, 2012

Chronic Health Indicators

Category	MSA[1] (%)	U.S. (%)
Adults who have ever been told they had a heart attack	4.3	4.5
Adults who have ever been told they had a stroke	2.4	2.9
Adults who have been told they currently have asthma	11.8	8.9
Adults who have ever been told they have arthritis	24.5	25.7
Adults who have ever been told they have diabetes[2]	9.0	9.7
Adults who have ever been told they had skin cancer	5.0	5.7
Adults who have ever been told they had any other types of cancer	5.7	6.5
Adults who have ever been told they have COPD	6.7	6.2
Adults who have ever been told they have kidney disease	2.0	2.5
Adults who have ever been told they have a form of depression	19.3	18.0

Note: Data as of 2012 unless otherwise noted; (1) Figures cover the Worcester, MA Metropolitan Statistical Area—see Appendix B for areas included; (2) Figures do not include pregnancy-related, borderline, or pre-diabetes
Source: Centers for Disease Control and Prevention, Behaviorial Risk Factor Surveillance System, SMART: Selected Metropolitan/Micropolitan Area Risk Trends, 2012

Mortality Rates for the Top 10 Causes of Death in the U.S.

ICD-10[a] Sub-Chapter	ICD-10[a] Code	Age-Adjusted Mortality Rate[1] per 100,000 population	
		County[2]	U.S.
Malignant neoplasms	C00-C97	183.8	174.2
Ischaemic heart diseases	I20-I25	100.5	119.1
Other forms of heart disease	I30-I51	50.8	49.6
Chronic lower respiratory diseases	J40-J47	40.3	43.2
Cerebrovascular diseases	I60-I69	38.8	40.3
Organic, including symptomatic, mental disorders	F01-F09	45.9	30.5
Other degenerative diseases of the nervous system	G30-G31	27.6	26.3
Other external causes of accidental injury	W00-X59	23.0	25.1
Diabetes mellitus	E10-E14	17.4	21.3
Hypertensive diseases	I10-I15	12.4	18.8

Note: (a) ICD-10 = International Classification of Diseases 10th Revision; (1) Mortality rates are a three year average covering 2008-2010; (2) Figures cover Worcester County
Source: Centers for Disease Control and Prevention, National Center for Health Statistics. Compressed Mortality File 1999-2010 on CDC WONDER Online Database, released January 2013. Data are compiled from the Compressed Mortality File 1999-2010, Series 20 No. 2P, 2013.

Mortality Rates for Selected Causes of Death

ICD-10[a] Sub-Chapter	ICD-10[a] Code	Age-Adjusted Mortality Rate[1] per 100,000 population	
		County[2]	U.S.
Assault	X85-Y09	1.9	5.5
Diseases of the liver	K70-K76	12.4	12.4
Human immunodeficiency virus (HIV) disease	B20-B24	1.5	3.0
Influenza and pneumonia	J09-J18	20.7	16.4
Intentional self-harm	X60-X84	7.3	11.8
Malnutrition	E40-E46	0.8	0.8
Obesity and other hyperalimentation	E65-E68	1.6	1.6
Renal failure	N17-N19	14.8	13.6
Transport accidents	V01-V99	7.5	12.6
Viral hepatitis	B15-B19	1.6	2.2

Note: (a) ICD-10 = International Classification of Diseases 10th Revision; (1) Mortality rates are a three year average covering 2008-2010; (2) Figures cover Worcester County
Source: Centers for Disease Control and Prevention, National Center for Health Statistics. Compressed Mortality File 1999-2010 on CDC WONDER Online Database, released January 2013. Data are compiled from the Compressed Mortality File 1999-2010, Series 20 No. 2P, 2013.

Health Insurance Coverage

Area	With Health Insurance	With Private Health Insurance	With Public Health Insurance	Without Health Insurance	Population Under Age 18 Without Health Insurance
City	95.0	62.8	42.1	5.0	1.9
MSA[1]	96.2	75.9	32.1	3.8	1.3
U.S.	84.9	65.4	30.4	15.1	7.5

Note: Figures are percentages that cover the civilian noninstitutionalized population; (1) Figures cover the Worcester, MA-CT Metropolitan Statistical Area—see Appendix B for areas included
Source: U.S. Census Bureau, 2010-2012 American Community Survey 3-Year Estimates

Number of Medical Professionals

Area[1]	MDs[2]	DOs[2,3]	Dentists	Podiatrists	Chiropractors	Optometrists
Local (number)	2,837	158	525	49	156	144
Local (rate[4])	353.1	19.7	65.2	6.1	19.4	17.9
U.S. (rate[4])	267.6	19.6	61.7	5.6	24.7	14.5

Note: Data as of 2012 unless noted; (1) Local data covers Worcester County; (2) Data as of 2011; (3) Doctor of Osteopathic Medicine; (4) rate per 100,000 population
Source: Area Resource File (ARF) 2012-2013. U.S. Department of Health and Human Services, Health Resources and Services Administration, Bureau of Health Professions

EDUCATION

Public School District Statistics

District Name	Schls	Pupils	Pupil/ Teacher Ratio	Minority Pupils[1] (%)	Free Lunch Eligible[2] (%)	IEP[3] (%)
Worcester	45	24,411	15.4	63.6	65.8	21.4

Note: Table includes school districts with 2,000 or more students; (1) Percentage of students that are not non-Hispanic white; (2) Percentage of students that are eligible for the free lunch program; (3) Percentage of students that have an Individualized Education Program.
Source: U.S. Department of Education, National Center for Education Statistics, Common Core of Data, Local Education Agency (School District) Universe Survey: School Year 2011-2012; U.S. Department of Education, National Center for Education Statistics, Common Core of Data, Public Elementary/Secondary School Universe Survey: School Year 2011-2012

Best High Schools

High School Name	Rank[1]	Grad. Rate[2] (%)	Coll.[3] (%)	AP/IB/ AICE Tests[4]	AP/IB/ AICE Score[5]	SAT Score[6]	ACT Score[6]
University Park Campus School	1437	91	100	0.2	2.2	1338	n/a

Note: (1) Public schools are ranked from 1 to 2,000 based on the following self-reported statistics (with the corresponding weight used in calculating their overall score). Schools that were newly founded and did not have a graduating senior class in 2012 were excluded; (2) Four-year, on-time graduation rate (25%); (3) Percent of 2011 graduates who were accepted to college (25%); (4) AP/IB/AICE tests taken per student (25%); (5) Average AP/IB/AICE exam score (10%); (6) Average SAT and/or ACT score (10%); Percent of students enrolled in at least one AP/IB/AICE course (5%)—data not shown; n/a not available
Source: Newsweek and The Daily Beast, "America's Best High Schools 2013"

Highest Level of Education

Area	Less than H.S.	H.S. Diploma	Some College, No Deg.	Associate Degree	Bachelor's Degree	Master's Degree	Prof. School Degree	Doctorate Degree
City	16.1	28.5	17.6	7.9	18.3	8.5	1.8	1.3
MSA[1]	10.8	28.4	18.0	9.1	20.8	9.8	1.8	1.4
U.S.	14.1	28.3	21.3	7.8	18.0	7.5	1.9	1.2

Note: Figures cover persons age 25 and over; (1) Figures cover the Worcester, MA-CT Metropolitan Statistical Area—see Appendix B for areas included
Source: U.S. Census Bureau, 2010-2012 American Community Survey 3-Year Estimates

Educational Attainment by Race

Area	High School Graduate or Higher (%)					Bachelor's Degree or Higher (%)				
	Total	White	Black	Asian	Hisp.[2]	Total	White	Black	Asian	Hisp.[2]
City	83.9	86.3	87.8	71.5	63.2	29.9	32.4	20.3	33.8	9.4
MSA[1]	89.2	90.7	86.7	83.1	66.4	33.7	34.2	23.7	55.6	13.5
U.S.	85.9	88.1	82.5	85.5	63.1	28.6	30.0	18.4	50.2	13.4

Note: Figures shown cover persons 25 years old and over; (1) Figures cover the Worcester, MA-CT Metropolitan Statistical Area—see Appendix B for areas included; (2) People of Hispanic origin can be of any race
Source: U.S. Census Bureau, 2010-2012 American Community Survey 3-Year Estimates

School Enrollment by Grade and Control

Area	Preschool (%)		Kindergarten (%)		Grades 1 - 4 (%)		Grades 5 - 8 (%)		Grades 9 - 12 (%)	
	Public	Private	Public	Private	Public	Private	Public	Private	Public	Private
City	70.2	29.8	93.0	7.0	89.7	10.3	85.6	14.4	87.7	12.3
MSA[1]	54.3	45.7	86.9	13.1	91.4	8.6	91.3	8.7	90.7	9.3
U.S.	56.9	43.1	87.8	12.2	89.9	10.1	90.0	10.0	90.8	9.2

Note: Figures shown cover persons 3 years old and over; (1) Figures cover the Worcester, MA-CT Metropolitan Statistical Area—see Appendix B for areas included
Source: U.S. Census Bureau, 2010-2012 American Community Survey 3-Year Estimates

Average Salaries of Public School Classroom Teachers

Area	2012-13		2013-14		Percent Change 2012-13 to 2013-14	Percent Change 2003-04 to 2013-14
	Dollars	Rank[1]	Dollars	Rank[1]		
Massachusetts	72,334	2	73,736	2	1.94	37.2
U.S. Average	56,103	–	56,689	–	1.04	21.8

Note: (1) State rank ranges from 1 to 51 where 1 indicates highest salary.
Source: National Education Association, Rankings & Estimates: Rankings of the States 2013 and Estimates of School Statistics 2014, March 2014

Higher Education

Four-Year Colleges			Two-Year Colleges			Medical Schools[1]	Law Schools[2]	Voc/ Tech[3]
Public	Private Non-profit	Private For-profit	Public	Private Non-profit	Private For-profit			
2	5	0	1	0	0	1	0	3

Note: Figures cover institutions located within the city limits and include main campuses only; (1) includes schools accredited by the Liaison Committee on Medical Education and the American Osteopathic Association's Commission on Osteopathic College Accreditation; (2) includes ABA-accredited schools, schools with provisional ABA accreditation, and state accredited schools; (3) includes all schools with programs that are less than 2 years.
Source: National Center for Education Statistics, Integrated Postsecondary Education System (IPEDS), 2012-13; Association of American Medical Colleges, Member List, April 24, 2014; American Osteopathic Association, Member List, April 24, 2014; Law School Admission Council, Official Guide to ABA-Approved Law Schools Online, April 24, 2014; Wikipedia, List of Medical Schools in the United States, April 24, 2014; Wikipedia, List of Law Schools in the United States, April 24, 2014

According to *U.S. News & World Report,* the Worcester, MA-CT metro area is home to two of the best national universities in the U.S.: **Worcester Polytechnic Institute** (#62); **Clark University** (#75). The indicators used to capture academic quality fall into a number of categories: assessment by administrators at peer institutions; retention of students; faculty resources; student selectivity; financial resources; alumni giving; high school counselor ratings of colleges; and graduation rate. *U.S. News & World Report, "America's Best Colleges 2014"*

According to *U.S. News & World Report,* the Worcester, MA-CT metro area is home to one of the best liberal arts colleges in the U.S.: **College of the Holy Cross** (#25). The indicators used to capture academic quality fall into a number of categories: assessment by administrators at peer institutions; retention of students; faculty resources; student selectivity; financial resources; alumni giving; high school counselor ratings of colleges; and graduation rate. *U.S. News & World Report, "America's Best Colleges 2014"*

PRESIDENTIAL ELECTION

2012 Presidential Election Results

Area	Obama	Romney	Other
Worcester County	53.7	44.5	1.8
U.S.	51.0	47.2	1.8

Note: Results are percentages and may not add to 100% due to rounding
Source: Dave Leip's Atlas of U.S. Presidential Elections

EMPLOYERS

Major Employers

Company Name	Industry
3M Co	Manufacturer
Abb Vie Bioresearch Center	Pharmaceutical research & development
Abrasives Marketing Group	Marketing
Affiliated Podiatrists	Healthcare
Allegro Micro Systems Inc	Manufacturer
Amica Mutual Insurance Co	Insurance
Assumption College	Education
Astra Zeneca	Pharmaceutical research & development
Babcock Power Environmental	Utility
Bj's Wholesale Club	Retail
Bny Mellon Wealth Management	Finance
College of the Holy Cross	Education
Commerce Insurance Co	Insurance
Community Healthlink	Healthcare
Hanover Insurance Co	Insurance
Hanover Insurance Group	Insurance
Integrated Genetics	Lab testing
Mapfre USA Corp	Insurance
Mt Wachusett Ski Area	Ski resort
P F Pc Inc	Finance
Saint-Gobain Abrasives	Manufacturer
Saint-Gobain Ceramic Materials	Manufacturer
St Vincent Hospital	Healthcare
Vna Care Network	Healthcare
Wachusett Mountain	Ski resort

Note: Companies shown are located within the Worcester, MA-CT Metropolitan Statistical Area.
Source: Hoovers.com; Wikipedia

PUBLIC SAFETY

Crime Rate

Area	All Crimes	Violent Crimes				Property Crimes		
		Murder	Forcible Rape	Robbery	Aggrav. Assault	Burglary	Larceny -Theft	Motor Vehicle Theft
City	4,469.4	4.4	18.0	228.7	708.3	1,113.3	2,143.0	253.8
Suburbs[1]	2,007.0	0.9	22.9	35.8	212.6	435.8	1,224.1	74.9
Metro[2]	2,537.1	1.6	21.9	77.3	319.3	581.7	1,421.9	113.4
U.S.	3,246.1	4.7	26.9	112.9	242.3	670.2	1,959.3	229.7

Note: Figures are crimes per 100,000 population; (1) All areas within the metro area that are located outside the city limits; (2) Figures cover the Worcester, MA-CT Metropolitan Statistical Area—see Appendix B for areas included
Source: FBI Uniform Crime Reports, 2012

Hate Crimes

Area	Number of Quarters Reported	Bias Motivation				
		Race	Religion	Sexual Orientation	Ethnicity	Disability
City	4	2	0	2	1	0
U.S.	4	2,797	1,099	1,135	667	92

Source: Federal Bureau of Investigation, Hate Crime Statistics 2012

Identity Theft Consumer Complaints

Area	Complaints	Complaints per 100,000 Population	Rank[2]
MSA[1]	519	56.6	233
U.S.	290,056	91.8	-

Note: (1) Figures cover the Worcester, MA-CT Metropolitan Statistical Area—see Appendix B for areas included; (2) Rank ranges from 1 to 377 where 1 indicates greatest number of identity theft complaints per 100,000 population
Source: Federal Trade Commission, Consumer Sentinel Network Data Book for January–December 2013

Fraud and Other Consumer Complaints

Area	Complaints	Complaints per 100,000 Population	Rank[2]
MSA[1]	3,332	363.4	183
U.S.	1,811,724	595.2	-

Note: (1) Figures cover the Worcester, MA-CT Metropolitan Statistical Area—see Appendix B for areas included; (2) Rank ranges from 1 to 377 where 1 indicates greatest number of identity theft complaints per 100,000 population
Source: Federal Trade Commission, Consumer Sentinel Network Data Book for January–December 2013

RECREATION

Culture

Dance[1]	Theatre[1]	Instrumental Music[1]	Vocal Music[1]	Series and Festivals	Museums and Art Galleries[2]	Zoos and Aquariums[3]
0	3	0	1	1	10	0

Note: (1) Number of professional perfoming groups; (2) Based on organizations with primary SIC code 8412; (3) AZA-accredited
Source: The Grey House Performing Arts Directory, 2013; Association of Zoos & Aquariums, AZA Member Zoos & Aquariums, April 2014; www.AccuLeads.com, May 1, 2014

Professional Sports Teams

Team Name	League	Year Established
No teams are located in the metro area		

Source: Wikipedia, Major Professional Sports Teams of the United States and Canada, April 25, 2014

CLIMATE

Average and Extreme Temperatures

Temperature	Jan	Feb	Mar	Apr	May	Jun	Jul	Aug	Sep	Oct	Nov	Dec	Yr.
Extreme High (°F)	67	67	81	91	92	98	96	97	99	85	79	70	99
Average High (°F)	32	34	42	55	66	75	79	77	69	59	47	35	56
Average Temp. (°F)	24	26	34	45	56	65	70	68	60	51	40	28	47
Average Low (°F)	16	18	25	35	46	55	61	59	51	41	32	21	38
Extreme Low (°F)	-13	-12	-6	11	28	36	43	38	30	20	6	-13	-13

Note: Figures cover the years 1949-1992
Source: National Climatic Data Center, International Station Meteorological Climate Summary, 9/96

Average Precipitation/Snowfall/Humidity

Precip./Humidity	Jan	Feb	Mar	Apr	May	Jun	Jul	Aug	Sep	Oct	Nov	Dec	Yr.
Avg. Precip. (in.)	3.6	3.4	4.1	4.0	4.3	3.7	3.7	4.1	4.0	4.1	4.5	4.1	47.6
Avg. Snowfall (in.)	16	16	11	3	Tr	0	0	0	Tr	1	4	13	62
Avg. Rel. Hum. 7am (%)	72	73	71	69	70	73	76	79	81	78	78	75	75
Avg. Rel. Hum. 4pm (%)	61	58	55	50	52	57	58	61	62	58	63	65	58

Note: Figures cover the years 1949-1992; Tr = Trace amounts (<0.05 in. of rain; <0.5 in. of snow)
Source: National Climatic Data Center, International Station Meteorological Climate Summary, 9/96

Weather Conditions

Temperature			Daytime Sky			Precipitation		
5°F & below	32°F & below	90°F & above	Clear	Partly cloudy	Cloudy	0.01 inch or more precip.	0.1 inch or more snow/ice	Thunder-storms
12	141	4	81	144	140	131	32	23

Note: Figures are average number of days per year and cover the years 1949-1992
Source: National Climatic Data Center, International Station Meteorological Climate Summary, 9/96

HAZARDOUS WASTE

Superfund Sites

Worcester has no sites on the EPA's Superfund Final National Priorities List.
U.S. Environmental Protection Agency, Final National Priorities List, April 26, 2014

AIR & WATER QUALITY

Air Quality Index

Area	Percent of Days when Air Quality was...[2]					AQI Statistics[2]	
	Good	Moderate	Unhealthy for Sensitive Groups	Unhealthy	Very Unhealthy	Maximum	Median
MSA[1]	80.8	19.2	0.0	0.0	0.0	97	38

Note: (1) Data covers the Worcester, MA-CT Metropolitan Statistical Area—see Appendix B for areas included; (2) Based on 365 days with AQI data in 2013. Air Quality Index (AQI) is an index for reporting daily air quality. EPA calculates the AQI for five major air pollutants regulated by the Clean Air Act: ground-level ozone, particle pollution (aka particulate matter), carbon monoxide, sulfur dioxide, and nitrogen dioxide. The AQI runs from 0 to 500. The higher the AQI value, the greater the level of air pollution and the greater the health concern. There are six AQI categories: "Good" AQI is between 0 and 50. Air quality is considered satisfactory; "Moderate" AQI is between 51 and 100. Air quality is acceptable; "Unhealthy for Sensitive Groups" When AQI values are between 101 and 150, members of sensitive groups may experience health effects; "Unhealthy" When AQI values are between 151 and 200 everyone may begin to experience health effects; "Very Unhealthy" AQI values between 201 and 300 trigger a health alert; "Hazardous" AQI values over 300 trigger warnings of emergency conditions (not shown).
Source: U.S. Environmental Protection Agency, Air Quality Index Report, 2013

Air Quality Index Pollutants

Area	Percent of Days when AQI Pollutant was...[2]					
	Carbon Monoxide	Nitrogen Dioxide	Ozone	Sulfur Dioxide	Particulate Matter 2.5	Particulate Matter 10
MSA[1]	0.0	3.3	48.8	0.0	47.1	0.8

Note: (1) Data covers the Worcester, MA-CT Metropolitan Statistical Area—see Appendix B for areas included; (2) Based on 365 days with AQI data in 2013. The Air Quality Index (AQI) is an index for reporting daily air quality. EPA calculates the AQI for five major air pollutants regulated by the Clean Air Act: ground-level ozone, particle pollution (also known as particulate matter), carbon monoxide, sulfur dioxide, and nitrogen dioxide. The AQI runs from 0 to 500. The higher the AQI value, the greater the level of air pollution and the greater the health concern.
Source: U.S. Environmental Protection Agency, Air Quality Index Report, 2013

Air Quality Trends: Ozone

	2003	2004	2005	2006	2007	2008	2009	2010	2011	2012
MSA[1]	0.080	0.074	0.085	0.077	0.089	0.081	0.077	0.070	0.065	0.070

Note: (1) Data covers the Worcester, MA-CT Metropolitan Statistical Area—see Appendix B for areas included. The values shown are the composite ozone concentration averages among trend sites based on the highest fourth daily maximum 8-hour concentration in parts per million. These trends are based on sites having an adequate record of monitoring data during the trend period. Data from exceptional events are included.
Source: U.S. Environmental Protection Agency, Air Quality Monitoring Information, "Air Quality Trends by City, 2000-2012"

Maximum Air Pollutant Concentrations: Particulate Matter, Ozone, CO and Lead

	Particulate Matter 10 (ug/m^3)	Particulate Matter 2.5 Wtd AM (ug/m^3)	Particulate Matter 2.5 24-Hr (ug/m^3)	Ozone (ppm)	Carbon Monoxide (ppm)	Lead (ug/m^3)
MSA[1] Level	38	8.8	20	0.07	2	n/a
NAAQS[2]	150	15	35	0.075	9	0.15
Met NAAQS[2]	Yes	Yes	Yes	Yes	Yes	n/a

Note: (1) Data covers the Worcester, MA-CT Metropolitan Statistical Area—see Appendix B for areas included; Data from exceptional events are included; (2) National Ambient Air Quality Standards; ppm = parts per million; ug/m^3 = micrograms per cubic meter; n/a not available.
Concentrations: Particulate Matter 10 (coarse particulate)—highest second maximum 24-hour concentration; Particulate Matter 2.5 Wtd AM (fine particulate)—highest weighted annual mean concentration; Particulate Matter 2.5 24-Hour (fine particulate)—highest 98th percentile 24-hour concentration; Ozone—highest fourth daily maximum 8-hour concentration; Carbon Monoxide—highest second maximum non-overlapping 8-hour concentration; Lead—maximum running 3-month average
Source: U.S. Environmental Protection Agency, Air Quality Monitoring Information, "Air Quality Statistics by City, 2012"

Maximum Air Pollutant Concentrations: Nitrogen Dioxide and Sulfur Dioxide

	Nitrogen Dioxide AM (ppb)	Nitrogen Dioxide 1-Hr (ppb)	Sulfur Dioxide AM (ppb)	Sulfur Dioxide 1-Hr (ppb)	Sulfur Dioxide 24-Hr (ppb)
MSA[1] Level	13	45	n/a	9	n/a
NAAQS[2]	53	100	30	75	140
Met NAAQS[2]	Yes	Yes	n/a	Yes	n/a

Note: (1) Data covers the Worcester, MA-CT Metropolitan Statistical Area—see Appendix B for areas included; Data from exceptional events are included; (2) National Ambient Air Quality Standards; ppm = parts per million; ug/m³ = micrograms per cubic meter; n/a not available.
Concentrations: Nitrogen Dioxide AM—highest arithmetic mean concentration; Nitrogen Dioxide 1-Hr—highest 98th percentile 1-hour daily maximum concentration; Sulfur Dioxide AM—highest annual mean concentration; Sulfur Dioxide 1-Hr—highest 99th percentile 1-hour daily maximum concentration; Sulfur Dioxide 24-Hr—highest second maximum 24-hour concentration
Source: U.S. Environmental Protection Agency, Air Quality Monitoring Information, "Air Quality Statistics by City, 2012"

Drinking Water

Water System Name	Pop. Served	Primary Water Source Type	Violations[1] Health Based	Violations[1] Monitoring/ Reporting
Worcester DPW, Water Supply Div.	181,045	Surface	0	0

Note: (1) Based on violation data from January 1, 2013 to December 31, 2013 (includes unresolved violations from earlier years)
Source: U.S. Environmental Protection Agency, Office of Ground Water and Drinking Water, Safe Drinking Water Information System (based on data extracted February 10, 2014)

Appendix A: Comparative Statistics

Population Growth: City

City	1990 Census	2000 Census	2010 Census	Population Growth (%) 1990-2000	2000-2010
Abilene, TX	106,927	115,930	117,063	8.4	1.0
Albuquerque, NM	388,375	448,607	545,852	15.5	21.7
Anchorage, AK	226,338	260,283	291,826	15.0	12.1
Ann Arbor, MI	111,018	114,024	113,934	2.7	-0.1
Athens, GA	86,561	100,266	115,452	15.8	15.1
Atlanta, GA	394,092	416,474	420,003	5.7	0.8
Austin, TX	499,053	656,562	790,390	31.6	20.4
Baltimore, MD	736,014	651,154	620,961	-11.5	-4.6
Billings, MT	81,812	89,847	104,170	9.8	15.9
Boise City, ID	144,317	185,787	205,671	28.7	10.7
Boston, MA	574,283	589,141	617,594	2.6	4.8
Boulder, CO	87,737	94,673	97,385	7.9	2.9
Cape Coral, FL	75,507	102,286	154,305	35.5	50.9
Cedar Rapids, IA	110,829	120,758	126,326	9.0	4.6
Charleston, SC	96,102	96,650	120,083	0.6	24.2
Charlotte, NC	428,283	540,828	731,424	26.3	35.2
Chicago, IL	2,783,726	2,896,016	2,695,598	4.0	-6.9
Cincinnati, OH	363,974	331,285	296,943	-9.0	-10.4
Clarksville, TN	78,569	103,455	132,929	31.7	28.5
Colorado Spgs, CO	283,798	360,890	416,427	27.2	15.4
Columbia, MO	71,069	84,531	108,500	18.9	28.4
Columbus, OH	648,656	711,470	787,033	9.7	10.6
Dallas, TX	1,006,971	1,188,580	1,197,816	18.0	0.8
Davenport, IA	95,705	98,359	99,685	2.8	1.3
Denver, CO	467,153	554,636	600,158	18.7	8.2
Des Moines, IA	193,569	198,682	203,433	2.6	2.4
Durham, NC	151,737	187,035	228,330	23.3	22.1
El Paso, TX	515,541	563,662	649,121	9.3	15.2
Erie, PA	108,718	103,717	101,786	-4.6	-1.9
Eugene, OR	118,073	137,893	156,185	16.8	13.3
Fargo, ND	74,372	90,599	105,549	21.8	16.5
Fayetteville, NC	118,247	121,015	200,564	2.3	65.7
Ft. Collins, CO	89,555	118,652	143,986	32.5	21.4
Ft. Wayne, IN	205,671	205,727	253,691	0.0	23.3
Ft. Worth, TX	448,311	534,694	741,206	19.3	38.6
Gainesville, FL	90,519	95,447	124,354	5.4	30.3
Grand Rapids, MI	189,145	197,800	188,040	4.6	-4.9
Green Bay, WI	96,466	102,313	104,057	6.1	1.7
Greensboro, NC	193,389	223,891	269,666	15.8	20.4
Honolulu, HI	376,465	371,657	337,256	-1.3	-9.3
Houston, TX	1,697,610	1,953,631	2,099,451	15.1	7.5
Huntsville, AL	161,842	158,216	180,105	-2.2	13.8
Indianapolis, IN	730,993	781,870	820,445	7.0	4.9
Jacksonville, FL	635,221	735,617	821,784	15.8	11.7
Kansas City, MO	434,967	441,545	459,787	1.5	4.1
Lafayette, LA	104,735	110,257	120,623	5.3	9.4
Las Vegas, NV	261,374	478,434	583,756	83.0	22.0
Lexington, KY	225,366	260,512	295,803	15.6	13.5
Lincoln, NE	193,629	225,581	258,379	16.5	14.5
Little Rock, AR	177,519	183,133	193,524	3.2	5.7
Los Angeles, CA	3,487,671	3,694,820	3,792,621	5.9	2.6
Louisville, KY	269,160	256,231	597,337	-4.8	133.1
Lubbock, TX	187,170	199,564	229,573	6.6	15.0
Madison, WI	193,451	208,054	233,209	7.5	12.1
Manchester, NH	99,567	107,006	109,565	7.5	2.4

Table continued on next page.

City	1990 Census	2000 Census	2010 Census	Population Growth (%) 1990-2000	2000-2010
McAllen, TX	86,145	106,414	129,877	23.5	22.0
Miami, FL	358,843	362,470	399,457	1.0	10.2
Midland, TX	89,358	94,996	111,147	6.3	17.0
Minneapolis, MN	368,383	382,618	382,578	3.9	-0.0
Montgomery, AL	190,866	201,568	205,764	5.6	2.1
Nashville, TN	488,364	545,524	601,222	11.7	10.2
New Orleans, LA	496,938	484,674	343,829	-2.5	-29.1
New York, NY	7,322,552	8,008,278	8,175,133	9.4	2.1
Oklahoma City, OK	445,065	506,132	579,999	13.7	14.6
Omaha, NE	371,972	390,007	408,958	4.8	4.9
Orlando, FL	161,172	185,951	238,300	15.4	28.2
Oxnard, CA	143,271	170,358	197,899	18.9	16.2
Peoria, IL	114,341	112,936	115,007	-1.2	1.8
Philadelphia, PA	1,585,577	1,517,550	1,526,006	-4.3	0.6
Phoenix, AZ	989,873	1,321,045	1,445,632	33.5	9.4
Pittsburgh, PA	369,785	334,563	305,704	-9.5	-8.6
Portland, OR	485,833	529,121	583,776	8.9	10.3
Providence, RI	160,734	173,618	178,042	8.0	2.5
Provo, UT	87,148	105,166	112,488	20.7	7.0
Raleigh, NC	226,841	276,093	403,892	21.7	46.3
Reno, NV	139,950	180,480	225,221	29.0	24.8
Richmond, VA	202,783	197,790	204,214	-2.5	3.2
Riverside, CA	226,232	255,166	303,871	12.8	19.1
Rochester, MN	74,151	85,806	106,769	15.7	24.4
Salem, OR	112,046	136,924	154,637	22.2	12.9
Salt Lake City, UT	159,796	181,743	186,440	13.7	2.6
San Antonio, TX	997,258	1,144,646	1,327,407	14.8	16.0
San Diego, CA	1,111,048	1,223,400	1,307,402	10.1	6.9
San Francisco, CA	723,959	776,733	805,235	7.3	3.7
San Jose, CA	784,324	894,943	945,942	14.1	5.7
Santa Rosa, CA	123,297	147,595	167,815	19.7	13.7
Savannah, GA	138,038	131,510	136,286	-4.7	3.6
Seattle, WA	516,262	563,374	608,660	9.1	8.0
Sioux Falls, SD	102,262	123,975	153,888	21.2	24.1
Spokane, WA	178,202	195,629	208,916	9.8	6.8
Springfield, MO	142,557	151,580	159,498	6.3	5.2
Tallahassee, FL	128,014	150,624	181,376	17.7	20.4
Tampa, FL	279,960	303,447	335,709	8.4	10.6
Topeka, KS	121,197	122,377	127,473	1.0	4.2
Tulsa, OK	367,241	393,049	391,906	7.0	-0.3
Virginia Beach, VA	393,069	425,257	437,994	8.2	3.0
Washington, DC	606,900	572,059	601,723	-5.7	5.2
Wichita, KS	313,693	344,284	382,368	9.8	11.1
Wilmington, NC	64,609	75,838	106,476	17.4	40.4
Worcester, MA	169,759	172,648	181,045	1.7	4.9
U.S.	248,709,873	281,421,906	308,745,538	13.2	9.7

Source: U.S. Census Bureau, Census 2010, 2000, 1990

Population Growth: Metro Area

Metro Area	1990 Census	2000 Census	2010 Census	Population Growth (%) 1990-2000	Population Growth (%) 2000-2010
Abilene, TX	148,004	160,245	165,252	8.3	3.1
Albuquerque, NM	599,416	729,649	887,077	21.7	21.6
Anchorage, AK	266,021	319,605	380,821	20.1	19.2
Ann Arbor, MI	282,937	322,895	344,791	14.1	6.8
Athens, GA	136,025	166,079	192,541	22.1	15.9
Atlanta, GA	3,069,411	4,247,981	5,268,860	38.4	24.0
Austin, TX	846,217	1,249,763	1,716,289	47.7	37.3
Baltimore, MD	2,382,172	2,552,994	2,710,489	7.2	6.2
Billings, MT	121,499	138,904	158,050	14.3	13.8
Boise City, ID	319,596	464,840	616,561	45.4	32.6
Boston, MA	4,133,895	4,391,344	4,552,402	6.2	3.7
Boulder, CO	208,898	269,758	294,567	29.1	9.2
Cape Coral, FL	335,113	440,888	618,754	31.6	40.3
Cedar Rapids, IA	210,640	237,230	257,940	12.6	8.7
Charleston, SC	506,875	549,033	664,607	8.3	21.1
Charlotte, NC	1,024,331	1,330,448	1,758,038	29.9	32.1
Chicago, IL	8,182,076	9,098,316	9,461,105	11.2	4.0
Cincinnati, OH	1,844,917	2,009,632	2,130,151	8.9	6.0
Clarksville, TN	189,277	232,000	273,949	22.6	18.1
Colorado Spgs, CO	409,482	537,484	645,613	31.3	20.1
Columbia, MO	122,010	145,666	172,786	19.4	18.6
Columbus, OH	1,405,176	1,612,694	1,836,536	14.8	13.9
Dallas, TX	3,989,294	5,161,544	6,371,773	29.4	23.4
Davenport, IA	368,151	376,019	379,690	2.1	1.0
Denver, CO	1,666,935	2,179,296	2,543,482	30.7	16.7
Des Moines, IA	416,346	481,394	569,633	15.6	18.3
Durham, NC	344,646	426,493	504,357	23.7	18.3
El Paso, TX	591,610	679,622	800,647	14.9	17.8
Erie, PA	275,603	280,843	280,566	1.9	-0.1
Eugene, OR	282,912	322,959	351,715	14.2	8.9
Fargo, ND	153,296	174,367	208,777	13.7	19.7
Fayetteville, NC	297,422	336,609	366,383	13.2	8.8
Ft. Collins, CO	186,136	251,494	299,630	35.1	19.1
Ft. Wayne, IN	354,435	390,156	416,257	10.1	6.7
Ft. Worth, TX	3,989,294	5,161,544	6,371,773	29.4	23.4
Gainesville, FL	191,263	232,392	264,275	21.5	13.7
Grand Rapids, MI	645,914	740,482	774,160	14.6	4.5
Green Bay, WI	243,698	282,599	306,241	16.0	8.4
Greensboro, NC	540,257	643,430	723,801	19.1	12.5
Honolulu, HI	836,231	876,156	953,207	4.8	8.8
Houston, TX	3,767,335	4,715,407	5,946,800	25.2	26.1
Huntsville, AL	293,047	342,376	417,593	16.8	22.0
Indianapolis, IN	1,294,217	1,525,104	1,756,241	17.8	15.2
Jacksonville, FL	925,213	1,122,750	1,345,596	21.4	19.8
Kansas City, MO	1,636,528	1,836,038	2,035,334	12.2	10.9
Lafayette, LA	208,740	239,086	273,738	14.5	14.5
Las Vegas, NV	741,459	1,375,765	1,951,269	85.5	41.8
Lexington, KY	348,428	408,326	472,099	17.2	15.6
Lincoln, NE	229,091	266,787	302,157	16.5	13.3
Little Rock, AR	535,034	610,518	699,757	14.1	14.6
Los Angeles, CA	11,273,720	12,365,627	12,828,837	9.7	3.7
Louisville, KY	1,055,973	1,161,975	1,283,566	10.0	10.5
Lubbock, TX	229,940	249,700	284,890	8.6	14.1
Madison, WI	432,323	501,774	568,593	16.1	13.3
Manchester, NH	336,073	380,841	400,721	13.3	5.2

Table continued on next page.

Metro Area	1990 Census	2000 Census	2010 Census	Population Growth (%) 1990-2000	Population Growth (%) 2000-2010
McAllen, TX	383,545	569,463	774,769	48.5	36.1
Miami, FL	4,056,100	5,007,564	5,564,635	23.5	11.1
Midland, TX	106,611	116,009	136,872	8.8	18.0
Minneapolis, MN	2,538,834	2,968,806	3,279,833	16.9	10.5
Montgomery, AL	305,175	346,528	374,536	13.6	8.1
Nashville, TN	1,048,218	1,311,789	1,589,934	25.1	21.2
New Orleans, LA	1,264,391	1,316,510	1,167,764	4.1	-11.3
New York, NY	16,845,992	18,323,002	18,897,109	8.8	3.1
Oklahoma City, OK	971,042	1,095,421	1,252,987	12.8	14.4
Omaha, NE	685,797	767,041	865,350	11.8	12.8
Orlando, FL	1,224,852	1,644,561	2,134,411	34.3	29.8
Oxnard, CA	669,016	753,197	823,318	12.6	9.3
Peoria, IL	358,552	366,899	379,186	2.3	3.3
Philadelphia, PA	5,435,470	5,687,147	5,965,343	4.6	4.9
Phoenix, AZ	2,238,480	3,251,876	4,192,887	45.3	28.9
Pittsburgh, PA	2,468,289	2,431,087	2,356,285	-1.5	-3.1
Portland, OR	1,523,741	1,927,881	2,226,009	26.5	15.5
Providence, RI	1,509,789	1,582,997	1,600,852	4.8	1.1
Provo, UT	269,407	376,774	526,810	39.9	39.8
Raleigh, NC	541,081	797,071	1,130,490	47.3	41.8
Reno, NV	257,193	342,885	425,417	33.3	24.1
Richmond, VA	949,244	1,096,957	1,258,251	15.6	14.7
Riverside, CA	2,588,793	3,254,821	4,224,851	25.7	29.8
Rochester, MN	141,945	163,618	186,011	15.3	13.7
Salem, OR	278,024	347,214	390,738	24.9	12.5
Salt Lake City, UT	768,075	968,858	1,124,197	26.1	16.0
San Antonio, TX	1,407,745	1,711,703	2,142,508	21.6	25.2
San Diego, CA	2,498,016	2,813,833	3,095,313	12.6	10.0
San Francisco, CA	3,686,592	4,123,740	4,335,391	11.9	5.1
San Jose, CA	1,534,280	1,735,819	1,836,911	13.1	5.8
Santa Rosa, CA	388,222	458,614	483,878	18.1	5.5
Savannah, GA	258,060	293,000	347,611	13.5	18.6
Seattle, WA	2,559,164	3,043,878	3,439,809	18.9	13.0
Sioux Falls, SD	153,500	187,093	228,261	21.9	22.0
Spokane, WA	361,364	417,939	471,221	15.7	12.7
Springfield, MO	298,818	368,374	436,712	23.3	18.6
Tallahassee, FL	259,096	320,304	367,413	23.6	14.7
Tampa, FL	2,067,959	2,395,997	2,783,243	15.9	16.2
Topeka, KS	210,257	224,551	233,870	6.8	4.2
Tulsa, OK	761,019	859,532	937,478	12.9	9.1
Virginia Beach, VA	1,449,389	1,576,370	1,671,683	8.8	6.0
Washington, DC	4,122,914	4,796,183	5,582,170	16.3	16.4
Wichita, KS	511,111	571,166	623,061	11.7	9.1
Wilmington, NC	200,124	274,532	362,315	37.2	32.0
Worcester, MA	709,728	750,963	798,552	5.8	6.3
U.S.	248,709,873	281,421,906	308,745,538	13.2	9.7

Note: Figures cover the Metropolitan Statistical Area (MSA)—see Appendix B for areas included
Source: U.S. Census Bureau, Census 2010, 2000, 1990

Household Size: City

City	Persons in Household (%)							Average Household Size
	One	Two	Three	Four	Five	Six	Seven or More	
Abilene, TX	29.2	35.3	15.0	11.7	5.3	2.4	1.1	2.55
Albuquerque, NM	33.1	32.6	15.1	11.4	5.0	1.9	0.8	2.43
Anchorage, AK	26.2	32.6	17.6	12.8	5.8	2.7	2.3	2.73
Ann Arbor, MI	38.9	33.4	13.7	9.3	2.3	2.0	0.4	2.24
Athens, GA	32.8	34.3	13.8	12.8	4.1	1.7	0.6	2.66
Atlanta, GA	45.6	29.2	11.8	7.8	3.2	1.6	0.7	2.27
Austin, TX	34.0	32.4	14.9	11.0	4.8	1.6	1.3	2.44
Baltimore, MD	39.4	28.1	15.2	9.1	4.9	1.8	1.6	2.48
Billings, MT	32.5	36.0	13.9	10.5	4.5	1.8	0.8	2.33
Boise City, ID	31.2	34.7	15.3	11.6	4.4	2.0	0.7	2.37
Boston, MA	38.2	31.0	14.5	9.8	3.8	1.7	1.0	2.34
Boulder, CO	32.9	35.5	16.3	11.0	3.6	0.7	0.2	2.24
Cape Coral, FL	22.5	41.3	15.7	11.6	6.1	1.7	1.0	2.84
Cedar Rapids, IA	32.3	34.8	13.9	12.5	4.2	1.7	0.6	2.37
Charleston, SC	35.8	36.2	14.4	9.8	2.9	0.6	0.4	2.25
Charlotte, NC	31.4	31.2	16.0	12.7	5.7	2.2	0.9	2.54
Chicago, IL	36.2	28.0	14.2	10.8	5.8	2.6	2.4	2.59
Cincinnati, OH	43.4	29.1	13.0	8.1	3.2	2.0	1.1	2.22
Clarksville, TN	22.4	31.1	20.8	15.0	6.6	2.4	1.7	2.71
Colorado Spgs, CO	30.0	33.6	15.0	12.6	5.3	2.3	1.1	2.50
Columbia, MO	33.5	32.2	15.5	13.5	3.5	1.3	0.4	2.35
Columbus, OH	36.4	30.7	14.3	10.1	5.4	1.8	1.2	2.40
Dallas, TX	34.7	28.1	13.8	11.5	6.6	3.0	2.3	2.63
Davenport, IA	34.0	34.2	15.6	8.4	5.7	1.2	1.0	2.39
Denver, CO	40.4	31.5	12.3	8.3	4.2	2.0	1.4	2.27
Des Moines, IA	32.2	30.8	15.5	11.6	6.1	2.2	1.6	2.46
Durham, NC	32.2	34.0	15.5	10.6	4.7	2.0	1.0	2.34
El Paso, TX	22.4	26.6	19.0	16.8	9.2	3.7	2.3	3.02
Erie, PA	36.9	31.7	13.9	9.7	4.8	1.5	1.5	2.33
Eugene, OR	32.0	37.7	14.8	9.5	3.7	1.5	0.8	2.28
Fargo, ND	37.9	34.6	14.2	8.5	3.5	1.0	0.3	2.15
Fayetteville, NC	29.7	33.4	17.2	12.5	4.9	1.2	1.0	2.49
Ft. Collins, CO	26.7	36.1	18.1	12.0	4.8	1.5	0.8	2.46
Ft. Wayne, IN	32.2	31.5	16.0	11.4	5.4	2.3	1.2	2.48
Ft. Worth, TX	27.8	27.7	15.7	15.0	8.0	3.5	2.3	2.83
Gainesville, FL	37.0	35.6	14.9	9.1	2.2	0.8	0.3	2.39
Grand Rapids, MI	33.2	30.2	14.3	12.1	5.7	2.6	1.9	2.49
Green Bay, WI	34.9	32.5	12.9	11.1	4.8	2.2	1.6	2.37
Greensboro, NC	34.7	32.7	14.8	10.6	4.5	1.8	0.9	2.35
Honolulu, HI	33.8	31.3	14.5	10.4	4.5	2.4	3.1	2.58
Houston, TX	32.2	28.5	15.3	12.1	7.0	2.8	2.2	2.73
Huntsville, AL	36.7	33.8	13.7	10.2	3.7	1.1	0.6	2.33
Indianapolis, IN	34.3	31.9	14.5	10.5	5.3	2.4	1.2	2.49
Jacksonville, FL	30.6	33.1	16.6	11.7	4.9	2.0	1.2	2.61
Kansas City, MO	35.8	32.2	14.6	10.1	4.5	1.7	1.1	2.38
Lafayette, LA	35.4	32.7	15.4	10.8	3.8	0.7	1.1	2.38
Las Vegas, NV	28.5	31.6	14.8	13.2	6.9	3.0	2.1	2.76
Lexington, KY	33.2	32.7	16.0	11.8	3.9	1.6	0.7	2.36
Lincoln, NE	30.4	36.4	13.5	11.8	4.9	1.8	1.2	2.37
Little Rock, AR	36.0	34.0	14.7	9.1	4.6	0.9	0.7	2.42
Los Angeles, CA	30.4	27.7	15.3	13.2	7.2	3.2	3.1	2.84
Louisville, KY	32.7	32.0	15.7	11.8	5.1	1.7	0.9	2.43
Lubbock, TX	30.1	32.8	15.7	12.3	5.4	2.3	1.4	2.51
Madison, WI	35.6	34.5	14.1	10.6	3.2	1.3	0.6	2.22

Table continued on next page.

City	Persons in Household (%)							Average Household Size
	One	Two	Three	Four	Five	Six	Seven or More	
Manchester, NH	31.3	33.7	16.0	11.5	4.9	1.6	1.0	2.40
McAllen, TX	22.0	26.6	18.7	15.1	10.1	5.2	2.3	3.12
Miami, FL	36.5	29.2	15.7	10.5	4.6	2.1	1.5	2.67
Midland, TX	24.7	33.0	18.4	12.9	7.1	2.5	1.4	2.77
Minneapolis, MN	40.8	31.9	11.1	9.1	3.9	1.3	1.9	2.25
Montgomery, AL	31.5	31.4	17.8	10.7	5.3	1.9	1.3	2.51
Nashville, TN	36.2	32.7	14.1	9.9	4.3	1.6	1.2	2.40
New Orleans, LA	39.1	30.1	14.9	8.8	4.5	1.4	1.3	2.37
New York, NY	32.7	27.9	16.0	12.5	6.0	2.6	2.2	2.65
Oklahoma City, OK	30.5	32.7	15.6	11.5	6.1	2.3	1.2	2.56
Omaha, NE	33.8	32.2	13.2	10.8	6.5	1.8	1.6	2.47
Orlando, FL	36.3	33.5	14.4	9.9	3.7	1.3	0.7	2.42
Oxnard, CA	14.7	21.4	16.0	17.6	13.7	7.4	9.2	3.96
Peoria, IL	35.9	31.7	14.0	10.3	4.9	2.3	1.0	2.34
Philadelphia, PA	39.6	27.7	14.6	9.7	4.9	2.0	1.5	2.58
Phoenix, AZ	28.8	30.1	15.1	13.0	7.0	3.3	2.7	2.81
Pittsburgh, PA	41.7	32.7	13.2	7.9	2.9	1.0	0.6	2.14
Portland, OR	35.4	34.2	14.1	9.8	3.8	1.6	1.2	2.33
Providence, RI	30.5	26.2	18.4	15.2	5.4	2.7	1.6	2.71
Provo, UT	14.9	30.9	16.4	17.9	9.7	6.8	3.4	3.30
Raleigh, NC	33.5	30.9	15.8	12.6	4.6	1.7	0.9	2.45
Reno, NV	33.2	32.8	13.6	11.3	5.5	2.4	1.1	2.50
Richmond, VA	41.8	31.0	13.7	8.3	3.4	1.0	0.8	2.35
Riverside, CA	22.2	25.6	16.2	15.3	10.2	6.1	4.5	3.34
Rochester, MN	31.2	33.5	13.5	13.6	5.5	1.8	1.0	2.44
Salem, OR	29.8	32.2	14.6	12.2	6.1	3.6	1.6	2.57
Salt Lake City, UT	36.6	29.6	14.1	9.9	4.8	2.7	2.4	2.47
San Antonio, TX	28.4	29.5	16.3	13.2	7.2	3.2	2.3	2.80
San Diego, CA	29.2	32.2	15.4	12.7	5.9	2.6	2.0	2.73
San Francisco, CA	39.0	32.8	12.4	9.2	3.4	1.7	1.5	2.33
San Jose, CA	19.6	27.6	18.6	17.9	8.8	3.7	3.7	3.12
Santa Rosa, CA	28.5	32.8	15.5	12.7	6.6	1.8	2.0	2.67
Savannah, GA	36.1	31.2	15.5	9.8	4.6	1.7	1.1	2.57
Seattle, WA	41.9	33.0	12.3	8.4	2.6	1.0	0.7	2.10
Sioux Falls, SD	29.8	35.9	14.0	11.9	4.7	2.2	1.5	2.43
Spokane, WA	34.4	33.4	14.1	10.7	4.6	1.8	1.0	2.30
Springfield, MO	37.7	35.3	13.6	9.6	2.6	0.8	0.4	2.14
Tallahassee, FL	33.9	33.8	17.3	10.9	2.3	1.2	0.7	2.35
Tampa, FL	36.6	31.2	15.1	10.6	4.2	1.4	0.9	2.44
Topeka, KS	36.3	31.9	12.9	10.1	4.5	2.5	1.9	2.32
Tulsa, OK	35.0	32.5	14.1	10.0	5.0	2.1	1.1	2.37
Virginia Beach, VA	23.7	34.7	18.2	13.8	6.3	2.0	1.3	2.64
Washington, DC	46.9	29.1	11.6	7.1	3.0	1.5	0.8	2.21
Wichita, KS	32.2	32.4	14.1	11.3	5.9	2.4	1.7	2.53
Wilmington, NC	34.7	35.6	15.7	10.4	2.2	1.0	0.5	2.23
Worcester, MA	33.4	29.9	15.8	12.4	5.7	1.7	1.1	2.49
U.S.	27.6	33.5	15.7	13.2	6.1	2.4	1.5	2.63

U.S. Census Bureau, 2010-2012 American Community Survey 3-Year Estimates

Household Size: Metro Area

Metro Area	Persons in Household (%)							Average Household Size
	One	Two	Three	Four	Five	Six	Seven or More	
Abilene, TX	28.5	36.8	14.7	11.4	5.4	2.2	1.0	2.55
Albuquerque, NM	29.6	33.5	15.4	12.4	5.7	2.1	1.3	2.56
Anchorage, AK	25.2	33.6	17.4	13.0	5.8	2.7	2.5	2.76
Ann Arbor, MI	32.2	32.7	15.6	12.7	4.4	1.7	0.7	2.45
Athens, GA	27.9	35.3	15.0	14.2	4.8	1.9	0.9	2.75
Atlanta, GA	26.6	31.2	16.8	14.8	6.6	2.5	1.6	2.78
Austin, TX	27.7	32.8	15.7	13.8	6.2	2.3	1.5	2.65
Baltimore, MD	28.6	32.4	16.5	13.2	6.1	2.0	1.2	2.60
Billings, MT	30.0	37.4	13.3	11.6	4.9	1.8	1.0	2.40
Boise City, ID	24.1	34.9	14.7	14.2	7.1	3.2	1.8	2.70
Boston, MA	28.7	32.3	16.0	14.4	5.8	1.9	0.9	2.53
Boulder, CO	28.2	35.5	15.5	13.8	5.0	1.4	0.6	2.42
Cape Coral, FL	28.4	43.5	12.0	9.4	4.1	1.7	0.8	2.62
Cedar Rapids, IA	28.6	36.4	14.4	13.1	5.0	1.8	0.7	2.43
Charleston, SC	28.4	34.4	16.9	12.7	4.9	1.8	0.9	2.57
Charlotte, NC	27.1	32.6	17.0	13.7	6.1	2.3	1.1	2.64
Chicago, IL	28.0	29.8	15.9	14.4	7.1	2.8	1.9	2.73
Cincinnati, OH	28.1	33.8	15.9	13.1	5.7	2.2	1.1	2.57
Clarksville, TN	22.8	32.4	18.9	14.3	7.2	2.6	1.7	2.68
Colorado Spgs, CO	26.4	34.7	15.6	13.6	6.0	2.6	1.2	2.60
Columbia, MO	30.5	33.7	16.5	13.0	4.4	1.3	0.5	2.41
Columbus, OH	29.3	32.8	15.4	13.3	6.0	2.0	1.1	2.54
Dallas, TX	25.3	30.4	16.7	15.1	7.6	3.0	1.9	2.80
Davenport, IA	31.5	35.6	14.4	10.8	5.3	1.4	1.0	2.41
Denver, CO	29.5	33.2	15.1	12.8	5.7	2.3	1.4	2.54
Des Moines, IA	26.9	34.2	16.1	13.7	6.2	1.9	1.0	2.52
Durham, NC	29.7	35.7	15.8	11.6	4.7	1.5	1.0	2.41
El Paso, TX	20.5	25.8	19.3	17.4	10.1	4.1	2.8	3.13
Erie, PA	30.5	34.7	14.8	12.1	5.1	1.7	1.0	2.45
Eugene, OR	28.7	38.7	15.2	10.2	4.5	1.6	1.1	2.38
Fargo, ND	32.9	34.7	14.4	11.4	4.8	1.4	0.4	2.32
Fayetteville, NC	27.3	32.1	18.3	13.7	5.8	1.7	1.2	2.63
Ft. Collins, CO	25.3	39.4	15.9	12.2	4.9	1.5	0.7	2.45
Ft. Wayne, IN	28.2	33.5	15.9	12.8	6.1	2.3	1.2	2.55
Ft. Worth, TX	25.3	30.4	16.7	15.1	7.6	3.0	1.9	2.80
Gainesville, FL	31.6	37.1	15.7	10.1	3.7	1.1	0.7	2.48
Grand Rapids, MI	25.9	33.9	15.5	14.0	6.9	2.6	1.3	2.61
Green Bay, WI	27.9	35.9	14.6	13.2	5.5	1.8	1.0	2.46
Greensboro, NC	29.2	34.4	16.6	12.1	4.8	1.9	1.0	2.47
Honolulu, HI	23.9	30.8	16.8	13.7	6.9	3.4	4.4	3.01
Houston, TX	24.4	29.8	16.9	15.3	8.1	3.2	2.2	2.92
Huntsville, AL	29.4	34.7	15.9	12.7	5.0	1.5	0.8	2.51
Indianapolis, IN	28.4	33.1	16.0	13.1	6.0	2.2	1.1	2.58
Jacksonville, FL	27.6	35.2	16.3	12.7	5.3	1.9	1.0	2.63
Kansas City, MO	28.6	33.9	15.5	13.0	5.8	2.1	1.2	2.54
Lafayette, LA	30.3	32.5	16.7	12.8	5.2	1.4	1.1	2.58
Las Vegas, NV	27.2	32.4	15.5	12.9	6.9	3.1	2.0	2.77
Lexington, KY	30.1	33.7	16.8	12.5	4.5	1.7	0.8	2.43
Lincoln, NE	29.0	36.8	13.6	12.2	5.3	1.9	1.2	2.41
Little Rock, AR	28.9	36.9	15.2	11.9	5.1	1.2	0.8	2.53
Los Angeles, CA	24.7	27.9	16.4	15.4	8.4	3.8	3.4	3.03
Louisville, KY	28.7	34.2	16.2	13.0	5.4	1.7	0.8	2.51
Lubbock, TX	28.0	33.0	16.2	12.8	6.1	2.4	1.5	2.57
Madison, WI	30.1	36.0	14.8	12.2	4.5	1.7	0.7	2.36

Table continued on next page.

Metro Area	Persons in Household (%)							Average Household Size
	One	Two	Three	Four	Five	Six	Seven or More	
Manchester, NH	25.1	35.2	15.9	15.3	5.9	1.7	0.9	2.56
McAllen, TX	15.4	24.1	17.3	17.1	12.8	7.6	5.7	3.61
Miami, FL	29.0	31.9	16.5	13.3	5.7	2.3	1.3	2.78
Midland, TX	24.5	32.8	17.9	13.9	7.1	2.5	1.3	2.78
Minneapolis, MN	28.0	33.6	14.9	14.1	6.0	2.1	1.3	2.54
Montgomery, AL	28.3	33.3	17.8	12.3	5.4	1.7	1.3	2.57
Nashville, TN	27.6	34.1	16.1	13.4	5.7	1.8	1.2	2.60
New Orleans, LA	30.7	32.2	16.6	11.7	5.7	2.0	1.1	2.56
New York, NY	28.0	28.9	16.8	14.8	6.9	2.7	2.0	2.74
Oklahoma City, OK	28.1	34.0	15.9	12.9	5.9	2.2	1.0	2.58
Omaha, NE	28.3	34.1	14.4	13.1	6.6	2.1	1.3	2.55
Orlando, FL	25.9	35.2	16.6	13.3	5.9	2.0	1.0	2.80
Oxnard, CA	20.8	30.6	17.4	15.5	8.5	3.7	3.4	3.07
Peoria, IL	28.8	36.4	14.3	12.2	5.3	1.9	1.1	2.44
Philadelphia, PA	29.5	31.3	16.2	13.6	6.2	2.1	1.2	2.62
Phoenix, AZ	26.6	34.6	14.4	12.8	6.4	3.0	2.2	2.74
Pittsburgh, PA	32.3	35.4	14.8	11.4	4.2	1.3	0.6	2.33
Portland, OR	27.7	34.8	15.3	13.0	5.5	2.1	1.5	2.57
Providence, RI	29.7	32.9	16.3	13.3	5.3	1.6	0.9	2.49
Provo, UT	12.4	26.2	15.9	17.2	12.7	9.0	6.7	3.62
Raleigh, NC	26.2	32.0	17.3	15.1	6.2	2.0	1.1	2.65
Reno, NV	29.0	35.4	14.2	12.4	5.2	2.2	1.6	2.57
Richmond, VA	28.0	34.2	16.4	13.8	5.1	1.6	0.9	2.59
Riverside, CA	20.0	28.0	16.2	16.0	10.3	5.2	4.3	3.30
Rochester, MN	27.6	35.2	13.9	14.7	5.9	1.8	0.8	2.51
Salem, OR	25.3	33.9	15.3	12.6	7.2	3.8	1.9	2.70
Salt Lake City, UT	22.8	29.6	16.0	14.4	8.5	4.7	3.9	3.02
San Antonio, TX	25.1	31.2	16.5	14.2	7.4	3.2	2.3	2.83
San Diego, CA	25.1	32.3	16.3	14.3	6.8	3.0	2.1	2.86
San Francisco, CA	28.7	31.4	15.9	13.9	5.8	2.5	1.8	2.67
San Jose, CA	21.7	29.2	18.5	17.3	7.7	3.0	2.7	2.94
Santa Rosa, CA	28.0	35.1	15.2	12.8	5.8	1.6	1.6	2.60
Savannah, GA	29.8	33.9	15.4	12.9	5.3	1.7	1.0	2.63
Seattle, WA	29.4	33.1	15.9	13.3	5.1	2.0	1.2	2.52
Sioux Falls, SD	27.0	36.0	14.3	13.2	5.8	2.3	1.5	2.52
Spokane, WA	28.9	35.4	14.9	11.9	5.6	2.3	1.0	2.44
Springfield, MO	27.9	37.1	15.7	12.1	4.4	1.6	1.3	2.43
Tallahassee, FL	29.4	35.0	17.0	12.2	3.6	1.7	1.0	2.46
Tampa, FL	32.0	36.0	14.4	10.9	4.2	1.5	0.9	2.48
Topeka, KS	29.4	36.1	13.6	11.9	5.1	2.2	1.7	2.44
Tulsa, OK	28.0	34.6	16.0	12.0	5.9	2.4	1.1	2.54
Virginia Beach, VA	25.9	34.5	17.7	12.9	5.8	1.8	1.3	2.62
Washington, DC	27.6	30.7	16.6	14.4	6.5	2.6	1.6	2.72
Wichita, KS	29.3	33.7	14.1	12.5	6.2	2.8	1.5	2.59
Wilmington, NC	28.2	39.5	15.7	11.0	4.1	1.1	0.4	2.37
Worcester, MA	27.0	32.1	16.7	15.5	6.0	1.9	0.8	2.60
U.S.	27.6	33.5	15.7	13.2	6.1	2.4	1.5	2.63

Note: Figures cover the Metropolitan Statistical Area (MSA)—see Appendix B for areas included
Source: U.S. Census Bureau, 2010-2012 American Community Survey 3-Year Estimates

Race: City

City	White Alone[1] (%)	Black Alone[1] (%)	Asian Alone[1] (%)	AIAN[2] Alone[1] (%)	NHOPI[3] Alone[1] (%)	Other Race Alone[1] (%)	Two or More Races (%)
Abilene, TX	80.3	10.3	1.8	0.5	0.0	4.2	2.9
Albuquerque, NM	69.3	3.3	2.4	4.2	0.1	16.4	4.2
Anchorage, AK	66.1	6.0	8.4	6.7	2.1	1.4	9.3
Ann Arbor, MI	73.9	6.7	14.3	0.2	0.0	0.8	4.1
Athens, GA	65.8	26.2	4.0	0.2	0.0	1.3	2.4
Atlanta, GA	39.3	53.4	3.6	0.2	0.0	1.5	1.9
Austin, TX	72.7	7.9	6.4	0.6	0.1	9.3	2.9
Baltimore, MD	30.1	63.4	2.4	0.3	0.0	1.5	2.3
Billings, MT	89.6	0.8	1.2	4.2	0.1	1.9	2.2
Boise City, ID	89.8	1.5	3.5	0.7	0.2	1.2	3.1
Boston, MA	53.8	25.6	9.2	0.3	0.0	6.7	4.5
Boulder, CO	88.4	1.2	4.4	0.2	0.0	2.5	3.2
Cape Coral, FL	91.2	3.5	1.6	0.5	0.0	1.7	1.4
Cedar Rapids, IA	87.5	6.2	2.0	0.3	0.0	0.9	3.0
Charleston, SC	71.0	25.5	1.3	0.1	0.1	0.4	1.5
Charlotte, NC	53.1	34.8	5.2	0.5	0.1	3.7	2.7
Chicago, IL	47.7	32.5	5.6	0.3	0.0	11.8	2.1
Cincinnati, OH	50.1	44.2	1.9	0.4	0.0	0.9	2.5
Clarksville, TN	66.6	23.0	2.4	1.1	0.4	1.8	4.7
Colorado Spgs, CO	80.6	6.4	2.9	0.6	0.3	4.5	4.8
Columbia, MO	78.8	10.8	5.3	0.2	0.1	1.2	3.7
Columbus, OH	62.1	27.7	4.4	0.2	0.0	2.1	3.5
Dallas, TX	56.5	24.4	2.9	0.3	0.0	13.8	2.0
Davenport, IA	81.4	11.0	2.1	0.4	0.0	1.2	3.8
Denver, CO	72.2	10.0	3.5	1.2	0.1	9.7	3.3
Des Moines, IA	77.9	10.5	4.9	0.5	0.1	3.1	3.1
Durham, NC	46.8	40.2	4.8	0.5	0.1	4.8	2.9
El Paso, TX	81.8	3.4	1.3	0.5	0.1	10.8	2.1
Erie, PA	75.7	16.2	2.1	0.5	0.0	1.8	3.7
Eugene, OR	86.6	1.4	4.1	0.8	0.2	1.9	4.9
Fargo, ND	90.1	2.4	2.7	1.4	0.0	0.7	2.8
Fayetteville, NC	47.1	40.7	2.8	0.8	0.4	2.9	5.2
Ft. Collins, CO	89.6	1.4	2.9	0.4	0.1	1.8	3.7
Ft. Wayne, IN	74.4	16.1	3.2	0.4	0.1	2.3	3.4
Ft. Worth, TX	66.6	18.9	3.8	0.7	0.2	7.5	2.4
Gainesville, FL	65.8	22.8	6.9	0.3	0.1	1.1	3.0
Grand Rapids, MI	69.2	21.0	2.1	0.5	0.0	2.6	4.5
Green Bay, WI	83.7	3.7	4.1	2.8	0.0	1.9	3.9
Greensboro, NC	49.8	40.5	4.2	0.4	0.1	2.6	2.5
Honolulu, HI	17.7	1.7	55.0	0.1	8.1	0.6	16.7
Houston, TX	57.5	23.3	6.1	0.4	0.0	10.9	1.7
Huntsville, AL	62.2	31.0	2.3	0.4	0.1	1.0	3.0
Indianapolis, IN	62.4	27.6	2.1	0.3	0.0	4.7	2.9
Jacksonville, FL	60.5	30.5	4.3	0.3	0.1	1.2	3.2
Kansas City, MO	59.3	29.3	2.6	0.5	0.2	4.4	3.6
Lafayette, LA	64.7	30.7	2.1	0.2	0.0	0.5	1.7
Las Vegas, NV	67.9	10.9	6.2	0.6	0.5	9.4	4.5
Lexington, KY	76.3	14.1	3.4	0.2	0.0	3.0	2.9
Lincoln, NE	87.8	4.0	4.0	0.7	0.1	0.6	2.8
Little Rock, AR	51.4	43.2	3.2	0.3	0.0	0.7	1.1
Los Angeles, CA	52.6	9.4	11.5	0.4	0.2	22.5	3.4
Louisville, KY	71.4	22.7	2.2	0.1	0.0	0.8	2.7
Lubbock, TX	77.3	8.0	2.5	0.5	0.1	8.4	3.2
Madison, WI	79.9	7.6	7.8	0.3	0.0	1.3	3.1

Table continued on next page.

City	White Alone[1] (%)	Black Alone[1] (%)	Asian Alone[1] (%)	AIAN[2] Alone[1] (%)	NHOPI[3] Alone[1] (%)	Other Race Alone[1] (%)	Two or More Races (%)
Manchester, NH	85.9	4.5	4.2	0.2	0.0	2.7	2.5
McAllen, TX	87.6	1.1	2.8	0.5	0.0	6.6	1.3
Miami, FL	74.8	19.6	0.9	0.1	0.0	3.5	1.0
Midland, TX	83.2	8.0	1.9	0.3	0.0	4.9	1.7
Minneapolis, MN	67.6	17.7	5.6	1.5	0.1	3.0	4.4
Montgomery, AL	37.9	56.8	2.3	0.3	0.0	1.2	1.4
Nashville, TN	60.9	28.5	3.1	0.2	0.0	4.9	2.5
New Orleans, LA	33.5	60.0	2.9	0.3	0.0	1.7	1.6
New York, NY	44.0	24.9	12.9	0.4	0.1	14.7	3.1
Oklahoma City, OK	66.9	14.4	3.9	3.1	0.1	4.5	7.0
Omaha, NE	75.8	13.1	2.6	0.8	0.0	4.7	3.0
Orlando, FL	58.3	29.2	3.4	0.3	0.1	6.1	2.7
Oxnard, CA	73.3	2.6	8.0	0.8	0.2	11.4	3.6
Peoria, IL	63.3	27.7	4.8	0.5	0.0	1.0	2.7
Philadelphia, PA	41.3	43.2	6.4	0.3	0.1	6.0	2.6
Phoenix, AZ	77.7	6.8	3.2	1.8	0.2	7.7	2.6
Pittsburgh, PA	66.4	25.1	4.7	0.2	0.0	0.5	3.0
Portland, OR	77.4	6.4	7.3	0.7	0.5	3.6	4.0
Providence, RI	50.4	15.3	6.5	0.9	0.2	22.5	4.3
Provo, UT	87.4	0.8	2.5	0.6	1.3	4.2	3.2
Raleigh, NC	61.0	29.8	4.2	0.3	0.0	2.9	1.9
Reno, NV	78.9	3.2	5.9	1.0	0.7	6.8	3.5
Richmond, VA	43.3	49.5	2.2	0.3	0.0	1.3	3.3
Riverside, CA	66.9	6.2	6.9	1.2	0.2	14.1	4.5
Rochester, MN	82.7	6.3	6.9	0.2	0.0	0.8	3.0
Salem, OR	79.5	1.3	3.0	1.1	1.1	9.7	4.3
Salt Lake City, UT	75.9	3.1	4.7	1.5	2.0	10.3	2.6
San Antonio, TX	75.2	6.7	2.2	0.8	0.1	12.3	2.6
San Diego, CA	63.9	6.8	16.5	0.6	0.4	7.0	4.8
San Francisco, CA	50.3	5.9	33.4	0.4	0.4	5.3	4.1
San Jose, CA	46.6	3.1	32.8	0.7	0.4	11.6	4.7
Santa Rosa, CA	78.7	2.4	5.1	1.4	0.7	8.2	3.6
Savannah, GA	40.8	54.1	2.4	0.3	0.1	0.7	1.7
Seattle, WA	69.9	7.8	14.4	0.8	0.3	1.6	5.2
Sioux Falls, SD	86.4	4.5	2.2	2.9	0.0	2.4	1.6
Spokane, WA	87.1	2.6	2.9	1.8	0.3	1.2	4.1
Springfield, MO	88.9	4.0	2.1	0.7	0.2	0.9	3.2
Tallahassee, FL	57.2	34.8	3.8	0.4	0.0	1.3	2.5
Tampa, FL	63.6	26.4	3.5	1.1	0.1	2.6	2.9
Topeka, KS	75.8	11.1	1.6	1.3	0.0	4.5	5.8
Tulsa, OK	67.0	15.3	2.4	4.3	0.1	4.2	6.6
Virginia Beach, VA	68.4	19.2	6.5	0.3	0.1	1.2	4.4
Washington, DC	39.9	50.3	3.5	0.3	0.0	3.7	2.2
Wichita, KS	74.9	10.9	5.0	1.0	0.0	3.6	4.6
Wilmington, NC	75.3	20.1	1.6	0.3	0.0	1.6	1.2
Worcester, MA	74.3	11.4	6.1	0.3	0.0	3.9	3.9
U.S.	74.0	12.6	4.9	0.8	0.2	4.7	2.8

Note: (1) Alone is defined as not being in combination with one or more other races; (2) American Indian and Alaska Native; (3) Native Hawaiian and Other Pacific Islander
Source: U.S. Census Bureau, 2010-2012 American Community Survey 3-Year Estimates

Race: Metro Area

Metro Area	White Alone[1] (%)	Black Alone[1] (%)	Asian Alone[1] (%)	AIAN[2] Alone[1] (%)	NHOPI[3] Alone[1] (%)	Other Race Alone[1] (%)	Two or More Races (%)
Abilene, TX	83.7	8.1	1.5	0.4	0.0	3.7	2.6
Albuquerque, NM	69.6	2.7	1.8	5.6	0.1	16.4	3.7
Anchorage, AK	70.7	4.8	6.7	6.5	1.7	1.2	8.6
Ann Arbor, MI	74.4	12.2	7.9	0.3	0.0	0.9	4.2
Athens, GA	73.9	19.3	3.2	0.2	0.0	1.2	2.2
Atlanta, GA	56.2	32.7	5.0	0.3	0.0	3.8	2.1
Austin, TX	77.3	7.4	4.9	0.5	0.1	7.2	2.7
Baltimore, MD	62.2	28.7	4.7	0.2	0.0	1.5	2.5
Billings, MT	90.8	0.6	0.9	3.9	0.1	1.6	2.2
Boise City, ID	91.8	0.8	1.9	0.7	0.1	1.8	2.8
Boston, MA	78.7	7.7	6.7	0.2	0.0	3.9	2.8
Boulder, CO	88.0	1.0	4.0	0.3	0.0	3.6	3.0
Cape Coral, FL	84.1	8.2	1.6	0.4	0.0	4.1	1.6
Cedar Rapids, IA	91.6	3.7	1.6	0.3	0.0	0.8	2.1
Charleston, SC	67.0	27.4	1.6	0.4	0.1	1.2	2.3
Charlotte, NC	67.1	23.9	3.3	0.4	0.1	2.8	2.3
Chicago, IL	66.6	17.2	5.8	0.3	0.0	8.1	2.1
Cincinnati, OH	83.1	12.1	2.0	0.2	0.0	0.8	1.8
Clarksville, TN	74.2	18.0	1.7	0.8	0.4	1.3	3.6
Colorado Spgs, CO	82.1	5.9	2.5	0.6	0.3	3.4	5.1
Columbia, MO	83.3	8.9	3.7	0.2	0.0	0.9	3.0
Columbus, OH	77.7	14.9	3.2	0.2	0.0	1.3	2.7
Dallas, TX	69.2	15.0	5.5	0.5	0.1	7.1	2.6
Davenport, IA	86.2	7.1	1.6	0.3	0.0	2.2	2.6
Denver, CO	81.1	5.6	3.7	0.9	0.1	5.3	3.4
Des Moines, IA	87.5	4.7	3.2	0.2	0.1	2.0	2.3
Durham, NC	62.1	26.8	4.4	0.4	0.0	3.8	2.4
El Paso, TX	80.4	3.3	1.1	0.5	0.1	12.4	2.2
Erie, PA	88.3	7.1	1.2	0.3	0.0	0.9	2.2
Eugene, OR	88.9	0.9	2.5	1.1	0.2	2.1	4.2
Fargo, ND	91.5	2.2	1.9	1.2	0.0	0.7	2.4
Fayetteville, NC	51.4	35.8	2.1	2.1	0.3	2.9	5.3
Ft. Collins, CO	90.8	0.9	1.9	0.6	0.1	2.8	2.9
Ft. Wayne, IN	82.6	10.2	2.4	0.3	0.1	1.8	2.6
Ft. Worth, TX	69.2	15.0	5.5	0.5	0.1	7.1	2.6
Gainesville, FL	71.3	19.4	5.1	0.3	0.1	1.0	2.8
Grand Rapids, MI	85.0	8.0	1.9	0.4	0.0	1.8	2.9
Green Bay, WI	90.4	1.9	2.3	2.0	0.0	1.0	2.5
Greensboro, NC	66.0	25.6	3.1	0.4	0.0	2.6	2.2
Honolulu, HI	21.1	2.2	43.7	0.2	9.6	0.9	22.3
Houston, TX	65.7	17.2	6.7	0.4	0.1	7.9	2.0
Huntsville, AL	71.6	22.0	2.1	0.7	0.1	1.2	2.5
Indianapolis, IN	77.5	14.9	2.2	0.2	0.0	2.7	2.4
Jacksonville, FL	70.8	21.6	3.5	0.3	0.1	1.0	2.8
Kansas City, MO	79.4	12.4	2.4	0.5	0.1	2.3	2.8
Lafayette, LA	69.4	26.3	1.4	0.3	0.0	0.5	2.0
Las Vegas, NV	66.6	10.5	8.8	0.6	0.7	8.4	4.4
Lexington, KY	81.8	10.8	2.4	0.2	0.0	2.5	2.3
Lincoln, NE	89.2	3.5	3.6	0.6	0.1	0.5	2.6
Little Rock, AR	73.1	22.6	1.6	0.5	0.0	0.8	1.5
Los Angeles, CA	55.7	6.8	14.9	0.4	0.3	18.2	3.7
Louisville, KY	81.4	13.7	1.6	0.1	0.0	0.9	2.2
Lubbock, TX	79.2	7.2	2.1	0.4	0.1	8.0	3.0
Madison, WI	87.1	4.7	4.3	0.3	0.0	1.2	2.4

Table continued on next page.

Metro Area	White Alone[1] (%)	Black Alone[1] (%)	Asian Alone[1] (%)	AIAN[2] Alone[1] (%)	NHOPI[3] Alone[1] (%)	Other Race Alone[1] (%)	Two or More Races (%)
Manchester, NH	91.1	2.1	3.3	0.2	0.0	1.3	2.0
McAllen, TX	90.8	0.6	1.0	0.4	0.0	6.5	0.7
Miami, FL	71.8	21.1	2.3	0.2	0.0	2.7	1.8
Midland, TX	85.1	6.7	1.6	0.4	0.0	4.7	1.5
Minneapolis, MN	81.5	7.5	5.8	0.6	0.0	1.6	2.9
Montgomery, AL	53.0	42.8	1.6	0.3	0.0	0.9	1.4
Nashville, TN	77.5	15.4	2.3	0.3	0.0	2.5	1.9
New Orleans, LA	58.4	34.3	2.8	0.4	0.1	2.2	1.7
New York, NY	59.3	17.4	10.1	0.3	0.0	10.1	2.8
Oklahoma City, OK	74.2	10.1	2.9	3.6	0.1	2.9	6.3
Omaha, NE	84.3	7.7	2.1	0.6	0.1	2.6	2.5
Orlando, FL	72.4	16.2	4.0	0.3	0.1	4.2	2.9
Oxnard, CA	76.3	1.9	6.9	0.7	0.2	10.0	4.1
Peoria, IL	86.0	9.3	1.9	0.2	0.0	0.7	1.8
Philadelphia, PA	68.5	20.8	5.1	0.2	0.1	3.1	2.3
Phoenix, AZ	80.7	5.1	3.3	2.2	0.2	5.7	2.7
Pittsburgh, PA	87.6	8.2	1.8	0.1	0.0	0.3	1.9
Portland, OR	81.9	2.9	5.9	0.8	0.5	4.2	3.8
Providence, RI	84.1	5.3	2.7	0.3	0.0	4.9	2.6
Provo, UT	91.6	0.6	1.3	0.6	0.9	2.6	2.4
Raleigh, NC	69.9	20.3	4.5	0.3	0.0	2.7	2.2
Reno, NV	81.5	2.4	5.1	1.6	0.6	5.3	3.4
Richmond, VA	63.0	30.0	3.1	0.4	0.0	1.1	2.3
Riverside, CA	64.9	7.4	6.2	1.0	0.3	16.0	4.2
Rochester, MN	88.9	3.9	4.3	0.1	0.0	0.6	2.2
Salem, OR	80.5	0.9	2.0	1.4	0.6	10.5	4.1
Salt Lake City, UT	85.6	1.6	3.2	0.8	1.4	4.8	2.6
San Antonio, TX	77.7	6.4	2.1	0.7	0.1	10.1	2.9
San Diego, CA	71.1	5.1	11.1	0.7	0.4	6.9	4.7
San Francisco, CA	55.0	8.2	23.5	0.5	0.8	7.0	5.1
San Jose, CA	51.4	2.6	31.7	0.6	0.4	9.0	4.4
Santa Rosa, CA	80.2	1.6	4.1	1.3	0.4	8.8	3.6
Savannah, GA	60.8	33.9	2.2	0.3	0.1	1.0	1.7
Seattle, WA	73.0	5.6	11.6	0.9	0.8	2.6	5.5
Sioux Falls, SD	89.9	3.2	1.6	2.1	0.0	1.7	1.5
Spokane, WA	89.1	1.9	2.4	1.4	0.3	1.2	3.7
Springfield, MO	93.2	2.1	1.1	0.5	0.1	0.5	2.4
Tallahassee, FL	61.0	32.5	2.4	0.4	0.0	1.7	2.1
Tampa, FL	79.9	11.9	2.9	0.5	0.1	2.2	2.5
Topeka, KS	84.5	6.3	1.0	1.4	0.0	2.6	4.1
Tulsa, OK	72.9	8.2	1.8	6.9	0.1	2.4	7.7
Virginia Beach, VA	60.2	31.1	3.7	0.3	0.1	1.1	3.5
Washington, DC	55.8	25.6	9.4	0.4	0.0	5.3	3.6
Wichita, KS	81.8	7.5	3.4	0.9	0.0	2.6	3.9
Wilmington, NC	81.3	13.9	0.9	0.4	0.1	1.5	1.9
Worcester, MA	85.8	4.1	4.1	0.2	0.0	3.1	2.6
U.S.	74.0	12.6	4.9	0.8	0.2	4.7	2.8

Note: (1) Figures cover the Metropolitan Statistical Area (MSA)—see Appendix B for areas included; (1) Alone is defined as not being in combination with one or more other races; (2) American Indian and Alaska Native; (3) Native Hawaiian and Other Pacific Islander
Source: U.S. Census Bureau, 2010-2012 American Community Survey 3-Year Estimates

Hispanic Origin: City

City	Hispanic or Latino (%)	Mexican (%)	Puerto Rican (%)	Cuban (%)	Other Hispanic or Latino (%)
Abilene, TX	25.1	22.4	0.5	0.1	2.1
Albuquerque, NM	47.0	24.3	0.4	0.6	21.7
Anchorage, AK	7.9	4.4	1.2	0.2	2.1
Ann Arbor, MI	4.8	2.5	0.2	0.1	2.0
Athens, GA	10.6	7.3	0.3	0.4	2.6
Atlanta, GA	5.7	3.3	0.6	0.2	1.5
Austin, TX	35.0	29.9	0.5	0.5	4.1
Baltimore, MD	4.3	1.3	0.6	0.2	2.3
Billings, MT	5.2	3.8	0.3	0.0	1.1
Boise City, ID	7.5	6.2	0.1	0.1	1.1
Boston, MA	17.7	1.1	5.0	0.4	11.2
Boulder, CO	9.1	6.3	0.2	0.4	2.1
Cape Coral, FL	18.2	1.8	5.3	5.9	5.3
Cedar Rapids, IA	3.6	2.7	0.3	0.0	0.5
Charleston, SC	3.0	1.0	1.0	0.4	0.6
Charlotte, NC	13.2	5.4	1.1	0.4	6.4
Chicago, IL	28.8	21.5	3.8	0.3	3.2
Cincinnati, OH	2.9	1.3	0.3	0.1	1.2
Clarksville, TN	9.7	5.0	2.5	0.1	2.1
Colorado Spgs, CO	16.5	11.1	1.1	0.2	4.2
Columbia, MO	3.6	1.9	0.4	0.4	0.9
Columbus, OH	5.6	3.2	0.7	0.1	1.6
Dallas, TX	42.2	37.5	0.3	0.2	4.3
Davenport, IA	7.9	7.0	0.3	0.1	0.6
Denver, CO	31.7	27.2	0.6	0.1	3.7
Des Moines, IA	11.9	9.7	0.3	0.0	1.9
Durham, NC	13.6	8.0	0.8	0.3	4.6
El Paso, TX	80.0	76.2	1.0	0.3	2.5
Erie, PA	6.7	1.4	4.3	0.1	0.9
Eugene, OR	7.8	6.4	0.3	0.0	1.2
Fargo, ND	2.8	2.0	0.2	0.1	0.5
Fayetteville, NC	10.6	4.2	3.5	0.2	2.7
Ft. Collins, CO	10.5	7.3	0.8	0.2	2.3
Ft. Wayne, IN	7.9	6.2	0.4	0.1	1.2
Ft. Worth, TX	33.9	30.6	0.7	0.2	2.5
Gainesville, FL	10.2	1.2	2.1	2.7	4.1
Grand Rapids, MI	15.6	9.8	1.7	0.3	3.8
Green Bay, WI	12.2	9.6	1.0	0.1	1.6
Greensboro, NC	7.4	4.6	0.6	0.2	2.1
Honolulu, HI	5.6	1.4	1.7	0.1	2.4
Houston, TX	43.9	33.3	0.5	0.3	9.8
Huntsville, AL	6.0	4.0	0.7	0.1	1.2
Indianapolis, IN	9.6	7.3	0.4	0.1	1.9
Jacksonville, FL	8.1	1.8	2.6	1.1	2.6
Kansas City, MO	10.0	7.7	0.4	0.4	1.5
Lafayette, LA	4.4	1.5	0.2	0.2	2.4
Las Vegas, NV	31.8	24.5	1.0	1.1	5.3
Lexington, KY	6.9	5.3	0.3	0.2	1.2
Lincoln, NE	6.4	4.7	0.2	0.1	1.4
Little Rock, AR	5.9	4.1	0.3	0.0	1.5
Los Angeles, CA	48.5	32.7	0.5	0.4	15.0
Louisville, KY	4.6	2.0	0.3	1.4	0.9
Lubbock, TX	33.0	28.5	0.2	0.0	4.3
Madison, WI	6.9	4.6	0.9	0.2	1.1
Manchester, NH	8.5	3.7	2.0	0.1	2.8

Table continued on next page.

City	Hispanic or Latino (%)	Mexican (%)	Puerto Rican (%)	Cuban (%)	Other Hispanic or Latino (%)
McAllen, TX	85.1	80.8	0.3	0.2	3.8
Miami, FL	70.4	2.0	2.9	35.0	30.5
Midland, TX	39.6	37.7	0.0	0.1	1.7
Minneapolis, MN	10.0	6.6	0.5	0.1	2.7
Montgomery, AL	3.7	2.3	0.4	0.1	1.0
Nashville, TN	10.1	6.3	0.5	0.3	2.9
New Orleans, LA	5.3	1.6	0.2	0.4	3.1
New York, NY	28.8	3.9	9.0	0.5	15.4
Oklahoma City, OK	17.7	15.1	0.3	0.1	2.2
Omaha, NE	13.4	10.8	0.4	0.0	2.2
Orlando, FL	26.7	2.9	13.3	1.8	8.7
Oxnard, CA	73.5	69.9	0.4	0.1	3.1
Peoria, IL	5.3	4.5	0.2	0.1	0.6
Philadelphia, PA	12.7	0.9	8.5	0.3	3.0
Phoenix, AZ	39.9	37.0	0.4	0.3	2.2
Pittsburgh, PA	2.6	0.9	0.6	0.2	0.9
Portland, OR	9.9	7.5	0.4	0.3	1.7
Providence, RI	40.2	2.1	8.3	0.4	29.4
Provo, UT	17.2	11.2	0.3	0.2	5.5
Raleigh, NC	11.3	5.2	1.2	0.3	4.6
Reno, NV	25.4	20.3	0.8	0.1	4.2
Richmond, VA	6.3	2.1	0.5	0.1	3.6
Riverside, CA	51.0	45.7	0.5	0.3	4.4
Rochester, MN	5.3	4.2	0.1	0.2	0.8
Salem, OR	20.6	19.0	0.1	0.1	1.5
Salt Lake City, UT	20.9	16.8	0.3	0.0	3.8
San Antonio, TX	63.3	57.4	1.1	0.2	4.6
San Diego, CA	29.5	26.2	0.6	0.2	2.5
San Francisco, CA	15.3	7.4	0.5	0.2	7.1
San Jose, CA	33.3	28.7	0.5	0.2	3.9
Santa Rosa, CA	28.7	24.4	0.5	0.1	3.8
Savannah, GA	5.2	3.1	0.8	0.1	1.3
Seattle, WA	6.5	4.2	0.4	0.2	1.8
Sioux Falls, SD	4.8	2.4	0.1	0.0	2.3
Spokane, WA	5.3	3.8	0.3	0.2	1.1
Springfield, MO	3.9	2.7	0.4	0.0	0.9
Tallahassee, FL	6.4	1.5	1.5	1.2	2.3
Tampa, FL	22.7	2.5	7.2	6.7	6.3
Topeka, KS	13.9	12.3	0.5	0.0	1.0
Tulsa, OK	14.5	12.3	0.4	0.1	1.6
Virginia Beach, VA	6.9	2.1	2.4	0.2	2.3
Washington, DC	9.5	1.5	0.6	0.3	7.2
Wichita, KS	15.5	13.7	0.5	0.1	1.2
Wilmington, NC	5.1	3.2	0.7	0.1	1.1
Worcester, MA	19.9	0.7	12.3	0.1	6.7
U.S.	16.6	10.7	1.6	0.6	3.7

Note: Persons of Hispanic or Latino origin can be of any race
Source: U.S. Census Bureau, 2010-2012 American Community Survey 3-Year Estimates

Hispanic Origin: Metro Area

Metro Area	Hispanic or Latino (%)	Mexican (%)	Puerto Rican (%)	Cuban (%)	Other Hispanic or Latino (%)
Abilene, TX	21.7	19.3	0.4	0.1	1.9
Albuquerque, NM	47.1	23.8	0.4	0.4	22.5
Anchorage, AK	6.9	4.0	1.0	0.2	1.8
Ann Arbor, MI	4.2	2.2	0.4	0.1	1.5
Athens, GA	8.1	5.5	0.4	0.3	2.0
Atlanta, GA	10.5	6.0	0.9	0.4	3.2
Austin, TX	31.7	26.5	0.5	0.4	4.3
Baltimore, MD	4.8	1.3	0.7	0.1	2.6
Billings, MT	4.7	3.6	0.3	0.0	0.8
Boise City, ID	12.7	10.8	0.4	0.1	1.5
Boston, MA	9.3	0.6	2.6	0.2	5.8
Boulder, CO	13.5	10.3	0.3	0.3	2.6
Cape Coral, FL	18.6	5.8	4.3	3.8	4.8
Cedar Rapids, IA	2.5	1.7	0.2	0.0	0.6
Charleston, SC	5.4	3.1	0.8	0.2	1.3
Charlotte, NC	10.0	4.8	0.9	0.3	4.1
Chicago, IL	21.0	16.7	2.1	0.2	2.0
Cincinnati, OH	2.7	1.4	0.3	0.1	0.9
Clarksville, TN	7.2	3.9	1.7	0.0	1.5
Colorado Spgs, CO	15.0	9.6	1.1	0.2	4.1
Columbia, MO	3.0	1.6	0.3	0.3	0.8
Columbus, OH	3.7	2.1	0.5	0.1	1.0
Dallas, TX	27.8	23.8	0.5	0.2	3.3
Davenport, IA	7.9	7.0	0.4	0.1	0.4
Denver, CO	22.7	18.2	0.5	0.1	3.8
Des Moines, IA	6.8	5.3	0.2	0.1	1.3
Durham, NC	11.3	7.0	0.7	0.2	3.4
El Paso, TX	81.7	78.1	0.9	0.2	2.4
Erie, PA	3.5	0.9	1.9	0.1	0.6
Eugene, OR	7.6	6.4	0.3	0.0	1.0
Fargo, ND	2.6	1.9	0.1	0.0	0.4
Fayetteville, NC	10.2	4.1	3.4	0.3	2.4
Ft. Collins, CO	10.7	7.6	0.5	0.1	2.5
Ft. Wayne, IN	6.0	4.7	0.4	0.1	0.8
Ft. Worth, TX	27.8	23.8	0.5	0.2	3.3
Gainesville, FL	8.4	1.3	2.0	2.0	3.2
Grand Rapids, MI	8.6	5.7	0.9	0.2	1.8
Green Bay, WI	6.4	4.7	0.4	0.1	1.1
Greensboro, NC	7.7	5.4	0.7	0.2	1.4
Honolulu, HI	8.5	2.4	2.9	0.1	3.1
Houston, TX	35.7	27.7	0.5	0.3	7.1
Huntsville, AL	4.9	3.4	0.6	0.1	0.8
Indianapolis, IN	6.3	4.6	0.3	0.1	1.3
Jacksonville, FL	7.2	1.6	2.3	0.9	2.3
Kansas City, MO	8.3	6.4	0.3	0.2	1.4
Lafayette, LA	3.7	1.7	0.1	0.1	1.7
Las Vegas, NV	29.5	22.5	1.0	1.1	4.9
Lexington, KY	5.9	4.6	0.3	0.1	0.9
Lincoln, NE	5.8	4.3	0.2	0.1	1.2
Little Rock, AR	4.9	3.7	0.2	0.0	1.0
Los Angeles, CA	44.7	34.9	0.5	0.4	8.9
Louisville, KY	4.1	2.2	0.3	0.7	0.8
Lubbock, TX	33.0	28.8	0.2	0.0	4.0
Madison, WI	5.5	3.9	0.6	0.1	0.9
Manchester, NH	5.5	1.9	1.5	0.1	2.0

Table continued on next page.

Metro Area	Hispanic or Latino (%)	Mexican (%)	Puerto Rican (%)	Cuban (%)	Other Hispanic or Latino (%)
McAllen, TX	90.8	88.4	0.2	0.1	2.0
Miami, FL	41.9	2.4	3.7	18.1	17.7
Midland, TX	38.8	36.8	0.1	0.1	1.8
Minneapolis, MN	5.5	3.8	0.3	0.1	1.3
Montgomery, AL	3.1	2.0	0.3	0.1	0.7
Nashville, TN	6.7	4.2	0.5	0.2	1.8
New Orleans, LA	8.1	2.0	0.5	0.5	5.0
New York, NY	23.3	3.0	6.4	0.7	13.1
Oklahoma City, OK	11.7	9.8	0.3	0.1	1.5
Omaha, NE	9.2	7.3	0.3	0.0	1.5
Orlando, FL	26.1	3.2	13.1	2.0	7.7
Oxnard, CA	40.8	36.2	0.5	0.2	4.0
Peoria, IL	2.9	2.3	0.2	0.0	0.4
Philadelphia, PA	8.1	1.7	4.2	0.2	2.0
Phoenix, AZ	29.7	26.8	0.5	0.2	2.2
Pittsburgh, PA	1.4	0.5	0.4	0.1	0.4
Portland, OR	11.0	8.9	0.3	0.2	1.7
Providence, RI	10.6	0.8	3.4	0.1	6.2
Provo, UT	10.8	7.1	0.2	0.1	3.4
Raleigh, NC	10.3	6.0	1.0	0.3	3.0
Reno, NV	22.5	18.2	0.5	0.2	3.6
Richmond, VA	5.1	1.7	0.8	0.1	2.5
Riverside, CA	47.9	42.3	0.6	0.3	4.6
Rochester, MN	4.2	3.2	0.2	0.1	0.6
Salem, OR	22.3	20.3	0.2	0.0	1.7
Salt Lake City, UT	16.9	12.8	0.3	0.1	3.6
San Antonio, TX	54.3	48.9	1.0	0.2	4.2
San Diego, CA	32.4	29.1	0.7	0.2	2.5
San Francisco, CA	21.8	14.8	0.6	0.2	6.2
San Jose, CA	27.8	23.5	0.4	0.1	3.7
Santa Rosa, CA	25.2	21.2	0.4	0.2	3.4
Savannah, GA	5.2	3.0	1.0	0.1	1.2
Seattle, WA	9.2	6.8	0.5	0.1	1.8
Sioux Falls, SD	3.5	1.8	0.1	0.0	1.7
Spokane, WA	4.7	3.4	0.3	0.1	0.9
Springfield, MO	2.8	1.9	0.2	0.0	0.7
Tallahassee, FL	6.1	2.1	1.2	1.1	1.7
Tampa, FL	16.7	3.5	5.3	3.3	4.5
Topeka, KS	9.1	7.9	0.4	0.0	0.7
Tulsa, OK	8.6	7.1	0.3	0.1	1.1
Virginia Beach, VA	5.6	1.8	1.7	0.2	1.9
Washington, DC	14.2	2.2	0.9	0.3	10.8
Wichita, KS	11.8	10.4	0.4	0.1	0.9
Wilmington, NC	5.4	3.6	0.6	0.1	1.1
Worcester, MA	9.7	0.6	5.3	0.1	3.7
U.S.	16.6	10.7	1.6	0.6	3.7

Note: Persons of Hispanic or Latino origin can be of any race; Figures cover the Metropolitan Statistical Area (MSA)—see Appendix B for areas included

Source: U.S. Census Bureau, 2010-2012 American Community Survey 3-Year Estimates

Age: City

City	Percent of Population							
	Under Age 5	Age 5–19	Age 20–34	Age 35–44	Age 45–54	Age 55–64	Age 65–74	Age 75–84
Abilene, TX	7.4	19.1	27.4	11.2	12.3	10.2	6.4	4.2
Albuquerque, NM	6.9	19.6	23.0	12.8	13.7	11.7	6.7	4.0
Anchorage, AK	7.5	20.8	24.5	13.1	14.7	11.6	4.8	2.3
Ann Arbor, MI	4.1	19.3	38.0	9.8	9.3	9.6	5.3	3.2
Athens, GA	5.9	20.8	37.9	10.2	8.7	7.8	4.9	2.8
Atlanta, GA	6.4	16.4	30.4	15.0	12.2	9.8	5.5	2.8
Austin, TX	7.1	18.3	31.4	15.1	11.9	9.0	4.0	2.2
Baltimore, MD	6.7	18.0	26.2	12.1	13.8	11.4	6.3	3.8
Billings, MT	7.0	18.6	21.5	11.8	13.3	13.0	7.4	4.9
Boise City, ID	6.3	18.2	23.8	13.4	14.1	12.2	6.7	3.4
Boston, MA	5.3	16.8	34.7	12.3	11.3	9.2	5.4	3.3
Boulder, CO	4.2	19.4	35.9	11.4	10.4	9.5	4.9	2.7
Cape Coral, FL	5.9	19.9	14.6	13.1	14.5	14.0	10.4	5.2
Cedar Rapids, IA	7.1	19.5	23.2	12.6	12.9	11.8	6.1	4.6
Charleston, SC	5.7	16.1	30.7	12.3	11.8	11.2	6.9	3.8
Charlotte, NC	7.6	20.1	24.8	15.5	13.3	9.9	4.9	2.7
Chicago, IL	7.0	18.7	27.2	14.1	12.5	10.1	5.7	3.3
Cincinnati, OH	7.2	19.0	27.4	11.3	13.1	11.1	5.8	3.5
Clarksville, TN	9.2	21.8	29.9	13.1	11.0	7.7	4.3	2.2
Colorado Spgs, CO	7.1	20.3	23.0	12.7	14.4	11.4	6.1	3.4
Columbia, MO	6.2	20.6	36.1	9.9	10.1	8.3	4.5	2.9
Columbus, OH	7.7	18.8	29.2	13.6	12.2	9.8	4.9	2.7
Dallas, TX	8.3	20.4	26.4	13.9	12.5	9.4	5.1	2.8
Davenport, IA	6.9	20.1	23.0	12.3	12.8	12.4	6.4	3.9
Denver, CO	7.3	16.6	28.4	15.1	11.8	10.5	5.5	3.2
Des Moines, IA	8.0	20.0	24.3	13.0	13.2	10.5	5.7	3.4
Durham, NC	7.7	18.9	28.1	13.9	12.0	10.1	5.1	2.7
El Paso, TX	7.8	23.9	21.6	12.7	12.8	10.0	6.0	3.9
Erie, PA	7.1	20.5	23.7	11.7	12.8	11.1	6.2	4.4
Eugene, OR	4.8	17.9	28.6	11.7	11.5	12.2	6.9	4.2
Fargo, ND	6.1	17.5	33.1	11.2	11.6	10.4	4.7	3.9
Fayetteville, NC	8.6	19.9	28.3	11.6	11.9	9.5	5.7	3.3
Ft. Collins, CO	6.0	19.8	32.7	11.5	11.5	9.8	4.7	2.5
Ft. Wayne, IN	7.7	21.6	21.0	12.5	13.2	11.5	6.2	4.2
Ft. Worth, TX	8.9	23.1	23.3	14.6	12.7	9.1	4.6	2.6
Gainesville, FL	4.3	18.1	44.0	8.1	7.9	9.2	3.9	3.1
Grand Rapids, MI	7.7	21.1	27.7	11.7	11.2	9.4	4.8	3.9
Green Bay, WI	7.6	20.1	24.1	12.1	13.4	10.9	5.5	3.9
Greensboro, NC	6.5	19.8	24.9	13.0	12.7	11.2	6.0	4.3
Honolulu, HI	5.2	14.8	22.9	12.3	13.7	13.1	8.2	6.2
Houston, TX	7.9	20.5	25.7	14.0	12.8	9.8	5.2	2.8
Huntsville, AL	6.1	18.8	23.0	12.1	14.9	11.1	7.6	4.4
Indianapolis, IN	7.6	20.1	23.9	13.0	13.7	10.9	5.6	3.4
Jacksonville, FL	7.0	19.3	23.0	13.3	14.4	11.7	6.4	3.4
Kansas City, MO	7.3	19.2	23.4	13.4	13.9	11.6	6.0	3.6
Lafayette, LA	5.3	19.9	25.6	12.3	13.9	10.5	6.8	4.0
Las Vegas, NV	7.0	20.4	20.5	14.3	13.7	11.1	7.5	4.1
Lexington, KY	6.4	18.3	27.1	13.3	13.1	11.2	5.9	3.4
Lincoln, NE	7.1	19.7	27.4	11.9	12.1	10.9	5.6	3.6
Little Rock, AR	7.4	19.2	23.3	13.0	13.0	12.3	6.3	3.7
Los Angeles, CA	6.6	19.1	25.3	14.8	13.3	10.2	5.7	3.4
Louisville, KY	6.8	19.3	21.1	12.8	14.6	12.6	6.7	4.2
Lubbock, TX	7.4	21.1	29.0	10.6	11.4	9.6	5.9	3.9
Madison, WI	6.0	17.1	34.6	11.7	11.1	10.0	4.9	3.1

Table continued on next page.

City	Percent of Population							
	Under Age 5	Age 5–19	Age 20–34	Age 35–44	Age 45–54	Age 55–64	Age 65–74	Age 75–84
Manchester, NH	6.3	17.7	23.5	14.5	14.2	11.7	6.7	3.3
McAllen, TX	7.7	23.8	21.3	13.7	13.0	9.8	6.2	3.1
Miami, FL	6.1	14.8	22.9	15.0	14.2	11.4	7.6	5.7
Midland, TX	8.2	21.8	23.6	11.6	12.6	10.9	5.5	4.3
Minneapolis, MN	7.0	17.1	32.0	13.3	12.1	10.1	4.6	2.5
Montgomery, AL	7.3	21.3	23.0	12.6	12.9	11.1	6.5	3.9
Nashville, TN	7.1	17.6	27.2	13.7	13.2	10.9	5.7	3.3
New Orleans, LA	6.6	17.8	26.0	12.3	13.7	12.5	6.3	3.3
New York, NY	6.4	17.6	25.0	14.0	13.4	11.1	6.7	3.9
Oklahoma City, OK	8.0	19.6	24.1	12.6	13.0	11.4	6.1	3.6
Omaha, NE	7.5	20.5	23.9	12.0	13.4	11.3	5.8	3.7
Orlando, FL	7.3	16.9	29.7	14.9	12.9	8.7	5.1	3.1
Oxnard, CA	8.7	23.5	24.6	13.4	12.3	8.9	4.7	2.7
Peoria, IL	7.1	21.3	23.4	11.8	12.1	11.2	6.6	4.4
Philadelphia, PA	6.8	19.1	26.1	12.2	12.7	10.9	6.3	4.0
Phoenix, AZ	7.9	22.7	22.9	14.5	13.3	10.0	5.1	2.6
Pittsburgh, PA	5.0	16.7	30.7	10.1	11.8	11.6	6.8	4.5
Portland, OR	6.0	15.3	26.8	16.2	12.9	12.0	5.8	3.1
Providence, RI	6.1	23.3	30.5	11.8	11.0	8.8	4.3	2.6
Provo, UT	8.6	22.8	44.7	7.0	5.9	5.1	2.9	1.8
Raleigh, NC	7.2	19.9	27.9	15.3	12.3	9.0	4.7	2.6
Reno, NV	6.9	19.5	24.9	12.5	13.0	11.2	6.8	3.6
Richmond, VA	6.5	17.1	30.2	11.5	12.3	11.3	5.8	3.5
Riverside, CA	7.2	23.7	25.2	12.6	13.0	8.9	5.1	2.8
Rochester, MN	7.4	19.3	23.0	12.5	13.8	10.8	6.6	4.3
Salem, OR	7.7	19.9	22.6	12.2	13.2	11.6	7.1	3.8
Salt Lake City, UT	7.7	18.1	31.2	13.4	10.7	9.4	5.0	3.0
San Antonio, TX	7.4	22.2	23.4	13.0	13.1	10.2	5.9	3.4
San Diego, CA	6.3	18.3	27.0	13.9	13.2	10.2	5.8	3.5
San Francisco, CA	4.4	11.0	28.4	16.5	13.7	12.2	6.9	4.7
San Jose, CA	7.1	19.6	22.3	15.5	14.5	10.5	5.9	3.3
Santa Rosa, CA	6.6	19.9	20.8	12.8	14.3	12.4	6.5	4.3
Savannah, GA	7.1	19.7	28.2	10.8	12.0	10.4	6.1	3.5
Seattle, WA	5.3	13.1	29.8	15.9	13.0	11.8	6.0	3.2
Sioux Falls, SD	8.4	18.4	24.8	12.5	13.2	11.4	5.7	3.9
Spokane, WA	7.1	18.1	24.3	12.3	12.8	11.8	6.7	4.8
Springfield, MO	6.2	16.8	29.6	10.8	11.9	10.3	6.8	4.8
Tallahassee, FL	5.1	20.5	38.4	10.0	9.6	8.3	4.2	2.5
Tampa, FL	6.4	19.7	24.5	13.7	14.3	10.5	5.8	3.7
Topeka, KS	7.5	20.0	21.9	11.5	13.0	12.0	6.8	5.1
Tulsa, OK	7.3	20.0	22.9	12.2	13.3	11.7	6.5	4.1
Virginia Beach, VA	6.6	19.6	24.0	13.3	14.5	11.1	6.1	3.5
Washington, DC	5.8	15.0	31.4	13.4	12.3	10.7	6.2	3.5
Wichita, KS	8.1	20.8	22.1	12.4	13.5	11.5	6.2	3.7
Wilmington, NC	5.4	18.0	27.6	11.1	12.7	11.6	7.4	4.3
Worcester, MA	7.0	19.6	25.4	12.3	12.8	10.5	6.1	3.8
U.S.	6.4	20.1	20.5	13.1	14.3	12.2	7.3	4.2

Source: U.S. Census Bureau, 2010-2012 American Community Survey 3-Year Estimates

Age: Metro Area

Metro Area	Percent of Population							
	Under Age 5	Age 5–19	Age 20–34	Age 35–44	Age 45–54	Age 55–64	Age 65–74	Age 75–84
Abilene, TX	6.9	19.9	23.6	11.5	13.0	11.3	7.4	4.7
Albuquerque, NM	6.7	20.3	21.0	12.6	14.1	12.5	7.3	3.9
Anchorage, AK	7.5	21.4	23.2	13.2	14.9	11.8	5.0	2.3
Ann Arbor, MI	5.4	20.3	26.3	12.4	13.4	11.6	6.1	3.0
Athens, GA	6.0	21.1	29.3	11.4	11.6	10.1	6.2	3.0
Atlanta, GA	7.0	21.9	20.9	15.5	14.6	10.8	5.7	2.7
Austin, TX	7.3	20.8	25.3	15.2	13.1	10.0	5.0	2.5
Baltimore, MD	6.2	19.4	20.8	13.0	15.3	12.4	7.0	4.1
Billings, MT	6.5	19.1	19.4	12.0	14.6	13.6	7.8	4.7
Boise City, ID	7.4	22.7	20.6	13.5	13.3	11.2	6.5	3.3
Boston, MA	5.6	18.8	21.1	13.5	15.3	12.3	7.0	4.3
Boulder, CO	5.4	19.9	23.7	13.6	14.5	12.3	6.1	3.0
Cape Coral, FL	5.2	16.3	16.0	11.2	13.0	14.1	13.6	7.5
Cedar Rapids, IA	6.4	20.6	19.7	12.9	14.5	12.1	7.2	4.7
Charleston, SC	6.8	19.1	23.2	13.0	13.8	12.0	7.2	3.4
Charlotte, NC	7.0	21.3	20.8	15.5	14.3	10.9	6.0	3.1
Chicago, IL	6.6	20.9	21.0	13.8	14.4	11.5	6.4	3.6
Cincinnati, OH	6.7	20.8	19.7	13.1	15.0	12.3	6.8	3.9
Clarksville, TN	8.6	21.3	26.3	12.8	12.0	9.4	5.6	3.0
Colorado Spgs, CO	7.0	21.4	22.2	12.8	14.6	11.5	6.1	3.2
Columbia, MO	6.1	20.4	30.1	11.0	12.2	10.3	5.3	3.1
Columbus, OH	6.8	20.4	22.2	14.0	14.2	11.4	6.1	3.4
Dallas, TX	7.6	22.6	21.6	14.8	14.1	10.2	5.4	2.7
Davenport, IA	6.4	19.6	18.7	12.1	14.3	13.3	8.2	4.9
Denver, CO	6.9	20.0	21.7	14.7	14.4	11.7	6.0	3.1
Des Moines, IA	7.5	20.8	21.4	13.8	13.8	11.3	6.2	3.6
Durham, NC	6.4	19.2	23.8	13.5	13.4	11.8	6.7	3.5
El Paso, TX	8.1	25.0	21.7	13.0	12.4	9.5	5.6	3.5
Erie, PA	5.9	20.2	19.9	11.8	14.4	13.2	7.5	4.9
Eugene, OR	5.1	18.0	22.4	11.4	13.2	14.4	8.5	5.0
Fargo, ND	6.8	19.6	28.2	11.9	12.3	10.6	5.3	3.7
Fayetteville, NC	8.6	21.5	25.5	12.5	12.6	9.9	5.5	2.8
Ft. Collins, CO	5.7	19.1	24.4	12.1	13.7	12.8	7.0	3.7
Ft. Wayne, IN	7.2	21.9	19.5	12.7	14.0	12.2	6.7	4.1
Ft. Worth, TX	7.6	22.6	21.6	14.8	14.1	10.2	5.4	2.7
Gainesville, FL	5.3	18.4	31.2	10.3	11.7	11.5	6.3	3.6
Grand Rapids, MI	7.0	21.4	20.9	12.6	14.5	11.8	6.4	3.8
Green Bay, WI	6.6	20.5	19.5	12.9	15.4	12.4	6.8	4.1
Greensboro, NC	6.1	20.2	19.8	13.6	14.4	12.4	7.5	4.5
Honolulu, HI	6.4	18.0	22.4	12.9	13.4	12.1	7.5	4.8
Houston, TX	7.8	22.6	21.9	14.4	13.8	10.6	5.3	2.6
Huntsville, AL	6.2	19.9	20.3	13.3	15.9	11.9	7.2	3.8
Indianapolis, IN	7.2	21.5	20.5	13.8	14.6	11.3	6.2	3.5
Jacksonville, FL	6.4	19.8	20.5	13.3	14.9	12.6	7.3	3.8
Kansas City, MO	7.0	20.7	20.0	13.3	14.7	12.0	6.7	3.8
Lafayette, LA	7.2	20.3	23.7	12.6	14.1	11.3	6.1	3.4
Las Vegas, NV	7.0	20.2	21.6	14.5	13.5	11.3	7.3	3.4
Lexington, KY	6.5	19.3	23.8	13.6	13.8	11.7	6.4	3.6
Lincoln, NE	6.9	20.2	25.5	11.9	12.7	11.4	5.9	3.7
Little Rock, AR	6.8	20.1	21.9	13.1	13.7	11.9	7.1	4.0
Los Angeles, CA	6.5	20.6	22.5	14.3	14.0	10.8	6.1	3.6
Louisville, KY	6.4	19.8	19.6	13.3	15.0	12.8	7.3	4.2
Lubbock, TX	7.1	21.6	26.9	11.0	11.9	10.1	6.1	3.8
Madison, WI	6.1	18.8	24.6	13.0	14.2	12.1	6.1	3.6

Table continued on next page.

Metro Area	Percent of Population							
	Under Age 5	Age 5–19	Age 20–34	Age 35–44	Age 45–54	Age 55–64	Age 65–74	Age 75–84
Manchester, NH	5.8	19.8	18.3	14.0	16.9	12.8	6.8	3.8
McAllen, TX	9.6	28.2	21.2	13.2	10.4	7.9	5.3	3.2
Miami, FL	5.7	18.0	19.4	13.9	14.9	11.8	8.1	5.5
Midland, TX	8.2	22.1	22.3	12.0	13.5	11.1	5.5	4.0
Minneapolis, MN	6.8	20.4	21.1	13.6	15.2	11.7	6.0	3.4
Montgomery, AL	6.8	20.9	21.3	13.2	14.0	11.6	7.0	3.9
Nashville, TN	6.8	20.1	21.8	14.2	14.5	11.6	6.4	3.3
New Orleans, LA	6.6	19.1	21.6	12.6	14.7	12.8	7.0	3.8
New York, NY	6.2	19.0	21.2	13.8	14.7	11.8	7.0	4.3
Oklahoma City, OK	7.2	20.4	22.7	12.5	13.5	11.5	6.7	3.8
Omaha, NE	7.6	21.2	21.6	12.9	14.0	11.5	6.1	3.5
Orlando, FL	6.0	20.0	22.0	13.8	14.3	11.2	7.1	4.0
Oxnard, CA	6.6	21.6	19.9	13.2	14.8	11.7	6.6	3.8
Peoria, IL	6.5	19.9	19.1	12.2	14.1	13.0	7.8	5.1
Philadelphia, PA	6.1	19.9	20.3	12.9	15.1	12.2	7.0	4.4
Phoenix, AZ	7.2	21.6	21.2	13.6	13.0	10.8	7.2	4.0
Pittsburgh, PA	5.1	17.5	18.4	12.0	15.4	14.3	8.5	6.0
Portland, OR	6.4	19.4	21.4	14.5	14.0	12.6	6.6	3.4
Providence, RI	5.4	19.2	19.6	13.0	15.4	12.7	7.4	4.7
Provo, UT	10.9	28.4	27.9	11.3	8.4	6.4	3.8	2.1
Raleigh, NC	7.0	21.6	21.1	15.9	14.5	10.5	5.6	2.7
Reno, NV	6.5	19.4	21.2	13.0	14.2	13.1	7.7	3.6
Richmond, VA	6.1	19.7	20.1	13.6	15.1	12.8	7.1	3.7
Riverside, CA	7.5	24.1	21.2	13.2	13.4	10.1	6.0	3.4
Rochester, MN	7.1	20.3	19.8	12.4	15.1	11.8	7.2	4.3
Salem, OR	7.1	21.7	20.5	12.3	12.6	12.1	7.4	4.2
Salt Lake City, UT	8.6	23.3	24.4	13.4	11.9	9.7	5.0	2.7
San Antonio, TX	7.2	22.3	21.5	13.3	13.5	11.0	6.3	3.5
San Diego, CA	6.6	19.6	24.1	13.4	13.7	11.0	6.1	3.7
San Francisco, CA	5.9	17.4	21.5	14.9	14.8	12.4	7.0	4.0
San Jose, CA	6.9	19.6	21.4	15.4	14.7	10.7	6.2	3.6
Santa Rosa, CA	5.8	18.8	19.4	12.3	14.8	14.5	7.9	4.3
Savannah, GA	6.9	20.2	23.6	12.8	13.2	11.4	6.8	3.6
Seattle, WA	6.4	18.6	22.2	14.6	14.9	12.1	6.2	3.3
Sioux Falls, SD	7.8	20.5	22.0	13.0	14.0	11.3	5.8	3.8
Spokane, WA	6.3	19.6	21.6	12.1	14.0	12.9	7.2	4.3
Springfield, MO	6.4	19.7	22.1	12.1	13.5	11.8	7.7	4.6
Tallahassee, FL	5.5	19.7	27.9	11.7	12.6	11.8	6.2	3.1
Tampa, FL	5.6	17.7	18.5	12.8	14.8	13.1	9.2	5.8
Topeka, KS	6.7	20.4	18.0	11.6	14.6	13.5	8.0	5.0
Tulsa, OK	7.0	21.0	19.9	12.8	14.0	12.1	7.4	4.1
Virginia Beach, VA	6.5	19.9	23.3	12.5	14.6	11.4	6.7	3.8
Washington, DC	6.7	19.5	22.1	14.8	15.1	11.5	6.0	3.0
Wichita, KS	7.6	21.9	20.3	12.1	14.0	11.8	6.4	4.0
Wilmington, NC	5.4	17.3	19.8	12.5	13.6	14.6	10.4	5.0
Worcester, MA	5.8	20.4	18.5	13.7	16.2	12.5	6.7	4.1
U.S.	6.4	20.1	20.5	13.1	14.3	12.2	7.3	4.2

Note: Figures cover the Metropolitan Statistical Area (MSA)—see Appendix B for areas included
Source: U.S. Census Bureau, 2010-2012 American Community Survey 3-Year Estimates

Segregation

Area	Black/White		Asian/White		Hispanic/White	
	Index[1]	Rank[2]	Index[1]	Rank[2]	Index[1]	Rank[2]
Abilene, TX	n/a	n/a	n/a	n/a	n/a	n/a
Albuquerque, NM	30.9	99	28.5	93	36.4	79
Anchorage, AK	n/a	n/a	n/a	n/a	n/a	n/a
Ann Arbor, MI	n/a	n/a	n/a	n/a	n/a	n/a
Athens, GA	n/a	n/a	n/a	n/a	n/a	n/a
Atlanta, GA	59.0	41	48.5	10	49.5	27
Austin, TX	50.1	70	41.2	49	43.2	51
Baltimore, MD	65.4	19	43.6	33	39.8	67
Billings, MT	n/a	n/a	n/a	n/a	n/a	n/a
Boise City, ID	30.2	101	27.6	95	36.2	80
Boston, MA	64.0	27	45.4	23	59.6	5
Boulder, CO	n/a	n/a	n/a	n/a	n/a	n/a
Cape Coral, FL	61.6	35	25.3	96	40.2	63
Cedar Rapids, IA	n/a	n/a	n/a	n/a	n/a	n/a
Charleston, SC	41.5	88	33.4	84	39.8	66
Charlotte, NC	53.8	56	43.6	34	47.6	35
Chicago, IL	76.4	3	44.9	26	56.3	10
Cincinnati, OH	69.4	8	46.0	21	36.9	77
Clarksville, TN	n/a	n/a	n/a	n/a	n/a	n/a
Colorado Spgs, CO	39.3	92	24.1	98	30.3	95
Columbia, MO	n/a	n/a	n/a	n/a	n/a	n/a
Columbus, OH	62.2	33	43.3	35	41.5	59
Dallas, TX	56.6	48	46.6	19	50.3	24
Davenport, IA	n/a	n/a	n/a	n/a	n/a	n/a
Denver, CO	62.6	31	33.4	83	48.8	31
Des Moines, IA	51.6	66	35.5	76	46.7	40
Durham, NC	48.1	75	44.0	30	48.0	33
El Paso, TX	30.7	100	22.2	100	43.3	50
Erie, PA	n/a	n/a	n/a	n/a	n/a	n/a
Eugene, OR	n/a	n/a	n/a	n/a	n/a	n/a
Fargo, ND	n/a	n/a	n/a	n/a	n/a	n/a
Fayetteville, NC	n/a	n/a	n/a	n/a	n/a	n/a
Ft. Collins, CO	n/a	n/a	n/a	n/a	n/a	n/a
Ft. Wayne, IN	n/a	n/a	n/a	n/a	n/a	n/a
Ft. Worth, TX	56.6	48	46.6	19	50.3	24
Gainesville, FL	n/a	n/a	n/a	n/a	n/a	n/a
Grand Rapids, MI	64.3	26	43.2	37	50.4	23
Green Bay, WI	n/a	n/a	n/a	n/a	n/a	n/a
Greensboro, NC	54.7	53	47.7	14	41.1	61
Honolulu, HI	36.9	95	42.1	44	31.9	91
Houston, TX	61.4	36	50.4	7	52.5	18
Huntsville, AL	n/a	n/a	n/a	n/a	n/a	n/a
Indianapolis, IN	66.4	15	41.6	47	47.3	37
Jacksonville, FL	53.1	59	37.5	71	27.6	98
Kansas City, MO	61.2	39	38.4	65	44.4	48
Lafayette, LA	n/a	n/a	n/a	n/a	n/a	n/a
Las Vegas, NV	37.6	94	28.8	92	42.0	58
Lexington, KY	n/a	n/a	n/a	n/a	n/a	n/a
Lincoln, NE	n/a	n/a	n/a	n/a	n/a	n/a
Little Rock, AR	58.8	42	39.7	59	39.7	68
Los Angeles, CA	67.8	10	48.4	12	62.2	2
Louisville, KY	58.1	43	42.2	43	38.7	73
Lubbock, TX	n/a	n/a	n/a	n/a	n/a	n/a
Madison, WI	49.6	71	44.2	29	40.1	65
Manchester, NH	n/a	n/a	n/a	n/a	n/a	n/a

Table continued on next page.

Area	Black/White		Asian/White		Hispanic/White	
	Index[1]	Rank[2]	Index[1]	Rank[2]	Index[1]	Rank[2]
McAllen, TX	40.7	90	46.7	17	39.2	69
Miami, FL	64.8	23	34.2	80	57.4	8
Midland, TX	n/a	n/a	n/a	n/a	n/a	n/a
Minneapolis, MN	52.9	60	42.8	39	42.5	54
Montgomery, AL	n/a	n/a	n/a	n/a	n/a	n/a
Nashville, TN	56.2	49	41.0	51	47.9	34
New Orleans, LA	63.9	28	48.6	9	38.3	74
New York, NY	78.0	2	51.9	3	62.0	3
Oklahoma City, OK	51.4	67	39.2	60	47.0	38
Omaha, NE	61.3	38	36.3	74	48.8	30
Orlando, FL	50.7	69	33.9	81	40.2	64
Oxnard, CA	39.9	91	31.2	87	54.6	13
Peoria, IL	n/a	n/a	n/a	n/a	n/a	n/a
Philadelphia, PA	68.4	9	42.3	42	55.1	12
Phoenix, AZ	43.6	86	32.7	85	49.3	28
Pittsburgh, PA	65.8	17	52.4	2	28.6	97
Portland, OR	46.0	81	35.8	75	34.3	83
Providence, RI	53.5	57	40.1	55	60.1	4
Provo, UT	21.9	102	28.2	94	30.9	93
Raleigh, NC	42.1	87	46.7	16	37.1	76
Reno, NV	n/a	n/a	n/a	n/a	n/a	n/a
Richmond, VA	52.4	63	43.9	32	44.9	46
Riverside, CA	45.7	82	40.7	53	42.4	55
Rochester, MN	n/a	n/a	n/a	n/a	n/a	n/a
Salem, OR	n/a	n/a	n/a	n/a	n/a	n/a
Salt Lake City, UT	39.3	93	31.0	88	42.9	53
San Antonio, TX	49.0	73	38.3	66	46.1	43
San Diego, CA	51.2	68	48.2	13	49.6	25
San Francisco, CA	62.0	34	46.6	18	49.6	26
San Jose, CA	40.9	89	45.0	25	47.6	36
Santa Rosa, CA	n/a	n/a	n/a	n/a	n/a	n/a
Savannah, GA	n/a	n/a	n/a	n/a	n/a	n/a
Seattle, WA	49.1	72	37.6	69	32.8	87
Sioux Falls, SD	n/a	n/a	n/a	n/a	n/a	n/a
Spokane, WA	n/a	n/a	n/a	n/a	n/a	n/a
Springfield, MO	n/a	n/a	n/a	n/a	n/a	n/a
Tallahassee, FL	n/a	n/a	n/a	n/a	n/a	n/a
Tampa, FL	56.2	50	35.3	78	40.7	62
Topeka, KS	n/a	n/a	n/a	n/a	n/a	n/a
Tulsa, OK	56.6	47	42.6	40	45.3	45
Virginia Beach, VA	47.8	76	34.3	79	32.2	90
Washington, DC	62.3	32	38.9	64	48.3	32
Wichita, KS	58.0	44	46.5	20	42.3	56
Wilmington, NC	n/a	n/a	n/a	n/a	n/a	n/a
Worcester, MA	52.6	61	45.8	22	52.7	17

Note: Figures are based on an analysis of 1990, 2000, and 2010 Census Decennial Census tract data by William H. Frey, Brookings Institution and the University of Michigan Social Science Data Analysis Network. In this analysis all racial groups (whites, blacks, and asians) are non-Hispanic members of those races. Hispanics are shown as a separate category; All figures cover the Metropolitan Statistical Area (see Appendix B for areas included); (1) Segregation Indices are Dissimilarity Indices that measure the degree to which the minority group is distributed differently than whites across census tracts. They range from 0 (complete integration) to 100 (complete [segregation] where the value indicates the percentage of the minority group that needs to move to be distributed exactly like whites; (2) Ranges from 1 (most segregated) to 102 (least segregated); n/a not available.
Source: www.CensusScope.org

Religious Groups by Family

Area[1]	Catholic	Baptist	Non-Den.	Methodist[2]	Lutheran	LDS[3]	Pente-costal	Presby-terian[4]	Muslim[5]	Judaism
Abilene, TX	5.3	40.3	4.7	6.3	1.1	1.0	1.7	1.0	<0.1	<0.1
Albuquerque, NM	27.2	3.8	4.2	1.5	1.0	2.4	1.5	1.1	0.2	0.3
Anchorage, AK	6.9	5.0	6.4	1.4	1.9	5.1	1.9	0.7	0.2	0.1
Ann Arbor, MI	12.4	2.2	1.6	3.1	2.9	0.9	1.9	3.0	1.3	0.9
Athens, GA	4.4	16.3	2.3	8.4	0.4	0.8	2.8	2.0	0.4	0.2
Atlanta, GA	7.5	17.5	6.9	7.9	0.5	0.8	2.6	1.8	0.8	0.6
Austin, TX	16.0	10.3	4.5	3.6	2.0	1.2	0.8	1.1	1.2	0.3
Baltimore, MD	16.7	4.2	4.8	6.1	2.1	0.5	1.1	1.3	0.5	1.8
Billings, MT	12.1	2.5	3.8	2.1	6.1	4.9	4.1	1.8	<0.1	0.1
Boise City, ID	8.0	2.9	4.2	2.1	1.2	15.9	2.3	0.6	0.1	0.1
Boston, MA	44.4	1.2	1.0	1.0	0.4	0.4	0.6	1.6	0.4	1.4
Boulder, CO	20.1	2.4	4.8	1.8	3.1	3.0	0.5	2.0	0.1	0.8
Cape Coral, FL	16.2	5.0	3.0	2.5	1.2	0.5	4.4	1.4	0.9	0.2
Cedar Rapids, IA	18.8	2.4	3.0	7.3	11.3	0.9	1.8	3.3	0.5	0.1
Charleston, SC	6.2	12.4	7.1	10.0	1.1	1.0	2.0	2.4	0.2	0.3
Charlotte, NC	5.9	17.3	6.8	8.6	1.3	0.8	3.3	4.5	0.2	0.3
Chicago, IL	34.2	3.2	4.5	1.9	3.0	0.4	1.2	1.9	3.3	0.8
Cincinnati, OH	19.1	9.6	3.7	3.9	1.2	0.6	2.2	1.6	0.2	0.5
Clarksville, TN	4.1	30.9	2.3	6.2	0.6	1.5	1.8	1.1	0.1	<0.1
Colorado Spgs, CO	8.4	4.3	7.4	2.4	2.0	3.0	1.1	2.1	0.1	0.1
Columbia, MO	6.6	14.7	5.4	4.3	1.7	1.4	1.1	2.3	0.3	0.3
Columbus, OH	11.8	5.3	3.6	4.7	2.4	0.7	2.0	2.0	0.8	0.5
Dallas, TX	13.3	18.7	7.8	5.3	0.8	1.2	2.2	1.0	2.4	0.4
Davenport, IA	14.9	5.0	2.7	5.3	8.7	0.8	1.4	3.0	0.9	0.1
Denver, CO	16.1	3.0	4.6	1.7	2.1	2.4	1.2	1.6	0.6	0.6
Des Moines, IA	13.6	4.8	3.3	7.0	8.2	1.0	2.4	3.0	0.3	0.3
Durham, NC	5.1	13.9	5.6	8.1	0.5	0.8	1.4	2.5	0.5	0.6
El Paso, TX	43.2	3.8	5.0	0.9	0.3	1.6	1.4	0.2	0.1	0.2
Erie, PA	33.5	2.2	1.7	5.7	3.0	0.6	2.2	2.1	0.7	0.2
Eugene, OR	6.2	3.1	1.9	0.9	1.4	3.7	3.3	0.6	0.1	0.4
Fargo, ND	17.4	0.4	0.5	3.3	32.5	0.6	1.5	1.9	0.1	<0.1
Fayetteville, NC	2.6	14.1	10.5	6.2	0.2	1.4	4.9	2.1	0.2	<0.1
Ft. Collins, CO	11.8	2.2	6.4	4.4	3.5	3.0	4.7	1.9	0.1	<0.1
Ft. Wayne, IN	14.2	6.1	6.8	5.1	8.5	0.4	1.5	1.7	0.3	0.1
Ft. Worth, TX	13.3	18.7	7.8	5.3	0.8	1.2	2.2	1.0	2.4	0.4
Gainesville, FL	7.6	12.3	4.3	6.4	0.5	1.0	3.5	1.1	1.1	0.4
Grand Rapids, MI	17.2	1.7	8.4	3.1	2.1	0.6	1.1	10.0	1.1	0.1
Green Bay, WI	42.0	0.7	3.4	2.2	12.7	0.4	0.6	1.0	0.1	0.1
Greensboro, NC	2.7	12.8	7.4	9.9	0.7	0.8	2.5	3.2	0.6	0.4
Honolulu, HI	18.2	1.9	2.2	0.8	0.3	5.1	4.2	1.5	<0.1	0.1
Houston, TX	17.1	16.0	7.3	4.9	1.1	1.1	1.5	0.9	2.7	0.4
Huntsville, AL	4.0	27.6	3.2	7.5	0.7	1.2	1.2	1.7	0.2	0.2
Indianapolis, IN	10.5	10.3	7.2	5.0	1.7	0.7	1.6	1.7	0.2	0.4
Jacksonville, FL	9.9	18.5	7.8	4.5	0.7	1.1	1.9	1.6	0.6	0.4
Kansas City, MO	12.7	13.2	5.2	5.9	2.3	2.5	2.6	1.6	0.3	0.4
Lafayette, LA	47.0	14.8	4.0	2.6	0.2	0.4	2.9	0.2	0.1	0.1
Las Vegas, NV	18.1	3.0	3.1	0.4	0.7	6.4	1.5	0.2	0.1	0.3
Lexington, KY	6.8	24.9	2.4	5.9	0.4	1.1	2.1	1.4	0.1	0.3
Lincoln, NE	14.8	2.4	1.9	7.2	11.3	1.2	1.4	3.9	0.2	0.2
Little Rock, AR	4.5	25.9	6.1	7.3	0.5	0.9	2.9	0.9	0.1	0.1
Los Angeles, CA	33.8	2.8	3.6	1.1	0.7	1.7	1.8	0.9	0.7	1.0
Louisville, KY	13.7	25.1	1.7	3.7	0.6	0.8	1.0	1.2	0.5	0.4
Lubbock, TX	13.4	22.4	7.3	6.6	0.5	1.4	1.9	0.8	1.8	0.1
Madison, WI	21.8	1.1	1.6	3.7	12.8	0.5	0.4	2.2	0.5	0.5
Manchester, NH	31.2	1.4	2.4	1.2	0.5	0.6	0.5	2.0	0.3	0.5

Table continued on next page.

Area[1]	Catholic	Baptist	Non-Den.	Methodist[2]	Lutheran	LDS[3]	Pentecostal	Presbyterian[4]	Muslim[5]	Judaism
McAllen, TX	34.7	4.5	2.8	1.3	0.4	1.3	1.2	0.2	1.0	<0.1
Miami, FL	18.6	5.4	4.2	1.3	0.5	0.5	1.8	0.7	0.9	1.6
Midland, TX	22.4	25.3	8.8	4.2	0.7	1.2	1.6	1.9	3.7	<0.1
Minneapolis, MN	21.7	2.5	3.0	2.8	14.5	0.6	1.8	1.9	0.4	0.7
Montgomery, AL	3.2	35.4	4.0	11.1	0.2	0.9	5.2	1.5	0.3	0.3
Nashville, TN	4.1	25.3	5.8	6.1	0.4	0.8	2.2	2.1	0.4	0.2
New Orleans, LA	31.6	8.4	3.7	2.7	0.8	0.6	2.1	0.5	0.5	0.5
New York, NY	36.9	1.9	1.8	1.3	0.8	0.4	0.9	1.1	2.3	4.8
Oklahoma City, OK	6.4	25.4	7.1	10.6	0.7	1.3	3.2	1.0	0.2	0.1
Omaha, NE	21.6	4.6	1.8	3.9	7.9	1.8	1.3	2.3	0.5	0.4
Orlando, FL	13.2	7.0	5.7	3.0	0.9	1.0	3.2	1.4	1.3	0.3
Oxnard, CA	28.2	1.9	4.1	1.1	1.5	2.5	1.3	0.7	0.4	0.7
Peoria, IL	11.5	5.5	5.3	5.0	6.1	0.5	1.5	2.8	5.2	0.1
Philadelphia, PA	33.5	3.9	2.9	3.0	1.9	0.3	0.9	2.1	1.3	1.4
Phoenix, AZ	13.4	3.5	5.2	1.0	1.6	6.1	2.9	0.6	0.2	0.3
Pittsburgh, PA	32.8	2.3	2.8	5.7	3.4	0.4	1.1	4.7	0.3	0.7
Portland, OR	10.6	2.3	4.5	1.0	1.6	3.8	2.0	1.0	0.1	0.3
Providence, RI	47.0	1.4	1.2	0.8	0.5	0.3	0.6	1.0	0.1	0.7
Provo, UT	1.3	0.1	0.1	0.2	<0.1	88.6	0.1	0.1	<0.1	<0.1
Raleigh, NC	9.2	12.1	6.0	6.7	0.9	0.9	2.3	2.3	0.9	0.3
Reno, NV	14.3	1.5	3.2	0.9	0.8	4.6	2.0	0.4	0.1	0.2
Richmond, VA	6.0	19.9	5.5	6.1	0.6	1.0	1.8	2.1	2.8	0.4
Riverside, CA	24.8	2.6	5.5	0.6	0.5	2.5	1.6	0.6	0.6	0.1
Rochester, MN	23.4	1.7	4.7	4.9	21.1	1.1	1.3	2.9	0.3	0.2
Salem, OR	16.7	2.2	3.0	1.2	1.7	3.9	3.4	0.7	<0.1	0.1
Salt Lake City, UT	8.9	0.8	0.5	0.5	0.5	58.9	0.7	0.4	0.4	0.1
San Antonio, TX	28.4	8.5	6.0	3.1	1.7	1.4	1.3	0.8	1.0	0.2
San Diego, CA	25.9	2.0	4.8	1.1	1.0	2.3	1.0	0.9	0.7	0.5
San Francisco, CA	20.8	2.5	2.5	2.0	0.6	1.6	1.2	1.1	1.2	0.9
San Jose, CA	26.0	1.4	4.3	1.1	0.6	1.4	1.2	0.7	1.0	0.7
Santa Rosa, CA	22.3	1.4	1.5	0.9	1.0	1.9	0.7	0.9	0.5	0.4
Savannah, GA	7.1	19.7	6.9	8.9	1.6	1.0	2.4	1.0	0.2	0.8
Seattle, WA	12.3	2.2	5.0	1.2	2.1	3.3	2.8	1.4	0.5	0.5
Sioux Falls, SD	14.9	3.0	1.5	3.9	21.4	0.7	1.1	6.2	0.3	0.1
Spokane, WA	13.1	1.9	4.3	1.0	2.9	5.2	2.9	1.5	0.1	0.2
Springfield, MO	4.4	23.2	3.9	4.7	1.4	1.2	9.3	1.1	0.1	0.1
Tallahassee, FL	4.8	16.1	6.8	9.2	0.5	1.0	2.2	1.6	0.9	0.4
Tampa, FL	10.9	7.1	3.8	3.5	1.0	0.6	2.1	1.0	1.3	0.5
Topeka, KS	12.8	9.1	4.1	7.3	3.6	1.5	2.0	1.7	0.1	0.1
Tulsa, OK	5.8	22.9	7.6	9.2	0.8	1.2	3.3	1.3	0.3	0.3
Virginia Beach, VA	6.4	11.6	6.2	5.3	0.7	0.9	1.9	2.0	2.1	0.4
Washington, DC	14.5	7.3	4.9	4.5	1.3	1.2	1.1	1.4	2.4	1.2
Wichita, KS	14.5	13.5	3.2	7.2	1.8	1.4	2.0	1.7	0.2	<0.1
Wilmington, NC	6.2	14.5	4.6	8.5	0.9	1.0	1.1	2.5	0.3	0.1
Worcester, MA	38.4	1.2	1.8	1.0	0.9	0.3	1.1	2.1	0.1	0.5
U.S.	19.1	9.3	4.0	4.0	2.3	2.0	1.9	1.6	0.8	0.7

Note: Figures are the number of adherents as a percentage of the total population; (1) Figures cover the Metropolitan Statistical Area—see Appendix B for areas included; (2) Methodist/Pietist; (3) Latter Day Saints; (4) Reformed; (5) Figures are estimates
Source: Association of Statisticians of American Religious Bodies, 2010 U.S. Religion Census: Religious Congregations & Membership Study

Religious Groups by Tradition

Area	Catholic	Evangelical Protestant	Mainline Protestant	Other Tradition	Black Protestant	Orthodox
Abilene, TX	5.3	47.4	9.0	1.1	0.4	<0.1
Albuquerque, NM	27.2	11.3	3.3	3.9	0.2	0.2
Anchorage, AK	6.9	15.7	3.6	6.8	0.3	0.6
Ann Arbor, MI	12.4	7.3	7.5	3.8	1.6	0.3
Athens, GA	4.4	21.1	9.8	1.7	2.5	0.1
Atlanta, GA	7.5	26.1	9.8	2.9	3.2	0.3
Austin, TX	16.0	16.1	6.3	3.9	1.4	0.1
Baltimore, MD	16.7	9.9	8.3	3.2	3.5	0.5
Billings, MT	12.1	13.7	8.2	5.2	0.1	0.1
Boise City, ID	8.0	13.0	4.4	16.7	<0.1	0.1
Boston, MA	44.4	3.2	4.5	3.4	0.2	1.1
Boulder, CO	20.1	9.8	6.5	4.9	<0.1	0.2
Cape Coral, FL	16.2	14.3	4.6	2.0	0.3	0.2
Cedar Rapids, IA	18.8	13.7	17.5	2.0	0.2	0.2
Charleston, SC	6.2	19.7	11.2	1.9	7.3	0.1
Charlotte, NC	5.9	27.6	13.3	1.7	2.8	0.5
Chicago, IL	34.2	9.8	5.1	5.1	2.1	0.9
Cincinnati, OH	19.1	15.5	7.2	1.6	1.2	0.2
Clarksville, TN	4.1	35.4	7.3	1.7	2.4	<0.1
Colorado Spgs, CO	8.4	15.2	5.4	3.7	0.4	0.1
Columbia, MO	6.6	19.9	10.5	2.3	0.5	0.1
Columbus, OH	11.8	11.9	9.5	3.1	1.1	0.3
Dallas, TX	13.3	28.3	7.0	4.8	1.8	0.2
Davenport, IA	14.9	11.4	15.1	2.4	1.6	0.1
Denver, CO	16.1	11.1	4.5	4.6	0.4	0.3
Des Moines, IA	13.6	12.4	16.8	1.9	0.9	0.1
Durham, NC	5.1	19.4	11.7	2.9	3.1	0.1
El Paso, TX	43.2	10.9	1.3	2.1	0.2	0.1
Erie, PA	33.5	8.4	11.7	1.6	0.9	0.3
Eugene, OR	6.2	9.7	3.4	5.5	0.1	0.1
Fargo, ND	17.4	10.7	30.8	0.9	<0.1	<0.1
Fayetteville, NC	2.6	26.7	7.9	1.8	4.3	0.1
Ft. Collins, CO	11.8	18.8	5.9	4.0	<0.1	0.1
Ft. Wayne, IN	14.2	24.6	9.2	1.0	2.4	0.2
Ft. Worth, TX	13.3	28.3	7.0	4.8	1.8	0.2
Gainesville, FL	7.6	20.4	7.0	4.2	2.2	0.1
Grand Rapids, MI	17.2	20.7	7.6	2.2	1.1	0.2
Green Bay, WI	42.0	14.1	8.1	0.6	<0.1	<0.1
Greensboro, NC	2.7	23.2	14.0	2.2	2.6	0.1
Honolulu, HI	18.2	9.7	2.9	8.4	<0.1	<0.1
Houston, TX	17.1	24.9	6.7	4.9	1.3	0.2
Huntsville, AL	4.0	33.3	9.7	1.9	1.8	0.1
Indianapolis, IN	10.5	18.3	9.6	1.7	1.9	0.3
Jacksonville, FL	9.9	27.1	5.7	2.9	4.2	0.3
Kansas City, MO	12.7	20.6	10.0	3.7	2.6	0.1
Lafayette, LA	47.0	12.8	3.2	0.8	9.3	0.1
Las Vegas, NV	18.1	7.7	1.4	7.6	0.4	0.4
Lexington, KY	6.8	28.3	10.3	1.7	2.1	0.2
Lincoln, NE	14.8	14.8	16.2	2.0	0.1	0.1
Little Rock, AR	4.5	33.9	8.2	1.7	3.5	0.1
Los Angeles, CA	33.8	9.0	2.4	4.6	0.9	0.6
Louisville, KY	13.7	24.5	7.1	2.0	3.0	0.1
Lubbock, TX	13.4	31.5	8.6	4.0	0.7	0.1
Madison, WI	21.8	7.3	15.4	2.3	0.1	0.1
Manchester, NH	31.2	5.1	4.4	1.8	<0.1	0.7

Table continued on next page.

Area	Catholic	Evangelical Protestant	Mainline Protestant	Other Tradition	Black Protestant	Orthodox
McAllen, TX	34.7	9.7	1.9	2.4	<0.1	<0.1
Miami, FL	18.6	11.4	2.5	3.5	1.7	0.3
Midland, TX	22.4	35.5	7.2	5.4	1.0	<0.1
Minneapolis, MN	21.7	12.9	14.5	2.3	0.5	0.2
Montgomery, AL	3.2	34.2	11.7	1.6	13.5	<0.1
Nashville, TN	4.1	33.0	8.0	1.7	3.4	0.5
New Orleans, LA	31.6	12.7	4.0	2.1	3.0	0.1
New York, NY	36.9	4.0	4.1	8.4	1.2	1.0
Oklahoma City, OK	6.4	39.1	9.9	2.8	1.9	0.2
Omaha, NE	21.6	12.1	10.8	3.3	1.5	0.1
Orlando, FL	13.2	17.8	4.8	3.3	1.2	0.3
Oxnard, CA	28.2	8.9	2.7	4.5	0.2	0.2
Peoria, IL	11.5	18.9	11.1	6.2	0.9	0.1
Philadelphia, PA	33.5	6.3	8.9	3.7	1.8	0.4
Phoenix, AZ	13.4	13.2	2.6	7.8	0.2	0.3
Pittsburgh, PA	32.8	7.4	13.8	2.1	0.9	0.7
Portland, OR	10.6	11.7	3.7	5.2	0.2	0.3
Providence, RI	47.0	2.8	4.7	1.6	0.1	0.6
Provo, UT	1.3	0.5	0.1	88.9	<0.1	<0.1
Raleigh, NC	9.2	19.9	10.1	3.3	1.7	0.2
Reno, NV	14.3	7.7	1.9	5.1	0.2	0.1
Richmond, VA	6.0	23.7	13.3	4.6	2.4	0.2
Riverside, CA	24.8	11.5	1.3	3.7	0.8	0.2
Rochester, MN	23.4	19.0	21.1	2.1	<0.1	0.1
Salem, OR	16.7	14.1	3.8	4.2	<0.1	<0.1
Salt Lake City, UT	8.9	2.6	1.3	60.1	0.1	0.5
San Antonio, TX	28.4	17.0	5.0	3.2	0.4	0.1
San Diego, CA	25.9	9.8	2.4	5.2	0.4	0.3
San Francisco, CA	20.8	6.2	3.8	5.2	1.1	0.7
San Jose, CA	26.0	8.2	2.5	6.9	0.1	0.4
Santa Rosa, CA	22.3	5.3	2.4	4.8	<0.1	0.3
Savannah, GA	7.1	25.1	9.5	2.6	8.6	0.1
Seattle, WA	12.3	11.9	4.7	5.9	0.4	0.4
Sioux Falls, SD	14.9	12.9	28.1	1.2	0.1	0.1
Spokane, WA	13.1	12.4	4.9	6.3	0.1	0.2
Springfield, MO	4.4	38.0	7.7	1.4	0.1	<0.1
Tallahassee, FL	4.8	21.9	6.4	3.0	9.2	0.2
Tampa, FL	10.9	13.6	5.2	3.1	1.2	0.8
Topeka, KS	12.8	15.5	12.9	1.8	2.8	<0.1
Tulsa, OK	5.8	34.6	11.3	2.2	1.6	0.1
Virginia Beach, VA	6.4	18.0	9.4	4.0	2.3	0.3
Washington, DC	14.5	12.4	8.8	5.9	2.3	0.6
Wichita, KS	14.5	20.7	11.1	2.4	1.9	0.2
Wilmington, NC	6.2	20.4	10.8	1.7	3.1	0.1
Worcester, MA	38.4	4.7	5.4	2.4	0.1	1.0
U.S.	19.1	16.2	7.3	4.3	1.6	0.3

Note: Figures are the number of adherents as a percentage of the total population; (1) Figures cover the Metropolitan Statistical Area—see Appendix B for areas included; Source: Association of Statisticians of American Religious Bodies, 2010 U.S. Religion Census: Religious Congregations & Membership Study

Ancestry: City

City	German	Irish	English	American	Italian	Polish	French[1]	Scottish	Dutch
Abilene, TX	12.4	9.2	7.3	6.0	1.3	0.6	2.0	1.6	0.8
Albuquerque, NM	10.5	7.8	6.8	3.6	3.2	1.3	2.1	1.8	1.1
Anchorage, AK	17.8	10.9	8.8	5.2	3.4	1.9	3.1	3.0	1.7
Ann Arbor, MI	18.9	9.5	10.3	5.2	5.2	6.5	3.7	3.1	2.4
Athens, GA	9.6	8.1	8.5	10.2	2.0	2.2	1.6	3.5	0.8
Atlanta, GA	6.2	5.0	6.5	7.1	1.9	1.3	1.3	2.1	0.6
Austin, TX	12.6	8.6	8.4	4.0	2.9	1.5	3.1	2.3	0.9
Baltimore, MD	7.5	6.6	3.5	2.3	3.4	2.5	0.7	0.8	0.6
Billings, MT	30.2	12.5	10.3	12.5	3.3	1.7	2.9	2.5	1.8
Boise City, ID	16.6	9.9	13.9	7.2	4.4	1.6	2.3	3.5	2.0
Boston, MA	4.8	15.5	5.3	4.8	8.4	2.6	1.9	1.3	0.5
Boulder, CO	22.6	13.7	13.1	4.7	6.9	4.3	4.3	3.3	2.1
Cape Coral, FL	19.2	16.0	8.9	10.6	12.3	4.5	3.1	1.4	1.4
Cedar Rapids, IA	38.2	17.1	8.8	5.2	2.3	1.7	2.8	1.9	2.4
Charleston, SC	12.2	11.3	11.9	11.4	4.3	1.9	3.0	3.4	1.2
Charlotte, NC	9.9	7.8	7.8	5.0	3.5	1.7	1.5	2.3	0.8
Chicago, IL	7.4	7.5	2.3	1.8	3.9	6.1	0.9	0.6	0.6
Cincinnati, OH	19.1	10.3	5.3	5.2	3.5	1.4	1.5	1.1	0.9
Clarksville, TN	13.7	10.9	6.5	11.9	2.9	1.8	1.8	1.4	1.1
Colorado Spgs, CO	22.1	12.7	10.3	5.7	5.8	2.6	3.3	2.9	2.1
Columbia, MO	27.2	12.0	11.6	4.8	4.2	2.3	3.2	3.4	1.3
Columbus, OH	20.4	12.6	6.8	4.9	5.4	2.2	1.8	1.6	1.2
Dallas, TX	5.9	4.4	5.0	3.2	1.4	0.8	1.4	1.1	0.5
Davenport, IA	33.8	14.9	7.0	6.4	2.4	2.4	2.7	1.0	1.9
Denver, CO	14.5	10.2	8.0	3.2	4.3	2.4	2.4	2.0	1.4
Des Moines, IA	22.9	12.3	8.1	4.7	3.7	1.1	2.0	1.6	3.8
Durham, NC	7.3	5.3	7.6	4.3	2.6	1.6	1.5	1.6	0.8
El Paso, TX	3.7	2.8	1.8	4.3	1.1	0.4	0.7	0.5	0.2
Erie, PA	23.5	14.8	4.5	2.8	12.6	12.6	1.8	0.8	1.3
Eugene, OR	19.6	13.7	11.8	4.7	4.3	2.4	4.0	3.1	2.4
Fargo, ND	41.1	9.4	5.0	2.0	1.3	2.9	3.7	1.1	1.0
Fayetteville, NC	11.0	8.0	5.2	4.7	2.7	1.3	1.5	2.0	0.7
Ft. Collins, CO	27.2	14.1	12.6	4.0	6.3	3.2	3.7	3.2	2.9
Ft. Wayne, IN	26.1	9.3	7.0	14.5	2.3	2.1	3.4	1.3	1.4
Ft. Worth, TX	9.0	7.3	5.7	7.4	1.8	1.0	1.5	1.6	0.8
Gainesville, FL	11.6	10.8	8.5	4.1	5.8	3.2	2.7	2.1	0.7
Grand Rapids, MI	15.9	9.3	6.9	2.8	2.7	7.2	3.0	1.5	14.4
Green Bay, WI	33.5	9.8	3.7	3.5	2.3	10.5	5.5	0.7	3.6
Greensboro, NC	7.7	6.1	8.1	5.2	2.4	1.0	1.2	2.2	0.7
Honolulu, HI	4.0	3.3	2.9	1.2	1.7	0.6	1.2	0.8	0.5
Houston, TX	5.4	3.7	3.9	3.3	1.5	0.9	1.7	0.9	0.5
Huntsville, AL	9.8	8.4	9.5	10.8	2.5	1.1	2.0	2.6	1.1
Indianapolis, IN	16.8	10.5	7.0	7.2	2.3	1.5	1.8	1.5	1.2
Jacksonville, FL	9.4	9.9	8.4	6.0	4.0	1.4	2.2	1.7	0.9
Kansas City, MO	17.0	11.3	7.7	11.1	3.1	1.4	2.3	1.7	1.5
Lafayette, LA	9.8	5.7	6.3	7.0	3.6	0.5	19.8	1.4	0.5
Las Vegas, NV	10.3	8.5	6.1	3.5	6.2	2.7	2.2	1.2	0.9
Lexington, KY	13.8	12.6	11.6	15.7	3.0	1.3	2.0	2.5	1.1
Lincoln, NE	40.7	13.2	9.5	4.4	1.9	2.7	2.7	1.4	2.1
Little Rock, AR	8.2	8.2	8.8	5.5	1.4	0.6	1.6	2.0	0.8
Los Angeles, CA	4.5	3.8	3.2	2.5	2.6	1.6	1.3	0.7	0.5
Louisville, KY	17.1	13.0	8.1	13.5	2.6	0.8	2.0	1.6	1.2
Lubbock, TX	11.9	9.0	7.4	7.2	1.5	0.9	1.5	1.7	0.9
Madison, WI	33.5	12.7	8.7	2.8	4.5	5.2	2.8	1.8	2.1
Manchester, NH	7.6	20.5	9.8	3.1	7.9	4.2	18.1	2.1	0.5
McAllen, TX	4.3	2.5	2.5	1.6	1.2	0.3	2.8	0.2	0.2

Table continued on next page.

City	German	Irish	English	American	Italian	Polish	French[1]	Scottish	Dutch
Miami, FL	2.0	1.7	1.2	4.0	2.2	0.8	0.9	0.2	0.4
Midland, TX	10.5	7.5	8.1	6.9	1.1	0.5	1.4	1.5	0.9
Minneapolis, MN	22.6	10.7	6.0	2.1	2.4	3.8	3.1	1.5	1.6
Montgomery, AL	3.8	3.5	4.8	13.1	0.8	0.5	1.1	1.3	0.3
Nashville, TN	9.9	9.5	8.4	8.3	2.5	1.1	2.0	2.0	0.9
New Orleans, LA	6.8	5.9	4.1	3.7	4.2	0.8	6.3	1.0	0.4
New York, NY	3.1	4.9	1.7	3.7	7.0	2.6	0.8	0.4	0.3
Oklahoma City, OK	12.6	9.8	7.5	7.5	1.5	0.9	2.0	1.9	1.3
Omaha, NE	27.4	15.2	7.9	3.7	4.6	4.3	2.5	1.1	1.6
Orlando, FL	8.4	7.0	5.7	6.7	4.1	1.4	1.6	1.2	0.6
Oxnard, CA	4.3	3.2	2.5	1.4	1.7	0.6	0.8	0.7	0.5
Peoria, IL	21.2	11.5	7.6	4.4	3.2	2.2	2.2	1.1	1.1
Philadelphia, PA	7.6	12.3	2.8	2.2	8.0	3.4	0.7	0.6	0.4
Phoenix, AZ	12.2	8.3	6.5	4.3	4.0	2.3	1.8	1.3	1.1
Pittsburgh, PA	19.6	16.0	4.9	3.7	13.1	7.7	1.6	1.5	0.7
Portland, OR	18.0	12.0	10.9	5.3	4.4	2.1	3.1	3.3	1.8
Providence, RI	3.5	8.8	4.1	1.9	10.1	2.1	3.5	1.2	0.4
Provo, UT	11.1	5.4	23.3	4.4	2.5	0.7	2.6	4.6	1.3
Raleigh, NC	9.7	8.1	9.9	10.0	3.9	1.8	1.8	2.3	0.8
Reno, NV	14.4	12.7	8.3	5.0	7.5	1.8	3.1	1.7	1.4
Richmond, VA	7.0	6.7	8.1	4.0	2.6	1.2	1.6	1.6	0.5
Riverside, CA	8.4	6.6	5.4	3.2	3.5	1.3	2.2	1.2	0.9
Rochester, MN	31.6	10.0	6.2	4.4	1.7	3.4	3.1	1.2	2.1
Salem, OR	20.5	11.6	11.4	4.9	3.2	0.9	3.1	2.7	2.2
Salt Lake City, UT	11.0	6.5	16.2	3.9	3.1	1.1	1.8	3.7	2.2
San Antonio, TX	8.4	4.7	4.0	3.9	1.8	1.1	1.5	1.0	0.5
San Diego, CA	9.7	7.6	6.0	3.2	4.1	1.8	2.1	1.5	0.9
San Francisco, CA	8.0	7.8	5.0	2.1	4.9	1.8	2.2	1.5	0.8
San Jose, CA	6.2	4.6	4.2	1.6	4.2	0.9	1.4	0.9	0.7
Santa Rosa, CA	12.7	10.5	9.1	4.5	8.2	1.3	3.1	2.5	1.9
Savannah, GA	5.0	6.3	5.1	3.8	2.1	0.8	1.5	1.3	0.6
Seattle, WA	15.9	11.4	11.1	3.4	4.4	2.4	3.2	3.2	2.0
Sioux Falls, SD	37.4	10.9	4.8	3.6	1.0	1.6	2.0	1.0	7.3
Spokane, WA	22.7	13.8	10.7	4.9	5.1	1.7	3.4	3.0	1.8
Springfield, MO	18.2	11.9	9.7	24.1	2.7	1.3	2.6	1.7	2.2
Tallahassee, FL	8.9	9.7	9.6	4.9	4.7	1.9	2.3	2.2	0.9
Tampa, FL	8.7	8.0	5.7	5.0	5.9	1.8	1.9	1.4	1.1
Topeka, KS	26.4	14.1	9.7	4.8	2.2	1.0	3.2	1.9	1.9
Tulsa, OK	13.3	11.4	8.8	7.8	1.7	1.0	2.4	2.2	1.7
Virginia Beach, VA	12.9	11.3	9.2	15.0	6.3	2.7	2.7	2.2	1.2
Washington, DC	6.5	6.7	5.3	2.2	3.3	1.8	1.6	1.3	0.5
Wichita, KS	21.3	10.3	8.5	10.0	1.9	0.9	2.6	1.8	1.6
Wilmington, NC	10.6	10.5	10.5	21.0	4.3	1.5	2.3	3.2	1.5
Worcester, MA	3.1	17.3	4.9	2.7	11.1	4.8	8.3	1.2	0.3
U.S.	15.2	11.1	8.2	7.2	5.6	3.1	2.8	1.7	1.4

Note: Figures are the percentage of the total population reporting a particular ancestry. The nine most commonly reported ancestries in the U.S. are shown. Figures include multiple ancestries (e.g. if a person reported being Irish and Italian, they were included in both columns);
(1) Excludes Basque
Source: U.S. Census Bureau, 2010-2012 American Community Survey 3-Year Estimates

Ancestry: Metro Area

Metro Area	German	Irish	English	American	Italian	Polish	French[1]	Scottish	Dutch
Abilene, TX	12.1	9.7	7.9	7.3	1.4	0.5	1.9	1.7	0.8
Albuquerque, NM	10.9	7.7	7.0	4.4	3.2	1.5	2.1	1.7	1.0
Anchorage, AK	19.1	11.7	9.0	5.2	3.4	2.2	3.3	3.2	1.9
Ann Arbor, MI	20.8	11.5	10.3	7.0	5.0	6.6	3.4	2.7	2.3
Athens, GA	9.5	9.1	9.7	15.7	2.0	1.6	1.7	3.3	0.7
Atlanta, GA	7.7	7.6	7.6	9.8	2.6	1.3	1.5	1.8	0.8
Austin, TX	15.0	9.1	9.0	4.7	2.9	1.6	2.8	2.2	1.0
Baltimore, MD	18.2	13.6	8.6	5.3	6.5	4.6	1.7	1.7	1.0
Billings, MT	30.7	12.1	10.3	14.2	2.9	1.8	3.0	2.4	2.0
Boise City, ID	16.3	8.8	12.6	12.3	3.2	1.3	2.2	3.0	1.9
Boston, MA	6.4	24.2	10.9	4.5	15.0	3.8	5.7	2.6	0.6
Boulder, CO	22.3	14.0	13.2	5.0	6.1	3.8	3.9	3.6	2.1
Cape Coral, FL	15.8	12.6	9.5	13.6	8.1	3.8	2.9	1.6	1.3
Cedar Rapids, IA	41.7	17.1	9.6	5.7	2.2	1.5	2.9	1.7	2.6
Charleston, SC	11.7	10.3	9.0	13.2	3.6	1.9	2.7	2.6	1.1
Charlotte, NC	11.8	9.5	8.6	8.8	3.8	1.7	1.7	2.5	1.0
Chicago, IL	15.7	12.0	4.5	2.9	7.2	9.5	1.5	1.0	1.3
Cincinnati, OH	29.9	14.4	9.2	11.3	4.1	1.5	2.1	1.8	1.2
Clarksville, TN	13.0	10.5	7.8	16.9	2.8	1.6	1.8	1.9	1.2
Colorado Spgs, CO	22.4	13.2	10.6	6.2	5.2	2.7	3.4	2.9	2.1
Columbia, MO	28.4	12.8	11.4	6.5	3.6	1.7	3.1	3.2	1.3
Columbus, OH	25.5	14.5	9.6	8.0	5.7	2.4	2.2	2.1	1.6
Dallas, TX	10.5	8.2	7.6	6.8	2.2	1.1	2.0	1.7	1.0
Davenport, IA	29.6	14.9	8.7	6.4	2.9	2.4	2.4	1.3	2.1
Denver, CO	19.8	11.8	10.1	5.2	5.3	2.7	2.8	2.4	1.7
Des Moines, IA	30.0	14.0	9.6	5.4	3.2	1.4	2.5	1.6	4.1
Durham, NC	9.6	8.1	11.4	6.9	2.9	1.7	2.0	2.2	1.0
El Paso, TX	3.3	2.6	1.6	3.9	1.0	0.4	0.6	0.4	0.2
Erie, PA	29.5	17.4	7.9	4.9	13.2	12.5	1.8	1.6	1.5
Eugene, OR	19.7	13.3	12.4	5.7	4.1	2.3	3.8	3.0	2.7
Fargo, ND	40.2	8.5	4.6	2.0	1.3	3.1	3.7	1.0	1.0
Fayetteville, NC	9.9	8.1	5.9	7.0	2.9	1.3	1.7	2.1	0.9
Ft. Collins, CO	29.5	13.9	13.5	4.4	5.5	2.9	3.8	3.2	2.8
Ft. Wayne, IN	30.0	9.5	7.5	14.9	2.2	2.3	3.4	1.4	1.5
Ft. Worth, TX	10.5	8.2	7.6	6.8	2.2	1.1	2.0	1.7	1.0
Gainesville, FL	13.3	11.2	10.2	6.1	5.0	2.8	2.7	2.0	1.3
Grand Rapids, MI	21.9	11.5	10.2	5.6	3.0	7.1	3.5	2.0	17.0
Green Bay, WI	39.5	9.8	3.6	4.2	2.5	10.9	5.1	0.8	5.0
Greensboro, NC	8.9	7.0	9.5	10.0	2.4	0.9	1.3	2.2	0.8
Honolulu, HI	5.3	4.1	3.3	1.3	1.9	0.8	1.1	0.8	0.6
Houston, TX	8.9	6.1	5.5	5.0	2.0	1.3	2.3	1.2	0.7
Huntsville, AL	9.5	8.9	9.5	15.8	2.1	1.1	2.1	2.1	1.0
Indianapolis, IN	20.8	12.0	9.8	9.5	2.8	1.9	2.1	2.0	1.7
Jacksonville, FL	11.2	11.8	9.8	8.3	5.1	1.9	2.6	2.1	1.0
Kansas City, MO	23.3	13.7	10.3	9.1	3.4	1.7	2.7	2.1	1.7
Lafayette, LA	8.9	4.9	4.6	8.9	3.1	0.4	22.0	1.1	0.3
Las Vegas, NV	10.8	8.5	6.5	3.8	6.2	2.5	2.2	1.4	1.0
Lexington, KY	13.9	12.8	11.5	20.0	2.6	1.2	1.9	2.6	1.1
Lincoln, NE	42.2	12.8	9.4	4.6	2.0	2.7	2.6	1.5	2.2
Little Rock, AR	10.8	10.8	10.3	11.1	1.8	1.0	2.2	2.0	1.2
Los Angeles, CA	6.2	4.9	4.5	3.1	3.0	1.3	1.5	1.0	0.7
Louisville, KY	19.0	13.5	9.6	17.4	2.3	1.0	2.2	1.7	1.3
Lubbock, TX	12.0	9.4	7.4	7.6	1.4	0.9	1.6	1.7	1.0
Madison, WI	40.5	14.0	9.1	3.4	3.6	4.9	2.9	1.6	2.1
Manchester, NH	8.5	21.9	14.0	4.3	9.9	4.6	15.8	3.4	1.0
McAllen, TX	2.7	1.4	1.3	1.1	0.5	0.2	1.0	0.3	0.2

Table continued on next page.

Metro Area	German	Irish	English	American	Italian	Polish	French[1]	Scottish	Dutch
Miami, FL	5.5	5.3	3.4	5.4	5.6	2.4	1.4	0.7	0.5
Midland, TX	10.2	8.0	7.8	6.9	0.9	0.4	1.4	1.7	1.0
Minneapolis, MN	32.6	12.0	6.1	3.4	2.8	4.7	3.8	1.3	1.6
Montgomery, AL	5.5	6.3	6.4	14.9	1.1	0.5	1.3	1.7	0.5
Nashville, TN	11.1	11.5	10.6	14.0	2.7	1.2	2.2	2.4	1.1
New Orleans, LA	11.3	8.6	5.1	6.0	8.8	0.6	14.9	0.9	0.5
New York, NY	7.1	10.6	3.1	4.0	13.8	4.4	1.0	0.7	0.6
Oklahoma City, OK	14.1	11.4	8.3	9.4	1.8	0.9	2.1	1.9	1.6
Omaha, NE	32.6	15.6	9.0	4.5	4.5	4.1	2.6	1.3	2.0
Orlando, FL	10.9	8.9	7.6	8.3	5.6	2.2	2.3	1.6	1.0
Oxnard, CA	11.7	8.6	8.5	3.4	5.1	1.9	2.3	1.9	1.3
Peoria, IL	32.1	13.7	10.1	9.1	3.9	2.4	2.7	1.7	1.7
Philadelphia, PA	16.8	20.5	7.9	3.5	14.0	5.4	1.5	1.4	1.0
Phoenix, AZ	14.7	9.7	8.4	6.7	4.6	2.6	2.4	1.7	1.4
Pittsburgh, PA	29.0	19.1	8.4	4.6	16.3	9.1	1.9	2.0	1.4
Portland, OR	19.9	11.9	11.3	5.1	4.0	1.9	3.3	3.2	2.2
Providence, RI	5.2	19.0	11.9	3.0	15.5	4.1	11.6	2.0	0.5
Provo, UT	12.0	5.0	28.6	5.4	2.3	0.7	2.1	5.4	2.0
Raleigh, NC	10.7	9.7	11.3	12.2	4.5	2.2	1.9	2.6	1.1
Reno, NV	15.1	12.6	9.6	5.4	7.3	2.0	3.2	2.1	1.5
Richmond, VA	10.3	8.8	12.3	9.1	3.5	1.8	1.9	2.2	0.8
Riverside, CA	8.9	6.4	5.8	3.6	3.4	1.2	1.9	1.2	1.2
Rochester, MN	37.6	10.6	6.5	4.4	1.6	3.2	2.8	1.3	2.3
Salem, OR	20.1	10.5	10.9	5.0	2.7	1.1	3.1	2.5	2.3
Salt Lake City, UT	11.7	6.3	22.0	5.8	3.1	1.0	1.8	4.1	2.5
San Antonio, TX	12.2	6.1	5.5	4.3	1.9	1.6	2.0	1.2	0.6
San Diego, CA	11.0	8.3	8.4	3.1	4.3	1.8	2.3	1.6	1.1
San Francisco, CA	8.6	7.9	6.4	2.6	5.3	1.5	2.0	1.6	0.9
San Jose, CA	7.6	5.7	5.4	2.0	4.6	1.2	1.7	1.2	0.9
Santa Rosa, CA	14.4	12.4	10.1	4.4	9.2	1.7	3.6	2.6	1.8
Savannah, GA	9.4	9.3	8.3	6.9	2.9	1.1	1.9	2.0	0.9
Seattle, WA	17.1	11.1	10.5	4.6	3.8	2.0	3.3	2.8	1.8
Sioux Falls, SD	40.8	10.6	4.7	4.0	1.0	1.6	2.0	0.9	7.5
Spokane, WA	23.8	13.1	11.7	5.4	4.9	1.6	3.6	3.0	1.9
Springfield, MO	20.2	12.1	10.8	19.0	2.6	1.2	2.9	1.8	2.0
Tallahassee, FL	9.5	10.0	9.0	6.4	4.2	1.6	2.6	2.7	1.1
Tampa, FL	13.4	12.0	9.0	8.8	7.8	3.0	3.1	1.8	1.3
Topeka, KS	30.7	14.7	10.4	6.9	2.3	1.2	3.4	1.8	2.1
Tulsa, OK	15.0	12.7	8.9	9.2	1.9	1.0	2.4	2.1	1.8
Virginia Beach, VA	10.9	9.6	9.7	11.6	4.5	2.0	2.1	2.2	1.0
Washington, DC	10.9	9.5	7.8	4.6	4.4	2.3	1.8	1.8	0.8
Wichita, KS	25.2	11.4	9.4	10.8	1.9	1.0	3.0	2.0	1.9
Wilmington, NC	12.0	11.9	11.9	17.8	4.8	1.9	2.5	3.1	1.1
Worcester, MA	6.3	21.6	10.4	3.9	13.8	6.3	14.7	2.4	0.7
U.S.	15.2	11.1	8.2	7.2	5.6	3.1	2.8	1.7	1.4

Note: Figures are the percentage of the total population reporting a particular ancestry. The nine most commonly reported ancestries in the U.S. are shown. Figures include multiple ancestries (e.g. if a person reported being Irish and Italian, they were included in both columns); Figures cover the Metropolitan Statistical Area—see Appendix B for areas included; (1) Excludes Basque
Source: U.S. Census Bureau, 2010-2012 American Community Survey 3-Year Estimates

Foreign-Born Population: City

City	Any Foreign Country	Mexico	Asia	Europe	Carribean	South America	Central America[1]	Africa	Canada
Abilene, TX	n/a	n/a	n/a	n/a	n/a	n/a	n/a	n/a	n/a
Albuquerque, NM	10.5	5.9	2.2	0.9	0.5	0.4	0.3	0.2	0.2
Anchorage, AK	9.4	0.8	5.5	1.2	0.4	0.2	0.3	0.4	0.3
Ann Arbor, MI	17.6	0.3	11.0	3.5	0.2	0.8	0.3	0.6	0.9
Athens, GA	n/a	n/a	n/a	n/a	n/a	n/a	n/a	n/a	n/a
Atlanta, GA	8.2	1.8	2.7	1.3	0.6	0.5	0.3	0.7	0.1
Austin, TX	18.5	9.6	4.7	1.2	0.4	0.4	1.5	0.4	0.2
Baltimore, MD	7.3	0.7	1.9	1.0	1.1	0.5	1.0	1.0	0.1
Billings, MT	n/a	n/a	n/a	n/a	n/a	n/a	n/a	n/a	n/a
Boise City, ID	7.2	1.3	3.0	1.7	0.0	0.1	0.2	0.4	0.4
Boston, MA	26.6	0.4	6.9	3.6	7.9	2.0	2.8	2.6	0.4
Boulder, CO	10.0	2.4	3.5	2.9	0.1	0.4	0.2	0.1	0.3
Cape Coral, FL	13.6	0.5	1.3	3.1	5.1	2.4	0.9	0.1	0.3
Cedar Rapids, IA	n/a	n/a	n/a	n/a	n/a	n/a	n/a	n/a	n/a
Charleston, SC	n/a	n/a	n/a	n/a	n/a	n/a	n/a	n/a	n/a
Charlotte, NC	14.7	3.0	4.1	1.5	0.9	1.3	2.4	1.2	0.2
Chicago, IL	21.1	9.6	4.4	3.8	0.4	1.0	0.9	0.7	0.2
Cincinnati, OH	5.3	0.5	1.6	0.6	0.2	0.2	0.6	1.5	0.2
Clarksville, TN	n/a	n/a	n/a	n/a	n/a	n/a	n/a	n/a	n/a
Colorado Spgs, CO	8.4	2.4	2.2	1.8	0.2	0.3	0.5	0.3	0.4
Columbia, MO	n/a	n/a	n/a	n/a	n/a	n/a	n/a	n/a	n/a
Columbus, OH	10.9	1.6	3.8	0.9	0.5	0.5	0.4	3.1	0.1
Dallas, TX	24.8	17.1	2.6	0.8	0.2	0.5	2.2	1.3	0.2
Davenport, IA	n/a	n/a	n/a	n/a	n/a	n/a	n/a	n/a	n/a
Denver, CO	16.0	9.2	2.7	1.6	0.2	0.3	0.4	1.2	0.3
Des Moines, IA	n/a	n/a	n/a	n/a	n/a	n/a	n/a	n/a	n/a
Durham, NC	14.5	4.5	3.7	1.0	0.3	0.6	2.5	1.4	0.3
El Paso, TX	24.6	22.2	1.0	0.5	0.3	0.2	0.3	0.1	0.1
Erie, PA	n/a	n/a	n/a	n/a	n/a	n/a	n/a	n/a	n/a
Eugene, OR	8.1	2.1	3.6	1.1	0.0	0.2	0.2	0.1	0.5
Fargo, ND	n/a	n/a	n/a	n/a	n/a	n/a	n/a	n/a	n/a
Fayetteville, NC	6.4	0.7	2.2	1.3	0.5	0.6	0.7	0.3	0.1
Ft. Collins, CO	6.0	1.3	2.5	1.0	0.0	0.2	0.3	0.2	0.3
Ft. Wayne, IN	7.3	2.2	2.9	0.9	0.2	0.2	0.5	0.3	0.2
Ft. Worth, TX	17.6	11.5	3.2	0.8	0.2	0.4	0.7	0.6	0.1
Gainesville, FL	12.7	0.4	5.4	1.7	2.0	2.0	0.4	0.4	0.3
Grand Rapids, MI	9.3	3.3	1.9	0.8	0.4	0.2	1.5	0.8	0.4
Green Bay, WI	n/a	n/a	n/a	n/a	n/a	n/a	n/a	n/a	n/a
Greensboro, NC	11.1	2.6	3.6	1.0	0.3	0.6	0.8	1.9	0.2
Honolulu, HI	28.6	0.2	23.8	1.2	0.1	0.2	0.1	0.1	0.3
Houston, TX	28.1	13.4	5.4	1.1	0.5	1.0	5.4	1.1	0.2
Huntsville, AL	6.5	1.6	2.0	0.8	0.5	0.2	0.4	0.9	0.1
Indianapolis, IN	8.4	3.6	2.0	0.5	0.2	0.2	0.8	1.0	0.1
Jacksonville, FL	9.6	0.5	3.7	1.7	1.6	0.9	0.6	0.6	0.2
Kansas City, MO	7.6	2.3	2.0	0.7	0.5	0.3	0.4	1.1	0.1
Lafayette, LA	n/a	n/a	n/a	n/a	n/a	n/a	n/a	n/a	n/a
Las Vegas, NV	21.2	10.3	5.0	1.5	0.8	0.6	2.1	0.4	0.4
Lexington, KY	8.9	3.0	3.2	0.8	0.2	0.3	0.5	0.6	0.2
Lincoln, NE	7.8	1.2	3.9	1.1	0.1	0.2	0.4	0.6	0.1
Little Rock, AR	n/a	n/a	n/a	n/a	n/a	n/a	n/a	n/a	n/a
Los Angeles, CA	38.9	14.2	11.2	2.4	0.3	1.1	8.5	0.7	0.3
Louisville, KY	6.7	0.9	2.1	0.9	1.3	0.2	0.2	0.9	0.1
Lubbock, TX	n/a	n/a	n/a	n/a	n/a	n/a	n/a	n/a	n/a
Madison, WI	11.0	1.8	5.9	1.4	0.1	0.7	0.1	0.7	0.4

Table continued on next page.

City	Any Foreign Country	Mexico	Asia	Europe	Carribean	South America	Central America[1]	Africa	Canada
Manchester, NH	13.0	1.5	3.8	2.5	0.9	1.4	0.3	1.5	1.0
McAllen, TX	n/a	n/a	n/a	n/a	n/a	n/a	n/a	n/a	n/a
Miami, FL	58.3	1.1	1.0	1.5	34.0	7.7	12.5	0.2	0.2
Midland, TX	n/a	n/a	n/a	n/a	n/a	n/a	n/a	n/a	n/a
Minneapolis, MN	14.7	3.0	3.7	1.3	0.2	1.5	0.5	4.3	0.3
Montgomery, AL	n/a	n/a	n/a	n/a	n/a	n/a	n/a	n/a	n/a
Nashville, TN	12.0	3.4	3.3	0.9	0.3	0.4	1.6	1.9	0.2
New Orleans, LA	5.8	0.6	2.0	0.8	0.2	0.4	1.4	0.3	0.1
New York, NY	37.3	2.3	10.3	5.8	10.5	5.1	1.5	1.5	0.3
Oklahoma City, OK	12.2	6.7	3.1	0.4	0.1	0.2	0.9	0.5	0.1
Omaha, NE	9.7	4.5	2.3	0.7	0.1	0.2	0.9	1.0	0.1
Orlando, FL	18.9	1.3	2.6	1.3	6.5	5.5	0.8	0.6	0.3
Oxnard, CA	n/a	n/a	n/a	n/a	n/a	n/a	n/a	n/a	n/a
Peoria, IL	n/a	n/a	n/a	n/a	n/a	n/a	n/a	n/a	n/a
Philadelphia, PA	12.0	0.4	4.7	2.3	2.1	0.8	0.4	1.1	0.1
Phoenix, AZ	20.1	13.3	2.9	1.5	0.3	0.3	0.6	0.6	0.3
Pittsburgh, PA	7.2	0.3	3.9	1.7	0.2	0.3	0.1	0.5	0.2
Portland, OR	13.8	3.0	5.5	2.7	0.2	0.2	0.5	0.8	0.5
Providence, RI	29.8	0.5	4.6	2.2	10.6	1.6	7.5	2.6	0.2
Provo, UT	n/a	n/a	n/a	n/a	n/a	n/a	n/a	n/a	n/a
Raleigh, NC	13.9	3.1	3.7	1.2	0.8	1.0	1.7	2.1	0.3
Reno, NV	16.3	7.7	4.7	1.4	0.1	0.3	1.5	0.2	0.2
Richmond, VA	7.5	1.2	1.6	0.8	0.3	0.3	2.0	1.0	0.2
Riverside, CA	23.4	14.5	4.7	0.8	0.3	0.6	2.0	0.2	0.2
Rochester, MN	12.7	1.6	5.2	1.5	0.2	0.4	0.2	2.8	0.5
Salem, OR	n/a	n/a	n/a	n/a	n/a	n/a	n/a	n/a	n/a
Salt Lake City, UT	17.5	7.0	3.6	2.4	0.3	1.0	0.8	1.2	0.3
San Antonio, TX	14.3	10.0	2.1	0.7	0.2	0.3	0.8	0.3	0.1
San Diego, CA	26.3	9.5	11.8	2.3	0.2	0.6	0.5	0.9	0.4
San Francisco, CA	36.1	2.7	22.8	4.7	0.2	1.2	3.0	0.4	0.6
San Jose, CA	38.5	10.1	23.4	2.0	0.1	0.5	1.1	0.6	0.4
Santa Rosa, CA	18.0	9.9	3.5	1.4	0.1	0.3	1.2	0.8	0.3
Savannah, GA	6.2	2.0	1.9	0.6	0.4	0.4	0.2	0.4	0.2
Seattle, WA	18.1	1.3	10.0	2.5	0.2	0.4	0.4	2.2	0.9
Sioux Falls, SD	n/a	n/a	n/a	n/a	n/a	n/a	n/a	n/a	n/a
Spokane, WA	7.2	0.4	2.4	3.1	0.1	0.2	0.2	0.3	0.5
Springfield, MO	n/a	n/a	n/a	n/a	n/a	n/a	n/a	n/a	n/a
Tallahassee, FL	7.9	0.4	2.9	1.1	1.9	0.7	0.2	0.5	0.2
Tampa, FL	15.6	1.1	2.8	1.5	6.3	1.6	1.2	0.7	0.4
Topeka, KS	n/a	n/a	n/a	n/a	n/a	n/a	n/a	n/a	n/a
Tulsa, OK	10.0	5.7	2.2	0.5	0.1	0.3	0.7	0.3	0.2
Virginia Beach, VA	8.8	0.4	4.6	1.6	0.7	0.5	0.4	0.4	0.2
Washington, DC	13.8	0.5	2.6	2.5	1.3	1.1	3.2	2.2	0.2
Wichita, KS	10.4	4.7	3.8	0.4	0.1	0.2	0.5	0.6	0.1
Wilmington, NC	n/a	n/a	n/a	n/a	n/a	n/a	n/a	n/a	n/a
Worcester, MA	20.3	0.4	5.8	3.7	2.6	2.6	1.0	4.0	0.2
U.S.	13.0	3.7	3.7	1.6	1.2	0.9	1.0	0.5	0.3

Note: (1) Excludes Mexico
Source: U.S. Census Bureau, 2010-2012 American Community Survey 3-Year Estimates

Foreign-Born Population: Metro Area

Metro Area	Percent of Population Born in								
	Any Foreign Country	Mexico	Asia	Europe	Carribean	South America	Central America[1]	Africa	Canada
Abilene, TX	n/a	n/a	n/a	n/a	n/a	n/a	n/a	n/a	n/a
Albuquerque, NM	9.6	6.0	1.6	0.8	0.3	0.3	0.2	0.1	0.2
Anchorage, AK	8.1	0.6	4.5	1.4	0.3	0.2	0.2	0.3	0.3
Ann Arbor, MI	11.2	0.5	6.3	2.0	0.2	0.4	0.4	0.8	0.6
Athens, GA	7.6	2.9	2.3	0.7	0.1	0.5	0.7	0.3	0.2
Atlanta, GA	13.3	3.2	3.9	1.2	1.5	0.9	1.1	1.3	0.2
Austin, TX	14.6	7.5	3.6	1.1	0.3	0.4	1.0	0.4	0.3
Baltimore, MD	9.3	0.5	3.7	1.3	0.7	0.5	1.1	1.2	0.2
Billings, MT	n/a	n/a	n/a	n/a	n/a	n/a	n/a	n/a	n/a
Boise City, ID	6.6	2.9	1.5	1.2	0.1	0.2	0.2	0.2	0.3
Boston, MA	16.8	0.2	5.3	3.3	2.9	1.9	1.4	1.3	0.5
Boulder, CO	10.5	3.7	3.2	2.2	0.1	0.3	0.3	0.2	0.3
Cape Coral, FL	14.9	2.8	1.2	2.3	4.4	1.7	1.4	0.1	0.9
Cedar Rapids, IA	n/a	n/a	n/a	n/a	n/a	n/a	n/a	n/a	n/a
Charleston, SC	5.2	1.5	1.2	1.0	0.3	0.3	0.5	0.1	0.2
Charlotte, NC	10.2	2.6	2.5	1.2	0.6	0.9	1.4	0.7	0.2
Chicago, IL	17.7	7.1	4.6	3.9	0.3	0.6	0.5	0.5	0.2
Cincinnati, OH	4.0	0.5	1.6	0.8	0.1	0.2	0.3	0.5	0.1
Clarksville, TN	n/a	n/a	n/a	n/a	n/a	n/a	n/a	n/a	n/a
Colorado Spgs, CO	7.2	1.8	1.9	1.8	0.2	0.3	0.5	0.3	0.4
Columbia, MO	n/a	n/a	n/a	n/a	n/a	n/a	n/a	n/a	n/a
Columbus, OH	7.0	0.9	2.7	0.8	0.2	0.3	0.3	1.6	0.2
Dallas, TX	17.6	9.2	4.3	0.8	0.2	0.5	1.3	1.0	0.2
Davenport, IA	4.7	1.8	1.3	0.7	0.0	0.2	0.1	0.5	0.1
Denver, CO	12.2	5.6	2.8	1.5	0.1	0.3	0.5	0.9	0.3
Des Moines, IA	7.4	2.0	2.3	1.4	0.0	0.1	0.4	0.8	0.2
Durham, NC	12.3	3.9	3.3	1.2	0.3	0.5	1.8	0.9	0.3
El Paso, TX	25.7	23.5	0.9	0.4	0.2	0.2	0.3	0.0	0.1
Erie, PA	4.1	0.2	1.3	1.7	0.1	0.1	0.1	0.4	0.2
Eugene, OR	5.9	1.9	2.0	1.0	0.0	0.2	0.1	0.1	0.4
Fargo, ND	n/a	n/a	n/a	n/a	n/a	n/a	n/a	n/a	n/a
Fayetteville, NC	5.9	1.1	1.7	1.1	0.5	0.5	0.7	0.3	0.1
Ft. Collins, CO	5.0	1.6	1.5	1.0	0.1	0.2	0.2	0.1	0.2
Ft. Wayne, IN	5.2	1.5	2.0	0.8	0.1	0.1	0.3	0.2	0.1
Ft. Worth, TX	17.6	9.2	4.3	0.8	0.2	0.5	1.3	1.0	0.2
Gainesville, FL	10.3	0.4	3.9	1.6	1.6	1.6	0.4	0.4	0.3
Grand Rapids, MI	6.1	1.6	1.6	1.1	0.4	0.2	0.6	0.4	0.3
Green Bay, WI	4.4	2.0	1.3	0.3	0.1	0.1	0.3	0.2	0.1
Greensboro, NC	8.4	3.0	2.4	0.7	0.2	0.4	0.6	0.9	0.1
Honolulu, HI	19.7	0.2	16.1	0.8	0.2	0.2	0.1	0.1	0.3
Houston, TX	22.1	9.9	5.3	1.0	0.5	0.9	3.4	0.9	0.2
Huntsville, AL	5.1	1.4	1.7	0.7	0.3	0.2	0.2	0.4	0.1
Indianapolis, IN	6.3	2.1	2.0	0.6	0.2	0.2	0.4	0.7	0.1
Jacksonville, FL	7.9	0.4	2.9	1.6	1.2	0.8	0.4	0.4	0.2
Kansas City, MO	6.2	2.1	1.9	0.6	0.2	0.2	0.4	0.6	0.1
Lafayette, LA	n/a	n/a	n/a	n/a	n/a	n/a	n/a	n/a	n/a
Las Vegas, NV	21.7	9.1	6.6	1.7	0.8	0.6	1.8	0.6	0.3
Lexington, KY	6.8	2.5	2.2	0.7	0.2	0.2	0.4	0.4	0.1
Lincoln, NE	6.9	1.1	3.4	1.1	0.1	0.2	0.3	0.5	0.1
Little Rock, AR	4.0	1.6	1.3	0.3	0.1	0.1	0.3	0.1	0.1
Los Angeles, CA	34.1	13.4	12.3	1.7	0.3	0.9	4.3	0.5	0.3
Louisville, KY	4.9	1.0	1.5	0.7	0.7	0.2	0.2	0.5	0.1
Lubbock, TX	5.8	2.7	1.8	0.4	0.1	0.2	0.3	0.3	0.1
Madison, WI	7.1	1.6	3.2	1.0	0.1	0.5	0.1	0.4	0.3

Table continued on next page.

Metro Area	Any Foreign Country	Mexico	Asia	Europe	Carribean	South America	Central America[1]	Africa	Canada
Manchester, NH	8.5	0.7	2.7	1.8	0.5	0.9	0.3	0.6	0.9
McAllen, TX	29.4	27.4	0.8	0.2	0.1	0.2	0.4	0.0	0.3
Miami, FL	38.5	1.2	1.9	2.2	20.3	7.7	4.2	0.4	0.6
Midland, TX	n/a	n/a	n/a	n/a	n/a	n/a	n/a	n/a	n/a
Minneapolis, MN	9.6	1.5	3.8	1.1	0.1	0.5	0.4	2.0	0.3
Montgomery, AL	n/a	n/a	n/a	n/a	n/a	n/a	n/a	n/a	n/a
Nashville, TN	7.4	2.1	2.2	0.7	0.2	0.3	0.9	0.9	0.2
New Orleans, LA	7.0	0.6	2.0	0.6	0.5	0.4	2.5	0.2	0.1
New York, NY	29.0	1.7	8.1	4.8	6.7	4.4	1.9	1.1	0.2
Oklahoma City, OK	7.9	3.8	2.3	0.5	0.1	0.2	0.5	0.4	0.1
Omaha, NE	6.8	2.8	1.9	0.6	0.1	0.1	0.6	0.6	0.1
Orlando, FL	16.2	1.3	2.8	1.7	4.9	3.7	0.9	0.5	0.4
Oxnard, CA	22.8	13.3	5.2	1.6	0.1	0.6	1.3	0.2	0.5
Peoria, IL	3.1	0.6	1.6	0.5	0.1	0.1	0.1	0.1	0.1
Philadelphia, PA	9.7	0.9	3.9	2.0	1.1	0.6	0.4	0.8	0.1
Phoenix, AZ	14.4	8.1	2.8	1.4	0.2	0.3	0.5	0.4	0.6
Pittsburgh, PA	3.2	0.1	1.5	1.0	0.1	0.1	0.1	0.2	0.1
Portland, OR	12.4	3.7	4.4	2.4	0.1	0.2	0.4	0.4	0.5
Providence, RI	12.7	0.2	2.1	4.4	1.8	1.0	1.5	1.4	0.3
Provo, UT	7.2	3.0	1.0	0.6	0.1	1.3	0.5	0.1	0.4
Raleigh, NC	11.8	3.3	3.7	1.1	0.5	0.7	1.1	1.1	0.3
Reno, NV	14.7	7.2	3.9	1.4	0.1	0.2	1.2	0.2	0.3
Richmond, VA	7.2	0.8	2.6	1.1	0.3	0.4	1.1	0.7	0.2
Riverside, CA	21.6	13.1	4.5	0.9	0.2	0.5	1.6	0.3	0.3
Rochester, MN	8.0	1.0	3.2	1.1	0.1	0.2	0.2	1.6	0.3
Salem, OR	12.0	7.9	1.5	1.1	0.1	0.2	0.5	0.2	0.3
Salt Lake City, UT	11.7	4.8	2.4	1.4	0.2	1.0	0.6	0.4	0.3
San Antonio, TX	12.0	8.1	1.8	0.7	0.2	0.3	0.7	0.2	0.1
San Diego, CA	23.4	10.7	8.5	1.9	0.2	0.5	0.5	0.6	0.4
San Francisco, CA	29.9	5.8	16.1	2.9	0.2	1.0	2.5	0.5	0.4
San Jose, CA	36.6	8.2	22.6	2.9	0.1	0.7	1.0	0.5	0.5
Santa Rosa, CA	16.4	9.1	2.9	1.9	0.1	0.3	1.0	0.5	0.3
Savannah, GA	5.9	1.5	1.9	0.6	0.5	0.3	0.3	0.6	0.1
Seattle, WA	17.0	2.6	8.4	2.9	0.1	0.3	0.4	1.2	0.8
Sioux Falls, SD	n/a	n/a	n/a	n/a	n/a	n/a	n/a	n/a	n/a
Spokane, WA	5.7	0.4	1.9	2.3	0.0	0.1	0.1	0.2	0.5
Springfield, MO	2.5	0.4	0.9	0.6	0.1	0.1	0.1	0.2	0.1
Tallahassee, FL	6.2	0.7	1.9	0.9	1.3	0.6	0.3	0.4	0.2
Tampa, FL	12.7	1.4	2.4	2.4	3.2	1.6	0.6	0.4	0.7
Topeka, KS	n/a	n/a	n/a	n/a	n/a	n/a	n/a	n/a	n/a
Tulsa, OK	5.8	2.9	1.5	0.4	0.1	0.2	0.4	0.2	0.2
Virginia Beach, VA	6.2	0.4	2.7	1.1	0.5	0.4	0.5	0.4	0.2
Washington, DC	21.9	0.8	7.8	1.9	1.0	2.3	4.7	3.0	0.2
Wichita, KS	7.3	3.2	2.6	0.5	0.1	0.2	0.3	0.4	0.1
Wilmington, NC	5.0	2.0	0.7	1.0	0.2	0.2	0.5	0.1	0.2
Worcester, MA	11.1	0.2	3.4	2.3	1.0	1.6	0.6	1.4	0.6
U.S.	13.0	3.7	3.7	1.6	1.2	0.9	1.0	0.5	0.3

Note: Figures cover the Metropolitan Statistical Area—see Appendix B for areas included; (1) Excludes Mexico
Source: U.S. Census Bureau, 2010-2012 American Community Survey 3 Year Estimates

Marital Status: City

City	Never Married	Now Married[1]	Separated	Widowed	Divorced
Abilene, TX	35.3	43.2	2.4	6.8	12.2
Albuquerque, NM	35.7	43.0	1.8	5.1	14.4
Anchorage, AK	33.8	47.6	1.7	3.7	13.2
Ann Arbor, MI	56.0	32.7	0.6	3.5	7.2
Athens, GA	56.5	30.1	1.7	4.0	7.7
Atlanta, GA	54.2	26.8	2.6	5.4	11.1
Austin, TX	43.8	39.1	2.3	3.4	11.5
Baltimore, MD	52.1	25.9	4.2	7.1	10.8
Billings, MT	30.3	46.6	1.8	6.6	14.7
Boise City, ID	32.1	47.8	1.1	5.0	14.0
Boston, MA	56.8	28.3	2.9	4.1	7.9
Boulder, CO	54.8	33.7	0.8	2.6	8.0
Cape Coral, FL	25.1	52.3	1.9	7.1	13.7
Cedar Rapids, IA	34.4	46.2	1.8	5.8	11.7
Charleston, SC	44.2	38.1	2.6	5.5	9.5
Charlotte, NC	38.7	43.1	3.2	4.6	10.5
Chicago, IL	48.6	34.3	2.6	5.6	8.8
Cincinnati, OH	51.1	27.7	3.0	5.7	12.6
Clarksville, TN	29.2	52.5	2.8	3.7	11.7
Colorado Spgs, CO	28.8	51.3	2.2	4.7	13.1
Columbia, MO	50.9	35.6	1.4	3.3	8.8
Columbus, OH	43.2	36.8	2.6	4.5	12.8
Dallas, TX	40.5	39.7	3.6	4.9	11.3
Davenport, IA	35.8	43.4	1.2	6.1	13.5
Denver, CO	41.9	38.3	2.3	4.5	13.0
Des Moines, IA	34.9	43.1	2.6	5.9	13.5
Durham, NC	42.0	40.3	2.9	4.7	10.2
El Paso, TX	31.6	47.8	3.5	5.7	11.4
Erie, PA	42.2	36.4	3.5	6.9	11.1
Eugene, OR	42.7	38.0	1.3	5.3	12.7
Fargo, ND	44.2	41.8	0.9	4.3	8.8
Fayetteville, NC	32.8	44.4	3.6	5.7	13.5
Ft. Collins, CO	43.3	43.4	0.7	3.2	9.4
Ft. Wayne, IN	34.3	44.8	1.4	6.2	13.2
Ft. Worth, TX	33.4	46.6	3.1	4.7	12.3
Gainesville, FL	62.5	24.1	1.6	4.0	7.7
Grand Rapids, MI	44.8	36.5	2.5	5.4	10.8
Green Bay, WI	37.3	43.9	1.2	5.4	12.1
Greensboro, NC	41.2	39.4	2.9	5.7	10.7
Honolulu, HI	37.1	43.7	1.5	7.4	10.3
Houston, TX	39.3	41.5	3.6	4.9	10.7
Huntsville, AL	35.3	42.8	2.4	6.2	13.4
Indianapolis, IN	39.0	39.5	2.4	5.4	13.7
Jacksonville, FL	33.5	43.6	2.8	6.0	14.1
Kansas City, MO	38.4	40.4	2.4	5.5	13.2
Lafayette, LA	40.2	38.6	2.2	6.0	13.0
Las Vegas, NV	32.3	44.0	3.0	5.6	15.0
Lexington, KY	37.5	43.3	1.9	4.5	12.8
Lincoln, NE	37.0	46.3	1.4	4.2	11.2
Little Rock, AR	37.0	40.2	2.7	6.0	14.0
Los Angeles, CA	45.5	38.4	2.9	4.7	8.5
Louisville, KY	35.0	42.5	2.4	6.5	13.6
Lubbock, TX	39.9	41.4	2.2	5.7	10.9
Madison, WI	48.2	38.4	1.2	3.3	8.9
Manchester, NH	36.3	43.1	2.2	5.3	13.2
McAllen, TX	30.7	50.0	3.9	6.1	9.4

Table continued on next page.

City	Never Married	Now Married[1]	Separated	Widowed	Divorced
Miami, FL	39.9	34.5	4.6	6.9	14.0
Midland, TX	30.1	51.8	2.0	5.3	10.8
Minneapolis, MN	52.3	32.3	1.6	3.5	10.3
Montgomery, AL	39.2	38.3	3.2	6.2	13.1
Nashville, TN	40.5	39.1	2.5	5.2	12.7
New Orleans, LA	48.8	29.7	2.8	6.3	12.3
New York, NY	44.1	38.6	3.4	5.7	8.1
Oklahoma City, OK	30.7	48.2	2.6	5.4	13.1
Omaha, NE	37.3	42.9	1.9	5.8	12.1
Orlando, FL	43.3	34.9	3.6	5.1	13.0
Oxnard, CA	38.4	46.2	2.7	4.5	8.2
Peoria, IL	40.0	40.5	1.8	6.2	11.4
Philadelphia, PA	51.7	28.9	3.5	7.0	8.9
Phoenix, AZ	38.2	42.8	2.3	4.2	12.5
Pittsburgh, PA	51.5	30.4	2.6	6.7	8.8
Portland, OR	41.0	39.8	1.7	4.6	12.9
Providence, RI	54.3	28.2	3.6	4.8	9.1
Provo, UT	48.8	42.8	0.9	2.3	5.2
Raleigh, NC	41.7	40.8	2.9	4.1	10.5
Reno, NV	35.3	42.4	2.5	4.9	14.9
Richmond, VA	52.3	25.4	4.3	5.9	12.1
Riverside, CA	39.2	43.5	2.6	4.6	10.1
Rochester, MN	32.1	52.3	1.2	4.7	9.7
Salem, OR	30.9	46.5	2.6	5.3	14.7
Salt Lake City, UT	41.7	39.6	2.1	4.4	12.2
San Antonio, TX	35.5	43.4	3.1	5.5	12.5
San Diego, CA	40.8	42.7	2.1	4.6	9.9
San Francisco, CA	47.0	37.8	1.7	5.2	8.2
San Jose, CA	34.3	50.9	1.9	4.5	8.4
Santa Rosa, CA	34.4	45.6	2.1	5.4	12.6
Savannah, GA	46.9	30.3	2.8	7.0	13.0
Seattle, WA	44.0	39.3	1.3	4.2	11.2
Sioux Falls, SD	33.0	49.3	1.2	5.1	11.4
Spokane, WA	33.5	44.1	1.6	6.3	14.4
Springfield, MO	38.3	37.9	2.1	7.1	14.7
Tallahassee, FL	56.4	29.0	1.5	3.8	9.4
Tampa, FL	41.2	36.4	3.3	5.6	13.5
Topeka, KS	31.6	43.4	1.7	7.1	16.2
Tulsa, OK	33.3	42.9	2.6	6.1	15.1
Virginia Beach, VA	30.5	51.0	2.7	4.7	11.0
Washington, DC	58.0	25.1	2.4	5.0	9.5
Wichita, KS	31.7	47.1	2.2	5.6	13.4
Wilmington, NC	41.9	37.9	3.0	5.1	12.2
Worcester, MA	43.5	36.0	2.6	6.5	11.4
U.S.	32.4	48.4	2.2	6.0	11.0

Note: Figures are percentages and cover the population 15 years of age and older; (1) Excludes separated
Source: U.S. Census Bureau, 2010-2012 American Community Survey 3-Year Estimates

Marital Status: Metro Area

Metro Area	Never Married	Now Married[1]	Separated	Widowed	Divorced
Abilene, TX	31.3	46.9	2.3	7.0	12.5
Albuquerque, NM	33.7	45.6	1.8	5.2	13.7
Anchorage, AK	32.4	48.8	1.8	3.7	13.2
Ann Arbor, MI	42.0	43.8	0.9	4.2	9.1
Athens, GA	44.1	40.7	1.7	4.9	8.6
Atlanta, GA	33.9	47.9	2.4	4.7	11.0
Austin, TX	35.8	47.7	2.0	3.6	11.0
Baltimore, MD	35.5	45.7	2.6	6.2	10.1
Billings, MT	27.6	50.7	1.6	6.2	13.9
Boise City, ID	27.0	54.6	1.3	4.7	12.4
Boston, MA	36.2	47.3	1.9	5.6	9.1
Boulder, CO	36.9	48.1	1.1	3.4	10.5
Cape Coral, FL	25.9	50.4	2.1	8.2	13.4
Cedar Rapids, IA	28.8	52.6	1.5	5.8	11.3
Charleston, SC	33.7	46.5	3.2	5.7	10.9
Charlotte, NC	32.1	49.7	3.0	5.1	10.1
Chicago, IL	36.1	47.1	1.9	5.7	9.2
Cincinnati, OH	31.1	49.6	1.9	5.9	11.6
Clarksville, TN	26.5	54.7	2.5	5.1	11.2
Colorado Spgs, CO	27.9	53.7	2.0	4.3	12.0
Columbia, MO	42.0	42.9	1.5	4.2	9.4
Columbus, OH	33.4	47.8	2.0	5.0	11.9
Dallas, TX	31.2	50.7	2.6	4.5	11.1
Davenport, IA	28.9	50.3	1.3	6.9	12.6
Denver, CO	31.5	49.9	1.8	4.3	12.4
Des Moines, IA	28.6	53.4	1.6	5.0	11.4
Durham, NC	37.4	45.4	2.4	5.0	9.8
El Paso, TX	32.1	47.8	3.8	5.5	10.8
Erie, PA	34.3	46.4	2.6	6.9	9.8
Eugene, OR	32.9	45.3	1.6	5.9	14.4
Fargo, ND	38.3	47.9	0.7	4.3	8.8
Fayetteville, NC	31.1	47.2	3.6	5.6	12.6
Ft. Collins, CO	33.1	51.4	1.0	4.0	10.5
Ft. Wayne, IN	29.9	50.9	1.3	5.8	12.1
Ft. Worth, TX	31.2	50.7	2.6	4.5	11.1
Gainesville, FL	45.6	37.9	1.7	4.8	9.9
Grand Rapids, MI	31.5	51.5	1.4	5.0	10.6
Green Bay, WI	30.2	53.6	0.9	5.3	10.0
Greensboro, NC	32.2	47.5	3.3	6.3	10.7
Honolulu, HI	33.8	49.7	1.4	6.2	9.0
Houston, TX	32.4	49.7	2.9	4.6	10.3
Huntsville, AL	29.2	51.1	1.9	5.9	11.9
Indianapolis, IN	31.2	49.2	1.8	5.1	12.7
Jacksonville, FL	30.4	47.6	2.4	5.9	13.7
Kansas City, MO	29.3	50.9	1.9	5.5	12.4
Lafayette, LA	34.6	45.1	2.2	5.8	12.3
Las Vegas, NV	33.2	45.0	2.7	5.1	14.0
Lexington, KY	32.9	47.3	2.1	4.9	12.8
Lincoln, NE	35.2	48.8	1.3	4.1	10.6
Little Rock, AR	29.4	49.1	2.3	5.9	13.2
Los Angeles, CA	39.6	44.2	2.5	5.0	8.7
Louisville, KY	30.2	48.5	2.0	6.2	13.1
Lubbock, TX	37.0	44.3	2.2	5.9	10.6
Madison, WI	35.5	49.3	1.2	4.1	9.8
Manchester, NH	29.5	52.6	1.5	5.1	11.4
McAllen, TX	31.6	52.4	4.2	5.1	6.8

Table continued on next page.

Metro Area	Never Married	Now Married[1]	Separated	Widowed	Divorced
Miami, FL	33.9	43.3	3.1	7.0	12.8
Midland, TX	28.9	53.3	2.1	5.1	10.6
Minneapolis, MN	33.1	51.3	1.3	4.4	10.0
Montgomery, AL	33.4	44.4	3.0	6.5	12.7
Nashville, TN	31.0	49.6	2.0	5.3	12.1
New Orleans, LA	36.8	42.0	2.5	6.5	12.2
New York, NY	37.8	45.5	2.6	6.1	8.0
Oklahoma City, OK	29.4	50.0	2.2	5.7	12.7
Omaha, NE	31.0	51.3	1.5	5.3	11.0
Orlando, FL	34.2	45.9	2.7	5.5	11.7
Oxnard, CA	32.2	50.5	1.9	5.1	10.4
Peoria, IL	28.6	52.0	1.5	6.3	11.5
Philadelphia, PA	36.9	45.4	2.3	6.6	8.9
Phoenix, AZ	33.0	48.0	1.8	5.1	12.2
Pittsburgh, PA	31.6	48.5	2.1	8.1	9.7
Portland, OR	31.4	49.4	1.8	4.8	12.7
Providence, RI	35.0	45.0	2.0	6.7	11.3
Provo, UT	31.8	58.4	1.1	2.6	6.0
Raleigh, NC	31.2	52.2	2.8	4.5	9.4
Reno, NV	30.7	48.0	2.1	4.8	14.4
Richmond, VA	33.7	46.8	2.9	5.8	10.8
Riverside, CA	34.4	47.5	2.7	5.0	10.3
Rochester, MN	28.2	56.5	1.0	4.9	9.4
Salem, OR	29.1	50.9	2.5	5.4	12.2
Salt Lake City, UT	30.8	52.7	1.8	3.9	10.8
San Antonio, TX	31.8	48.7	2.6	5.3	11.6
San Diego, CA	36.0	46.9	1.9	5.0	10.2
San Francisco, CA	36.1	47.2	2.0	5.2	9.5
San Jose, CA	32.6	52.9	1.7	4.6	8.3
Santa Rosa, CA	32.1	47.8	1.9	5.3	13.0
Savannah, GA	35.3	43.7	2.4	6.0	12.8
Seattle, WA	32.2	49.6	1.7	4.5	12.0
Sioux Falls, SD	30.1	53.6	0.9	5.1	10.3
Spokane, WA	30.3	49.5	1.5	5.6	13.2
Springfield, MO	27.6	52.1	1.7	6.4	12.2
Tallahassee, FL	43.0	39.3	1.9	4.6	11.1
Tampa, FL	29.8	46.1	2.5	7.5	14.1
Topeka, KS	26.3	52.3	1.3	6.3	13.8
Tulsa, OK	27.1	51.1	2.1	6.2	13.5
Virginia Beach, VA	32.8	47.6	3.0	5.5	11.0
Washington, DC	36.1	48.2	2.3	4.5	8.9
Wichita, KS	28.5	51.1	1.8	5.8	12.8
Wilmington, NC	28.2	50.9	2.8	6.0	12.1
Worcester, MA	32.8	48.6	1.8	6.1	10.7
U.S.	32.4	48.4	2.2	6.0	11.0

Note: Figures are percentages and cover the population 15 years of age and older; Figures cover the Metropolitan Statistical Area—see Appendix B for areas included; (1) Excludes separated
Source: U.S. Census Bureau, 2010-2012 American Community Survey 3-Year Estimates

Male/Female Ratio: City

City	Males	Females	Males per 100 Females
Abilene, TX	61,444	58,583	104.9
Albuquerque, NM	267,458	284,139	94.1
Anchorage, AK	150,377	145,662	103.2
Ann Arbor, MI	57,616	57,508	100.2
Athens, GA	55,698	61,633	90.4
Atlanta, GA	214,757	217,995	98.5
Austin, TX	413,718	404,518	102.3
Baltimore, MD	292,411	328,432	89.0
Billings, MT	51,343	54,305	94.5
Boise City, ID	104,400	104,892	99.5
Boston, MA	299,769	328,596	91.2
Boulder, CO	50,506	49,897	101.2
Cape Coral, FL	78,211	79,722	98.1
Cedar Rapids, IA	62,523	64,980	96.2
Charleston, SC	58,093	65,133	89.2
Charlotte, NC	363,181	393,544	92.3
Chicago, IL	1,311,742	1,394,239	94.1
Cincinnati, OH	140,714	155,729	90.4
Clarksville, TN	67,056	70,532	95.1
Colorado Spgs, CO	209,996	215,729	97.3
Columbia, MO	52,890	58,314	90.7
Columbus, OH	389,045	410,312	94.8
Dallas, TX	612,684	607,195	100.9
Davenport, IA	49,079	51,564	95.2
Denver, CO	309,777	309,239	100.2
Des Moines, IA	99,913	105,709	94.5
Durham, NC	110,168	123,992	88.9
El Paso, TX	317,940	344,767	92.2
Erie, PA	49,329	52,090	94.7
Eugene, OR	77,558	79,638	97.4
Fargo, ND	53,572	54,180	98.9
Fayetteville, NC	98,609	102,725	96.0
Ft. Collins, CO	72,332	73,903	97.9
Ft. Wayne, IN	122,482	131,313	93.3
Ft. Worth, TX	369,818	392,044	94.3
Gainesville, FL	60,145	65,128	92.3
Grand Rapids, MI	91,725	97,437	94.1
Green Bay, WI	50,917	53,577	95.0
Greensboro, NC	129,218	144,423	89.5
Honolulu, HI	169,148	173,042	97.7
Houston, TX	1,069,485	1,060,631	100.8
Huntsville, AL	88,848	92,886	95.7
Indianapolis, IN	398,657	428,982	92.9
Jacksonville, FL	401,863	427,672	94.0
Kansas City, MO	222,575	239,717	92.8
Lafayette, LA	59,849	61,895	96.7
Las Vegas, NV	298,726	290,815	102.7
Lexington, KY	148,398	152,813	97.1
Lincoln, NE	131,120	131,094	100.0
Little Rock, AR	92,211	103,031	89.5
Los Angeles, CA	1,900,258	1,925,395	98.7
Louisville, KY	291,167	310,503	93.8
Lubbock, TX	115,293	118,182	97.6
Madison, WI	117,449	119,687	98.1
Manchester, NH	54,671	55,208	99.0

Table continued on next page.

City	Males	Females	Males per 100 Females
McAllen, TX	64,587	68,133	94.8
Miami, FL	202,143	206,179	98.0
Midland, TX	55,547	59,258	93.7
Minneapolis, MN	196,165	191,889	102.2
Montgomery, AL	97,117	109,229	88.9
Nashville, TN	297,280	316,549	93.9
New Orleans, LA	173,088	186,042	93.0
New York, NY	3,932,715	4,332,730	90.8
Oklahoma City, OK	291,687	298,605	97.7
Omaha, NE	203,256	213,118	95.4
Orlando, FL	118,191	125,704	94.0
Oxnard, CA	101,827	98,188	103.7
Peoria, IL	54,704	59,694	91.6
Philadelphia, PA	726,023	812,188	89.4
Phoenix, AZ	736,219	731,181	100.7
Pittsburgh, PA	148,144	157,862	93.8
Portland, OR	294,006	300,518	97.8
Providence, RI	86,626	91,673	94.5
Provo, UT	56,618	57,849	97.9
Raleigh, NC	199,292	215,081	92.7
Reno, NV	116,573	112,085	104.0
Richmond, VA	98,377	108,559	90.6
Riverside, CA	154,521	155,272	99.5
Rochester, MN	53,057	54,967	96.5
Salem, OR	76,947	79,208	97.1
Salt Lake City, UT	95,493	92,471	103.3
San Antonio, TX	661,308	696,835	94.9
San Diego, CA	665,894	655,651	101.6
San Francisco, CA	414,137	401,097	103.3
San Jose, CA	487,819	481,505	101.3
Santa Rosa, CA	84,372	85,004	99.3
Savannah, GA	66,795	72,872	91.7
Seattle, WA	308,107	314,166	98.1
Sioux Falls, SD	78,242	78,755	99.3
Spokane, WA	101,738	107,608	94.5
Springfield, MO	77,852	82,896	93.9
Tallahassee, FL	87,994	96,085	91.6
Tampa, FL	168,972	174,705	96.7
Topeka, KS	61,493	66,402	92.6
Tulsa, OK	190,081	203,043	93.6
Virginia Beach, VA	217,519	225,583	96.4
Washington, DC	292,559	326,218	89.7
Wichita, KS	189,420	194,605	97.3
Wilmington, NC	51,786	56,534	91.6
Worcester, MA	85,543	96,801	88.4
U.S.	153,276,055	158,333,314	96.8

Source: U.S. Census Bureau, 2010-2012 American Community Survey 3-Year Estimates

Male/Female Ratio: Metro Area

Metro Area	Males	Females	Males per 100 Females
Abilene, TX	83,952	82,388	101.9
Albuquerque, NM	440,882	455,314	96.8
Anchorage, AK	197,949	189,967	104.2
Ann Arbor, MI	171,853	176,458	97.4
Athens, GA	93,538	101,323	92.3
Atlanta, GA	2,609,093	2,752,059	94.8
Austin, TX	892,059	888,831	100.4
Baltimore, MD	1,316,630	1,417,508	92.9
Billings, MT	78,541	81,633	96.2
Boise City, ID	313,178	314,667	99.5
Boston, MA	2,229,374	2,373,295	93.9
Boulder, CO	150,911	149,770	100.8
Cape Coral, FL	310,415	322,084	96.4
Cedar Rapids, IA	128,955	131,385	98.2
Charleston, SC	333,074	349,170	95.4
Charlotte, NC	872,208	924,551	94.3
Chicago, IL	4,642,475	4,854,112	95.6
Cincinnati, OH	1,046,009	1,092,127	95.8
Clarksville, TN	139,821	140,411	99.6
Colorado Spgs, CO	330,119	329,300	100.2
Columbia, MO	85,543	90,514	94.5
Columbus, OH	912,971	946,726	96.4
Dallas, TX	3,216,334	3,303,515	97.4
Davenport, IA	187,118	194,249	96.3
Denver, CO	1,293,188	1,306,087	99.0
Des Moines, IA	285,448	295,124	96.7
Durham, NC	246,272	267,934	91.9
El Paso, TX	397,109	419,186	94.7
Erie, PA	138,077	142,717	96.7
Eugene, OR	173,728	179,587	96.7
Fargo, ND	106,873	105,898	100.9
Fayetteville, NC	180,157	191,549	94.1
Ft. Collins, CO	151,988	153,347	99.1
Ft. Wayne, IN	204,982	214,270	95.7
Ft. Worth, TX	3,216,334	3,303,515	97.4
Gainesville, FL	129,927	136,437	95.2
Grand Rapids, MI	386,335	393,347	98.2
Green Bay, WI	154,016	154,862	99.5
Greensboro, NC	351,105	379,472	92.5
Honolulu, HI	485,338	481,067	100.9
Houston, TX	3,027,722	3,058,151	99.0
Huntsville, AL	210,052	215,057	97.7
Indianapolis, IN	868,952	910,487	95.4
Jacksonville, FL	663,092	699,558	94.8
Kansas City, MO	1,005,603	1,046,192	96.1
Lafayette, LA	135,466	141,595	95.7
Las Vegas, NV	992,784	981,252	101.2
Lexington, KY	235,376	243,766	96.6
Lincoln, NE	153,781	152,845	100.6
Little Rock, AR	344,604	365,717	94.2
Los Angeles, CA	6,389,104	6,558,230	97.4
Louisville, KY	632,215	661,616	95.6
Lubbock, TX	143,217	146,468	97.8
Madison, WI	286,516	290,329	98.7
Manchester, NH	198,957	202,976	98.0

Table continued on next page.

Metro Area	Males	Females	Males per 100 Females
McAllen, TX	386,944	406,368	95.2
Miami, FL	2,753,497	2,923,911	94.2
Midland, TX	69,616	71,591	97.2
Minneapolis, MN	1,641,004	1,679,186	97.7
Montgomery, AL	180,522	196,442	91.9
Nashville, TN	791,205	827,614	95.6
New Orleans, LA	578,837	611,325	94.7
New York, NY	9,183,572	9,864,595	93.1
Oklahoma City, OK	629,988	646,783	97.4
Omaha, NE	432,704	444,267	97.4
Orlando, FL	1,066,934	1,112,486	95.9
Oxnard, CA	412,614	418,214	98.7
Peoria, IL	185,644	194,274	95.6
Philadelphia, PA	2,894,285	3,101,816	93.3
Phoenix, AZ	2,120,250	2,143,413	98.9
Pittsburgh, PA	1,141,730	1,217,495	93.8
Portland, OR	1,117,800	1,143,348	97.8
Providence, RI	774,756	826,452	93.7
Provo, UT	271,300	269,158	100.8
Raleigh, NC	567,822	595,047	95.4
Reno, NV	216,628	213,213	101.6
Richmond, VA	615,392	655,343	93.9
Riverside, CA	2,139,026	2,159,615	99.0
Rochester, MN	92,501	95,065	97.3
Salem, OR	195,208	198,724	98.2
Salt Lake City, UT	575,758	569,031	101.2
San Antonio, TX	1,078,236	1,114,703	96.7
San Diego, CA	1,576,317	1,563,409	100.8
San Francisco, CA	2,170,877	2,228,334	97.4
San Jose, CA	937,812	930,353	100.8
Santa Rosa, CA	239,948	248,289	96.6
Savannah, GA	172,578	182,961	94.3
Seattle, WA	1,743,562	1,756,070	99.3
Sioux Falls, SD	116,736	116,562	100.1
Spokane, WA	234,592	239,201	98.1
Springfield, MO	215,697	225,114	95.8
Tallahassee, FL	180,521	191,406	94.3
Tampa, FL	1,366,313	1,453,069	94.0
Topeka, KS	114,562	119,954	95.5
Tulsa, OK	464,528	481,216	96.5
Virginia Beach, VA	827,442	856,569	96.6
Washington, DC	2,782,107	2,928,736	95.0
Wichita, KS	309,440	316,500	97.8
Wilmington, NC	180,599	189,112	95.5
Worcester, MA	396,216	407,213	97.3
U.S.	153,276,055	158,333,314	96.8

Note: Figures cover the Metropolitan Statistical Area (MSA)—see Appendix B for areas included
Source: U.S. Census Bureau, 2010-2012 American Community Survey 3-Year Estimates

Gross Metropolitan Product

MSA[1]	2011	2012	2013	2014	Rank[2]
Abilene, TX	5.6	6.0	6.2	6.5	244
Albuquerque, NM	37.9	38.8	39.6	41.5	61
Anchorage, AK	27.9	28.6	29.0	29.6	84
Ann Arbor, MI	18.7	19.3	19.7	20.5	112
Athens, GA	6.6	6.8	7.0	7.3	224
Atlanta, GA	282.0	294.0	304.9	320.9	10
Austin, TX	91.5	98.7	103.2	109.3	31
Baltimore, MD	149.8	157.3	162.1	168.7	19
Billings, MT	8.2	8.5	8.6	8.9	206
Boise City, ID	26.5	27.5	28.2	29.5	85
Boston, MA	323.3	336.2	346.4	361.4	9
Boulder, CO	19.3	20.3	21.0	22.0	105
Cape Coral, FL	20.1	20.9	21.4	22.4	100
Cedar Rapids, IA	14.3	14.8	15.1	15.5	142
Charleston, SC	29.7	31.0	31.8	33.4	74
Charlotte, NC	117.4	125.2	130.5	137.0	22
Chicago, IL	548.5	571.0	585.9	610.4	3
Cincinnati, OH	103.8	108.4	111.2	115.7	29
Clarksville, TN	11.5	11.8	11.9	12.5	163
Colorado Spgs, CO	27.2	28.0	28.6	29.9	83
Columbia, MO	7.0	7.3	7.5	8.0	216
Columbus, OH	95.3	99.7	102.1	106.7	32
Dallas, TX	397.0	418.6	436.4	460.9	6
Davenport, IA	17.9	18.6	18.9	19.4	116
Denver, CO	161.8	167.9	173.3	182.2	18
Des Moines, IA	40.0	42.1	43.9	45.7	57
Durham, NC	38.0	39.7	41.5	43.8	59
El Paso, TX	29.0	29.6	29.8	31.2	78
Erie, PA	9.7	10.0	10.1	10.5	182
Eugene, OR	11.8	12.2	12.4	12.8	160
Fargo, ND	12.3	13.2	14.1	15.0	144
Fayetteville, NC	18.4	18.7	18.8	19.4	116
Ft. Collins, CO	11.9	12.4	12.8	13.4	156
Ft. Wayne, IN	18.2	19.0	19.5	20.1	114
Ft. Worth, TX	397.0	418.6	436.4	460.9	6
Gainesville, FL	10.3	10.5	10.7	11.1	176
Grand Rapids, MI	33.3	35.3	36.8	38.6	65
Green Bay, WI	15.3	15.9	16.3	17.1	131
Greensboro, NC	35.3	36.9	37.9	39.5	64
Honolulu, HI	54.4	56.6	57.6	59.7	51
Houston, TX	425.5	449.7	463.7	488.7	4
Huntsville, AL	21.4	21.7	21.9	22.8	98
Indianapolis, IN	107.2	112.8	116.1	120.9	27
Jacksonville, FL	59.8	62.3	65.1	68.2	47
Kansas City, MO	109.1	113.8	116.6	121.7	25
Lafayette, LA	19.2	17.7	17.2	17.8	126
Las Vegas, NV	92.6	95.6	98.4	103.3	34
Lexington, KY	23.4	23.9	24.7	25.9	90
Lincoln, NE	15.2	15.9	16.2	16.8	133
Little Rock, AR	33.6	34.4	35.1	36.5	68
Los Angeles, CA	732.2	765.7	792.4	827.6	2
Louisville, KY	60.3	63.8	66.5	69.4	46
Lubbock, TX	10.3	10.9	11.3	11.7	171
Madison, WI	36.8	38.0	39.2	40.9	63
Manchester, NH	22.1	22.2	22.3	23.2	97
McAllen, TX	15.5	16.0	16.5	17.3	130

Table continued on next page.

MSA[1]	2011	2012	2013	2014	Rank[2]
Miami, FL	260.7	274.1	283.4	296.1	11
Midland, TX	14.7	16.2	17.5	18.7	119
Minneapolis, MN	207.0	218.5	228.0	237.7	13
Montgomery, AL	15.3	15.4	15.5	16.0	139
Nashville, TN	84.9	91.1	95.5	100.3	35
New Orleans, LA	74.3	80.2	83.0	86.2	40
New York, NY	1,294.2	1,335.1	1,379.7	1,431.3	1
Oklahoma City, OK	61.5	63.3	64.3	66.9	48
Omaha, NE	50.0	51.9	53.1	55.8	52
Orlando, FL	101.5	106.1	109.8	115.6	30
Oxnard, CA	38.3	39.1	39.7	41.5	61
Peoria, IL	19.5	21.3	21.6	22.3	101
Philadelphia, PA	352.3	364.0	373.9	388.4	8
Phoenix, AZ	192.3	201.7	210.1	221.0	14
Pittsburgh, PA	119.3	123.6	126.5	131.5	23
Portland, OR	138.5	147.0	152.6	160.9	20
Providence, RI	67.3	69.5	71.2	73.9	44
Provo, UT	16.1	17.0	17.7	18.7	119
Raleigh, NC	59.0	61.4	63.2	66.8	49
Reno, NV	20.0	20.4	20.7	21.5	108
Richmond, VA	66.6	70.0	71.7	74.4	43
Riverside, CA	110.3	114.0	115.7	121.4	26
Rochester, MN	9.3	9.7	10.0	10.4	185
Salem, OR	12.4	12.7	13.1	13.6	154
Salt Lake City, UT	70.9	74.8	77.5	81.5	42
San Antonio, TX	87.2	92.0	94.1	99.0	36
San Diego, CA	169.9	177.4	182.6	191.7	16
San Francisco, CA	331.0	360.4	377.2	395.4	7
San Jose, CA	167.8	173.9	181.2	191.0	17
Santa Rosa, CA	20.1	20.3	20.6	21.4	110
Savannah, GA	13.5	14.1	14.3	14.8	147
Seattle, WA	243.8	258.8	268.5	281.0	12
Sioux Falls, SD	16.0	16.6	17.6	18.3	123
Spokane, WA	18.6	19.3	19.9	20.7	111
Springfield, MO	15.4	16.2	16.9	17.6	128
Tallahassee, FL	13.3	13.4	13.7	14.2	149
Tampa, FL	114.4	119.9	125.5	131.5	23
Topeka, KS	9.6	9.9	9.9	10.2	192
Tulsa, OK	47.3	47.9	48.2	50.3	54
Virginia Beach, VA	82.1	85.2	87.2	90.2	39
Washington, DC	437.2	446.9	455.8	477.5	5
Wichita, KS	28.6	29.4	29.6	30.8	81
Wilmington, NC	15.1	15.4	15.9	16.6	135
Worcester, MA	29.7	30.5	31.1	32.2	75

Note: Figures are in billions of dollars; (1) Metropolitan Statistical Area—see Appendix B for areas included; (2) Rank is based on 2014 data and ranges from 1 to 363.
Source: The United States Conference of Mayors, U.S. Metro Economies: Outlook—Gross Metropolitan Product, with Metro Employment Projections, November 2013

Income: City

City	Per Capita ($)	Median Household ($)	Average Household ($)
Abilene, TX	20,195	41,460	54,290
Albuquerque, NM	26,277	46,060	62,606
Anchorage, AK	35,525	74,648	94,517
Ann Arbor, MI	33,992	53,351	76,144
Athens, GA	18,760	32,809	50,939
Atlanta, GA	34,041	44,784	78,505
Austin, TX	30,880	51,668	74,860
Baltimore, MD	23,326	39,788	56,287
Billings, MT	26,568	46,655	62,330
Boise City, ID	27,063	45,985	63,852
Boston, MA	32,886	51,452	78,420
Boulder, CO	36,016	56,205	86,325
Cape Coral, FL	22,522	47,586	59,540
Cedar Rapids, IA	27,884	52,455	65,965
Charleston, SC	31,728	50,602	72,430
Charlotte, NC	30,710	51,209	76,914
Chicago, IL	27,237	45,483	68,868
Cincinnati, OH	24,106	32,591	53,215
Clarksville, TN	20,493	44,760	54,454
Colorado Spgs, CO	28,270	52,896	69,844
Columbia, MO	25,171	41,576	62,641
Columbus, OH	23,609	42,491	55,908
Dallas, TX	26,294	41,745	67,684
Davenport, IA	23,966	42,451	57,089
Denver, CO	32,508	49,049	73,299
Des Moines, IA	23,186	44,292	57,027
Durham, NC	27,001	46,924	65,249
El Paso, TX	19,472	40,920	57,117
Erie, PA	18,207	31,838	42,773
Eugene, OR	25,282	40,435	58,847
Fargo, ND	29,887	45,644	65,527
Fayetteville, NC	22,889	44,472	56,003
Ft. Collins, CO	27,499	51,830	69,242
Ft. Wayne, IN	23,283	43,673	57,396
Ft. Worth, TX	23,597	50,129	65,747
Gainesville, FL	19,445	31,294	48,531
Grand Rapids, MI	19,616	37,791	49,277
Green Bay, WI	23,323	41,404	55,576
Greensboro, NC	24,608	40,323	58,528
Honolulu, HI	29,446	57,452	75,157
Houston, TX	26,335	43,792	69,421
Huntsville, AL	29,484	46,821	68,794
Indianapolis, IN	22,983	40,167	56,113
Jacksonville, FL	24,483	45,577	62,009
Kansas City, MO	26,360	44,277	61,822
Lafayette, LA	27,580	43,928	64,837
Las Vegas, NV	25,045	49,726	66,373
Lexington, KY	28,369	47,785	68,100
Lincoln, NE	25,770	48,295	63,302
Little Rock, AR	28,352	45,267	66,836
Los Angeles, CA	26,913	47,742	74,525
Louisville, KY	25,192	42,609	60,786
Lubbock, TX	23,003	42,139	58,725
Madison, WI	30,386	52,599	69,567
Manchester, NH	27,095	54,122	65,035
McAllen, TX	21,406	41,375	64,900

Table continued on next page.

City	Per Capita ($)	Median Household ($)	Average Household ($)
Miami, FL	20,104	28,935	49,640
Midland, TX	31,846	59,336	86,405
Minneapolis, MN	30,560	48,228	69,624
Montgomery, AL	23,655	42,403	59,186
Nashville, TN	26,412	44,271	62,441
New Orleans, LA	25,654	36,004	59,897
New York, NY	30,826	50,711	79,740
Oklahoma City, OK	24,994	44,519	62,585
Omaha, NE	26,376	46,202	64,411
Orlando, FL	24,936	41,266	58,471
Oxnard, CA	19,835	60,667	74,150
Peoria, IL	26,948	44,061	64,118
Philadelphia, PA	21,292	35,581	52,296
Phoenix, AZ	23,091	44,649	62,918
Pittsburgh, PA	25,927	37,280	57,505
Portland, OR	30,517	49,958	70,209
Providence, RI	21,262	37,654	58,512
Provo, UT	16,506	38,338	55,633
Raleigh, NC	29,277	52,709	72,867
Reno, NV	25,113	44,318	61,643
Richmond, VA	26,231	40,001	60,594
Riverside, CA	21,615	53,893	70,403
Rochester, MN	31,673	61,547	77,129
Salem, OR	22,905	45,215	59,755
Salt Lake City, UT	26,176	42,267	64,133
San Antonio, TX	22,171	45,074	60,254
San Diego, CA	32,086	63,034	85,370
San Francisco, CA	46,580	72,888	106,350
San Jose, CA	32,974	80,155	101,431
Santa Rosa, CA	28,733	58,893	75,670
Savannah, GA	18,889	34,832	46,779
Seattle, WA	41,518	62,617	88,590
Sioux Falls, SD	27,099	50,295	66,148
Spokane, WA	23,567	41,593	54,915
Springfield, MO	20,176	32,359	44,751
Tallahassee, FL	23,722	38,865	57,787
Tampa, FL	28,262	41,524	68,107
Topeka, KS	22,875	39,118	53,735
Tulsa, OK	26,374	40,359	62,060
Virginia Beach, VA	31,431	65,169	82,301
Washington, DC	44,670	64,610	99,781
Wichita, KS	24,123	44,612	60,053
Wilmington, NC	28,552	41,554	64,656
Worcester, MA	23,946	43,999	60,512
U.S.	27,385	51,771	71,579

Source: U.S. Census Bureau, 2010-2012 American Community Survey 3-Year Estimates

Income: Metro Area

Metro Area	Per Capita ($)	Median Household ($)	Average Household ($)
Abilene, TX	21,548	42,724	57,470
Albuquerque, NM	25,545	47,604	64,264
Anchorage, AK	34,076	73,218	91,789
Ann Arbor, MI	32,675	57,548	79,863
Athens, GA	21,698	41,339	59,744
Atlanta, GA	27,642	54,807	75,230
Austin, TX	30,365	58,821	79,799
Baltimore, MD	34,097	67,340	88,089
Billings, MT	26,768	49,610	64,081
Boise City, ID	23,354	48,188	62,610
Boston, MA	37,800	71,375	96,583
Boulder, CO	37,539	66,783	92,309
Cape Coral, FL	26,278	46,022	65,020
Cedar Rapids, IA	28,954	56,667	70,824
Charleston, SC	26,490	50,660	67,011
Charlotte, NC	28,421	52,346	74,162
Chicago, IL	30,112	59,496	81,061
Cincinnati, OH	27,761	53,475	70,905
Clarksville, TN	21,098	44,361	55,912
Colorado Spgs, CO	28,342	55,649	73,248
Columbia, MO	26,057	45,156	65,102
Columbus, OH	28,259	53,717	71,707
Dallas, TX	28,421	57,109	78,238
Davenport, IA	26,698	49,197	64,300
Denver, CO	32,657	61,392	82,057
Des Moines, IA	29,457	59,047	74,101
Durham, NC	29,028	49,965	72,098
El Paso, TX	18,183	39,821	55,130
Erie, PA	23,650	44,475	58,689
Eugene, OR	23,532	41,465	56,155
Fargo, ND	28,997	52,655	68,593
Fayetteville, NC	22,026	44,680	56,594
Ft. Collins, CO	29,717	56,274	73,196
Ft. Wayne, IN	24,905	49,305	63,277
Ft. Worth, TX	28,421	57,109	78,238
Gainesville, FL	24,223	41,405	60,928
Grand Rapids, MI	24,499	50,286	64,332
Green Bay, WI	26,693	51,795	66,183
Greensboro, NC	23,568	42,235	58,207
Honolulu, HI	29,475	70,541	86,889
Houston, TX	28,059	56,080	79,881
Huntsville, AL	29,599	54,407	74,576
Indianapolis, IN	27,291	51,626	70,011
Jacksonville, FL	26,938	50,952	69,112
Kansas City, MO	28,853	55,320	72,650
Lafayette, LA	26,809	47,146	67,314
Las Vegas, NV	25,380	50,943	67,662
Lexington, KY	27,294	48,446	67,120
Lincoln, NE	26,708	51,101	66,578
Little Rock, AR	25,520	47,969	63,248
Los Angeles, CA	28,329	58,377	83,636
Louisville, KY	26,032	47,961	64,793
Lubbock, TX	23,133	43,414	60,467
Madison, WI	32,007	60,308	76,451
Manchester, NH	33,635	69,395	86,470
McAllen, TX	14,073	33,549	48,908

Table continued on next page.

Metro Area	Per Capita ($)	Median Household ($)	Average Household ($)
Miami, FL	26,277	46,867	69,526
Midland, TX	31,602	58,875	86,027
Minneapolis, MN	33,262	65,756	84,643
Montgomery, AL	23,860	46,058	61,625
Nashville, TN	27,474	51,178	70,435
New Orleans, LA	26,159	46,087	65,519
New York, NY	34,738	64,344	93,767
Oklahoma City, OK	25,782	48,618	65,833
Omaha, NE	28,360	55,984	72,066
Orlando, FL	24,156	47,228	64,869
Oxnard, CA	31,960	74,458	96,240
Peoria, IL	27,493	52,705	67,442
Philadelphia, PA	31,569	60,444	82,361
Phoenix, AZ	25,836	51,695	69,492
Pittsburgh, PA	28,881	49,973	67,445
Portland, OR	29,114	56,236	73,797
Providence, RI	29,018	54,674	72,588
Provo, UT	20,109	58,513	72,129
Raleigh, NC	30,039	60,332	79,164
Reno, NV	27,898	51,033	70,341
Richmond, VA	29,527	57,234	76,042
Riverside, CA	21,759	53,855	69,495
Rochester, MN	31,897	63,610	79,757
Salem, OR	21,959	46,214	59,213
Salt Lake City, UT	25,549	59,641	75,575
San Antonio, TX	24,522	51,087	68,110
San Diego, CA	29,483	61,364	81,993
San Francisco, CA	40,165	75,168	105,452
San Jose, CA	39,806	88,446	116,236
Santa Rosa, CA	31,386	61,491	80,775
Savannah, GA	24,759	47,998	63,523
Seattle, WA	34,317	65,710	85,890
Sioux Falls, SD	27,191	54,682	68,473
Spokane, WA	25,279	49,059	62,536
Springfield, MO	22,496	42,305	55,395
Tallahassee, FL	24,196	44,647	61,518
Tampa, FL	26,123	44,959	62,781
Topeka, KS	25,323	48,297	62,038
Tulsa, OK	25,551	47,160	64,227
Virginia Beach, VA	28,418	58,241	73,852
Washington, DC	42,624	88,689	114,231
Wichita, KS	24,782	49,096	63,430
Wilmington, NC	27,541	47,452	65,184
Worcester, MA	30,969	63,687	80,951
U.S.	27,385	51,771	71,579

Note: Figures cover the Metropolitan Statistical Area (MSA)—see Appendix B for areas included
Source: U.S. Census Bureau, 2010-2012 American Community Survey 3-Year Estimates

Household Income Distribution: City

City	Percent of Households Earning							
	Under $15,000	$15,000 -24,999	$25,000 -34,999	$35,000 -49,999	$50,000 -74,999	$75,000 -99,000	$100,000 -149,999	$150,000 and up
Abilene, TX	16.4	13.3	12.7	15.9	19.3	9.8	8.4	4.3
Albuquerque, NM	15.3	12.1	11.8	14.0	17.8	11.1	11.1	6.8
Anchorage, AK	6.3	6.7	7.4	12.1	17.7	14.6	18.6	16.6
Ann Arbor, MI	15.6	9.3	10.7	11.6	17.2	9.8	13.3	12.6
Athens, GA	28.0	13.3	10.7	12.8	15.1	7.1	6.9	6.1
Atlanta, GA	21.5	10.9	9.9	10.9	15.4	8.7	10.2	12.5
Austin, TX	13.4	10.0	10.5	14.8	17.2	11.3	12.3	10.5
Baltimore, MD	22.0	12.6	10.9	13.5	17.2	9.0	8.9	6.0
Billings, MT	13.7	12.3	11.6	15.2	18.9	12.2	10.3	6.0
Boise City, ID	13.4	11.6	12.9	15.9	17.4	10.3	11.3	7.2
Boston, MA	20.6	10.2	7.5	10.8	14.8	10.6	13.1	12.6
Boulder, CO	17.1	9.5	8.5	10.5	15.5	9.5	13.0	16.4
Cape Coral, FL	11.3	11.7	12.9	16.2	20.6	11.9	10.6	4.9
Cedar Rapids, IA	11.5	10.6	10.2	14.4	21.1	14.3	12.3	5.7
Charleston, SC	17.6	9.8	9.6	12.4	16.5	11.8	11.5	10.6
Charlotte, NC	12.8	10.5	10.9	14.6	18.3	11.0	11.7	10.2
Chicago, IL	17.9	12.0	10.5	13.0	16.2	10.4	10.6	9.3
Cincinnati, OH	27.1	14.3	10.7	12.3	14.4	8.2	7.3	5.7
Clarksville, TN	13.9	10.6	12.7	17.8	22.3	11.2	8.4	3.2
Colorado Spgs, CO	11.9	10.8	10.2	14.0	19.6	11.7	13.6	8.2
Columbia, MO	19.7	12.9	10.3	15.0	15.2	9.4	10.5	7.2
Columbus, OH	17.3	12.2	11.8	15.3	18.9	10.8	9.3	4.5
Dallas, TX	16.4	12.9	13.1	14.6	17.1	8.3	8.7	8.9
Davenport, IA	15.3	11.9	14.2	16.1	17.2	11.7	9.9	3.7
Denver, CO	15.2	11.3	10.6	13.7	16.6	11.1	10.9	10.5
Des Moines, IA	14.8	12.3	12.2	15.7	19.6	12.4	9.1	4.0
Durham, NC	14.6	12.2	11.8	14.8	16.7	10.8	11.5	7.7
El Paso, TX	17.4	13.9	12.1	15.5	16.9	9.6	9.2	5.4
Erie, PA	24.4	15.9	13.0	15.6	15.6	8.3	5.3	2.0
Eugene, OR	20.8	11.5	12.2	13.5	16.3	9.7	10.3	5.6
Fargo, ND	12.9	12.1	12.2	16.5	17.8	10.8	10.0	7.7
Fayetteville, NC	14.8	10.3	12.7	17.7	20.9	11.0	8.5	4.1
Ft. Collins, CO	14.0	11.3	8.8	14.2	18.5	12.6	12.5	8.2
Ft. Wayne, IN	14.4	12.2	12.8	16.5	20.7	10.7	8.6	4.1
Ft. Worth, TX	13.6	11.6	10.9	13.7	19.1	12.6	11.7	6.8
Gainesville, FL	27.6	14.0	12.5	12.3	14.5	6.8	7.7	4.5
Grand Rapids, MI	19.0	14.4	12.7	16.1	18.4	9.1	7.7	2.7
Green Bay, WI	15.5	13.2	13.3	18.4	18.2	9.9	7.2	4.4
Greensboro, NC	15.9	14.6	13.8	15.5	16.9	8.9	8.5	6.0
Honolulu, HI	11.9	8.5	9.3	13.9	18.6	13.3	14.3	10.4
Houston, TX	16.1	12.9	12.1	14.0	15.8	9.9	9.7	9.4
Huntsville, AL	16.2	11.7	11.1	13.2	15.8	10.6	12.4	9.1
Indianapolis, IN	16.8	13.5	13.5	15.1	16.9	10.6	8.9	4.7
Jacksonville, FL	15.2	12.1	11.6	14.8	18.6	11.4	10.9	5.5
Kansas City, MO	17.2	11.5	11.6	15.0	17.4	10.7	10.4	6.4
Lafayette, LA	18.5	13.3	9.0	14.0	16.2	9.6	11.0	8.3
Las Vegas, NV	12.7	11.3	11.2	15.1	19.1	12.7	10.6	7.3
Lexington, KY	15.9	11.2	10.8	14.0	16.8	11.1	11.9	8.3
Lincoln, NE	13.6	11.0	12.3	14.9	18.8	12.4	10.7	6.5
Little Rock, AR	16.8	13.4	11.1	12.6	16.4	10.5	10.3	9.0
Los Angeles, CA	15.8	12.1	10.5	13.2	16.2	10.3	11.3	10.7
Louisville, KY	16.9	13.0	11.8	14.7	17.3	10.2	9.9	6.3
Lubbock, TX	17.5	13.6	12.1	13.6	18.0	10.4	9.1	5.7
Madison, WI	14.4	9.7	10.6	12.9	18.4	13.1	12.3	8.5

Table continued on next page.

City	Percent of Households Earning							
	Under $15,000	$15,000 -24,999	$25,000 -34,999	$35,000 -49,999	$50,000 -74,999	$75,000 -99,000	$100,000 -149,999	$150,000 and up
Manchester, NH	11.7	10.5	11.5	12.3	21.6	12.7	13.5	6.2
McAllen, TX	19.3	13.2	11.0	14.7	15.0	9.5	9.5	7.7
Miami, FL	28.4	16.3	12.4	12.7	12.7	6.0	5.8	5.7
Midland, TX	10.1	9.2	10.0	12.0	20.8	12.3	13.8	12.0
Minneapolis, MN	17.1	10.9	9.7	13.6	16.4	11.1	12.2	9.0
Montgomery, AL	18.6	12.7	10.3	15.8	17.3	9.7	10.0	5.6
Nashville, TN	15.6	12.1	12.0	15.6	18.5	10.3	9.1	6.8
New Orleans, LA	24.5	13.3	11.2	12.7	13.9	8.8	8.3	7.2
New York, NY	17.1	11.0	9.4	11.9	15.9	10.5	12.1	12.0
Oklahoma City, OK	14.8	12.3	12.7	15.0	18.1	10.6	10.5	6.1
Omaha, NE	14.3	12.2	12.2	14.5	18.5	11.5	10.4	6.4
Orlando, FL	15.4	14.2	12.8	16.0	19.2	8.1	8.3	5.8
Oxnard, CA	8.7	9.5	8.4	14.5	20.2	14.6	14.9	9.1
Peoria, IL	17.2	12.7	10.7	14.1	17.1	11.2	10.5	6.5
Philadelphia, PA	23.9	13.6	11.8	13.2	15.9	8.9	7.8	4.8
Phoenix, AZ	15.4	11.7	12.1	15.1	17.2	10.7	10.8	7.0
Pittsburgh, PA	21.4	14.5	11.7	13.2	16.5	8.5	7.8	6.5
Portland, OR	15.4	10.6	10.7	13.3	17.2	11.5	12.4	8.9
Providence, RI	25.0	12.6	9.8	13.4	16.2	8.8	8.1	6.1
Provo, UT	18.8	14.3	12.8	14.7	18.8	9.0	7.0	4.5
Raleigh, NC	11.5	9.4	11.8	14.1	19.2	12.2	12.1	9.6
Reno, NV	15.6	12.8	11.7	14.9	17.9	10.1	10.4	6.6
Richmond, VA	20.9	12.8	11.5	15.1	15.8	9.6	7.7	6.5
Riverside, CA	11.5	11.1	10.2	13.5	19.4	12.2	12.9	9.0
Rochester, MN	9.0	9.8	8.9	12.9	19.1	15.4	15.0	9.9
Salem, OR	14.6	11.7	12.3	16.3	19.2	11.1	10.0	4.8
Salt Lake City, UT	17.3	13.2	11.3	14.3	16.9	10.1	9.2	7.7
San Antonio, TX	15.2	12.5	11.9	15.2	18.5	10.8	10.0	5.9
San Diego, CA	11.2	9.0	8.3	12.0	16.8	13.2	15.3	14.2
San Francisco, CA	13.2	8.5	6.9	8.7	13.6	10.7	16.1	22.2
San Jose, CA	8.1	7.5	7.1	10.2	14.4	12.7	18.5	21.4
Santa Rosa, CA	8.9	10.8	9.2	14.5	19.1	13.3	14.2	10.0
Savannah, GA	23.0	13.8	13.3	15.1	18.4	7.5	5.7	3.2
Seattle, WA	12.5	7.8	8.6	11.9	17.0	11.9	15.3	15.2
Sioux Falls, SD	10.7	10.7	12.0	16.3	19.7	13.1	11.1	6.5
Spokane, WA	16.6	13.6	12.8	14.7	19.0	11.0	8.0	4.4
Springfield, MO	20.6	17.8	15.5	15.2	16.6	6.8	4.7	2.9
Tallahassee, FL	24.4	11.7	10.6	14.5	14.7	8.5	9.3	6.3
Tampa, FL	19.0	12.9	11.8	13.3	15.9	8.5	9.2	9.3
Topeka, KS	16.9	13.3	14.2	16.6	18.1	9.5	7.9	3.5
Tulsa, OK	16.8	13.5	13.4	15.7	17.1	8.5	8.0	7.2
Virginia Beach, VA	7.1	6.6	8.6	14.1	21.1	14.7	16.9	11.1
Washington, DC	15.1	7.8	7.1	10.5	14.9	10.8	14.8	19.0
Wichita, KS	14.0	13.0	12.6	15.3	18.6	11.5	9.8	5.2
Wilmington, NC	18.5	13.3	12.4	13.9	15.7	8.5	9.9	7.9
Worcester, MA	18.7	12.6	10.1	13.3	17.5	10.4	10.7	6.7
U.S.	13.1	11.0	10.5	13.7	18.1	11.9	12.5	9.1

Source: U.S. Census Bureau, 2010-2012 American Community Survey 3-Year Estimates

Household Income Distribution: Metro Area

Metro Area	Under $15,000	$15,000 -24,999	$25,000 -34,999	$35,000 -49,999	$50,000 -74,999	$75,000 -99,000	$100,000 -149,999	$150,000 and up
				Percent of Households Earning				
Abilene, TX	15.3	13.3	12.5	15.4	19.6	9.8	9.1	4.9
Albuquerque, NM	14.7	11.9	11.3	14.1	18.1	11.2	11.5	7.2
Anchorage, AK	6.8	7.2	7.3	11.7	18.2	14.6	18.7	15.5
Ann Arbor, MI	12.3	9.5	10.0	12.2	16.7	11.7	14.8	12.9
Athens, GA	20.9	12.3	10.7	13.4	16.4	9.8	9.1	7.4
Atlanta, GA	12.0	9.9	10.1	13.7	18.6	12.0	13.3	10.4
Austin, TX	10.9	8.9	9.4	13.8	18.2	12.8	14.6	11.4
Baltimore, MD	10.3	7.8	8.0	11.1	17.7	13.0	17.1	15.1
Billings, MT	12.5	11.5	11.3	15.0	19.6	12.9	11.4	5.8
Boise City, ID	12.4	11.4	12.2	15.6	20.6	11.3	10.6	6.0
Boston, MA	10.9	7.9	7.3	10.3	15.7	12.8	17.5	17.6
Boulder, CO	10.8	8.4	7.8	12.6	15.2	11.7	16.5	16.9
Cape Coral, FL	11.9	12.5	13.2	16.2	18.9	10.4	10.1	6.8
Cedar Rapids, IA	9.6	9.6	10.1	13.8	21.1	14.5	14.1	7.1
Charleston, SC	13.7	10.9	10.4	14.3	19.4	11.9	11.6	7.9
Charlotte, NC	12.2	10.5	10.4	14.5	18.6	11.8	12.4	9.5
Chicago, IL	11.3	9.6	9.2	12.5	17.8	12.9	14.6	12.1
Cincinnati, OH	12.9	10.6	10.0	13.4	18.7	12.7	12.8	8.8
Clarksville, TN	13.8	12.3	12.6	16.8	21.0	11.4	8.4	3.7
Colorado Spgs, CO	10.6	10.1	9.5	13.9	19.7	12.3	14.9	8.9
Columbia, MO	16.9	12.1	10.4	14.5	17.0	11.4	10.8	6.9
Columbus, OH	12.5	10.2	10.1	13.7	18.9	12.5	13.0	9.0
Dallas, TX	10.4	9.7	10.2	13.6	18.5	12.1	14.4	11.0
Davenport, IA	11.9	11.2	12.1	15.6	19.5	12.5	11.2	6.1
Denver, CO	10.1	8.7	9.2	12.8	18.5	13.1	15.4	12.2
Des Moines, IA	9.4	9.1	10.1	13.6	20.0	14.2	15.0	8.5
Durham, NC	13.8	11.3	11.0	13.9	16.8	11.2	12.2	9.8
El Paso, TX	17.8	14.3	12.7	15.2	17.1	9.3	8.5	5.0
Erie, PA	15.9	12.6	11.5	14.8	19.2	11.3	9.9	4.6
Eugene, OR	17.0	13.1	12.2	15.1	17.9	11.0	9.1	4.5
Fargo, ND	11.5	10.8	11.1	14.5	19.3	13.2	12.4	7.2
Fayetteville, NC	14.9	11.2	12.5	16.3	19.7	11.6	9.7	4.0
Ft. Collins, CO	11.2	10.5	9.1	13.7	18.9	13.7	13.8	9.1
Ft. Wayne, IN	11.6	10.9	11.7	16.5	21.7	12.4	10.2	5.1
Ft. Worth, TX	10.4	9.7	10.2	13.6	18.5	12.1	14.4	11.0
Gainesville, FL	20.6	12.3	10.8	12.8	16.1	10.1	10.5	6.7
Grand Rapids, MI	11.9	11.4	11.6	14.8	20.7	12.8	10.8	5.9
Green Bay, WI	10.7	11.4	10.7	15.3	20.5	13.5	11.7	6.2
Greensboro, NC	15.2	13.1	13.5	15.1	18.2	10.5	9.2	5.4
Honolulu, HI	8.8	6.4	7.4	11.9	18.3	14.5	18.9	13.6
Houston, TX	11.5	10.1	10.2	13.0	17.3	12.0	13.8	12.1
Huntsville, AL	12.5	10.3	9.8	13.6	16.5	12.1	14.7	10.4
Indianapolis, IN	11.9	10.7	11.2	14.5	18.2	12.7	12.8	7.9
Jacksonville, FL	13.2	10.8	10.7	14.5	19.1	12.2	12.1	7.4
Kansas City, MO	11.3	9.7	10.0	14.1	19.1	13.1	14.0	8.6
Lafayette, LA	16.9	12.3	9.7	12.9	17.1	11.0	11.5	8.6
Las Vegas, NV	11.5	10.7	11.7	15.2	19.8	12.6	11.4	7.2
Lexington, KY	15.3	11.0	10.9	14.2	17.4	11.6	12.2	7.4
Lincoln, NE	12.6	10.3	11.7	14.5	19.0	13.0	11.8	7.2
Little Rock, AR	13.7	12.1	11.4	14.4	18.5	12.5	11.3	6.1
Los Angeles, CA	11.7	10.1	9.3	12.6	16.9	11.9	14.4	13.2
Louisville, KY	13.8	11.7	11.2	14.9	18.6	11.9	11.4	6.6
Lubbock, TX	16.7	13.4	12.0	13.8	17.8	10.7	9.7	6.0
Madison, WI	10.3	8.6	9.7	13.1	18.9	14.8	15.3	9.3

Table continued on next page.

Metro Area	Percent of Households Earning							
	Under $15,000	$15,000 -24,999	$25,000 -34,999	$35,000 -49,999	$50,000 -74,999	$75,000 -99,000	$100,000 -149,999	$150,000 and up
Manchester, NH	7.8	8.1	8.3	11.1	18.4	14.5	18.4	13.3
McAllen, TX	23.7	15.8	12.2	14.2	15.1	8.1	7.0	3.8
Miami, FL	15.0	12.1	11.3	14.2	17.2	10.5	11.1	8.7
Midland, TX	9.2	9.2	10.4	13.1	20.3	12.0	13.6	12.1
Minneapolis, MN	9.1	8.0	8.4	12.5	18.5	14.5	16.9	12.2
Montgomery, AL	16.1	11.4	10.8	14.9	18.4	10.8	12.0	5.6
Nashville, TN	12.2	10.6	10.8	15.2	18.8	12.3	11.9	8.2
New Orleans, LA	16.8	11.8	11.2	13.6	16.4	11.2	11.4	7.7
New York, NY	12.3	9.1	8.2	10.8	15.8	11.7	15.4	16.8
Oklahoma City, OK	13.4	11.7	11.6	14.5	18.9	11.6	11.4	6.9
Omaha, NE	10.9	9.8	10.3	13.8	19.5	13.9	13.8	7.9
Orlando, FL	12.4	12.0	12.5	15.4	19.1	11.1	10.7	6.8
Oxnard, CA	7.4	7.8	7.1	11.4	16.8	13.8	18.3	17.5
Peoria, IL	11.4	10.8	10.1	14.6	20.2	13.5	13.4	6.1
Philadelphia, PA	12.1	9.2	9.0	11.9	17.0	12.5	15.2	13.0
Phoenix, AZ	11.9	10.6	11.0	14.9	18.8	12.0	12.8	8.1
Pittsburgh, PA	13.2	12.1	11.1	13.7	18.7	11.9	11.8	7.5
Portland, OR	11.3	9.3	9.9	13.9	19.3	13.2	14.0	9.1
Providence, RI	13.9	10.5	9.1	12.5	17.7	12.4	14.3	9.6
Provo, UT	9.3	9.2	9.1	14.4	23.2	13.9	13.6	7.4
Raleigh, NC	9.6	8.5	10.2	13.1	18.8	13.0	15.2	11.7
Reno, NV	12.6	11.3	10.9	14.3	18.7	11.5	13.2	7.6
Richmond, VA	10.5	8.8	9.9	14.2	18.8	13.2	14.8	9.8
Riverside, CA	11.4	11.0	10.3	13.9	18.6	13.0	13.5	8.4
Rochester, MN	8.4	8.9	8.7	13.3	19.1	15.5	15.9	10.2
Salem, OR	13.5	11.9	12.2	16.0	20.0	11.6	10.5	4.4
Salt Lake City, UT	9.3	9.3	9.3	13.5	21.4	14.1	14.5	8.6
San Antonio, TX	12.7	10.9	10.7	14.6	19.0	12.0	12.3	7.7
San Diego, CA	11.0	8.9	9.2	12.6	17.3	12.8	15.2	13.0
San Francisco, CA	9.6	7.6	7.0	10.1	15.5	11.7	17.2	21.3
San Jose, CA	7.3	6.6	6.3	9.4	13.7	12.0	18.9	25.8
Santa Rosa, CA	8.7	10.0	8.8	13.7	18.2	13.2	15.6	11.8
Savannah, GA	14.6	11.3	11.0	14.8	19.1	11.3	11.3	6.6
Seattle, WA	9.3	7.9	8.3	12.5	18.3	13.6	16.9	13.2
Sioux Falls, SD	9.6	9.5	11.2	15.5	20.3	15.0	12.5	6.4
Spokane, WA	13.8	11.7	11.3	14.1	19.8	12.8	10.7	5.9
Springfield, MO	14.5	13.8	13.1	16.2	19.9	10.4	7.8	4.2
Tallahassee, FL	19.0	10.8	10.7	14.2	17.1	10.9	11.1	6.2
Tampa, FL	14.1	12.9	12.2	15.3	18.2	10.7	9.9	6.6
Topeka, KS	12.8	10.8	12.2	15.9	20.0	12.1	11.3	5.0
Tulsa, OK	13.6	11.8	11.9	15.1	19.0	11.4	10.7	6.5
Virginia Beach, VA	10.1	8.8	9.7	14.2	20.0	13.9	14.7	8.8
Washington, DC	6.5	5.2	5.5	9.3	15.8	13.3	19.9	24.5
Wichita, KS	11.8	12.0	11.6	15.5	19.2	12.9	11.6	5.4
Wilmington, NC	14.4	11.5	11.9	14.4	18.5	11.4	11.7	6.2
Worcester, MA	11.1	9.3	8.3	11.6	17.0	13.5	16.5	12.7
U.S.	13.1	11.0	10.5	13.7	18.1	11.9	12.5	9.1

Note: Figures cover the Metropolitan Statistical Area (MSA)—see Appendix B for areas included
Source: Source: U.S. Census Bureau, 2010-2012 American Community Survey 3-Year Estimates

Poverty Rate: City

City	All Ages	Under 18 Years Old	18 to 64 Years Old	65 Years and Over
Abilene, TX	20.3	23.5	20.9	11.2
Albuquerque, NM	18.3	25.6	17.3	9.0
Anchorage, AK	8.5	12.1	7.4	4.9
Ann Arbor, MI	22.6	14.1	26.8	5.9
Athens, GA	35.8	34.7	39.3	11.2
Atlanta, GA	26.0	39.2	23.1	20.1
Austin, TX	20.1	28.4	18.6	9.3
Baltimore, MD	25.2	36.5	22.8	18.0
Billings, MT	14.5	20.5	13.7	8.5
Boise City, ID	16.1	21.1	16.0	7.1
Boston, MA	22.7	30.4	21.2	20.4
Boulder, CO	23.4	12.2	27.9	6.1
Cape Coral, FL	15.1	21.6	14.5	8.7
Cedar Rapids, IA	12.0	14.0	12.7	5.4
Charleston, SC	21.2	28.8	21.3	10.0
Charlotte, NC	17.8	24.9	16.3	8.2
Chicago, IL	23.3	34.6	20.4	17.2
Cincinnati, OH	31.4	48.1	28.6	13.3
Clarksville, TN	18.9	27.8	16.0	10.2
Colorado Spgs, CO	14.4	20.6	13.1	7.6
Columbia, MO	24.5	17.2	28.9	7.1
Columbus, OH	22.4	31.9	20.7	10.4
Dallas, TX	24.2	37.9	19.9	15.4
Davenport, IA	17.4	25.4	16.4	6.5
Denver, CO	19.7	29.5	17.6	12.8
Des Moines, IA	19.5	29.1	17.8	6.6
Durham, NC	21.1	28.7	19.9	10.1
El Paso, TX	21.9	30.5	18.5	18.4
Erie, PA	28.1	43.1	25.2	14.0
Eugene, OR	25.1	24.1	28.4	10.1
Fargo, ND	15.5	15.1	16.9	6.9
Fayetteville, NC	18.2	26.2	16.2	10.0
Ft. Collins, CO	18.5	13.5	21.5	5.6
Ft. Wayne, IN	18.9	27.5	17.3	8.4
Ft. Worth, TX	19.5	27.0	16.8	12.3
Gainesville, FL	36.1	29.7	40.4	8.9
Grand Rapids, MI	28.3	41.2	26.2	10.2
Green Bay, WI	17.3	24.2	15.8	10.9
Greensboro, NC	19.9	26.3	19.6	9.4
Honolulu, HI	12.1	16.7	11.8	8.6
Houston, TX	23.5	36.3	19.7	14.4
Huntsville, AL	16.6	24.9	15.8	7.3
Indianapolis, IN	21.6	32.5	19.3	9.5
Jacksonville, FL	17.7	25.5	16.2	9.6
Kansas City, MO	20.0	30.4	18.0	9.6
Lafayette, LA	20.6	26.7	20.7	9.4
Las Vegas, NV	17.7	25.7	16.1	10.0
Lexington, KY	18.5	22.1	19.0	7.9
Lincoln, NE	16.3	20.4	16.6	5.6
Little Rock, AR	18.7	27.8	17.1	8.4
Los Angeles, CA	22.5	32.5	20.1	16.1
Louisville, KY	19.3	28.8	17.4	11.1
Lubbock, TX	22.6	28.5	23.0	7.1
Madison, WI	19.4	21.1	21.1	3.7
Manchester, NH	14.2	24.7	12.0	7.7

Table continued on next page.

City	All Ages	Under 18 Years Old	18 to 64 Years Old	65 Years and Over
McAllen, TX	27.2	35.9	24.2	22.1
Miami, FL	31.5	45.6	27.0	33.7
Midland, TX	12.2	18.9	9.6	9.9
Minneapolis, MN	23.1	32.2	21.3	15.9
Montgomery, AL	23.3	34.7	21.5	8.7
Nashville, TN	19.9	31.8	17.6	9.6
New Orleans, LA	28.5	42.4	26.0	16.5
New York, NY	20.8	30.4	18.1	18.5
Oklahoma City, OK	18.7	28.2	16.7	8.0
Omaha, NE	17.5	25.7	15.8	8.7
Orlando, FL	20.0	31.8	17.1	14.1
Oxnard, CA	16.5	23.9	14.0	9.5
Peoria, IL	23.4	34.5	21.9	8.9
Philadelphia, PA	27.3	37.7	25.6	17.2
Phoenix, AZ	23.1	33.1	20.4	11.5
Pittsburgh, PA	22.9	31.7	22.7	13.2
Portland, OR	18.6	24.7	18.0	11.0
Providence, RI	30.0	40.8	27.6	18.2
Provo, UT	32.7	27.4	36.9	4.2
Raleigh, NC	17.3	24.8	15.9	7.4
Reno, NV	19.5	25.0	19.1	10.6
Richmond, VA	26.4	39.0	24.7	15.0
Riverside, CA	19.5	25.7	18.1	11.3
Rochester, MN	10.0	10.9	10.1	7.7
Salem, OR	20.4	29.5	18.9	9.1
Salt Lake City, UT	21.9	28.2	20.9	13.4
San Antonio, TX	20.4	29.7	17.6	13.4
San Diego, CA	16.1	21.8	15.3	9.6
San Francisco, CA	13.8	13.9	13.6	14.8
San Jose, CA	12.5	15.4	11.7	10.4
Santa Rosa, CA	13.5	15.5	14.0	7.3
Savannah, GA	27.4	42.2	25.1	11.4
Seattle, WA	14.4	14.7	14.4	14.0
Sioux Falls, SD	11.7	15.3	11.1	7.5
Spokane, WA	18.7	23.2	18.9	10.4
Springfield, MO	25.2	35.2	25.9	9.5
Tallahassee, FL	32.2	30.3	35.2	9.7
Tampa, FL	22.7	31.8	20.2	18.6
Topeka, KS	21.4	32.1	20.4	6.5
Tulsa, OK	20.3	31.7	18.0	9.6
Virginia Beach, VA	8.3	12.8	7.2	5.0
Washington, DC	18.8	29.3	17.2	12.6
Wichita, KS	17.9	26.0	16.0	9.5
Wilmington, NC	23.1	34.6	22.9	7.8
Worcester, MA	21.3	30.4	19.3	15.1
U.S.	15.7	22.2	14.6	9.3

Note: Figures are percentage of people whose income during the past 12 months was below the poverty level;
Source: U.S. Census Bureau, 2010-2012 American Community Survey 3-Year Estimates

Poverty Rate: Metro Area

Metro Area	All Ages	Under 18 Years Old	18 to 64 Years Old	65 Years and Over
Abilene, TX	18.4	22.2	18.5	11.2
Albuquerque, NM	18.7	26.6	17.4	10.0
Anchorage, AK	8.9	12.6	8.0	4.7
Ann Arbor, MI	15.4	15.9	16.9	5.8
Athens, GA	26.1	24.5	29.3	9.3
Atlanta, GA	16.0	22.5	14.2	9.8
Austin, TX	15.4	20.1	14.7	6.8
Baltimore, MD	11.3	15.2	10.4	8.5
Billings, MT	12.8	17.5	12.1	8.1
Boise City, ID	16.1	21.3	15.4	7.5
Boston, MA	10.5	12.8	10.1	9.1
Boulder, CO	14.4	13.6	16.0	5.4
Cape Coral, FL	16.1	27.3	16.3	6.9
Cedar Rapids, IA	9.7	11.2	9.9	5.7
Charleston, SC	16.1	22.6	15.0	9.2
Charlotte, NC	15.2	20.7	14.1	8.0
Chicago, IL	14.2	20.5	12.7	9.1
Cincinnati, OH	14.3	20.3	13.3	7.4
Clarksville, TN	18.2	26.5	15.9	9.1
Colorado Spgs, CO	12.9	18.2	11.7	7.0
Columbia, MO	19.9	18.1	22.4	7.4
Columbus, OH	15.3	21.0	14.6	7.0
Dallas, TX	15.1	21.8	13.0	9.0
Davenport, IA	12.6	18.8	11.7	6.3
Denver, CO	12.7	17.5	11.6	7.8
Des Moines, IA	11.2	15.5	10.5	5.0
Durham, NC	18.4	24.6	18.1	7.9
El Paso, TX	24.0	33.4	20.2	19.3
Erie, PA	16.6	24.7	15.4	9.1
Eugene, OR	20.8	24.2	22.9	7.9
Fargo, ND	12.4	11.9	13.5	7.1
Fayetteville, NC	18.1	25.0	16.1	11.1
Ft. Collins, CO	14.0	13.7	15.7	5.5
Ft. Wayne, IN	14.7	21.3	13.5	6.6
Ft. Worth, TX	15.1	21.8	13.0	9.0
Gainesville, FL	25.5	25.0	28.5	8.8
Grand Rapids, MI	15.8	22.4	14.8	6.5
Green Bay, WI	11.1	15.1	10.0	8.4
Greensboro, NC	18.0	25.6	17.0	9.7
Honolulu, HI	9.8	13.2	9.3	7.0
Houston, TX	16.8	24.6	14.2	10.5
Huntsville, AL	13.0	18.0	12.2	7.3
Indianapolis, IN	14.4	20.5	13.1	7.1
Jacksonville, FL	15.2	21.1	14.4	8.4
Kansas City, MO	12.8	18.6	11.7	6.5
Lafayette, LA	18.5	25.3	16.9	11.6
Las Vegas, NV	16.1	23.3	14.6	8.8
Lexington, KY	17.2	22.1	17.1	8.4
Lincoln, NE	14.6	17.7	15.1	5.3
Little Rock, AR	14.9	20.4	14.2	7.7
Los Angeles, CA	17.0	23.9	15.3	11.9
Louisville, KY	15.6	22.9	14.1	9.2
Lubbock, TX	21.5	27.6	21.5	7.4
Madison, WI	12.4	14.2	13.1	4.9
Manchester, NH	8.3	12.6	7.3	5.9

Table continued on next page.

Metro Area	All Ages	Under 18 Years Old	18 to 64 Years Old	65 Years and Over
McAllen, TX	35.4	47.2	30.0	24.8
Miami, FL	17.3	24.3	15.6	14.7
Midland, TX	10.8	16.3	8.8	8.5
Minneapolis, MN	10.8	14.4	10.1	7.2
Montgomery, AL	18.9	27.7	17.3	9.1
Nashville, TN	14.8	21.4	13.4	8.4
New Orleans, LA	18.8	27.4	17.1	11.5
New York, NY	14.3	20.1	12.8	11.6
Oklahoma City, OK	16.2	22.7	15.2	7.9
Omaha, NE	12.6	18.1	11.2	7.3
Orlando, FL	15.9	22.6	14.8	9.0
Oxnard, CA	11.1	16.0	9.8	7.4
Peoria, IL	13.6	19.7	12.9	6.6
Philadelphia, PA	13.2	17.8	12.5	8.7
Phoenix, AZ	16.9	24.2	15.8	7.7
Pittsburgh, PA	12.3	17.6	11.9	7.8
Portland, OR	14.1	18.7	13.6	7.9
Providence, RI	13.6	19.1	12.7	9.8
Provo, UT	14.3	12.9	16.3	4.7
Raleigh, NC	12.6	17.5	11.4	7.4
Reno, NV	15.9	22.2	15.1	8.2
Richmond, VA	11.8	15.5	11.4	7.4
Riverside, CA	18.0	25.0	16.3	10.1
Rochester, MN	8.6	9.9	8.3	7.3
Salem, OR	19.3	28.4	18.2	6.7
Salt Lake City, UT	13.3	17.4	12.3	6.3
San Antonio, TX	16.8	24.4	14.6	11.1
San Diego, CA	14.9	19.2	14.4	9.0
San Francisco, CA	11.5	14.2	11.2	9.1
San Jose, CA	10.6	12.8	10.1	8.8
Santa Rosa, CA	12.4	15.2	12.8	6.7
Savannah, GA	18.0	27.3	16.1	9.0
Seattle, WA	11.8	15.6	11.1	8.2
Sioux Falls, SD	9.9	12.3	9.2	8.4
Spokane, WA	15.2	18.1	15.6	8.6
Springfield, MO	17.0	23.4	16.6	8.5
Tallahassee, FL	23.8	26.3	25.3	9.5
Tampa, FL	16.1	22.9	15.7	9.3
Topeka, KS	14.8	22.1	14.2	5.1
Tulsa, OK	15.3	22.4	13.8	8.3
Virginia Beach, VA	11.9	18.0	10.7	6.5
Washington, DC	8.3	10.7	7.8	6.6
Wichita, KS	14.7	20.7	13.3	7.8
Wilmington, NC	16.8	24.4	17.1	7.0
Worcester, MA	11.3	15.1	10.5	8.4
U.S.	15.7	22.2	14.6	9.3

Note: Figures are percentage of people whose income during the past 12 months was below the poverty level; Figures cover the Metropolitan Statistical Area—see Appendix B for areas included
Source: U.S. Census Bureau, 2010-2012 American Community Survey 3-Year Estimates

Personal Bankruptcy Filing Rate

City	Area Covered	2008	2009	2010	2011	2012	2013
Abilene, TX	Taylor County	2.48	2.42	2.09	2.10	1.87	1.54
Albuquerque, NM	Bernalillo County	2.67	3.44	3.65	3.16	2.73	2.57
Anchorage, AK	Anchorage Borough	1.68	1.79	1.93	1.72	1.19	0.96
Ann Arbor, MI	Washtenaw County	3.98	4.82	4.96	4.03	3.32	2.74
Athens, GA	Clarke County	2.89	3.46	3.52	3.77	3.43	3.31
Atlanta, GA	Fulton County	5.68	7.45	8.21	7.57	6.23	5.48
Austin, TX	Travis County	1.35	1.81	1.86	1.52	1.37	1.08
Baltimore, MD	Baltimore city County	3.08	4.25	5.03	4.87	5.29	5.52
Billings, MT	Yellowstone County	2.34	2.60	3.34	3.32	2.29	2.01
Boise City, ID	Ada County	4.26	6.17	6.11	5.57	4.31	3.75
Boston, MA	Suffolk County	1.95	2.32	2.70	2.32	1.89	1.30
Boulder, CO	Boulder County	2.98	3.92	4.31	3.94	3.10	2.43
Cape Coral, FL	Lee County	4.92	7.38	7.32	5.30	3.73	2.92
Cedar Rapids, IA	Linn County	2.60	3.44	3.17	2.54	2.06	1.93
Charleston, SC	Charleston County	1.45	1.71	1.88	1.51	1.36	1.36
Charlotte, NC	Mecklenburg County	1.98	2.50	2.67	2.23	2.02	1.76
Chicago, IL	Cook County	4.72	6.40	7.44	6.69	6.72	6.90
Cincinnati, OH	Hamilton County	4.67	5.49	5.78	5.14	4.70	4.10
Clarksville, TN	Montgomery County	4.14	4.65	5.02	4.47	4.25	4.24
Colorado Spgs, CO	El Paso County	4.56	5.53	6.05	5.03	4.69	4.11
Columbia, MO	Boone County	5.43	6.39	5.70	4.68	4.19	3.46
Columbus, OH	Franklin County	5.41	6.20	6.22	5.47	4.80	4.46
Dallas, TX	Dallas County	2.39	2.90	2.86	2.64	2.74	2.20
Davenport, IA	Scott County	3.14	3.93	3.91	3.01	2.26	2.23
Denver, CO	Denver County	4.36	5.51	6.28	6.08	5.16	4.60
Des Moines, IA	Polk County	3.92	4.58	4.81	3.51	2.91	2.61
Durham, NC	Durham County	2.35	2.80	2.97	2.70	2.41	2.08
El Paso, TX	El Paso County	2.87	3.71	3.41	3.13	2.99	2.61
Erie, PA	Erie County	3.69	3.33	3.56	3.23	2.70	2.43
Eugene, OR	Lane County	3.25	4.30	4.92	4.14	3.48	3.37
Fargo, ND	Cass County	2.81	3.42	3.29	2.61	2.24	1.88
Fayetteville, NC	Cumberland County	2.87	3.25	3.25	2.99	2.59	2.60
Ft. Collins, CO	Larimer County	4.28	5.37	6.23	5.28	4.39	3.57
Ft. Wayne, IN	Allen County	6.64	8.22	7.67	6.72	5.93	5.90
Ft. Worth, TX	Tarrant County	3.02	3.74	3.76	3.20	3.11	2.57
Gainesville, FL	Alachua County	1.46	1.90	1.99	1.81	1.62	1.29
Grand Rapids, MI	Kent County	3.51	4.78	4.85	3.95	3.51	3.13
Green Bay, WI	Brown County	3.98	4.59	5.02	4.04	3.47	3.17
Greensboro, NC	Guilford County	2.28	2.68	2.54	2.27	2.10	1.87
Honolulu, HI	Honolulu County	1.44	1.98	2.41	2.05	1.65	1.31
Houston, TX	Harris County	1.52	1.78	2.08	1.95	1.64	1.36
Huntsville, AL	Madison County	4.45	4.94	5.11	4.78	4.60	4.26
Indianapolis, IN	Marion County	7.37	8.44	8.65	7.26	6.77	6.22
Jacksonville, FL	Duval County	4.44	5.80	5.97	5.13	4.36	4.39
Kansas City, MO	Jackson County	5.21	5.89	6.43	5.45	5.29	4.67
Lafayette, LA	Lafayette Parish	2.50	2.97	3.00	2.75	2.52	2.25
Las Vegas, NV	Clark County	8.25	12.68	12.54	10.25	7.30	5.54
Lexington, KY	Fayette County	3.59	4.58	4.57	3.93	3.65	3.42
Lincoln, NE	Lancaster County	4.02	4.37	4.43	4.01	3.38	2.79
Little Rock, AR	Pulaski County	6.10	6.81	7.14	6.71	6.38	6.42
Los Angeles, CA	Los Angeles County	3.43	5.57	7.35	6.88	5.49	3.90
Louisville, KY	Jefferson County	5.43	6.05	6.21	5.90	5.35	4.84
Lubbock, TX	Lubbock County	1.36	1.50	1.50	1.34	1.33	0.96
Madison, WI	Dane County	2.66	3.37	3.71	3.00	2.69	2.47
Manchester, NH	Hillsborough County	3.31	3.99	4.62	3.94	3.20	2.50
McAllen, TX	Hidalgo County	1.18	1.35	1.30	1.18	0.99	0.82

Table continued on next page.

City	Area Covered	2008	2009	2010	2011	2012	2013
Miami, FL	Miami-Dade County	n/a	n/a	n/a	n/a	n/a	n/a
Midland, TX	Midland County	0.73	0.94	1.17	0.88	0.81	0.38
Minneapolis, MN	Hennepin County	2.96	3.89	4.22	3.76	3.30	2.82
Montgomery, AL	Montgomery County	5.88	7.24	6.89	6.83	7.46	7.61
Nashville, TN	Davidson County	6.61	7.29	6.84	6.49	6.17	5.38
New Orleans, LA	Orleans Parish	1.59	2.12	2.31	2.23	2.04	2.01
New York, NY	Bronx County	2.01	2.36	2.34	2.21	1.86	1.74
New York, NY	Kings County	1.49	1.82	1.85	1.65	1.29	1.16
New York, NY	New York County	1.42	2.15	1.96	1.77	1.42	1.06
New York, NY	Queens County	1.99	2.56	2.74	2.41	1.94	1.69
New York, NY	Richmond County	1.92	2.85	3.03	2.73	2.23	1.91
Oklahoma City, OK	Oklahoma County	3.76	4.54	4.67	4.15	3.88	3.35
Omaha, NE	Douglas County	4.39	4.43	4.65	4.02	3.69	3.45
Orlando, FL	Orange County	3.83	6.51	7.70	6.36	5.42	5.04
Oxnard, CA	Ventura County	3.17	5.04	6.37	5.96	4.68	3.06
Peoria, IL	Peoria County	5.69	6.14	5.54	4.83	4.07	3.68
Philadelphia, PA	Philadelphia County	2.02	1.88	2.32	2.04	1.97	2.09
Phoenix, AZ	Maricopa County	3.47	6.22	7.82	6.61	5.02	4.11
Pittsburgh, PA	Allegheny County	3.54	3.83	3.70	3.19	2.54	2.39
Portland, OR	Multnomah County	3.18	4.30	4.82	4.40	3.85	3.27
Providence, RI	Providence County	4.49	5.23	5.59	5.09	4.20	3.62
Provo, UT	Utah County	2.64	4.59	5.94	5.78	4.73	3.90
Raleigh, NC	Wake County	2.66	3.45	3.08	2.85	2.68	2.15
Reno, NV	Washoe County	4.27	7.89	8.37	6.59	4.76	3.92
Richmond, VA	Richmond city County	4.41	4.77	5.80	5.13	4.55	4.54
Riverside, CA	Riverside County	5.32	8.64	10.86	9.81	7.19	5.08
Rochester, MN	Olmsted County	2.40	2.87	2.88	2.44	2.09	1.78
Salem, OR	Marion County	4.17	5.37	5.74	4.54	4.49	4.21
Salt Lake City, UT	Salt Lake County	4.10	6.22	7.45	7.58	6.72	6.00
San Antonio, TX	Bexar County	1.91	2.39	2.32	2.04	1.80	1.57
San Diego, CA	San Diego County	4.46	6.50	7.23	6.49	5.22	3.83
San Francisco, CA	San Francisco County	1.52	2.29	2.74	2.29	1.75	1.32
San Jose, CA	Santa Clara County	2.36	3.99	4.91	4.47	3.48	2.40
Santa Rosa, CA	Sonoma County	3.34	4.77	5.38	4.96	3.80	2.62
Savannah, GA	Chatham County	6.33	6.98	6.53	6.21	5.74	5.60
Seattle, WA	King County	2.42	3.76	4.32	4.07	3.48	2.88
Sioux Falls, SD	Minnehaha County	2.84	3.22	3.58	3.23	2.72	2.34
Spokane, WA	Spokane County	4.18	5.42	5.51	4.62	4.11	3.82
Springfield, MO	Christian County	4.51	5.01	5.48	4.36	4.33	3.60
Tallahassee, FL	Leon County	2.17	2.68	2.70	2.44	1.89	1.72
Tampa, FL	Hillsborough County	4.09	5.55	6.26	4.84	4.01	3.72
Topeka, KS	Shawnee County	5.91	6.66	6.65	5.93	5.96	5.24
Tulsa, OK	Tulsa County	3.30	4.23	4.51	3.82	3.54	3.05
Virginia Beach, VA	Virginia Beach city County	4.06	4.99	5.46	5.01	4.57	4.03
Washington, DC	District of Columbia	1.46	1.94	2.13	1.56	1.36	1.27
Wichita, KS	Sedgwick County	3.63	4.42	4.55	4.20	4.00	3.85
Wilmington, NC	New Hanover County	1.90	2.95	3.05	3.12	2.77	2.19
Worcester, MA	Worcester County	3.44	4.37	4.88	3.90	3.24	2.35
U.S.	U.S.	3.53	4.61	4.97	4.37	3.76	3.29

Note: Numbers are per 1,000 population and include Chapter 7 and Chapter 13 filings; n/a not available
Source: Federal Deposit Insurance Corporation, Regional Economic Conditions, March 20, 2014

Building Permits: City

City	Single-Family			Multi-Family			Total		
	2012	2013	Pct. Chg.	2012	2013	Pct. Chg.	2012	2013	Pct. Chg.
Abilene, TX	233	280	20.2	206	2	-99.0	439	282	-35.8
Albuquerque, NM	455	434	-4.6	744	1,040	39.8	1,199	1,474	22.9
Anchorage, AK	497	475	-4.4	35	58	65.7	532	533	0.2
Ann Arbor, MI	12	27	125.0	2	198	9,800.0	14	225	1,507.1
Athens, GA	185	143	-22.7	168	351	108.9	353	494	39.9
Atlanta, GA	359	473	31.8	1,764	5,070	187.4	2,123	5,543	161.1
Austin, TX	2,539	2,573	1.3	7,671	9,261	20.7	10,210	11,834	15.9
Baltimore, MD	164	220	34.1	566	1,037	83.2	730	1,257	72.2
Billings, MT	406	481	18.5	181	558	208.3	587	1,039	77.0
Boise City, ID	580	498	-14.1	157	222	41.4	737	720	-2.3
Boston, MA	40	34	-15.0	1,736	2,527	45.6	1,776	2,561	44.2
Boulder, CO	59	89	50.8	356	789	121.6	415	878	111.6
Cape Coral, FL	330	492	49.1	16	6	-62.5	346	498	43.9
Cedar Rapids, IA	289	242	-16.3	72	245	240.3	361	487	34.9
Charleston, SC	477	576	20.8	338	351	3.8	815	927	13.7
Charlotte, NC	n/a	n/a	n/a	n/a	n/a	n/a	n/a	n/a	n/a
Chicago, IL	317	448	41.3	1,673	2,577	54.0	1,990	3,025	52.0
Cincinnati, OH	83	90	8.4	367	74	-79.8	450	164	-63.6
Clarksville, TN	937	779	-16.9	421	580	37.8	1,358	1,359	0.1
Colorado Spgs, CO	n/a	n/a	n/a	n/a	n/a	n/a	n/a	n/a	n/a
Columbia, MO	733	631	-13.9	304	378	24.3	1,037	1,009	-2.7
Columbus, OH	723	770	6.5	3,286	3,565	8.5	4,009	4,335	8.1
Dallas, TX	936	1,075	14.9	6,149	7,559	22.9	7,085	8,634	21.9
Davenport, IA	128	114	-10.9	60	16	-73.3	188	130	-30.9
Denver, CO	1,056	1,284	21.6	4,522	4,586	1.4	5,578	5,870	5.2
Des Moines, IA	128	184	43.8	236	559	136.9	364	743	104.1
Durham, NC	874	1,112	27.2	1,719	2,636	53.3	2,593	3,748	44.5
El Paso, TX	2,815	2,271	-19.3	1,177	1,408	19.6	3,992	3,679	-7.8
Erie, PA	40	2	-95.0	0	0	-	40	2	-95.0
Eugene, OR	120	182	51.7	383	733	91.4	503	915	81.9
Fargo, ND	403	509	26.3	694	1,146	65.1	1,097	1,655	50.9
Fayetteville, NC	527	437	-17.1	1,356	288	-78.8	1,883	725	-61.5
Ft. Collins, CO	470	612	30.2	674	779	15.6	1,144	1,391	21.6
Ft. Wayne, IN	n/a	n/a	n/a	n/a	n/a	n/a	n/a	n/a	n/a
Ft. Worth, TX	2,716	3,321	22.3	1,485	2,334	57.2	4,201	5,655	34.6
Gainesville, FL	51	63	23.5	225	240	6.7	276	303	9.8
Grand Rapids, MI	45	59	31.1	174	96	-44.8	219	155	-29.2
Green Bay, WI	48	71	47.9	26	105	303.8	74	176	137.8
Greensboro, NC	323	354	9.6	481	614	27.7	804	968	20.4
Honolulu, HI	n/a	n/a	n/a	n/a	n/a	n/a	n/a	n/a	n/a
Houston, TX	3,513	5,198	48.0	9,020	8,845	-1.9	12,533	14,043	12.0
Huntsville, AL	960	1,000	4.2	420	306	-27.1	1,380	1,306	-5.4
Indianapolis, IN	472	562	19.1	79	671	749.4	551	1,233	123.8
Jacksonville, FL	1,310	1,844	40.8	2,499	709	-71.6	3,809	2,553	-33.0
Kansas City, MO	536	703	31.2	525	827	57.5	1,061	1,530	44.2
Lafayette, LA	n/a	n/a	n/a	n/a	n/a	n/a	n/a	n/a	n/a
Las Vegas, NV	1,233	1,517	23.0	75	0	-100.0	1,308	1,517	16.0
Lexington, KY	750	676	-9.9	1,066	223	-79.1	1,816	899	-50.5
Lincoln, NE	704	844	19.9	388	531	36.9	1,092	1,375	25.9
Little Rock, AR	347	356	2.6	323	252	-22.0	670	608	-9.3
Los Angeles, CA	870	1,144	31.5	5,830	7,248	24.3	6,700	8,392	25.3
Louisville, KY	851	938	10.2	1,185	1,289	8.8	2,036	2,227	9.4
Lubbock, TX	697	938	34.6	715	1,039	45.3	1,412	1,977	40.0
Madison, WI	161	217	34.8	1,047	1,018	-2.8	1,208	1,235	2.2

Table continued on next page.

City	Single-Family			Multi-Family			Total		
	2012	2013	Pct. Chg.	2012	2013	Pct. Chg.	2012	2013	Pct. Chg.
Manchester, NH	61	49	-19.7	61	38	-37.7	122	87	-28.7
McAllen, TX	433	374	-13.6	96	145	51.0	529	519	-1.9
Miami, FL	40	115	187.5	911	4,371	379.8	951	4,486	371.7
Midland, TX	599	732	22.2	410	1,092	166.3	1,009	1,824	80.8
Minneapolis, MN	76	146	92.1	3,227	3,176	-1.6	3,303	3,322	0.6
Montgomery, AL	218	265	21.6	0	0	-	218	265	21.6
Nashville, TN	1,305	1,824	39.8	1,529	2,142	40.1	2,834	3,966	39.9
New Orleans, LA	690	736	6.7	276	159	-42.4	966	895	-7.3
New York, NY	280	402	43.6	10,054	17,593	75.0	10,334	17,995	74.1
Oklahoma City, OK	3,260	3,609	10.7	70	804	1,048.6	3,330	4,413	32.5
Omaha, NE	1,305	1,567	20.1	610	1,003	64.4	1,915	2,570	34.2
Orlando, FL	815	1,037	27.2	1,070	1,850	72.9	1,885	2,887	53.2
Oxnard, CA	77	94	22.1	223	276	23.8	300	370	23.3
Peoria, IL	220	147	-33.2	14	6	-57.1	234	153	-34.6
Philadelphia, PA	566	632	11.7	1,609	2,183	35.7	2,175	2,815	29.4
Phoenix, AZ	1,650	1,673	1.4	2,784	1,458	-47.6	4,434	3,131	-29.4
Pittsburgh, PA	137	100	-27.0	0	0	-	137	100	-27.0
Portland, OR	644	763	18.5	1,654	2,992	80.9	2,298	3,755	63.4
Providence, RI	12	16	33.3	3	26	766.7	15	42	180.0
Provo, UT	67	136	103.0	46	51	10.9	113	187	65.5
Raleigh, NC	1,414	1,662	17.5	3,596	2,138	-40.5	5,010	3,800	-24.2
Reno, NV	443	687	55.1	68	426	526.5	511	1,113	117.8
Richmond, VA	119	106	-10.9	721	743	3.1	840	849	1.1
Riverside, CA	190	70	-63.2	168	51	-69.6	358	121	-66.2
Rochester, MN	299	323	8.0	62	44	-29.0	361	367	1.7
Salem, OR	179	283	58.1	200	294	47.0	379	577	52.2
Salt Lake City, UT	41	80	95.1	321	178	-44.5	362	258	-28.7
San Antonio, TX	1,896	2,102	10.9	2,747	16	-99.4	4,643	2,118	-54.4
San Diego, CA	535	821	53.5	2,548	4,487	76.1	3,083	5,308	72.2
San Francisco, CA	22	54	145.5	3,067	4,420	44.1	3,089	4,474	44.8
San Jose, CA	186	274	47.3	3,312	3,429	3.5	3,498	3,703	5.9
Santa Rosa, CA	103	138	34.0	134	347	159.0	237	485	104.6
Savannah, GA	223	265	18.8	160	18	-88.8	383	283	-26.1
Seattle, WA	498	822	65.1	6,799	5,855	-13.9	7,297	6,677	-8.5
Sioux Falls, SD	882	1,025	16.2	459	986	114.8	1,341	2,011	50.0
Spokane, WA	207	321	55.1	176	142	-19.3	383	463	20.9
Springfield, MO	126	152	20.6	646	816	26.3	772	968	25.4
Tallahassee, FL	216	293	35.6	692	648	-6.4	908	941	3.6
Tampa, FL	547	686	25.4	1,945	1,168	-39.9	2,492	1,854	-25.6
Topeka, KS	88	84	-4.5	34	2	-94.1	122	86	-29.5
Tulsa, OK	577	436	-24.4	594	164	-72.4	1,171	600	-48.8
Virginia Beach, VA	594	733	23.4	523	929	77.6	1,117	1,662	48.8
Washington, DC	271	333	22.9	3,552	2,922	-17.7	3,823	3,255	-14.9
Wichita, KS	415	536	29.2	322	200	-37.9	737	736	-0.1
Wilmington, NC	n/a	n/a	n/a	n/a	n/a	n/a	n/a	n/a	n/a
Worcester, MA	44	53	20.5	20	8	-60.0	64	61	-4.7
U.S.	518,695	620,802	19.7	310,963	370,020	19.0	829,658	990,822	19.4

Note: Figures represent new, privately-owned housing units authorized (unadjusted data); All permit data are based on estimates with imputation

Source: U.S. Census Bureau, Manufacturing, Mining, and Construction Statistics, Building Permits, 2012, 2013

Building Permits: Metro Area

Metro Area	Single-Family			Multi-Family			Total		
	2012	2013	Pct. Chg.	2012	2013	Pct. Chg.	2012	2013	Pct. Chg.
Abilene, TX	241	292	21.2	214	14	-93.5	455	306	-32.7
Albuquerque, NM	1,259	1,456	15.6	825	1,150	39.4	2,084	2,606	25.0
Anchorage, AK	530	500	-5.7	45	76	68.9	575	576	0.2
Ann Arbor, MI	262	394	50.4	14	364	2,500.0	276	758	174.6
Athens, GA	447	698	56.2	172	381	121.5	619	1,079	74.3
Atlanta, GA	9,167	14,824	61.7	5,213	9,473	81.7	14,380	24,297	69.0
Austin, TX	8,229	8,941	8.7	11,334	11,911	5.1	19,563	20,852	6.6
Baltimore, MD	3,895	4,617	18.5	2,061	3,452	67.5	5,956	8,069	35.5
Billings, MT	419	974	132.5	202	1,128	458.4	621	2,102	238.5
Boise City, ID	2,887	3,522	22.0	669	843	26.0	3,556	4,365	22.8
Boston, MA	4,126	4,953	20.0	4,725	7,068	49.6	8,851	12,021	35.8
Boulder, CO	471	591	25.5	824	1,034	25.5	1,295	1,625	25.5
Cape Coral, FL	1,806	2,531	40.1	237	645	172.2	2,043	3,176	55.5
Cedar Rapids, IA	617	625	1.3	171	324	89.5	788	949	20.4
Charleston, SC	3,132	3,779	20.7	1,461	1,638	12.1	4,593	5,417	17.9
Charlotte, NC	6,703	8,792	31.2	5,544	5,217	-5.9	12,247	14,009	14.4
Chicago, IL	5,658	7,261	28.3	3,699	4,366	18.0	9,357	11,627	24.3
Cincinnati, OH	2,641	3,308	25.3	963	1,022	6.1	3,604	4,330	20.1
Clarksville, TN	1,387	1,256	-9.4	509	586	15.1	1,896	1,842	-2.8
Colorado Spgs, CO	2,410	2,885	19.7	601	702	16.8	3,011	3,587	19.1
Columbia, MO	916	836	-8.7	312	396	26.9	1,228	1,232	0.3
Columbus, OH	2,913	3,495	20.0	3,898	4,868	24.9	6,811	8,363	22.8
Dallas, TX	18,090	21,224	17.3	16,952	16,686	-1.6	35,042	37,910	8.2
Davenport, IA	545	510	-6.4	141	107	-24.1	686	617	-10.1
Denver, CO	5,606	6,965	24.2	8,154	8,510	4.4	13,760	15,475	12.5
Des Moines, IA	2,809	3,307	17.7	1,358	1,614	18.9	4,167	4,921	18.1
Durham, NC	1,595	1,969	23.4	1,719	2,725	58.5	3,314	4,694	41.6
El Paso, TX	3,176	2,613	-17.7	1,179	1,484	25.9	4,355	4,097	-5.9
Erie, PA	216	258	19.4	272	209	-23.2	488	467	-4.3
Eugene, OR	417	506	21.3	385	743	93.0	802	1,249	55.7
Fargo, ND	1,037	1,395	34.5	1,174	1,698	44.6	2,211	3,093	39.9
Fayetteville, NC	1,376	1,269	-7.8	1,664	621	-62.7	3,040	1,890	-37.8
Ft. Collins, CO	1,139	1,489	30.7	729	888	21.8	1,868	2,377	27.2
Ft. Wayne, IN	694	960	38.3	536	75	-86.0	1,230	1,035	-15.9
Ft. Worth, TX	18,090	21,224	17.3	16,952	16,686	-1.6	35,042	37,910	8.2
Gainesville, FL	397	558	40.6	227	242	6.6	624	800	28.2
Grand Rapids, MI	1,098	1,319	20.1	188	162	-13.8	1,286	1,481	15.2
Green Bay, WI	648	719	11.0	275	551	100.4	923	1,270	37.6
Greensboro, NC	1,183	1,416	19.7	704	616	-12.5	1,887	2,032	7.7
Honolulu, HI	994	1,137	14.4	730	1,504	106.0	1,724	2,641	53.2
Houston, TX	28,628	34,542	20.7	14,662	16,791	14.5	43,290	51,333	18.6
Huntsville, AL	1,927	1,944	0.9	420	306	-27.1	2,347	2,250	-4.1
Indianapolis, IN	4,004	5,014	25.2	990	3,137	216.9	4,994	8,151	63.2
Jacksonville, FL	4,579	6,281	37.2	2,587	1,077	-58.4	7,166	7,358	2.7
Kansas City, MO	3,299	4,229	28.2	1,682	3,303	96.4	4,981	7,532	51.2
Lafayette, LA	1,198	1,399	16.8	145	155	6.9	1,343	1,554	15.7
Las Vegas, NV	6,108	7,067	15.7	1,267	1,506	18.9	7,375	8,573	16.2
Lexington, KY	1,218	1,335	9.6	1,100	319	-71.0	2,318	1,654	-28.6
Lincoln, NE	859	1,052	22.5	390	535	37.2	1,249	1,587	27.1
Little Rock, AR	1,851	1,681	-9.2	1,462	814	-44.3	3,313	2,495	-24.7
Los Angeles, CA	4,946	7,509	51.8	12,501	17,689	41.5	17,447	25,198	44.4
Louisville, KY	2,365	2,551	7.9	1,306	1,466	12.3	3,671	4,017	9.4
Lubbock, TX	752	1,009	34.2	715	1,039	45.3	1,467	2,048	39.6
Madison, WI	865	1,212	40.1	1,577	1,754	11.2	2,442	2,966	21.5

Table continued on next page.

Metro Area	Single-Family			Multi-Family			Total		
	2012	2013	Pct. Chg.	2012	2013	Pct. Chg.	2012	2013	Pct. Chg.
Manchester, NH	365	468	28.2	255	99	-61.2	620	567	-8.5
McAllen, TX	2,833	2,545	-10.2	659	749	13.7	3,492	3,294	-5.7
Miami, FL	5,089	6,369	25.2	8,172	13,552	65.8	13,261	19,921	50.2
Midland, TX	599	732	22.2	410	1,092	166.3	1,009	1,824	80.8
Minneapolis, MN	5,750	7,174	24.8	5,743	4,859	-15.4	11,493	12,033	4.7
Montgomery, AL	776	744	-4.1	474	110	-76.8	1,250	854	-31.7
Nashville, TN	5,340	7,020	31.5	2,907	3,869	33.1	8,247	10,889	32.0
New Orleans, LA	2,015	2,441	21.1	278	175	-37.1	2,293	2,616	14.1
New York, NY	6,815	10,139	48.8	20,097	29,685	47.7	26,912	39,824	48.0
Oklahoma City, OK	5,474	6,359	16.2	1,103	1,146	3.9	6,577	7,505	14.1
Omaha, NE	2,479	3,039	22.6	983	1,425	45.0	3,462	4,464	28.9
Orlando, FL	7,322	9,222	25.9	4,684	6,341	35.4	12,006	15,563	29.6
Oxnard, CA	278	430	54.7	288	571	98.3	566	1,001	76.9
Peoria, IL	638	538	-15.7	89	80	-10.1	727	618	-15.0
Philadelphia, PA	5,175	6,252	20.8	4,095	4,965	21.2	9,270	11,217	21.0
Phoenix, AZ	11,931	12,959	8.6	4,036	5,778	43.2	15,967	18,737	17.3
Pittsburgh, PA	2,918	3,251	11.4	548	1,312	139.4	3,466	4,563	31.7
Portland, OR	4,501	5,717	27.0	3,284	6,013	83.1	7,785	11,730	50.7
Providence, RI	1,144	1,465	28.1	217	509	134.6	1,361	1,974	45.0
Provo, UT	2,226	2,675	20.2	213	748	251.2	2,439	3,423	40.3
Raleigh, NC	6,425	8,034	25.0	6,501	3,397	-47.7	12,926	11,431	-11.6
Reno, NV	777	1,243	60.0	68	477	601.5	845	1,720	103.6
Richmond, VA	2,840	3,555	25.2	1,431	1,450	1.3	4,271	5,005	17.2
Riverside, CA	4,488	6,472	44.2	1,461	2,876	96.9	5,949	9,348	57.1
Rochester, MN	464	594	28.0	62	44	-29.0	526	638	21.3
Salem, OR	395	646	63.5	326	304	-6.7	721	950	31.8
Salt Lake City, UT	2,826	3,447	22.0	1,078	2,081	93.0	3,904	5,528	41.6
San Antonio, TX	5,102	5,827	14.2	2,902	301	-89.6	8,004	6,128	-23.4
San Diego, CA	2,197	2,565	16.8	3,469	5,699	64.3	5,666	8,264	45.9
San Francisco, CA	3,095	3,659	18.2	6,068	7,263	19.7	9,163	10,922	19.2
San Jose, CA	1,501	1,870	24.6	4,031	5,894	46.2	5,532	7,764	40.3
Santa Rosa, CA	312	453	45.2	248	593	139.1	560	1,046	86.8
Savannah, GA	1,263	1,517	20.1	277	233	-15.9	1,540	1,750	13.6
Seattle, WA	8,047	8,773	9.0	9,619	10,744	11.7	17,666	19,517	10.5
Sioux Falls, SD	1,104	1,330	20.5	483	1,079	123.4	1,587	2,409	51.8
Spokane, WA	963	1,299	34.9	390	335	-14.1	1,353	1,634	20.8
Springfield, MO	906	1,098	21.2	660	877	32.9	1,566	1,975	26.1
Tallahassee, FL	468	628	34.2	766	652	-14.9	1,234	1,280	3.7
Tampa, FL	5,883	7,314	24.3	4,278	4,838	13.1	10,161	12,152	19.6
Topeka, KS	270	272	0.7	42	10	-76.2	312	282	-9.6
Tulsa, OK	2,699	3,008	11.4	737	717	-2.7	3,436	3,725	8.4
Virginia Beach, VA	3,534	4,104	16.1	1,849	3,273	77.0	5,383	7,377	37.0
Washington, DC	10,980	13,274	20.9	11,424	10,759	-5.8	22,404	24,033	7.3
Wichita, KS	845	1,163	37.6	465	341	-26.7	1,310	1,504	14.8
Wilmington, NC	2,045	3,141	53.6	1,018	916	-10.0	3,063	4,057	32.5
Worcester, MA	867	1,164	34.3	258	177	-31.4	1,125	1,341	19.2
U.S.	518,695	620,802	19.7	310,963	370,020	19.0	829,658	990,822	19.4

Note: Figures cover the Metropolitan Statistical Area—see Appendix B for areas included; Figures represent new, privately-owned housing units authorized (unadjusted data); All permit data are based on estimates with imputation
Source: U.S. Census Bureau, Manufacturing, Mining, and Construction Statistics, Building Permits, 2012, 2013

Homeownership Rate

Metro Area	2006	2007	2008	2009	2010	2011	2012	2013
Abilene, TX	n/a	n/a	n/a	n/a	n/a	n/a	n/a	n/a
Albuquerque, NM	70.0	70.5	68.2	65.7	65.5	67.1	62.8	65.9
Anchorage, AK	n/a	n/a	n/a	n/a	n/a	n/a	n/a	n/a
Ann Arbor, MI	n/a	n/a	n/a	n/a	n/a	n/a	n/a	n/a
Athens, GA	n/a	n/a	n/a	n/a	n/a	n/a	n/a	n/a
Atlanta, GA	67.9	66.4	67.5	67.7	67.2	65.8	62.1	61.6
Austin, TX	66.7	66.4	65.5	64.0	65.8	58.4	60.1	59.6
Baltimore, MD	72.9	71.2	69.3	67.7	65.7	66.8	66.1	66.0
Billings, MT	n/a	n/a	n/a	n/a	n/a	n/a	n/a	n/a
Boise City, ID	n/a	n/a	n/a	n/a	n/a	n/a	n/a	n/a
Boston, MA	64.7	64.8	66.2	65.5	66.0	65.5	66.0	66.3
Boulder, CO	n/a	n/a	n/a	n/a	n/a	n/a	n/a	n/a
Cape Coral, FL	n/a	n/a	n/a	n/a	n/a	n/a	n/a	n/a
Cedar Rapids, IA	n/a	n/a	n/a	n/a	n/a	n/a	n/a	n/a
Charleston, SC	n/a	n/a	n/a	n/a	n/a	n/a	n/a	n/a
Charlotte, NC	66.1	66.5	65.4	66.1	66.1	63.6	58.3	58.9
Chicago, IL	69.6	69.0	68.4	69.2	68.2	67.7	67.1	68.2
Cincinnati, OH	65.5	67.6	64.7	62.4	62.8	65.2	63.4	63.3
Clarksville, TN	n/a	n/a	n/a	n/a	n/a	n/a	n/a	n/a
Colorado Spgs, CO	n/a	n/a	n/a	n/a	n/a	n/a	n/a	n/a
Columbia, MO	n/a	n/a	n/a	n/a	n/a	n/a	n/a	n/a
Columbus, OH	65.8	66.1	61.2	61.5	62.2	59.7	60.7	60.5
Dallas, TX	60.7	60.9	60.9	61.6	63.8	62.6	61.8	59.9
Davenport, IA	n/a	n/a	n/a	n/a	n/a	n/a	n/a	n/a
Denver, CO	70.0	69.5	66.9	65.3	65.7	63.0	61.8	61.0
Des Moines, IA	n/a	n/a	n/a	n/a	n/a	n/a	n/a	n/a
Durham, NC	n/a	n/a	n/a	n/a	n/a	n/a	n/a	n/a
El Paso, TX	65.0	68.2	64.8	63.8	70.1	72.0	67.4	69.3
Erie, PA	n/a	n/a	n/a	n/a	n/a	n/a	n/a	n/a
Eugene, OR	n/a	n/a	n/a	n/a	n/a	n/a	n/a	n/a
Fargo, ND	n/a	n/a	n/a	n/a	n/a	n/a	n/a	n/a
Fayetteville, NC	n/a	n/a	n/a	n/a	n/a	n/a	n/a	n/a
Ft. Collins, CO	n/a	n/a	n/a	n/a	n/a	n/a	n/a	n/a
Ft. Wayne, IN	n/a	n/a	n/a	n/a	n/a	n/a	n/a	n/a
Ft. Worth, TX	60.7	60.9	60.9	61.6	63.8	62.6	61.8	59.9
Gainesville, FL	n/a	n/a	n/a	n/a	n/a	n/a	n/a	n/a
Grand Rapids, MI	76.5	78.6	77.6	75.6	76.4	76.4	76.9	73.7
Green Bay, WI	n/a	n/a	n/a	n/a	n/a	n/a	n/a	n/a
Greensboro, NC	62.2	62.1	68.0	70.7	68.8	62.7	64.9	67.9
Honolulu, HI	58.4	58.8	57.2	57.6	54.9	54.1	56.1	57.9
Houston, TX	63.5	64.5	64.8	63.6	61.4	61.3	62.1	60.5
Huntsville, AL	n/a	n/a	n/a	n/a	n/a	n/a	n/a	n/a
Indianapolis, IN	79.0	75.9	75.0	71.0	68.8	68.3	67.1	67.5
Jacksonville, FL	70.0	70.9	72.1	72.6	70.0	68.0	66.6	69.9
Kansas City, MO	69.5	71.3	70.2	69.5	68.8	68.5	65.1	65.6
Lafayette, LA	n/a	n/a	n/a	n/a	n/a	n/a	n/a	n/a
Las Vegas, NV	63.3	60.5	60.3	59.0	55.7	52.9	52.6	52.8
Lexington, KY	n/a	n/a	n/a	n/a	n/a	n/a	n/a	n/a
Lincoln, NE	n/a	n/a	n/a	n/a	n/a	n/a	n/a	n/a
Little Rock, AR	n/a	n/a	n/a	n/a	n/a	n/a	n/a	n/a
Los Angeles, CA	54.4	52.3	52.1	50.4	49.7	50.1	49.9	48.7
Louisville, KY	66.4	67.2	67.9	67.7	63.4	61.7	63.3	64.5
Lubbock, TX	n/a	n/a	n/a	n/a	n/a	n/a	n/a	n/a
Madison, WI	n/a	n/a	n/a	n/a	n/a	n/a	n/a	n/a
Manchester, NH	n/a	n/a	n/a	n/a	n/a	n/a	n/a	n/a
McAllen, TX	n/a	n/a	n/a	n/a	n/a	n/a	n/a	n/a

Table continued on next page.

Metro Area	2006	2007	2008	2009	2010	2011	2012	2013
Miami, FL	67.4	66.6	66.0	67.1	63.8	64.2	61.8	60.1
Midland, TX	n/a	n/a	n/a	n/a	n/a	n/a	n/a	n/a
Minneapolis, MN	73.4	70.7	69.9	70.9	71.2	69.1	70.8	71.7
Montgomery, AL	n/a	n/a	n/a	n/a	n/a	n/a	n/a	n/a
Nashville, TN	72.4	70.0	71.3	71.8	70.4	69.6	64.9	63.9
New Orleans, LA	70.3	67.8	68.0	68.2	66.9	63.9	62.4	61.4
New York, NY	53.6	53.8	52.6	51.7	51.6	50.9	51.5	50.6
Oklahoma City, OK	71.8	68.2	69.5	69.0	70.0	69.6	67.3	67.6
Omaha, NE	68.1	67.9	72.5	73.1	73.2	71.6	72.4	70.6
Orlando, FL	71.1	71.8	70.5	72.4	70.8	68.6	68.0	65.5
Oxnard, CA	69.8	71.4	71.7	73.1	67.1	67.0	66.1	66.8
Peoria, IL	n/a	n/a	n/a	n/a	n/a	n/a	n/a	n/a
Philadelphia, PA	73.1	73.1	71.8	69.7	70.7	69.7	69.5	69.1
Phoenix, AZ	72.5	70.8	70.2	69.8	66.5	63.3	63.1	62.2
Pittsburgh, PA	72.2	73.6	73.2	71.7	70.4	70.3	67.9	68.3
Portland, OR	66.0	61.2	62.6	64.0	63.7	63.7	63.9	60.9
Providence, RI	65.5	64.1	63.9	61.7	61.0	61.3	61.7	60.1
Provo, UT	n/a	n/a	n/a	n/a	n/a	n/a	n/a	n/a
Raleigh, NC	71.1	72.8	70.7	65.7	65.9	66.7	67.7	65.5
Reno, NV	n/a	n/a	n/a	n/a	n/a	n/a	n/a	n/a
Richmond, VA	68.9	72.7	72.4	72.2	68.1	65.2	67.0	65.4
Riverside, CA	68.3	66.6	65.8	65.9	63.9	59.2	58.2	56.3
Rochester, MN	n/a	n/a	n/a	n/a	n/a	n/a	n/a	n/a
Salem, OR	n/a	n/a	n/a	n/a	n/a	n/a	n/a	n/a
Salt Lake City, UT	69.6	71.8	72.0	68.8	65.5	66.4	66.9	66.8
San Antonio, TX	62.6	62.4	66.1	69.8	70.1	66.5	67.5	70.1
San Diego, CA	61.2	59.6	57.1	56.4	54.4	55.2	55.4	55.0
San Francisco, CA	59.4	58.0	56.4	57.3	58.0	56.1	53.2	55.2
San Jose, CA	59.4	57.6	54.6	57.2	58.9	60.4	58.6	56.4
Santa Rosa, CA	n/a	n/a	n/a	n/a	n/a	n/a	n/a	n/a
Savannah, GA	n/a	n/a	n/a	n/a	n/a	n/a	n/a	n/a
Seattle, WA	63.7	62.8	61.3	61.2	60.9	60.7	60.4	61.0
Sioux Falls, SD	n/a	n/a	n/a	n/a	n/a	n/a	n/a	n/a
Spokane, WA	n/a	n/a	n/a	n/a	n/a	n/a	n/a	n/a
Springfield, MO	n/a	n/a	n/a	n/a	n/a	n/a	n/a	n/a
Tallahassee, FL	n/a	n/a	n/a	n/a	n/a	n/a	n/a	n/a
Tampa, FL	71.6	72.9	70.5	68.3	68.3	68.3	67.0	65.3
Topeka, KS	n/a	n/a	n/a	n/a	n/a	n/a	n/a	n/a
Tulsa, OK	67.9	66.7	66.8	67.8	64.2	64.4	66.5	64.1
Virginia Beach, VA	68.3	66.0	63.9	63.5	61.4	62.3	62.0	63.3
Washington, DC	68.9	69.2	68.1	67.2	67.3	67.6	66.9	66.0
Wichita, KS	n/a	n/a	n/a	n/a	n/a	n/a	n/a	n/a
Wilmington, NC	n/a	n/a	n/a	n/a	n/a	n/a	n/a	n/a
Worcester, MA	71.0	67.8	68.5	64.4	64.1	65.8	61.9	63.3
U.S.	68.8	68.1	67.8	67.4	66.9	66.1	65.4	65.1

Note: Figures are percentages and cover the Metropolitan Statistical Area—see Appendix B for areas included
Source: U.S. Census Bureau, Housing Vacancies and Homeownership Annual Statistics: 2013

Housing Vacancy Rates

Metro Area[1]	Gross Vacancy Rate[2] (%)			Year-Round Vacancy Rate[3] (%)			Rental Vacancy Rate[4] (%)			Homeowner Vacancy Rate[5] (%)		
	2011	2012	2013	2011	2012	2013	2011	2012	2013	2011	2012	2013
Abilene, TX	n/a	n/a	n/a	n/a	n/a	n/a	n/a	n/a	n/a	n/a	n/a	n/a
Albuquerque, NM	7.1	7.1	8.4	6.3	6.5	7.7	6.9	5.1	7.8	1.4	2.2	2.4
Anchorage, AK	n/a	n/a	n/a	n/a	n/a	n/a	n/a	n/a	n/a	n/a	n/a	n/a
Ann Arbor, MI	n/a	n/a	n/a	n/a	n/a	n/a	n/a	n/a	n/a	n/a	n/a	n/a
Athens, GA	n/a	n/a	n/a	n/a	n/a	n/a	n/a	n/a	n/a	n/a	n/a	n/a
Atlanta, GA	12.8	12.5	12.4	12.4	12.2	11.8	11.6	10.6	10.2	4.3	2.6	2.1
Austin, TX	12.6	12.7	12.5	11.7	11.9	11.9	6.4	9.6	12.1	0.6	1.3	1.1
Baltimore, MD	11.7	11.7	10.5	11.6	11.4	10.2	10.7	9.7	9.5	2.8	2.2	1.8
Billings, MT	n/a	n/a	n/a	n/a	n/a	n/a	n/a	n/a	n/a	n/a	n/a	n/a
Boise City, ID	n/a	n/a	n/a	n/a	n/a	n/a	n/a	n/a	n/a	n/a	n/a	n/a
Boston, MA	8.7	8.6	7.8	6.9	6.9	6.2	5.5	5.9	6.8	1.4	1.3	1.1
Boulder, CO	n/a	n/a	n/a	n/a	n/a	n/a	n/a	n/a	n/a	n/a	n/a	n/a
Cape Coral, FL	n/a	n/a	n/a	n/a	n/a	n/a	n/a	n/a	n/a	n/a	n/a	n/a
Cedar Rapids, IA	n/a	n/a	n/a	n/a	n/a	n/a	n/a	n/a	n/a	n/a	n/a	n/a
Charleston, SC	n/a	n/a	n/a	n/a	n/a	n/a	n/a	n/a	n/a	n/a	n/a	n/a
Charlotte, NC	9.2	8.0	9.3	9.1	7.7	8.7	10.1	6.4	6.4	1.9	1.3	3.5
Chicago, IL	11.8	10.8	10.5	11.6	10.6	10.3	9.9	9.7	10.9	3.6	2.8	2.8
Cincinnati, OH	13.2	11.2	11.2	11.8	9.6	10.0	11.1	9.3	8.9	3.0	1.8	2.6
Clarksville, TN	n/a	n/a	n/a	n/a	n/a	n/a	n/a	n/a	n/a	n/a	n/a	n/a
Colorado Spgs, CO	n/a	n/a	n/a	n/a	n/a	n/a	n/a	n/a	n/a	n/a	n/a	n/a
Columbia, MO	n/a	n/a	n/a	n/a	n/a	n/a	n/a	n/a	n/a	n/a	n/a	n/a
Columbus, OH	11.8	13.7	9.8	11.7	13.7	9.8	8.2	8.3	6.3	3.2	2.3	1.1
Dallas, TX	9.8	8.7	9.0	9.6	8.4	8.8	11.8	9.2	8.2	2.0	2.1	1.9
Davenport, IA	n/a	n/a	n/a	n/a	n/a	n/a	n/a	n/a	n/a	n/a	n/a	n/a
Denver, CO	7.0	6.3	6.3	6.5	5.9	5.5	6.8	4.7	5.3	1.8	1.5	1.2
Des Moines, IA	n/a	n/a	n/a	n/a	n/a	n/a	n/a	n/a	n/a	n/a	n/a	n/a
Durham, NC	n/a	n/a	n/a	n/a	n/a	n/a	n/a	n/a	n/a	n/a	n/a	n/a
El Paso, TX	6.5	4.3	8.8	5.9	4.3	8.6	9.2	8.2	7.9	1.3	0.1	2.9
Erie, PA	n/a	n/a	n/a	n/a	n/a	n/a	n/a	n/a	n/a	n/a	n/a	n/a
Eugene, OR	n/a	n/a	n/a	n/a	n/a	n/a	n/a	n/a	n/a	n/a	n/a	n/a
Fargo, ND	n/a	n/a	n/a	n/a	n/a	n/a	n/a	n/a	n/a	n/a	n/a	n/a
Fayetteville, NC	n/a	n/a	n/a	n/a	n/a	n/a	n/a	n/a	n/a	n/a	n/a	n/a
Ft. Collins, CO	n/a	n/a	n/a	n/a	n/a	n/a	n/a	n/a	n/a	n/a	n/a	n/a
Ft. Wayne, IN	n/a	n/a	n/a	n/a	n/a	n/a	n/a	n/a	n/a	n/a	n/a	n/a
Ft. Worth, TX	9.8	8.7	9.0	9.6	8.4	8.8	11.8	9.2	8.2	2.0	2.1	1.9
Gainesville, FL	n/a	n/a	n/a	n/a	n/a	n/a	n/a	n/a	n/a	n/a	n/a	n/a
Grand Rapids, MI	11.0	8.8	7.2	7.8	6.4	6.2	6.1	5.6	5.1	2.6	2.4	2.5
Green Bay, WI	n/a	n/a	n/a	n/a	n/a	n/a	n/a	n/a	n/a	n/a	n/a	n/a
Greensboro, NC	12.4	12.1	12.5	12.4	12.0	12.4	11.9	7.6	9.6	3.0	3.5	3.0
Honolulu, HI	12.1	10.2	10.9	10.9	8.8	8.6	6.9	6.3	6.0	0.7	1.3	0.9
Houston, TX	11.8	9.8	9.6	11.4	9.4	9.0	16.5	11.4	10.0	2.0	1.9	2.3
Huntsville, AL	n/a	n/a	n/a	n/a	n/a	n/a	n/a	n/a	n/a	n/a	n/a	n/a
Indianapolis, IN	12.4	10.5	9.2	11.9	9.5	8.7	13.1	11.1	10.9	3.4	1.8	1.5
Jacksonville, FL	14.7	15.4	14.2	14.1	14.4	12.7	13.3	11.7	8.4	2.8	1.9	1.5
Kansas City, MO	11.1	10.5	10.8	10.9	10.3	10.4	12.1	11.2	10.1	2.7	1.6	2.0
Lafayette, LA	n/a	n/a	n/a	n/a	n/a	n/a	n/a	n/a	n/a	n/a	n/a	n/a
Las Vegas, NV	16.4	16.2	16.6	16.0	15.0	15.5	12.1	12.8	14.1	4.1	3.4	3.0
Lexington, KY	n/a	n/a	n/a	n/a	n/a	n/a	n/a	n/a	n/a	n/a	n/a	n/a
Lincoln, NE	n/a	n/a	n/a	n/a	n/a	n/a	n/a	n/a	n/a	n/a	n/a	n/a
Little Rock, AR	n/a	n/a	n/a	n/a	n/a	n/a	n/a	n/a	n/a	n/a	n/a	n/a
Los Angeles, CA	6.7	6.2	6.2	6.4	5.9	5.7	5.3	4.9	4.2	1.8	1.3	1.2
Louisville, KY	10.8	10.6	11.0	10.8	10.6	11.0	10.2	7.2	7.8	2.4	2.4	0.8
Lubbock, TX	n/a	n/a	n/a	n/a	n/a	n/a	n/a	n/a	n/a	n/a	n/a	n/a
Madison, WI	n/a	n/a	n/a	n/a	n/a	n/a	n/a	n/a	n/a	n/a	n/a	n/a

Table continued on next page.

Metro Area[1]	Gross Vacancy Rate[2] (%)			Year-Round Vacancy Rate[3] (%)			Rental Vacancy Rate[4] (%)			Homeowner Vacancy Rate[5] (%)		
	2011	2012	2013	2011	2012	2013	2011	2012	2013	2011	2012	2013
Manchester, NH	n/a	n/a	n/a	n/a	n/a	n/a	n/a	n/a	n/a	n/a	n/a	n/a
McAllen, TX	n/a	n/a	n/a	n/a	n/a	n/a	n/a	n/a	n/a	n/a	n/a	n/a
Miami, FL	21.0	20.1	20.2	11.7	10.1	10.3	11.8	8.2	6.7	1.8	0.9	1.7
Midland, TX	n/a	n/a	n/a	n/a	n/a	n/a	n/a	n/a	n/a	n/a	n/a	n/a
Minneapolis, MN	6.6	5.8	5.7	6.1	5.2	5.1	6.7	5.3	5.4	1.8	1.2	0.9
Montgomery, AL	n/a	n/a	n/a	n/a	n/a	n/a	n/a	n/a	n/a	n/a	n/a	n/a
Nashville, TN	9.0	8.7	6.6	8.3	8.2	6.4	8.2	8.4	5.3	2.2	1.6	0.9
New Orleans, LA	10.7	13.6	13.3	10.3	13.4	12.7	13.1	15.9	11.1	2.1	2.9	1.9
New York, NY	10.0	9.8	9.5	8.7	8.4	8.1	6.4	6.4	5.4	2.6	2.2	2.1
Oklahoma City, OK	15.1	12.8	13.0	14.8	12.6	12.6	9.9	10.2	8.7	3.9	2.5	2.0
Omaha, NE	9.3	8.3	7.5	9.0	7.9	6.5	11.1	9.5	6.1	1.9	1.2	1.3
Orlando, FL	20.1	21.2	20.5	14.0	14.3	15.5	19.0	18.5	14.7	2.5	2.2	2.8
Oxnard, CA	7.1	5.5	7.4	4.7	4.6	5.6	3.2	2.3	5.3	0.5	0.5	1.7
Peoria, IL	n/a	n/a	n/a	n/a	n/a	n/a	n/a	n/a	n/a	n/a	n/a	n/a
Philadelphia, PA	10.5	10.2	10.4	10.1	9.8	10.2	12.7	12.6	11.6	1.6	1.9	1.6
Phoenix, AZ	16.7	16.6	18.4	10.8	9.8	11.5	10.9	10.3	9.7	3.1	2.7	2.4
Pittsburgh, PA	12.3	14.4	12.7	11.6	14.1	12.5	6.3	6.4	7.8	2.2	1.3	1.7
Portland, OR	6.5	7.0	6.5	6.3	6.6	6.1	3.4	5.0	3.1	2.0	1.9	1.2
Providence, RI	13.7	13.8	12.3	10.8	10.9	8.9	8.8	8.0	6.6	2.2	2.9	2.3
Provo, UT	n/a	n/a	n/a	n/a	n/a	n/a	n/a	n/a	n/a	n/a	n/a	n/a
Raleigh, NC	9.2	8.5	7.3	9.1	8.2	7.2	8.9	8.8	6.9	2.9	1.9	1.8
Reno, NV	n/a	n/a	n/a	n/a	n/a	n/a	n/a	n/a	n/a	n/a	n/a	n/a
Richmond, VA	12.4	13.8	14.5	12.0	13.0	13.6	13.7	17.5	11.4	2.4	1.4	2.4
Riverside, CA	17.7	17.9	16.2	11.4	12.5	12.9	8.4	9.0	8.6	3.5	3.3	1.8
Rochester, MN	n/a	n/a	n/a	n/a	n/a	n/a	n/a	n/a	n/a	n/a	n/a	n/a
Salem, OR	n/a	n/a	n/a	n/a	n/a	n/a	n/a	n/a	n/a	n/a	n/a	n/a
Salt Lake City, UT	7.5	7.9	7.4	6.4	7.3	6.8	7.4	7.3	6.7	2.2	0.8	1.5
San Antonio, TX	11.2	11.3	9.0	10.2	10.4	8.3	9.2	9.0	9.1	1.5	2.7	1.4
San Diego, CA	9.9	9.1	7.8	9.5	8.6	7.4	6.9	7.1	5.5	1.9	1.4	1.2
San Francisco, CA	8.3	6.9	6.5	8.1	6.8	6.4	6.8	3.2	3.9	1.8	1.0	1.1
San Jose, CA	5.3	3.8	5.0	5.3	3.7	4.9	4.8	3.8	3.0	0.9	0.9	0.6
Santa Rosa, CA	n/a	n/a	n/a	n/a	n/a	n/a	n/a	n/a	n/a	n/a	n/a	n/a
Savannah, GA	n/a	n/a	n/a	n/a	n/a	n/a	n/a	n/a	n/a	n/a	n/a	n/a
Seattle, WA	8.6	8.1	6.9	8.3	8.0	6.6	6.7	5.7	4.3	2.6	2.3	1.7
Sioux Falls, SD	n/a	n/a	n/a	n/a	n/a	n/a	n/a	n/a	n/a	n/a	n/a	n/a
Spokane, WA	n/a	n/a	n/a	n/a	n/a	n/a	n/a	n/a	n/a	n/a	n/a	n/a
Springfield, MO	n/a	n/a	n/a	n/a	n/a	n/a	n/a	n/a	n/a	n/a	n/a	n/a
Tallahassee, FL	n/a	n/a	n/a	n/a	n/a	n/a	n/a	n/a	n/a	n/a	n/a	n/a
Tampa, FL	20.4	20.8	18.4	14.5	14.2	12.1	11.7	13.0	9.2	3.8	2.0	2.1
Topeka, KS	n/a	n/a	n/a	n/a	n/a	n/a	n/a	n/a	n/a	n/a	n/a	n/a
Tulsa, OK	13.2	13.3	12.0	12.7	12.8	11.5	13.0	9.5	10.5	2.5	2.4	2.4
Virginia Beach, VA	10.8	10.8	9.6	10.3	9.5	8.7	9.4	8.7	7.0	3.2	2.9	2.5
Washington, DC	9.6	8.1	8.3	9.4	7.9	8.2	7.9	6.4	7.2	1.8	1.3	1.3
Wichita, KS	n/a	n/a	n/a	n/a	n/a	n/a	n/a	n/a	n/a	n/a	n/a	n/a
Wilmington, NC	n/a	n/a	n/a	n/a	n/a	n/a	n/a	n/a	n/a	n/a	n/a	n/a
Worcester, MA	10.3	10.3	10.8	9.5	9.5	8.6	4.9	3.7	6.4	1.3	2.4	3.1
U.S.	14.2	13.8	13.8	11.1	10.8	10.7	9.5	8.7	8.3	2.5	2.0	2.0

Note: (1) Metropolitan Statistical Area—see Appendix B for areas included; (2) The percentage of the total housing inventory that is vacant; (3) The percentage of the housing inventory (excluding seasonal units) that is year-round vacant; (4) The percentage of rental inventory that is vacant for rent; (5) The percentage of homeowner inventory that is vacant for sale; n/a not available
Source: U.S. Census Bureau, Housing Vacancies and Homeownership Annual Statistics: 2013

Employment by Industry

Metro Area[1]	(A)	(B)	(C)	(D)	(E)	(F)	(G)	(H)	(I)	(J)	(K)	(L)	(M)
Abilene, TX	n/a	19.3	5.6	18.7	1.8	11.2	4.0	n/a	4.1	7.7	12.7	2.8	4.1
Albuquerque, NM	n/a	15.6	4.9	22.6	2.0	10.2	4.5	n/a	3.1	14.6	11.6	2.7	3.0
Anchorage, AK	5.7	16.6	4.6	20.1	2.5	10.0	1.3	2.1	3.8	12.0	12.1	6.5	2.8
Ann Arbor, MI	n/a	12.5	3.9	37.8	1.9	7.3	6.6	n/a	3.4	12.6	8.2	1.8	2.5
Athens, GA	n/a	n/a	n/a	34.6	n/a	10.0	n/a	n/a	n/a	7.9	10.8	n/a	n/a
Atlanta, GA	3.9	12.2	6.5	13.0	3.5	10.2	6.2	<0.1	3.8	18.0	11.1	5.4	6.2
Austin, TX	n/a	11.4	5.6	19.2	2.7	11.8	6.0	n/a	4.3	15.7	11.2	1.7	5.2
Baltimore, MD	n/a	18.9	5.7	17.2	1.2	9.0	4.2	n/a	4.0	16.3	10.8	3.4	3.8
Billings, MT	n/a	17.5	n/a	11.8	n/a	12.6	n/a	n/a	n/a	10.8	n/a	n/a	n/a
Boise City, ID	n/a	15.2	5.3	16.3	1.6	9.2	8.8	n/a	3.5	13.9	12.6	3.1	4.8
Boston, MA[4]	3.1	22.9	8.0	11.3	3.3	9.4	5.2	<0.1	3.9	18.6	8.7	2.3	3.3
Boulder, CO	n/a	12.7	4.2	19.7	4.8	10.6	9.7	n/a	3.2	18.7	9.6	1.0	3.2
Cape Coral, FL	n/a	11.3	5.2	17.5	1.4	15.6	2.2	n/a	4.1	13.0	17.0	1.9	3.0
Cedar Rapids, IA	n/a	14.1	7.4	11.9	3.5	7.9	14.3	n/a	3.6	9.6	12.3	6.6	4.0
Charleston, SC	n/a	11.6	4.1	20.1	1.7	12.1	7.8	n/a	4.2	14.3	12.3	4.5	2.6
Charlotte, NC	n/a	10.1	8.4	14.0	2.5	10.8	8.2	n/a	3.6	16.6	11.4	4.4	5.3
Chicago, IL[2]	3.0	15.5	6.8	12.3	2.0	9.3	8.3	<0.1	4.3	17.9	10.3	4.9	5.4
Cincinnati, OH	n/a	15.4	6.4	12.6	1.4	10.2	10.3	n/a	3.9	16.1	10.4	3.9	5.8
Clarksville, TN	n/a	12.8	3.4	23.6	1.2	12.1	11.1	n/a	3.4	9.7	13.6	2.6	n/a
Colorado Spgs, CO	n/a	12.8	6.4	19.0	2.7	12.4	4.5	n/a	5.9	15.9	11.9	1.7	1.9
Columbia, MO	n/a	n/a	n/a	32.3	n/a	n/a	n/a	n/a	n/a	n/a	12.0	n/a	n/a
Columbus, OH	n/a	14.0	7.6	16.7	1.8	9.8	6.8	n/a	3.8	16.5	10.7	5.0	4.0
Dallas, TX[2]	n/a	12.2	9.0	12.4	3.0	9.7	7.4	n/a	3.5	17.4	10.5	3.9	5.9
Davenport, IA	n/a	n/a	n/a	n/a	n/a	n/a	n/a	n/a	n/a	n/a	n/a	n/a	n/a
Denver, CO	n/a	12.5	7.3	14.3	3.3	10.7	4.9	n/a	3.9	18.0	10.1	3.8	5.0
Des Moines, IA	n/a	14.2	15.3	13.3	2.0	8.6	5.8	n/a	3.9	12.3	11.6	3.0	5.4
Durham, NC	n/a	21.6	4.4	22.5	1.3	8.7	10.3	n/a	3.5	12.4	8.3	1.5	3.2
El Paso, TX	n/a	13.6	4.2	24.0	2.0	10.5	6.0	n/a	3.3	10.3	13.6	4.8	3.4
Erie, PA	n/a	21.3	4.8	12.8	1.0	10.1	17.0	n/a	4.8	7.4	12.2	2.5	3.0
Eugene, OR	3.4	15.8	4.9	21.1	2.2	10.0	8.5	0.6	3.2	10.5	13.5	2.4	3.9
Fargo, ND	n/a	16.2	7.3	13.6	2.4	9.6	7.6	n/a	3.9	11.3	11.9	3.6	6.7
Fayetteville, NC	n/a	11.0	2.8	29.9	1.1	11.2	8.6	n/a	3.8	9.7	13.1	3.6	1.8
Ft. Collins, CO	n/a	9.8	4.1	24.8	1.6	12.0	8.0	n/a	3.7	13.4	12.3	1.8	2.6
Ft. Wayne, IN	n/a	17.9	5.5	10.3	1.5	9.0	16.5	n/a	5.0	9.7	11.1	4.4	5.0
Ft. Worth, TX[2]	n/a	12.6	5.8	13.7	1.4	11.0	10.0	n/a	3.9	11.6	11.4	7.3	4.7
Gainesville, FL	n/a	18.2	4.7	32.4	1.1	10.6	3.5	n/a	3.0	8.7	10.6	2.1	2.1
Grand Rapids, MI	n/a	17.3	5.2	8.1	1.1	9.1	16.9	n/a	4.2	16.6	9.7	2.6	5.6
Green Bay, WI	n/a	13.4	8.1	12.7	1.1	9.3	16.9	n/a	4.7	11.1	9.9	4.6	4.4
Greensboro, NC	n/a	14.0	5.2	13.0	1.4	8.8	15.0	n/a	3.6	14.4	11.0	4.7	5.4
Honolulu, HI	n/a	13.3	4.4	21.8	1.5	14.4	2.5	n/a	4.6	13.8	10.9	4.7	3.1
Houston, TX	6.7	12.0	5.0	13.3	1.2	9.8	9.0	3.8	3.5	15.2	10.5	4.8	5.4
Huntsville, AL	n/a	9.0	2.9	22.9	1.3	8.5	10.7	n/a	3.3	22.7	11.2	1.3	2.7
Indianapolis, IN	4.4	14.5	6.4	12.9	1.7	9.9	8.9	0.1	4.2	15.4	10.7	6.1	4.8
Jacksonville, FL	5.0	14.6	9.8	12.1	1.5	12.0	4.5	0.1	3.3	15.9	12.0	5.2	4.0
Kansas City, MO	n/a	13.8	7.4	14.8	3.0	9.3	7.2	n/a	4.2	16.1	10.7	4.6	5.1
Lafayette, LA	4.3	15.0	5.6	10.4	1.5	10.4	7.7	10.7	3.1	12.0	12.1	2.6	4.7
Las Vegas, NV	4.7	9.4	5.1	11.3	1.1	30.8	2.4	<0.1	2.8	13.1	12.6	4.3	2.4
Lexington, KY	n/a	12.8	3.7	20.7	2.1	9.8	11.2	n/a	3.5	14.1	11.0	3.5	3.7
Lincoln, NE	n/a	15.9	7.8	21.8	1.4	8.8	7.5	n/a	3.8	9.9	11.0	5.9	2.2
Little Rock, AR	n/a	14.8	5.9	20.8	2.1	9.0	5.7	n/a	4.5	13.1	10.9	4.2	4.5
Los Angeles, CA[2]	2.9	17.5	5.0	13.3	4.8	10.5	8.6	0.1	3.5	14.5	10.3	3.8	5.2
Louisville, KY	n/a	13.5	7.0	13.3	1.5	10.1	11.7	n/a	4.0	13.0	10.3	7.3	4.7
Lubbock, TX	n/a	16.0	5.2	21.1	2.9	12.8	3.6	n/a	4.1	8.1	13.3	3.6	4.6
Madison, WI	n/a	11.5	7.8	23.8	3.5	8.4	7.9	n/a	4.9	11.8	10.7	2.4	3.6
Manchester, NH[3]	n/a	19.9	7.1	11.2	3.0	8.4	7.5	n/a	4.5	14.3	13.2	2.6	4.0
McAllen, TX	n/a	25.6	3.8	23.6	0.9	8.9	2.8	n/a	2.6	6.5	14.9	3.5	3.0

Table continued on next page.

Metro Area[1]	(A)	(B)	(C)	(D)	(E)	(F)	(G)	(H)	(I)	(J)	(K)	(L)	(M)
Miami, FL[2]	3.2	15.3	6.8	13.1	1.7	11.8	3.4	<0.1	4.4	13.8	13.8	6.1	6.8
Midland, TX	n/a	7.8	4.9	9.8	1.0	9.2	4.2	n/a	3.5	10.0	10.1	5.2	5.7
Minneapolis, MN	n/a	16.7	7.8	13.3	2.1	9.0	10.2	n/a	4.3	15.2	10.1	3.5	4.5
Montgomery, AL	n/a	11.0	4.3	25.3	1.3	9.1	10.8	n/a	4.2	12.3	11.4	3.6	3.1
Nashville, TN	n/a	15.4	6.1	12.8	2.5	10.7	8.8	n/a	4.0	15.5	10.8	4.3	4.9
New Orleans, LA	5.6	15.4	5.0	13.7	1.5	14.5	5.3	1.4	3.7	13.2	11.4	5.0	4.2
New York, NY[2]	n/a	20.0	9.9	13.6	3.9	9.0	2.9	n/a	4.3	15.9	9.9	3.4	4.1
Oklahoma City, OK	4.5	14.4	5.6	20.9	1.3	10.8	5.8	3.2	3.5	12.1	10.8	2.7	4.4
Omaha, NE	n/a	15.6	8.7	13.5	2.3	9.1	6.7	n/a	3.7	14.8	11.5	5.7	3.5
Orlando, FL	4.9	12.1	6.5	10.9	2.2	20.6	3.6	<0.1	3.3	16.4	12.8	3.0	3.7
Oxnard, CA	4.2	13.8	6.4	15.2	1.7	11.7	10.2	0.4	3.3	12.6	14.1	2.0	4.4
Peoria, IL	n/a	19.1	4.1	11.9	1.2	9.8	15.2	n/a	4.5	11.5	10.3	4.4	4.1
Philadelphia, PA[2]	n/a	22.8	6.8	11.3	1.9	8.6	6.6	n/a	4.4	16.1	10.4	3.3	4.3
Phoenix, AZ	5.0	14.5	8.9	12.8	1.8	10.4	6.3	0.2	3.5	16.4	12.1	3.5	4.5
Pittsburgh, PA	4.5	20.7	6.1	10.5	1.6	9.4	7.6	0.9	4.4	15.0	11.3	3.9	3.9
Portland, OR	4.9	14.7	6.0	13.9	2.2	10.0	11.0	0.1	3.5	14.6	10.8	3.3	5.0
Providence, RI[3]	3.5	22.0	6.2	12.8	1.8	10.8	9.1	<0.1	4.6	11.5	11.7	2.5	3.6
Provo, UT	n/a	22.3	3.3	14.4	4.7	7.3	8.8	n/a	2.2	13.0	12.5	1.3	2.8
Raleigh, NC	n/a	11.9	4.8	16.8	3.3	10.9	5.5	n/a	4.1	19.7	11.5	1.8	4.2
Reno, NV	5.4	11.4	4.7	14.5	0.9	17.2	6.0	0.1	2.9	13.8	11.7	6.9	4.5
Richmond, VA	n/a	14.5	7.5	17.9	1.2	8.9	5.0	n/a	4.9	15.3	11.4	3.3	4.4
Riverside, CA	5.7	14.7	3.3	18.1	0.9	11.4	6.8	0.1	3.2	10.9	14.0	6.5	4.5
Rochester, MN	n/a	40.6	2.4	10.3	1.6	8.5	9.0	n/a	3.5	5.1	11.5	2.3	2.1
Salem, OR	4.4	15.7	4.8	27.9	0.7	8.9	7.4	0.9	3.4	8.5	12.2	2.7	2.4
Salt Lake City, UT	n/a	11.1	7.8	15.3	2.8	9.7	8.2	n/a	3.0	16.3	11.1	4.8	4.7
San Antonio, TX	4.6	15.3	8.3	17.7	2.3	12.7	5.1	0.7	3.7	12.1	11.6	2.6	3.3
San Diego, CA	4.8	13.8	5.4	17.5	1.8	12.5	7.1	<0.1	3.7	16.7	11.2	2.1	3.3
San Francisco, CA[2]	3.6	13.3	7.0	12.4	4.8	13.3	3.5	<0.1	3.9	23.1	8.9	3.8	2.5
San Jose, CA	4.0	15.2	3.4	9.7	6.1	8.8	16.1	<0.1	2.6	19.7	9.2	1.5	3.7
Santa Rosa, CA	5.2	15.9	4.0	17.6	1.4	12.0	10.7	0.1	3.5	10.2	13.1	2.4	4.0
Savannah, GA	n/a	14.7	4.1	14.3	0.8	14.0	9.4	n/a	4.4	12.6	12.2	6.7	3.8
Seattle, WA[2]	4.6	13.1	5.5	13.5	5.7	9.5	11.1	0.1	3.6	15.0	10.7	3.2	4.6
Sioux Falls, SD	n/a	20.6	11.5	9.3	1.9	8.5	9.3	n/a	3.3	9.4	12.6	3.5	5.3
Spokane, WA	n/a	20.9	6.1	16.8	1.3	8.6	7.0	n/a	4.2	10.6	12.3	3.1	4.6
Springfield, MO	n/a	19.2	5.7	14.7	1.9	9.4	6.9	n/a	3.6	12.3	12.7	5.1	5.1
Tallahassee, FL	n/a	11.6	4.3	35.8	2.0	10.6	1.8	n/a	5.2	10.9	11.0	1.2	2.0
Tampa, FL	4.8	15.8	8.4	12.8	2.2	10.9	5.1	<0.1	3.5	16.9	12.9	2.4	4.2
Topeka, KS	n/a	16.0	6.4	23.5	1.3	8.1	6.3	n/a	4.2	11.8	9.9	4.1	3.1
Tulsa, OK	5.0	15.2	5.2	13.5	1.8	8.9	11.7	1.8	3.8	13.3	11.5	4.7	3.6
Virginia Beach, VA	n/a	14.2	4.8	21.0	1.5	10.6	7.2	n/a	4.7	13.6	12.0	3.2	2.6
Washington, DC[2]	n/a	12.7	4.5	23.1	2.4	9.5	1.2	n/a	6.3	22.9	8.7	2.3	2.0
Wichita, KS	n/a	15.2	3.7	14.1	1.5	10.0	17.7	n/a	3.6	11.1	11.3	3.2	3.2
Wilmington, NC	n/a	12.7	4.6	19.3	2.0	14.5	5.1	n/a	3.7	11.7	14.6	3.1	3.2
Worcester, MA[3]	n/a	24.3	5.4	14.9	1.4	8.5	9.5	n/a	3.1	10.2	11.6	3.9	3.9
U.S.	4.2	15.5	5.7	16.1	1.9	10.2	8.7	0.6	3.9	13.7	11.4	3.8	4.2

Note: All figures are percentages covering non-farm employment as of December 2013 and are not seasonally adjusted;
(1) Figures cover the Metropolitan Statistical Area (MSA) except where noted. See Appendix B for areas included; (2) Metropolitan Division; (3) New England City and Town Area; (4) New England City and Town Area Division; (A) Construction; (B) Education and Health Services; (C) Financial Activities; (D) Government; (E) Information; (F) Leisure and Hospitality; (G) Manufacturing; (H) Mining and Logging; (I) Other Services; (J) Professional and Business Services; (K) Retail Trade; (L) Transportation and Utilities; (M) Wholesale Trade; n/a not available
Source: Bureau of Labor Statistics, Current Employment Statistics, Employment, Hours, and Earnings

Labor Force, Employment and Job Growth: City

City	Civilian Labor Force			Workers Employed		
	Dec. 2012	Dec. 2013	% Chg.	Dec. 2012	Dec. 2013	% Chg.
Abilene, TX	58,388	59,322	1.6	55,629	56,690	1.9
Albuquerque, NM	257,503	253,224	-1.7	241,594	238,036	-1.5
Anchorage, AK	159,323	158,797	-0.3	151,276	151,438	0.1
Ann Arbor, MI	63,061	63,412	0.6	59,552	59,918	0.6
Athens, GA	69,635	68,686	-1.4	64,973	64,893	-0.1
Atlanta, GA	197,605	193,652	-2.0	176,010	176,555	0.3
Austin, TX	464,387	475,873	2.5	442,621	455,863	3.0
Baltimore, MD	280,654	276,345	-1.5	253,248	252,991	-0.1
Billings, MT	59,074	60,167	1.9	56,680	57,893	2.1
Boise City, ID	111,833	112,063	0.2	105,525	106,950	1.4
Boston, MA	320,515	322,960	0.8	301,058	303,051	0.7
Boulder, CO	61,750	61,918	0.3	58,701	59,321	1.1
Cape Coral, FL	79,099	79,040	-0.1	72,936	74,536	2.2
Cedar Rapids, IA	70,359	72,469	3.0	66,625	69,140	3.8
Charleston, SC	61,564	61,147	-0.7	57,591	58,429	1.5
Charlotte, NC	394,698	391,422	-0.8	363,056	368,591	1.5
Chicago, IL	1,276,070	1,271,227	-0.4	1,151,796	1,150,079	-0.1
Cincinnati, OH	139,839	139,879	0.0	130,211	130,389	0.1
Clarksville, TN	58,343	56,734	-2.8	53,866	52,473	-2.6
Colorado Spgs, CO	208,029	204,653	-1.6	190,227	190,029	-0.1
Columbia, MO	61,533	62,817	2.1	59,235	60,685	2.4
Columbus, OH	426,552	430,423	0.9	403,825	407,115	0.8
Dallas, TX	586,561	596,415	1.7	549,042	561,247	2.2
Davenport, IA	50,302	52,034	3.4	46,893	48,803	4.1
Denver, CO	329,615	328,452	-0.4	303,556	308,202	1.5
Des Moines, IA	104,991	108,232	3.1	98,223	102,321	4.2
Durham, NC	123,995	122,692	-1.1	115,431	116,919	1.3
El Paso, TX	271,850	270,705	-0.4	250,664	251,186	0.2
Erie, PA	48,156	48,060	-0.2	43,940	44,643	1.6
Eugene, OR	80,117	78,516	-2.0	74,788	73,815	-1.3
Fargo, ND	59,587	58,473	-1.9	57,621	56,929	-1.2
Fayetteville, NC	89,479	87,203	-2.5	82,694	82,364	-0.4
Ft. Collins, CO	88,053	86,935	-1.3	82,897	83,067	0.2
Ft. Wayne, IN	121,687	122,979	1.1	111,316	115,180	3.5
Ft. Worth, TX	360,346	368,237	2.2	339,337	348,449	2.7
Gainesville, FL	65,566	65,672	0.2	61,555	62,366	1.3
Grand Rapids, MI	99,786	102,834	3.1	91,273	95,032	4.1
Green Bay, WI	59,228	59,530	0.5	54,082	55,069	1.8
Greensboro, NC	139,545	136,564	-2.1	127,146	127,851	0.6
Honolulu, HI	n/a	n/a	n/a	n/a	n/a	n/a
Houston, TX	1,038,662	1,062,784	2.3	974,997	1,004,714	3.0
Huntsville, AL	90,433	88,011	-2.7	85,419	83,636	-2.1
Indianapolis, IN	422,888	423,668	0.2	385,789	396,511	2.8
Jacksonville, FL	423,087	419,389	-0.9	390,776	395,150	1.1
Kansas City, MO	227,690	227,284	-0.2	210,655	212,790	1.0
Lafayette, LA	63,962	65,811	2.9	61,411	63,563	3.5
Las Vegas, NV	286,848	285,073	-0.6	257,678	259,462	0.7
Lexington, KY	159,498	156,989	-1.6	150,161	148,265	-1.3
Lincoln, NE	152,026	150,990	-0.7	146,998	146,410	-0.4
Little Rock, AR	94,582	93,794	-0.8	88,565	87,934	-0.7
Los Angeles, CA	1,916,100	1,929,831	0.7	1,699,953	1,742,272	2.5
Louisville, KY	368,679	359,327	-2.5	339,507	333,783	-1.7
Lubbock, TX	119,336	122,325	2.5	113,737	117,178	3.0
Madison, WI	144,993	147,223	1.5	138,815	141,727	2.1
Manchester, NH	62,477	61,692	-1.3	58,772	58,550	-0.4

Table continued on next page.

City	Civilian Labor Force			Workers Employed		
	Dec. 2012	Dec. 2013	% Chg.	Dec. 2012	Dec. 2013	% Chg.
McAllen, TX	61,590	61,903	0.5	57,452	58,083	1.1
Miami, FL	184,999	181,547	-1.9	166,485	167,760	0.8
Midland, TX	75,394	79,562	5.5	73,233	77,357	5.6
Minneapolis, MN	215,809	217,300	0.7	204,947	208,040	1.5
Montgomery, AL	93,234	91,988	-1.3	86,867	86,386	-0.6
Nashville, TN	340,174	331,727	-2.5	319,549	312,959	-2.1
New Orleans, LA	150,567	150,127	-0.3	140,613	141,677	0.8
New York, NY	4,028,164	4,037,749	0.2	3,669,066	3,732,938	1.7
Oklahoma City, OK	274,105	280,247	2.2	261,489	266,736	2.0
Omaha, NE	218,683	217,335	-0.6	209,462	208,721	-0.4
Orlando, FL	137,813	138,700	0.6	127,752	131,373	2.8
Oxnard, CA	92,145	91,124	-1.1	81,363	82,560	1.5
Peoria, IL	57,119	55,791	-2.3	51,804	49,990	-3.5
Philadelphia, PA	660,276	642,317	-2.7	590,748	588,476	-0.4
Phoenix, AZ	728,773	725,352	-0.5	677,980	679,012	0.2
Pittsburgh, PA	155,902	153,811	-1.3	144,809	145,348	0.4
Portland, OR	321,366	318,514	-0.9	298,490	299,668	0.4
Providence, RI	81,449	79,843	-2.0	72,508	71,452	-1.5
Provo, UT	55,250	59,507	7.7	52,695	57,575	9.3
Raleigh, NC	222,597	220,426	-1.0	207,564	210,461	1.4
Reno, NV	117,068	115,588	-1.3	105,711	105,752	0.0
Richmond, VA	100,762	101,449	0.7	92,647	94,314	1.8
Riverside, CA	167,284	165,242	-1.2	148,554	150,084	1.0
Rochester, MN	59,183	59,094	-0.2	56,700	56,881	0.3
Salem, OR	74,334	71,837	-3.4	67,821	66,692	-1.7
Salt Lake City, UT	104,296	109,681	5.2	99,376	106,050	6.7
San Antonio, TX	627,542	630,554	0.5	592,131	596,914	0.8
San Diego, CA	715,817	712,880	-0.4	657,354	667,464	1.5
San Francisco, CA	482,376	484,247	0.4	451,368	461,193	2.2
San Jose, CA	480,781	484,451	0.8	440,174	453,654	3.1
Santa Rosa, CA	81,629	81,500	-0.2	75,258	76,868	2.1
Savannah, GA	66,322	64,048	-3.4	59,995	58,835	-1.9
Seattle, WA	372,822	381,488	2.3	352,010	364,929	3.7
Sioux Falls, SD	89,696	91,923	2.5	86,001	88,892	3.4
Spokane, WA	103,149	99,692	-3.4	94,465	92,436	-2.1
Springfield, MO	81,901	82,481	0.7	77,427	78,681	1.6
Tallahassee, FL	94,691	95,773	1.1	88,425	90,725	2.6
Tampa, FL	163,559	164,309	0.5	150,171	154,202	2.7
Topeka, KS	65,108	63,782	-2.0	60,510	60,054	-0.8
Tulsa, OK	191,828	194,571	1.4	182,396	184,737	1.3
Virginia Beach, VA	226,742	228,375	0.7	214,384	217,580	1.5
Washington, DC	371,456	365,540	-1.6	339,415	340,486	0.3
Wichita, KS	184,363	181,136	-1.8	172,236	170,662	-0.9
Wilmington, NC	53,923	52,649	-2.4	49,369	49,596	0.5
Worcester, MA	84,235	84,090	-0.2	77,626	77,344	-0.4
U.S.	154,904,000	154,408,000	-0.3	143,060,000	144,423,000	1.0

Note: Data is not seasonally adjusted and covers workers 16 years of age and older
Source: Bureau of Labor Statistics, Local Area Unemployment Statistics

Labor Force, Employment and Job Growth: Metro Area

Metro Area[1]	Civilian Labor Force			Workers Employed		
	Dec. 2012	Dec. 2013	% Chg.	Dec. 2012	Dec. 2013	% Chg.
Abilene, TX	84,362	85,707	1.6	80,437	81,972	1.9
Albuquerque, NM	400,580	393,881	-1.7	373,825	368,319	-1.5
Anchorage, AK	203,758	203,084	-0.3	192,298	192,504	0.1
Ann Arbor, MI	183,130	184,155	0.6	173,585	174,651	0.6
Athens, GA	114,803	113,199	-1.4	107,437	107,305	-0.1
Atlanta, GA	2,773,421	2,734,954	-1.4	2,540,260	2,548,119	0.3
Austin, TX	972,339	996,173	2.5	923,238	950,857	3.0
Baltimore, MD	1,483,033	1,465,478	-1.2	1,380,763	1,379,362	-0.1
Billings, MT	89,120	90,847	1.9	85,498	87,328	2.1
Boise City, ID	307,922	308,593	0.2	289,070	292,972	1.3
Boston, MA[2]	1,550,680	1,562,753	0.8	1,466,586	1,476,295	0.7
Boulder, CO	181,087	180,906	-0.1	171,073	172,879	1.1
Cape Coral, FL	288,827	288,702	-0.0	266,079	271,916	2.2
Cedar Rapids, IA	142,934	147,236	3.0	135,381	140,490	3.8
Charleston, SC	330,542	328,726	-0.5	307,190	311,663	1.5
Charlotte, NC	928,564	916,145	-1.3	841,635	855,842	1.7
Chicago, IL[2]	4,112,381	4,098,575	-0.3	3,747,045	3,760,120	0.3
Cincinnati, OH	1,081,111	1,073,366	-0.7	1,011,041	1,006,980	-0.4
Clarksville, TN	117,691	114,501	-2.7	108,121	105,574	-2.4
Colorado Spgs, CO	312,941	307,585	-1.7	285,719	285,422	-0.1
Columbia, MO	97,647	99,565	2.0	93,600	95,891	2.4
Columbus, OH	967,106	975,987	0.9	915,289	922,747	0.8
Dallas, TX[2]	2,245,884	2,285,469	1.8	2,113,329	2,160,308	2.2
Davenport, IA	197,858	198,667	0.4	184,080	185,069	0.5
Denver, CO	1,421,045	1,417,353	-0.3	1,315,711	1,335,851	1.5
Des Moines, IA	308,244	318,220	3.2	292,159	304,347	4.2
Durham, NC	276,816	273,704	-1.1	257,103	260,417	1.3
El Paso, TX	323,811	322,443	-0.4	296,188	296,805	0.2
Erie, PA	140,809	140,694	-0.1	129,605	131,678	1.6
Eugene, OR	175,947	171,484	-2.5	162,019	159,911	-1.3
Fargo, ND	118,466	117,176	-1.1	114,045	113,657	-0.3
Fayetteville, NC	165,633	160,669	-3.0	148,798	148,205	-0.4
Ft. Collins, CO	180,270	178,459	-1.0	169,533	169,880	0.2
Ft. Wayne, IN	204,345	206,341	1.0	187,655	194,169	3.5
Ft. Worth, TX[2]	1,123,153	1,148,399	2.2	1,059,051	1,087,543	2.7
Gainesville, FL	142,757	142,789	0.0	134,185	135,953	1.3
Grand Rapids, MI	389,082	402,103	3.3	364,397	379,403	4.1
Green Bay, WI	172,384	174,169	1.0	161,898	164,854	1.8
Greensboro, NC	373,892	364,290	-2.6	337,407	339,279	0.6
Honolulu, HI	459,870	463,811	0.9	440,370	446,131	1.3
Houston, TX	3,055,533	3,131,593	2.5	2,872,966	2,960,533	3.0
Huntsville, AL	211,330	205,600	-2.7	199,598	195,434	-2.1
Indianapolis, IN	903,457	907,894	0.5	832,410	855,545	2.8
Jacksonville, FL	699,589	694,256	-0.8	648,259	655,515	1.1
Kansas City, MO	1,034,701	1,031,930	-0.3	968,609	975,741	0.7
Lafayette, LA	141,028	145,012	2.8	135,418	140,163	3.5
Las Vegas, NV	987,932	983,147	-0.5	889,559	895,716	0.7
Lexington, KY	247,670	243,841	-1.5	232,678	229,740	-1.3
Lincoln, NE	176,663	175,515	-0.6	170,687	170,004	-0.4
Little Rock, AR	340,341	338,060	-0.7	319,225	316,950	-0.7
Los Angeles, CA[2]	4,941,671	4,941,492	-0.0	4,438,759	4,508,710	1.6
Louisville, KY	637,024	626,298	-1.7	588,310	583,770	-0.8
Lubbock, TX	146,387	150,127	2.6	139,492	143,712	3.0
Madison, WI	344,939	349,831	1.4	328,830	335,728	2.1
Manchester, NH	107,832	106,653	-1.1	102,005	101,619	-0.4

Table continued on next page.

Metro Area[1]	Civilian Labor Force			Workers Employed		
	Dec. 2012	Dec. 2013	% Chg.	Dec. 2012	Dec. 2013	% Chg.
McAllen, TX	317,468	320,758	1.0	284,246	287,367	1.1
Miami, FL[2]	1,295,038	1,282,132	-1.0	1,174,459	1,194,364	1.7
Midland, TX	92,254	97,358	5.5	89,593	94,639	5.6
Minneapolis, MN	1,858,152	1,870,263	0.7	1,762,494	1,790,025	1.6
Montgomery, AL	168,280	165,988	-1.4	157,029	156,160	-0.6
Nashville, TN	863,413	841,403	-2.5	811,941	795,197	-2.1
New Orleans, LA	544,227	543,640	-0.1	514,276	518,168	0.8
New York, NY[2]	5,745,485	5,742,363	-0.1	5,247,273	5,334,716	1.7
Oklahoma City, OK	600,367	613,490	2.2	572,314	583,803	2.0
Omaha, NE	461,488	460,949	-0.1	442,331	443,173	0.2
Orlando, FL	1,149,261	1,156,473	0.6	1,062,530	1,092,651	2.8
Oxnard, CA	440,772	438,900	-0.4	402,857	408,786	1.5
Peoria, IL	201,110	196,205	-2.4	184,634	178,165	-3.5
Philadelphia, PA[2]	2,005,235	1,960,037	-2.3	1,843,376	1,836,286	-0.4
Phoenix, AZ	2,042,749	2,033,400	-0.5	1,904,463	1,907,362	0.2
Pittsburgh, PA	1,261,313	1,244,990	-1.3	1,170,044	1,174,397	0.4
Portland, OR	1,178,537	1,164,828	-1.2	1,091,135	1,092,460	0.1
Providence, RI	698,341	687,582	-1.5	632,386	624,667	-1.2
Provo, UT	232,500	250,146	7.6	221,010	241,475	9.3
Raleigh, NC	602,263	595,803	-1.1	557,064	564,840	1.4
Reno, NV	223,265	220,352	-1.3	201,721	201,799	0.0
Richmond, VA	659,432	665,236	0.9	619,573	630,722	1.8
Riverside, CA	1,819,256	1,795,514	-1.3	1,619,017	1,635,688	1.0
Rochester, MN	104,165	103,879	-0.3	99,590	99,909	0.3
Salem, OR	190,388	184,194	-3.3	173,577	170,689	-1.7
Salt Lake City, UT	613,413	645,340	5.2	583,405	622,582	6.7
San Antonio, TX	1,024,714	1,028,922	0.4	966,143	973,947	0.8
San Diego, CA	1,603,528	1,596,937	-0.4	1,472,508	1,495,156	1.5
San Francisco, CA[2]	1,023,133	1,028,522	0.5	960,281	981,184	2.2
San Jose, CA	944,587	953,544	0.9	871,335	898,019	3.1
Santa Rosa, CA	257,011	256,586	-0.2	236,895	241,961	2.1
Savannah, GA	183,298	177,195	-3.3	168,509	165,250	-1.9
Seattle, WA[2]	1,517,566	1,535,481	1.2	1,430,711	1,460,104	2.1
Sioux Falls, SD	131,241	134,415	2.4	125,996	130,230	3.4
Spokane, WA	233,657	226,034	-3.3	214,042	209,444	-2.1
Springfield, MO	223,052	224,783	0.8	210,940	214,358	1.6
Tallahassee, FL	187,562	189,428	1.0	174,929	179,480	2.6
Tampa, FL	1,331,021	1,338,701	0.6	1,226,191	1,259,105	2.7
Topeka, KS	120,621	118,404	-1.8	113,380	112,525	-0.8
Tulsa, OK	450,802	456,837	1.3	426,833	432,310	1.3
Virginia Beach, VA	824,175	828,953	0.6	773,629	785,007	1.5
Washington, DC[2]	2,521,100	2,514,981	-0.2	2,385,023	2,396,147	0.5
Wichita, KS	301,071	295,940	-1.7	283,080	280,493	-0.9
Wilmington, NC	184,167	179,204	-2.7	165,773	166,535	0.5
Worcester, MA	292,613	291,563	-0.4	271,522	270,674	-0.3
U.S.	154,904,000	154,408,000	-0.3	143,060,000	144,423,000	1.0

Note: Data is not seasonally adjusted and covers workers 16 years of age and older; (1) Figures cover the Metropolitan Statistical Area (MSA) except where noted. See Appendix B for areas included; (2) Metropolitan Division; (3) New England City and Town Area; (4) New England City and Town Area Division
Source: Bureau of Labor Statistics, Local Area Unemployment Statistics

Unemployment Rate: City

City	2013											
	Jan.	Feb.	Mar.	Apr.	May	Jun.	Jul.	Aug.	Sep.	Oct.	Nov.	Dec.
Abilene, TX	5.5	5.1	5.0	4.8	5.4	5.9	5.6	5.1	5.1	4.8	4.6	4.4
Albuquerque, NM	6.6	7.0	6.6	5.9	6.2	7.2	7.1	6.3	6.1	6.1	5.7	6.0
Anchorage, AK	5.5	5.1	4.9	4.8	4.7	5.3	4.9	4.7	4.4	4.7	4.6	4.6
Ann Arbor, MI	5.7	5.6	5.4	5.4	6.3	7.2	7.8	6.6	6.0	6.4	5.7	5.5
Athens, GA	6.9	6.4	6.2	5.9	6.6	7.7	7.3	6.6	6.1	6.2	5.4	5.5
Atlanta, GA	11.1	10.3	9.9	9.6	10.4	11.4	10.9	10.4	9.6	9.8	9.1	8.8
Austin, TX	5.5	5.0	4.9	4.7	5.0	5.4	5.2	4.8	5.0	4.8	4.4	4.2
Baltimore, MD	10.5	9.7	9.5	9.3	10.0	11.1	10.7	10.3	9.4	9.9	9.0	8.5
Billings, MT	4.6	4.4	4.4	3.9	3.8	4.4	3.8	3.7	3.6	3.6	3.6	3.8
Boise City, ID	6.3	6.0	5.8	5.5	5.3	5.9	5.7	5.8	5.8	5.7	4.7	4.6
Boston, MA	6.7	5.8	5.8	5.9	6.8	7.8	7.5	7.1	7.0	6.9	6.3	6.2
Boulder, CO	4.9	5.2	5.1	5.0	4.9	6.4	5.5	5.0	4.9	4.7	4.5	4.2
Cape Coral, FL	8.0	7.4	6.9	6.6	6.7	7.1	7.2	6.9	6.5	6.2	6.2	5.7
Cedar Rapids, IA	6.1	5.5	5.1	4.6	4.9	5.1	5.1	5.1	4.6	4.3	4.4	4.6
Charleston, SC	6.6	6.0	5.6	5.2	5.8	6.8	6.1	6.3	5.6	5.2	4.8	4.4
Charlotte, NC	8.5	8.0	7.7	7.4	7.9	8.4	8.4	7.5	6.8	6.9	6.1	5.8
Chicago, IL	10.9	11.3	10.4	10.3	10.7	11.6	11.2	10.9	10.1	9.9	9.6	9.5
Cincinnati, OH	8.6	7.8	7.4	6.9	7.6	8.3	8.0	7.7	8.1	8.1	7.8	6.8
Clarksville, TN	8.2	7.7	7.9	7.5	7.8	9.0	8.3	8.1	8.2	8.9	8.0	7.5
Colorado Spgs, CO	8.7	8.6	8.5	8.0	7.8	9.0	8.3	8.0	7.7	7.4	7.2	7.1
Columbia, MO	4.6	4.5	4.4	4.2	4.6	5.1	5.3	4.9	3.8	3.7	3.5	3.4
Columbus, OH	6.8	6.3	6.1	5.7	6.0	6.4	6.3	6.1	6.5	6.2	6.1	5.4
Dallas, TX	7.3	6.9	6.7	6.5	6.9	7.2	6.9	6.5	6.7	6.4	6.1	5.9
Davenport, IA	7.8	7.3	6.2	5.9	6.0	6.6	6.6	6.1	6.3	6.0	6.2	6.2
Denver, CO	8.1	8.1	7.8	7.3	7.0	7.7	7.2	7.0	6.8	6.3	6.2	6.2
Des Moines, IA	7.3	6.7	6.0	5.4	5.2	5.5	5.4	5.7	5.1	4.8	5.0	5.5
Durham, NC	7.3	6.6	6.4	6.1	6.6	7.0	7.1	6.4	5.6	5.7	4.9	4.7
El Paso, TX	8.7	8.3	8.1	8.0	8.5	9.0	8.6	8.0	8.1	7.8	7.5	7.2
Erie, PA	10.1	9.1	8.7	7.7	7.8	8.7	8.5	8.6	7.6	7.7	8.0	7.1
Eugene, OR	7.8	7.6	7.3	6.8	6.6	7.6	7.8	7.5	6.3	6.2	5.9	6.0
Fargo, ND	4.2	3.8	3.8	3.6	3.0	3.6	3.2	2.9	2.3	2.3	2.3	2.6
Fayetteville, NC	8.2	7.5	7.1	6.8	7.5	8.0	8.1	7.3	6.5	6.5	5.8	5.5
Ft. Collins, CO	6.0	6.1	5.8	5.4	5.2	6.3	5.6	5.2	5.1	4.9	4.7	4.4
Ft. Wayne, IN	9.4	9.2	9.2	8.1	8.1	8.6	9.0	7.5	7.4	7.1	7.2	6.3
Ft. Worth, TX	6.7	6.3	6.3	6.0	6.5	6.9	6.6	6.2	6.1	5.9	5.6	5.4
Gainesville, FL	6.2	5.7	5.4	4.8	5.5	6.3	6.5	5.7	5.5	4.8	5.1	5.0
Grand Rapids, MI	8.8	8.8	8.3	7.9	8.9	9.7	10.0	8.8	8.2	8.7	7.7	7.6
Green Bay, WI	10.1	10.2	9.8	9.2	8.6	9.1	8.6	7.7	7.4	7.3	7.5	7.5
Greensboro, NC	9.8	8.6	8.3	8.0	8.8	9.4	9.2	8.3	7.4	7.6	6.7	6.4
Honolulu, HI	n/a	n/a	n/a	n/a	n/a	n/a	n/a	n/a	n/a	n/a	n/a	n/a
Houston, TX	6.9	6.4	6.2	6.1	6.5	6.9	6.6	6.2	6.3	6.0	5.7	5.5
Huntsville, AL	6.7	6.9	6.0	5.2	5.6	6.2	5.9	5.9	5.6	5.6	4.9	5.0
Indianapolis, IN	9.5	9.3	9.2	8.3	8.4	8.8	8.5	7.9	7.3	7.4	7.4	6.4
Jacksonville, FL	7.9	7.4	6.8	6.7	6.9	7.5	6.9	7.3	6.6	6.3	6.1	5.8
Kansas City, MO	7.5	8.0	7.4	6.8	7.6	7.8	8.4	9.0	7.1	6.5	6.2	6.4
Lafayette, LA	5.5	4.2	4.3	4.6	5.5	6.1	5.4	5.4	4.9	4.7	4.3	3.4
Las Vegas, NV	10.4	10.0	10.0	9.7	9.6	10.4	10.0	10.0	9.7	9.6	8.8	9.0
Lexington, KY	6.5	6.6	6.6	5.9	6.4	7.1	6.4	6.1	6.2	6.4	6.1	5.6
Lincoln, NE	4.0	3.6	3.3	3.2	3.4	3.9	3.9	3.2	3.2	2.9	2.8	3.0
Little Rock, AR	7.2	7.1	6.8	6.4	6.8	7.1	7.1	6.7	6.5	6.4	6.1	6.2
Los Angeles, CA	12.0	11.4	11.0	10.2	10.2	11.3	11.9	11.3	10.3	10.4	10.4	9.7
Louisville, KY	8.3	8.3	8.4	7.5	8.4	9.0	8.7	7.8	7.8	7.8	7.6	7.1
Lubbock, TX	5.4	5.0	5.1	4.7	5.1	6.0	5.7	5.0	4.9	4.6	4.4	4.2
Madison, WI	5.2	5.3	4.7	4.7	4.8	5.1	5.0	4.6	4.2	4.1	4.0	3.7
Manchester, NH	7.0	6.6	6.4	5.5	5.5	5.5	5.4	5.2	5.1	5.2	5.1	5.1

Table continued on next page.

City	2013											
	Jan.	Feb.	Mar.	Apr.	May	Jun.	Jul.	Aug.	Sep.	Oct.	Nov.	Dec.
McAllen, TX	7.6	7.3	7.2	7.1	7.3	7.7	7.5	6.9	7.0	6.8	6.4	6.2
Miami, FL	10.5	10.6	10.3	9.7	9.7	9.8	9.3	9.4	9.2	9.5	7.9	7.6
Midland, TX	3.4	3.2	3.1	3.0	3.4	3.6	3.4	3.2	3.3	3.0	2.9	2.8
Minneapolis, MN	5.7	5.1	5.0	4.7	5.0	5.4	5.3	5.1	4.9	4.5	4.3	4.3
Montgomery, AL	7.9	7.8	7.1	6.2	6.5	7.1	7.0	7.1	7.0	6.8	6.0	6.1
Nashville, TN	6.5	6.3	6.2	6.5	6.7	7.0	6.7	6.9	6.7	6.7	5.8	5.7
New Orleans, LA	8.6	7.0	7.1	7.3	8.2	9.6	9.0	9.0	8.3	7.6	6.8	5.6
New York, NY	9.7	9.2	8.6	8.2	8.6	8.9	9.1	8.8	8.5	8.7	8.0	7.5
Oklahoma City, OK	5.1	4.9	4.6	4.0	4.9	5.4	4.7	4.7	5.0	5.3	4.7	4.8
Omaha, NE	5.0	4.6	4.4	4.1	4.3	4.8	4.8	4.4	4.1	4.0	3.6	4.0
Orlando, FL	7.6	7.1	6.7	6.5	6.6	6.6	6.5	6.4	6.1	5.8	5.5	5.3
Oxnard, CA	12.2	11.1	10.6	9.5	9.1	10.1	10.9	10.7	10.1	10.0	9.9	9.4
Peoria, IL	10.8	11.0	9.6	8.5	8.9	9.9	10.6	9.9	9.7	9.9	10.3	10.4
Philadelphia, PA	11.8	10.6	10.1	9.6	10.1	10.4	10.9	11.1	10.2	10.2	9.6	8.4
Phoenix, AZ	7.3	6.7	6.8	6.8	6.3	7.2	7.1	7.5	7.3	6.9	6.1	6.4
Pittsburgh, PA	8.2	7.3	6.9	6.5	7.0	7.6	7.6	7.9	6.7	6.5	6.4	5.5
Portland, OR	7.9	7.8	7.4	6.7	6.8	7.2	7.2	6.8	6.1	6.2	5.9	5.9
Providence, RI	12.1	11.0	11.0	10.4	11.4	11.0	11.7	11.5	10.8	10.4	9.8	10.5
Provo, UT	5.1	4.9	4.2	4.2	4.6	5.5	4.6	5.0	4.3	4.0	3.1	3.2
Raleigh, NC	7.2	6.6	6.3	6.0	6.6	6.9	6.7	6.2	5.5	5.4	4.8	4.5
Reno, NV	10.6	10.2	10.1	9.9	9.5	10.0	9.4	9.3	9.0	8.9	8.3	8.5
Richmond, VA	8.9	8.0	7.4	7.2	7.7	8.2	8.3	8.1	7.6	7.8	7.3	7.0
Riverside, CA	11.6	11.0	10.6	9.7	9.2	10.3	11.2	10.9	10.2	10.2	9.7	9.2
Rochester, MN	5.2	4.8	4.6	4.4	4.3	4.5	4.4	4.1	4.1	3.6	3.5	3.7
Salem, OR	10.1	9.8	9.4	8.5	8.2	8.8	8.8	8.5	7.3	7.3	7.0	7.2
Salt Lake City, UT	5.1	4.8	4.3	4.1	4.3	4.9	4.2	4.3	4.2	3.9	3.4	3.3
San Antonio, TX	6.5	6.0	5.8	5.6	6.1	6.5	6.4	5.9	6.1	5.8	5.6	5.3
San Diego, CA	8.6	8.0	7.7	7.0	6.8	7.4	7.8	7.5	7.0	7.1	6.9	6.4
San Francisco, CA	6.9	6.3	6.1	5.4	5.3	5.8	6.0	5.7	5.3	5.4	5.2	4.8
San Jose, CA	8.9	8.3	8.0	7.2	6.9	7.6	7.9	7.5	7.1	7.1	6.9	6.4
Santa Rosa, CA	8.3	7.6	7.3	6.5	6.1	6.7	7.1	6.6	6.0	6.1	6.0	5.7
Savannah, GA	9.7	9.0	8.6	8.1	9.0	10.6	10.4	9.3	8.6	8.7	8.1	8.1
Seattle, WA	5.9	5.3	4.7	4.1	4.0	4.8	4.7	5.3	5.0	5.2	4.7	4.3
Sioux Falls, SD	4.6	4.6	4.2	3.7	3.4	3.4	3.2	3.2	3.1	3.0	3.0	3.3
Spokane, WA	9.7	9.7	9.0	7.6	7.8	8.0	8.0	7.2	6.6	6.7	6.7	7.3
Springfield, MO	6.2	6.0	5.7	5.5	5.9	6.2	6.3	6.3	5.1	4.9	4.7	4.6
Tallahassee, FL	6.8	6.4	6.0	5.7	6.3	6.9	6.9	6.2	5.9	5.3	5.4	5.3
Tampa, FL	8.4	7.9	7.4	7.1	7.3	7.8	7.9	7.4	7.0	6.6	6.5	6.2
Topeka, KS	8.1	7.7	7.8	7.0	7.5	7.2	7.7	7.5	7.0	6.4	5.7	5.8
Tulsa, OK	5.5	5.2	5.0	4.4	5.3	5.6	5.0	4.9	5.2	5.5	4.9	5.1
Virginia Beach, VA	5.8	5.4	4.9	4.7	5.3	5.6	5.5	5.2	5.1	5.3	4.9	4.7
Washington, DC	9.4	8.7	8.4	7.9	8.2	8.9	8.9	8.3	8.1	9.0	7.1	6.9
Wichita, KS	7.7	7.2	7.3	6.6	7.3	7.4	7.8	7.5	7.0	6.5	5.6	5.8
Wilmington, NC	9.5	8.8	8.0	7.7	8.2	8.4	8.3	7.4	6.8	7.1	6.1	5.8
Worcester, MA	8.4	7.8	7.9	7.8	8.8	9.8	9.3	8.9	8.7	8.5	8.2	8.0
U.S.	8.5	8.1	7.6	7.1	7.3	7.8	7.7	7.3	7.0	7.0	6.6	6.5

Note: Data is not seasonally adjusted and covers workers 16 years of age and older; All figures are percentages
Source: Bureau of Labor Statistics, Local Area Unemployment Statistics

Unemployment Rate: Metro Area

Metro Area[1]	2013											
	Jan.	Feb.	Mar.	Apr.	May	Jun.	Jul.	Aug.	Sep.	Oct.	Nov.	Dec.
Abilene, TX	5.4	5.1	4.9	4.8	5.3	5.7	5.5	5.0	5.0	4.7	4.5	4.4
Albuquerque, NM	7.2	7.6	7.1	6.4	6.6	7.8	7.8	6.9	6.6	6.6	6.3	6.5
Anchorage, AK	6.3	5.8	5.5	5.3	5.1	5.7	5.3	5.0	4.8	5.0	5.1	5.2
Ann Arbor, MI	5.3	5.3	5.1	5.1	5.9	6.8	7.3	6.2	5.6	6.0	5.3	5.2
Athens, GA	6.5	6.1	5.9	5.5	6.2	7.2	6.9	6.1	5.6	5.8	5.0	5.2
Atlanta, GA	8.7	8.3	7.9	7.6	8.2	8.8	8.6	7.9	7.4	7.7	7.0	6.8
Austin, TX	5.8	5.4	5.3	5.1	5.4	5.8	5.6	5.2	5.3	5.1	4.7	4.5
Baltimore, MD	7.5	7.1	6.9	6.7	7.2	7.9	7.5	7.1	6.6	7.0	6.3	5.9
Billings, MT	4.7	4.6	4.5	3.9	3.7	4.4	3.9	3.8	3.6	3.6	3.6	3.9
Boise City, ID	7.0	6.6	6.1	5.8	5.7	6.2	6.1	6.1	5.9	5.8	5.1	5.1
Boston, MA[2]	6.0	5.4	5.3	5.2	5.7	6.5	6.2	5.8	6.0	6.0	5.5	5.5
Boulder, CO	5.5	5.7	5.4	5.1	5.1	6.1	5.4	5.1	5.0	4.9	4.7	4.4
Cape Coral, FL	7.9	7.4	6.8	6.7	7.0	7.5	7.6	7.3	7.0	6.5	6.3	5.8
Cedar Rapids, IA	6.3	5.7	5.3	4.8	4.6	4.9	4.8	4.9	4.3	4.2	4.2	4.6
Charleston, SC	7.3	6.8	6.4	5.9	6.4	7.3	6.7	6.9	6.3	6.0	5.5	5.2
Charlotte, NC	10.0	9.4	8.8	8.4	8.9	9.3	9.2	8.3	7.6	7.5	6.9	6.6
Chicago, IL[2]	10.0	9.8	9.3	9.1	9.2	10.1	9.6	9.1	8.5	8.5	8.3	8.3
Cincinnati, OH	8.0	7.5	7.2	6.5	6.8	7.3	7.1	6.8	7.1	7.0	6.8	6.2
Clarksville, TN	9.0	8.6	8.4	8.4	8.8	9.5	9.4	8.9	8.7	8.9	8.1	7.8
Colorado Spgs, CO	8.8	8.7	8.6	8.1	7.9	9.1	8.4	8.0	7.8	7.5	7.3	7.2
Columbia, MO	5.1	4.9	4.8	4.4	4.7	5.3	5.5	5.0	4.0	3.9	3.7	3.7
Columbus, OH	7.0	6.4	6.2	5.7	6.0	6.4	6.3	6.0	6.4	6.1	6.1	5.5
Dallas, TX[2]	6.7	6.4	6.2	6.0	6.3	6.7	6.4	6.0	6.1	5.9	5.7	5.5
Davenport, IA	8.3	8.2	7.2	6.2	6.3	6.7	6.9	6.5	6.7	6.7	6.4	6.8
Denver, CO	7.4	7.4	7.2	6.7	6.6	7.3	6.7	6.5	6.4	6.0	5.8	5.8
Des Moines, IA	6.0	5.5	5.0	4.4	4.3	4.7	4.5	4.7	4.2	4.0	4.0	4.4
Durham, NC	7.7	7.0	6.6	6.3	6.8	7.2	7.1	6.4	5.7	5.7	5.1	4.9
El Paso, TX	9.5	9.1	8.9	8.7	9.2	9.8	9.3	8.7	8.8	8.5	8.2	8.0
Erie, PA	9.2	8.2	7.8	7.2	7.1	7.7	7.5	7.6	6.6	6.7	7.1	6.4
Eugene, OR	9.1	8.8	8.4	7.6	7.3	8.1	8.3	8.1	6.9	6.9	6.6	6.7
Fargo, ND	4.7	4.2	4.2	3.9	3.1	3.6	3.2	3.0	2.5	2.3	2.5	3.0
Fayetteville, NC	10.8	10.0	9.6	9.3	9.9	10.4	10.6	9.8	8.9	8.9	8.2	7.8
Ft. Collins, CO	6.2	6.4	6.0	5.5	5.3	6.2	5.6	5.3	5.2	5.1	5.0	4.8
Ft. Wayne, IN	9.1	8.9	8.8	7.6	7.7	8.2	8.5	7.0	7.0	6.6	6.7	5.9
Ft. Worth, TX[2]	6.8	6.2	6.1	5.8	6.2	6.6	6.3	5.9	5.9	5.7	5.5	5.3
Gainesville, FL	6.1	5.6	5.2	4.8	5.3	6.0	6.0	5.5	5.3	4.8	4.9	4.8
Grand Rapids, MI	6.6	6.6	6.2	5.9	6.5	7.1	7.5	6.4	6.0	6.3	5.6	5.6
Green Bay, WI	7.3	7.5	7.0	6.7	6.2	6.5	6.2	5.7	5.4	5.1	5.3	5.3
Greensboro, NC	10.6	9.9	9.4	8.9	9.4	9.7	9.6	8.6	7.9	7.9	7.2	6.9
Honolulu, HI	4.8	4.5	4.4	3.9	4.0	4.7	4.2	3.8	4.1	4.2	4.2	3.8
Houston, TX	6.7	6.3	6.1	6.0	6.3	6.7	6.5	6.1	6.2	5.9	5.6	5.5
Huntsville, AL	6.6	6.8	5.9	5.2	5.5	5.9	5.6	5.8	5.6	5.6	4.8	4.9
Indianapolis, IN	8.7	8.5	8.3	7.4	7.4	7.9	7.5	6.9	6.4	6.5	6.6	5.8
Jacksonville, FL	7.5	7.1	6.5	6.4	6.6	7.0	7.0	6.8	6.4	6.1	5.9	5.6
Kansas City, MO	6.9	7.1	6.6	6.1	6.5	6.6	7.1	7.3	6.0	5.7	5.3	5.4
Lafayette, LA	5.4	4.2	4.3	4.6	5.3	6.0	5.4	5.3	4.8	4.6	4.2	3.3
Las Vegas, NV	10.2	9.8	9.8	9.5	9.3	10.1	9.7	9.6	9.4	9.4	8.6	8.9
Lexington, KY	6.8	6.8	6.8	6.0	6.5	7.3	6.6	6.2	6.4	6.6	6.3	5.8
Lincoln, NE	4.2	3.8	3.4	3.3	3.5	4.0	4.0	3.3	3.2	3.1	2.9	3.1
Little Rock, AR	7.1	7.0	6.7	6.2	6.6	6.7	6.8	6.5	6.4	6.5	6.2	6.2
Los Angeles, CA[2]	10.9	10.2	9.9	9.4	9.7	10.3	10.7	10.2	9.6	9.6	9.1	8.8
Louisville, KY	8.4	8.4	8.3	7.4	8.0	8.5	8.2	7.4	7.4	7.6	7.3	6.8
Lubbock, TX	5.5	5.1	5.3	4.8	5.3	6.1	5.8	5.0	5.0	4.7	4.5	4.3
Madison, WI	5.9	5.9	5.4	5.2	5.0	5.2	4.9	4.5	4.3	4.1	4.1	4.0
Manchester, NH	6.3	6.0	5.8	4.9	4.9	5.0	5.1	4.8	4.7	4.9	4.7	4.7

Table continued on next page.

Metro Area[1]	2013											
	Jan.	Feb.	Mar.	Apr.	May	Jun.	Jul.	Aug.	Sep.	Oct.	Nov.	Dec.
McAllen, TX	11.6	11.0	10.6	10.5	10.9	11.5	11.3	10.8	10.7	10.1	10.3	10.4
Miami, FL[2]	9.5	9.0	8.8	8.6	8.7	9.2	8.6	8.6	8.1	8.1	6.9	6.8
Midland, TX	3.4	3.2	3.1	3.0	3.4	3.7	3.5	3.2	3.3	3.1	2.9	2.8
Minneapolis, MN	6.0	5.5	5.4	5.0	4.7	5.1	5.0	4.7	4.5	4.1	4.0	4.3
Montgomery, AL	7.9	7.9	7.0	6.1	6.3	6.9	6.7	7.0	6.8	6.7	5.8	5.9
Nashville, TN	6.6	6.4	6.3	6.4	6.7	7.0	6.8	6.8	6.5	6.6	5.6	5.5
New Orleans, LA	7.2	5.9	6.0	6.2	7.0	7.9	7.2	7.2	6.7	6.3	5.7	4.7
New York, NY[2]	9.7	9.0	8.4	7.7	8.1	8.5	8.4	8.4	8.2	8.4	7.5	7.1
Oklahoma City, OK	5.2	4.9	4.7	4.1	5.0	5.5	4.8	4.7	5.0	5.4	4.7	4.8
Omaha, NE	5.0	4.6	4.3	4.0	4.1	4.6	4.6	4.2	4.0	3.8	3.6	3.9
Orlando, FL	7.7	7.2	6.7	6.4	6.6	6.9	6.9	6.6	6.3	6.0	5.9	5.5
Oxnard, CA	9.0	8.2	7.8	6.9	6.7	7.4	8.0	7.8	7.4	7.3	7.2	6.9
Peoria, IL	10.1	10.3	8.9	7.9	7.8	8.8	9.4	8.7	8.5	8.7	8.9	9.2
Philadelphia, PA[2]	9.3	8.5	8.0	7.5	7.9	8.2	8.3	8.4	7.5	7.5	7.2	6.3
Phoenix, AZ	7.2	6.7	6.7	6.6	6.2	7.2	7.0	7.4	7.1	6.7	6.0	6.2
Pittsburgh, PA	8.6	7.8	7.1	6.4	6.6	7.2	7.0	7.2	6.2	6.1	6.2	5.7
Portland, OR	8.7	8.5	8.0	7.2	7.1	7.6	7.6	7.3	6.4	6.5	6.3	6.2
Providence, RI	10.6	10.0	9.9	8.9	9.3	8.7	9.4	9.6	8.9	8.6	8.6	9.2
Provo, UT	5.5	5.3	4.5	4.3	4.6	5.3	4.6	4.9	4.3	4.0	3.4	3.5
Raleigh, NC	8.0	7.5	7.1	6.7	7.2	7.5	7.3	6.7	6.1	6.0	5.5	5.2
Reno, NV	10.5	10.1	10.0	9.7	9.3	9.8	9.3	9.1	8.8	8.8	8.2	8.4
Richmond, VA	6.6	6.1	5.6	5.4	6.0	6.3	6.2	6.0	5.7	5.8	5.3	5.2
Riverside, CA	11.5	10.9	10.5	9.6	9.3	10.3	11.0	10.5	9.8	9.8	9.4	8.9
Rochester, MN	5.5	5.1	4.9	4.6	4.3	4.5	4.4	4.1	3.9	3.5	3.4	3.8
Salem, OR	10.1	9.7	9.2	8.4	8.1	8.7	8.6	8.2	7.1	7.3	7.1	7.3
Salt Lake City, UT	5.3	5.0	4.5	4.2	4.4	5.0	4.3	4.5	4.3	4.0	3.5	3.5
San Antonio, TX	6.6	6.1	6.0	5.8	6.2	6.6	6.5	6.0	6.1	5.8	5.6	5.3
San Diego, CA	8.6	8.0	7.7	7.0	6.8	7.4	7.8	7.5	7.0	7.1	6.9	6.4
San Francisco, CA[2]	6.5	6.0	5.8	5.2	5.0	5.6	5.8	5.5	5.1	5.2	5.0	4.6
San Jose, CA	8.2	7.6	7.4	6.6	6.3	6.9	7.2	6.8	6.4	6.4	6.3	5.8
Santa Rosa, CA	8.3	7.6	7.3	6.5	6.1	6.7	7.1	6.6	6.1	6.1	6.0	5.7
Savannah, GA	8.3	7.7	7.4	7.1	7.9	8.8	8.6	7.8	7.3	7.5	6.7	6.7
Seattle, WA[2]	6.1	5.7	5.3	4.8	5.0	5.7	5.6	5.5	5.4	5.5	5.2	4.9
Sioux Falls, SD	4.4	4.4	4.0	3.5	3.3	3.3	3.0	3.0	2.9	2.9	2.9	3.1
Spokane, WA	9.7	9.8	9.0	7.5	7.6	7.9	7.9	7.1	6.6	6.7	6.8	7.3
Springfield, MO	6.2	6.1	5.8	5.4	5.7	6.1	6.2	6.1	5.0	4.7	4.6	4.6
Tallahassee, FL	6.8	6.4	5.9	5.6	6.1	6.7	6.7	6.2	5.8	5.3	5.4	5.3
Tampa, FL	8.0	7.5	6.9	6.7	6.9	7.3	7.3	7.0	6.7	6.4	6.3	5.9
Topeka, KS	7.1	6.7	6.7	6.0	6.5	6.3	6.7	6.4	5.9	5.5	4.8	5.0
Tulsa, OK	5.9	5.7	5.3	4.7	5.6	5.9	5.3	5.2	5.5	5.8	5.3	5.4
Virginia Beach, VA	6.8	6.2	5.7	5.4	6.0	6.3	6.2	5.9	5.7	6.0	5.5	5.3
Washington, DC[2]	5.8	5.5	5.2	5.0	5.5	6.0	5.8	5.5	5.4	5.9	4.9	4.7
Wichita, KS	7.0	6.6	6.7	6.0	6.7	6.6	7.1	6.8	6.3	5.8	5.1	5.2
Wilmington, NC	11.1	10.3	9.2	8.7	9.1	9.4	9.1	8.3	7.7	7.7	7.2	7.1
Worcester, MA	7.9	7.3	7.3	7.0	7.4	8.2	8.0	7.6	7.5	7.5	7.1	7.2
U.S.	8.5	8.1	7.6	7.1	7.3	7.8	7.7	7.3	7.0	7.0	6.6	6.5

Note: Data is not seasonally adjusted and covers workers 16 years of age and older; All figures are percentages; (1) Figures cover the Metropolitan Statistical Area (MSA) except where noted. See Appendix B for areas included; (2) Metropolitan Division; (3) New England City and Town Area; (4) New England City and Town Area Division
Source: Bureau of Labor Statistics, Local Area Unemployment Statistics

Average Hourly Wages: Occupations A – C

Metro Area	Accountants/ Auditors	Automotive Mechanics	Book-keepers	Carpenters	Cashiers	Clerks, Gen. Office	Clerks, Recep./Info.
Abilene, TX	27.43	16.42	14.82	12.98	9.17	13.24	10.53
Albuquerque, NM	30.19	18.65	17.01	18.15	10.12	12.20	12.24
Anchorage, AK	36.17	23.37	20.46	31.31	11.75	19.03	15.50
Ann Arbor, MI	29.53	17.46	17.39	24.50	10.26	14.17	13.07
Athens, GA	26.22	19.62	15.14	13.35	9.24	11.17	12.30
Atlanta, GA	36.56	19.69	18.07	21.86	9.32	13.52	13.47
Austin, TX	32.18	19.17	18.54	17.33	10.12	15.40	12.42
Baltimore, MD	36.00	20.24	20.50	20.24	10.05	15.04	13.46
Billings, MT	33.26	19.76	16.60	19.04	9.90	14.02	12.41
Boise City, ID	31.72	18.99	16.60	16.39	9.96	13.64	12.66
Boston, MA	38.28	21.67	21.66	28.99	10.63	17.12	15.11
Boulder, CO	35.08	18.51	18.63	18.27	10.90	17.84	14.04
Cape Coral, FL	32.91	18.63	16.17	19.17	9.72	13.10	12.80
Cedar Rapids, IA	28.85	17.67	16.95	20.72	8.92	15.50	11.69
Charleston, SC	28.92	20.06	16.48	17.86	9.45	12.58	13.41
Charlotte, NC	35.75	20.32	17.69	17.12	9.50	13.74	13.53
Chicago, IL	35.80	20.80	19.31	28.75	10.46	15.22	14.01
Cincinnati, OH	32.92	16.95	17.65	20.92	9.78	14.81	12.84
Clarksville, TN	28.37	17.07	15.56	18.13	9.05	13.06	11.27
Colorado Spgs, CO	30.13	20.15	16.87	20.22	10.09	14.90	13.08
Columbia, MO	30.34	16.56	18.60	22.31	9.30	13.82	12.84
Columbus, OH	32.32	18.75	20.46	21.36	9.64	14.62	12.91
Dallas, TX	37.07	19.69	18.75	14.51	9.45	15.35	12.97
Davenport, IA	29.86	18.61	15.87	21.53	9.41	13.70	12.43
Denver, CO	35.95	20.23	18.55	19.23	10.44	17.13	14.91
Des Moines, IA	32.54	19.67	17.45	20.38	9.23	15.42	13.64
Durham, NC	35.16	18.90	18.59	18.11	9.33	13.79	13.22
El Paso, TX	28.26	15.93	15.14	13.85	8.90	11.88	10.48
Erie, PA	28.43	15.68	15.06	18.21	8.83	12.89	11.20
Eugene, OR	30.59	17.92	17.64	21.59	10.76	14.63	12.61
Fargo, ND	27.37	19.40	17.12	19.68	9.17	12.50	12.79
Fayetteville, NC	31.00	17.52	15.79	16.06	8.99	12.92	10.88
Ft. Collins, CO	30.42	20.91	16.78	17.36	9.85	15.20	13.23
Ft. Wayne, IN	30.11	17.98	16.19	18.43	8.84	12.35	12.48
Ft. Worth, TX	34.18	19.54	17.62	14.67	10.01	14.85	12.80
Gainesville, FL	27.91	18.50	16.42	17.40	8.96	12.60	11.14
Grand Rapids, MI	34.32	18.09	17.06	19.73	9.35	14.17	13.72
Green Bay, WI	30.58	18.53	16.65	21.53	8.98	14.33	13.62
Greensboro, NC	32.99	20.17	16.88	14.58	8.85	13.23	12.77
Honolulu, HI	29.88	22.71	17.92	33.80	10.80	15.06	13.96
Houston, TX	38.74	19.17	18.62	16.62	9.40	15.80	12.86
Huntsville, AL	32.82	18.14	17.17	16.52	8.84	11.15	11.72
Indianapolis, IN	33.44	22.45	17.96	20.95	9.28	13.29	13.16
Jacksonville, FL	34.05	18.24	16.66	14.81	9.16	13.20	13.25
Kansas City, MO	31.24	19.09	18.28	25.07	9.53	15.10	13.44
Lafayette, LA	31.37	19.07	16.45	17.49	8.98	11.42	11.29
Las Vegas, NV	30.08	20.31	17.75	24.10	10.67	15.05	13.05
Lexington, KY	33.61	17.21	16.87	17.87	9.08	14.05	12.73
Lincoln, NE	29.13	19.63	15.79	16.05	9.12	10.78	12.82
Little Rock, AR	30.95	17.97	16.09	17.27	8.95	12.05	11.66
Los Angeles, CA	37.55	17.81	19.63	25.42	10.79	15.07	13.97
Louisville, KY	30.07	17.02	16.92	18.09	9.39	14.04	12.93
Lubbock, TX	29.12	14.24	14.57	15.94	8.83	13.01	10.76
Madison, WI	33.33	18.35	18.38	24.10	9.61	15.44	13.35
Manchester, NH	34.23	20.10	19.97	22.32	9.31	16.38	13.43

Table continued on next page.

Metro Area	Accountants/ Auditors	Automotive Mechanics	Book-keepers	Carpenters	Cashiers	Clerks, Gen. Office	Clerks, Recep./Info.
McAllen, TX	26.81	16.00	13.56	13.93	8.78	11.14	9.94
Miami, FL	33.25	16.83	16.90	17.61	9.40	13.15	12.06
Midland, TX	34.93	20.63	18.08	16.48	9.68	16.26	13.36
Minneapolis, MN	32.84	19.00	19.10	25.54	10.12	15.43	14.23
Montgomery, AL	29.11	19.72	16.48	15.44	8.81	11.66	11.50
Nashville, TN	32.17	16.82	17.50	17.16	9.55	15.14	13.64
New Orleans, LA	32.37	18.87	17.21	18.99	9.15	12.00	11.82
New York, NY	44.94	20.68	20.95	31.17	10.15	14.82	14.70
Oklahoma City, OK	31.09	18.76	15.97	17.26	9.10	13.43	13.13
Omaha, NE	32.68	19.42	16.45	17.79	9.47	12.68	12.47
Orlando, FL	31.58	16.84	16.23	16.93	9.20	13.53	12.58
Oxnard, CA	35.77	20.57	21.02	23.41	11.68	15.50	14.00
Peoria, IL	35.52	18.17	16.67	24.90	9.92	13.40	12.01
Philadelphia, PA	37.58	19.91	19.61	25.03	10.24	16.19	13.60
Phoenix, AZ	31.32	20.60	17.55	19.17	10.39	16.07	13.44
Pittsburgh, PA	32.64	17.37	16.84	21.51	9.06	14.42	12.31
Portland, OR	31.75	21.10	18.80	20.95	11.73	15.79	13.96
Providence, RI	36.01	18.48	18.82	22.21	10.02	15.77	13.92
Provo, UT	31.69	16.22	16.64	17.39	9.40	12.88	11.93
Raleigh, NC	31.96	21.92	17.94	16.13	9.22	14.19	13.40
Reno, NV	29.02	20.32	18.21	22.23	10.64	16.17	13.46
Richmond, VA	33.61	19.92	17.74	18.44	9.61	14.44	13.22
Riverside, CA	32.45	18.79	18.50	27.31	10.63	14.04	13.07
Rochester, MN	28.78	17.72	18.69	21.97	9.18	13.57	12.60
Salem, OR	30.00	21.24	18.27	19.55	10.96	15.60	13.45
Salt Lake City, UT	34.38	18.42	17.07	17.16	9.72	13.39	12.55
San Antonio, TX	33.35	18.10	17.72	16.84	9.44	14.41	11.73
San Diego, CA	37.37	20.54	19.64	22.65	11.10	14.91	13.74
San Francisco, CA	41.51	26.04	23.77	30.01	12.81	18.99	17.83
San Jose, CA	41.89	24.36	23.39	29.47	12.29	18.73	16.42
Santa Rosa, CA	33.81	21.73	21.06	30.54	12.87	17.20	16.73
Savannah, GA	33.25	20.02	16.14	19.48	9.74	12.40	12.80
Seattle, WA	37.17	22.23	20.39	25.57	13.50	15.80	15.53
Sioux Falls, SD	29.73	19.18	14.71	16.05	9.27	11.41	11.92
Spokane, WA	28.98	20.54	17.42	22.57	11.96	14.21	13.64
Springfield, MO	27.75	15.40	14.45	20.46	9.23	12.72	11.24
Tallahassee, FL	26.01	15.45	15.91	16.16	9.16	11.39	12.28
Tampa, FL	31.71	17.66	15.77	16.90	9.29	13.20	12.99
Topeka, KS	27.11	17.70	15.82	18.91	8.92	13.79	11.64
Tulsa, OK	30.46	17.97	16.51	15.09	8.97	13.00	12.26
Virginia Beach, VA	33.02	20.84	16.69	18.84	9.04	13.39	12.61
Washington, DC	40.82	22.96	21.52	22.03	10.52	17.50	14.93
Wichita, KS	31.45	18.57	16.36	16.62	9.26	13.51	12.50
Wilmington, NC	32.27	20.30	16.48	16.21	9.01	12.75	12.07
Worcester, MA	35.61	20.23	19.02	22.84	10.60	14.94	14.29

Notes: Wage data is for May 2013 and covers the Metropolitan Statistical Area—see Appendix B for areas included; n/a not available
Source: Bureau of Labor Statistics, May 2013 Metro Area Occupational Employment and Wage Estimates

Average Hourly Wages: Occupations C – E

Metro Area	Clerks, Ship./Rec.	Computer Programmers	Computer Systems Analysts	Comp. User Support Specialists	Cooks, Restaurant	Dentists	Electrical Engineers
Abilene, TX	13.69	27.23	32.18	17.64	9.42	103.87	37.88
Albuquerque, NM	13.54	47.92	36.61	21.63	10.71	80.23	49.12
Anchorage, AK	17.87	36.95	36.76	25.36	14.45	104.89	52.25
Ann Arbor, MI	16.95	31.55	35.52	19.32	11.43	77.01	44.17
Athens, GA	13.86	26.99	30.82	17.19	9.71	n/a	33.72
Atlanta, GA	14.19	45.14	36.84	24.72	10.64	91.04	41.62
Austin, TX	13.46	41.66	39.12	23.74	11.05	99.44	47.89
Baltimore, MD	15.88	40.57	42.83	25.20	12.96	88.28	47.30
Billings, MT	13.89	27.07	35.36	20.87	10.53	79.34	35.78
Boise City, ID	13.83	37.50	37.21	19.70	9.63	84.71	44.82
Boston, MA	17.35	40.17	41.42	30.58	13.94	83.35	49.66
Boulder, CO	15.11	54.80	42.01	25.96	11.08	82.37	42.59
Cape Coral, FL	12.50	44.91	45.79	19.67	11.37	47.08	32.63
Cedar Rapids, IA	16.01	31.33	35.96	21.13	9.87	103.77	39.12
Charleston, SC	15.68	32.89	31.81	22.77	10.15	88.16	38.32
Charlotte, NC	14.93	39.57	42.61	24.91	10.66	75.21	42.52
Chicago, IL	15.03	36.41	38.63	25.25	10.92	62.86	43.03
Cincinnati, OH	14.76	34.51	40.85	23.82	10.04	84.46	38.69
Clarksville, TN	15.98	27.53	32.31	18.56	9.56	n/a	35.58
Colorado Spgs, CO	14.64	36.76	45.24	24.10	10.88	94.04	47.09
Columbia, MO	12.88	30.13	37.64	18.56	9.82	73.83	31.64
Columbus, OH	13.64	34.99	38.04	24.30	11.15	91.49	35.80
Dallas, TX	14.76	38.38	41.14	23.30	11.30	103.85	46.81
Davenport, IA	15.24	33.99	39.27	17.76	10.19	n/a	40.13
Denver, CO	15.54	43.75	45.80	26.49	11.49	69.78	42.32
Des Moines, IA	16.41	32.66	37.50	21.53	9.86	87.24	32.11
Durham, NC	14.73	37.11	40.26	27.13	10.37	65.26	40.44
El Paso, TX	12.21	33.64	34.01	21.32	9.33	104.40	45.11
Erie, PA	13.62	36.17	30.92	18.99	10.73	75.00	37.20
Eugene, OR	13.89	28.98	35.12	22.23	10.96	102.79	34.76
Fargo, ND	15.13	24.40	n/a	22.81	10.55	95.87	37.58
Fayetteville, NC	14.96	29.95	34.22	22.55	10.15	96.55	51.65
Ft. Collins, CO	13.21	38.45	43.42	26.39	11.20	70.26	42.77
Ft. Wayne, IN	13.01	29.98	31.36	19.47	9.40	90.74	37.60
Ft. Worth, TX	14.27	39.47	38.95	24.54	10.68	77.20	44.46
Gainesville, FL	14.29	27.73	37.77	19.94	10.26	75.62	36.41
Grand Rapids, MI	15.06	31.17	37.87	22.12	10.84	95.40	39.30
Green Bay, WI	15.06	30.62	32.19	21.37	9.93	92.83	31.83
Greensboro, NC	14.49	36.40	39.01	22.68	10.21	103.71	45.86
Honolulu, HI	15.40	31.10	37.24	24.72	12.49	81.39	40.45
Houston, TX	14.39	39.02	49.83	27.90	10.16	80.85	49.20
Huntsville, AL	15.17	43.90	43.34	21.85	9.95	88.17	48.64
Indianapolis, IN	14.40	31.15	35.31	21.97	11.15	64.38	39.77
Jacksonville, FL	14.27	33.68	37.38	20.85	11.17	75.89	41.44
Kansas City, MO	14.84	34.26	38.11	24.42	10.53	69.78	39.61
Lafayette, LA	14.48	23.56	29.34	22.37	10.05	75.83	n/a
Las Vegas, NV	14.84	35.55	41.40	22.75	13.64	52.27	39.56
Lexington, KY	14.70	30.61	36.66	16.81	10.30	101.69	41.91
Lincoln, NE	14.12	30.60	33.56	20.21	10.52	83.33	38.58
Little Rock, AR	14.06	30.79	32.63	21.07	9.90	93.18	42.51
Los Angeles, CA	14.10	44.05	44.23	26.28	11.18	62.76	53.18
Louisville, KY	14.50	30.71	36.69	21.44	9.81	70.32	39.73
Lubbock, TX	13.38	28.78	32.41	18.01	9.23	64.36	36.33
Madison, WI	14.62	36.41	33.43	22.70	11.37	94.32	37.20
Manchester, NH	15.01	29.13	35.94	23.82	12.00	99.35	41.16

Table continued on next page.

Metro Area	Clerks, Ship./Rec.	Computer Programmers	Computer Systems Analysts	Comp. User Support Specialists	Cooks, Restaurant	Dentists	Electrical Engineers
McAllen, TX	11.27	28.68	29.92	18.42	9.23	96.37	n/a
Miami, FL	13.24	45.85	48.29	22.69	11.73	83.10	45.51
Midland, TX	n/a	35.91	31.03	23.54	11.41	n/a	44.31
Minneapolis, MN	16.20	38.60	39.98	25.36	11.52	91.74	43.80
Montgomery, AL	14.13	37.10	32.06	22.00	9.21	83.38	50.27
Nashville, TN	14.89	38.24	33.90	21.17	10.74	96.86	38.25
New Orleans, LA	15.83	34.95	31.13	22.56	11.37	92.33	49.53
New York, NY	15.85	43.75	47.55	28.67	13.46	69.88	46.38
Oklahoma City, OK	14.49	32.23	34.02	20.60	10.12	57.11	38.18
Omaha, NE	15.05	38.16	36.31	23.39	11.37	90.09	38.09
Orlando, FL	12.90	36.73	43.11	20.29	11.56	89.42	35.43
Oxnard, CA	15.40	43.41	47.37	26.96	11.39	67.98	45.60
Peoria, IL	14.51	31.01	46.10	22.48	10.20	56.10	43.45
Philadelphia, PA	16.57	38.63	44.47	24.11	13.74	85.38	46.41
Phoenix, AZ	14.79	38.36	40.32	23.83	13.64	73.29	47.03
Pittsburgh, PA	15.46	30.77	33.58	22.75	11.71	72.66	41.29
Portland, OR	15.66	35.47	42.35	22.71	11.19	80.83	41.94
Providence, RI	15.08	38.04	38.00	22.97	11.89	n/a	45.34
Provo, UT	12.87	34.15	35.91	21.12	10.55	55.57	38.94
Raleigh, NC	14.05	38.60	40.47	24.88	10.69	92.29	41.46
Reno, NV	15.08	38.61	31.73	20.76	11.56	101.97	41.21
Richmond, VA	15.43	38.28	38.59	24.88	10.79	78.56	40.88
Riverside, CA	14.65	37.70	37.14	24.30	11.10	68.42	46.03
Rochester, MN	14.64	45.51	30.54	23.06	11.93	118.24	41.11
Salem, OR	14.03	36.34	36.82	23.44	11.26	100.20	46.72
Salt Lake City, UT	14.15	38.31	35.07	23.17	12.23	59.22	45.53
San Antonio, TX	13.09	39.12	36.21	20.90	9.96	89.68	41.41
San Diego, CA	16.27	39.34	42.87	24.83	12.10	78.93	49.74
San Francisco, CA	17.20	47.86	49.87	33.43	13.91	79.51	51.79
San Jose, CA	16.72	45.14	50.02	33.75	12.35	70.50	58.37
Santa Rosa, CA	16.13	41.37	39.95	28.35	12.21	89.18	49.08
Savannah, GA	17.46	35.54	36.03	24.38	9.81	107.80	43.91
Seattle, WA	17.86	55.54	48.03	29.07	12.88	94.76	48.66
Sioux Falls, SD	13.65	26.68	31.34	17.35	11.06	87.04	37.79
Spokane, WA	14.45	28.12	36.41	21.15	11.57	118.72	38.21
Springfield, MO	14.37	28.95	28.21	19.79	9.32	79.34	44.48
Tallahassee, FL	13.00	28.72	40.01	18.19	10.65	101.64	42.41
Tampa, FL	13.32	35.91	40.50	22.02	11.10	70.66	42.83
Topeka, KS	18.87	32.30	33.78	20.01	9.14	74.33	38.72
Tulsa, OK	15.09	30.98	34.64	22.38	10.48	78.06	36.72
Virginia Beach, VA	15.44	32.13	39.10	22.42	12.75	73.45	38.98
Washington, DC	16.29	39.90	51.34	29.12	12.80	73.33	52.63
Wichita, KS	14.81	35.15	37.73	17.54	10.18	85.45	43.84
Wilmington, NC	13.42	39.39	37.39	22.14	11.53	87.19	52.57
Worcester, MA	16.08	38.85	41.52	23.76	12.05	88.51	59.16

Notes: Wage data is for May 2013 and covers the Metropolitan Statistical Area—see Appendix B for areas included; n/a not available
Source: Bureau of Labor Statistics, May 2013 Metro Area Occupational Employment and Wage Estimates

Average Hourly Wages: Occupations E – I

Metro Area	Electricians	Financial Managers	First-Line Supervisors/ Mgrs., Sales	Food Preparation Workers	General/ Operations Managers	Hairdressers/ Cosmetolo- gists	Internists
Abilene, TX	18.68	56.69	22.73	9.26	43.14	11.06	n/a
Albuquerque, NM	21.11	50.83	18.13	10.29	47.76	12.28	n/a
Anchorage, AK	35.47	57.95	20.16	12.03	52.42	12.91	94.74
Ann Arbor, MI	33.61	50.43	21.34	11.17	53.18	12.36	n/a
Athens, GA	18.25	48.93	17.60	9.44	43.42	14.05	n/a
Atlanta, GA	22.84	61.89	20.29	10.03	57.36	12.42	112.68
Austin, TX	22.17	65.02	20.04	10.21	57.84	12.37	119.07
Baltimore, MD	26.52	59.94	21.63	11.09	62.50	13.92	101.04
Billings, MT	28.66	55.10	19.36	9.38	45.84	14.66	n/a
Boise City, ID	21.01	46.12	17.49	10.01	40.44	10.09	n/a
Boston, MA	32.11	64.39	22.24	11.68	67.32	15.96	98.46
Boulder, CO	23.32	64.93	20.56	10.22	63.79	15.06	n/a
Cape Coral, FL	16.91	49.70	20.90	10.08	52.27	15.40	102.76
Cedar Rapids, IA	26.44	57.15	19.93	9.74	48.16	11.86	n/a
Charleston, SC	18.98	50.16	19.38	10.20	50.21	11.03	73.51
Charlotte, NC	18.07	67.43	21.23	9.65	63.70	13.62	116.54
Chicago, IL	34.76	63.80	19.83	9.70	52.40	13.91	78.25
Cincinnati, OH	23.81	54.26	18.37	10.45	54.22	12.62	71.31
Clarksville, TN	20.80	29.29	17.04	9.33	36.00	11.81	n/a
Colorado Spgs, CO	22.70	67.65	20.01	10.13	52.86	12.83	n/a
Columbia, MO	25.25	49.57	17.27	9.05	35.78	14.23	n/a
Columbus, OH	22.13	60.47	18.15	10.62	53.60	12.27	87.91
Dallas, TX	20.44	65.14	21.17	9.81	63.07	13.42	94.24
Davenport, IA	28.86	44.57	17.44	9.57	41.80	10.89	n/a
Denver, CO	23.62	69.42	19.79	11.22	63.61	14.12	107.52
Des Moines, IA	24.93	56.76	19.36	9.20	49.48	15.72	100.89
Durham, NC	19.44	61.38	19.43	11.11	64.84	16.36	n/a
El Paso, TX	18.79	48.22	20.29	8.84	47.02	9.84	n/a
Erie, PA	24.09	48.31	18.73	10.73	50.50	11.14	n/a
Eugene, OR	25.78	46.63	18.21	10.19	41.27	13.45	n/a
Fargo, ND	21.93	47.63	18.87	11.81	49.40	12.70	n/a
Fayetteville, NC	20.60	55.58	17.83	10.22	58.29	11.66	n/a
Ft. Collins, CO	22.88	61.98	19.28	11.16	47.99	12.34	n/a
Ft. Wayne, IN	25.72	46.93	19.15	9.80	53.56	11.29	n/a
Ft. Worth, TX	19.21	57.15	21.00	9.59	55.07	12.29	104.23
Gainesville, FL	19.03	61.28	18.58	10.19	50.33	12.75	101.18
Grand Rapids, MI	23.20	46.55	19.01	10.06	52.41	12.20	43.94
Green Bay, WI	24.35	49.56	18.39	10.27	48.10	11.71	n/a
Greensboro, NC	18.65	59.93	20.13	9.69	59.17	12.52	109.09
Honolulu, HI	32.59	45.95	23.31	11.19	48.16	17.49	113.81
Houston, TX	22.65	68.99	21.30	9.38	63.07	14.85	84.76
Huntsville, AL	22.76	57.94	19.98	8.46	65.79	13.19	n/a
Indianapolis, IN	27.18	54.25	19.32	9.40	56.65	13.18	111.80
Jacksonville, FL	19.69	60.52	19.05	9.83	55.77	13.48	100.97
Kansas City, MO	26.99	55.22	18.97	9.93	50.32	10.98	99.62
Lafayette, LA	21.20	44.84	17.49	8.84	56.92	11.98	n/a
Las Vegas, NV	27.14	53.11	20.76	14.18	51.02	10.48	80.44
Lexington, KY	20.66	48.10	17.37	10.18	45.17	13.08	78.65
Lincoln, NE	22.04	58.13	18.37	9.30	50.94	10.89	n/a
Little Rock, AR	21.55	52.25	16.61	8.88	43.41	13.57	82.59
Los Angeles, CA	30.15	70.50	20.81	9.78	61.50	13.44	88.31
Louisville, KY	24.00	48.03	18.48	10.02	46.33	13.37	89.70
Lubbock, TX	19.77	43.63	20.57	9.10	47.36	10.62	n/a
Madison, WI	27.53	55.09	18.93	9.80	52.70	13.76	120.68
Manchester, NH	25.00	55.30	21.01	13.44	56.50	13.23	n/a

Table continued on next page.

Metro Area	Electricians	Financial Managers	First-Line Supervisors/ Mgrs., Sales	Food Preparation Workers	General/ Operations Managers	Hairdressers/ Cosmetologists	Internists
McAllen, TX	15.29	45.55	18.37	8.74	39.42	12.01	n/a
Miami, FL	19.99	70.12	20.88	10.36	61.15	12.33	98.51
Midland, TX	21.13	65.76	22.28	10.27	58.38	13.68	n/a
Minneapolis, MN	28.89	60.96	19.57	11.41	54.40	13.76	95.42
Montgomery, AL	19.77	52.29	17.77	9.45	55.87	14.09	n/a
Nashville, TN	20.69	56.15	19.81	9.49	50.70	13.99	83.91
New Orleans, LA	23.96	45.67	19.27	8.63	52.05	12.66	106.75
New York, NY	37.44	87.96	23.97	11.96	77.74	15.36	80.33
Oklahoma City, OK	20.82	49.30	18.69	9.02	48.80	10.80	77.20
Omaha, NE	22.41	60.10	20.28	8.92	53.69	13.49	98.70
Orlando, FL	19.06	62.20	19.56	10.38	54.68	11.54	75.20
Oxnard, CA	28.21	57.60	23.20	10.59	58.41	13.05	96.37
Peoria, IL	30.48	56.22	17.98	9.69	48.60	9.84	102.78
Philadelphia, PA	30.89	72.36	25.25	11.01	67.69	13.27	101.37
Phoenix, AZ	20.96	54.93	19.12	10.08	52.02	11.97	107.00
Pittsburgh, PA	24.73	60.75	21.60	9.91	57.93	11.63	105.49
Portland, OR	34.72	53.72	19.15	10.58	51.33	14.63	106.69
Providence, RI	26.50	62.42	21.71	11.22	65.06	13.37	79.79
Provo, UT	22.62	55.80	17.68	9.02	40.52	12.61	n/a
Raleigh, NC	18.70	61.21	20.55	10.38	64.35	15.50	120.51
Reno, NV	26.36	47.58	19.88	9.80	51.67	10.72	n/a
Richmond, VA	21.48	61.79	20.33	10.36	58.75	17.09	98.97
Riverside, CA	28.74	53.90	21.11	9.84	52.10	10.26	88.55
Rochester, MN	28.95	51.80	17.51	11.98	41.65	13.47	n/a
Salem, OR	26.97	47.20	18.42	10.34	42.44	13.24	105.60
Salt Lake City, UT	23.13	55.44	20.40	9.67	46.16	14.99	69.36
San Antonio, TX	20.30	59.79	22.31	9.66	52.56	13.02	n/a
San Diego, CA	30.01	62.91	23.00	10.04	58.63	15.76	94.95
San Francisco, CA	40.01	80.75	22.84	11.42	71.88	18.86	73.44
San Jose, CA	30.81	77.44	23.11	10.98	71.60	11.43	88.19
Santa Rosa, CA	33.56	56.45	21.60	10.39	53.03	11.40	118.57
Savannah, GA	21.99	53.44	16.91	9.75	45.85	11.05	n/a
Seattle, WA	33.06	60.02	22.52	12.05	63.97	18.84	97.49
Sioux Falls, SD	20.71	61.26	20.74	9.36	59.52	13.91	n/a
Spokane, WA	23.89	49.78	20.28	10.19	46.58	12.64	78.06
Springfield, MO	21.43	52.66	18.14	8.73	37.73	11.79	n/a
Tallahassee, FL	17.49	53.63	19.46	9.33	52.68	12.38	n/a
Tampa, FL	17.90	57.97	20.55	9.91	58.67	12.21	104.44
Topeka, KS	22.07	48.80	17.77	8.73	42.34	13.85	n/a
Tulsa, OK	22.07	52.38	17.13	9.66	48.38	12.24	84.59
Virginia Beach, VA	21.45	57.11	19.19	9.99	55.74	15.88	89.75
Washington, DC	26.69	69.14	22.09	10.87	68.59	17.40	103.67
Wichita, KS	23.87	45.98	18.79	8.79	50.05	11.93	n/a
Wilmington, NC	18.64	52.06	21.03	10.41	59.01	10.83	n/a
Worcester, MA	32.10	56.15	21.73	10.81	60.60	16.18	n/a

Notes: Wage data is for May 2013 and covers the Metropolitan Statistical Area—see Appendix B for areas included; n/a not available
Source: Bureau of Labor Statistics, May 2013 Metro Area Occupational Employment and Wage Estimates

Average Hourly Wages: Occupations J – N

Metro Area	Janitors/ Cleaners	Landscapers	Lawyers	Maids/ House- keepers	Main- tenance Repairers	Marketing Managers	Nuclear Medicine Technologists
Abilene, TX	9.79	10.35	50.25	8.54	13.87	n/a	n/a
Albuquerque, NM	10.75	11.45	43.99	9.10	17.08	40.40	35.11
Anchorage, AK	13.87	14.07	59.01	10.81	21.64	40.58	n/a
Ann Arbor, MI	12.94	13.36	55.32	10.29	18.10	53.22	32.69
Athens, GA	10.93	10.04	58.06	9.62	16.79	53.90	n/a
Atlanta, GA	11.69	12.60	69.70	9.14	18.34	64.06	34.66
Austin, TX	10.43	12.05	59.97	9.40	17.03	67.44	32.88
Baltimore, MD	11.93	13.56	58.38	10.50	19.11	56.97	38.66
Billings, MT	12.08	12.57	33.40	9.80	15.25	n/a	n/a
Boise City, ID	10.53	12.28	54.04	9.83	15.21	48.83	n/a
Boston, MA	15.25	16.90	67.33	13.66	22.26	67.72	37.12
Boulder, CO	13.23	13.24	63.60	10.02	19.31	69.69	n/a
Cape Coral, FL	11.52	11.41	40.19	10.00	15.96	51.96	36.35
Cedar Rapids, IA	12.63	13.08	46.71	9.96	19.80	53.67	n/a
Charleston, SC	10.54	10.92	48.58	9.35	17.87	53.11	32.35
Charlotte, NC	10.35	10.88	55.60	8.93	18.46	63.83	32.42
Chicago, IL	13.12	12.72	65.83	11.62	20.04	55.55	35.48
Cincinnati, OH	11.35	12.28	54.21	10.52	19.13	57.28	30.29
Clarksville, TN	11.03	11.47	40.52	8.59	16.48	42.15	n/a
Colorado Spgs, CO	13.13	11.67	51.72	9.38	17.31	62.23	n/a
Columbia, MO	12.40	10.68	47.69	9.13	15.74	47.96	n/a
Columbus, OH	11.87	11.91	55.29	9.76	18.14	63.14	31.93
Dallas, TX	10.00	11.31	65.75	9.06	17.50	66.23	33.14
Davenport, IA	11.91	12.11	43.51	9.64	17.03	41.86	n/a
Denver, CO	11.56	13.81	69.19	10.17	18.95	66.34	39.26
Des Moines, IA	11.57	14.89	65.93	10.06	17.28	65.18	32.00
Durham, NC	11.12	13.26	53.74	10.28	20.22	70.91	n/a
El Paso, TX	9.82	9.83	64.13	8.80	12.72	55.22	n/a
Erie, PA	10.54	11.09	56.25	8.84	15.58	56.19	n/a
Eugene, OR	12.52	14.05	45.90	9.99	18.10	36.20	n/a
Fargo, ND	12.26	12.40	52.72	9.71	16.61	47.97	n/a
Fayetteville, NC	10.01	10.33	53.27	8.58	17.19	n/a	28.73
Ft. Collins, CO	11.69	12.64	57.33	9.81	17.22	63.23	n/a
Ft. Wayne, IN	11.19	12.11	60.17	8.75	18.83	45.97	28.70
Ft. Worth, TX	10.62	11.14	54.57	9.18	16.15	53.94	35.60
Gainesville, FL	10.22	11.02	51.94	9.44	16.67	53.76	n/a
Grand Rapids, MI	11.34	12.19	51.01	9.81	18.14	50.88	31.32
Green Bay, WI	11.76	13.86	54.59	9.27	18.63	51.30	n/a
Greensboro, NC	9.70	11.98	56.20	9.06	18.38	62.14	31.19
Honolulu, HI	12.14	13.83	52.23	15.55	20.38	45.86	40.27
Houston, TX	9.66	11.34	76.17	8.98	17.78	70.33	33.26
Huntsville, AL	9.75	10.62	59.69	9.14	19.52	56.43	25.22
Indianapolis, IN	11.70	11.45	49.17	9.14	17.86	52.08	33.00
Jacksonville, FL	11.28	11.69	55.10	9.35	17.27	59.89	34.31
Kansas City, MO	12.04	12.68	60.63	9.63	18.27	53.69	31.60
Lafayette, LA	9.85	10.53	52.48	8.58	17.89	39.76	n/a
Las Vegas, NV	13.88	13.00	59.54	15.10	22.67	55.75	40.01
Lexington, KY	11.35	11.35	47.19	9.22	16.36	49.27	28.83
Lincoln, NE	10.89	11.84	51.53	9.20	18.60	47.20	31.66
Little Rock, AR	10.15	11.41	45.53	8.67	15.30	46.84	32.36
Los Angeles, CA	12.89	13.58	79.15	11.46	20.16	65.55	45.43
Louisville, KY	11.18	12.56	46.86	9.34	18.32	54.14	29.28
Lubbock, TX	10.31	10.92	53.47	8.45	14.17	56.59	n/a
Madison, WI	12.32	14.36	46.97	9.65	18.85	51.85	n/a
Manchester, NH	11.87	17.02	61.67	10.32	20.45	50.26	n/a

Table continued on next page.

Metro Area	Janitors/ Cleaners	Landscapers	Lawyers	Maids/ House- keepers	Main- tenance Repairers	Marketing Managers	Nuclear Medicine Technologists
McAllen, TX	10.13	9.71	61.72	8.40	11.30	n/a	n/a
Miami, FL	10.23	11.48	72.84	9.54	15.19	59.68	35.08
Midland, TX	10.86	13.04	61.47	9.36	18.71	50.77	n/a
Minneapolis, MN	12.43	14.03	63.74	11.09	20.88	61.66	35.28
Montgomery, AL	9.88	10.90	46.64	8.80	17.80	54.81	n/a
Nashville, TN	10.51	11.95	52.06	9.28	17.70	48.43	29.04
New Orleans, LA	10.96	10.52	60.17	9.58	16.78	55.25	33.10
New York, NY	15.78	15.65	79.66	17.16	20.80	85.29	39.70
Oklahoma City, OK	10.13	11.82	47.01	9.21	16.24	45.66	33.57
Omaha, NE	11.13	12.19	49.32	9.46	17.77	52.74	30.46
Orlando, FL	10.20	11.32	65.35	9.85	15.16	55.71	34.18
Oxnard, CA	14.04	14.09	74.49	10.60	19.22	71.85	51.71
Peoria, IL	11.22	12.37	65.50	10.33	19.32	52.74	31.85
Philadelphia, PA	13.88	14.88	68.56	11.45	19.63	80.57	34.14
Phoenix, AZ	11.03	11.21	67.95	9.72	17.62	55.64	38.06
Pittsburgh, PA	12.61	12.40	68.07	10.06	18.75	69.89	27.40
Portland, OR	12.88	13.80	55.70	11.28	19.94	50.31	38.71
Providence, RI	13.33	13.96	47.45	12.21	19.51	58.72	40.30
Provo, UT	10.22	11.48	55.41	9.15	16.24	51.92	n/a
Raleigh, NC	10.37	11.56	58.36	9.57	18.32	64.08	32.80
Reno, NV	10.41	13.39	61.68	10.44	18.21	48.54	n/a
Richmond, VA	11.00	12.01	56.65	9.60	18.31	62.98	30.90
Riverside, CA	13.09	11.85	57.55	10.91	18.73	64.22	46.06
Rochester, MN	13.96	13.84	51.27	12.26	18.91	59.61	n/a
Salem, OR	13.04	12.88	56.65	11.17	17.37	36.97	n/a
Salt Lake City, UT	10.12	12.31	57.91	9.47	17.62	62.76	31.06
San Antonio, TX	10.50	10.98	54.75	9.38	14.83	53.91	32.77
San Diego, CA	12.99	12.94	72.34	10.58	18.90	68.45	36.68
San Francisco, CA	13.55	20.09	81.42	16.90	23.90	83.57	50.86
San Jose, CA	13.14	15.06	94.01	13.74	23.14	88.36	55.61
Santa Rosa, CA	13.39	15.11	77.12	13.34	21.88	61.72	n/a
Savannah, GA	10.94	11.83	51.02	8.61	17.38	48.96	n/a
Seattle, WA	14.60	15.57	62.33	12.07	20.33	67.55	42.21
Sioux Falls, SD	10.88	12.52	48.61	9.38	16.02	51.58	25.69
Spokane, WA	13.46	13.65	48.67	10.56	17.96	54.55	35.02
Springfield, MO	10.85	11.91	42.05	9.03	14.69	39.92	34.09
Tallahassee, FL	9.91	10.83	52.36	8.98	14.97	50.22	n/a
Tampa, FL	10.34	10.76	54.49	9.39	15.55	51.59	36.09
Topeka, KS	11.82	12.38	38.64	9.08	17.69	60.60	n/a
Tulsa, OK	10.41	10.89	57.64	9.03	16.72	46.31	33.07
Virginia Beach, VA	10.22	11.32	61.05	9.68	16.63	55.08	32.47
Washington, DC	12.45	13.26	75.70	11.90	21.37	73.15	38.43
Wichita, KS	10.45	11.56	46.81	9.05	15.68	57.49	32.20
Wilmington, NC	10.91	11.00	45.17	9.04	17.82	50.19	n/a
Worcester, MA	14.17	13.49	60.66	12.18	20.42	62.04	n/a

Notes: Wage data is for May 2013 and covers the Metropolitan Statistical Area—see Appendix B for areas included; n/a not available
Source: Bureau of Labor Statistics, May 2013 Metro Area Occupational Employment and Wage Estimates

Average Hourly Wages: Occupations N – R

Metro Area	Nurses, Licensed Practical	Nurses, Registered	Nursing Assistants	Packers/ Packagers	Physical Therapists	Postal Mail Carriers	R.E. Brokers
Abilene, TX	18.56	28.14	10.88	9.20	40.86	24.24	n/a
Albuquerque, NM	21.69	31.78	13.52	12.32	40.02	24.89	n/a
Anchorage, AK	25.13	40.64	16.92	12.77	48.59	25.49	30.29
Ann Arbor, MI	22.43	32.94	13.87	9.73	37.94	24.63	n/a
Athens, GA	18.64	29.33	9.81	9.29	36.78	23.23	n/a
Atlanta, GA	19.02	30.95	11.11	10.47	37.96	24.72	43.11
Austin, TX	22.05	30.98	11.67	11.34	41.88	25.00	30.32
Baltimore, MD	24.87	34.24	13.96	10.58	39.05	24.68	37.94
Billings, MT	18.43	31.61	12.53	10.98	33.13	24.73	n/a
Boise City, ID	19.45	29.33	11.20	11.43	36.48	24.35	n/a
Boston, MA	25.49	42.35	14.96	10.99	38.80	25.95	63.74
Boulder, CO	21.53	34.08	13.27	10.59	34.04	24.89	29.50
Cape Coral, FL	19.78	28.94	12.72	9.05	40.30	24.25	n/a
Cedar Rapids, IA	17.69	25.65	11.93	8.74	34.36	24.58	n/a
Charleston, SC	20.18	32.16	11.10	9.94	36.90	23.89	26.30
Charlotte, NC	19.86	28.52	11.23	10.76	37.91	24.31	35.01
Chicago, IL	22.53	34.46	12.48	11.00	36.84	25.01	49.15
Cincinnati, OH	20.64	30.08	12.21	10.64	38.29	24.51	23.98
Clarksville, TN	18.75	27.23	11.76	12.86	36.69	24.34	n/a
Colorado Spgs, CO	21.21	31.37	12.78	9.86	37.23	24.74	20.86
Columbia, MO	18.45	27.81	10.90	9.75	31.91	24.25	n/a
Columbus, OH	20.13	30.64	12.13	11.04	36.90	24.08	34.29
Dallas, TX	22.36	33.65	12.32	10.29	45.06	24.91	n/a
Davenport, IA	17.55	26.26	11.72	11.16	37.48	23.98	n/a
Denver, CO	22.89	34.42	14.42	10.29	35.19	24.82	41.76
Des Moines, IA	19.29	26.79	12.14	10.00	36.62	24.62	n/a
Durham, NC	21.76	31.62	12.82	9.49	36.49	24.41	26.03
El Paso, TX	20.50	31.00	10.82	9.06	48.95	23.89	n/a
Erie, PA	18.48	26.75	12.25	11.76	37.13	23.58	n/a
Eugene, OR	22.40	37.50	13.39	10.26	41.40	24.28	31.03
Fargo, ND	18.17	27.67	13.43	8.64	31.95	24.04	n/a
Fayetteville, NC	19.57	29.81	11.33	10.02	38.64	24.08	19.47
Ft. Collins, CO	21.17	30.50	13.44	9.34	32.86	24.95	27.79
Ft. Wayne, IN	18.40	25.17	10.78	10.17	38.22	24.68	n/a
Ft. Worth, TX	22.36	33.60	11.89	11.04	41.45	24.79	n/a
Gainesville, FL	19.90	28.53	10.88	10.59	36.44	23.80	n/a
Grand Rapids, MI	19.05	28.64	12.14	10.98	35.42	23.99	n/a
Green Bay, WI	18.02	27.82	12.31	11.78	39.45	23.63	n/a
Greensboro, NC	19.67	28.80	10.89	9.28	35.43	24.12	22.44
Honolulu, HI	22.43	42.55	13.98	10.44	38.58	26.07	41.96
Houston, TX	22.88	36.56	12.06	11.38	42.08	24.51	48.51
Huntsville, AL	18.73	26.74	10.86	10.78	38.44	23.71	n/a
Indianapolis, IN	20.27	29.90	12.24	11.26	39.04	24.13	60.38
Jacksonville, FL	20.51	30.37	11.57	9.32	46.60	24.69	n/a
Kansas City, MO	19.06	29.88	11.81	11.54	34.37	24.30	24.96
Lafayette, LA	18.72	27.89	9.24	9.32	38.84	24.57	23.35
Las Vegas, NV	26.07	39.12	16.52	11.27	59.64	24.87	54.44
Lexington, KY	18.63	27.91	11.95	9.82	39.27	24.65	n/a
Lincoln, NE	18.23	26.73	12.12	10.11	34.88	24.54	n/a
Little Rock, AR	17.95	28.67	11.01	9.05	35.78	24.18	n/a
Los Angeles, CA	24.62	44.26	13.71	10.33	42.31	25.76	64.57
Louisville, KY	18.93	28.80	11.91	10.54	38.82	24.11	n/a
Lubbock, TX	20.57	27.47	10.95	8.89	38.23	24.89	n/a
Madison, WI	20.97	34.97	13.89	15.06	36.29	24.44	20.83
Manchester, NH	23.10	31.99	13.91	10.50	37.48	25.09	47.44

Table continued on next page.

Metro Area	Nurses, Licensed Practical	Nurses, Registered	Nursing Assistants	Packers/ Packagers	Physical Therapists	Postal Mail Carriers	R.E. Brokers
McAllen, TX	21.91	31.97	9.83	8.67	46.12	24.38	n/a
Miami, FL	20.23	29.53	11.04	9.31	35.27	25.08	n/a
Midland, TX	21.31	30.14	12.55	9.45	n/a	25.01	22.83
Minneapolis, MN	21.08	35.30	14.12	11.24	36.81	24.41	n/a
Montgomery, AL	18.35	29.68	11.00	9.85	38.82	23.87	26.74
Nashville, TN	18.85	28.42	11.87	9.83	36.18	24.52	n/a
New Orleans, LA	19.23	31.68	10.85	11.23	40.70	24.16	n/a
New York, NY	24.60	40.44	16.20	10.81	40.71	25.37	54.98
Oklahoma City, OK	18.99	28.13	10.89	10.81	35.86	24.41	18.85
Omaha, NE	19.69	28.43	13.09	10.20	35.87	24.53	37.40
Orlando, FL	19.43	29.70	11.53	10.74	38.33	24.73	47.52
Oxnard, CA	25.15	36.37	13.40	10.84	41.90	25.49	n/a
Peoria, IL	21.95	26.81	11.43	11.56	33.61	24.34	n/a
Philadelphia, PA	23.18	35.07	13.96	11.90	37.78	24.81	64.60
Phoenix, AZ	25.24	35.12	13.79	11.06	38.46	25.01	44.12
Pittsburgh, PA	19.78	30.04	13.16	12.27	39.28	24.65	71.36
Portland, OR	24.17	40.58	13.87	11.50	37.84	24.51	32.04
Providence, RI	24.60	35.47	13.75	10.48	38.50	24.81	n/a
Provo, UT	19.31	27.31	11.26	10.26	36.46	24.53	21.19
Raleigh, NC	21.13	28.43	11.67	10.48	35.21	24.14	25.34
Reno, NV	26.51	35.25	13.49	11.17	45.80	24.51	n/a
Richmond, VA	19.23	30.32	11.44	12.84	39.35	23.71	27.71
Riverside, CA	22.18	42.37	13.43	11.81	41.17	25.31	n/a
Rochester, MN	22.02	n/a	15.25	10.63	39.57	25.04	n/a
Salem, OR	21.94	37.37	13.40	10.81	40.09	23.63	22.52
Salt Lake City, UT	21.32	29.89	11.31	10.16	40.42	25.05	n/a
San Antonio, TX	20.50	31.82	11.69	10.18	43.27	24.66	28.51
San Diego, CA	23.18	40.60	13.60	10.31	43.73	25.26	36.79
San Francisco, CA	29.97	61.38	20.10	12.74	49.25	26.44	26.40
San Jose, CA	27.94	59.23	16.42	11.17	45.42	26.36	50.01
Santa Rosa, CA	25.85	48.36	15.79	10.34	41.42	25.12	48.60
Savannah, GA	18.50	28.25	10.72	9.29	42.55	24.73	28.35
Seattle, WA	25.93	39.68	14.93	13.41	40.75	25.22	32.78
Sioux Falls, SD	16.79	25.78	11.84	10.60	31.95	24.04	n/a
Spokane, WA	21.55	34.37	12.87	11.06	36.73	24.55	23.22
Springfield, MO	17.12	24.94	10.55	10.77	39.63	24.12	n/a
Tallahassee, FL	19.16	27.41	10.92	8.94	40.08	24.26	n/a
Tampa, FL	19.97	30.28	11.44	9.45	37.93	24.66	n/a
Topeka, KS	19.06	29.36	10.93	15.60	38.36	23.60	n/a
Tulsa, OK	18.83	27.73	10.91	9.53	36.27	24.47	n/a
Virginia Beach, VA	18.26	28.80	11.22	10.43	39.84	24.73	32.08
Washington, DC	22.95	35.74	13.77	10.30	38.69	24.66	34.45
Wichita, KS	19.29	25.51	11.03	9.15	36.26	24.34	26.38
Wilmington, NC	18.86	26.83	11.21	9.61	41.89	23.50	37.64
Worcester, MA	26.36	43.05	15.10	10.06	39.78	24.22	n/a

Notes: Wage data is for May 2013 and covers the Metropolitan Statistical Area—see Appendix B for areas included; n/a not available
Source: Bureau of Labor Statistics, May 2013 Metro Area Occupational Employment and Wage Estimates

Average Hourly Wages: Occupations R – T

Metro Area	Retail Salespersons	Sales Reps., Except Tech./Scien.	Sales Reps., Tech./Scien.	Secretaries, Exc. Leg./ Med./Exec.	Security Guards	Surgeons	Teacher Assistants
Abilene, TX	13.62	23.66	36.44	12.92	10.71	n/a	9.90
Albuquerque, NM	11.74	26.90	39.81	13.97	11.55	n/a	10.10
Anchorage, AK	13.18	25.83	36.45	16.96	13.31	n/a	17.30
Ann Arbor, MI	12.14	32.93	41.15	17.22	16.96	n/a	13.10
Athens, GA	10.51	24.97	n/a	14.32	13.49	n/a	8.70
Atlanta, GA	11.95	30.79	38.95	16.85	11.48	120.81	10.30
Austin, TX	12.53	29.84	37.48	15.77	12.42	n/a	10.60
Baltimore, MD	11.89	33.94	42.30	17.78	14.58	110.84	14.30
Billings, MT	13.88	26.55	n/a	14.44	12.86	n/a	13.50
Boise City, ID	11.90	27.45	29.67	14.49	12.89	n/a	11.10
Boston, MA	12.39	43.10	44.47	21.16	15.06	n/a	14.50
Boulder, CO	13.89	37.59	35.67	17.37	15.01	103.03	15.10
Cape Coral, FL	11.83	24.18	29.78	14.54	11.15	n/a	13.20
Cedar Rapids, IA	11.85	31.08	44.18	14.30	n/a	n/a	12.60
Charleston, SC	11.52	27.76	40.46	15.32	13.52	n/a	11.50
Charlotte, NC	12.10	31.41	40.29	17.10	11.31	n/a	11.20
Chicago, IL	12.33	33.29	37.20	16.95	13.02	115.47	12.30
Cincinnati, OH	11.78	31.64	39.93	15.94	16.47	109.54	12.70
Clarksville, TN	11.36	23.44	52.26	13.22	13.43	n/a	11.10
Colorado Spgs, CO	12.79	30.52	35.26	15.58	13.48	107.95	11.90
Columbia, MO	10.64	23.27	28.42	14.58	13.91	n/a	10.70
Columbus, OH	12.03	29.62	36.19	16.87	12.43	119.77	13.10
Dallas, TX	12.58	33.78	36.24	16.42	13.08	95.05	10.70
Davenport, IA	12.71	28.28	33.17	14.44	12.50	116.62	11.70
Denver, CO	12.80	36.54	48.36	17.96	13.89	111.18	13.30
Des Moines, IA	12.84	35.92	37.24	16.32	16.53	91.11	10.70
Durham, NC	10.89	31.22	45.63	17.51	12.77	113.39	12.20
El Paso, TX	10.96	21.60	38.11	12.87	10.13	n/a	10.60
Erie, PA	11.39	30.08	39.28	13.84	11.23	115.46	10.00
Eugene, OR	13.02	25.11	39.96	16.19	12.41	n/a	13.80
Fargo, ND	13.09	26.62	42.24	15.68	11.95	104.49	12.90
Fayetteville, NC	10.56	24.42	39.94	14.77	15.30	n/a	10.00
Ft. Collins, CO	12.25	26.89	40.29	15.92	10.31	110.38	12.50
Ft. Wayne, IN	11.55	28.96	39.16	15.47	14.83	n/a	11.10
Ft. Worth, TX	11.78	32.63	36.55	15.36	14.30	n/a	8.90
Gainesville, FL	11.11	22.34	33.50	13.86	12.24	n/a	9.40
Grand Rapids, MI	11.77	28.24	37.72	16.53	11.30	n/a	13.00
Green Bay, WI	11.45	32.44	33.42	16.18	13.78	n/a	14.40
Greensboro, NC	12.20	30.40	33.29	15.60	11.06	n/a	10.90
Honolulu, HI	12.25	21.44	33.40	18.43	12.68	n/a	13.40
Houston, TX	12.40	35.33	46.06	16.39	11.75	84.40	9.90
Huntsville, AL	11.46	31.78	37.45	16.94	12.32	n/a	8.70
Indianapolis, IN	12.06	32.67	46.55	16.61	12.49	n/a	11.20
Jacksonville, FL	11.47	28.88	35.44	14.98	10.35	118.25	12.40
Kansas City, MO	12.08	32.16	45.48	15.81	13.84	n/a	11.60
Lafayette, LA	11.24	28.84	31.88	14.31	11.22	71.35	10.20
Las Vegas, NV	13.07	28.96	42.72	18.64	13.22	113.49	15.90
Lexington, KY	11.71	24.93	35.03	15.59	10.51	114.35	14.70
Lincoln, NE	11.07	26.63	n/a	15.31	14.98	n/a	11.80
Little Rock, AR	12.75	27.25	29.86	14.42	12.41	113.90	9.40
Los Angeles, CA	12.39	29.73	38.84	18.27	12.81	111.49	14.10
Louisville, KY	11.51	30.69	44.89	15.00	13.37	118.16	13.80
Lubbock, TX	11.69	28.05	29.00	13.35	11.87	90.44	8.80
Madison, WI	12.09	30.06	41.70	17.17	11.48	n/a	12.80
Manchester, NH	11.99	31.44	38.83	15.96	11.92	105.45	12.90

Table continued on next page.

Metro Area	Retail Salespersons	Sales Reps., Except Tech./Scien.	Sales Reps., Tech./Scien.	Secretaries, Exc. Leg./ Med./Exec.	Security Guards	Surgeons	Teacher Assistants
McAllen, TX	9.57	25.44	n/a	12.71	10.59	n/a	10.30
Miami, FL	11.23	26.45	32.81	14.60	10.97	n/a	11.20
Midland, TX	14.55	33.58	48.05	15.43	12.50	n/a	9.20
Minneapolis, MN	11.44	36.68	44.11	18.95	14.94	119.63	14.40
Montgomery, AL	12.49	29.59	35.75	16.22	12.16	n/a	9.00
Nashville, TN	12.46	27.75	34.29	15.16	12.46	n/a	11.10
New Orleans, LA	12.89	29.58	37.42	15.19	13.36	n/a	11.10
New York, NY	12.84	38.77	46.37	19.00	15.18	98.64	13.90
Oklahoma City, OK	12.73	30.44	32.95	14.90	12.67	114.30	9.70
Omaha, NE	12.29	28.02	34.52	15.61	13.38	n/a	10.20
Orlando, FL	11.24	25.68	37.45	14.66	11.65	n/a	11.60
Oxnard, CA	12.75	32.68	42.86	18.21	12.65	119.04	14.50
Peoria, IL	11.79	28.49	33.56	14.65	16.04	n/a	11.20
Philadelphia, PA	13.07	32.23	49.82	17.47	12.30	120.27	12.90
Phoenix, AZ	11.61	29.76	42.58	16.43	13.52	114.05	11.20
Pittsburgh, PA	12.50	31.81	42.81	15.24	11.90	113.69	11.50
Portland, OR	12.93	32.81	41.56	17.50	13.80	n/a	14.70
Providence, RI	12.48	32.76	41.15	17.93	12.83	116.46	14.50
Provo, UT	12.37	29.40	33.72	14.45	14.08	110.65	11.00
Raleigh, NC	11.79	29.45	41.18	16.28	12.44	n/a	10.80
Reno, NV	12.74	27.70	39.48	17.62	11.51	115.67	12.30
Richmond, VA	12.43	34.63	44.28	16.41	12.89	112.78	10.90
Riverside, CA	12.10	29.92	40.45	17.31	11.51	106.75	14.00
Rochester, MN	11.24	27.21	32.56	17.40	13.32	n/a	12.40
Salem, OR	12.92	25.36	40.96	15.61	14.60	n/a	16.30
Salt Lake City, UT	12.67	34.62	46.90	15.93	14.32	115.18	11.40
San Antonio, TX	12.42	27.83	41.84	15.25	11.83	84.64	10.80
San Diego, CA	13.73	28.45	39.02	18.35	14.03	83.21	14.00
San Francisco, CA	14.53	31.29	47.92	20.71	15.27	93.98	16.60
San Jose, CA	12.94	32.85	58.34	20.56	15.17	114.84	14.40
Santa Rosa, CA	13.67	30.64	46.30	19.16	14.00	118.83	14.30
Savannah, GA	11.52	28.61	30.20	15.65	14.44	n/a	10.50
Seattle, WA	14.69	35.29	45.11	19.62	15.73	115.08	15.80
Sioux Falls, SD	12.34	27.49	43.01	13.16	12.24	n/a	10.90
Spokane, WA	13.16	25.87	46.81	16.12	13.45	n/a	12.90
Springfield, MO	11.82	22.81	30.02	13.13	12.99	n/a	10.40
Tallahassee, FL	11.02	21.94	33.81	14.09	11.27	n/a	11.90
Tampa, FL	12.01	30.42	33.10	14.48	10.79	103.26	10.20
Topeka, KS	11.52	27.70	40.10	14.09	13.94	n/a	10.90
Tulsa, OK	13.25	28.32	41.58	14.04	12.17	79.61	11.00
Virginia Beach, VA	11.29	28.23	42.31	15.60	12.89	111.83	11.80
Washington, DC	12.12	34.08	47.52	20.61	17.82	116.42	14.00
Wichita, KS	12.36	31.22	43.32	14.57	13.43	117.05	10.60
Wilmington, NC	11.87	29.03	35.81	15.03	11.81	n/a	11.60
Worcester, MA	11.90	35.68	38.33	19.68	14.47	116.75	13.60

Notes: Wage data is for May 2013 and covers the Metropolitan Statistical Area—see Appendix B for areas included; hourly wages for teacher assistants were calculated by the editors from annual wage data assuming a 40 hour work week; n/a not available
Source: Bureau of Labor Statistics, May 2013 Metro Area Occupational Employment and Wage Estimates

Average Hourly Wages: Occupations T – Z

Metro Area	Teachers, Elementary School	Teachers, Secondary School	Tele-marketers	Truck Driv., Heavy/ Trac. Trail.	Truck Drivers, Light	Waiters/ Waitresses
Abilene, TX	21.30	22.00	n/a	18.97	11.41	8.74
Albuquerque, NM	21.70	22.40	n/a	19.03	14.14	10.88
Anchorage, AK	32.60	32.60	n/a	25.87	19.18	10.72
Ann Arbor, MI	27.70	29.70	n/a	19.63	17.05	10.14
Athens, GA	25.30	25.30	8.69	20.40	15.44	9.03
Atlanta, GA	26.20	27.10	13.99	20.41	16.93	9.19
Austin, TX	22.70	23.50	13.90	18.67	16.53	9.34
Baltimore, MD	29.50	29.30	12.90	19.80	17.45	9.18
Billings, MT	23.80	26.10	13.73	21.13	16.18	8.99
Boise City, ID	23.60	24.30	12.58	18.08	14.07	8.96
Boston, MA	34.30	35.10	17.08	23.41	18.17	13.50
Boulder, CO	26.60	27.20	12.08	20.68	16.73	12.33
Cape Coral, FL	23.40	24.10	9.65	16.06	14.10	9.67
Cedar Rapids, IA	24.00	23.80	10.54	20.03	16.20	8.74
Charleston, SC	24.70	25.40	9.57	19.36	15.63	9.42
Charlotte, NC	22.10	22.40	13.66	19.37	16.05	9.34
Chicago, IL	28.80	35.80	13.34	23.42	18.67	10.50
Cincinnati, OH	27.20	27.40	13.51	20.10	16.71	9.15
Clarksville, TN	26.60	26.40	n/a	15.41	13.76	9.12
Colorado Spgs, CO	21.60	22.20	12.60	19.36	13.99	9.94
Columbia, MO	21.60	20.90	10.63	19.62	13.15	9.53
Columbus, OH	29.10	29.90	11.74	19.02	16.63	9.37
Dallas, TX	25.00	25.80	n/a	19.20	15.72	10.24
Davenport, IA	26.60	26.10	10.50	19.13	15.78	10.29
Denver, CO	25.50	26.90	13.50	21.35	16.33	10.53
Des Moines, IA	25.20	25.70	15.07	21.18	16.38	9.00
Durham, NC	20.70	21.40	15.76	17.58	17.67	9.40
El Paso, TX	24.60	24.80	9.49	17.61	14.03	8.51
Erie, PA	27.00	24.10	8.65	18.04	15.28	9.07
Eugene, OR	26.90	24.70	12.52	17.32	16.40	10.84
Fargo, ND	24.40	24.00	11.26	18.84	14.90	10.12
Fayetteville, NC	19.20	19.10	8.90	15.43	15.54	9.09
Ft. Collins, CO	22.80	23.30	11.00	17.26	16.25	9.16
Ft. Wayne, IN	24.60	24.80	9.79	19.81	15.74	8.95
Ft. Worth, TX	25.40	26.30	11.19	19.47	15.61	9.29
Gainesville, FL	22.10	24.90	9.47	15.04	15.26	9.90
Grand Rapids, MI	32.70	28.90	11.93	18.72	16.07	9.52
Green Bay, WI	25.70	24.60	12.38	19.49	15.22	8.80
Greensboro, NC	21.60	21.80	11.11	18.90	15.37	8.67
Honolulu, HI	26.30	27.20	11.62	21.37	14.70	12.93
Houston, TX	24.90	25.50	12.17	22.66	16.51	9.73
Huntsville, AL	24.60	24.00	9.29	16.39	14.79	9.19
Indianapolis, IN	25.40	26.00	17.93	20.12	17.28	9.54
Jacksonville, FL	24.10	24.50	10.58	18.75	15.81	9.66
Kansas City, MO	24.30	24.10	13.16	21.38	17.06	9.39
Lafayette, LA	27.40	n/a	11.24	19.29	13.58	8.97
Las Vegas, NV	25.80	26.00	11.88	19.78	16.43	11.11
Lexington, KY	24.00	24.60	n/a	18.81	16.17	8.84
Lincoln, NE	25.10	25.10	10.56	n/a	13.26	8.98
Little Rock, AR	21.80	23.60	8.82	18.66	14.19	8.30
Los Angeles, CA	34.80	33.30	12.66	20.29	16.24	11.07
Louisville, KY	26.60	26.90	12.10	20.93	17.63	9.31
Lubbock, TX	21.40	22.50	n/a	17.79	14.21	9.03
Madison, WI	25.00	27.50	10.87	21.43	17.75	10.35
Manchester, NH	26.30	26.70	15.57	18.63	15.08	11.33

Table continued on next page.

Metro Area	Teachers, Elementary School	Teachers, Secondary School	Tele-marketers	Truck Driv., Heavy/ Trac. Trail.	Truck Drivers, Light	Waiters/ Waitresses
McAllen, TX	23.70	25.20	10.62	17.51	11.63	8.79
Miami, FL	23.20	26.50	11.81	17.53	14.08	9.76
Midland, TX	23.60	25.80	n/a	20.49	15.87	9.80
Minneapolis, MN	31.90	31.20	13.07	21.93	17.93	9.32
Montgomery, AL	22.80	22.10	8.45	18.26	15.61	8.60
Nashville, TN	22.70	23.40	15.24	19.93	15.34	8.90
New Orleans, LA	22.90	24.70	14.81	19.65	16.09	10.29
New York, NY	35.30	37.40	14.62	22.08	17.98	11.50
Oklahoma City, OK	20.80	22.90	10.30	19.01	15.82	9.25
Omaha, NE	22.40	23.40	12.21	19.11	14.67	8.85
Orlando, FL	22.80	22.10	10.95	17.46	15.16	10.98
Oxnard, CA	32.90	31.90	15.69	21.54	18.09	10.01
Peoria, IL	23.80	28.10	12.83	17.46	16.87	10.32
Philadelphia, PA	30.40	31.60	14.56	20.89	17.51	10.38
Phoenix, AZ	20.90	21.00	13.39	20.36	15.72	9.96
Pittsburgh, PA	27.90	29.00	12.88	20.52	15.69	9.69
Portland, OR	27.50	28.00	13.33	19.52	17.07	10.65
Providence, RI	34.70	33.60	15.11	20.27	17.91	10.34
Provo, UT	22.00	23.60	14.09	22.75	13.60	11.15
Raleigh, NC	21.60	22.00	14.65	19.28	16.30	9.47
Reno, NV	25.00	24.10	13.63	21.84	15.47	8.65
Richmond, VA	26.30	26.40	14.06	18.70	16.58	10.48
Riverside, CA	35.10	33.70	11.98	21.73	17.91	9.63
Rochester, MN	25.10	25.20	n/a	18.85	17.53	8.26
Salem, OR	27.20	26.60	10.52	18.24	16.75	10.21
Salt Lake City, UT	26.30	27.50	12.07	19.99	15.18	11.23
San Antonio, TX	26.60	27.20	n/a	16.40	14.14	9.32
San Diego, CA	30.80	33.20	11.55	19.27	16.58	9.95
San Francisco, CA	32.10	33.60	13.93	22.04	19.81	12.13
San Jose, CA	33.30	34.90	14.14	22.03	17.27	10.96
Santa Rosa, CA	22.70	31.00	11.71	22.34	18.16	10.51
Savannah, GA	26.30	n/a	13.15	18.66	16.33	10.07
Seattle, WA	29.10	30.30	13.18	21.75	17.79	14.14
Sioux Falls, SD	20.10	20.00	13.45	19.13	15.04	8.79
Spokane, WA	28.80	29.80	11.23	19.70	17.33	13.14
Springfield, MO	20.70	19.20	10.22	20.44	13.81	9.07
Tallahassee, FL	21.90	22.10	13.78	15.22	14.76	9.61
Tampa, FL	21.00	21.00	12.29	17.96	16.34	9.73
Topeka, KS	24.40	24.70	n/a	17.10	15.21	8.53
Tulsa, OK	22.20	21.60	12.19	19.26	14.05	8.88
Virginia Beach, VA	26.30	27.10	10.10	17.82	15.15	11.28
Washington, DC	32.60	33.60	12.50	19.86	19.19	11.87
Wichita, KS	20.60	23.80	n/a	17.82	13.07	8.96
Wilmington, NC	19.90	19.90	11.55	18.87	15.55	8.84
Worcester, MA	31.10	32.60	18.18	22.87	17.81	12.77

Notes: Wage data is for May 2013 and covers the Metropolitan Statistical Area—see Appendix B for areas included; hourly wages for elementary and secondary school teachers were calculated by the editors from annual wage data assuming a 40 hour work week; n/a not available
Source: Bureau of Labor Statistics, May 2013 Metro Area Occupational Employment and Wage Estimates

Means of Transportation to Work: City

City	Car/Truck/Van		Public Transportation			Bicycle	Walked	Other Means	Worked at Home
	Drove Alone	Car-pooled	Bus	Subway	Railroad				
Abilene, TX	80.3	10.2	1.1	0.0	0.0	0.2	2.9	2.7	2.5
Albuquerque, NM	80.4	9.1	1.9	0.0	0.2	1.2	2.2	1.2	3.8
Anchorage, AK	74.5	12.8	1.9	0.0	0.0	1.3	2.8	2.6	4.0
Ann Arbor, MI	58.4	5.9	9.7	0.1	0.0	4.4	15.4	0.4	5.8
Athens, GA	72.5	10.5	3.0	0.0	0.0	2.1	5.7	1.9	4.2
Atlanta, GA	67.4	7.8	7.0	2.9	0.3	1.0	4.8	1.6	7.3
Austin, TX	72.4	10.6	4.1	0.0	0.1	1.5	2.8	1.9	6.6
Baltimore, MD	59.8	10.2	15.4	1.5	1.0	0.9	6.8	1.7	2.8
Billings, MT	78.8	10.6	1.3	0.0	0.0	1.2	4.0	0.9	3.3
Boise City, ID	78.5	7.4	0.6	0.0	0.0	3.2	3.2	1.3	5.7
Boston, MA	38.1	7.2	13.3	17.7	1.1	1.8	15.3	1.8	3.8
Boulder, CO	52.0	5.8	8.1	0.0	0.0	10.5	9.8	1.4	12.3
Cape Coral, FL	83.7	9.0	0.6	0.0	0.0	0.5	0.8	1.5	4.0
Cedar Rapids, IA	80.3	9.5	1.6	0.0	0.0	0.6	2.9	1.3	3.7
Charleston, SC	76.4	7.2	2.9	0.0	0.0	2.5	5.6	1.1	4.3
Charlotte, NC	76.8	10.1	3.3	0.4	0.1	0.2	2.2	1.1	5.8
Chicago, IL	50.1	9.2	14.1	10.6	1.8	1.4	6.6	1.7	4.4
Cincinnati, OH	72.1	9.7	7.8	0.0	0.0	0.4	5.0	0.8	4.1
Clarksville, TN	84.8	9.8	0.5	0.0	0.0	0.1	2.1	1.1	1.5
Colorado Spgs, CO	79.9	9.9	0.7	0.0	0.0	0.6	2.7	1.1	5.2
Columbia, MO	77.4	9.7	0.9	0.0	0.0	1.5	6.3	0.6	3.6
Columbus, OH	80.3	8.6	3.0	0.0	0.0	0.7	3.0	1.0	3.4
Dallas, TX	77.7	10.7	3.3	0.3	0.3	0.2	1.8	1.6	4.1
Davenport, IA	85.8	7.5	0.7	0.0	0.0	0.4	2.1	0.9	2.6
Denver, CO	69.7	9.4	5.6	0.6	0.3	2.5	4.5	1.3	6.0
Des Moines, IA	79.1	11.7	2.1	0.0	0.0	0.4	2.4	0.8	3.5
Durham, NC	74.8	11.9	3.7	0.0	0.0	1.0	3.3	1.4	4.0
El Paso, TX	79.5	11.2	2.0	0.0	0.0	0.1	1.9	2.6	2.7
Erie, PA	75.7	10.9	4.7	0.0	0.0	0.3	5.4	1.0	2.0
Eugene, OR	66.1	8.2	3.8	0.0	0.0	8.1	6.9	0.8	6.1
Fargo, ND	82.5	7.4	1.1	0.0	0.0	0.9	4.1	1.0	2.9
Fayetteville, NC	80.5	9.8	0.8	0.0	0.0	0.2	4.5	1.3	2.9
Ft. Collins, CO	72.9	8.2	1.5	0.0	0.0	6.4	3.8	1.1	6.1
Ft. Wayne, IN	85.4	7.6	0.7	0.0	0.0	0.3	1.5	0.8	3.7
Ft. Worth, TX	82.0	10.9	0.7	0.0	0.3	0.2	1.2	1.5	3.2
Gainesville, FL	63.4	11.8	7.4	0.0	0.0	6.3	5.2	1.7	4.1
Grand Rapids, MI	74.9	11.4	3.9	0.0	0.0	0.7	3.8	0.7	4.7
Green Bay, WI	81.0	9.4	1.4	0.0	0.0	0.7	2.6	1.9	3.0
Greensboro, NC	81.2	9.6	2.2	0.0	0.0	0.3	2.3	0.9	3.5
Honolulu, HI	57.5	12.6	12.5	0.0	0.0	1.7	9.1	3.4	3.3
Houston, TX	75.8	12.2	4.3	0.0	0.0	0.4	2.1	2.0	3.1
Huntsville, AL	84.7	8.0	0.6	0.0	0.0	0.1	1.3	2.0	3.2
Indianapolis, IN	81.9	9.7	2.0	0.0	0.0	0.5	2.1	0.9	2.9
Jacksonville, FL	80.6	10.3	1.8	0.0	0.0	0.4	1.3	1.1	4.4
Kansas City, MO	80.5	8.5	3.3	0.0	0.0	0.3	2.1	1.2	4.0
Lafayette, LA	80.0	12.2	1.0	0.0	0.0	0.9	1.9	1.2	2.8
Las Vegas, NV	78.1	11.3	3.9	0.0	0.0	0.4	1.8	1.4	3.1
Lexington, KY	79.8	9.8	1.5	0.0	0.0	1.1	3.8	0.7	3.4
Lincoln, NE	80.7	9.9	1.1	0.0	0.0	1.8	2.6	0.6	3.3
Little Rock, AR	84.2	10.6	0.9	0.0	0.0	0.1	1.2	0.6	2.5
Los Angeles, CA	67.0	10.0	10.4	0.6	0.1	1.0	3.7	1.5	5.8
Louisville, KY	81.6	8.3	3.3	0.0	0.0	0.3	2.1	1.3	3.0
Lubbock, TX	82.2	10.5	0.9	0.0	0.0	0.5	2.0	0.9	3.0
Madison, WI	63.6	8.7	8.7	0.0	0.0	5.6	8.9	0.7	3.8

Table continued on next page.

City	Car/Truck/Van		Public Transportation			Bicycle	Walked	Other Means	Worked at Home
	Drove Alone	Car-pooled	Bus	Subway	Railroad				
Manchester, NH	81.0	10.4	1.3	0.1	0.0	0.1	2.9	0.7	3.6
McAllen, TX	75.4	9.5	0.8	0.0	0.0	0.1	1.5	6.7	6.0
Miami, FL	69.4	10.4	10.0	0.7	0.2	0.9	4.1	1.4	3.0
Midland, TX	83.9	11.2	0.3	0.0	0.0	0.2	1.1	1.1	2.3
Minneapolis, MN	61.5	8.0	12.8	0.4	0.5	3.8	6.5	1.2	5.4
Montgomery, AL	85.4	9.8	0.8	0.0	0.0	0.2	1.4	0.3	2.1
Nashville, TN	79.2	10.9	2.2	0.0	0.1	0.3	1.9	1.1	4.3
New Orleans, LA	70.1	10.4	6.5	0.0	0.0	2.2	5.3	2.3	3.1
New York, NY	22.4	4.8	11.7	42.1	1.7	0.9	10.2	2.3	4.0
Oklahoma City, OK	81.9	11.4	0.5	0.0	0.0	0.2	1.7	0.9	3.4
Omaha, NE	81.8	10.2	1.4	0.0	0.0	0.2	2.6	0.8	3.0
Orlando, FL	78.7	8.9	4.8	0.0	0.0	0.4	2.0	1.6	3.5
Oxnard, CA	71.5	21.2	1.5	0.0	0.1	0.6	1.6	0.9	2.6
Peoria, IL	81.3	8.9	3.0	0.0	0.0	0.5	2.6	1.2	2.5
Philadelphia, PA	49.9	9.0	18.7	4.4	2.7	2.0	8.6	1.5	3.0
Phoenix, AZ	75.0	12.1	3.2	0.1	0.0	0.7	1.9	1.8	5.1
Pittsburgh, PA	54.1	10.4	17.3	0.2	0.2	1.5	10.9	1.8	3.8
Portland, OR	58.3	9.0	9.7	0.7	0.2	6.2	5.7	2.5	7.7
Providence, RI	58.8	13.8	7.9	0.1	1.0	1.3	10.2	2.4	4.2
Provo, UT	60.8	14.2	1.7	0.0	0.0	3.4	13.1	1.2	5.7
Raleigh, NC	80.7	9.0	1.8	0.0	0.0	0.6	1.7	1.0	5.1
Reno, NV	76.7	10.4	3.2	0.0	0.0	1.1	3.2	1.9	3.4
Richmond, VA	71.9	10.5	5.3	0.1	0.0	2.1	4.3	1.4	4.4
Riverside, CA	77.1	11.6	2.0	0.0	1.2	0.9	2.7	1.0	3.5
Rochester, MN	75.1	10.2	4.7	0.1	0.0	0.8	3.8	1.1	4.2
Salem, OR	74.7	12.1	1.7	0.0	0.0	1.7	4.8	1.1	3.9
Salt Lake City, UT	67.9	12.5	5.3	0.3	0.2	2.9	5.2	2.6	3.3
San Antonio, TX	79.3	11.0	3.2	0.0	0.0	0.2	2.0	1.1	3.1
San Diego, CA	74.9	9.5	3.7	0.0	0.1	1.0	2.9	1.3	6.6
San Francisco, CA	36.6	7.6	23.4	6.2	1.2	3.6	9.6	4.5	7.1
San Jose, CA	78.4	10.5	2.4	0.1	0.6	0.9	1.6	1.5	4.0
Santa Rosa, CA	78.6	10.3	1.9	0.0	0.0	1.0	2.9	0.8	4.6
Savannah, GA	75.8	11.1	3.8	0.0	0.0	1.2	4.1	0.8	3.2
Seattle, WA	52.0	8.8	17.7	0.4	0.1	3.8	9.1	1.5	6.6
Sioux Falls, SD	84.3	7.8	1.2	0.0	0.0	0.5	2.1	1.3	2.7
Spokane, WA	75.6	10.3	4.0	0.0	0.0	1.1	3.8	0.7	4.5
Springfield, MO	81.9	8.8	0.8	0.0	0.0	0.7	3.4	1.3	3.1
Tallahassee, FL	81.0	8.2	2.2	0.0	0.0	0.9	3.4	1.2	3.1
Tampa, FL	76.5	9.5	3.0	0.1	0.0	1.6	2.4	1.6	5.3
Topeka, KS	80.9	11.9	1.1	0.0	0.0	0.3	2.2	0.8	2.8
Tulsa, OK	81.5	10.8	0.9	0.0	0.0	0.3	1.9	1.1	3.6
Virginia Beach, VA	81.7	8.5	0.8	0.0	0.0	0.6	2.4	1.0	4.9
Washington, DC	34.0	5.9	17.2	20.9	0.4	3.6	11.9	1.3	4.8
Wichita, KS	84.6	9.1	0.6	0.0	0.0	0.3	1.3	1.0	3.0
Wilmington, NC	78.2	9.7	0.7	0.0	0.0	1.4	3.1	1.6	5.3
Worcester, MA	74.7	10.3	2.7	0.2	0.6	0.2	6.3	1.1	3.9
U.S.	76.4	9.7	2.6	1.7	0.5	0.6	2.8	1.3	4.3

Note: Figures are percentages and cover workers 16 years of age and older
Source: U.S. Census Bureau, 2010-2012 American Community Survey 3-Year Estimates

Means of Transportation to Work: Metro Area

Metro Area	Car/Truck/Van		Public Transportation			Bicycle	Walked	Other Means	Worked at Home
	Drove Alone	Car-pooled	Bus	Subway	Railroad				
Abilene, TX	80.1	11.1	0.8	0.0	0.0	0.2	2.5	2.7	2.4
Albuquerque, NM	80.2	9.4	1.4	0.0	0.3	0.9	2.0	1.2	4.5
Anchorage, AK	74.1	12.9	1.8	0.0	0.0	1.1	2.6	3.1	4.4
Ann Arbor, MI	73.0	8.2	4.8	0.0	0.0	1.7	6.6	0.6	5.1
Athens, GA	77.3	9.4	1.8	0.0	0.0	1.3	3.9	1.6	4.7
Atlanta, GA	77.8	10.4	2.3	0.7	0.1	0.2	1.4	1.4	5.7
Austin, TX	75.4	10.9	2.2	0.0	0.1	0.8	2.0	1.6	7.0
Baltimore, MD	76.4	9.4	4.4	0.9	0.8	0.2	2.6	1.1	4.1
Billings, MT	79.4	10.5	1.0	0.0	0.0	0.8	3.6	1.0	3.6
Boise City, ID	78.9	8.5	0.4	0.0	0.0	1.4	2.0	1.8	6.9
Boston, MA	68.8	7.7	4.0	5.5	2.0	0.8	5.4	1.3	4.5
Boulder, CO	65.1	8.2	5.1	0.0	0.0	4.3	4.9	1.3	11.1
Cape Coral, FL	76.6	12.1	1.3	0.0	0.0	1.0	1.0	2.2	5.8
Cedar Rapids, IA	81.2	9.0	1.0	0.0	0.0	0.4	2.7	1.3	4.5
Charleston, SC	80.4	9.0	1.3	0.0	0.0	0.9	3.0	0.9	4.4
Charlotte, NC	79.8	10.0	1.8	0.2	0.1	0.2	1.5	0.9	5.4
Chicago, IL	70.9	8.6	4.6	3.5	3.1	0.6	3.2	1.1	4.3
Cincinnati, OH	83.3	8.2	2.0	0.0	0.0	0.1	2.1	0.6	3.7
Clarksville, TN	82.3	10.4	0.5	0.0	0.0	0.1	2.8	1.2	2.7
Colorado Spgs, CO	77.7	9.7	0.6	0.0	0.0	0.4	4.7	1.0	5.8
Columbia, MO	79.2	10.3	0.6	0.0	0.0	1.0	4.5	0.7	3.7
Columbus, OH	82.4	8.0	1.6	0.0	0.0	0.4	2.2	0.9	4.4
Dallas, TX	81.1	10.2	1.0	0.1	0.3	0.2	1.2	1.3	4.6
Davenport, IA	84.0	8.5	0.9	0.0	0.0	0.4	1.9	1.0	3.3
Denver, CO	76.2	9.3	3.6	0.4	0.2	0.9	2.1	1.2	6.1
Des Moines, IA	83.0	9.2	1.1	0.0	0.0	0.2	1.5	0.7	4.3
Durham, NC	74.0	11.0	4.0	0.0	0.0	1.1	3.0	1.6	5.2
El Paso, TX	79.1	11.2	1.8	0.0	0.0	0.1	2.1	2.8	2.9
Erie, PA	81.2	9.0	1.8	0.0	0.0	0.2	3.9	0.8	3.1
Eugene, OR	71.1	9.8	3.0	0.0	0.0	4.5	4.8	0.9	5.9
Fargo, ND	82.2	7.6	0.8	0.0	0.0	0.6	4.0	0.8	3.9
Fayetteville, NC	82.7	9.6	0.5	0.0	0.0	0.2	3.1	1.5	2.3
Ft. Collins, CO	76.1	8.4	1.0	0.0	0.0	3.8	2.8	1.2	6.8
Ft. Wayne, IN	85.5	7.4	0.4	0.0	0.0	0.3	1.3	0.8	4.2
Ft. Worth, TX	81.1	10.2	1.0	0.1	0.3	0.2	1.2	1.3	4.6
Gainesville, FL	72.9	11.1	4.2	0.0	0.0	3.2	3.1	1.3	4.3
Grand Rapids, MI	82.8	8.9	1.4	0.0	0.0	0.4	1.8	0.6	4.1
Green Bay, WI	82.8	8.2	0.7	0.0	0.0	0.3	2.4	1.1	4.5
Greensboro, NC	83.2	9.7	1.1	0.0	0.0	0.1	1.7	0.7	3.6
Honolulu, HI	64.4	14.7	8.2	0.0	0.0	1.0	5.4	2.8	3.5
Houston, TX	79.9	11.1	2.4	0.0	0.0	0.3	1.4	1.6	3.4
Huntsville, AL	86.3	7.9	0.3	0.1	0.0	0.1	1.1	1.3	2.8
Indianapolis, IN	83.8	8.6	1.1	0.0	0.0	0.3	1.6	0.8	3.7
Jacksonville, FL	81.3	9.8	1.2	0.0	0.0	0.6	1.3	1.2	4.7
Kansas City, MO	83.2	9.0	1.1	0.0	0.0	0.2	1.3	1.0	4.2
Lafayette, LA	82.6	11.1	0.7	0.0	0.0	0.4	1.7	1.2	2.2
Las Vegas, NV	78.8	10.7	3.8	0.0	0.0	0.4	1.8	1.5	3.0
Lexington, KY	80.7	10.0	1.0	0.0	0.0	0.7	3.2	0.6	3.7
Lincoln, NE	80.5	9.9	1.0	0.0	0.0	1.6	2.6	0.6	3.8
Little Rock, AR	84.7	9.9	0.6	0.0	0.0	0.1	1.2	0.9	2.6
Los Angeles, CA	73.8	10.4	5.5	0.3	0.2	0.9	2.7	1.2	5.0
Louisville, KY	83.5	8.8	1.9	0.0	0.0	0.2	1.6	1.0	3.0
Lubbock, TX	82.1	10.5	0.8	0.0	0.0	0.4	1.9	0.9	3.4
Madison, WI	73.9	8.8	4.2	0.0	0.0	2.7	5.1	0.9	4.5

Table continued on next page.

Metro Area	Car/Truck/Van Drove Alone	Car/Truck/Van Car-pooled	Public Transportation Bus	Public Transportation Subway	Public Transportation Railroad	Bicycle	Walked	Other Means	Worked at Home
Manchester, NH	82.1	8.2	0.8	0.0	0.1	0.0	2.0	0.7	6.1
McAllen, TX	78.4	11.5	0.2	0.0	0.0	0.1	1.2	4.0	4.5
Miami, FL	78.3	9.6	3.3	0.3	0.2	0.6	1.8	1.4	4.6
Midland, TX	84.3	10.1	0.2	0.0	0.0	0.2	1.0	1.0	3.3
Minneapolis, MN	78.2	8.4	4.3	0.1	0.1	0.8	2.2	0.9	4.9
Montgomery, AL	85.8	9.3	0.5	0.0	0.0	0.1	1.1	0.8	2.4
Nashville, TN	81.9	10.0	1.1	0.0	0.1	0.2	1.2	1.0	4.6
New Orleans, LA	78.9	10.5	2.6	0.0	0.0	0.9	2.6	2.0	2.5
New York, NY	50.1	6.7	8.2	18.8	3.6	0.5	6.1	2.0	4.0
Oklahoma City, OK	82.7	10.5	0.4	0.0	0.0	0.3	1.7	1.1	3.4
Omaha, NE	83.4	9.5	0.9	0.0	0.0	0.2	1.8	0.8	3.5
Orlando, FL	81.2	9.1	2.0	0.0	0.0	0.5	1.2	1.6	4.4
Oxnard, CA	75.7	13.3	1.0	0.0	0.3	0.8	2.1	1.1	5.6
Peoria, IL	84.6	8.5	1.1	0.0	0.0	0.3	2.0	0.7	2.9
Philadelphia, PA	73.6	8.0	5.5	1.5	2.2	0.6	3.7	0.9	4.0
Phoenix, AZ	76.6	11.6	1.9	0.1	0.0	0.8	1.5	1.8	5.8
Pittsburgh, PA	77.1	9.1	5.0	0.1	0.0	0.3	3.5	1.3	3.6
Portland, OR	71.2	9.4	4.7	0.5	0.2	2.3	3.5	1.7	6.4
Providence, RI	80.7	8.7	1.7	0.2	0.8	0.3	3.2	1.0	3.3
Provo, UT	73.1	12.8	1.6	0.0	0.0	1.2	4.3	1.0	6.0
Raleigh, NC	81.0	9.1	0.9	0.0	0.0	0.3	1.2	1.2	6.2
Reno, NV	77.8	10.6	2.3	0.0	0.0	0.8	2.2	1.9	4.4
Richmond, VA	81.7	9.4	1.6	0.0	0.0	0.4	1.3	0.8	4.6
Riverside, CA	76.9	14.0	1.1	0.0	0.4	0.4	1.6	1.2	4.3
Rochester, MN	76.9	10.5	3.4	0.1	0.0	0.5	3.0	0.9	4.7
Salem, OR	74.2	13.8	1.3	0.0	0.0	1.1	4.2	1.0	4.3
Salt Lake City, UT	76.2	11.9	2.5	0.2	0.3	0.8	2.1	1.6	4.4
San Antonio, TX	79.4	11.1	2.2	0.0	0.0	0.2	1.9	1.2	4.1
San Diego, CA	76.3	10.0	2.6	0.0	0.3	0.8	2.7	1.3	6.2
San Francisco, CA	61.2	10.1	7.8	5.5	0.9	1.8	4.3	2.1	6.2
San Jose, CA	76.8	10.3	2.1	0.1	0.9	1.8	1.9	1.3	4.8
Santa Rosa, CA	76.3	10.0	1.6	0.0	0.0	1.0	3.0	1.2	6.8
Savannah, GA	81.5	9.3	1.7	0.0	0.0	0.5	2.0	1.1	3.8
Seattle, WA	70.2	10.3	7.7	0.1	0.4	1.1	3.6	1.2	5.4
Sioux Falls, SD	83.4	8.1	0.8	0.0	0.0	0.4	2.2	1.2	3.8
Spokane, WA	76.4	10.3	2.7	0.0	0.0	0.7	3.1	1.0	5.8
Springfield, MO	82.2	9.9	0.4	0.0	0.0	0.3	2.1	1.1	4.0
Tallahassee, FL	81.8	10.0	1.4	0.0	0.0	0.5	2.2	1.2	3.1
Tampa, FL	80.3	9.5	1.3	0.0	0.0	0.8	1.5	1.4	5.2
Topeka, KS	81.6	11.4	0.6	0.0	0.0	0.2	2.0	0.6	3.5
Tulsa, OK	83.0	10.2	0.5	0.0	0.0	0.2	1.3	1.1	3.6
Virginia Beach, VA	80.7	8.7	1.8	0.0	0.0	0.4	2.9	1.1	4.4
Washington, DC	65.8	10.3	5.7	7.8	0.7	0.7	3.3	1.0	4.8
Wichita, KS	85.2	8.6	0.4	0.0	0.0	0.3	1.3	0.9	3.2
Wilmington, NC	79.5	11.8	0.4	0.0	0.0	0.6	1.5	1.3	4.8
Worcester, MA	82.0	8.7	0.8	0.1	0.7	0.2	2.8	0.8	3.9
U.S.	76.4	9.7	2.6	1.7	0.5	0.6	2.8	1.3	4.3

Note: Figures are percentages and cover workers 16 years of age and older; (1) Figures cover the Metropolitan Statistical Area—see Appendix B for areas included
Source: U.S. Census Bureau, 2010-2012 American Community Survey 3-Year Estimates

Travel Time to Work: City

City	Less Than 10 Minutes	10 to 19 Minutes	20 to 29 Minutes	30 to 44 Minutes	45 to 59 Minutes	60 to 89 Minutes	90 Minutes or More
Abilene, TX	24.2	56.3	11.3	3.9	1.7	1.6	1.1
Albuquerque, NM	10.6	37.3	28.6	16.7	3.3	2.0	1.6
Anchorage, AK	16.0	42.9	22.7	12.7	2.7	1.3	1.6
Ann Arbor, MI	17.9	44.4	18.2	10.8	4.7	3.1	0.7
Athens, GA	17.5	49.9	17.2	7.7	2.8	2.9	2.0
Atlanta, GA	8.9	31.5	26.6	20.5	5.6	4.2	2.7
Austin, TX	11.5	34.6	24.1	20.6	4.5	3.2	1.6
Baltimore, MD	7.2	25.6	23.1	23.8	7.5	7.7	5.2
Billings, MT	20.9	50.2	18.8	5.4	1.6	0.8	2.4
Boise City, ID	17.1	45.9	22.4	10.6	1.4	1.2	1.3
Boston, MA	7.9	22.5	20.8	28.3	10.4	8.3	1.8
Boulder, CO	19.8	43.6	16.4	10.6	5.5	2.8	1.2
Cape Coral, FL	8.3	25.9	23.0	26.4	10.1	4.0	2.3
Cedar Rapids, IA	20.5	46.6	17.3	10.5	2.5	1.3	1.3
Charleston, SC	13.0	35.0	28.2	16.0	3.5	2.7	1.6
Charlotte, NC	10.0	30.2	26.5	23.2	5.4	2.5	2.2
Chicago, IL	5.3	18.3	18.6	29.2	13.7	11.2	3.6
Cincinnati, OH	11.7	35.1	26.7	17.7	4.2	2.6	2.0
Clarksville, TN	12.9	35.8	25.5	15.8	5.2	4.0	0.9
Colorado Spgs, CO	14.0	38.6	26.4	14.4	2.9	2.3	1.4
Columbia, MO	18.9	53.2	14.4	8.6	2.8	1.1	1.0
Columbus, OH	10.3	34.7	30.7	18.6	2.8	1.7	1.2
Dallas, TX	9.0	29.6	23.1	25.3	7.0	4.4	1.7
Davenport, IA	18.5	49.3	21.1	7.4	1.6	1.1	1.0
Denver, CO	9.7	31.1	25.2	22.2	6.6	3.8	1.5
Des Moines, IA	15.6	41.3	28.3	10.0	2.6	1.2	0.9
Durham, NC	12.7	40.7	23.6	15.8	3.1	2.2	1.8
El Paso, TX	9.5	32.5	29.2	21.5	3.9	2.1	1.3
Erie, PA	20.0	50.8	15.7	8.8	2.5	1.4	0.7
Eugene, OR	18.8	49.0	20.4	6.9	2.0	2.0	0.9
Fargo, ND	24.7	54.7	13.3	3.2	1.4	1.4	1.3
Fayetteville, NC	17.0	38.5	24.2	12.5	3.8	1.8	2.0
Ft. Collins, CO	18.4	45.3	17.7	10.2	3.2	3.0	2.1
Ft. Wayne, IN	11.2	43.4	29.2	11.1	2.4	1.5	1.2
Ft. Worth, TX	9.2	29.2	23.2	23.3	8.0	5.7	1.5
Gainesville, FL	18.1	50.9	19.3	8.1	1.8	1.2	0.6
Grand Rapids, MI	15.8	44.5	23.2	9.2	3.2	2.9	1.3
Green Bay, WI	18.0	50.0	17.2	8.5	2.8	2.2	1.3
Greensboro, NC	13.0	45.0	22.6	13.4	2.3	1.8	1.9
Honolulu, HI	8.9	36.0	24.7	22.4	4.3	2.9	0.8
Houston, TX	8.6	28.0	24.4	25.2	7.2	5.0	1.7
Huntsville, AL	14.5	45.2	24.9	11.4	1.9	1.0	1.0
Indianapolis, IN	10.9	31.0	29.1	21.1	4.3	2.5	1.0
Jacksonville, FL	8.2	31.3	30.1	22.1	4.7	2.5	1.1
Kansas City, MO	12.1	35.4	26.7	19.3	3.5	1.8	1.2
Lafayette, LA	18.2	44.5	18.9	11.4	1.9	2.6	2.5
Las Vegas, NV	7.7	25.6	28.9	28.6	4.6	2.7	1.9
Lexington, KY	13.0	42.9	25.6	13.1	2.7	1.8	0.9
Lincoln, NE	16.8	46.8	23.0	8.0	2.3	1.9	1.1
Little Rock, AR	15.2	43.8	26.1	10.8	2.1	1.5	0.6
Los Angeles, CA	7.3	24.7	20.3	26.9	9.4	8.5	3.0
Louisville, KY	9.9	33.4	29.7	19.7	3.5	2.0	1.7
Lubbock, TX	20.4	58.1	12.9	5.0	1.5	1.0	1.0
Madison, WI	15.0	42.1	24.6	12.5	2.6	2.0	1.1
Manchester, NH	12.5	41.3	19.3	14.6	5.0	5.0	2.2

Table continued on next page.

City	Less Than 10 Minutes	10 to 19 Minutes	20 to 29 Minutes	30 to 44 Minutes	45 to 59 Minutes	60 to 89 Minutes	90 Minutes or More
McAllen, TX	17.2	44.4	21.7	10.6	2.1	1.7	2.4
Miami, FL	6.3	25.3	28.1	26.3	7.2	5.0	1.8
Midland, TX	19.8	48.0	15.8	10.4	1.8	1.8	2.3
Minneapolis, MN	8.3	35.0	30.4	18.5	3.7	2.8	1.3
Montgomery, AL	13.0	45.7	26.0	10.9	2.1	1.4	0.9
Nashville, TN	8.9	30.8	28.0	23.8	5.2	2.1	1.1
New Orleans, LA	10.9	35.5	24.9	18.2	4.5	4.2	1.9
New York, NY	4.5	13.9	14.7	27.4	15.2	17.9	6.4
Oklahoma City, OK	13.3	37.5	28.3	16.1	2.3	1.3	1.2
Omaha, NE	15.1	43.1	27.0	11.1	1.4	1.3	1.0
Orlando, FL	8.6	33.7	25.7	20.8	5.6	3.0	2.5
Oxnard, CA	9.8	36.8	24.2	19.7	4.6	3.2	1.8
Peoria, IL	16.4	47.4	24.3	6.7	2.4	2.0	0.7
Philadelphia, PA	6.3	20.8	20.1	27.0	12.9	9.2	3.7
Phoenix, AZ	9.1	29.1	25.1	25.8	6.2	3.4	1.3
Pittsburgh, PA	10.9	32.7	25.6	20.5	5.8	3.1	1.4
Portland, OR	9.0	31.3	26.6	21.8	5.9	3.8	1.7
Providence, RI	15.9	41.6	18.4	13.4	4.3	4.3	2.1
Provo, UT	25.3	44.6	16.5	7.0	3.0	2.4	1.2
Raleigh, NC	12.0	36.6	27.3	17.4	3.3	2.2	1.0
Reno, NV	14.8	45.3	22.9	9.2	3.4	3.0	1.4
Richmond, VA	11.6	38.5	26.8	14.9	3.9	2.4	1.9
Riverside, CA	11.1	28.5	19.7	19.2	7.9	8.4	5.2
Rochester, MN	19.9	57.7	12.5	4.7	1.9	2.1	1.2
Salem, OR	17.2	41.3	20.2	12.0	3.9	3.8	1.6
Salt Lake City, UT	14.8	45.9	20.3	11.7	3.6	2.2	1.4
San Antonio, TX	10.2	32.0	27.4	21.4	4.6	2.7	1.6
San Diego, CA	9.1	35.3	28.4	19.5	3.7	2.5	1.5
San Francisco, CA	5.0	22.4	21.6	28.3	10.9	9.4	2.3
San Jose, CA	7.0	28.5	26.0	24.5	6.9	5.4	1.7
Santa Rosa, CA	14.5	41.1	19.6	12.3	4.4	5.3	2.8
Savannah, GA	11.5	42.9	28.3	11.2	3.6	1.6	1.0
Seattle, WA	9.0	28.1	24.4	25.5	7.8	3.8	1.4
Sioux Falls, SD	16.1	55.0	20.4	4.5	1.7	1.5	0.9
Spokane, WA	16.9	39.7	24.2	13.2	2.9	1.6	1.5
Springfield, MO	19.1	46.6	22.7	6.9	2.0	1.7	1.0
Tallahassee, FL	15.6	43.8	23.5	13.0	1.9	1.5	0.7
Tampa, FL	13.0	34.1	22.6	19.5	5.6	3.4	1.7
Topeka, KS	19.3	55.2	15.3	6.3	1.2	1.8	0.9
Tulsa, OK	15.9	43.1	25.1	11.2	2.0	1.5	1.2
Virginia Beach, VA	10.8	31.5	26.1	23.4	5.0	2.2	1.0
Washington, DC	5.3	20.4	23.5	30.8	10.8	6.9	2.2
Wichita, KS	14.0	48.7	24.4	9.7	1.4	1.2	0.7
Wilmington, NC	18.3	50.0	18.1	7.3	3.1	2.1	1.1
Worcester, MA	12.5	39.0	19.2	16.2	6.0	5.2	1.9
U.S.	13.5	29.8	20.9	20.1	7.5	5.6	2.5

Note: Figures are percentages and include workers 16 years old and over
Source: U.S. Census Bureau, 2010-2012 American Community Survey 3-Year Estimates

Travel Time to Work: Metro Area

Metro Area	Less Than 10 Minutes	10 to 19 Minutes	20 to 29 Minutes	30 to 44 Minutes	45 to 59 Minutes	60 to 89 Minutes	90 Minutes or More
Abilene, TX	24.2	47.2	15.5	7.6	2.3	1.8	1.5
Albuquerque, NM	11.1	33.1	25.2	20.0	5.9	2.9	1.8
Anchorage, AK	15.7	40.1	20.9	12.6	4.4	4.2	2.1
Ann Arbor, MI	13.0	34.8	22.9	17.7	6.6	3.9	1.1
Athens, GA	13.7	42.7	21.4	13.1	3.5	3.2	2.4
Atlanta, GA	8.0	23.3	20.2	25.3	11.7	8.6	2.9
Austin, TX	11.3	29.2	22.3	22.9	7.8	4.7	1.8
Baltimore, MD	8.2	23.7	21.5	24.4	10.2	8.1	3.7
Billings, MT	19.2	43.4	21.9	9.0	2.2	1.4	2.9
Boise City, ID	14.6	35.0	25.1	17.6	4.1	2.2	1.3
Boston, MA	10.6	24.1	18.7	24.0	10.9	8.9	2.7
Boulder, CO	15.7	35.3	20.9	16.9	6.0	3.7	1.4
Cape Coral, FL	9.1	28.2	21.6	25.5	8.7	4.4	2.6
Cedar Rapids, IA	19.7	38.1	20.9	13.5	4.3	2.3	1.2
Charleston, SC	10.2	29.8	25.7	21.9	7.5	3.3	1.6
Charlotte, NC	10.3	28.8	23.8	24.1	7.6	3.3	2.0
Chicago, IL	9.1	22.6	18.7	24.8	11.7	9.9	3.2
Cincinnati, OH	11.4	29.1	25.4	22.6	6.9	3.3	1.4
Clarksville, TN	14.8	32.9	23.1	17.7	6.2	3.8	1.5
Colorado Spgs, CO	14.2	35.1	25.2	16.8	4.4	2.7	1.7
Columbia, MO	16.2	45.2	19.4	13.2	3.7	1.2	1.1
Columbus, OH	12.2	30.3	27.0	21.3	5.3	2.5	1.3
Dallas, TX	10.0	26.7	21.3	25.1	9.5	5.6	1.8
Davenport, IA	18.1	39.1	23.8	12.9	2.9	1.8	1.4
Denver, CO	9.1	26.4	23.7	25.6	8.6	4.8	1.9
Des Moines, IA	15.4	36.3	28.5	14.1	3.2	1.5	1.1
Durham, NC	11.4	34.6	25.1	18.9	5.6	3.0	1.5
El Paso, TX	9.8	31.2	28.3	22.5	4.3	2.6	1.4
Erie, PA	19.3	39.2	21.9	14.0	3.1	1.4	1.1
Eugene, OR	17.6	42.2	21.7	11.3	3.0	2.5	1.7
Fargo, ND	22.4	48.6	16.6	7.1	2.2	1.7	1.4
Fayetteville, NC	13.6	33.7	25.7	17.8	4.9	2.1	2.1
Ft. Collins, CO	15.9	38.9	19.2	14.4	5.0	4.2	2.5
Ft. Wayne, IN	12.7	37.0	29.6	14.4	3.4	1.6	1.3
Ft. Worth, TX	10.0	26.7	21.3	25.1	9.5	5.6	1.8
Gainesville, FL	14.0	39.7	23.1	15.8	4.0	2.2	1.2
Grand Rapids, MI	14.5	35.0	25.0	15.9	5.2	2.9	1.5
Green Bay, WI	17.9	40.8	22.0	12.9	3.3	1.9	1.3
Greensboro, NC	12.6	37.6	24.3	17.2	4.3	2.0	1.9
Honolulu, HI	9.7	25.9	20.6	26.6	8.7	6.6	1.8
Houston, TX	8.7	25.2	21.1	25.5	10.3	7.1	2.0
Huntsville, AL	11.6	34.5	27.4	19.1	4.4	1.9	1.1
Indianapolis, IN	11.5	27.3	25.0	24.2	7.4	3.3	1.4
Jacksonville, FL	9.5	28.1	25.9	23.8	7.8	3.7	1.2
Kansas City, MO	13.4	31.4	25.1	20.7	5.8	2.4	1.2
Lafayette, LA	14.5	37.0	22.9	15.7	4.1	2.6	3.2
Las Vegas, NV	8.6	28.8	29.5	24.4	4.4	2.5	1.9
Lexington, KY	15.0	37.3	24.3	16.2	4.1	1.9	1.2
Lincoln, NE	16.7	43.6	23.8	10.2	2.7	2.0	1.2
Little Rock, AR	13.5	33.8	23.4	19.6	5.7	2.7	1.2
Los Angeles, CA	8.3	26.5	20.5	24.8	9.0	8.0	2.9
Louisville, KY	10.5	30.5	27.2	21.6	5.9	2.8	1.7
Lubbock, TX	19.5	53.5	15.6	7.5	1.9	1.0	1.1
Madison, WI	15.5	34.5	24.9	17.0	4.3	2.4	1.4
Manchester, NH	11.0	31.0	20.3	20.0	7.9	7.0	2.8

Table continued on next page.

Metro Area	Less Than 10 Minutes	10 to 19 Minutes	20 to 29 Minutes	30 to 44 Minutes	45 to 59 Minutes	60 to 89 Minutes	90 Minutes or More
McAllen, TX	14.3	38.4	23.0	17.7	2.7	1.8	2.1
Miami, FL	7.7	25.1	23.3	27.2	8.8	5.9	2.0
Midland, TX	18.2	46.7	17.3	11.1	2.5	1.9	2.3
Minneapolis, MN	10.9	28.4	25.1	22.9	7.5	3.9	1.3
Montgomery, AL	11.4	34.2	25.9	19.2	5.7	2.4	1.3
Nashville, TN	10.0	27.3	23.0	23.8	9.7	4.5	1.7
New Orleans, LA	11.1	31.5	21.5	20.1	7.7	5.8	2.2
New York, NY	7.8	19.9	16.8	23.7	11.9	14.0	5.9
Oklahoma City, OK	14.5	33.4	25.0	19.1	4.7	2.0	1.4
Omaha, NE	14.7	37.3	27.1	15.2	3.0	1.6	1.0
Orlando, FL	7.6	27.7	23.8	24.8	9.7	4.4	1.9
Oxnard, CA	14.7	31.7	20.6	18.7	6.4	5.3	2.7
Peoria, IL	16.8	34.9	26.6	14.9	3.4	2.0	1.3
Philadelphia, PA	10.2	25.8	20.3	22.9	10.4	7.4	2.9
Phoenix, AZ	10.0	27.3	23.0	25.3	8.4	4.5	1.5
Pittsburgh, PA	12.8	27.6	21.5	21.6	8.8	5.7	2.0
Portland, OR	11.5	29.1	23.5	22.1	7.7	4.3	1.8
Providence, RI	13.8	32.2	21.2	18.2	6.8	5.3	2.5
Provo, UT	18.9	35.5	20.4	14.3	5.9	3.5	1.5
Raleigh, NC	10.6	29.5	25.6	22.2	7.1	3.5	1.5
Reno, NV	13.0	38.9	25.7	14.0	3.7	2.9	1.8
Richmond, VA	9.4	30.4	27.1	21.9	6.1	2.9	2.2
Riverside, CA	11.0	27.8	17.7	18.7	8.7	10.2	5.9
Rochester, MN	18.6	44.9	20.5	9.7	2.9	2.0	1.5
Salem, OR	17.6	33.9	21.5	15.7	5.2	4.3	1.8
Salt Lake City, UT	11.0	34.1	25.8	19.9	5.2	2.6	1.4
San Antonio, TX	10.8	29.1	24.7	22.8	6.9	3.8	1.9
San Diego, CA	9.6	31.9	26.0	21.0	5.9	3.7	1.9
San Francisco, CA	8.2	25.7	19.2	24.2	10.8	9.3	2.6
San Jose, CA	8.9	30.6	25.1	21.8	6.9	5.0	1.6
Santa Rosa, CA	15.5	33.0	19.3	15.5	6.3	6.5	3.9
Savannah, GA	9.3	31.5	29.1	20.1	6.3	2.2	1.4
Seattle, WA	9.5	25.5	22.1	24.8	9.4	6.3	2.3
Sioux Falls, SD	16.7	45.7	23.9	8.7	2.4	1.5	1.1
Spokane, WA	14.6	36.1	25.0	16.7	4.3	2.0	1.4
Springfield, MO	14.8	35.6	24.0	16.9	4.9	2.1	1.6
Tallahassee, FL	11.4	34.4	24.7	20.8	5.7	2.1	0.9
Tampa, FL	10.5	29.2	22.6	22.6	8.8	4.6	1.8
Topeka, KS	16.9	42.5	21.6	11.6	3.7	2.7	1.2
Tulsa, OK	15.0	33.8	26.0	17.4	4.2	2.3	1.3
Virginia Beach, VA	10.9	32.7	23.6	21.4	6.5	3.3	1.5
Washington, DC	6.4	19.1	18.0	25.7	13.7	12.6	4.3
Wichita, KS	16.1	40.9	24.9	13.8	2.4	1.1	0.8
Wilmington, NC	13.9	38.2	22.7	15.4	4.9	3.1	1.8
Worcester, MA	12.7	27.1	19.4	20.5	9.1	8.4	2.9
U.S.	13.5	29.8	20.9	20.1	7.5	5.6	2.5

Note: Figures are percentages and include workers 16 years old and over; Figures cover the Metropolitan Statistical Area—see Appendix B for areas included
Source: U.S. Census Bureau, 2010-2012 American Community Survey 3-Year Estimates

2012 Presidential Election Results

City	Area Covered	Obama	Romney	Other
Abilene, TX	Taylor County	22.5	76.1	1.4
Albuquerque, NM	Bernalillo County	55.6	39.3	5.1
Anchorage, AK	Districts 18 – 32	41.5	54.5	4.0
Ann Arbor, MI	Washtenaw County	67.0	31.3	1.7
Athens, GA	Clarke County	63.3	34.4	2.4
Atlanta, GA	Fulton County	64.3	34.5	1.2
Austin, TX	Travis County	60.1	36.2	3.6
Baltimore, MD	Baltimore City	87.0	11.3	1.7
Billings, MT	Yellowstone County	38.4	58.9	2.8
Boise City, ID	Ada County	42.7	54.0	3.2
Boston, MA	Suffolk County	77.6	20.8	1.6
Boulder, CO	Boulder County	69.7	27.9	2.4
Cape Coral, FL	Lee County	41.4	57.9	0.7
Cedar Rapids, IA	Linn County	57.9	40.2	1.9
Charleston, SC	Charleston County	50.4	48.0	1.6
Charlotte, NC	Mecklenburg County	60.7	38.2	1.1
Chicago, IL	Cook County	74.0	24.6	1.3
Cincinnati, OH	Hamilton County	51.8	46.9	1.3
Clarksville, TN	Montgomery County	44.0	54.5	1.5
Colorado Spgs, CO	El Paso County	38.1	59.4	2.5
Columbia, MO	Boone County	50.2	47.1	2.7
Columbus, OH	Franklin County	60.1	38.4	1.5
Dallas, TX	Dallas County	57.1	41.7	1.2
Davenport, IA	Scott County	56.1	42.4	1.5
Denver, CO	Denver County	73.5	24.4	2.1
Des Moines, IA	Polk County	56.1	42.0	1.9
Durham, NC	Durham County	75.8	23.0	1.2
El Paso, TX	El Paso County	65.6	33.0	1.3
Erie, PA	Erie County	57.4	41.3	1.3
Eugene, OR	Lane County	59.7	36.4	3.9
Fargo, ND	Cass County	47.0	49.9	3.1
Fayetteville, NC	Cumberland County	59.4	39.7	0.9
Ft. Collins, CO	Larimer County	51.4	45.8	2.7
Ft. Wayne, IN	Allen County	40.9	57.6	1.5
Ft. Worth, TX	Tarrant County	41.4	57.1	1.4
Gainesville, FL	Alachua County	57.9	40.5	1.6
Grand Rapids, MI	Kent County	45.5	53.4	1.0
Green Bay, WI	Brown County	48.6	50.4	1.0
Greensboro, NC	Guilford County	57.7	41.2	1.1
Honolulu, HI	Honolulu County	68.9	29.8	1.3
Houston, TX	Harris County	49.4	49.3	1.3
Huntsville, AL	Madison County	40.0	58.6	1.4
Indianapolis, IN	Marion County	60.2	38.1	1.7
Jacksonville, FL	Duval County	47.8	51.4	0.8
Kansas City, MO	Jackson County	58.7	39.7	1.6
Lafayette, LA	Lafayette Parish	32.2	65.9	1.9
Las Vegas, NV	Clark County	56.4	41.9	1.8
Lexington, KY	Fayette County	49.3	48.3	2.3
Lincoln, NE	Lancaster County	49.0	49.3	1.7
Little Rock, AR	Pulaski County	54.7	43.3	2.0
Los Angeles, CA	Los Angeles County	68.6	29.1	2.3
Louisville, KY	Jefferson County	54.8	43.7	1.4
Lubbock, TX	Lubbock County	28.8	69.6	1.6
Madison, WI	Dane County	71.1	27.6	1.3
Manchester, NH	Hillsborough County	49.7	48.6	1.6
McAllen, TX	Hidalgo County	70.4	28.6	1.0

Table continued on next page.

City	Area Covered	Obama	Romney	Other
Miami, FL	Miami-Dade County	61.6	37.9	0.4
Midland, TX	Midland County	18.6	80.1	1.4
Minneapolis, MN	Hennepin County	62.3	35.3	2.4
Montgomery, AL	Montgomery County	61.9	37.6	0.5
Nashville, TN	Davidson County	58.4	39.9	1.7
New Orleans, LA	Orleans Parish	80.3	17.7	2.0
New York, NY	Bronx County	91.4	8.1	0.5
New York, NY	Kings County	82.0	16.9	1.1
New York, NY	New York County	83.7	14.9	1.3
New York, NY	Queens County	79.1	19.9	1.0
New York, NY	Richmond County	50.7	48.1	1.2
Oklahoma City, OK	Oklahoma County	41.7	58.3	0.0
Omaha, NE	Douglas County	47.2	51.4	1.4
Orlando, FL	Orange County	58.7	40.4	0.9
Oxnard, CA	Ventura County	51.7	46.1	2.2
Peoria, IL	Peoria County	51.3	46.9	1.8
Philadelphia, PA	Philadelphia County	85.3	14.0	0.7
Phoenix, AZ	Maricopa County	43.1	54.9	2.0
Pittsburgh, PA	Allegheny County	56.6	42.2	1.2
Portland, OR	Multnomah County	75.3	20.7	4.0
Providence, RI	Providence County	66.5	31.6	1.9
Provo, UT	Utah County	9.8	88.3	2.0
Raleigh, NC	Wake County	54.9	43.5	1.6
Reno, NV	Washoe County	50.7	47.2	2.1
Richmond, VA	Richmond City	77.0	21.4	1.6
Riverside, CA	Riverside County	48.8	49.2	2.0
Rochester, MN	Olmsted County	50.2	47.0	2.7
Salem, OR	Marion County	46.7	50.2	3.1
Salt Lake City, UT	Salt Lake County	38.8	58.2	3.0
San Antonio, TX	Bexar County	51.6	47.0	1.4
San Diego, CA	San Diego County	51.7	46.2	2.1
San Francisco, CA	San Francisco County	83.4	13.3	3.3
San Jose, CA	Santa Clara County	69.9	27.6	2.5
Santa Rosa, CA	Sonoma County	70.8	26.0	3.2
Savannah, GA	Chatham County	55.5	43.5	1.0
Seattle, WA	King County	68.8	28.8	2.3
Sioux Falls, SD	Minnehaha County	45.3	52.7	2.0
Spokane, WA	Spokane County	45.6	51.6	2.8
Springfield, MO	Christian County	25.8	72.4	1.8
Tallahassee, FL	Leon County	61.3	37.6	1.1
Tampa, FL	Hillsborough County	52.8	46.2	1.0
Topeka, KS	Shawnee County	48.0	49.7	2.2
Tulsa, OK	Tulsa County	36.3	63.7	0.0
Virginia Beach, VA	Virginia Beach City	48.0	50.5	1.6
Washington, DC	District of Columbia	91.1	7.1	1.8
Wichita, KS	Sedgwick County	39.0	58.7	2.3
Wilmington, NC	New Hanover County	47.0	51.5	1.5
Worcester, MA	Worcester County	53.7	44.5	1.8
U.S.	U.S.	51.0	47.2	1.8

Note: Results are percentages and may not add to 100% due to rounding
Source: Dave Leip's Atlas of U.S. Presidential Elections

House Price Index (HPI)

Metro Area[1]	National Ranking[3]	Quarterly Change (%)	One-Year Change (%)	Five-Year Change (%)
Abilene, TX	n/r	n/a	5.43	6.70
Albuquerque, NM	192	-0.50	0.73	-12.18
Anchorage, AK	100	1.15	4.18	4.32
Ann Arbor, MI	53	1.67	9.78	3.91
Athens, GA	85	2.17	5.31	-12.78
Atlanta, GA	66	1.07	7.12	-13.81
Austin, TX	46	2.40	10.34	12.60
Baltimore, MD	144	0.25	2.06	-11.68
Billings, MT	110	-1.21	3.64	4.89
Boise City, ID	31	2.08	13.31	-13.87
Boston, MA[2]	92	1.62	4.78	-0.62
Boulder, CO	57	1.56	9.37	9.08
Cape Coral, FL	39	2.14	11.67	4.86
Cedar Rapids, IA	204	-0.14	0.46	0.69
Charleston, SC	95	-0.30	4.62	-10.06
Charlotte, NC	91	0.84	4.85	-8.42
Chicago, IL[2]	114	1.08	3.37	-17.11
Cincinnati, OH	232	-0.85	-0.23	-6.61
Clarksville, TN	n/r	n/a	-0.03	2.36
Colorado Spgs, CO	116	-0.69	3.14	-2.78
Columbia, MO	175	0.87	1.29	3.61
Columbus, OH	125	0.05	2.90	-2.47
Dallas, TX[2]	70	1.18	6.77	6.22
Davenport, IA	180	-0.64	1.13	2.89
Denver, CO	44	1.58	10.95	11.71
Des Moines, IA	135	0.28	2.38	-0.87
Durham, NC	166	0.37	1.51	-2.44
El Paso, TX	203	-1.67	0.47	-5.06
Erie, PA	n/r	n/a	5.98	9.28
Eugene, OR	71	2.05	6.34	-11.52
Fargo, ND	64	1.47	7.30	11.67
Fayetteville, NC	280	1.32	-3.52	-4.73
Ft. Collins, CO	59	1.58	8.49	9.83
Ft. Wayne, IN	184	0.51	0.97	-0.07
Ft. Worth, TX[2]	82	0.99	5.42	4.04
Gainesville, FL	n/r	n/a	1.04	-23.19
Grand Rapids, MI	76	0.36	5.85	-1.98
Green Bay, WI	260	-0.49	-1.41	-7.47
Greensboro, NC	244	-1.22	-0.57	-6.33
Honolulu, HI	n/a	n/a	n/a	n/a
Houston, TX	69	1.85	6.81	9.89
Huntsville, AL	275	-2.36	-2.87	-6.81
Indianapolis, IN	156	-0.19	1.77	-0.89
Jacksonville, FL	65	1.46	7.30	-18.23
Kansas City, MO	177	-0.52	1.21	-5.53
Lafayette, LA	142	-0.08	2.15	3.31
Las Vegas, NV	5	5.14	24.65	-12.67
Lexington, KY	234	-1.83	-0.28	-2.31
Lincoln, NE	130	0.82	2.64	3.99
Little Rock, AR	221	-0.96	0.08	-0.55
Los Angeles, CA[2]	24	3.91	15.85	6.34
Louisville, KY	155	0.51	1.79	-0.61
Lubbock, TX	109	2.74	3.67	8.35
Madison, WI	164	-0.58	1.61	-3.32
Manchester, NH	158	0.42	1.76	-10.15

Table continued on next page.

Metro Area[1]	National Ranking[3]	Quarterly Change (%)	One-Year Change (%)	Five-Year Change (%)
McAllen, TX	n/r	n/a	0.43	-1.17
Miami, FL[2]	40	3.08	11.63	-7.55
Midland, TX	n/r	n/a	11.37	26.16
Minneapolis, MN	68	0.20	7.00	-7.57
Montgomery, AL	230	-0.17	-0.14	-10.39
Nashville, TN	77	1.56	5.74	-0.52
New Orleans, LA	137	-0.36	2.30	-0.81
New York, NY[2]	146	0.50	2.00	-9.63
Oklahoma City, OK	167	-0.62	1.47	3.64
Omaha, NE	131	0.99	2.60	1.08
Orlando, FL	43	1.92	11.31	-20.16
Oxnard, CA	20	3.60	16.68	6.98
Peoria, IL	217	0.07	0.16	0.07
Philadelphia, PA[2]	138	0.85	2.28	-4.79
Phoenix, AZ	14	3.72	18.13	-6.11
Pittsburgh, PA	132	-0.32	2.57	7.92
Portland, OR	52	1.20	9.84	-6.70
Providence, RI	224	-0.59	0.06	-12.41
Provo, UT	49	1.49	10.02	-7.51
Raleigh, NC	123	-0.09	2.97	-4.52
Reno, NV	11	3.13	20.69	-16.61
Richmond, VA	151	0.26	1.90	-13.49
Riverside, CA	6	5.73	23.29	9.91
Rochester, MN	153	-0.62	1.85	-2.65
Salem, OR	78	1.89	5.73	-16.87
Salt Lake City, UT	56	1.25	9.43	-4.31
San Antonio, TX	117	2.81	3.13	6.38
San Diego, CA	17	3.42	17.14	11.12
San Francisco, CA[2]	21	2.24	16.57	11.98
San Jose, CA	16	2.74	17.32	14.40
Santa Rosa, CA	9	5.16	21.72	6.99
Savannah, GA	93	1.96	4.73	-12.97
Seattle, WA[2]	48	1.67	10.02	-8.70
Sioux Falls, SD	122	-0.09	2.98	3.66
Spokane, WA	195	-1.18	0.66	-15.61
Springfield, MO	190	0.39	0.76	-5.12
Tallahassee, FL	106	-0.37	3.76	-20.12
Tampa, FL	47	2.63	10.17	-11.07
Topeka, KS	174	1.89	1.29	-0.51
Tulsa, OK	241	-1.56	-0.46	0.01
Virginia Beach, VA	237	-0.24	-0.35	-14.40
Washington, DC[2]	90	0.58	5.01	1.34
Wichita, KS	238	-0.82	-0.38	-1.58
Wilmington, NC	179	-0.87	1.20	-19.03
Worcester, MA[2]	168	0.84	1.46	-8.55
U.S.[4]	—	1.20	7.69	4.18

Note: The HPI is a weighted repeat sales index. It measures average price changes in repeat sales or refinancings on the same properties. This information is obtained by reviewing repeat mortgage transactions on single-family properties whose mortgages have been purchased or securitized by Fannie Mae or Freddie Mac in January 1975; (1) figures cover the Metropolitan Statistical Area (MSA) unless noted otherwise—see Appendix B for areas included; (2) Metropolitan Division—see Appendix B for areas included; (3) Rankings are based on annual percentage change, for all MSAs containing at least 15,000 transactions over the last 10 years and ranges from 1 to 283; (4) figures based on a weighted division average; all figures are for the period ended December 31, 2013; n/a not available; n/r not ranked
Source: Federal Housing Finance Agency, House Price Index, February 25, 2014

Year Housing Structure Built: City

City	2010 or Later	2000 -2009	1990 -1999	1980 -1989	1970 -1979	1960 -1969	1950 -1959	Before 1950	Median Year
Abilene, TX	0.7	9.8	8.9	17.2	13.7	12.4	20.4	16.8	1970
Albuquerque, NM	0.2	17.6	15.6	14.8	20.3	10.5	13.1	7.9	1979
Anchorage, AK	0.4	13.2	10.9	24.5	29.9	12.7	6.4	2.0	1980
Ann Arbor, MI	0.0	7.2	10.7	10.2	17.5	19.8	13.5	21.1	1968
Athens, GA	0.2	18.0	19.4	20.9	17.8	10.3	5.8	7.6	1984
Atlanta, GA	0.7	25.2	10.6	8.3	9.5	13.3	12.6	19.8	1975
Austin, TX	0.8	22.5	15.6	20.9	19.7	8.2	6.3	6.1	1985
Baltimore, MD	0.1	3.6	3.3	4.7	5.8	8.6	15.8	58.1	1944
Billings, MT	0.7	14.1	10.4	12.6	20.0	9.3	16.7	16.2	1974
Boise City, ID	0.3	13.5	22.6	14.4	22.3	6.9	7.9	12.1	1981
Boston, MA	0.3	6.7	4.2	5.6	7.0	7.5	7.3	61.4	<1940
Boulder, CO	0.9	10.2	10.3	16.0	24.2	17.6	9.7	11.2	1975
Cape Coral, FL	0.2	45.2	14.5	20.6	12.5	6.1	0.6	0.4	1997
Cedar Rapids, IA	0.4	14.3	13.8	6.9	13.8	14.3	13.8	22.7	1969
Charleston, SC	0.7	25.4	12.5	13.9	9.6	11.0	7.3	19.6	1982
Charlotte, NC	0.7	25.4	20.6	15.7	13.8	10.4	7.3	6.1	1988
Chicago, IL	0.2	8.8	4.1	3.6	6.6	9.7	12.6	54.3	1945
Cincinnati, OH	0.3	4.0	3.3	4.2	8.1	14.2	13.0	52.9	1947
Clarksville, TN	1.7	27.8	22.1	14.5	13.7	9.2	5.8	5.2	1991
Colorado Spgs, CO	0.4	18.2	15.2	19.1	19.3	11.0	8.1	8.6	1982
Columbia, MO	0.7	24.7	18.5	13.8	13.6	13.4	6.5	8.7	1986
Columbus, OH	0.4	12.4	15.7	13.3	14.8	13.5	11.7	18.2	1974
Dallas, TX	0.6	12.8	9.2	17.3	19.7	14.8	13.8	11.8	1975
Davenport, IA	0.3	9.0	6.4	5.3	12.0	12.0	17.2	37.9	1957
Denver, CO	0.8	14.2	6.6	8.3	14.6	12.4	15.6	27.6	1966
Des Moines, IA	0.2	7.9	7.1	6.1	13.3	10.5	15.9	38.9	1957
Durham, NC	1.1	21.7	18.6	17.9	11.4	11.4	6.9	11.0	1985
El Paso, TX	1.5	16.7	13.3	15.2	18.4	12.8	12.9	9.1	1978
Erie, PA	0.1	3.7	2.6	4.3	10.1	7.7	17.9	53.6	1947
Eugene, OR	0.4	13.6	17.5	8.8	23.0	13.4	9.5	13.6	1976
Fargo, ND	0.5	17.8	20.6	14.8	16.6	8.0	8.1	13.6	1983
Fayetteville, NC	0.7	17.7	18.1	16.7	18.9	14.3	8.7	4.9	1982
Ft. Collins, CO	0.4	21.1	20.2	18.4	20.7	7.9	3.5	7.9	1985
Ft. Wayne, IN	0.2	5.9	14.8	12.7	14.2	16.3	12.4	23.5	1969
Ft. Worth, TX	1.1	27.9	11.0	14.8	10.7	9.3	11.9	13.2	1983
Gainesville, FL	0.3	15.4	14.3	19.6	22.8	13.1	7.1	7.3	1980
Grand Rapids, MI	0.2	5.4	6.3	7.0	8.1	10.5	16.9	45.7	1953
Green Bay, WI	0.2	6.8	10.9	10.5	16.0	11.8	17.3	26.6	1965
Greensboro, NC	0.4	15.9	19.2	17.1	16.2	11.7	10.2	9.3	1982
Honolulu, HI	0.5	7.5	8.3	10.0	26.1	22.3	13.2	12.0	1971
Houston, TX	0.7	15.7	8.9	13.9	25.2	14.9	11.2	9.5	1976
Huntsville, AL	0.7	15.3	10.9	16.1	15.4	24.0	10.3	7.3	1975
Indianapolis, IN	0.3	10.5	12.4	11.4	13.5	14.6	14.1	23.3	1969
Jacksonville, FL	0.4	20.9	15.0	16.0	13.8	11.1	12.0	10.8	1981
Kansas City, MO	0.3	11.5	8.8	9.1	11.9	14.4	15.1	29.0	1964
Lafayette, LA	0.7	14.2	12.4	16.9	21.6	14.3	11.3	8.6	1977
Las Vegas, NV	0.4	23.9	33.0	18.4	11.3	7.3	4.5	1.3	1992
Lexington, KY	0.7	16.9	16.2	15.6	15.7	13.4	10.1	11.3	1980
Lincoln, NE	0.3	16.7	14.6	10.2	15.8	11.8	11.9	18.6	1975
Little Rock, AR	0.2	11.4	12.8	17.7	20.9	13.7	10.8	12.6	1976
Los Angeles, CA	0.3	6.4	5.5	10.3	13.5	14.5	18.2	31.3	1960
Louisville, KY	0.2	12.6	11.2	7.2	13.7	14.3	14.8	26.0	1966
Lubbock, TX	0.8	17.5	11.6	15.5	18.6	14.1	14.1	7.7	1978
Madison, WI	0.6	17.2	12.3	10.2	16.2	12.4	11.8	19.4	1974
Manchester, NH	0.1	6.2	6.1	14.2	10.1	6.9	10.1	46.5	1954

Table continued on next page.

City	2010 or Later	2000 -2009	1990 -1999	1980 -1989	1970 -1979	1960 -1969	1950 -1959	Before 1950	Median Year
McAllen, TX	1.1	27.9	20.7	18.5	18.0	5.6	5.5	2.7	1990
Miami, FL	0.6	20.1	5.4	7.6	13.1	10.3	16.1	26.8	1967
Midland, TX	0.7	12.0	8.4	22.1	18.1	11.9	20.5	6.3	1976
Minneapolis, MN	0.2	7.4	3.5	6.7	9.5	7.9	9.7	55.3	1943
Montgomery, AL	0.2	11.6	16.1	13.9	20.8	13.1	11.6	12.8	1976
Nashville, TN	0.6	15.5	11.8	17.2	18.0	13.2	11.8	11.8	1977
New Orleans, LA	0.8	8.5	3.8	7.2	15.0	11.1	12.3	41.3	1957
New York, NY	0.3	6.3	3.5	4.4	7.2	12.5	13.8	52.0	1948
Oklahoma City, OK	1.0	14.3	9.7	15.7	17.4	14.4	11.8	15.7	1975
Omaha, NE	0.2	5.4	9.1	10.2	18.7	15.6	12.9	27.9	1966
Orlando, FL	0.2	25.3	15.9	18.1	13.6	8.3	10.8	7.8	1985
Oxnard, CA	0.2	13.8	9.5	11.6	19.2	22.5	15.8	7.5	1972
Peoria, IL	0.7	9.3	7.8	6.8	15.8	12.6	14.7	32.4	1962
Philadelphia, PA	0.2	3.5	2.7	3.8	7.0	10.7	16.8	55.4	1946
Phoenix, AZ	0.3	18.3	16.2	18.8	20.7	10.0	10.5	5.2	1982
Pittsburgh, PA	0.1	3.9	2.7	4.5	5.8	8.1	13.0	62.0	<1940
Portland, OR	0.3	11.8	8.5	5.6	11.8	9.7	13.1	39.3	1958
Providence, RI	0.1	4.6	2.7	5.3	8.2	6.5	8.4	64.3	<1940
Provo, UT	0.5	14.4	18.5	12.2	19.9	11.6	8.1	14.8	1978
Raleigh, NC	0.8	29.4	21.1	18.4	11.4	8.2	5.3	5.6	1991
Reno, NV	0.7	21.7	18.2	13.8	21.5	9.6	7.0	7.6	1983
Richmond, VA	0.3	6.4	3.7	6.5	12.2	12.3	16.1	42.6	1955
Riverside, CA	0.3	13.1	10.1	14.2	19.8	11.8	18.4	12.2	1974
Rochester, MN	0.7	19.3	15.3	13.7	13.4	13.3	11.3	13.0	1979
Salem, OR	0.3	15.1	16.5	11.8	21.3	9.0	10.4	15.5	1977
Salt Lake City, UT	0.2	6.4	4.9	8.8	12.9	9.3	14.5	42.9	1955
San Antonio, TX	0.7	18.6	12.5	17.4	17.7	11.2	10.5	11.3	1980
San Diego, CA	0.4	10.7	10.9	17.7	22.2	13.2	12.9	12.1	1975
San Francisco, CA	0.2	6.9	4.4	5.1	6.8	8.1	9.5	58.9	1941
San Jose, CA	0.2	10.3	10.4	13.3	24.7	19.9	12.2	8.9	1974
Santa Rosa, CA	0.1	14.0	14.1	17.0	24.0	11.5	8.3	11.0	1978
Savannah, GA	0.8	11.1	7.7	10.6	16.6	13.9	15.3	23.9	1968
Seattle, WA	0.7	14.3	7.8	7.9	9.6	9.6	11.2	39.0	1960
Sioux Falls, SD	1.5	23.1	15.8	11.5	15.8	8.4	8.7	15.1	1982
Spokane, WA	0.3	8.3	9.0	8.4	14.4	6.0	15.8	37.8	1958
Springfield, MO	0.4	12.4	12.8	12.6	18.2	13.6	12.2	17.8	1974
Tallahassee, FL	0.4	20.8	17.5	19.7	17.9	10.1	7.9	5.7	1984
Tampa, FL	0.6	18.4	10.6	13.2	13.7	12.9	16.1	14.4	1975
Topeka, KS	0.3	7.8	8.5	10.8	14.1	16.8	17.0	24.7	1965
Tulsa, OK	0.4	6.4	8.6	14.4	21.6	14.6	17.2	16.7	1971
Virginia Beach, VA	0.4	11.5	13.6	28.7	23.0	13.7	6.6	2.6	1981
Washington, DC	0.3	8.2	3.0	4.4	7.5	12.8	14.0	49.8	1950
Wichita, KS	0.3	11.1	12.1	12.1	13.2	9.1	21.0	21.0	1969
Wilmington, NC	0.4	15.9	23.3	15.5	10.3	9.5	7.6	17.5	1983
Worcester, MA	0.3	4.6	4.4	9.4	8.6	6.3	9.7	56.8	1942
U.S.	0.5	14.9	13.8	13.9	15.9	11.1	10.9	19.0	1976

Note: Figures are percentages except for Median Year
Source: U.S. Census Bureau, 2010-2012 American Community Survey 3-Year Estimates

Year Housing Structure Built: Metro Area

Metro Area	2010 or Later	2000 -2009	1990 -1999	1980 -1989	1970 -1979	1960 -1969	1950 -1959	Before 1950	Median Year
Abilene, TX	0.9	11.2	9.1	17.6	14.9	11.0	17.1	18.1	1973
Albuquerque, NM	0.3	19.1	18.3	16.8	18.4	9.4	10.4	7.4	1983
Anchorage, AK	0.5	18.4	12.5	24.9	26.0	10.4	5.3	1.9	1983
Ann Arbor, MI	0.2	14.8	15.8	10.8	17.5	13.3	11.0	16.5	1975
Athens, GA	0.2	18.8	20.7	20.2	17.6	9.2	5.1	8.2	1985
Atlanta, GA	0.5	27.0	22.3	18.5	13.5	7.9	5.1	5.2	1990
Austin, TX	1.3	31.2	18.9	19.3	14.7	5.5	4.3	4.8	1991
Baltimore, MD	0.4	10.3	13.2	14.2	13.5	10.5	13.9	24.1	1971
Billings, MT	0.8	15.6	11.6	12.7	21.1	7.7	13.1	17.3	1976
Boise City, ID	0.6	28.5	22.8	10.3	17.9	5.0	5.2	9.8	1991
Boston, MA	0.3	8.1	7.1	10.6	11.0	10.4	11.2	41.3	1958
Boulder, CO	0.6	13.5	20.8	16.2	22.6	11.7	5.3	9.2	1981
Cape Coral, FL	0.2	34.4	18.1	21.6	15.8	5.7	2.8	1.4	1992
Cedar Rapids, IA	0.5	15.9	15.2	6.8	14.5	12.1	11.4	23.6	1972
Charleston, SC	0.8	26.3	16.3	17.4	15.9	9.5	6.3	7.5	1986
Charlotte, NC	0.8	27.0	20.8	15.4	12.5	9.2	7.0	7.3	1989
Chicago, IL	0.2	12.1	10.6	8.7	13.8	11.9	13.7	28.9	1966
Cincinnati, OH	0.4	12.8	14.4	10.8	13.3	11.5	12.7	24.2	1971
Clarksville, TN	1.3	23.3	21.8	13.6	14.7	10.2	6.8	8.3	1987
Colorado Spgs, CO	0.7	20.9	16.8	18.3	18.4	9.9	7.2	7.7	1984
Columbia, MO	0.4	21.5	19.6	13.9	17.4	11.7	5.7	9.7	1984
Columbus, OH	0.4	15.5	17.0	11.9	14.6	12.5	11.0	17.1	1976
Dallas, TX	0.9	23.6	16.2	19.7	15.6	9.7	7.9	6.3	1985
Davenport, IA	0.3	8.6	7.5	6.3	13.9	13.4	15.2	34.9	1960
Denver, CO	0.5	18.6	15.5	15.3	19.5	10.5	9.9	10.3	1980
Des Moines, IA	1.2	18.8	14.6	9.3	14.2	9.2	9.9	22.8	1976
Durham, NC	0.9	20.9	19.5	17.7	13.8	10.7	7.3	9.3	1985
El Paso, TX	1.8	19.1	14.6	16.0	17.4	11.5	11.5	8.4	1981
Erie, PA	0.1	7.1	8.8	8.9	14.7	9.7	15.2	35.4	1960
Eugene, OR	0.5	12.9	15.8	9.4	23.4	13.6	9.7	14.7	1975
Fargo, ND	1.0	20.2	17.2	11.4	18.3	8.1	9.0	14.7	1980
Fayetteville, NC	1.4	21.5	21.1	16.3	17.0	11.2	7.2	4.3	1986
Ft. Collins, CO	0.8	21.0	20.3	15.1	21.4	8.0	4.0	9.4	1985
Ft. Wayne, IN	0.4	10.6	15.4	11.5	14.3	14.0	11.2	22.7	1972
Ft. Worth, TX	0.9	23.6	16.2	19.7	15.6	9.7	7.9	6.3	1985
Gainesville, FL	0.5	21.3	20.2	19.8	18.1	9.4	5.5	5.1	1986
Grand Rapids, MI	0.3	12.6	15.5	11.8	13.5	10.4	12.0	23.9	1973
Green Bay, WI	0.5	15.5	16.6	11.2	15.6	9.7	10.2	20.7	1976
Greensboro, NC	0.5	16.4	19.1	15.7	15.4	11.4	10.3	11.2	1981
Honolulu, HI	0.5	11.1	12.5	12.6	25.1	19.3	11.3	7.6	1975
Houston, TX	1.2	25.3	14.4	16.5	20.2	9.6	6.9	5.8	1985
Huntsville, AL	1.2	21.9	18.8	17.5	12.3	15.2	7.3	5.8	1985
Indianapolis, IN	0.7	17.8	17.0	10.9	13.3	11.8	11.0	17.6	1977
Jacksonville, FL	0.5	24.6	17.3	17.8	13.7	8.8	8.9	8.3	1986
Kansas City, MO	0.3	15.0	14.1	12.8	15.8	12.4	12.3	17.3	1975
Lafayette, LA	1.6	18.9	15.6	18.4	19.6	10.7	7.8	7.4	1982
Las Vegas, NV	0.7	34.6	27.9	15.6	12.6	5.3	2.4	0.9	1995
Lexington, KY	0.7	18.5	17.2	15.0	15.6	11.8	8.9	12.3	1981
Lincoln, NE	0.4	16.7	15.0	9.8	16.3	11.2	10.9	19.7	1975
Little Rock, AR	1.2	19.9	17.9	16.7	18.2	10.8	7.8	7.6	1983
Los Angeles, CA	0.3	7.0	7.4	12.7	16.5	16.1	18.9	21.1	1966
Louisville, KY	0.3	15.0	14.6	10.0	15.6	12.7	12.3	19.4	1974
Lubbock, TX	0.8	17.3	12.4	15.6	18.0	13.5	13.9	8.7	1978
Madison, WI	0.5	18.1	15.4	11.0	16.8	10.2	9.1	18.8	1977
Manchester, NH	0.3	10.1	9.7	20.6	15.8	9.5	7.7	26.3	1974

Table continued on next page.

Metro Area	2010 or Later	2000 -2009	1990 -1999	1980 -1989	1970 -1979	1960 -1969	1950 -1959	Before 1950	Median Year
McAllen, TX	1.1	32.1	23.4	19.2	12.2	4.8	3.6	3.5	1993
Miami, FL	0.2	14.0	14.9	20.0	22.1	12.8	10.5	5.5	1980
Midland, TX	0.8	13.6	11.5	22.5	16.5	11.0	17.8	6.2	1979
Minneapolis, MN	0.3	15.3	14.5	14.9	15.5	10.2	10.2	19.1	1977
Montgomery, AL	0.7	17.2	19.8	13.9	18.5	11.6	8.5	9.7	1981
Nashville, TN	0.8	21.8	18.8	16.3	15.8	10.4	7.6	8.6	1985
New Orleans, LA	0.6	13.1	9.6	14.3	19.7	13.8	10.1	18.7	1974
New York, NY	0.3	7.3	5.8	7.4	9.8	13.9	16.8	38.7	1957
Oklahoma City, OK	1.0	16.2	10.7	16.3	18.6	13.6	10.9	12.7	1977
Omaha, NE	0.7	15.8	12.5	10.3	16.1	12.4	9.8	22.4	1973
Orlando, FL	0.4	27.0	21.0	22.3	13.8	6.5	5.9	3.1	1989
Oxnard, CA	0.2	11.4	10.6	16.9	22.7	20.8	10.8	6.6	1975
Peoria, IL	0.3	10.5	8.7	5.8	17.5	12.5	16.1	28.6	1964
Philadelphia, PA	0.3	8.4	8.9	10.0	12.5	12.3	16.1	31.5	1962
Phoenix, AZ	0.5	28.0	20.8	18.6	17.1	7.0	5.5	2.5	1990
Pittsburgh, PA	0.2	6.7	7.5	7.6	11.9	11.1	16.8	38.1	1957
Portland, OR	0.4	16.3	19.0	11.6	18.2	9.3	7.5	17.6	1979
Providence, RI	0.2	6.7	7.5	10.3	12.1	10.3	11.4	41.5	1957
Provo, UT	1.0	31.2	20.8	9.6	15.4	5.8	6.4	9.9	1991
Raleigh, NC	1.0	30.5	25.4	16.8	10.8	6.5	4.1	4.9	1993
Reno, NV	0.5	22.9	19.9	15.9	21.1	8.7	5.5	5.4	1986
Richmond, VA	0.6	16.3	15.3	16.5	16.6	11.0	9.7	13.9	1979
Riverside, CA	0.4	21.8	14.5	22.6	16.4	9.3	8.7	6.2	1984
Rochester, MN	0.6	19.4	15.7	12.3	14.6	11.3	8.9	17.2	1979
Salem, OR	0.5	15.3	18.4	10.5	23.2	9.8	8.4	13.9	1978
Salt Lake City, UT	0.7	17.9	16.9	14.4	19.9	8.6	9.1	12.4	1980
San Antonio, TX	1.2	23.9	14.8	16.2	16.4	9.6	8.3	9.5	1984
San Diego, CA	0.4	12.0	12.1	19.2	24.1	13.0	11.0	8.3	1977
San Francisco, CA	0.3	8.2	7.8	10.6	15.7	13.6	14.5	29.3	1965
San Jose, CA	0.3	9.8	10.5	12.4	22.5	19.1	15.7	9.5	1973
Santa Rosa, CA	0.2	10.8	13.1	18.5	22.1	11.2	9.4	14.7	1977
Savannah, GA	0.8	24.4	16.6	14.9	13.4	8.6	8.6	12.7	1985
Seattle, WA	0.7	16.9	15.7	15.5	15.6	11.8	7.9	15.8	1979
Sioux Falls, SD	1.3	22.8	16.4	10.1	15.0	7.8	8.1	18.5	1981
Spokane, WA	0.6	15.3	13.2	10.2	18.8	6.7	11.8	23.3	1974
Springfield, MO	0.6	21.6	18.6	13.4	16.3	9.0	7.4	13.0	1983
Tallahassee, FL	0.5	20.7	21.0	20.9	15.8	8.4	6.9	5.9	1986
Tampa, FL	0.4	17.0	14.5	21.7	21.8	11.2	8.6	4.7	1982
Topeka, KS	0.3	9.7	11.1	11.0	17.4	14.6	13.0	22.8	1970
Tulsa, OK	0.8	14.9	12.5	15.3	20.5	11.5	11.4	13.3	1977
Virginia Beach, VA	0.5	13.3	14.7	19.5	16.9	13.2	10.6	11.2	1979
Washington, DC	0.6	15.6	14.1	16.7	15.1	13.2	10.2	14.5	1978
Wichita, KS	0.5	12.5	13.6	12.2	13.6	8.5	18.9	20.1	1972
Wilmington, NC	0.6	28.2	24.1	18.0	11.3	6.5	4.5	6.8	1991
Worcester, MA	0.3	8.8	9.4	12.4	10.9	8.2	10.7	39.4	1960
U.S.	0.5	14.9	13.8	13.9	15.9	11.1	10.9	19.0	1976

Note: Figures are percentages except for Median Year; Figures cover the Metropolitan Statistical Area—see Appendix B for areas included
Source: U.S. Census Bureau, 2010-2012 American Community Survey 3-Year Estimates

Highest Level of Education: City

City	Less than H.S.	H.S. Diploma	Some College, No Deg.	Associate Degree	Bachelors Degree	Masters Degree	Profess. School Degree	Doctorate Degree
Abilene, TX	17.7	28.2	25.4	6.6	14.8	5.1	1.3	1.0
Albuquerque, NM	11.3	23.1	25.0	7.7	18.5	9.8	2.4	2.3
Anchorage, AK	7.7	23.2	28.1	8.4	20.5	8.3	2.4	1.3
Ann Arbor, MI	4.0	8.5	13.1	5.0	29.1	24.0	6.4	9.8
Athens, GA	14.2	22.5	17.9	5.0	19.8	12.1	3.1	5.3
Atlanta, GA	12.1	20.4	16.7	4.3	27.7	12.3	4.5	2.0
Austin, TX	13.6	16.8	19.3	5.4	28.5	11.3	2.8	2.3
Baltimore, MD	20.7	29.4	19.5	4.3	14.1	7.7	2.5	1.7
Billings, MT	6.9	30.1	25.4	6.9	22.3	5.3	2.2	1.0
Boise City, ID	6.4	21.2	26.9	8.0	23.8	9.4	2.8	1.5
Boston, MA	15.2	22.7	14.3	4.4	23.8	12.6	4.3	2.7
Boulder, CO	4.3	7.2	13.5	3.6	34.6	22.3	5.7	8.8
Cape Coral, FL	10.2	38.6	23.6	8.0	12.8	4.9	1.1	0.7
Cedar Rapids, IA	7.1	27.0	24.1	10.4	21.8	6.9	1.6	1.0
Charleston, SC	7.7	18.4	18.9	6.9	30.3	11.0	4.4	2.5
Charlotte, NC	11.7	20.4	21.0	7.1	27.3	9.3	2.3	0.8
Chicago, IL	19.2	23.3	18.4	5.4	20.5	9.1	2.9	1.3
Cincinnati, OH	15.5	26.4	20.2	6.7	18.5	8.5	2.6	1.7
Clarksville, TN	8.8	30.6	28.1	8.6	16.0	6.0	1.0	0.8
Colorado Spgs, CO	6.9	21.4	25.2	10.4	22.0	11.0	1.8	1.2
Columbia, MO	6.0	15.1	17.5	5.4	31.1	15.3	3.9	5.6
Columbus, OH	11.7	26.7	22.3	6.9	21.4	7.7	1.8	1.4
Dallas, TX	26.2	22.4	17.8	4.4	18.4	7.0	2.7	1.1
Davenport, IA	9.2	29.6	22.9	12.3	18.2	5.7	1.6	0.5
Denver, CO	14.7	18.6	18.7	5.1	26.2	11.1	3.9	1.7
Des Moines, IA	13.0	32.1	21.8	8.3	17.6	5.2	1.5	0.7
Durham, NC	12.9	17.0	18.2	6.0	25.0	12.8	3.6	4.4
El Paso, TX	23.4	23.9	23.0	7.2	15.1	5.4	1.3	0.7
Erie, PA	13.6	42.4	17.1	6.7	13.2	4.9	1.0	1.2
Eugene, OR	6.7	18.4	28.2	7.4	22.8	10.9	2.8	2.9
Fargo, ND	4.6	19.3	25.6	11.3	25.5	8.4	2.9	2.4
Fayetteville, NC	9.2	25.6	29.5	10.8	16.5	6.1	1.4	1.0
Ft. Collins, CO	4.3	13.5	21.1	9.2	31.9	13.9	2.6	3.5
Ft. Wayne, IN	11.9	29.5	24.1	9.2	17.1	5.9	1.4	0.8
Ft. Worth, TX	20.6	24.3	23.5	5.8	17.7	6.0	1.4	0.8
Gainesville, FL	8.7	20.3	17.8	10.5	20.6	12.0	3.9	6.2
Grand Rapids, MI	16.0	25.2	22.8	7.1	18.9	7.3	1.6	1.0
Green Bay, WI	12.9	33.5	21.5	9.7	16.2	4.6	0.9	0.6
Greensboro, NC	12.6	23.7	21.6	6.5	23.9	8.6	1.7	1.4
Honolulu, HI	11.9	24.7	20.1	8.7	22.6	7.6	2.7	1.7
Houston, TX	24.8	22.4	19.3	4.6	18.0	7.0	2.3	1.5
Huntsville, AL	10.3	20.5	23.4	7.3	23.4	11.0	2.4	1.8
Indianapolis, IN	15.8	29.5	20.7	7.2	17.7	6.4	1.8	0.9
Jacksonville, FL	12.5	29.8	23.8	9.2	17.3	5.1	1.5	0.8
Kansas City, MO	12.5	25.9	23.5	6.8	19.6	8.4	2.3	1.1
Lafayette, LA	13.4	25.8	22.7	5.3	22.2	6.8	2.5	1.3
Las Vegas, NV	17.2	29.7	24.4	7.4	14.0	5.0	1.6	0.7
Lexington, KY	11.3	21.3	20.5	7.1	22.9	10.1	3.6	3.2
Lincoln, NE	6.8	22.8	23.9	10.6	23.3	7.7	2.0	2.8
Little Rock, AR	10.0	22.9	22.3	6.2	23.6	9.0	4.1	1.9
Los Angeles, CA	25.5	19.5	18.1	5.9	20.6	6.5	2.7	1.2
Louisville, KY	13.5	29.9	22.8	6.9	16.0	7.8	2.0	1.2
Lubbock, TX	14.3	24.9	25.2	6.2	19.1	6.6	2.0	1.7
Madison, WI	4.9	16.4	16.8	8.0	29.3	15.5	4.0	5.1
Manchester, NH	13.7	33.0	18.7	8.4	17.9	6.4	1.1	0.7

Table continued on next page.

City	Less than H.S.	H.S. Diploma	Some College, No Deg.	Associate Degree	Bachelors Degree	Masters Degree	Profess. School Degree	Doctorate Degree
McAllen, TX	26.1	20.4	21.5	5.3	18.7	4.9	2.4	0.6
Miami, FL	29.6	29.8	11.0	7.2	14.2	4.6	2.7	0.9
Midland, TX	18.0	23.3	28.3	7.2	16.7	4.8	1.1	0.6
Minneapolis, MN	11.7	17.1	18.4	6.7	29.1	11.0	3.7	2.4
Montgomery, AL	14.5	25.6	22.7	5.7	19.2	9.2	1.8	1.3
Nashville, TN	14.2	25.0	20.6	5.6	21.7	8.3	2.5	2.0
New Orleans, LA	15.9	24.4	22.3	4.4	19.1	7.8	3.9	2.2
New York, NY	20.4	24.8	14.7	6.1	20.2	9.5	3.0	1.3
Oklahoma City, OK	15.0	25.5	25.1	6.4	18.9	6.3	2.0	0.9
Omaha, NE	12.1	23.8	24.8	6.5	21.7	7.4	2.4	1.4
Orlando, FL	11.9	25.2	20.5	10.3	21.1	7.7	2.3	1.0
Oxnard, CA	36.7	20.0	20.3	7.2	11.3	3.3	0.8	0.4
Peoria, IL	11.2	28.1	21.2	7.7	19.3	8.8	2.5	1.2
Philadelphia, PA	19.3	34.7	17.4	5.0	13.6	6.3	2.3	1.3
Phoenix, AZ	19.4	24.3	23.0	7.3	17.1	6.3	1.8	0.8
Pittsburgh, PA	9.7	29.9	17.3	7.7	18.0	10.3	3.4	3.7
Portland, OR	9.6	17.6	22.8	6.8	26.0	11.3	3.9	2.0
Providence, RI	28.2	22.5	16.0	5.4	14.6	7.5	2.9	2.9
Provo, UT	10.2	14.3	28.8	8.3	26.5	7.7	1.7	2.5
Raleigh, NC	10.0	16.4	20.1	7.6	30.8	10.5	2.6	1.9
Reno, NV	15.0	23.7	26.4	6.5	17.8	6.5	2.3	1.8
Richmond, VA	18.8	22.8	18.7	5.4	21.0	9.0	2.9	1.4
Riverside, CA	22.5	23.3	25.0	7.4	12.5	6.4	1.4	1.6
Rochester, MN	6.7	21.1	20.0	11.3	24.4	9.9	4.4	2.2
Salem, OR	13.7	24.4	27.0	8.0	16.4	7.5	2.1	0.9
Salt Lake City, UT	14.7	16.9	21.1	6.5	23.8	9.7	4.0	3.2
San Antonio, TX	19.6	25.2	23.9	7.0	15.5	6.1	1.7	1.0
San Diego, CA	13.0	16.5	21.3	7.9	24.6	10.3	3.3	3.0
San Francisco, CA	13.9	13.6	15.1	5.3	32.1	13.0	4.9	2.2
San Jose, CA	17.5	18.7	18.9	7.6	23.6	10.3	1.7	1.7
Santa Rosa, CA	14.5	20.9	26.0	8.7	19.0	7.3	2.8	0.9
Savannah, GA	15.7	31.2	22.4	5.6	16.6	5.7	1.6	1.2
Seattle, WA	7.0	11.8	17.3	7.2	33.6	14.9	4.7	3.4
Sioux Falls, SD	9.6	28.4	20.1	9.9	21.4	7.2	1.9	1.4
Spokane, WA	8.4	25.1	27.2	10.7	17.8	7.5	2.2	1.3
Springfield, MO	12.5	27.4	26.5	7.2	17.5	5.8	1.7	1.5
Tallahassee, FL	7.5	16.4	19.3	8.9	27.1	13.4	3.9	3.4
Tampa, FL	14.2	27.3	18.2	7.7	20.2	7.8	3.2	1.5
Topeka, KS	11.1	32.3	22.4	7.0	17.1	6.8	2.4	0.9
Tulsa, OK	13.4	25.8	23.8	7.4	19.5	6.6	2.5	1.1
Virginia Beach, VA	6.6	23.2	27.6	10.1	21.1	8.4	2.0	0.9
Washington, DC	12.3	19.0	14.0	3.0	23.1	16.7	8.2	3.7
Wichita, KS	13.0	26.9	25.8	6.4	18.9	6.7	1.4	0.9
Wilmington, NC	11.2	19.5	19.1	10.4	26.2	9.5	2.4	1.7
Worcester, MA	16.1	28.5	17.6	7.9	18.3	8.5	1.8	1.3
U.S.	14.1	28.3	21.3	7.8	18.0	7.5	1.9	1.2

Note: Figures cover persons age 25 and over
Source: U.S. Census Bureau, 2010-2012 American Community Survey 3-Year Estimates

Highest Level of Education: Metro Area

Metro Area	Less than H.S.	H.S. Diploma	Some College, No Deg.	Associate Degree	Bachelors Degree	Masters Degree	Profess. School Degree	Doctorate Degree
Abilene, TX	16.8	30.4	25.5	6.3	14.1	4.8	1.2	0.9
Albuquerque, NM	12.6	25.1	24.8	7.8	16.7	8.9	2.0	2.1
Anchorage, AK	7.7	25.2	28.7	8.6	19.0	7.5	2.2	1.2
Ann Arbor, MI	6.2	16.5	20.0	6.9	24.7	16.0	4.6	5.1
Athens, GA	14.5	26.6	18.9	5.3	17.7	10.5	2.7	3.8
Atlanta, GA	12.5	24.9	20.9	7.0	22.6	8.7	2.2	1.3
Austin, TX	12.1	19.4	21.7	6.5	26.6	9.7	2.3	1.7
Baltimore, MD	11.4	26.5	20.0	6.4	20.4	10.8	2.6	1.9
Billings, MT	7.2	31.3	25.7	7.0	21.1	4.8	2.0	0.9
Boise City, ID	10.0	25.5	27.0	8.2	19.8	6.6	1.8	1.1
Boston, MA	9.4	24.7	15.7	7.2	24.0	13.1	3.2	2.7
Boulder, CO	5.8	13.2	17.5	5.4	32.2	17.0	3.6	5.2
Cape Coral, FL	13.2	33.0	22.0	7.8	15.0	6.0	1.9	1.1
Cedar Rapids, IA	6.6	29.5	23.3	11.4	20.8	6.1	1.5	0.8
Charleston, SC	12.2	26.1	22.3	8.4	20.2	7.8	1.9	1.2
Charlotte, NC	12.8	24.3	21.8	8.1	22.9	7.7	1.7	0.8
Chicago, IL	13.4	25.2	20.3	6.7	21.3	9.4	2.5	1.2
Cincinnati, OH	11.2	31.3	20.2	7.8	18.7	7.9	1.7	1.2
Clarksville, TN	11.6	33.0	27.1	8.2	13.3	5.2	1.1	0.7
Colorado Spgs, CO	6.1	22.3	26.1	10.8	21.3	10.5	1.7	1.3
Columbia, MO	7.1	20.7	18.7	6.2	27.8	12.3	3.2	4.0
Columbus, OH	9.9	28.7	20.8	7.3	21.6	8.2	2.0	1.5
Dallas, TX	16.3	23.0	22.8	6.5	21.2	7.7	1.6	1.0
Davenport, IA	9.9	31.1	23.7	10.5	16.3	6.5	1.4	0.6
Denver, CO	10.5	21.3	21.8	7.5	25.2	10.0	2.5	1.3
Des Moines, IA	7.7	27.2	20.9	10.0	24.3	7.0	1.9	1.0
Durham, NC	12.5	20.1	17.7	6.5	22.7	12.1	3.6	4.7
El Paso, TX	25.8	24.0	22.6	7.0	13.9	4.9	1.1	0.6
Erie, PA	9.5	41.2	16.9	8.0	15.3	6.4	1.6	1.1
Eugene, OR	9.3	25.4	29.8	7.9	16.8	7.2	1.7	1.8
Fargo, ND	5.2	22.4	24.3	12.5	24.6	7.1	2.1	1.8
Fayetteville, NC	11.6	27.1	28.4	10.9	14.8	5.4	1.1	0.7
Ft. Collins, CO	5.3	18.6	23.0	8.9	27.4	11.7	2.3	2.7
Ft. Wayne, IN	10.5	32.4	22.9	9.5	16.3	6.2	1.4	0.7
Ft. Worth, TX	16.3	23.0	22.8	6.5	21.2	7.7	1.6	1.0
Gainesville, FL	9.5	23.0	18.5	10.7	20.0	10.0	3.8	4.6
Grand Rapids, MI	10.7	30.0	23.1	8.6	18.2	6.9	1.6	0.8
Green Bay, WI	9.6	35.0	20.7	10.8	17.0	5.3	1.0	0.6
Greensboro, NC	15.2	29.1	21.6	7.8	18.1	6.2	1.2	0.9
Honolulu, HI	9.7	26.8	22.0	9.9	20.9	7.1	2.3	1.3
Houston, TX	19.0	23.8	22.0	6.2	19.0	6.8	1.9	1.3
Huntsville, AL	11.7	23.7	22.5	7.3	21.7	10.2	1.6	1.4
Indianapolis, IN	11.4	29.6	20.3	7.5	20.4	7.5	2.1	1.2
Jacksonville, FL	11.3	28.9	23.4	9.2	18.8	6.0	1.6	1.0
Kansas City, MO	9.5	26.7	23.6	7.3	21.1	8.7	2.1	1.0
Lafayette, LA	15.9	33.5	21.3	4.6	17.5	4.7	1.6	0.9
Las Vegas, NV	16.1	29.7	25.1	7.1	14.7	4.9	1.6	0.7
Lexington, KY	13.0	25.6	20.7	7.0	19.9	8.7	3.0	2.3
Lincoln, NE	6.6	23.5	23.7	11.0	23.0	7.7	2.0	2.7
Little Rock, AR	11.4	30.7	23.5	6.6	18.1	6.4	2.0	1.2
Los Angeles, CA	21.8	20.0	19.9	7.0	20.5	7.1	2.5	1.3
Louisville, KY	12.7	31.4	22.6	7.4	15.8	7.3	1.9	0.9
Lubbock, TX	15.6	25.7	25.1	6.0	18.0	6.2	1.9	1.5
Madison, WI	5.5	22.6	19.4	9.7	25.3	11.5	3.1	3.0
Manchester, NH	9.2	27.3	18.4	9.6	22.6	10.2	1.5	1.2

Table continued on next page.

Metro Area	Less than H.S.	H.S. Diploma	Some College, No Deg.	Associate Degree	Bachelors Degree	Masters Degree	Profess. School Degree	Doctorate Degree
McAllen, TX	37.7	24.2	17.6	4.4	11.2	3.4	1.0	0.5
Miami, FL	16.4	27.9	18.4	8.5	18.2	6.7	2.7	1.2
Midland, TX	18.5	23.8	27.5	7.3	16.3	4.9	1.0	0.6
Minneapolis, MN	7.0	22.9	21.8	9.6	25.9	9.0	2.5	1.4
Montgomery, AL	14.8	29.4	22.1	6.7	16.9	7.7	1.5	0.9
Nashville, TN	12.8	29.0	21.0	6.3	20.3	7.1	2.0	1.5
New Orleans, LA	15.5	29.7	22.9	5.5	17.0	5.7	2.5	1.2
New York, NY	15.2	26.2	15.7	6.4	21.5	10.5	3.0	1.4
Oklahoma City, OK	12.4	27.4	25.3	6.6	18.5	6.7	1.8	1.2
Omaha, NE	8.9	25.6	24.4	8.1	22.1	7.7	2.0	1.1
Orlando, FL	12.6	28.5	21.3	9.8	18.4	6.8	1.7	0.9
Oxnard, CA	17.5	18.6	24.1	8.5	20.0	7.9	2.3	1.2
Peoria, IL	8.9	32.4	23.5	9.4	17.2	6.4	1.4	0.8
Philadelphia, PA	11.3	31.0	17.9	6.5	20.2	9.0	2.5	1.6
Phoenix, AZ	13.8	24.1	25.5	8.3	18.5	7.1	1.7	1.0
Pittsburgh, PA	8.2	35.9	16.9	9.2	18.5	8.0	1.9	1.4
Portland, OR	9.5	22.4	25.7	8.3	21.6	8.7	2.4	1.4
Providence, RI	16.2	28.1	18.2	8.3	18.0	8.2	1.8	1.2
Provo, UT	6.6	17.9	29.1	10.6	25.1	7.4	1.5	1.8
Raleigh, NC	10.2	20.1	19.6	8.8	27.4	10.0	2.0	1.9
Reno, NV	13.7	25.1	26.8	7.2	17.2	6.3	2.2	1.4
Richmond, VA	13.4	27.1	20.9	6.6	20.4	8.5	2.0	1.2
Riverside, CA	21.4	25.7	25.7	7.7	12.6	4.8	1.3	0.8
Rochester, MN	6.4	25.3	21.1	11.9	22.1	8.3	3.4	1.6
Salem, OR	15.5	26.9	26.9	8.2	14.4	5.9	1.5	0.7
Salt Lake City, UT	11.1	23.3	26.2	8.5	20.2	7.3	2.0	1.4
San Antonio, TX	17.1	25.4	24.0	7.5	16.7	6.7	1.6	1.0
San Diego, CA	14.7	19.2	22.6	9.5	21.1	8.4	2.5	2.0
San Francisco, CA	12.5	17.4	19.1	6.8	26.8	11.4	3.5	2.4
San Jose, CA	13.6	16.0	17.5	7.1	25.6	14.3	2.6	3.2
Santa Rosa, CA	13.1	20.7	25.5	8.7	20.7	7.5	2.7	1.2
Savannah, GA	12.6	28.7	22.8	7.0	18.9	6.9	1.9	1.1
Seattle, WA	8.6	21.6	23.4	9.2	23.8	9.5	2.4	1.6
Sioux Falls, SD	8.4	30.0	20.5	11.0	20.7	6.5	1.7	1.1
Spokane, WA	7.3	25.2	27.4	11.3	18.3	7.4	1.9	1.1
Springfield, MO	11.0	30.6	25.9	7.1	17.2	5.6	1.5	1.1
Tallahassee, FL	11.0	24.7	20.2	7.9	21.0	10.2	2.5	2.5
Tampa, FL	12.5	30.8	21.6	9.1	17.3	6.1	1.7	0.9
Topeka, KS	8.7	34.3	23.5	6.8	17.3	6.6	2.0	0.8
Tulsa, OK	11.9	29.8	24.1	8.4	17.8	5.6	1.6	0.8
Virginia Beach, VA	10.3	26.2	26.0	8.8	18.0	8.0	1.7	1.0
Washington, DC	10.0	19.4	17.4	5.6	24.8	15.5	4.3	2.9
Wichita, KS	11.1	27.8	26.2	7.2	18.9	6.8	1.3	0.8
Wilmington, NC	11.4	25.5	22.6	9.6	20.8	7.3	1.8	1.2
Worcester, MA	10.8	28.4	18.0	9.1	20.8	9.8	1.8	1.4
U.S.	14.1	28.3	21.3	7.8	18.0	7.5	1.9	1.2

Note: Figures cover persons age 25 and over; Figures cover the Metropolitan Statistical Area—see Appendix B for areas included
Source: U.S. Census Bureau, 2010-2012 American Community Survey 3-Year Estimates

School Enrollment by Grade and Control: City

City	Preschool (%)		Kindergarten (%)		Grades 1 - 4 (%)		Grades 5 - 8 (%)		Grades 9 - 12 (%)	
	Public	Private	Public	Private	Public	Private	Public	Private	Public	Private
Abilene, TX	78.7	21.3	99.0	1.0	94.3	5.7	91.9	8.1	94.9	5.1
Albuquerque, NM	58.7	41.3	89.8	10.2	88.7	11.3	89.1	10.9	89.4	10.6
Anchorage, AK	45.2	54.8	89.6	10.4	91.6	8.4	91.8	8.2	91.4	8.6
Ann Arbor, MI	25.6	74.4	88.7	11.3	88.5	11.5	85.1	14.9	89.7	10.3
Athens, GA	60.5	39.5	84.6	15.4	93.9	6.1	86.0	14.0	90.8	9.2
Atlanta, GA	54.6	45.4	82.9	17.1	85.2	14.8	83.6	16.4	81.6	18.4
Austin, TX	48.3	51.7	88.7	11.3	90.4	9.6	90.9	9.1	93.0	7.0
Baltimore, MD	71.0	29.0	83.2	16.8	88.5	11.5	85.3	14.7	87.8	12.2
Billings, MT	40.9	59.1	93.1	6.9	93.8	6.2	93.4	6.6	91.4	8.6
Boise City, ID	58.5	41.5	92.6	7.4	94.7	5.3	95.8	4.2	93.5	6.5
Boston, MA	53.7	46.3	79.9	20.1	84.8	15.2	84.9	15.1	86.5	13.5
Boulder, CO	29.0	71.0	86.2	13.8	87.0	13.0	85.0	15.0	92.8	7.2
Cape Coral, FL	65.6	34.4	92.8	7.2	92.3	7.7	95.2	4.8	93.6	6.4
Cedar Rapids, IA	54.0	46.0	90.3	9.7	83.9	16.1	89.2	10.8	88.7	11.3
Charleston, SC	35.2	64.8	80.4	19.6	81.3	18.7	81.4	18.6	84.2	15.8
Charlotte, NC	39.9	60.1	89.8	10.2	89.0	11.0	87.2	12.8	89.4	10.6
Chicago, IL	65.5	34.5	82.7	17.3	86.8	13.2	87.2	12.8	88.3	11.7
Cincinnati, OH	62.9	37.1	88.1	11.9	78.1	21.9	79.4	20.6	82.1	17.9
Clarksville, TN	60.5	39.5	93.0	7.0	92.8	7.2	94.3	5.7	90.1	9.9
Colorado Spgs, CO	56.9	43.1	93.5	6.5	95.1	4.9	94.7	5.3	92.3	7.7
Columbia, MO	45.8	54.2	85.0	15.0	88.4	11.6	82.6	17.4	93.6	6.4
Columbus, OH	52.3	47.7	88.4	11.6	87.6	12.4	87.4	12.6	88.6	11.4
Dallas, TX	70.8	29.2	89.1	10.9	91.7	8.3	90.3	9.7	90.8	9.2
Davenport, IA	56.5	43.5	87.8	12.2	91.7	8.3	87.4	12.6	94.5	5.5
Denver, CO	57.8	42.2	87.1	12.9	88.8	11.2	87.6	12.4	90.1	9.9
Des Moines, IA	58.2	41.8	87.4	12.6	89.4	10.6	90.2	9.8	92.9	7.1
Durham, NC	48.6	51.4	93.4	6.6	92.0	8.0	88.8	11.2	92.5	7.5
El Paso, TX	80.9	19.1	94.7	5.3	93.9	6.1	94.5	5.5	95.4	4.6
Erie, PA	48.2	51.8	80.9	19.1	85.4	14.6	85.6	14.4	83.3	16.7
Eugene, OR	43.3	56.7	84.2	15.8	86.2	13.8	89.5	10.5	88.7	11.3
Fargo, ND	38.6	61.4	84.2	15.8	80.1	19.9	85.1	14.9	92.1	7.9
Fayetteville, NC	81.6	18.4	92.7	7.3	91.7	8.3	90.0	10.0	90.0	10.0
Ft. Collins, CO	26.0	74.0	96.7	3.3	91.1	8.9	87.6	12.4	98.0	2.0
Ft. Wayne, IN	52.5	47.5	80.8	19.2	83.5	16.5	81.2	18.8	86.7	13.3
Ft. Worth, TX	62.5	37.5	92.7	7.3	91.9	8.1	92.1	7.9	93.2	6.8
Gainesville, FL	51.6	48.4	74.4	25.6	89.6	10.4	90.7	9.3	93.9	6.1
Grand Rapids, MI	71.7	28.3	78.0	22.0	83.7	16.3	84.3	15.7	81.0	19.0
Green Bay, WI	78.5	21.5	88.0	12.0	91.8	8.2	90.6	9.4	90.5	9.5
Greensboro, NC	51.9	48.1	90.9	9.1	92.6	7.4	91.0	9.0	91.0	9.0
Honolulu, HI	34.3	65.7	82.0	18.0	79.3	20.7	78.4	21.6	76.0	24.0
Houston, TX	67.0	33.0	92.2	7.8	93.5	6.5	93.7	6.3	93.1	6.9
Huntsville, AL	37.5	62.5	86.6	13.4	84.7	15.3	81.9	18.1	85.8	14.2
Indianapolis, IN	42.1	57.9	82.3	17.7	89.0	11.0	88.2	11.8	88.3	11.7
Jacksonville, FL	54.8	45.2	84.1	15.9	85.9	14.1	85.3	14.7	84.2	15.8
Kansas City, MO	55.7	44.3	84.4	15.6	84.7	15.3	84.5	15.5	86.4	13.6
Lafayette, LA	50.0	50.0	81.3	18.7	78.2	21.8	67.4	32.6	76.3	23.7
Las Vegas, NV	45.7	54.3	92.5	7.5	93.0	7.0	91.5	8.5	93.9	6.1
Lexington, KY	41.5	58.5	85.4	14.6	86.8	13.2	85.4	14.6	87.7	12.3
Lincoln, NE	45.6	54.4	83.4	16.6	83.5	16.5	84.1	15.9	87.8	12.2
Little Rock, AR	54.1	45.9	88.6	11.4	86.0	14.0	79.6	20.4	82.2	17.8
Los Angeles, CA	63.1	36.9	87.1	12.9	89.3	10.7	88.9	11.1	90.0	10.0
Louisville, KY	45.6	54.4	82.8	17.2	80.4	19.6	80.0	20.0	79.9	20.1
Lubbock, TX	64.5	35.5	88.2	11.8	93.0	7.0	95.8	4.2	97.0	3.0
Madison, WI	37.2	62.8	89.5	10.5	90.8	9.2	88.2	11.8	94.8	5.2
Manchester, NH	50.0	50.0	78.9	21.1	89.9	10.1	91.5	8.5	96.6	3.4

Table continued on next page.

City	Preschool (%)		Kindergarten (%)		Grades 1 - 4 (%)		Grades 5 - 8 (%)		Grades 9 - 12 (%)	
	Public	Private	Public	Private	Public	Private	Public	Private	Public	Private
McAllen, TX	74.5	25.5	90.7	9.3	95.6	4.4	93.2	6.8	94.5	5.5
Miami, FL	59.5	40.5	84.8	15.2	87.9	12.1	89.7	10.3	91.2	8.8
Midland, TX	38.2	61.8	77.7	22.3	89.1	10.9	88.0	12.0	89.3	10.7
Minneapolis, MN	59.1	40.9	86.4	13.6	89.2	10.8	86.9	13.1	90.5	9.5
Montgomery, AL	52.1	47.9	85.9	14.1	86.4	13.6	83.5	16.5	79.4	20.6
Nashville, TN	56.3	43.7	89.2	10.8	87.2	12.8	82.8	17.2	82.4	17.6
New Orleans, LA	55.7	44.3	70.5	29.5	79.6	20.4	77.4	22.6	79.2	20.8
New York, NY	55.0	45.0	79.3	20.7	82.3	17.7	82.3	17.7	83.4	16.6
Oklahoma City, OK	69.8	30.2	91.9	8.1	91.2	8.8	91.2	8.8	91.4	8.6
Omaha, NE	58.1	41.9	80.4	19.6	84.4	15.6	85.2	14.8	88.3	11.7
Orlando, FL	49.6	50.4	79.9	20.1	87.1	12.9	88.8	11.2	89.9	10.1
Oxnard, CA	75.0	25.0	98.0	2.0	94.2	5.8	94.3	5.7	95.9	4.1
Peoria, IL	63.8	36.2	91.6	8.4	84.6	15.4	82.1	17.9	91.8	8.2
Philadelphia, PA	59.2	40.8	82.6	17.4	80.8	19.2	79.1	20.9	82.7	17.3
Phoenix, AZ	59.2	40.8	91.6	8.4	94.1	5.9	94.6	5.4	93.1	6.9
Pittsburgh, PA	61.3	38.7	78.9	21.1	80.8	19.2	78.5	21.5	82.4	17.6
Portland, OR	40.2	59.8	84.7	15.3	89.2	10.8	90.4	9.6	88.3	11.7
Providence, RI	67.8	32.2	84.1	15.9	90.4	9.6	86.3	13.7	86.6	13.4
Provo, UT	44.6	55.4	91.6	8.4	94.3	5.7	92.3	7.7	89.5	10.5
Raleigh, NC	32.1	67.9	88.9	11.1	90.6	9.4	90.7	9.3	93.0	7.0
Reno, NV	57.9	42.1	90.4	9.6	92.6	7.4	93.5	6.5	95.5	4.5
Richmond, VA	52.7	47.3	86.4	13.6	87.2	12.8	87.1	12.9	86.7	13.3
Riverside, CA	72.7	27.3	91.5	8.5	92.9	7.1	93.1	6.9	95.6	4.4
Rochester, MN	50.8	49.2	78.8	21.2	85.8	14.2	88.1	11.9	91.0	9.0
Salem, OR	59.6	40.4	87.5	12.5	94.5	5.5	94.0	6.0	93.7	6.3
Salt Lake City, UT	48.3	51.7	88.3	11.7	92.7	7.3	91.8	8.2	90.5	9.5
San Antonio, TX	64.7	35.3	88.9	11.1	93.6	6.4	92.8	7.2	93.2	6.8
San Diego, CA	54.4	45.6	90.2	9.8	91.4	8.6	93.0	7.0	93.2	6.8
San Francisco, CA	34.6	65.4	70.9	29.1	71.6	28.4	69.9	30.1	81.4	18.6
San Jose, CA	43.6	56.4	83.3	16.7	89.1	10.9	90.7	9.3	90.5	9.5
Santa Rosa, CA	53.8	46.2	90.6	9.4	97.3	2.7	95.6	4.4	91.6	8.4
Savannah, GA	72.1	27.9	89.2	10.8	92.7	7.3	88.2	11.8	85.9	14.1
Seattle, WA	31.8	68.2	75.2	24.8	78.7	21.3	80.3	19.7	80.1	19.9
Sioux Falls, SD	51.9	48.1	84.6	15.4	87.8	12.2	90.8	9.2	92.9	7.1
Spokane, WA	41.1	58.9	85.2	14.8	84.9	15.1	87.9	12.1	91.7	8.3
Springfield, MO	60.8	39.2	90.5	9.5	90.2	9.8	91.5	8.5	91.8	8.2
Tallahassee, FL	44.3	55.7	80.1	19.9	86.5	13.5	89.7	10.3	90.5	9.5
Tampa, FL	56.7	43.3	92.0	8.0	90.7	9.3	85.7	14.3	92.9	7.1
Topeka, KS	71.4	28.6	99.2	0.8	88.4	11.6	90.8	9.2	89.7	10.3
Tulsa, OK	72.5	27.5	88.7	11.3	89.0	11.0	87.8	12.2	87.3	12.7
Virginia Beach, VA	32.8	67.2	81.6	18.4	88.6	11.4	90.6	9.4	92.9	7.1
Washington, DC	71.3	28.7	83.8	16.2	84.0	16.0	79.0	21.0	84.5	15.5
Wichita, KS	66.3	33.7	85.3	14.7	87.2	12.8	86.1	13.9	83.1	16.9
Wilmington, NC	41.8	58.2	82.9	17.1	90.0	10.0	84.2	15.8	86.8	13.2
Worcester, MA	70.2	29.8	93.0	7.0	89.7	10.3	85.6	14.4	87.7	12.3
U.S.	56.9	43.1	87.8	12.2	89.9	10.1	90.0	10.0	90.8	9.2

Note: Figures shown cover persons 3 years old and over
Source: U.S. Census Bureau, 2010-2012 American Community Survey 3-Year Estimates

School Enrollment by Grade and Control: Metro Area

Metro Area	Preschool (%)		Kindergarten (%)		Grades 1 - 4 (%)		Grades 5 - 8 (%)		Grades 9 - 12 (%)	
	Public	Private	Public	Private	Public	Private	Public	Private	Public	Private
Abilene, TX	78.5	21.5	98.4	1.6	94.3	5.7	93.2	6.8	93.9	6.1
Albuquerque, NM	63.1	36.9	88.5	11.5	89.8	10.2	90.3	9.7	90.8	9.2
Anchorage, AK	48.9	51.1	89.2	10.8	90.1	9.9	90.5	9.5	90.3	9.7
Ann Arbor, MI	44.9	55.1	83.7	16.3	88.3	11.7	88.6	11.4	91.2	8.8
Athens, GA	64.4	35.6	87.3	12.7	93.9	6.1	85.7	14.3	89.9	10.1
Atlanta, GA	53.5	46.5	88.5	11.5	90.4	9.6	89.6	10.4	90.9	9.1
Austin, TX	50.8	49.2	88.7	11.3	92.4	7.6	92.4	7.6	93.5	6.5
Baltimore, MD	48.4	51.6	84.3	15.7	87.1	12.9	85.2	14.8	85.5	14.5
Billings, MT	45.7	54.3	92.6	7.4	93.2	6.8	90.8	9.2	89.5	10.5
Boise City, ID	44.8	55.2	92.7	7.3	93.7	6.3	94.4	5.6	93.8	6.2
Boston, MA	41.6	58.4	86.1	13.9	90.4	9.6	88.9	11.1	86.8	13.2
Boulder, CO	44.0	56.0	92.9	7.1	90.8	9.2	88.6	11.4	94.5	5.5
Cape Coral, FL	61.1	38.9	93.7	6.3	93.3	6.7	90.3	9.7	92.5	7.5
Cedar Rapids, IA	57.1	42.9	86.5	13.5	85.3	14.7	89.9	10.1	91.3	8.7
Charleston, SC	46.5	53.5	84.2	15.8	88.2	11.8	89.8	10.2	90.2	9.8
Charlotte, NC	43.5	56.5	90.2	9.8	89.9	10.1	89.3	10.7	89.6	10.4
Chicago, IL	56.7	43.3	85.2	14.8	88.6	11.4	88.8	11.2	91.0	9.0
Cincinnati, OH	48.7	51.3	84.3	15.7	83.4	16.6	82.5	17.5	83.6	16.4
Clarksville, TN	66.8	33.2	88.4	11.6	89.5	10.5	91.4	8.6	89.4	10.6
Colorado Spgs, CO	59.1	40.9	92.1	7.9	92.8	7.2	93.2	6.8	92.6	7.4
Columbia, MO	46.7	53.3	90.6	9.4	89.8	10.2	85.9	14.1	92.3	7.7
Columbus, OH	47.8	52.2	86.4	13.6	88.3	11.7	88.2	11.8	89.8	10.2
Dallas, TX	55.6	44.4	90.2	9.8	92.2	7.8	92.4	7.6	92.7	7.3
Davenport, IA	64.6	35.4	90.4	9.6	92.5	7.5	90.0	10.0	92.6	7.4
Denver, CO	55.9	44.1	89.3	10.7	91.7	8.3	91.4	8.6	91.9	8.1
Des Moines, IA	56.5	43.5	86.2	13.8	90.8	9.2	91.7	8.3	91.5	8.5
Durham, NC	42.9	57.1	92.4	7.6	91.9	8.1	89.8	10.2	91.5	8.5
El Paso, TX	83.8	16.2	95.5	4.5	95.1	4.9	95.4	4.6	96.3	3.7
Erie, PA	50.1	49.9	84.9	15.1	89.2	10.8	89.1	10.9	86.8	13.2
Eugene, OR	49.9	50.1	85.0	15.0	90.9	9.1	91.8	8.2	91.1	8.9
Fargo, ND	50.9	49.1	90.4	9.6	87.5	12.5	91.7	8.3	92.3	7.7
Fayetteville, NC	78.0	22.0	93.6	6.4	91.0	9.0	90.6	9.4	90.4	9.6
Ft. Collins, CO	28.4	71.6	86.2	13.8	92.0	8.0	90.5	9.5	97.1	2.9
Ft. Wayne, IN	47.9	52.1	78.6	21.4	81.8	18.2	80.9	19.1	88.4	11.6
Ft. Worth, TX	55.6	44.4	90.2	9.8	92.2	7.8	92.4	7.6	92.7	7.3
Gainesville, FL	46.5	53.5	82.1	17.9	86.2	13.8	87.8	12.2	86.0	14.0
Grand Rapids, MI	63.4	36.6	85.2	14.8	87.9	12.1	86.3	13.7	86.9	13.1
Green Bay, WI	75.6	24.4	88.7	11.3	89.9	10.1	90.6	9.4	93.0	7.0
Greensboro, NC	57.3	42.7	89.6	10.4	91.8	8.2	91.1	8.9	90.5	9.5
Honolulu, HI	35.2	64.8	82.5	17.5	82.1	17.9	78.4	21.6	76.6	23.4
Houston, TX	57.0	43.0	90.6	9.4	93.8	6.2	94.4	5.6	93.9	6.1
Huntsville, AL	43.8	56.2	84.2	15.8	86.0	14.0	87.4	12.6	87.0	13.0
Indianapolis, IN	43.7	56.3	83.7	16.3	88.8	11.2	90.2	9.8	88.7	11.3
Jacksonville, FL	51.8	48.2	84.9	15.1	86.4	13.6	87.1	12.9	87.3	12.7
Kansas City, MO	52.6	47.4	85.7	14.3	89.0	11.0	88.5	11.5	89.1	10.9
Lafayette, LA	49.1	50.9	82.4	17.6	77.5	22.5	74.3	25.7	79.6	20.4
Las Vegas, NV	53.5	46.5	91.1	8.9	93.7	6.3	94.6	5.4	95.5	4.5
Lexington, KY	45.6	54.4	86.4	13.6	86.6	13.4	85.5	14.5	87.0	13.0
Lincoln, NE	46.2	53.8	82.2	17.8	82.5	17.5	83.5	16.5	87.8	12.2
Little Rock, AR	57.1	42.9	90.0	10.0	88.2	11.8	88.5	11.5	87.7	12.3
Los Angeles, CA	58.9	41.1	88.4	11.6	90.3	9.7	90.7	9.3	92.2	7.8
Louisville, KY	48.3	51.7	84.7	15.3	83.7	16.3	83.2	16.8	83.8	16.2
Lubbock, TX	64.2	35.8	87.3	12.7	92.5	7.5	95.3	4.7	95.6	4.4
Madison, WI	48.9	51.1	89.5	10.5	90.2	9.8	89.3	10.7	94.6	5.4
Manchester, NH	41.4	58.6	74.9	25.1	89.6	10.4	89.7	10.3	91.3	8.7

Table continued on next page.

Metro Area	Preschool (%)		Kindergarten (%)		Grades 1 - 4 (%)		Grades 5 - 8 (%)		Grades 9 - 12 (%)	
	Public	Private	Public	Private	Public	Private	Public	Private	Public	Private
McAllen, TX	89.3	10.7	96.7	3.3	97.6	2.4	97.4	2.6	97.1	2.9
Miami, FL	48.7	51.3	82.6	17.4	86.9	13.1	88.2	11.8	88.1	11.9
Midland, TX	43.2	56.8	81.3	18.7	90.9	9.1	88.7	11.3	87.9	12.1
Minneapolis, MN	52.5	47.5	87.2	12.8	87.5	12.5	88.2	11.8	91.1	8.9
Montgomery, AL	49.3	50.7	80.1	19.9	83.7	16.3	82.1	17.9	78.0	22.0
Nashville, TN	48.4	51.6	89.4	10.6	88.8	11.2	86.4	13.6	85.8	14.2
New Orleans, LA	54.2	45.8	72.6	27.4	77.5	22.5	75.8	24.2	75.0	25.0
New York, NY	49.6	50.4	82.0	18.0	86.1	13.9	86.3	13.7	86.1	13.9
Oklahoma City, OK	71.9	28.1	91.2	8.8	91.8	8.2	91.3	8.7	92.0	8.0
Omaha, NE	53.2	46.8	84.6	15.4	86.6	13.4	86.9	13.1	87.2	12.8
Orlando, FL	48.6	51.4	85.4	14.6	88.5	11.5	88.0	12.0	90.7	9.3
Oxnard, CA	50.8	49.2	90.1	9.9	90.9	9.1	90.3	9.7	90.9	9.1
Peoria, IL	63.8	36.2	90.7	9.3	87.9	12.1	86.7	13.3	92.7	7.3
Philadelphia, PA	43.5	56.5	79.4	20.6	84.3	15.7	83.3	16.7	84.0	16.0
Phoenix, AZ	56.9	43.1	91.3	8.7	93.2	6.8	94.9	5.1	94.1	5.9
Pittsburgh, PA	47.4	52.6	86.1	13.9	87.9	12.1	87.8	12.2	90.4	9.6
Portland, OR	37.7	62.3	84.3	15.7	90.2	9.8	91.6	8.4	91.6	8.4
Providence, RI	49.7	50.3	85.0	15.0	89.3	10.7	90.3	9.7	87.9	12.1
Provo, UT	43.0	57.0	92.7	7.3	95.1	4.9	94.5	5.5	96.0	4.0
Raleigh, NC	33.1	66.9	88.5	11.5	89.9	10.1	89.7	10.3	91.2	8.8
Reno, NV	50.9	49.1	88.6	11.4	92.4	7.6	93.3	6.7	93.6	6.4
Richmond, VA	38.5	61.5	89.4	10.6	90.9	9.1	92.0	8.0	91.4	8.6
Riverside, CA	65.5	34.5	93.1	6.9	94.5	5.5	94.3	5.7	94.6	5.4
Rochester, MN	60.1	39.9	83.3	16.7	88.1	11.9	89.4	10.6	91.9	8.1
Salem, OR	56.4	43.6	88.1	11.9	90.6	9.4	90.4	9.6	93.1	6.9
Salt Lake City, UT	47.3	52.7	90.5	9.5	92.8	7.2	93.2	6.8	93.2	6.8
San Antonio, TX	62.1	37.9	90.1	9.9	92.7	7.3	92.8	7.2	93.1	6.9
San Diego, CA	53.2	46.8	90.8	9.2	92.0	8.0	92.6	7.4	93.4	6.6
San Francisco, CA	40.7	59.3	82.7	17.3	85.2	14.8	85.9	14.1	88.4	11.6
San Jose, CA	34.1	65.9	82.5	17.5	87.1	12.9	88.3	11.7	89.4	10.6
Santa Rosa, CA	43.7	56.3	88.4	11.6	91.9	8.1	92.3	7.7	92.3	7.7
Savannah, GA	56.0	44.0	91.8	8.2	90.2	9.8	88.3	11.7	85.5	14.5
Seattle, WA	40.7	59.3	83.3	16.7	88.9	11.1	89.4	10.6	91.1	8.9
Sioux Falls, SD	53.9	46.1	89.0	11.0	89.2	10.8	90.3	9.7	93.0	7.0
Spokane, WA	39.8	60.2	84.1	15.9	89.0	11.0	89.0	11.0	92.0	8.0
Springfield, MO	63.9	36.1	92.6	7.4	88.8	11.2	88.3	11.7	90.4	9.6
Tallahassee, FL	55.8	44.2	79.3	20.7	87.2	12.8	86.9	13.1	86.7	13.3
Tampa, FL	58.8	41.2	89.1	10.9	89.4	10.6	88.0	12.0	91.7	8.3
Topeka, KS	74.2	25.8	94.8	5.2	88.4	11.6	90.3	9.7	91.1	8.9
Tulsa, OK	71.4	28.6	88.9	11.1	90.9	9.1	89.6	10.4	89.4	10.6
Virginia Beach, VA	53.1	46.9	85.7	14.3	90.2	9.8	91.2	8.8	93.1	6.9
Washington, DC	40.1	59.9	83.6	16.4	87.2	12.8	87.2	12.8	89.0	11.0
Wichita, KS	64.0	36.0	86.1	13.9	88.0	12.0	87.9	12.1	86.7	13.3
Wilmington, NC	46.3	53.7	88.7	11.3	90.2	9.8	91.9	8.1	90.7	9.3
Worcester, MA	54.3	45.7	86.9	13.1	91.4	8.6	91.3	8.7	90.7	9.3
U.S.	56.9	43.1	87.8	12.2	89.9	10.1	90.0	10.0	90.8	9.2

Note: Figures shown cover persons 3 years old and over; Figures cover the Metropolitan Statistical Area—see Appendix B for areas included;

Source: U.S. Census Bureau, 2010-2012 American Community Survey 3-Year Estimates

Educational Attainment by Race: City

City	High School Graduate or Higher (%)					Bachelor's Degree or Higher (%)				
	Total	White	Black	Asian	Hisp.[1]	Total	White	Black	Asian	Hisp.[1]
Abilene, TX	82.3	84.7	71.7	82.6	61.7	22.1	24.2	9.1	30.6	6.8
Albuquerque, NM	88.7	91.4	89.6	83.9	79.1	32.9	37.3	29.6	43.8	17.8
Anchorage, AK	92.3	95.5	87.6	78.1	81.9	32.5	37.3	24.9	23.5	21.2
Ann Arbor, MI	96.0	96.7	91.2	96.3	92.9	69.3	70.0	38.7	84.4	55.8
Athens, GA	85.8	89.8	77.1	92.0	55.6	40.4	52.5	10.9	70.5	10.5
Atlanta, GA	87.9	95.8	81.2	95.6	74.1	46.5	73.0	22.5	82.2	36.2
Austin, TX	86.4	89.2	88.1	92.9	62.5	44.9	49.2	20.9	69.1	17.8
Baltimore, MD	79.3	84.5	76.7	91.5	57.7	26.1	47.1	13.0	70.4	20.1
Billings, MT	93.1	93.9	n/a	76.6	80.9	30.8	31.8	n/a	17.3	13.5
Boise City, ID	93.6	94.5	81.8	83.5	77.9	37.5	38.1	14.0	49.4	17.8
Boston, MA	84.8	91.9	79.7	75.8	66.1	43.4	58.5	17.3	45.8	17.0
Boulder, CO	95.7	97.3	n/a	97.0	61.4	71.3	73.5	n/a	75.0	29.0
Cape Coral, FL	89.8	90.2	88.9	75.9	75.1	19.5	19.9	10.4	29.0	15.3
Cedar Rapids, IA	92.9	93.5	83.3	90.6	65.6	31.4	31.6	14.5	59.1	12.0
Charleston, SC	92.3	96.2	80.1	n/a	89.1	48.2	57.8	15.8	n/a	30.3
Charlotte, NC	88.3	91.5	86.9	84.4	57.5	39.8	50.0	22.8	55.2	15.5
Chicago, IL	80.8	85.1	81.1	85.8	59.3	33.8	45.1	17.6	58.3	12.4
Cincinnati, OH	84.5	89.2	78.3	96.4	57.4	31.3	45.2	11.2	78.1	25.9
Clarksville, TN	91.2	92.4	89.2	86.1	82.3	23.9	25.2	19.4	32.2	17.8
Colorado Spgs, CO	93.1	94.7	91.0	88.5	79.2	36.1	38.7	20.4	36.7	14.7
Columbia, MO	94.0	95.7	84.8	91.0	78.9	56.0	59.0	27.6	71.6	43.1
Columbus, OH	88.3	90.3	85.6	88.6	64.4	32.4	37.2	16.3	63.5	18.5
Dallas, TX	73.8	75.3	82.9	83.1	44.3	29.2	38.0	15.0	56.5	8.2
Davenport, IA	90.8	92.1	85.4	65.1	76.9	26.0	27.7	12.5	23.2	12.4
Denver, CO	85.3	88.7	87.1	77.6	59.0	42.8	49.3	22.1	45.1	10.7
Des Moines, IA	87.0	89.7	82.8	70.9	51.6	24.9	26.7	15.1	25.9	7.0
Durham, NC	87.1	90.2	86.7	94.9	45.1	45.9	58.7	29.6	76.9	13.1
El Paso, TX	76.6	77.4	92.2	87.7	71.6	22.6	22.8	28.6	49.1	17.9
Erie, PA	86.4	88.3	80.9	62.1	71.6	20.3	21.5	13.6	29.9	11.4
Eugene, OR	93.3	93.9	97.5	94.3	68.7	39.4	39.5	21.3	60.3	20.8
Fargo, ND	95.4	96.4	80.7	90.8	83.5	39.2	39.5	33.7	61.7	15.9
Fayetteville, NC	90.8	93.5	88.3	83.4	90.1	25.0	27.9	21.2	37.6	17.0
Ft. Collins, CO	95.7	96.3	86.8	95.3	79.0	51.9	52.9	37.7	59.6	27.0
Ft. Wayne, IN	88.1	90.9	82.3	61.5	61.9	25.3	27.7	11.4	34.2	16.1
Ft. Worth, TX	79.4	81.1	85.2	79.7	51.3	25.9	29.8	16.2	37.5	8.6
Gainesville, FL	91.3	94.3	82.4	95.6	89.3	42.8	50.0	13.6	77.3	43.4
Grand Rapids, MI	84.0	87.5	74.7	64.2	51.7	28.9	34.0	11.2	32.2	8.8
Green Bay, WI	87.1	88.4	85.4	75.7	40.9	22.4	23.9	5.9	19.2	7.4
Greensboro, NC	87.4	91.6	85.6	62.0	53.3	35.6	45.1	23.3	31.7	11.8
Honolulu, HI	88.1	96.4	95.2	85.1	90.2	34.7	48.6	36.9	33.4	26.1
Houston, TX	75.2	75.2	84.4	84.0	51.2	28.9	33.6	19.0	53.4	10.1
Huntsville, AL	89.7	91.7	85.6	89.7	61.3	38.6	44.1	23.7	54.6	19.9
Indianapolis, IN	84.2	86.7	83.3	80.6	49.9	26.9	31.8	14.8	53.9	8.0
Jacksonville, FL	87.5	89.1	84.5	86.0	80.7	24.7	27.2	16.0	44.7	21.0
Kansas City, MO	87.5	91.9	82.4	76.7	64.4	31.3	39.7	14.6	38.5	13.9
Lafayette, LA	86.6	90.8	77.1	87.2	77.2	32.8	39.9	14.7	37.4	28.7
Las Vegas, NV	82.8	84.5	87.3	89.2	57.6	21.4	22.4	16.0	38.2	8.3
Lexington, KY	88.7	91.0	84.1	90.9	51.8	39.8	43.5	17.3	71.1	13.3
Lincoln, NE	93.2	94.6	85.8	72.7	67.5	35.8	36.6	21.5	41.1	19.4
Little Rock, AR	90.0	93.2	85.4	92.1	71.3	38.7	49.6	20.6	64.8	16.2
Los Angeles, CA	74.5	78.7	86.6	89.2	50.5	31.0	36.3	22.6	50.7	9.6
Louisville, KY	86.5	88.2	81.8	74.6	77.0	27.0	29.3	16.5	52.6	22.0
Lubbock, TX	85.7	88.3	81.9	86.9	68.7	29.5	32.0	12.2	69.7	10.2
Madison, WI	95.1	96.4	87.7	88.9	80.4	54.0	55.2	24.7	72.7	30.1
Manchester, NH	86.3	88.2	73.3	68.1	64.7	26.2	26.8	20.2	28.1	13.8

Table continued on next page.

City	High School Graduate or Higher (%)					Bachelor's Degree or Higher (%)				
	Total	White	Black	Asian	Hisp.[1]	Total	White	Black	Asian	Hisp.[1]
McAllen, TX	73.9	74.3	91.8	97.5	69.4	26.7	26.3	35.5	69.0	22.4
Miami, FL	70.4	71.7	65.4	75.7	66.6	22.4	24.8	9.7	58.8	18.4
Midland, TX	82.0	83.0	84.0	76.7	59.4	23.2	24.3	15.5	43.1	6.1
Minneapolis, MN	88.3	93.3	73.7	76.5	53.8	46.2	54.6	14.7	44.9	16.5
Montgomery, AL	85.5	91.5	81.1	86.4	59.3	31.5	43.0	21.2	50.6	20.2
Nashville, TN	85.8	89.0	84.2	80.3	54.9	34.5	40.0	23.3	48.7	11.3
New Orleans, LA	84.1	94.7	78.4	71.1	71.4	33.0	59.3	15.1	38.3	29.6
New York, NY	79.6	86.2	80.5	74.1	63.6	34.0	45.1	20.9	40.5	15.1
Oklahoma City, OK	85.0	87.3	87.6	76.4	49.1	28.1	31.4	18.7	34.9	8.0
Omaha, NE	87.9	91.2	81.7	73.0	48.4	32.8	36.2	15.0	52.2	10.8
Orlando, FL	88.1	91.6	81.8	85.6	79.7	32.1	38.3	16.6	50.4	21.6
Oxnard, CA	63.3	59.9	89.0	89.5	48.4	15.8	14.2	16.4	35.9	7.1
Peoria, IL	88.8	92.1	78.6	93.4	69.2	31.9	35.5	10.2	83.6	12.4
Philadelphia, PA	80.7	86.1	79.9	67.5	60.6	23.5	33.6	12.8	34.3	10.6
Phoenix, AZ	80.6	82.0	85.6	83.9	56.5	26.0	27.4	17.4	50.6	8.3
Pittsburgh, PA	90.3	92.0	84.3	93.0	85.8	35.4	39.8	14.6	79.4	40.6
Portland, OR	90.4	93.4	85.0	77.1	61.7	43.2	46.8	17.7	38.1	20.1
Providence, RI	71.8	79.5	74.2	63.7	54.0	27.9	40.4	15.5	36.1	7.4
Provo, UT	89.8	91.9	n/a	84.4	65.8	38.3	39.3	n/a	48.2	16.7
Raleigh, NC	90.0	93.0	89.0	82.4	50.5	45.9	55.4	28.4	45.0	11.8
Reno, NV	85.0	87.0	83.5	89.1	50.3	28.4	30.3	12.1	39.9	9.1
Richmond, VA	81.2	89.1	74.8	82.9	40.8	34.3	57.1	12.3	59.6	11.2
Riverside, CA	77.5	78.8	92.9	87.6	59.3	21.9	22.0	26.4	43.8	9.2
Rochester, MN	93.3	94.9	72.1	87.4	69.5	41.0	41.6	19.1	51.2	25.6
Salem, OR	86.3	90.4	91.6	90.1	49.5	26.9	29.4	24.7	27.4	10.3
Salt Lake City, UT	85.3	90.8	78.3	83.6	50.9	40.8	44.7	26.8	57.3	12.1
San Antonio, TX	80.4	82.1	87.6	85.4	71.5	24.3	26.0	21.5	51.6	13.6
San Diego, CA	87.0	89.1	89.1	87.4	65.3	41.3	44.7	20.4	47.0	17.3
San Francisco, CA	86.1	94.3	86.8	74.8	74.9	52.2	65.5	23.3	40.4	29.6
San Jose, CA	82.5	84.5	91.9	84.6	63.7	37.3	35.3	28.1	49.7	11.9
Santa Rosa, CA	85.5	88.8	85.0	79.4	59.2	29.9	31.7	26.4	37.5	9.9
Savannah, GA	84.3	90.3	79.6	77.5	58.6	25.1	36.7	14.6	32.4	25.5
Seattle, WA	93.0	96.5	82.4	81.1	78.7	56.6	63.1	21.5	46.1	37.7
Sioux Falls, SD	90.4	92.9	71.4	65.0	52.4	31.9	33.7	13.8	37.5	12.1
Spokane, WA	91.6	92.3	98.7	74.4	78.0	28.7	29.4	25.5	28.4	15.7
Springfield, MO	87.5	88.3	88.1	77.4	63.8	26.4	27.1	17.4	33.9	17.4
Tallahassee, FL	92.5	96.0	85.9	94.1	88.7	47.8	56.0	29.1	77.1	39.2
Tampa, FL	85.8	89.4	78.3	84.7	74.5	32.6	39.2	12.2	55.7	17.3
Topeka, KS	88.9	90.5	85.3	89.1	63.3	27.2	30.0	10.3	61.3	8.3
Tulsa, OK	86.6	88.7	86.7	81.3	55.4	29.6	33.5	16.7	44.0	7.9
Virginia Beach, VA	93.4	94.6	90.1	90.6	91.2	32.5	34.4	23.8	38.3	20.3
Washington, DC	87.7	95.5	82.0	90.5	64.9	51.7	83.6	22.9	76.8	35.7
Wichita, KS	87.0	88.9	86.8	76.9	57.4	27.9	30.4	16.9	28.5	9.6
Wilmington, NC	88.8	92.8	75.0	86.4	56.5	39.8	47.1	10.4	55.7	16.0
Worcester, MA	83.9	86.3	87.8	71.5	63.2	29.9	32.4	20.3	33.8	9.4
U.S.	85.9	88.1	82.5	85.5	63.1	28.6	30.0	18.4	50.2	13.4

Note: Figures shown cover persons 25 years old and over; (1) People of Hispanic origin can be of any race
Source: U.S. Census Bureau, 2010-2012 American Community Survey 3-Year Estimates

Educational Attainment by Race: Metro Area

Metro Area	High School Graduate or Higher (%)					Bachelor's Degree or Higher (%)				
	Total	White	Black	Asian	Hisp.[1]	Total	White	Black	Asian	Hisp.[1]
Abilene, TX	83.2	85.5	69.5	83.4	61.4	20.9	22.4	8.4	31.8	6.2
Albuquerque, NM	87.4	90.3	90.9	85.4	77.2	29.7	33.9	31.5	44.5	15.6
Anchorage, AK	92.3	94.9	87.5	78.2	83.3	29.9	33.3	24.4	23.1	21.5
Ann Arbor, MI	93.8	94.8	88.0	95.5	83.9	50.4	52.1	23.9	79.9	32.2
Athens, GA	85.5	88.7	75.2	89.6	57.2	34.8	40.2	11.2	66.6	10.7
Atlanta, GA	87.5	89.0	88.2	86.9	59.7	34.7	38.5	26.9	52.5	15.6
Austin, TX	87.9	90.0	89.1	92.1	65.8	40.2	42.6	23.1	66.0	17.3
Baltimore, MD	88.6	91.2	83.6	91.1	68.7	35.7	39.9	21.8	61.8	25.4
Billings, MT	92.8	93.3	n/a	79.8	80.1	28.8	29.5	n/a	22.6	10.0
Boise City, ID	90.0	90.8	84.6	84.3	62.8	29.2	29.7	17.4	48.3	9.7
Boston, MA	90.6	93.3	82.1	83.4	68.5	43.0	45.2	22.6	56.7	19.2
Boulder, CO	94.2	95.6	85.4	95.2	62.9	58.1	59.6	37.6	73.2	22.8
Cape Coral, FL	86.8	89.3	71.0	80.9	64.7	24.1	25.6	10.2	37.4	11.3
Cedar Rapids, IA	93.4	93.9	84.3	88.6	72.3	29.1	29.1	17.8	57.9	19.2
Charleston, SC	87.8	91.7	79.0	81.8	70.1	31.1	37.6	14.2	38.4	19.8
Charlotte, NC	87.2	89.1	85.3	84.3	59.0	33.1	36.6	21.7	53.3	15.3
Chicago, IL	86.6	89.7	84.5	90.0	61.6	34.4	37.8	19.8	62.1	12.4
Cincinnati, OH	88.8	89.7	82.8	92.0	69.9	29.5	30.6	15.5	63.8	24.1
Clarksville, TN	88.4	88.9	87.1	85.0	82.0	20.2	20.8	16.0	35.4	14.4
Colorado Spgs, CO	93.9	95.2	92.0	86.6	82.4	34.8	36.8	20.9	36.2	15.5
Columbia, MO	92.9	94.0	84.5	88.8	80.4	47.3	48.4	26.1	68.5	40.7
Columbus, OH	90.1	91.3	85.9	90.2	69.2	33.3	34.7	18.9	67.2	21.8
Dallas, TX	83.7	85.4	88.4	86.9	54.7	31.4	33.4	23.0	54.3	10.9
Davenport, IA	90.1	91.6	80.6	81.2	65.7	24.8	25.5	14.0	53.6	11.0
Denver, CO	89.5	91.5	89.0	84.4	64.6	38.9	41.4	24.4	44.3	12.6
Des Moines, IA	92.3	93.9	85.7	82.2	54.8	34.2	35.3	18.7	43.3	12.4
Durham, NC	87.5	90.3	84.4	91.7	49.4	43.1	49.8	25.6	76.1	12.7
El Paso, TX	74.2	75.4	92.6	88.1	69.1	20.6	21.0	28.2	49.1	16.1
Erie, PA	90.5	91.6	81.7	70.5	74.7	24.4	25.1	13.8	36.3	14.6
Eugene, OR	90.7	91.3	93.9	86.5	66.7	27.5	27.7	22.9	46.8	14.5
Fargo, ND	94.8	95.6	79.2	89.2	81.6	35.6	36.0	27.2	52.6	12.9
Fayetteville, NC	88.4	90.4	87.4	83.3	82.4	22.0	24.3	19.6	32.9	15.0
Ft. Collins, CO	94.7	95.6	89.4	94.8	75.3	44.2	45.1	31.7	54.9	22.1
Ft. Wayne, IN	89.5	91.4	82.7	67.5	64.1	24.6	25.8	12.2	38.5	15.1
Ft. Worth, TX	83.7	85.4	88.4	86.9	54.7	31.4	33.4	23.0	54.3	10.9
Gainesville, FL	90.5	92.9	80.5	93.2	89.3	38.3	42.3	13.0	71.7	44.9
Grand Rapids, MI	89.3	91.0	78.0	70.5	62.3	27.5	28.9	13.1	38.5	11.6
Green Bay, WI	90.4	91.0	81.2	83.6	48.1	23.9	24.2	7.1	36.4	9.6
Greensboro, NC	84.8	86.7	83.8	70.2	54.2	26.4	28.4	20.8	35.9	10.9
Honolulu, HI	90.3	96.4	95.4	87.4	89.4	31.6	43.0	27.8	32.8	20.5
Houston, TX	81.0	81.9	87.6	85.1	57.2	29.0	30.3	23.3	50.6	11.6
Huntsville, AL	88.3	89.0	87.0	85.1	62.5	34.8	36.5	27.2	54.4	19.8
Indianapolis, IN	88.6	90.3	84.3	86.4	56.2	31.2	33.5	17.2	59.0	13.0
Jacksonville, FL	88.7	90.0	84.6	87.5	82.7	27.3	29.4	16.4	45.2	23.7
Kansas City, MO	90.5	92.2	85.4	83.6	66.2	33.0	35.4	17.7	51.0	16.3
Lafayette, LA	84.1	88.0	73.4	77.1	70.1	24.7	28.8	12.2	31.3	16.9
Las Vegas, NV	83.9	85.3	87.8	88.9	60.6	22.0	22.5	16.4	36.8	8.6
Lexington, KY	87.0	88.5	84.3	90.9	51.9	33.8	35.7	16.3	69.2	11.7
Lincoln, NE	93.4	94.6	85.9	72.8	68.5	35.3	35.9	21.4	41.5	21.1
Little Rock, AR	88.6	89.8	85.0	86.1	68.2	27.7	29.6	19.3	52.6	13.8
Los Angeles, CA	78.2	80.9	88.3	86.9	56.6	31.3	33.2	23.8	49.8	10.7
Louisville, KY	87.3	88.2	83.1	80.5	70.1	25.9	26.9	17.0	53.9	17.4
Lubbock, TX	84.4	87.0	79.2	87.5	66.0	27.6	29.8	11.3	68.8	9.4
Madison, WI	94.5	95.3	87.4	89.4	73.3	42.9	43.1	22.8	67.1	23.5
Manchester, NH	90.8	91.5	83.5	84.2	70.1	35.5	35.1	29.5	55.3	19.0

Table continued on next page.

Metro Area	High School Graduate or Higher (%)					Bachelor's Degree or Higher (%)				
	Total	White	Black	Asian	Hisp.[1]	Total	White	Black	Asian	Hisp.[1]
McAllen, TX	62.3	62.9	78.1	93.7	58.3	16.1	16.0	25.2	66.5	13.5
Miami, FL	83.6	85.3	77.9	86.7	76.2	28.8	31.4	17.0	48.5	23.4
Midland, TX	81.5	82.4	83.8	77.6	59.2	22.8	23.8	15.3	45.4	6.8
Minneapolis, MN	93.0	95.2	81.4	79.7	65.1	38.7	40.4	19.8	44.3	17.8
Montgomery, AL	85.2	89.7	79.0	86.0	61.4	27.0	32.3	18.4	48.6	19.7
Nashville, TN	87.2	88.7	84.1	86.0	59.9	30.9	32.3	23.6	46.3	12.9
New Orleans, LA	84.5	88.9	78.5	72.8	71.3	26.3	32.1	14.7	35.6	19.7
New York, NY	84.8	89.3	82.4	82.0	66.8	36.5	41.4	21.9	52.3	16.0
Oklahoma City, OK	87.6	89.1	88.1	79.8	54.8	28.2	29.9	19.9	42.7	10.1
Omaha, NE	91.1	93.0	84.1	78.7	55.6	32.9	34.3	17.9	52.2	12.5
Orlando, FL	87.4	89.3	82.6	85.4	79.2	27.8	29.4	18.4	45.6	19.1
Oxnard, CA	82.5	83.7	93.8	92.1	57.8	31.3	31.4	33.4	56.9	10.8
Peoria, IL	91.1	92.1	79.0	94.2	74.9	25.7	25.9	10.9	76.7	15.8
Philadelphia, PA	88.7	91.6	83.6	82.1	66.3	33.4	37.2	17.3	53.5	14.4
Phoenix, AZ	86.2	87.6	89.1	87.3	62.8	28.4	29.2	22.0	52.7	10.4
Pittsburgh, PA	91.8	92.3	86.7	89.7	84.1	29.8	30.1	15.8	70.5	34.0
Portland, OR	90.5	92.6	86.4	85.4	60.6	34.1	35.0	22.9	45.6	13.8
Providence, RI	83.8	85.5	77.3	78.4	60.4	29.2	30.4	18.9	42.2	11.6
Provo, UT	93.4	94.3	95.5	91.2	71.4	35.7	36.1	50.6	52.5	18.8
Raleigh, NC	89.8	91.9	86.5	91.1	53.2	41.3	44.8	26.2	66.5	12.9
Reno, NV	86.3	87.9	86.1	89.8	52.7	27.2	28.5	14.7	37.1	9.3
Richmond, VA	86.6	89.9	80.5	85.2	55.5	32.0	37.4	17.9	56.6	16.6
Riverside, CA	78.6	80.7	88.3	88.4	60.6	19.4	19.4	20.0	47.1	8.0
Rochester, MN	93.6	94.7	73.4	86.5	71.1	35.4	35.4	18.3	50.2	25.8
Salem, OR	84.5	88.8	93.4	86.7	47.2	22.5	24.5	32.9	32.1	7.7
Salt Lake City, UT	88.9	91.2	81.6	82.2	61.8	31.0	32.1	19.4	44.8	11.4
San Antonio, TX	82.9	84.5	89.3	83.8	72.5	26.0	27.5	23.8	48.5	14.2
San Diego, CA	85.3	86.7	89.7	88.1	62.9	34.1	35.3	21.4	45.0	14.7
San Francisco, CA	87.5	90.9	89.1	84.5	67.5	44.2	48.5	23.6	49.5	18.0
San Jose, CA	86.4	87.7	92.3	89.2	64.8	45.7	43.0	30.0	60.7	13.5
Santa Rosa, CA	86.9	89.8	83.5	82.8	58.4	32.0	34.1	30.2	39.8	10.3
Savannah, GA	87.4	90.1	82.9	78.7	64.5	28.8	33.7	17.8	37.4	25.6
Seattle, WA	91.4	93.5	87.8	85.6	69.7	37.3	38.4	19.9	46.7	17.6
Sioux Falls, SD	91.6	93.5	72.5	66.7	54.4	30.0	31.2	13.3	35.9	13.3
Spokane, WA	92.7	93.4	95.1	80.6	79.1	28.8	29.3	20.1	33.3	15.3
Springfield, MO	89.0	89.4	85.1	85.7	66.2	25.4	25.6	17.4	37.4	19.8
Tallahassee, FL	89.0	93.1	80.8	92.9	77.9	36.3	41.6	22.6	72.0	28.6
Tampa, FL	87.5	88.8	82.6	83.9	75.7	26.0	26.5	18.1	47.4	17.3
Topeka, KS	91.3	92.4	85.8	85.1	66.8	26.7	28.2	10.8	59.1	10.0
Tulsa, OK	88.1	89.4	87.0	82.6	60.7	25.8	27.5	18.5	39.3	10.9
Virginia Beach, VA	89.7	92.2	84.5	88.8	83.3	28.6	32.5	18.8	41.9	21.0
Washington, DC	90.0	93.0	89.5	90.4	64.5	47.6	55.3	30.5	61.6	22.7
Wichita, KS	88.9	90.4	86.3	77.9	61.9	27.8	29.3	17.1	30.1	10.9
Wilmington, NC	88.6	90.5	80.5	92.0	58.5	31.0	34.3	11.1	61.6	12.3
Worcester, MA	89.2	90.7	86.7	83.1	66.4	33.7	34.2	23.7	55.6	13.5
U.S.	85.9	88.1	82.5	85.5	63.1	28.6	30.0	18.4	50.2	13.4

Note: Figures shown cover persons 25 years old and over; Figures cover the Metropolitan Statistical Area—see Appendix B for areas included; (1) People of Hispanic origin can be of any race
Source: U.S. Census Bureau, 2010-2012 American Community Survey 3-Year Estimates

Cost of Living Index

Urban Area	Composite	Groceries	Housing	Utilities	Transp.	Health	Misc.
Abilene, TX	n/a	n/a	n/a	n/a	n/a	n/a	n/a
Albuquerque, NM[1]	92.7	89.8	82.6	89.1	99.9	97.8	99.4
Anchorage, AK	125.7	112.6	154.1	98.9	107.0	139.0	121.8
Ann Arbor, MI	101.7	85.8	112.7	106.6	105.0	99.2	97.0
Athens, GA	n/a	n/a	n/a	n/a	n/a	n/a	n/a
Atlanta, GA	94.9	91.2	87.1	92.0	102.0	102.5	99.6
Austin, TX	92.9	84.0	86.0	91.1	97.2	99.4	99.8
Baltimore, MD	112.6	105.0	154.6	102.5	98.7	95.0	93.4
Billings, MT	n/a	n/a	n/a	n/a	n/a	n/a	n/a
Boise City, ID	93.2	85.6	86.7	87.9	103.7	103.8	97.3
Boston, MA	139.1	125.5	175.3	144.3	104.1	126.1	129.7
Boulder, CO	n/a	n/a	n/a	n/a	n/a	n/a	n/a
Cape Coral, FL	97.4	91.9	93.2	98.1	109.1	98.1	98.3
Cedar Rapids, IA	91.6	86.5	82.1	102.2	94.6	101.5	95.2
Charleston, SC	99.8	104.9	88.8	113.5	95.7	103.0	103.4
Charlotte, NC	95.4	101.6	83.7	106.6	98.4	98.2	97.0
Chicago, IL	114.8	98.1	135.3	98.9	124.1	97.7	109.2
Cincinnati, OH	91.4	92.0	79.0	86.8	105.2	99.8	95.8
Clarksville, TN	n/a	n/a	n/a	n/a	n/a	n/a	n/a
Colorado Springs, CO	95.7	93.5	94.4	101.0	94.4	102.4	95.6
Columbia, MO	95.6	91.3	88.3	98.0	94.3	101.7	102.1
Columbus, OH	86.9	86.5	77.1	96.4	96.2	95.1	87.2
Dallas, TX	95.6	92.3	75.5	106.9	102.2	99.1	106.2
Davenport, IA	95.4	86.6	100.2	85.5	111.2	94.9	92.1
Denver, CO	103.8	93.4	115.5	101.3	94.8	103.7	103.0
Des Moines, IA	90.0	85.2	85.4	89.5	96.1	93.6	92.8
Durham, NC	92.3	100.4	80.2	83.5	98.6	101.7	97.5
El Paso, TX	91.2	90.8	84.0	87.2	97.5	89.9	96.1
Erie, PA	97.8	97.5	94.8	97.1	100.5	94.6	99.9
Eugene, OR	n/a	n/a	n/a	n/a	n/a	n/a	n/a
Fargo, ND	93.5	97.6	83.6	89.4	95.6	111.8	97.4
Fayetteville, NC	n/a	n/a	n/a	n/a	n/a	n/a	n/a
Fort Collins, CO	n/a	n/a	n/a	n/a	n/a	n/a	n/a
Fort Wayne, IN	91.3	82.5	85.0	89.5	104.3	95.8	94.7
Fort Worth, TX	97.1	93.6	85.6	99.6	101.8	104.1	103.9
Gainesville, FL	98.7	97.3	94.1	106.1	104.1	101.2	98.1
Grand Rapids, MI	92.7	84.4	77.6	99.4	106.6	91.8	100.9
Green Bay, WI	93.3	86.4	83.9	101.2	99.5	106.1	96.9
Greensboro, NC[2]	88.1	98.0	69.5	100.3	85.3	102.9	94.0
Honolulu, HI	168.3	154.7	262.4	171.4	126.5	111.3	123.1
Houston, TX	98.8	79.5	107.3	103.2	95.4	96.4	100.2
Huntsville, AL	94.2	89.4	79.1	103.7	98.7	96.2	103.2
Indianapolis, IN	91.6	85.5	80.9	91.3	99.4	115.7	96.1
Jacksonville, FL	94.9	95.2	83.3	105.7	104.7	85.1	98.4
Kansas City, MO	98.9	95.6	91.7	110.6	98.2	96.3	102.9
Lafayette, LA	95.9	90.5	101.5	87.8	104.1	84.8	94.6
Las Vegas, NV	100.4	96.5	99.7	85.3	100.9	103.4	106.4
Lexington, KY	89.4	86.1	75.6	101.0	97.9	94.3	94.1
Lincoln, NE	89.3	87.6	75.6	92.3	96.6	95.0	96.3
Little Rock, AR	97.9	89.2	96.6	110.3	93.3	83.9	102.5
Los Angeles, CA	129.8	102.8	196.8	108.0	111.0	109.5	104.8
Louisville, KY	91.0	85.3	81.6	87.2	101.0	91.2	98.1
Lubbock, TX	89.2	90.4	81.4	78.4	95.0	95.6	95.0
Madison, WI	105.2	90.5	110.4	104.2	106.1	123.9	104.2
Manchester, NH	120.2	98.5	137.9	122.7	101.2	117.7	121.9
McAllen, TX	87.9	83.3	78.8	99.9	94.6	88.6	90.5

Table continued on next page.

Urban Area	Composite	Groceries	Housing	Utilities	Transp.	Health	Misc.
Miami, FL	107.2	99.9	118.0	95.7	110.4	104.4	104.3
Midland, TX	99.4	88.3	100.2	93.2	104.7	95.0	103.7
Minneapolis, MN	109.7	115.4	116.5	97.8	103.6	98.9	109.4
Montgomery, AL	94.4	95.2	85.6	110.2	96.7	84.7	96.7
Nashville, TN	87.3	87.8	74.3	87.0	94.1	81.4	95.8
New Orleans, LA	98.4	97.9	95.1	91.3	100.0	103.2	102.1
New York, NY	170.7	118.7	320.3	124.0	111.9	110.3	119.2
Oklahoma City, OK	89.9	87.8	82.2	91.6	98.9	98.1	91.7
Omaha, NE	86.9	84.3	78.4	91.1	96.6	100.6	87.6
Orlando, FL	96.0	96.7	78.6	104.4	98.5	99.3	105.6
Oxnard, CA	n/a	n/a	n/a	n/a	n/a	n/a	n/a
Peoria, IL	99.2	89.0	100.0	95.9	108.2	95.8	100.8
Philadelphia, PA	120.8	112.8	141.9	128.2	105.1	100.0	114.3
Phoenix, AZ	95.6	93.4	96.2	97.6	95.5	95.8	95.4
Pittsburgh, PA	93.6	94.2	79.3	94.9	104.2	100.9	99.1
Portland, OR	117.1	102.7	142.3	96.6	115.1	117.2	110.1
Providence, RI	125.2	106.9	138.8	133.1	104.2	118.2	128.4
Provo, UT	95.5	88.3	87.1	91.0	111.3	93.1	100.8
Raleigh, NC	93.3	101.7	76.1	105.7	97.8	101.7	96.6
Reno, NV	89.8	90.1	88.1	73.0	103.1	93.3	90.4
Richmond, VA	101.4	98.2	89.4	107.6	99.7	106.5	110.1
Riverside, CA	112.1	104.2	133.9	111.7	111.8	101.3	99.9
Rochester, MN	100.6	95.9	99.3	101.8	101.9	104.8	102.0
Salem, OR	n/a	n/a	n/a	n/a	n/a	n/a	n/a
Salt Lake City, UT	94.1	88.4	90.0	84.2	98.8	96.7	100.5
San Antonio, TX	88.4	81.4	79.5	82.6	95.5	93.7	96.6
San Diego, CA	129.4	101.6	199.0	97.7	113.3	109.7	104.5
San Francisco, CA	160.8	119.2	293.5	95.0	114.9	119.9	116.4
San Jose, CA	148.6	110.4	255.6	123.2	112.1	114.6	106.5
Santa Rosa, CA	n/a	n/a	n/a	n/a	n/a	n/a	n/a
Savannah, GA	92.5	91.2	71.5	111.5	102.0	100.1	99.2
Seattle, WA	118.6	102.6	140.1	97.0	118.3	118.9	114.7
Sioux Falls, SD	97.1	86.3	92.5	107.1	93.7	101.3	102.8
Spokane, WA	95.6	91.8	88.4	91.2	99.5	109.8	100.5
Springfield, MO	88.2	89.8	74.6	92.6	92.5	100.6	93.6
Tallahassee, FL	98.1	99.2	98.2	88.7	101.1	101.4	98.6
Tampa, FL	92.8	92.7	78.4	93.9	102.3	95.6	99.8
Topeka, KS	93.4	87.5	91.4	84.0	94.3	91.8	100.2
Tulsa, OK	88.0	85.5	65.0	96.5	96.3	95.5	100.3
Virginia Beach, VA	n/a	n/a	n/a	n/a	n/a	n/a	n/a
Washington, DC	139.4	107.9	247.5	104.1	105.6	98.6	96.6
Wichita, KS	91.6	88.2	75.6	107.7	96.9	94.8	98.2
Wilmington, NC	98.2	104.8	84.9	107.8	97.8	107.4	102.0
Worcester, MA[3]	104.2	94.3	97.7	117.6	103.8	123.4	106.6
U.S.	100.0	100.0	100.0	100.0	100.0	100.0	100.0

Note: The Cost of Living Index measures regional differences in the cost of consumer goods and services, excluding taxes and non-consumer expenditures, for professional and managerial households in the top income quintile. It is based on more than 50,000 prices covering almost 60 different items for which prices are collected three times a year by chambers of commerce, economic development organizations or university applied economic centers in each participating urban area. The numbers shown should be read as a percentage above or below the national average of 100. For example, a value of 115.4 in the groceries column indicates that grocery prices are 15.4% higher than the national average. Small differences in the index numbers should not be interpreted as significant. In cases where data is not available for the city, data for the metro area or for a neighboring city has been provided and noted below; (1) Rio Rancho NM; (2) Winston-Salem NC; (3) Fitchburg-Leominster MA
Source: The Council for Community and Economic Research (formerly ACCRA), Cost of Living Index, 2013

Grocery Prices

Urban Area	T-Bone Steak ($/pound)	Frying Chicken ($/pound)	Whole Milk ($/half gal.)	Eggs ($/dozen)	Orange Juice ($/64 oz.)	Coffee ($/11.5 oz.)
Abilene, TX	n/a	n/a	n/a	n/a	n/a	n/a
Albuquerque, NM[1]	9.99	0.99	2.38	2.00	3.03	4.59
Anchorage, AK	11.19	1.24	2.43	2.50	4.68	5.50
Ann Arbor, MI	10.09	1.02	2.08	1.70	3.03	4.50
Athens, GA	n/a	n/a	n/a	n/a	n/a	n/a
Atlanta, GA	11.52	1.09	2.22	1.66	3.41	4.93
Austin, TX	8.95	1.25	2.13	1.70	3.17	3.57
Baltimore, MD	10.49	1.39	2.55	2.28	3.57	4.85
Billings, MT	n/a	n/a	n/a	n/a	n/a	n/a
Boise City, ID	9.42	1.02	1.75	1.45	3.38	4.50
Boston, MA	11.49	1.64	2.79	2.99	3.85	5.07
Boulder, CO	n/a	n/a	n/a	n/a	n/a	n/a
Cape Coral, FL	10.66	1.13	2.60	1.79	3.42	4.11
Cedar Rapids, IA	9.76	1.28	1.96	1.63	3.22	4.04
Charleston, SC	10.12	1.46	2.73	1.76	3.54	4.31
Charlotte, NC	9.59	1.42	2.71	1.79	3.44	3.85
Chicago, IL	10.63	1.48	2.11	1.84	3.72	5.86
Cincinnati, OH	10.80	1.40	1.86	1.69	3.62	4.77
Clarksville, TN	n/a	n/a	n/a	n/a	n/a	n/a
Colorado Springs, CO	10.79	1.18	2.05	1.95	3.32	4.90
Columbia, MO	10.53	1.11	2.39	1.69	3.35	4.41
Columbus, OH	10.70	1.11	1.99	1.74	3.27	4.70
Dallas, TX	10.54	1.19	2.18	1.71	3.61	4.46
Davenport, IA	9.57	1.13	2.19	1.52	3.38	4.45
Denver, CO	11.46	1.32	1.98	1.89	3.84	5.11
Des Moines, IA	9.22	1.28	2.03	1.48	3.36	4.20
Durham, NC	10.14	1.46	2.65	1.85	3.46	4.08
El Paso, TX	10.28	1.15	2.13	1.66	3.25	4.96
Erie, PA	10.33	1.33	2.06	1.80	3.29	4.76
Eugene, OR	n/a	n/a	n/a	n/a	n/a	n/a
Fargo, ND	10.24	1.45	2.81	1.58	3.52	4.48
Fayetteville, NC	n/a	n/a	n/a	n/a	n/a	n/a
Fort Collins, CO	n/a	n/a	n/a	n/a	n/a	n/a
Fort Wayne, IN	11.06	0.99	2.05	1.69	3.55	4.60
Fort Worth, TX	9.66	1.29	2.33	1.74	3.35	4.06
Gainesville, FL	10.33	1.31	2.70	1.93	3.67	4.19
Grand Rapids, MI	10.51	1.09	2.10	1.67	3.33	3.89
Green Bay, WI	10.41	1.36	2.27	1.38	3.19	4.02
Greensboro, NC[2]	10.89	1.37	2.68	1.86	3.28	3.75
Honolulu, HI	9.99	2.28	3.56	3.39	5.12	7.32
Houston, TX	9.80	1.00	2.11	1.52	3.16	4.01
Huntsville, AL	10.28	1.19	2.21	1.55	3.35	4.14
Indianapolis, IN	9.71	1.11	2.00	1.71	3.31	4.26
Jacksonville, FL	10.37	1.50	2.66	1.94	3.49	4.07
Kansas City, MO	10.77	1.23	2.55	1.67	3.26	4.39
Lafayette, LA	9.58	1.13	2.81	1.65	3.40	4.00
Las Vegas, NV	9.07	1.26	2.21	1.91	4.03	5.14
Lexington, KY	9.99	1.01	2.11	1.81	3.44	4.09
Lincoln, NE	10.54	1.14	2.04	1.51	3.76	4.79
Little Rock, AR	10.64	1.07	2.08	1.79	3.36	4.00
Los Angeles, CA	10.46	1.48	2.22	2.21	3.50	5.56
Louisville, KY	9.24	0.97	1.99	1.86	3.15	4.42
Lubbock, TX	9.86	1.05	2.63	1.73	3.16	4.04
Madison, WI	10.69	1.47	2.13	1.32	3.53	4.38
Manchester, NH	10.68	1.26	2.22	1.88	2.88	3.81

Table continued on next page.

Urban Area	T-Bone Steak ($/pound)	Frying Chicken ($/pound)	Whole Milk ($/half gal.)	Eggs ($/dozen)	Orange Juice ($/64 oz.)	Coffee ($/11.5 oz.)
McAllen, TX	9.82	1.08	2.70	1.59	3.20	3.85
Miami, FL	11.10	1.43	2.66	1.91	3.45	3.43
Midland, TX	9.55	1.09	2.05	1.92	3.51	3.94
Minneapolis, MN	14.82	2.09	2.34	1.95	3.62	4.68
Montgomery, AL	9.42	1.29	2.63	1.95	3.13	3.65
Nashville, TN	10.63	1.08	2.05	1.73	3.24	4.11
New Orleans, LA	10.81	1.33	2.86	1.87	3.65	3.91
New York, NY	12.32	1.73	2.26	2.61	4.18	5.13
Oklahoma City, OK	9.69	1.26	2.31	1.64	3.40	4.48
Omaha, NE	9.95	1.16	2.09	1.50	3.58	4.35
Orlando, FL	10.72	1.43	2.67	1.94	3.77	3.86
Oxnard, CA	n/a	n/a	n/a	n/a	n/a	n/a
Peoria, IL	10.02	1.02	2.06	1.74	3.60	4.13
Philadelphia, PA	10.56	1.73	2.10	2.30	3.89	4.64
Phoenix, AZ	11.36	1.50	1.87	1.83	3.58	4.83
Pittsburgh, PA	10.53	1.43	2.05	1.69	3.56	4.51
Portland, OR	10.34	1.41	2.00	1.77	3.96	5.20
Providence, RI	11.56	1.36	2.94	2.26	3.29	4.51
Provo, UT	9.31	1.24	2.37	1.73	3.39	6.00
Raleigh, NC	10.51	1.50	2.61	1.98	3.70	4.00
Reno, NV	9.27	1.33	2.10	1.66	3.46	4.72
Richmond, VA	10.12	1.30	2.36	1.74	3.08	4.30
Riverside, CA	9.58	1.47	2.14	2.27	3.81	5.50
Rochester, MN	10.98	1.51	2.08	1.75	3.56	4.62
Salem, OR	n/a	n/a	n/a	n/a	n/a	n/a
Salt Lake City, UT	10.24	1.16	2.09	1.74	3.41	4.97
San Antonio, TX	9.67	0.99	2.16	1.56	3.38	3.89
San Diego, CA	9.77	1.55	2.16	2.09	3.43	5.33
San Francisco, CA	10.46	1.55	2.66	2.86	3.87	6.04
San Jose, CA	10.80	1.29	2.32	2.74	4.03	6.58
Santa Rosa, CA	n/a	n/a	n/a	n/a	n/a	n/a
Savannah, GA	9.54	1.25	2.63	1.65	3.32	4.02
Seattle, WA	11.01	1.52	1.91	1.75	3.97	5.30
Sioux Falls, SD	8.95	1.23	1.97	1.43	3.48	4.10
Spokane, WA	10.08	1.29	2.07	1.63	3.31	4.71
Springfield, MO	10.85	1.17	2.31	1.64	3.45	4.24
Tallahassee, FL	10.76	1.37	2.75	1.95	3.58	4.24
Tampa, FL	10.61	1.33	2.58	1.73	3.16	3.60
Topeka, KS	10.15	1.11	2.17	1.63	3.43	4.23
Tulsa, OK	9.31	1.09	2.34	1.62	3.63	4.01
Virginia Beach, VA	n/a	n/a	n/a	n/a	n/a	n/a
Washington, DC	10.52	1.57	2.58	2.36	3.65	4.93
Wichita, KS	9.47	1.21	2.38	1.68	3.49	4.11
Wilmington, NC	10.88	1.39	2.62	2.10	3.42	4.33
Worcester, MA[3]	9.82	1.41	1.86	1.51	3.28	4.69
Average*	10.19	1.28	2.34	1.81	3.48	4.39
Minimum*	8.56	0.94	1.44	1.19	2.78	3.40
Maximum*	14.82	2.28	3.56	3.73	6.23	7.32

Note: **T-Bone Steak** (price per pound); **Frying Chicken** (price per pound, whole fryer); **Whole Milk** (half gallon carton); **Eggs** (price per dozen, Grade A, large); **Orange Juice** (64 oz. Tropicana or Florida Natural); **Coffee** (11.5 oz. can, vacuum-packed, Maxwell House, Hills Bros, or Folgers); (*) Values for the local area are compared with the average, minimum, and maximum values for all 327 areas in the Cost of Living Index report; n/a not available; In cases where data is not available for the city, data for the metro area or for a neighboring city has been provided and noted below; (1) Rio Rancho NM; (2) Winston-Salem NC; (3) Fitchburg-Leominster MA
Source: The Council for Community and Economic Research (formerly ACCRA), Cost of Living Index, 2013

Housing and Utility Costs

Urban Area	New Home Price ($)	Apartment Rent ($/month)	All Electric ($/month)	Part Electric ($/month)	Other Energy ($/month)	Telephone ($/month)
Abilene, TX	n/a	n/a	n/a	n/a	n/a	n/a
Albuquerque, NM[1]	243,339	759	-	102.21	54.04	22.15
Anchorage, AK	476,652	1,277	-	71.12	96.57	26.01
Ann Arbor, MI	338,760	952	-	111.57	68.48	28.21
Athens, GA	n/a	n/a	n/a	n/a	n/a	n/a
Atlanta, GA	239,252	964	-	94.08	58.37	25.06
Austin, TX	234,211	970	-	89.15	36.67	30.94
Baltimore, MD	447,890	1,432	-	90.68	78.22	28.11
Billings, MT	n/a	n/a	n/a	n/a	n/a	n/a
Boise City, ID	260,775	743	-	90.33	59.21	22.95
Boston, MA	482,267	1,863	-	105.74	137.62	38.25
Boulder, CO	n/a	n/a	n/a	n/a	n/a	n/a
Cape Coral, FL	271,536	847	189.95	-	-	20.00
Cedar Rapids, IA	245,521	766	-	96.44	64.02	29.99
Charleston, SC	238,131	1,058	196.23	-	-	28.92
Charlotte, NC	244,676	829	164.64	-	-	31.94
Chicago, IL	398,795	1,175	-	86.36	64.58	30.04
Cincinnati, OH	217,051	847	-	84.01	61.24	23.27
Clarksville, TN	n/a	n/a	n/a	n/a	n/a	n/a
Colorado Springs, CO	270,912	902	-	66.42	59.93	37.45
Columbia, MO	268,483	749	-	88.84	66.30	28.45
Columbus, OH	217,589	784	-	90.95	61.53	27.99
Dallas, TX	214,062	818	-	134.32	46.62	28.15
Davenport, IA	316,168	750	-	66.26	70.13	24.52
Denver, CO	349,490	1,009	-	103.82	63.88	27.61
Des Moines, IA	275,275	636	-	68.04	69.09	27.10
Durham, NC	232,103	802	148.11	-	-	20.37
El Paso, TX	232,054	922	-	97.59	33.67	26.95
Erie, PA	295,090	684	-	98.71	80.68	21.95
Eugene, OR	n/a	n/a	n/a	n/a	n/a	n/a
Fargo, ND	247,098	792	-	63.42	61.61	29.95
Fayetteville, NC	n/a	n/a	n/a	n/a	n/a	n/a
Fort Collins, CO	n/a	n/a	n/a	n/a	n/a	n/a
Fort Wayne, IN	265,671	614	-	66.05	54.95	30.99
Fort Worth, TX	214,551	1,179	-	133.76	46.62	23.34
Gainesville, FL	271,646	900	-	121.68	45.26	31.06
Grand Rapids, MI	220,542	789	-	87.62	73.18	28.01
Green Bay, WI	266,845	624	-	78.44	74.27	31.21
Greensboro, NC[2]	202,750	659	157.77	-	-	29.33
Honolulu, HI	742,651	2,733	364.83	-	-	26.95
Houston, TX	248,558	1,435	-	119.33	45.38	29.59
Huntsville, AL	225,591	815	146.54	-	-	34.39
Indianapolis, IN	224,970	894	-	81.37	66.38	25.68
Jacksonville, FL	216,016	1,037	171.80	-	-	29.58
Kansas City, MO	270,041	845	-	91.98	76.65	33.67
Lafayette, LA	298,091	940	-	91.54	44.89	26.12
Las Vegas, NV	303,436	797	-	117.68	39.76	19.32
Lexington, KY	210,972	792	-	83.74	52.77	34.99
Lincoln, NE	229,001	670	-	69.72	82.55	25.25
Little Rock, AR	291,639	755	-	79.66	64.28	39.47
Los Angeles, CA	552,280	2,051	-	104.77	59.89	32.90
Louisville, KY	233,107	793	-	58.52	65.67	28.66
Lubbock, TX	242,341	720	-	79.41	39.42	24.00
Madison, WI	346,950	866	-	103.82	78.52	25.99
Manchester, NH	389,899	1,378	-	106.64	84.83	36.25

Table continued on next page.

Urban Area	New Home Price ($)	Apartment Rent ($/month)	All Electric ($/month)	Part Electric ($/month)	Other Energy ($/month)	Telephone ($/month)
McAllen, TX	220,129	795	-	136.74	54.28	21.01
Miami, FL	325,413	1,290	150.39	-	-	28.01
Midland, TX	260,386	1,215	-	115.78	40.33	24.95
Minneapolis, MN	342,058	1,100	-	84.79	83.48	25.07
Montgomery, AL	265,245	673	182.72	-	-	29.99
Nashville, TN	200,706	811	-	84.68	57.33	24.16
New Orleans, LA	277,938	861	-	97.49	54.79	24.59
New York, NY	990,514	2,493	-	116.34	103.28	30.33
Oklahoma City, OK	245,212	767	-	78.90	60.11	28.01
Omaha, NE	238,755	688	-	83.48	59.70	26.68
Orlando, FL	214,602	857	171.11	-	-	28.86
Oxnard, CA	n/a	n/a	n/a	n/a	n/a	n/a
Peoria, IL	314,209	723	-	88.85	57.31	29.23
Philadelphia, PA	413,372	1,263	-	123.19	74.37	38.50
Phoenix, AZ	291,667	843	184.23	-	-	21.08
Pittsburgh, PA	220,334	855	-	83.58	77.16	24.95
Portland, OR	345,844	2,029	-	84.72	73.80	26.67
Providence, RI	386,097	1,450	-	117.64	102.89	36.19
Provo, UT	239,391	793	-	63.98	65.56	29.92
Raleigh, NC	228,372	649	-	94.58	65.98	32.33
Reno, NV	249,678	841	-	71.66	51.08	19.43
Richmond, VA	249,778	871	-	85.49	75.66	33.45
Riverside, CA	403,163	1,199	-	110.75	68.55	31.79
Rochester, MN	248,270	1,143	-	79.14	99.35	25.32
Salem, OR	n/a	n/a	n/a	n/a	n/a	n/a
Salt Lake City, UT	257,032	846	-	68.04	62.19	25.17
San Antonio, TX	222,574	838	-	92.24	36.48	24.49
San Diego, CA	584,280	1,790	-	85.70	50.15	32.90
San Francisco, CA	820,479	2,925	-	107.76	57.54	23.96
San Jose, CA	805,160	1,734	-	171.40	57.42	27.52
Santa Rosa, CA	n/a	n/a	n/a	n/a	n/a	n/a
Savannah, GA	205,496	726	170.47	-	-	33.80
Seattle, WA	382,151	1,643	162.36	-	-	25.99
Sioux Falls, SD	287,840	730	-	82.59	67.82	35.71
Spokane, WA	257,960	724	-	55.24	74.78	29.98
Springfield, MO	225,591	652	-	68.72	49.28	33.84
Tallahassee, FL	305,099	820	164.06	-	-	20.00
Tampa, FL	221,461	818	158.03	-	-	24.99
Topeka, KS	270,615	854	-	73.04	65.65	22.99
Tulsa, OK	192,729	604	-	65.78	61.84	34.13
Virginia Beach, VA	n/a	n/a	n/a	n/a	n/a	n/a
Washington, DC	767,485	1,961	-	78.65	97.87	27.32
Wichita, KS	223,589	673	-	85.02	65.61	36.09
Wilmington, NC	259,686	713	181.99	-	-	28.53
Worcester, MA[3]	288,809	881	-	93.43	109.81	29.99
Average*	295,864	900	171.38	91.82	70.12	27.73
Minimum*	185,506	458	117.80	48.81	33.67	17.16
Maximum*	1,358,917	3,783	441.68	171.40	372.65	39.47

*Note: **New Home Price** (2,400 sf living area, 8,000 sf lot, in urban area with full utilities); **Apartment Rent** (950 sf 2 bedroom/1.5 or 2 bath, unfurnished, excluding all utilities except water); **All Electric** (average monthly cost for an all-electric home); **Part Electric** (average monthly cost for a part-electric home); **Other Energy** (average monthly cost for natural gas, fuel oil, coal, wood, and any other forms of energy except electricity); **Telephone** (price includes basic monthly rate for a private residential line plus additional local usage charges incurred by a family of four); (*) Values for the local area are compared with the average, minimum, and maximum values for all 327 areas in the Cost of Living Index report; n/a not available; In cases where data is not available for the city, data for the metro area or for a neighboring city has been provided and noted below; (1) Rio Rancho NM; (2) Winston-Salem NC; (3) Fitchburg-Leominster MA*
Source: The Council for Community and Economic Research (formerly ACCRA), Cost of Living Index, 2013

Health Care, Transportation, and Other Costs

Urban Area	Doctor ($/visit)	Dentist ($/visit)	Optometrist ($/visit)	Gasoline ($/gallon)	Beauty Salon ($/visit)	Men's Shirt ($)
Abilene, TX	n/a	n/a	n/a	n/a	n/a	n/a
Albuquerque, NM[1]	94.25	95.69	100.00	3.21	22.75	35.86
Anchorage, AK	164.15	125.00	171.58	3.75	44.53	28.42
Ann Arbor, MI	91.51	90.47	98.94	3.62	37.00	23.87
Athens, GA	n/a	n/a	n/a	n/a	n/a	n/a
Atlanta, GA	97.60	99.69	76.89	3.42	42.10	24.19
Austin, TX	100.74	94.53	112.08	3.30	42.60	30.48
Baltimore, MD	82.09	84.36	70.43	3.48	43.32	26.88
Billings, MT	n/a	n/a	n/a	n/a	n/a	n/a
Boise City, ID	116.44	81.53	111.68	3.41	23.14	38.22
Boston, MA	149.00	114.07	120.73	3.61	44.00	36.52
Boulder, CO	n/a	n/a	n/a	n/a	n/a	n/a
Cape Coral, FL	85.97	85.69	86.36	3.54	35.31	20.52
Cedar Rapids, IA	125.28	72.79	105.33	3.32	30.34	25.41
Charleston, SC	95.15	92.47	105.89	3.28	42.50	31.50
Charlotte, NC	98.80	85.07	114.83	3.47	38.80	18.52
Chicago, IL	86.39	99.00	91.00	4.09	40.00	27.30
Cincinnati, OH	98.24	84.06	91.67	3.53	37.20	23.38
Clarksville, TN	n/a	n/a	n/a	n/a	n/a	n/a
Colorado Springs, CO	103.23	91.98	101.47	3.19	36.40	27.29
Columbia, MO	108.83	87.00	86.14	3.28	32.61	23.33
Columbus, OH	99.04	79.19	63.62	3.39	35.40	24.51
Dallas, TX	106.67	86.19	93.70	3.40	39.02	35.25
Davenport, IA	82.50	87.81	73.78	3.38	26.07	23.53
Denver, CO	124.47	80.09	101.09	3.23	39.82	26.93
Des Moines, IA	95.45	76.76	81.53	3.28	27.76	16.82
Durham, NC	95.42	84.50	115.08	3.46	43.75	19.39
El Paso, TX	83.33	77.83	83.33	3.27	32.17	24.94
Erie, PA	94.94	78.51	80.86	3.53	35.71	33.33
Eugene, OR	n/a	n/a	n/a	n/a	n/a	n/a
Fargo, ND	140.61	90.47	78.13	3.30	26.20	27.35
Fayetteville, NC	n/a	n/a	n/a	n/a	n/a	n/a
Fort Collins, CO	n/a	n/a	n/a	n/a	n/a	n/a
Fort Wayne, IN	86.33	85.38	97.33	3.53	20.48	25.77
Fort Worth, TX	96.72	100.50	82.11	3.35	38.39	36.00
Gainesville, FL	93.97	94.69	78.59	3.59	37.00	31.95
Grand Rapids, MI	90.33	77.00	85.60	3.50	37.50	21.91
Green Bay, WI	130.29	82.84	62.79	3.51	27.80	33.15
Greensboro, NC[2]	107.75	83.20	95.40	3.36	36.53	30.24
Honolulu, HI	109.87	86.91	141.39	4.18	51.83	52.03
Houston, TX	90.61	86.57	89.60	3.38	46.10	24.22
Huntsville, AL	79.53	82.56	133.61	3.30	33.00	35.98
Indianapolis, IN	104.10	120.45	85.33	3.45	31.37	30.05
Jacksonville, FL	67.03	88.43	61.02	3.52	43.07	23.47
Kansas City, MO	93.19	86.80	87.96	3.24	24.62	39.97
Lafayette, LA	70.27	72.80	65.20	3.33	32.40	24.46
Las Vegas, NV	112.39	90.21	104.58	3.44	53.46	38.97
Lexington, KY	89.24	89.27	68.33	3.48	37.40	22.79
Lincoln, NE	102.75	72.57	96.67	3.27	28.31	28.81
Little Rock, AR	102.61	50.83	89.44	3.28	40.27	29.29
Los Angeles, CA	100.60	98.13	118.90	3.91	60.61	28.08
Louisville, KY	86.27	86.30	78.43	3.58	33.20	27.66
Lubbock, TX	99.08	77.20	96.47	3.20	35.93	26.92
Madison, WI	182.71	93.56	53.35	3.43	40.07	23.96
Manchester, NH	149.00	98.13	102.96	3.55	38.13	35.78

Table continued on next page.

Urban Area	Doctor ($/visit)	Dentist ($/visit)	Optometrist ($/visit)	Gasoline ($/gallon)	Beauty Salon ($/visit)	Men's Shirt ($)
McAllen, TX	70.00	75.33	85.44	3.29	30.83	18.66
Miami, FL	108.85	98.88	91.33	3.57	58.07	18.10
Midland, TX	92.67	82.00	94.33	3.32	34.95	22.93
Minneapolis, MN	117.48	80.26	79.95	3.40	36.37	24.62
Montgomery, AL	77.11	62.45	82.44	3.26	38.33	33.60
Nashville, TN	78.53	78.20	78.31	3.34	31.00	25.59
New Orleans, LA	77.67	103.40	77.06	3.30	37.45	32.69
New York, NY	108.35	114.81	76.87	3.82	57.93	31.16
Oklahoma City, OK	85.75	102.30	98.78	3.32	35.57	23.89
Omaha, NE	129.33	66.10	98.53	3.24	30.67	18.04
Orlando, FL	75.96	84.18	62.50	3.34	42.59	36.62
Oxnard, CA	n/a	n/a	n/a	n/a	n/a	n/a
Peoria, IL	101.85	71.93	94.85	3.48	23.41	23.01
Philadelphia, PA	118.09	94.76	100.24	3.48	52.14	39.08
Phoenix, AZ	96.94	87.54	89.72	3.37	40.80	19.48
Pittsburgh, PA	94.13	85.40	97.27	3.63	38.37	23.92
Portland, OR	141.65	96.40	123.95	3.77	41.70	31.32
Providence, RI	149.00	96.22	116.67	3.68	45.48	39.46
Provo, UT	98.23	68.48	88.94	3.60	32.11	31.84
Raleigh, NC	97.60	104.92	97.55	3.34	36.53	22.47
Reno, NV	79.00	92.47	108.25	3.61	32.00	19.59
Richmond, VA	90.42	103.67	119.17	3.37	51.78	22.08
Riverside, CA	86.21	92.23	89.25	3.92	36.36	35.82
Rochester, MN	127.22	83.58	86.12	3.43	31.53	27.66
Salem, OR	n/a	n/a	n/a	n/a	n/a	n/a
Salt Lake City, UT	90.00	82.17	90.04	3.27	47.36	21.09
San Antonio, TX	96.00	88.07	85.55	3.33	41.27	27.57
San Diego, CA	103.86	99.93	102.65	3.90	55.35	25.65
San Francisco, CA	130.96	115.18	123.11	3.98	58.61	33.95
San Jose, CA	105.54	113.00	130.31	3.85	46.61	23.88
Santa Rosa, CA	n/a	n/a	n/a	n/a	n/a	n/a
Savannah, GA	113.42	75.53	71.90	3.40	37.25	22.48
Seattle, WA	110.21	116.74	153.83	3.80	47.22	26.09
Sioux Falls, SD	113.50	81.80	97.97	3.32	27.88	25.12
Spokane, WA	127.03	97.07	112.56	3.43	33.95	21.19
Springfield, MO	116.72	78.95	88.78	3.20	30.83	23.74
Tallahassee, FL	102.20	90.72	81.84	3.52	35.06	36.57
Tampa, FL	80.31	89.27	78.38	3.41	39.23	23.60
Topeka, KS	77.57	75.22	110.67	3.21	25.20	34.50
Tulsa, OK	102.58	71.00	79.70	3.08	33.33	23.72
Virginia Beach, VA	n/a	n/a	n/a	n/a	n/a	n/a
Washington, DC	84.40	89.47	72.98	3.73	51.00	26.52
Wichita, KS	89.26	78.01	129.04	3.34	35.62	44.69
Wilmington, NC	120.42	109.38	94.42	3.45	40.62	31.96
Worcester, MA[3]	178.33	105.00	96.94	3.54	31.52	31.35
Average*	101.40	86.48	96.16	3.44	33.87	26.55
Minimum*	61.67	50.83	50.12	3.08	18.92	12.48
Maximum*	182.71	152.50	223.78	4.33	68.22	52.03

Note: **Doctor** *(general practitioners routine exam of an established patient);* **Dentist** *(adult teeth cleaning and periodic oral examination);* **Optometrist** *(full vision eye exam for established adult patient);* **Gasoline** *(one gallon regular unleaded, national brand, including all taxes, cash price at self-service pump if available);* **Beauty Salon** *(woman's shampoo, trim, and blow-dry);* **Men's Shirt** *(cotton/polyester dress shirt, pinpoint weave, long sleeves); (*) Values for the local area are compared with the average, minimum, and maximum values for all 327 areas in the Cost of Living Index report; n/a not available; In cases where data is not available for the city, data for the metro area or for a neighboring city has been provided and noted below; (1) Rio Rancho NM; (2) Winston-Salem NC; (3) Fitchburg-Leominster MA*
Source: The Council for Community and Economic Research (formerly ACCRA), Cost of Living Index, 2013

Number of Medical Professionals

City	Area Covered	MDs[1]	DOs[1,2]	Dentists	Podiatrists	Chiropractors	Optometrists
Abilene, TX	Taylor County	205.7	21.8	62.7	6.0	17.2	17.2
Albuquerque, NM	Bernalillo County	404.4	18.8	73.2	7.9	21.7	15.5
Anchorage, AK	Anchorage Borough	305.8	25.7	102.2	4.4	44.9	23.1
Ann Arbor, MI	Washtenaw County	1,125.8	32.4	148.1	5.4	22.5	14.8
Athens, GA	Clarke County	276.6	8.4	52.4	5.0	19.1	16.6
Atlanta, GA	Fulton County	482.7	8.5	64.0	3.9	45.5	13.8
Austin, TX	Travis County	292.5	15.1	62.0	4.5	29.6	15.1
Baltimore, MD	Baltimore City	918.1	15.9	54.5	5.6	9.8	11.1
Billings, MT	Yellowstone County	343.7	18.0	82.3	7.2	32.3	25.0
Boise City, ID	Ada County	274.3	18.0	78.5	3.2	49.4	18.1
Boston, MA	Suffolk County	1,362.0	13.6	166.6	8.8	14.3	28.8
Boulder, CO	Boulder County	360.1	22.0	91.7	4.6	66.5	23.9
Cape Coral, FL	Lee County	176.5	27.3	43.3	7.8	25.9	13.5
Cedar Rapids, IA	Linn County	183.7	15.4	68.8	7.9	49.7	16.3
Charleston, SC	Charleston County	758.6	24.9	100.2	4.9	41.4	19.2
Charlotte, NC	Mecklenburg County	299.1	8.9	65.0	3.3	30.5	12.6
Chicago, IL	Cook County	406.7	22.0	77.9	10.7	23.9	17.0
Cincinnati, OH	Hamilton County	548.1	21.5	66.9	7.7	18.9	16.3
Clarksville, TN	Montgomery County	104.1	18.1	37.3	2.2	14.6	15.1
Colorado Spgs, CO	El Paso County	182.0	25.6	95.6	3.7	36.9	20.5
Columbia, MO	Boone County	763.4	48.8	58.7	5.3	26.7	23.7
Columbus, OH	Franklin County	398.5	59.7	80.5	6.7	22.4	24.2
Dallas, TX	Dallas County	309.1	19.5	71.8	3.7	31.1	11.9
Davenport, IA	Scott County	218.0	47.9	66.4	4.1	155.3	15.4
Denver, CO	Denver County	561.9	25.6	65.4	6.5	28.8	13.7
Des Moines, IA	Polk County	226.4	105.3	65.3	9.5	42.1	22.1
Durham, NC	Durham County	1,118.0	12.0	70.2	5.0	16.0	12.4
El Paso, TX	El Paso County	175.5	13.1	35.4	3.6	8.3	7.7
Erie, PA	Erie County	169.4	97.2	61.6	11.0	35.3	14.6
Eugene, OR	Lane County	244.7	10.5	64.3	2.8	25.4	16.1
Fargo, ND	Cass County	390.2	9.2	70.2	3.2	54.9	26.8
Fayetteville, NC	Cumberland County	193.6	19.5	85.1	6.5	9.6	18.0
Ft. Collins, CO	Larimer County	230.7	24.3	71.8	4.2	50.2	20.0
Ft. Wayne, IN	Allen County	244.6	16.2	56.6	5.0	18.0	21.1
Ft. Worth, TX	Tarrant County	172.6	36.6	51.7	4.1	22.5	12.6
Gainesville, FL	Alachua County	851.6	27.2	153.3	4.4	25.0	13.1
Grand Rapids, MI	Kent County	302.4	54.1	65.8	4.7	27.4	20.7
Green Bay, WI	Brown County	224.0	18.0	63.6	3.6	39.1	18.2
Greensboro, NC	Guilford County	254.1	6.5	52.7	3.8	13.0	10.2
Honolulu, HI	Honolulu County	321.8	13.0	90.4	2.9	15.9	20.9
Houston, TX	Harris County	295.8	9.1	59.9	4.5	20.4	16.9
Huntsville, AL	Madison County	253.8	10.6	54.6	4.1	20.4	16.0
Indianapolis, IN	Marion County	431.2	16.6	76.9	5.3	14.6	17.1
Jacksonville, FL	Duval County	337.6	24.3	65.7	7.6	20.7	14.4
Kansas City, MO	Jackson County	271.3	62.6	73.8	5.3	37.8	16.5
Lafayette, LA	Lafayette Parish	352.3	4.0	61.7	4.0	30.0	13.2
Las Vegas, NV	Clark County	169.5	23.0	55.4	3.6	18.7	11.2
Lexington, KY	Fayette County	679.0	22.9	121.5	7.2	21.3	17.7
Lincoln, NE	Lancaster County	215.7	10.4	87.6	4.4	37.8	19.1
Little Rock, AR	Pulaski County	668.6	11.6	67.9	4.4	17.5	16.2
Los Angeles, CA	Los Angeles County	280.6	10.2	76.0	5.7	25.8	14.9
Louisville, KY	Jefferson County	464.0	12.9	92.2	7.6	28.0	11.6
Lubbock, TX	Lubbock County	359.6	12.7	50.4	3.1	15.7	15.7
Madison, WI	Dane County	554.1	16.5	64.5	4.8	39.7	17.1
Manchester, NH	Hillsborough County	226.7	17.9	73.2	4.7	23.3	17.1
McAllen, TX	Hidalgo County	107.2	2.6	23.6	1.2	8.7	6.2

Table continued on next page.

City	Area Covered	MDs[1]	DOs[1,2]	Dentists	Podiatrists	Chiropractors	Optometrists
Miami, FL	Miami-Dade County	319.4	14.2	54.2	9.0	17.0	11.4
Midland, TX	Midland County	205.7	5.7	46.3	2.7	15.0	12.3
Minneapolis, MN	Hennepin County	471.1	12.8	85.4	3.6	61.1	17.2
Montgomery, AL	Montgomery County	259.6	15.1	61.9	7.0	16.1	15.3
Nashville, TN	Davidson County	592.0	9.4	72.1	3.9	20.3	14.2
New Orleans, LA	Orleans Parish	705.9	13.0	59.5	3.8	6.8	6.2
New York, NY	Kings County	300.2	11.5	59.1	12.3	9.9	9.0
Oklahoma City, OK	Oklahoma County	383.7	41.2	92.8	4.8	24.0	17.9
Omaha, NE	Douglas County	506.9	22.1	81.5	4.3	33.3	17.5
Orlando, FL	Orange County	267.1	17.5	42.8	4.0	22.3	11.7
Oxnard, CA	Ventura County	213.0	8.2	77.5	4.9	33.3	14.7
Peoria, IL	Peoria County	483.1	39.6	64.1	6.9	44.9	18.7
Philadelphia, PA	Philadelphia County	519.0	46.8	62.8	15.8	14.7	14.4
Phoenix, AZ	Maricopa County	234.1	32.0	62.4	5.5	33.1	13.5
Pittsburgh, PA	Allegheny County	598.2	35.3	83.1	10.4	38.9	17.9
Portland, OR	Multnomah County	572.1	29.5	86.3	4.9	60.5	20.6
Providence, RI	Providence County	458.5	15.5	57.1	9.1	18.5	16.1
Provo, UT	Utah County	121.1	14.1	64.3	3.5	23.3	9.1
Raleigh, NC	Wake County	261.0	7.3	63.5	3.2	24.2	15.4
Reno, NV	Washoe County	270.4	17.9	61.3	4.0	25.9	17.5
Richmond, VA	Richmond City	679.8	17.9	123.8	10.0	6.6	12.8
Riverside, CA	Riverside County	113.2	9.6	47.1	2.2	16.2	10.9
Rochester, MN	Olmsted County	2,244.3	48.0	76.1	6.1	35.3	21.1
Salem, OR	Marion County	178.7	10.7	72.5	4.4	26.4	14.3
Salt Lake City, UT	Salt Lake County	354.0	10.4	72.2	5.2	24.3	12.2
San Antonio, TX	Bexar County	313.3	18.6	76.3	5.5	14.6	13.5
San Diego, CA	San Diego County	294.9	14.0	77.4	4.0	30.2	15.6
San Francisco, CA	San Francisco County	790.3	10.3	136.6	9.3	34.8	23.1
San Jose, CA	Santa Clara County	386.0	6.4	104.1	5.4	37.8	22.8
Santa Rosa, CA	Sonoma County	247.8	12.3	84.6	6.1	35.3	15.1
Savannah, GA	Chatham County	342.2	18.4	59.6	6.5	15.2	13.7
Seattle, WA	King County	461.0	12.7	99.1	6.4	41.9	19.2
Sioux Falls, SD	Minnehaha County	330.8	21.5	51.9	4.6	53.0	19.4
Spokane, WA	Spokane County	269.9	20.3	71.2	5.0	27.9	18.5
Springfield, MO	Christian County	96.6	21.6	27.6	0.0	13.8	10.0
Tallahassee, FL	Leon County	252.6	7.2	34.9	3.9	17.6	16.9
Tampa, FL	Hillsborough County	313.9	26.4	48.4	4.8	22.2	11.2
Topeka, KS	Shawnee County	215.7	21.8	58.1	5.6	23.5	26.2
Tulsa, OK	Tulsa County	273.9	104.8	65.6	3.4	36.1	19.9
Virginia Beach, VA	Virginia Beach City	245.2	10.4	69.4	6.7	24.9	13.9
Washington, DC	The District County	797.7	16.8	113.7	8.4	7.6	12.8
Wichita, KS	Sedgwick County	253.2	34.0	55.0	2.2	35.8	24.6
Wilmington, NC	New Hanover County	341.7	20.9	71.2	6.7	32.0	17.2
Worcester, MA	Worcester County	353.1	19.7	65.2	6.1	19.4	17.9
U.S.	U.S.	267.6	19.6	61.7	5.6	24.7	14.5

Note: All figures are rates per 100,000 population; Data as of 2012 unless noted; (1) Data as of 2011; (2) Doctor of Osteopathic Medicine;
Source: Area Resource File (ARF) 2012-2013. U.S. Department of Health and Human Services, Health Resources and Services
Administration, Bureau of Health Professions

Health Insurance Coverage: City

City	With Health Insurance	With Private Health Insurance	With Public Health Insurance	Without Health Insurance	Population Under Age 18 Without Health Insurance
Abilene, TX	80.8	59.8	33.3	19.2	9.4
Albuquerque, NM	83.9	60.5	34.0	16.1	7.4
Anchorage, AK	83.1	68.2	23.6	16.9	10.1
Ann Arbor, MI	93.9	86.4	17.3	6.1	2.7
Athens, GA	83.5	68.3	22.5	16.5	6.8
Atlanta, GA	80.7	59.8	27.6	19.3	7.2
Austin, TX	78.9	63.0	22.3	21.1	11.2
Baltimore, MD	86.6	54.2	42.1	13.4	5.3
Billings, MT	84.2	67.1	31.3	15.8	9.9
Boise City, ID	84.3	70.9	24.5	15.7	9.6
Boston, MA	94.6	66.0	35.6	5.4	1.5
Boulder, CO	90.9	83.4	14.4	9.1	6.6
Cape Coral, FL	78.8	57.5	34.3	21.2	11.9
Cedar Rapids, IA	91.3	76.1	28.0	8.7	3.0
Charleston, SC	87.2	73.3	24.9	12.8	7.2
Charlotte, NC	82.4	64.7	25.0	17.6	6.9
Chicago, IL	79.9	52.4	33.6	20.1	4.9
Cincinnati, OH	84.2	56.3	36.1	15.8	6.2
Clarksville, TN	87.1	70.7	28.5	12.9	4.0
Colorado Spgs, CO	84.7	69.1	27.0	15.3	8.4
Columbia, MO	89.9	79.7	18.3	10.1	7.0
Columbus, OH	84.5	63.2	29.0	15.5	6.6
Dallas, TX	69.0	45.0	29.9	31.0	16.7
Davenport, IA	87.3	69.2	30.5	12.7	7.3
Denver, CO	82.5	60.7	29.3	17.5	10.2
Des Moines, IA	88.5	64.2	36.3	11.5	4.5
Durham, NC	81.9	63.6	26.5	18.1	9.4
El Paso, TX	73.4	48.1	32.7	26.6	12.8
Erie, PA	88.5	57.2	44.6	11.5	3.5
Eugene, OR	84.4	68.4	27.7	15.6	6.9
Fargo, ND	89.4	79.3	20.4	10.6	6.1
Fayetteville, NC	85.8	66.1	33.0	14.2	5.0
Ft. Collins, CO	88.6	78.0	18.8	11.4	4.8
Ft. Wayne, IN	83.1	61.9	30.8	16.9	10.4
Ft. Worth, TX	75.8	54.8	26.9	24.2	13.0
Gainesville, FL	82.1	69.2	20.1	17.9	7.5
Grand Rapids, MI	87.0	59.5	39.0	13.0	2.6
Green Bay, WI	86.4	61.7	35.2	13.6	6.9
Greensboro, NC	82.6	63.2	28.0	17.4	7.1
Honolulu, HI	92.6	76.0	30.7	7.4	2.9
Houston, TX	70.5	46.4	30.0	29.5	16.7
Huntsville, AL	84.1	69.4	28.6	15.9	4.9
Indianapolis, IN	82.4	58.7	33.1	17.6	9.4
Jacksonville, FL	82.4	62.0	30.1	17.6	8.9
Kansas City, MO	82.8	64.0	28.0	17.2	7.9
Lafayette, LA	82.0	64.1	29.0	18.0	4.3
Las Vegas, NV	76.6	60.1	26.0	23.4	16.5
Lexington, KY	85.6	71.4	23.5	14.4	6.4
Lincoln, NE	88.7	74.6	24.4	11.3	5.6
Little Rock, AR	85.1	63.7	31.7	14.9	6.2
Los Angeles, CA	73.9	48.4	31.2	26.1	10.4
Louisville, KY	85.7	66.1	31.4	14.3	4.9
Lubbock, TX	81.7	63.6	28.0	18.3	9.7
Madison, WI	92.1	80.2	21.9	7.9	3.4
Manchester, NH	86.0	67.0	29.4	14.0	4.0

Table continued on next page.

City	With Health Insurance	With Private Health Insurance	With Public Health Insurance	Without Health Insurance	Population Under Age 18 Without Health Insurance
McAllen, TX	64.4	40.0	29.0	35.6	19.4
Miami, FL	64.7	32.5	35.4	35.3	14.5
Midland, TX	79.5	66.3	22.6	20.5	14.6
Minneapolis, MN	87.4	64.3	30.3	12.6	7.0
Montgomery, AL	85.3	62.2	35.8	14.7	4.9
Nashville, TN	82.6	62.5	28.8	17.4	7.6
New Orleans, LA	80.8	52.4	36.4	19.2	5.5
New York, NY	85.5	54.1	39.1	14.5	4.3
Oklahoma City, OK	79.3	59.7	29.5	20.7	9.6
Omaha, NE	85.1	66.2	28.8	14.9	7.0
Orlando, FL	75.2	55.0	26.0	24.8	12.9
Oxnard, CA	74.4	48.0	32.6	25.6	11.7
Peoria, IL	87.4	62.4	37.0	12.6	2.7
Philadelphia, PA	85.6	55.1	40.8	14.4	4.8
Phoenix, AZ	77.6	52.2	31.9	22.4	15.2
Pittsburgh, PA	89.8	68.7	33.4	10.2	2.9
Portland, OR	83.7	67.1	25.6	16.3	5.1
Providence, RI	79.3	50.9	35.0	20.7	6.0
Provo, UT	82.8	72.0	17.9	17.2	14.9
Raleigh, NC	83.4	68.6	22.5	16.6	9.9
Reno, NV	74.9	60.5	23.5	25.1	22.5
Richmond, VA	83.0	59.0	32.9	17.0	4.7
Riverside, CA	78.1	55.1	29.0	21.9	11.1
Rochester, MN	92.3	78.7	25.3	7.7	3.9
Salem, OR	82.7	62.8	31.9	17.3	7.4
Salt Lake City, UT	78.6	62.3	24.0	21.4	16.0
San Antonio, TX	78.3	57.1	31.4	21.7	11.1
San Diego, CA	82.9	65.9	25.0	17.1	8.5
San Francisco, CA	88.8	70.3	27.0	11.2	4.1
San Jose, CA	85.9	66.7	26.0	14.1	4.7
Santa Rosa, CA	84.2	63.1	31.9	15.8	8.3
Savannah, GA	78.0	55.8	30.7	22.0	8.9
Seattle, WA	88.2	76.4	20.3	11.8	4.9
Sioux Falls, SD	88.7	75.7	24.1	11.3	6.2
Spokane, WA	85.1	61.7	35.5	14.9	5.6
Springfield, MO	82.3	60.9	32.9	17.7	5.4
Tallahassee, FL	85.6	72.8	20.1	14.4	5.7
Tampa, FL	80.2	56.6	31.0	19.8	9.8
Topeka, KS	83.3	63.8	32.6	16.7	9.5
Tulsa, OK	77.6	56.9	30.9	22.4	11.2
Virginia Beach, VA	89.3	80.3	20.4	10.7	4.8
Washington, DC	93.2	69.9	35.0	6.8	2.6
Wichita, KS	83.6	65.3	28.5	16.4	7.0
Wilmington, NC	82.9	65.1	30.3	17.1	6.1
Worcester, MA	95.0	62.8	42.1	5.0	1.9
U.S.	84.9	65.4	30.4	15.1	7.5

Note: Figures are percentages that cover the civilian noninstitutionalized population
Source: U.S. Census Bureau, 2010-2012 American Community Survey 3-Year Estimates

Health Insurance Coverage: Metro Area

Metro Area	With Health Insurance	With Private Health Insurance	With Public Health Insurance	Without Health Insurance	Population Under Age 18 Without Health Insurance
Abilene, TX	80.5	60.3	32.9	19.5	10.8
Albuquerque, NM	83.6	59.7	34.6	16.4	7.4
Anchorage, AK	82.4	67.0	24.1	17.6	10.8
Ann Arbor, MI	92.5	80.9	22.7	7.5	2.3
Athens, GA	84.7	68.9	24.2	15.3	6.1
Atlanta, GA	80.8	65.0	23.5	19.2	9.7
Austin, TX	81.2	67.1	21.9	18.8	10.4
Baltimore, MD	90.8	74.2	28.2	9.2	4.0
Billings, MT	84.5	68.9	29.1	15.5	9.3
Boise City, ID	84.0	68.3	26.4	16.0	8.5
Boston, MA	95.4	77.1	29.4	4.6	1.7
Boulder, CO	89.0	79.0	18.3	11.0	6.8
Cape Coral, FL	78.7	56.6	39.4	21.3	14.2
Cedar Rapids, IA	92.6	78.8	26.9	7.4	2.5
Charleston, SC	82.9	66.7	27.5	17.1	9.8
Charlotte, NC	83.5	66.7	25.5	16.5	7.2
Chicago, IL	85.6	66.4	28.1	14.4	4.2
Cincinnati, OH	88.9	72.6	26.7	11.1	4.9
Clarksville, TN	85.9	69.3	28.8	14.1	6.4
Colorado Spgs, CO	86.1	71.7	25.7	13.9	7.5
Columbia, MO	89.9	78.2	20.7	10.1	5.9
Columbus, OH	88.3	71.4	26.4	11.7	5.0
Dallas, TX	77.7	61.1	23.3	22.3	13.3
Davenport, IA	89.9	72.9	31.9	10.1	4.3
Denver, CO	84.8	69.6	23.6	15.2	9.5
Des Moines, IA	91.9	77.1	26.6	8.1	3.4
Durham, NC	84.5	68.3	26.1	15.5	8.4
El Paso, TX	71.8	45.4	33.0	28.2	13.7
Erie, PA	90.9	69.6	35.9	9.1	2.8
Eugene, OR	83.7	64.3	33.3	16.3	6.9
Fargo, ND	91.4	81.3	20.7	8.6	4.7
Fayetteville, NC	85.2	64.6	32.9	14.8	5.9
Ft. Collins, CO	87.7	75.0	23.3	12.3	6.0
Ft. Wayne, IN	85.6	68.0	27.8	14.4	9.4
Ft. Worth, TX	77.7	61.1	23.3	22.3	13.3
Gainesville, FL	83.8	68.3	25.3	16.2	8.5
Grand Rapids, MI	89.1	70.7	30.7	10.9	3.6
Green Bay, WI	91.1	72.5	29.6	8.9	4.1
Greensboro, NC	83.2	62.5	30.7	16.8	8.0
Honolulu, HI	93.9	79.2	28.8	6.1	2.9
Houston, TX	75.7	57.0	25.0	24.3	14.4
Huntsville, AL	87.4	73.8	26.2	12.6	3.6
Indianapolis, IN	86.2	69.3	26.7	13.8	7.4
Jacksonville, FL	84.1	65.9	29.2	15.9	8.3
Kansas City, MO	86.9	72.9	24.8	13.1	6.8
Lafayette, LA	83.2	63.8	29.0	16.8	4.1
Las Vegas, NV	77.4	62.5	23.9	22.6	16.3
Lexington, KY	85.9	70.4	25.4	14.1	5.9
Lincoln, NE	89.6	76.4	23.6	10.4	5.2
Little Rock, AR	85.3	65.8	31.2	14.7	5.8
Los Angeles, CA	78.6	56.1	28.7	21.4	9.3
Louisville, KY	87.0	70.6	28.7	13.0	5.3
Lubbock, TX	81.2	62.5	28.6	18.8	10.0
Madison, WI	93.1	81.2	23.1	6.9	3.2
Manchester, NH	90.3	76.9	23.6	9.7	2.7

Table continued on next page.

Metro Area	With Health Insurance	With Private Health Insurance	With Public Health Insurance	Without Health Insurance	Population Under Age 18 Without Health Insurance
McAllen, TX	63.5	30.4	37.6	36.5	16.6
Miami, FL	74.3	51.8	30.0	25.7	14.0
Midland, TX	78.3	65.8	21.5	21.7	18.2
Minneapolis, MN	91.5	77.5	24.3	8.5	5.6
Montgomery, AL	87.0	67.2	32.4	13.0	4.5
Nashville, TN	86.1	68.8	26.4	13.9	6.0
New Orleans, LA	82.9	58.9	33.1	17.1	4.8
New York, NY	86.8	64.8	31.3	13.2	4.7
Oklahoma City, OK	82.5	65.0	28.4	17.5	8.5
Omaha, NE	88.8	74.1	25.1	11.2	5.3
Orlando, FL	79.3	60.8	27.5	20.7	11.6
Oxnard, CA	83.7	66.7	26.4	16.3	7.4
Peoria, IL	90.2	72.4	31.6	9.8	2.9
Philadelphia, PA	90.0	72.3	29.4	10.0	4.1
Phoenix, AZ	82.7	61.9	30.7	17.3	12.3
Pittsburgh, PA	91.9	75.5	32.3	8.1	2.8
Portland, OR	85.5	69.9	26.2	14.5	6.4
Providence, RI	91.0	70.6	33.0	9.0	3.5
Provo, UT	86.3	76.3	17.4	13.7	9.7
Raleigh, NC	85.3	71.7	21.9	14.7	8.6
Reno, NV	78.1	63.9	24.0	21.9	18.9
Richmond, VA	87.2	73.1	25.0	12.8	6.3
Riverside, CA	79.2	54.9	31.5	20.8	10.6
Rochester, MN	92.9	80.0	25.0	7.1	4.3
Salem, OR	82.7	62.6	32.9	17.3	7.9
Salt Lake City, UT	83.9	72.0	19.7	16.1	11.6
San Antonio, TX	80.4	61.4	29.7	19.6	10.3
San Diego, CA	82.7	65.6	25.8	17.3	8.8
San Francisco, CA	88.1	71.9	25.7	11.9	5.3
San Jose, CA	88.1	72.2	23.8	11.9	4.2
Santa Rosa, CA	85.6	68.2	29.2	14.4	6.8
Savannah, GA	80.9	63.8	26.5	19.1	10.1
Seattle, WA	87.0	72.8	24.1	13.0	5.5
Sioux Falls, SD	90.5	79.2	22.0	9.5	5.1
Spokane, WA	86.8	66.5	32.9	13.2	4.9
Springfield, MO	84.4	65.8	30.1	15.6	9.9
Tallahassee, FL	85.5	69.6	25.2	14.5	6.0
Tampa, FL	81.8	59.9	34.0	18.2	9.4
Topeka, KS	87.5	72.2	29.8	12.5	7.5
Tulsa, OK	82.0	63.7	29.5	18.0	9.6
Virginia Beach, VA	88.1	74.9	25.2	11.9	5.0
Washington, DC	88.2	76.9	20.7	11.8	5.2
Wichita, KS	85.9	69.7	26.9	14.1	6.5
Wilmington, NC	83.7	66.2	32.5	16.3	7.6
Worcester, MA	96.2	75.9	32.1	3.8	1.3
U.S.	84.9	65.4	30.4	15.1	7.5

Note: Figures are percentages that cover the civilian noninstitutionalized population; Figures cover the Metropolitan Statistical Area (MSA)—see Appendix B for areas included
Source: U.S. Census Bureau, 2010-2012 American Community Survey 3-Year Estimates

Crime Rate: City

City	All Crimes	Violent Crimes				Property Crimes		
		Murder	Forcible Rape	Robbery	Aggrav. Assault	Burglary	Larceny -Theft	Motor Vehicle Theft
Abilene, TX	4,058.0	2.5	31.7	105.9	253.6	865.0	2,656.7	142.6
Albuquerque, NM	6,117.0	7.4	50.2	197.2	494.9	1,205.9	3,666.0	495.4
Anchorage, AK	4,353.1	5.0	101.3	163.1	559.3	387.1	2,859.5	277.8
Ann Arbor, MI	2,567.6	0.9	30.4	43.5	122.6	620.8	1,650.3	99.1
Athens, GA	4,304.6	4.3	40.9	134.5	207.7	978.2	2,732.9	206.0
Atlanta, GA	7,912.5	19.0	25.9	520.8	813.4	1,416.8	3,938.3	1,178.4
Austin, TX	5,628.2	3.7	25.1	117.4	262.6	869.7	4,071.7	277.9
Baltimore, MD	6,065.5	34.9	50.4	576.4	743.6	1,242.3	2,781.4	636.6
Billings, MT	4,871.6	2.8	35.7	63.9	245.4	745.5	3,391.9	386.4
Boise City, ID	2,792.9	0.5	35.4	30.3	201.8	431.5	2,019.2	74.2
Boston, MA	3,744.6	9.0	39.5	302.9	483.6	527.2	2,124.8	257.5
Boulder, CO	3,177.8	0.0	31.9	47.9	168.6	470.8	2,331.0	127.7
Cape Coral, FL	2,349.3	2.5	10.0	25.7	105.2	538.8	1,595.6	71.4
Cedar Rapids, IA	3,955.6	2.3	33.5	75.5	165.9	752.3	2,728.2	197.8
Charleston, SC	2,962.3	9.7	15.3	84.0	130.0	302.0	2,231.6	189.7
Charlotte, NC[1]	4,660.7	7.1	27.6	204.2	367.5	1,081.2	2,707.0	266.1
Chicago, IL	n/a	18.5	n/a	497.6	453.1	839.9	2,684.9	627.7
Cincinnati, OH	7,110.0	15.5	63.5	582.4	313.3	1,851.1	3,912.8	371.4
Clarksville, TN	3,360.6	7.3	33.5	72.1	524.2	710.6	1,891.4	121.6
Colorado Springs, CO	4,595.8	4.2	82.8	121.0	247.3	842.3	2,881.4	416.9
Columbia, MO	4,245.1	2.7	37.1	146.4	244.0	708.6	2,977.1	129.2
Columbus, OH[1]	6,885.1	11.0	71.7	411.9	163.7	1,926.0	3,841.9	459.0
Dallas, TX	5,048.5	12.4	39.1	329.7	293.7	1,296.0	2,508.8	568.8
Davenport, IA	4,636.7	4.0	39.5	149.2	404.2	879.5	2,877.7	282.6
Denver, CO	4,329.7	6.2	59.8	185.3	364.5	816.0	2,313.9	583.9
Des Moines, IA	5,450.3	3.4	48.2	120.5	355.4	1,212.2	3,333.7	377.0
Durham, NC	5,089.5	8.9	26.7	261.1	429.2	1,394.1	2,670.6	298.9
El Paso, TX	2,852.5	3.4	27.2	69.7	322.9	270.3	1,987.3	171.7
Erie, PA	3,891.3	7.8	62.8	168.7	209.9	1,073.8	2,266.3	102.0
Eugene, OR	5,336.5	0.0	45.6	124.0	102.5	958.6	3,830.6	275.2
Fargo, ND	2,940.5	1.8	62.8	41.9	252.2	410.7	2,029.8	141.1
Fayetteville, NC	6,966.7	10.7	34.0	271.9	259.3	1,995.0	4,028.8	367.1
Fort Collins, CO	3,031.1	1.3	29.6	26.9	205.0	401.9	2,271.0	95.4
Fort Wayne, IN	4,070.5	8.6	36.2	174.2	143.8	789.1	2,756.2	162.5
Fort Worth, TX	4,809.5	5.7	50.8	166.2	364.8	1,096.2	2,811.1	314.8
Gainesville, FL	4,764.0	4.7	58.3	134.6	472.3	794.3	3,111.7	188.1
Grand Rapids, MI[1]	4,028.2	5.3	43.1	246.9	447.1	1,038.9	2,074.0	173.0
Green Bay, WI	3,291.9	0.9	41.5	82.0	360.1	621.2	2,083.3	102.8
Greensboro, NC	4,932.0	7.6	25.4	201.4	328.8	1,211.4	2,952.6	205.0
Honolulu, HI	n/a	n/a	n/a	n/a	n/a	n/a	n/a	n/a
Houston, TX	5,938.1	10.0	30.5	431.0	521.0	1,223.1	3,122.2	600.3
Huntsville, AL	5,964.9	7.6	39.2	248.2	628.2	1,178.6	3,476.5	386.5
Indianapolis, IN	6,777.6	11.6	52.0	410.4	711.5	1,761.6	3,282.1	548.4
Jacksonville, FL	4,741.9	11.1	40.6	163.1	402.5	907.9	3,021.8	195.0
Kansas City, MO	6,788.6	22.6	53.0	354.9	832.6	1,500.6	3,251.2	773.6
Lafayette, LA	6,181.4	9.0	9.0	164.4	451.8	1,082.6	4,268.6	196.2
Las Vegas, NV	3,922.2	5.1	40.3	258.5	480.1	961.2	1,725.2	451.9
Lexington, KY	4,784.5	4.0	33.7	200.4	114.4	944.0	3,188.9	299.0
Lincoln, NE	4,247.6	1.1	68.9	74.6	252.9	611.7	3,120.7	117.7
Little Rock, AR	9,376.5	23.0	69.9	411.6	811.0	2,164.7	5,337.8	558.5
Los Angeles, CA	2,750.2	7.8	24.3	233.0	216.1	425.1	1,452.8	391.3
Louisville, KY	4,892.7	9.3	27.5	209.2	352.7	1,051.9	2,913.7	328.3
Lubbock, TX	6,000.2	4.6	43.8	137.0	641.5	1,306.3	3,552.9	314.0
Madison, WI	3,642.0	1.3	48.0	101.5	226.9	674.1	2,483.3	106.9

Table continued on next page.

City	All Crimes	Violent Crimes				Property Crimes		
		Murder	Forcible Rape	Robbery	Aggrav. Assault	Burglary	Larceny -Theft	Motor Vehicle Theft
Manchester, NH	4,064.0	0.9	65.4	186.3	314.4	771.5	2,588.1	137.2
McAllen, TX	4,148.2	0.7	2.2	41.3	78.1	370.5	3,499.9	155.4
Miami, FL	6,547.2	16.7	15.7	505.9	633.8	1,027.0	3,693.9	654.3
Midland, TX	2,945.4	3.5	18.2	45.0	277.6	483.4	2,000.2	117.6
Minneapolis, MN	5,953.0	10.0	103.3	440.5	438.4	1,225.4	3,269.8	465.6
Montgomery, AL	6,164.5	21.1	19.6	219.6	135.4	1,631.0	3,611.2	526.7
Nashville, TN	5,411.9	10.0	50.1	277.7	878.3	923.8	3,041.6	230.5
New Orleans, LA	4,587.5	53.2	37.5	293.5	431.0	943.3	2,218.7	610.4
New York, NY	2,361.5	5.1	14.0	243.7	376.5	224.8	1,398.6	98.8
Oklahoma City, OK	6,860.9	14.3	65.3	203.0	636.5	1,654.4	3,553.0	734.4
Omaha, NE	5,182.9	9.8	44.7	195.0	345.0	792.2	3,139.0	657.2
Orlando, FL	7,631.2	9.7	41.8	244.6	721.3	1,532.6	4,552.3	529.0
Oxnard, CA	2,316.2	4.5	4.0	150.6	139.7	420.2	1,326.6	270.6
Peoria, IL	5,153.2	8.7	21.7	281.0	485.7	1,231.7	2,923.1	201.2
Philadelphia, PA	4,863.7	21.5	57.2	518.8	562.6	780.0	2,507.7	415.9
Phoenix, AZ	4,728.0	8.3	37.4	236.7	354.3	1,205.8	2,401.7	483.8
Pittsburgh, PA	4,177.3	13.1	15.1	363.3	360.4	812.8	2,438.2	174.3
Portland, OR	5,609.5	3.3	38.6	158.9	316.4	747.6	3,745.3	599.5
Providence, RI	5,121.4	9.6	47.2	203.5	376.7	1,084.4	2,745.6	654.4
Provo, UT	2,236.5	0.0	30.8	16.3	80.4	257.5	1,754.8	96.7
Raleigh, NC	3,699.3	4.0	26.9	158.1	234.2	721.8	2,332.9	221.4
Reno, NV	3,737.8	3.0	14.3	141.9	357.9	708.5	2,129.8	382.2
Richmond, VA	5,029.4	20.2	18.3	304.6	305.6	976.9	2,953.8	450.0
Riverside, CA	3,893.4	5.1	24.2	164.9	248.8	716.7	2,262.9	470.8
Rochester, MN	n/a	1.8	n/a	50.7	95.8	455.9	1,968.1	82.0
Salem, OR	4,636.1	4.4	25.4	87.7	240.9	662.8	3,150.9	463.9
Salt Lake City, UT	8,135.0	4.2	63.4	164.2	443.7	947.7	5,625.4	886.4
San Antonio, TX	6,493.0	6.4	39.8	135.1	321.8	1,135.3	4,393.3	461.3
San Diego, CA	2,781.4	3.5	22.7	113.3	273.5	440.9	1,433.6	493.8
San Francisco, CA	5,445.8	8.4	13.2	424.7	257.9	648.1	3,442.6	650.8
San Jose, CA	3,278.2	4.6	28.7	123.7	206.3	533.2	1,484.8	897.0
Santa Rosa, CA	2,606.8	1.2	39.2	73.7	258.1	424.3	1,625.3	184.9
Savannah, GA	3,979.1	9.9	10.8	212.3	146.6	900.6	2,413.9	284.9
Seattle, WA	5,691.3	3.7	19.0	226.7	348.2	1,040.6	3,485.9	567.3
Sioux Falls, SD	3,581.8	1.3	87.8	44.2	265.2	567.7	2,426.8	188.8
Spokane, WA	9,375.3	6.1	38.2	253.1	347.8	1,803.8	5,938.8	987.4
Springfield, MO	10,002.4	9.9	87.6	219.3	674.7	1,376.1	6,981.8	652.9
Tallahassee, FL	5,499.3	6.5	62.0	283.1	501.5	1,418.1	2,945.6	282.5
Tampa, FL	3,452.2	6.6	12.3	163.4	434.2	705.9	1,956.9	173.1
Topeka, KS	5,908.7	11.6	30.3	183.9	373.3	991.1	3,855.1	463.4
Tulsa, OK	6,206.0	10.5	79.2	266.2	634.0	1,563.0	3,048.9	604.2
Virginia Beach, VA	2,787.2	4.7	13.0	72.8	78.9	351.4	2,158.7	107.7
Washington, DC	5,805.9	13.9	37.3	589.1	537.5	556.5	3,510.2	561.3
Wichita, KS	6,195.2	6.0	59.0	128.1	549.4	1,014.2	3,967.6	471.0
Wilmington, NC	5,968.7	7.3	21.0	238.6	298.1	1,548.9	3,513.8	341.0
Worcester, MA	4,469.4	4.4	18.0	228.7	708.3	1,113.3	2,143.0	253.8
U.S.	3,246.1	4.7	26.9	112.9	242.3	670.2	1,959.3	229.7

Note: Figures are crimes per 100,000 population in 2012 except where noted; n/a not available; (1) 2011 data
Source: FBI Uniform Crime Reports, 2012

Crime Rate: Suburbs

Suburbs[1]	All Crimes	Violent Crimes				Property Crimes		
		Murder	Forcible Rape	Robbery	Aggrav. Assault	Burglary	Larceny -Theft	Motor Vehicle Theft
Abilene, TX	1,570.7	0.0	14.3	18.4	136.7	424.3	909.8	67.3
Albuquerque, NM	n/a	3.5	26.8	39.6	407.9	n/a	n/a	203.0
Anchorage, AK	6,012.8	0.0	27.8	55.6	361.5	542.2	4,733.8	292.0
Ann Arbor, MI	2,813.0	1.7	48.5	58.7	233.7	694.7	1,635.9	139.8
Athens, GA	2,849.0	1.3	26.9	26.9	164.3	537.7	1,955.8	136.0
Atlanta, GA	3,431.7	5.0	19.6	122.2	177.0	824.3	1,978.8	304.9
Austin, TX	2,101.1	0.8	25.0	22.2	145.8	402.0	1,434.1	71.2
Baltimore, MD	2,883.2	2.1	16.7	107.8	264.4	456.0	1,886.6	149.5
Billings, MT	1,856.0	0.0	9.0	1.8	152.6	369.8	1,173.9	149.0
Boise City, ID	1,876.3	1.4	28.1	12.6	140.6	408.2	1,221.1	64.2
Boston, MA	2,153.3	1.1	20.2	74.3	235.1	417.0	1,304.8	100.9
Boulder, CO	2,229.6	0.0	20.2	26.6	131.4	342.9	1,609.7	98.9
Cape Coral, FL	2,811.7	8.5	19.4	106.6	282.9	689.3	1,536.5	168.4
Cedar Rapids, IA	n/a	0.8	20.3	3.8	56.3	n/a	757.6	59.3
Charleston, SC	3,850.5	6.4	31.7	91.0	333.2	708.1	2,393.3	286.9
Charlotte, NC[2]	3,228.5	3.0	22.2	60.5	200.4	686.7	2,117.4	138.3
Chicago, IL	n/a	2.1	n/a	59.5	89.8	384.0	1,532.4	94.0
Cincinnati, OH	3,035.0	1.6	27.1	58.7	85.3	623.0	2,145.0	94.3
Clarksville, TN	2,736.0	5.4	30.3	58.2	138.9	676.8	1,699.0	127.3
Colorado Springs, CO	n/a	0.8	37.5	18.6	180.0	n/a	1,051.6	116.4
Columbia, MO	2,658.6	0.0	9.0	32.6	224.3	432.3	1,857.4	103.1
Columbus, OH[2]	2,783.7	1.6	24.5	49.9	64.8	593.9	1,979.6	69.3
Dallas, TX	2,786.9	1.3	20.0	52.8	115.4	573.7	1,846.4	177.1
Davenport, IA	2,352.8	2.1	27.4	33.5	228.2	386.6	1,614.1	60.9
Denver, CO	2,694.1	3.2	38.6	52.8	155.8	400.3	1,836.5	206.9
Des Moines, IA	n/a	0.3	20.8	9.1	127.4	n/a	1,380.7	81.0
Durham, NC	2,848.2	2.1	16.6	38.9	120.7	845.7	1,724.3	99.8
El Paso, TX	2,117.7	3.1	22.4	23.0	237.2	344.1	1,365.0	123.0
Erie, PA	2,267.8	1.7	16.2	28.4	84.7	397.3	1,680.0	59.6
Eugene, OR	3,004.8	3.5	27.3	32.8	144.5	558.9	2,021.9	215.8
Fargo, ND	n/a	0.0	n/a	12.2	116.7	327.6	1,378.9	76.2
Fayetteville, NC	4,535.2	4.7	14.5	112.3	279.8	1,626.5	2,345.6	151.8
Fort Collins, CO	2,363.9	0.6	26.1	21.7	149.7	311.9	1,786.2	67.7
Fort Wayne, IN	1,674.2	1.2	11.6	15.2	61.5	312.5	1,183.7	88.3
Fort Worth, TX	3,143.3	2.6	25.4	63.9	182.3	641.5	2,058.6	168.9
Gainesville, FL	3,054.6	2.8	44.8	58.1	395.2	700.9	1,759.1	93.7
Grand Rapids, MI[2]	2,215.9	1.7	42.7	34.8	138.8	501.1	1,407.6	89.1
Green Bay, WI	1,509.4	2.9	11.8	6.4	78.4	296.8	1,068.7	44.6
Greensboro, NC	3,311.6	5.0	14.5	64.9	169.0	878.4	2,036.5	143.3
Honolulu, HI	n/a	n/a	n/a	n/a	n/a	n/a	n/a	n/a
Houston, TX	n/a	3.3	21.0	104.2	196.8	n/a	1,848.3	256.8
Huntsville, AL	2,284.6	3.3	15.2	37.8	162.2	595.5	1,361.8	108.8
Indianapolis, IN	2,321.3	1.6	15.4	29.1	97.2	388.2	1,675.5	114.4
Jacksonville, FL	2,769.3	3.2	15.8	44.4	287.8	488.2	1,845.6	84.4
Kansas City, MO	3,128.3	3.3	28.1	49.3	178.3	531.9	2,064.1	273.4
Lafayette, LA	n/a	6.6	21.9	66.7	n/a	720.4	1,778.0	n/a
Las Vegas, NV	2,918.4	3.7	27.7	115.8	298.8	642.8	1,532.5	297.1
Lexington, KY	3,732.8	3.4	33.1	53.9	115.1	826.4	2,570.1	130.8
Lincoln, NE	1,819.2	2.2	31.5	9.0	51.7	368.8	1,306.5	49.5
Little Rock, AR	4,463.8	3.9	36.2	76.5	301.6	1,082.0	2,714.2	249.4
Los Angeles, CA	2,788.2	4.9	17.0	162.3	240.4	534.1	1,413.7	415.8
Louisville, KY	2,765.2	2.7	15.8	54.4	153.8	596.5	1,794.6	147.3
Lubbock, TX	2,393.8	1.6	63.4	6.3	247.3	559.6	1,377.6	137.9
Madison, WI	1,998.3	3.2	15.9	14.8	65.7	302.3	1,545.0	51.4

Table continued on next page.

Suburbs[1]	All Crimes	Violent Crimes				Property Crimes		
		Murder	Forcible Rape	Robbery	Aggrav. Assault	Burglary	Larceny -Theft	Motor Vehicle Theft
Manchester, NH	1,982.7	0.0	24.3	24.3	78.7	302.0	1,486.5	67.0
McAllen, TX	4,075.7	4.3	29.5	62.0	263.1	884.6	2,652.8	179.5
Miami, FL	4,768.9	6.5	23.2	179.7	356.8	774.8	3,117.7	310.2
Midland, TX	2,400.9	3.1	6.3	6.3	191.9	487.7	1,447.5	258.0
Minneapolis, MN	n/a	1.2	n/a	45.2	103.0	n/a	1,950.4	158.5
Montgomery, AL	3,134.8	5.3	26.9	55.5	212.7	873.1	1,804.1	157.2
Nashville, TN	2,553.5	2.3	23.4	42.1	285.3	479.9	1,613.9	106.7
New Orleans, LA	3,373.8	6.8	17.4	76.6	241.7	630.4	2,230.2	170.6
New York, NY	n/a	1.9	9.2	94.5	n/a	350.9	1,255.8	102.4
Oklahoma City, OK	3,237.7	2.6	30.0	39.1	157.2	734.5	2,066.9	207.4
Omaha, NE	2,510.9	0.4	31.8	26.7	179.6	470.0	1,579.7	222.6
Orlando, FL	3,577.0	4.3	29.3	105.9	347.0	897.3	1,990.7	202.4
Oxnard, CA	2,024.7	1.9	14.4	49.1	101.0	355.2	1,368.5	134.5
Peoria, IL	2,268.9	3.0	27.2	29.9	183.0	492.0	1,475.9	57.9
Philadelphia, PA	n/a	5.0	15.2	143.1	n/a	418.8	1,822.6	107.3
Phoenix, AZ	n/a	3.7	22.4	69.8	190.0	617.1	2,222.6	n/a
Pittsburgh, PA	n/a	2.9	15.2	48.3	n/a	335.5	1,271.5	61.5
Portland, OR	2,656.0	2.0	29.3	49.4	96.7	451.1	1,785.1	242.5
Providence, RI	2,549.9	1.5	26.8	73.3	201.1	538.3	1,550.7	158.3
Provo, UT	1,846.4	0.9	10.9	11.4	32.2	235.1	1,496.8	59.1
Raleigh, NC	2,170.5	0.5	12.2	30.2	105.8	557.2	1,379.2	85.4
Reno, NV	2,235.1	2.4	25.4	43.5	187.1	513.3	1,286.0	177.3
Richmond, VA	2,356.0	4.1	11.9	51.9	93.3	416.8	1,669.2	108.7
Riverside, CA	3,350.9	4.0	16.6	117.9	224.4	884.2	1,626.9	476.9
Rochester, MN	n/a	1.0	n/a	4.0	60.3	278.5	628.2	57.3
Salem, OR	2,670.7	2.5	20.4	25.8	108.6	475.2	1,812.2	226.0
Salt Lake City, UT	3,936.1	1.8	40.8	54.5	158.5	561.3	2,827.4	291.8
San Antonio, TX	2,776.2	2.9	30.9	30.0	143.8	581.5	1,845.9	141.2
San Diego, CA	2,416.2	3.3	21.2	91.9	228.3	446.5	1,323.2	301.9
San Francisco, CA	2,375.4	1.4	14.7	78.8	158.7	457.4	1,445.3	219.1
San Jose, CA	2,445.6	1.2	15.1	51.2	110.3	451.4	1,557.9	258.4
Santa Rosa, CA	1,818.6	0.6	26.4	32.9	299.3	342.2	996.0	121.2
Savannah, GA	2,521.7	1.6	27.3	50.0	154.6	538.7	1,626.3	123.4
Seattle, WA	3,581.4	2.3	29.2	75.4	115.3	781.6	2,175.9	401.7
Sioux Falls, SD	1,117.5	0.0	24.8	0.0	82.1	301.2	650.7	58.7
Spokane, WA	3,595.3	2.5	21.0	38.7	89.4	868.4	2,292.2	283.1
Springfield, MO	2,288.9	2.1	16.4	8.2	161.4	542.8	1,432.1	125.7
Tallahassee, FL	2,719.9	5.3	26.4	45.9	301.0	765.3	1,475.1	100.9
Tampa, FL	3,246.9	3.5	26.2	85.1	265.6	672.7	2,043.3	150.5
Topeka, KS	2,257.9	2.8	10.3	8.4	174.8	552.3	1,371.0	138.3
Tulsa, OK	2,144.1	2.2	27.8	24.9	165.7	494.1	1,301.5	127.8
Virginia Beach, VA	3,622.0	7.6	23.2	112.7	204.1	598.0	2,516.7	159.6
Washington, DC	2,319.9	2.7	14.9	102.1	118.8	286.0	1,595.7	199.6
Wichita, KS	2,420.4	0.4	24.0	12.4	162.7	528.0	1,582.7	110.3
Wilmington, NC	2,931.5	1.3	22.3	36.0	168.2	641.4	1,949.1	113.2
Worcester, MA	2,007.0	0.9	22.9	35.8	212.6	435.8	1,224.1	74.9
U.S.	3,246.1	4.7	26.9	112.9	242.3	670.2	1,959.3	229.7

Note: Figures are crimes per 100,000 population in 2012 except where noted; n/a not available; (1) All areas within the metro area that are located outside the city limits; (2) 2011 data
Source: FBI Uniform Crime Reports, 2012

Crime Rate: Metro Area

Metro Area[1]	All Crimes	Violent Crimes				Property Crimes		
		Murder	Forcible Rape	Robbery	Aggrav. Assault	Burglary	Larceny -Theft	Motor Vehicle Theft
Abilene, TX	3,336.1	1.8	26.6	80.5	219.6	737.1	2,149.7	120.8
Albuquerque, NM	n/a	5.9	41.2	136.5	461.4	n/a	n/a	382.9
Anchorage, AK	4,429.3	4.8	97.9	158.2	550.2	394.2	2,945.5	278.4
Ann Arbor, MI	2,731.9	1.4	42.5	53.7	197.0	670.3	1,640.7	126.4
Athens, GA	3,724.0	3.1	35.3	91.6	190.4	802.5	2,423.0	178.1
Atlanta, GA	3,792.0	6.1	20.1	154.2	228.2	871.9	2,136.4	375.1
Austin, TX	3,723.9	2.2	25.0	66.0	199.5	617.2	2,647.7	166.3
Baltimore, MD	3,605.5	9.5	24.4	214.2	373.2	634.5	2,089.7	260.1
Billings, MT	3,835.1	1.9	26.5	42.6	213.5	616.4	2,629.5	304.8
Boise City, ID	2,183.2	1.1	30.5	18.5	161.1	416.0	1,488.3	67.6
Boston, MA[2]	2,675.7	3.7	26.5	149.4	316.7	453.2	1,574.0	152.3
Boulder, CO	2,542.8	0.0	24.1	33.6	143.6	385.1	1,848.0	108.4
Cape Coral, FL	2,696.3	7.0	17.0	86.4	238.6	651.8	1,551.2	144.2
Cedar Rapids, IA	n/a	1.5	26.8	39.0	110.1	n/a	1,724.9	127.3
Charleston, SC	3,690.8	7.0	28.8	89.7	296.7	635.1	2,364.2	269.4
Charlotte, NC[3]	3,863.7	4.8	24.6	124.2	274.5	861.7	2,378.9	195.0
Chicago, IL[2]	n/a	8.2	n/a	222.0	224.6	553.1	1,959.9	292.0
Cincinnati, OH	3,603.4	3.5	32.2	131.8	117.1	794.3	2,391.6	133.0
Clarksville, TN	3,058.3	6.4	31.9	65.4	337.7	694.2	1,798.3	124.3
Colorado Springs, CO	n/a	3.0	66.8	84.7	223.5	n/a	2,233.2	310.4
Columbia, MO	3,716.4	1.8	27.7	108.5	237.4	616.5	2,604.0	120.5
Columbus, OH[3]	4,541.3	5.7	44.7	205.0	107.2	1,164.8	2,777.7	236.3
Dallas, TX[2]	3,424.2	4.4	25.4	130.9	165.7	777.2	2,033.1	287.5
Davenport, IA	2,957.7	2.6	30.6	64.1	274.8	517.2	1,948.8	119.6
Denver, CO	3,084.2	3.9	43.6	84.4	205.6	499.5	1,950.4	296.8
Des Moines, IA	n/a	1.4	30.6	48.8	208.6	n/a	2,076.0	186.4
Durham, NC	3,867.3	5.2	21.2	139.9	261.0	1,095.0	2,154.6	190.3
El Paso, TX	2,711.1	3.3	26.3	60.7	306.4	284.5	1,867.5	162.3
Erie, PA	2,856.0	3.9	33.0	79.2	130.0	642.4	1,892.4	75.0
Eugene, OR	4,040.2	2.0	35.4	73.3	125.9	736.4	2,825.0	242.2
Fargo, ND	n/a	0.9	n/a	27.3	185.6	369.8	1,709.7	109.2
Fayetteville, NC	5,860.6	7.9	25.1	199.3	268.6	1,827.4	3,263.1	269.1
Fort Collins, CO	2,684.4	1.0	27.8	24.2	176.3	355.1	2,019.0	81.0
Fort Wayne, IN	3,135.7	5.7	26.6	112.2	111.7	603.2	2,142.8	133.6
Fort Worth, TX[2]	3,707.5	3.6	34.0	98.6	244.1	795.5	2,313.4	218.3
Gainesville, FL	3,858.8	3.7	51.1	94.1	431.5	744.8	2,395.5	138.1
Grand Rapids, MI[3]	2,656.1	2.6	42.8	86.4	213.7	631.7	1,569.5	109.5
Green Bay, WI	2,118.9	2.3	21.9	32.2	174.7	407.7	1,415.6	64.5
Greensboro, NC	3,917.7	6.0	18.6	116.0	228.8	1,003.0	2,379.1	166.3
Honolulu, HI	3,600.7	2.0	22.9	93.8	149.4	606.1	2,315.9	410.5
Houston, TX	n/a	5.7	24.4	219.9	311.6	n/a	2,299.3	378.4
Huntsville, AL	3,867.1	5.1	25.5	128.3	362.6	846.2	2,271.1	228.2
Indianapolis, IN	4,272.0	6.0	31.4	196.0	366.1	989.4	2,378.8	304.4
Jacksonville, FL	3,972.0	8.0	30.9	116.8	357.8	744.0	2,562.7	151.8
Kansas City, MO	3,963.8	7.7	33.8	119.1	327.7	753.0	2,335.0	387.6
Lafayette, LA	n/a	7.2	18.6	92.0	n/a	814.4	2,423.8	n/a
Las Vegas, NV	3,662.5	4.8	37.0	221.6	433.2	878.8	1,675.3	411.8
Lexington, KY	4,394.6	3.7	33.5	146.1	114.7	900.4	2,959.5	236.6
Lincoln, NE	3,897.7	1.3	63.5	65.1	223.9	576.7	2,859.3	107.9
Little Rock, AR	5,815.4	9.1	45.5	168.7	441.8	1,379.9	3,436.0	334.4
Los Angeles, CA[2]	2,773.6	6.0	19.8	189.6	231.0	492.0	1,428.8	406.3
Louisville, KY	3,900.3	6.2	22.0	137.0	260.0	839.5	2,391.7	243.9
Lubbock, TX	5,242.7	4.0	47.9	109.5	558.7	1,149.4	3,096.0	277.0
Madison, WI	2,633.2	2.4	28.3	48.3	128.0	445.9	1,907.4	72.9

Table continued on next page.

Metro Area[1]	All Crimes	Violent Crimes				Property Crimes		
		Murder	Forcible Rape	Robbery	Aggrav. Assault	Burglary	Larceny -Theft	Motor Vehicle Theft
Manchester, NH	2,551.8	0.2	35.5	68.6	143.1	430.3	1,787.7	86.2
McAllen, TX	4,087.9	3.7	24.9	58.5	232.0	798.4	2,794.8	175.5
Miami, FL[2]	5,053.4	8.1	22.0	231.9	401.1	815.1	3,209.9	365.3
Midland, TX	2,828.0	3.4	15.6	36.6	259.1	484.3	1,881.1	147.9
Minneapolis, MN	n/a	2.2	n/a	90.5	141.4	n/a	2,101.5	193.7
Montgomery, AL	4,800.7	13.9	22.9	145.7	170.2	1,289.8	2,797.7	360.4
Nashville, TN	3,589.7	5.1	33.0	127.5	500.3	640.8	2,131.5	151.6
New Orleans, LA	3,734.8	20.6	23.4	141.1	298.0	723.5	2,226.8	301.4
New York, NY[2]	n/a	3.8	12.0	182.6	n/a	276.5	1,340.1	100.3
Oklahoma City, OK	4,915.9	8.0	46.3	115.0	379.2	1,160.6	2,755.3	451.5
Omaha, NE	3,775.9	4.9	37.9	106.4	257.9	622.5	2,317.9	428.4
Orlando, FL	4,031.1	5.0	30.7	121.4	389.0	968.5	2,277.6	238.9
Oxnard, CA	2,094.7	2.5	11.9	73.5	110.3	370.8	1,358.5	167.2
Peoria, IL	3,144.6	4.7	25.5	106.1	274.9	716.6	1,915.3	101.4
Philadelphia, PA[2]	n/a	16.8	45.3	412.6	n/a	678.0	2,314.1	328.7
Phoenix, AZ	n/a	5.3	27.6	127.3	246.6	820.0	2,284.3	n/a
Pittsburgh, PA	n/a	4.2	15.2	89.9	n/a	398.5	1,425.6	76.4
Portland, OR	3,430.8	2.4	31.8	78.1	154.3	528.8	2,299.3	336.1
Providence, RI	2,835.1	2.4	29.1	87.7	220.6	598.8	1,683.2	213.3
Provo, UT	1,929.6	0.7	15.1	12.4	42.5	239.9	1,551.8	67.1
Raleigh, NC	2,717.7	1.8	17.4	76.0	151.7	616.1	1,720.5	134.0
Reno, NV	3,030.9	2.8	19.5	95.6	277.6	616.7	1,732.9	285.8
Richmond, VA	2,806.7	6.8	13.0	94.5	129.1	511.3	1,885.8	166.3
Riverside, CA	3,390.1	4.1	17.1	121.3	226.2	872.1	1,672.8	476.4
Rochester, MN	n/a	1.4	n/a	28.1	78.6	370.3	1,321.6	70.1
Salem, OR	3,448.3	3.3	22.4	50.3	160.9	549.5	2,341.9	320.1
Salt Lake City, UT	4,655.5	2.2	44.7	73.3	207.3	627.5	3,306.8	393.7
San Antonio, TX	5,078.7	5.1	36.4	95.1	254.1	924.5	3,424.0	339.5
San Diego, CA	2,570.5	3.4	21.8	101.0	247.4	444.2	1,369.8	382.9
San Francisco, CA[2]	3,995.9	5.1	13.9	261.3	211.1	558.1	2,499.5	446.9
San Jose, CA	2,877.4	3.0	22.1	88.8	160.1	493.8	1,520.0	589.6
Santa Rosa, CA	2,092.0	0.8	30.9	47.1	285.0	370.7	1,214.3	143.3
Savannah, GA	3,459.7	7.0	16.7	154.4	149.4	771.6	2,133.2	227.3
Seattle, WA[2]	4,067.9	2.6	26.8	110.3	169.0	841.3	2,478.0	439.9
Sioux Falls, SD	2,777.8	0.9	67.2	29.8	205.5	480.8	1,847.3	146.4
Spokane, WA	5,885.8	3.9	27.8	123.6	191.8	1,239.1	3,737.3	562.2
Springfield, MO	5,104.4	5.0	42.4	85.3	348.8	847.0	3,457.8	318.2
Tallahassee, FL	4,095.2	5.9	44.0	163.3	400.2	1,088.3	2,202.8	190.8
Tampa, FL	3,272.0	3.9	24.5	94.7	286.2	676.7	2,032.7	153.3
Topeka, KS	4,252.4	7.6	21.2	104.3	283.2	792.0	2,728.1	315.9
Tulsa, OK	3,844.7	5.7	49.3	125.9	361.8	941.7	2,033.1	327.3
Virginia Beach, VA	3,402.7	6.8	20.5	102.3	171.2	533.2	2,422.7	146.0
Washington, DC[2]	2,800.3	4.3	18.0	169.2	176.5	323.3	1,859.6	249.4
Wichita, KS	4,711.6	3.8	45.2	82.6	397.4	823.1	3,030.2	329.2
Wilmington, NC	4,198.6	3.8	21.7	120.5	222.4	1,020.0	2,601.8	208.3
Worcester, MA	2,537.1	1.6	21.9	77.3	319.3	581.7	1,421.9	113.4
U.S.	3,246.1	4.7	26.9	112.9	242.3	670.2	1,959.3	229.7

Note: Figures are crimes per 100,000 population in 2012 except where noted; n/a not available; (1) Figures cover the Metropolitan Statistical Area except where noted, (2) Metropolitan Division (MD); See Appendix B for counties included in MSAs and MDs; (3) 2011 data
Source: FBI Uniform Crime Reports, 2012

Temperature & Precipitation: Yearly Averages and Extremes

City	Extreme Low (°F)	Average Low (°F)	Average Temp. (°F)	Average High (°F)	Extreme High (°F)	Average Precip. (in.)	Average Snow (in.)
Abilene, TX	-7	53	65	76	110	23.6	5
Albuquerque, NM	-17	43	57	70	105	8.5	11
Anchorage, AK	-34	29	36	43	85	15.7	71
Ann Arbor, MI	-21	39	49	58	104	32.4	41
Athens, GA	-8	52	62	72	105	49.8	2
Atlanta, GA	-8	52	62	72	105	49.8	2
Austin, TX	-2	58	69	79	109	31.1	1
Baltimore, MD	-7	45	56	65	105	41.2	21
Billings, MT	-32	36	47	59	105	14.6	59
Boise City, ID	-25	39	51	63	111	11.8	22
Boston, MA	-12	44	52	59	102	42.9	41
Boulder, CO	-25	37	51	64	103	15.5	63
Cape Coral, FL	26	65	75	84	103	53.9	0
Cedar Rapids, IA	-34	36	47	57	105	34.4	33
Charleston, SC	6	55	66	76	104	52.1	1
Charlotte, NC	-5	50	61	71	104	42.8	6
Chicago, IL	-27	40	49	59	104	35.4	39
Cincinnati, OH	-25	44	54	64	103	40.9	23
Clarksville, TN	-17	49	60	70	107	47.4	11
Colorado Springs, CO	-24	36	49	62	99	17.0	48
Columbia, MO	-20	44	54	64	111	40.6	25
Columbus, OH	-19	42	52	62	104	37.9	28
Dallas, TX	-2	56	67	77	112	33.9	3
Davenport, IA	-24	40	50	60	108	31.8	33
Denver, CO	-25	37	51	64	103	15.5	63
Des Moines, IA	-24	40	50	60	108	31.8	33
Durham, NC	-9	48	60	71	105	42.0	8
El Paso, TX	-8	50	64	78	114	8.6	6
Erie, PA	-18	41	49	57	100	40.5	83
Eugene, OR	-12	42	53	63	108	47.3	7
Fargo, ND	-36	31	41	52	106	19.6	40
Fayetteville, NC	-9	48	60	71	105	42.0	8
Fort Collins, CO	-25	37	51	64	103	15.5	63
Fort Wayne, IN	-22	40	50	60	106	35.9	33
Fort Worth, TX	-1	55	66	76	113	32.3	3
Gainesville, FL	10	58	69	79	102	50.9	Trace
Grand Rapids, MI	-22	38	48	57	102	34.7	73
Green Bay, WI	-31	34	44	54	99	28.3	46
Greensboro, NC	-8	47	58	69	103	42.5	10
Honolulu, HI	52	70	77	84	94	22.4	0
Houston, TX	7	58	69	79	107	46.9	Trace
Huntsville, AL	-11	50	61	71	104	56.8	4
Indianapolis, IN	-23	42	53	62	104	40.2	25
Jacksonville, FL	7	58	69	79	103	52.0	0
Kansas City, MO	-23	44	54	64	109	38.1	21
Lafayette, LA	8	57	68	78	103	58.5	Trace
Las Vegas, NV	8	53	67	80	116	4.0	1
Lexington, KY	-21	45	55	65	103	45.1	17
Lincoln, NE	-33	39	51	62	108	29.1	27
Little Rock, AR	-5	51	62	73	112	50.7	5
Los Angeles, CA	27	55	63	70	110	11.3	Trace
Louisville, KY	-20	46	57	67	105	43.9	17
Lubbock, TX	-16	47	60	74	110	18.4	10
Madison, WI	-37	35	46	57	104	31.1	42
Manchester, NH	-33	34	46	57	102	36.9	63

Table continued on next page.

City	Extreme Low (°F)	Average Low (°F)	Average Temp. (°F)	Average High (°F)	Extreme High (°F)	Average Precip. (in.)	Average Snow (in.)
McAllen, TX	16	65	74	83	106	25.8	Trace
Miami, FL	30	69	76	83	98	57.1	0
Midland, TX	-11	50	64	77	116	14.6	4
Minneapolis, MN	-34	35	45	54	105	27.1	52
Montgomery, AL	0	54	65	76	105	52.7	Trace
Nashville, TN	-17	49	60	70	107	47.4	11
New Orleans, LA	11	59	69	78	102	60.6	Trace
New York, NY	-2	47	55	62	104	47.0	23
Oklahoma City, OK	-8	49	60	71	110	32.8	10
Omaha, NE	-23	40	51	62	110	30.1	29
Orlando, FL	19	62	72	82	100	47.7	Trace
Oxnard, CA	27	51	60	68	105	12.0	0
Peoria, IL	-26	41	51	61	113	35.4	23
Philadelphia, PA	-7	45	55	64	104	41.4	22
Phoenix, AZ	17	59	72	86	122	7.3	Trace
Pittsburgh, PA	-18	41	51	60	103	37.1	43
Portland, OR	-3	45	54	62	107	37.5	7
Providence, RI	-13	42	51	60	104	45.3	35
Provo, UT	-22	40	52	64	107	15.6	63
Raleigh, NC	-9	48	60	71	105	42.0	8
Reno, NV	-16	33	50	67	105	7.2	24
Richmond, VA	-8	48	58	69	105	43.0	13
Riverside, CA	24	53	66	78	114	n/a	n/a
Rochester, MN	-40	34	44	54	102	29.4	47
Salem, OR	-12	41	52	63	108	40.2	7
Salt Lake City, UT	-22	40	52	64	107	15.6	63
San Antonio, TX	0	58	69	80	108	29.6	1
San Diego, CA	29	57	64	71	111	9.5	Trace
San Francisco, CA	24	49	57	65	106	19.3	Trace
San Jose, CA	21	50	59	68	105	13.5	Trace
Santa Rosa, CA	23	42	57	71	109	29.0	n/a
Savannah, GA	3	56	67	77	105	50.3	Trace
Seattle, WA	0	44	52	59	99	38.4	13
Sioux Falls, SD	-36	35	46	57	110	24.6	38
Spokane, WA	-25	37	47	57	108	17.0	51
Springfield, MO	-17	45	56	67	113	42.0	18
Tallahassee, FL	6	56	68	79	103	63.3	Trace
Tampa, FL	18	63	73	82	99	46.7	Trace
Topeka, KS	-26	43	55	66	110	34.4	21
Tulsa, OK	-8	50	61	71	112	38.9	10
Virginia Beach, VA	-3	51	60	69	104	44.8	8
Washington, DC	-5	49	58	67	104	39.5	18
Wichita, KS	-21	45	57	68	113	29.3	17
Wilmington, NC	0	53	64	74	104	55.0	2
Worcester, MA	-13	38	47	56	99	47.6	62

Source: National Climatic Data Center, International Station Meteorological Climate Summary, 9/96

Weather Conditions

City	Temperature			Daytime Sky			Precipitation		
	10°F & below	32°F & below	90°F & above	Clear	Partly cloudy	Cloudy	0.01 inch or more precip.	1.0 inch or more snow/ice	Thunder-storms
Abilene, TX	2	52	102	141	125	99	65	4	43
Albuquerque, NM	4	114	65	140	161	64	60	9	38
Anchorage, AK	n/a	194	n/a	50	115	200	113	49	2
Ann Arbor, MI	n/a	136	12	74	134	157	135	38	32
Athens, GA	1	49	38	98	147	120	116	3	48
Atlanta, GA	1	49	38	98	147	120	116	3	48
Austin, TX	< 1	20	111	105	148	112	83	1	41
Baltimore, MD	6	97	31	91	143	131	113	13	27
Billings, MT	n/a	149	29	75	163	127	97	41	27
Boise City, ID	n/a	124	45	106	133	126	91	22	14
Boston, MA	n/a	97	12	88	127	150	253	48	18
Boulder, CO	24	155	33	99	177	89	90	38	39
Cape Coral, FL	n/a	n/a	115	93	220	52	110	0	92
Cedar Rapids, IA	n/a	156	16	89	132	144	109	28	42
Charleston, SC	< 1	33	53	89	162	114	114	1	59
Charlotte, NC	1	65	44	98	142	125	113	3	41
Chicago, IL	n/a	132	17	83	136	146	125	31	38
Cincinnati, OH	14	107	23	80	126	159	127	25	39
Clarksville, TN	5	76	51	98	135	132	119	8	54
Colorado Springs, CO	21	161	18	108	157	100	98	33	49
Columbia, MO	17	108	36	99	127	139	110	17	52
Columbus, OH	n/a	118	19	72	137	156	136	29	40
Dallas, TX	1	34	102	108	160	97	78	2	49
Davenport, IA	n/a	137	26	99	129	137	106	25	46
Denver, CO	24	155	33	99	177	89	90	38	39
Des Moines, IA	n/a	137	26	99	129	137	106	25	46
Durham, NC	n/a	n/a	39	98	143	124	110	3	42
El Paso, TX	1	59	106	147	164	54	49	3	35
Erie, PA	n/a	124	3	57	128	180	165	55	36
Eugene, OR	n/a	n/a	15	75	115	175	136	4	3
Fargo, ND	n/a	180	15	81	145	139	100	38	31
Fayetteville, NC	n/a	n/a	39	98	143	124	110	3	42
Fort Collins, CO	24	155	33	99	177	89	90	38	39
Fort Wayne, IN	n/a	131	16	75	140	150	131	31	39
Fort Worth, TX	1	40	100	123	136	106	79	3	47
Gainesville, FL	n/a	n/a	77	88	196	81	119	0	78
Grand Rapids, MI	n/a	146	11	67	119	179	142	57	34
Green Bay, WI	n/a	163	7	86	125	154	120	40	33
Greensboro, NC	3	85	32	94	143	128	113	5	43
Honolulu, HI	n/a	n/a	23	25	286	54	98	0	7
Houston, TX	n/a	n/a	96	83	168	114	101	1	62
Huntsville, AL	2	66	49	70	118	177	116	2	54
Indianapolis, IN	19	119	19	83	128	154	127	24	43
Jacksonville, FL	< 1	16	83	86	181	98	114	1	65
Kansas City, MO	22	110	39	112	134	119	103	17	51
Lafayette, LA	< 1	21	86	99	150	116	113	< 1	73
Las Vegas, NV	< 1	37	134	185	132	48	27	2	13
Lexington, KY	11	96	22	86	136	143	129	17	44
Lincoln, NE	n/a	145	40	108	135	122	94	19	46
Little Rock, AR	1	57	73	110	142	113	104	4	57
Los Angeles, CA	0	< 1	5	131	125	109	34	0	1
Louisville, KY	8	90	35	82	143	140	125	15	45
Lubbock, TX	5	93	79	134	150	81	62	8	48
Madison, WI	n/a	161	14	88	119	158	118	38	40

Table continued on next page.

City	Temperature			Daytime Sky			Precipitation		
	10°F & below	32°F & below	90°F & above	Clear	Partly cloudy	Cloudy	0.01 inch or more precip.	1.0 inch or more snow/ice	Thunder-storms
Manchester, NH	n/a	171	12	87	131	147	125	32	19
McAllen, TX	n/a	n/a	116	86	180	99	72	0	27
Miami, FL	n/a	n/a	55	48	263	54	128	0	74
Midland, TX	1	62	102	144	138	83	52	3	38
Minneapolis, MN	n/a	156	16	93	125	147	113	41	37
Montgomery, AL	< 1	38	82	97	152	116	109	< 1	59
Nashville, TN	5	76	51	98	135	132	119	8	54
New Orleans, LA	0	13	70	90	169	106	114	1	69
New York, NY	n/a	n/a	18	85	166	114	120	11	20
Oklahoma City, OK	5	79	70	124	131	110	80	8	50
Omaha, NE	n/a	139	35	100	142	123	97	20	46
Orlando, FL	n/a	n/a	90	76	208	81	115	0	80
Oxnard, CA	0	1	2	114	155	96	34	< 1	1
Peoria, IL	n/a	127	27	89	127	149	115	22	49
Philadelphia, PA	5	94	23	81	146	138	117	14	27
Phoenix, AZ	0	10	167	186	125	54	37	< 1	23
Pittsburgh, PA	n/a	121	8	62	137	166	154	42	35
Portland, OR	n/a	37	11	67	116	182	152	4	7
Providence, RI	n/a	117	9	85	134	146	123	21	21
Provo, UT	n/a	128	56	94	152	119	92	38	38
Raleigh, NC	n/a	n/a	39	98	143	124	110	3	42
Reno, NV	14	178	50	143	139	83	50	17	14
Richmond, VA	3	79	41	90	147	128	115	7	43
Riverside, CA	0	4	82	124	178	63	n/a	n/a	5
Rochester, MN	n/a	165	9	87	126	152	114	40	41
Salem, OR	n/a	66	16	78	119	168	146	6	5
Salt Lake City, UT	n/a	128	56	94	152	119	92	38	38
San Antonio, TX	n/a	n/a	112	97	153	115	81	1	36
San Diego, CA	0	< 1	4	115	126	124	40	0	5
San Francisco, CA	0	6	4	136	130	99	63	< 1	5
San Jose, CA	0	5	5	106	180	79	57	< 1	6
Santa Rosa, CA	n/a	43	30	n/a	365	n/a	n/a	n/a	2
Savannah, GA	< 1	29	70	97	155	113	111	< 1	63
Seattle, WA	n/a	38	3	57	121	187	157	8	8
Sioux Falls, SD	n/a	n/a	n/a	95	136	134	n/a	n/a	n/a
Spokane, WA	n/a	140	18	78	135	152	113	37	11
Springfield, MO	12	102	42	113	119	133	109	14	55
Tallahassee, FL	< 1	31	86	93	175	97	114	1	83
Tampa, FL	n/a	n/a	85	81	204	80	107	< 1	87
Topeka, KS	20	123	45	110	128	127	96	15	54
Tulsa, OK	6	78	74	117	141	107	88	8	50
Virginia Beach, VA	< 1	53	33	89	149	127	115	5	38
Washington, DC	2	71	34	84	144	137	112	9	30
Wichita, KS	13	110	63	117	132	116	87	13	54
Wilmington, NC	< 1	42	46	96	150	119	115	1	47
Worcester, MA	n/a	141	4	81	144	140	131	32	23

Note: Figures are average number of days per year
Source: National Climatic Data Center, International Station Meteorological Climate Summary, 9/96

Air Quality Index

| MSA[1] (Days[2]) | Percent of Days when Air Quality was... | | | | | AQI Statistics | |
	Good	Moderate	Unhealthy for Sensitive Groups	Unhealthy	Very Unhealthy	Maximum	Median
Abilene, TX (n/a)	n/a	n/a	n/a	n/a	n/a	n/a	n/a
Albuquerque, NM (365)	48.5	50.7	0.8	0.0	0.0	145	51
Anchorage, AK (365)	77.8	20.8	1.1	0.3	0.0	151	29
Ann Arbor, MI (365)	88.2	11.8	0.0	0.0	0.0	87	34
Athens, GA (365)	74.5	25.5	0.0	0.0	0.0	91	39
Atlanta, GA (365)	47.9	51.2	0.5	0.3	0.0	151	52
Austin, TX (365)	73.7	26.0	0.3	0.0	0.0	109	41
Baltimore, MD (365)	58.4	40.3	1.4	0.0	0.0	111	46
Billings, MT (365)	93.2	6.6	0.3	0.0	0.0	101	24
Boise City, ID (365)	80.5	16.2	2.5	0.8	0.0	188	36
Boston, MA (365)	61.1	37.5	1.4	0.0	0.0	116	47
Boulder, CO (363)	81.5	17.4	1.1	0.0	0.0	127	42
Cape Coral, FL (365)	90.1	9.9	0.0	0.0	0.0	77	33
Cedar Rapids, IA (365)	70.1	29.6	0.3	0.0	0.0	122	42
Charleston, SC (365)	83.3	16.7	0.0	0.0	0.0	73	36
Charlotte, NC (365)	76.2	23.8	0.0	0.0	0.0	87	42
Chicago, IL (365)	19.7	77.0	3.0	0.3	0.0	186	60
Cincinnati, OH (365)	42.7	54.2	3.0	0.0	0.0	123	54
Clarksville, TN (365)	76.2	23.8	0.0	0.0	0.0	100	41
Colorado Spgs, CO (365)	69.6	29.0	1.4	0.0	0.0	116	44
Columbia, MO (214)	94.9	5.1	0.0	0.0	0.0	80	37.5
Columbus, OH (365)	66.6	32.9	0.5	0.0	0.0	114	43
Dallas, TX (365)	42.7	48.2	8.8	0.3	0.0	161	54
Davenport, IA (365)	37.5	61.6	0.8	0.0	0.0	126	55
Denver, CO (365)	41.9	51.8	6.3	0.0	0.0	145	54
Des Moines, IA (365)	73.2	26.8	0.0	0.0	0.0	99	41
Durham, NC (365)	84.9	15.1	0.0	0.0	0.0	90	35
El Paso, TX (365)	49.0	48.2	1.9	0.8	0.0	168	51
Erie, PA (365)	54.8	45.2	0.0	0.0	0.0	88	48
Eugene, OR (365)	66.3	27.7	5.8	0.3	0.0	161	36
Fargo, ND (355)	86.8	13.2	0.0	0.0	0.0	88	35
Fayetteville, NC (336)	84.8	15.2	0.0	0.0	0.0	90	37
Ft. Collins, CO (365)	72.3	25.8	1.9	0.0	0.0	140	46
Ft. Wayne, IN (365)	60.0	39.7	0.3	0.0	0.0	104	47
Ft. Worth, TX (365)	42.7	48.2	8.8	0.3	0.0	161	54
Gainesville, FL (365)	91.8	8.2	0.0	0.0	0.0	84	33
Grand Rapids, MI (365)	73.2	26.3	0.5	0.0	0.0	138	39
Green Bay, WI (365)	72.1	26.6	1.4	0.0	0.0	114	40
Greensboro, NC (338)	81.7	18.3	0.0	0.0	0.0	90	38
Honolulu, HI (365)	95.1	4.9	0.0	0.0	0.0	67	30
Houston, TX (365)	46.8	47.9	4.9	0.3	0.0	172	52
Huntsville, AL (336)	90.8	9.2	0.0	0.0	0.0	74	37
Indianapolis, IN (365)	29.0	67.9	3.0	0.0	0.0	124	59
Jacksonville, FL (365)	82.2	17.3	0.5	0.0	0.0	111	38
Kansas City, MO (365)	31.5	57.0	11.2	0.3	0.0	162	58
Lafayette, LA (365)	63.0	36.7	0.3	0.0	0.0	101	44
Las Vegas, NV (365)	43.0	52.6	4.1	0.3	0.0	157	54
Lexington, KY (365)	70.4	29.6	0.0	0.0	0.0	81	42
Lincoln, NE (259)	90.3	9.7	0.0	0.0	0.0	74	34
Little Rock, AR (365)	57.8	41.9	0.3	0.0	0.0	103	47
Los Angeles, CA (365)	7.1	71.5	20.3	1.1	0.0	172	73
Louisville, KY (365)	37.8	57.3	4.9	0.0	0.0	144	55
Lubbock, TX (334)	92.8	6.9	0.0	0.3	0.0	165	26
Madison, WI (365)	68.5	31.5	0.0	0.0	0.0	87	42

Table continued on next page.

MSA[1] (Days[2])	Percent of Days when Air Quality was...					AQI Statistics	
	Good	Moderate	Unhealthy for Sensitive Groups	Unhealthy	Very Unhealthy	Maximum	Median
Manchester, NH (365)	89.6	10.4	0.0	0.0	0.0	84	36
McAllen, TX (365)	78.4	21.4	0.3	0.0	0.0	106	36
Miami, FL (365)	76.4	22.7	0.8	0.0	0.0	118	41
Midland, TX (n/a)	n/a	n/a	n/a	n/a	n/a	n/a	n/a
Minneapolis, MN (365)	63.8	35.6	0.5	0.0	0.0	106	44
Montgomery, AL (285)	87.7	12.3	0.0	0.0	0.0	73	37
Nashville, TN (365)	74.2	25.5	0.3	0.0	0.0	112	43
New Orleans, LA (365)	61.4	31.8	6.0	0.8	0.0	200	45
New York, NY (365)	44.1	51.8	4.1	0.0	0.0	135	53
Oklahoma City, OK (365)	60.8	38.4	0.8	0.0	0.0	122	47
Omaha, NE (365)	54.0	44.9	1.1	0.0	0.0	128	48
Orlando, FL (365)	89.3	10.7	0.0	0.0	0.0	97	36
Oxnard, CA (365)	57.0	41.6	1.4	0.0	0.0	135	48
Peoria, IL (365)	56.7	36.2	5.8	1.4	0.0	183	48
Philadelphia, PA (365)	30.1	66.8	3.0	0.0	0.0	133	57
Phoenix, AZ (365)	9.9	66.3	16.4	5.2	2.2	902	74
Pittsburgh, PA (365)	33.7	61.4	4.7	0.3	0.0	164	56
Portland, OR (365)	66.0	29.6	3.3	1.1	0.0	157	38
Providence, RI (365)	64.1	33.4	2.5	0.0	0.0	145	45
Provo, UT (365)	60.0	29.9	5.8	4.4	0.0	189	47
Raleigh, NC (365)	68.8	31.2	0.0	0.0	0.0	90	43
Reno, NV (365)	50.7	40.5	3.8	1.1	3.8	895	50
Richmond, VA (365)	81.6	18.1	0.3	0.0	0.0	124	39
Riverside, CA (365)	8.2	56.4	27.7	6.8	0.8	455	84
Rochester, MN (365)	80.8	19.2	0.0	0.0	0.0	99	37
Salem, OR (361)	78.7	19.9	1.4	0.0	0.0	123	31
Salt Lake City, UT (365)	61.1	26.6	9.9	2.5	0.0	160	47
San Antonio, TX (365)	68.2	29.0	2.7	0.0	0.0	129	45
San Diego, CA (365)	18.9	75.9	4.7	0.3	0.3	617	61
San Francisco, CA (365)	44.4	53.7	1.9	0.0	0.0	133	53
San Jose, CA (365)	55.9	41.9	1.9	0.3	0.0	152	48
Santa Rosa, CA (365)	81.1	18.9	0.0	0.0	0.0	85	35
Savannah, GA (365)	68.2	29.0	2.7	0.0	0.0	131	40
Seattle, WA (365)	53.4	44.4	2.2	0.0	0.0	149	49
Sioux Falls, SD (365)	77.0	22.7	0.3	0.0	0.0	109	39
Spokane, WA (365)	70.4	29.0	0.3	0.3	0.0	175	39
Springfield, MO (365)	80.8	19.2	0.0	0.0	0.0	80	39
Tallahassee, FL (365)	83.8	15.3	0.5	0.0	0.3	222	36
Tampa, FL (365)	71.2	27.9	0.8	0.0	0.0	104	43
Topeka, KS (365)	90.4	9.6	0.0	0.0	0.0	77	36
Tulsa, OK (365)	54.2	43.8	1.9	0.0	0.0	114	48
Virginia Beach, VA (365)	80.3	19.7	0.0	0.0	0.0	100	39
Washington, DC (365)	53.2	45.5	1.4	0.0	0.0	104	49
Wichita, KS (365)	79.7	20.3	0.0	0.0	0.0	100	39
Wilmington, NC (344)	79.1	20.9	0.0	0.0	0.0	80	38
Worcester, MA (365)	80.8	19.2	0.0	0.0	0.0	97	38

Note: The Air Quality Index (AQI) is an index for reporting daily air quality. EPA calculates the AQI for five major air pollutants regulated by the Clean Air Act: ground-level ozone, particle pollution (also known as particulate matter), carbon monoxide, sulfur dioxide, and nitrogen dioxide. The AQI runs from 0 to 500. The higher the AQI value, the greater the level of air pollution and the greater the health concern. There are six AQI categories; "Good" The AQI is between 0 and 50. Air quality is considered satisfactory; "Moderate" The AQI is between 51 and 100. Air quality is acceptable; "Unhealthy for Sensitive Groups" When AQI values are between 101 and 150, members of sensitive groups may experience health effects; "Unhealthy" When AQI values are between 151 and 200 everyone may begin to experience health effects; "Very Unhealthy" AQI values between 201 and 300 trigger a health alert; "Hazardous" AQI values over 300 trigger health warnings of emergency conditions; Data covers the entire county unless noted otherwise; (1) Data covers the Metropolitan Statistical Area—see Appendix B for areas included; (2) Number of days with AQI data in 2013
Source: U.S. Environmental Protection Agency, Air Quality Index Report, 2013

Air Quality Index Pollutants

MSA[1] (Days[2])	Percent of Days when AQI Pollutant was...					
	Carbon Monoxide	Nitrogen Dioxide	Ozone	Sulfur Dioxide	Particulate Matter 2.5	Particulate Matter 10
Abilene, TX (n/a)	n/a	n/a	n/a	n/a	n/a	n/a
Albuquerque, NM (365)	0.0	0.3	49.0	0.0	33.7	17.0
Anchorage, AK (365)	0.5	0.0	0.0	0.0	69.6	29.9
Ann Arbor, MI (365)	0.0	0.0	83.8	0.0	16.2	0.0
Athens, GA (365)	0.0	0.0	21.6	0.0	78.4	0.0
Atlanta, GA (365)	0.0	1.9	20.8	0.0	77.3	0.0
Austin, TX (365)	0.0	0.3	51.5	0.0	48.2	0.0
Baltimore, MD (365)	0.0	4.4	37.5	0.3	57.8	0.0
Billings, MT (365)	0.0	0.0	0.0	55.1	44.9	0.0
Boise City, ID (365)	0.0	21.6	43.0	0.0	17.0	18.4
Boston, MA (365)	0.0	5.5	21.4	0.8	72.1	0.3
Boulder, CO (363)	0.0	0.0	91.7	0.0	8.0	0.3
Cape Coral, FL (365)	0.0	0.0	57.3	0.0	42.7	0.0
Cedar Rapids, IA (365)	0.0	0.0	28.5	0.0	71.0	0.5
Charleston, SC (365)	0.0	2.5	20.8	0.5	76.2	0.0
Charlotte, NC (365)	0.0	2.7	41.4	0.0	55.3	0.5
Chicago, IL (365)	0.0	7.4	10.7	6.8	69.3	5.8
Cincinnati, OH (365)	0.0	0.8	23.8	15.9	58.1	1.4
Clarksville, TN (365)	0.0	0.0	43.3	1.9	54.8	0.0
Colorado Spgs, CO (365)	0.0	0.0	87.4	9.0	2.7	0.8
Columbia, MO (214)	0.0	0.0	100.0	0.0	0.0	0.0
Columbus, OH (365)	0.0	1.1	34.8	0.0	64.1	0.0
Dallas, TX (365)	0.0	4.7	38.4	0.0	55.6	1.4
Davenport, IA (365)	0.0	0.0	8.5	0.0	65.8	25.8
Denver, CO (365)	0.0	23.0	53.4	1.9	18.1	3.6
Des Moines, IA (365)	0.0	2.2	31.2	0.0	66.6	0.0
Durham, NC (365)	0.0	0.0	31.5	0.3	68.2	0.0
El Paso, TX (365)	0.0	13.4	28.2	0.0	53.7	4.7
Erie, PA (365)	0.0	0.8	23.3	0.0	75.9	0.0
Eugene, OR (365)	0.0	0.0	31.5	0.0	67.9	0.5
Fargo, ND (355)	0.0	2.3	57.2	0.0	37.7	2.8
Fayetteville, NC (336)	0.0	0.0	36.0	0.0	64.0	0.0
Ft. Collins, CO (365)	0.0	0.0	93.7	0.0	4.9	1.4
Ft. Wayne, IN (365)	1.1	0.0	20.8	0.3	77.8	0.0
Ft. Worth, TX (365)	0.0	4.7	38.4	0.0	55.6	1.4
Gainesville, FL (365)	0.0	0.0	53.2	0.0	46.8	0.0
Grand Rapids, MI (365)	0.0	0.0	43.0	0.0	57.0	0.0
Green Bay, WI (365)	0.0	0.0	37.5	13.4	49.0	0.0
Greensboro, NC (338)	0.0	0.0	39.1	0.0	60.7	0.3
Honolulu, HI (365)	0.0	0.0	25.8	0.0	73.2	1.1
Houston, TX (365)	0.0	6.8	26.6	1.6	63.8	1.1
Huntsville, AL (336)	0.0	0.0	61.3	0.0	22.9	15.8
Indianapolis, IN (365)	0.0	0.3	11.2	19.5	69.0	0.0
Jacksonville, FL (365)	0.0	0.3	38.1	6.6	55.1	0.0
Kansas City, MO (365)	0.0	0.5	20.5	27.9	49.0	1.9
Lafayette, LA (365)	0.0	0.0	30.4	0.0	69.0	0.5
Las Vegas, NV (365)	0.0	2.5	59.5	0.0	35.1	3.0
Lexington, KY (365)	0.0	6.0	22.2	1.1	70.1	0.5
Lincoln, NE (259)	0.0	0.0	71.8	0.0	28.2	0.0
Little Rock, AR (365)	0.0	0.8	29.3	0.0	69.9	0.0
Los Angeles, CA (365)	0.0	4.4	33.4	0.0	60.8	1.4
Louisville, KY (365)	0.0	0.5	12.3	17.5	69.6	0.0
Lubbock, TX (334)	0.0	0.0	0.0	0.0	100.0	0.0
Madison, WI (365)	0.0	0.0	37.5	0.0	62.5	0.0

Table continued on next page.

MSA[1] (Days[2])	Percent of Days when AQI Pollutant was...					
	Carbon Monoxide	Nitrogen Dioxide	Ozone	Sulfur Dioxide	Particulate Matter 2.5	Particulate Matter 10
Manchester, NH (365)	0.0	0.0	79.5	0.0	20.5	0.0
McAllen, TX (365)	0.0	0.0	33.2	0.0	65.5	1.4
Miami, FL (365)	0.0	1.1	25.5	0.0	73.2	0.3
Midland, TX (n/a)	n/a	n/a	n/a	n/a	n/a	n/a
Minneapolis, MN (365)	0.0	3.8	36.7	0.5	55.3	3.6
Montgomery, AL (285)	0.0	0.0	66.7	0.0	33.3	0.0
Nashville, TN (365)	0.0	4.9	37.0	0.0	58.1	0.0
New Orleans, LA (365)	0.0	1.4	32.1	14.0	52.1	0.5
New York, NY (365)	0.0	15.1	25.2	0.0	59.7	0.0
Oklahoma City, OK (365)	0.0	5.8	47.9	0.0	46.3	0.0
Omaha, NE (365)	0.0	0.0	19.7	5.8	52.9	21.6
Orlando, FL (365)	0.0	0.3	55.6	0.0	44.1	0.0
Oxnard, CA (365)	0.0	1.6	45.5	0.0	50.4	2.5
Peoria, IL (365)	0.0	0.0	27.1	21.4	51.5	0.0
Philadelphia, PA (365)	0.0	1.6	15.6	0.3	81.9	0.5
Phoenix, AZ (365)	0.0	4.7	19.5	0.0	20.8	55.1
Pittsburgh, PA (365)	0.0	0.3	15.6	7.9	76.2	0.0
Portland, OR (365)	0.0	1.1	41.1	0.0	57.8	0.0
Providence, RI (365)	0.0	0.5	36.7	3.6	58.6	0.5
Provo, UT (365)	0.0	20.3	47.9	0.0	30.7	1.1
Raleigh, NC (365)	0.0	0.0	26.8	0.0	73.2	0.0
Reno, NV (365)	0.0	1.1	48.5	0.0	34.0	16.4
Richmond, VA (365)	0.0	8.2	46.3	1.4	44.1	0.0
Riverside, CA (365)	0.0	4.1	40.5	0.0	38.4	17.0
Rochester, MN (365)	0.0	0.0	40.8	0.0	59.2	0.0
Salem, OR (361)	0.0	0.0	36.0	0.0	64.0	0.0
Salt Lake City, UT (365)	0.0	12.1	54.0	1.4	31.8	0.8
San Antonio, TX (365)	0.0	0.8	51.0	0.3	47.9	0.0
San Diego, CA (365)	0.0	7.1	27.1	0.0	57.5	8.2
San Francisco, CA (365)	0.0	5.2	9.0	0.0	85.8	0.0
San Jose, CA (365)	0.0	0.5	40.5	0.0	58.1	0.8
Santa Rosa, CA (365)	0.0	0.8	51.5	0.0	46.8	0.8
Savannah, GA (365)	0.0	0.0	18.4	25.8	55.9	0.0
Seattle, WA (365)	0.0	0.0	19.5	0.0	80.5	0.0
Sioux Falls, SD (365)	0.0	0.5	58.9	0.0	39.2	1.4
Spokane, WA (365)	0.5	0.0	32.9	0.0	64.1	2.5
Springfield, MO (365)	0.0	0.0	36.7	8.8	54.2	0.3
Tallahassee, FL (365)	0.0	0.0	52.6	0.0	47.4	0.0
Tampa, FL (365)	0.0	0.0	34.0	6.6	59.5	0.0
Topeka, KS (365)	0.0	0.0	83.3	0.0	15.3	1.4
Tulsa, OK (365)	0.0	0.0	37.0	8.2	54.8	0.0
Virginia Beach, VA (365)	0.0	5.8	34.8	9.6	49.9	0.0
Washington, DC (365)	0.0	10.1	32.6	0.0	57.3	0.0
Wichita, KS (365)	0.0	7.9	71.2	0.0	15.3	5.5
Wilmington, NC (344)	0.0	0.0	29.4	6.7	64.0	0.0
Worcester, MA (365)	0.0	3.3	48.8	0.0	47.1	0.8

Note: The Air Quality Index (AQI) is an index for reporting daily air quality. EPA calculates the AQI for five major air pollutants regulated by the Clean Air Act: ground-level ozone, particle pollution (also known as particulate matter), carbon monoxide, sulfur dioxide, and nitrogen dioxide. The AQI runs from 0 to 500. The higher the AQI value, the greater the level of air pollution and the greater the health concern; (1) (1) Data covers the Metropolitan Statistical Area—see Appendix B for areas included; (2) Number of days with AQI data in 2013
Source: U.S. Environmental Protection Agency, Air Quality Index Report, 2013

Air Quality Trends: Ozone

MSA[1]	2003	2004	2005	2006	2007	2008	2009	2010	2011	2012
Abilene, TX	n/a	n/a	n/a	n/a	n/a	n/a	n/a	n/a	n/a	n/a
Albuquerque, NM	0.076	0.071	0.074	0.071	0.070	0.066	0.065	0.066	0.070	0.070
Anchorage, AK	n/a	n/a	n/a	n/a	n/a	n/a	n/a	n/a	n/a	n/a
Ann Arbor, MI	0.091	0.071	0.083	0.076	0.077	0.069	0.065	0.066	0.077	0.085
Athens, GA	0.072	0.078	0.082	0.086	0.083	0.077	0.067	0.073	0.075	0.071
Atlanta, GA	0.083	0.081	0.085	0.092	0.091	0.080	0.072	0.074	0.078	0.077
Austin, TX	0.083	0.081	0.081	0.083	0.073	0.072	0.073	0.072	0.074	0.075
Baltimore, MD	0.083	0.082	0.089	0.089	0.086	0.084	0.072	0.085	0.087	0.083
Billings, MT	n/a	n/a	n/a	n/a	n/a	n/a	n/a	n/a	n/a	n/a
Boise City, ID	n/a	n/a	n/a	n/a	n/a	n/a	n/a	n/a	n/a	n/a
Boston, MA	0.079	0.075	0.082	0.077	0.081	0.072	0.070	0.069	0.066	0.068
Boulder, CO	0.082	0.068	0.076	0.082	0.085	0.076	0.073	0.072	0.076	0.076
Cape Coral, FL	0.074	0.072	0.070	0.070	0.069	0.068	0.062	0.064	0.062	0.063
Cedar Rapids, IA	0.068	0.063	0.073	0.065	0.076	0.063	0.061	0.064	0.064	0.071
Charleston, SC	0.072	0.072	0.073	0.071	0.065	0.069	0.059	0.067	0.066	0.063
Charlotte, NC	0.081	0.078	0.085	0.084	0.088	0.081	0.067	0.076	0.078	0.076
Chicago, IL	0.077	0.067	0.083	0.070	0.079	0.064	0.065	0.070	0.071	0.081
Cincinnati, OH	0.088	0.075	0.085	0.078	0.086	0.075	0.070	0.076	0.080	0.083
Clarksville, TN	n/a	n/a	n/a	n/a	n/a	n/a	n/a	n/a	n/a	n/a
Colorado Spgs, CO	0.077	0.070	0.077	0.072	0.072	0.070	0.060	0.068	0.074	0.075
Columbia, MO	n/a	n/a	n/a	n/a	n/a	n/a	n/a	n/a	n/a	n/a
Columbus, OH	0.088	0.075	0.085	0.077	0.081	0.073	0.070	0.074	0.078	0.079
Dallas, TX	0.089	0.087	0.093	0.089	0.081	0.077	0.080	0.076	0.085	0.083
Davenport, IA	0.072	0.064	0.071	0.065	0.072	0.061	0.061	0.061	0.059	0.069
Denver, CO	0.084	0.068	0.075	0.080	0.079	0.075	0.070	0.072	0.078	0.080
Des Moines, IA	0.061	0.051	0.072	0.064	0.069	0.059	0.061	0.064	0.063	0.070
Durham, NC	0.079	0.072	0.079	0.073	0.077	0.075	0.064	0.072	0.070	0.068
El Paso, TX	0.071	0.074	0.077	0.077	0.074	0.074	0.068	0.068	0.069	0.067
Erie, PA	0.091	0.074	0.086	0.077	0.084	0.074	0.069	0.075	0.072	0.082
Eugene, OR	0.075	0.066	0.068	0.073	0.060	0.059	0.065	0.058	0.059	0.061
Fargo, ND	0.065	0.056	0.061	0.065	0.055	0.055	0.057	0.063	0.057	0.063
Fayetteville, NC	0.084	0.075	0.088	0.073	0.081	0.075	0.066	0.072	0.075	0.069
Ft. Collins, CO	0.081	0.069	0.076	0.077	0.074	0.071	0.066	0.072	0.073	0.077
Ft. Wayne, IN	0.087	0.071	0.081	0.072	0.079	0.068	0.065	0.067	0.071	0.076
Ft. Worth, TX	0.089	0.087	0.093	0.089	0.081	0.077	0.080	0.076	0.085	0.083
Gainesville, FL	0.071	0.075	0.073	0.075	0.078	0.069	0.056	0.069	0.064	0.064
Grand Rapids, MI	0.089	0.070	0.083	0.082	0.085	0.068	0.069	0.068	0.076	0.080
Green Bay, WI	0.087	0.072	0.084	0.072	0.084	0.064	0.068	0.072	0.068	0.083
Greensboro, NC	0.083	0.074	0.078	0.075	0.082	0.084	0.068	0.074	0.071	0.076
Honolulu, HI	0.038	0.046	0.042	0.040	0.033	0.041	0.048	0.047	0.046	0.043
Houston, TX	0.097	0.092	0.087	0.090	0.079	0.074	0.079	0.078	0.082	0.081
Huntsville, AL	0.079	0.077	0.075	0.079	0.082	0.073	0.066	0.071	0.072	0.076
Indianapolis, IN	0.084	0.071	0.080	0.076	0.081	0.070	0.070	0.068	0.071	0.075
Jacksonville, FL	0.071	0.074	0.072	0.074	0.073	0.069	0.061	0.067	0.066	0.060
Kansas City, MO	0.085	0.066	0.082	0.085	0.076	0.067	0.068	0.068	0.074	0.082
Lafayette, LA	n/a	n/a	n/a	n/a	n/a	n/a	n/a	n/a	n/a	n/a
Las Vegas, NV	0.081	0.077	0.082	0.081	0.080	0.073	0.072	0.070	0.074	0.076
Lexington, KY	0.071	0.064	0.078	0.070	0.079	0.070	0.064	0.070	0.074	0.078
Lincoln, NE	0.060	0.056	0.056	0.056	0.054	0.051	0.053	0.050	0.053	0.058
Little Rock, AR	0.075	0.073	0.083	0.083	0.081	0.068	0.072	0.072	0.078	0.078
Los Angeles, CA	0.097	0.088	0.083	0.088	0.084	0.088	0.085	0.073	0.077	0.078
Louisville, KY	0.077	0.071	0.083	0.076	0.083	0.074	0.068	0.075	0.081	0.085
Lubbock, TX	n/a	n/a	n/a	n/a	n/a	n/a	n/a	n/a	n/a	n/a
Madison, WI	0.078	0.065	0.079	0.066	0.079	0.064	0.063	0.062	0.068	0.074
Manchester, NH	0.070	0.071	0.071	0.068	0.074	0.064	0.060	0.063	0.063	0.063
McAllen, TX	0.073	0.070	0.069	0.060	0.055	0.058	0.060	0.065	0.062	0.061

Table continued on next page.

MSA[1]	2003	2004	2005	2006	2007	2008	2009	2010	2011	2012
Miami, FL	0.066	0.063	0.064	0.074	0.066	0.067	0.062	0.064	0.060	0.062
Midland, TX	n/a	n/a	n/a	n/a	n/a	n/a	n/a	n/a	n/a	n/a
Minneapolis, MN	0.073	0.062	0.073	0.068	0.073	0.060	0.062	0.065	0.064	0.068
Montgomery, AL	0.069	0.068	0.069	0.073	0.077	0.069	0.063	0.073	0.069	0.066
Nashville, TN	0.076	0.072	0.078	0.078	0.083	0.072	0.064	0.073	0.071	0.077
New Orleans, LA	0.083	0.076	0.076	0.078	0.079	0.070	0.073	0.075	0.073	0.072
New York, NY	0.089	0.079	0.092	0.087	0.086	0.081	0.072	0.081	0.081	0.079
Oklahoma City, OK	0.079	0.072	0.076	0.081	0.073	0.071	0.072	0.071	0.082	0.078
Omaha, NE	0.067	0.068	0.072	0.070	0.063	0.057	0.057	0.061	0.059	0.068
Orlando, FL	0.075	0.074	0.080	0.078	0.075	0.069	0.064	0.068	0.072	0.069
Oxnard, CA	0.085	0.082	0.077	0.078	0.073	0.077	0.076	0.072	0.072	0.069
Peoria, IL	0.072	0.064	0.075	0.069	0.078	0.064	0.061	0.064	0.068	0.072
Philadelphia, PA	0.085	0.080	0.088	0.083	0.086	0.082	0.069	0.082	0.082	0.081
Phoenix, AZ	0.080	0.073	0.078	0.078	0.073	0.076	0.069	0.072	0.076	0.076
Pittsburgh, PA	0.085	0.074	0.085	0.077	0.078	0.075	0.068	0.075	0.072	0.079
Portland, OR	0.071	0.060	0.059	0.067	0.058	0.062	0.064	0.056	0.056	0.059
Providence, RI	0.089	0.081	0.087	0.082	0.084	0.078	0.068	0.076	0.075	0.077
Provo, UT	0.078	0.069	0.079	0.077	0.077	0.072	0.069	0.070	0.067	0.075
Raleigh, NC	0.086	0.076	0.083	0.074	0.081	0.078	0.067	0.072	0.075	0.073
Reno, NV	0.071	0.069	0.067	0.071	0.069	0.074	0.064	0.067	0.064	0.070
Richmond, VA	0.082	0.076	0.082	0.082	0.081	0.082	0.065	0.078	0.076	0.076
Riverside, CA	0.113	0.102	0.101	0.103	0.100	0.103	0.094	0.092	0.094	0.093
Rochester, MN	n/a	n/a	n/a	n/a	n/a	n/a	n/a	n/a	n/a	n/a
Salem, OR	0.072	0.062	0.063	0.075	0.060	0.066	0.069	0.057	0.057	0.063
Salt Lake City, UT	0.079	0.072	0.084	0.082	0.081	0.075	0.074	0.072	0.074	0.079
San Antonio, TX	0.082	0.085	0.082	0.083	0.071	0.075	0.070	0.072	0.075	0.079
San Diego, CA	0.072	0.076	0.070	0.073	0.073	0.080	0.071	0.069	0.067	0.066
San Francisco, CA	0.067	0.063	0.057	0.067	0.058	0.067	0.066	0.063	0.061	0.059
San Jose, CA	0.080	0.072	0.066	0.080	0.068	0.074	0.072	0.074	0.066	0.065
Santa Rosa, CA	0.057	0.053	0.049	0.053	0.054	0.058	0.052	0.054	0.050	0.050
Savannah, GA	0.070	0.071	0.068	0.069	0.065	0.067	0.062	0.065	0.065	0.063
Seattle, WA	0.072	0.065	0.055	0.068	0.059	0.058	0.061	0.056	0.053	0.058
Sioux Falls, SD	n/a	n/a	n/a	n/a	n/a	n/a	n/a	n/a	n/a	n/a
Spokane, WA	0.074	0.065	0.063	0.066	0.064	0.058	0.057	0.058	0.056	0.063
Springfield, MO	0.072	0.064	0.077	0.074	0.080	0.067	0.062	0.066	0.073	0.075
Tallahassee, FL	0.074	0.071	0.070	0.071	0.072	0.071	0.058	0.066	0.065	0.066
Tampa, FL	0.077	0.074	0.075	0.074	0.076	0.075	0.064	0.067	0.071	0.066
Topeka, KS	n/a	n/a	n/a	n/a	n/a	n/a	n/a	n/a	n/a	n/a
Tulsa, OK	0.083	0.071	0.080	0.082	0.072	0.071	0.071	0.071	0.083	0.084
Virginia Beach, VA	0.081	0.075	0.078	0.074	0.077	0.078	0.065	0.074	0.075	0.069
Washington, DC	0.084	0.080	0.082	0.086	0.084	0.077	0.067	0.080	0.080	0.079
Wichita, KS	0.076	0.061	0.072	0.073	0.063	0.065	0.071	0.073	0.075	0.076
Wilmington, NC	0.076	0.070	0.075	0.072	0.071	0.063	0.060	0.062	0.064	0.064
Worcester, MA	0.080	0.074	0.085	0.077	0.089	0.081	0.077	0.070	0.065	0.070

Note: (1) Data covers the Metropolitan Statistical Area—see Appendix B for areas included; n/a not available. The values shown are the composite ozone concentration averages among trend sites based on the highest fourth daily maximum 8-hour concentration in parts per million. These trends are based on sites having an adequate record of monitoring data during the trend period. Data from exceptional events are included.
Source: U.S. Environmental Protection Agency, Air Quality Monitoring Information, "Air Quality Trends by City, 2000-2012"

Maximum Air Pollutant Concentrations: Particulate Matter, Ozone, CO and Lead

Metro Aea	PM 10 (ug/m³)	PM 2.5 Wtd AM (ug/m³)	PM 2.5 24-Hr (ug/m³)	Ozone (ppm)	Carbon Monoxide (ppm)	Lead (ug/m³)
Abilene, TX	n/a	n/a	n/a	n/a	n/a	n/a
Albuquerque, NM	227	7.4	20	0.077	2	0.01
Anchorage, AK	121	8	33	0.048	6	0.07
Ann Arbor, MI	n/a	9.2	23	0.085	n/a	n/a
Athens, GA	n/a	n/a	n/a	0.071	n/a	n/a
Atlanta, GA	38	11	21	0.088	1	0.03
Austin, TX	32	7.8	17	0.076	0	n/a
Baltimore, MD	31	11.1	25	0.087	2	n/a
Billings, MT	n/a	n/a	n/a	n/a	n/a	n/a
Boise City, ID	182	10.4	41	0.073	2	n/a
Boston, MA	37	9.5	24	0.074	2	n/a
Boulder, CO	43	n/a	n/a	0.076	n/a	n/a
Cape Coral, FL	57	6.7	14	0.065	n/a	n/a
Cedar Rapids, IA	53	9.5	23	0.072	2	n/a
Charleston, SC	41	8.5	21	0.064	n/a	n/a
Charlotte, NC	38	9.6	21	0.085	2	n/a
Chicago, IL	153	11.9	32	0.093	2	0.13
Cincinnati, OH	105	13.9	28	0.091	1	0.01
Clarksville, TN	29	9.9	20	0.078	n/a	n/a
Colorado Spgs, CO	51	n/a	n/a	0.075	1	n/a
Columbia, MO	n/a	n/a	n/a	0.078	n/a	n/a
Columbus, OH	62	10.7	22	0.082	2	0.01
Dallas, TX	66	10.7	22	0.092	1	0.42
Davenport, IA	137	10.4	25	0.072	1	0.02
Denver, CO	103	n/a	37	0.086	2	0.02
Des Moines, IA	49	9.2	21	0.07	1	n/a
Durham, NC	30	8.3	18	0.076	n/a	n/a
El Paso, TX	643	9.9	21	0.074	4	0.03
Erie, PA	32	11.2	25	0.082	1	n/a
Eugene, OR	41	7.6	38	0.062	n/a	n/a
Fargo, ND	92	7.5	23	0.063	0	n/a
Fayetteville, NC	26	8.9	18	0.069	n/a	n/a
Ft. Collins, CO	91	n/a	n/a	0.08	2	n/a
Ft. Wayne, IN	n/a	9.9	26	0.077	2	n/a
Ft. Worth, TX	66	10.7	22	0.092	1	0.42
Gainesville, FL	n/a	7	17	0.064	n/a	n/a
Grand Rapids, MI	35	9.6	29	0.081	1	0.06
Green Bay, WI	n/a	8.7	25	0.086	n/a	n/a
Greensboro, NC	24	8.5	20	0.078	n/a	n/a
Honolulu, HI	36	7.1	15	0.048	1	0
Houston, TX	128	11.8	26	0.087	2	0.01
Huntsville, AL	38	9.3	19	0.076	n/a	0.01
Indianapolis, IN	71	11.7	26	0.084	2	0.04
Jacksonville, FL	55	8	22	0.061	1	n/a
Kansas City, MO	82	9.6	20	0.086	2	0.01
Lafayette, LA	73	8.6	18	0.07	n/a	n/a
Las Vegas, NV	139	8.6	21	0.085	3	n/a
Lexington, KY	30	9.8	19	0.078	n/a	n/a
Lincoln, NE	n/a	8.7	20	0.058	n/a	n/a
Little Rock, AR	36	11.6	27	0.08	1	n/a
Los Angeles, CA	74	12.5	32	0.102	4	0.15
Louisville, KY	46	11.9	24	0.092	2	n/a
Lubbock, TX	n/a	n/a	n/a	n/a	n/a	n/a
Madison, WI	36	9.4	27	0.074	n/a	n/a
Manchester, NH	20	8.2	23	0.073	0	n/a

Table continued on next page.

Metro Aea	PM 10 (ug/m^3)	PM 2.5 Wtd AM (ug/m^3)	PM 2.5 24-Hr (ug/m^3)	Ozone (ppm)	Carbon Monoxide (ppm)	Lead (ug/m^3)
McAllen, TX	69	n/a	n/a	0.061	n/a	n/a
Miami, FL	73	8.3	20	0.064	2	n/a
Midland, TX	n/a	n/a	n/a	n/a	n/a	n/a
Minneapolis, MN	70	9.9	25	0.074	2	0.11
Montgomery, AL	28	10.6	20	0.066	n/a	n/a
Nashville, TN	34	10.3	19	0.083	2	n/a
New Orleans, LA	63	12.9	19	0.077	n/a	0.04
New York, NY	73	11.7	26	0.085	3	0.03
Oklahoma City, OK	73	9.8	19	0.081	1	n/a
Omaha, NE	181	11.7	29	0.077	2	0.2
Orlando, FL	41	7.1	19	0.072	1	n/a
Oxnard, CA	76	9.6	19	0.081	n/a	n/a
Peoria, IL	n/a	9.8	21	0.078	2	0.01
Philadelphia, PA	66	16.5	31	0.092	2	0.05
Phoenix, AZ	504	12	29	0.083	3	n/a
Pittsburgh, PA	75	14.3	43	0.085	2	0.19
Portland, OR	33	7.3	23	0.065	2	0.05
Providence, RI	32	7.8	20	0.082	1	n/a
Provo, UT	67	8.1	34	0.077	2	n/a
Raleigh, NC	29	8.5	19	0.075	1	n/a
Reno, NV	194	9.1	26	0.072	2	n/a
Richmond, VA	29	8.9	20	0.078	2	0.01
Riverside, CA	334	15.1	36	0.106	2	0.01
Rochester, MN	n/a	7.8	19	0.069	n/a	n/a
Salem, OR	n/a	n/a	n/a	0.063	n/a	n/a
Salt Lake City, UT	81	8.9	29	0.08	2	0.05
San Antonio, TX	50	8.7	23	0.087	n/a	n/a
San Diego, CA	193	11.1	24	0.08	2	0.17
San Francisco, CA	46	9.5	22	0.072	2	0.33
San Jose, CA	56	9	32	0.072	2	0.12
Santa Rosa, CA	30	8.2	19	0.058	1	n/a
Savannah, GA	27	10	24	0.063	n/a	n/a
Seattle, WA	27	9.7	28	0.071	1	0.06
Sioux Falls, SD	72	8.7	21	0.072	1	n/a
Spokane, WA	84	n/a	n/a	0.063	2	n/a
Springfield, MO	33	10.1	22	0.08	n/a	n/a
Tallahassee, FL	n/a	8.7	18	0.067	n/a	n/a
Tampa, FL	55	6.9	16	0.074	1	0.98
Topeka, KS	47	8.6	18	0.079	n/a	n/a
Tulsa, OK	139	9.7	20	0.085	1	0.01
Virginia Beach, VA	32	8.2	23	0.074	1	n/a
Washington, DC	38	10.3	28	0.09	3	0
Wichita, KS	94	9.3	18	0.081	1	n/a
Wilmington, NC	n/a	6.6	16	0.064	n/a	n/a
Worcester, MA	38	8.8	20	0.07	2	n/a
NAAQS[1]	150	15	35	0.075	9	0.15

Note: Data from exceptional events are included; Data covers the Metropolitan Statistical Area—see Appendix B for areas included; (1) National Ambient Air Quality Standards; ppm = parts per million; ug/m^3 = micrograms per cubic meter; n/a not available
Concentrations: Particulate Matter 10 (coarse particulate)—highest second maximum 24-hour concentration; Particulate Matter 2.5 Wtd AM (fine particulate)—highest weighted annual mean concentration; Particulate Matter 2.5 24-Hour (fine particulate)—highest 98th percentile 24-hour concentration; Ozone—highest fourth daily maximum 8-hour concentration; Carbon Monoxide—highest second maximum non-overlapping 8-hour concentration; Lead—maximum running 3-month average
Source: U.S. Environmental Protection Agency, Air Quality Monitoring Information, "Air Quality Statistics by City, 2012"

Maximum Air Pollutant Concentrations: Nitrogen Dioxide and Sulfur Dioxide

Metro Area	Nitrogen Dioxide AM (ppb)	Nitrogen Dioxide 1-Hr (ppb)	Sulfur Dioxide AM (ppb)	Sulfur Dioxide 1-Hr (ppb)	Sulfur Dioxide 24-Hr (ppb)
Abilene, TX	n/a	n/a	n/a	n/a	n/a
Albuquerque, NM	14	49	n/a	6	n/a
Anchorage, AK	n/a	n/a	n/a	n/a	n/a
Ann Arbor, MI	n/a	n/a	n/a	n/a	n/a
Athens, GA	n/a	n/a	n/a	n/a	n/a
Atlanta, GA	12	53	n/a	11	n/a
Austin, TX	n/a	n/a	n/a	n/a	n/a
Baltimore, MD	16	56	n/a	19	n/a
Billings, MT	n/a	n/a	n/a	70	n/a
Boise City, ID	n/a	n/a	n/a	6	n/a
Boston, MA	19	49	n/a	21	n/a
Boulder, CO	n/a	n/a	n/a	n/a	n/a
Cape Coral, FL	n/a	n/a	n/a	n/a	n/a
Cedar Rapids, IA	n/a	n/a	n/a	29	n/a
Charleston, SC	7	n/a	n/a	17	n/a
Charlotte, NC	9	n/a	n/a	8	n/a
Chicago, IL	22	63	n/a	108	n/a
Cincinnati, OH	4	29	n/a	85	n/a
Clarksville, TN	n/a	n/a	n/a	55	n/a
Colorado Spgs, CO	n/a	n/a	n/a	n/a	n/a
Columbia, MO	n/a	n/a	n/a	n/a	n/a
Columbus, OH	n/a	n/a	n/a	n/a	n/a
Dallas, TX	12	53	n/a	15	n/a
Davenport, IA	8	34	n/a	12	n/a
Denver, CO	25	72	n/a	39	n/a
Des Moines, IA	8	40	n/a	1	n/a
Durham, NC	n/a	n/a	n/a	n/a	n/a
El Paso, TX	16	59	n/a	5	n/a
Erie, PA	6	31	n/a	19	n/a
Eugene, OR	n/a	n/a	n/a	n/a	n/a
Fargo, ND	5	34	n/a	4	n/a
Fayetteville, NC	n/a	n/a	n/a	4	n/a
Ft. Collins, CO	n/a	n/a	n/a	n/a	n/a
Ft. Wayne, IN	n/a	n/a	n/a	n/a	n/a
Ft. Worth, TX	12	53	n/a	15	n/a
Gainesville, FL	n/a	n/a	n/a	n/a	n/a
Grand Rapids, MI	n/a	n/a	n/a	10	n/a
Green Bay, WI	n/a	n/a	n/a	72	n/a
Greensboro, NC	n/a	n/a	n/a	n/a	n/a
Honolulu, HI	3	19	n/a	16	n/a
Houston, TX	15	60	n/a	29	n/a
Huntsville, AL	n/a	n/a	n/a	n/a	n/a
Indianapolis, IN	10	n/a	n/a	92	n/a
Jacksonville, FL	8	37	n/a	54	n/a
Kansas City, MO	14	53	n/a	167	n/a
Lafayette, LA	n/a	n/a	n/a	n/a	n/a
Las Vegas, NV	14	59	n/a	9	n/a
Lexington, KY	8	45	n/a	15	n/a
Lincoln, NE	n/a	n/a	n/a	n/a	n/a
Little Rock, AR	11	55	n/a	10	n/a
Los Angeles, CA	21	63	n/a	3	n/a
Louisville, KY	11	45	n/a	147	n/a
Lubbock, TX	n/a	n/a	n/a	n/a	n/a
Madison, WI	n/a	n/a	n/a	n/a	n/a
Manchester, NH	n/a	n/a	n/a	4	n/a

Table continued on next page.

Metro Area	Nitrogen Dioxide AM (ppb)	Nitrogen Dioxide 1-Hr (ppb)	Sulfur Dioxide AM (ppb)	Sulfur Dioxide 1-Hr (ppb)	Sulfur Dioxide 24-Hr (ppb)
McAllen, TX	n/a	n/a	n/a	n/a	n/a
Miami, FL	8	46	n/a	27	n/a
Midland, TX	n/a	n/a	n/a	n/a	n/a
Minneapolis, MN	11	57	n/a	16	n/a
Montgomery, AL	n/a	n/a	n/a	n/a	n/a
Nashville, TN	12	42	n/a	11	n/a
New Orleans, LA	8	46	n/a	217	n/a
New York, NY	22	67	n/a	32	n/a
Oklahoma City, OK	9	60	n/a	5	n/a
Omaha, NE	n/a	n/a	n/a	73	n/a
Orlando, FL	5	35	n/a	5	n/a
Oxnard, CA	10	38	n/a	n/a	n/a
Peoria, IL	n/a	n/a	n/a	245	n/a
Philadelphia, PA	18	56	n/a	29	n/a
Phoenix, AZ	26	65	n/a	9	n/a
Pittsburgh, PA	14	50	n/a	117	n/a
Portland, OR	9	36	n/a	5	n/a
Providence, RI	10	40	n/a	65	n/a
Provo, UT	17	66	n/a	n/a	n/a
Raleigh, NC	n/a	n/a	n/a	13	n/a
Reno, NV	14	53	n/a	6	n/a
Richmond, VA	10	51	n/a	21	n/a
Riverside, CA	22	96	n/a	5	n/a
Rochester, MN	n/a	n/a	n/a	n/a	n/a
Salem, OR	n/a	n/a	n/a	n/a	n/a
Salt Lake City, UT	16	54	n/a	20	n/a
San Antonio, TX	4	34	n/a	n/a	n/a
San Diego, CA	20	72	n/a	1	n/a
San Francisco, CA	15	66	n/a	15	n/a
San Jose, CA	13	52	n/a	13	n/a
Santa Rosa, CA	9	36	n/a	n/a	n/a
Savannah, GA	n/a	n/a	n/a	78	n/a
Seattle, WA	n/a	n/a	n/a	19	n/a
Sioux Falls, SD	6	37	n/a	6	n/a
Spokane, WA	n/a	n/a	n/a	n/a	n/a
Springfield, MO	n/a	n/a	n/a	52	n/a
Tallahassee, FL	n/a	n/a	n/a	n/a	n/a
Tampa, FL	5	34	n/a	110	n/a
Topeka, KS	n/a	n/a	n/a	n/a	n/a
Tulsa, OK	9	42	n/a	55	n/a
Virginia Beach, VA	8	41	n/a	56	n/a
Washington, DC	17	51	n/a	12	n/a
Wichita, KS	10	85	n/a	n/a	n/a
Wilmington, NC	n/a	n/a	n/a	47	n/a
Worcester, MA	13	45	n/a	9	n/a
NAAQS[1]	53	100	30	75	140

Note: Data from exceptional events are included; Data covers the Metropolitan Statistical Area—see Appendix B for areas included; (1) National Ambient Air Quality Standards; ppb = parts per billion; n/a not available
Concentrations: Nitrogen Dioxide AM—highest arithmetic mean concentration; Nitrogen Dioxide 1-Hr—highest 98th percentile 1-hour daily maximum concentration; Sulfur Dioxide AM—highest annual mean concentration; Sulfur Dioxide 1-Hr—highest 99th percentile 1-hour daily maximum concentration; Sulfur Dioxide 24 Hr—highest second maximum 24-hour concentration
Source: U.S. Environmental Protection Agency, Air Quality Monitoring Information, "Air Quality Statistics by City, 2012"

Table continued on next page.

Appendix B: Metropolitan Area Definitions

Metropolitan Statistical Areas (MSA), Metropolitan Divisions (MD), New England City and Town Areas (NECTA), and New England City and Town Area Divisions (NECTAD)

Note: In February 2013, the Office of Management and Budget (OMB) announced changes to metropolitan and micropolitan statistical area definitions. Both current and historical definitions are shown below. If the change only affected the name of the metro area, the counties included were not repeated.

Abilene, TX MSA
Callahan, Jones, and Taylor Counties

Albuquerque, NM MSA
Bernalillo, Sandoval, Torrance, and Valencia Counties

Anchorage, AK MSA
Anchorage Municipality and Matanuska-Susitna Borough

Ann Arbor, MI MSA
Washtenaw County

Athens-Clarke County, GA MSA
Clarke, Madison, Oconee, and Oglethorpe Counties

Atlanta-Sandy Springs-Roswell, GA MSA
Barrow, Bartow, Butts, Carroll, Cherokee, Clayton, Cobb, Coweta, Dawson, DeKalb, Douglas, Fayette, Forsyth, Fulton, Gwinnett, Haralson, Heard, Henry, Jasper, Lamar, Meriwether, Morgan, Newton, Paulding, Pickens, Pike, Rockdale, Spalding, and Walton Counties
Previously Atlanta-Sandy Springs-Marietta, GA MSA
Barrow, Bartow, Butts, Carroll, Cherokee, Clayton, Cobb, Coweta, Dawson, DeKalb, Douglas, Fayette, Forsyth, Fulton, Gwinnett, Haralson, Heard, Henry, Jasper, Lamar, Meriwether, Newton, Paulding, Pickens, Pike, Rockdale, Spalding, and Walton Counties

Austin-Round Rock, TX MSA
Previously Austin-Round Rock-San Marcos, TX MSA
Bastrop, Caldwell, Hays, Travis, and Williamson Counties

Baltimore-Columbia-Towson, MD MSA
Previously Baltimore-Towson, MD MSA
Baltimore city; Anne Arundel, Baltimore, Carroll, Harford, Howard, and Queen Anne's Counties

Billings, MT MSA
Carbon and Yellowstone Counties

Boise City, ID MSA
Previously Boise City-Nampa, ID MSA
Ada, Boise, Canyon, Gem, and Owyhee Counties

Boston, MA

Boston-Cambridge-Newton, MA-NH MSA
Peviously Boston-Cambridge-Quincy, MA-NH MSA
Essex, Middlesex, Norfolk, Plymouth, and Suffolk Counties, MA; Rockingham and Strafford Counties, NH

Boston, MA MD
Previously Boston-Quincy, MA MD
Norfolk, Plymouth, and Suffolk Counties

Boston-Cambridge-Nashua, MA-NH NECTA
Includes 157 cities and towns in Massachusetts and 34 cities and towns in New Hampshire
Previously Boston-Cambridge-Quincy, MA-NH NECTA
Includes 155 cities and towns in Massachusetts and 38 cities and towns in New Hampshire

Boston-Cambridge-Newton, MA NECTA Division
Includes 92 cities and towns in Massachusetts
Previously Boston-Cambridge-Quincy, MA NECTA Division
Includes 97 cities and towns in Massachusetts

Boulder, CO MSA
Boulder County

Cape Coral-Fort Myers, FL MSA
Lee County

Cedar Rapids, IA, MSA
Benton, Jones, and Linn Counties

Charleston-North Charleston, SC MSA
Previously Charleston-North Charleston- Summerville, SC MSA
Berkeley, Charleston, and Dorchester Counties

Charlotte-Concord-Gastonia, NC-SC MSA
Cabarrus, Gaston, Iredell, Lincoln, Mecklenburg, Rowan, and Union Counties, NC; Chester, Lancaster, and York Counties, SC
Previously Charlotte-Gastonia-Rock Hill, NC-SC MSA
Anson, Cabarrus, Gaston, Mecklenburg, and Union Counties, NC; York County, SC

Chicago, IL

Chicago-Naperville-Elgin, IL-IN-WI MSA
Previously Chicago-Joliet-Naperville, IL-IN-WI MSA
Cook, DeKalb, DuPage, Grundy, Kane, Kendall, Lake, McHenry, and Will Counties, IL; Jasper, Lake, Newton, and Porter Counties, IN; Kenosha County, WI

Chicago-Naperville-Arlington Heights, IL MD
Cook, DuPage, Grundy, Kendall, McHenry, and Will Counties
Previously Chicago-Joliet-Naperville, IL MD
Cook, DeKalb, DuPage, Grundy, Kane, Kendall, McHenry, and Will Counties

Lake County-Kenosha County, IL-WI MD
Lake County, IL; Kenosha County, WI

Cincinnati, OH-KY-IN MSA
Previously Cincinnati-Middletown, OH-KY-IN MSA
Dearborn, Ohio, and Union Counties, OH; Boone, Bracken, Campbell, Gallatin, Grant, Kenton, and Pendleton County, KY; Brown, Butler, Clermont, Hamilton, and Warren Counties, IN

Clarksville, TN-KY MSA
Mongomery and Stewart Counties, TN; Christian and Trigg Counties, KY

Colorado Springs, CO MSA
El Paso and Teller Counties

Columbia, MO MSA
Boone and Howard Counties

Columbus, OH MSA
Delaware, Fairfield, Franklin, Licking, Madison, Morrow, Pickaway, and Union Counties

Dallas, TX

Dallas-Fort Worth-Arlington, TX MSA
Collin, Dallas, Denton, Ellis, Hunt, Johnson, Kaufman, Parker, Rockwall, Tarrant, and Wise Counties

Dallas-Plano-Irving, TX MD
Collin, Dallas, Denton, Ellis, Hunt, Kaufman, and Rockwall Counties

Davenport-Moline-Rock Island, IA-IL MSA
Henry, Mercer, and Rock Island Counties, IA; Scott County, IL

Denver-Aurora-Lakewood, CO MSA
Previously Denver-Aurora-Broomfield, CO MSA
Adams, Arapahoe, Broomfield, Clear Creek, Denver, Douglas, Elbert, Gilpin, Jefferson, and Park Counties

Des Moines-West Des Moines, IA MSA
Dallas, Guthrie, Madison, Polk, and Warren Counties

Durham-Chapel Hill, NC MSA
Chatham, Durham, Orange, and and Person Counties

El Paso, TX MSA
El Paso County

Erie, PA MSA
Erie County

Eugene, OR MSA
Previously Eugene-Springfield, OR MSA
Lane County

Fargo, ND-MN MSA
Cass County, ND; Clay County, MN

Fayetteville, NC MSA
Cumberland, and Hoke Counties

Fort Collins, CO MSA
Previously Fort Collins-Loveland, CO MSA
Larimer County

Fort Wayne, IN MSA
Allen, Wells, and Whitley Counties

Fort Worth, TX

Dallas-Fort Worth-Arlington, TX MSA
Collin, Dallas, Denton, Ellis, Hunt, Johnson, Kaufman, Parker, Rockwall, Tarrant, and Wise Counties

Fort Worth-Arlington, TX MD
Hood, Johnson, Parker, Somervell, Tarrant, and Wise Counties

Gainesville, FL MSA
Alachua, and Gilchrist Counties

Grand Rapids-Wyoming, MI MSA
Barry, Kent, Montcalm, and Ottawa Counties

Green Bay, WI MSA
Brown, Kewaunee, and Oconto Counties

Greensboro-High Point, NC MSA
Guilford, Randolph, and Rockingham Counties

Honolulu, HI MSA
Honolulu County

Houston-The Woodlands-Sugar Land-Baytown, TX MSA
Austin, Brazoria, Chambers, Fort Bend, Galveston, Harris, Liberty, Montgomery, and Waller Counties
Previously Houston-Sugar Land-Baytown, TX MSA
Austin, Brazoria, Chambers, Fort Bend, Galveston, Harris, Liberty, Montgomery, San Jacinto, and Waller Counties

Huntsville, AL MSA
Limestone and Madison Counties

Indianapolis-Carmel, IN MSA
Boone, Brown, Hamilton, Hancock, Hendricks, Johnson, Marion, Morgan, Putnam, and Shelby Counties

Jacksonville, FL MSA
Baker, Clay, Duval, Nassau, and St. Johns Counties

Kansas City, MO-KS MSA
Franklin, Johnson, Leavenworth, Linn, Miami, and Wyandotte Counties, KS; Bates, Caldwell, Cass, Clay, Clinton, Jackson, Lafayette, Platte, and Ray Counties, MO

Lafayette, LA MSA
Acadia, Iberia, Lafayette, St. Martin, and Vermilion Parishes

Las Vegas-Henderson-Paradise, NV MSA
Previously Las Vegas-Paradise, NV MSA
Clark County

Lexington-Fayette, KY MSA
Bourbon, Clark, Fayette, Jessamine, Scott, and Woodford Counties

Lincoln, NE MSA
Lancaster and Seward Counties

Little Rock-North Little Rock-Conway, AR MSA
Faulkner, Grant, Lonoke, Perry, Pulaski and Saline Counties, AR

Los Angeles, CA

Los Angeles-Long Beach-Anaheim, CA MSA
Previously Los Angeles-Long Beach-Santa Ana, CA MSA
Los Angeles and Orange Counties

Los Angeles-Long Beach-Glendale, CA MD
Los Angeles County

Anaheim-Santa Ana-Irvine, CA MD
Previously Santa Ana-Anaheim-Irvine, CA MD
Orange County

Louisville/Jefferson, KY-IN MSA
Clark, Floyd, Harrison, Scott, and Washington Counties, IN; Bullitt, Henry, Jefferson, Oldham, Shelby, Spencer, and Trimble Counties, KY

Lubbock, TX MSA
Crosby, Lubbock, and Lynn Counties

Madison, WI MSA
Columbia, Dane, and Iowa Counties

Manchester, NH

Manchester-Nashua, NH MSA
Hillsborough County

Manchester, NH NECTA
Includes 11 cities and towns in New Hampshire
Previously Manchester, NH NECTA
Includes 9 cities and towns in New Hampshire

McAllen-Edinburg-Mission, TX
Hidalgo County

Miami, FL

Miami-Fort Lauderdale-West Palm Beach, FL MSA
Previously Miami-Fort Lauderdale-Pompano Beach, FL MSA
Broward, Miami-Dade, and Palm Beach Counties

Miami-Miami Beach-Kendall, FL MD
Miami-Dade County

Midland, TX MSA
Martin, and Midland Counties

Minneapolis-St. Paul-Bloomington, MN-WI MSA
Anoka, Carver, Chisago, Dakota, Hennepin, Isanti, Le Sueur, Mille
Lacs, Ramsey, Scott, Sherburne, Sibley, Washington, and Wright
Counties, MN; Pierce and St. Croix Counties, WI

Montgomery, AL MSA
Autauga, Elmore, Lowndes, and Montgomery Counties

Nashville-Davidson-Murfreesboro-Franklin, TN MSA
Cannon, Cheatham, Davidson, Dickson, Hickman, Macon, Robertson,
Rutherford, Smith, Sumner, Trousdale, Williamson, and Wilson
Counties

New Orleans-Metairie-Kenner, LA MSA
Jefferson, Orleans, Plaquemines, St. Bernard, St. Charles, St. James,
St. John the Baptist, and St. Tammany Parish
Previously New Orleans-Metairie-Kenner, LA MSA
Jefferson, Orleans, Plaquemines, St. Bernard, St. Charles, St. John the
Baptist, and St. Tammany Parish

New York, NY

New York-Newark-Jersey City, NY-NJ-PA MSA
Bergen, Essex, Hudson, Hunterdon, Middlesex, Monmouth, Morris,
Ocean, Passaic, Somerset, Sussex, and Union Counties, NJ; Bronx,
Dutchess, Kings, Nassau, New York, Orange, Putnam, Queens,
Richmond, Rockland, Suffolk, and Westchester Counties, NY; Pike
County, PA
Previously New York-Northern New Jersey-Long Island, NY-NJ-PA
MSA
Bergen, Essex, Hudson, Hunterdon, Middlesex, Monmouth, Morris,
Ocean, Passaic, Somerset, Sussex, and Union Counties, NJ; Bronx,
Kings, Nassau, New York, Putnam, Queens, Richmond, Rockland,
Suffolk, and Westchester Counties, NY; Pike County, PA

New York-Jersey City-White Plains, NY-NJ MD
Bergen, Hudson, Middlesex, Monmouth, Ocean, and Passaic
Counties, NJ; Bronx, Kings, New York, Putnam, Queens, Richmond,
Rockland, and Westchester Counties, NY
Previously New York-Wayne-White Plains, NY-NJ MD
Bergen, Hudson, and Passaic Counties, NJ; Bronx, Kings, New York,
Putnam, Queens, Richmond, Rockland, and Westchester Counties,
NY

Nassau-Suffolk, NY MD
Nassau and Suffolk Counties

Oklahoma City, OK MSA
Canadian, Cleveland, Grady, Lincoln, Logan, McClain, and Oklahoma
Counties

Omaha-Council Bluffs, NE-IA MSA
Harrison, Mills, and Pottawattamie Counties, IA; Cass, Douglas,
Sarpy, Saunders, and Washington Counties, NE

Orlando-Kissimmee-Sanford, FL MSA
Lake, Orange, Osceola, and Seminole Counties

Oxnard-Thousand Oaks-Ventura, CA MSA
Ventura County

Peoria, IL MSA
Marshall, Peoria, Stark, Tazewell, and Woodford Counties

Philadelphia, PA

Philadelphia-Camden-Wilmington, PA-NJ-DE-MD MSA
New Castle County, DE; Cecil County, MD; Burlington, Camden,
Gloucester, and Salem Counties, NJ; Bucks, Chester, Delaware,
Montgomery, and Philadelphia Counties, PA

Philadelphia, PA MD
Delaware and Philadelphia Counties
Previously Philadelphia, PA MD
Bucks, Chester, Delaware, Montgomery, and Philadelphia Counties

Phoenix-Mesa-Scottsdale, AZ MSA
Previously Phoenix-Mesa-Glendale, AZ MSA
Maricopa and Pinal Counties

Pittsburgh, PA MSA
Allegheny, Armstrong, Beaver, Butler, Fayette, Washington, and
Westmoreland Counties

Portland-Vancouver-Hillsboro, OR-WA MSA
Clackamas, Columbia, Multnomah, Washington, and Yamhill
Counties, OR; Clark and Skamania Counties, WA

Providence, RI

Providence-New Bedford-Fall River, RI-MA MSA
Previously Providence-New Bedford-Fall River, RI-MA MSA
Bristol County, MA; Bristol, Kent, Newport, Providence, and
Washington Counties, RI

Providence-Warwick, RI-MA NECTA
Includes 12 cities and towns in Massachusetts and 36 cities and towns
in Rhode Island
Previously Providence-Fall River-Warwick, RI-MA NECTA
Includes 12 cities and towns in Massachusetts and 37 cities and towns
in Rhode Island

Provo-Orem, UT MSA
Juab and Utah Counties

Raleigh, NC MSA
Previously Raleigh-Cary, NC MSA
Franklin, Johnston, and Wake Counties

Reno, NV MSA
Previously Reno-Sparks, NV MSA
Storey and Washoe Counties

Richmond, VA MSA
Amelia, Caroline, Charles City, Chesterfield, Dinwiddie, Goochland,
Hanover, Henrico, King William, New Kent, Powhatan, Prince
George, and Sussex Counties; Colonial Heights, Hopewell,
Petersburg, and Richmond Cities

Riverside-San Bernardino-Ontario, CA MSA
Riverside and San Bernardino Counties

Rochester, MN MSA
Dodge, Fillmore, Olmsted, and Wabasha Counties

Salem, OR MSA
Marion and Polk Counties

Salt Lake City, UT MSA
Salt Lake and Tooele Counties

San Antonio-New Braunfels, TX MSA
Atascosa, Bandera, Bexar, Comal, Guadalupe, Kendall, Medina, and Wilson Counties

San Diego-Carlsbad, CA MSA
Previously San Diego-Carlsbad-San Marcos, CA MSA
San Diego County

San Francisco, CA

San Francisco-Oakland-Hayward, CA MSA
Previously San Francisco-Oakland- Fremont, CA MSA
Alameda, Contra Costa, Marin, San Francisco, and San Mateo Counties

San Francisco-Redwood City-South San Francisco, CA MD
San Francisco and San Mateo Counties

Previously San Francisco-San Mateo-Redwood City, CA MD
Marin, San Francisco, and San Mateo Counties

San Jose-Sunnyvale-Santa Clara, CA MSA
San Benito and Santa Clara Counties

Santa Rosa, CA MSA
Previously Santa Rosa-Petaluma, CA MSA
Sonoma County

Savannah, GA MSA
Bryan, Chatham, and Effingham Counties

Seattle, WA

Seattle-Tacoma-Bellevue, WA MSA
King, Pierce, and Snohomish Counties

Seattle-Bellevue-Everett, WA MD
King and Snohomish Counties

Sioux Falls, SD MSA
Lincoln, McCook, Minnehaha, and Turner Counties

Spokane-Spokane Valley, WA MSA
Pend Oreille, Spokane, and Stevens Counties
Previously Spokane, WA MSA
Spokane County

Springfield, MO MSA
Christian, Dallas, Greene, Polk, and Webster Counties

Tallahassee, FL MSA
Gadsden, Jefferson, Leon, and Wakulla Counties

Tampa-St. Petersburg-Clearwater, FL MSA
Hernando, Hillsborough, Pasco, and Pinellas Counties

Topeka, KS MSA
Jackson, Jefferson, Osage, Shawnee, and Wabaunsee Counties

Tulsa, OK MSA
Creek, Okmulgee, Osage, Pawnee, Rogers, Tulsa, and Wagoner Counties

Virginia Beach-Norfolk-Newport News, VA-NC MSA
Currituck County, NC; Chesapeake, Hampton, Newport News, Norfolk, Poquoson, Portsmouth, Suffolk, Virginia Beach and Williamsburg cities, VA; Gloucester, Isle of Wight, James City, Mathews, Surry, and York Counties, VA

Washington, DC

Washington-Arlington-Alexandria, DC-VA-MD-WV MSA
District of Columbia; Calvert, Charles, Frederick, Montgomery, and Prince George's Counties, MD; Alexandria, Fairfax, Falls Church, Fredericksburg, Manassas Park, and Manassas cities, VA; Arlington, Clarke, Culpepper, Fairfax, Fauquier, Loudoun, Prince William, Rappahannock, Spotsylvania, Stafford, and Warren Counties, VA; Jefferson County, WV
Previously Washington-Arlington-Alexandria, DC-VA-MD-WV MSA
District of Columbia; Calvert, Charles, Frederick, Montgomery, and Prince George's Counties, MD; Alexandria, Fairfax, Falls Church, Fredericksburg, Manassas Park, and Manassas cities, VA; Arlington, Clarke, Fairfax, Fauquier, Loudoun, Prince William, Spotsylvania, Stafford, and Warren Counties, VA; Jefferson County, WV

Washington-Arlington-Alexandria, DC-VA-MD-WV MD
District of Columbia; Calvert, Charles, and Prince George's Counties, MD; Alexandria, Fairfax, Falls Church, Fredericksburg, Manassas Park, and Manassas cities, VA; Arlington, Clarke, Culpepper, Fairfax, Fauquier, Loudoun, Prince William, Rappahannock, Spotsylvania, Stafford, and Warren Counties, VA; Jefferson County, WV
Previously Washington-Arlington-Alexandria, DC-VA-MD-WV MD
District of Columbia; Calvert, Charles, and Prince George's Counties, MD; Alexandria, Fairfax, Falls Church, Fredericksburg, Manassas Park, and Manassas cities, VA; Arlington, Clarke, Fairfax, Fauquier, Loudoun, Prince William, Spotsylvania, Stafford, and Warren Counties, VA; Jefferson County, WV

Wichita, KS MSA
Butler, Harvey, Kingman, Sedgwick, and Sumner Counties

Wilmington, NC MSA
New Hanover and Pender Counties

Worcester, MA

Worcester, MA-CT MSA
Windham County, CT; Worcester County, MA
Previously Worcester, MA MSA
Worcester County

Worcester, MA-CT NECTA
Includes 40 cities and towns in Massachusetts and 8 cities and towns in Connecticut
Previously Worcester, MA-CT NECTA
Includes 37 cities and towns in Massachusetts and 3 cities and towns in Connecticut

Appendix C: Government Type and Primary County

This appendix includes the government structure of each place included in this book. It also includes the county or county equivalent in which each place is located. If a place spans more that one county, the county in which the majority of the population resides is shown.

Abilene, TX
Government Type: City
County: Taylor

Albuquerque, NM
Government Type: City
County: Bernalillo

Anchorage, AK
Government Type: Municipality
Borough: Anchorage

Ann Arbor, MI
Government Type: City
County: Washtenaw

Athens, GA
Government Type: Consolidated
  city-county
County: Clarke

Atlanta, GA
Government Type: City
County: Fulton

Austin, TX
Government Type: City
County: Travis

Baltimore, MD
Government Type: Independent city
County: Baltimore city

Billings, MT
Government Type: City
County: Yellowstone

Boise City, ID
Government Type: City
County: Ada

Boston, MA
Government Type: City
County: Suffolk

Boulder, CO
Government Type: City
County: Boulder

Cape Coral, FL
Government Type: City
County: Lee

Cedar Rapids, IA
Government Type: City
County: Linn

Charleston, SC
Government Type: City
County: Charleston

Charlotte, NC
Government Type: City
County: Mecklenburg

Chicago, IL
Government Type: City
County: Cook

Cincinnati, OH
Government Type: City
County: Hamilton

Clarksville, TN
Government Type: City
County: Montgomery

Colorado Springs, CO
Government Type: City
County: El Paso

Columbia, MO
Government Type: City
County: Boone

Columbus, OH
Government Type: City
County: Franklin

Dallas, TX
Government Type: City
County: Dallas

Davenport, IA
Government Type: City
County: Scott

Denver, CO
Government Type: City
County: Denver

Des Moines, IA
Government Type: City
County: Polk

Durham, NC
Government Type: City
County: Durham

El Paso, TX
Government Type: City
County: El Paso

Erie, PA
Government Type: City
County: Erie

Eugene, OR
Government Type: City
County: Lane

Fargo, ND
Government Type: City
County: Cass

Fayetteville, NC
Government Type: City
County: Cumberland

Fort Collins, CO
Government Type: City
County: Larimer

Fort Wayne, IN
Government Type: City
County: Allen

Fort Worth, TX
Government Type: City
County: Tarrant

Gainesville, FL
Government Type: City
County: Alachua

Grand Rapids, MI
Government Type: City
County: Kent

Green Bay, WI
Government Type: City
County: Brown

Greensboro, NC
Government Type: City
County: Guilford

Honolulu, HI
Government Type: Census Designated Place
  (CDP)
County: Honolulu

Houston, TX
Government Type: City
County: Harris

Huntsville, AL
Government Type: City
County: Madison

Indianapolis, IN
Government Type: City
County: Marion

Jacksonville, FL
Government Type: City
County: Duval

Kansas City, MO
Government Type: City
County: Jackson

Lafayette, LA
Government Type: City
Parish: Lafayette

Las Vegas, NV
Government Type: City
County: Clark

Lexington, KY
Government Type: Consolidated city-county
County: Fayette

Lincoln, NE
Government Type: City
County: Lancaster

Little Rock, AR
Government Type: City
County: Pulaski

Los Angeles, CA
Government Type: City
County: Los Angeles

Louisville, KY
Government Type: Consolidated city-county
County: Jefferson

Lubbock, TX
Government Type: City
County: Lubbock

Madison, WI
Government Type: City
County: Dane

Manchester, NH
Government Type: City
County: Hillsborough

McAllen, TX
Government Type: City
County: Hidalgo

Miami, FL
Government Type: City
County: Miami-Dade

Midland, TX
Government Type: City
County: Midland

Minneapolis, MN
Government Type: City
County: Hennepin

Montgomery, AL
Government Type: City
County: Montgomery

Nashville, TN
Government Type: Consolidated city-county
County: Davidson

New Orleans, LA
Government Type: City
Parish: Orleans

New York, NY
Government Type: City
Counties: Bronx; Kings; New York; Queens;
  Staten Island

Oklahoma City, OK
Government Type: City
County: Oklahoma

Omaha, NE
Government Type: City
County: Douglas

Orlando, FL
Government Type: City
County: Orange

Oxnard, CA
Government Type: City
County: Ventura

Peoria, IL
Government Type: City
County: Peoria

Philadelphia, PA
Government Type: City
County: Philadelphia

Phoenix, AZ
Government Type: City
County: Maricopa

Pittsburgh, PA
Government Type: City
County: Allegheny

Portland, OR
Government Type: City
County: Multnomah

Providence, RI
Government Type: City
County: Providence

Provo, UT
Government Type: City
County: Utah

Raleigh, NC
Government Type: City
County: Wake

Reno, NV
Government Type: City
County: Washoe

Richmond, VA
Government Type: Independent city
County: Richmond city

Riverside, CA
Government Type: City
County: Riverside

Rochester, MN
Government Type: City
County: Olmsted

Salem, OR
Government Type: City
County: Marion

Salt Lake City, UT
Government Type: City
County: Salt Lake

San Antonio, TX
Government Type: City
County: Bexar

San Diego, CA
Government Type: City
County: San Diego

San Francisco, CA
Government Type: City
County: San Francisco

San Jose, CA
Government Type: City
County: Santa Clara

Santa Rosa, CA
Government Type: City
County: Sonoma

Savannah, GA
Government Type: City
County: Chatham

Seattle, WA
Government Type: City
County: King

Sioux Falls, SD
Government Type: City
County: Minnehaha

Spokane, WA
Government Type: City
County: Spokane

Springfield, MO
Government Type: City
County: Christian

Tallahassee, FL
Government Type: City
County: Leon

Tampa, FL
Government Type: City
County: Hillsborough

Topeka, KS
Government Type: City
County: Shawnee

Tulsa, OK
Government Type: City
County: Tulsa

Virginia Beach, VA
Government Type: Independent city
County: Virginia Beach city

Washington, DC
Government Type: City
County: District of Columbia

Wichita, KS
Government Type: City
County: Sedgwick

Wilmington, NC
Government Type: City
County: New Hanover

Worcester, MA
Government Type: City
County: Worcester

Appendix D: Chambers of Commerce & Economic Development Offices

Abilene, TX
Abilene Chamber of Commerce
174 Cypress Street
Suite 200
Abilene, TX 79601
Phone: (325) 677-7241
Fax: (325) 677-0622
www.abilenechamber.com

Albuquerque, NM
Albuquerque Chamber of Commerce
P.O. Box 25100
Albuquerque, NM 87125
Phone: (505) 764-3700
Fax: (505) 764-3714
www.abqchamber.com

Albuquerque Economic Development Dept
851 University Blvd SE
Suite 203
Albuquerque, NM 87106
Phone: (505) 246-6200
Fax: (505) 246-6219
www.cabq.gov/econdev

Anchorage, AK
Anchorage Chamber of Commerce
1016 W Sixth Avenue
Suite 303
Anchorage, AK 99501
Phone: (907) 272-2401
Fax: (907) 272-4117
www.anchoragechamber.org

Anchorage Economic Development
Department
900 W 5th Avenue
Suite 300
Anchorage, AK 99501
Phone: (907) 258-3700
Fax: (907) 258-6646
www.aedcweb.com/aedcdig

Ann Arbor, MI
Ann Arbor Area Chamber of Commerce
115 West Huron
3rd Floor
Ann Arbor, MI 48104
Phone: (734) 665-4433
Fax: (734) 665-4191
www.annarborchamber.org

Ann Arbor Economic Development
Department
201 S Division
Suite 430
Ann Arbor, MI 48104
Phone: (734) 761-9317
www.annarborspark.org

Athens, GA
Athens Area Chamber of Commerce
246 W Hancock Avenue
Athens, GA 30601
Phone: (706) 549-6800
Fax: (706) 549-5636
www.aacoc.org

Athens-Clarke Economic Development
150 E. Hancock Avenue
P.O. Box 1692
Athens, GA 30603
Phone: (706) 613-3810
Fax: (706) 613-3812
www.athensbusiness.org/contact.aspx

Atlanta, GA
Metro Atlanta Chamber of Commerce
235 Andrew Young International Blvd NW
Atlanta, GA 30303
Phone: (404) 880-9000
Fax: (404) 586-8464
www.metroatlantachamber.com/contact_us.
html

Austin, TX
Greater Austin Chamber of Commerce
210 Barton Springs Road
Suite 400
Austin, TX 78704
Phone: (512) 478-9383
Fax: (512) 478-6389
www.austin-chamber.org

Baltimore, MD
Baltimore City Chamber of Commerce
312 Martin Luther King Jr Blvd
Baltimore, MD 21201
Phone: (410) 837-7101
Fax: (410) 837-7104
www.baltimorecitychamber.com

City of Baltimore Development Corporation
36 South Charles Street
Suite 1600
Baltimore, MD 21201
Phone: (410) 837-9305
Fax: (410) 837-6363
www.baltimoredevelopment.com

Billings, MT
Billings Area Chamber of Commerce
815 S 27th St
Billings, MT 59101
Phone: (406) 245-4111
Fax: (406) 2457333
www.billingschamber.com

Boise City, ID
Boise Metro Chamber of Commerce
250 S 5th Street
Suite 800
Boise City, ID 83701
Phone: (208) 472-5200
Fax: (208) 472-5201
www.boisechamber.org

Boston, MA
Greater Boston Chamber of Commerce
265 Franklin Street
12th Floor
Boston, MA 02110
Phone: (617) 227-4500
Fax: (617) 227-7505
www.bostonchamber.com

Boulder, CO
Boulder Chamber of Commerce
2440 Pearl Street
Boulder, CO 80302
Phone: (303) 442-1044
Fax: (303) 938-8837
www.boulderchamber.com

City of Boulder Economic Vitality Program
P.O. Box 791
Boulder, CO 80306
Phone: (303) 441-3090
www.bouldercolorado.gov

Cape Coral, FL
Chamber of Commerce of Cape Coral
2051 Cape Coral Parkway East
Cape Coral, FL 33904
Phone: (239) 549-6900
Fax: (239) 549-9609
www.capecoralchamber.com

Cedar Rapids, IA
Cedar Rapids Chamber of Commerce
424 First Avenue NE
Cedar Rapids, IA 52401
Phone: (319) 398-5317
Fax: (319) 398-5228
www.cedarrapids.org

Cedar Rapids Economic Development
50 Second Avenue Bridge, Sixth Floor
Cedar Rapids, IA 52401-1256
Phone: (319) 286-5041
Fax: (319) 286-5141
www.cedar-rapids.org

Charleston, SC
Charleston Metro Chamber of Commerce
P.O. Box 975
Charleston, SC 29402
Phone: (843) 577-2510
www.charlestonchamber.net

Charlotte, NC
Charlotte Chamber of Commerce
330 S Tryon Street
Charlotte, NC 28232
Phone: (704) 378-1300
Fax: (704) 374-1903
www.charlottechamber.com

Charlotte Regional Partnership
1001 Morehead Square Drive
Suite 200
Charlotte, NC 28203
Phone: (704) 347-8942
Fax: (704) 347-8981
www.charlotteusa.com

Chicago, IL
Chicagoland Chamber of Commerce
200 E Randolph Street
Suite 2200
Chicago, IL 60601-6436
Phone: (312) 494-6700
Fax: (312) 861-0660
www.chicagolandchamber.org

City of Chicago Department of Planning
and Development
City Hall, Room 1000
121 North La Salle Street
Chicago, IL 60602
Phone: (312) 744-4190
Fax: (312) 744-2271
www.egov.cityofchicago.org

Cincinnati, OH
Greater Cincinnati Chamber of Commerce
441 Vine Street
Suite 300
Cincinnati, OH 45202
Phone: (513) 579-3100
Fax: (513) 579-3101
www.cincinnatichamber.com

Clarksville, TN
Clarksville Area Chamber of Commerce
25 Jefferson Street
Suite 300
Clarksville, TN 37040
Phone: (931) 647-2331
www.clarksvillechamber.com

Colorado Springs, CO
Greater Colorado Springs Chamber of
Commerce
6 S. Tejon Street
Suite 700
Colorado Springs, CO 80903
Phone: (719) 635-1551
Fax: (719) 635-1571
www.gcsco.wliinc3.com

Greater Colorado Springs Economic
Development Corp
90 South Cascade Avenue
Suite 1050
Colorado Springs, CO 80903
Phone: (719) 471-8183
Fax: (719) 471-9733
www.coloradosprings.org

Columbia, MO
Columbia Chamber of Commerce
300 South Providence Rd.
PO Box 1016
Columbia, MO 65205-1016
Phone: (573) 874-1132
Fax: (573)443-3986
www.columbiamochamber.com

Columbus, OH
Greater Columbus Chamber
37 North High Street
Columbus, OH 43215
Phone: (614) 221-1321
Fax: (614) 221-1408
www.columbus.org

Dallas, TX
City of Dallas Economic Development
Department
1500 Marilla Street
5C South
Dallas, TX 75201
Phone: (214) 670-1685
Fax: (214) 670-0158
www.dallas-edd.org

Greater Dallas Chamber of Commerce
700 North Pearl Street
Suite1200
Dallas, TX 75201
Phone: (214) 746-6600
Fax: (214) 746-6799
www.dallaschamber.org

Davenport, IA
Quad Cities Chamber
331 W. 3rd St.,
Davenport, IA 52801
Phone: (563) 322-1706
www.quadcitieschamber.com

Denver, CO
Denver Metro Chamber of Commerce
1445 Market Street
Denver, CO 80202
Phone: (303) 534-8500
Fax: (303) 534-3200
www.denverchamber.org

Downtown Denver Partnership
511 16th Street
Suite 200
Denver, CO 80202
Phone: (303) 534-6161
Fax: (303) 534-2803
www.downtowndenver.com

Des Moines, IA
Des Moines Downtown Chamber
301 Grand Ave
Des Moines, IA 50309
Phone: (515) 309-3229
www.desmoinesdowtownchamber.com

Greater Des Moines Partnership
700 Locust Street
Suite 100
Des Moines, IA 50309
Phone: (515) 286-4950
Fax: (515) 286-4974
www.desmoinesmetro.com

Durham, NC
Durham Chamber of Commerce
PO Box 3829
Durham, NC 27702
Phone: (919) 682-2133
Fax: (919) 688-8351
www.durhamchamber.org

North Carolina Institute of Minority
Economic Development
114 W Parish Street
Durham, NC 27701
Phone: (919) 956-8889
Fax: (919) 688-7668
www.ncimed.com

El Paso, TX
City of El Paso Department of Economic
Development
2 Civic Center Plaza
El Paso, TX 79901
Phone: (915) 541-4000
Fax: (915) 541-1316
www.elpasotexas.gov

Greater El Paso Chamber of Commerce
10 Civic Center Plaza
El Paso, TX 79901
Phone: (915) 534-0500
Fax: (915) 534-0510
www.elpaso.org

Erie, PA
Erie Regional Chamber and Growth
Partnership
208 E. Bayfront Parkway
Suite 100
Erie, PA 16507
Phone: (814) 454-7191
www.eriepa.com

Eugene, OR
Eugene Area Chamber of Commerce
1401 Williamette Street
Eugene, OR 97401
Phone: (541) 484-1314
Fax: (541) 484-4942
www.eugenechamber.com

Fargo, ND
Chamber of Commerce of Fargo Moorhead
202 First Avenue North
Fargo, ND 56560
Phone: (218) 233-1100
Fax: (218) 233-1200
www.fmchamber.com

Greater Fargo-Moorhead Economic
Development Corporation
51 Broadway, Suite 500
Fargo, ND 58102
Phone: (701) 364-1900
Fax: (701) 293-7819
www.gfmedc.com

Fayetteville, NC
Fayetteville Regional Chamber
1019 Hay Street
Fayetteville, NC 28305
Phone: (910) 483-8133
Fax: (910) 483-0263
www.fayettevillencchamber.org

Fort Collins, CO
Fort Collins Chamber of Commerce
225 South Meldrum
Fort Collins, CO 80521
Phone: (970) 482-3746
Fax: (970) 482-3774
www.fcchamber.org

Fort Wayne, IN
City of Fort Wayne Economic Development
1 Main St
1 Main Street
Fort Wayne, IN 46802
Phone: (260) 427-1111
Fax: (260) 427-1375
www.cityoffortwayne.org

Greater Fort Wayne Chamber of Commerce
826 Ewing Street
Fort Wayne, IN 46802
Phone: (260) 424-1435
Fax: (260) 426-7232
www.fwchamber.org

Fort Worth, TX
City of Fort Worth Economic Development
City Hall
900 Monroe Street, Suite 301
Fort Worth, TX 76102
Phone: (817) 392-6103
Fax: (817) 392-2431
www.fortworthgov.org

Fort Worth Chamber of Commerce
777 Taylor Street
Suite 900
Fort Worth, TX 76102-4997
Phone: (817) 336-2491
Fax: (817) 877-4034
www.fortworthchamber.com

Gainesville, FL
Gainesville Area Chamber of Commerce
300 East University Avenue
Suite 100
Gainesville, FL 32601
Phone: (352) 334-7100
Fax: (352) 334-7141
www.gainesvillechamber.com

Grand Rapids, MI
Grands Rapids Area Chamber of Commerce
111 Pearl Street N.W.
Grand Rapids, MI 49503
Phone: (616) 771-0300
Fax: (616) 771-0318
www.grandrapids.org

Green Bay, WI
Economic Development
100 N Jefferson St
Room 202
Green Bay, WI 54301
Phone: (920) 448-3397
Fax: (920) 448-3063
www.ci.green-bay.wi.us

Green Bay Area Chamber of Commerce
300 N. Broadway
Suite 3A
Green Bay, WI 54305-1660
Phone: (920) 437-8704
Fax: (920) 593-3468
www.titletown.org

Greensboro, NC
Greensboro Area Chamber of Commerce
342 N Elm St.
Greensboro, NC 27401
Phone: (336) 387-8301
Fax: (336) 275-9299
www.greensboro.org

Honolulu, HI
The Chamber of Commerce of Hawaii
1132 Bishop Street
Suite 402
Honolulu, HI 96813
Phone: (808) 545-4300
Fax: (808) 545-4369
www.cochawaii.com

Houston, TX
Greater Houston Partnership
1200 Smith Street
Suite 700
Houston, TX 77002-4400
Phone: (713) 844-3600
Fax: (713) 844-0200
www.houston.org

Huntsville, AL
Chamber of Commerce of
Huntsville/Madison County
225 Church Street
Huntsville, AL 35801
Phone: (256) 535-2000
Fax: (256) 535-2015
www.huntsvillealabamausa.com

Indianapolis, IN
Greater Indianapolis Chamber of Commerce
111 Monument Circle
Suite 1950
Indianapolis, IN 46204
Phone: (317) 464-2222
Fax: (317) 464-2217
www.indychamber.com

The Indy Partnership
111 Monument Circle
Suite 1800
Indianapolis, IN 46204
Phone: (317) 236-6262
Fax: (317) 236-6275
www.indypartnership.com

Jacksonville, FL
Jacksonville Chamber of Commerce
3 Independent Drive
Jacksonville, FL 32202
Phone: (904) 366-6600
Fax: (904) 632-0617
www.myjaxchamber.com

Kansas City, MO
Greater Kansas City Chamber of Commerce
2600 Commerce Tower
911 Main Street
Kansas City, MO 64105
Phone: (816) 221-2424
Fax: (816) 221-7440
www.kcchamber.com

Kansas City Area Development Council
2600 Commerce Tower
911 Main Street
Kansas City, MO 64105
Phone: (816) 221-2121
Fax: (816) 842-2865
www.thinkkc.com

Lafayette, LA
Greater Lafayette Chamber of Commerce
804 East Saint Mary Blvd.
Lafayette, LA 70503
Phone: (337) 233-2705
Fax: (337) 234-8671
www.lafchamber.org

Las Vegas, NV
Las Vegas Chamber of Commerce
6671 Las Vegas Blvd South
Suite 300
Las Vegas, NV 89119
Phone: (702) 735-1616
Fax: (702) 735-0406
www.lvchamber.org

Las Vegas Office of Business Development
400 Stewart Avenue
City Hall
Las Vegas, NV 89101
Phone: (702) 229-6011
Fax: (702) 385-3128
www.lasvegasnevada.gov

Lexington, KY
Greater Lexington Chamber of Commerce
330 East Main Street
Suite 100
Lexington, KY 40507
Phone: (859) 254-4447
Fax: (859) 233-3304
www.commercelexington.com

Lexington Downtown Development
Authority
101 East Vine Street
Suite 500
Lexington, KY 40507
Phone: (859) 425-2296
Fax: (859) 425-2292
www.lexingtondda.com

Lincoln, NE
Lincoln Chamber of Commerce
1135 M Street
Suite 200
Lincoln, NE 68508
Phone: (402) 436-2350
Fax: (402) 436-2360
www.lcoc.com

Little Rock, AR
Little Rock Regional Chamber of
Commerce
One Chamber Plaza
Little Rock, AR 72201-1618
Phone: (501) 374-2001
www.littlerockchamber.com

Los Angeles, CA
Los Angeles Area Chamber of Commerce
350 South Bixel Street
Los Angeles, CA 90017
Phone: (213) 580-7500
Fax: (213) 580-7511
www.lachamber.org

Los Angeles County Economic
Development Corporation
444 South Flower Street
34th Floor
Los Angeles, CA 90071
Phone: (213) 622-4300
Fax: (213) 622-7100
www.laedc.org

Louisville, KY
The Greater Louisville Chamber of
Commerce
614 West Main Street
Suite 6000
Louisville, KY 40202
Phone: (502) 625-0000
Fax: (502) 625-0010
www.greaterlouisville.com

Lubbock, TX
Lubbock Chamber of Commerce
1500 Broadway
Suite 101
Lubbock, TX 79401
Phone: (806) 761-7000
Fax: (806) 761-7013
www.lubbockchamber.com

Madison, WI
Greater Madison Chamber of Commerce
615 East Washington Avenue
P.O. Box 71
Madison, WI 53701-0071
Phone: (608) 256-8348
Fax: (608) 256-0333
www.greatermadisonchamber.com

Manchester, NH
Greater Manchester Chamber of Commerce
889 Elm Street
Manchester, NH 03101
Phone: (603) 666-6600
Fax: (603) 626-0910
www.manchester-chamber.org

Manchester Economic Development Office
One City Hall Plaza
Manchester, NH 03101
Phone: (603) 624-6505
Fax: (603) 624-6308
www.yourmanchesternh.com

Miami, FL
Greater Miami Chamber of Commerce
1601 Biscayne Boulevard
Ballroom Level
Miami, FL 33132-1260
Phone: (305) 350-7700
Fax: (305) 374-6902
www.greatermiami.com

The Beacon Council
80 Southwest 8th Street
Suite 2400
Miami, FL 33130
Phone: (305) 579-1300
Fax: (305) 375-0271
www.beaconcouncil.com

Midland, TX
Midland Chamber of Commerce
109 N. Main
Midland, TX 79701
Phone: (432) 683-3381
Fax: (432) 686-3556
www.midlandtxchamber.com

Minneapolis, MN
Minneapolis Community Development
Agency
Crown Roller Mill
105 5th Avenue South, Suite 200
Minneapolis, MN 55401
Phone: (612) 673-5095
Fax: (612) 673-5100
www.ci.minneapolis.mn.us

Minneapolis Regional Chamber
81 South Ninth Street
Suite 200
Minneapolis, MN 55402
Phone: (612) 370-9100
Fax: (612) 370-9195
www.minneapolischamber.org

Montgomery, AL
Montgomery Area Chamber of Commerce
41 Commerce Street
Montgomery, AL 36104
Phone: (334) 834-5200
www.montgomerychamber.com

Nashville, TN
Nashville Area Chamber of Commerce
211 Commerce Street, Suite 100
Nashville, TN 37201
Phone: (615) 743-3000
Fax: (615) 256-3074
www.nashvillechamber.cm

Tennessee Valley Authority Economic
Development Corp.
P.O. Box 292409
Nashville, TN 37229-2409
Phone: (615) 232-6225
www.tvaed.com

New Orleans, LA
New Orleans Chamber of Commerce
1515 Poydras St, Suite 1010
New Orleans, LA 70112
Phone: (504) 799-4260
Fax: (504) 799-4259
www.neworleanschamber.org

New York, NY
New York City Economic Development
Corporation
110 William Street
New York, NY 10038
Phone: (212) 619-5000
www.nycedc.com

The Partnership for New York City
One Battery Park Plaza
5th Floor
New York, NY 10004
Phone: (212) 493-7400
Fax: (212) 344-3344
www.pfnyc.org

Oklahoma City, OK
Greater Oklahoma City Chamber of
Commerce
123 Park Avenue
Oklahoma City, OK 73102
Phone: (405) 297-8900
Fax: (405) 297-8916
www.okcchamber.com

Omaha, NE
Omaha Chamber of Commerce
1301 Harney Street
Omaha, NE 68102
Phone: (402) 346-5000
Fax: (402) 346-7050
www.omahachamber.org

Orlando, FL
Metro Orlando Economic Development
Commission of Mid-Florida
301 East Pine Street
Suite 900
Orlando, FL 32801
Phone: (407) 422-7159
Fax: (407) 425.6428
www.orlandoedc.com

Orlando Regional Chamber of Commerce
75 South Ivanhoe Boulevard
PO Box 1234
Orlando, FL 32802
Phone: (407) 425-1234
Fax: (407) 839-5020
www.orlando.org

Oxnard, CA
Oxnard Chamber of Commerce
400 E Esplanade Drive
Suite 302
Oxnard, CA 93036
Phone: (805) 983-6118
Fax: (805) 604-7331
www.oxnardchamber.org

Peoria, IL
Peoria Area Chamber
100 SW Water St.
Peoria, IL 61602
Phone: (309) 495-5900
www.peoriachamber.org

Philadelphia, PA
Greater Philadelphia Chamber of
Commerce
200 South Broad Street
Suite 700
Philadelphia, PA 19102
Phone: (215) 545-1234
Fax: (215) 790-3600
www.greaterphilachamber.com

Phoenix, AZ
Greater Phoenix Chamber of Commerce
201 North Central Avenue
27th Floor
Phoenix, AZ 85073
Phone: (602) 495-2195
Fax: (602) 495-8913
www.phoenixchamber.com

Greater Phoenix Economic Council
2 North Central Avenue
Suite 2500
Phoenix, AZ 85004
Phone: (602) 256-7700
Fax: (602) 256-7744
www.gpec.org

Pittsburgh, PA
Allegheny County Industrial Development
Authority
425 6th Avenue
Suite 800
Pittsburgh, PA 15219
Phone: (412) 350-1067
Fax: (412) 642-2217
www.alleghenycounty.us

Greater Pittsburgh Chamber of Commerce
425 6th Avenue
12th Floor
Pittsburgh, PA 15219
Phone: (412) 392-4500
Fax: (412) 392-4520
www.alleghenyconference.org

Portland, OR
Portland Business Alliance
200 SW Market Street
Suite 1770
Portland, OR 97201
Phone: (503) 224-8684
Fax: (503) 323-9186
www.portlandalliance.com

Providence, RI
Greater Providence Chamber of Commerce
30 Exchange Terrace
Fourth Floor
Providence, RI 02903
Phone: (401) 521-5000
Fax: (401) 351-2090
www.provchamber.com

Rhode Island Economic Development
Corporation
Providence City Hall
25 Dorrance Street
Providence, RI 02903
Phone: (401) 421-7740
Fax: (401) 751-0203
www.providenceri.com

Provo, UT
Provo-Orem Chamber of Commerce
51 South University Avenue
Suite 215
Provo, UT 84601
Phone: (801) 851-2555
Fax: (801) 851-2557
www.thechamber.org

Raleigh, NC
Greater Raleigh Chamber of Commerce
800 South Salisbury Street
Raleigh, NC 27601-2978
Phone: (919) 664-7000
Fax: (919) 664-7099
www.raleighchamber.org

Reno, NV
Greater Reno-Sparks Chamber of
Commerce
1 East First Street
16th Floor
Reno, NV 89505
Phone: (775) 337-3030
Fax: (775) 337-3038
www.reno-sparkschamber.org

The Chamber Reno-Sparks-Northern
Nevada
449 S. Virginia St.
2nd Floor
Reno, NV 89501
Phone: (775) 636-9550
www.thechambernv.org

Richmond, VA
Greater Richmond Chamber
600 East Main Street
Suite 700
Richmond, VA 23219
Phone: (804) 648-1234
www.grcc.com

Greater Richmond Partnership
901 East Byrd Street
Suite 801
Richmond, VA 23219-4070
Phone: (804) 643-3227
Fax: (804) 343-7167
www.grpva.com

Riverside, CA
Greater Riverside Chamber of Commerce
3985 University Avenue
Riverside, CA 92501
Phone: (951) 683-7100
Fax: (951) 683-2670
www.riverside-chamber.com

Rochester, MN
Rochester Area Chamber of Commerce
220 South Broadway
Suite 100
Rochester, MN 55904
Phone: (507) 288-1122
Fax: (507) 282-8960
www.rochestermnchamber.com

Salem, OR
Salem Area Chamber of Commerce
1110 Commercial Street NE
Salem, OR 97301
Phone: (503) 581-1466
Fax: (503) 581-0972
www.salemchamber.org

Salt Lake City, UT
Department of Economic Development
451 South State Street, Room 345
Salt Lake City, UT 84111
Phone: (801) 535-6306
Fax: (801) 535-6331
www.slcgov.com/mayor/ED

Salt Lake Chamber
175 E. University Blvd. (400 S)
Suite 600
Salt Lake City, UT 84111
Phone: (801) 364-3631
www.slchamber.com

San Antonio, TX
San Antonio Economic Development
Department
P.O. Box 839966
San Antonio, TX 78283-3966
Phone: (210) 207-8080
Fax: (210) 207-8151
www.sanantonio.gov/edd

The Greater San Antonio Chamber of
Commerce
602 E. Commerce Street
San Antonio, TX 78205
Phone: (210) 229-2100
Fax: (210) 229-1600
www.sachamber.org

San Diego, CA
San Diego Economic Development Corp.
401 B Street
Suite 1100
San Diego, CA 92101
Phone: (619) 234-8484
Fax: (619) 234-1935
www.sandiegobusiness.org

San Diego Regional Chamber of Commerce
402 West Broadway
Suite 1000
San Diego, CA 92101-3585
Phone: (619) 544-1300
Fax: (619) 744-7481
www.sdchamber.org

San Francisco, CA
San Francisco Chamber of Commerce
235 Montgomery Street
12th Floor
San Francisco, CA 94104
Phone: (415) 392-4520
Fax: (415) 392-0485
www.sfchamber.com

San Jose, CA
Office of Economic Development
60 South Market Street
Suite 470
San Jose, CA 95113
Phone: (408) 277-5880
Fax: (408) 277-3615
www.sba.gov

San Jose-Silicon Valley Chamber of
Commerce
310 South First Street
San Jose, CA 95113
Phone: (408) 291-5250
Fax: (408) 286-5019
www.sjchamber.com

Santa Rosa, CA
Santa Rosa Chamber of Commerce
1260 North Dutton Avenue
Suite 272
Santa Rosa, CA 95401
Phone: (707) 545-1414
www.santarosachamber.com

Savannah, GA
Economic Development Authority
131 Hutchinson Island Road
4th Floor
Savannah, GA 31421
Phone: (912) 447-8450
Fax: (912) 447-8455
www.seda.org

Savannah Chamber of Commerce
101 E. Bay Street
Savannah, GA 31402
Phone: (912) 644-6400
Fax: (912) 644-6499
www.savannahchamber.com

Seattle, WA
Greater Seattle Chamber of Commerce
1301 Fifth Avenue
Suite 2500
Seattle, WA 98101
Phone: (206) 389-7200
Fax: (206) 389-7288
www.seattlechamber.com

Sioux Falls, SD
Sioux Falls Area Chamber of Commerce
200 N. Phillips Avenue
Suite 102
Sioux Falls, SD 57104
Phone: (605) 336-1620
Fax: (605) 336-6499
www.siouxfallschamber.com

Spokane, WA
Greater Spokane
801 W Riverside
Suite 100
Spokane, WA 99201
Phone: (509) 624-1393
Fax: (509) 747-0077
www.spokanechamber.org

Springfield, MO
Springfield Area Chamber of Commerce
202 S. John Q. Hammons Parkway
PO Box 1687
Springfield, MO 65806
Phone: (417) 862-5567
www.springfieldchamber.com

Tallahassee, FL
Greater Tallahassee Chamber of Commerce
300 E. Park Avenue
PO Box 1638
Tallahassee, FL 32301
Phone: (850) 224-8116
Fax: (850) 561-3860
www.talchamber.com

Tampa, FL
Greater Tampa Chamber of Commerce
P.O. Box 420
Tampa, FL 33601-0420
Phone: (813) 276-9401
Fax: (813) 229-7855
www.tampachamber.com

Topeka, KS
Greater Topeka Chamber of Commerce/
GO Topeka
120 SE Sixth Avenue
Suite 110
Topeka, KS 66603
Phone: (785) 234-2644
Fax: (785) 234-8656
www.topekachamber.org

Tulsa, OK
Tulsa Regional Chamber
1 West 3rd Street
Suite 100
Tulsa, OK 74103
Phone: (918) 585-1201
Fax: (918) 585-8016
www.tulsachamber.com

Virginia Beach, VA
Hampton Roads Chamber of Commerce
500 East Main St
Suite 700
Virginia Beach, VA 23510
Phone: (757) 664-2531
www.hamptonroadschamber.com

Washington, DC
District of Columbia Chamber of
Commerce
1213 K Street NW
Washington, DC 20005
Phone: (202) 347-7201
Fax: (202) 638-6762
www.dcchamber.org

District of Columbia Office of Planning and
Economic Development
J.A. Wilson Building
1350 Pennsylvania Ave NW, Suite 317
Washington, DC 20004
Phone: (202) 727-6365
Fax: (202) 727-6703
www.dcbiz.dc.gov

Wichita, KS
City of Wichita Economic Development
Department
City Hall, 12th Floor
455 North Main Street
Wichita, KS 67202
Phone: (316) 268-4524
Fax: (316) 268-4656
www.wichitagov.org

Wichita Metro Chamber of Commerce
350 West Douglas Avenue
Wichita, KS 67202
Phone: (316) 265-7771
www.wichitachamber.org

Wilmington, NC
Wilmington Chamber of Commerce
One Estell Lee Place
Wilmington, NC 28401
Phone: (910) 762-2611
www.wilmingtonchamber.org

Worcester, MA
Worcester Regional Chamber of Commerce
446 Main St
Suite 200
Worcester, MA 1608
Phone: (508) 753-2924
Fax: (508) 754-8560
www.worcesterchamber.org

Appendix E: State Departments of Labor

Alabama
Alabama Department of Labor
P.O. Box 303500
Montgomery, AL 36130-3500
Phone: (334) 242-3072
www.Alalabor.state.al.us

Alaska
Dept of Labor and Workforce Devel.
P.O. Box 11149
Juneau, AK 99822-2249
Phone: (907) 465-2700
www.labor.state.AK.us

Arizona
Arizona Industrial Commission
800 West Washington Street
Phoenix, AZ 85007
Phone: (602) 542-4515
www.ica.state.AZ.us

Arkansas
Department of Labor
10421 West Markham
Little Rock, AR 72205
Phone: (501) 682-4500
www.Arkansas.gov/labor

California
Labor and Workforce Development
445 Golden Gate Ave., 10th Floor
San Francisco, CA 94102
Phone: (916) 263-1811
www.labor.CA.gov

Colorado
Dept of Labor and Employment
633 17th St., 2nd Floor
Denver, CO 80202-3660
Phone: (888) 390-7936
www.COworkforce.com

Connecticut
Department of Labor
200 Folly Brook Blvd.
Wethersfield, CT 06109-1114
Phone: (860) 263-6000
www.CT.gov/dol

Delaware
Department of Labor
4425 N. Market St., 4th Floor
Wilmington, DE 19802
Phone: (302) 451-3423
www.Delawareworks.com

District of Columbia
Employment Services Department
614 New York Ave., NE, Suite 300
Washington, DC 20002
Phone: (202) 671-1900
www.DOES.DC.gov

Florida
Agency for Workforce Innovation
The Caldwell Building
107 East Madison St. Suite 100
Tallahassee, FL 32399-4120
Phone: (800) 342-3450
www.Floridajobs.org

Georgia
Department of Labor
Sussex Place, Room 600
148 Andrew Young Intl Blvd., NE
Atlanta, GA 30303
Phone: (404) 656-3011
www.dol.state.GA.us

Hawaii
Dept of Labor & Industrial Relations
830 Punchbowl Street
Honolulu, HI 96813
Phone: (808) 586-8842
wwwHawaii.gov/labor

Idaho
Department of Labor
317 W. Main St.
Boise, ID 83735-0001
Phone: (208) 332-3579
www.labor.Idaho.gov

Illinois
Department of Labor
160 N. LaSalle Street, 13th Floor
Suite C-1300
Chicago, IL 60601
Phone: (312) 793-2800
www.state.IL.us/agency/idol

Indiana
Indiana Government Center South
402 W. Washington Street
Room W195
Indianapolis, IN 46204
Phone: (317) 232-2655
www.IN.gov/labor

Iowa
Iowa Workforce Development
1000 East Grand Avenue
Des Moines, IA 50319-0209
Phone: (515) 242-5870
www.Iowaworkforce.org/labor

Kansas
Department of Labor
401 S.W. Topeka Blvd.
Topeka, KS 66603-3182
Phone: (785) 296-5000
www.dol.KS.gov

Kentucky
Philip Anderson, Commissioner
Department of Labor
1047 U.S. Hwy 127 South, Suite 4
Frankfort, KY 40601-4381
Phone: (502) 564-3070
www.labor.KY.gov

Louisiana
Department of Labor
P.O. Box 94094
Baton Rouge, LA 70804-9094
Phone: (225) 342-3111
www.LAworks.net

Maine
Department of Labor
45 Commerce Street
Augusta, ME 04330
Phone: (207) 623-7900
www.state.ME.us/labor

Maryland
Department of Labor and Industry
500 N. Calvert Street
Suite 401
Baltimore, MD 21202
Phone: (410) 767-2357
www.dllr.state.MD.us

Massachusetts
Dept of Labor & Work Force Devel.
One Ashburton Place
Room 2112
Boston, MA 02108
Phone: (617) 626-7100
www.Mass.gov/eolwd

Michigan
Dept of Labor & Economic Growth
P.O. Box 30004
Lansing, MI 48909
Phone: (517) 335-0400
www.Michigan.gov/cis

Minnesota
Dept of Labor and Industry
443 Lafayette Road North
Saint Paul, MN 55155
Phone: (651) 284-5070
www.doli.state.MN.us

Mississippi
Dept of Employment Security
P.O. Box 1699
Jackson, MS 39215-1699
Phone: (601) 321-6000
www.mdes.MS.gov

Missouri
Labor and Industrial Relations
P.O. Box 599
3315 W. Truman Boulevard
Jefferson City, MO 65102-0599
Phone: (573) 751-7500
www.dolir.MO.gov/lirc

Montana
Dept of Labor and Industry
P.O. Box 1728
Helena, MT 59624-1728
Phone: (406) 444-9091
www.dli.MT.gov

Nebraska
Department of Labor
550 South 16th Street
Box 94600
Lincoln, NE 68509-4600
Phone: (402) 471-9000
www.Nebraskaworkforce.com

Nevada
Dept of Business and Industry
555 E. Washington Ave.
Suite 4100
Las Vegas, NV 89101-1050
Phone: (702) 486-2650
www.laborcommissioner.com

New Hampshire
Department of Labor
State Office Park South
95 Pleasant Street
Concord, NH 03301
Phone: (603) 271-3176
www.labor.state.NH.us

New Jersey
Department of Labor
John Fitch Plaza, 13th Floor
Suite D
Trenton, NJ 08625-0110
Phone: (609) 777-3200
lwd.dol.state.nj.us/labor

New Mexico
Department of Labor
401 Broadway, NE
Albuquerque, NM 87103-1928
Phone: (505) 841-8450
www.dol.state.NM.us

New York
Department of Labor
State Office Bldg. # 12
W.A. Harriman Campus
Albany, NY 12240
Phone: (518) 457-5519
www.labor.state.NY.us

North Carolina
Department of Labor
4 West Edenton Street
Raleigh, NC 27601-1092
Phone: (919) 733-7166
www.nclabor.com

North Dakota
Department of Labor
State Capitol Building
600 East Boulevard, Dept 406
Bismark, ND 58505-0340
Phone: (701) 328-2660
www.nd.gov/labor

Ohio
Department of Commerce
77 South High Street, 22nd Floor
Columbus, OH 43215
Phone: (614) 644-2239
www.com.state.OH.us

Oklahoma
Department of Labor
4001 N. Lincoln Blvd.
Oklahoma City, OK 73105-5212
Phone: (405) 528-1500
www.state.OK.us/~okdol

Oregon
Bureau of Labor and Industries
800 NE Oregon St., #32
Portland, OR 97232
Phone: (971) 673-0761
www.Oregon.gov/boli

Pennsylvania
Dept of Labor and Industry
1700 Labor and Industry Bldg
7th and Forster Streets
Harrisburg, PA 17120
Phone: (717) 787-5279
www.dli.state.PA.us

Rhode Island
Department of Labor and Training
1511 Pontiac Avenue
Cranston, RI 02920
Phone: (401) 462-8000
www.dlt.state.RI.us

South Carolina
Dept of Labor, Licensing & Regulations
P.O. Box 11329
Columbia, SC 29211-1329
Phone: (803) 896-4300
www.llr.state.SC.us

South Dakota
Department of Labor
700 Governors Drive
Pierre, SD 57501-2291
Phone: (605) 773-3682
www.state.SD.us

Tennessee
Dept of Labor & Workforce Development
Andrew Johnson Tower
710 James Robertson Pkwy
Nashville, TN 37243-0655
Phone: (615) 741-6642
www.state.TN.us/labor-wfd

Texas
Texas Workforce Commission
101 East 15th St.
Austin, TX 78778
Phone: (512) 475-2670
www.twc.state.TX.us

Utah
Utah Labor Commission
P.O. Box 146610
Salt Lake City, UT 84114-6610
Phone: (801) 530-6800
Laborcommission.Utah.gov

Vermont
Department of Labor
5 Green Mountain Drive
P.O. Box 488
Montpelier, VT 05601-0488
Phone: (802) 828-4000
www.labor.verMont.gov

Virginia
Dept of Labor and Industry
Powers-Taylor Building
13 S. 13th Street
Richmond, VA 23219
Phone: (804) 371-2327
www.doli.Virginia.gov

Washington
Dept of Labor and Industries
P.O. Box 44001
Olympia, WA 98504-4001
Phone: (360) 902-4200
www.lni.WA.gov

West Virginia
Division of Labor
State Capitol Complex, Building #6
1900 Kanawha Blvd.
Charleston, WV 25305
Phone: (304) 558-7890
www.labor.state.WV.us

Wisconsin
Dept of Workforce Development
201 E. Washington Ave., #A400
P.O. Box 7946
Madison, WI 53707-7946
Phone: (608) 266-6861
www.dwd.state.WI.us

Wyoming
Department of Employment
1510 East Pershing Blvd.
Cheyenne, WY 82002
Phone: (307) 777-7261
www.doe.state.WY.us

Source: U.S. Department of Labor

General Reference

America's College Museums
American Environmental Leaders: From Colonial Times to the Present
An African Biographical Dictionary
An Encyclopedia of Human Rights in the United States
Constitutional Amendments
Encyclopedia of African-American Writing
Encyclopedia of the Continental Congress
Encyclopedia of Gun Control & Gun Rights
Encyclopedia of Invasions & Conquests
Encyclopedia of Prisoners of War & Internment
Encyclopedia of Religion & Law in America
Encyclopedia of Rural America
Encyclopedia of the United States Cabinet, 1789-2010
Encyclopedia of War Journalism
Encyclopedia of Warrior Peoples & Fighting Groups
From Suffrage to the Senate: America's Political Women
Nations of the World
Political Corruption in America
Speakers of the House of Representatives, 1789-2009
The Environmental Debate: A Documentary History
The Evolution Wars: A Guide to the Debates
The Religious Right: A Reference Handbook
The Value of a Dollar: 1860-2009
The Value of a Dollar: Colonial Era
This is Who We Were: A Companion to the 1940 Census
This is Who We Were: The 1920s
This is Who We Were: The 1950s
This is Who We Were: The 1960s
US Land & Natural Resource Policy
Working Americans 1770-1869 Vol. IX: Revolutionary War to the Civil War
Working Americans 1880-1999 Vol. I: The Working Class
Working Americans 1880-1999 Vol. II: The Middle Class
Working Americans 1880-1999 Vol. III: The Upper Class
Working Americans 1880-1999 Vol. IV: Their Children
Working Americans 1880-2003 Vol. V: At War
Working Americans 1880-2005 Vol. VI: Women at Work
Working Americans 1880-2006 Vol. VII: Social Movements
Working Americans 1880-2007 Vol. VIII: Immigrants
Working Americans 1880-2009 Vol. X: Sports & Recreation
Working Americans 1880-2010 Vol. XI: Inventors & Entrepreneurs
Working Americans 1880-2011 Vol. XII: Our History through Music
Working Americans 1880-2012 Vol. XIII: Education & Educators
World Cultural Leaders of the 20th & 21st Centuries

Business Information

Complete Television, Radio & Cable Industry Directory
Directory of Business Information Resources
Directory of Mail Order Catalogs
Directory of Venture Capital & Private Equity Firms
Environmental Resource Handbook
Food & Beverage Market Place
Grey House Homeland Security Directory
Grey House Performing Arts Directory
Hudson's Washington News Media Contacts Directory
New York State Directory
Sports Market Place Directory

Education Information

Charter School Movement
Comparative Guide to American Elementary & Secondary Schools
Complete Learning Disabilities Directory
Educators Resource Directory
Special Education

Health Information

Comparative Guide to American Hospitals
Complete Directory for Pediatric Disorders
Complete Directory for People with Chronic Illness
Complete Directory for People with Disabilities
Complete Mental Health Directory
Diabetes in America: A Geographic & Demographic Analysis
Directory of Health Care Group Purchasing Organizations
Directory of Hospital Personnel
HMO/PPO Directory
Medical Device Register
Older Americans Information Directory

Statistics & Demographics

America's Top-Rated Cities
America's Top-Rated Small Towns & Cities
America's Top-Rated Smaller Cities
American Tally
Ancestry & Ethnicity in America
Comparative Guide to American Hospitals
Comparative Guide to American Suburbs
Profiles of America
Profiles of... Series – State Handbooks
The Hispanic Databook
Weather America

Financial Ratings Series

TheStreet.com Ratings Guide to Bond & Money Market Mutual Funds
TheStreet.com Ratings Guide to Common Stocks
TheStreet.com Ratings Guide to Exchange-Traded Funds
TheStreet.com Ratings Guide to Stock Mutual Funds
TheStreet.com Ratings Ultimate Guided Tour of Stock Investing
Weiss Ratings Consumer Guides
Weiss Ratings Guide to Banks & Thrifts
Weiss Ratings Guide to Credit Unions
Weiss Ratings Guide to Health Insurers
Weiss Ratings Guide to Life & Annuity Insurers
Weiss Ratings Guide to Property & Casualty Insurers

Bowker's Books In Print®Titles

Books In Print®
Books In Print® Supplement
American Book Publishing Record® Annual
American Book Publishing Record® Monthly
Books Out Loud™
Bowker's Complete Video Directory™
Children's Books In Print®
El-Hi Textbooks & Serials In Print®
Forthcoming Books®
Law Books & Serials In Print™
Medical & Health Care Books In Print™
Publishers, Distributors & Wholesalers of the US™
Subject Guide to Books In Print®
Subject Guide to Children's Books In Print®

Canadian General Reference

Associations Canada
Canadian Almanac & Directory
Canadian Environmental Resource Guide
Canadian Parliamentary Guide
Financial Services Canada
Governments Canada
Health Services Canada
Libraries Canada
Major Canadian Cities
The History of Canada

Grey House Publishing | Salem Press | H.W. Wilson
4919 Route, 22 PO Box 56, Amenia NY 12501-0056

2014 Title List

Visit **www.SalemPress.com** for Product Information, Table of Contents and Sample Pages

Literature

American Ethnic Writers
Critical Insights: Authors
Critical Insights: New Literary Collection Bundles
Critical Insights: Themes
Critical Insights: Works
Critical Survey of Drama
Critical Survey of Graphic Novels: Heroes & Super Heroes
Critical Survey of Graphic Novels: History, Theme & Technique
Critical Survey of Graphic Novels: Independents & Underground Classics
Critical Survey of Graphic Novels: Manga
Critical Survey of Long Fiction
Critical Survey of Mystery & Detective Fiction
Critical Survey of Mythology and Folklore: Heroes and Heroines
Critical Survey of Mythology and Folklore: Love, Sexuality & Desire
Critical Survey of Mythology and Folklore: World Mythology
Critical Survey of Poetry
Critical Survey of Poetry: American Poetry
Critical Survey of Poetry: British, Irish & Commonwealth Poets
Critical Survey of Poetry: European Poets
Critical Survey of Poetry: European Poets
Critical Survey of Poetry: Topical Essays
Critical Survey of Poetry: World Poets
Critical Survey of Science Fiction & Fantasy Literature
Critical Survey of Shakespeare's Sonnets
Critical Survey of Short Fiction
Critical Survey of Short Fiction: American Writers
Critical Survey of Short Fiction: British, Irish & Commonwealth Poets
Critical Survey of Short Fiction: European Writers
Critical Survey of Short Fiction: Topical Essays
Critical Survey of Short Fiction: World Writers
Cyclopedia of Literary Characters
Introduction to Literary Context: American Post-Modernist Novels
Introduction to Literary Context: American Short Fiction
Introduction to Literary Context: English Literature
Introduction to Literary Context: World Literature
Magill's Literary Annual 2014
Magill's Survey of American Literature
Magill's Survey of World Literature
Masterplots
Masterplots II: African American Literature
Masterplots II: Christian Literature
Masterplots II: Drama Series
Masterplots II: Short Story Series
Notable African American Writers
Notable American Novelists
Notable Playwrights
Short Story Writers

Science, Careers & Mathematics

Applied Science
Applied Science: Engineering & Mathematics
Applied Science: Science & Medicine
Applied Science: Technology
Biomes and Ecosystems
Careers in Chemistry
Careers in Communications & Media
Careers in Healthcare
Careers in Hospitality & Tourism
Careers in Law & Criminology
Careers in Physics
Computer Technology Inventors
Contemporary Biographies in Chemistry
Contemporary Biographies in Communications & Media
Contemporary Biographies in Healthcare
Contemporary Biographies in Hospitality & Tourism
Contemporary Biographies in Law & Criminology
Contemporary Biographies in Physics
Earth Science
Earth Science: Earth Materials & Resources
Earth Science: Earth's Surface and History
Earth Science: Physics & Chemistry of the Earth
Earth Science: Weather, Water & Atmosphere
Encyclopedia of Energy
Encyclopedia of Environmental Issues
Encyclopedia of Global Resources
Encyclopedia of Global Warming
Encyclopedia of Mathematics and Society
Encyclopedia of the Ancient World
Forensic Science
Internet Innovators
Introduction to Chemistry
Magill's Encyclopedia of Science: Animal Life
Magill's Encyclopedia of Science: Plant life
Magill's Medical Guide
Notable Natural Disasters
Solar System

Health

Addictions & Substance Abuse
Cancer
Complementary & Alternative Medicine
Genetics & Inherited Conditions
Infectious Diseases & Conditions
Magill's Medical Guide
Psychology & Mental Health
Psychology Basics

Grey House Publishing | Salem Press | H.W. Wilson
4919 Route, 22 PO Box 56, Amenia NY 12501-0056

2014 Title List

Visit **www.SalemPress.com** for Product Information, Table of Contents and Sample Pages

History and Social Science

A 2000s in America
50 States
African American History
Agriculture in History (check)
American First Ladies
American Heroes
American Indian Tribes
American Presidents
American Villains
Ancient Greece
Bill of Rights, The
Cold War, The
Defining Documents: American Revolution 1754-1805
Defining Documents: Civil War 1860-1865
Defining Documents: Emergence of Modern America, 1868-1918
Defining Documents: Exploration & Colonial America 1492-1755
Defining Documents: Manifest Destiny 1803-1860
Defining Documents: Reconstruction, 1865-1880
Defining Documents: The 1920s
Defining Documents: The 1930s
Defining Documents: World War I
Eighties in America
Encyclopedia of American Immigration
Fifties in America
Forties in America
Great Athletes
Great Events from History: 17th Century
Great Events from History: 18th Century
Great Events from History: 19th Century
Great Events from History: 20th Century, 1901-1940
Great Events from History: 20th Century, 1941-1970
Great Events from History: 20th Century, 1971-200
Great Events from History: Ancient World
Great Events from History: Middle Ages
Great Events from History: Modern Scandals
Great Events from History: Renaissance & Early Modern Era
Great Lives from History: 17th Century
Great Lives from History: 18th Century
Great Lives from History: 19th Century
Great Lives from History: 20th Century
Great Lives from History: African Americans
Great Lives from History: Ancient World
Great Lives from History: Asian & Pacific Islander Americans
Great Lives from History: Incredibly Wealthy
Great Lives from History: Inventors & Inventions
Great Lives from History: Jewish Americans
Great Lives from History: Latinos
Great Lives from History: Middle Ages
Great Lives from History: Notorious Lives
Great Lives from History: Renaissance & Early Modern Era
Great Lives from History: Scientists & Science
Historical Encyclopedia of American Business
Immigration in U.S. History
Magill's Guide to Military History
Milestone Documents in African American History
Milestone Documents in American History
Milestone Documents in World History
Milestone Documents of American Leaders
Milestone Documents of World Religions
Musicians & Composers 20th Century
Nineties in America
Seventies in America

Sixties in America
Survey of American Industry and Careers
Thirties in America
Twenties in America
U.S. Court Cases
U.S. Laws, Acts, and Treaties
U.S. Legal System
U.S. Supreme Court
United States at War
USA in Space
Weapons and Warfare
World Conflicts: Asia and the Middle East

Grey House Publishing | Salem Press | H.W. Wilson
4919 Route, 22 PO Box 56, Amenia NY 12501-0056

Current Biography

Current Biography Cumulative Index 1946-2013
Current Biography Magazine
Current Biography Yearbook-2004
Current Biography Yearbook-2005
Current Biography Yearbook-2006
Current Biography Yearbook-2007
Current Biography Yearbook-2008
Current Biography Yearbook-2009
Current Biography Yearbook-2010
Current Biography Yearbook-2011
Current Biography Yearbook-2012
Current Biography Yearbook-2013
Current Biography Yearbook-2014

Core Collections

Senior High Core Collection
Middle & Junior High School Core
Children's Core Collection
Fiction Core Collection
Public Library Core Collection: Nonfiction

Sears List

Sears List of Subject Headings
Sears: Lista de Encabezamientos de Materia

The Reference Shelf

Aging in America
Revisiting Gender
The U.S. National Debate Topic, 2014/2015
Embracing New Paradigms in education
Marijuana Reform
Representative American Speeches 2013-2014
Reality Television
The Business of Food
The Future of U.S. Economic Relations: Mexico, Cuba, and Venezuela
Sports in America
Global Climate Change
Representative American Speeches, 2012-2013
Conspiracy Theories
The Arab Spring
U.S. National Debate Topic: Transportation Infrastructure
Families: Traditional and New Structures
Faith & Science
Representative American Speeches 2011-2012
Social Networking
Dinosaurs
Space Exploration & Development
U.S. Infrastructure
Politics of the Ocean
Representative American Speeches 2010-2011
Robotics
The News and its Future
American Military Presence Overseas
Russia
Graphic Novels and Comic Books
Representative American Speeches 2009-2010

Readers' Guide

Readers Guide to Periodicals Literature
Abridged Readers' Guide to Periodical Literature
Short Story Index

Indexes

Short Story Index
Index to Legal Periodicals & Books

Facts About Series

Facts About the Presidents, Eighth Edition
Facts About China
Facts About the 20th Century
Facts About American Immigration
Facts About World's Languages

Nobel Prize Winners

Nobel Prize Winners, 2002-2013

World Authors

World Authors 2000-2005
World Authors 2006-2013

Famous First Facts

Famous First Facts, Seventh Edition
Famous First Facts About American Politics
Famous First Facts About Sports
Famous First Facts About the Environment
Famous First Facts, International Edition

American Book of Days

The American Book of Days, Fifth Edition
The International Book of Days

Junior Authors & Illustrators

Tenth Book of Junior Authors & Illustrations

Monographs

The Barnhart Dictionary of Etymology
Celebrate the World
Indexing from A to Z
Radical Change: Books for Youth in a Digital Age
The Poetry Break
Guide to the Ancient World

Wilson Chronology

Wilson Chronology of Asia and the Pacific
Wilson Chronology of Human Rights
Wilson Chronology of Ideas
Wilson Chronology of the Arts
Wilson Chronology of the World's Religions
Wilson Chronology of Women's Achievements

Book Review Digest

Book Review Digest, 2014

Grey House Publishing | Salem Press | H.W. Wilson
4919 Route, 22 PO Box 56, Amenia NY 12501-0056